THE COMPLETE
SERMONS ON SEVERAL OCCASIONS
VOL. 1-4

JOHN WESLEY

LONDON:
JOHN MASON
1838

CROSSREACH PUBLICATIONS

Hope. Inspiration. Trust.

WE'RE SOCIAL! FOLLOW US FOR NEW TITLES AND DEALS:
FaceBook.com/CrossReachPublications
@CrossReachPub

AVAILABLE IN PAPERBACK AND eBOOK EDITIONS
PLEASE GO ONLINE FOR MORE GREAT TITLES
AVAILABLE THROUGH CrossReach PUBLICATIONS.
AND IF YOU ENJOYED THIS BOOK PLEASE CONSIDER LEAVING A
REVIEW ON AMAZON. THAT HELPS US OUT A LOT. THANKS.

CONTENTS

Preface...11

First Series

1. Salvation by Faith 13
2. The Almost Christian 16
3. Awake, Thou That Sleepest...19
4. Scriptural Christianity 23
5. Justification by Faith..29
6. The Righteousness of Faith 33
7. The Way to the Kingdom 38
8. The First Fruits of the Spirit 41
9. The Spirit of Bondage and of Adoption 45
10. The Witness of the Spirit Discourse I..50
11. The Witness of the Spirit Discourse II 54
12. The Witness of our own Spirit 58
13. On Sin in Believers 62
14. The Repentance of Believers 66
15. The Great Assize [I.E., The Last Judgment—GL]..............................71
16. The Means of Grace 78
17. The Circumcision of the Heart...84
18. The Marks of the New Birth 88
19. The Great Privilege of those that are Born of God..............................92
20. The Lord our Righteousness 95
21. Upon our Lord's Sermon on the Mount Discourse 1.........................100
22. Upon our Lord's Sermon on the Mount Discourse 2.........................105
23. Upon our Lord's Sermon on the Mount Discourse 3.........................111
24. Upon our Lord's Sermon on the Mount Discourse 4.........................117
25. Upon our Lord's Sermon on the Mount Discourse 5.........................122
26. Upon our Lord's Sermon on the Mount Discourse 6.........................129
27. Upon our Lord's Sermon on the Mount Discourse 7.........................134
28. Upon our Lord's Sermon on the Mount Discourse 8.........................141
29. Upon our Lord's Sermon on the Mount Discourse 9.........................147
30. Upon our Lord's Sermon on the Mount Discourse 10.......................152
31. Upon our Lord's Sermon on the Mount Discourse 11 156
32. Upon our Lord's Sermon on the Mount Discourse 12.......................159
33. Upon Our Lord's Sermon on the Mount Discourse 13.......................163
34. The Original, Nature, Property, and Use of the Law.........................166
35. The Law Established through Faith Discourse I.................................171
36. The Law Established through Faith Discourse 2................................175
37. The Nature of Enthusiasm...179
38. A Caution against Bigotry 183
39. Catholic Spirit...188

40. Christian Perfection 193
41. Wandering Thoughts 201
42. Satan's Devices 204
43. The Scripture Way of Salvation 208
44. Original Sin 212
45. The New Birth 216
46. The Wilderness State 220
47. Heaviness through Manifold Temptations 225
48. Self-Denial 229
49. The Cure of Evil-Speaking 233
50. The Use of Money 237
51. The Good Steward 241
52. 246
53. On the Death of the Rev. Mr. George Whitefield 253

Second Series

54. On Eternity 258
55. On the Trinity 262
56. God's Approbation of His Works 264
57. On the Fall of Man 268
58. On Predestination 271
59. God's Love to Fallen Man 273
60. The General Deliverance 277
61. The Mystery of Iniquity 281
62. The End of Christ's Coming 286
63. The General Spread of the Gospel 290
64. The New Creation 294
65. The Duty of Reproving our Neighbour 297
66. The Signs of the Times 300
67. On Divine Providence 303
69. The Imperfection of Human Knowledge 308
70. The Case of Reason impartially Considered 312
71. Of Good Angels 316
72. Of Evil Angels 319
73. Of Hell 323
74. Of the Church 327
75. On Schism 331
76. On Perfection 334
77. Spiritual Worship 339
78. Spiritual Idolatry 343
79. On Dissipation 346
80. On Friendship with the World 349
81. In what Sense we are to Leave the World 353
82. On Temptation 357
83. On Patience 361
84. The Important Question 364

85. On Working out our own Salvation 368
86. A Call to Backsliders 371
87. The Danger of Riches 376
88. On Dress 381
89. The More Excellent Way 385
90. An Israelite Indeed 389
91. On Charity 392
92. On Zeal 396
93. On Redeeming the Time 400
94. On Family Religion 403
95. On the Education of Children 406
96. On Obedience to Parents 411
97. On Obedience to Pastors 414
98. On Visiting the Sick 418
99. The Reward of the Righteous 421
100. On Pleasing All Men 425
101. The Duty of Constant Communion J.W. 428
102. Of Former Times 432
103. What is Man? 436
104. On Attending the Church Service 438
105. "On Conscience" 442
106. On Faith 446
107. On God's Vineyard 448
108. On Riches 452

Third Series

109. What is Man? 455
110. On the Discoveries of Faith 458
111. On the Omnipresence of God 460
112. The Rich Man and Lazarus 463
113. The Difference between Walking by Sight, and Walking by Faith 467
114. The Unity of the Divine Being 470
115. The Ministerial Office** 473
116. Causes of the Inefficacy of Christianity 476
117. On Knowing Christ sfter the Flesh 480
118. On a Single Eye 482
119. On Worldly Folly 485
120. On the Wedding Garment 487
121. Human Life a Dream 489
122. On Faith 492
123. The Deceitfulness of the Human Heart 495
124. The Heavenly Treasure in Earthen Vessels 498
125. On Living without God 500
126. On the Danger of Increasing Riches 502

Fourth Series

127. The Trouble and Rest of Good Men 505
128. Free Grace* 508

129. The Cause and Cure of Earthquakes...513

130. National Sins and Miseries 518

131. The Late Work of God in North America...521

132. On Laying the Foundation of the New Chapel, near the City-Road, London 525

133. Preached on Occasion of the Death of the Rev. Mr. John Fletcher, Vicar of Madeley, Shropshire 529

Fifth Series

134. True Christianity Defended...536

135. On Mourning for the Dead..540

136. On Corrupting the Word of God 542

137. On the Resurrection of the Dead 544

138. On Grieving the Holy Spirit 548

139. On Love*...550

140. On Public Diversions 553

141. On the Holy Spirit 556

About CrossReach Publications...561

Bestselling Titles from CrossReach..561

Title Index

Almost Christian, The (Sermon 2)—Acts 26:28

Awake, Thou That Sleepest (Sermon 3)—Eph 5:14

Call to Backsliders, A (Sermon 86)—Ps 77:7–8

Case of Reason Impartially Considered, The (Sermon 70)—1 Cor 14:20

Catholic Spirit (Sermon 39)—2 Ki 10:15

Cause and Cure of Earthquakes, The (Sermon 129)—Ps 46:8

Causes of the Inefficiency of Christianity (Sermon 116)—Jer 8:22

Caution against Bigotry, A (Sermon 38)—Mark 9:38–39

Christian Perfection (Sermon 40)—Phil 3:12

Circumcision of the Heart, The (Sermon 17)—Rom 2:29

Cure of Evil Speaking, The (Sermon 49)—Matt 18:15–17

Danger of Riches, The (Sermon 87)—1 Tim 6:9

Duty of Constant Communion, The (Sermon 101)—Luke 22:19

Duty of Reproving our Neighbor, The (Sermon 65)—Lev 19:17

End of Christ's Coming, The (Sermon 62)—1 Joh 3:8

First Fruits of the Spirit, The (Sermon 8)—Rom 8:1

Free Grace (Sermon 128)—Rom 8:32

General Deliverence, The (Sermon 60)—Rom 8:19–22

General Spread of the Gospel, The (Sermon 63)—Is 11:9

God's Approbation of his Works (Sermon 56)—Gen 1:31

God's Love to Fallen Man (Sermon 59)—Rom 5:15

Good Steward, The (Sermon 51)—Luke 21:2

Great Assize, The (Sermon 15)—Rom 14:10

Great Privilege of Those that are Born of God (Sermon 19)—1 John 3:9

Heavenly Treasure in Earthen Vessels, The (Sermon 124)—2 Cor 9:7

Heaviness through Manifold Temptations (Sermon 47)—1 Pet 1:6

Human Life a Dream (Sermon 121)—Ps 73:20

Imperfection of Human Knowledge (Sermon 69)—1 Cor 13:9

Important Question, The (Sermon 84)—Matt 16:26

In What Sense We Are to Leave the World (Sermon 81)—2 Cor 6:17–18

Israelite Indeed, An (Sermon 90)—John 1:47

Justification by Faith (Sermon 5)—Rom 4:5

Law Established through Faith, 1, The (Sermon 35)—Rom 3:31

Law Established through Faith, 2, The (Sermon 36)—Rom 3:31

Lord Our Righteousness, The (Sermon 20)—Jer 23:6

Marks of the New Birth, The (Sermon 18)—John 3:8

Means of Grace, The (Sermon 16)—Mal 3:7

Ministerial Office, The (Sermon 115)—Heb 5:4

More Excellent Way, The (Sermon 89)—1 Cor 12:31

Mystery of Iniquity, The (Sermon 61)—2 Thes 2:7

National Sins and Miseries (Sermon 130)—2 Sam 24:17

Nature of Enthusiasm, The (Sermon 37)—Acts 26:24

New Birth, The (Sermon 45)—John 3:7

New Creation, The (Sermon 64)—Rev 21:5

Of Evil Angels (Sermon 72)—Eph 6:12

Of Former Times (Sermon 102)—Ecc 7:10

Of Good Angels (Sermon 71)—Heb 1:14

Of Hell (Sermon 73)—Mark 9:48

Of the Church (Sermon 74)—Eph 4:1–6

On Attending the Church Service (Sermon 104)—1 Sam 2:17

On Charity (Sermon 91)—1 Cor 13:1–3

On Conscience (Sermon 105)—2 Cor 1:12

On Corrupting the Word of God (Sermon 136)—2 Cor 2:17

On Dissipation (Sermon 79)—1 Cor 7:35

On Divine Providence (Sermon 67)—Luke 12:7

On Dress (Sermon 88)—1 Pet 3:3–4

On Eternity (Sermon 54)—Ps 90:2

On Faith (Sermon 122)—Heb 11:1

On Faith (Sermon 106)—Heb 11:6

On Family Religion (Sermon 94)—Josh 24:15

On Friendship with the World (Sermon 80)—Jas 4:4

On God's Vineyard (Sermon 107)—Isa 5:4

On Grieving the Holy Spirit (Sermon 138)—Eph 4:30

On Knowing Christ after the Flesh (Sermon 117)—2 Cor 5:16

On Laying the Foundation of the New Chapel (Sermon 132)—Num 23:23

On Living without God (Sermon 125)—Eph 2:12

On Love (Sermon 139)—1 Cor 13:3

On Mourning the Dead (Sermon 135)—2 Sam 12:23

On Obedience to Parents (Sermon 96)—Col 3:20

On Obedience to Pastors (Sermon 97)—Heb 13:17

On Patience (Sermon 83)—Jas 1:4

On Perfection (Sermon 76)—Heb 6:1

On Pleasing all Men (Sermon 100)—Rom 15:2

On Predestination (Sermon 58)—Rom 8:29–30

On Public Diversions (Sermon 140)—Amos 3:6

On Redeeming the Time (Sermon 93)—Eph 5:16

On Riches (Sermon 108)—Matt 19:24

On Schism (Sermon 75)—1 Cor 12:5

On Sin in Believers (Sermon 13)—2 Cor 5:17

On Temptation (Sermon 82)—1 Cor 10:13

On Visiting the Sick (Sermon 98)—Matt 25:36

On Working out Own Salvation (Sermon 85)—Phil 2:12–13

On Worldly Folly (Sermon 119)—Luke 22:20

On Zeal (Sermon 92)—Gal 4:18

On the Danger of Increasing Riches (Sermon 126)—Ps 62:10

On the Death of Mr. Whitefield (Sermon 53)—Num 23:10

On the Death of Rev. Mr. John Fletcher (Sermon 133)—Ps 37:37

On the Deceitfulness of the Human Heart (Sermon 123)—Jer 17:9

On the Discoveries of Faith (Sermon 110)—Heb 11:1

On the Education of Children (Sermon 95)—Prov 22:6

On the Fall of Man (Sermon 57)—Gen 3:19

On the Holy Spirit (Sermon 141)—2 Cor 3:17

On the Omnipresence of God (Sermon 111)—Jer 23:24

On the Resurrection of the Dead (Sermon 137)—1 Cor 15:35

On the Single Eye (Sermon 118)—Matt 6:22–23

On the Trinity (Sermon 55)—1 John 5:7

On the Wedding Garment (Sermon 120)—Matt 22:12

Original Sin (Sermon 44)—Gen 6:5

Original, Nature, Property, and Use of Law (Sermon 34)—Rom 7:12

Reformation of Manners, The (Sermon 52)—Ps 94:16

Repentance of Believers, The (Sermon 14)—Mark 1:15

Reward of Righteousness, The (Sermon 99)—Matt 25:34

Rich Man and Lazarus, The (Sermon 112)—Luke 16:31

Righteousness of Faith, The (Sermon 6)—Rom 10:5–8

Salvation by Faith (Sermon 1)—Eph 2:8

Satan's Devices (Sermon 42)—2 Cor 2:11

Scriptural Christianity (Sermon 4)—Acts 4:31

Scripture Way of Salvation, The (Sermon 43)—Eph 2:8

Self-Denial (Sermon 48)—Luke 9:23

Sermon on the Mount, 1 (Sermon 21)—Matt 5:1–4

Sermon on the Mount, 10 (Sermon 30)—Matt 7:1–12

Sermon on the Mount, 11 (Sermon 31)—Matt 7:13–14

Sermon on the Mount, 12 (Sermon 32)—Matt 7:15–20

Sermon on the Mount, 13 (Sermon 33)—Matt 7:21–27

Sermon on the Mount, 2 (Sermon 22)—Matt 5:5–7

Sermon on the Mount, 3 (Sermon 23)—Matt 5:8–12

Sermon on the Mount, 4 (Sermon 24)—Matt 5:13–16

Sermon on the Mount, 5 (Sermon 25)—Matt 5:17–20

Sermon on the Mount, 6 (Sermon 26)—Matt 6:1–15

Sermon on the Mount, 7 (Sermon 27)—Matt 6:16–18

Sermon on the Mount, 8 (Sermon 28)—Matt 6:19–23

Sermon on the Mount, 9 (Sermon 29)—Matt 6:24–34

Signs of the Times, The (Sermon 66)—Matt 16:3

Some Account of the Late Work of God … (Sermon 131)—Ezek 1:16

Spirit of Bondage and of Adoption, The (Sermon 9)—Rom 8:15

Spiritual Idolatry (Sermon 78)—1 John 5:21

Spiritual Worship (Sermon 77)—1 John 5:20

Trouble and Rest of Good Men, The (Sermon 127)—Job 3:17

True Christianity Defended (Sermon 134)—Isa 1:21

Unity of the Divine Being, The (Sermon 114)—Mark 12:32

Use of Money, The (Sermon 50)—Luke 16:9

Walking by Sight, and Walking by Faith (Sermon 113)—2 Cor 5:7

Wandering Thoughts (Sermon 41)—2 Cor 10:5

Way of the Kingdom, The (Sermon 7)—Mark 1:15

What is Man? (Sermon 103)—Ps 8:3–4

What is Man? (Sermon 109)—Ps 8:4

Wilderness State, The (Sermon 46)—John 16:22

Wisdom of God's Counsels, The (Sermon 68)—Rom 11:33

Witness of our own Spirit, The (Sermon 12)—2 Cor 1:12

Witness of the Spirit, 1, The (Sermon 10)—Rom 8:16

Witness of the Spirit, 2, The (Sermon 11)—2 Cor 1:12

Number Index

1. Salvation by Faith—Eph 2:8
2. Almost Christian, The—Acts 26:28
3. Awake, Thou That Sleepest—Eph 5:14
4. Scriptural Christianity—Acts 4:31
5. Justification by Faith—Rom 4:5
6. Righteousness of Faith, The—Rom 10:5–8

7. Way of the Kingdom, The—Mark 1:15

8. First Fruits of the Spirit, The—Rom 8:1

9. Spirit of Bondage and of Adoption, The—Rom 8:15

10. Witness of the Spirit, 1, The—Rom 8:16

11. Witness of the Spirit, 2, The—2 Cor 1:12

12. Witness of our own Spirit, The—2 Cor 1:12

13. On Sin in Believers—2 Cor 5:17

14. Repentance of Believers, The—Mark 1:15

15. Great Assize, The—Rom 14:10

16. Means of Grace, The—Mal 3:7

17. Circumcision of the Heart, The—Rom 2:29

18. Marks of the New Birth, The—John 3:8

19. Great Privilege of Those that are Born of God—1 John 3:9

20. Lord Our Righteousness, The—Jer 23:6

21. Sermon on the Mount, 1—Matt 5:1–4

22. Sermon on the Mount, 2—Matt 5:5–7

23. Sermon on the Mount, 3—Matt 5:8–12

24. Sermon on the Mount, 4—Matt 5:13–16

25. Sermon on the Mount, 5—Matt 5:17–20

26. Sermon on the Mount, 6—Matt 6:1–15

27. Sermon on the Mount, 7—Matt 6:16–18

28. Sermon on the Mount, 8—Matt 6:19–23

29. Sermon on the Mount, 9—Matt 6:24–34

30. Sermon on the Mount, 10—Matt 7:1–12

31. Sermon on the Mount, 11—Matt 7:13–14

32. Sermon on the Mount, 12—Matt 7:15–20

33. Sermon on the Mount, 13—Matt 7:21–27

34. Original, Nature, Property, and Use of Law—Rom 7:12

35. Law Established through Faith, 1, The—Rom 3:31

36. Law Established through Faith, 2, The—Rom 3:31

37. Nature of Enthusiasm, The—Acts 26:24

38. Caution against Bigotry, A—Mark 9:38–39

39. Catholic Spirit—2 Ki 10:15

40. Christian Perfection—Phil 3:12

41. Wandering Thoughts—2 Cor 10:5

42. Satan's Devices—2 Cor 2:11

43. Scripture Way of Salvation, The—Eph 2:8

44. Original Sin—Gen 6:5

45. New Birth, The—John 3:7

46. Wilderness State, The—John 16:22

47. Heaviness through Manifold Temptations—1 Pet 1:6

48. Self-Denial—Luke 9:23

49. Cure of Evil Speaking, The—Matt 18:15–17

50. Use of Money, The—Luke 16:9

51. Good Steward, The—Luke 21:2

52. Reformation of Manners, The—Ps 94:16

53. On the Death of Mr. Whitefield—Num 23:10

54. On Eternity—Ps 90:2

55. On the Trinity—1 John 5:7

56. God's Approbation of his Works—Gen 1:31

57. On the Fall of Man—Gen 3:19

58. On Predestination—Rom 8:29–30

59. God's Love to Fallen Man—Rom 5:15

60. General Deliverence, The—Rom 8:19–22

61. Mystery of Iniquity, The—2 Thes 2:7

62. End of Christ's Coming, The—1 Joh 3:8

63. General Spread of the Gospel, The—Is 11:9

64. New Creation, The—Rev 21:5

65. Duty of Reproving our Neighbor, The—Lev 19:17

66. Signs of the Times, The—Matt 16:3

67. On Divine Providence—Luke 12:7

68. Wisdom of God's Counsels, The—Rom 11:33

69. Imperfection of Human Knowledge—1 Cor 13:9

70. Case of Reason Impartially Considered, The—1 Cor 14:20

71. Of Good Angels—Heb 1:14

72. Of Evil Angels—Eph 6:12

73. Of Hell—Mark 9:48

74. Of the Church—Eph 4:1–6

75. On Schism—1 Cor 12:5

76. On Perfection—Heb 6:1

77. Spiritual Worship—1 John 5:20

78. Spiritual Idolatry—1 John 5:21

79. On Dissipation—1 Cor 7:35

80. On Friendship with the World—Jas 4:4

81. In What Sense We Are to Leave the World—2 Cor 6:17–18

82. On Temptation—1 Cor 10:13

83. On Patience—Jas 1:4

84. Important Question, The—Matt 16:26

85. On Working out Own Salvation—Phil 2:12–13

86. Call to Backsliders, A—Ps 77:7–8

87. Danger of Riches, The—1 Tim 6:9

88. On Dress—1 Pet 3:3–4

89. More Excellent Way, The—1 Cor 12:31

90. Israelite Indeed, An—John 1:47

91. On Charity—1 Cor 13:1–3

92. On Zeal—Gal 4:18

93. On Redeeming the Time—Eph 5:16

94. On Family Religion—Josh 24:15

95. On the Education of Children—Prov 22:6

96. On Obedience to Parents—Col 3:20

97. On Obedience to Pastors—Heb 13:17

98. On Visiting the Sick—Matt 25:36

99. Reward of Righteousness, The—Matt 25:34

100. On Pleasing all Men—Rom 15:2

101. Duty of Constant Communion, The—Luke 22:19

102. Of Former Times—Ecc 7:10

103. What is Man?—Ps 8:3–4

104. On Attending the Church Service—1 Sam 2:17

105. On Conscience—2 Cor 1:12

106. On Faith—Heb 11:6

107. On God's Vineyard—Isa 5:4

108. On Riches—Matt 19:24

109. What is Man?—Ps 8:4

110. On the Discoveries of Faith—Heb 11:1

111. On the Omnipresence of God—Jer 23:24

112. Rich Man and Lazarus, The—Luke 16:31

113. Walking by Sight, and Walking by Faith—2 Cor 5:7

114. Unity of the Divine Being, The—Mark 12:32

115. Ministerial Office, The—Heb 5:4

116. Causes of the Inefficiency of Christianity—Jer 8:22

117. On Knowing Christ after the Flesh—2 Cor 5:16

118. On the Single Eye—Matt 6:22–23

119. On Worldly Folly—Luke 22:20

120. On the Wedding Garment—Matt 22:12

121. Human Life a Dream—Ps 73:20

122. On Faith—Heb 11:1

123. On the Deceitfulness of the Human Heart—Jer 17:9

124. Heavenly Treasure in Earthen Vessels, The—2 Cor 9:7

125. On Living without God—Eph 2:12

126. On the Danger of Increasing Riches—Ps 62:10

127. Trouble and Rest of Good Men, The—Job 3:17

128. Free Grace—Rom 8:32

129. Cause and Cure of Earthquakes, The—Ps 46:8

130. National Sins and Miseries—2 Sam 24:17

131. Some Account of the Late Work of God....—Ezek 1:16

132. On Laying the Foundation of the New Chapel—Num 23:23

133. On the Death of Rev. Mr. John Fletcher—Ps 37:37

134. True Christianity Defended—Isa 1:21

135. On Mourning the Dead—2 Sam 12:23

136. On Corrupting the Word of God—2 Cor 2:17

137. On the Resurrection of the Dead—1 Cor 15:35

138. On Grieving the Holy Spirit—Eph 4:30

139. On Love—1 Cor 13:3

140. On Public Diversions—Amos 3:6

141. On the Holy Spirit—2 Cor 3:17

Preface

First Series

Consisting of Fifty-Three Discourses
[Sermons 1–53]

1. The following Sermons contain the substance of what I have been preaching for between eight and nine years last past. [In the year 1747.] During that time I have frequently spoken in public, on every subject in the ensuing collection; and I am not conscious, that there is any one point of doctrine, on which I am accustomed to speak in public, which is not here, incidentally, if not professedly, laid before every Christian reader. Every serious man who peruses these, will therefore see, in the clearest manner, what these doctrines are which I embrace and teach as the essentials of true religion.

2. But I am throughly sensible, these are not proposed in such a manner as some may expect. Nothing here appears in an elaborate, elegant, or oratorical dress. If it had been my desire or design to write thus, my leisure would not permit. But, in truth, I, at present, designed nothing less; for I now write, as I generally speak, *ad populum*,—to the bulk of mankind, to those who neither relish nor understand the art of speaking; but who, notwithstanding, are competent judges of those truths which are necessary to present and future happiness. I mention this, that curious readers may spare themselves the labour of seeking for what they will not find.

3. I design plain truth for plain people: Therefore, of set purpose, I abstain from all nice and philosophical speculations; from all perplexed and intricate reasonings; and, as far as possible, from even the show of learning, unless in sometimes citing the original Scripture. I labour to avoid all words which are not easy to be understood, all which are not used in common life; and, in particular, those kinds of technical terms that so frequently occur in Bodies of Divinity; those modes of speaking which men of reading are intimately acquainted with, but which to common people are an unknown tongue. Yet I am not assured, that I do not sometimes slide into them unawares: It is so extremely natural to imagine, that a word which is familiar to ourselves is so to all the world.

4. Nay, my design is, in some sense, to forget all that ever I have read in my life. I mean to speak, in the general, as if I had never read one author, ancient or modern (always excepting the inspired). I am persuaded, that, on the one hand, this may be a means of enabling me more clearly to express the sentiments of my heart, while I simply follow the chain of my own thoughts, without entangling myself with those of other men; and that, on the other, I shall come with fewer weights upon my mind, with less of prejudice and prepossession, either to search for myself, or to deliver to others, the naked truths of the gospel.

5. To candid, reasonable men, I am not afraid to lay open what have been the inmost thoughts of my heart. I have thought, I am a creature of a day, passing through life as an arrow through the air. I am a spirit come from God, and returning to God: Just hovering over the great gulf; till, a few moments hence, I am no more seen; I drop into an unchangeable eternity! I want to know one thing,—the way to heaven; how to land safe on that happy shore. God himself has condescended to teach the way: For this very end he came from heaven. He hath written it down in a book. O give me that book! At any price, give me the book of God! I have it: Here is knowledge enough for me. Let me be *homo unius libri.* [A man of one book.] Here then I am, far from the busy ways of men. I sit down alone: Only God is here. In his presence I open, I read his book; for this end, to find the way to heaven. Is there a doubt concerning the meaning of what I read? Does anything appear dark or intricate? I lift up my heart to the Father of Lights:—"Lord, is it not thy word, 'If any man lack wisdom, let him ask of God?' Thou 'givest liberally, and upbraidest not.' Thou hast said, 'If any be willing to do thy will, he shall know.' I am willing to do, let me know, thy will." I then search after and consider parallel passages of Scripture, "comparing spiritual things with spiritual." I meditate thereon with all the attention and earnestness of which my mind is capable. If any doubt still remains, I consult those who are experienced in the things of God; and then the writings whereby, being dead, they yet speak. And what I thus learn, that I teach.

6. I have accordingly set down in the following sermons what I find in the Bible concerning the way to heaven; with a view to distinguish this way of God from all those which are the inventions of men. I have endeavoured to describe the true, the scriptural, experimental religion, so as to omit nothing which is a real part thereof, and to add nothing thereto which is not. And herein it is more especially my desire, First, to guard those who are just setting their faces toward heaven, (and who, having little acquaintance with the things of God, are the more liable to be turned out of the way,) from formality, from mere outside religion, which has almost driven heart-religion out of the world; and, Secondly, to warn those who know the religion of the heart, the faith which worketh by love, lest at any time they make void the law through faith, and so fall back into the snare of the devil.

7. By the advice and at the request of some of my friends, I have prefixed to the other sermons contained in this volume, three sermons of my own, and one of my Brother's, preached before the University of Oxford. My design required some discourses on those heads; and I preferred these before any others, as being a stronger answer than any which can be drawn up now, to those who have frequently asserted that we have changed our doctrine of late, and do not preach now what we did some years ago. Any man of understanding may now judge for himself, when he has compared the latter with the former sermons.

8. But some may say, I have mistaken the way myself, although I take upon me to teach it to others. It is probable many will think this, and it is very possible that I have. But I trust, whereinsoever I have mistaken, my mind is open to conviction. I sincerely desire to be better informed. I say to God and man, "What I know not, teach thou me!"

9. Are you persuaded you see more clearly than me? It is not unlikely that you may. Then treat me as you would desire to

be treated yourself upon a change of circumstances. Point me out a better way than I have yet known. Show me it is so, by plain proof of Scripture. And if I linger in the path I have been accustomed to tread, and am therefore unwilling to leave it, labour with me a little; take me by the hand, and lead me as I am able to bear. But be not displeased if I entreat you not to beat me down in order to quicken my pace: I can go but feebly and slowly at best; then, I should not be able to go at all. May I not request of you, further, not to give me hard names in order to bring me into the right way. Suppose I were ever so much in the wrong, I doubt this would not set me right. Rather, it would make me run so much the farther from you, and so get more and more out of the way.

10. Nay, perhaps, if you are angry, so shall I be too; and then there will be small hopes of finding the truth. If once anger arise, *Eute kapnos*, (as Homer somewhere expresses it,) this smoke will so dim the eyes of my soul, that I shall be able to see nothing clearly. For God's sake, if it be possible to avoid it, let us not provoke one another to wrath. Let us not kindle in each other this fire of hell; much less blow it up into a flame. If we could discern truth by that dreadful light, would it not be loss, rather than gain? For, how far is love, even with many wrong opinions, to be preferred before truth itself without love! We may die without the knowledge of many truths, and yet be carried into Abraham's bosom. But, if we die without love, what will knowledge avail? Just as much as it avails the devil and his angels!

The God of love forbid we should ever make the trial! May he prepare us for the knowledge of all truth, by filling our hearts with his love, and with all joy and peace in believing!

SECOND SERIES

Consisting of Fifty-Five Discourses, [Sermons 54–108]*

1. A gentleman in the west of England informed me a few days ago, that a Clergyman in his neighbourhood designed to print, in two or three volumes, the Sermons which had been published in the ten volumes of the Arminian Magazine. I had been frequently solicited to do this myself, and had as often answered, "I leave this for my executors." But if it must be done before I go hence, methinks I am the properest person to do it.

2. I intend, therefore, to set about it without delay: And if it pleases God to continue to me a little longer the use of my understanding and memory, I know not that I can employ them better. And perhaps I may be better able than another to revise my own writings; in order either to retrench what is redundant, to supply what is wanting, or to make any farther alterations which shall appear needful.

3. To make these plain Discourses more useful, I purpose now to range them in proper order; placing those first which are intended to throw light on some important Christian doctrines; and afterwards those which more directly relate to some branch of Christian practice: And I shall endeavour to place them all in such an order that one may illustrate and confirm the other. There may be the greater need of this, because they were occasionally written, during a course of years, without any order or connexion at all; just as this or the other subject either occurred to my own mind, or was suggested to me at various times by one or another friend.

4. To complete the number of twelve Sermons in every volume, I have added six Sermons to those printed in the Magazines; and I did this the rather, because the subjects were important, and cannot be too much insisted on.

5. Is there need to apologize to sensible persons for the plainness of my style? A gentleman, whom I much love and respect, lately informed me, with much tenderness and courtesy, that men of candour made great allowance for the decay of my faculties; and did not expect me to write now, either with regard to sentiment or language, as I did thirty or forty years ago. Perhaps they are decayed; though I am not conscious of it. But is not this a fit occasion to explain myself concerning the style I use from choice, not necessity? I could even now write as floridly and rhetorically as ever the admired Dr. B—; but I dare not; because I seek the honour that cometh of God only. What is the praise of man to *me*, that have one foot in the grave, and am stepping into the land whence I shall not return? Therefore, I dare no more write in a *fine style* than wear a fine coat. But were it otherwise, had I time to spare, I should still write just as I do. I should purposely decline, what many admire, an highly ornamental style. I cannot admire French oratory: I despise it from my heart. Let those that please be in raptures at the pretty, elegant sentences of Massillon or Bourdabue; but give me the plain, nervous style of Dr. South, Dr. Bates, or Mr. John Howe: And for elegance, show me any French writer who exceeds Dean Young, or Mr. Seed. Let who will admire the French frippery, I am still for plain, sound English.

6. I think a preacher or a writer of Sermons has lost his way when he imitates any of the French orators; even the most famous of them; even Massillon, or Bourdabue. Only let his language be plain, proper, and clear, and it is enough. God himself has told us how to speak, both as to the matter and the manner: "If any man speak," in the name of God, "let him speak as the oracles of God;" and if he would imitate any part of these above the rest, let it be the First Epistle of St. John. This is the style, the most excellent style, for every gospel preacher. And let him aim at no more ornament than he finds in that sentence, which is the sum of the whole gospel, "We love Him, because He first loved us."

London,
January 1, 1788.

THIRD SERIES

[Sermons 109–126]*

---

* Most of which were first inserted in the Arminian magazine, and afterwards revised, and published in four volumes, Duodecimo, in the year 1788.

* Consisting of eighteen discourses, which were written for insertion in the Arminian magazine, but which were never revised by Mr. Wesley after their publication.

12

FOURTH SERIES*

[Sermons 127–133]

FIFTH SERIES*

[Sermons 134–141]

[Most of these Discourses, it will be observed, were written before Mr. Wesley obtained correct views of the way of salvation; and as they were not published either with his knowledge or by his appointment, he should not be made responsible for the sentiments which they contain. That on the resurrection of the body was only revised and abridged by him; and it is probable that some others of them were not his composition.

The first Sermon of the series, however, entitled, "True Christianity Defended," is every way worthy of its author. It seems to have been intended as a kind of *Concio ad Clerum*; and contains a faithful exposure of that departure from the pure doctrines of Protestantism which then prevailed in the Church of England, and of that laxity of discipline and of morals which was so awfully manifest in the University of Oxford, as well as in general society. To deliver such a sermon before that learned body must have required no small degree of pious resolution; and is a striking display of that spirit of sacrifice by which Mr. Wesley was actuated.—Edit.]

FIRST SERIES

1. SALVATION BY FAITH*

"By grace are ye saved through faith."

Eph. 2:8.

1. All the blessings which God hath bestowed upon man are of his mere grace, bounty, or favour; his free, undeserved favour; favour altogether undeserved; man having no claim to the least of his mercies. It was free grace that "formed man of the dust of the ground, and breathed into him a living soul," and stamped on that soul the image of God, and "put all things under his feet." The same free grace continues to us, at this day, life, and breath, and all things. For there is nothing we are, or have, or do, which can deserve the least thing at God's hand. "All our works, Thou, O God, hast wrought in us." These, therefore, are so many more instances of free mercy: and whatever righteousness may be found in man, this is also the gift of God.

2. Wherewithal then shall a sinful man atone for any the least of his sins? With his own works? No. Were they ever so many or holy, they are not his own, but God's. But indeed they are all unholy and sinful themselves, so that every one of them needs a fresh atonement. Only corrupt fruit grows on a corrupt tree. And his heart is altogether corrupt and abominable; being "come short of the glory of God," the glorious righteousness at first impressed on his soul, after the image of his great Creator. Therefore, having nothing, neither righteousness nor works, to plead, his mouth is utterly stopped before God.

3. If then sinful men find favour with God, it is "grace upon grace!" If God vouchsafe still to pour fresh blessings upon us, yea, the greatest of all blessings, salvation; what can we say to these things, but, "Thanks be unto God for his unspeakable gift!" And thus it is herein "God commendeth his love toward us, in that, while we were yet sinners, Christ died" to save us "By grace" then "are ye saved through faith." Grace is the source, faith the condition, of salvation.

Now, that we fall not short of the grace of God, it concerns us carefully to inquire,—

I.   What faith it is through which we are saved.
II.   What is the salvation which is through faith.
III.   How we may answer some objections.

I. What faith it is through which we are saved.

1. And, first, it is not barely the faith of a heathen. Now, God requireth of a heathen to believe, "that God is; that he is a rewarder of them that diligently seek him;" and that he is to be sought by glorifying him as God, by giving him thanks for all things, and by a careful practice of moral virtue, of justice, mercy, and truth, toward their fellow creatures. A Greek or Roman, therefore, yea, a Scythian or Indian, was without excuse if he did not believe thus much: the being and attributes of God, a future state of reward and punishment, and the obligatory nature of moral virtue. For this is barely the faith of a heathen.

2. Nor, secondly, is it the faith of a devil, though this goes much farther than that of a heathen. For the devil believes, not only that there is a wise and powerful God, gracious to reward, and just to punish; but also, that Jesus is the Son of God, the Christ, the Saviour of the world. So we find him declaring, in express terms, "I know Thee who Thou art; the Holy One of God" (Luke 4:34). Nor can we doubt but that unhappy spirit believes all those words which came out of the mouth of the Holy One, yea, and whatsoever else was written by those holy men of old, of two of whom he was compelled to give that glorious testimony, "These men are the servants of the most high God, who show unto you the way of salvation." Thus much, then, the great enemy of God and man believes, and trembles in believing,—that God was made manifest in the flesh; that he will "tread all enemies under his feet;" and that "all Scripture was given by inspiration of God." Thus far goeth the faith of a devil.

3. Thirdly. The faith through which we are saved, in that sense of the word which will hereafter be explained, is not barely that which the Apostles themselves had while Christ was yet upon earth; though they so believed on him as to

---

* Consisting of seven discourses which were published by Mr. Wesley only in a separate form, and were never, by him, embodied in any collection of his sermons.

* Consisting of eight discourses which were published from Mr. Wesley's manuscripts after his death, but never designed by him for publication.

* Preached at St. Mary's, Oxford, before the University, on June 18, 1738.

"leave all and follow him;" although they had then power to work miracles, to "heal all manner of sickness, and all manner of disease;" yea, they had then "power and authority over all devils;" and, which is beyond all this, were sent by their Master to "preach the kingdom of God."

4. What faith is it then through which we are saved? It may be answered, first, in general, it is a faith in Christ: Christ, and God through Christ, are the proper objects of it. herein, therefore, it is sufficiently, absolutely distinguished from the faith either of ancient or modern heathens. And from the faith of a devil it is fully distinguished by this: it is not barely a speculative, rational thing, a cold, lifeless assent, a train of ideas in the head; but also a disposition of the heart. For thus saith the Scripture, "With the heart man believeth unto righteousness;" and, "If thou shalt confess with thy mouth the Lord Jesus, and shalt believe in thy heart that God hath raised him from the dead, thou shalt be saved."

5. And herein does it differ from that faith which the Apostles themselves had while our Lord was on earth, that it acknowledges the necessity and merit of his death, and the power of his resurrection. It acknowledges his death as the only sufficient means of redeeming man from death eternal, and his resurrection as the restoration of us all to life and immortality; inasmuch as he "was delivered for our sins, and rose again for our justification." Christian faith is then, not only an assent to the whole gospel of Christ, but also a full reliance on the blood of Christ; a trust in the merits of his life, death, and resurrection; a recumbency upon him as our atonement and our life, as given for us, and living in us; and, in consequence hereof, a closing with him, and cleaving to him, as our "wisdom, righteousness, sanctification, and redemption," or, in one word, our salvation.

II. What salvation it is, which is through this faith, is the Second thing to be considered.

1. And, First, whatsoever else it imply, it is a present salvation. It is something attainable, yea, actually attained, on earth, by those who are partakers of this faith. For thus saith the Apostle to the believers at Ephesus, and in them to the believers of all ages, not, *Ye shall be* (though that also is true), but, "*Ye are saved through faith.*"

2. *Ye are saved* (to comprise all in one word) from sin. This is the salvation which is through faith. This is that great salvation foretold by the angel, before God brought his First-begotten into the world: "Thou shalt call his name Jesus; for he shall save his people from their sins." And neither here, nor in other parts of holy writ, is there any limitation or restriction. All his people, or, as it is elsewhere expressed, "all that believe in him," he will save from all their sins; from original and actual, past and present sin, "of the flesh and of the spirit." Through faith that is in him, they are saved both from the guilt and from the power of it.

3. First. From the guilt of all past sin: for, whereas all the world is guilty before God, insomuch that should he "be extreme to mark what is done amiss, there is none that could abide it;" and whereas, "by the law is" only "the knowledge of sin," but no deliverance from it, so that, "by" fulfilling "the deeds of the law, no flesh can be justified in his sight": now, "the righteousness of God, which is by faith of Jesus Christ,

is manifested unto all that believe." Now, "they are justified freely by his grace, through the redemption that is in Jesus Christ." "Him God hath set forth to be a propitiation through faith in his blood, to declare his righteousness for (or by) the remission of the sins that are past." Now hath Christ taken away "the curse of the law, being made a curse for us." he hath "blotted out the handwriting that was against us, taking it out of the way, nailing it to his cross." "There is therefore no condemnation now to them which" believe "in Christ Jesus."

4. And being saved from guilt, they are saved from fear. Not indeed from a filial fear of offending; but from all servile fear; from that fear which hath torment; from fear of punishment; from fear of the wrath of God, whom they now no longer regard as a severe Master, but as an indulgent Father. "They have not received again the spirit of bondage, but the Spirit of adoption, whereby they cry, Abba, Father: the Spirit itself also bearing witness with their spirits, that they are the children of God." They are also saved from the fear, though not from the possibility, of falling away from the grace of God, and coming short of the great and precious promises. Thus have they "peace with God through our Lord Jesus Christ. They rejoice in hope of the glory of God. And the love of God is shed abroad in their hearts, through the Holy Ghost, which is given unto them." And hereby they are persuaded (though perhaps not at all times, nor with the same fullness of persuasion), that "neither death, nor life, nor things present, nor things to come, nor height, nor depth, nor any other creature, shall be able to separate them from the love of God, which is in Christ Jesus our Lord."

5. Again: through this faith they are saved from the power of sin, as well as from the guilt of it. So the Apostle declares, "Ye know that he was manifested to take away our sins; and in him is no sin. Whosoever abideth in him sinneth not" (1 John 3:5ff.). Again, "Little children, let no man deceive you. he that committeth sin is of the devil. Whosoever believeth is born of God. And whosoever is born of God doth not commit sin; for his seed remaineth in him: and he cannot sin, because he is born of God." Once more: "We know that whosoever is born of God sinneth not; but he that is begotten of God keepeth himself, and that wicked one toucheth him not" (1 John 5:18).

6. he that is, by faith, born of God sinneth not (1.) by any habitual sin; for all habitual sin is sin reigning: But sin cannot reign in any that believeth. Nor (2.) by any wilful sin: for his will, while he abideth in the faith, is utterly set against all sin, and abhorreth it as deadly poison. Nor (3.) By any sinful desire; for he continually desireth the holy and perfect will of God. and any tendency to an unholy desire, he by the grace of God, stifleth in the birth. Nor (4.) Doth he sin by infirmities, whether in act, word, or thought; for his infirmities have no concurrence of his will; and without this they are not properly sins. Thus, "he that is born of God doth not commit sin": and though he cannot say he hath not sinned, yet now "he sinneth not."

7. This then is the salvation which is through faith, even in the present world: a salvation from sin, and the consequences of sin, both often expressed in the word *justification*; which,

taken in the largest sense, implies a deliverance from guilt and punishment, by the atonement of Christ actually applied to the soul of the sinner now believing on him, and a deliverance from the power of sin, through Christ *formed in his heart.* So that he who is thus justified, or saved by faith, is indeed *born again.* he is *born again of the Spirit* unto a new life, which "is hid with Christ in God." And as a new-born babe he gladly receives the *adolon,* "*sincere* milk of the word, and grows thereby;" going on in the might of the Lord his God, from faith to faith, from grace to grace, until at length, he come unto "a perfect man, unto the measure of the stature of the fullness of Christ."

III. The first usual objection to this is,

1. That to preach salvation or justification, by faith only, is to preach against holiness and good works. To which a short answer might be given: "It would be so, if we spake, as some do, of a faith which was separate from these; but we speak of a faith which is not so, but productive of all good works, and all holiness."

2. But it may be of use to consider it more at large; especially since it is no new objection, but as old as St. Paul's time. For even then it was asked, "Do we not make void the law through faith?" We answer, First, all who preach not faith do manifestly make void the law; either directly and grossly, by limitations and comments that eat out all the spirit of the text; or indirectly, by not pointing out the only means whereby it is possible to perform it. Whereas, Secondly, "we establish the law," both by showing its full extent and spiritual meaning; and by calling all to that living way, whereby "the righteousness of the law may be fulfilled in them." These, while they trust in the blood of Christ alone, use all the ordinances which he hath appointed, do all the "good works which he had before prepared that they should walk therein," and enjoy and manifest all holy and heavenly tempers, even the same mind that was in Christ Jesus.

3. But does not preaching this faith lead men into pride? We answer, Accidentally it may: therefore ought every believer to be earnestly cautioned, in the words of the great Apostle "Because of unbelief," the first branches "were broken off: and thou standest by faith. Be not high-minded, but fear. If God spared not the natural branches, take heed lest he spare not thee. Behold therefore the goodness and severity of God! On them which fell, severity; but towards thee, goodness, if thou continue in his goodness; otherwise thou also shalt be cut off." And while he continues therein, he will remember those words of St. Paul, foreseeing and answering this very objection (Rom. 3:27), "Where is boasting then? It is excluded. By what law? of works? Nay: but by the law of faith." If a man were justified by his works, he would have whereof to glory. But there is no glorying for him "that worketh not, but believeth on him that justifieth the ungodly" (Rom. 4:5). To the same effect are the words both preceding and following the text (Eph. 2:4ff.): "God, who is rich in mercy, even when we were dead in sins, hath quickened us together with Christ (by grace ye are saved), that he might show the exceeding riches of his grace in his kindness toward us through Christ Jesus. For by grace are ye saved through faith; and that not of yourselves." Of yourselves cometh neither your faith nor your salvation: "it is the gift of God;" the free, undeserved gift; the faith through which ye are saved, as well as the salvation which he of his own good pleasure, his mere favour, annexes thereto. That ye believe, is one instance of his grace; that believing ye are saved, another. "Not of works, lest any man should boast." For all our works, all our righteousness, which were before our believing, merited nothing of God but condemnation; so far were they from deserving faith, which therefore, whenever given, is not of works. Neither is salvation of the works we do when we believe, for it is then God that worketh in us: and, therefore, that he giveth us a reward for what he himself worketh, only commendeth the riches of his mercy, but leaveth us nothing whereof to glory.

4. "However, may not the speaking thus of the mercy of God, as saving or justifying freely by faith only, encourage men in sin?" Indeed, it may and will: Many will "continue in sin that grace may abound:" But their blood is upon their own head. The goodness of God ought to lead them to repentance; and so it will those who are sincere of heart. When they know there is yet forgiveness with him, they will cry aloud that he would blot out their sins also, through faith which is in Jesus. And if they earnestly cry, and faint not, it they seek him in all the means he hath appointed; if they refuse to be comforted till he come; "he will come, and will not tarry." And he can do much work in a short time. Many are the examples, in the Acts of the Apostles, of God's working this faith in men's hearts, even like lightning falling from heaven. So in the same hour that Paul and Silas began to preach, the jailer repented, believed, and was baptized; as were three thousand, by St. Peter, on the day of Pentecost, who all repented and believed at his first preaching And, blessed be God, there are now many living proofs that he is still "mighty to save."

5. Yet to the same truth, placed in another view, a quite contrary objection is made: "If a man cannot be saved by all that he can do, this will drive men to despair." True, to despair of being saved by their own works, their own merits, or righteousness. And so it ought; for none can trust in the merits of Christ, till he has utterly renounced his own. he that "goeth about to stablish his own righteousness" cannot receive the righteousness of God. The righteousness which is of faith cannot be given him while he trusteth in that which is of the law.

6. But this, it is said, is an uncomfortable doctrine. The devil spoke like himself, that is, without either truth or shame, when he dared to suggest to men that it is such. It is the only comfortable one, it is "very full of comfort," to all self-destroyed, self-condemned sinners. That "whosoever believeth on him shall not be ashamed that the same Lord over all is rich unto all that call upon him": here is comfort, high as heaven, stronger than death! What! Mercy for all? For Zacchaeus, a public robber? For Mary Magdalene, a common harlot? Methinks I hear one say "Then I, even I, may hope for mercy!" And so thou mayest, thou afflicted one, whom none hath comforted! God will not cast out thy prayer. Nay, perhaps he may say the next hour, "Be of good cheer, thy sins are forgiven thee;" so forgiven, that they shall reign over thee

no more; yea, and that "the Holy Spirit shall bear witness with thy spirit that thou art a child of God." O glad tidings! tidings of great joy, which are sent unto all people! "Ho, every one that thirsteth, come ye to the waters: Come ye, and buy, without money and without price." Whatsoever your sins be, "though red like crimson," though more than the hairs of your head, "return ye unto the Lord, and he will have mercy upon you, and to our God, for he will abundantly pardon."

7. When no more objections occur, then we are simply told that salvation by faith only ought not to be preached as the first doctrine, or, at least, not to be preached at all. But what saith the Holy Ghost? "Other foundation can no man lay than that which is laid, even Jesus Christ." So then, that "whosoever believeth on him shall be saved," is, and must be, the foundation of all our preaching; that is, must be preached first. "Well, but not to all." To whom, then are we not to preach it? Whom shall we except? The poor? Nay; they have a peculiar right to have the gospel preached unto them. The unlearned? No. God hath revealed these things unto unlearned and ignorant men from the beginning. The young? By no means. "Suffer these," in any wise, "to come unto Christ, and forbid them not." The sinners? Least of all. "He came not to call the righteous, but sinners to repentance." Why then, if any, we are to except the rich, the learned, the reputable, the moral men. And, it is true, they too often except themselves from hearing; yet we must speak the words of our Lord. For thus the tenor of our commission runs, "Go and preach the gospel to every creature." If any man wrest it, or any part of it, to his destruction, he must bear his own burden. But still, "as the Lord liveth, whatsoever the Lord saith unto us, that we will speak."

8. At this time, more especially, will we speak, that "by grace are ye saved through faith": because, never was the maintaining this doctrine more seasonable than it is at this day. Nothing but this can effectually prevent the increase of the Romish delusion among us. It is endless to attack, one by one, all the errors of that Church. But salvation by faith strikes at the root, and all fall at once where this is established. It was this doctrine, which our Church justly calls *the strong rock and foundation of the Christian religion*, that first drove Popery out of these kingdoms; and it is this alone can keep it out. Nothing but this can give a check to that immorality which hath "overspread the land as a flood." Can you empty the great deep, drop by drop? Then you may reform us by dissuasives from particular vices. But let the "righteousness which is of God by faith be brought in, and so shall its proud waves be stayed. Nothing but this can stop the mouths of those who "glory in their shame, and openly deny the Lord that bought them." They can talk as sublimely of the law, as he that hath it written by God in his heart To hear them speak on this head might incline one to think they were not far from the kingdom of God: but take them out of the law into the gospel; begin with the righteousness of faith; with Christ, "the end of the law to every one that believeth;" and those who but now appeared almost, if not altogether, Christians, stand confessed the sons of perdition; as far from

life and salvation (God be merciful unto them!) as the depth of hell from the height of heaven.

9. For this reason the adversary so rages whenever "salvation by faith" is declared to the world: for this reason did he stir up earth and hell, to destroy those who first preached it. And for the same reason, knowing that faith alone could overturn the foundations of his kingdom, did he call forth all his forces, and employ all his arts of lies and calumny, to affright Martin Luther from reviving it. Nor can we wonder thereat; for, as that man of God observes, "How would it enrage a proud, strong man armed, to be stopped and set at nought by a little child coming against him with a reed in his hand!" especially when he knew that little child would surely overthrow him, and tread him under foot. Even so, Lord Jesus! Thus hath Thy strength been ever "made perfect in weakness!" Go forth then, thou little child that believest in him, and his "right hand shall teach thee terrible things!" Though thou art helpless and weak as an infant of days, the strong man shall not be able to stand before thee. Thou shalt prevail over him, and subdue him, and overthrow him and trample him under thy feet. Thou shalt march on, under the great Captain of thy salvation, "conquering and to conquer," until all thine enemies are destroyed, and "death is swallowed up in victory."

Now, thanks be to God, which giveth us the victory through our Lord Jesus Christ; to whom, with the Father and the Holy Ghost, be blessing, and glory, and wisdom, and thanksgiving, and honour, and power, and might, for ever and ever. Amen

2* THE ALMOST CHRISTIAN*

"Almost thou persuadest me to be a Christian."

Acts 26:28.

AND many there are who go thus far: ever since the Christian religion was in the world, there have been many in every age and nation who were almost persuaded to be Christians. But seeing it avails nothing before God to go *only thus far*, it highly imports us to consider,

First. What is implied in being *almost*,

Secondly. What in being *altogether, a Christian*.

I. (I.) 1. Now, in the being *almost a Christian* is implied, First, heathen honesty. No one, I suppose, will make any question of this; especially, since by heathen honesty here, I mean, not that which is recommended in the writings of their philosophers only, but such as the common heathens expected one of another, and many of them actually practised. By the rules of this they were taught that they ought not to be unjust; not to take away their neighbour's goods, either by robbery or theft; not to oppress the poor, neither to use extortion toward any; not to cheat or overreach either the poor or rich, in whatsoever commerce they had with them; to defraud no man of his right; and, if it were possible, to owe no man anything.

2. Again: the common heathens allowed, that some regard was to be paid to truth, as well as to justice. And, accordingly,

---

they not only held him in abomination who was forsworn, who called God to witness to a lie; but him also who was known to be a slanderer of his neighbour, who falsely accused any man. And indeed, little better did they esteem wilful liars of any sort, accounting them the disgrace of human kind, and the pests of society.

3. Yet again: there was a sort of love and assistance which they expected one from another. They expected whatever assistance any one could give another, without prejudice to himself. And this they extended not only to those little offices of humanity which are performed without any expense or labour, but likewise to the feeding the hungry, if they had food to spare; the clothing the naked with their own superfluous raiment; and, in general the giving, to any that needed, such things as they needed not themselves. Thus far, in the lowest account of it, heathen honesty went; the first thing implied in the being *almost a Christian.*

(II.) 4. A second thing implied in the being *almost a Christian*, is, the having a form of godliness; of that godliness which is prescribed in the gospel of Christ; the having the *outside of a real Christian.* Accordingly, the almost Christian does nothing which the gospel forbids he taketh not the name of God in vain; he blesseth, and curseth not; he sweareth not at all, but his communication is, yea, yea; nay, nay he profanes not the day of the Lord, nor suffers it to be profaned, even by the stranger that is within his gates he not only avoids all actual adultery, fornication, and uncleanness, but every word or look that either directly or indirectly tends thereto; nay, and all idle words, abstaining both from detraction, backbiting, talebearing, evil speaking, and from "all foolish talking and jesting"—*eutrapelia*, a kind of virtue in the heathen moralist's account;—briefly, from all conversation that is not "good to the use of edifying," and that, consequently, "grieves the Holy Spirit of God, whereby we are sealed to the day of redemption."

5. He abstains from "wine wherein is excess"; from revellings and gluttony. He avoids, as much as in him lies, all strife and contention, continually endeavouring to live peaceably with all men. And, if he suffer wrong, he avengeth not himself, neither returns evil for evil he is no railer, no brawler, no scoffer, either at the faults or infirmities of his neighbour. he does not willingly wrong, hurt, or grieve any man; but in all things act and speaks by that plain rule, "Whatsoever thou wouldest not he should do unto thee, that do not thou to another."

6. And in doing good, he does not confine himself to cheap and easy offices of kindness, but labours and suffers for the profit of many, that by all means he may help some. In spite of toil or pain, "whatsoever his hand findeth to do, he doeth it with his might;" whether it be for his friends, or for his enemies; for the evil, or for the good. For being "not slothful" in this, or in any "business," as he "hath opportunity" he doeth "good," all manner of good, "to all men;" and to their souls as well as their bodies. he reproves the wicked, instructs the ignorant, confirms the wavering, quickens the good, and comforts the afflicted. he labours to awaken those that sleep; to lead those whom God hath already awakened to the "Fountain opened for sin and for uncleanness," that they may wash therein and be clean; and to stir up those who are saved through faith, to adorn the gospel of Christ in all things.

7. he that hath the form of godliness uses also the means of grace; yea, all of them, and at all opportunities. he constantly frequents the house of God; and that, not as the manner of some is, who come into the presence of the Most High, either loaded with gold and costly apparel, or in all the gaudy vanity of dress, and either by their unseasonable civilities to each other, or the impertinent gaiety of their behaviour, disclaim all pretensions to the form as well as to the power of godliness. Would to God there were none even among ourselves who fall under the same condemnation! who come into this house, it may be, gazing about, or with all the signs of the most listless, careless indifference, though sometimes they may *seem* to use a prayer to God for his blessing on what they are entering upon; who, during that awful service, are either asleep, or reclined in the most convenient posture for it; or, as though they supposed God was asleep, talking with one another, or looking round, as utterly void of employment. Neither let these be accused of the form of godliness. No; he who has even this, behaves with seriousness and attention, in every part of that solemn service. More especially, when he approaches the table of the Lord, it is not with a light or careless behaviour, but with an air, gesture, and deportment which speaks nothing else but "God be merciful to me a sinner!"

8. To this, if we add the constant use of family prayer, by those who are masters of families, and the setting times apart for private addresses to God, with a daily seriousness of behaviour; he who uniformly practises this outward religion, has the form of godliness. There needs but one thing more in order to his being *almost a Christian*, and that is, sincerity.

(III.) 9. By sincerity I mean, a real, inward principle of religion, from whence these outward actions flow. And, indeed if we have not this, we have not heathen honesty; no, not so much of it as will answer the demand of a heathen Epicurean poet. Even this poor wretch, in his sober intervals, is able to testify,

> Oderunt peccare boni, virtutis amore;
> Oderunt peccare mali, formidine poenae.
> [Good men avoid sin from the love of virtue;
> Wicked men avoid sin from a fear of punishment.]

So that, if a man only abstains from doing evil in order to avoid punishment, *Non pasces in cruce corvos*, [Thou shalt not be hanged.], saith the Pagan; there, "thou hast thy reward." But even he will not allow such a harmless man as this to be so much as a *good heathen.* If, then, any man, from the same motive, viz., to avoid punishment, to avoid the loss of his friends, or his gain, or his reputation, should not only abstain from doing evil, but also do ever so much good; yea, and use all the means of grace; yet we could not with any propriety say, this man is even *almost a Christian.* If he has no better principle in his heart, he is only a hypocrite altogether.

10. Sincerity, therefore, is necessarily implied in the being *almost a Christian*; a real design to serve God, a hearty desire to do his will. It is necessarily implied, that a man have a sincere view of pleasing God in all things; in all his

conversation; in all his actions; in all he does or leaves undone. This design, if any man be *almost a Christian*, runs through the whole tenor of his life. This is the moving principle, both in his doing good, his abstaining from evil, and his using the ordinances of God.

11. But here it will probably be inquired, "Is it possible that any man living should go so far as this, and, nevertheless, be *only almost a Christian*"? What more than this, can be implied in the being *a Christian altogether*? I answer, First, that it is possible to go thus far, and yet be but *almost a Christian*, I learn, not only from the oracles of God, but also from the sure testimony of experience.

12. Brethren, great is "my boldness towards you in this behalf." And "forgive me this wrong," if I declare my own folly upon the house-top, for yours and the gospel's sake.— Suffer me, then, to speak freely of myself, even as of another man. I am content to be abased, so ye may be exalted, and to be yet more vile for the glory of my Lord.

13. I did go thus far for many years, as many of this place can testify; using diligence to eschew all evil, and to have a conscience void of offence; redeeming the time; buying up every opportunity of doing all good to all men; constantly and carefully using all the public and all the private means of grace; endeavouring after a steady seriousness of behaviour, at all times, and in all places; and, God is my record, before whom I stand, doing all this in sincerity; having a real design to serve God; a hearty desire to do his will in all things; to please him who had called me to "fight the good fight," and to "lay hold of eternal life." Yet my own conscience beareth me witness in the Holy Ghost, that all this time I was but *almost a Christian*.

II. If it be inquired, "What more than this is implied in the being *altogether a Christian?*" I answer,

(I.) 1. First. The love of God. For thus saith his word, "Thou shalt love the Lord thy God with all thy heart, and with all thy soul, and with all thy mind, and with all thy strength." Such a love is this, as engrosses the whole heart, as rakes up all the affections, as fills the entire capacity of the soul and employs the utmost extent of all its faculties. he that thus loves the Lord his God, his spirit continually "rejoiceth in God his Saviour." his delight is in the Lord, his Lord and his All, to whom "in everything he giveth thanks. All his desire is unto God, and to the remembrance of his name." his heart is ever crying out, "Whom have I in heaven but Thee? and there is none upon earth that I desire beside Thee." Indeed, what can he desire beside God? Not the world, or the things of the world: for he is "crucified to the world, and the world crucified to him." he is crucified to "the desire of the flesh, the desire of the eye, and the pride of life." Yea, he is dead to pride of every kind: for "love is not puffed up" but "he that dwelling in love, dwelleth in God, and God in him," is less than nothing in his own eyes.

(II.) 2. The Second thing implied in the being *altogether a Christian* is, the love of our neighbour. For thus said our Lord in the following words, "Thou shalt love thy neighbour as thyself." If any man ask, "Who is my neighbour?" we reply, Every man in the world; every child of his who is the Father of the spirits of all flesh. Nor may we in any wise except our

enemies or the enemies of God and their own souls. But every Christian loveth these also as himself, yea, "as Christ loved us." he that would more fully understand what manner of love this is, may consider St. Paul's description of it. It is "long-suffering and kind." It "envieth not." It is not rash or hasty in judging. It "is not puffed up;" but maketh him that loves, the least, the servant of all. Love "doth not behave itself unseemly," but becometh "all things to all men." She "seeketh not her own;" but only the good of others, that they may be saved. "Love is not provoked." It casteth out wrath, which he who hath is wanting in love. "It thinketh no evil. It rejoiceth not in iniquity, but rejoiceth in the truth. It covereth all things, believeth all things, hopeth all things, endureth all things."

(III.) 3. There is yet one thing more that may be separately considered, though it cannot actually be separate from the preceding, which is implied in the being *altogether a Christian*; and that is the ground of all, even faith. Very excellent things are spoken of this throughout the oracles of God. "Every one," saith the beloved disciple, "that believeth is born of God." "To as many as received him, gave he power to become the sons of God. even to them that believe on his name." And "this is the victory that overcometh the world, even our faith." Yea, our Lord himself declares, "He that believeth in the Son hath everlasting life; and cometh not into condemnation, but is passed from death unto life."

4. But here let no man deceive his own soul. "It is diligently to be noted, the faith which bringeth not forth repentance, and love, and all good works, is not that right living faith, but a dead and devilish one. For, even the devils believe that Christ was born of a virgin: that he wrought all kinds of miracles, declaring himself very God: that, for our sakes, he suffered a most painful death, to redeem us from death everlasting; that he rose again the third day: that he ascended into heaven, and sitteth at the right hand of the Father and at the end of the world shall come again to judge both the quick and dead. These articles of our faith the devils believe, and so they believe all that is written in the Old and New Testament. And yet for all this faith, they be but devils. They remain still in their damnable estate lacking the very true Christian faith." [Homily on the Salvation of Man.]

5. "The right and true Christian faith is" (to go on the words of our own Church), "not only to believe that Holy Scripture and the Articles of our Faith are true, but also to have a sure trust and confidence to be saved from everlasting damnation by Christ. It is a sure trust and confidence which a man hath in God, that, by the merits of Christ, his sins are forgiven, and he reconciled to the favour of God; whereof doth follow a loving heart, to obey his commandments."

6. Now, whosoever has this faith, which "purifies the heart" (by the power of God, who dwelleth therein) from "pride, anger, desire, from all unrighteousness" from "all filthiness of flesh and spirit;" which fills it with love stronger than death, both to God and to all mankind; love that doeth the works of God, glorying to spend and to be spent for all men, and that endureth with joy, not only the reproach of Christ, the being mocked, despised, and hated of all men, but whatsoever the wisdom of God permits the malice of men or

devils to inflict,—whosoever has this faith thus working by love is not almost only, but altogether, a Christian.

7. But who are the living witnesses of these things? I beseech you, brethren, as in the presence of that God before whom "hell and destruction are without a covering—how much more the hearts of the children of men?"—that each of you would ask his own heart, "Am I of that number? Do I so far practise justice, mercy, and truth, as even the rules of heathen honesty require? If so, have I the very *outside* of a Christian? the form of godliness? Do I abstain from evil,—from whatsoever is forbidden in the written Word of God? Do I, whatever good my hand findeth to do, do it with my might? Do I seriously use all the ordinances of God at all opportunities? And is all this done with a sincere design and desire to please God in all things?"

8. Are not many of you conscious, that you never came thus far; that you have not been even *almost a Christian*; that you have not come up to the standard of heathen honesty; at least, not to the form of Christian godliness?—much less hath God seen sincerity in you, a real design of pleasing him in all things. You never so much as intended to devote all your words and works. your business, studies, diversions, to his glory. You never even designed or desired, that whatsoever you did should be done "in the name of the Lord Jesus," and as such should be "a spiritual sacrifice, acceptable to God through Christ."

9. But, supposing you had, do good designs and good desires make a Christian? By no means, unless they are brought to good effect. "Hell is paved," saith one, "with good intentions." The great question of all, then, still remains. Is the love of God shed abroad in your heart? Can you cry out, "My God, and my All"? Do you desire nothing but him? Are you happy in God? Is he your glory, your delight, your crown of rejoicing? And is this commandment written in your heart, "That he who loveth God love his brother also"? Do you then love your neighbour as yourself? Do you love every man, even your enemies, even the enemies of God, as your own soul? as Christ loved you? Yea, dost thou believe that Christ loved thee, and gave himself for thee? Hast thou faith in his blood? Believest thou the Lamb of God hath taken away thy sins, and cast them as a stone into the depth of the sea? that he hath blotted out the handwriting that was against thee, taking it out of the way, nailing it to his cross? Hast thou indeed redemption through his blood, even the remission of thy sins? And doth his Spirit bear witness with thy spirit, that thou art a child of God?

10. The God and Father of our Lord Jesus Christ, who now standeth in the midst of us, knoweth, that if any man die without this faith and this love, good it were for him that he had never been born. Awake, then, thou that sleepest, and call upon thy God: call in the day when he may be found. Let him not rest, till he make his "goodness to pass before thee;" till he proclaim unto thee the name of the Lord, "The Lord, the Lord God, merciful and gracious, long-suffering, and abundant in goodness and truth, keeping mercy for thousands, forgiving iniquity, and transgression, and sin."

Let no man persuade thee, by vain words, to rest short of this prize of thy high calling. But cry unto him day and night, who, "while we were without strength, died for the ungodly," until thou knowest in whom thou hast believed, and canst say, "My Lord, and my God!" Remember, "always to pray, and not to faint," till thou also canst lift up thy hand unto heaven, and declare to him that liveth for ever and ever, "Lord, Thou knowest all things, Thou knowest that I love Thee."

11. May we all thus experience what it is to be, not almost only; but altogether Christians; being justified freely by his grace, through the redemption that is in Jesus; knowing we have peace with God through Jesus Christ; rejoicing in hope of the glory of God; and having the love of God shed abroad in our hearts, by the Holy Ghost given unto us!

3* AWAKE, THOU THAT SLEEPEST*

"Awake, thou that sleepest, and arise from the dead, and Christ shall give thee light."

Eph. 5:14.

IN discoursing on these words, I shall, with the help of God,—

First. Describe the sleepers, to whom they are spoken:

Secondly. Enforce the exhortation, "Awake, thou that sleepest, and arise from the dead:" And,

Thirdly. Explain the promise made to such as do awake and arise: "Christ shall give thee light."

I. 1. And first, as to the sleepers here spoken to. By sleep is signified the natural state of man; that deep sleep of the soul, into which the sin of Adam hath cast all who spring from his loins: That supineness, indolence, and stupidity, that insensibility of his real condition, wherein every man comes Into the world, and continues till the voice of God awakes him.

2. Now, "they that sleep, sleep in the night." The state of nature is a state of utter darkness; a state wherein "darkness covers the earth, and gross darkness the people." The poor unawakened sinner, how much knowledge soever he may have as to other things, has no knowledge of himself: in this respect "he knoweth nothing yet as he ought to know." He knows not that he is a fallen spirit, whose only business in the present world, is to recover from his fall, to regain that image of God wherein he was created. he sees *no necessity* for the *one thing needful*, even that inward universal change, that "birth from above," figured out by baptism, which is the beginning of that total renovation. that sanctification of spirit, soul, and body, "without which no man shall see the Lord."

3. Full of all diseases as he is, he fancies himself in perfect health. Fast bound in misery and iron, he dreams that he is at liberty. he says, "Peace! Peace!" while the devil, as "a strong, man armed," is in full possession of his soul. he sleeps on still and takes his rest, though hell is moved from beneath to meet him; though the pit from whence there is no return hath opened its mouth to swallow him up. A fire is kindled around

---

* (text from the 1872 edition)

him, yet he knoweth it not; yea, it burns him, yet he lays it not to heart.

4. By one who sleeps, we are, therefore, to understand (and would to God we might all understand it!) a sinner satisfied in his sins; contented to remain in his fallen state, to live and die without the image of God; one who is ignorant both of his disease, and of the only remedy for it; one who never was warned, or never regarded the warning voice of God, "to flee from the wrath to come;" one that never yet saw he was in danger of hell-fire, or cried out in the earnestness of his soul, "What must I do to be saved?"

5. If this sleeper be not outwardly vicious, his sleep is usually the deepest of all: whether he be of the Laodicean spirit, "neither cold nor hot," but a quiet, rational, inoffensive, good-natured professor of the religion of his fathers; or whether he be zealous and orthodox, and, "after the most straitest sect of our religion," live "a Pharisee;" that is, according to the scriptural account, one that justifies himself; one that labours to establish his own righteousness, as the ground of his acceptance with God.

6. This is he, who, "having a form of godliness, denies the power thereof;" yea, and probably reviles it, wheresoever it is found, as mere extravagance and delusion. Meanwhile, the wretched self-deceiver thanks God, that he is "not as other men are; adulterers, unjust, extortioners": no, he doeth no wrong to any man. he "fasts twice in a week," uses all the means of grace, is constant at church and sacrament, yea, and "gives tithes of all that he has;" does all the good that he can "touching the righteousness of the law," he is "blameless": he wants nothing of godliness, but the power; nothing of religion, but the spirit; nothing of Christianity, but the truth and the life.

7. But know ye not, that, however highly esteemed among men such a Christian as this may be, he is an abomination in the sight of God, and an heir of every woe which the Son of God, yesterday, to-day, and for ever, denounces against "scribes and Pharisees, hypocrites"? he hath "made clean the outside of the cup and the platter," but within is full of all filthiness. "An evil disease cleaveth still unto him, so that his inward parts are very wickedness." Our Lord fitly compares him to a "painted sepulchre," which "appears beautiful without;" but, nevertheless, is "full of dead men's bones, and of all uncleanness." The bones indeed are no longer dry; the sinews and flesh are come upon them, and the skin covers them above: but there is no breath in them, no Spirit of the living God. And, "if any man have not the Spirit of Christ, he is none of his." "Ye are Christ's, if so be that the Spirit of God dwell in you": but, if not, God knoweth that ye abide in death, even until now.

8. This is another character of the sleeper here spoken to. he abides in death, though he knows it not. he is dead unto God, "dead in trespasses and sins." For, "to be carnally minded is death" Even as it is written, "By one man sin entered into the world, and death by sin; and so death passed upon all men;" not only temporal death, but likewise spiritual and eternal. "In that day that thou eatest," said God to Adam, "thou shalt surely die;" not bodily (unless as he then became mortal), but spiritually: thou shalt lose the life of thy soul; thou shalt die

to God: shalt be separated from him, thy essential life and happiness.

9. Thus first was dissolved the vital union of our soul with God; insomuch that "in the midst of" natural "life, we are" now in spiritual "death." And herein we remain till the Second Adam becomes a quickening Spirit to us; till he raises the dead, the dead in sin, in pleasure, riches or honours. But, before any dead soul can live, he "hears" (hearkens to) "the voice of the Son of God": he is made sensible of his lost estate, and receives the sentence of death in himself. he knows himself to be "dead while he liveth;" dead to God, and all the things of God; having no more power to perform the actions of a living Christian, than a dead body to perform the functions of a living man.

10. And most certain it is, that one dead in sin has not "senses exercised to discern spiritual good and evil." "Having eyes, he sees not; he hath ears, and hears not." he doth not "taste and see that the Lord is gracious." he "hath not seen God at any time," nor "heard his voice," nor "handled the word of life." In vain is the name of Jesus "like ointment poured forth, and all his garments smell of myrrh, aloes, and cassia." The soul that sleepeth in death hath no perception of any objects of this kind. his heart is "past feeling," and understandeth none of these things.

11. And hence, having no spiritual senses, no inlets of spiritual knowledge, the natural man receiveth not the things of the Spirit of God; nay, he is so far from receiving them, that whatsoever is spiritually discerned is mere foolishness unto him. he is not content with being utterly ignorant of spiritual things, but he denies the very existence of them. And spiritual sensation itself is to him the foolishness of folly. "How," saith he, "can these things be? How can any man *know* that he is alive to God?" Even as you know that your body is now alive. Faith is the life of the soul; and if ye have this life abiding in you, ye want no marks to evidence it *to yourself*, but *elegchos pneumatos*, that divine consciousness, that *witness* of God, which is more and greater than ten thousand human witnesses.

12. If he doth not now bear witness with thy spirit, that thou art a child of God, O that he might convince thee, thou poor unawakened sinner, by his demonstration and power, that thou art a child of the devil! O that, as I prophesy, there might now be "a noise and a shaking;" and may "the bones come together, bone to his bone!" Then "come from the four winds, O Breath! and breathe on these slain, that they may live!" And do not ye harden your hearts, and resist the Holy Ghost, who even now is come to convince you of sin, "because you believe not on the name of the only begotten Son of God."

II. 1. Wherefore, "awake, thou that sleepest, and arise from the dead." God calleth thee now by my mouth; and bids thee know thyself, thou fallen spirit, thy true state and only concern below. "What meanest thou, O sleeper? Arise! Call upon thy God, if so be thy God will think upon thee, that thou perish not." A mighty tempest is stirred up round about thee, and thou art sinking into the depths of perdition, the gulf of God's judgements. If thou wouldest escape them, cast thyself into them. "Judge thyself, and thou shalt not be judged of the Lord."

2. Awake, awake! Stand up this moment, lest thou "drink at the Lord's hand the cup of his fury." Stir up thyself to lay hold on the Lord, the Lord thy Righteousness, mighty to save! "Shake thyself from the dust." At least, let the earthquake of God's threatenings shake thee. Awake, and cry out with the trembling jailer, "What must I do to be saved?" And never rest till thou believest on the Lord Jesus, with a faith which is his gift, by the operation of his Spirit.

3. If I speak to any one of you, more than to another, it is to thee, who thinkest thyself unconcerned in this exhortation. "I have a message from God unto thee." In his name, I warn thee "to flee from the wrath to come." Thou unholy soul, see thy picture in condemned Peter, lying in the dark dungeon, between the soldiers, bound with two chains, the keepers before the door keeping the prison. The night is far spent, the morning is at hand, when thou art to be brought forth to execution. And in these dreadful circumstances, thou art fast asleep; thou art fast asleep in the devil's arms, on the brink of the pit, in the jaws of everlasting destruction!

4. O may the Angel of the Lord come upon thee, and the light shine into thy prison! And mayest thou feel the stroke of an Almighty Hand, raising thee, with, "Arise up quickly, gird thyself, and bind on thy sandals, cast thy garment about thee, and follow Me."

5. Awake, thou everlasting spirit, out of thy dream of worldly happiness! Did not God create thee for himself? Then thou canst not rest till thou restest in him. Return, thou wanderer! Fly back to thy ark, This is not thy home. Think not of building tabernacles here. Thou art but a stranger, a sojourner upon earth; a creature of a day, but just launching out into an unchangeable state. Make haste. Eternity is at hand. Eternity depends on this moment. An eternity of happiness, or an eternity of misery!

6. In what state is thy soul? Was God, while I am yet speaking, to require it of thee, art thou ready to meet death and judgement? Canst thou stand in his sight, who is of "purer eyes than to behold iniquity"? Art thou "meet to be partaker of the inheritance of the saints in light"? Hast thou "fought a good fight, and kept the faith"? Hast thou secured the one thing needful? Hast thou recovered the image of God, even righteousness and true holiness? Hast thou put off the old man, and put on the new? Art thou clothed upon with Christ?

7. Hast thou oil in thy lamp? grace in thy heart? Dost thou "love the Lord thy God with all thy heart, and with all thy mind and with all thy soul, and with all thy strength"? Is that mind in thee, which was also in Christ Jesus? Art thou a Christian indeed, that is, a new creature? Are old things passed away, and all things become new?

8. Art thou a "partaker of the divine nature"? Knowest thou not, that "Christ is in thee, except thou be reprobate"? Knowest thou, that God "dwelleth in thee, and thou in God, by his Spirit, which he hath given thee"? Knowest thou not that "thy body is a temple of the Holy Ghost, which thou hast of God"? Hast thou the witness in thyself? the earnest of thine inheritance? Hast thou "received the Holy Ghost"? Or

dost thou start at the question, not knowing "whether there be any Holy Ghost"?

9. If it offends thee, be thou assured, that thou neither art a Christian, nor desirest to be one. Nay, thy very prayer is turned into sin; and thou hast solemnly mocked God this very day, by praying for the inspiration of his Holy Spirit, when thou didst not believe there was any such thing to be received.

10. Yet, on the authority of God's Word, and our own Church, I must repeat the question, "Hast thou received the Holy Ghost?" If thou hast not, thou art not yet a Christian. For a Christian is a man that is "anointed with the Holy Ghost and with power." Thou art not yet made a partaker of pure religion and undefiled. Dost thou know what religion is?—that it is a participation of the divine nature; the life of God in the soul of man; Christ formed in the heart; "Christ in thee, the hope of glory;" happiness and holiness; heaven begun upon earth; "a kingdom of God within thee; not meat and drink," no outward thing; "but righteousness, and peace, and joy in the Holy Ghost;" an everlasting kingdom brought into thy soul; a "peace of God that passeth all understanding;" a "joy unspeakable, and full of glory"?

11. Knowest thou, that "in Jesus Christ, neither circumcision availeth anything, nor uncircumcision; but faith that worketh by love;" but a new creation? Seest thou the necessity of that inward change, that spiritual birth, that life from the dead, that holiness? And art thou throughly convinced, that without it no man shall see the Lord? Art thou labouring after it?—"giving all diligence to make thy calling and election sure," "working out thy salvation with fear and trembling," "agonizing to enter in at the strait gate"? Art thou in earnest about thy soul? And canst thou tell the Searcher of hearts, "Thou, O God, art the thing that I long for! Lord, Thou knowest all things; Thou knowest that I *would* love Thee!"

12. Thou hopest to be saved; but what reason hast thou to give of the hope that is in thee? Is it because thou hast done no harm? or, because thou hast done much good? or, because thou art not like other men; but wise, or learned, or honest, and morally good; esteemed of men, and of a fair reputation? Alas! all this will never bring thee to God. It is in his account lighter than vanity. Dost thou know Jesus Christ, whom he hath sent? Hath he taught thee, that "by grace we are saved through faith; and that not of ourselves: it is the gift of God: not of works, lest any man should boast"? Hast thou received the faithful saying as the whole foundation of thy hope, "that Jesus Christ came into the world to save sinners"? Hast thou learned what that meaneth, "I came not to call the righteous, but sinners to repentance? I am not sent, but unto the lost sheep"? Art thou (he that heareth, let him understand!) lost, dead, *damned already?* Dost thou know thy deserts? Dost thou feel thy wants? Art thou "poor in spirit"? mourning for God, and refusing to be comforted? Is the prodigal "come to himself," and well content to be therefore thought beside himself" by those who are still feeding upon the husks which he hath left? Art thou willing to live godly in Christ Jesus? And dost thou therefore suffer persecution? Do men say all manner of evil against thee falsely, for the Son of Man's sake?

13. O that in all these questions ye may hear the voice that wakes the dead; and feel that hammer of the Word, which breaketh the rocks in pieces! "If ye will hear his voice to-day, while it is called to-day, harden not your hearts." Now, "awake, thou that sleepest" in spiritual death, that thou sleep not in death eternal! Feel thy lost estate, and "arise from the dead." Leave thine old companions in sin and death. Follow thou Jesus, and let the dead bury their dead. "Save thyself from this untoward generation." "Come out from among them, and be thou separate, and touch not the unclean thing, and the Lord shall receive thee." "Christ shall give thee light."

III. 1. This promise, I come, lastly, to explain. And how encouraging a consideration is this, that whosoever thou art, who obeyest his call, thou canst not seek his face in vain! If thou even now "awakest, and arisest from the dead," he hath bound himself to "give thee light." "The Lord shall give thee grace and glory;" the light of his grace here, and the light of his glory when thou receivest the crown that fadeth not away. "Thy light shall break forth as the morning, and thy darkness be as the noon-day." "God, who commanded the light to shine out of darkness, shall shine in thy heart; to give the knowledge of the glory of God in the face of Jesus Christ." On them that fear the Lord shall "the Sun of Righteousness arise with healing in his wings." And in that day it shall be said unto thee, "Arise, shine; for thy light is come, and the glory of the Lord is risen upon thee." For Christ shall reveal himself in thee: and he is the true Light.

2. God is light, and will give himself to every awakened sinner that waiteth for him; and thou shalt then be a temple of the living God, and Christ shall "dwell in thy heart by faith;" and, "being rooted and grounded in love, thou shalt be able to comprehend with all saints, what is the breadth, and length, and depth, and height of that love of Christ which passeth knowledge."

3. Ye see your calling, brethren. We are called to be "an habitation of God through his Spirit;" and, through his Spirit dwelling in us, to be saints here, and partakers of the inheritance of the saints in light. So exceeding great are the promises which are given unto us, actually given unto us who believe! For by faith "we receive, not the spirit of the world, but the Spirit which is of God"—the sum of all the promises—"that we may know the things that are freely given to us of God."

4. The Spirit of Christ is that great gift of God, which at sundry times, and in divers manners, he hath promised to man, and hath fully bestowed since the time that Christ was glorified. Those promises, before made to the fathers, he hath thus fulfilled: "I will put My spirit within you, and cause you to walk in My statutes" (Ezek. 36:27). "I will pour water upon him that is thirsty, and floods upon the dry ground; I will pour My Spirit upon thy seed, and My blessing upon thine offspring (Isa. 44:3).

5. Ye may all be living witnesses of these things; of remission of sins, and the gift of the Holy Ghost. "If thou canst believe, all things are possible to him that believeth." "Who among you is there that feareth the Lord, and" yet walketh on "in darkness, and hath no light?" I ask thee, in the name of Jesus, Believest thou that his arm is not shortened at all? that he is still mighty to save? that he is the same yesterday, to-day, and for ever? that he hath now power on earth to forgive sins? "Son, be of good cheer; thy sins are forgiven." God, for Christ's sake, hath forgiven thee. Receive this, "not as the word of man; but as it is indeed, the word of God;" and thou art justified freely through faith. Thou shalt be sanctified also through faith which is in Jesus, and shalt set to thy seal, even thine, that "God hath given unto us eternal life, and this life is in his Son."

6. Men and brethren, let me freely speak unto you, and suffer ye the word of exhortation, even from one the least esteemed in the Church. Your conscience beareth you witness in the Holy Ghost, that these things are so, if so be ye have tasted that the Lord is gracious. "This is eternal life, to know the only true God, and Jesus Christ, whom he hath sent." This experimental knowledge, and this alone, is true Christianity. he is a Christian who hath received the Spirit of Christ. he is not a Christian who hath not received him. Neither is it possible to have received him, and not know it. "For, at that day" (when he cometh, saith our Lord), "ye shall know that I am in My Father, and you in Me, and I in you." This is that "Spirit of Truth, whom the world cannot receive, because it seeth him not, neither knoweth him: but ye know him; for he dwelleth with you, and shall be in you" (John 14:17).

7. The world cannot receive him, but utterly reject the Promise of the Father, contradicting and blaspheming. But every spirit which confesseth not this is not of God. Yea, "this is that spirit of Antichrist, whereof ye have heard that it should come into the world; and even now it is in the world." he is Antichrist whosoever denies the inspiration of the Holy Ghost, or that the indwelling Spirit of God is the common privilege of all believers, the blessing of the gospel, the unspeakable gift, the universal promise, the criterion of a real Christian.

8. It nothing helps them to say, "We do not deny the *assistance* of God's Spirit; but only this *inspiration*, this *receiving the Holy Ghost*: and being *sensible* of it. It is only this *feeling of the* Spirit, this being *moved* by the Spirit, or *filled* with it, which we deny to have any place in sound religion." But, in *only denying this*, you deny the whole Scriptures; the whole truth, and promise, and testimony of God.

9. Our own excellent Church knows nothing of this devilish distinction; but speaks plainly of "feeling the Spirit of Christ" [Article 17]; of being "moved by the Holy Ghost" [Office of consecrating Priests] and knowing and "feeling there is no other name than that of Jesus," [Visitation of the Sick] whereby we can receive" life and salvation. She teaches us all to pray for the "inspiration of the Holy Spirit" [Collect before Holy Communion]; yea, that we may be "filled with the Holy Ghost" [Order of Confirmation]. Nay, and every Presbyter of hers professes to receive the Holy Ghost by the imposition of hands. Therefore, to deny any of these, is, in effect, to renounce the Church of England, as well as the whole Christian revelation.

10. But "the wisdom of God" was always "foolishness with men." No marvel, then, that the great mystery of the gospel should be now also "hid from the wise and prudent," as well

as in the days of old; that it should be almost universally denied, ridiculed, and exploded, as mere frenzy; and that all who dare avow it still are branded with the names of madmen and enthusiasts! This is "that falling away" which was to come—that general apostasy of all orders and degrees of men, which we even now find to have overspread the earth. "Run to and fro in the streets of Jerusalem, and see if ye can find a man," a man that loveth the Lord his God with all his heart, and serveth him with all his strength. How does our own land mourn (that we look no farther) under the overflowings of ungodliness! What villanies of every kind are committed day by day; yea, too often with impunity, by those who sin with a high hand, and glory in their shame! Who can reckon up the oaths, curses, profaneness blasphemies; the lying, slandering, evil-speaking; the Sabbath-breaking, gluttony, drunkenness, revenge; the whoredoms, adulteries, and various uncleanness; the frauds, injustice, oppression, extortion, which overspread our land as a flood?

11. And even among those who have kept themselves pure from those grosser abominations; how much anger and pride how much sloth and idleness, how much softness and effeminacy how much luxury and self-indulgence, how much covetousness and ambition, how much thirst of praise, how much love of the world, how much fear of man, is to be found! Meanwhile, how little of true religion! For, where is he that loveth either God or his neighbour, as he hath given us commandment? On the one hand, are those who have not so much as the form of godliness; on the other, those who have the form only: there stands the *open*, there the *painted*, sepulchre. So that in very deed, whosoever were earnestly to behold any public gathering together of the people (I fear those in our churches are not to be excepted) might easily perceive, "that the one part were Sadducees, and the other Pharisees": the one having almost as little concern about religion, as if there were "no resurrection, neither angel nor spirit;" and the other making it a mere lifeless form, a dull round of external performances, without either true faith, or the love of God, or joy in the Holy Ghost!

12. Would to God I could except *us* of this place! "Brethren, my heart's desire, and prayer to God, for you is, that ye may be saved" from this overflowing of ungodliness; and that here may its proud waves be stayed! But is it so indeed? God knoweth, yea, and our own consciences, it is not. Ye have not kept yourselves pure. Corrupt are we also and abominable; and few are there that understand any more; few that worship God in spirit and in truth. We, too, are "a generation that set not our hearts aright, and whose spirit cleaveth not steadfastly unto God." he hath appointed us indeed to be "the salt of the earth: but if the salt hath lost its savour, it is thenceforth good for nothing; but to be cast out, and to be trodden underfoot of men."

13. And "shall I not visit for these things, saith the Lord? Shall not My soul be avenged on such a nation as this?" Yea, we know not how soon he may say to the sword, "Sword, go through this land!" he hath given us long space to repent. he lets us alone this year also: but he warns and awakens us by thunder. his judgements are abroad in the earth; and we have all reason to expect the heaviest of all, even that he "should come unto us quickly, and remove our candlestick out of its place, except we repent and do the first works;" unless we return to the principles of the Reformation, the truth and simplicity of the gospel. Perhaps we are now resisting the last effort of divine grace to save us. Perhaps we have well-nigh "filled up the measure of our iniquities," by rejecting the counsel of God against ourselves, and casting out his messengers.

14. O God, "in the midst of wrath, remember mercy!" Be glorified in our reformation, not in our destruction! Let us "hear the rod, and him that appointed it!" Now that Thy "judgements are abroad in the earth," let the inhabitants of the world "learn righteousness!"

15. My brethren, it is high time for us to awake out of sleep before the "great trumpet of the Lord be blown," and our land become a field of blood. O may we speedily see the things that make for our peace, before they are hid from our eyes! "Turn Thou us, O good Lord, and let Thine anger cease from us. O Lord, look down from heaven, behold and visit this vine;" and cause us to know "the time of our visitation." "Help us, O God of our salvation, for the glory of Thy name! O deliver us, and be merciful to our sins, for Thy name's sake! And so we will not go back from Thee. O let us live, and we shall call upon Thy name. Turn us again, O Lord God of Hosts! Show the light of Thy countenance, and we shall be whole."

"Now unto him that is able to do exceeding abundantly above all that we can ask or think, according to the power that worketh in us, unto him be glory in the church by Christ Jesus throughout all ages; world without end.—Amen!"

4* SCRIPTURAL CHRISTIANITY**

"Whosoever heareth the sound of the trumpet, and taketh not warning; if the sword come, and take him away, his blood shall be upon his own head."

Ezek. 33:4.

"And they were all filled with the Holy Ghost."

Acts 4:31.

1. The same expression occurs in the second chapter, where we read, "When the day of Pentecost was fully come, they were all" (the Apostles, with the women, and the mother of Jesus, and his brethren) "with one accord in one place. And suddenly there came a sound from heaven as of a rushing mighty wind. And there appeared unto them cloven tongues like as of fire, and it sat upon each of them. And they were all filled with the Holy Ghost:" one immediate effect whereof was, they "began to speak with other tongues;" insomuch that both the Parthians, Medes, Elamites, and the other strangers who "came together, when this was noised abroad, heard them speak, in their several tongues, the wonderful works of God" (Acts 2:1–6).

2. In this chapter we read, that when the Apostles and brethren had been praying, and praising God, "the place was

---

* (text of the 1872 edition)

shaken where they were assembled together, and they were all filled with the Holy Ghost." Not that we find any visible appearance here, such as had been in the former instance: nor are we informed that the *extraordinary gifts* of the Holy Ghost were then given to all or any of them; such as the gifts of "healing, of working" other "miracles, of prophecy, of discerning spirits, the speaking with divers kinds of tongues, and the interpretation of tongues (1 Cor. 12:9, 10).

3. Whether these gifts of the Holy Ghost were designed to remain in the church throughout all ages, and whether or no they will be restored at the nearer approach of the "restitution of all things," are questions which it is not needful to decide. But it is needful to observe this, that, even in the infancy of the church, God divided them with a sparing hand. Were all even then prophets? Were all workers of miracles? Had all the gifts of healing? Did all speak with tongues? No, in no wise. Perhaps not one in a thousand. Probably none but the teachers in the church, and only some of them (1 Cor. 12:28–30). It was therefore, for a more excellent purpose than this, that "they were all filled with the Holy Ghost."

4. It was, to give them (what none can deny to be essential to all Christians in all ages) the mind which was in Christ, those holy fruits of the Spirit, which whosoever hath not, is none of his; to fill them with "love, joy, peace, long-suffering, gentleness, goodness" (Gal. 5:22–24); to endue them with faith (perhaps it might be rendered, *fidelity*), with meekness and temperance; to enable them to crucify the flesh, with its affections and lusts, its passions and desires; and in consequence of that inward change, to fulfil all outward righteousness; to "walk as Christ also walked," in "the work of faith, in the patience of hope, the labour of love" (1 Thess. 1:3).

5. Without busying ourselves, then, in curious, needless inquiries, touching those *extraordinary gifts* of the Spirit, let us take a nearer view of these his *ordinary* fruits, which we are assured will remain throughout all ages;—of that great work of God among the children of men, which we are used to express by one word, "Christianity;" not as it implies a set of opinions, a system of doctrines, but as it refers to men's hearts and lives. And this Christianity it may be useful to consider under three distinct views:

I.   As beginning to exist in individuals:
II.   As spreading from one to another:
III.   As covering the earth.

I design to close these considerations with a plain, practical application.

I. 1. And, first, let us consider Christianity in its rise, as beginning to exist in individuals.

Suppose, then, one of those who heard the Apostle Peter preaching repentance and remission of sins, was pricked to the heart, was convinced of sin, repented, and then believed in Jesus. By this faith of the operation of God, which was the very substance, or subsistence, of things hoped for (Heb. 11:1,) the demonstrative evidence of invisible things, he instantly received the Spirit of adoption, whereby he now cried, "Abba, Father" (Rom. 8:15). Now first it was that he could call Jesus Lord, by the Holy Ghost (1 Cor. 12:3), the Spirit itself bearing witness with his spirit, that he was a child of God (Rom. 8:16). Now it was that he could truly say, "I live not, but Christ liveth in me; and the life which I now live in the flesh, I live by faith in the Son of God, who loved me, and gave himself for me" (Gal. 2:20).

2. This, then, was the very essence of his faith, a divine *elegchos* (*evidence* or *conviction*) of the love of God the Father, through the Son of his love, to him a sinner, now accepted in the Beloved. And, being justified by faith, he had peace with God (Rom. 5:1), yea, the peace of God ruling in his heart; a peace, which passing all understanding (*panta noun*, all barely rational conception), kept his heart and mind from all doubt and fear, through the knowledge of him in whom he had believed. he could not, therefore, "be afraid of any evil tidings;" for his "heart stood fast, believing in the Lord." he feared not what man could do unto him, knowing the very hairs of his head were all numbered. he feared not all the powers of darkness, whom God was daily bruising under his feet. Least of all was he afraid to die; nay, he desired to "depart, and to be with Christ" (Phil. 1:23); who, "through death, had destroyed him that had the power of death, even the devil; and delivered them who, through fear of death, were all their life-time," till then, "subject to bondage" (Heb. 2:15).

3. his soul, therefore, magnified the Lord, and his spirit rejoiced in God his Saviour. "He rejoiced in him with joy unspeakable," who had reconciled him to God, even the Father; "in whom he had redemption through his blood, the forgiveness of sins." he rejoiced in that witness of God's Spirit with his spirit, that he was a child of God; and more abundantly, "in hope of the glory of God;" in hope of the glorious image of God, and full renewal of his soul in righteousness and true holiness, and in hope of that crown of glory, that "inheritance, incorruptible, undefiled, and that fadeth not away."

4. "The love of God was also shed abroad in his heart by the Holy Ghost which was given unto him" (Rom. 5:5). "Because he was a son God had sent forth the Spirit of his Son into his heart, crying Abba, Father!" (Gal. 4:6). And that filial love of God was continually increased by the witness he had in himself (1 John 5:10) of God's pardoning love to him; by "beholding what manner of love it was which the Father had bestowed upon him, that he should be called a child of God" (1 John 3:1). So that God was the. desire of his eyes, and the joy of his heart; his portion in time and in eternity.

5. he that thus *loved* God could not but love his brother also; and "not in word only, but in deed and in truth." "If God," said he, "so loved us, we ought also to love one another" (1 John 4:11); yea, every soul of man, as "the mercy of God is over all his works" (Ps. 145:9). Agreeably hereto, the affection of this lover of God embraced all mankind for his sake; not excepting those whom he had never seen in the flesh, or those of whom he knew nothing more than that they were "the offspring of God," for whose souls his Son had died; not excepting the "evil" and "unthankful," and least of all his enemies, those who hated, or persecuted, or despitefully used him for his Master's sake. These had a peculiar place, both in his heart and in his prayers. he loved them "even as Christ loved us."

6. And "love is not puffed up" (1 Cor. 13:4). It abases to the dust every soul wherein it dwells. Accordingly, he was lowly of heart, little, mean, and vile in his own eyes. he neither sought nor received the praise of men, but that which cometh of God only. he was meek and long-suffering, gentle to all, and easy to be entreated. Faithfulness and truth never forsook him: they were "bound about his neck, and wrote on the table of his heart." By the same spirit he was enabled to be temperate in all things, refraining his soul even as a weaned child. he was "crucified to the world, and the world crucified to him;" superior to "the desire of the flesh, the desire of the eye, and the pride of life." By the same almighty love was he saved, both from passion and pride; from lust and vanity; from ambition and covetousness; and from every temper which was not in Christ.

7. It may be easily believed, he who had this love in his heart would work no evil to his neighbour. It was impossible for him, knowingly and designedly, to do harm to any man. he was at the greatest distance from cruelty and wrong, from any unjust or unkind action. With the same care did he "set a watch before his mouth, and keep the door of his lips," lest he should offend in tongue, either against justice, or against mercy or truth. he put away all lying, falsehood; and fraud; neither was guile found in his mouth. he spake evil of no man; nor did an unkind word ever come out of his lips.

8. And as he was deeply sensible of the truth of that word "Without me ye can do nothing," and, consequently, of the need he had to be watered of God every moment; so he continued daily in all the ordinances of God, the stated channels of his grace to man: "in the Apostles' doctrine," or teaching, receiving that food of the soul with all readiness of heart; in "the breaking of bread," which he found to be the communion of the body of Christ; and "in the prayers" and praises offered up by the great congregation. And thus, he daily grew in grace, increasing in strength, in the knowledge and love of God.

9. But it did not satisfy him, barely to abstain from doing evil. his soul was athirst to do good. The language of his heart continually was, " 'My Father worketh hitherto, and I work.' My Lord went about doing good; and shall not I tread in his steps?" As he had opportunity therefore, if he could do no good of a higher kind, he fed the hungry, clothed the naked, helped the fatherless or stranger, visited and assisted them that were sick or in prison. he gave all his goods to feed the poor. he rejoiced to labour or to suffer for them; and whereinsoever he might profit another, there especially to "deny himself." he counted nothing too dear to part with for them, as well remembering the word of his Lord, "Inasmuch as ye have done it unto one of the least of these My brethren, ye have done it unto Me" (Matt. 25:40).

10. Such was Christianity in its rise. Such was a Christian in ancient days. Such was every one of those who, when they heard the threatenings of the chief priests and elders, "lifted up their voice to God with one accord, and were all filled with the Holy Ghost. The multitude of them that believed were of one heart and of one soul:" So did the love of him in whom they had believed constrain them to love one another! "Neither said any of them that aught of the things which he possessed was his own but they had all things common:" So fully were they crucified to the world, and the world crucified to them! "And they continued steadfastly with one accord in the Apostles" doctrine, and in the breaking of bread, and in prayers" (Acts 2:42). "And great grace was upon them all; neither was there any among them that lacked: for as many as were possessors of lands or houses sold them, and brought the prices of the things that were sold, and laid them down at the Apostles' feet: And distribution was made unto every man according as he had need." (Acts 4:31–35.)

II. 1. Let us take a view, in the Second place, of this Christianity, as spreading from one to another, and so gradually making its way into the world: For such was the will of God concerning it, who did not "light a candle to put it under a bushel, but that it might give light to all that were in the house." And this our Lord had declared to his first disciples, "Ye are the salt of the earth," "the light of the world;" at the same time that he gave that general command, "Let your light so shine before men, that they may see your good works, and glorify your Father which is in heaven." (Matt. 5:13–16).

2. And, indeed, supposing a few of these lovers of mankind to see "the whole world lying in wickedness," can we believe they would be unconcerned at the sight, at the misery of those for whom their Lord died? Would not their bowels yearn over them, and their hearts melt away for very trouble? Could they then stand idle all the day long, even were there no command from him whom they loved? Rather, would they not labour by all possible means, to pluck some of these brands out of the burning? Undoubtedly they would: they would spare no pains to bring back whomsoever they could of those poor "sheep that had gone astray, to the great Shepherd and Bishop of their souls" (1 Pet. 2:25).

3. So the Christians of old did. They laboured, having opportunity, "to do good unto all men" (Gal. 6:10), warning them to flee from the wrath to come; now, now to escape the damnation of hell. They declared, "The times of ignorance God winked at; but now he calleth all men everywhere to repent." (Acts 17:30) They cried aloud, Turn ye, turn ye, from your evil ways: "so iniquity shall not be your ruin" (Ezek. 18:30). They "reasoned" with them of "temperance, and righteousness," or justice—of the virtues opposite to their reigning sins; "and of judgement to come,"—of the wrath of God which would surely be executed on evildoers in that day when he should judge the world (Acts 24:25).

4. They endeavoured herein to speak to every man severally as he had need. To the careless, to those who lay unconcerned in darkness and in the shadow of death, they thundered, "Awake thou that sleepest; arise from the dead, and Christ shall give thee light." But to those who were already awakened out of sleep, and groaning under a sense of the wrath of God, their language was, "We have an Advocate with the Father; he is the propitiation for our sins." Meantime, those who had believed, they provoked to love and to good works; to patient continuance in well-doing; and to abound more and more in that holiness without which no man can see the Lord. (Heb 12:14)

5. And their labour was not in vain in the Lord. his word ran and was glorified. It grew mightily and prevailed. But so much the more did offences prevail also. The world in general were offended, "because they testified of it, that the works thereof were evil" (John 7:7). The men of pleasure were offended, not only because these men were made, as it were, to reprove their thoughts ("He professeth," said they, "to have the knowledge of God; he calleth himself the child of the Lord, his life is not like other men's; his ways are of another fashion; he abstaineth from our ways, as from filthiness; he maketh his boast, that God is his Father" Wis. 2:13–16;) but much more, because so many of their companions were taken away, and would no more run with them to "the same excess of riot." (1 Pet. 4:4.) The men of reputation were offended, because, as the gospel spread, they declined in the esteem of the people; and because many no longer dared to give them flattering titles, or to pay man the homage due to God only. The men of trade called one another together, and said, "Sirs, ye know that by this craft we have our wealth: but ye see and hear that these men have persuaded and turned away much people; so that this our craft is in danger to be set at nought" (Acts 19:25ff.). Above all, the men of religion, so called, the men of *outside* religion, "the saints of the world," were offended, and ready at every opportunity to cry out, "Men of Israel, help! We have found these men pestilent fellows, movers of sedition throughout the world" (Acts 24:5). "These are the men that teach all men everywhere against the people, and against this place" (Acts 21:28).

6. Thus it was that the heavens grew black with clouds, and the storm gathered amain. For the more Christianity spread, the more hurt was done, in the account of those who received it not; and the number increased of those who were more and more enraged at these "men who thus turned the world upside down;" (Acts 17:6;) insomuch that more and more cried out, "Away with such fellows from the earth; it is not fit that they should live;" yea, and sincerely believed, that whosoever should kill them would do God service.

7. Meanwhile they did not fail to cast out their name as evil; (Luke 6:22;) so that this "sect was everywhere spoken against." (Acts 27:22.) Men said all manner of evil of them, even as had been done of the prophets that were before them (Matt. 5:12). And whatsoever any would affirm, others would believe; so that offences grew as the stars of heaven for multitude. And hence arose, at the time fore-ordained of the Father, persecution in all its forms. Some, for a season, suffered only shame and reproach; some, "the spoiling of their goods;" "some had trial of mocking and scourging; some of bonds and imprisonment;" and others "resisted unto blood" (Heb. 10:34; 11:36ff.)

8. Now it was that the pillars of hell were shaken, and the kingdom of God spread more and more. Sinners were everywhere "turned from darkness to light, and from the power of Satan unto God." he gave his children "such a mouth, and such wisdom, as all their adversaries could not resist;" and their lives were of equal force with their words. But above all, their sufferings spake to all the world. They "approved themselves the servants of God, in afflictions, in necessities, in distresses, in stripes, in imprisonments, in tumults, in labours; in perils in the sea, in perils in the wilderness, in weariness and painfulness, in hunger and thirst, in cold and nakedness" (2 Cor. 6:4ff.). And when, having fought the good fight, they were led as sheep to the slaughter, and offered up on the sacrifice and service of their faith, then the blood of each found a voice, and the heathen owned, "He being dead, yet speaketh."

9. Thus did Christianity spread itself in the earth. But how soon did the tares appear with the wheat, and the *mystery of iniquity* work, as well as the *mystery of godliness!* How soon did Satan find a seat, even *in the temple of God*, "till the woman fled into the wilderness," and "the faithful were again minished from the children of men!" here we tread a beaten path: the still unceasing corruptions of the succeeding generations have been largely described, from time to time, by those witnesses God raised up, to show that he had "built his church upon a rock, and the gates of hell should not" wholly "prevail against her." (Matt. 16:18.)

III. 1. But shall we not see greater things than these? Yea, greater than have been yet from the beginning of the world. Can Satan cause the truth of God to fail, or his promises to be of none effect? If not, the time will come when Christianity will prevail over all, and cover the earth. Let us stand a little, and survey (the Third thing which was proposed) this strange sight, a *Christian World*. Of this the Prophets of old inquired and searched diligently (1 Pet. 1:10, 11ff.:) of this the Spirit which was in them testified: "It shall come to pass in the last days, that the mountain of the Lord's house shall be established in the top of the mountains, and shall be exalted above the hills; and all nations shall flow unto it. And they shall beat their swords into ploughshares, and their spears into pruning-hooks. Nation shall not lift up sword against nation; neither shall they learn war any more." (Isa. 2:1–4.) "In that day there shall be a Root of Jesse, which shall stand for an Ensign of the people. To it shall the Gentiles seek: and his rest shall be glorious. And it shall come to pass in that day, that the Lord shall set his hand again to recover the remnant of his people; and he shall set up an Ensign for the nations, and shall assemble the outcasts of Israel, and gather together the dispersed of Judah, from the four corners of the earth." (Isa. 11:10–12.) "The wolf shall then dwell with the lamb, and the leopard shall lie down with the kid; and the calf and the young lion and the fatling together; and a little child shall lead them. They shall not hurt nor destroy, saith the Lord, in all my holy mountain. For the earth shall be full of the knowledge of the Lord, as the waters cover the sea" (Isa. 11:6–9).

2. To the same effect are the words of the great Apostle, which it is evident have never yet been fulfilled. "Hath God cast away his people? God forbid." "But through their fall salvation is come to the Gentiles." "And if the diminishing of them be the riches of the Gentiles, how much more their fullness?" "For I would not, brethren, that ye should be ignorant of this mystery; that blindness in part is happened to Israel, until the fullness of the Gentiles be come in: And so all Israel shall be saved." (Rom. 11:1, 11, 25, 26.)

3. Suppose now the fullness of time to be come, and the prophecies to be accomplished. What a prospect is this! All is peace, "quietness, and assurance for ever." here is no din of arms, no "confused noise," no "garments rolled in blood." "Destructions are come to a perpetual end." Wars are ceased from the earth. Neither are there any intestine jars remaining; no brother rising up against brother; no country or city divided against itself, and tearing out its own bowels. Civil discord is at an end for evermore, and none is left either to destroy or hurt his neighbour. here is no oppression to "make" even "the wise man mad;" no extortion to "grind the face of the poor;" no robbery or wrong; no rapine or injustice; for all are "content with such things as they possess." Thus "righteousness and peace have kissed each other;" (Ps. 85:10;) they have "taken root and filled the land;" "righteousness flourishing out of the earth;" and "peace looking down from heaven."

4. And with righteousness or justice, mercy is also found. The earth is no longer full of cruel habitations. The Lord hath destroyed both the blood-thirsty and malicious, the envious and revengeful man. Were there any provocation, there is none that now knoweth to return evil for evil; but indeed there is none that doeth evil, no, not one; for all are harmless as doves. And being filled with peace and joy in believing, and united in one body, by one Spirit, they all love as brethren, they are all of one heart and of one soul. "Neither saith any of them, that aught of the things which he possesseth is his own." There is none among them that lacketh: for every man loveth his neighbour as himself. And all walk by one rule: "Whatever ye would that men should do unto you, even so do unto them."

5. It follows, that no unkind word can ever be heard among them, no strife of tongues, no contention of any kind, no railing or evil-speaking, but every one "opens his mouth with wisdom, and in his tongue there is the law of kindness." Equally incapable are they of fraud or guile: their love is without dissimulation: Their words are always the just expression of their thoughts, opening a window into their breast, that whosoever desires may look into their hearts, and see that only love and God are there.

6. Thus, where the Lord Omnipotent taketh to himself his mighty power and reigneth, doth he "subdue all things to himself," cause every heart to overflow with love, and fill every mouth with praise. "Happy are the people that are in such a case: yea, blessed are the people who have the Lord for their God" (Psalm 144:15.) "Arise, shine;" (saith the Lord;) "for thy light is come, and the glory of the Lord is risen upon thee." "Thou hast known that I the Lord am thy Saviour and thy Redeemer, the mighty God of Jacob. I have made thy officers peace, and thy exactors righteousness. Violence shall no more be heard in thy land, wasting nor destruction within thy borders; but thou shalt call thy walls Salvation and thy gates Praise." "Thy people are all righteous; they shall inherit the land for ever; the branch of my planting, the work of my hands, that I may be glorified." "The sun shall be no more thy light by day; neither for brightness shall the moon give light unto thee: but the Lord shall be unto thee an everlasting light, and thy God thy glory" (Isa. 60:1, 16–19).

IV. Having thus briefly considered Christianity, as beginning, as going on, and as covering the earth, it remains only that I should close the whole with a plain, practical application.

1. And, first, I would ask, Where does this Christianity now exist? Where, I pray, do the Christians live? Which is the country, the inhabitants whereof are all thus filled with the Holy Ghost?—are all of one heart and of one soul? cannot suffer one among them to lack anything, but continually give to every man as he hath need; who, one and all, have the love of God filling their hearts, and constraining them to love their neighbour as themselves; who have all "put on bowels of mercy, humbleness of mind, gentleness, long-suffering?" who offend not in any kind, either by word or deed, against justice, mercy, or truth; but in every point do unto all men; as they would these should do unto them? With what propriety can we term any a Christian country, which does not answer this description? Why then, let us confess we have never yet seen a Christian country upon earth.

2. I beseech you, brethren, by the mercies of God, if ye do account me a madman or a fool, yet, *as a fool bear with me.* It is utterly needful that some one should use great plainness of speech towards you. It is more especially needful at *this* time; for who knoweth but it is the *last?* Who knoweth how soon the righteous Judge may say, "I will no more be entreated for this people?" "Though Noah, Daniel, and Job were in this land, they should but deliver their own souls." And who will use this plainness, if I do not? Therefore I, even I, will speak. And I adjure you, by the living God, that ye steel not your breasts against receiving a blessing at *my* hands. Do not say in your hearts, *Non persuadebis, etiamsi persuaseris;*" [Your persuasions shall not prevail with us, even though they should really convince us.—EDIT.] or, in other words, "Lord, thou shalt not *send by whom thou wilt send;* let me rather perish in my blood, than be saved by this man!"

3. Brethren, "I am persuaded better things of you, though I thus speak." Let me ask you then, in tender love, and in the spirit of meekness, Is this city a Christian city? Is Christianity, scriptural Christianity, found here? Are we, considered as a community of men, so "filled with the Holy Ghost," as to enjoy in our hearts, and show forth in our lives, the genuine fruits of that Spirit? Are all the Magistrates, all heads and Governors of Colleges and Halls, and their respective Societies (not to speak of the inhabitants of the town), "of one heart "and one soul?" Is "the love of God shed abroad in our hearts?" Are our tempers the same that were in him? And are our lives agreeable thereto? Are we "holy as he who hath called us is holy in all manner of conversation?"

4. I entreat you to observe, that here are no peculiar notions now under consideration; that the question moved is not concerning *doubtful opinions* of one kind or another, but concerning the undoubted, fundamental branches (if there be any such) of our common Christianity. And for the decision thereof, I appeal to your own conscience, guided by the Word of God. he therefore that is not condemned by his own heart, let him go free.

5. In the fear, then, and in the presence of the great God, before whom both you and I shall shortly appear, I pray you

that are in authority over us, whom I reverence for your office sake, to consider (and not after the manner of dissemblers with God), are you "filled with the Holy Ghost?" Are you lively portraitures of him whom ye are appointed to represent among men? "I have said, Ye are gods," ye magistrates and rulers; ye are by office so nearly allied to the God of heaven! In your several stations and degrees, ye are to show forth unto us "the Lord our Governor." Are all the thoughts of your hearts, all your tempers and desires, suitable to your high calling? Are all your words like unto those which come out of the mouth of God? Is there in all your actions dignity and love?—a greatness which words cannot express, which can flow only from a heart "full of God;" and yet consistent with the character of "man that is a worm, and the son of man that is a worm?"

6. Ye venerable men, who are more especially called to form the tender minds of youth, to dispel thence the shades of ignorance and error, and train them up to be wise unto salvation, are you "filled with the Holy Ghost?" with all those "fruits of the Spirit," which your important office so indispensably requires? Is your heart whole with God? full of love and zeal to set up his kingdom on earth? Do you continually remind those under your care, that the one rational end of all our studies, is to know, love and serve "the only true God, and Jesus Christ whom he hath sent?" Do you inculcate upon them day by day, that love alone never faileth (whereas, whether there be tongues, they shall fail, or philosophical knowledge, it shall vanish away); and that without love, all learning is but splendid ignorance, pompous folly, vexation of spirit? Has all you teach an actual tendency to the love of God, and of all mankind for his sake? Have you an eye to this end in whatever you prescribe, touching the kind, the manner, and the measure of their studies; desiring and labouring that, wherever the lot of these young soldiers of Christ is cast, they may be so many burning and shining lights, adorning the gospel of Christ in all things? And permit me to ask, Do you put forth all your strength in the vast work you have undertaken? Do you labour herein with all your might? exerting every faculty of your soul, using every talent which God hath lent you, and that to the uttermost of your power?

7. Let it not be said, that I speak here, as if all under your care were intended to be clergymen. Not so: I only speak as if they were all intended to be Christians. But what example is set them by us who enjoy the beneficence of our forefathers?—by Fellows, Students, Scholars; more especially those who are of some rank and eminence? Do ye, brethren, abound in the fruits of the Spirit, in lowliness of mind, in self-denial and mortification, in seriousness and composure of spirit, in patience, meekness, sobriety, temperance; and in unwearied, restless endeavours to do good in every kind unto all men, to relieve their outward wants, and to bring their souls to the true knowledge and love of God? Is this the general character of Fellows of Colleges? I fear it is not. Rather, have not pride and haughtiness of spirit, impatience and peevishness, sloth and indolence, gluttony and sensuality, and even a proverbial uselessness, been objected to us, perhaps not always by our enemies, nor wholly without ground? O that God would roll away this reproach from us, that the very memory of it might perish for ever!

8. Many of us are more immediately consecrated to God, called to minister in holy things. Are we then patterns to the rest, "in word, in conversation, in charity, in spirit, in faith, in purity" (1 Tim. 4:12)? Is there written on our forehead and on our heart, "Holiness to the Lord?" From what motives did we enter upon this office? Was it indeed with a single eye "to serve God, trusting that we were inwardly moved by the Holy Ghost to take upon us this ministration, for the promoting of his glory, and the edifying of his people?" And have we "clearly determined, by God's grace, to give ourselves wholly to this office?" Do we forsake and set aside, as much as in us lies, all worldly cares and studies? Do we apply ourselves wholly to this one thing, and draw all our cares and studies this way? Are we apt to teach? Are we taught of God, that we may be able to teach others also? Do we know God? Do we know Jesus Christ? Hath "God revealed his Son in us?" And hath he "made us able ministers of the new covenant?" Where then are the "seals of our apostleship?" Who, that were dead in trespasses and sins, have been quickened by our word? Have we a burning zeal to save souls from death, so that for their sake we often forget even to eat our bread? Do we speak plain, "by manifestation of the truth commending ourselves to every man's conscience in the sight of God" (2 Cor. 4:2)? Are we dead to the world, and the things of the world, "laying up all our treasure in heaven?" Do we lord over God's heritage? Or are we the least, the servants of all? When we bear the reproach of Christ, does it sit heavy upon us? Or do we rejoice therein? When we are smitten on the one cheek, do we resent it? Are we impatient of affronts? Or do we turn the other also; not resisting the evil, but overcoming evil with good? Have we a bitter zeal, inciting us to strive sharply and passionately with them that are out of the way? Or is our zeal the flame of love, so as to direct all our words with sweetness, lowliness, and meekness of wisdom?

9. Once more: what shall we say concerning the youth of this place? Have you either the form or the power of Christian godliness? Are you humble, teachable, advisable; or stubborn, self-willed, heady, and highminded? Are you obedient to your superiors as to parents? Or do you despise those to whom you owe the tenderest reverence? Are you diligent in your easy business, pursuing your studies with all your strength? Do you redeem the time, crowding as much work into every day as it can contain? Rather, are ye not conscious to yourselves, that you waste away day after day, either in reading what has no tendency to Christianity, or in gaming, or in—you know not what? Are you better managers of your fortune than of your time? Do you, out of principle, take care to owe no man anything? Do you "remember the Sabbath day, to keep it holy;" to spend it in the more immediate worship of God? When you are in his house, do you consider that God is there? Do you behave "as seeing him that is invisible?" Do you know how to possess your bodies in sanctification and honour?" Are not drunkenness and uncleanness found among you? Yea, are there not of you who "glory in their shame?" Do not many of you "take the name

of God in vain," perhaps habitually, without either remorse or fear? Yea, are there not a multitude of you that are forsworn? I fear, a swiftly-increasing multitude. Be not surprised, brethren. Before God and this congregation, I own myself to have been of the number, solemnly swearing to observe all those customs, which I then knew nothing of; and those statutes, which I did not so much as read over, either then, or for some years after. What is perjury, if this is not? But if it be, O what a weight of sin, yea, sin of no common dye, lieth upon us! And doth not the Most High regard it?

10. May it not be one of the consequences of this, that so many of you are a generation of triflers; triflers with God, with one another, and with your own souls? For, how few of you spend, from one week to another, a single hour in private prayer! How few have any thought of God in the general tenor of your conversation! Who of you is in any degree acquainted with the work of his Spirit, his supernatural work in the souls of men? Can you bear, unless now and then in a church, any talk of the Holy Ghost? Would you not take it for granted, if one began such a conversation, that it was either hypocrisy or enthusiasm? In the name of the Lord God Almighty, I ask, what religion are you of? Even the talk of Christianity, ye cannot, will not bear. O my brethren, what a Christian city is this! "It is time for Thee, Lord, to lay to Thine hand!"

11. For, indeed, what probability, what possibility, rather (speaking after the manner of men), is there that Christianity, scriptural Christianity, should be again the religion of this place? that all orders of men among us should speak and live as men "filled with the Holy Ghost?" By whom should this Christianity be restored? By those of you that are in authority? Are you convinced then that this is scriptural Christianity? Are you desirous it should be restored? And do ye not count your fortune, liberty, life, dear unto yourselves, so ye may be instrumental in the restoring of it? But suppose ye have this desire, who hath any power proportioned to the effect? Perhaps some of you have made a few faint attempts, but with how small success! Shall Christianity then be restored by young, unknown, inconsiderable men? I know not whether ye yourselves could suffer it. Would not some of you cry out, "Young man, in so doing thou reproachest us?" But there is no danger of your being put to the proof; so hath iniquity overspread us like a flood. Whom then shall God send?—the famine, the pestilence (the last messengers of God to a guilty land), or the sword, "the armies of the" Romish "aliens," to reform us into our first love? Nay, "rather let us fall into thy hand, O Lord, and let us not fall into the hand of man." Lord, save, or we perish! Take us out of the mire, that we sink not! O help us against these enemies! for vain is the help of man. Unto thee all things are possible. According to the greatness of thy power, preserve thou those that are appointed to die; and preserve us in the manner that seemeth to thee good; not as we will, but as thou wilt!

5* JUSTIFICATION BY FAITH

---

* (text from the 1872 edition)

"To him that worketh not, but believeth on him that justifieth the ungodly, his faith is counted for righteousness."

Romans 4:5.

1. How a sinner may be justified before God, the Lord and Judge of all, is a question of no common importance to every child of man. It contains the foundation of all our hope, inasmuch as while we are at enmity with God, there can be no true peace, no solid joy, either in time or in eternity. What peace can there be, while our own heart condemns us; and much more, He that is "greater than our heart, and knoweth all things?" What solid joy, either in this world or that to come, while "the wrath of God abideth on us?"

2. And yet how little hath this important question been understood! What confused notions have many had concerning it! Indeed, not only confused, but often utterly false; contrary to the truth, as light to darkness; notions absolutely inconsistent with the oracles of God, and with the whole analogy of faith. And hence, erring concerning the very foundation, they could not possibly build thereon; at least, not "gold, silver, or precious stones," which would endure when tried as by fire; but only "hay and stubble," neither acceptable to God, nor profitable to man.

3. In order to justice, in far as in me lies, to the vast importance of the subject, to save those that seek the truth in sincerity from "vain jangling and strife of words," to clear the confusedness of thought into which so many have already been led thereby, and to give them true and just conceptions of this great mystery of godliness, I shall endeavour to show,

First. What is the general ground of this whole doctrine of justification.

Secondly. What justification is.

Thirdly. Who they are that are justified. And,

Fourthly. On what terms they are justified. I. I am, First, to show, what is the general ground of this whole doctrine of justification.

1. In the image of God was man made, holy as he that created him is holy; merciful as the Author of all is merciful; perfect as his Father in heaven is perfect. As God is love, so man, dwelling in love, dwelt in God, and God in him. God made him to be an "image of his own eternity," an incorruptible picture of the God of glory. He was accordingly pure, as God is pure, from every spot of sin. He knew not evil in any kind or degree, but was inwardly and outwardly sinless and undefiled. He "loved the Lord his God with all his heart, and with all his mind, and soul, and strength."

2. To man thus upright and perfect, God gave a perfect law, to which he required full and perfect obedience. He required full obedience in every point, and this to be performed without any intermission, from the moment man became a living soul, till the time of his trial should be ended. No allowance was made for any falling short: As, indeed, there was no need of any; man being altogether equal to the task assigned, and thoroughly furnished for every good word and work.

3. To the entire law of love which was written in his heart, (against which, perhaps, he could not sin directly,) it seemed good to the sovereign wisdom of God to superadd one positive law: "Thou shalt not eat of the fruit of the tree that groweth in the midst of the garden;" annexing that penalty thereto, "In the day that thou eatest thereof, thou shalt surely die."

4. Such, then, was the state of man in Paradise. By the free, unmerited love of God, he was holy and happy: He knew, loved, enjoyed God, which is, in substance, life everlasting. And in this life of love, he was to continue for ever, if he continued to obey God in all things; but, if he disobeyed him in any, he was to forfeit all. "In that day," said God, "thou shalt surely die."

5. Man did disobey God. He "ate of the tree, of which God commanded him, saying, Thou shalt not eat of it." And in that day he was condemned by the righteous judgment of God. Then also the sentence whereof he was warned before, began to take place upon him. For the moment he tasted that fruit, he died. His soul died, was separated from God; separate from whom the soul has no more life than the body has when separate from the soul. His body, likewise, became corruptible and mortal; so that death then took hold on this also. And being already dead in spirit, dead to God, dead in sin, he hastened on to death everlasting; to the destruction both of body and soul, in the fire never to be quenched

6. Thus "by one man sin entered into the world, and death by sin. And so death passed upon all men," as being contained in him who was the common father and representative of us all. Thus, "through the offence of one," all are dead, dead to God, dead in sin, dwelling in a corruptible, mortal body, shortly to be dissolved, and under the sentence of death eternal. For as, "by one man's disobedience," all "were made sinners;" so, by that offence of one, "judgment came upon all men to condemnation." (Romans 5:12)

7. In this state we were, even all mankind, when "God so loved the world, that he gave his only-begotten Son, to the end we might not perish, but have everlasting life." In the fullness of time he was made Man, another common Head of mankind, a second general Parent and Representative of the whole human race. And as such it was that "he bore our griefs," "the Lord laying upon him the iniquities of us all." Then was he "wounded for our transgressions, and bruised for our iniquities." "He made his soul an offering for sin:" He poured out his blood for the transgressors: He "bare our sins in his own body on the tree," that by his stripes we might be healed: And by that one oblation of himself, once offered, he hath redeemed me and all mankind; having thereby "made a full, perfect, and sufficient sacrifice and satisfaction for the sins of the whole world."

8. In consideration of this, that the Son of God hath "tasted death for every man," God hath now "reconciled the world to himself, not imputing to them their" former "trespasses." And thus, "as by the offence of one judgment came upon all men to condemnation, even so by the righteousness of one the free gift came upon all men unto justification." So that, for the sake of his well-beloved Son, of what he hath done and suffered for us, God now vouchsafes, on one only condition, (which himself also enables us to perform,) both to remit the punishment due to our sins, to reinstate us in his favour, and to restore our dead souls to spiritual life, as the earnest of life eternal.

9. This, therefore, is the general ground of the whole doctrine of justification. By the sin of the first Adam, who was not only the father, but likewise the representative, of us all, we all fell short of the favour of God; we all became children of wrath; or, as the Apostle expresses it, "judgment came upon all men to condemnation." Even so, by the sacrifice for sin made by the Second Adam, as the Representative of us all, God is so far reconciled to all the world, that he hath given them a new covenant; the plain condition whereof being once fulfilled, "there is no more condemnation" for us, but "we are justified freely by his grace, through the redemption that is in Jesus Christ."

II. 1. But what is it to be "justified?" What is "justification?" This was the Second thing which I proposed to show. And it is evident, from what has been already observed, that it is not the being made actually just and righteous. This is "sanctification;" which is, indeed, in some degree, the immediate fruit of justification, but, nevertheless, is a distinct gift of God, and of a totally different nature. The one implies what God does for us through his Son; the other, what he works in us by his Spirit. So that, although some rare instances may be found, wherein the term "justified" or "justification" is used in so wide a sense as to include "sanctification" also; yet, in general use, they are sufficiently distinguished from each other, both by St. Paul and the other inspired writers.

2. Neither is that far-fetched conceit, that justification is the clearing us from accusation, particularly that of Satan, easily provable from any clear text of holy writ. In the whole scriptural account of this matter, as above laid down, neither that accuser nor his accusation appears to be at all taken in. It can not indeed be denied, that he is the "accuser" of men, emphatically so called. But it does in nowise appear, that the great Apostle hath any reference to this, more or less, in all he hath written touching justification, either to the Romans or the Galatians.

3. It is also far easier to take for granted, than to prove from any clear scripture testimony, that justification is the clearing us from the accusation brought against us by the law: At least if this forced, unnatural way of speaking mean either more or less than this, that, whereas we have transgressed the law of God, and thereby deserved the damnation of hell, God does not inflict on those who are justified the punishment which they had deserved.

4. Least of all does justification imply, that God is deceived in those whom he justifies; that he thinks them to be what, in fact, they are not; that he accounts them to be otherwise than they are. It does by no means imply, that God judges concerning us contrary to the real nature of things; that he esteems us better than we really are, or believes us righteous when we are unrighteous. Surely no. The judgment of the all-wise God is always according to truth. Neither can it ever consist with his unerring wisdom, to think that I am

innocent, to judge that I am righteous or holy, because another is so. He can no more, in this manner, confound me with Christ, than with David or Abraham. Let any man to whom God hath given understanding, weigh this without prejudice; and he cannot but perceive, that such a notion of justification is neither reconcilable to reason nor Scripture.

5. The plain scriptural notion of justification is pardon, the forgiveness of sins. It is that act of God the Father, hereby, for the sake of the propitiation made by the blood of his Son, he "showeth forth his righteousness (or mercy) by the remission of the sins that are past." This is the easy, natural account of it given by St. Paul, throughout this whole epistle. So he explains it himself, more particularly in this and in the following chapter. Thus, in the next verses but one to the text, "Blessed are they," saith he, "whose iniquities are forgiven, and whose sins are covered: Blessed is the man to whom the Lord will not impute sin." To him that is justified or forgiven, God "will not impute sin" to his condemnation. He will not condemn him on that account, either in this world or in that which is to come. His sins, all his past sins, in thought, word, and deed, are covered, are blotted out, shall not be remembered or mentioned against him, any more than if they had not been. God will not inflict on that sinner what he deserved to suffer, because the Son of his love hath suffered for him. And from the time we are "accepted through the Beloved," "reconciled to God through his blood," he loves, and blesses, and watches over us for good, even as if we had never sinned.

Indeed the Apostle in one place seems to extend the meaning of the word much farther, where he says, "Not the hearers of the law, but the doers of the law, shall be justified." Here he appears to refer our justification to the sentence of the great day. And so our Lord himself unquestionably doth, when he says, "By thy words thou shalt be justified;" proving hereby, that "for every idle word men shall speak, they shall give an account in the day of judgment." But perhaps we can hardly produce another instance of St. Paul's using the word in that distant sense. In the general tenor of his writings, it is evident he doth not; and least of all in the text before us, which undeniably speaks, not of those who have already "finished their course," but of those who are now just "setting out," just beginning to "run the race which is set before them."

III. 1. But this is the third thing which was to be considered, namely, Who are they that are justified? And the Apostle tells us expressly, the ungodly: "He (that is, God) justifieth the ungodly;" the ungodly of every kind and degree; and none but the ungodly. As "they that are righteous need no repentance," so they need no forgiveness. It is only sinners that have any occasion for pardon: It is sin alone which admits of being forgiven. Forgiveness, therefore, has an immediate reference to sin, and, in this respect, to nothing else. It is our "unrighteousness" to which the pardoning God is "merciful:" It is our "iniquity" which he "remembereth no more."

2. This seems not to be at all considered by those who so vehemently contend that a man must be sanctified, that is, holy, before he can be justified; especially by such of them as affirm, that universal holiness or obedience must precede justification. (Unless they mean that justification at the last day, which is wholly out of the present question.) So far from it, that the very supposition is not only flatly impossible, (for where there is no love of God, there is no holiness, and there is no love of God but from a sense of his loving us,) but also grossly, intrinsically absurd, contradictory to itself. For it is not a saint but a sinner that is forgiven, and under the notion of a sinner. God justifieth not the godly, but the ungodly; not those that are holy already, but the unholy. Upon what condition he doeth this, will be considered quickly: but whatever it is, it cannot be holiness. To assert this, is to say the Lamb of God takes away only those sins which were taken away before.

3. Does then the good Shepherd seek and save only those that are found already? No: He seeks and saves that which is lost. He pardons those who need his pardoning mercy. He saves from the guilt of sin, (and, at the same time, from the power,) sinners of every kind, of every degree: men who, till then, were altogether ungodly; in whom the love of the Father was not; and, consequently, in whom dwelt no good thing, no good or truly Christian temper,—but all such as were evil and abominable,—pride, anger, love of the world,—the genuine fruits of that "carnal mind" which is "enmity against God."

4. These who are sick, the burden of whose sins is intolerable, are they that need a Physician; these who are guilty, who groan under the wrath of God, are they that need a pardon. These who are "condemned already," not only by God, but also by their own conscience, as by a thousand witnesses, of all their ungodliness, both in thought, and word, and work, cry aloud for Him that "justifieth the ungodly," through the redemption that is in Jesus;—the ungodly, and "him that worketh not;" that worketh not, before he is justified, anything that is good, that is truly virtuous or holy, but only evil continually. For his heart is necessarily, essentially evil, till the love of God is shed abroad therein. And while the tree is corrupt, so are the fruits; "for an evil tree cannot bring forth good fruit."

5. If it be objected, "Nay, but a man, before he is justified, may feed the hungry, or clothe the naked; and these are good works;" the answer is easy: He may do these, even before he is justified; and these are, in one sense, "good works;" they are "good and profitable to men." But it does not follow, that they are, strictly speaking, good in themselves, or good in the sight of God. All truly "good works" (to use the words of our Church) "follow after justification;" and they are therefore good and "acceptable to God in Christ," because they "spring out of a true and living faith." By a parity of reason, all "works done before justification are not good," in the Christian sense, "forasmuch as they spring not of faith in Jesus Christ;" (though from some kind of faith in God they may spring;) "yea, rather, for that they are not done as God hath willed and commanded them to be done, we doubt not" (how strange soever it may appear to some) "but they have the nature of sin."

6. Perhaps those who doubt of this have not duly considered the weighty reason which is here assigned, why no works

done before justification can be truly and properly good. The argument plainly runs thus:—

No works are good, which are not done as God hath willed and commanded them to be done.

But no works done before justification are done as God hath willed and commanded them to be done:

Therefore, no works done before justification are good.

The first proposition is self-evident; and the second, that no works done before justification are done as God hath willed and commanded them to be done, will appear equally plain and undeniable, if we only consider, God hath willed and commanded that "all our works" should "be done in charity;" (*en agape*) in love, in that love to God which produces love to all mankind. But none of our works can be done in this love, while the love of the Father (of God as our Father) is not in us; and this love can not be in us till we receive the Spirit of Adoption, crying in, our hearts, Abba, Father. If, therefore, God doth not justify the ungodly, and him that (in this sense) worketh not, then hath Christ died in vain; then, notwithstanding his death, can no flesh living be justified.

IV. 1. But on what terms, then, is he justified who is altogether "ungodly," and till that time "worketh not?" on one alone; which is faith: he "believeth is him that justifieth the ungodly." And "he that believeth is not condemned;" yea, he is "passed from death unto life." "For the righteousness (or mercy) of God is by faith of Jesus Christ unto all and upon all them that believe: Whom God hath set forth for a propitiation, through faith in his blood; that he might be just, and" (consistently with his justice) "the Justifier of him which believeth in Jesus:" "Therefore we conclude that a man is justified by faith without the deeds of the law;" without previous obedience to the moral law, which, indeed, he could not, till now, perform. That it is the moral law, and that alone, which is here intended, appears evidently from the words that follow: "Do we then make void the law through faith? God forbid: Yea, we establish the law. What law do we establish by faith? Not the ritual law: Not the ceremonial law of Moses. In nowise; but the great, unchangeable law of love, the holy love of God and of our neighbour."

2. Faith in general is a divine, supernatural "*elegchos,*" "evidence" or "conviction," "of things not seen," not discoverable by our bodily senses, as being either past, future, or spiritual. Justifying faith implies, not only a divine evidence or conviction that "God was in Christ, reconciling the world unto himself;" but a sure trust and confidence that Christ died for "my" sins, that he loved "me," and gave himself for "me." And at what time soever a sinner thus believes, be it in early childhood, in the strength of his years, or when he is old and hoary-haired, God justifieth that ungodly one: God, for the sake of his Son, pardoneth and absolveth him, who had in him, till then, no good thing. Repentance, indeed, God had given him before; but that repentance was neither more nor less than a deep sense of the want of all good, and the presence of all evil. And whatever good he hath, or doeth, from that hour when he first believes in God through Christ, faith does not "find," but "bring." This is the fruit of faith. First the tree is good, and then the fruit is good also.

3. I cannot describe the nature of this faith better than in the words of our own Church: "The only instrument of salvation" (whereof justification is one branch) "is faith; that is, a sure trust and confidence that God both hath and will forgive our sins, that he hath accepted us again into His favour, for the merits of Christ's death and passion.—But here we must take heed that we do not halt with God, through an inconstant, wavering faith: Peter, coming to Christ upon the water, because he fainted in faith, was in danger of drowning; so we, if we begin to waver or doubt, it is to be feared that we shall sink as Peter did, not into the water, but into the bottomless pit of hell fire." ("Second Sermon on the Passion")

"Therefore, have a sure and constant faith, not only that the death of Christ is available for all the world, but that he hath made a full and sufficient sacrifice for "thee," a perfect cleansing of "thy" sins, so that thou mayest say, with the Apostle, he loved "thee," and gave himself for "thee." For this is to make Christ "thine own," and to apply his merits unto "thyself." ("Sermon on the Sacrament, First Part")

4. By affirming that this faith is the term or "condition of justification," I mean, First, that there is no justification without it. "He that believeth not is condemned already;" and so long as he believeth not, that condemnation cannot be removed, but "the wrath of God abideth on him." As "there is no other name given under heaven," than that of Jesus of Nazareth, no other merit whereby a condemned sinner can ever be saved from the guilt of sin; so there is no other way of obtaining a share in his merit, than "by faith in his name." So that as long as we are without this faith, we are "strangers to the covenant of promise," we are "aliens from the commonwealth of Israel, and without God in the world." Whatsoever virtues (so called) a man may have,—I speak of those unto whom the gospel is preached; for "what have I to do to judge them that are without?"—whatsoever good works (so accounted) he may do, it profiteth not; he is still a "child of wrath," still under the curse, till he believes in Jesus.

5. Faith, therefore, is the "necessary" condition of justification; yea, and the "only necessary" condition thereof. This is the Second point carefully to be observed; that, the very moment God giveth faith (for "it is the gift of God") to the "ungodly" that "worketh not," that "faith is counted to him for righteousness." He hath no righteousness at all, antecedent to this, not so much as negative righteousness, or innocence. But "faith is imputed to him for righteousness," the very moment that he believeth. Not that God (as was observed before) thinketh him to be what he is not. But as "he made Christ to be sin for us," that is, treated him as a sinner, punishing him for our sins; so he counteth us righteous, from the time we believe in him: That is, he doth not punish us for our sins; yea, treats us as though we are guiltless and righteous.

6. Surely the difficulty of assenting to this proposition, that "faith is the "only condition" of justification," must arise from not understanding it. We mean thereby thus much, that it is the only thing without which none is justified; the only thing that is immediately, indispensably, absolutely requisite in order to pardon. As, on the one hand, though a man

should have every thing else without faith, yet he cannot be justified; so, on the other, though he be supposed to want everything else, yet if he hath faith, he cannot but be justified. For suppose a sinner of any kind or degree, in a full sense of his total ungodliness, of his utter inability to think, speak, or do good, and his absolute meetness for hell-fire; suppose, I say, this sinner, helpless and hopeless, casts himself wholly on the mercy of God in Christ, (which indeed he cannot do but by the grace of God,) who can doubt but he is forgiven in that moment? Who will affirm that any more is "indispensably required" before that sinner can be justified? Now, if there ever was one such instance from the beginning of the world, (and have there not been, and are there not, ten thousand times ten thousand?) it plainly follows, that faith is, in the above sense, the sole condition of justification.

7. It does not become poor, guilty, sinful worms, who receive whatsoever blessings they enjoy, (from the least drop of water that cools our tongue, to the immense riches of glory in eternity,) of grace, of mere favour, and not of debt, to ask of God the reasons of his conduct. It is not meet for us to call Him in question "who giveth account to none of his ways;" to demand, "Why didst thou make faith the condition, the only condition, of justification? Wherefore didst thou decree, "He that believeth," and he only, "shall be saved?" This is the very point on which St. Paul so strongly insists in the ninth chapter of this Epistle, viz., That the terms of pardon and acceptance must depend, not on us, but "on him that calleth us;" that there is no "unrighteousness with God," in fixing his own terms, not according to ours, but his own good pleasure; who may justly say, "I will have mercy on whom I will have mercy;" namely, on him who believeth in Jesus. "So then it is not of him that willeth, nor of him that runneth," to choose the condition on which he shall find acceptance; "but of God that showeth mercy;" that accepteth none at all, but of his own free love, his unmerited goodness. "Therefore hath he mercy on whom he will have mercy," viz., on those who believe on the Son of his love; "and whom he will," that is, those who believe not, "he hardeneth," leaves at last to the hardness of their hearts.

8. One reason, however, we may humbly conceive, of God's fixing this condition of justification, "If thou believest in the Lord Jesus Christ, thou shalt be saved," was to "hide pride from man." Pride had already destroyed the very angels of God, had cast down "a third part of the stars of heaven." It was likewise in great measure owing to this, when the tempter said, "Ye shall be as gods," that Adam fell from his own steadfastness, and brought sin and death into the world. It was therefore an instance of wisdom worthy of God, to appoint such a condition of reconciliation for him and all his posterity as might effectually humble, might abase them to the dust. And such is faith. It is peculiarly fitted for this end: For he that cometh unto God by this faith, must fix his eye singly on his own wickedness, on his guilt and helplessness, without having the least regard to any supposed good in himself, to any virtue or righteousness whatsoever. He must come as a "mere sinner," inwardly and outwardly, self-destroyed and self-condemned, bringing nothing to God but ungodliness only, pleading nothing of his own but sin and misery. Thus it is, and thus alone, when his "mouth is stopped," and he stands utterly "guilty before" God, that he can "look unto Jesus," as the whole and sole "Propitiation for his sins." Thus only can he be "found in him," and receive the "righteousness which is of God by faith."

9. Thou ungodly one, who hearest or readest these words! thou vile, helpless, miserable sinner! I charge thee before God, the Judge of all, go straight unto him, with all thy ungodliness. Take heed thou destroy not thy own soul by pleading thy righteousness, more or less. Go as altogether ungodly, guilty, lost, destroyed, deserving and dropping into hell; and thou shalt then find favour in his sight, and know that he justifieth the ungodly. As such thou shalt be brought unto the "blood of sprinkling," as an undone, helpless, damned sinner. Thus "look unto Jesus!" There is "the Lamb of God," who "taketh away thy sins!" Plead thou no works, no righteousness of thine own! no humility, contrition, sincerity! In nowise. That were, in very deed, to deny the Lord that bought thee. No: Plead thou, singly, the blood of the covenant, the ransom paid for thy proud, stubborn, sinful soul. Who art thou, that now seest and feelest both thine inward and outward ungodliness? Thou art the man! I want thee for my Lord! I challenge "thee" for a child of God by faith! The Lord hath need of thee. Thou who feelest thou art just fit for hell, art just fit to advance his glory; the glory of his free grace, justifying the ungodly and him that worketh not. O come quickly! Believe in the Lord Jesus; and thou, even thou, art reconciled to God.

6*. THE RIGHTEOUSNESS OF FAITH

"Moses describeth the righteousness which is of the law, That the man which doeth those things shall live by them. But the righteousness which is of faith speaketh on this wise, Say not in thine heart, Who shall ascend into heaven? (that is, to bring Christ down from above:) Or, Who shall descend into the deep? (that is, to bring up Christ again from the dead.) But what saith it? The word is nigh thee, even in thy mouth, and in thy heart: That is, the word of faith, which we preach."

Rom. 10:5–8.

1. The Apostle does not here oppose the covenant given by Moses, to the covenant given by Christ. If we ever imagined this, it was for want of observing, that the latter as well as the former part of these words were spoken by Moses himself to the people of Israel, and that concerning the covenant which then was. (Deut. 30:11, 12, 14.) But it is the covenant of grace, which God, through Christ, hath established with men in all ages, (as well before and under the Jewish dispensation, as since God was manifest in the flesh,) which St. Paul here opposes to the covenant of works, made with Adam while in Paradise, but commonly supposed to be the only covenant which God had made with man, particularly by those Jews of whom the Apostle writes.

---

* [text from the 1872 edition]

2. Of these it was that he so affectionately speaks in the beginning of this chapter: "My heart's desire and prayer to God for Israel is, that they may be saved. For I bear them record, that they have a zeal for God, but not according to knowledge. For they being ignorant of God's righteousness," (of the justification that flows from his mere grace and mercy, freely forgiving our sins through the Son of his love, through the redemption which is in Jesus,) "and seeking to establish their own righteousness," (their own holiness, antecedent to faith in "him that justifieth the ungodly," as the ground of their pardon and acceptance,) "have not submitted themselves unto the righteousness of God," and consequently seek death in the error of their life.

3. They were ignorant that "Christ is the end of the law for righteousness to every one that believeth;"—that, by the oblation of himself once offered, he had put an end to the first law or covenant, (which, indeed, was not given by God to Moses, but to Adam in his state of innocence,) the strict tenor whereof, without any abatement, was, "Do this, and live;" and, at the same time, purchased for us that better covenant," Believe, and live;" believe, and thou shalt be saved; now saved, both from the guilt and power of sin, and, of consequence, from the wages of it.

4. And how many are equally ignorant now, even among those who are called by the name of Christ! How many who have now a "zeal for God," yet have it not "according to knowledge;" but are still seeking "to establish their own righteousness," as the ground of their pardon and acceptance; and therefore, vehemently refuse to "submit themselves unto the righteousness of God!" Surely my heart's desire, and prayer to God for you, brethren, is, that ye may be saved. And, in order to remove this grand stumbling-block out of your way, I will endeavour to show, First, what the righteousness *is*, which is of the law; and what "the righteousness which is of faith;" Secondly, the folly of trusting in the righteousness of the law, and the wisdom of submitting to that which is of faith.

I. 1. And, First, "the righteousness which is of the law saith, The man which doeth these things shall live by them." Constantly and perfectly observe all these things to do them, and then thou shalt live for ever. This law, or covenant, (usually called the Covenant of Works,) given by God to man in Paradise, required an obedience perfect in all its parts, entire and wanting nothing, as the condition of his eternal continuance in the holiness and happiness wherein he was created.

2. It required that man should fulfil all righteousness, inward and outward, negative and positive: That he should not only abstain from every idle word, and avoid every evil work, but should keep every affection, every desire, every thought, in obedience to the will of God: That he should continue holy, as he which had created him was holy, both in heart, and in all manner of conversation: That he should be pure in heart, even as God is pure; perfect as his Father in heaven was perfect: That he should love the Lord his God with all his heart, with all his soul, with all his mind, and with all his strength; that he should love every soul which God had made, even as God had loved him: That by this universal benevolence, he should dwell in God, (who is love,) and God in him: That he should serve the Lord his God with all his strength, and in all things singly aim at his glory.

3. These were the things which the righteousness of the law required, that he who did them might live thereby. But it farther required, that this entire obedience to God, this inward and outward holiness, this conformity both of heart and life to his will, should be perfect in *degree*. No abatement, no allowance could possibly be made, for falling short in any degree, as to any jot or tittle, either of the outward or the inward law. If every commandment, relating to outward things, was obeyed, yet that was not sufficient unless every one was obeyed with all the strength, in the highest measure, and most perfect manner. Nor did it answer the demand of this covenant, to love God with every power and faculty, unless he were loved with the full capacity of each, with the whole possibility of the soul.

4. One thing more was indispensably required by the righteousness of the law, namely, that this universal obedience, this perfect holiness both of heart and life, should be perfectly uninterrupted also, should continue without any intermission, from the moment wherein God created man, and breathed into his nostrils the breath of life, until the days of his trial should be ended, and he should be confirmed in life everlasting.

5. The righteousness, then, which is of the law, speaketh on this wise: "Thou, O man of God, stand fast in love, in the image of God wherein thou art made. If thou wilt remain in life, keep the commandments, which are now written in thy heart. Love the Lord thy God with all thy heart. Love, as thyself, every soul that he hath made. Desire nothing but God. Aim at God in every thought, in every word and work. Swerve not, in one motion of body or soul, from him, thy mark, and the prize of thy high calling; and let all that is in thee praise his holy name, every power and faculty of thy soul, in every kind, in every degree, and at every moment of thine existence. 'This do, and thou shalt live:' Thy light shall shine, thy love shall flame more and more, till thou art received up into the house of God in the heavens, to reign with him for ever and ever."

6. "But the righteousness which is of faith speaketh on this wise: Say not in thine heart, Who shall ascend into heaven? that is, to bring down Christ from above;" (as though it were some impossible task which God required thee previously to perform in order to thine acceptance;) "or, Who shall descend into the deep? that is, to bring up Christ from the dead;" (as though that were still remaining to be done, for the sake of which thou wert to be accepted;) "but what saith it? The word," according to the tenor of which thou mayest now be accepted as an heir of life eternal, "is nigh thee, even in thy mouth, and in thy heart; that is, the word of faith which we preach,"—the new covenant which God hath now established with sinful man, through Christ Jesus.

7. By "the righteousness which is of faith" is meant, that condition of justification, (and, in consequence, of present and final salvation, if we endure therein unto the end,) which was given by God to *fallen man*, through the merits and mediation of his only-begotten Son. This was in part revealed

to Adam, soon after his fall; being contained in the original promise, made to him and his seed, concerning the Seed of the Woman, who should "bruise the serpent's head." (Gen. 3:15.) It was a little more clearly revealed to Abraham, by the angel of God from heaven, saying, "By myself have I sworn, saith the Lord, that in thy seed shall all the nations of the world be blessed." (Gen. 12:15, 18.) It was yet more fully made known to Moses, to David, and to the Prophets that followed; and, through them, to many of the people of God in their respective generations. But still the bulk even of these were ignorant of it; and very few understood it clearly. Still "life and immortality" were not so "brought to light" to the Jews of old, as they are now unto us "by the gospel."

8. Now, this covenant saith not to sinful man, "Perform unsinning obedience, and live." If this were the term, he would have no more benefit by all which Christ hath done and suffered for him, than if he was required, in order to life, to "ascend into heaven, and bring down Christ from above;" or to "descend into the deep," into the invisible world, and "bring up Christ from the dead." It doth not require any impossibility to be done: (Although to mere man, what it requires would be impossible; but not to man assisted by the Spirit of God:) This were only to mock human weakness. Indeed, strictly speaking, the covenant of *grace* doth not require us to *do* anything at all, as absolutely and indispensably necessary in order to our justification; but only, to *believe* in Him who, for the sake of his Son, and the propitiation which he hath made, "justifieth the ungodly that worketh not," and imputes his faith to him for righteousness. Even so Abraham "believed in the Lord, and he counted it to him for righteousness." (Gen. 15:6.) "And he received the sign of circumcision, a seal of the righteousness of faith,—that he might be the father of all them that believe,—that righteousness might be imputed unto them also." (Rom. 4:11.) "Now it was not written for his sake alone, that it," *i.e.*, faith, "was imputed to him; but for us also, to whom it shall be imputed," to whom faith shall be imputed for righteousness, shall stand in the stead of perfect obedience, in order to our acceptance with God, "if we believe on him who raised up Jesus our Lord from the dead; who was delivered" to death "for our offences, and was raised again for our justification:" (Rom. 4:23–25:) For the assurance of the remission of our sins, and of a second life to come, to them that believe.

9. What saith then the covenant of forgiveness, of unmerited love, of pardoning mercy? "Believe in the Lord Jesus Christ, and thou shalt be saved." In the day thou believest, thou shalt surely live. Thou shalt be restored to the favour of God; and in his pleasure is life. Thou shalt be saved from the curse, and from the wrath of God. Thou shalt be quickened, from the death of sin into the life of righteousness. And if thou endure to the end, believing in Jesus, thou shalt never taste the second death; but, having suffered with thy Lord, shalt also live and reign with him for ever and ever.

10. Now, "this word is nigh thee." This condition of life is plain, easy, always at hand. "It is in thy mouth, and in thy heart," through the operation of the Spirit of God. The moment "thou believest in thine heart" in him whom God "hath raised from the dead," and "confessest with thy mouth the Lord Jesus," as *thy* Lord and *thy* God, "thou shalt be saved" from condemnation, from the guilt and punishment of thy former sins, and shalt have power to serve God in true holiness all the remaining days of thy life.

11. What is the difference then between the "righteousness which is of the law," and the "righteousness which is of faith?—between the first covenant, or the covenant of works, and the second, the covenant of grace? The essential, unchangeable difference is this: The one supposes him to whom it is given to be already holy and happy, created in the image and enjoying the favour of God; and prescribes the condition whereon he may continue therein, in love and joy, life and immortality: The other supposes him to whom it is given to be now unholy and unhappy, fallen short of the glorious image of God, having the wrath of God abiding on him, and hastening, through sin, whereby his soul is dead, to bodily death, and death everlasting; and to man in this state it prescribes the condition whereon he may regain the pearl he has lost, may recover the favour and image of God, may retrieve the life of God in his soul, and be restored to the knowledge and the love of God, which is the beginning of life eternal.

12. Again: The covenant of works, in order to man's *continuance* in the favour of God, in his knowledge and love, in holiness and happiness, required of perfect man a *perfect* and uninterrupted *obedience* to every point of the law of God. Whereas, the covenant of grace, in order to man's *recovery* of the favour and the life of God, requires only *faith*; living faith in Him who, through God, justifies him that obeyed not.

13. Yet, again: The covenant of works required of Adam and all his children, to pay the price themselves, in consideration of which they were to receive all the future blessings of God. But, in the covenant of grace, seeing we have nothing to pay, God "frankly forgives us all:" Provided only, that we believe in Him who hath paid the price for us; who hath given himself a "Propitiation for our sins, for the sins of the whole world."

14. Thus the first covenant required what is now *afar off* from all the children of men; namely, unsinning obedience, which is far from those who are "conceived and born in sin." Whereas, the second requires what is nigh at hand; as though it should say, "Thou art sin! God is love! Thou by sin art fallen short of the glory of God; yet there is mercy with him. Bring then all thy sins to the pardoning God, and they shall vanish away as a cloud. If thou wert not ungodly, there would be no room for him to justify thee as ungodly. But now draw near, in full assurance of faith. He speaketh, and it is done. Fear not, only believe; for even the just God justifieth all that believe in Jesus."

II. 1. These things considered, it would be easy to show, as I proposed to do in the Second place, the folly of trusting in the "righteousness which is of the law," and the wisdom of submitting to "the righteousness which is of faith."

The folly of those who still trust in the "righteousness which is of the law," the terms of which are, "Do this, and live," may abundantly appear from hence: They set out wrong;

their very first step is a fundamental mistake: For, before they can ever think of claiming any blessing on the terms of this covenant, they must suppose themselves to be in his state with whom this covenant was made. But how vain a supposition is this; since it was made with Adam in a state of innocence! How weak, therefore, must that whole building be, which stands on such a foundation! And how foolish are they who thus build on the sand! who seem never to have considered, that the covenant of works was not given to man when he was "dead in trespasses and sins," but when he was alive to God, when he knew no sin, but was holy as God is holy; who forget, that it was never designed for the *recovery* of the favour and life of God once lost, but only for the *continuance* and increase thereof, till it should be complete in life everlasting.

2. Neither do they consider, who are thus seeking to establish their "own righteousness, which is of the law," what manner of obedience or righteousness that is which the law indispensably requires. It must be perfect and entire in every point, or it answers not the demand of the law. But which of you is able to perform such obedience; or, consequently, to live thereby? Who among you fulfils every jot and tittle even of the outward commandments of God? doing nothing, great or small, which God forbids? leaving nothing undone which he enjoins? speaking no *idle word?* having your conversation always "meet to minister grace to the hearers?" and, "whether you eat or drink, or whatever you do, doing all to the glory of God?" And how much less are you able to fulfil all the inward commandments of God! those which require that every temper and motion of your soul should be holiness unto the Lord! Are you able to "love God with all your heart?" to love all mankind as your own soul? to "pray without ceasing? in every thing to give thanks?" to have God always before you? and to keep every affection, desire, and thought, in obedience to his law?

3. You should farther consider, that the righteousness of the law requires, not only the obeying every command of God, negative and positive, internal and external, but likewise in the perfect degree. In every instance whatever, the voice of the law is, "Thou shalt serve the Lord thy God with all thy strength." It allows no abatement of any kind: It excuses no defect: It condemns every coming short of the full measure of obedience, and immediately pronounces a curse on the offender: It regards only the invariable rules of justice, and saith, "I know not to show mercy."

4. Who then can appear before such a Judge, who is "extreme to mark what is done amiss?" How weak are they who desire to be tried at the bar where "no flesh living can be justified!"—none of the offspring of Adam. For, suppose we did now keep every commandment with all our strength; yet one single breach which ever was, utterly destroys our whole claim to life. If we have ever offended in any one point, this righteousness is at an end. For the law condemns all who do not perform uninterrupted as well as perfect obedience. So that, according to the sentence of this, for him who hath once sinned, in any degree, "there remaineth only a fearful looking for of fiery indignation, which shall devour the adversaries" of God.

5. Is it not then the very foolishness of folly, for fallen man to seek life by this righteousness? for man, who was "shapen in wickedness, and in sin did his mother conceive him?" man, who is, by nature, all "earthly, sensual, devilish;" altogether corrupt and abominable;" in whom, till he find grace, "dwelleth no good thing;" nay, who cannot of himself think one good thought; who is indeed all sin, a mere lump of ungodliness, and who commits sin in every breath he draws; whose actual transgressions, in word and deed, are more in number than the hairs of his head? What stupidity, what senselessness must it be for such an unclean, guilty, helpless worm as this, to dream of seeking acceptance by his own righteousness, of living by "the righteousness which is of the law!"

6. Now, whatsoever considerations prove the folly of trusting in the "righteousness which is of the law," prove equally the wisdom of submitting to the "righteousness which is of God by faith." This were easy to be shown with regard to each of the preceding considerations. But, to wave this, the wisdom of the first step hereto, the disclaiming our own righteousness, plainly appears from hence, that it is acting according to truth, to the real nature of things. For, what is it more, than to acknowledge, with our heart as well as lips, the true state wherein we are? to acknowledge that we bring with us into the world a corrupt, sinful nature; more corrupt, indeed, than we can easily conceive, or find words to express? that hereby we are prone to all that is evil, and averse from all that is good; that we are full of pride, self will, unruly passions, foolish desires, vile and inordinate affections; lovers of the world, lovers of pleasure more than lovers of God? that our lives have been no better than our hearts, but many ways ungodly and unholy; insomuch that our actual sins, both in word and deed, have been as the stars of heaven for multitude; that, on all these accounts, we are displeasing to Him who is of purer eyes than to behold iniquity, and deserve nothing from him but indignation and wrath and death, the due wages of sin? that we cannot, by any of our righteousness, (for indeed we have none at all,) nor by any of our works, (for they are as the tree upon which they grow,) appease the wrath of God, or avert the punishment we have justly deserved; yea, that, if left to ourselves, we shall only wax worse and worse, sink deeper and deeper into sin, offend God more and more, both with our evil works, and with the evil tempers of our carnal mind, till we fill up the measure of our iniquities, and bring upon ourselves swift destruction? And is not this the very state wherein by nature we are? To acknowledge this, then, both with our heart and lips, that is, to disclaim our own righteousness, "the righteousness which is of the law," is to act according to the real nature of things, and, consequently, is an instance of true wisdom.

7. The wisdom of submitting to "the righteousness of faith" appears farther, from this consideration, that it is the righteousness of God: I mean here, it is that method of reconciliation with God which hath been chosen and established by God himself, not only as he is the God of wisdom, but as he is the sovereign Lord of heaven and earth, and of every creature which he hath made. Now, as it is not meet for man to say unto God, "What doest thou?"—as none

who is not utterly void of understanding, will contend with One that is mightier than he, with Him whose kingdom ruleth over all; so it is true wisdom, it is a mark of sound understanding, to acquiesce in whatever he hath chosen; to say in this, as in all things, "It is the Lord: Let him do what seemeth him good."

8. It may be farther considered, that it was of mere grace, of free love, of undeserved mercy, that God hath vouchsafed to sinful man any way of reconciliation with himself, that we were not cut away from his hand, and utterly blotted out of his remembrance. Therefore, whatever method he is pleased to appoint, of his tender mercy, of his unmerited goodness, whereby his enemies, who have so deeply revolted from him, so long and obstinately rebelled against him, may still find favour in his sight, it is doubtless our wisdom to accept it with all thankfulness.

9. To mention but one consideration more. It is wisdom to aim at the best end by the best means. Now the best end which any creature can pursue is, happiness in God. And the best end a fallen creature can pursue is, the recovery of the favour and image of God. But the best, indeed the only, means under heaven given to a man, whereby he may regain the favour of God, which is better than life itself, or the image of God, which is the true life of the soul, is the submitting to the "righteousness which is of faith," the believing in the only-begotten Son of God.

III. 1. Whosoever therefore thou art, who desirest to be forgiven and reconciled to the favour of God, do not say in thy heart, "I must *first do this*; I must *first* conquer every sin; break off every evil word and work, and do all good to all men; or, I must *first* go to church, receive the Lord's Supper, hear more sermons, and say more prayers." Alas, my brother! Thou art clean gone out of the way. Thou art still "ignorant of the righteousness of God," and art "seeking to establish thy own righteousness," as the ground of thy reconciliation. Knowest thou not, that thou canst do nothing but sin, till thou art reconciled to God? Wherefore, then, dost thou say," I must do this and this *first*, and then I shall believe?" Nay, but *first believe!* Believe in the Lord Jesus Christ, the Propitiation for thy sins. Let this good foundation first be laid, and then thou shalt do all things well.

2. Neither say in thy heart, "I cannot be accepted yet, because I am not *good enough*." Who is *good enough*—who ever was—to merit acceptance at God's hands? Was ever any child of Adam *good enough* for this? or will any till the consummation of all things? And as for thee, thou art not good at all: There dwelleth in thee no good thing. And thou never wilt be, till thou believe in Jesus. Rather, thou wilt find thyself worse and worse. But is there any need of being worse, in order to be accepted? Art thou not *bad enough* already? Indeed thou art, and that God knoweth. And thou thyself canst not deny it. Then delay not. All things are now ready. "Arise, and wash away thy sins." The fountain is open. Now is the time to wash thee white in the blood of the Lamb. Now he shall "purge" thee as "with hyssop," and thou shalt "be clean:" He shall "wash" thee, and thou shalt "be whiter than snow."

3. Do not say, "But I am not *contrite enough:* I am not *sensible enough* of my sins." I know it. I would to God thou wert more *sensible* of them, more *contrite* a thousand fold than thou art. But do not stay for this. It may be, God will make thee so, not before thou believest, but by believing. It may be, thou wilt not weep much till thou lovest much because thou hast had much forgiven. In the mean time, look unto Jesus. Behold, how he loveth thee! What could he have done more for thee which he hath not done?

O Lamb of God, was ever pain,
Was ever love like thine?

Look steadily upon him, till he looks on thee, and breaks thy hard heart. Then shall thy "head" be "waters," and thy "eyes fountains of tears."

4. Nor yet do thou say, "I must *do* something more *before* I come to Christ." I grant, supposing thy Lord should delay his coming, it were meet and right to wait for his appearing, in doing, so far as thou hast power, whatsoever he hath commanded thee. But there is no necessity for making such a supposition. How knowest thou that he will delay? Perhaps he will appear, as the day-spring from on high, before the morning light. O do not set him a time! Expect him every hour. Now he is nigh! even at the door!

5. And to what end wouldest thou wait for *more sincerity, before* thy sins are blotted out? to make thee more worthy of the grace of God? Alas, thou art still "establishing thy own righteousness." He will have mercy, not because thou art worthy of it, but because his compassions fail not; not because thou art righteous, but because Jesus Christ hath atoned for thy sins.

Again, if there be anything good in *sincerity,* why dost thou expect it *before* thou hast faith?—seeing faith itself is the only root of whatever is really good and holy.

Above all, how long wilt thou forget, that whatsoever thou doest, or whatsoever thou hast, before thy sins are forgiven thee, it avails nothing with God toward the procuring of thy forgiveness? yea, and that it must all be cast behind thy back, trampled under foot, made no account of, or thou wilt never find favour in God's sight; because, until then, thou canst not ask it, as a mere sinner, guilty, lost, undone, having nothing to plead, nothing to offer to God, but only the merits of his well-beloved Son, "who loved *thee,* and gave himself for *thee!*"

6. To conclude. Whosoever thou art, O man, who hast the sentence of death in thyself, who feelest thyself a condemned sinner, and hast the wrath of God abiding on thee: Unto thee saith the Lord, not, "Do this,"—perfectly obey all my commands,—"and live;" but, "Believe in the Lord Jesus Christ, and thou shalt be saved." "The word of faith is nigh unto thee:" Now, at this instant, in the present moment, and in thy present state, sinner as thou art, just as thou art, believe the gospel; and "I will be merciful unto *thy* unrighteousness, and *thy* iniquities will I remember no more."

7*. THE WAY TO THE KINGDOM

"The kingdom of God is at hand: repent ye, and believe the gospel."

Mark 1:15

These words naturally lead us to consider, First, the nature of true religion, here termed by our Lord, "the kingdom of God," which, saith he, "is at hand;" and, Secondly, the way thereto, which he points out in those words, "Repent ye, and believe the gospel."

I. 1. We are, First, to consider the nature of true religion, here termed by our Lord, "the kingdom of God." The same expression the great Apostle uses in his Epistle to the Romans, where he likewise explains his Lord's words, saying, "The kingdom of God is not meat and drink; but righteousness, and peace, and joy in the Holy Ghost." (Rom. 14:17.)

2. "The kingdom of God," or true religion, "is not meat and drink." It is well known that not only the unconverted Jews, but great numbers of those who had received the faith of Christ, were, notwithstanding "zealous of the law," (Acts 21:20,) even the ceremonial law of Moses. Whatsoever, therefore, they found written therein, either concerning meat and drink offerings, or the distinction between clean and unclean meats, they not only observed themselves, but vehemently pressed the same even on those "among the Gentiles" (or heathens) "who were turned to God;" yea, to such a degree, that some of them taught, wheresoever they came among them, "Except ye be circumcised, and keep the law," (the whole ritual law,) "ye cannot be saved." (Acts 15:1, 24.)

3. In opposition to these, the Apostle declares, both here and in many other places, that true religion does not consist in *meat* and *drink*, or in any ritual observances; nor, indeed in any outward thing whatever; in anything exterior to the heart; the whole substance thereof lying in "righteousness, peace, and joy in the Holy Ghost."

4. Not in any *outward thing*; such as *forms*, or *ceremonies*, even of the most excellent kind. Supposing these to be ever so decent and significant, ever so expressive of inward things: supposing them ever so helpful, not only to the vulgar, whose thought reaches little farther than their sight; but even to men of understanding, men of strong capacities, as doubtless they may sometimes be: Yea, supposing them, as in the case of the Jews, to be appointed by God himself; yet even during the period of time wherein that appointment remains in force, true religion does not principally consist therein; nay, strictly speaking, not at all. How much more must this hold concerning such rites and forms as are only of human appointment! The religion of Christ rises infinitely higher, and lies immensely deeper, than all these. These are good in their place; just so far as they are in fact subservient to true religion. And it were superstition to object against them, while they are applied only as occasional helps to human weakness. But let no man carry them farther. Let no man dream that they have any intrinsic worth; or that religion cannot subsist without them. This were to make them an abomination to the Lord.

5. The nature of religion is so far from consisting in these, in forms of worship, or rites and ceremonies, that it does not properly consist in any outward actions, of what kind so ever. It is true, a man cannot have any religion who is guilty of vicious, immoral actions; or who does to others what he would not they should do to him, if he were in the same circumstance. And it is also true, that he can have no real religion who "knows to do good, and doth it not." Yet may a man both abstain from outward evil, and do good, and still have no religion. Yea, two persons may do the same outward work; suppose, feeding the hungry, or clothing the naked; and, in the meantime, one of these may be truly religious, and the other have no religion at all: For the one may act from the love of God, and the other from the love of praise. So manifest it is, that although true religion naturally leads to every good word and work, yet the real nature thereof lies deeper still, even in "the hidden man of the heart."

6. I say of *the heart*. For neither does religion consist Orthodoxy, or right opinions; which, although they are not properly outward things, are not in the heart, but the understanding. A man may be orthodox in every point; he may not only espouse right opinions, but zealously defend them against all opposers; he may think justly concerning the incarnation of our Lord, concerning the ever-blessed Trinity, and every other doctrine contained in the oracles of God; he may assent to all the three creeds,—that called the Apostles', the Nicene, and the Athanasian; and yet it is possible he may have no religion at all, no more than a Jew, Turk, or pagan. He may be almost as orthodox—as the devil, (though, indeed, not altogether; for every man errs in something; whereas we can't well conceive him to hold any erroneous opinion,) and may, all the while be as great a stranger as he to the religion of the heart.

7. This alone is religion, truly so called: This alone is in the sight of God of great price. The Apostle sums it all up in three particulars, "righteousness, and peace, and joy in the Holy Ghost." And, First, *righteousness*. We cannot be at a loss concerning this, if we remember the words of our Lord, describing the two grand branches thereof, on which "hang all the law and the prophets;" "Thou shalt love the Lord thy God with all thy heart, and with all thy mind, and with all thy soul, and with all thy strength: This is the first and great commandment;" (Mark 12:30;) the first and great branch of Christian righteousness. Thou shalt delight thyself in the Lord thy God; thou shalt seek and find all happiness in him. He shall be "thy shield, and thy exceeding great reward," in time and in eternity. All thy bones shall say, "Whom have I in heaven but thee? And there is none upon earth that I desire beside thee!" Thou shalt hear and fulfil His word who saith, "My son, give me thy heart." And, having given him thy heart, thy inmost soul, to reign there without a rival, thou mayest well cry out, in the fullness of thy heart, "I will love thee, O Lord, my strength. The Lord is my strong rock, and my defence; my Saviour, my God, and my might, in whom

---

* [text from the 1872 edition]

I will trust; my buckler, the horn also of my salvation, and my refuge."

8. And the second commandment is like unto this; the Second great branch of Christian righteousness is closely and inseparably connected therewith; even, "Thou shalt love thy neighbour as thyself." *Thou shalt love*,—thou shalt embrace with the most tender good-will, the most earnest and cordial affection, the most inflamed desires of preventing or removing all evil, and of procuring for him every possible good,—*Thy neighbour*,—that is, not only thy friend, thy kinsman, or thy acquaintance; not only the virtuous, the friendly, him that loves thee, that prevents or returns thy kindness; but every child of man, every human creature, every soul which God hath made; not excepting him whom thou never hast seen in the flesh, whom thou knowest not, either by face or name; not excepting him whom thou knowest to be evil and unthankful, him that still despitefully uses and persecutes thee: Him thou shalt love *as thyself*, with the same invariable thirst after his happiness in every kind; the same unwearied care to screen him from whatever might grieve or hurt either his soul or body.

9. Now is not this love "the fulfilling of the law?" the sum of all Christian righteousness?—of all inward righteousness; for it necessarily implies "bowels of mercies, humbleness of mind," (seeing "love is not puffed up,") "gentleness, meekness, long-suffering:" (for love "is not provoked;" but "believeth, hopeth, endureth all things:") And of all outward righteousness; for "love worketh no evil to his neighbour," either by word or deed. It cannot willingly hurt or grieve any one. And it is zealous of good works. Every lover of mankind, as he hath opportunity, "doth good unto all men," being (without partiality and without hypocrisy) "full of mercy and good fruits."

10. But true religion, or a heart right toward God and man, implies happiness as well as holiness. For it is not only "righteousness," but also "peace and joy in the Holy Ghost." What peace? "The peace of God," which God only can give, and the world cannot take away; the peace which "passeth all under-standing," all barely rational conception; being a supernatural sensation, a divine taste, of "the powers of the world to come;" such as the natural man knoweth not, how wise soever in the things of this world; nor, indeed, can he know it, in his present state, "because it is spiritually discerned." It is a peace that banishes all doubt, all painful uncertainty; the Spirit of God bearing witness with the spirit of a Christian, that he is "a child of God." And it banishes fear, all such fear as hath torment; the fear of the wrath of God; the fear of hell; the fear of the devil; and, in particular, the fear of death: he that hath the peace of God, desiring, if it were the will of God, "to depart, and to be with Christ."

11. With this peace of God, wherever it is fixed in the soul, there is also "joy in the Holy Ghost;" joy wrought in the heart by the Holy Ghost, by the ever-blessed Spirit of God. He it is that worketh in us that calm, humble rejoicing in God, through Christ Jesus, "by whom we have now received the atonement," *katallagen*, the reconciliation with God; and that enables us boldly to confirm the truth of the royal Psalmists declaration, Blessed is the man (or rather, *happy*) whose unrighteousness is forgiven, and whose sin is covered. he it is that inspires the Christian soul with that even, solid joy, which arises from the testimony of the Spirit that he is a child of God; and that gives him to rejoice with joy unspeakable, in hope of the glory of God; hope both of the glorious image of God, which is in part and shall be fully "revealed in him;" and of that crown of glory which fadeth not away, reserved in heaven for him.

12. This holiness and happiness, joined in one, are sometimes styled, in the inspired writings, "the kingdom of God," (as by our Lord in the text,) and sometimes, "the kingdom of heaven." It is termed "the kingdom of God," because it is the immediate fruit of Gods reigning in the soul. So soon as ever he takes unto himself his mighty power, and sets up his throne in our hearts, they are instantly filled with this "righteousness, and peace, and joy in the holy Ghost." It is called "the kingdom of heaven" because it is (in a degree) heaven opened in the soul. For whosoever they are that experience this, they can aver before angels and men,

everlasting life is won,
Glory is on earth begun,

according to the constant tenor of Scripture, which everywhere bears record, God "hath given unto us eternal life, and this life is in his Son. he that hath the Son" (reigning in his heart) "hath life," even life everlasting. (1 John 5:11, 12.) For "this is life eternal, to know thee, the only true God, and Jesus Christ, whom thou hast sent." (John 17:3.) And they, to whom this is given, may confidently address God, though they were in the midst of a fiery furnace,

Thee, Lord, safe shielded by thy power,
Thee, Son of God, Jehovah, we adore;
In form of man descending to appear:
To thee be ceaseless hallelujahs given,
Praise, as in heaven thy throne, we offer here;
For where thy presence is displayd, is heaven.

13. And this "kingdom of God," or of heaven, "is at hand." As these words were originally spoken, they implied that "the time" was then fulfilled, God being "made manifest in the flesh," when he would set up his kingdom among men, and reign in the hearts of his people. And is not the time now fulfilled? For, "Lo! (saith he,) I am with you always," you who preach remission of sins in my name, "even unto the end of the world." (Matt. 28:20.) Wheresoever, therefore, the gospel of Christ is preached, this his "kingdom is nigh at hand." It is not far from every one of you. Ye may this hour enter thereinto, if so be ye hearken to his voice, "Repent ye, and believe the gospel."

II. 1. This is the way: walk ye in it. And, First, "repent;" that is, know yourselves. This is the first repentance, previous to faith; even conviction, or self-knowledge. Awake, then, thou that sleepest. Know thyself to be a sinner, and what manner of sinner thou art. Know that corruption of thy inmost nature, whereby thou art very far gone from original righteousness, whereby "the flesh lusteth" always "contrary to the Spirit," through that "carnal mind" which "is enmity against God," which "is not subject to the law of God, neither indeed can be." Know that thou art corrupted in every power, in every faculty of thy soul; that thou art totally corrupted in every one of these, all the foundations being out of course. The eyes of thine understanding are darkened, so that they cannot discern God, or the things of God. The clouds of ignorance and error rest upon thee, and cover thee with the shadow of death. Thou knowest nothing yet as thou oughtest to know, neither God, nor the world, nor thyself. Thy will is no longer the will of God, but is utterly perverse and distorted, averse from all good, from all which God loves, and prone to all evil, to every abomination which God hateth. Thy affections are alienated from God, and scattered abroad over all the earth. All thy passions, both thy desires and aversions, thy joys and sorrows, thy hopes and fears, are out of frame, are either undue in their degree, or placed on undue objects. So that there is no soundness in thy soul; but "from the crown of the head, to the sole of the foot," (to use the strong expression of the Prophet,) there are only "wounds, and bruises, and putrefying sores."

2. Such is the inbred corruption of thy heart, of thy very inmost nature. And what manner of branches canst thou expect to grow from such an evil root? Hence springs unbelief; ever departing from the living God; saying, "Who is the Lord, that I should serve him? Tush! Thou, God, carest not for it." Hence independence; affecting to be like the Most High. Hence pride, in all its forms; teaching thee to say, "I am rich, and increased in goods, and have need of nothing." From this evil fountain flow forth the bitter streams of vanity, thirst of praise, ambition, covetousness, the lust of the flesh, the lust of the eye, and the pride of life. From this arise anger, hatred, malice, revenge, envy, jealousy, evil surmisings: From this, all the foolish and hurtful lusts that now "pierce thee through with many sorrows," and if not timely prevented, will at length drown thy soul in everlasting perdition.

3. And what fruits can grow on such branches as these? only such as are bitter and evil continually. of pride comethcontention, vain boasting, seeking and receiving praise of men, and so robbing God of that glory which he cannot give unto another. of the lust of the flesh, come gluttony or drunkenness, luxury or sensuality, fornication, uncleanness; variously defiling that body which was designed for a temple of the Holy Ghost: of unbelief, every evil word and work. But the time would fail, shouldst thou reckon up all; all the idle words thou hast spoken, provoking the Most High, grieving the Holy One of Israel; all the evil works thou hast done, either wholly evil in themselves, or, at least, not done to the glory of God. For thy actual sins are more than thou art able to express, more than the hairs of thy head. Who can number the sands of the sea, or the drops of rain, or thy iniquities?

4. And knowest thou not that "the wages of sin is death?" death, not only temporal, but eternal. "The soul that sinneth, it shall die;" for the mouth of the Lord hath spoken it." It shall die the second death. This is the sentence, to "be punished" with never-ending death, "with everlasting destruction from the presence of the Lord, and from the glory of his power." Knowest thou not that every sinner, *enochos estai eis ten geennan tou pyros*, not properly, "is in danger of hell-fire" is far too weak; but rather, "is under the sentence of hell-fire;" doomed already, just dragging to execution. Thou

art guilty of everlasting death. It is the just reward of thy inward and outward wickedness. It is just that the sentence should now take place. Dost thou see, dost thou feel this? Art thou thoroughly convinced that thou deservest God's wrath, and everlasting damnation? Would God do thee no wrong, if he now commanded the earth to open, and swallow thee up? if thou wert now to go down quick into the pit, into the fire that never shall be quenched? If God hath given thee truly to repent, thou hast a deep sense that these things are so; and that it is of his mere mercy thou art not consumed, swept away from the face of the earth.

5. And what wilt thou do to appease the wrath of God, to atone for all thy sins, and to escape the punishment thou hast so justly deserved? Alas, thou canst do nothing; nothing that will in anywise make amends to God for one evil work, or word, or thought. If thou couldst now do all things well, if from this very hour, till thy soul should return to God thou couldst perform perfect, uninterrupted obedience, even this would not atone for what is past. The not increasing thy debt would not discharge it. It would still remain as great as ever. Yea, the present and future obedience of all the men upon earth, and all the angels in heaven, would never make satisfaction to the justice of God for one single sin. How vain, then, was the thought of atoning for thy own sins, by anything thou couldest do! It costeth far more to redeem one soul, than all mankind is able to pay. So that were there no other help for a guilty sinner, without doubt he must have perished everlastingly.

6. But suppose perfect obedience, for the time to come, could atone for the sins that are past, this would profit thee nothing; for thou art not able to perform it; no, not in any one point. Begin now: Make the trial. Shake off that outward sin that so easily besetteth thee. Thou canst not. How then wilt thou change thy life from all evil to all good? Indeed, it is impossible to be done, unless first thy heart be changed. For, so long as the tree remains evil, it cannot bring forth good fruit. But art thou able to change thy own heart, from all sin to all holiness? to quicken a soul that is dead in sin,— dead to God and alive only to the world? No more than thou art able to quicken a dead body, to raise to life him that lieth in the grave. Yea, thou art not able to quicken thy soul in any degree, no more than to give any degree of life to the dead body. Thou canst do nothing, more or less, in this matter; thou art utterly without strength. To be deeply sensible of this, how helpless thou art, as well as how guilty and how sinful,—this is that "repentance not to be repented of," which is the forerunner of the kingdom of God.

7. If to this lively conviction of thy inward and outward sins, of thy utter guiltiness and helplessness, there be added suitable affections,—sorrow of heart, for having despised thy own mercies,—remorse, and self-condemnation, having thy mouth stopped,—shame to lift up thine eyes to heaven,— fear of the wrath of God abiding on thee, of his curse hanging over thy head, and of the fiery indignation ready to devour those who forget God, and obey not our Lord Jesus Christ,— earnest desire to escape from that indignation, to cease from evil, and learn to do well;—then I say unto thee, in the name of the Lord, "Thou art not far from the kingdom of God."

One step more and thou shalt enter in. Thou dost "repent." Now, "believe the gospel."

8. *The gospel*, (that is, good tidings, good news for guilty, helpless sinners,) in the largest sense of the word, means, the whole revelation made to men by Jesus Christ; and sometimes the whole account of what our Lord did and suffered while he tabernacled among men. The substance of all is, "Jesus Christ came into the world to save sinners;" or, "God so loved the world that he gave his only-begotten Son, to the end we might not perish, but have everlasting life;" or, "He was bruised for our transgressions, he was wounded for our iniquities; the chastisement of our peace was upon him; and with his stripes we are healed."

9. *Believe* this, and the kingdom of God is thine. By faith thou attainest the promise. "He pardoneth and absolveth all that truly repent, and unfeignedly believe his holy gospel." As soon as ever God hath spoken to thy heart, "Be of good cheer, thy sins are forgiven thee," his kingdom comes: Thou hast "righteousness, and peace, and joy in the Holy Ghost."

10. Only beware thou do not deceive thy own soul with regard to the nature of this faith. It is not, as some have fondly conceived, a bare assent to the truth of the Bible, of the articles of our creed, or of all that is contained in the Old and New Testament. The devils believe this, as well as I or thou! And yet they are devils still. But it is, over and above this, a sure trust in the mercy of God, through Christ Jesus. It is a confidence in a pardoning God. It is a divine evidence or conviction that "God was in Christ, reconciling the world to himself, not imputing to them their" former "trespasses;" and, in particular, that the Son of God hath loved *me*, and given himself for *me*; and that I, even I, am now reconciled to God by the blood of the cross.

11. Dost thou thus believe? Then the peace of God is in thy heart, and sorrow and sighing flee away. Thou art no longer in doubt of the love of God; it is clear as the noon-day sun. Thou criest out, "My song shall be always of the loving-kindness of the Lord: With my mouth will I ever be telling of thy truth, from one generation to another." Thou art no longer afraid of hell, or death, or him that had once the power of death, the devil; no, nor painfully afraid of God himself; only thou hast a tender, filial fear of offending him. Dost thou believe? Then thy "soul doth magnify the Lord," and thy "spirit rejoiceth in God thy Saviour." Thou rejoicest in that thou hast "redemption through his blood, even the forgiveness of sins." Thou rejoicest in that "Spirit of adoption," which crieth in thy heart, "Abba, Father!" Thou rejoicest in a "hope full of immortality;" in reaching forth unto the "mark of the prize of thy high calling;" in an earnest expectation of all the good things which God hath prepared for them that love him.

12. Dost thou now believe? Then "the love of God is" now "shed abroad in thy heart." Thou lovest him, because he first loved us. And because thou lovest God, thou lovest thy brother also. And being filled with "love, peace, joy," thou art also filled with "long-suffering, gentleness, fidelity, goodness, meekness, temperance," and all the other fruits of the same Spirit; in a word, with whatever dispositions are holy, are heavenly or divine. For while thou "beholdest with open," uncovered "face" (the veil now being taken away) "the glory of the Lord," his glorious love, and the glorious image wherein thou wast created, thou art "changed into the same image, from glory to glory, by the Spirit of the Lord."

13. This repentance, this faith, this peace, joy, love, this change from glory to glory, is what the wisdom of the world has voted to be madness, mere enthusiasm, utter distraction. But thou, O man of God, regard them not; be thou moved by none of these things. Thou knowest in whom thou hast believed. See that no man take thy crown. Whereunto thou hast already attained, hold fast, and follow, till thou attain all the great and precious promises. And thou who hast not yet known him, let not vain men make thee ashamed of the gospel of Christ. Be thou in nothing terrified by those who speak evil of the things which they know not. God will soon turn thy heaviness into joy. O let not thy hands hang down! Yet a little longer, and he will take away thy fears, and give thee the spirit of a sound mind. He is nigh "that justifieth: Who is he that condemneth? It is Christ that died, yea rather, that rose again, who is even now at the right hand of God, making intercession" for thee.

"Now cast thyself on the Lamb of God, with all thy sins, how many soever they be; and "an entrance shall" now "be ministered unto thee, into the kingdom of our Lord and Saviour Jesus Christ!"

8.* THE FIRST FRUITS OF THE SPIRIT

"There is therefore now no condemnation to them which are in Christ Jesus, who walk not after the flesh, but after the Spirit."

Rom. 8:1

1. By "them which are in Christ Jesus," St. Paul evidently means, those who truly believe in him; those who, "being justified by faith, have peace with God through our Lord Jesus Christ." They who thus believe do no longer "walk after the flesh," no longer follow the motions of corrupt nature, but "after the Spirit"; both their thoughts, words, and works are under the direction of the blessed Spirit of God.

2. "There is therefore now no condemnation to" these. There is no condemnation to them from God; for he hath *justified* them "freely by his grace, through the redemption that is in Jesus." he hath forgiven all their iniquities, and blotted out all their sins. And there is no condemnation to them from within; for they "have received, not the spirit of the world, but the Spirit which is of God; that they might know the things which are freely given to them of God" (1 Cor. 2:12); which Spirit "beareth witness with their spirits, that they are the children of God." And to this is added the testimony of their conscience, "that in simplicity and godly sincerity, not with fleshly wisdom, but by the grace of God, they have had their conversation in the world" (2 Cor. 1:12).

3. But because this scripture has been so frequently misunderstood, and that in so dangerous a manner; because

---

* (text of the 1872 edition)

such multitudes of "unlearned and unstable men" (*hoi amatheis kai asteriktoi*, men untaught of God, and consequently unestablished in the truth which is after godliness) have wrested it to their own destruction; I propose to show, as clearly as I can, first who those are which are in Christ Jesus, and walk not after the flesh, but after the Spirit: and, secondly, how there is no condemnation to these. I shall conclude with some practical inferences.

I. 1. First, I am to show, who those are that "are in Christ Jesus." And are they not those who believe in his name? those who are "found in him, not having their own righteousness, but the righteousness which is of God by faith?" these, "who have redemption through his blood," are properly said to be *in him*; for they dwell in Christ, and Christ in them. They are joined unto the Lord in one Spirit. They are ingrafted into him as branches into the vine. They are united, as members to their head, in a manner which words cannot express, nor could it before enter into their hearts to conceive.

2. Now "whosoever abideth in him, sinneth not"; "walketh not after the flesh." The flesh, in the usual language of St. Paul, signifies corrupt nature. In this sense he uses the word, writing to the Galatians, "The works of the flesh are manifest" (Gal. 5:19); and a little before, "Walk in the Spirit, and ye shall not fulfil the lust" (or desire) "of the flesh" (v. 16). To prove which, namely, that those who "walk by the Spirit,"do not "fulfil the lusts of the flesh," he immediately adds, "For the flesh lusteth against the Spirit, and the Spirit lusteth against the flesh (for these are contrary to each other); that ye may not do the things which ye would." So the words are literally translated; *hina me ha an thelete, tauta poiete*, not, "So that ye cannot do the things that ye would"; as if the flesh overcame the Spirit: a translation which hath not only nothing to do with the original text of the Apostle, but likewise makes his whole argument nothing worth; yea, asserts just the reverse of what he is proving.

3. They who are of Christ, who abide in him, "have crucified the flesh with its affections and lusts." They abstain from all those works of the flesh; from "adultery and fornication"; from "uncleanness and lasciviousness"; from "idolatry, witchcraft, hatred, variance" from "emulations, wrath, strife, sedition, heresies, envyings, murders, drunkenness, revellings"; from every design, and word, and work, to which the corruption of nature leads. Although they feel the root of bitterness in themselves, yet are they endued with power from on high to trample it continually under foot, so that it cannot "spring up to trouble them"; insomuch that every fresh assault which they undergo, only gives them fresh occasion of praise, of crying out, "Thanks be unto God, who giveth us the victory through Jesus Christ our Lord."

4. They now "walk after the Spirit," both in their hearts and lives. They are taught of him to love God and their neighbour, with a love which is as "a well of water, springing up into everlasting life." And by him they are led into every holy desire, into every divine and heavenly temper, till every thought which arises in their heart is holiness unto the Lord.

5. They who "walk after the Spirit," are also led by him into all holiness of conversation. Their "speech is always in grace, seasoned with salt"; with the love and fear of God. "No corrupt communication comes out of their mouth; but only that which is good," that which is "to the use of edifying," which is "meet to minister grace to the hearers." And herein likewise do they exercise themselves day and night, to do only the things which please God; in all their outward behaviour to follow him "who left us an example that we might tread in his steps"; in all their intercourse with their neighbour, to walk in justice, mercy, and truth; and "whatsoever they do," in every circumstances of life, to "do all to the glory of God.

6. These are they who indeed "walk after the Spirit." Being filled with faith and with the holy Ghost, they possess in their hearts, and show forth in their lives, in the whole course of their words and actions, the genuine fruits of the Spirit of God, namely, "love, joy, peace, long-suffering, gentleness, goodness, fidelity, meekness, temperance," and whatsoever else is lovely or praiseworthy. "They adorn in all things the gospel of God our Saviour"; and give full proof to all mankind, that they are indeed actuated by the same Spirit "which raised up Jesus from the dead."

II. 1. I proposed to show, in the second place, how "there is no condemnation to them which are" thus "in Christ Jesus," and thus "walk not after the flesh, but after the Spirit." And, first, to believers in Christ, walking thus, "there is no condemnation" on account of their past sins. God condemneth them not for any of these; they are as though they had never been; they are cast "as a stone into the depth of the sea," and he remembereth them no more. God, having "set forth his Son to be a propitiation "for them, "through faith in his blood," hath declared unto them "his righteousness for the remission of the sins that are past." he layeth therefore none of these to their charge; their memorial is perished with them.

2. And there is no condemnation in their own breast; no sense of guilt, or dread of the wrath of God. They "have the witness in themselves:" they are conscious of their interest in the blood of sprinkling. "They have not received again the spirit of bondage unto fear," unto doubt and racking uncertainty; but they "have received the Spirit of adoption," crying in their heart, "Abba, Father." Thus, being "justified by faith," they have the peace of God ruling in their hearts; flowing from a continual sense of his pardoning mercy, and "the answer of a good conscience toward God."

3. If it be said, "But sometimes a believer in Christ may lose his sight of the mercy of God; sometimes such darkness may fall upon him that he no longer sees him that is invisible, no longer feels that witness in himself of his part in the atoning blood; and then he is inwardly condemned, he hath again "the sentence of death in himself": I answer, supposing it so to be, supposing him not to see the mercy of God, then he is not a believer: For faith implies light, the light of God shining upon the soul. So far, therefore, as any one loses this light, he, for the time, loses his faith. And, no doubt, a true believer in Christ may lose the light of faith; and so far as this is lost, he may, for a time, fall again into condemnation. But this is not the case of them who now "are in Christ Jesus," who now believe in his name. For so long as they believe, and walk after the Spirit, neither God condemns them, nor their own heart.

4. They are not condemned, secondly, for any present sins, for now transgressing the commandments of God. For they do not transgress them: they do not "walk after the flesh, but after the Spirit." This is the continual proof of their "love of God, that they keep his commandments"; even as St. John bears witness. "Whosoever is born of God doth not commit sin. For his seed remaineth in him, and he cannot sin, because he is born of God:" he cannot, so long as that seed of God, that loving, holy faith remaineth in him. So long as "he keepeth himself" herein, "that wicked one toucheth him not." Now it is evident, he is not condemned for the sins which he doth not commit at all. They, therefore, who are thus "led by the Spirit, are not under the law" (Gal. 5:18): not under the curse or condemnation of it; for it condemns none but those who break it. Thus, that law of God, "Thou shalt not steal," condemns none but those who do steal. Thus, "Remember the Sabbath-day to keep it holy," condemns those only who do not keep it holy. But against the fruits of the Spirit "there is no law" (5:23); as the Apostle more largely declares in those memorable words of his former epistle to Timothy: "We know that the law is good, if a man use it lawfully; knowing this," (if, while he uses the law of God, in order either to convince or direct, he know and remember this), *hoti dikaio nomos ou keitai*, (not, "that the law is not made for a righteous man," but) "that the law does not lie against a righteous man:" it has no force against him, no power to condemn him; "but against the lawless and disobedient, against the ungodly and sinners, against the unholy and profane; according to the glorious gospel of the blessed God." (1 Tim. 1:8, 9, 11).

5. They are not condemned, thirdly, for inward sin, even though it does now remain. That the corruption of nature does still remain, even in those who are the children of God by faith; that they have in them the seeds of pride and vanity, of anger, lust, and evil desire, yea, sin of every kind; is too plain to be denied, being matter of daily experience. And on this account it is, that St. Paul, speaking to those whom he had just before witnessed to be "in Christ Jesus," (1 Cor. 1:2, 9), to have been "called of God into the fellowship" (or participation) "of his Son Jesus Christ"; yet declares, "Brethren, I could not speak unto you as unto spiritual, but as unto carnal, even as unto babes in Christ" (1 Cor. 3:1): "babes in Christ"; so we see they were "in Christ"; they were believers in a low degree. And yet how much of sin remained in them! of that "carnal mind, which is not subject to the law of God!"

6. And yet, for all this, they are not condemned. Although they feel the flesh, the evil nature, in them; although they are more sensible, day by day, that their "heart is deceitful and desperately wicked"; yet, so long as they do not yield thereto; so long as they give no place to the devil; so long as they maintain a continual war with all sin, with pride, anger, desire, so that the flesh hath not dominion over them, but they still "walk after the Spirit"; "there is no condemnation to them which are in Christ Jesus." God is well pleased with their sincere, though imperfect. obedience; and they "have confidence toward God," knowing they are his, "by the Spirit which he hath given" them. (1 John 3:24).

7. Nay, fourthly, although they are continually convinced of sin cleaving to all they do; although they are conscious of not fulfilling the perfect law, either in their thoughts, or words, or works; although they know they do not love the Lord their God with all their heart, and mind, and soul, and strength; although they feel more or less of pride, or self-will, stealing in, and mixing with their best duties; although even in their more immediate intercourse with God, when they assemble themselves with the great congregation, and when they pour out their souls in secret to him who seeth all the thoughts and intents of the heart, they are continually ashamed of their wandering thoughts, or of the deadness and dulness of their affections; yet there is no condemnation to them still, either from God or from their own heart. The consideration of these manifold defects only gives them a deeper sense, that they have always need of that blood of sprinkling which speaks for them in the ears of God, and that Advocate with the Father "who ever liveth to make intercession for them." So far are these from driving them away from him in whom they have believed, that they rather drive them the closer to him whom they feel the want of every moment. And, at the same time, the deeper sense they have of this want, the more earnest desire do they feel, and the more diligent they are, as they "have received the Lord Jesus, so to walk in him."

8. They are not condemned, fifthly, for sins of infirmity, as they are usually called. Perhaps it were advisable rather to call them *infirmities*: that we may not seem to give any countenance to sin, or to extenuate it in any degree, by thus coupling it with infirmity. But (if we must retain so ambiguous and dangerous an expression), by sins of infirmity I would mean, such involuntary failings as the saying a thing we believe true, though, in fact, it prove to be false; or, the hurting our neighbour without knowing or designing it, perhaps when we designed to do him good. Though these are deviations from the holy, and acceptable, and perfect will of God, yet they are not properly sins, nor do they bring any guilt on the conscience of "them which are in Christ Jesus." They separate not between God and them, neither intercept the light of his countenance; as being no ways inconsistent with their general character of "walking not after the flesh, but after the Spirit."

9. Lastly. "There is no condemnation "to them for anything whatever which it is not in their power to help; whether it be of an inward or outward nature, and whether it be doing something or leaving something undone. For instance, the Lord's Supper is to be administered; but you do not partake thereof. Why do you not? You are confined by sickness; therefore, you cannot help omitting it; and for the same reason you are not condemned. There is no guilt, because there is no choice. As there "is a willing mind, it is accepted according to that a man hath, not according to that he hath not."

10. A believer, indeed, may sometimes be *grieved*: because he cannot do what his soul longs for. He may cry out, when he is detained from worshipping God in the great congregation, "Like as the hart panteth after the water-brooks, so panteth my soul after thee, O God. My soul is athirst for God, yea, even for the living God: When shall I come to appear in the

presence of God?" he may earnestly desire (only still saying in his heart, "Not as I will, but as thou wilt") to "go again with the multitude, and bring them forth into the house of God." But still, if he cannot go, he feels no condemnation, no guilt, no sense of God's displeasure; but can cheerfully yield up those desires with, "O my soul, put thy trust in God! for I will yet give him thanks, who is the help of my countenance and my God."

11. It is more difficult to determine concerning those which are usually styled sins of surprise: as when one who commonly in patience possesses his soul, on a sudden and violent temptation, speaks or acts in a manner not consistent with the royal law, "Thou shalt love thy neighbour as thyself." Perhaps it is not easy to fix a general rule concerning transgressions of this nature. We cannot say, either that men are, or that they are not, condemned for sins of surprise in general: but it seems, whenever a believer is by surprise overtaken in a fault, there is more or less condemnation, as there is more or less concurrence of his will. In proportion as a sinful desire, or word, or action is more or less voluntary, so we may conceive God is more or less displeased, and there is more or less guilt upon the soul.

12. But if so, then there may be some sins of surprise which bring much guilt and condemnation. For, in some instances, our being surprised is owing to some wilful and culpable neglect; or, to a sleepiness of soul which might have been prevented, or shaken off before the temptation came. A man may be previously warned either of God or man, that trials and dangers are at hand; and yet may say in his heart, "A little more slumber, a little more folding of the hands to rest." Now, if such an one afterwards fall, though unawares, into the snare which he might have avoided,—that he fell unawares, is no excuse; he might have foreseen and have shunned the danger. The falling, even by surprise, in such an instance as this, is, in effect, a wilful sin; and, as such, must expose the sinner to condemnation, both from God and his own conscience.

13. On the other hand, there may be sudden assaults, either from the world, or the god of this world, and frequently from our own evil hearts, which we did not, and hardly could, foresee. And by these even a believer, while weak in faith, may possibly be borne down, suppose into a degree of anger, or thinking evil of another, with scarce any concurrence of his will. Now in such a case, the jealous God would undoubtedly show him that he had done foolishly. He would be convinced of having swerved from the perfect law, from the mind which was in Christ, and consequently, *grieved* with a godly sorrow, and lovingly *ashamed* before God. Yet need he not come into condemnation. God layeth not folly to his charge, but hath compassion upon him, "even as a father pitieth his own children." And his heart condemneth him not: in the midst of that sorrow and shame he can still say, "I will trust and not be afraid; for the Lord Jehovah is my strength and my song; he also is become my salvation."

III. 1. It remains only to draw some practical inferences from the preceding considerations. And, first, if there be "no condemnation to them which are in Christ Jesus," and "walk not after the flesh, but after the Spirit," on account of their past sin; then why art thou fearful, O thou of little faith? Though thy sins were once more in number than the sand, what is that to thee, now thou art in Christ Jesus? "Who shall lay anything to the charge of God's elect? It is God that justifieth: Who is he that condemneth?" all the sins thou hast committed from thy youth up, until the hour when thou wast "accepted in the Beloved," are driven away as chaff, are gone, are lost, swallowed up, remembered no more. Thou art now "born of the Spirit:" wilt thou be troubled or afraid of what is done before thou wert born? Away with thy fears! thou art not called to fear, but to the "spirit of love and of a sound mind." know thy calling! rejoice in God thy Saviour, and give thanks to God thy Father through him!

2. Wilt thou say, "But I have again committed sin, since I had redemption through his blood? And therefore it is, that "I abhor myself, and repent in dust and ashes." It is meet thou shouldest abhor thyself; and it is God who hath wrought thee to this self-same thing. But, dost thou now believe? hath he again enabled thee to say, "I know that my Redeemer liveth"; "and the life which I now live, I live by faith in the Son of God?" Then that faith again cancels all that is past, and there is no condemnation to thee. At whatsoever time thou truly believest in the name of the Son of God, all thy sins, antecedent to that hour, vanish away as the morning dew. Now then, "stand thou fast in the liberty wherewith Christ hath made thee free." he hath once more made thee free from the power of sin, as well as from the guilt and punishment of it. O "be not entangled again with the yoke of bondage!"— neither the vile, devilish bondage of sin, of evil desires, evil tempers, or words, or works, the most grievous yoke on this side hell; nor the bondage of slavish, tormenting fear, of guilt and self-condemnation.

3. But secondly, do all they which abide "in Christ Jesus, walk not after the flesh, but after the Spirit?" Then we cannot but infer, that whosoever now committeth sin, hath no part or lot in this matter. He is even now condemned by his own heart. But, "if our heart condemn us," if our own conscience beareth witness that we are guilty, undoubtedly God doth; for "He is greater than our heart, and knoweth all things" so that we cannot deceive him, if we can ourselves. And think not to say, "I was justified once; my sins were once forgiven me:" I know not that; neither will I dispute whether they were or no. Perhaps, at this distance of time, it is next to impossible to know, with any tolerable degree of certainty, whether that was a true, genuine work of God, or whether thou didst only deceive thy own soul. But this I know, with the utmost degree of certainty, "he that committeth sin is of the devil." Therefore, thou art of thy father the devil. It cannot be denied: for the works of thy father thou doest. O flatter not thyself with vain hopes! Say not to thy soul, "Peace peace!" For there is no peace. Cry aloud! Cry unto God out of the deep; if haply he may hear thy voice. Come unto him as at first, as wretched and poor, as sinful, miserable, blind and naked! And beware thou suffer thy soul to take no rest, till his pardoning love be again revealed; till he "heal thy backslidings," and fill thee again with the "faith that worketh by love."

4. Thirdly. Is there no condemnation to them which "walk after the Spirit," by reason of *inward sin* still remaining, so long as they do not give way thereto; nor by reason of *sin cleaving* to all they do? Then fret not thyself because of ungodliness, though it still remain in thy heart. Repine not, because thou still comest short of the glorious image of God; nor yet because pride, self-will, or unbelief, cleave to all thy words and works. And be not afraid to know all this evil of thy heart, to know thyself as also thou art known. Yea, desire of God, that thou mayest not think of thyself more highly than thou oughtest to think. Let thy continual prayer be,

> Show me, as my soul can bear,
> The depth of inbred sin;
> All the unbelief declare,
> The pride that lurks within.

But when he heareth thy prayer, and unveils thy heart; when he shows thee throughly what spirit thou art of; then beware that thy faith fail thee not, that thou suffer not thy shield to be torn from thee. Be abased. Be humbled in the dust. See thyself nothing, less than nothing, and vanity. But still, "Let not thy heart be troubled, neither let it be afraid." Still hold fast, "I, even I, have an Advocate with the Father, Jesus Christ the righteous." "And as the heavens are higher than the earth, so is his love higher than even my sins." Therefore, God is merciful to thee a sinner! such a sinner as thou art! God is love; and Christ hath died! Therefore, the Father himself loveth thee! Thou art his child! Therefore he will withhold from thee no manner of thing that is good. Is it good, that the whole body of sin, which is now crucified in thee, should be destroyed? It shall be done! Thou shalt be "cleansed from all filthiness, both of flesh and spirit." Is it good, that nothing should remain in thy heart but the pure love of God alone? Be of good cheer! "Thou shalt love the Lord thy God, with all thy heart, and mind, and soul, and strength." "Faithful is he that hath promised, who also will do it." It is thy part, patiently to continue in the work of faith, and in the labour of love; and in cheerful peace, in humble confidence, with calm and resigned and yet earnest expectation, to wait till the zeal of the Lord of hosts shall perform this.

5. Fourthly. If they that "are in Christ," and "walk after the Spirit," are not condemned for *sins of infirmity*: as neither for *involuntary failings*, nor for anything whatever which they are not able to help; then beware, O thou that hast faith in his blood, that Satan herein gain no advantage over thee. Thou art still foolish and weak, blind and ignorant; more weak than any words can express; more foolish than it call yet enter into thy heart to conceive; knowing nothing yet as thou oughtest to know. Yet let not all thy weakness and folly, or any fruit thereof, which thou art not yet able to avoid, shake thy faith, thy filial trust in God, or disturb thy peace or joy in the Lord. The rule which some give, as to wilful sins, and which, in that case, may perhaps be dangerous, is undoubtedly wise and safe if it be applied only to the case of weakness and infirmities. Art thou fallen, O man of God? yet, do not lie there, fretting thyself and bemoaning thy weakness; but meekly say, "Lord, I shall fall every moment, unless thou uphold me with thy hand." And then arise! Leap and walk! Go on thy way! "run with patience the race that is set before Thee."

6. Lastly. Since a believer need not come into condemnation, even though he be *surprised* into what his soul abhors; (suppose his being surprised is not owing to any carelessness or wilful neglect of his own); if thou who believest art thus overtaken in a fault, then grieve unto the Lord; it shall be a precious balm. Pour out thy heart before him, and show him of thy trouble, and pray with all thy might to him who is "touched with the feeling of thy infirmities,"that he would establish, and strengthen and settle thy soul, and suffer thee to fall no more. But still he condemneth thee not. Wherefore shouldest thou fear? Thou hast no need of any "fear that hath torment." Thou shalt love him that loveth thee, and it sufficeth: more love will bring more strength. And, as soon as thou lovest him with all thy heart, thou shalt be perfect and entire, lacking nothing." Wait in peace for that hour, when the God of peace shall sanctify thee wholly, so that thy whole spirit and soul and body may be preserved blameless unto the coming of our Lord Jesus Christ!"

9.* THE SPIRIT OF BONDAGE AND OF ADOPTION

"Ye have not received the spirit of bondage again unto fear; but ye have received the Spirit of adoption, whereby we cry Abba, Father."

Romans 8:15.

1. ST. PAUL here speaks to those who are the children of God by faith. "Ye," saith he, who are indeed his children, have drank into his Spirit; "ye have not received the spirit of bondage again unto fear;" "but, because ye are sons, God hath sent forth the Spirit of his Son into your hearts." "Ye have received the Spirit of adoption, whereby we cry, Abba, Father."

2. The spirit of bondage and fear is widely distant from this loving Spirit of adoption: Those who are influenced only by slavish fear, cannot be termed "the sons of God;" yet some of them may be styled his servants, and are "not far from the kingdom of heaven."

3. But it is to be feared, the bulk of mankind, yea, of what is called the Christian world, have not attained even this; but are still afar off, "neither is God in all their thoughts." A few names may be found of those who love God; a few more there are that fear him; but the greater part have neither the fear of God before their eyes, nor the love of God in their hearts.

4. Perhaps most of you, who, by the mercy of God, now partake of a better spirit, may remember the time when ye were as they, when ye were under the same condemnation. But at first ye knew it not, though ye were wallowing daily in your sins and in your blood; till, in due time, ye "received the spirit of fear;" (*ye received*, for this also is the gift of God;) and afterwards, fear vanished away, and the Spirit of love filled your hearts.

* (text from the 1872 edition)

5. One who is in the first state of mind, without fear of love, is in Scripture termed a "natural man:" One who is under the spirit of bondage and fear, is sometimes said to be "under the law:" (Although that expression more frequently signifies one who is under the Jewish dispensation, or who thinks himself obliged to observe all the rites and ceremonies of the Jewish law:) But one who has exchanged the spirit of fear for the Spirit of love, is properly said to be "under grace."

Now, because it highly imports us to know what spirit we are of, I shall endeavour to point out distinctly, First, the state of a "natural man:" Secondly, that of one who is "under the law:" And Thirdly, of one who is "under grace."

I. 1. And, First, the state of a *natural man*. This the Scripture represents as a state of sleep: The voice of God to him is, "Awake thou that sleepest." For his soul is in a deep sleep: His spiritual senses are not awake; They discern neither spiritual good nor evil. The eyes of his understanding are closed; They are sealed together, and see not. Clouds and darkness continually rest upon them; for he lies in the valley of the shadow of death. Hence having no inlets for the knowledge of spiritual things, all the avenues of his soul being shut up, he is in gross, stupid ignorance of whatever he is most concerned to know. He is utterly ignorant of God, knowing nothing concerning him as he ought to know. He is totally a stranger to the law of God, as to its true, inward, spiritual meaning. He has no conception of that evangelical holiness, without which no man shall see the Lord; nor of the happiness which they only find whose "life is hid with Christ in God."

2. And for this very reason, because he is fast asleep, he is, in some sense, at rest. Because he is blind, he is also secure; He saith, "Tush, there shall no harm happen unto me." The darkness which covers him on every side, keeps him in a kind of peace; so far as peace can consist with the works of the devil, and with an earthly, devilish mind. He *sees* not that he stands on the edge of the pit, therefore he *fears* it not. He cannot *tremble* at the danger he does not *know*. He has not understanding enough to fear. Why is it that he is in no dread of God? Because he is totally ignorant of him: If not saying in his heart, "There is no God;" or, that "he sitteth on the circle of the heavens, and humbleth" not "himself to behold the things which are done on earth:" yet satisfying himself as well to all Epicurean intents and purposes, by saying, "God is merciful;" confounding and swallowing up all at once in that unwieldy idea of mercy, all his holiness and essential hatred of sin; all his justice, wisdom, and truth. He is in no dread of the vengeance denounced against those who obey not the blessed law of God, because he understands it not. He imagines the main point is to *do thus*, to be *outwardly* blameless; and sees not that it extends to every temper, desire, thought, motion of the heart. Or he fancies that the obligation hereto is ceased; that Christ came to "destroy the Law and the Prophets;" to save his people *in*, not *from* their sins; to bring them to heaven without holiness:—Notwithstanding his own words, "Not one jot or tittle of the law shall pass away, till all things are fulfilled;" and "Not every one that saith unto me, Lord, Lord! shall enter into the kingdom of heaven; but he that doeth the will of my Father which is in heaven."

3. He is secure, because he is utterly ignorant of himself. Hence he talks of "repenting by and by;" he does not indeed exactly know when, but some time or other before he dies; taking it for granted, that this is quite in his own power. For what should hinder his doing it, if he will? if he does but once set a resolution, no fear but he will make it good!

4. But this ignorance never so strongly glares, as in those who are termed, *men of learning*. If a natural man be one of these, he can talk at large of his rational faculties, of the freedom of his will, and the absolute necessity of such freedom, in order to constitute man a moral agent. He reads, and argues, and proves to a demonstration, that every man may do as he will; may dispose his own heart to evil or good, as it seems best in his own eyes. Thus the god of this world spreads a double veil of blindness over his heart, lest, by any means, "the light of the glorious gospel of Christ should shine" upon it.

5. From the same ignorance of himself and God, there may sometimes arise, in the natural man, a kind of *joy*, in congratulating himself upon his own wisdom and goodness: And what the world calls joy, he may often possess. He may have pleasure in various kinds; either in gratifying the desires of the flesh, or the desire of the eye, or the pride of life; particularly if he has large possessions; if he enjoy an affluent fortune; then he may "clothe" himself "in purple and fine linen, and fare sumptuously every day." And so long as he thus doeth well unto himself, men will doubtless speak good of him. They will say, "He is a happy man." For, indeed, this is the sum of worldly happiness; to dress, and visit, and talk, and eat, and drink, and rise up to play.

6. It in not surprising, if one in such circumstances as these, dosed with the opiates of flattery and sin, should imagine, among his other waking dreams, that he walks in great *liberty*. How easily may he persuade himself, that he is at liberty from all *vulgar errors*, and from the *prejudice* of education; judging exactly right, and keeping clear of all extremes. "I am free," may he say, "from all the *enthusiasm* of weak and narrow souls; from *superstition*, the disease of fools and cowards, always righteous over much; and from *bigotry*, continually incident to those who have not a free and generous way of thinking." And too sure it is, that he is altogether free from the "wisdom which cometh from above," from holiness, from the religion of the heart, from the whole mind which was in Christ.

7. For all this time he is the servant of sin. He commits sin, more or less, day by day. Yet he is not troubled: He "is in no bondage," as some speak; he feels no condemnation. He contents himself (even though he should profess to believe that the Christian Revelation is of God) with, "Man is frail. We are all weak. Every man has his infirmity." Perhaps he quotes Scripture: "Why, does not Solomon say,—The righteous man falls into sin seven times a day!—And, doubtless, they are all hypocrites or enthusiasts who pretend to be better than their neighbours." If, at any time, a serious thought fix upon him, he stifles it as soon as possible, with, "Why should I fear, since God is merciful, and Christ died for sinners?" Thus, he remains a willing servant of sin,

content with the bondage of corruption; inwardly and outwardly unholy, and satisfied therewith; not only not conquering sin, but not striving to conquer, particularly that sin which doth so easily beset him.

8. Such is the state of every *natural man*; whether he be a gross, scandalous transgressor, or a more reputable and decent sinner, having the form, though not the power of godliness. But how can such an one be *convinced of sin?* How is he brought to repent? To be *under the law?* To receive the *spirit of bondage unto fear?* This is the point which in next to be considered.

II. 1. By some awful providence, or by his word applied with the demonstration of his Spirit, God touches the heart of him that lay asleep in darkness and in the shadow of death. He is terribly shaken out of his sleep, and awakes into a consciousness of his danger. Perhaps in a moment, perhaps by degrees, the eyes of his understanding are opened, and now first (the veil being in part removed) discern the real state he is in. Horrid light breaks in upon his soul; such light, as may be conceived to gleam from the bottomless pit, from the lowest deep, from a lake of fire burning with brimstone. He at last sees the loving, the merciful God is also "a consuming fire;" that he is a just God and a terrible, rendering to every man according to his words, entering into judgment with the ungodly for every idle word, yea, and for the imaginations of the heart. He now clearly perceives, that the great and holy God is "of purer eyes than to behold iniquity;" that he is an avenger of every one who rebelleth against him, and repayeth the wicked to his face; and that "it is a fearful thing to fall into the hands of the living God."

2. The inward, spiritual meaning of the law of God now begins to glare upon him. He perceives "the commandment is exceeding broad," and there is "nothing hid from the light thereof." He is convinced, that every part of it relates, not barely to outward sin or obedience, but to what passes in the secret recesses of the soul, which no eye but God's can penetrate. If he now hears, "Thou shalt not kill," God speaks in thunder, "He that hateth his brother is a murderer;" "he that saith unto his brother, Thou fool, is obnoxious to hell-fire." If the law say, "Thou shalt not commit adultery," the voice of the Lord sounds in his ears, "He that looketh on a woman to lust after he hath committed adultery with her already in his heart." And thus, in every point, he feels the word of God "quick and powerful, sharper than a two-edged sword." It "pierces even to the dividing asunder of his soul and spirit, his joints and marrow." And so much the more, because he is conscious to himself of having neglected so great salvation; of having "trodden under foot the son of God," who would have saved him from his sins, and "counted the blood of the covenant an unholy," a common, unsanctifying thing.

3. And as he knows, "all things are naked and open unto the eyes of him with whom we have to do," so he sees himself naked, stripped of all the fig-leaves which he had sewed together, of all his poor pretenses to religion or virtue, and his wretched excuses for sinning against God. He now sets himself like the ancient sacrifices, cleft in sunder, as it were, from the neck downward, so that all within him stands confessed. His heart is bare, and he sees it is all sin, "deceitful above all things, desperately wicked;" that it is altogether corrupt and abominable, more than it is possible for tongue to express; that there dwelleth therein no good thing, but unrighteousness and ungodliness only; every motion thereof, every temper and thought, being only evil continually.

4. And he not only sees, but feels in himself, by an emotion of soul which he cannot describe, that for the sins of his heart were his life without blame, (which yet it is not, and cannot be; seeing "an evil tree cannot bring forth good fruit,") he deserves to be cast into the fire that never shall be quenched. He feels that "the wages," the just reward "of sin," of his sin above all, "is death;" even the second death; the death which dieth not; the destruction of body and soul in hell.

5. Here ends his pleasing dream, his delusive rest, his false peace, his vain security. His joy now vanishes as a cloud; pleasures, once loved, delight no more. They pall upon the taste: He loathes the nauseous sweet; he is weary to bear them. The shadows of happiness flee away, and sink into oblivion: So that he is stripped of all, and wanders to and fro, seeking rest, but finding none.

6. The fumes of those opiates being now dispelled, he feels the anguish of a wounded spirit. He finds that sin let loose upon the soul (whether it be pride, anger, or evil desire, whether self-will, malice, envy, revenge, or any other) is perfect misery: He feels sorrow of heart for the blessings he has lost, and the curse which is come upon him: remorse for having thus destroyed himself, and despised his own mercies; fear, from a lively sense of the wrath of God, and of the consequences of his wrath, of the punishment which he has justly deserved, and which he sees hanging over is head;—fear of death, as being to him the gate of hell, the entrance of death eternal;—fear of the devil, the executioner of the wrath and righteous vengeance of God;—fear of men, who, if they were able to kill his body, would thereby plunge both body and soul into hell; fear, sometimes arising to such a height, that the poor, sinful, guilty soul, is terrified with everything, with nothing, with shades, with a leaf shaken of the wind. Yea, sometimes it may even border upon distraction, making a man "drunken though not with wine," suspending the exercise of the memory, of the understanding, of all the natural faculties. Sometimes it may approach to the very brink of despair; so that he who trembles at the name of death, may yet be ready to plunge into it every moment, to "choose strangling rather than life." Well may such a man roar, like him of old, for the very disquietness of his heart. Well may he cry out, "The spirit of a man may sustain his infirmities; but a wounded spirit who can bear?"

7. Now he truly desires to break loose from sin, and begins to struggle with it. But though he strive with all his might, he cannot conquer: Sin is mightier than he. He would fain escape; but he is so fast in prison, that he cannot get forth. He resolved against sin, but yet sins on: He sees the snare, and abhors, and runs into it. So much does his boasted reason avail,—only to enhance his guilt, and increase his misery! Such is the freedom of his will; free only to evil; free to "drink in iniquity like water;" to wander farther and farther from the living God, and do more "despite to the Spirit of grace!"

8. The more he strive, wishes, labours to be free, the more does he feel his chains, the grievous chains of sin, wherewith Satan binds and "leads him captive at his will;" his servant he is, though he repine ever so much; though he rebel, he cannot prevail. He is still in bondage and fear, by reason of sin: Generally, of some outward sin, to which he is peculiarly disposed, either, by nature, custom, or outward circumstance; but always, of some inward sin, some evil temper or unholy affection. And the more he frets against it, the more it prevails; he may bite but cannot break his chain. Thus he toils without end, repenting and sinning, and repenting and sinning again, till at length the poor, sinful, helpless wretch is even at his wit's end and can barely groan, "O wretched man that I am! who shall deliver me from the body of this death?"

9. This whole struggle of one who is "under the law," under the "spirit of fear and bondage," is beautifully described by the Apostle in the foregoing chapter, speaking in the person of an awakened man. "I," saith he, "was alive without the law once:" (Verse 9:) I had much life, wisdom, strength, and virtue; so I thought: "But, when the commandment came, sin revived, and I died:" When the commandment, in its spiritual meaning, came to my heart, with the power of God, my inbred sin was stirred up, fretted, inflamed, and all my virtue died away. "And the commandment, which was ordained to life, I found to be unto death. For sin taking occasion by the commandment, deceived me, and by it slew me:" (Verses 10, 11:) It came upon me unaware; slew all my hopes; and plainly showed, in the midst of life I was in death. "Wherefore the law is holy, and the commandment holy, and just, and good:" (Verse 12:) I no longer lay the blame on this, but on the corruption of my own heart. I acknowledge that "the law is spiritual; but I am carnal, sold under sin:" (Verse 14:) I now see both the spiritual nature of the law; and my own carnal, devilish heart "sold under sin," totally enslaved: (Like slave bought with money, who were absolutely at their master's disposal:) "For that which I do, I allow not; for what I would, I do not, but what I hate, that I do:" (Verse 15:) Such is the bondage under which I groan; such the tyranny of my hard master. "To will is present with me, but how to perform that which is good I find not. For the good that I would, I do not; but the evil which I would not, that I do:" (Verses 18, 19:) "I find a law," an inward constraining power, "that when I would do good, evil is present with me. For I delight in "or consent to "the law of God, after the inward man:" (Verses 21, 22:) In my "mind:" (So the Apostle explains himself in the words that immediately follow; and so, *o eso anthropos, the inward man*, is understood in all other Greek writers:) But I see another law in my members, another constraining power, warring against the law of my mind, or inward man, and bringing me into captivity to the law or power "of sin:" (Verse 23:) Dragging me, as it were, at my conquerors chariot-wheels, into the very thing which my soul abhors. "o wretched man that I am! who shall deliver me from the body of this death?" (Verse 24.) Who shall deliver me from this helpless, dying life, from this bondage of sin and misery? Till this is done, "I myself" (or rather, *that I, autos ego*, that man I am now personating) "with the mind,"

or inward man, "serve the law of God;" my mind, my conscience is on God's side; "but with my flesh," with my body, "the law of sin," (verse 25,) being hurried away by a force I cannot resist.

10. How lively a portraiture is this of one "under the law;" one who feels the burden he cannot shake off; who pants after liberty, power, and love, but is in fear and bondage still! until the time that God answers the wretched man, crying out, "Who shall deliver me" from this bondage of sin, from this body of death?—"The grace of God, through Jesus Christ thy Lord."

III. 1. Them it is that this miserable bondage ends, and he is no more "under the law, but under grace." This state we are, Thirdly, to consider; the state of one who has found *grace* or favour in the sight of God, even the Father, and who has the *grace* or power of the Holy Ghost, reigning in his heart; who has received, in the language of the Apostle, the "Spirit of adoption, whereby" he now cries, "Abba, Father!"

2. "He cried unto the Lord in his trouble, and God delivers him out of his distress." His eyes are opened in quite another manner than before, even to see a loving, gracious God. While he is calling, "I beseech thee, show me thy glory!"—he hears a voice in the inmost soul, "I will make all my goodness pass before thee, and I will proclaim the name of the Lord: I will be gracious to whom I will be gracious, and I will show mercy to whom I will show mercy." And, it is not long before "the Lord" descends in the cloud, and proclaims the name of the Lord." Then he sees, but not with eyes of flesh and blood, "The Lord, the Lord God, merciful and gracious, long-suffering, and abundant in goodness and truth; keeping mercy for thousands, and forgiving iniquities, and transgressions and sin."

3. Heavenly, healing light now breaks in upon his soul. He "looks on him whom he had pierced;" and "God, who out of darkness commanded light to shine, shineth in his heart." He sees the light of the glorious love of God, in the face of Jesus Christ. He hath a divine "evidence of things not seen" by sense, even of the "deep things of God;" more particularly of the love of God, of his pardoning love to him that believes in Jesus. Overpowered with the sight, his whole soul cried out, "My Lord and my God;" For he sees all his iniquities laid on Him, who "bare them in his own body on the tree;" he beholds the Lamb of God taking away his sins. How clearly now does he discern, that "God was in Christ, reconciling the world unto himself; making him sin for us, who knew no sin, that we might be made the righteousness of God through him;"—and that he himself is reconciled to God, by that blood of the covenant!

4. Here end both the guilt and power of sin. He can now say, "I am crucified with Christ: Nevertheless I live; yet not I but Christ liveth in me: And the life which I now live in the flesh," (even in this mortal body,) "I live by faith in the Son of God, who loved me, and gave himself for me." Here end remorse, and sorrow of heart, and the anguish of a wounded spirit. "God turneth his heaviness into joy." He made sore, and now his hands bind up. Here ends also that bondage unto fear; for "his heart standeth fast, believing in the Lord." He cannot fear any longer the wrath of God; for he knows it

is now turned away from him, and looks upon Him no more as an angry Judge, but as a loving Father. He cannot fear the devil, knowing he has "no power, except it be given him from above." He fears not hell; being an heir of the kingdom of heaven: Consequently, he has no fear of death; by reason whereof he was in time past, for so many years, "subject to bondage." Rather, knowing that "if the earthly house of this tabernacle be dissolved, he hath a building of God, a house not made with hands, eternal in the heavens; he groaneth earnestly, desiring to be clothed upon with that house which is from heaven." He groans to shake off this house of earth, that "mortality" may be "swallowed up of life;" knowing that God "hath wrought him for the self-same thing; who hath also given him the earnest of his Spirit."

5. And "where the Spirit of the Lord is, there is liberty;" liberty, not only from guilt and fear, but from sin, from that heaviest of all yokes, that basest of all bondage. His labour is not now in vain. The snare is broken, and he is delivered. He not only strives, but likewise prevails; he not only fights, but conquers also. "Henceforth he does not serve sin." (Chap. 6:6) He is "dead unto sin, and alive unto God;" "sin doth not now reign," even "in his mortal body," nor doth he "obey it in the desires thereof." He does not "yield his members as instruments of unrighteousness unto sin, but as instruments of righteousness unto God." For "being now made free from sin, he is become the servant of righteousness."

6. Thus, "having peace with God, through our Lord Jesus Christ," "rejoicing in hope of the glory of God," and having power over all sin, over every evil desire, and temper, and word, and work, he is a living witness of the "glorious liberty of the sons of God;" all of whom, being partakers of like precious faith, bear record with one voice, "We have received the Spirit of adoption, whereby we cry, Abba, Father!"

7. It is this spirit which continually, "worketh in them, both to will and to do of his good pleasure." It is he that sheds the love of God abroad in their hears, and the love of all mankind; thereby purifying their hearts from the love of world, from the lust of the flesh, the lust of the eye, and the pride of life. It is by him they are delivered from anger and pride, from all vile and inordinate affections. In consequence, they are delivered from evil words and works, from all unholiness of conversation; doing no evil to any child of man, and being zealous of all good works.

8. To sum up all: the *natural* man neither fears nor loves God; one *under the law*, fears,—one *under grace*, loves him. The first has no light in the things of God, but walks in utter darkness; the second sees the painful light of hell; the third, the joyous light of heaven. He that sleeps in death, has a false peace; he that is awakened, has no peace at all; he that believes, has true peace,—the peace of God filling and ruling his heart. The Heathen, baptized or unbaptized, hath a fancied liberty, which is indeed licentiousness; the Jew, or one under the Jewish dispensation, is in heavy, grievous bondage; the Christian enjoys the true glorious liberty of the sons of God. An unawakened child of the devil sins willingly, one that is awakened sins unwillingly; a child of God "sinneth not," but "keepeth himself, and the wicked one toucheth him not." To conclude: the natural man neither conquers nor fights; the man under the law fights with sin, but cannot conquer; the man under grace fights and conquers, yea, is "more than conqueror, through him that loveth him."

IV. 1. From this plain account of the three-fold state of man, the *natural*, the *legal*, and the *evangelical*, it appears that it is not sufficient to divide mankind into sincere and insincere. A man may be sincere in any of these states; not only when he has the "Spirit of adoption," but while he has the "spirit of bondage unto fear;" yea, while he has neither this fear, nor love. For undoubtedly there may be sincere Heathens, as well as sincere Jews, or Christians. This circumstance, them does by no means prove, that, a man is in a state of acceptance with God.

"Examine yourselves, therefore," not only whether ye are sincere, but "whether ye be in the faith." Examine narrowly, (for it imports you much,) what is the ruling principle in your soul! Is it the love of God? Is it the fear of God? Or is it neither one nor the other? Is it not rather the love of the world? the love of pleasure, or gain? of ease, or reputation? If so, you are not come so far as a Jew. You are but a Heathen still. Have you heaven in your heart? Have you the Spirit of adoption, ever crying, Abba, Father? Or do you cry unto God, as "out of the belly of hell," overwhelmed with sorrow and fear? Or are you a stranger to this whole affair, and cannot imagine what I mean? Heathen, pull off the mask! Thou hast never put on Christ! Stand barefaced! Look up to heaven; and own before Him that liveth for ever and ever, thou hast no part, either among the sons of servants of God! Whosoever thou art: Dost thou commit sin, or dost thou not? If thou dost, is it willingly, or unwillingly? In either case, God hath told thee whose thou art: "He that committeth sin is of the devil." If thou committest it willingly, thou art his faithful servant: He will not fail to reward thy labour. If unwillingly, still thou art his servant. God deliver thee out of his hands!

Art thou daily fighting against all sin? And daily more than conqueror? I acknowledge thee for a child of God. O stand fast in thy glorious liberty! Art thou fighting, but not conquering? striving for the mastery, but not able to attain? Then thou art not yet a believer in Christ; but follow on, and thou shalt know the Lord. Art thou not fighting at all, but leading an easy, indolent, fashionable life! O how hast thou dared to name the name of Christ, only to make it a reproach among the Heathen? Awake, thou sleeper! Call upon thy God before the deep swallow thee up!

2. Perhaps one reason why so many think of themselves more highly than they ought to think, why they do not discern what state they are in, is because these several states of soul are often mingled together, and in some measure meet in one and the same person. Thus experience shows, that the legal state, or state of fear, is frequently mixed with the natural; for few men are so fast asleep in sin, but they are sometimes more or less awakened. As the Spirit of God does not "wait for the call of man," so, at some times he *will* be heard. He puts them in fear, so that, for a season at least, the Heathen "know themselves to be but men." They feel the burden of sin, and earnestly desire to flee from the wrath to come. But not long:

They seldom suffer the arrows of conviction to go deep into their souls; but quickly stifle the grace of God, and return to their wallowing in the mire.

In like manner, the evangelical state, or state of love, is frequently mixed with the legal. For few of those who have the spirit of bondage and fear, remain always without hope. The wise and gracious God rarely suffers this; "for he remembereth that we are but dust;" and he willeth not that "the flesh should fail before him, or the spirit which he hath made." Therefore, at such times as he seeth good, he gives a dawning of light unto them that sit in darkness. He cause a part of his goodness to pass before them, and shows he is a "God that heareth the prayer." They see the promise, which is by faith in Christ Jesus, though it be yet afar off; and hereby they are encouraged to "run with patience the race which is set before them."

3. Another reason why many deceive themselves, is, because they do not consider how far a man may go, and yet be in a natural, or, at best, a legal state. A man may be of a compassionate and a benevolent temper; he may be affable, courteous, generous, friendly; he may have some degree of meekness, patience, temperance, and of many other moral virtues. He may feel many desires of shaking off all vice, and of attaining higher degrees of virtue. He may abstain from much evil; perhaps from all that is grossly contrary to justice, mercy, or truth. He may do much good, may feed the hungry, clothe the naked, relieve the widow and fatherless. He may attend public worship, use prayer in private, read many books of devotion; and yet, for all this, he may be a mere natural man, knowing neither himself nor God; equally a stranger to the spirit of fear and to that of love; having neither repented, nor believed the gospel.

But suppose there were added to all this a deep conviction of sin, with much fear of the wrath of God; vehement desires to cast off every sin, and to fulfill all righteousness; frequent rejoicing in hope, and touches of love often glancing upon the soul; yet neither do these prove a man to be *under grace*, to have true, living, Christian faith, unless the Spirit of adoption abide in his heart, unless he can continually cry, "Abba, Father!"

4. Beware, then, thou who art called by the name of Christ, that thou come not short of the mark of thy high calling. Beware thou rest, not, either in a natural state with too many that are accounted *good Christians*; or in a legal state, wherein those who are highly esteemed of men are generally content to live and die. Nay, but God hath prepared better things for thee, if thou follow on till thou attain. Thou art not called to fear and tremble like devils; but to rejoice and love, like the angels of God. "Thou shalt love the lord thy God will all thy heart, and with all thy soul, and with all thy mind, and with all thy strength." Thou shalt "rejoice evermore;" thou shalt "pray without ceasing:" thou shalt "in everything give thanks." Thou shalt do the will of God on earth as it is done in heaven. O prove thou "what is that good, and acceptable, and perfect will of God!" Now present thyself "a living sacrifice, holy, acceptable to God." "Whereunto thou hast already attained, hold fast," by "reaching forth unto those things which are before:" until "the God of peace make thee perfect in every good work, working in thee that which is well-pleasing in his sight through Jesus Christ: To whom be glory for ever and ever! Amen!"

10.* THE WITNESS OF THE SPIRIT DISCOURSE
I

"The Spirit itself beareth witness with our spirit, that we are the children of God."

Rom. 8:16

1. How many vain men, not understanding what they spake, neither whereof they affirmed, have wrested this Scripture to the great loss if not the destruction of their souls! How many have mistaken the voice of their own imagination for this witness of the Spirit of God, and thence idly presumed they were the children of God while they were doing the works of the devil! These are truly and properly enthusiasts; and, indeed, in the worst sense of the word. But with what difficulty are they convinced thereof, especially if they have drank deep into that spirit of error! All endeavours to bring them to the knowledge of themselves they will then account fighting against God; and that vehemence and impetuosity of spirit which they call "contending earnestly for the faith," sets them so far above all the usual methods of conviction that we may well say, "With men it is impossible."

2. Who can then be surprised if many reasonable men, seeing the dreadful effects of this delusion, and labouring to keep at the utmost distance from it, should sometimes lean toward another extreme?—if they are not forward to believe any who speak of having this witness concerning which others have so grievously erred?—if they are almost ready to set all down for enthusiasts, who use the expressions which have been so terribly abused?—yea, if they should question whether the witness or testimony here spoken of, be the privilege of *ordinary* Christians, and not, rather, one of those *extraordinary* gifts which they suppose belonged only to the apostolic age?

3. But is there any necessity laid upon us of running either into one extreme or the other? May we not steer a middle course?—keep a sufficient distance from that spirit of error and enthusiasm, without denying the gift of God, and giving up the great privilege of his children? Surely we may. In order thereto, let us consider, in the presence and fear of God,

First. What is this witness or testimony of our spirit; what is the testimony of God's Spirit; and, how does he "bear witness with our spirit that we are the children of God?"

Secondly. How is this joint testimony of God's Spirit and our own, clearly and solidly distinguished from the presumption of a natural mind, and from the delusion of the devil?

I. 1. Let us first consider, what is the witness or testimony of our spirit. But here I cannot but desire all those who are for swallowing up the testimony of the Spirit of God, in the rational testimony of our own spirit, to observe, that in this text the Apostle is so far from speaking of the testimony of

---

* [text from the 1872 edition]

our own spirit *only*, that it may be questioned whether he speaks of it *at all*,—whether he does not speak *only* of the testimony of God's Spirit. It does not appear but the original text may fairly be understood thus. The Apostle had just said, in the preceding verse, "Ye have received the Spirit of adoption, whereby we cry, Abba, Father;" and immediately subjoins, *Auto to pneuma* (some copies read *to auto pneuma*) *symmartyrei toi pneumati hemon, hoti esmen tekna Theou,* which may be translated, The same Spirit beareth witness to our spirit that we are the children of God (the preposition *syn* only denoting that he witnesses this *at the same* time that he enables us to cry Abba, Father.) But I contend not; seeing so many other texts, with the experience of all real Christians, sufficiently evince, that there is in every believer, both the testimony of God's Spirit, and the testimony of his own, that he is a child of God.

2. With regard to the latter, the foundation thereof is laid in those numerous texts of Scripture which describe the marks of the children of God; and that so plain, that he which runneth may read them. These are also collected together, and placed in the strongest light, by many both ancient and modern writers. If any need farther light, he may receive it by attending on the ministry of God's Word; by meditating thereon before God in secret; and by conversing with those who have the knowledge of his ways. And by the reason or understanding that God has given him, which religion was designed not to extinguish, but to perfect;—according to that of the Apostle, "Brethren, be not children in understanding; in malice" or wickedness "be ye children; but in understanding be ye men;" (1 Cor. 14:20;)—every man applying those scriptural marks to himself, may know whether he is a child of God. Thus, if he know, First, "as many as are led by the Spirit of God," into all holy tempers and actions, "they are the sons of God;" (for which he has the infallible assurance of holy writ;) Secondly, I am thus "led by the Spirit of God;" he will easily conclude,—"Therefore I am a son of God."

3. Agreeable to this are all those plain declarations of St. John, in his First Epistle: "Hereby we know that we do know him, if we keep his commandments." (1 John 2:3.) "Whoso keepeth his word, in him verily is the love of God perfected; Hereby know we that we are in him;" that we are indeed the children of God. (1 John 2:5.) "If ye know that he is righteous, ye know that everyone that doeth righteousness is born of him." (1 John 2:29.) "We know that we have passed from death unto life, because we love the brethren." (1 John 3:14) "Hereby we know that we are of the truth, and shall assure our hearts before him;" namely, because we "love one another not in word, neither in tongue, but in deed and in truth." "Hereby know we that we dwell in him, because he hath given us of his" loving "Spirit." (1 John 4:13.) And, "hereby we know that he abideth in us, by the" obedient "spirit which he hath given us." (1 John 3:24.)

4. It is highly probable there never were any children of God, from the beginning of the world unto this day, who were farther advanced in the grace of God and the knowledge of our Lord Jesus Christ, than the Apostle John, at the time when he wrote these words, and the fathers in Christ to whom he wrote. Notwithstanding which, it is evident both the Apostle himself, and all those pillars in God's temple, were very far from despising these marks of their being the children of God; and that they applied them to their own souls for the confirmation of their faith. Yet all this is no other than rational evidence, the witness of our spirit, our reason or understanding. It all resolves into this: Those who have these marks are the children of God: But we have these marks. Therefore we are children of God.

5. But how does it appear, that we have these marks? This is a question which still remains. How does it appear, that we do love God and our neighbour, and that we keep his commandments? Observe, that the meaning of the question is, How does it appear to *ourselves*, not to *others?* I would ask him, then, that proposes this question, How does it appear to you that you are alive, and that you are now in ease, and not in pain? Are you not immediately conscious of it? By the same immediate consciousness, you will know if your soul is alive to God; if you are saved from the pain of proud wrath, and have the ease of a meek and quiet spirit. By the same means you cannot but perceive if you love, rejoice, and delight in God. By the same you must be directly assured, if you love your neighbour as yourself; if you are kindly affectioned to all mankind, and full of gentleness and longsuffering. And with regard to the outward mark of the children of God, which is, according to St. John, the keeping his commandments, you undoubtedly know in your own breast, if, by the grace of God, it belongs to you. Your conscience informs you from day to day, if you do not take the name of God within your lips unless with seriousness and devotion, with reverence and godly fear; if you remember the Sabbath-day to keep it holy; if you honour your father and mother; if you do to all as you would they should do unto you; if you possess your body in sanctification and honour; and if, whether you eat or drink, you are temperate therein, and do all to the glory of God.

6. Now this is properly the testimony of our own spirit; even the testimony of our conscience, that God hath given us to be holy of heart, and holy in outward conversation. It is a consciousness of our having received, in and by the Spirit of adoption, the tempers mentioned in the Word of God as belonging to his adopted children; even a loving heart toward God and toward all mankind; hanging with childlike confidence on God our Father, desiring nothing but him, casting all our care upon him, and embracing every child of man with earnest, tender affection:—A consciousness that we are inwardly conformed, by the Spirit of God, to the image of his Son, and that we walk before him in justice, mercy, and truth, doing the things which are pleasing in his sight.

7. But what is that testimony of God's Spirit, which is superadded to, and conjoined with, this? How does he "bear witness with our spirit that we are the children of God?" It is hard to find words in the language of men to explain "the deep things of God." Indeed, there are none that will adequately express what the children of God experience. But perhaps one might say, (desiring any who are taught of God to correct, to soften or strengthen the expression,) The testimony of the Spirit is an inward impression on the soul,

whereby the Spirit of God directly witnesses to my spirit, that I am a child of God; that Jesus Christ hath loved me, and given himself for me; and that all my sins are blotted out, and I, even I, am reconciled to God.

8. That this testimony of the Spirit of God must needs, in the very nature of things, be antecedent to the testimony of our own spirit, may appear from this single consideration: We must be holy of heart, and holy in life before we can be conscious that we are so; before we can have the testimony of our spirit, that we are inwardly and outwardly holy. But we must love God, before we can be holy at all; this being the root of all holiness. Now we cannot love God, till we know he loves us. "We love him, because he first loved us." And we cannot know his pardoning love to us, till his Spirit witnesses it to our spirit. Since, therefore, this testimony of his Spirit must precede the love of God and all holiness, of consequence it must precede our inward consciousness thereof, or the testimony of our spirit concerning them.

9. Then, and not till then,—when the Spirit of God beareth that witness to our spirit, "God hath loved thee, and given his own Son to be the propitiation for thy sins; the Son of God hath loved thee, and hath washed thee from thy sins in his blood,"—"we love God, because he first loved us;" and, for his sake, we love our brother also. And of this we cannot but be conscious to ourselves: We "know the things that are freely given to us of God." We know that we love God and keep his commandments; and "hereby also we know that we are of God." This is that testimony of our own spirit, which, so long as we continue to love God and keep his commandments, continues joined with the testimony of God's Spirit, "that we are the children of God."

10. Not that I would by any means be understood, by anything which has been spoken concerning it, to exclude the operation of the Spirit of God, even from the testimony of our own spirit. In no wise. It is he that not only worketh in us every manner of thing that is good, but also shines upon his own work, and clearly shows what he has wrought. Accordingly, this is spoken of by St. Paul, as one great end of our receiving the Spirit, "that we may know the things which are freely given to us of God:" That he may strengthen the testimony of our conscience, touching our 'simplicity and godly sincerity;" and give us to discern, in a fuller and stronger light, that we now do the things which please him.

11. Should it still be inquired, "How does the Spirit of God bear witness with our spirit, that we are the children of God,' so as to exclude all doubt, and evince the reality of our sonship?"—the answer is clear from what has been observed above. And, First, as to the witness of our spirit: The soul as intimately and evidently perceives when it loves, delights, and rejoices in God, as when it loves and delights in anything on earth. And it can no more doubt, whether it loves, delights, and rejoices or no, than whether it exists or no. If, therefore this be just reasoning,

He that now loves God, that delights and rejoices in him with an humble joy, and holy delight, and an obedient love, is a child of God;

But I thus love, delight, and rejoice in God;

Therefore, I am a child of God:—Then a Christian can in no wise doubt of his being a child of God. Of the former proposition he has as full an assurance as he has that the Scriptures are of God; and of his thus loving God, he has an inward proof, which is nothing short of self-evidence. Thus, the testimony of our own spirit is with the most intimate conviction manifested to our hearts, in such a manner, as beyond all reasonable doubt to evince the reality of our sonship.

12. The manner how the *divine* testimony is manifested to the heart, I do not take upon me to explain. Such knowledge is too wonderful and excellent for me: I cannot attain unto it. The wind bloweth, and I hear the sound thereof; but I cannot tell how it cometh, or whither it goeth. As no one knoweth the things of a man, save the spirit of a man that is in him; so the *manner* of the things of God knoweth no one, save the Spirit of God. But the fact we know; namely, that the Spirit of God does give a believer such a testimony of his adoption that while it is present to the soul, he can no more doubt the reality of his sonship, than he can doubt of the shining of the sun, while he stands full blaze of his beams.

II. 1. How this joint testimony of God's Spirit and our spirit may be clearly and solidly distinguished from the presumption of a natural mind, and from the delusion of the devil, is the next thing to be considered. And it highly imports all who desire the salvation of God, to consider it with the deepest attention, as they would not deceive their own souls. An error in this is generally observed to have the most fatal consequences; the rather, because he that errs, seldom discovers his mistake till it is too late to remedy it.

2. And, First, how is this testimony to be distinguished from the presumption of a natural mind? It is certain, one who was never convinced of sin, is always ready to flatter himself, and to think of himself, especially in spiritual things, more highly than he ought to think. And hence, it is in no wise strange, if one who is vainly puffed up by his fleshly mind, when he hears of this privilege of true Christians, among whom he undoubtedly ranks himself, should soon work himself up into a persuasion that he is already possessed thereof. Such instances now abound in the world, and have abounded in all ages. How then may the real testimony of the Spirit with our spirit, be distinguished from this damning presumption?

3. I answer, the Holy Scriptures abound with marks, whereby the one may be distinguished from the other. They describe, in the plainest manner, the circumstances which go before, which accompany, and which follow, the true, genuine testimony of the Spirit of God with the spirit of a believer. Whoever carefully weighs and attends to these will not need to put darkness for light. He will perceive so wide a difference, with respect to all these, between the real and the pretended witness of the Spirit, that there will be no danger, I might say, no possibility, of confounding the one with the other.

4. By these, one who vainly presumes on the gift of God might surely know, if he really desired it, that he hath been hitherto "given up to a strong delusion," and suffered to believe a lie. For the Scriptures lay down those clear, obvious marks, as preceding, accompanying, and following that gift,

which a little reflection would convince him, beyond all doubt, were never found in his soul. For instance: The Scripture describes repentance, or conviction of sin, as constantly going before this witness of pardon. So, "Repent; for the kingdom of heaven is at hand." (Matt. 3:2.) "Repent ye, and believe the gospel." (Mark 1:15.) "Repent, and be baptized every one of you for the remission of sins." (Acts 2:38.) "Repent ye therefore, and be converted, that your sins may be blotted out." (Acts 3:19.) In conformity whereto, our Church also continually places repentance before pardon, or the witness of it. "He pardoneth and absolveth all them that truly repent, and unfeignedly believe his holy gospel." "Almighty God—hath promised forgiveness of sins to all them, who, with hearty repentance and true faith, turn unto him." But he is a stranger even to this repentance: He hath never known a broken and a contrite heart: "The remembrance of his sins" was never "grievous unto him," nor "the burden of them intolerable." In repeating those words, he never meant what he said; he merely paid a compliment to God. And were it only from the want of this previous work of God, he hath too great reason to believe that he hath grasped a mere shadow, and never yet known the real privilege of the sons of God.

5. Again, the Scriptures describe the being born of God, which must precede the witness that we are his children, as a vast and mighty change; a change "from darkness to light," as well as "from the power of Satan unto God;" as a "passing from death unto life," a resurrection from the dead. Thus the Apostle to the Ephesians: "You hath he quickened who were dead in trespasses and sins." (Eph. 2:1.) And again, "when we were dead in sins, he hath quickened us together with Christ; and hath raised us up together, and made us sit together in heavenly places in Christ Jesus." (Eph. 2:5, 6.) But what knoweth he, concerning whom we now speak, of any such change as this? He is altogether unacquainted with this whole matter. This is a language which he does not understand. He tells you he always was a Christian. He knows no time when he had need of such a change. By this also, if he give himself leave to think, may he know, that he is not born of the Spirit; that he has never yet known God; but has mistaken the voice of nature for the voice of God.

6. But waving the consideration of whatever he has or has not experienced in time past; by the present marks may we easily distinguish a child of God from a presumptuous self-deceiver. The Scriptures describe that joy in the Lord which accompanies the witness of his Spirit, as a humble joy; a joy that abases to the dust, that makes a pardoned sinner cry out, "I am vile! What am I, or my father's house? Now mine eye seeth thee, I abhor myself in dust and ashes!" And wherever lowliness is, there is meekness, patience, gentleness, long-suffering. There is a soft, yielding spirit; a mildness and sweetness, a tenderness of soul, which words cannot express. But do these fruits attend that *supposed* testimony of the Spirit in a presumptuous man? Just the reverse. The more confident he is of the favour of God, the more is he lifted up; the more does he exalt himself, the more haughty and assuming is his whole behaviour. The stronger witness he imagines himself to have, the more overbearing is he to all around him; the more incapable of receiving any reproof; the more impatient of contradiction. Instead of being more meek, and gentle, and teachable, more "swift to hear, and slow to speak," he is more slow to hear, and swift to speak; more unready to learn of anyone; more fiery and vehement in his temper, and eager in his conversation. Yea, perhaps, there will sometimes appear a kind of fierceness in his air, his manner of speaking, his whole deportment, as if he were just going to take the matter out of God's hands, and himself to "devour the adversaries."

7. Once more: the Scriptures teach, "This is the love of God," the sure mark thereof, "that we keep his commandments." (1 John 5:3.) And our Lord himself saith, "He that keepeth my commandments, he it is that loveth me." (John 14:21.) Love rejoices to obey; to do, in every point whatever is acceptable to the beloved. A true lover of God hastens to do his will on earth as it is done in heaven. But is this the character of the presumptuous pretender to the love of God? Nay, but his love gives him a liberty to disobey, to break, not keep, the commandments of God. Perhaps, when he was in fear of the wrath of God, he did labour to do his will. But now, looking on himself as "not under the law," he thinks he is no longer obliged to observe it. He is therefore less zealous of good works: less careful to abstain from evil; less watchful over his own heart; less jealous over his tongue. He is less earnest to deny himself, and to take up his cross daily. In a word, the whole form of his life is changed since he has fancied himself to be *at liberty*. He is no longer "exercising himself unto godliness;" "wrestling not only with flesh and blood, but with principalities and powers," enduring hardships, "agonizing to enter in at the strait gate." No; he has found an easier way to heaven; a broad, smooth flowery path, in which he can say to his soul, "Soul, take thy ease; eat, drink, and be merry." It follows, with undeniable evidence, that he has not the true testimony of his own spirit. He cannot be conscious of having those marks which he hath not; that lowliness, meekness, and obedience: Nor yet can the Spirit of the God of truth bear witness to a lie; or testify that he is a child of God when he is manifestly a child of the devil.

8. Discover thyself, thou poor self-deceiver!—thou who art confident of being a child of God; thou who sayest, "I have the witness in myself," and therefore defiest all thy enemies. Thou art weighed in the balance and found wanting; even in the balance of the sanctuary. The word of the Lord hath tried thy soul, and proved thee to be reprobate silver. Thou art not lowly of heart; therefore thou hast not received the Spirit of Jesus unto this day. Thou art not gentle and meek; therefore thy joy is nothing worth: It is not joy in the Lord. Thou dost not keep his commandments; therefore thou lovest him not, neither art thou partaker of the Holy Ghost. It is consequently as certain and as evident, as the Oracles of God can make it, his Spirit doth not bear witness with thy spirit that thou art a child of God. O cry unto him, that the scales may fall off thine eyes; that thou mayst know thyself as thou art known; that thou mayest receive the sentence of death in thyself, till thou hear the voice that raises the dead, saying, "Be of good cheer: Thy sins are forgiven; thy faith hath made thee whole."

9. "But how may one who has the real witness in himself distinguish it from presumption?" How, I pray, do you distinguish day from night? How do you distinguish light from darkness; or the light of a star, or glimmering taper, from the light of the noonday sun? Is there not an inherent, obvious, essential difference between the one and the other? And do you not immediately and directly perceive that difference, provided your senses are rightly disposed? In like manner, there is an inherent, essential difference between spiritual light and spiritual darkness; and between the light wherewith the Sun of righteousness shines upon our heart, and that glimmering light which arises only from "sparks of our own kindling:" And this difference also is immediately and directly perceived, if our spiritual senses are rightly disposed.

10. To require a more minute and philosophical account of the manner whereby we distinguish these, and of the *criteria*, or intrinsic marks, whereby we know the voice of God, is to make a demand which can never be answered; no, not by one who has the deepest knowledge of God. Suppose when Paul answered before Agrippa, the wise Roman had said, "Thou talkest of hearing the voice of the Son of God. How dost thou know it was his voice? By what *criteria*, what intrinsic marks, dost thou know the voice of God? Explain to me the *manner* of distinguishing this from a human or angelic voice." Can you believe the Apostle himself would have once attempted to answer so idle a demand? And yet, doubtless, the moment he heard that voice he knew it was the voice of God. But *how* he knew this, who is able to explain? Perhaps neither man nor angel.

11. To come yet closer: Suppose God were now to speak to any soul, "Thy sins are forgiven thee,"—he must be willing that soul should know his voice; otherwise he would speak in vain. And he is able to effect this; for, whenever he wills, to do is present with him. And he does effect it: That soul is absolutely assured, "this voice is the voice of God." But yet he who hath that witness in himself, cannot explain it to one who hath it not: Nor indeed is it to be expected that he should. Were there any natural medium to prove, or natural method to explain, the things of God to unexperienced men, then the natural man might discern and know the things of the Spirit of God. But this is utterly contrary to the assertion of the Apostle, that "he cannot know them, because they are spiritually discerned;" [1 Cor. 2:14] even by spiritual senses, which the natural man hath not.

12. "But how shall I know that my spiritual senses are rightly disposed?" This also is a question of vast importance; for if a man mistake in this, he may run on in endless error and delusion. "And how am I assured that this is not my case; and that I do not mistake the voice of the Spirit?" Even by the testimony of your own spirit; by "the answer of a good conscience toward God." [Acts 23:1] By the fruits which he hath wrought in your spirit, you shall know the testimony of the Spirit of God. Hereby you shall know, that you are in no delusion, that you have not deceived your own soul. The immediate fruits of the Spirit ruling in the heart, are "love, joy, peace, bowels of mercies, humbleness of mind, meekness, gentleness, long-suffering." [Gal. 5:22, 23] And the outward fruits are, the doing good to all men; the doing no evil to any; and the walking in the light, [1 John 1:7]—a zealous, uniform obedience to all the commandments of God.

13. By the same fruits shall you distinguish this voice of God, from any delusion of the devil. That proud spirit cannot humble thee before God. He neither can nor would soften thy heart, and melt it first into earnest mourning after God, and then into filial love. It is not the adversary of God and man that enables thee to love thy neighbour; or to put on meekness, gentleness, patience, temperance, and the whole armour of God. [see Col. 3:12–14;Eph. 6:11] He is not divided against himself, or a destroyer of sin, his own work. No; it is none but the Son of God who cometh to "destroy the works of the devil." [1 John 3:8] As surely therefore as holiness is of God, and as sin is the work of the devil, so surely the witness thou hast in thyself is not of Satan, but of God.

14. Well then mayst thou say, "Thanks be unto God for his unspeakable gift!" [2 Cor. 9:15] Thanks be unto God, who giveth me to "know in whom I have believed;" [2 Tim. 1:12] who hath "sent forth the Spirit of his Son into my heart, crying, Abba, Father," [Gal. 4:6] and even now, "bearing witness with my spirit that I am a child of God!" [Rom. 8:16] And see, that not only thy lips, but thy life show forth his praise. He hath sealed thee for his own; glorify him then in thy body and thy spirit, which are his. [1 Cor. 6:20] Beloved, if thou hast this hope in thyself, purify thyself as he is pure. While thou beholdest what manner of love the Father hath given thee, that thou shouldst be called a child of God; [1 John 3:1] cleanse thyself "from all filthiness of flesh and Spirit, perfecting holiness in the fear of God;" [2 Cor. 7:1] and let all thy thoughts, words, and works be a spiritual sacrifice, holy, acceptable to God through Christ Jesus! [Rom. 12:1, 2]

11. THE WITNESS OF THE SPIRIT DISCOURSE II

"The Spirit itself beareth witness with our spirit, that we are the children of God."

Rom. 8:16

I. 1. None who believe the Scriptures to be the word of God, can doubt the importance of such a truth as this;—a truth revealed therein, not once only, not obscurely, not incidentally; but frequently, and that in express terms; but solemnly and of set purpose, as denoting one of the peculiar privileges of the children of God.

2. And it is the more necessary to explain and defend this truth, because there is a danger on the right hand and on the left. If we deny it, there is a danger lest our religion degenerate into mere formality; lest, "having a form of godliness," we neglect, if not "deny, the power of it." If we allow it, but do not understand what we allow, we are liable to run into all the wildness of enthusiasm. It is therefore needful, in the highest degree, to guard those who fear God from both those dangers by a scriptural and rational illustration and confirmation of this momentous truth.

3. It may seem, something of this kind is the more needful, because so little has been wrote on the subject with any

clearness; unless some discourses on the wrong side of the question, which explain it quite away. And it cannot be doubted, but these were occasioned, at least in a great measure, by the crude, unscriptural, irrational explication of others, who "knew not what they spake, nor whereof they affirmed."

4. It more nearly concerns the Methodists, so called, clearly to understand, explain, and defend this doctrine; because it is one grand part of the testimony which God has given them to bear to all mankind. It is by this peculiar blessing upon them in searching the Scriptures, confirmed by the experience of his children, that this great evangelical truth has been recovered, which had been or many years well nigh lost and forgotten.

II. 1. But what is the witness of the Spirit? The original word *martyria* may be rendered either (as it is in several places) *the witness*, or less ambiguously, *the testimony*, or *the record*: So it is rendered in our translation, (1 John 5:11,) This is the record, the testimony, the sum of what God testifies in all the inspired writings, that God hath given unto us eternal life, and this life is in his Son. The testimony now under consideration is given by the Spirit of God to and with our spirit: he is the Person testifying. What he testifies to us is, that we are the children of God. The immediate result of this testimony is, "the fruit of the Spirit;" namely, "love, joy, peace, long-suffering, gentleness, goodness:" and without these, the testimony itself cannot continue. For it is inevitably destroyed, not only by the commission of any outward sin, or the omission of known duty, but by giving way to any inward sin; in a word, by whatever grieves the holy Spirit of God.

2. I observed many years ago, "It is hard to find words in the language of men, to explain the deep things of God. Indeed there are none that will adequately express what the Spirit of God works in his children. But perhaps one might say, (desiring any who are taught of God, to correct, soften, or strengthen the expression,) By the testimony of the Spirit, I mean, an inward impression on the soul whereby the Spirit of God immediately and directly witnesses to my spirit, that I am a child of God; that Jesus Christ hath loved me, and given himself for me; that all my sins are blotted out, and I, even I, am reconciled to God."

3. After twenty years' further consideration, I see no cause to retract any part of this. Neither do I conceive how any of these expressions may be altered, so as to make them more intelligible. I can only add, that if any of the children of God will point out any other expressions, which are more clear, or more agreeable to the word of God, I will readily lay these aside.

4. Meantime let it be observed, I do not mean hereby, that the Spirit of God testifies this by any outward voice; no, nor always by an inward voice, although he may do this sometimes. Neither do I suppose, that he always applies to the heart (though he often may) one or more texts of Scripture. But he so works upon the soul by his immediate influence, and by a strong, though inexplicable operation, that the stormy wind and troubled waves subside, and there is a sweet calm; the heart resting as in the arms of Jesus, and

the sinner being clearly satisfied that God is reconciled, that all his "iniquities are forgiven, and his sins covered."

5. Now what is the matter of dispute concerning this? Not whether there be a witness or testimony of the Spirit. Not whether the Spirit does testify with our spirit, that we are the children of God. None can deny this, without flatly contradicting the Scriptures, and charging a lie upon the God of truth. Therefore, that there is a testimony of the Spirit is acknowledged by all parties.

6. Neither is it questioned whether there is an *indirect* witness or testimony, that we are the children of God. This is nearly, if not exactly, the same with the testimony of a good conscience towards God; and is the result of reason, or reflection on what we feel in our own souls. Strictly speaking, it is a conclusion drawn partly from the word of God, and partly from our own experience. The word of God says, every one who has the fruit of the Spirit is a child of God; experience, or inward consciousness, tells me, that I have the fruit of the Spirit; and hence I rationally conclude, "Therefore I am a child of God." This is likewise allowed on all hands, and so is no matter of controversy.

7. Nor do we assert, that there can be any real testimony of the Spirit without the fruit of the Spirit. We assert, on the contrary, that the fruit of the Spirit immediately springs from this testimony; not always indeed in the same degree, even when the testimony is first given: and much less afterwards neither joy nor peace is always at one stay; no, nor love; as neither is the testimony itself always equally strong and clear.

8. But the point in question is, whether there be any *direct* testimony of the Spirit at all; whether there be any other testimony of the Spirit, than that which arises from a consciousness of the fruit.

III. 1. I believe there is; because that is the plain, natural meaning of the text, "The Spirit itself beareth witness with our spirit, that we are the children of God." It is manifest, here are two witnesses mentioned, who together testify the same thing; the Spirit of God, and our own spirit. The late Bishop of London, in his sermon on this text, seems astonished that any one can doubt of this, which appears upon the very face of the words. Now, "The testimony of our own spirit," says the Bishop, "is one, which is the consciousness of our own sincerity;" or, to express the same thing a little more clearly, the consciousness of the fruit of the Spirit. When our spirit is conscious of this, of love, peace, long-suffering, gentleness, goodness, it easily infers from these premises, that we are the children of God.

2. It is true, that great man supposed the other witness to be, "The consciousness of our won good works." This, he affirms, is the testimony of Gods Spirit. But this is included in the testimony of our own spirit; yea, and in sincerity, even according to the common sense of the word. So the Apostle, "our rejoicing in this, the testimony our conscience, that in simplicity and godly sincerity refers to our words and actions, as least as much as to our inward dispositions. So that this is not another witness, but the very same that he mentioned before; the consciousness of our good works being only one branch of the consciousness of our sincerity. Consequently here is only one witness still. If therefore the text speaks of

two witnesses, one of these is not the consciousness of our good works, neither of our sincerity; all this being manifestly contained in the testimony of our spirit.

3. What then is the other witness? This might easily be learned, if the text itself were not sufficiently clear, from the verse immediately preceding: Ye have received, not the spirit of bondage, but the Spirit of adoption, whereby we cry, Abba, Father: It follows, The Spirit itself beareth witness with our spirit, that we are the children of God.

4. This is farther explained by the parallel text, (Gal. 4:6,) "Because ye are sons, God hath sent forth the Spirit of his Son into your hearts, crying Abba, Father." Is not this something *immediate* and *direct*, not the result of reflection or argumentation? Does not his Spirit cry, "Abba, Father," in our hearts the moment it is given, antecedently to any reflection upon our sincerity; yea, to any reasoning whatsoever? And is not this the plain natural sense of the words, which strikes any one as soon as he hears them? All these texts then, in their most obvious meaning, describe a direct testimony of the Spirit.

5. That the testimony of the Spirit of God must, in the very nature of things, be antecedent to the testimony of our own spirit, may appear from this single consideration: We must be holy in heart and life before we can be conscious that we are so. But we must love God before we can be holy at all, this being the root of holiness. Now we cannot love God, till we know he loves us: We love him, because he first loved us: And we cannot know his love to us, till his Spirit witnesses it to our spirit. Till then we cannot believe it; we cannot say, "The life which I now live, I live by faith in the Son of God, who loved me, and gave himself for me."

> Then, only then we feel
> our interest in his blood,
> And cry, with joy unspeakable,
> Thou art my Lord, my God!

Since, therefore, the testimony of his Spirit must precede the love of God, and all holiness, of consequence it must precede our consciousness thereof.

6. And here properly comes in, to confirm this scriptural doctrine, the experience of the children of God; the experience not of two or three, not of a few, but of a great multitude which no man can number. It has been confirmed, both in this, and in all ages, by "a cloud" of living and dying "witnesses." It is confirmed by *your* experience and *mine*. The Spirit itself bore witness to my spirit that I was a child of God, gave me an evidence hereof, and I immediately cried, "Abba, Father!" And this I did, (and so did you,) before I reflected on, or was conscious of, any fruit of the Spirit. It was from this testimony received, that love, joy, peace, and the whole fruit of the Spirit flowed. First, I heard,

> Thy sins are forgiven! Accepted thou art!
> I listen and heaven sprung up in my heart.

7. But this is confirmed, not only by experience of the children of God; thousands of whom can declare that they never did know themselves to be in the favour of God till it was directly witnessed to them by his Spirit;—but by all those who are convinced of sin, who feel the wrath of God abiding on them. These cannot be satisfied with any thing less than a direct testimony from his Spirit, that he is "merciful to their unrighteousness, and remembers their sins and iniquities no more." Tell any of these, "You are to know you are a child, by reflecting on what he has wrought in you, on your love, joy, and peace; and will he not immediately reply, "By all this I know I am a child of the devil? I have no more love to God than the devil has; my carnal mind is enmity against God. I have no joy in the holy Ghost; my soul is sorrowful even unto death. I have no peace; my heart is a troubled sea; I am all storm and tempest." And which way can these souls possibly be comforted, but by a divine testimony not that they are good, or sincere, or conformable to the Scripture in heart and life, but) that God *justifieth the ungodly?*—him that, till the moment he is justified, is all ungodly, void of all true holiness; him that worketh not, that worketh nothing that is truly good, till he is conscious that he is accepted, not for any works of righteousness which he hath done, but by the mere, free mercy of God; wholly and solely for what the Son of God hath done and suffered for him. And can it be any otherwise, if "a man is justified by faith, without the works of the law?" If so, what inward or outward goodness can he be conscious of, antecedent to his justification? Nay, is not the having nothing to pay, that is, the being conscious that "there dwelleth in us no good thing," neither inward nor outward goodness, essentially, indispensably necessary, before we can be "justified freely, through the redemption that is in Jesus Christ?" Was ever any man justified since his coming into the world, or can any man ever be justified, till he is brought to that point,

> I give up every plea beside,—
> Lord, I am damnd; but Thou has died?

8. every one, therefore, who denies the existence of such a testimony, does in effect deny justification by faith. It follows, that either he never experienced this, either he never was justified, or that be has forgotten, as St. Peter speaks, *ta katharismou ton palai autou hamartion, the purification from his former sins*, the experience he then had himself; the manner wherein God wrought in his own soul, when his former sins were blotted out.

9. And the experience even of the children of the world here confirms that of the children of God. Many of these have a desire to please God: Some of them take much pains to please him: But do they not, one and all, count it the highest absurdity for any to talk of *knowing* his sins are forgiven? Which of *them* even pretends to any such thing? And yet many of them are conscious of their own sincerity. Many of them undoubtedly have, in a degree, the testimony of their own spirit, a consciousness of their own uprightness. But this brings them no consciousness that they are forgiven; no knowledge that they are the children of God. Yea, the more sincere they are, the more uneasy they generally are, for want of knowing it; plainly showing that this cannot be known, in a satisfactory manner, by the bare testimony of our own spirit, without God's directly testifying that we are his children.

IV. But abundance of objections have been made to this; the chief of which it may be well to consider.

1. It is objected, First, "Experience is not sufficient to prove a doctrine which is not founded on Scripture." This is undoubtedly true; and it is an important truth; but it does not affect the present question; for it has been shown, that this doctrine is founded on Scripture: Therefore experience is properly alleged to confirm it.

2. But madmen, French prophets, and enthusiasts of every kind, have imagined they experienced this witness. They have so; and perhaps not a few of them did, although they did not retain it long: But if they did not, this is no proof at all that others have not experienced it; as a madman's imagining himself a king, does not prove that there are no *real* kings. "Nay, many who pleaded strongly for this, have utterly decried the Bible." Perhaps so; but this was no necessary consequence: Thousands plead for it who have the highest esteem for the Bible.

"Yea, but many have fatally deceived themselves hereby, and got above all conviction."

And yet a scriptural doctrine is no worse though men abuse it to their own destruction.

3. "But I lay it down as an undoubted truth, the fruit of the Spirit is the witness of the Spirit." Not undoubted; thousands doubt of, yea, flatly deny it: But let that pass. If this witness be sufficient, there is no need of any other. But it is sufficient, unless in one of these cases, 1. The *total absence* of the fruit of the Spirit. And this is the case, when the direct witness is first given. 2. The *not perceiving it*. But to contend for it in this case, is to contend for being in the favour of God, and not knowing it. True; not knowing it at that time any otherwise than by the testimony which is given for that end. And this we do contend for; we contend that the direct witness may shine clear, even while the indirect one is under a cloud.

4. It is objected, Secondly, "The design of the witness contended for is, to prove that the profession we make is genuine. But it does not prove this. I answer, the proving this is not the design of it. It is antecedent to our making any profession at all, but that of being lost, undone, guilty, helpless sinners. It is designed to assure those to whom it is given, that they are the children of God; that they are "justified freely by his grace, through the redemption that is in Jesus Christ." And this does not suppose that their preceding thoughts, words, and actions, are conformable to the rule of Scripture; it supposes quite the reverse; namely, that they are sinners all over; sinners both in heart and life. Were it otherwise, God would *justify the godly* and *their own works* would be *counted to them for righteousness*. And I cannot but fear that a supposition of our being justified by works is at the root of all these objections; for, whoever cordially believes that God imputes to all that are justified *righteousness without works*, will find no difficulty in allowing the witness of his Spirit, preceding the fruit of it.

5. It is objected, Thirdly, "One Evangelist says, 'Your heavenly Father will give the Holy Spirit to them that ask him.' The other Evangelist calls the same thing 'good gifts;' abundantly demonstrating that the Spirit's way of bearing witness is by giving good gifts." Nay, here is nothing at all about *bearing witness*, either in the one text or the other.

Therefore till this demonstration is better demonstrated, I let it stand as it is.

6. It is objected, Fourthly, "The Scripture says, 'The tree is known by its fruits. Prove all things. Try the spirits. Examine yourselves.'" Most true: Therefore, let every man who believes he hath the witness in himself, try whether it be of God; if the fruit follow, it is; otherwise it is not. For certainly "the tree is known by its fruit:" Hereby we *prove* if it be of God. "But the direct witness is never referred to in the Book of God." Not as standing alone; not as a single witness; but as connected with the other; as giving a *joint testimony*, testifying *with our spirit*, that we are children of God. And who is able to prove, that it is not *thus* referred to in this very Scripture? "Examine yourselves whether ye be in the faith; prove your own selves. Know ye not your ownselves, that Jesus Christ is in you?" It is by no means clear, that they did not know this by a *direct* as well as a *remote* witness. How is it proved, that they did not know it, First, by an inward consciousness; and Then, by love, joy and peace?

7. "But the testimony arising from the internal and external change is constantly referred to in the Bible. It is so: And we constantly refer thereto, to confirm the testimony of the Spirit.

"Nay, all the marks *you* have given, whereby to distinguish the operations of God's Spirit from delusion, refer to the change wrought in us and upon us. This, likewise, is undoubtedly true.

8. It is objected, Fifthly, that "the direct witness of the Spirit does not secure us from the greatest delusion. And is that a witness fit to be trusted, whose testimony cannot be depended on? That is forced to fly to something else, to prove what it asserts?" I answer: To secure us from all delusion, God gives us two witnesses that we are his children. And this they testify conjointly. Therefore, "what God hath joined together, let no man put asunder." And while they are joined, we cannot be deluded: Their testimony can be depended on. They are fit to be trusted in the highest degree, and need nothing else to prove what they assert.

"Nay, the direct witness only asserts, but does not prove, any thing." By two witnesses shall every word be established. And when the Spirit witnesses with our spirit, as God designs it to do, then it fully proves that we are children of God.

9. It is objected, Sixthly, You own the change wrought is a sufficient testimony, unless in the case of severe trials, such as that of our Saviour upon the cross; but none of us can be tried in that manner. But you or I may be tried in such a manner, and so may any other child of God, that it will be impossible for us to keep our filial confidence in God without the direct witness of his Spirit.

10. It is objected, Lastly, "The greatest contenders for it are some of the proudest and most uncharitable of men." Perhaps some of the *hottest* contenders for it are both proud and uncharitable; but many of the *firmest* contenders for it are eminently meek and lowly in heart; and, indeed, in all other respects also,

True followers of their lamb-like Lord.

The preceding objections are the most considerable that I have heard, and I believe contain the strength of the cause.

Yet I apprehend whoever calmly and impartially considers those objections and the answers together, will easily see that they do not destroy, no, nor weaken, the evidence of that great truth, that the Spirit of God does *directly* as well as *indirectly*, testify that we are children of God.

V. 1. The sum of all this is: The testimony of the Spirit is an inward impression on the souls of believers, whereby the Spirit of God directly testifies to their spirit, that they are children of God. And it is not questioned, whether there is a testimony of the Spirit; but whether there is an *direct* testimony; whether there is any other than that which arises from a consciousness of the fruit of the Spirit. We believe there is; because this is the plain natural meaning of the text, illustrated both by the preceding words, and by the parallel passage in the Epistle to the Galatians; because, in the nature of the thing, the testimony must precede the fruit which springs from it and because this plain meaning of the word of God is confirmed by the experience of innumerable children of God; yea, and by the experience of all who are convinced of sin, who can never rest till they have a direct witness; and even of the children of the world, who, not having the witness in themselves, one and all declare, none can *know* his sins forgiven.

2. And whereas it is objected, that experience is not sufficient to prove a doctrine unsupported by Scripture;—that madmen and enthusiasts of every kind have imagined such a witness that the design of that witness is to prove our profession genuine, which design it does not answer;—that the Scripture says, "The tree is known by its fruit;" "examine yourselves; prove your ownselves;" and, meantime, the direct witness is never referred to in all the Book of God;—that it does not secure us from the greatest delusions; and, Lastly, that the change wrought in us is a sufficient testimony, unless in such trials as Christ alone suffered:—We answer, 1. Experience is sufficient to *confirm* a doctrine which is grounded on Scripture. 2. Though many fancy they experience what they do not, this is no prejudice to real experience. 3. The design of that witness is, to assure us we are children of God; and this design it does answer. 4. The true witness of the Spirit is known by its fruit, "love, peace, joy;" not indeed preceding, but following it. 5. It cannot be proved, that the direct as well as the indirect witness is not referred to in that very text, "Know ye not your ownselves, that Jesus Christ is in you? 6. The Spirit of God, witnessing with our spirit, does secure us from all delusion: And, Lastly, we are all liable to trials, wherein the testimony of our own spirit is not sufficient; wherein nothing less than the direct testimony of God's Spirit can assure us that we are his children.

3. Two inferences may be drawn from the whole: The First, let none ever presume to rest in any supposed testimony of the Spirit which is separate from the fruit of it. If the Spirit of God does really testify that we are the children of God, the immediate consequence will be the fruit of the Spirit, even "love, joy, peace, long-suffering, gentleness, goodness, fidelity, meekness, temperance." And however this fruit may be clouded for a while, during the time of strong temptation, so that it does not appear to the tempted person, while Satan is sifting him as wheat; yet the substantial part of it remains, even under the thickest cloud. It is true, joy in the Holy Ghost may be withdrawn, during the hour of trial; yea, the soul may be "exceeding sorrowful," while "the hour and power of darkness" continue; but even this is generally restored with increase, till we rejoice "with joy unspeakable and full of glory."

4. The Second inference, is, let none rest in any supposed fruit of the Spirit without the witness. There may be foretastes of the Spirit without the witness. There may be foretastes of joy, of peace, of love, and those not delusive, but really from God, long before we have the witness in ourselves; before the Spirit of God witnesses with our spirits that we have "redemption in the blood of Jesus, even the forgiveness of sins." Yea, there may be a degree of long-suffering, of gentleness, of fidelity, meekness, temperance, (not a shadow thereof, but a real degree, by the preventing grace of God,) before we "are accepted in the Beloved," and, consequently, before we have a testimony of our acceptance: But it is by no means advisable to rest here; it is at the peril of our souls if we do. If we are wise, we shall be continually crying to God, until his Spirit cry in our heart, "Abba, Father!" This is the privilege of all the children of God, and without this we can never be assured that we are his children. Without this we cannot retain a steady peace, nor avoid perplexing doubts and fears. But when we have once received this Spirit of adoption, this "peace which passeth all understanding," and which expels all painful doubt and fear, will "keep our hearts and minds in Christ Jesus." And when this has brought forth its genuine fruit, all inward and outward holiness, it is undoubtedly the will of Him that calleth us, to give us always what he has once given; so that there is no need that we should ever more be deprived of either the testimony of God's Spirit, or the testimony of our own, the consciousness of our walking in all righteousness and true holiness. *Newry, April 4, 1767.*

12.* THE WITNESS OF OUR OWN SPIRIT

"This is our rejoicing, the testimony of out conscience, that in simplicity and godly sincerity, not with fleshly wisdom, but by the grace of God, we have had our conversation in the world."

2 Cor. 1:12

1. Such is the voice of every true believer in Christ, so long as he abides in faith and love. "He that followeth me," saith our Lord, "walketh not in darkness:" And while he hath the light, he rejoiceth therein. As he hath "received the Lord Jesus Christ," so he walketh in him; and while he walketh in him, the exhortation of the Apostle takes place in his soul, day by day, "Rejoice in the Lord always; and again I say, Rejoice."

2. But that we may not build our house upon the sand, (lest when the rains descend, and the winds blow, and the floods arise and beat up it, it fall and great be the fall thereof,) I

---

* [text of the 1872 edition]

intend in the following discourse to show, what is the nature and ground of a Christian's joy. We know, in general, it is that happy peace, that calm satisfaction of spirit, which arises from such a testimony of his conscience, as is here described by the Apostle. But, in order to understand this the more thoroughly, it will be requisite to weigh all his words; whence will easily appear, both what we are to understand by *conscience*, and what by the *testimony* thereof; and also, how he that hath this testimony rejoiceth evermore.

3. And, First, what are we to understand by *conscience*? What is the meaning of this word that is in every one's mouth? One would imagine it was an exceedingly difficult thing to discover this, when we consider how large and numerous volumes have been from time to time wrote on this subject; and how all the treasures of ancient and modern learning have been ransacked, in order to explain it. And yet it is to be feared, it has not received much light from all those elaborate inquiries. Rather, have not most of those writers puzzled the cause; "darkening counsel by words without knowledge;" perplexing a subject, plain in itself, and easy to be understood? For, set aside but hard words, and every man of an honest heart will soon understand the thing.

4. God has made us thinking beings, capable of perceiving what is present, and of reflecting or looking back on what is past. In particular, we are capable of perceiving whatsoever passes in our own hearts or lives; of knowing whatsoever we feel or do; and that either while it passes, or when it is past. This we mean when we say, man is a *conscious* being: He hath a *consciousness*, or inward perception, both of things present and past, relating to himself, of his own tempers and outward behavior. But what we usually term *conscience*, implies somewhat more than this. It is not barely the knowledge of our present or the remembrance of our preceding life. To remember, to bear witness either of past or present things, is only one, and the least office of conscience: Its main business is to excuse or accuse, to approve or disapprove, to acquit or condemn.

5. Some latter writers indeed have given a new name to this, and have chose to style it a *moral sense*. But the old word seems preferable to the new, were it only on this account, that it is more common and familiar among men, and therefore easier to be understood. And to Christians it is undeniably preferable, on another account also; namely, because it is scriptural; because it is the word which the wisdom of God hath chose to use in the inspired writings.

And according to the meaning wherein it is generally used there, particularly in the Epistles of St. Paul, we may understand by conscience, a faculty or power, implanted by God in every soul that comes into the world, of perceiving what is right or wrong in his own heart or life, in his tempers, thoughts, words, and actions.

6. But what is the rule whereby men are to judge of right and wrong? Whereby their conscience is to be directed? The rule of Heathens, as the Apostle teaches elsewhere is "the law written in their hearts;" by the finger of God; "their conscience also bearing witness," whether they walk by this rule or not, "and their thoughts the mean while accusing, or even excusing," acquitting, defending them; *he kai*

apologoumenon. (Rom. 2:14, 15.) But the Christian rule of right and wrong is the word of God, the writings of the old and New Testament; all that the Prophets and holy men of old wrote as they were moved by the holy Ghost; all that Scripture which was given by inspiration of God, and which is indeed profitable for doctrine, or teaching the whole will of God; for reproof of what is contrary thereto; for correction or error; and for instruction, or training us up, in righteousness. (2 Tim. 3:16.)

This is a lantern unto a Christians feet, and a light in all his paths. This alone he receives as his rule of right or wrong, of whatever is really good or evil. he esteems nothing good, but what is here enjoined, either directly or by plain consequence, he accounts nothing evil but what is here forbidden, either in terms, or by undeniable inference. Whatever the Scripture neither forbids nor enjoins, either directly or by plain consequence, he believes to be of an indifferent nature; to be in itself neither good nor evil; this being the whole and sole outward rule whereby his conscience is to be directed in all things.

7. And if it be directed thereby, in fact, then hath he the answer of a good conscience toward God. "A good conscience is what is elsewhere termed by the Apostle, "a conscience void of offense." So, what he at one time expresses thus, "I have lived in all good conscience before God until this day;" (Acts 23:1;) he denotes at another, by that expression, "herein do I exercise myself, to have always a conscience void of offense toward God, and toward men." (Acts 24:16.) Now in order to this there is absolutely required, First, a right understanding of the word of God, or his "holy, and acceptable, and perfect will" concerning us, as it is revealed therein. For it is impossible we should walk by a rule, if we do not know what it means. There is, Secondly, required (which how few have attained!) a true knowledge of ourselves; a knowledge both of our hearts and lives, or our inward tempers and outward conversation: Seeing, if we know them not, it is not possible that we should compare them with our rule. There is required, Thirdly, an agreement of our hearts and lives, or our tempers and conversation, or our thoughts, and words, and works, with that rule, with the written word of God. For, without this, if we have any conscience at all, it can be only an evil conscience. There is, Fourthly, required, an inward perception of this agreement with our rule: And this habitual perception, this inward consciousness itself, is properly *a good conscience*; or, in other phrase of the Apostle, "a conscience void of offense, toward God, and toward men."

8. But whoever desires to have a conscience thus void of offence, let him see that he lay the right foundation. Let him remember, "other foundation" of this "can no man lay, than that which is laid, even Jesus Christ." And let him also be mindful, that no man buildeth on him but by a living faith; that no man is a partaker of Christ, until he can clearly testify, "The life which I now live, I live by faith in the Son of God;" in him who is now *revealed* in my heart; who "loved me, and gave himself for me." Faith alone is that evidence, that conviction, that demonstration of things invisible, whereby the eyes of our understanding being opened, and divine light

poured in upon them, we "see the wondrous things of Gods law;" the excellency and purity of it; the height, and depth, and length, and breadth thereof, and of every commandment contained therein. It is by faith that, beholding "the light of the glory of God in the face of Jesus Christ," we perceive, as in a glass, all that is in ourselves, yea, the inmost motions of our souls. And by this alone can that blessed love of God be "shed abroad in our hearts," which enables us so to love one another as Christ loved us. By this is that gracious promise fulfilled unto all the Israel of God, "I will put my laws into their mind, and write" (or engrave) "them in their hearts;" (Heb. 8:10;) hereby producing in their souls an entire agreement with his holy and perfect law, and "bringing into captivity every thought to the obedience of Christ."

And, as an evil tree cannot bring forth good fruit, so a good tree cannot bring forth evil fruit. As the heart therefore of a believer, so likewise his life, is thoroughly conformed to the rule of Gods commandments; in a consciousness whereof, he can give glory to God, and say with the Apostle, "This is our rejoicing, the testimony of our conscience, that in simplicity and godly sincerity, not with fleshly wisdom, but by the grace of God, we have had our conversation in the world."

9. "We have had our conversation:" The Apostle in the original expresses this by one single word, *anestaphemen*, but the meaning thereof is exceeding broad, taking in our whole deportment, yea, every inward as well as outward circumstance, whether relating to our soul or body. It includes every motion of our heart, of our tongue, or our hands, and bodily members. It extends to all our actions and words; to the employment of all our powers and faculties; to the manner of using every talent we have received, with respect either to God or man.

10. "We have had our conversation in the world;" even in the world of the ungodly: Not only among the children of God; (that were comparatively a little thing;) but among the children of the devil, among those that lie in wickedness, *en toi poneroi, in the wicked one*. What a world is this! how thoroughly impregnated with the spirit it continually breathes. As our God is good, and doeth good, so the god of this world and all his children, are evil, and do evil (so far as they are suffered) to all the children of God. Like their father, they are always lying in wait, or walking about, seeking whom they may devour; using fraud or force, secret wiles or open violence, to destroy those who are not of the world; continually warring against our souls, and, by old or new weapons, and devices of every kind, labouring to bring them back into the snare of the devil, into the broad road that leadeth to destruction.

11. We have had our whole conversation, in such a world, "in simplicity and godly sincerity." First, in simplicity: This is what our Lord recommends, under the name of a "single eye." "The light of the body," saith he, "is the eye. If therefore thine eye be single, the whole body shall be full of light." The meaning whereof is this: What the eye is to the body, that the intention is to all the words and actions: If therefore this eye of thy soul be single, all thy actions and conversation shall be "full of light," of the light of heaven, of love, and peace, and joy in the holy Ghost.

We are then simple of heart, when the eye of our mind is singly fixed on God; when in all things we aim at God alone, as our God, our portion, our strength, our happiness, our exceeding great reward, our all, in time and eternity. This is simplicity; when a steady view, a single intention of promoting his glory, of doing and suffering his blessed will, runs through our whole soul, fills all our heart, and is the constant spring of all our thoughts, desires, and purposes.

12. "We have had our conversation in the world," Secondly, "in godly sincerity." the difference between simplicity and sincerity seems to be chiefly this: Simplicity regards the intention itself, sincerity the execution of it; and this sincerity relates not barely to our words, but to our whole conversation, as described above. It is not here to be understood in that narrow sense, wherein St. Paul himself sometimes uses it, for speaking the truth, or abstaining from guile, from craft, and dissimulation; but in a more extensive meaning, as actually hitting the mark, which we aim at by simplicity. Accordingly, it implies in this place, that we do, in fact, speak and do all to the glory of God; that all our words are not only pointed at this, but actually conducive thereto; that all our actions flow on in an even stream, uniformly subservient to this great end; and that, in our whole lives, we are moving straight toward God, and that continually; walking steadily on in the highway of holiness, in the paths of justice, mercy, and truth.

13. This sincerity is termed by the Apostle, godly sincerity, or the sincerity of God; *eilikrineiai Theou*, to prevent our mistaking or confounding it with the sincerity of the Heathens; (for they had also a kind of sincerity among them, for which they professed no small veneration;) likewise to denote the object and end of this, as of every Christian virtue, seeing whatever does not ultimately tend to God, sinks among "the beggarly elements of the world." By styling it the sincerity of God, he also points out the Author or it, the "Father of lights, from whom every good and perfect gift descendeth;" which is still more clearly declared in the following words, "Not with fleshly wisdom, but by the grace of God."

14. "Not with fleshly wisdom:" As if he had said, "We cannot thus converse in the world, by any natural strength of understanding, neither by any naturally acquired knowledge or wisdom. We cannot gain this simplicity, or practise this sincerity, by the force either of good sense, good nature, or good breeding. It overshoots all our native courage and resolution, as well as all our precepts of philosophy. The power of custom is not able to train us up to this, nor the most exquisite rules of human education. Neither could I Paul ever attain hereto, notwithstanding all the advantages I enjoyed, so long as I was *in the flesh*, in my natural state, and pursued it only by *fleshly*, natural *wisdom*."

And yet surely, if any man could, Paul himself might have attained thereto by that wisdom: For we can hardly conceive any who was more highly favoured with all the gifts both of nature and education. Besides his natural abilities, probably not inferior to those of any person then up the earth, he had all the benefits of learning, studying at the University of Tarsus, afterwards brought up at the feet of Gamaliel, a person of the greatest account, both for knowledge and integrity, that was then in the whole Jewish nation. And he had all the possible advantages of religious education, being a Pharisee, the son of a Pharisee, trained up in the very straitest sect or profession, distinguished from all others by a more eminent strictness. And herein he had "profited above many" others, "who were his equals" in years, "being more abundantly zealous" of whatever he thought would please God, and "as touching the righteousness of the law, blameless." But it could not be, that he should hereby attain this simplicity and godly sincerity. It was all but lost labour; in a deep, piercing sense of which he was at length constrained to cry out, "The things which were gain to me, those I counted loss, for the excellency of the knowledge of Christ Jesus my Lord." (Phil. 3:7, 8.)

15. It could not be that ever he should attain to this but by the "excellent knowledge of Jesus Christ" our Lord; or, "by the grace of God,"—another expression of nearly the same import. By "the grace of God" is sometimes to be understood that free love, that unmerited mercy, by which I a sinner, through the merits of Christ, am now reconciled to God. But in this place it rather means that power of God the Holy Ghost, which "worketh in us both to will and to do of his good pleasure." As soon as ever the grace of God in the former sense, his pardoning love, is manifested to our souls, the grace of God in the latter sense, the power of his Spirit, takes place therein. And now we can perform, through God, what to man was impossible. Now we can order our conversation aright. We can do all things in the light and power of that love, through Christ which strengtheneth us. We now have "the testimony of our conscience," which we could never have by fleshly wisdom, "that in simplicity and godly sincerity, we have our conversation in the world."

16. This is properly the ground of a Christian's joy. We may now therefore readily conceive, how he that hath this testimony in himself rejoiceth evermore. "My soul," may he say, "doth magnify the Lord, and my spirit rejoiceth in God my Saviour." I rejoice in him, who, of his own unmerited love, of his own free and tender mercy, "hath called me into this state of salvation," wherein, through his power, I now stand. I rejoice, because his spirit beareth witness to my spirit, that I am bought with the blood of the Lamb; and that, believing in him, "I am a member of Christ, a child of God, and an inheritor of the kingdom of heaven." I rejoice, because the sense of God's love to me hath, by the same Spirit, wrought in me to love him, and to love for his sake every child of man, every soul that hath made. I rejoice, because he gives me to feel in myself "the mind that was in Christ:"— Simplicity, a single eye to him, in every motion of my heart; power always to fix the loving eye of my soul on Him who "loved me, and gave himself for me;" to aim at him alone, at his glorious will, in all I think, or speak, or do:—Purity, desiring nothing more but God; "crucifying the flesh with its affections and lusts;" "setting my affections on things above, not on things of the earth:"—Holiness, a recovery of the image of God, a renewal of soul "after his likeness:"—And Godly Sincerity, directing all my words and works, so as to conduce to his glory. In this I likewise rejoice, yea, and will

rejoice, because my conscience beareth me witness in the Holy Ghost, by the light he continually pours in upon it, that "walk worthy of the vocation wherewith I am called;" that I "abstain from all appearance of evil," fleeing from sin as from the face of a serpent; that as I have opportunity I do all possible good, in every kind, to all men; that I follow my Lord in all my steps, and do what is acceptable in his sight. I rejoice, because I both see and feel, through the inspiration of God's Holy Spirit, that all my works are wrought in him, yea, and that it is He who worketh all my works in me. I rejoice in seeing through the light of God, which shines in my heart, that I have power to walk in his ways; and that, through his grace, I turn not therefrom, to the right hand or to the left.

17. Such is the ground and the nature of that joy whereby an adult Christian rejoiceth evermore. And from all this we may easily infer, First, that this is not a *natural* joy. It does not arise from any natural cause: Not from any sudden flow of spirits. This may give a transient start of joy; but the Christian *rejoiceth always.* It cannot be owing to bodily health or ease; to strength and soundness of constitution: For it is equally strong in sickness and pain; yea, perhaps far stronger than before. Many Christians have never experienced any joy, to be compared with that which then filled their soul, when the body was well nigh worn out with pain, or consumed away with pining sickness. Least of all can it be ascribed to outward prosperity, to the favour of men, or plenty of worldly goods; for then, chiefly, when their faith has been tried as with fire, by all manner of outward afflictions, have the children of God rejoiced in Him, whom unseen they loved, even with joy unspeakable. And never surely did men rejoice like those who were used as "the filth and off scouring of the world;" who wandered to and fro, being in want of all things; in hunger, in cold, in nakedness; who had trials, not only of "cruel mockings," but, "moreover of bonds and imprisonments;" yea, who, at last, "counted not their lives dear unto themselves, so they might finish their course with joy."

18. From the preceding considerations, we may Secondly, infer, that the joy of a Christian does not arise from any blindness of conscience, from his not being able to discern good from evil. So far from it, that he was an utter stranger to this joy, till the eyes of his understanding were opened; that he knew it not, until he had spiritual senses, fitted to discern spiritual good and evil. And now the eye of his soul waxeth not dim: He was never so sharp-sighted before: He has so quick a perception of the smallest things, as is quite amazing to the natural man. As a mote is visible in the sunbeam, so to him who is walking in the light, in the beams of the uncreated Sun, every mote of sin is visible. Nor does he close the eyes of his conscience any more: That sleep is departed from him. His soul is always broad awake: No more slumber or folding of the hands to rest! He is always standing on the tower, and hearkening what his lord will say concerning him; and always rejoicing in this very thing, in "seeing him that is invisible."

19. Neither does the joy of a Christian arise, Thirdly, from any dulness or callousness of conscience. A kind of joy, it is

true, may arise from this, in those whose "foolish hearts are darkened;" whose heart is callous, unfeeling, dull of sense, and, consequently, without spiritual understanding. Because of their senseless, unfeeling hearts, they may rejoice even in committing sin; and this they may probably call *liberty!*—which is indeed mere drunkenness of soul, a fatal numbness of spirit, the stupid insensibility of a sacred conscience. On the contrary, a Christian has the most exquisite sensibility; such as he could not have conceived before. He never had such a tenderness of conscience as he has had, since the love of God has reigned in his heart. And this also is his glory and joy, that God hath heard his daily prayer:—

> O that my tender soul might fly
> > The first abhorr'd approach of ill;
> Quick, as the apple of an eye,
> > The slightest touch of sin to feel.

20. To conclude. Christian joy is joy in obedience; joy in loving God and keeping his commandments: And yet not in keeping them, as if we were thereby to fulfil the terms of the covenant of works; as if by any works or righteousness of ours, we were to procure pardon and acceptance with God. Not so: We are already pardoned and accepted through the mercy of God in Christ Jesus. Not as if we were by our own obedience to procure life, life from the death of sin: This also we have already through the grace of God. Us "hath he quickened, who were dead in sins;" and now we are "alive to God, through Jesus Christ our Lord." But we rejoice in walking according to the covenant of grace, in holy love and happy obedience. We rejoice in knowing that, "being justified through his grace," we have "not received that grace of God in vain: "that God having freely (not for the sake of our willing or running, but through the blood of the Lamb) reconciled us to himself, we run, in the strength which he hath given us, the way of his commandments. He hath "girded us with strength unto the war," and we gladly "fight the good fight of faith." We rejoice through him who liveth in our hearts by faith, to "lay hold of eternal life." This is our rejoicing, that as our "Father worketh hitherto," so (not by our own might or wisdom, but through the power of his Spirit, freely given in Christ Jesus) we also work the works of God. And may he work in us whatsoever is well-pleasing in his sight! To whom be the praise for ever and ever!

[It may easily be observed, that the preceding discourse describes the experience of those that are *strong* in faith: But hereby those that are *weak* in faith may be discouraged; to prevent which, the following discourse may be of use.]

13. ON SIN IN BELIEVERS

"If any man be in Christ, he is a new creature."

2 Cor. 5:17.

I. 1. Is there then sin in him that is in Christ? Does sin *remain* in one that believes in him? Is there any sin in them that are born of God, or are they wholly delivered from it? Let no one imagine this to be a question of mere curiosity; or that it is of little importance whether it be determined one way or the other. Rather it is a point of the utmost moment to every serious Christian; the resolving of which very nearly concerns both his present and eternal happiness.

2. And yet I do not know that ever it was controverted in the primitive Church. Indeed there was no room for disputing concerning it, as all Christians were agreed. And so far as I have observed, the whole body of ancient Christians, who have left us anything in writing, declare with one voice, that even believers in Christ, till they are "strong in the Lord, and in the power of his might," have need to "wrestle with flesh and blood," with an evil nature, as well as "with principalities and powers."

3. And herein our own Church (as indeed in most points) exactly copies after the primitive; declaring in her Ninth Article, "Original sin is the corruption of the nature of every man, whereby man is in his own nature inclined to evil, so that the flesh lusteth contrary to the Spirit. And this infection of nature doth remain, yea, in them that are regenerated; whereby the lust of the flesh, called in Greek *phronema sarkos*, is not subject to the law of God. And although there is no condemnation for them that believe, yet this lust hath of itself the nature of sin."

4. The same testimony is given by all other Churches; not only by the Greek and Romish Church, but by every Reformed Church in europe, of whatever denomination. Indeed some of these seem to carry the thing too far; so describing the corruption of heart in a believer, as scarce to allow that he has dominion over it, but rather is in bondage thereto; and, by this means, they leave hardly any distinction between a believer and an unbeliever.

5. To avoid this extreme, many well-meaning men, particularly those under the direction of the late Count Zinzendorf, ran into another; affirming, that all true believers are not only saved from the *dominion* of sin, but from the *being* of inward as well as outward sin, so that it no longer *remains* in them: And from them, about twenty years ago, many of our countrymen imbibed the same opinion, that even the corruption of nature *is no more*, in those who believe in Christ.

6. It is true that, when the Germans were pressed upon this head, they soon allowed, (many of them at least,) that sin did still remain *in the flesh*, but not *in the heart* of a believer; and, after a time, when the absurdity of this was shown, they fairly gave up the point; allowing that sin did still remain, though not reign, in him that is born of God.

7. But the english, who had received it from them, (some directly, some at second or third hand,) were not so easily prevailed upon to part with a favourite opinion: And even when the generality of them were convinced it was utterly indefensible, a few could not be persuaded to give it up, but maintain it to this day.

II. 1. For the sake of these who really fear God, and desire to know the truth as it is in Jesus," it may not be amiss to consider the point with calmness and impartiality. In doing this, I use indifferently the words, *regenerate, justified*, or *believers*; since, though they have not precisely the same meaning, (the First implying an inward, actual change, the Second a relative one, and the Third the means whereby both the one and the other are wrought,) yet they come to one and the same thing; as everyone that believes, is both justified and born of God.

2. By sin, I here understand inward sin; any sinful temper, passion, or affection; such as pride, self-will, love of the world, in any kind or degree; such as lust, anger, peevishness; any disposition contrary to the mind which was in Christ.

3. The question is not concerning *outward sin*; whether a child of God *commits sin* or no. We all agree and earnestly maintain, "he that committeth sin is of the devil." We agree, "Whosoever is born of God doth not commit sin." Neither do we now inquire whether inward sin will *always* remain in the children of God; whether sin will continue in the soul as long as it continues in the body: Nor yet do we inquire whether a justified person may *relapse* either into inward or outward sin; but simply this, Is a justified or regenerate man freed from *all sin* as soon as he is justified? Is there then no sin in his heart? nor ever after, unless he fall from grace?

4. We allow that the state of a justified person is inexpressibly great and glorious. he is born again, "not of blood, nor of the flesh, nor of the will of man, but of God." he is a child of God, a member of Christ, an heir of the kingdom of heaven. "The peace of God, which passeth all understanding, keepeth his heart and mind in Christ Jesus." His very body is a "temple of the Holy Ghost," and an "habitation of God through the Spirit." He is "created anew in Christ Jesus:" He is *washed*, he is *sanctified*. His heart is purified by faith; he is cleansed "from the corruption that is in the world;" "the love of God is shed abroad in his heart by the Holy Ghost which is given unto him." And so long as he "walketh in love," (which he may always do,) he worships God in spirit and in truth. He keepeth the commandments of God, and doeth those things that are pleasing in his sight; so exercising himself as to "have a conscience void of offence, toward God and toward man:" And he has power both over outward and inward sin, even from the moment he is justified.

III. 1. "But was he not then freed from all sin, so that there is no sin in his heart?" I cannot say this; I cannot believe it; because St. Paul says the contrary. He is speaking to believers, and describing the state of believers in general, when he says, "The flesh lusteth against the Spirit, and the Spirit against the flesh: These are contrary the one to the other." (Gal. 5:17) Nothing can be more express. The Apostle here directly affirms that the flesh, evil nature, opposes the Spirit, even in believers; that even in the regenerate there are two principles, "contrary the one to the other."

2. Again: When he writes to the believers at Corinth, to those who were sanctified in Christ Jesus, (1 Cor. 1:2) he says, "I, brethren, could not speak unto you, as unto spiritual, but as unto carnal, as unto babes in Christ. Ye are yet carnal: For whereas there is among you envying and strife, are ye not carnal?" (1 Cor. 3:13) Now here the Apostle speaks unto those who were unquestionably believers, whom, in the same breath, he styles his brethren in Christ,—as being still, in a measure, carnal. He affirms, there was envying, (an evil temper,) occasioning strife among them, and yet does not give the least intimation that they had lost their faith. Nay, he manifestly declares they had not; for then they would not have been babes in Christ. And (what is most remarkable of all) he speaks of being carnal, and babes in Christ, as one and the same thing; plainly showing that every believer is (in a degree) carnal, while he is only a babe in Christ.

3. Indeed this grand point, that there are two contrary principles in believers,—nature and grace, the flesh and the Spirit, runs through all the epistles of St. Paul, yea, through all the Holy Scriptures; almost all the directions and exhortations therein are founded on this supposition; pointing at wrong tempers or practices in those who are, notwithstanding, acknowledged by the inspired writers to be believers. And they are continually exhorted to fight with and conquer these, by the power of the faith which was in them.

4. And who can doubt, but there was faith in the angel of the church of ephesus, when our Lord said to him, "I know thy works, and thy labour, and thy patience: Thou hast patience, and for my names sake hast laboured, and hast not fainted?" (Rev. 2:24.) But was there, meantime, no sin in his heart? Yea, or Christ would not have added, "Nevertheless, I have somewhat against thee, because thou hast left thy first love." This was real sin which God saw in his heart; of which, accordingly, he is exhorted to *repent:* And yet we have no authority to say, that even then he had no faith.

5. Nay, the angel of the church at Pergamos, also, is exhorted to *repent*, which implies sin, though our Lord expressly says, "Thou hast not denied my faith." (Rev. 2:13, 16) And to the angel of the church in Sardis, he says, "Strengthen the things which remain, that are ready to die." The good which remained was *ready to die*, but was not actually dead. (Rev. 3:2) So there was still a spark of faith even in him; which he is accordingly commanded to *hold fast*. (Rev. 3:3.)

6. once more: When the Apostle exhorts believers to "cleanse themselves from all filthiness of flesh and spirit," (2 Cor. 7:1,) he plainly teaches, that those believers were not yet cleansed therefrom.

Will you answer, "He that abstains from all appearance of evil, does *ipso facto* cleanse himself from all filthiness?" Not in any wise. For instance: A man reviles me: I feel resentment, which is filthiness of spirit; yet I say not a word. Here I "abstain from all appearance of evil;" but this does not cleanse me from that filthiness of spirit, as I experience to my sorrow.

7. And as this position, "There is no sin in a believer, no carnal mind, no bent to backsliding," is thus contrary to the word of God, so it is to the experience of his children. These continually feel an heart bent to backsliding; a natural tendency to evil; a proneness to depart from God, and cleave to the things of earth. They are daily sensible of sin remaining in their heart,—pride, self-will, unbelief; and of sin cleaving to all they speak and do, even their best actions and holiest duties. Yet at the same time they "know that they are of God;" they cannot doubt of it for a moment. They feel his Spirit clearly "witnessing with their spirit, that they are the children of God." They "rejoice in God through Christ Jesus, by whom they have now received the atonement." So that they are equally assured, that sin is in them, and that "Christ is in them the hope of glory."

8. "But can Christ be in the same heart where sin is?" Undoubtedly he can; otherwise it never could be saved therefrom. Where the sickness is, there is the Physician,

Carrying on his work within,
Striving till he cast out sin.

Christ indeed cannot *reign*, where sin *reigns*; neither will he *dwell* where any sin is *allowed*. But he *is* and *dwells* in the heart of every believer, who is *fighting against* all sin; although it be not yet purified, according to the purification of the sanctuary.

9. It has been observed before, that the opposite doctrine,—That there is no sin in believers,—is quite new in the church of Christ; that it was never heard of for seventeen hundred years; never till it was discovered by Count Zinzendorf. I do not remember to have seen the least intimation of it, either in any ancient or modern writer; unless perhaps in some of the wild, ranting Antinomians. And these likewise say and unsay, acknowledging there is sin *in their flesh*, although no *sin in their heart*. But whatever doctrine is *new* must be wrong; for the *old* religion is the only *true one*; and no doctrine can be right, unless it is the very same "which was from the beginning."

10. one argument more against this new, unscriptural doctrine may be drawn from the dreadful consequences of it. one says, "I felt anger to-day." Must I reply, "Then you have no faith?" Another says, "I know what you advise is good, but my will is quite averse to it." Must I tell him, "Then you are an unbeliever, under the wrath and the curse of God?" What will be the natural consequence of this? Why, if he believe what I say, his soul will not only be grieved and wounded, but perhaps utterly destroyed; inasmuch as he will "cast away" that "confidence which hath great recompense of reward:" And having cast away his shield, how shall he "quench the fiery darts of the wicked one?" How shall he overcome the world?—seeing "this is the victory that overcometh the world, even our faith." He stands disarmed in the midst of his enemies, open to all their assaults. What wonder then, if he be utterly overthrown; if they take him captive at their will; yea, if he fall from one wickedness to another, and never see good any more? I cannot, therefore, by any means receive this assertion, that there is no sin in a believer from the moment he is justified; First, because it is contrary to the whole tenor of Scripture;—Secondly, because it is contrary to the experience of the children of God;—Thirdly, because it is absolutely new, never heard of in the world till yesterday;—and Lastly, because it is naturally attended with the most fatal consequences; not only grieving those whom God hath not grieved, but perhaps dragging them into everlasting perdition.

IV. 1. However, let us give a fair hearing to the chief arguments of those who endeavour to support it. And it is, First, from Scripture they attempt to prove that there is no sin in a believer. They argue thus: "The Scripture says, every believer is born of God, is clean, is holy, is sanctified, is pure in heart, has a new heart, is a temple of the Holy Ghost. Now, as that which is born of the flesh is flesh, is altogether evil, so that which is born of the Spirit is spirit, is altogether good. Again: A man cannot be clean, sanctified, holy, and at the same time unclean, unsanctified, unholy. He cannot be pure and impure, or have a new and an old heart together. Neither can his soul be unholy, while it is a temple of the Holy Ghost.

I have put this objection as strong as possible, that its full weight may appear. Let us now examine it, part by part. And, 1. "That which is born of the Spirit is spirit, is altogether good." I allow the text, but not the comment. For the text affirms this, and no more,—that every man who is "born of the Spirit," is a spiritual man. He is so: But so he may be, and yet not be altogether spiritual. The Christians at Corinth were spiritual men; else they had been no Christians at all; and yet they were not altogether spiritual: they were still, in part, carnal.—"But they were fallen from grace." St. Paul says, No. They were even then babes in Christ. 2. "But a man cannot be clean, sanctified, holy, and at the same time unclean, unsanctified, unholy." Indeed he may. So the Corinthians were. "Ye are washed," says the Apostle, "ye are sanctified;" namely, cleansed from "fornication, idolatry, drunkenness," and all other outward sin; (1 Cor. 6:9, 10, 11;) and yet at the same time, in another sense of the word, they were unsanctified; they were not washed, not inwardly cleansed from envy, evil surmising, partiality.—"But sure, they had not a new heart and an old heart together." It is most sure they had, for at that very time, their hearts were *truly*, yet not *entirely*, renewed. Their carnal mind was nailed to the cross; yet it was not wholly destroyed.—"But could they be unholy while they were temples of the Holy Ghost?' " Yes; that they were temples of the Holy Ghost, is certain; (1 Cor. 6:19;) and it is equally certain, they were, in some degree, carnal, that is, unholy.

2. "However, there is one Scripture more which will put the matter out of question: 'If any man be' a believer 'in Christ, he is a new creature. old things are passed away; behold, all things are become new.' (2 Cor. 5:17.) Now certainly a man cannot be a new creature and an old creature at once." Yes, he may: He may be partly renewed, which was the very case with those at Corinth. They were doubtless "renewed in the spirit of their mind," or they could not have been so much as "babes in Christ." yet they had not the whole mind which was in Christ, for they envied one another. "But it is said expressly, 'old things are passed away: All things are become new.' " But we must not so interpret the Apostle's words, as to make him contradict himself. And if we will make him consistent with himself, the plain meaning of the words is this: His old judgment concerning justification, holiness, happiness, indeed concerning the things of God in general, is now passed away; so are his old desires, designs, affections, tempers, and conversation. All these are undeniably become new, greatly changed from what they were; and yet, though they are new, they are not wholly new. Still he feels, to his sorrow and shame, remains of the old man, too manifest taints of his former tempers and affections, though they cannot gain any advantage over him, as long as he watches unto prayer.

3. This whole argument, "If he is clean, he is clean;" "If he is holy, he is holy;" (and twenty more expressions of the same kind may easily be heaped together;) is really no better than playing upon words: It is the fallacy of arguing from a *particular to a general*; of inferring a general conclusion from particular premises. Propose the sentence entire, and it runs thus: "If he is holy *at all*, he is holy *altogether*." That does not

follow: Every babe in Christ is holy, and yet not altogether so. He is saved from sin; yet not entirely: It *remains*, though it does not *reign*. If you think it does not *remain*, (in babes at least, whatever be the case with young men, or fathers) you certainly have not considered the height, and depth, and length, and breadth of the law of God; (even the law of love, laid down by St. Paul in the thirteenth of Corinthians;) and that *every anomia*, disconformity to, or deviation from, this law *is sin*. Now, is there no disconformity to this in the heart or life of a believer? What may be in an adult Christian, is another question; but what a stranger must he be to human nature, who can possibly imagine, that this is the case with every babe in Christ!

4. "But believers walk after the Spirit, [What follows for some pages is an answer to a paper, published in the Christian Magazine, p. 577–582. I am surprised Mr. Dodd should give such a paper a place in his Magazine, which is directly contrary to our Ninth Article.—editor] (Rom. 8:1,) and the Spirit of God dwells in them; consequently, they are delivered from the guilt, the power, or, in one word, the being of sin."

These are coupled together, as if they were the same thing. But they are not the same thing. The *guilt* is one thing, the *power* another, and the *being* yet another. That believers are delivered from the *guilt* and *power* of sin we allow; that they are delivered from the *being* of it we deny. Nor does it in any wise follow from these texts. A man may have the Spirit of God dwelling in him, and may "walk after the Spirit," though he still feels "the flesh lusting against the Spirit."

5. "But the 'church is the body of Christ;' (Col. 1:24;) this implies, that its members are washed from all filthiness; otherwise it will follow, that Christ and Belial are incorporated with each other."

Nay, it will not follow from hence, "Those who are the mystical body of Christ, still feel the flesh lusting against the Spirit," that Christ has any fellowship with the devil; or with that sin which he enables them to resist and overcome.

6. "But are not Christians 'come to the heavenly Jerusalem,' where 'nothing defiled can enter?' " (Heb. 12:22.) Yes; "and to an innumerable company of angels, and to the spirits of just men made perfect:" That is,

> Earth and heaven all agree;
> All is one great family.

And they are likewise holy and undefiled, while they "walk after the Spirit;" although sensible there is another principle in them, and that "these are contrary to each other."

7. "But Christians are reconciled to God. Now this could not be, if any of the carnal mind remained; for this is enmity against God: Consequently, no reconciliation can be effected, but by its total destruction."

We are "reconciled to God through the blood of the cross:" And in that moment the *phronema sarkos*, the corruption of nature, which is enmity with God, is put under our feet; the flesh has no more dominion over us. But it still *exists*; and it is still in its nature enmity with God, lusting against his Spirit.

8. But they that are Christ's have crucified the flesh, with its affections and lusts. (Gal. 5:24.) They have so; yet it remains in them still, and often struggles to break from the cross. Nay, but they have put off the old man with his deeds. (Col. 3:9.) They have; and, in the sense above described, old things are passed away; all things are become new. A hundred texts may be cited to the same effect; and they will all admit of the same answer. "But, to say all in one word, Christ gave himself for the Church, that it might be holy and without blemish.' " (Eph. 5:25, 27.) And so it will be in the end: But it never was yet, from the beginning to this day.

9. "But let experience speak: All who are justified do at that time find an absolute freedom from all sin." That I doubt; But, if they do, do they find it ever after? else you gain nothing. "If they do not, it is their own fault." That remains to be proved.

10. "But, in the very nature of things, can a man have pride in him, and not be proud; anger, and yet not be angry?"

A man may have *pride* in him, may think of himself in some particulars above what he ought to think, (and so be proud in that particular,) and yet not be a proud man in his general character. he may have *anger* in him, yea, and a strong propensity to furious anger, without *giving way* to it.—"But can anger and pride be in that heart, where *only* meekness and humility are felt?" No; but *some* pride and anger may be in that heart, where there is much humility and meekness. "It avails not to say, These tempers are there, but they do not *reign*: For sin cannot, in any kind or degree, exist where it does not reign; for *guilt* and *power* are essential properties of sin. Therefore, where one of them is, all must be."

Strange indeed! "Sin cannot, in any kind or degree, *exist* where it does not *reign?*" Absolutely contrary this to all experience, all Scripture, all common sense. Resentment of an affront is sin; it is *anomia*, disconformity to the law of love. This has existed in me a thousand times. Yet it did not, and does not, *reign*.—"But *guilt* and *power* are essential properties of sin; therefore where one is, all must be." No: In the instance before us, if the resentment I feel is not yielded to, even for a moment, there is no guilt at all, no condemnation from God upon that account. And in this case, it has no *power*: though it "lusteth against the Spirit," it cannot prevail. Here, therefore, as in ten thousand instances, there is *sin* without either *guilt* or *power*.

11. "But the supposing sin in a believer is pregnant with everything frightful and discouraging. It implies the contending with a power that has the possession of our strength; maintains his usurpation of our hearts; and there prosecutes the war in defiance of our Redeemer." Not so: The supposing sin is in us, does not imply that it has the possession of our strength; no more than a man crucified has the possession of those that crucify him. As little does it imply, that "sin maintains its usurpation of our hearts." The usurper is dethroned. He remains indeed where he once reigned; but remains *in chains*. So that he does, in some sense, "prosecute the war," yet he grows weaker and weaker; while the believer goes on from strength to strength, conquering and to conquer.

12. "I am not satisfied yet: He that has sin in him, is a slave to sin. Therefore you suppose a man to be justified, while he is a slave to sin. Now, if you allow men may be justified while

they have pride, anger, or unbelief in them; nay, if you aver, these are (at least for a time) in all that are justified; what wonder that we have so many proud, angry, unbelieving believers!

I do not suppose any man who is justified is a slave to sin: Yet I do suppose sin remains (at least for a time) in all that are justified.

"But, if sin remains in a believer, he is a sinful man: If pride, for instance, then he is proud; if self-will, then he is self-willed; if unbelief, then he is an unbeliever; consequently, no believer at all. How then does he differ from unbelievers, from unregenerate men?" This is still mere playing upon words. It means no more than, if there is sin, pride, self-will in him, then—there is sin, pride, self-will. And this nobody can deny. In that sense then he is proud, or self-willed. But he is not proud or self-willed in the same sense that unbelievers are; that is, *governed* by pride or self-will. Herein he differs from unregenerate men. They *obey* sin; he does not. Flesh is in them both. But they "walk after the flesh;" he "walks after the Spirit."

"But how can *unbelief* be in a believer?" That word has two meanings. It means either no faith, or little faith; either the *absence* of faith or the *weakness* of it. In the former sense, unbelief is not in a believer; in the latter, it is in all babes. Their faith is commonly mixed with doubt or fear; that is, in the latter sense, with unbelief. "Why are ye fearful," says our Lord, "O ye of little faith?" Again: "O thou of little faith, wherefore didst thou doubt?" You see here was *unbelief* in *believers*; little faith and much unbelief.

13. "But this doctrine, that sin remains in a believer; that a man may be in the favour of God, while he has sin in his heart; certainly tends to encourage men in sin." Understand the proposition right, and no such consequence follows. A man may be in God's favour though he feel sin; but not if he *yields* to it. *Having sin* does not forfeit the favour of God; *giving way to sin* does. Though the flesh in you "lust against the Spirit," you may still be a child of God; but if you "walk after the flesh," you are a child of the devil. Now this doctrine does not encourage to *obey* sin, but to resist it with all our might.

V. 1. The sum of all is this: There are in every person, even after he is justified, two contrary principles, nature and grace, termed by St. Paul the *flesh* and the *Spirit*. Hence, although even babes in Christ are *sanctified*, yet it is only in part. In a degree, according to the measure of their faith, they are spiritual; yet, in a degree they are carnal. Accordingly, believers are continually exhorted to watch against the flesh, as well as the world and the devil. And to this agrees the constant experience of the children of God. While they feel this witness in themselves, they feel a will not wholly resigned to the will of God. They know they are in him; and yet find an heart ready to depart from him, a proneness to evil in many instances, and a backwardness to that which is good. The contrary doctrine is wholly new; never heard of in the church of Christ, from the time of his coming into the world, till the time of Count Zinzendorf; and it is attended with the most fatal consequences. It cuts off all watching against our evil nature, against the Delilah which we are told is gone, though she is still lying in our bosom. It tears away the shield of weak believers, deprives them of their faith and so leaves them exposed to all the assaults of the world, the flesh, and the devil.

2. Let us, therefore, hold fast the sound doctrine "once delivered to the saints," and delivered down by them with the written word to all succeeding generations: That although we are renewed, cleansed, purified, sanctified, the moment we truly believe in Christ, yet we are not then renewed, cleansed, purified altogether; but the flesh, the evil nature, still *remains* (though subdued) and wars against the Spirit. So much the more let us use all diligence in "fighting the good fight of faith." So much the more earnestly let us "watch and pray" against the enemy within. The more carefully let us take to ourselves, and "put on, the whole armor of God;" that, although "we wrestle" both "with flesh, and blood, and with the principalities, and with powers, and wicked spirits in high places," we may be able to withstand in the evil day, and having done all, to stand."

14. THE REPENTANCE OF BELIEVERS

"Repent ye, and believe the gospel."

Mark 1:15.

1. It is generally supposed, that repentance and faith are only the gate of religion; that they are necessary only at the beginning of our Christian course, when we are setting out in the way to the kingdom. And this may seem to be confirmed by the great Apostle, where, exhorting the Hebrew Christians to "go on to perfection," he teaches them to *leave* these first "principles of the doctrine of Christ;" "not laying again the foundation of repentance from dead works, and of faith towards God;" which must at least mean, that they should comparatively leave these, that at first took up all their thoughts, in order to "press forward toward the prize of the high calling of God in Christ Jesus."

2. And this is undoubtedly true, that there is a repentance and a faith, which are, more especially, necessary at the beginning: a repentance, which is a conviction of our utter sinfulness, and guiltiness, and helplessness; and which precedes our receiving that kingdom of God, which, our Lord observes, is "within us;" and a faith, whereby we receive that kingdom, even "righteousness, and peace, and joy in the Holy Ghost."

3. But, notwithstanding this, there is also a repentance and a faith (taking the words in another sense, a sense not quite the same, nor yet entirely different) which are requisite after we have "believed the gospel;" yea, and in every subsequent stage of our Christian course, or we cannot "run the race which is set before us." And this repentance and faith are full as necessary, in order to our *continuance* and *growth* in grace, as the former faith and repentance were, in order to our *entering* into the kingdom of God.

But in what sense are we to repent and believe, after we are justified? This is an important question, and worthy of being considered with the utmost attention.

I. And, First, in what sense are we to repent?

1. Repentance frequently means an inward change, a change of mind from sin to holiness. But we now speak of it in a quite different sense, as it is one kind of self-knowledge, the knowing ourselves sinners, yea, guilty, helpless sinners, even though we know we are children of God.

2. Indeed when we first know this; when we first find the redemption in the blood of Jesus; when the love of God is first shed abroad in our hearts, and his kingdom set up therein; it is natural to suppose that we are no longer sinners, that all our sins are not only covered but destroyed. As we do not then feel any evil in our hearts, we readily imagine none is there. Nay, some well-meaning men have imagined this not only at that time, but ever after; having persuaded themselves, that when they were justified, they were entirely sanctified: yea, they have laid it down as a general rule, in spite of Scripture, reason, and experience. These sincerely believe, and earnestly maintain, that all sin is destroyed when we are justified; and that there is no sin in the heart of a believer; but that it is altogether clean from that moment. But though we readily acknowledge, "he that believeth is born of God," and "he that is born of God doth not commit sin;" yet we cannot allow that he does not *feel* it from within: it does not *reign*, but it does remain. And a conviction of the sin which *remains* in our heart, is one great branch of the repentance we are now speaking of.

3. For it is seldom long before he who imagined all sin was gone, feels there is still *pride* in his heart. He is convinced both that in many respects he has thought of himself more highly than he ought to think, and that he has taken to himself the praise of something he had received, and gloried in it as though he had not received it; and yet he knows he is in the favour of God. He cannot, and ought not to, "cast away his confidence." "The Spirit" still "witnesses with" his "spirit, that he is a child of God."

4. Nor is it long before he feels *self-will* in his heart; even a will contrary to the will of God. A will every man must inevitably have, as long as he has an understanding. This is an essential part of human nature, indeed of the nature of every intelligent being. Our blessed Lord himself had a will as a man; otherwise he had not been a man. But his human will was invariably subject to the will of his Father. At all times, and on all occasions, even in the deepest affliction, he could say, "Not as I will, but as thou wilt." But this is not the case at all times, even with a true believer in Christ. He frequently finds his will more or less exalting itself against the will of God. He wills something, because it is pleasing to nature, which is not pleasing to God; and he nills (is averse from) something, because it is painful to nature, which is the will of God concerning him. Indeed, suppose he continues in the faith, he fights against it with all his might: but this very thing implies that it really exists, and that he is conscious of it.

5. Now self-will, as well as pride, is a species of *idolatry* and both are directly contrary to the love of God. The same observation may be made concerning the *love of the world.* But this likewise even true believers are liable to feel in themselves; and every one of them does feel it, more or less, sooner or later, in one branch or another. It is true, when he

first "passes from death unto life," he desires nothing more but God. He can truly say, "All my desire is unto Thee, and unto the remembrance of Thy name:" "Whom have I in heaven but Thee? and there is none upon earth that I desire beside Thee." But it is not so always. In process of time he will feel again, though perhaps only for a few moments, either "the desire of the flesh," or "the desire of the eye," or "the pride of life." Nay, if he does not continually watch and pray, he may find *lust* reviving; yea, and thrusting sore at him that he may fall, till he has scarce any strength left in him. He may feel the assaults of *inordinate affection*; yea, a strong propensity to "love the creature more than the Creator;" whether it be a child, a parent, a husband, or wife, or "the friend that is as his own soul." He may feel, in a thousand various ways, a desire of earthly things or pleasures. In the same proportion he will forget God, not seeking his happiness in him, and consequently being a "lover of pleasure more than a lover of God."

6. If he does not keep himself every moment, he will again feel *the desire of the eye*; the desire of gratifying his imagination with something great, or beautiful, or uncommon. In how many ways does this desire assault the soul! Perhaps with regard to the poorest trifles, such as dress, or furniture; things never designed to satisfy the appetite of an immortal spirit. Yet, how natural is it for us, even after we have "tasted of the powers of the world to come," to sink again into these foolish, low desires of things that perish in the using! How hard is it, even for those who know in whom they have believed, to conquer but one branch of the desire of the eye, *curiosity*; constantly to trample it under their feet; to desire nothing merely because it is new!

7. And how hard is it even for the children of God wholly to conquer the *pride of life!* St. John seems to mean by this nearly the same with what the world terms "the sense of honour." This is no other than a desire of, and delight in, "the honour that cometh of men;" a desire and love of praise; and, which is always joined with it, a proportionable *fear of dispraise.* Nearly allied to this is *evil shame*; the being ashamed of that wherein we ought to glory. And this is seldom divided from the *fear of man*, which brings a thousand snares upon the soul. Now where is he, even among those that seem strong in the faith, who does not find in himself a degree of all these evil tempers? So that even these are but in part "crucified to the world;" for the evil root still remains in their heart.

8. And do we not feel other tempers, which are as contrary to the love of our neighbour as these are to the love of God? The love of our neighbour "thinketh no evil." Do not we find anything of the kind? Do we never find any *jealousies*, any *evil surmisings*, any groundless or unreasonable suspicions? He that is clear in these respects, let him cast the first stone at his neighbour. Who does not sometimes feel other tempers or inward motions, which he knows are contrary to brotherly love? If nothing of *malice, hatred*, or *bitterness*, is there no touch of *envy*; particularly toward those who enjoy some real or supposed good, which we desire, but cannot attain? Do we never find any degree of *resentment*, when we are injured or affronted; especially by those whom we peculiarly loved, and

whom we had most laboured to help or oblige? Does injustice or ingratitude never excite in us any desire of *revenge*? any desire of returning evil for evil, instead of "overcoming evil with good?" This also shows, how much is still in our heart, which is contrary to the love of our neighbour.

9. *Covetousness*, in every kind and degree, is certainly as contrary to this as to the love of God; whether, *philargyri, the love of money*, which is too frequently the root of all evil; or *pleonexia*, literally, a desire of *having more*, or increasing in substance. And how few, even of the real children of God, are entirely free from both! Indeed one great man, Martin Luther, used to say, he "never had any covetousness in him" (not only in his converted state, but) "ever since he was born." But, if so, I would not scruple to say, he was the only man born of a woman (except him that was God as well as man,) who had not, who was born without it. Nay, I believe, never was any one born of God, that lived any considerable time after, who did not feel more or less of it many times, especially in the latter sense. We may therefore set it down as an undoubted truth, that covetousness, together with pride, and self-will, and anger, remain in the hearts even of them that are justified.

10. It is their experiencing this, which has inclined so many serious persons to understand the latter part of the seventh chapter to the Romans, not of them that are "under the law," that are convinced of sin, which is undoubtedly the meaning of the Apostle, but of them that are "under grace;" that are "justified freely through the redemption that is in Christ." And it is most certain, they are thus far right,—there does still *remain*, even in them that are justified, a *mind* which is in some measure *carnal* (so the Apostle tells even the believers at Corinth, "Ye are carnal;") an *heart bent to backsliding*, still ever ready to "depart from the living God;" a propensity to pride, self-will, anger, revenge, love of the world, yea, and all evil: a root of bitterness, which, if the restraint were taken off for a moment, would instantly spring up; yea, such a depth of corruption, as, without clear light from God, we cannot possibly conceive. And a conviction of all this sin *remaining* in *their hearts* is the repentance which belongs to them that are justified.

11. But we should likewise be convinced, that as sin remains in our hearts, so it *cleaves* to all our words and actions. Indeed it is to be feared, that many of our words are more than mixed with sin; that they are sinful altogether; for such undoubtedly is all *uncharitable conversation*; all which does not spring from brotherly love; all which does not agree with that golden rule, "What ye would that others should do to you, even so do unto them." Of this kind is all backbiting, all tale-bearing, all whispering, all evil-speaking, that is, repeating the faults of absent persons; for none would have others repeat his faults when he is absent. Now how few are there, even among believers, who are in no degree guilty of this; who steadily observe the good old rule, "Of the dead and the absent, nothing but good!" And suppose they do, do they likewise abstain from *unprofitable conversation?* Yet all this is unquestionably sinful, and "grieves the Holy Spirit of God:" Yea, and "for every idle word that men shall speak, they shall give an account in the day of judgement."

12. But let it be supposed, that they continually "watch and pray," and so do "not enter into" this "temptation;" that they constantly set a watch before their mouth, and keep the door of their lips; suppose they exercise themselves herein, that *all* their "conversation may be in grace, seasoned with salt, and meet to minister grace to the hearers:" yet do they not daily slide into useless discourse, notwithstanding all their caution? And even when they endeavour to speak for God, are their words pure, free from unholy mixtures? Do they find nothing wrong in their very *intention?* Do they speak merely to please God, and not partly to please themselves? Is it wholly to do the will of God, and not their own will also? Or, if they begin with a single eye, do they go on "looking unto Jesus," and talking with him all the time they are talking with their neighbour? When they are reproving sin, do they feel no anger or unkind temper to the sinner? When they are instructing the ignorant, do they not find any pride, any self-preference? When they are comforting the afflicted, or provoking one another to love and to good works, do they never perceive any inward self-commendation: *"Now you have spoken well?"* Or any vanity—a desire that others should think so, and esteem them on the account? In some or all of these respects, how much sin cleaves to the best *conversation* even of believers! The conviction of which is another branch of the repentance which belongs to them that are justified.

13. And how much sin, if their conscience is thoroughly awake, may they find cleaving to *their actions* also! Nay, are there not many of these, which, though they are such as the world would not condemn, yet cannot be commended, no, nor excused, if we judge by the Word of God? Are there not many of their actions which, they themselves know, are not to the glory of God? many, wherein they did not even aim at this; which were not undertaken with an eye to God? And of those that were, are there not many, wherein their eye is not singly fixed on God—wherein they are doing their own will, at least as much as his; and seeking to please themselves as much, if not more, than to please God?—And while they are endeavouring to do good to their neighbour, do they not feel wrong tempers of various kinds? Hence their good actions, so called, are far from being strictly such; being polluted with such a mixture of evil: such are their works of *mercy*. And is there not the same mixture in their works of *piety?* While they are hearing the word which is able to save their souls, do they not frequently find such thoughts as make them afraid lest it should turn to their condemnation, rather than their salvation? Is it not often the same case, while they are endeavouring to offer up their prayers to God, whether in public or private? Nay, while they are engaged in the most solemn service, even while they are at the table of the Lord, what manner of thoughts arise in them! Are not their hearts sometimes wandering to the ends of the earth; sometimes filled with such imaginations, as make them fear lest all their sacrifice should be an abomination to the Lord? So that they are now more ashamed of their best duties, than they were once of their worst sins.

14. Again: How many *sins of omission* are they chargeable with! We know the words of the Apostle: "To him that

knoweth to do good, and doeth it not, to him it is sin." But do they not know a thousand instances, wherein they might have done good, to enemies, to strangers, to their brethren, either with regard to their bodies or their souls, and they did it not? How many omissions have they been guilty of, in their duty toward God! How many opportunities of communicating, of hearing his word, of public or private prayer, have they neglected! So great reason had even that holy man, Archbishop Usher, after all his labours for God, to cry out, almost with his dying breath, "Lord, forgive me my sins of omission!"

15. But besides these outward omissions, may they not find in themselves *inward defects* without number? defects of every kind: they have not the love, the fear, the confidence they ought to have, toward God. They have not the love which is due to their neighbour, to every child of man; no, nor even that which is due to their brethren, to every child of God, whether those that are at a distance from them, or those with whom they are immediately connected. They have no holy temper in the degree they ought; they are defective in everything,—in a deep consciousness of which they are ready to cry out, with M. De Renty, "I am a ground all overrun with thorns;" or, with Job, "I am vile: I abhor myself, and repent as in dust and ashes."

16. A conviction of their *guiltiness* is another branch of that repentance which belongs to the children of God. But this is cautiously to be understood, and in a peculiar sense. For it is certain, "there is no condemnation to them that are in Christ Jesus," that believe in him, and, in the power of that faith, "walk not after the flesh, but after the Spirit." Yet can they no more bear the *strict justice* of God now, than before they believed. This pronounces them to be still *worthy of death*, on all the preceding accounts. And it would absolutely condemn them thereto, were it not for the atoning blood. Therefore they are thoroughly convinced, that they still *deserve* punishment, although it is hereby turned aside from them. But here there are extremes on one hand and on the other, and few steer clear of them. Most men strike on one or the other, either thinking themselves condemned when they are not, or thinking they *deserve* to be acquitted. Nay, the truth lies between: they still *deserve*, strictly speaking only the damnation of hell. But what they deserve does not come upon them, because they "have an Advocate with the Father." His life, and death, and intercession still interpose between them and condemnation.

17. A conviction of their *utter helplessness* is yet another branch of this repentance. I mean hereby two things: first, that they are no more able now *of themselves* to think one good thought, to form one good desire, to speak one good word, or do one good work, than before they were justified; that they have still no kind or degree of strength *of their own*; no power either to do good, or resist evil; no ability to conquer or even withstand the world, the devil, or their own evil nature. They can, it is certain, do all these things; but it is not by their own strength. They have power to overcome all these enemies; for "sin hath no more dominion over them;" but it is not from nature, either in whole or in part; it is the *mere* gift of God: nor is it given all at once, as if they

had a stock laid up for many years; but from moment to moment.

18. By this helplessness I mean, Secondly, an absolute inability to deliver ourselves from that guiltiness or desert of punishment whereof we are still conscious; yea, and an inability to remove, by all the grace we have (to say nothing of our natural powers,) either the pride, self-will, love of the world, anger, and general proneness to depart from God, which we experimentally know to *remain* in the heart, even of them that are regenerate; or the evil which, in spite of all our endeavours, cleaves to all our words and actions. Add to this, an utter inability wholly to avoid uncharitable, and, much more, unprofitable, conversation: and an inability to avoid sins of omission, or to supply the numberless defects we are convinced of; especially the want of love, and other right tempers both to God and man.

19. If any man is not satisfied of this, if any believes that whoever is justified is able to remove these sins out of his heart and life, let him make the experiment. Let him try whether, by the grace he has already received, he can expel pride, self-will, or inbred sin in general. Let him try whether he can cleanse his words and actions from all mixture of evil; whether he can avoid all uncharitable and unprofitable conversation, with all sins of omission; and, lastly, whether he can supply the numberless defects which he still finds in himself. Let him not be discouraged by one or two experiments, but repeat the trial again and again; and the longer he tries, the more deeply will he be convinced of his utter helplessness in all these respects.

20. Indeed this is so evident a truth, that well nigh all the children of God, scattered abroad, however they differ in other points, yet generally agree in this;—that although we may "by the Spirit, mortify the deeds of the body," resist and conquer both outward and inward sin: although we may *weaken* our enemies day by day;—yet we cannot *drive them out*. By all the grace which is given at justification we cannot extirpate them. Though we watch and pray ever so much, we cannot wholly cleanse either our hearts or hands. Most sure we cannot, till it shall please our Lord to speak to our hearts again, to speak the second time, "Be clean:" and then only the leprosy is cleansed. Then only, the evil root, the carnal mind, is destroyed; and inbred sin subsists no more. But if there be no such second change, if there be no instantaneous deliverance after justification, if there be *none but* a gradual work of God (that there is a gradual work none denies,) then we must be content, as well as we can, to remain full of sin till death; and, if so, we must remain guilty till death, continually *deserving* punishment. For it is impossible the guilt, or desert of punishment, should be removed from us, as long as all this sin remains in our heart, and cleaves to our words and actions. Nay, in rigorous justice, all we think, and speak, and act, continually increases it.

II. 1. In this sense we are to *repent*, after we are justified. And till we do so, we can go no farther. For, till we are sensible of our disease, it admits of no cure. But, supposing we do thus repent, then are we called to "believe the gospel."

2. And this also is to be understood in a peculiar sense, different from that wherein we believed in order to

justification. Believe the glad tidings of great salvation, which God hath prepared for all people. Believe that he who is "the brightness of his Father's glory, the express image of his person," is "able to save unto the uttermost all that come unto God through him." He is able to save you from all the sin that still remains in your heart. He is able to save you from all the sin that cleaves to all your words and actions. He is able to save you from sins of omission, and to supply whatever is wanting in you. It is true, this is impossible with man; but with God-Man all things are possible. For what can be too hard for him who hath "all power in heaven and in earth?" Indeed, his bare power to do this is not a sufficient foundation for our faith that he will do it, that he will thus exert his power, unless he hath promised it. But this he has done: he has promised it over and over, in the strongest terms. he has given us these "exceeding great and precious promises," both in the Old and the New Testament. So we read in the law, in the most ancient part of the oracles of God, "The Lord thy God will circumcise thy heart, and the heart of thy seed, to love the Lord thy God with all thy heart, and with all thy soul." (Deut. 30:6.) So in the Psalms, "He shall redeem Israel," the Israel of God, "from all his sins." So in the Prophet, "Then will I sprinkle clean water upon you, and ye shall be clean: from all your filthiness, and from all your idols, will I cleanse you. And I will put My Spirit within you, and ye shall keep My judgements, and do them. I will also save you from all your uncleannesses" (Ezek. 36:25) So likewise in the New Testament, "Blessed be the Lord God of Israel; for he hath visited and redeemed his people, and hath raised up an horn of salvation for us,—to perform the oath which he sware to our father Abraham, that he would grant unto us, that we being delivered out of the hands of our enemies should serve him without fear, in holiness and righteousness before him, all the days of our life" (Luke 1:68)

3. You have therefore good reason to believe, he is not only able, but willing to do this; to cleanse you from all your filthiness of flesh and spirit; to "save you from all your uncleannesses." This is the thing which you now long for; this is the faith which you now particularly need, namely, that the Great Physician, the Lover of my soul, is willing to make me clean. But is he willing to do this to-morrow, or to-day? Let him answer for himself: "To-day, if ye will hear" My "voice, harden not your hearts." If you put it off till to-morrow, you harden your hearts; you refuse to hear his voice. Believe, therefore, that he is willing to save you *to-day*. He is willing to save you *now*. "Behold, now is the accepted time." He now saith, "Be thou clean!" Only believe, and you also will immediately find, "all things are possible to him that believeth."

4. Continue to believe in him that loved thee, and gave himself for thee; that bore all thy sins in his own body on the tree; and he saveth thee from all condemnation, by his blood continually applied. Thus it is that we continue in a justified state. And when we go "from faith to faith, when we have faith to be cleansed from indwelling sin, to be saved from all our uncleannesses, we are likewise saved from all that *guilt*, that *desert* of punishment, which we felt before. So that then we may say, not only,

Every moment, Lord, I *want*
The merit of thy death;
but, likewise, in the full assurance of faith,
Every moment, Lord, I *have*
The merit of thy death!

For, by that faith in his life, death, and intercession for us, renewed from moment to moment, we are every whit clean, and there is not only now no condemnation for us, but no such desert of punishment as was before, the Lord cleansing both our hearts and lives.

5. By the same faith we feel the power of Christ every moment resting upon us, whereby alone we are what we are; whereby we are enabled to continue in spiritual life, and without which, notwithstanding all our present holiness, we should be devils the next moment. But as long as we retain our faith in him, we "draw water out of the wells of salvation." Leaning on our Beloved, even Christ in us the hope of glory, who dwelleth in our hearts by faith, who likewise is ever interceding for us at the right hand of God, we receive help from him, to think, and speak, and act, what is acceptable in his sight. Thus does he "prevent" them that believe in all their "doings, and further them with his continual help;" so that all their designs, conversations, and actions are "begun, continued, and ended in him." Thus doth he "cleanse the thoughts of their hearts, by the inspiration of his Holy Spirit, that they may perfectly love him, and worthily magnify his holy name."

6. Thus it is, that in the children of God, repentance and faith exactly answer each other. By repentance we feel the sin remaining in our hearts, and cleaving to our words and actions: by faith, we receive the power of God in Christ, purifying our hearts, and cleansing our hands. By repentance, we are still sensible that we deserve punishment for all our tempers, and words, and actions: by faith, we are conscious that our Advocate with the Father is continually pleading for us, and thereby continually turning aside all condemnation and punishment from us. By repentance we have an abiding conviction that there is no help in us: by faith we receive not only mercy, "but grace to help in" *every* "time of need." Repentance disclaims the very possibility of any other help; faith accepts all the help we stand in need of, from him that hath all power in heaven and earth. Repentance says, "Without him I can do nothing:" Faith says, "I can do all things through Christ strengthening me." Through him I can not only overcome, but expel, all the enemies of my soul. Through him I can "love the Lord my God with all my heart, mind, soul, and strength;" yea, and "walk in holiness and righteousness before him all the days of my life."

III. 1. From what has been said we may easily learn the mischievousness of that opinion,—that we are *wholly* sanctified when we are justified; that our hearts are then cleansed from all sin. It is true, we are then delivered, as was observed before, from the dominion of outward sin; and, at the same time, the power of inward sin is so broken, that we need no longer follow, or be led by it: but it is by no means true, that inward sin is then totally destroyed; that the root of pride, self-will, anger, love of the world, is then taken out of the heart; or that the carnal mind, and the heart bent to backsliding, are entirely extirpated. And to suppose the contrary is not, as some may think, an innocent harmless mistake. No: it does immense harm: it entirely blocks up the way to any farther change; for it is manifest, "they that are whole not need a physician, but they that are sick." If, therefore, we think we are quite made whole already, there is no room to seek any further healing. On this supposition it is absurd to expect a farther deliverance from sin, whether gradual or instantaneous.

2. On the contrary, a deep conviction that we are not yet whole; that our hearts are not fully purified; that there is yet in us a "carnal mind," which is still in its nature "enmity against God;" that a whole body of sin remains in our heart, weakened indeed, but not destroyed; shows, beyond all possibility of doubt, the absolute necessity of a farther change. We allow, that at the very moment of justification, we are *born again*: In that instant we experience that inward change from "darkness into marvellous light;" from the image of the brute and the devil, into the image of God; from the earthly, sensual, devilish mind, to the mind which was in Christ Jesus. But are we then *entirely* changed? Are we *wholly* transformed into the image of him that created us? Far from it: we still retain a depth of sin; and it is the consciousness of this which constrains us to groan, for a full deliverance, to him that is mighty to save. Hence it is, that those believers who are not convinced of the deep corruption of their hearts, or but slightly, and, as it were, notionally convinced, have little concern about *entire sanctification*. They may possibly hold the opinion, that such a thing is to be, either at death, or some time they know not when, before it. But they have no great uneasiness for the want of it, and no great hunger or thirst after it. They cannot, until they know themselves better, until they repent in the sense above described, until God unveils the inbred monster's face, and shows them the real state of their souls. Then only, when they feel the burden, will they groan for deliverance from it. Then, and not till then, will they cry out, in the agony of their soul,

> Break off the yoke of inbred sin,
>   And fully set my spirit free!
> I cannot rest till pure within,
>   Till I am wholly lost in Thee.

3. We may learn from hence, secondly, that a deep conviction of our *demerit*, after we are accepted (which in one sense may be termed *guilt*,) is absolutely necessary, in order to our seeing the true value of the atoning blood; in order to our feeling that we need this as much, after we are justified as ever we did before. Without this conviction, we cannot but account the blood of the covenant *as a common thing*, something of which we have not now any great need, seeing all our past sins are blotted out. Yea, but if both our hearts and lives are thus unclean, there is a kind of guilt which we are contracting every moment, and which, of consequence, would every moment expose us to fresh condemnation, but that

> He ever lives above,
>   For us to intercede,—

His all-atoning love,
    His precious blood, to plead.

It is this repentance, and the faith intimately connected with it, which are expressed in those strong lines,—

> I sin in every breath I draw,
> Nor do Thy will, nor keep Thy law
>   On earth, as angels do above:
> But still the fountain open stands,
> Washes my feet, my heart, my hands,
>   Till I am perfected in love.

4. We may observe, Thirdly, a deep conviction of our utter *helplessness*, of our total inability to retain anything we have received, much more to deliver ourselves from the world of iniquity remaining both in our hearts and lives, teaches us truly to live upon Christ by faith, not only as our Priest, but as our King. Hereby we are brought to "magnify him," indeed; to "give Him all the glory of his grace;" to "make him a whole Christ, an entire Saviour; and truly to set the crown upon his head." These excellent words, as they have frequently been used, have little or no meaning; but they are fulfilled in a strong and deep sense, when we thus, as it were, go out of ourselves, in order to be swallowed up in him; when we sink into nothing, that he may be all in all. Then, his almighty grace having abolished "every high thing which exalted itself against him," every temper, and thought, and word, and work "is brought to the obedience of Christ."

Londonderry, April 24, 1767

15.* THE GREAT ASSIZE [I.E., THE LAST JUDGMENT—GL]*

"We shall all stand before the judgement-seat of Christ."
Rom. 14:10.

1. How many circumstances concur to raise the awfulness of the present solemnity!—The general *concourse* of people of every age, sex, rank, and condition of life, willingly or unwillingly gathered together, not only from the neighboring, but from distant, parts; *criminals*, speedily to be brought forth and having no way to escape; *officers*, waiting in their various posts, to execute the orders which shall be given; and the *representative* of our gracious *Sovereign*, whom we so highly reverence and honor. The *occasion* likewise of this assembly adds not a little to the solemnity of it: to hear and determine causes of every kind, some of which are of the most important nature; on which depends no less than life or death, death that uncovers the face of eternity! It was, doubtless, in order to increase the serious sense of these things, and not in the minds of the vulgar only that the wisdom of our forefathers did not disdain to appoint even several minute circumstances of this solemnity. For these also, by means of the eye or ear, may more deeply affect the heart: and when viewed in this light, trumpets, staves, apparel, are no longer trifling or insignificant, but

---

* (text of the 1872 edition)

subservient, in their kind and degree, to the most valuable ends of society.[1]

2. But, as awful as this solemnity is, one far more awful is at hand. For yet a little while, and "we shall all stand before the judgement-seat of Christ." "For, as I live, saith the Lord, every knee shall bow to Me, and every tongue shall confess to God." And in that day, "every one of us shall give account of himself to God."

3. Had all men a deep sense of this, how effectually would it secure the interests of society! For what more forcible motive can be conceived to the practice of genuine morality? to a steady pursuit of solid virtue? an uniform walking in justice, mercy, and truth? What could strengthen our hands in all that is good, and deter us from all evil, like a strong conviction of this, "The Judge standeth at the door;" and we are shortly to stand before him?

4. It may not therefore be improper, or unsuitable to the design of the present assembly, to consider,—

    I.   The chief circumstances which will precede our standing before the judgement-seat of Christ;

    II.   The judgement itself; and,

    III.   A few of the circumstances which will follow it.

I. 1. Let us, in the first place, consider the chief circumstances which will precede our standing before the judgement-seat of Christ.

And, first, God will show "signs in the earth beneath" (Acts 2:19); particularly He will "arise to shake terribly the earth." "The earth shall reel to and fro like a drunkard, and shall be removed like a cottage" (Isa. 24:20). "There shall be earthquakes," *kata topous* (not in divers only, but) "in all places;" not in one only, or a few, but in every part of the habitable world (Luke 21:2); even "such as were not since men were upon the earth, so mighty earthquakes and so great." In one of these "every island shall flee away, and the mountains will not be found" (Rev. 16:20). Meantime all the waters of the terraqueous globe will feel the violence of those concussions; "the sea and waves roaring" (Luke 21:25), with such an agitation as had never been known before, since the hour that "the fountains of the great deep were broken up," to destroy the earth, which then "stood out of the water and in the water." The air will be all storm and tempest, full of dark vapors and "pillars of smoke" (Joel 2:30); resounding with thunder from pole to pole, and torn with ten thousand lightnings. But the commotion will not stop in the region of the air; "the powers of heaven also shall be shaken. There shall be signs in the sun, and in the moon, and in the stars" (Luke 21:25, 26); those fixed, as well as those that move round them. "The sun shall be turned into darkness, and the moon into blood, before the great and terrible day of the Lord come" (Joel 2:31). "The stars shall withdraw their shining" (Joel 3:15), yea, and "fall from heaven" (Rev. 6:13), being thrown out of their orbits. And then shall be heard the universal *shout*, from all the companies of heaven, followed by the "voice of the archangel," proclaiming the approach of the Son of God and Man, "and the trumpet of God," sounding an alarm to all that sleep in the dust of the earth (1 Thess. 4:16). In consequence of this, all the graves shall open, and the bodies of men arise. The sea also shall give up the dead which are therein (Rev. 20:13), and every one shall rise with "his own body:" his own in substance, although so changed in its properties as we cannot now conceive. "For this corruptible will" then "put on incorruption, and this mortal put on immortality" (1 Cor. 15:53). Yea, "death and hades," the invisible world, shall "deliver up the dead that are in them" (Rev. 20:13). So that all who ever lived and died, since God created man, shall be raised incorruptible and immortal.[2]

2. At the same time, "the Son of Man shall send forth his angels" over all the earth; "and they shall gather his elect from the four winds, from one end of heaven to the other" (Matt. 24:31). And the Lord himself shall come with clouds, in his

---

[1] "Our gracious Sovereign" is George II. Wesley was always intensely loyal. In 1744 he wrote an Address from his Societies to the King in which he says, "we are ready to obey your Majesty to the uttermost, in all things which we conceive to be agreeable [to the Word of God]. And we earnestly exhort all with whom we converse, as they fear God to honor the King." The Address was not sent, mainly because it might have been taken to imply that the Methodists were "a body distinct from the National Church." in 1745, the year of the Young Pretenders's invasion of England, he wrote to the Mayor of Newcastle, "All I can do for his Majesty, whom I honor and love—I think not less than I did my own father—is this: I cry unto God, day by day, to put all his enemies to confusion," etc. When George II died in October 1760 he records in his *Journal* (October 25), "King George was gathered to his fathers. When will England have a better Prince?" One thinks of Carlyle (*Sartor* 1.9). "Has not your Red hanging-individual a horsehair wig, squirrel-skins, and a plush-gown, whereby all mortals know that he is a JUDGE. Society, which the more I think of it astonishes me the more, is founded upon Cloth." Wesley never despised form and ceremonial; he robed himself even for his Bible studies with his Societies in London and Bristol and for his open-air services.

[2] This paragraph, finely and impressively composed as it is, is a defiance of all sound exegesis. Some of the passages quoted refer to the invasion of Judah by the Assyrians, some to the coming of the Holy Ghost, some to the destruction of Jerusalem by the Romans, some to the downfall of Rome herself. All these were is a sense "days of Jehovah;" but there is no warrant for transferring all these signs to the final day of judgement, nor for their literal interpretation. This just remark on the difference between the present and the resurrection bodies is worked out in detail in Sermon 138, originally written by Benjamin Calamy and revised and abridged by Wesley in 1732. "Substance" and "properties" are here used in their philosophical sense" the body will be the same in essence (not composed of the same material particles), but it properties, i.e. its characteristics and qualities will be entirely changed. Above all, it will be a "pneumatical" and not a "physical" body, i.e. it will be well adapted for the use and manifestation of the spirit, as the present body is adapted for the use and manifestation of the psyche or animal soul.

"Hades" is a very properly substituted for the A.V. "hell," which is here, and indeed in all passages where is the translation of Sheol, or Hades, most misleading to the English reader. It is the world of departed spirits, not the place of punishment of the Devil and his angels.

own glory, and the glory of his Father, with ten thousand of his saints, even myriads of angels, and shall sit upon the throne of his glory. "And before him shall be gathered all nations; and he shall separate them one from another, and shall set the sheep," the good, "on his right hand, and the goats," the wicked, "upon the left" (Matt. 25:31, etc.). Concerning this general assembly it is, that the beloved disciple speaks thus: "I saw the dead," all that had been dead, "small and great, stand before God; and the books were opened" (a figurative expression, plainly referring to the manner of proceeding among men), "and the dead were judged out of those things which were written in the books, according to their works" (Rev. 20:12).[3]

II. These are the chief circumstances which are recorded in the oracles of God, as preceding the general judgement. We are, secondly, to consider the judgement itself, so far as it hath pleased God to reveal it.

1. The person by whom God will judge the world, is his only-begotten Son, whose "goings forth are from everlasting;" "who is God over all, blessed for ever." Unto him, being "the outbeaming of his Father's glory, the express image of his person" (Heb. 1:3), the Father "hath committed all judgement, because he is the Son of Man" (John 5:22, 27); because, though he was "in the form of God, and thought it not robbery to be equal with God, yet he emptied himself, taking upon him the form of a servant, being made in the likeness of men" (Phil. 2:6, 7); yea, because, "being found in fashion as a man, he humbled himself" yet farther, "becoming obedient unto death, even the death of the cross. Wherefore God hath highly exalted him," even in his human nature, and "ordained him," as Man, to try the children of men, "to be the Judge both of the quick and the dead;" both of those who shall be found alive at his coming, and of those who were before gathered to their fathers.[4]

2. The time, termed by the prophet, "the great and the terrible day," is usually, in Scripture, styled *the day of the Lord*. The space from the creation of man upon the earth, to the end of all things, is *the day of the sons of men*; the time that is now passing over us is properly *our day*; when this is ended, *the day of the Lord* will begin. But who can say how long it will continue? "With the Lord one day is as a thousand years, and a thousand years as one day" (2 Pet. 3:8). And from this very expression, some of the ancient fathers drew that inference, that, what is commonly called the day of judgement would be indeed a thousand years: and it seems they did not go beyond the truth; nay, probably they did not come up to it. For, if we consider the number of persons who are to be judged, and of actions which are to be inquired into, it does not appear that a thousand years will suffice for the transactions of that day; so that it may not improbably comprise several thousand years. But God shall reveal this also in its season.[5]

3. With regard to the place where mankind will be judged, we have no explicit account in Scripture. An eminent writer (but not he alone; many have been of the same opinion) supposes it will be on earth, where the works were done, according to which they shall be judged; and that God will, in order thereto, employ the angels of his strength—.

> To smooth and lengthen out the boundless space,
> And spread an area for all human race.

But perhaps it is more agreeable to our Lord's own account of his coming in the clouds, to suppose it will be above the earth, if not "twice a planetary height." And this supposition is not a little favored by what St. Paul writes to the Thessalonians: "The dead in Christ shall rise first. Then we who remain alive shall be caught up together with them in the clouds, to meet the Lord in the air" (1 Thess. 4:16, 17). So that it seems most probable, the great white throne will be high exalted above the earth.[6]

4. The persons to be judged, who can count, any more than the drops of rain, or the sands of the sea? "I beheld," saith St. John, "a great multitude which no man can number, clothed with white robes, and palms in their hands." How immense then must be the total multitude of all nations, and kindreds, and people, and tongues; of all that have sprung from the loins of Adam, since the world began, till time shall be no more! If we admit the common supposition, which seems no ways absurd, that the earth bears, at any one time, no less than four hundred millions of living souls, men, women, and children; what a congregation must all those generations make, who have succeeded each other for seven thousand years!

---

[3] "All nations"—more exactly "all the Gentiles." This account of the judgement refers only to the judgement of the heathen nations, who have not heard of Christ; and the standard of judgement is according not their relation to Him, but their fulfillment of the common human duties of kindliness and charity there set out. It is a supplement to the three preceding parables of the Steward, the Virgins, and the Talents; the first describing the judgement of the Christian minister, the second and third the two sides of the judgment of those who have heard the gospel; first from the point of view of faith, second from the point of view of works.

"The beloved disciple." Wesley of course accepts the Johannine authorship of the Apocalypse.

[4] "Outbeaming," more exact than the A.V. "brightness." The Son is to the Father as the rays of light are to the sun. "Thought it not robbery:" better, "thought it not an object to be grasped at" to be equal with God. He laid aside for the time His equality with the Father, which was therefore restored to Him when God gave Him the name that is above every name.

[5] Pole quotes from Joseph Mede, "*Quod jam dixi diem judicii, non intelligi velim de die brevi, sive paucarum horarum; sed de spatio mile annorum quibus dies illa durabit*; i.e. The day of judgement is not to be understood as a short day of a few hours, but as the space of a thousand years, during which that day will last."

[6] The "eminent writer" is Edward Young, the author of *Night Thoughts*. The quotation is from his poem, "The Last Day" (1721), 2.19. The original runs:

> To smooth and lengthen out reached before the Society
> for Ref
> th' unbounded space.
> Twice a planetary height.

Young, 2:282 says: Now the descending triumph stops its flight From earth full twice a planetary height. Presumably he means twice as far from the earth as the farthest planet. All this seems rather solemn trifling.

> Great Xerxes' world in arms, proud Cannae's host,
> They all are here; and here they all are lost.
> Their numbers swell to be discern'd in vain;
> Lost as a drop in the unbounded main.

Every man, every woman, every infant of days, that ever breathed the vital air, will then hear the voice of the Son of God, and start into life, and appear before him. And this seems to be the natural import of that expression, "the dead, small and great:" all universally, all without exception, all of every age, sex, or degree; all that ever lived and died, or underwent such a change as will be equivalent with death. For long before that day, the phantom of human greatness disappears, and sinks into nothing. Even in the moment of death, that vanishes away. Who is rich or great in the grave?[7]

5. And every man shall there "give an account of his own works;" yea, a full and true account of all that he ever did while in the body, whether it was good or evil. O what a scene will then be disclosed, in the sight of angels and men!—while not the fabled Rhadamanthus, but the Lord God Almighty, who knoweth all things in heaven and in earth,—

> Castigatque, auditque dolos; subigitque fateri
> Quae quis apud superos, furto laetatus inani,
> Distulit in seram commissa piacula mortem.
>
> [O'er these drear realms stern Rhadamanthus reigns,
> Detects each artful villain, and constrains
> To own the crimes long veil'd from human sight:
> In vain! Now all stand forth in hated light.]

Nor will all the actions alone of every child of man be then brought to open view, but all their words; seeing "every idle word which men shall speak, they shall give account thereof in the day of judgement" (Matt. 12:36, 37); so that "by thy words," as well as works, "thou shalt be justified; and by thy words thou shalt be condemned." Will not God then bring to light every circumstance also that accompanied every word or action, and if not altered the nature, yet lessened or increased the goodness or badness, of them? And how easy is this to him who is "about our bed, and about our path, and spieth out all our ways!" We know "the darkness is no darkness to him, but the night shineth as the day."[8]

6. Yea, he will bring to light, not the hidden works of darkness only, but the very thoughts and intents of the heart. And what marvel? For he "searcheth the reins, and understandeth all our thoughts." "All things are naked and open to the eyes of him with whom we have to do." "Hell and destruction are before him without a covering. How much more the hearts of the children of men!"

7. And in that day shall be discovered every inward working of every human soul; every appetite, passion, inclination, affection, with the various combinations of them, with every temper and disposition that constitute the whole complex character of each individual. So shall it be clearly and infallibly seen, who was righteous, and who unrighteous; and in what degree every action, or person, or character was either good or evil.

8. "Then the King will say to them upon his right hand, Come, ye blessed of My Father. For I was hungry, and ye gave Me meat; thirsty, and ye gave Me drink: I was a stranger, and ye took Me in; naked, and ye clothed me." In like manner, all the good they did upon earth will be recited before men and angels; whatsoever they had done, either in word or deed, in the name, or for the sake, of the Lord Jesus. All their good desires, intentions, thoughts, all their holy dispositions, will also be then remembered; and it will appear, that though they were unknown or forgotten among men, yet God noted them in his book. All their sufferings likewise for the name of Jesus, and for the testimony of a good conscience, will be displayed unto their praise from the righteous Judge, their honor before saints and angels, and the increase of that "far more exceeding and eternal weight of glory."

9. But will their evil deeds too (since, if we take in his whole life, there is not a man on earth who liveth and sinneth, not), will these be remembered in that day, and mentioned in the great congregation? Many believe they will not; and ask, "Would not this imply, that their sufferings were not at an end, even when life ended?—seeing they would still have sorrow, and shame, and confusion of face to endure." They ask farther, "How can this be reconciled with God's declaration by the Prophet,—'If the wicked will turn from all his sins that he hath committed, and keep all My statutes, and do that which is lawful and right; all his transgressions that he hath committed, they shall not be once mentioned unto him?' (Ezek. 18:21, 22). How is it consistent with the promise which God has made to all who accept of the gospel covenant, 'I will forgive their iniquities, and remember their sin no more?' (Jer. 31:34) Or, as the Apostle expresses it, 'I will be merciful to their unrighteousness, and their sins and iniquities will I remember no more?' " (Heb. 8:12).

10. It may be answered, It is apparently and absolutely necessary, for the full display of the glory of God; for the clear and perfect manifestation of his wisdom, justice, power, and mercy, toward the heirs of salvation; that all the circumstances of their life should be placed in open view,

---

[7] "Four hundred millions;" it is now estimated as, more or less, fifteen hundred millions. But a few millions more or less are not worth considering in such an altogether indeterminate calculation as this.
The quotation is again from Young, 2.193. Wesley protest vigorously against any one altering his own or his brother's verse; but he never hesitates to do the same thing to other people's; the original passage in Young runs—

> Great Xerxes' world in arms, proud Cannae's field.
> Where Carthage taught victorious Rome to yield,
> Immortal Blenheim, fam'd Ramillia's host.

> They all are here, and here they are lost.
> Their millions sell to be discerned in vain,
> Lost as a billow in th' unbounded main.

[8] The quotation is from Virgil's *Aeneid*, 6.567. The subject of the verbs is Rhadamanthus, the mythical judge of the dead. No translation is furnished in the 1771 ed. Modern editions give Dryden's version. The meaning is "Rhadamanthus of Gnosus here holds his iron sway, and scourges them and hears their guile, and compels each man to confess the expiations put off till death (alas! too late!) which were due for the crimes he committed on earth, rejoicing in the vain hope that they might be concealed."

together with all their tempers, and all the desires, thoughts, and intents of their hearts: otherwise, how would it appear out of what a depth of sin and misery the grace of God had delivered them? And, indeed, if the whole lives of all the children of men were not manifestly discovered, the whole amazing contexture of divine providence could not be manifested; nor should we yet be able, in a thousand instances, "to justify the ways of God to man." Unless our Lord's words were fulfilled in their utmost sense, without any restriction or limitation," There is nothing covered, that shall not be revealed; or hid, that shall not be known" (Matt. 10:26); abundance of God's dispensations under the sun would still appear without their reasons. And then only when God hath brought to light all the hidden things of darkness, whosoever were the actors therein, will it be seen that wise and good were all his ways; that he saw through the thick cloud, and governed all things by the wise counsel of his own will; that nothing was left to chance or the caprice of men, but God disposed all strongly and sweetly, and wrought all into one connected chain of justice, mercy, and truth.[9]

11. And in the discovery of the divine perfections, the righteous will rejoice with joy unspeakable; far from feeling any painful sorrow or shame, for any of those past transgressions which were long since blotted out as a cloud, washed away by the blood of the Lamb. It will be abundantly sufficient for them, that all the transgressions which they had committed shall not be once mentioned unto them to their disadvantaged that their sins, and transgressions, and iniquities shall be remembered no more to their condemnation. This is the plain meaning of the promise; and this all the children of God shall find true, to their everlasting comfort.

12. After the righteous are judged, the King will turn to them upon his left hand; and they shall also be judged, every man according to his works. But not only their outward works will be brought into the account, but all the evil words which they have ever spoken; yea, all the evil desires, affections, tempers, which have, or have had, a place in their souls; and all the evil thoughts or designs which were ever cherished in their hearts. The joyful sentence of acquittal will then be pronounced Upon those upon the right hand; the dreadful sentence of condemnation upon those on the left; both of which must remain fixed and unmovable as the throne of God.

III. 1. We may, in the Third place, consider a few of the circumstances which will follow the general judgement. And the first is the execution of the sentence pronounced on the evil and on the good: "These shall go away into eternal punishment, and the righteous into life eternal." It should be observed, it is the very same word which is used, both in the former and the latter clause. It follows, that either the punishment lasts for ever, or the reward too will come to an end:—No, never, unless God could come to an end, or his mercy and truth could fail. "Then shall the righteous shine forth as the sun in the kingdom of their Father," "and shall drink of those rivers of pleasure which are at God's right hand for evermore." But here all description falls short; all human language fails! Only one who is caught up into the third heaven can have a just conception of it. But even such a one cannot express what he hath seen: these things it is not possible for man to utter.

The wicked, meantime, shall be turned into hell, even all the people that forget God. They will be "punished with everlasting destruction from the presence of the Lord, and from the glory of his power." They will be "cast into the lake of fire burning with brimstone," originally "prepared for the devil and his angels;" where they will gnaw their tongues for anguish and pain; they will curse God and look upward. There the dogs of hell—pride, malice, revenge, rage, horror, despair—continually devour them. There "they have no rest, day or night, but the smoke of their torment ascendeth for ever and ever!" For "their worm dieth not, and the fire is not quenched."[10]

2. Then the heavens will be shrivelled up as a parchment scroll, and pass away with a great noise: they will "flee from the face of him that sitteth on the throne, and there will be found no place for them" (Rev. 20:11). The very manner of their passing away is disclosed to us by the Apostle Peter: "In the day of God, the heavens, being on fire, shall be dissolved" (2 Pet. 3:12). The whole beautiful fabric will be overthrown by that raging element, the connexion of all its parts destroyed, and every atom torn asunder from the others. By the same, "the earth also, and the works that are therein, shall be burned up" (verse 10). The enormous works of nature, the everlasting hills, mountains that have defied the rage of time, and stood unmoved so many thousand years, will sink down in fiery ruin. How much less will the works of art, though of the most durable kind, the utmost efforts of human industry—tombs, pillars, triumphal arches, castles, pyramids—be able to withstand the flaming conqueror! All, all will die, perish, vanish away, like a dream when one awaketh![11]

---

[9] "To justify the way of God to man:" from Milton's *Paradise Lost*, 1.26. In the original the last line is "men."

[10] "The third heaven" Paul (2 Cor. 12:2) tells how he was caught up into the third heave, or paradise, and heard unutterable words which it is not in the power of man to speak, It is doubtful where he thought of three heavens only—viz. the heaven of the atmosphere and clouds, the heaven of the sun and stars, and the heaven of the blessed dead—or accepted the Jewish belief in seven heavens, of which Paradise was the third in order from below. Wesley admits of no hope for the finally impenitent, and interprets literally these passages which speak of their doom. In the first, however, Hell is Sheol, and all that the Psalmist says is that all the nations (no the people) that forget God will depart in to the world of the dead. In the Sermon 73, on Hell, he is quite explicit as to his belief in the endless torment of the wicked in material fire. Neither of these sermons are, however, part of the standard Methodist doctrine.

[11] The finale destruction of the earth by means of fires is quite within the bounds of possibility. The impact of some wandering star would generate heat enough for the purpose; of it may be that gravitation will at last overcome the centrifugal force and the arch will fall into the sun. But such speculations are as fruitless as they are uncertain; and the idea in the next paragraph of the origin of the sea of glass is merely grotesque.

3. It has indeed been imagined by some great and good men, that as it requires that same almighty power to annihilate things as to create; to speak into nothing or out of nothing; so no part of, no atom in, the universe, will be totally or finally destroyed. Rather, they suppose that, as the last operation of fire, which we have yet been able to observe, is to reduce into glass what, by a smaller force, it had reduced to ashes; so, in the day God hath ordained, the whole earth, if not the material heavens also, will undergo this change, after which the fire can have no farther power over them. And they believe this is intimated by that expression in the Revelation made to St. John: "Before the throne there was a sea of glass, like unto crystal" (Rev. 4:6). We cannot now either affirm or deny this; but we shall know hereafter.

4. If it be inquired by the scoffers, the minute philosophers, "How can these things be? Whence should come such an immense quantity of fire as would consume the heavens and the whole terraqueous globe?" we would beg leave, first, to remind them, that this difficulty is not peculiar to the Christian system. The same opinion almost universally obtained among the *unbigoted* Heathens. So one of these celebrated *freethinkers* speaks, according to the generally received sentiment,—

> Esse quoque in fatis reminiscitur, affore tempus,
> Quo mare, quo tellus, correptaque regia coeli
> Ardeat, et mundi moles operosa laboret.

[The following is Dryden's translation of this quotation from Ovid:—

> Rememb'ring, in the fates, a time when fire
> Should to the battlements of heaven aspire;
> And all the blazing world above should burn,
> And all the' inferior globe to cinders turn.—EDIT.]

But, Secondly, it is easy to answer, even from our slight and superficial acquaintance with natural things, that there are abundant magazines of fire ready prepared, and treasured up against the day of the Lord. How soon may a comet, commissioned by him, travel down from the most distant parts of the universe! And were it to fix upon the earth in its return from the sun, when it is some thousand times hotter than a red-hot cannon ball, who does not see what must be the immediate consequence? But, not to ascend so high as the ethereal heavens, might not the same lightnings which "give shine to the world," if commanded by the Lord of nature, give ruin and utter destruction? Or, to go no farther than the globe itself; who knows what huge reservoirs of liquid fire are from age to age contained in the bowels of the earth? Aetna, Hecla, Vesuvius, and all the other volcanoes that belch out flames and coals of fire, what are they, but so many proofs and mouths of those fiery furnaces; and at the same time so many evidences that God hath in readiness wherewith to fulfil his word? Yea, were we to observe no more than the surface of the earth, and the things that surround us on every side, it is most certain (as a thousand experiments prove, beyond all possibility of denial) that we ourselves, our whole bodies, are full of fire, as well as everything round about us. Is it not easy to make this ethereal fire visible even to the naked eye, and to produce thereby the very same effects on combustible matter, which are produced by culinary fire? Needs there then any more than for God to unloose that secret chain, whereby this irresistible agent is now bound down, and lies quiescent in every particle of matter? And how soon would it tear the universal frame in pieces, and involve all in one common ruin![12]

5. There is one circumstance more which will follow the judgement, that deserves our serious consideration: "We look," says the Apostle, "according to his promise, for new heavens and a new earth, wherein dwelleth righteousness" (2 Pet. 3:13). The promise stands in the prophecy of Isaiah: "Behold, I create new heavens and a new earth: and the former shall not be remembered" (Isa. 65:17), so great shall the glory of the latter be! These St. John did behold in the visions of God. "I saw," saith he, "a new heaven and a new earth; for the first heaven and the first earth were passed away" (Rev. 21:1). And only righteousness dwelt therein: accordingly, he adds, "And I heard a great voice from" the third "heaven, saying, Behold, the tabernacle of God is with men, and he will dwell with them, and they shall be his people, and God himself shall be with them, and be their God" (21:3). Of necessity, therefore, they will all be happy: "God shall wipe away all tears from their eyes; and there shall be no more death, neither sorrow, nor crying, neither shall there be any more pain" (21:4). "There shall be no more curse; but they shall see his face" (21:3, 4),—shall have the nearest access to, and thence the highest, resemblance of, him. This is the strongest expression in the language of Scripture, to denote the most perfect happiness. "And his name shall be on their foreheads;" they shall be openly acknowledged as God's own property, and his glorious nature shall most visibly shine forth in them. "And there shall be no night there; and they need no candle, neither light of

---

[12] Cicero is the author of the phrase "minute philosophers." He speaks in *de Senect=* 23 of "*Quidam minuti philosophi*," meaning trifling, insignificant. In English use it rather means meticulous, over-precise, speculators. All this discussion as to quantity of fire is absurd: fire is not a thing, but a state of violent chemical combination; a match is quite enough to kindle a conflagration if there be fuel enough. Wesley was keenly interested in electrical phenomena, and was the first man in England to make use of it as a curative agent. His pamphlet called *The Desideratum; or, Electricity made Plain, and Useful,* published in 1760, details many of Franklin's experiments, such as drawing sparks out of the human body or from the fur of a cat. This is what he is thinking of when he says that our bodies are full of fire.

"Freethinker" was a name claimed by the Deists and other rejecters of the Christian revelation at the beginning of the eighteenth century. Here Wesley uses it of Ovid, the Roman poet, with a kind of suggestion that the modern freethinkers were akin to him in their religious views. The quotation is from the *Metamorphoses*, 1.256, where Jupiter, preparing to hurl his thunderbolts, hesitates to do so lest he should set the ether aflame, "for he remembers that it is amongst the decrees of the Fates that a time will come when the sea, the earth, and the palace of heaven shall catch fire and blaze, and the mass of the world, so laboriously constructed, shall be imperilled."

the sun; for the Lord God giveth them light: and they shall reign for ever and ever."

IV. It remains only to apply the preceding considerations to all who are here before God. And are we not directly led so to do, by the present solemnity, which so naturally points us to that day, when the Lord will judge the world in righteousness? This, therefore, by reminding us of that more awful season, may furnish many lessons of instruction. A few of these I may be permitted just to touch on. May God write them on all our hearts!

1. And, First, how beautiful are the feet of those who are sent by the wise and gracious providence of God, to execute justice on earth, to defend the injured, and punish the wrongdoer! Are they not the ministers of God to us for good; the grand supporters of the public tranquillity; the patrons of innocence and virtue; the great security of all our temporal blessings? And does not every one of these represent, not only an earthly prince, but the Judge of the earth? Him whose "name is written upon his thigh, King of kings, and Lord of lords?" O that all these sons of the right hand of the Most High may be as holy as he is holy! wise with the wisdom that sitteth by his throne, like him who is the eternal Wisdom of the Father! no respecters of persons, as he is none; but rendering to every man according to his works; like him inflexibly, inexorably just, though pitiful and of tender mercy! So shall they be terrible indeed to them that do evil, as not bearing the sword in vain. So shall the laws of our land have their full use and due honor, and the throne of our King be still established in righteousness.

2. Ye truly honorable men, whom God and the King have commissioned, in a lower degree, to administer justice; may not ye be compared to those ministering spirits who will attend the Judge coming in the clouds? May you, like them, burn with love to God and man! May you love righteousness and hate iniquity! May ye all minister, in your several spheres (such honor hath God given you also to them that shall be heirs of salvation, and to the glory of your great sovereign! May ye remain the establishers of peace, the blessing and ornaments of your country, the protectors of a guilty land, the guardian angels of all that are round about you!

3. You, whose office it is to execute what is given you in charge by him before whom you stand; how nearly are you concerned to resemble those that stand before the face of the Son of Man, those servants of his that do his pleasure, and hearken to the voice of his words! Does it not highly import you, to be as uncorrupt as them? to approve yourselves the servants of God? to do justly, and love mercy? to do to all as ye would they should do to you? So shall that great Judge, under whose eye you continually stand, say to you also, "Well done, good and faithful servants: enter ye into the joy of your Lord!"

4. Suffer me to add a few words to all of you who are at this day present before the Lord. Should not you bear it in your minds all the day long, that a more awful day is coming? A large assembly this! But what is it to that which every eye will then behold, the general assembly of all the children of men that ever lived on the face of the whole earth? A few will stand at the judgement-seat this day, to be judged touching what shall be laid to their charge; and they are now reserved in prison, perhaps in chains, till they are brought forth to be tried and sentenced. But we shall all, I that speak and you that hear, "stand at the judgement-seat of Christ." And we are now reserved on this earth, which is not our home, in this prison of flesh and blood, perhaps many of us in chains of darkness too, till we are ordered to be brought forth. Here a man is questioned concerning one or two facts, which he is supposed to have committed: there we are to give an account of all our works, from the cradle to the grave; of all our words; of all our desires and tempers, all the thoughts and intents of our hearts; of all the use we have made of our various talents, whether of mind, body, or fortune, till God said, "Give an account of thy stewardship, for thou mayest be no longer steward." In this court, it is possible, some who are guilty may escape for want of evidence; but there is no want of evidence in that court. All men, with whom you had the most secret intercourse, who were privy to all your designs and actions, are ready before your face. So are all the spirits of darkness, who inspired evil designs and assisted in the execution of them. So are all the angels of God; those eyes of the Lord, that run to and fro over all the earth, who watched over your soul, and labored for your good, so far as you would permit. So is your own conscience, a thousand witnesses in one, now no more capable of being either blinded or silenced, but constrained to know and to speak the naked truth, touching all your thoughts, and words, and actions. And is conscience as a thousand witnesses?—yea, but God is as a thousand consciences! O, who can stand before the face of the great God, even our Savior Jesus Christ!

See! See! He cometh! He maketh the clouds his chariots! He rideth upon the wings of the wind! A devouring fire goeth before him, and after him a flame burneth! See! He sitteth upon his throne, clothed with light as with a garment, arrayed with majesty and honor! Behold, his eyes are as a flame of fire, his voice as the sound of many waters! How will ye escape? Will ye call to the mountains to fall, on you, the rocks to cover you? Alas, the mountains themselves, the rocks, the earth, the heavens, are just ready to flee away! Can ye prevent the sentence? Wherewith? With all the substance of thy house, with thousands of gold and, silver? Blind wretch! Thou camest naked from thy mother's womb, and more naked into eternity. Hear the Lord, the Judge! "Come, ye blessed of my Father, inherit the kingdom prepared for you from the foundation of the world." Joyful sound! How widely different from that voice which echoes, through the expanse of heaven, "Depart, ye cursed, into everlasting fire, prepared for the devil and his angels!" And who is he that can prevent or retard the full execution of either sentence? Vain hope! Lo, hell is moved from beneath to receive those who are ripe for destruction. And the everlasting doors lift up their heads, that the heirs of glory may come in![13]

5. "What manner of persons then ought we to be, in all holy conversation and godliness!" We know it cannot be long before the Lord will descend with the voice of the archangel, and the trumpet of God; when every one of us shall appear before him, and give account of his own works. "Wherefore, beloved, seeing ye look for these things," seeing ye know he will come and will not tarry, "be diligent, that ye may be found of him in peace, without spot and blameless." Why should ye not? Why should one of you be found on the left hand at his appearing? He willeth not that any should perish, but that all should come to repentance; by repentance, to faith in a bleeding Lord; by faith, to spotless love, to the full image of God renewed in the heart, and producing all holiness of conversation. Can you doubt of this, when you remember, the Judge of all is likewise the Savior of all? Hath he not bought you with his own blood, that ye might not perish, but have everlasting life? O make proof of his mercy, rather than his justice; of his love, rather than the thunder of his power! He is not far from every one of us; and he is now come, not to condemn, but to save the world he standeth in the midst! Sinner, doth he not now, even now, knock at the door of thy heart? O that thou mayest know, at least in this thy day, the things that belong unto thy peace! O that ye may now give yourselves to him who gave himself for you, in humble faith, in holy, active, patient love! So shall ye rejoice with exceeding joy in his day, when he cometh in the clouds of heaven.

16.* THE MEANS OF GRACE

"Ye are gone away from mine ordinances, and have not kept them."

Mal. 3:7.

I. 1. But are there any *ordinances* now, since life and immortality were brought to light by the gospel? Are there, under the Christian dispensation, any *means ordained* of God, as the usual channels of his grace? This question could never have been proposed in the apostolical church, unless by one who openly avowed himself to be a Heathen; the whole body of Christians being agreed, that Christ had ordained certain outward means, for conveying his grace into the souls of men. Their constant practice set this beyond all dispute; for so long as "all that believed were together, and had all things common," (Acts 2:44,) "they continued steadfastly in the teaching of the Apostles, and in the breaking of bread, and in prayers." (Acts 2:42.)

2. But in process of time, when "the love of many waxed cold," some began to mistake the *means* for the *end*, and to place religion rather in doing those outward works, than in a heart renewed after the image of God. They forgot that "the end of" every "commandment is love, out of a pure heart,"

with "faith unfeigned;" the loving the Lord their God with all their heart, and their neighbour as themselves; and the being purified from pride, anger, and evil desire, by a "faith of the operation of God." Others seemed to imagine, that though religion did not principally consist in these outward means, yet there was something in them wherewith God was well pleased: something that would still make them acceptable in his sight, though they were not exact in the weightier matters of the law, in justice, mercy, and the love of God.

3. It is evident, in those who abused them thus, they did not conduce to the end for which they were ordained: Rather, the things which should have been for their health, were to them an occasion of falling. They were so far from receiving any blessing therein, that they only drew down a curse upon their head; so far from growing more heavenly in heart and life, that they were two-fold more the children of hell than before. Others, clearly perceiving that these means did not convey the grace of God to those children of the devil, began, from this particular case, to draw a general conclusion,—that they were not means of conveying the grace of God.

4. Yet the number of those who *abused* the ordinances of God, was far greater than of those who *despised* them, till certain men arose, not only of great understanding, (sometimes joined with considerable learning,) but who likewise appeared to be men of love, experimentally acquainted with true, inward religion. Some of these were burning and shining lights, persons famous in their generations, and such as had well deserved of the church of Christ, for standing in the gap against the overflowings of ungodliness.

It cannot be supposed, that these holy and venerable men intended any more, at first, than to show that outward religion is nothing worth, without the religion of the heart; that "God is a Spirit, and they who worship him must worship him in spirit and in truth;" that, therefore, external worship is lost labour, without a heart devoted to God; that the outward ordinances of God then profit much, when they advance inward holiness, but, when they advance it not, are unprofitable and void, are lighter than vanity; yea, that when they are used, as it were *in the place* of this, they are an utter abomination to the Lord.

5. Yet is it not strange, if some of these, being strongly convinced of that horrid profanation of the ordinances of God, which had spread itself over the whole church, and well nigh driven true religion out of the world,—in their fervent zeal for the glory of God, and the recovery of souls from that fatal delusion,—spake as if outward religion were absolutely nothing, as if it had no place in the religion of Christ. It is not surprising at all, if they should not always have expressed themselves with sufficient caution; so that unwary hearers might believe they condemned all outward means, as altogether unprofitable, and as not designed of God to be the

---

[13] "Your in conscience;" so the author of the old Kentish *Poema Morale* says: *Elch man sceal him then biclupien and eacch sceal him demen; His aye weorc and his ithanc to witnesse he sceal temen,* which is, being interpreted, Every man shall accuse himself there, and every man shall judge himself; His own work and his conscience he shall bring to witness.

"See! See! He cometh!" One of Wesley's finest and most impassioned perorations.

* [text of the 1872 edition]

ordinary channels of conveying his grace into the souls of men.

Nay, it is not impossible, some of these holy men did, at length, themselves fall into this opinion; in particular those who, not by choice, but by the providence of God, were cut off from all these ordinances; perhaps wandering up and down, having no certain abiding-place, or dwelling in dens and caves of the earth. These, experiencing the grace of God in themselves, though they were deprived of all outward means, might infer that the same grace would be given to them who of set purpose abstained from them.

6. And experience shows how easily this notion spreads, and insinuates itself into the minds of men; especially of those who are throughly awakened out of the sleep of death, and begin to feel the weight of their sins a burden too heavy to be borne. These are usually impatient of their present state; and, trying every way to escape from it, they are always ready to catch at any new thing, any new proposal of ease or happiness. They have probably tried most outward means, and found no ease in them; it may be, more and more of remorse, and fear, and sorrow, and condemnation. It is easy, therefore, to persuade these, that it is better for them to abstain from all those means. They are already weary of striving (as it seems) in vain, of labouring in the fire; and are therefore glad of any pretence to cast aside that wherein their soul has no pleasure, to give over the painful strife, and sink down into an indolent inactivity.

II. 1. In the following discourse, I propose to examine at large, whether there are any means of grace.

By "means of grace" I understand outward signs, words, or actions, ordained of God, and appointed for this end, to be the ordinary channels whereby he might convey to men, preventing, justifying, or sanctifying grace.

I use this expression, means of grace, because I know none better; and because it has been generally used in the Christian church for many ages;—in particular by our own Church, which directs us to bless God both for the means of grace, and hope of glory; and teaches us, that a sacrament is "an outward sign of inward grace, and a means whereby we receive the same."

The chief of these means are prayer, whether in secret or with the great congregation; searching the Scriptures; (which implies reading, hearing, and meditating thereon;) and receiving the Lord's Supper, eating bread and drinking wine in remembrance of Him: And these we believe to be ordained of God, as the ordinary channels of conveying his grace to the souls of men.

2. But we allow, that the whole value of the means depends on their actual subservience to the end of religion; that, consequently, all these means, when separate from the end, are less than nothing and vanity; that if they do not actually conduce to the knowledge and love of God, they are not acceptable in his sight; yea, rather, they are an abomination before him, a stink in his nostrils; he is weary to bear them. Above all, if they are used as a kind of *commutation* for the religion they were designed to subserve, it is not easy to find words for the enormous folly and wickedness of thus turning God's arms against himself; of keeping Christianity out of the heart by those very means which were ordained for the bringing it in.

3. We allow, likewise, that all outward means whatever, if separate from the Spirit of God, cannot profit at all, cannot conduce, in any degree, either to the knowledge or love of God. Without controversy, the help that is done upon earth, He doeth it himself. It is He alone who, by his own almighty power, worketh in us what is pleasing in his sight; and all outward things, unless He work in them and by them, are mere weak and beggarly elements. Whosoever, therefore, imagines there is any intrinsic power in any means whatsoever, does greatly err, not knowing the Scriptures, neither the power of God. We know that there is no inherent power in the words that are spoken in prayer, in the letter of Scripture read, the sound thereof heard, or the bread and wine received in the Lord's Supper; but that it is God alone who is the Giver of every good gift, the Author of all grace; that the whole power is of him, whereby, through any of these, there is any blessing conveyed to our soul. We know, likewise, that he is able to give the same grace, though there were no means on the face of the earth. In this sense, we may affirm, that, with regard to God, there is no such thing as means; seeing he is equally able to work whatsoever pleaseth him, by any, or by none at all.

4. We allow farther, that the use of all means whatever will never atone for one sin; that it is the blood of Christ alone, whereby any sinner can be reconciled to God; there being no other propitiation for our sins, no other fountain for sin and uncleanness. Every believer in Christ is deeply convinced that there is no merit but in Him; that there is no merit in any of his own works; not in uttering the prayer, or searching the Scripture, or hearing the word of God, or eating of that bread and drinking of that cup. So that if no more be intended by the expression some have used, "Christ is the only means of grace," than this,—that He is the only meritorious cause of it, it cannot be gainsayed by any who know the grace of God.

5. Yet once more: We allow, though it is a melancholy truth, that a large proportion of those who are called Christians, do to this day abuse the means of grace to the destruction of their souls. This is doubtless the case with all those who rest content in the form of godliness, without the power. Either they fondly presume they are Christians already, because they do thus and thus,—although Christ was never yet revealed in their hearts, nor the love of God shed abroad therein:—Or else they suppose they shall infallibly be so barely because they use these means; idly dreaming, (though perhaps hardly conscious thereof,) either that there is some kind of *power* therein, whereby, sooner or later, (they know not when,) they shall certainly be made holy; or that there is a sort of *merit* in using them, which will surely move God to give them holiness, or accept them without it.

6. So little do they understand that great foundation of the whole Christian building, "By grace are ye saved:" Ye are saved from your sins, from the guilt and power thereof, ye are restored to the favour and image of God, not for any works, merits, or deservings of yours, but by the free grace, the mere mercy of God, through the merits of his well-beloved Son: Ye are thus saved, not by any power, wisdom, or strength,

which is in you, or in any other creature; but merely through the grace or power of the Holy Ghost, which worketh all in all.

7. But the main question remains: "We know this salvation is the gift and the work of God; but how (may one say who is convinced he hath it not) may I attain thereto?" If you say, "Believe, and thou shalt be saved!" he answers, "True; but how shall I believe?" You reply, "Wait upon God." "Well; but how am I to wait? In the means of grace, or out of them? Am I to wait for the grace of God which bringeth salvation, by using these means, or by laying them aside?"

8. It cannot possibly be conceived, that the word of God should give no direction in so important a point; or, that the Son of God, who came down from heaven for us men and for our salvation, should have left us undetermined with regard to a question wherein our salvation is so nearly concerned.

And, in fact, he hath not left us undetermined; he hath shown us the way wherein we should go. We have only to consult the oracles of God; to inquire what is written there; and, if we simply abide by their decision, there can no possible doubt remain.

III. 1. According to this, according to the decision of holy writ all who desire the grace of God are to wait for it in the means which he hath ordained; in using, not in laying them aside.

And, First, all who desire the grace of God are to wait for it in the way of prayer. This is the express direction of our Lord himself. In his Sermon upon the Mount, after explaining at large wherein religion consists, and describing the main branches of it, he adds, "Ask, and it shall be given you; seek, and ye shall find; knock, and it shall be opened unto you: For everyone that asketh receiveth; and he that seeketh findeth; and to him that knocketh it shall be opened." (Matt. 7:7, 8.) Here we are in the plainest manner directed to ask, in order to, or as a means of, receiving; to seek, in order to find, the grace of God, the pearl of great price; and to knock, to continue asking and seeking, if we would enter into his kingdom.

2. That no doubt might remain, our Lord labours this point in a more peculiar manner. He appeals to every man's own heart: "What man is there of you, who, if his son ask bread, will give him a stone? Or, if he ask a fish, will he give him a serpent? If ye then, being evil, know how to give good gifts unto your children, how much more shall your Father which is in heaven," the Father of angels and men, the Father of the spirits of all flesh, "give good things to them that ask him?" (Matt. 7:9–11.) Or, as he expresses himself on another occasion, including all good things in one, "How much more shall your heavenly Father give the Holy Spirit to them that ask him?" (Luke 11:13.) It should be particularly observed here, that the persons directed to ask had not then received the Holy Spirit: Nevertheless our Lord directs them to use this means, and promises that it should be effectual; that upon asking they should receive the Holy Spirit, from him whose mercy is over all his works.

3. The absolute necessity of using this means, if we would receive any gift from God, yet farther appears from that remarkable passage which immediately precedes these words: "And he said unto them," whom he had just been teaching how to pray, "Which of you shall have a friend, and shall go unto him at midnight, and shall say unto him, Friend, lend me three loaves: And he from within shall answer, Trouble me not; I cannot rise and give thee. I say unto you, though he will not rise and give him, because he is his friend, yet because of his importunity, he will rise, and give him as many as he needeth. And I say unto you, Ask, and it shall be given you." (Luke 11:5, 7–9.) "Though he will not give him, because he is his friend, yet because of his importunity he will rise and give him as many as he needeth." How could our blessed Lord more plainly declare, that we may receive of God, by this means, by importunately asking, what otherwise we should not receive at all?

4. "He spake also another parable, to this end, that men ought always to pray, and not to faint," till through this means they should receive of God whatsoever petition they asked of him: "There was in a city a judge which feared not God, neither regarded man. And there was a widow in that city, and she came unto him, saying, Avenge me of my adversary. And he would not for a while; but afterward he said within himself, Though I fear not God, nor regard man, yet because this widow troubleth me, I will avenge her, lest, by her continual coming, she weary me." (Luke 18:1–5.) The application of this our Lord himself hath made: "Hear what the unjust judge saith!" Because she continues to ask, because she will take no denial, therefore I will avenge her. "And shall not God avenge his own elect, which cry day and night unto him? I tell you he will avenge them speedily," if they pray and faint not.

5. A direction, equally full and express, to wait for the blessings of God in private prayer, together with a positive promise, that, by this means, we shall obtain the request of our lips, he hath given us in those well-known words: "Enter into thy closet, and, when thou hast shut thy door, pray to thy Father which is in secret; and thy Father, which seeth in secret, shall reward thee openly." (Matt. 6:6.)

6. If it be possible for any direction to be more clear, it is that which God hath given us by the Apostle, with regard to prayer of every kind, public or private, and the blessing annexed thereto: "If any of you lack wisdom, let him ask of God, that giveth to all men liberally," (if they ask; otherwise "ye have not, because ye ask not," (James 4:2,) "and upbraideth not; and it shall be given him." (James 1:5).

If it be objected, "But this is no direction to unbelievers; to them who know not the pardoning grace of God: For the Apostle adds, 'But let him ask in faith;' otherwise, 'let him not think that he shall receive any thing of the Lord:' " I answer, The meaning of the word *faith*, in this place, is fixed by the Apostle himself, as if it were on purpose to obviate this objection, in the following: "Let him ask in faith, nothing wavering," nothing *doubting, meden dikrinomenos*. Not doubting but God heareth his prayer, and will fulfil the desire of his heart.

The gross, blasphemous absurdity of supposing *faith*, in this place, to be taken in the full Christian meaning, appears hence: It is supposing the holy Ghost to direct a man who knows he has not faith, (which is here termed *wisdom*,) to ask it of God, with a positive promise that it shall be given him; and then immediately to subjoin, that it shall not be given him, unless he have it before he asks for it! But who can bear such a supposition? From this scripture, therefore, as well as those cited above, we must infer, that all who desire the grace of God are to wait for it in the way of prayer.

7. Secondly. All who desire the grace of God are to wait for it in searching the Scriptures.

our Lords direction, with regard to the use of this means, is likewise plain and clear. Search the Scriptures, saith he to the unbelieving Jews, for they testify of me. (John 5:39.) And for this very end did he direct them to search the Scriptures, that they might believe in him.

The objection, that "this is not a command, but only an assertion, that they did search the Scriptures," is shamelessly false. I desire those who urge it, to let us know how a command can be more clearly expressed, than in those terms, *ereunate tas graphas*. It is as peremptory as so many words can make it.

And what a blessing from God attends the use of this means, appears from what is recorded concerning the Bereans; who, after hearing St. Paul, "searched the Scriptures daily, whether those things were so. Therefore many of them believed;" found the grace of God, in the way which he had ordained. (Acts 17:11, 12.)

It is probable, indeed, that in some of those who had "received the word with all readiness of mind," "faith came," as the same Apostle speaks, "by hearing," and was only confirmed by reading the Scriptures: But it was observed above, that under the general term of searching the Scriptures, both hearing, reading, and meditating are contained.

8. And that this is a means whereby God not only gives, but also confirms and increases, true wisdom, we learn from the words of St. Paul to Timothy: "From a child thou hast known the holy Scriptures, which are able to make thee wise unto salvation through faith which is in Christ Jesus." (2 Tim. 3:15.) The same truth (namely, that this is the great means God has ordained for conveying his manifold grace to man) is delivered, in the fullest manner that can be conceived, in the words which immediately follow: "All Scripture is given by inspiration of God;" consequently, all Scripture is infallibly true; "and is profitable for doctrine, for reproof, for correction, for instruction in righteousness;" to the end "that the man of God may be perfect, throughly furnished unto all good works." (2 Tim. 3:16, 17.)

9. It should be observed, that this is spoken primarily and directly of the Scriptures which Timothy had known from a child; which must have been those of the old Testament, for the New was not then wrote. how far then was St. Paul (though he was "not a whit behind the very chief of the Apostles," nor, therefore, I presume, behind any man now upon earth) from making light of the old Testament! Behold this, lest ye one day "wonder and perish," ye who make so small account of one half of the oracles of God! Yea, and that half of which the Holy Ghost expressly declares, that it is "profitable," as a means ordained of God, for this very thing, "for doctrine, for reproof, for correction, for instruction in righteousness;" to the end, "the man of God may be perfect, throughly furnished unto all good works."

10. Nor is this profitable only for the men of God, for those who walk already in the light of his countenance; but also for those who are yet in darkness, seeking him whom they know not. Thus St. Peter, "We have also a more sure word of prophecy:" Literally, "And we have the prophetic word more sure;" *Kai echomen bebaioteron ton prophetikon logon*, confirmed by our being eye-witnesses of his Majesty, and hearing the voice which came from the excellent glory; unto which prophetic word; so he styles the holy Scriptures—ye do well that ye take heed, as unto a light that shineth in a dark place, until the day dawn, and the Day-star arise in your hearts. (2 Peter 1:19.) Let all, therefore, who desire that day to dawn upon their hearts, wait for it in searching the Scriptures.

11. Thirdly. All who desire an increase of the grace of God are to wait for it in partaking of the Lords Supper: For this also is a direction himself hath given. "The same night in which he was betrayed, he took bread, and brake it, and said, Take, eat; this is my body;" that is, the sacred sign of my body: "This do in remembrance of me." Likewise, "he took the cup, saying, This cup is the new testament," or covenant, "in my blood;" the sacred sign of that covenant; "this do ye in remembrance of me." "For as often as ye eat this bread, and drink this cup, ye do show forth the Lords death till he come:" (1 Cor. 11:23) Ye openly exhibit the same by, these visible signs, before God, and angels, and men; ye manifest your solemn remembrance of his death, till he cometh in the clouds of heaven.

only "let a man" first "examine himself," whether he understand the nature and design of this holy institution, and whether he really desire to be himself made conformable to the death of Christ; and so, nothing doubting, "let him eat of that bread, and drink of that cup." (1 Cor. 11:28.) Here, then, the direction first given by our Lord is expressly repeated by the Apostle: "Let him eat; let him drink;" *esthieto, pineto*, both in the imperative mood;) words not implying a bare permission only, but a clear, explicit command; a command to all those either who already are filled with peace and joy in believing, or who can truly say, "The remembrance of our sins is grievous unto us, the burden of them is intolerable."

12. And that this is also an ordinary, stated means of receiving the grace of God, is evident from those words of the Apostle, which occur in the preceding chapter: "The cup of blessing which we bless, is it not the communion," or *communication*, "of the blood of Christ? The bread which we break, is it not the communion of the body of Christ?" (1 Cor. 10:16.) Is not the eating of that bread, and the drinking of that cup, the outward, visible means, whereby God conveys into our souls all that spiritual grace, that righteousness, and peace, and joy in the Holy Ghost, which were purchased by the body of Christ once broken and the blood of Christ once shed for us? Let all, therefore, who truly desire the grace of God, eat of that bread, and drink of that cup.

IV. 1. But as plainly as God hath pointed out the way wherein he will be inquired after, innumerable are the objections which men, wise in their own eyes, have, from time to time, raised against it. It may be needful to consider a few of these; not because they are of weight in themselves, but because they have so often been used, especially of late years, to turn the lame out of the way; yea, to trouble and subvert those who did run well, till Satan appeared as an angel of light.

The first and chief of these is, "You cannot use these means (as you call them) without *trusting* in them." I pray, where is this written? I expect you should show me plain Scripture for your assertion: Otherwise I dare not receive it; because I am not convinced that you are wiser than God.

If it really had been as you assert, it is certain Christ must have known it. And if he had known it, he would surely have warned us; he would have revealed it long ago. Therefore, because he has not, because there is no tittle of this in the whole revelation of Jesus Christ, I am as fully assured your assertion is false, as that this revelation is of God.

"However, leave them off for a short time, to see whether you trusted in them or no." So I am to disobey God, in order to know whether I trust in obeying him! And do you avow this advice? Do you deliberately teach to "do evil, that good may come?" O tremble at the sentence of God against such teachers! Their "damnation is just."

"Nay, if you are troubled when you leave them off, it is plain you trusted in them." By no means. If I am troubled when I wilfully disobey God, it is plain his Spirit is still striving with me; but if I am not troubled at wilful sin, it is plain I am given up to a reprobate mind.

But what do you mean by *"trusting* in them?"—looking for the blessing of God therein? believing, that if I wait in this way, I shall attain what otherwise I should not? So I do. And so I will, God being my helper, even to my life's end. By the grace of God I will *thus* trust in them, till the day of my death; that is, I will believe, that whatever God hath promised, he is faithful also to perform. And seeing he hath promised to bless me in this way, I *trust* it shall be according to his word.

2. It has been, Secondly, objected, "This is seeking salvation by works." Do you know the meaning of the expression you use? What is seeking salvation by works? In the writings of St. Paul, it means, either seeking to be saved by observing the ritual works of the Mosaic law; or expecting salvation for the sake of our own works, by the merit of our own righteousness. But how is either of these implied in my waiting in the way God has ordained, and expecting that he will meet me there, because he has promised so to do?

I do expect that he will fulfil his word, that he will meet and bless me in this way. Yet not for the sake of any works which I have done, nor for the merit of my righteousness; but merely through the merits, and sufferings, and love of his Son, in whom he is always well pleased.

3. It has been vehemently objected, Thirdly, "that Christ is the only means of grace." I answer, this is mere playing upon words. Explain your term, and the objection vanishes away. When we say, "Prayer is a means of grace," we understand a channel through which the grace of God is conveyed. When you say, "Christ is the means of grace," you understand the sole price and purchaser of it; or, that "no man cometh unto the Father, but through him." And who denies it? But this is utterly wide of the question.

4. "But does not the Scripture" (it has been objected, Fourthly) "direct us to *wait* for salvation? Does not David say, 'My soul waiteth upon God, for of him cometh my salvation?' And does not Isaiah teach us the same thing, saying, 'O Lord, we have waited for thee?' " All this cannot be denied. Seeing it is the gift of God, we are undoubtedly to *wait* on him for salvation. But how shall we wait? If God himself has appointed a way, can you find a better way of waiting for him? But that he hath appointed a way hath been shown at large, and also what that way is. The very words of the Prophet, which you cite, put this out of the question. For the whole sentence runs thus:—"In the way of thy judgments," or ordinances, "O Lord, have we waited for thee." (Isaiah 26:8.) And in the very same way did David wait, as his own words abundantly testify: "I have waited for thy saving health, O Lord, and have kept thy law. Teach me, O Lord, the way of thy statutes, and I shall to keep it unto the end."

5. "Yea," say some, "but God has appointed another way.— 'Stand still, and see the salvation of God.' "

Let us examine the Scriptures to which you refer. The first of them, with the context, runs thus:—

"And when Pharaoh drew nigh, the children of Israel lifted up their eyes; and they were sore afraid. And they said unto Moses, Because there were no graves in Egypt, hast thou taken us away to die in the wilderness? And Moses said unto the people, Fear ye not; stand still, and see the salvation of the Lord. And the Lord said unto Moses, Speak unto the children of Israel that they go forward. But lift thou up thy rod, and stretch out thine hand over the sea, and divide it. And the children of Israel shall go on dry ground through the midst of the sea." (Exod. 14:10)

This was the *salvation of God*, which they *stood still* to see, by *marching forward* with all their might!

The other passage, wherein this expression occurs stands thus: "There came some that told Jehoshaphat, saying, There cometh a great multitude against thee, from beyond the sea. And Jehoshaphat feared, and set himself to seek the Lord, and proclaimed a fast throughout all Judah. And Judah gathered themselves together to ask help of the Lord: Even out of all the cities they came to seek the Lord. And Jehoshaphat stood in the congregation, in the house of the Lord.—Then upon Jahaziel came the Spirit of the Lord. And he said, Be not dismayed by reason of this great multitude. To-morrow go ye down against them: Ye shall not need to fight in this battle. Set yourselves: Stand ye still, and see the salvation of the Lord. And they rose early in the morning, and went forth. And when they began to sing and to praise, the Lord set ambushments against the children of Moab, Ammon, and mount Seir:—and everyone helped to destroy another." (2 Chron. 20:2)

Such was the salvation which the children of Judah saw. But how does all this prove, that we ought not to wait for the grace of God in the means which he hath ordained?

6. I shall mention but one objection more, which, indeed, does not properly belong to this head: Nevertheless, because it has been so frequently urged, I may not wholly pass it by. "Does not St. Paul say, 'If ye be dead with Christ, why are ye subject to ordinances?' (Col. 2:20.) Therefore a Christian, one that is dead with Christ, need not use the ordinances any more."

So you say, "If I am a Christian, I am not subject to the ordinances of Christ!" Surely, by the absurdity of this, you must see at the first glance, that the ordinances here mentioned cannot be the ordinances of Christ: That they must needs be the Jeish ordinances, to which it is certain a Christian is no longer subject.

And the same undeniably appears from the words immediately following, "Touch not, taste not, handle not;" all evidently referring to the ancient ordinances of the Jewish law.

So that this objection is the weakest of all. And, in spite of all, that great truth must stand unshaken;—that all who desire the grace of God, are to wait for it in the means which he hath ordained.

V. 1. But this being allowed, that all who desire the grace of God are to wait for it in the means he hath ordained; it may still be inquired, how those means should be used, both as to the order and the manner of using them.

With regard to the former, we may observe, there is a kind of order, wherein God himself is generally pleased to use these means in bringing a sinner to salvation. A stupid, senseless wretch is going on in his own way, not having God in all his thoughts, when God comes upon him unawares, perhaps by an awakening sermon or conversation, perhaps by some awful providence, or, it may be, an immediate stroke of his convincing Spirit, without any outward means at all. Having now a desire to flee from the wrath to come, he purposely goes to *hear* how it may be done. If he finds a preacher who speaks to the heart, he is amazed, and begins searching the Scriptures, whether these things are so? The more he *hears* and *reads*, the more convinced he is; and the more he meditates thereon day and night. Perhaps he finds some other book which explains and enforces what he has heard and read in Scripture. And by all these means, the arrows of conviction sink deeper into his! soul. He begins also to *talk* of the things of God, which are ever uppermost in his thoughts; yea, and to talk with God; to *pray* to him; although, through fear and shame, he scarce knows what to say. But whether he can speak or no, he cannot but pray, were it only in "groans which cannot be uttered." Yet, being in doubt, whether "the high and lofty One that inhabiteth eternity" will regard such a sinner as him, he wants to pray with those who know God, with the faithful, in the great congregation. But here he observes others go up to the table of the Lord. He considers, "Christ has said, 'Do this!' How is it that I do not? I am too great a sinner. I am not fit. I am not worthy." After struggling with these scruples a while, he breaks through. And thus he continues in God's way, in hearing, reading, meditating, praying, and partaking of the Lord's Supper, till God, in the manner that pleases him, speaks to his heart, "Thy faith hath saved thee. Go in peace."

2. By observing this order of God, we may learn what means to recommend to any particular soul. If any of these will reach a stupid, careless sinner, it is probably hearing, or conversation. To such, therefore, we might recommend these, if he has ever any thought about salvation. To one who begins to feel the weight of his sins, not only hearing the Word of God, but reading it too, and perhaps other serious books, may be a means of deeper conviction. May you not advise him also, to meditate on what he reads, that it may have its full force upon his heart? Yea, and to speak thereof, and not be ashamed, particularly among those who walk in the same path. When trouble and heaviness take hold upon him, should you not then earnestly exhort him to pour out his soul before God; "always to pray and not to faint;" and when he feels the worthlessness of his own prayers, are you not to work together with God, and remind him of going up into the house of the Lord, and praying with all! that fear him? But if he does this, the dying word of his Lord will soon be brought to his remembrance; a plain intimation that this is the time when we should second the motions of the blessed Spirit. And thus may we lead him, step by step, through all the means which God has ordained; not according to our own will, but just as the Providence and the Spirit of God go before and open the way.

3. Yet, as we find no command in holy writ for any particular order to be observed herein, so neither do the providence and the Spirit of god adhere to any without variation; but the means into which different men are led, and in which they find the blessing of God, are varied, transposed, and combined together, a thousand different ways. Yet still our wisdom is to follow the leadings of his providence and his Spirit; to be guided herein, (more especially as to the means wherein we ourselves seek the grace of God,) partly by his outward providence, giving us the opportunity of using sometimes one means, sometimes another, partly by our experience, which it is whereby his free Spirit is pleased most to work in our heart. And in the mean time, the sure and general rule for all who groan for the salvation of God is this,—whenever opportunity serves, use all the means which God has ordained; for who knows in which God will meet thee with the grace that bringeth salvation?

4. As to the manner of using them, whereon indeed it wholly depends whether they should convey any grace at all to the user; it behoves us, First, always to retain a lively sense, that God is above all means. Have a care, therefore, of limiting the Almighty. He doeth whatsoever and whensoever it pleaseth him. He can convey his grace, either in or out of any of the means which he hath appointed. Perhaps he will. "Who hath known the mind of the Lord? or who hath been his counsellor?" Look then every moment for his appearing! Be it at the hour you are employed in his ordinances; or before, or after that hour; or when you are hindered therefrom: He is not hindered. He is always ready, always able, always willing to save. "It is the Lord: Let him do what seemeth him good!"

Secondly. Before you use any means, let it be deeply impressed on your soul;—there is no *power* in this. It is, in itself, a poor, dead, empty thing: Separate from God, it is a dry leaf, a shadow. Neither is there any *merit* in my using this; nothing intrinsically pleasing to God; nothing whereby I deserve any favour at his hands, no, not a drop of water to cool my tongue. But, because God bids, therefore I do; because he directs me to wait in this way, therefore here I wait for his free mercy, whereof cometh my salvation.

Settle this in your heart, that the *opus operatum*, the mere *work done*, profiteth nothing; that there is no *power* to save, but in the Spirit of God, no *merit*, but in the blood of Christ; that, consequently, even what God ordains, conveys no grace to the soul, if you trust not in Him alone. On the other hand, he that does truly trust in Him, cannot fall short of the grace of God, even though he were cut off from every outward ordinance, though he were shut up in the centre of the earth.

Thirdly. In using all means, seek God alone. In and through every outward thing, look singly to the *power* of his Spirit; and the *merits* of his Son. Beware you do not stick in the *work* itself; if you do, it is all lost labour. Nothing short of God can satisfy your soul. Therefore, eye him in all, through all, and above all.

Remember also, to use all means, *as means*; as ordained, not for their own sake, but in order to the renewal of your soul in righteousness and true holiness. If, therefore, they actually tend to this, well; but if not, they are dung and dross.

Lastly. After you have used any of these, take care how you value yourself thereon: How you congratulate yourself as having done some great thing. This is turning all into poison. Think, "If God was not there, what does this avail? Have I not been adding sin to sin? How long? O Lord! save, or I perish! O lay not this sin to my charge!" If God was there, if his love flowed into your heart, you have forgot, as it were, the outward work. You see, you know, you feel, God is all in all. Be abased. Sink down before him. Give him all the praise. "Let God in all things be glorified through Christ Jesus". Let all your bones cry out," My song shall be always of the loving-kindness of the Lord: With my mouth will I ever be telling of thy truth, from one generation to another!"

17.* THE CIRCUMCISION OF THE HEART*

"Circumcision is that of the heart, in the spirit, and not in the letter."

Romans 2:29.

1. It is the melancholy remark of an excellent man, that he who now preaches the most essential duties of Christianity, runs the hazard of being esteemed, by a great part of his hearers, "a setter forth of new doctrines." Most men have so *lived away* the substance of that religion, the profession whereof they still retain, that no sooner are any of those truths proposed which difference the Spirit of Christ from the spirit of the world, than they cry out, "Thou bringest strange things to our ears; we would know what these things mean:"—Though he is only preaching to them "Jesus and the resurrection," with the necessary consequence of it,—If

Christ be risen, ye ought then to die unto the world, and to live wholly unto God.

2. A hard saying this to the natural man, Who is alive unto the world, and dead unto God; and one that he will not readily be persuaded to receive as the truth of God, unless it be so qualified in the interpretation, as to have neither use nor significance left. He "receiveth not the" word "of the Spirit of God," taken in their plain and obvious meaning; "they are foolishness unto him: Neither" indeed "can he know them, because they are spiritually discerned:"—They are perceivable only by that spiritual sense, which in him was never yet awakened for want of which he must reject, as idle fancies of men, what are both the wisdom and the power of God.

3. That "circumcision is that of the heart, in the spirit, and not in the letter;"—that the distinguishing mark of a true follower of Christ, of one who is in a state of acceptance with God, is not either outward circumcision, or baptism, or any other outward form, but a right state of soul, a mind and spirit renewed after the image of Him that created it;—is one of those important truths that can only be spiritually discerned. And this the Apostle himself intimates in the next words,—"Whose praise is not of men, but of God." As if he had said, "Expect not, whoever thou art, who thus followest thy great Master, that the world, the one who follow him not, will say, 'Well done, good and faithful servant!' Know that the circumcision of the heart, the seal of thy calling, is foolishness with the world. Be content to wait for thy applause till the day of thy Lord's appearing. In that day shalt thou have praise of God, in the great assembly of men and angels."

I design First, particularly to inquire, wherein this circumcision of the heart consists; and, Secondly, to mention some reflections that naturally arise from such an inquiry.

I. 1. I am, First, to inquire, wherein that circumcision of the heart consists, which will receive the praise of God. In general we may observe, it is that habitual disposition of soul which, in the sacred writings, is termed holiness; and which directly implies, the being cleansed from sin, "from all filthiness both of flesh and spirit;" and, by consequence, the being endued with those virtues which were also in Christ Jesus; the being so "renewed in the spirit of our mind," as to be "perfect as our Father in heaven is perfect."

2. To be more particular: Circumcision of heart implies humility, faith, hope, and charity. Humility, a right judgment of ourselves, cleanses our minds from those high conceits of our own perfection, from that undue opinion of our own abilities and attainments, which are the genuine fruit of a corrupted nature. This entirely cuts off that vain thought, "I am rich, and wise, and have need of nothing;" and convinces us that we are by nature wretched, and poor, and miserable, and blind, and naked. "It convinces us, that in our best estate we are, of ourselves, all sin and vanity; that confusion, and ignorance, and error reign over our understanding; that unreasonable, earthly, sensual, devilish passions usurp authority over our will; in a word, that there

---

* (text from the 1872 edition)

is no whole part in our soul, that all the foundations of our nature are out of course.

3. At the same time we are convinced, that we are not sufficient of ourselves to help ourselves; that, without the Spirit of God, we can do nothing but add sin to sin; that it is He alone who worketh in us by his almighty power, either to will or do that which is good; it being as impossible for us even to think a good thought, without the supernatural assistance of his Spirit, as to create ourselves, or to renew our whole souls in righteousness and true holiness.

4. A sure effect of our having formed this right judgment of the sinfulness and helplessness of our nature, is a disregard of that "honor which cometh of man," which is usually paid to some supposed excellency in us. He who knows himself, neither desires nor values the applause which he knows he deserves not. It is therefore "a very small thing with him, to be judged by man's judgment." He has all reason to think, by comparing what it has said, either for or against him, with what he feels in his own breast, that the world, as well as the god of this world, was "a liar form the beginning." And even as to those who are not of the world; thought he would choose, if it were the will of God, that they should account of him as of one desirous to be found a faithful steward of his Lord's goods, if haply this might be a means of enabling him to be of more use to his fellow-servants, yet as this is the one end of his wishing for their approbation, so he does not at all rest upon it: For he is assured, that whatever God wills, he can never want instruments to perform; since he is able, even of these stones, to raise up servants to do his pleasure.

5. this is that lowliness of mind, which they have learned of Christ, who follow his example and tread in his steps. And this knowledge of their disease, whereby they are more and more cleansed from one part of it, pride and vanity, disposes them to embrace, with a willing mind, the second thing implied in circumcision of the heart,—that faith which alone is able to make them whole, which is the one medicine given under heaven to heal their sickness.

6. The best guide of the blind, the surest light of them that are in darkness, the most perfect instructor of the foolish, is faith. But it must be such a faith as is "mighty through God, to the pulling down of strong-holds,"—to the overturning all the prejudices of corrupt reason, all the false maxims revered among men, all evil customs and habits, all that "wisdom of the world which is foolishness with God;" as "casteth down imaginations," reasoning, "and every high thing that exalteth itself against the knowledge of God, and bringeth into captivity every thought to the obedience of Christ."

7. "All things are possible to him that" thus "believeth." "The eyes of his understanding being enlightened," he sees what is his calling; even to glorify God, who hath bought him with so high a price, in his body and in his spirit, which now are God's by redemption, as well as by creation. He feels what is "the exceeding greatness of this power," who, as he raise up Christ from the dead, so is able to-quicken us, dead in sin," by his Spirit which dwelleth in us." "This is the victory which overcometh the world, even our faith;" that faith, which is not only an unshaken assent to all that God hath revealed in Scripture,—and in particular to those important truths, "Jesus Christ came into the world to save sinners;" "He bare our sins in his own body on the tree;" "He is the propitiation for our sins, and not for ours only, but also for the sins of the whole world;" *—but likewise the revelation of Christ in our hearts; a divine evidence or conviction of his love, his free, unmerited love to me a sinner; a sure confidence in his pardoning mercy, wrought in us by the Holy Ghost; a confidence, whereby every true believer is enabled to bear witness, "I know that my Redeemer liveth," that I have an "Advocate with the Father," and that "Jesus Christ the righteous" is my Lord, and "the propitiation for my sins,"—I know he hath "loved me, and given himself for me,"—He hath reconciled me, even me, to God; and I "have redemption through his blood, even the forgiveness of sins."

8. Such a faith as this cannot fail to show evidently the power of Him that inspires it, by delivering his children from the yoke of sin, and "purging their consciences from dead works;" by strengthening them so, that they are no longer constrained to obey sin in the desires there of; but instead of yielding their members unto it, as instruments of unrighteousness," they now "yield themselves" entirely "unto God, as those that are alive from the dead."

9. Those who are thus by faith born of God, have also strong consolation through hope. This is the next thing which the circumcision of the heart implies; even the testimony of their own spirit with the Spirit which witnesses in their hearts that* they are the children of God. Indeed it is the same Spirit who works in them that clear and cheerful confidence that their heart is upright toward God; that good assurance, that they now do, through his grace, the things which are acceptable in his sight; that they are now in the path which leadeth to life, and shall, by the mercy of God, endure therein to the end. It is He who giveth them a lively expectation of receiving all good things at God's hand; a joyous prospect of that crown of glory, which is reserved in heaven for them. By this anchor a Christian is kept steady in the midst of the waves of this troublesome world, and preserved from striking upon either of those fatal rocks,—presumption or despair. He is neither discouraged by the misconceived severity of his Lord, nor does He despise the riches of his goodness." He neither apprehends the difficulties of the race set before him to be greater than he has strength to conquer, nor expects there to be so little as to yield in the conquest, till he has put forth all strength. The experience he already has in the Christian warfare, as it assures him his "labor is not in vain," if "whatever his findeth to do, he doeth it with his might;" so it forbids his entertaining so vain a thought, as that he can otherwise gain any advantage, as that any virtue can be shown, any praise attained, by faint hearts and feeble hands; or, indeed, by any but those who pursue the same course with the great Apostle of the Gentiles—"I," says he, "so run, not as uncertainly; so fight I, not as one that beateth the air: But

* N. B. The following part of this paragraph is now added to the Sermon formerly preached.

I keep under my body, and bring it into subjection; lest, by any means, when I have preached to others, I myself should be a castaway." 10. By the same discipline is every good soldier of Christ to inure himself to endure hardship. Confirmed and strengthened by this, he will be able not only to renounce the works of darkness, but every appetite too, and every affection, which is no subject to the law of God. For "every one," saith St. John, "who hath this hope, purifieth himself even as He is pure." It is his daily care, by the grace of God in Christ, and through the blood of the covenant, to purge the inmost recesses of his soul from the lusts that before possessed and defiled it; from uncleanness, and envy, and malice, and wrath; from every passion and temper that is after the flesh, that either springs from or cherishes his native corruption: as well knowing, that he whose very body is the temple of God, ought to admit into it nothing common or unclean; and that holiness becometh that house for ever, where the Spirit of holiness vouchsafes to dwell. 11. Yet lackest thou one thing, whosoever thou art, that to a deep humility, and a steadfast faith, hast joined a lively hope, and thereby in a good measure cleansed thy heart from its inbred pollution. If thou wilt be perfect, add to all these, charity; add love, and thou hast the circumcision of the heart "Love is the fulfilling of the law, the end of the commandment." Very excellent things are spoken of love; it is the essence, the spirit, the life of all virtue. It is not only the first and great command, but it is all the commandments in one. "Whatsoever things are just, whatsoever things are pure, whatsoever things are amiable," or honorable; "if there be any virtue, if there be any praise," they are all comprised in this one word,—love. In this is perfection, and glory, and happiness. The royal law of heaven and earth is this, "Thou shalt love the Lord thy God with all thy heart, and with all thy soul, and with all thy mind, and with all thy strength." 12. Not that this forbids us to love anything besides God: It implies that we love our brother also. Nor yet does it forbid us (as some have strangely imagined) to take pleasure in any thing but God. To suppose this, is to suppose the Fountain of holiness is directly the author of sin; since he has inseparably annexed pleasure to the use of those creatures, which are necessary to sustain the life he has given us. This, therefore, can never be the meaning of his command. What the real sense of it is, both our blessed Lord and his Apostles tell us too frequently, and too plainly, to be misunderstood. They all with one mouth bear witness, that the true meaning of those several declarations, "The Lord thy God is one Lord;" "Thou shalt have no other Gods but me;" "Thou shalt love the Lord thy God with all thy strength" "Thou shalt cleave unto him;" "The desire of thy soul shall be to His name;"—is no other than this: The one perfect Good shall be your one ultimate end. One thing shall ye desire for its own sake,—the fruition of Him that is All in All. One happiness shall ye propose to your souls, even an union with Him that made them; the having "fellowship with the Father and the Son;" the being joined to the Lord in one Spirit. One design you are to pursue to the end of time,—the enjoyment of God in time and in eternity. Desire other things, so far as they tend to this. Love the creature as it leads to the Creator.

But in every step you take, be this the glorious point that terminates your view. Let every affection, and thought, and word, and work, be subordinate to this. Whatever ye desire or fear, whatever ye seek or shun, whatever ye think, speak, or do, be it in order to your happiness in God, the sole End, as well as Source, of your being. 13. Have no end, to ultimate end, but God. Thus our Lord: "One thing is needful:" And if thine eye be singly fixed on this one thing, "thy whole body shall be full of light." Thus St. Paul: "This one thing I do; I press toward the mark, for the prize of the high calling in Christ Jesus." Thus St. James: "Cleanse your hands, ye sinners, and purify your hearts, ye double-minded." Thus St. John: "love not the world, neither the things that are in the world. For all that is in the world, the lust of the flesh, the lust of the eye, and the pride of life, is not of the Father, but is of the world." The seeking happiness in what gratifies either the desire of the flesh, by agreeably striking upon the outward senses; the desire of the eye, of the imagination, by its novelty, greatness, or beauty; or the pride of life, whether by pomp, grandeur, power, or, the usual consequence of them, applause and admiration;—"is not of the Father," cometh not from, neither is approved by, the Father of spirits; "but of the world:" It is the distinguishing mark of those who will not have Him to reign over them.

II. 1. Thus have I particularly inquired, what that circumcision of heart is, which will obtain the praise of God. I am, in the Second place, to mention some reflections that naturally arise from such an inquiry, as a plain rule whereby every man may judge of himself, whether he be of the world or of God. And, First, it is clear from what has been said, that no man has a title to the praise of God, unless his heart is circumcised by humility; unless he is little, and base, and vile in his own eyes; unless he is deeply convinced of that inbred "corruption of his nature," "whereby he is very far gone from original righteousness," being prone to all evil, averse to all good, corrupt and abominable; having a "carnal mind which is enmity against God, and is not subject to the law of God, nor indeed can be," unless he continually feels in his inmost soul, that without the Spirit of God resting upon him, he can neither think, nor desire, nor speak, nor act anything good, or well-pleasing in his sight. No man I say, has A title to the praise of God, till he feels his want of God; nor indeed, till he seeketh that "honor which cometh of God only;" and neither desires nor pursues that which cometh of man, unless so far only as it tends to this.

2. Another truth, which naturally follows from what has been said, is, that none shall obtain the honor that cometh of God, unless his heart be circumcised by faith; even a "faith of the operation of God:" Unless, refusing to be any longer led by his senses, appetites, or passions, or even by that blind leader of the blind, so idolized by the world, natural reason, he lives and walks by faith; directs every step, as "seeking Him that is invisible;" "looks not at the things that are seen, which are temporal, but at the things that are not seen, which are eternal;" and governs all his desires, designs, and thoughts, all his actions and conversations, as one who is entered in within the veil, where Jesus sits at the right hand of God.

3. It were to be wished, that they were better acquainted with this faith, who employ much of their time and pains in laying another foundation; in grounding religion on the eternal *fitness* of things on the intrinsic *excellence* of virtue, and the *beauty* of actions flowing from it; on the *reasons* as they term them, of good and evil, and the *relations* of beings to each other. Either these accounts of the grounds of Christian duty coincide with the scriptural, or not. If they do, why are well meaning men perplexed, and drawn from the weightier matters of the law, by a cloud of terms, whereby the easiest truths are explained into obscurity? If they are not, then it behooves them to consider who is the author of this new doctrine; whether he is likely to be an angel from heaven, who preacheth another gospel than that of Christ Jesus; though, if he were, God, not we, hath pronounced his sentence: "Let him be accursed."

4. Our gospel, as it knows no other foundation of good works than faith, or of faith than Christ, so it clearly informs us, we are not his disciples while we either deny him to be the Author, or his Spirit to be the Inspirer an Perfecter, both of our faith and works. "If any man have not the spirit of Christ, he is none of his." He alone can quicken those Who are dead unto God, can breathe into them the breath of Christian life. and so prevent, accompany, and follow them with his grace, as to bring their good desires to good effect. And, as many as are thus led by the Spirit of God, they are the sons of God." This is God's short and plain account of true religion and virtue; and "other foundation can no man lay."

5. From what has been said, we may, Thirdly, learn, that it none is truly "led by the Spirit," unless that "Spirit bear witness with his spirit, that he is a child of God;" unless he see the prize and the crown before him, and "rejoice in hope of the glory of God." So greatly have they erred who have taught that, in serving God, we ought not to have a view to own happiness! Nay, but we are often and expressly taught of God, to have "respect unto the recompense of reward;" to balance toil with the "joy set before us," these "light afflictions" with that "exceeding weight of glory." Yea, we are "aliens to the covenant of promise," we are "without God in the world," until God, "of his abundant mercy, hath begotten us again unto a living hope of the inheritance incorruptible, undefiled, and that fadeth not away.

6. But if these things are so, it is high time for those persons to deal faithfully with their own souls who are so far from finding in themselves this joyful assurance that they fulfil the terms, and shall obtain the promises, of that covenant, as to quarrel with the covenant itself, and blaspheme the terms of it; to complain, they are too severe; and that no man ever did or shall live up to them. What is this but to reproach God, as if He were a hard Master, requiring of his servants more than he enables them to perform?—as if he had mocked the helpless works of his hands, by binding them to impossibilities; by commanding them to overcome, where neither their own strength nor grace was sufficient for them.?

7. These blasphemers might almost persuade those to imagine themselves guiltless, who, in the contrary extreme, hope to fulfil the commands of God, without taking any pains at all. Vain hope! that a child of Adam should ever expect to see the kingdom of Christ and of God, without striving, without *agonizing*, first "to enter in at the strait gate;"—that one who v. as "conceived and born in sin," and whose "inward parts are very wickedness," should once entertain a thought of being "purified as his Lord is pure," unless he tread in His steps, and "take up his cross daily;" unless he "cut off His right hand," and "pluck out the right eye, and cast it from him;"—that he should ever dream of shaking off his old opinions, passions, tempers, of being "sanctified throughout in spirit, soul, and body," without a constant and continued course of general self-denial!

8. What lees than this can we possibly infer from the above-cited words of St. Paul, who, living "ill infirmities, in reproaches, in necessities, in persecutions, in distresses" for Christ's sake;—who, being full of "signs, and wonders, and mighty deeds,"—who, having been "caught up into the third heaven;"—yet reckoned, as a late author strongly expresses it, that all his virtues would be insecure, and even his salvation in danger, without this constant self-denial? "So run I," says he, "not as uncertainly; so fight I, not as one that beateth the air which he plainly teaches us, that he who does not thus run, who does not thus deny himself daily, does run uncertainly, and fighteth to as little purpose as he that "beateth the air."

9. To as little purpose does He talk of "fighting the fight of faith," as vainly hope to attain the crown of incorruption, (as we may, Lastly, infer from the preceding observations,) whose heart is not circumcised by love. Love, cutting off both the lust of the flesh, the lust of the eye, and the pride of life,—engaging the whole man, body, soul, and spirit, in the ardent pursuit of that one object,—is so essential to a child of God, that, without it, whosoever liveth is counted dead before him. "Though I speak with the tongues of men and of angels, and have not love, I am as sounding brass, or a tinkling cymbal. Though I have the gift of prophecy, and understand all mysteries, and all knowledge; and though I have all faith, so as to remove mountains, and have not love, I am nothing." Nay, "though I give all my goods to feed the poor, and my body to be burned, and have not love, it profit me nothing."

10. Here, then, is the sum of the perfect law; this is the true circumcision of the heart. Let the spirit return to God that gave it, with the whole train of its affections. "Unto the place from whence all the rivers came thither let them flow again. Other sacrifices from us he would not; but the living sacrifice of the heart he hath chosen. Let it be continual offered up to God through Christ, in flames of holy love. And let no creature be suffered to share with him: For he is a jealous God. His throne will he not divide with another: He will reign without a rival. Be no design, no desire admitted there, but what has Him for its ultimate object. This is the way where in those children of God once walked, who, being dead, still speak to us:" Desire not to live, but to praise his name: Let all your thoughts, words, and works, tend to his glory. Set your heart firm on him, and on other things only as they are in and from him. Let your soul be filled with so entire a love of him, that you may love nothing but for his sake." "Have a pure intention of heart, a steadfast regard to his glory in all your actions." "Fix your eye upon the blessed

hope of your calling, and make all the things of the world minister unto it." For then, and not till then is that "mind in us which was also in Christ Jesus;" when, in every motion of our heart, in every word of our tongue, in every work of our hands, we "pursue nothing but in relation to him, and in subordination to his pleasure;" when we, too, neither think, nor speak, nor act, to fulfil our "own will, but the will of him that sent us;" when, whether we;' eat, or drink, or whatever we do, we do all to the glory of God."

18.* THE MARKS OF THE NEW BIRTH

"So is every one that is born of the Spirit."

John 3:8.

1. How is every one that is "born of the Spirit,"—that is, born again,—born of God? What is meant by the being born again, the being born of God, or being born of the Spirit? What is implied in the being a son or a child of God, or having the Spirit of adoption? That these privileges, by the free mercy of God, are ordinarily annexed to baptism (which is thence termed by our Lord in a preceding verse, the being "born of water and of the Spirit") we know; but we would know what these privileges are: What is the new birth?

2. Perhaps it is not needful to give a definition of this, seeing the Scripture gives none. But as the question is of the deepest concern to every child of man; since, "except a man be born again," born of the Spirit, "he cannot see the kingdom of God;" I propose to lay down the marks of it in the plainest manner, just as I find them laid down in Scripture.

I. 1. The First of these, and the foundation of all the rest, is faith. So St. Paul, "Ye are all the children of God by faith in Christ Jesus." (Gal. 3:26.) So St. John, "To them gave he power" (*exousian, right* or *privilege*, it might rather be translated) to become the sons of God, even to them that believe on his name; which were born, when they believed, not of blood, nor of the will of the flesh, not by natural generation, nor of the will of man, like those children adopted by men, in whom no inward change is thereby wrought, "but of God." (John 1:12, 13.) And again in his General epistle, "Whosoever believeth that Jesus is the Christ is born of God." (1 John 5:1.)

2. But it is not a barely notional or speculative faith that is here spoken of by the Apostles. It is not a bare assent to this proposition, Jesus is the Christ; nor indeed to all the propositions contained in our creed, or in the old and New Testament. It is not merely an assent to any or all these credible things, as credible. To say this, were to say (which who could hear?) that the devils were born of God; for they have this faith. They, trembling, believe, both that Jesus is the Christ, and that all Scripture, having been given by inspiration of God, is true as God is true. It is not only an assent to divine truth, upon the testimony of God, or upon the evidence of miracles; for *they* also heard the words of his mouth, and knew him to be a faithful and true witness. They could not but receive the testimony he gave, both of himself, and of the Father which sent him. They saw likewise the mighty works which he did, and thence believed that he "came forth from God." Yet, notwithstanding this faith, they are still "reserved in chains of darkness unto the judgment of the great day."

3. For all this is no more than a dead faith. The true, living, Christian faith, which whosoever hath, is born of God, is not only an assent, an act of the understanding; but a disposition, which God hath wrought in his heart; "a sure trust and confidence in God, that, through the merits of Christ, his sins are forgiven, and he reconciled to the favour of God." This implies, that a man first renounce himself; that, in order to be "found in Christ," to be accepted through him, he totally rejects all "confidence in the flesh;" that, "having nothing to pay," having no trust in his own works or righteousness of any kind, he comes to God as a lost, miserable, self-destroyed, self-condemned, undone, helpless sinner; as one whose mouth is utterly stopped, and who is altogether "guilty before God." Such a sense of sin, (commonly called despair, by those who speak evil of the things they know not,) together with a full conviction, such as no words can express, that of Christ only cometh our salvation, and an earnest desire of that salvation, must precede a living faith, a trust in him, who "for us paid our ransom by his death, and fulfilled the law of his life." This faith then, whereby we are born of God, is "not only a belief of all the articles of our faith, but also a true confidence of the mercy of God, through our Lord Jesus Christ."

4. An immediate and constant fruit of this faith whereby we are born of God, a fruit which can in no wise be separated from it, no, not for an hour, is power over sin; power over outward sin of every kind; over every evil word and work; for wheresoever the blood of Christ is thus applied, it "purgeth the conscience from dead works;" and over inward sin; for it purifieth the heart from every unholy desire and temper. This fruit of faith St. Paul has largely described, in the sixth chapter of his epistle to the Romans. "how shall we," saith he, "who" by faith "are dead to sin, live any longer therein?" "our old man is crucified with Christ, that the body of sin might be destroyed, that henceforth we should not serve sin."—"Likewise, reckon ye yourselves to be dead unto sin, but alive unto God, through Jesus Christ our Lord. Let not sin therefore reign" even "in your mortal body," "but yield yourselves unto God, as those that are alive from the dead." "For sin shall not have dominion over you.—God be thanked, that ye were the servants of sin,—but being made free,"—the plain meaning is, God be thanked that though ye were, in time past, the servants of sin, yet now—"being free from sin, ye are become the servants of righteousness."

5. The same invaluable privilege of the sons of God is as strongly asserted by St. John; particularly with regard to the former branch of it, namely, power over outward sin. After he had been crying out, as one astonished at the depth of the riches of the goodness of God,—"Behold, what manner of love the Father hath bestowed upon us, that we should be called the sons of God! Beloved, now are we the sons of God: And it doth not yet appear what we shall be; but we know,

---

* [text of the 1872 edition]

that when he shall appear, we shall be like him; for we shall see him as he is;" (1 John 3:1)—he soon adds, "Whosoever is born of God doth not commit sin; for his seed remaineth in him: And he cannot sin, because he is born of God." (1 John 3:9.) But some men will say, "True: Whosoever is born of God doth not commit sin *habitually.*" *habitually!* Whence is that? I read it not. It is not written in the Book. God plainly saith, "He doth not commit sin;" and thou addest, *habitually!* Who art thou that *mendest* the oracles of God?—that "addest to the words of this book?" Beware, I beseech thee, lest God "add to thee all the plagues that are written therein!" especially when the comment thou addest is such as quite swallows up the text: So that by this *methodeia planes*, artful method of deceiving, the precious promise is utterly lost; by this *kybeia anthropon*, tricking and shuffling of men, the word of God is made of none effect. o beware, thou that thus takest from the words of this book, that, taking away the whole meaning and spirit from them, leavest only what may indeed be termed a dead letter, lest God take away thy part out of the book of life!

6. Suffer we the Apostle to interpret his own words, by the whole tenor of his discourse. In the fifth verse of this chapter, he had said, Ye know that he, Christ, was manifested to take away our sins; and in him is no sin. What is the inference he draws from this? Whosoever abideth in him sinneth not. Whosoever sinneth hath not seen him, neither known him. (1 John 3:6.) To his enforcement of this important doctrine, he premises an highly necessary caution: "Little children, let no man deceive you;" (1 John 3:7;) for many will endeavor so to do; to persuade you that you may be unrighteous, that you may commit sin, and yet be children of God! "he that doeth righteousness is righteous, even as he is righteous. he that committeth sin is of the devil; for the devil sinneth from the beginning." Then follows, "Whosoever is born of God doth not commit sin; for his seed remaineth in him: And he cannot sin, because he is born of God. In this," adds the Apostle, "the children of God are manifest, and the children of the devil." By this plain mark (the committing or not committing sin) are they distinguished from each other. To the same effect are those words in his fifth chapter, "We know that whosoever is born of God sinneth not; but he that is begotten of God keepeth himself, and that wicked one toucheth him not." (1 John 3:18.)

7. Another fruit of this living faith is peace. For, "being justified by faith," having all our sins blotted out, "we have peace with God, through our Lord Jesus Christ." (Rom. 5:1.) This indeed our Lord himself, the night before his death, solemnly bequeathed to all his followers: "Peace," saith he, "I leave with you;" (you who "believe in God," and "believe also in me;") "my peace I give unto you:" "Not as the world giveth, give I unto you. Let not your heart be troubled, neither let it be afraid." (John 14:27.) And again, "These things have I spoken unto you, that in me ye might have peace." (John 16:33.) This is that "peace of God which passeth all understanding," that serenity of soul which it hath not entered into the heart of a natural man to conceive, and which it is not possible for even the spiritual man to utter. And it is a peace which all the powers of earth and hell are unable to take from him. Waves and storms beat upon it, but they shake it not; for it is founded upon a rock. It keepeth the hearts and minds of the children of God, at all times and in all places. Whether they are in ease or in pain, in sickness or health, in abundance or want, they are happy in God. In every state they have learned to be content, yea, to give thanks unto God through Christ Jesus; being well assured that "whatsoever is, is best," because it is His will concerning them: So that in all the vicissitudes of life their "heart standeth fast, believing in the Lord."

II. 1. A Second scriptural mark of those who are born of God, is hope. Thus St. Peter, speaking to all the children of God who were then scattered abroad, saith, "Blessed be the God and Father of our Lord Jesus Christ, which, according to his abundant mercy, hath begotten us again unto a lively hope." (1 Peter 1:3.) *elpida zosan*, a *lively* or *living* hope, saith the Apostle; because there is also a *dead* hope, as well as a dead faith; a hope which is not from God, but from the enemy of God and man;—as evidently appears by its fruits; for, as it is the offspring of pride, so it is the parent of every evil word and work; whereas, every man that hath in him this living hope, is "holy as He that calleth him is holy:" Every man that can truly say to his brethren in Christ, "Beloved, now are we the sons of God, and we shall see him as he is," "purifieth himself, even as He is pure."

2. This hope implies, First, the testimony of our own spirit or conscience, that we walk "in simplicity and godly sincerity;" Secondly, the testimony of the Spirit of God, "bearing witness with," or to, "our spirit, that we are the children of God," "and if children, then heirs, heirs of God, and joint-heirs with Christ."

3. Let us well observe what is here taught us by God himself, touching this glorious privilege of his children. Who is it that is here said to bear witness? Not our spirit only, but another; even the Spirit of God: He it is who "beareth witness with our spirit." What is it he beareth witness of? "That we are the children of God," "and if children, then heirs; heirs of God, and joint-heirs with Christ;" (Rom. 8:16, 17;) "if so be that we suffer with him," if we deny ourselves, if we take up our cross daily, if we cheerfully endure persecution or reproach for his sake, "that we may also be glorified together." And in whom doth the Spirit of God bear this witness? In all who are the children of God. By this very argument does the Apostle prove, in the preceding verses, that they are so: "As many," saith he, "as are led by the Spirit of God, they are the sons of God." "For ye have not received the spirit of bondage again to fear; but ye have received the Spirit of Adoption, whereby we cry, Abba, Father!" It follows, "The Spirit itself beareth witness with our spirit, that we are the children of God." (8:14–16.)

4. The variation of the phrase in the fifteenth verse is worthy our observation: "Ye have received the Spirit of Adoption, whereby we cry, Abba, Father!" *Ye*, as many as are the sons of God, have, in virtue of your sonship, received that selfsame Spirit of Adoption, whereby *we* cry, Abba, Father: *We*, the Apostles, Prophets, Teachers, (for so the word may not improperly be understood,) *we*, through whom you have believed, the "ministers of Christ, and stewards of the

mysteries of God." As *we* and *you* have one Lord, so we have one Spirit: As we have one faith, so we have one hope also. We and you are sealed with one "Spirit of promise," the earnest of *your* and of *our* inheritance: The same Spirit bearing witness with your and with our spirit, "that we are the children of God." (Rom. 8:14–16).

5. And thus is the Scripture fulfilled, "Blessed are they that mourn, for they shall be comforted." For it is easy to believe, that though sorrow may precede this witness of God's Spirit with our spirit; (indeed *must*, in some degree, while we groan under fear, and a sense of the wrath of God abiding on us;) yet, as soon as any man feeleth it in himself, his "sorrow is turned into joy." Whatsoever his pain may have been before; yet, as soon as that "hour is come, he remembereth the anguish no more, for joy" that he is born of God. It may be, many of *you* have now sorrow, because you are "aliens from the commonwealth of Israel;" because you are conscious to yourselves that you have not this Spirit; that you are "without hope and without God in the world." But when the Comforter is come, "then your heart shall rejoice;" yea, "your joy shall be full," and "that joy no man taketh from you." (John 16:22.) "We joy in God," will ye say, "through our Lord Jesus Christ, by whom we have now received the atonement;" "by whom we have access into this grace," this state of grace, of favour, or reconciliation with God, "wherein we stand, and rejoice in hope of the glory of God." (Rom. 5:2.) "Ye," saith St. Peter, whom God hath "begotten again unto a lively hope, are kept by the power of God unto salvation: Wherein ye greatly rejoice, though now for a season, if need be, ye are in heaviness through manifold temptations; that the trial of your faith may be found unto praise, and honour, and glory, at the appearing of Jesus Christ: In whom, though now ye see him not, ye rejoice with joy unspeakable and full of glory." (1 Peter 1:5.) Unspeakable indeed! It is not for the tongue of man to describe this joy in the Holy Ghost. It is "the hidden manna, which no man knoweth, save he that receiveth it." But this we know, it not only remains, but overflows, in the depth of affliction. "Are the consolations of God small" with his children, when all earthly comforts fail? Not so. But when sufferings most abound, the consolations of his Spirit do much more abound; insomuch that the sons of God "laugh at destruction when it cometh;" at want, pain, hell, and the grave; as knowing Him who "hath the keys of death and hell," and will shortly "cast them into the bottomless pit;" as hearing even now the great voice out of heaven, saying, "Behold, the tabernacle of God is with men, and he will dwell with them, and they shall be his people, and God himself shall be with them, and be their God. And God shall wipe away all tears from their eyes, and there shall be no more death, neither sorrow, nor crying, neither shall there be any more pain; for the former things are passed away." (Rev. 21:3, 4.)

III. 1. A Third scriptural mark of those who are born of God, and the greatest of all, is love; even "the love of God shed abroad in their hearts by the Holy Ghost which is given unto them." (Rom. 5:5.) "Because they are sons, God hath sent forth the Spirit of his Son in their hearts, crying, Abba, Father!" (Gal. 4:6.) By this Spirit, continually looking up to

God as their reconciled and loving Father, they cry to him for their daily bread, for all things needful, whether for their souls or bodies. They continually pour out their hearts before him, knowing "they have the petitions which they ask of him." (1 John 5:15.) Their delight is in him. He is the joy of their heart; their "shield," and their "exceeding great reward." The desire of their soul is toward him; it is their "meat and drink to do his will;" and they are "satisfied as with marrow and fatness, while their mouth praiseth him with joyful lips." (Psalm 63:5.)

2. And, in this sense also, "every one who loveth him that begat, loveth him that is begotten of him." (1 John 5:1.) His spirit rejoiceth in God his Saviour. He "loveth the Lord Jesus Christ in sincerity." He is so "joined unto the Lord," as to be one spirit. His soul hangeth upon Him, and chooseth Him as altogether lovely, "the chiefest among ten thousand." He knoweth, he feeleth what that means, "My Beloved is mine, and I am his." (Song 2:16.) "Thou art fairer than the children of men; full of grace are thy lips, because God hath anointed thee for ever!" (Psalm 45:2.)

3. The necessary fruit of this love of God is the love of our neighbour; of every soul which God hath made; not excepting our enemies; not excepting those who are now "despitefully using and persecuting us;"—a love whereby we love every man as ourselves; as we love our own souls. Nay, our Lord has expressed it still more strongly, teaching us to "love one another even as He hath loved us." Accordingly, the commandment written in the hearts of all those that love God, is no other than this, "As I have loved you, so love ye one another." Now, "herein perceive we the love of God, in that he laid down his life for us." (1 John 3:16.) "We ought," then, as the Apostle justly infers, "to lay down our lives for the brethren." If we feel ourselves ready to do this, then do we truly love our neighbour. Then "we know that we have passed from death unto life, because we" thus "love the brethren." (1 John 3:14.) "Hereby know we" that we are born of God, that we "dwell in him, and he in us, because he hath given us of his" loving "Spirit." (1 John 4:13.) For "love is of God; and every one that" thus "loveth is born of God, and knoweth God." (1 John 4:7.)

4. But some may possibly ask, "Does not the Apostle say, 'This is the love of God, that we keep his commandments?'" (1 John 5:3.) Yea, and this is the love of our neighbour also, in the same sense as it is the love of God. But what would you infer from hence? that the keeping the outward commandments is all that is implied in loving God with all your heart, with all your mind, and soul, and strength, and in loving your neighbour as yourself? that the love of God is not an affection of the soul, but merely an *outward service?* and that the love of our neighbour is not a disposition of heart, but barely a course of *outward works?* To mention so wild an interpretation of the Apostle's words, is sufficiently to confute it. The plain indisputable meaning of that text is,—this is the sign or proof of the love of God, of our keeping the first and great commandment, to keep the rest of his commandments. For true love, if it be once shed abroad in our heart, will constrain us so to do; since, whosoever loves

God with all his heart, cannot but serve him with all his strength.

5. A Second fruit then of the love of God (so far as it can be distinguished from it) is universal obedience to him we love, and conformity to his will; obedience to all the commands of God, internal and external; obedience of the heart and of the life; in every temper, and in all manner of conversation. And one of the tempers most obviously implied herein, is, the being "zealous of good works;" the hungering and thirsting to do good, in every possible kind, unto all men; the rejoicing to "spend and be spent for them," for every child of man; not looking for any recompence in this world, but only in the resurrection of the just.

IV. 1. Thus have I plainly laid down those marks of the new birth which I find laid down in Scripture. Thus doth God himself answer that weighty question, What is it to be born of God? Such, if the appeal be made to the oracles of God, is "every one that is born of the Spirit." This it is, in the judgment of the Spirit of God, to be a son or a child of God: It is, so to *believe* in God, through Christ, as "not to commit sin," and to enjoy at all times, and in all places, that "peace of God which passeth all understanding." It is, so to *hope* in God through the Son of his love, as to have not only the "testimony of a good conscience," but also the Spirit of God "bearing witness with your spirits, that ye are the children of God;" whence cannot but spring the rejoicing in Him, through whom ye "have received the atonement." It is, so to *love* God, who hath thus loved you, as you never did love any creature: So that ye are constrained to love all men as yourselves; with a love not only ever burning in your hearts, but flaming out in all your actions and conversations, and making your whole life one "labour of love," one continued obedience to those commands, "Be ye merciful, as God is merciful;" "Be ye holy, as I the Lord am holy:" "Be ye perfect, as your Father which is in heaven is perfect."

2. Who then are ye that are *thus* born of God? Ye "know the things which are given to you of God." Ye well know that ye are the children of God, and "can assure your hearts before him." And every one of you who has observed these words cannot but feel, and know of a truth, whether at this hour, (answer to God, and not to man!) you are thus a child of God or no. The question is not, what you was made in baptism; (do not evade;) but, What are you now? Is the Spirit of adoption now in your heart? To your own heart let the appeal be made. I ask not, whether you *was* born of water and of the Spirit; but are you *now* the temple of the Holy Ghost which dwelleth in you? I allow you was "circumcised with the circumcision of Christ;" (as St. Paul emphatically terms baptism;) but does the Spirit of Christ and of glory *now* rest upon you? Else "your circumcision is become uncircumcision."

3. Say not then in your heart, "I *was once* baptized, therefore I *am now* a child of God." Alas, that consequence will by no means hold. How many are the baptized gluttons and drunkards, the baptized liars and common swearers, the baptized railers and evil-speakers, the baptized whoremongers, thieves, extortioners? What think you? Are these now the children of God? Verily, I say unto you, whosoever you are, unto whom any one of the preceding characters belongs, "Ye are of your father the devil, and the works of your father ye do." Unto you I call, in the name of Him whom you crucify afresh, and in his words to your circumcised predecessors, "Ye serpents, ye generation of vipers, how can ye escape the damnation of hell?"

4. How, indeed, except ye be born again! For ye are now dead in trespasses and sins. To say, then, that ye cannot be born again, that there is no new birth but in baptism, is to seal you all under damnation, to consign you to hell, without help, without hope. And perhaps some may think this just and right. In their zeal for the Lord of hosts, they may say, "Yea, cut off the sinners, the Amalekites! Let these Gibeonites be utterly destroyed! They deserve no less." No; nor I, nor you. Mine and your desert, as well as theirs, is hell; and it is mere mercy, free, undeserved mercy, that *we* are not now in unquenchable fire. You will say, "But we are washed;" we were born again "of water and of the Spirit." So *were* they: This, therefore, hinders not at all, but that ye may *now* be even as they. Know ye not, that "what is highly esteemed of men is an abomination in the sight of God?" Come forth, ye "saints of the world," ye that are honoured of men, and see who will cast the first stone at them, at these wretches not fit to live upon the earth, these common harlots, adulterers, murderers. Only learn ye first what that meaneth, "He that hateth his brother is a murderer." (1 John 3:15.) "He that looketh on a woman, to lust after her, hath committed adultery with her already in his heart." (Matt. 5:28.) "Ye adulterers and adulteresses, know ye not that the friendship of the world is enmity with God?" (James 4:4.)

5. "Verily, verily, I say unto you, ye" also "must be born again." "Except ye" also "be born again, ye cannot see the kingdom of God." Lean no more on the staff of that broken reed, that ye *were* born again in baptism. Who denies that ye were then made children of God, and heirs of the kingdom of heaven? But, notwithstanding this, ye are now children of the devil. Therefore ye must be born again. And let not Satan put it into your heart to cavil at a word, when the thing is clear. Ye have heard what are the marks of the children of God: All ye who have them not on your souls, baptized or unbaptized, must needs receive them, or without doubt ye will perish everlastingly. And if ye have been baptized, your only hope is this,—that those who were made the children of God by baptism, but are now the children of the devil, may yet again receive "power to become the sons of God;" that they may receive again what they have lost, even the "Spirit of adoption, crying in their hearts, Abba, Father!" Amen, Lord Jesus! May every one who prepareth his heart yet again to seek thy face, receive again that Spirit of adoption, and cry out, "Abba, Father!" Let him now again have power so to believe in thy name as to become a child of God; as to know and feel he hath "redemption in thy blood, even the forgiveness of sins;" and that he "cannot commit sin, because he is born of God." Let him be now "begotten again unto a living hope," so as to "purify himself as thou art pure;" and "because he is a son," let the Spirit of love and of glory rest upon him, cleansing him "from all filthiness of flesh and

spirit," and teaching him to "perfect holiness in the fear of God!"

19.*THE GREAT PRIVILEGE OF THOSE THAT ARE BORN OF GOD

"Whosoever is born of God doth not commit sin."

1 John 3:9.

1. It has been frequently supposed, that the being born of God was all one with the being justified; that the new birth and justification were only different expressions, denoting the same thing: It being certain, on the one hand, that whoever is justified is also born of God; and, on the other, that whoever is born of God is also justified; yea, that both these gifts of God are given to every believer in one and the same moment. In one point of time his sins are blotted out, and he is born again of God.

2. But though it be allowed, that justification and the new birth are, in point of time, inseparable from each other, yet are they easily distinguished, as being not the same, but things of a widely different nature. Justification implies only a relative, the new birth a real, change. God in justifying us does something *for* us; in begetting us again, he does the work *in* us. The former changes our outward relation to God, so that of enemies we become children; by the latter our inmost souls are changed, so that of sinners we become saints. The one restores us to the favour, the other to the image, of God. The one is the taking away the guilt, the other the taking away the power, of sin: So that, although they are joined together in point of time, yet are they of wholly distinct natures.

3. The not discerning this, the not observing the wide difference there is between being justified and being born again, has occasioned exceeding great confusion of thought in many who have treated on this subject; particularly when they have attempted to explain this great privilege of the children of God; to show how "whosoever is born of God doth not commit sin."

4. In order to apprehend this clearly, it may be necessary, First, to consider what is the proper meaning of that expression, "Whosoever is born of God;" and, Secondly, to inquire, in what sense he "doth not commit sin."

I. 1. First, we are to consider, what is the proper meaning of that expression, "Whosoever is born of God." And, in general, from all the passages of holy writ wherein this expression, "the being born of God," occurs, we may learn that it implies not barely the being baptized, or any outward change whatever; but a vast inward change, a change wrought in the soul, by the operation of the Holy Ghost; a change in the whole manner of our existence; for, from the moment we are born of God, we live in quite another manner than we did before; we are, as it were, in another world.

2. The ground and reason of the expression is easy to be understood. When we undergo this great change, we may, with much propriety, be said to be born again, because there is so near a resemblance between the circumstances of the natural and of the spiritual birth; so that to consider the circumstances of the natural birth, is the most easy way to understand the spiritual.

3. The child which is not yet born subsists indeed by the air, as does everything which has life; but *feels* it not, nor any thing else, unless in a very dull and imperfect manner. It *hears* little, if at all; the organs of hearing being as yet closed up. It *sees* nothing; having its eyes fast shut, and being surrounded with utter darkness. There are, it may be, some faint beginnings of life, when the time of its birth draws nigh, and some motion consequent thereon, whereby it is distinguished from a mere mass of matter; but it has no *senses*; all these avenues of the soul are hitherto quite shut up. Of consequence, it has scarce any intercourse with this visible world; nor any knowledge, conception, or idea, of the things that occur therein.

4. The reason why he that is not yet born is wholly a stranger to the visible world, is, not because it is afar off; (it is very nigh; it surrounds him on every side;) but, partly, because he has not those senses, they are not yet opened in his soul, whereby alone it is possible to hold commerce with the material world; and partly, because so thick a veil is cast between, through which he can discern nothing.

5. But no sooner is the child born into the world, than he exists in a quite different manner. He now *feels* the air with which he is surrounded, and which pours into him from every side, as fast as he alternately breathes it back, to sustain the flame of life: And hence springs a continual increase of strength, of motion, and of sensation; all the bodily senses being now awakened, and furnished with their proper objects.

His eyes are now opened to perceive the light, which, silently flowing in upon them, discovers not only itself, but an infinite variety of things, with which before he was wholly unacquainted. His ears are unclosed, and sounds rush in with endless diversity. Every sense is employed upon such objects as are peculiarly suitable to it; and by these inlets the soul, having an open intercourse with the visible world, acquires more and more knowledge of sensible things, of all the things which are under the sun.

6. So it is with him that is born of God. Before that great change is wrought, although he subsists by Him, in whom all that have life "live, and move, and have their being," yet he is not *sensible* of God; he does not *feel*, he has no inward consciousness of His presence. He does not perceive that divine breath of life, without which he cannot subsist a moment: Nor is he sensible of any of the things of God; they make no impression upon his soul. God is continually calling to him from on high, but he heareth not; his ears are shut, so that the "voice of the charmer" is lost to him, "charm he never so wisely," He seeth not the things of the Spirit of God; the eyes of his understanding being closed, and utter darkness covering his whole soul, surrounding him on every side. It is true he may have some faint dawnings of life, some small beginnings of spiritual motion; but as yet he has no spiritual senses capable of discerning spiritual objects; consequently,

---

* [text from the 1872 edition]

he "discerneth not the things of the Spirit of God; he cannot know them, because they are spiritually discerned."

7. Hence he has scarce any knowledge of the invisible world, as he has scarce any intercourse with it. Not that it is afar off: No: He is in the midst of it; it encompasses him round about. The *other world*, as we usually term it, is not far from every one of us: It is above, and beneath, and on every side. Only the natural man discerneth it not; partly, because he has no spiritual senses, whereby alone we can discern the things of God; partly, because so thick a veil is interposed as he knows not how to penetrate.

8. But when he is born of God, born of the Spirit, how is the manner of his existence changed! His whole soul is now sensible of God, and he can say, by sure experience, "Thou art about my bed, and about my path;" I feel thee in all my ways: "Thou besettest me behind and before, and layest thy hand upon me." The Spirit or breath of God is immediately inspired, breathed into the new-born soul; and the same breath which comes from, returns to, God: As it is continually received by faith, so it is continually rendered back by love, by prayer, and praise, and thanksgiving; love and praise, and prayer being the breath of every soul which is truly born of God. And by this new kind of spiritual respiration, spiritual life is not only sustained, but increased day by day, together with spiritual strength, and motion, and sensation; all the senses of the soul being now awake, and capable of discerning spiritual good and evil.

9. "The eyes of his understanding" are now "open," and he "seeth Him that is invisible." He sees what is "the exceeding greatness of his power" and of his love toward them that believe. He sees that God is merciful to him a sinner, that he is reconciled through the Son of his love. He clearly perceives both the pardoning love of God, and all his "exceeding great and precious promises." "God, who commanded the light to shine out of the darkness, hath shined," and doth shine, "in his heart," to enlighten him with "the knowledge of the glory of God in the face of Jesus Christ." All the darkness is now passed away, and he abides in the light of God's countenance.

10. His ears are now opened, and the voice of God no longer calls in vain. He hears and obeys the heavenly calling: He knows the voice of his Shepherd. All his spiritual senses being now awakened, he has a clear intercourse with the invisible world; and hence he knows more and more of the things which before it could not "enter into his heart to conceive." He now knows what the peace of God is; what is joy in the Holy Ghost; what the love of God which is shed abroad in the heart of them that believe in him through Christ Jesus. Thus the veil being removed which before interrupted the light and voice, the knowledge and love of God, he who is born of the Spirit, dwelling in love, "dwelleth in God, and God in him."

II. 1. Having considered the meaning of that expression, "whosoever is born of God," it remains, in the Second place, to inquire, in what sense he "doth not commit sin."

Now one who is so born of God, as hath been above described, who continually receives into his soul the breath of life from God, the gracious influence of his Spirit, and continually renders it back; one who thus believes and loves, who by faith perceives the continual actings of God upon his spirit, and by a kind of spiritual re-action returns the grace he receives, in unceasing love, and praise, and prayer; not only doth not commit sin, while he thus keepeth himself, but so long as this "seed remaineth in him, he cannot sin, because he is born of God."

2. By sin, I here understand outward sin, according to the plain, common acceptation of the word; an actual, voluntary transgression of the law; of the revealed, written law of God; of any commandment of God, acknowledged to be such at the time that it is transgressed. But "whosoever is born of God," while he abideth in faith and love, and in the spirit of prayer and thanksgiving, not only doth not, but cannot, thus commit sin. So long as he thus believeth in God through Christ, and loves him, and is pouring out his heart before him, he cannot voluntarily transgress any command of God, either by speaking or acting what he knows God hath forbidden: So long that seed which remaineth in him, that loving, praying, thankful faith, compels him to refrain from whatsoever he knows to be an abomination in the sight of God.

3. But here a difficulty will immediately occur, and one that to many has appeared insuperable, and induced them to deny the plain assertion of the Apostle, and give up the privilege of the children of God.

It is plain, in fact, that those whom we cannot deny to have been truly born of God, (the Spirit of God having given us in his word this infallible testimony concerning them,) nevertheless, not only could, but did, commit sin, even gross, outward sin. They did transgress the plain, known laws of God, speaking or acting what they knew he had forbidden.

4. Thus David was unquestionably born of God or ever he was anointed king over Israel. He knew in whom he had believed; "he was strong in faith, giving glory to God." "The Lord," saith he, "is my Shepherd; therefore can I lack nothing. He shall feed me in green pastures, and lead me forth beside the waters of comfort. Yea, though I walk through the valley of the shadow of death, I will fear no evil; for thou art with me." (Psalm 23:1.) He was filled with love; such as often constrained him to cry out, "I will love thee, O Lord, my strength: The Lord is my stony rock, and my defence; the horn also of my salvation, and my refuge." (Psalm 28:1.) He was a man of prayer; pouring out his soul before God in all circumstances of life; and abundant in praises and thanksgiving. "Thy praise," saith he, "shall be ever in my mouth:" (Psalm 34:1:) "Thou art my God, and I will thank thee; thou art my God, and I will praise thee." (Psalm 118:28.) And yet such a child of God could and did commit sin; yea, the horrid sins of adultery and murder.

5. And even after the Holy Ghost was more largely given, after "life and immortality were brought to light by the gospel" we want not instances of the same melancholy kind, which were also doubtless written for our instruction. Thus he who (probably from his selling all that he had, and bringing the price for the relief of his poor brethren) was by the apostles themselves surnamed Barnabas, that is, the son of consolation; (Acts 4:36, 37;) who was so honoured at Antioch, as to be selected with Saul out of all the disciples, to

carry their relief unto the brethren in Judea; (Acts 11:29, 30;) this Barnabas, who, at his return from Judea, was, by the peculiar direction of the Holy Ghost, solemnly "separated from the other Prophets and Teachers, for the work whereunto God had called him," (Acts 13:1-4,) even to accompany the great Apostle among the Gentiles, and to be his fellow-labourer in every place;—nevertheless, was afterward so sharp, (Acts 15:35, 39,) in his contention with St. Paul, (because he "thought it not good to take with them John," in his visiting the brethren a second time, "who had departed from them from Pamphylia, and went not with them to the work,") that he himself also departed from the work; that he "took John, and sailed unto Cyprus;" (Acts 15:39;) forsaking him to whom he had been in so immediate a manner joined by the Holy Ghost.

6. An instance more astonishing than both these is given by St. Paul in his Epistle to the Galatians. When Peter, the aged, the zealous, the first of the apostles, one of the three most highly favoured by his Lord, "was come to Antioch, I withstood him to the face, because he was to be blamed. For before that certain came from James, he did eat with the Gentiles"—the Heathens converted to the Christian faith, as having been peculiarly taught of God, that he "should not call any man common or unclean." (Acts 10:28.) "But, when they were come, he separated himself, fearing them which were of the circumcision. And the other Jews dissembled likewise with him; insomuch that Barnabas also was carried away with their dissimulation. But when I saw that they walked not uprightly, according to the truth of the gospel, I said unto Peter, before them all, If thou, being a Jew, livest after the manner of the Gentiles,"—not regarding the ceremonial law of Moses,—"why compellest thou the Gentiles to live as do the Jews?" (Gal. 2:11.) Here is also plain, undeniable sin committed by one who was undoubtedly born of God. But how can this be reconciled with the assertion of St. John, if taken in the obvious literal meaning, that "whosoever is born of God, doth not commit sin?"

7. I answer, what has been long observed is this: so long as "he that is born of God keepeth himself," (which he is able to do, by the grace of God,) "the wicked one toucheth him not:" But if he keepeth not himself, if he abide not in the faith, he may commit sin even as another man.

It is easy therefore to understand, how any of these children of God might be moved from his own steadfastness, and yet the great truth of God, declared by the Apostle, remain steadfast and unshaken. He did not "keep himself," by that grace of God which was sufficient for him. He fell, step by step, First, into negative, inward sin, not "stirring up the gift of God which was in him," not "watching unto prayer," not "pressing on to the mark of the prize of his high calling:" Then, into positive inward sin, inclining to wickedness with his heart, giving way to some evil desire or temper: Next, he lost his faith, his sight of a pardoning God, and consequently his love of God; and, being then weak and like another man, he was capable of committing even outward sin.

8. To explain this by a particular instance: David was born of God, and saw God by faith. He loved God in sincerity. He

could truly say, "Whom have I in heaven but thee? and there is none upon earth," neither person nor thing, "that I desire in comparison of thee." But still there remained in his heart that corruption of nature, which is the seed of all evil. "He was walking upon the roof of his house," (2 Sam. 11:2,) probably praising the God whom his soul loved, when he looked down, and saw Bathsheba. He felt a temptation; a thought which tended to evil. The Spirit of God did not fail to convince him of this. He doubtless heard and knew the warning voice; but he yielded in some measure to the thought, and the temptation began to prevail over him. Hereby his spirit was sullied; he saw God still; but it was more dimly than before. He loved God still; but not in the same degree; not with the same strength and ardour of affection. Yet God checked him again, though his spirit was grieved; and his voice, though fainter and fainter, still whispered, "Sin lieth at the door; look unto me, and be thou saved." But he would not hear: He looked again, not unto God, but unto the forbidden object, till nature was superior to grace, and kindled lust in his soul.

The eye of his mind was now closed again, and God vanished out of his sight. Faith, the divine, supernatural intercourse with God, and the love of God, ceased together: He then rushed on as a horse into the battle, and knowingly committed the outward sin.

9. You see the unquestionable progress from grace to sin: Thus it goes on, from step to step. (1.) The divine seed of loving, conquering faith, remains in him that is born of God. "He keepeth himself," by the grace of God, and "cannot commit sin." (2.) A temptation arises; whether from the world, the flesh, or the devil, it matters not. (3.) The Spirit of God gives him warning that sin is near, and bids him more abundantly watch unto prayer. (4.) He gives way, in some degree, to the temptation, which now begins to grow pleasing to him. (5.) The Holy Spirit is grieved; his faith is weakened; and his love of God grows cold. (6.) The Spirit reproves him more sharply, and saith, "This is the way; walk thou in it." (7.) He turns away from the painful voice of God, and listens to the pleasing voice of the tempter. (8.) Evil desire begins and spreads in his soul, till faith and love vanish away: He is then capable of committing outward sin, the power of the Lord being departed from him.

10. To explain this by another instance: The Apostle Peter was full of faith and of the Holy Ghost; and hereby keeping himself, he had a conscience void of offence toward God and toward man.

Walking thus in simplicity and godly sincerity, "before that certain came from James, he did eat with the Gentiles," knowing that what God had cleansed was not common or unclean.

But "when they were come," a temptation arose in his heart, "to fear those of the circumcision," (the Jewish converts, who were zealous for circumcision and the other rites of the Mosaic law,) and regard the favour and praise of these men, more than the praise of God.

He was warned by the Spirit that sin was near: Nevertheless, he yielded to it in some degree, even to sinful fear of man, and his faith and love were proportionably weakened.

God reproved him again for giving place to the devil. Yet he would not hearken to the voice of his Shepherd; but gave himself up to that slavish fear, and thereby quenched the Spirit.

Then God disappeared, and, faith and love being extinct, he committed the outward sin. *Walking not uprightly,* not "according to the truth of the gospel," he "separated himself" from his Christian brethren, and by his evil example, if not advice also, "compelled even the Gentiles to live after the manner of the Jews;" to entangle themselves again with that "yoke of bondage," from which "Christ had set them free."

Thus it is unquestionably true, that he who is born of God, keeping himself, doth not, cannot commit sin; and yet, if he keepeth not himself, he may commit all manner of sin with greediness.

III. 1. From the preceding considerations we may learn, first, To give a clear and incontestable answer to a question which has frequently perplexed many who were sincere of heart. "Does sin precede or follow the loss of faith?" Does a child of God first commit sin, and thereby lose his faith? Or does he lose his faith first, before he can commit sin?"

I answer, Some sin of omission, at least, must necessarily precede the loss of faith; some inward sin: But the loss of faith must precede the committing outward sin.

The more any believer examines his own heart, the more will he be convinced of this: That faith working by love excludes both inward and outward sin from a soul watching unto prayer; that nevertheless we are even then liable to temptation, particularly to the sin that did easily beset us; that if the loving eye of the soul be steadily fixed on God, the temptation soon vanishes away: But if not, if we are *exelkomenoi,* (as the Apostle James speaks, James 1:14,) *drawn out* of God by *our own desire,* and *deleazomenoi, caught by the bait* of present or promised pleasure; then that desire, conceived in us, brings forth sin; and, having by that inward sin destroyed our faith, it casts us headlong into the snare of the devil, so that we may commit any outward sin whatever.

2. From what has been said, we may learn, Secondly, what the life of God in the soul of a believer is; wherein it properly consists; and what is immediately and necessarily implied therein. It immediately and necessarily implies the continual inspiration of God's Holy Spirit; God's breathing into the soul, and the soul's breathing back what it first receives from God; a continual action of God upon the soul, and a re-action of the soul upon God; an unceasing presence of God, the loving, pardoning God, manifested to the heart, and perceived by faith; and an unceasing return of love, praise, and prayer, offering up all the thoughts of our hearts, all the words of our tongues, all the works of our hands, all our body, soul, and spirit, to be a holy sacrifice, acceptable unto God in Christ Jesus.

3. And hence we may, Thirdly, infer the absolute necessity of this re-action of the soul, (whatsoever it be called,) in order to the continuance of the divine life therein. For it plainly appears, God does not continue to act upon the soul, unless the soul re-acts upon God. He prevents us indeed with the blessings of his goodness. He first loves us, and manifests himself unto us. While we are yet afar off, he calls us to himself, and shines upon our hearts. But if we do not then love him who first loved us; if we will not hearken to his voice; if we turn our eye away from him, and will not attend to the light which he pours upon us; his Spirit will not always strive: He will gradually withdraw, and leave us to the darkness of our own hearts. He will not continue to breathe into our soul, unless our soul breathes toward him again; unless our love, and prayer, and thanksgiving return to him, a sacrifice wherewith he is well pleased.

4. Let us learn, Lastly, to follow that direction of the great Apostle, "Be not high-minded, but fear." Let us fear sin, more than death or hell. Let us have a jealous (though not painful) fear, lest we should lean to our own deceitful hearts. "Let him that standeth take heed lest he fall." Even he who now standeth fast in the grace of God, in the faith that overcometh the world, may nevertheless fall into inward sin, and thereby "make shipwreck of his faith." And how easily then will outward sin regain its dominion over him! Thou, therefore, O man of God! watch always; that thou mayest always hear the voice of God! Watch, that thou mayest pray without ceasing, at all times, and in all places, pouring out thy heart before him! So shalt thou always believe, and always love, and never commit sin.

20.* THE LORD OUR RIGHTEOUSNESS

"This is his name whereby he shall be called, The Lord our righteousness."

Jer. 23:6.

1. How dreadful and how innumerable are the contests which have arisen about religion! And not only among the children of this world, among those who knew not what true religion was, but even among the children of God; those who had experienced "the kingdom of God within them;" who had tasted of "righteousness, and peace, and joy in the Holy Ghost." How many of these, in all ages, instead of joining together against the common enemy, have turned their weapons against each other, and so not only wasted their precious time, but hurt one another's spirits, weakened each other's hands, and so hindered the great work of their common Master! How many of the weak have hereby been offended!—How many of the lame turned out of the way! How many sinners confirmed in their disregard of all religion, and their contempt of those that profess it! And how many of "the excellent ones upon earth" have been constrained to "weep in secret places!"

2. What would not every lover of God and his neighbour do, what would he not suffer, to remedy this sore evil; to remove contention from the children of God; to restore or preserve peace among them? What but a good conscience would he think too dear to part with, in order to promote this valuable end? And suppose we cannot "make" these "wars to cease in

---

* (Preached at the chapel in West-Street, Seven Dials, on Sunday, Nov. 24, 1765)

all the world," suppose we cannot reconcile all the children of God to each other, however, let each do what he can, let him contribute, if it be but two mites, toward it. Happy are they who are able, in any degree, to promote "peace and good-will among men" especially among good men; among those that are all listed under the banner of "the Prince of Peace;" and are, therefore, peculiarly engaged, "as much as lies in them," to "live peaceably with all men."

3. It would be a considerable step toward this glorious end, if we could bring good men to understand one another. Abundance of disputes arise purely from the want of this; from mere misapprehension. Frequently neither of the contending parties understands what his opponent means; whence it follows, that each violently attacks the other, while there is no real difference between them. And yet it is not always an easy matter to convince them of this; particularly when their passions are moved: It is then attended with the utmost difficulty. However, it is not impossible; especially when we attempt it, not trusting in ourselves, but having all our dependence upon Him with whom all things are possible. How soon is he able to disperse the cloud, to shine upon their hearts, and to enable them both to understand each other, and "the truth as it is in Jesus!"

4. One very considerable article of this truth is contained in the words above recited, "This is his name whereby he shall be called, the LORD OUR RIGHTEOUSNESS;" a truth this, which enters deep into the nature of Christianity, and, in a manner, supports the whole frame of it. Of this, undoubtedly, may be affirmed, what Luther affirms of a truth closely connected with it: it is *articulus stantis vel cadentis ecclesiae*. The Christian church stands or falls with it. It is certainly the pillar and ground of that faith, of which alone cometh salvation; of that Catholic or universal faith which is found in all the children of God, and which "unless a man keep whole and undefiled, without doubt he shall perish everlastingly."

5. Might not one, therefore, reasonably expect, that, however they differed in others, all those who name the name of Christ should agree in this point? But how far is this from being the case! There is scarce any wherein they are so little agreed; wherein those who all profess to follow Christ, seem so widely and irreconcilably to differ. I say *seem*; because I am throughly convinced, that many of them *only seem* to differ. The disagreement is more in words than in sentiments: They are much nearer in judgment than in language. And a wide difference in language there certainly is, not only between Protestants and Papists, but between Protestant and Protestant; yea, even between those who all believe justification by faith; who agree, as well in this, as every other fundamental doctrine of the gospel.

6. But if the difference be more in *opinion*, than real *experience*, and more in *expression* than in *opinion*, how can it be, that even the children of God should so vehemently contend with each other on the point? Several reasons may be assigned for this: The chief is, their not understanding one another; joined with too keen an attachment to their opinions, and particular modes of expression.

In order to remove this, at least in some measure; in order to our understanding one another on this head; I shall, by the help of God, endeavour to show,

I. What is the righteousness of Christ:

II. When, and in what sense, it is imputed to us:

And conclude with a short and plain application.

And, I. What is the righteousness of Christ? It is twofold, either his divine or his human righteousness.

1. His divine righteousness belongs to his divine nature, as he is *ho on*, He that existeth; "over all, God blessed for ever;" the Supreme; the Eternal; "equal with the Father, as touching his Godhead, though inferior to the Father as touching his manhood." Now this is his eternal, essential, immutable holiness; his infinite justice, mercy, and truth; in all which, he and the Father are One.

But I do not apprehend that the divine righteousness of Christ is immediately concerned in the present question. I believe few, if any, do now contend for the imputation of this righteousness to us. Whoever believes the doctrine of imputation, understands it chiefly, if not solely, of his human righteousness.

2. The human righteousness of Christ belongs to him in his human nature; as he is the "Mediator between God and man, the Man Christ Jesus." This is either internal or external. His internal righteousness is the image of God, stamped on every power and faculty of his soul. It is a copy of his divine righteousness, as far as it can be imparted to a human spirit. It is a transcript of the divine purity, the divine justice, mercy, and truth. It includes love, reverence, resignation to his Father; humility, meekness, gentleness; love to lost mankind, and every other holy and heavenly temper; and all these in the highest degree, without any defect, or mixture of unholiness.

3. It was the least part of his external righteousness, that he did nothing amiss; that he knew no outward sin of any kind, neither was "guile found in his mouth;" that he never spoke one improper word, nor did one improper action. Thus far it is only a negative righteousness, though such an one as never did, nor ever can, belong to anyone that is born of a woman, save himself alone. But even his outward righteousness was positive too: He did all things well: In every word of his tongue, in every work of his hands, he did precisely the "will of Him that sent him." In the whole course of his life, he did the will of God on earth, as the angels do it in heaven. All he acted and spoke was exactly right in every circumstance. The whole and every part of his obedience was complete. "He fulfilled all righteousness."

4. But his obedience implied more than all this: It implied not only doing, but suffering; suffering the whole will of God, from the time he came into the world, till "he bore our sins in his own body upon the tree;" yea, till having made a full atonement for them, "he bowed his head, and gave up the ghost." This is usually termed the *passive* righteousness of Christ; the former, his *active* righteousness. But as the active and passive righteousness of Christ were never, in fact, separated from each other, so we never need separate them at all, either in speaking or even in thinking. And it is with

regard to both these conjointly that Jesus is called "the Lord our righteousness."

II. But when is it that any of us may truly say, "the Lord *our* righteousness?" In other words, when is it that the righteousness of Christ is *imputed* to us, and in what sense is it imputed?

1. Look through all the world, and all the men therein are either believers or unbelievers. The first thing, then, which admits of no dispute among reasonable men is this: To all believers the righteousness of Christ is imputed; to unbelievers it is not.

But when is it imputed? When they believe. In that very hour the righteousness of Christ is theirs. It is imputed to every one that believes, as soon as he believes: Faith and the righteousness of Christ are inseparable. For if he believes according to Scripture, he believes in the righteousness of Christ. There is no true faith, that is, justifying faith, which hath not the righteousness of Christ for its object.

2. It is true believers may not all speak alike; they may not all use the same language. It is not to be expected that they should: we cannot reasonably require it of them. A thousand circumstances may cause them to vary from each other, in the manner of expressing themselves: But a difference of expression does nor necessarily imply a difference of sentiment. Different persons may use different expressions, and yet mean the same thing. Nothing is more common than this, although we seldom make sufficient allowance for it. Nay, it is not easy for the same persons, when they speak of the same thing at a considerable distance of time, to use exactly the same expressions, even though they retain the same sentiments: How then can we be rigorous in requiring others to use just the same expressions with us?

3. We may go a step farther yet: Men may differ from us in their opinions, as well as their expressions, and nevertheless be partakers with us of the same precious faith. It is possible they may not have a distinct apprehension of the very blessing which they enjoy: Their ideas may not be so clear, and yet their experience may be as sound, as ours. There is a wide difference between the natural faculties of men, their understandings in particular; And that difference is exceedingly increased by the manner of their education. Indeed, this alone may occasion an inconceivable difference in their opinions of various kinds; and why not upon this head, as well as on any other? But still, though their opinions, as well as expressions, may be confused and inaccurate, their hearts may cleave to God through the Son of his love, and be truly interested in his righteousness.

4. Let us then make all that allowance to others, which, were we in their place, we would desire for ourselves. Who is ignorant (to touch again on that circumstance only) of the amazing power of education? And who that knows it, can expect, suppose, a member of the Church of Rome, either to think or speak clearly on this subject? And yet, if we had heard even dying Bellarmine cry out,—when he was asked, "Unto which of the saints wilt thou turn?"—*Fidere meritis Christi tutissimum*; "It is safest to trust in the merits of Christ;" would we have affirmed that, not withstanding his wrong opinions, he had no share in his righteousness?

5. But in what sense is this righteousness imputed to believers? In this: all believers are forgiven and accepted, not for the sake of anything in them, or of anything that ever was, that is, or ever can be done by them, but wholly and solely for the sake of what Christ hath done and suffered for them. I say again, not for the sake of anything in them, or done by them, of their own righteousness or works: "Not for works of righteousness which we have done, but of his own mercy he saved us." "By grace ye are saved through faith,—not of works, lest any man should boast;" but wholly and solely for the sake of what Christ hath done and suffered for us. We are "justified freely by his grace, through the redemption that is in Jesus Christ." And this is not only the means of our obtaining the favour of God, but of our continuing therein. It is thus we come to God at first; it is by the same we come unto him ever after. We walk in one and the same new and living way, till our spirit returns to God.

6. And this is the doctrine which I have constantly believed and taught, for near eight and twenty years. This I published to all the world in the year 1738, and ten or twelve times since, in those words, and many others to the same effect, extracted from the Homilies of our Church:—"These things must necessarily go together in our justification; upon God's part, his great mercy and grace; upon Christ's part, the satisfaction of God's justice; and on our part, faith in the merits of Christ. So that the grace of God doth not shut out the righteousness of God in our justification, but only shutteth out the righteousness of man, as to *deserving* our justification." "That we are justified by faith alone, is spoken to take away clearly all merit of our works, and wholly to ascribe the *merit* and *deserving* of our justification to Christ only. Our justification comes freely of the mere mercy of God. For whereas all the world was not able to pay any part toward our ransom, it pleased Him, without any of our deserving, to prepare for us Christ's body and blood, whereby our ransom might be paid, and his justice satisfied. Christ, therefore, is now the righteousness of all them that truly believe in him."

7. The Hymns published a year or two after this, and since republished several times, (a clear testimony that my judgment was still the same,) speak full to the same purpose. To cite all the passages to this effect, would be to transcribe a great part of the volumes. Take one for all, which was reprinted seven years ago, five years ago, two years ago, and some months since:—

> Jesus, thy blood and righteousness
> My beauty are, my glorious dress:
> 'Midst flaming worlds in these array'd,
> With joy shall I lift up my head.

The whole hymn expresses the same sentiment, from the beginning to the end.

8. In the Sermon on Justification, published nineteen, and again seven or eight, years ago, I express the same thing in these words: (P. 55) "In consideration of this,—that the Son of God hath 'tasted death for every man,' God hath now 'reconciled the world unto himself, not imputing to them their' former 'trespasses.' So that for the sake of his well-beloved Son, of what he hath done and suffered for us, God

now vouchsafes, on one only condition, (which himself also enables us to perform,) both to remit the punishment due to our sins, to re-instate us in his favour, and to restore our dead souls to spiritual life, as the earnest of life eternal."

9. This is more largely and particularly expressed in the Treatise on Justification, which I published last year: "If we take the phrase of imputing Christ's righteousness, for the bestowing (as it were) the righteousness of Christ, including his obedience, as well passive as active, in the return of it, that is, in the privileges, blessings, and benefits purchased it; so a believer may be said to be justified by the righteousness of Christ imputed. The meaning is, God justifies the believer for the sake of Christ's righteousness, and not for any righteousness of his own. So Calvin: (Institut. 1.2, c.17) 'Christ by his obedience, procured and merited for us grace or favour with God the Father.' Again: 'Christ, by his obedience, procured or purchased righteousness for us.' And yet again: 'All such expressions as these,—that we are justified by the grace of God, that Christ is our righteousness, that righteousness was procured for us by the death and resurrection of Christ, import the same thing; namely, that the righteousness of Christ, both his active and passive righteousness, is the meritorious cause of our justification, and has procured for us at God's hand, that, upon our believing, we should be accounted righteous by him.' " Page 5.

10. But perhaps some will object, "Nay, but you affirm that faith is imputed to us for righteousness. St. Paul affirms this over and over; therefore I affirm it too. Faith is imputed for righteousness to every believer; namely, faith in the righteousness of Christ; but this is exactly the same thing which has been said before; For by that expression I mean neither more nor less, than that we are justified by faith, not by works; or that every believer is forgiven and accepted, merely for the sake of what Christ has done and suffered.

11. But is not a believer invested or clothed with the righteousness of Christ? Undoubtedly he is. And accordingly the words above-recited are the language of every believing heart:

Jesu, thy blood and righteousness

My beauty are, my glorious dress. That is, "For the sake of thy active and passive righteousness, I am forgiven and accepted of God."

But must not we put off the filthy rags of our own righteousness, before we can put on the spotless righteousness of Christ? Certainly we must; that is, in plain terms, we must repent, before we can believe the gospel. We must be cut off from dependence upon ourselves, before we can truly depend upon Christ. We must cast away all confidence in our own righteousness, or we cannot have a true confidence in his. Till we are delivered from trusting in anything that we do, we cannot throughly trust in what he has done and suffered. First, we receive the sentence of death in ourselves: Then, we trust in Him that lived and died for us.

12. But do not you believe inherent righteousness? Yes, in its proper place; not as the ground of our acceptance with God, but as the fruit of it; not in the place of imputed righteousness, but as consequent upon it. That is, I believe God implants righteousness in every one to whom he has imputed it. I believe "Jesus Christ is made of God unto us sanctification," as well as "righteousness;" or, that God sanctifies, as well as justifies, all them that believe in him. They to whom the righteousness of Christ is imputed, are made righteous by the spirit of Christ, are renewed in the image of God, "after the likeness wherein they were created, in righteousness and true holiness."

13. But do not you put faith in the room of Christ, or of his righteousness? By no means: I take particular care to put each of these in its proper place. The righteousness of Christ is the whole and sole foundation of all our hope. It is by faith that the Holy Ghost enables us to build upon this foundation. God gives this faith; in that moment we are accepted of God; and yet, not for the sake of that faith, but of what Christ has done and suffered for us. You see, each of these has its proper place, and neither clashes with the other: we believe, we love, we endeavour to walk in all the commandments of the Lord blameless; yet,—

> While thus we bestow
> Our moments below,
> Ourselves we forsake,
> And refuge in Jesus's righteousness take.
> His passion alone,
> The foundation we own;
> And pardon we claim,
> And eternal redemption in Jesus's name.

14. I therefore no more deny the righteousness of Christ, than I deny the Godhead of Christ; and a man may full as justly charge me with denying the one as the other. Neither do I deny imputed righteousness: This is another unkind and unjust accusation. I always did, and do still continually affirm, that the righteousness of Christ is imputed to every believer. But who deny it? Why, all Infidels, whether baptized or unbaptized; all who affirm the glorious gospel of our Lord Jesus Christ to be a cunningly devised fable; all Socinians and Arians; all who deny the supreme Godhead of the Lord that bought them; they, of consequence, deny his divine righteousness, as they suppose him to be a mere creature; and they deny his human righteousness, as imputed to any man, seeing they believe everyone is accepted for his own righteousness.

15. The human righteousness of Christ, at least the imputation of it, as the whole and sole meritorious cause of the justification of a sinner before God, is likewise denied by the members of the Church of Rome; by all of them who are true to the principles of their own church. But undoubtedly there are many among them whose experience goes beyond their principles; who, though they are far from expressing themselves justly, yet feel what they know not how to express. Yea, although their conceptions of this great truth be as crude as their expressions, yet with their heart they Is believe: They rest on Christ alone, both unto present and eternal salvation

16. With these we may rank those even in the Reformed Churches, who are usually termed Mystics. One of the chief of these, in the present century, (at least in England,) was Mr. Law. It is well known that he absolutely and zealously denied the imputation of the righteousness of Christ, as zealously as

Robert Barclay, who scruples not to say, "Imputed righteousness!—imputed nonsense!" The body of the people known by the name of Quakers espouse the same sentiment. Nay, the generality of those who profess themselves members of the Church of England are either totally ignorant of the matter, and know nothing about imputed righteousness, or deny this and justification by faith together, as destructive of good works. To these we may add a considerable number of the people vulgarly styled Anabaptists, together with thousands of Presbyterians and Independents, lately enlightened by the writings of Dr. Taylor. On the last I am not called to pass any sentence: I leave them to Him that made them. But will anyone dare to affirm that all Mystics, (such as was Mr. Law in particular,) all Quakers, all Presbyterians or Independents, and all members of the Church of England who are not clear in their opinions or expressions, are void of all Christian experience?—that, consequently, they are all in a state of damnation, "without hope, without God in the world?" However confused their ideas may be, however improper their language, may there not be many of them whose heart is right toward God, and who effectually know "the Lord our righteousness?"

17. But, blessed be God, we are not among those who are so dark in their conceptions and expressions. We no more deny the phrase than the thing; but we are unwilling to obtrude it on other men. Let them use either this or such other expressions as they judge to be more exactly scriptural, provided their heart rests only on what Christ hath done and suffered, for pardon, grace, and glory. I cannot express this better than in Mr. Hervey's words, worthy to be wrote in letters of gold: "We are not solicitous as to any particular set of phrases. Only let men be humbled as repenting criminals at Christ's feet, let them rely as devoted pensioners on his merits and they are undoubtedly in the way to a blessed immortality."

18. Is there any need, is there any possibility, of saying more? Let us only abide by this declaration, and all the contention about this or that "particular phrase" is torn up by the roots. Keep to this,—"All who are humbled as repenting criminals at Christ's feet, and rely as devoted pensioners on his merits, are in the way to a blessed immortality;" And what room for dispute? Who denies this? Do we not all meet on this ground? What then shall we wrangle about? A man of peace here proposes terms of accommodation to all the contending parties. We desire no better: We accept of the terms: We subscribe to them with heart and hand. Whoever refuses so to do, set a mark upon that man! He is an enemy of peace, and a troubler of Israel, a disturber of the Church of God.

19. In the meantime what we are afraid of is this:—lest any should use the phrase, "The righteousness of Christ," or, "The righteousness of Christ is imputed to me," as a cover for his unrighteousness. We have known this done a thousand times. A man has been reproved, suppose for drunkenness: "O", said he, "I pretend to no righteousness of *my own*; Christ is *my righteousness*." Another has been told, that "the extortioner, the unjust, shall not inherit the kingdom of God:" He replies, with all assurance, "I am unjust in myself, but I have a spotless righteousness in Christ." And thus, though a man be as far from the practice as from the tempers of a Christian; though he neither has the mind which was in Christ, nor in any respect walks as he walked; yet he has armour of proof against all conviction, in what he calls the "righteousness of Christ."

20. It is the seeing so many deplorable instances of this kind, which makes us sparing in the use of these expressions. And I cannot but call upon all of you who use them frequently, and beseech you in the name of God, our Saviour, whose you are, and whom you serve, earnestly to guard all that hear you against this accursed abuse of them. O warn them (it may be they will hear *your* voice) against "continuing in sin that grace may abound!" Warn them against making "Christ the minister of sin;" against making void that solemn decree of God, "Without holiness no man shall see the Lord," by a vain imagination of being *holy in Christ!* O warn them that if they remain unrighteous, the righteousness of Christ will profit them nothing! Cry aloud, (is there not a cause?) that for this very end the righteousness of Christ is imputed to us, that "the righteousness of the law may be fulfilled in us;" and that we may "live soberly, religiously, and godly, in this present world."

It remains only to make a short and plain application. And, First, I would address myself to you who violently oppose these expressions, and are ready to condemn all that use them as Antinomians. But is not this bending the bow too much the other way? Why should you condemn all who do not speak just as you do? Why should you quarrel with them, for using the phrases they like, any more than they with you for taking the same liberty? Or, if they do quarrel with you upon that account, do not imitate the bigotry which you blame. At least, allow them the liberty which they ought to allow you. And why should you be angry at an expression? "O, it has been abused!" And what expression has not? However, the abuse may be removed, and, at the same time, the use remain. Above all, be sure to retain the important sense which is couched under that expression: "All the blessings I enjoy, all I hope for in time and in eternity, are given wholly and solely for the sake of what Christ has done and suffered for me."

I would, Secondly, add a few words to you who are fond of these expressions. And permit me to ask, Do not I allow enough? What can any reasonable man desire more? I allow the whole sense which you contend for; that we have every blessing through the righteousness of God our Saviour. I allow *you* to use whatever expressions you choose, and that a thousand times over; only guarding them against that dreadful abuse, which you are as deeply concerned to prevent as I am. I myself frequently use the expression in question,— imputed righteousness; and often put this and the like expressions into the mouth of a whole congregation. But allow me liberty of conscience herein: Allow me the right of private judgment. Allow me to use it just as often as I judge it preferable to any other expression; and be not angry with me if I cannot judge it proper to use any one expression every two minutes. You may, if you please; but do not condemn me because I do not. Do not, for this, represent me as a Papist, or "an enemy to the righteousness of Christ." Bear with me, as I do with you; else how shall we "fulfil the law of

Christ?" Do not make tragical outcries, as though I were "subverting the very foundations of Christianity." Whoever does this, does me much wrong: the Lord lay it not to his charge! I lay, and have done for many years, the very same foundation with you. And, indeed, "other foundation can no man lay, than that which is laid, even Jesus Christ." I build inward and outward holiness thereon, as you do, even by faith. Do not, therefore, suffer any distaste, or unkindness, no, nor any shyness or coldness in your heart. If there were a difference of opinion, where is our religion, if we cannot think and let think? What hinders but you may forgive me as easily as I may forgive you? How much more, when there is only a difference of expression? Nay, hardly so much as that? all the dispute being only, whether a particular mode of expression shall be used more or less frequently? Surely we must earnestly desire to contend with one another, before we can make this a bone of contention! O let us not any more, for such very trifles as these, give our common enemies room to blaspheme! Rather let us at length cut off occasion for them that seek occasion! Let us at length (O why was it not done before?) join hearts and hands in the service of our great Master. As we have "one Lord, one faith, one hope of our calling," let us all strengthen each other's hands in God, and with one heart and one mouth declare to all mankind, "THE LORD OUR RIGHTEOUSNESS."

21.* UPON OUR LORD'S SERMON ON THE MOUNT DISCOURSE 1

"And seeing the multitudes, he went up into a mountain: And when he was set, his disciples came unto him: And he opened his mouth, and taught them, saying, 'Blessed are the poor in spirit: For theirs is the kingdom of heaven. Blessed are they that mourn: For they shall be comforted."

Matt. 5:1–4.

1. Our Lord had now "gone about all Galilee," (Matt. 4:23,) beginning at the time "when John was cast into prison," (Matt. 4:12,) not only "teaching in their synagogues, and preaching the gospel of the kingdom," but likewise "healing all manner of sickness and all manner of disease among the people." It was a natural consequence of this, that "there followed him great multitudes from Galilee, and from Decapolis, and from Jerusalem, and from Judea, and from the region beyond Jordan." (Matt. 4:25.) "And seeing the multitudes," whom no synagogue could contain, even had there been any at hand, "he went up into a mountain," where there was room for all that came unto him, from every quarter. "And when he was set," as the manner of the Jews was, "his disciples came unto him. And he opened his mouth," (an expression denoting the beginning of a solemn discourse.) "and taught them, saying."—

2. Let us observe, who it is that is here speaking, that we may take heed how we hear. It is the Lord of heaven and earth, the Creator of all; who, as such, has a right to dispose of all his creatures; the Lord our Governor, whose kingdom is from everlasting, and ruleth over all; the great Lawgiver, who can well enforce all his laws, being "able to save and to destroy," yea, to punish with "everlasting destruction from his presence and from the glory of his power." It is the eternal Wisdom of the Father, who knoweth whereof we are made, and understands our inmost frame: who knows how we stand related to God, to one another, to every creature which God hath made, and, consequently, how to adapt every law he prescribes, to all the circumstances wherein he hath placed us. It is He who is "loving unto every man, whose mercy is over all his works;" the God of love, who, having emptied himself of his eternal glory, is come forth from his Father to declare his will to the children of men, and then goeth again to the Father; who is sent of God "to open the eyes of the blind, and to give light to them that sit in darkness." It is the great Prophet of the Lord, concerning whom God had solemnly declared long ago, "Whosoever will not hearken unto my words which he shall speak in my name, I will require it of him;" (Deut. 18:19;) or, as the Apostle expresses it, "Every soul which will not hear that Prophet, shall be destroyed from among the people." (Acts 3:23.)

3. And what is it which He is teaching? The Son of God, who came from heaven, is here showing us the way to heaven; to the place which he hath prepared for us; the glory he had before the world began. He is teaching us the true way to life everlasting; the royal way which leads to the kingdom; and the only true way,—for there is none besides; all other paths lead to destruction. From the character of the Speaker, we are well assured that he hath declared the full and perfect will of God. He hath uttered not one tittle too much,—nothing more than he had received of the Father; nor too little,—he hath not shunned to declare the whole counsel of God; much less hath he uttered anything wrong, anything contrary to the will of him that sent him. All his words are true and right concerning all things, and shall stand fast for ever and ever. And we may easily remark, that in explaining and confirming these faithful and true sayings, he takes care to refute not only the mistakes of the Scribes and Pharisees, which then were the false comments whereby the Jewish Teachers of that age had perverted the word of God, but all the practical mistakes that are inconsistent with salvation, which should ever arise in the Christian Church; all the comments whereby the Christian Teachers (so called) of any age or nation should pervert the word of God, and teach unwary souls to seek death in the error of their life.

4. And hence we are naturally led to observe, whom it is that he is here teaching. Not the Apostles alone; if so, he had no need to have gone up into the mountain. A room in the house of Matthew, or any of his disciples, would have contained the Twelve. Nor does it in anywise appear that the disciples who came unto him were the Twelve only. *hoi mathetai autou*, without any force put upon the expression, may be understood of all who desired to learn of him. But to put this out of all question, to make it undeniably plain that where it is said, he opened his mouth and taught them, the word *them* includes all the multitudes who went up with him into the

mountain, we need only observe the concluding verses of the seventh chapter: And it came to pass, when Jesus had ended these sayings, the multitudes (*hoi ochloi*) were astonished at his doctrine, or teaching; for he taught them, the multitudes, "as one having authority, and not as the Scribes." [Matt. 7:28–29]

Nor was it only those multitudes who were with him on the mount, to whom he now taught the way of salvation; but all the children of men; the whole race of mankind; the children that were yet unborn; all the generations to come, even to the end of the world, who should ever hear the words of this life.

5. And this all men allow, with regard to some parts of the ensuing discourse. No man, for instance, denies that what is said of poverty of spirit relates to all mankind. But many have supposed, that other parts concerned only the Apostles, or the first Christians, or the Ministers of Christ; and were never designed for the generality of men, who, consequently, have nothing at all to do with them.

But may we not justly inquire, who told them this, that some parts of this discourse concerned only the Apostles, or the Christians of the apostolic age, or the Ministers of Christ? Bare assertions are not a sufficient proof to establish a point of so great importance. has then our Lord himself taught us, that some parts of his discourse do not concern all mankind? Without doubt, had it been so, he would have told us; he could not have omitted so necessary an information. But has he told us so? Where? In the discourse itself? No: here is not the least intimation of it. Has he said so elsewhere? in any other of his discourses? Not one word so much as glancing this way, can we find in anything he ever spoke, either to the multitudes, or to his disciples. Has any one of the Apostles, or other inspired writers, left such an instruction upon record? No such thing. No assertion of this kind is to be found in all the oracles of God. Who then are the men who are so much wiser than God? wise so far above that is written?

6. Perhaps they will say, that the reason of the thing requires such a restriction to be made. If it does, it must be on one of these two accounts; because, without such a restriction, the discourse would either be apparently absurd, or would contradict some other scripture. But this is not the case. It will plainly appear, when we come to examine the several particulars, that there is no absurdity at all in applying all which our Lord hath here delivered to all mankind. Neither will it infer any contradiction to anything else he has delivered, nor to any other scripture whatever. Nay, it will farther appear, that either all the parts of this discourse are to be applied to men in general, or no part; seeing they are all connected together, all joined as the stones in an arch, of which you cannot take one away, without destroying the whole fabric.

7. We may, Lastly, observe, how our Lord teaches here. And surely, as at all times, so particularly at this, he speaks "as never man spake." Not as the holy men of old; although they also spoke "as they were moved by the Holy Ghost." Not as Peter, or James, or John, or Paul: They were indeed wise master-builders in his Church; but still in this, in the degrees of heavenly wisdom, the servant is not as his Lord. No, nor even as himself at any other time, or on any other occasion.

It does not appear, that it was ever his design, at any other time or place, to lay down at once the whole plan of his religion; to give us a full prospect of Christianity; to describe at large the nature of that holiness, without which no man shall see the Lord. Particular branches of this he has indeed described, on a thousand different occasions; but never, besides here, did he give, of set purpose, a general view of the whole. Nay, we have nothing else of this kind in all the Bible; unless one should except that short sketch of holiness delivered by God in those Ten Words or Commandments to Moses, on mount Sinai. But even here how wide a difference is there between one and the other! "even that which was made glorious had no glory in this respect, by reason of the glory that excelleth." (2 Cor. 3:10.)

8. Above all, with what amazing love does the Son of God here reveal his Fathers will to man! He does not bring us again "to the mount that burned with fire, nor unto blackness, and darkness, and tempest." He does not speak as when he "thundered out of heaven;" when the Highest "gave his thunder, hail-stones, and coals of fire." He now addresses us with his still, small voice, "Blessed," or happy, "are the poor in spirit." Happy are the mourners; the meek; those that hunger after righteousness; the merciful; the pure in heart: Happy in the end, and in the way; happy in this life, and in life everlasting! As if he had said, "Who is he that lusteth to live, and would fain see good days? Behold, I show you the thing which your soul longeth for! See the way you have so long sought in vain; the way of pleasantness; the path to calm, joyous peace, to heaven below and heaven above!"

9. At the same time, with what authority does he teach! Well might they say, "Not as the Scribes." observe the manner, (but it cannot be expressed in words,) the air, with which he speaks! Not as Moses, the servant of God; not as Abraham, his friend; not as any of the Prophets; nor as any of the sons of men. It is something more than human; more than can agree to any created being. It speaks the Creator of all! A God, a God appears! Yea, *o oN*, the Being of beings, JEHOVAH, the self-existent, the Supreme, the God who is over all, blessed for ever!

10. This divine discourse, delivered in the most excellent method, every subsequent part illustrating those that precede, is commonly, and not improperly, divided into three principal branches: The First, contained in the fifth,—the Second, in the sixth,—and the Third, in the seventh chapter. In the First, the sum of all true religion is laid down in eight particulars, which are explained, and guarded against the false glosses of man, in the following parts of the fifth chapter. In the Second are rules for that right intention which we are to preserve in all our outward actions, unmixed with worldly desires, or anxious cares for even the necessaries of life. In the Third are cautions against the main hinderances of religion, closed with an application of the whole.

I. 1. Our Lord, First, lays down the sum of all true religion in eight particulars, which he explains, and guards against the false glosses of men, to the end of the fifth chapter.

Some have supposed that he designed, in these, to point out the several stages of the Christian course; the steps which a Christian successively takes in his journey to the promised land;—others, that all the particulars here set down belong at all times to every Christian. And why may we not allow both the one and the other? What inconsistency is there between them? It is undoubtedly true, that both poverty of spirit, and every other temper which is here mentioned, are at all times found, in a greater or less degree, in every real Christian. And it is equally true, that real Christianity always begins in poverty of spirit, and goes on in the order here set down, till the "man of God is made perfect." We begin at the lowest of these gifts of God, yet so as not to relinquish this, when we are called of God to come up higher: But "whereunto we have already attained, we hold fast," while we press on to what is yet before, to the highest blessings of God in Christ Jesus.

2. The foundation of all is poverty of spirit: Here, therefore, our Lord begins: "Blessed," saith he, "are the poor in spirit; for theirs is the kingdom of heaven."

It may not improbably be supposed, that our Lord looked on those who were round about him, and, observing that not many rich were there, but rather the poor of the world, took occasion from thence to make a transition from temporal to spiritual things. "Blessed," saith he, (or *happy*,—so the word should be rendered, both in this and the following verses,) "are the poor in spirit." He does not say, they that are poor, as to outward circumstances,—it being not impossible, that some of these may be as far from happiness as a monarch upon his throne; but "the poor in spirit,"—they who, whatever their outward circumstances are, have that disposition of heart which is the first step to all real, substantial happiness, either in this world, or that which is to come.

3. Some have judged, that by the poor in spirit here, are meant those who love poverty; those who are free from covetousness, from the love of money; who fear, rather than desire, riches. Perhaps they have been induced so to judge, by wholly confining their thoughts to the very term; or by considering that weighty observation of St. Paul, that "the love of money is the root of all evil." And hence many have wholly divested themselves, not only of riches, but of all worldly goods. Hence also the vows of voluntary poverty seem to have arisen in the Romish Church; it being supposed, that so eminent a degree of this fundamental grace must be a large step toward the "kingdom of heaven."

But these do not seem to have observed, First, that the expression of St. Paul must be understood with some restriction; otherwise it is not true; for the love of money is not the root, the sole root, of all evil. There are a thousand other roots of evil in the world, as sad experience daily shows. His meaning can only be, it is the root of very many evils; perhaps of more than any single vice besides.—Secondly, that this sense of the expression, "poor in spirit," will by no means suit our Lord's present design, which is to lay a general foundation whereon the whole fabric of Christianity may be built; a design which would be in no wise answered by guarding against one particular vice: So that, if even this were supposed to be one part of his meaning, it could not possibly be the whole.—Thirdly, that it cannot be supposed to be any part of his meaning, unless we charge him with manifest tautology: Seeing, if poverty of spirit were only freedom from covetousness, from the love of money, or the desire of riches, it would coincide with what he afterwards mentions, it would be only a branch of purity of heart.

4. Who then are "the poor in spirit?" Without question, the humble; they who know themselves; who are convinced of sin; those to whom God hath given that first repentance, which is previous to faith in Christ.

One of these can no longer say, "I am rich, and increased in goods, and have need of nothing;" as now knowing, that he is "wretched, and poor, and miserable, and blind, and naked." He is convinced that he is spiritually poor indeed; having no spiritual good abiding in him. "In me," saith he, "dwelleth no good thing," but whatsoever is evil and abominable. He has a deep sense of the loathsome leprosy of sin, which be brought with him from his mother's womb, which overspreads his whole soul, and totally corrupts every power and faculty thereof. He sees more and more of the evil tempers which spring from that evil root; the pride and haughtiness of spirit, the constant bias to think of himself more highly than he ought to think; the vanity, the thirst after the esteem or honour that cometh from men, the hatred or envy, the jealousy or revenge, the anger, malice, or bitterness; the inbred enmity both against God and man, which appears in ten thousand shapes; the love of the world, the self-will, the foolish and hurtful desires, which cleave to his inmost soul. He is conscious how deeply he has offended by his tongue; if not by profane, immodest, untrue, or unkind words, yet by discourse which was not "good to the use of edifying," not "meet to minister grace to the hearers." which, consequently, was all corrupt in God's account, and grievous to his Holy Spirit. His evil works are now likewise ever in his sight: If he tells them, they are more than he is able to express. He may as well think to number the drops of rain, the sands of the sea, or the days of eternity.

5. His guilt is now also before his face: He knows the punishment he has deserved, were it only on account of his carnal mind, the entire, universal corruption of his nature; how much more, on account of all his evil desires and thoughts, of all his sinful words and actions! He cannot doubt for a moment, but the least of these deserves the damnation of hell,—"the worm that dieth not, and the fire that never shall be quenched." Above all, the guilt of "not believing on the name of the only-begotten Son of God" lies heavy upon him. How, saith he, shall I escape, who "neglect so great salvation!" "He that believeth not is condemned already," and "the wrath of God abideth on him."

6. But what shall he give in exchange for his soul, which is forfeited to the just vengeance of God? "Wherewithal shall he come before the Lord?" How shall he pay him that he oweth? Were he from this moment to perform the most perfect obedience to every command of God, this would make no amends for a single sin, for any one act of past disobedience; seeing he owes God all the service he is able to perform, from this moment to all eternity: Could he pay this, it would make no manner of amends for what he ought to have done before. He sees himself therefore utterly helpless with regard to atoning for his past sins; utterly unable to make any amends to God, to pay any ransom for his own soul.

But if God would forgive him all that is past, on this one condition, that he should sin no more; that for the time to come he should entirely and constantly obey all his commands; he well knows that this would profit him nothing, being a condition he could never perform. He knows and feels that he is not able to obey even the outward commands of God; seeing these cannot be obeyed while his heart remains in its natural sinfulness and corruption; inasmuch as an evil tree cannot bring forth good fruit. But he cannot cleanse a sinful heart: With men this is impossible: So that he is utterly at a loss even how to begin walking in the path of God's commandments. He knows not how to get one step forward in the way. Encompassed with sin, and sorrow, and fear, and finding no way to escape, he can only cry out, "Lord, save, or I perish!"

7. Poverty of spirit then, as it implies the first step we take in running the race which is set before us, is a just sense of our inward and outward sins, and of our guilt and helplessness. This some have monstrously styled, "the virtue of humility;" thus teaching us to be proud of knowing we deserve damnation! But our Lord's expression is quite of another kind; conveying no idea to the hearer, but that of mere want, of naked sin, of helpless guilt and misery.

8. The great Apostle, where he endeavours to bring sinners to God, speaks in a manner just answerable to this. "The wrath of God," saith he, "is revealed from heaven against all ungodliness and unrighteousness of men;" (Rom. 1:18.) a charge which he immediately fixes on the heathen world, and thereby proves they are under the wrath of God. He next shows that the Jews were no better than they, and were therefore under the same condemnation; and all this, not in order to their attaining "the noble virtue of humility," but "that every mouth might be stopped, and all the world become guilty before God."

He proceeds to show, that they were helpless as well as guilty, which is the plain purport of all those expressions: "Therefore by the deeds of the law there shall no flesh be justified:"—"But now the righteousness of God, which is by faith of Jesus Christ, without the law, is manifested:"—"We conclude, that a man is justified by faith, without the deeds of the law:"—Expressions all tending to the same point, even to "hide pride from man;" to humble him to the dust, without teaching him to reflect upon his humility as a virtue; to inspire him with that full, piercing conviction of his utter sinfulness, guilt, and helplessness, which casts the sinner, stripped of all, lost and undone, on his strong Helper, Jesus Christ the Righteous.

9. One cannot but observe here, that Christianity begins just where heathen morality ends; poverty of spirit, conviction of sin, the renouncing ourselves, the not having our own righteousness, (the very first point in the religion of Jesus Christ,) leaving all pagan religion behind. This was ever hid from the wise men of this world; insomuch that the whole Roman language, even with all the improvements of the Augustan age, does not afford so much as a name for *humility*; (the word from whence we borrow this, as is well known, bearing in Latin a quite different meaning;) no, nor was one found in all the copious language of Greece, till it was made by the great Apostle.

10. O that we may feel what they were not able to express! Sinner, awake! Know thyself! Know and feel, that thou wert "shapen in wickedness," and that "in sin did thy mother conceive thee;" and that thou thyself hast been heaping up sin upon sin, ever since thou couldst discern good from evil! Sink under the mighty hand of God, as guilty of death eternal; and cast off, renounce, abhor, all imagination of ever being able to help thyself! Be it all thy hope to be washed in His blood, and renewed by his almighty Spirit, who himself "bare all our sins in his own body on the tree!" So shalt thou witness, "Happy are the poor in spirit: For theirs is the kingdom of heaven."

11. This is that kingdom of heaven, or of God, which is within us; even "righteousness, and peace, and joy in the Holy Ghost." And what is "righteousness," but the life of God in the soul; the mind which was in Christ Jesus; the image of God stamped upon the heart, now renewed after the likeness of Him that created it? What is it but the love of God, because he first loved us, and the love of all mankind for his sake?

And what is this "peace," the peace of God, but that calm serenity of soul, that sweet repose in the blood of Jesus, which leaves no doubt of our acceptance in him; which excludes all fear, but the loving filial fear of offending our Father which is in heaven?

This inward kingdom implies also "joy in the Holy Ghost;" who seals upon our hearts "the redemption which is in Jesus," the righteousness of Christ imputed to us "for the remission of the sins that are past;" who giveth us now "the earnest of our inheritance," of the crown which the Lord, the righteous Judge, will give at that day. And well may this be termed, "the kingdom of heaven;" seeing it is heaven already opened in the soul; the first springing up of those rivers of pleasure which flow at God's right hand for evermore.

12. "Theirs is the kingdom of heaven." Whosoever thou art, to whom God hath given to be "poor in spirit," to feel thyself lost, thou hast a right thereto, through the gracious promise of Him who cannot lie. It is purchased for thee by the blood of the Lamb. It is very nigh: Thou art on the brink of heaven! Another step, and thou enterest into the kingdom of righteousness, and peace, and joy! Art thou all sin? "Behold the Lamb of God, who taketh away the sin of the world!"—all unholy? See thy "Advocate with the Father, Jesus Christ the Righteous!"—Art thou unable to atone for the least of thy sins? "He is the propitiation for" all thy "sins." Now believe on the Lord Jesus Christ, and all thy sins are blotted out!—Art thou totally unclean in soul and body? Here is the "fountain for sin and uncleanness!" "Arise, and wash away thy sins!" Stagger no more at the promise through unbelief! Give glory to God! Dare to believe! Now cry out, from the ground of thy heart,—

> Yes, I yield, I yield at last,
> Listen to thy speaking blood;
> Me with all my sins, I cast
> On my atoning God.

13. Then thou learnest of him to be "lowly of heart." And this is the true, genuine, Christian humility, which flows from a sense of the love of God, reconciled to us in Christ

Jesus. Poverty of spirit, in this meaning of the word, begins where a sense of guilt and of the wrath of God ends; and is a continual sense of our total dependence on him, for every good thought, or word, or work; of our utter inability to all good, unless he "water us every moment;" and an abhorrence of the praise of men, knowing that all praise is due unto God only. With this is joined a loving shame, a tender humiliation before God, even for the sins which we know he hath forgiven us, and for the sin which still remaineth in our hearts, although we know it is not imputed to our condemnation. Nevertheless, the conviction we feel of inbred sin is deeper and deeper every day. The more we grow in grace, the more do we see of the desperate wickedness of our heart. The more we advance in the knowledge and love of God, through our Lord Jesus Christ, (as great a mystery as this may appear to those who know not the power of God unto salvation,) the more do we discern of our alienation from God, of the enmity that is in our carnal mind, and the necessity of our being entirely renewed in righteousness and true holiness.

II. 1. It is true, he has scarce any conception of this who now begins to know the inward kingdom of heaven. "In his prosperity he saith, I shall never be moved; thou, Lord, hast made my hill so strong." Sin is so utterly bruised beneath his feet, that he can scarce believe it remaineth in him. Even temptation is silenced, and speaks not again: It cannot approach, but stands afar off. He is borne aloft in the chariots of joy and love: He soars, "as upon the wings of an eagle." But our Lord well knew that this triumphant state does not often continue long: He therefore presently subjoins, "Blessed are they that mourn; for they shall be comforted."

2. Not that we can imagine this promise belongs to those who mourn only on some worldly account; who are in sorrow and heaviness merely on account of some worldly trouble or disappointment,—such as the loss of their reputation or friends, or the impairing of their fortune. As little title to it have they who are afflicting themselves, through fear of some temporal evil; or who pine away with anxious care, or that desire of earthly things which "maketh the heart sick." Let us not think these "shall receive anything from the Lord:" He is not in all their thoughts. Therefore it is that they thus "walk in a vain shadow, and disquiet themselves in vain." "And this shall ye have of mine hand," saith the Lord, "ye shall lie down in sorrow."

3. The mourners of whom our Lord here speaks, are those that mourn on quite another account: They that mourn after God; after Him in whom they did "rejoice with joy unspeakable," when he gave them to "taste the good," the pardoning, "word, and the powers of the world to come." But he now "hides his face, and they are troubled:" They cannot see him through the dark cloud. But they see temptation and sin, which they fondly supposed were gone never to return, arising again, following after them amain, and holding them in on every side. It is not strange if their soul is now disquieted within them, and trouble and heaviness take hold upon them. Nor will their great enemy fail to improve the occasion; to ask, "Where is now thy God? Where is now the blessedness whereof thou spakest? the

beginning of the kingdom of heaven? Yea, hath God said, 'Thy sins are forgiven thee?' Surely God hath not said it. It was only a dream, a mere delusion, a creature of thy own imagination. If thy sins are forgiven, why art thou thus? Can a pardoned sinner be thus unholy?"—And, if then, instead of immediately crying to God, they reason with him that is wiser than they, they will be in heaviness indeed, in sorrow of heart, in anguish not to be expressed. Nay even when God shines again upon the soul, and takes away all doubt of his past mercy, still he that is weak in faith may be tempted and troubled on account of what is to come; especially when inward sin revives, and thrusts sore at him that he may fall. Then may he again cry out,

> I have a sin of fear, that when I've spun
> My last thread, I shall perish on the shore!—
> Lest I should make shipwreck of the faith,
> and my last state be worse than the first:—
> Lest all my bread of life should fail,
> And I sink down unchanged to hell!

4. Sure it is, that this "affliction," for the present, "is not joyous, but grievous; nevertheless afterward it bringeth forth peaceable fruit unto them that are exercised thereby." Blessed, therefore, are they that thus mourn, if they "tarry the Lord's leisure," and suffer not themselves to be turned out of the way, by the miserable comforters of the world; if they resolutely reject all the comforts of sin, of folly, and vanity; all the idle diversions and amusements of the world; all the pleasures which "perish in the using," and which only tend to benumb and stupefy the soul, that it may neither be sensible of itself nor God. Blessed are they who "follow on to know the Lord," and steadily refuse all other comfort. They shall be comforted by the consolations of his Spirit; by a fresh manifestation of his love; by such a witness of his accepting them in the Beloved, as shall never more be taken away from them. This "full assurance of faith" swallows up all doubt, as well as all tormenting fear; God now giving them a sure hope of an enduring substance, and "strong consolation through grace." Without disputing whether it be possible for any of those to "fall away, who were once enlightened and made partakers of the Holy Ghost," it suffices them to say, by the power now resting upon them, "Who shall separate us from the love of Christ?—I am persuaded, that neither death nor life, nor things present nor things to come, nor height nor depth, shall be able to separate us from the love of God, which is in Christ Jesus our Lord." (Rom. 8:35–39.)

5. This whole process, both of mourning for an absent God, and recovering the joy of his countenance, seems to be shadowed out in what our Lord spoke to his Apostles, the night before his passion: "Do ye inquire of that I said, A little while, and ye shall not see me: And again, a little while, and ye shall see me? Verily, verily, I say unto you, that ye shall weep and lament;" namely, when ye do not see me; "but the world shall rejoice;" shall triumph over you, as though your hope were now come to an end. "And ye shall be sorrowful," through doubt, through fear, through temptation, through vehement desire; "but your sorrow shall be turned into joy," by the return of Him whom your soul loveth. "A woman when she is in travail hath sorrow, because her hour is come.

But as soon as she is delivered of the child, she remembereth no more the anguish, for joy that a man is born into the world. And ye now have sorrow;" ye mourn and cannot be comforted; "but I will see you again; and your heart shall rejoice," with calm, inward joy, "and your joy no man taketh from you." (John 16:19–22.)

6. But although this mourning is at an end, is lost in holy joy, by the return of the Comforter, yet is there another, and a blessed mourning it is, which abides in the children of God. They still mourn for the sins and miseries of mankind: They "weep with them that weep." They weep for them that weep not for themselves, for the sinners against their own souls. They mourn for the weakness and unfaithfulness of those that are, in some measure, saved from their sins. "Who is weak, and they are not weak? Who is offended, and they burn not?" They are grieved for the dishonour continually done to the Majesty of heaven and earth. At all times they have an awful sense of this, which brings a deep seriousness upon their spirit; a seriousness which is not a little increased, since the eyes of their understanding were opened, by their continually seeing the vast ocean of eternity, without a bottom or a shore, which has already swallowed up millions of millions of men, and is gaping to devour them that yet remain. They see here the house of God eternal in the heavens; there, hell and destruction without a covering; and thence feel the importance of every moment, which just appears, and is gone for ever!

7. But all this wisdom of God is foolishness with the world. The whole affair of mourning and poverty of spirit is with them stupidity and dulness. Nay, it is well if they pass so favourable a judgment upon it; if they do not vote it to be mere moping and melancholy, if not downright lunacy and distraction. And it is no wonder at all, that this judgment should be passed by those who know not God. Suppose, as two persons were walking together, one should suddenly stop, and with the strongest signs of fear and amazement, cry out, "On what a precipice do we stand! See, we are on the point of being dashed in pieces! Another step, and we fall into that huge abyss! Stop! I will not go on for all the world!"—when the other, who seemed, to himself at least, equally sharp-sighted, looked forward and saw nothing of all this; what would he think of his companion, but that he was beside himself; that his head was out of order; that much religion (if he was not guilty of "much learning") had certainly made him mad!

8. But let not the children of God, "the mourners in Sion," be moved by any of these things. Ye, whose eyes are enlightened, be not troubled by those who walk on still in darkness. Ye do not walk on in a vain shadow: God and eternity are real things. Heaven and hell are in very deed open before you; and ye are on the edge of the great gulf. It has already swallowed up more than words can express, nations, and kindreds, and peoples, and tongues; and still yawns to devour, whether they see it or no, the giddy, miserable children of men. O cry aloud! Spare not! Lift up your voice to Him who grasps both time and eternity, both for

yourselves and your brethren, that ye may be counted worthy to escape the destruction that cometh as a whirlwind! that ye may be brought safe through all the waves and storms into the haven where you would be! Weep for yourselves, till he wipes away the tears from your eyes. And even then, weep for the miseries that come upon the earth, till the Lord of all shall put a period to misery and sin, shall wipe away the tears from all faces, and "the knowledge of the Lord shall cover the earth, as the waters cover the sea."

22.* Upon our Lord's Sermon on the Mount Discourse 2

"Blessed are the meek: For they shall inherit the earth. Blessed are they which do hunger and thirst after righteousness: For they shall be filled. Blessed are the merciful: For they shall obtain mercy."

Matt. 5:5–7

I. 1. When "the winter is past," when "the time of singing is come, and the voice of the turtle is heard in the land;" when He that comforts the mourners is now returned, "that he may abide with them for ever;" when, at the brightness of his presence, the clouds disperse, the dark clouds of doubt and uncertainty, the storms of fear flee away, the waves of sorrow subside, and their spirit again rejoiceth in God their Saviour; then is it that this word is eminently fulfilled; then those whom he hath comforted can bear witness, "Blessed," or happy, "are the meek; for they shall inherit the earth."

2. But who are "the meek?" Not those who grieve at nothing, because they know nothing; who are not discomposed at the evils that occur, because they discern not evil from good. Not those who are sheltered from the shocks of life by a stupid insensibility; who have, either by nature or art, the virtue of stocks and stones, and resent nothing, because they feel nothing. Brute philosophers are wholly unconcerned in this matter. Apathy is as far from meekness as from humanity. So that one would not easily conceive how any Christians of the purer ages, especially any of the Fathers of the Church, could confound these, and mistake one of the foulest errors of Heathenism for a branch of true Christianity.

3. Nor does Christian meekness imply, the being without zeal for God, any more than it does ignorance or insensibility. No; it keeps clear of every extreme, whether in excess or defect. It does not destroy but balance the affections, which the God of nature never designed should be rooted out by grace, but only brought and kept under due regulations. It poises the mind aright. It holds an even scale, with regard to anger, and sorrow, and fear; preserving the mean in every circumstance of life, and not declining either to the right hand or the left.

4. Meekness, therefore, seems properly to relate to ourselves[.] But it may be referred either to God or our neighbour. When this due composure of mind has reference to God, it is usually termed resignation; a calm acquiescence in whatsoever is his will concerning us, even though it may not be pleasing to nature; saying continually, "It is the Lord;

---

* [text of the 1872 edition]

let him do what seemeth him good." When we consider it more strictly with regard to ourselves, we style it patience or contentedness. When it is exerted toward other men, then it is mildness to the good, and gentleness to the evil.

5. They who are truly meek, can clearly discern what is evil; and they can also suffer it. They are sensible of everything of this kind, but still meekness holds the reins. They are exceeding "zealous for the Lord of hosts;" but their zeal is always guided by knowledge, and tempered, in every thought, and word, and work, with the love of man, as well as the love of God. They do not desire to extinguish any of the passions which God has for wise ends implanted in their nature; but they have the mastery of all: They hold them all in subjection, and employ them only in subservience to those ends. And thus even the harsher and more unpleasing passions are applicable to the noblest purposes; even hatred, and anger, and fear, when engaged against sin, and regulated by faith and love, are as walls and bulwarks to the soul, so that the wicked one cannot approach to hurt it.

6. It is evident, this divine temper is not only to abide but to increase in us day by day. Occasions of exercising, and thereby increasing it, will never be wanting while we remain upon earth. "We have need of patience, that after we have done" and suffered "the will of God, we may receive the promise." We have need of resignation, that we may in all circumstances say, "Not as I will, but as thou wilt." And we have need of "gentleness toward all men;" but especially toward the evil and unthankful: Otherwise we shall be overcome of evil, instead of overcoming evil with good.

7. Nor does meekness restrain only the outward act, as the Scribes and Pharisees taught of old, and the miserable Teachers who are not taught of God will not fail to do in all ages. Our Lord guards against this, and shows the true extent of it, in the following words: "Ye have heard that it was said by them of old time, Thou shalt not kill; and whosoever shall kill, shall be in danger of the judgment:" (Matt. 5:21.) "But I say unto you, That whosoever is angry with his brother without a cause, shall be in danger of the judgment: And whosoever shall say to his brother, Raca, shall be in danger of the council: But whosoever shall say, Thou fool, shall be in danger of hell-fire."

8. Our Lord here ranks under the head of murder, even that anger which goes no farther than the heart; which does not show itself by an outward unkindness, no, not so much as a passionate word. "Whosoever is angry with his brother," with any man living, seeing we are all brethren; whosoever feels any unkindness in his heart, any temper contrary to love; whosoever is angry without a cause, without a sufficient cause, or farther than that cause requires, "shall be in danger of the judgment;" _enochos estai, shall, in that moment, be obnoxious to the righteous judgment of God.

But would not one be inclined to prefer the reading of those copies which omit the word eike, without a cause? Is it not entirely superfluous? For if anger at persons be a temper contrary to love, how can there be a cause, a sufficient cause for it, any that will justify it in the sight of God?

Anger at sin we allow. In this sense we may be angry, and yet we sin not. In this sense our Lord himself is once recorded to have been angry: he looked round about upon them with anger, being grieved for the hardness of their hearts. he was grieved at the sinners, and angry at the sin. And this is undoubtedly right before God.

9. And whosoever shall say to his brother, Raca; whosoever shall give way to anger, so as to utter any contemptuous word. It is observed by commentators, that Raca is a Syriac word, which properly signifies, empty, vain, foolish; so that it is as inoffensive an expression as can well be used, toward one at whom we are displeased. And yet, whosoever shall use this, as our Lord assures us, shall be in danger of the council; rather, shall be obnoxious thereto: he shall be liable to a severer sentence from the Judge of all the earth. "But whosoever shall say, Thou fool;"—whosoever shall so give place to the devil, as to break out into reviling, into designedly reproachful and contumelious language, "shall be obnoxious to hell-fire;" shall, in that instant, be liable to the highest condemnation. It should be observed, that our Lord describes all these as obnoxious to capital punishment. The first, to strangling, usually inflicted on those who were condemned in one of the inferior courts; the second, to stoning, which was frequently inflicted on those who were condemned by the great Council at Jerusalem; the third, to burning alive, inflicted only on the highest offenders, in the "valley of the sons of Hinnom;" Ge Hennon, from which that word is evidently taken which we translate "hell."

10. And whereas men naturally imagine, that God will excuse their defect in some duties, for their exactness in others; our Lord next takes care to cut off that vain, though common imagination. He shows, that it is impossible for any sinner to commute with God; who will not accept one duty for another, nor take a part of obedience for the whole. He warns us, that the performing our duty to God will not excuse us from our duty to our neighbour; that works of piety, as they are called, will be so far from commending us to God, if we are wanting in charity, that, on the contrary, that want of charity will make all those works an abomination to the Lord. "Therefore, if thou bring thy gift to the altar, and there rememberest that thy brother hath aught against thee,"—on account of thy unkind behaviour toward him, of thy calling him "Raca," or, "Thou fool;" think not that thy gift will atone for thy anger; or that it will find any acceptance with God, so long as thy conscience is defiled with the guilt of unrepented sin. "Leave there thy gift before the altar, and go thy way; first be reconciled to thy brother," (at least do all that in thee lies toward being reconciled,) "and then come and offer thy gift." (Matt. 5:23, 24.)

11. And let there be no delay in what so nearly concerneth thy soul. "Agree with thine adversary quickly;"—now; upon the spot; "whiles thou art in the way with him;" if it be possible, before he go out of thy sight; "lest at any time the adversary deliver thee to the judge;" lest he appeal to God, the Judge of all; "and the judge deliver thee to the officer;" to Satan, the executioner of the wrath of God; "and thou be cast into prison;" into hell, there to be reserved to the judgment of the great day: "Verily, I say unto thee, Thou shalt by no means come out thence, till thou hast paid the uttermost farthing." But this it is impossible for thee ever to do; seeing

thou hast nothing to pay. Therefore, if thou art once in that prison, the smoke of thy torment must "ascend up for ever and ever."

12. Meantime "the meek shall inherit the earth." Such is the foolishness of worldly wisdom! The wise of the world had warned them again and again,—that if they did not resent such treatment, if they would tamely suffer themselves to be thus abused, there would be no living for them upon earth; that they would never be able to procure the common necessaries of life, nor to keep even what they had; that they could expect no peace, no quiet possession, no enjoyment of anything. Most true,—suppose there were no God in the world; or, suppose he did not concern himself with the children of men: But, "when God ariseth to judgment, and to help all the meek upon earth," how doth he laugh all this heathen wisdom to scorn, and turn the "fierceness of man to his praise!" He takes a peculiar care to provide them with all things needful for life and godliness; he secures to them the provision he hath made, in spite of the force, fraud, or malice of men; and what he secures he gives them richly to enjoy. It is sweet to them, be it little or much. As in patience they possess their souls, so they truly possess whatever God hath given them. They are always content, always pleased with what they have: It pleases them because it pleases God: So that while their heart, their desire, their joy is in heaven, they may truly be said to "inherit the earth."

13. But there seems to be a yet farther meaning in these words, even that they shall have a more eminent part in "the new earth, wherein dwelleth righteousness;" in that inheritance, a general description of which (and the particulars we shall know hereafter) St. John has given in the twentieth chapter of the Revelation: "And I saw an angel come down from heaven,—and he laid hold on the dragon, that old serpent,—and bound him a thousand years.—And I saw the souls of them that were beheaded for the witness of Jesus, and for the word of God, and of them which had not worshipped the Beast, neither his image, neither had received his mark upon their foreheads or in their hands; and they lived and reigned with Christ a thousand years. But the rest of the dead lived not again, until the thousand years were finished. This is the first resurrection. Blessed and holy is he that hath part in the first resurrection: on such the second death hath no power, but they shall be priests of God and of Christ, and shall reign with him a thousand years." [Rev. 20:6]

II. 1. our Lord has hitherto been more immediately employed in removing the hindrances of true religion: Such is pride, the first, grand hindrance of all religion, which is taken away by poverty of spirit; levity and thoughtlessness, which prevent any religion from taking root in the soul, till they are removed by holy mourning; such are anger, impatience, discontent, which are all healed by Christian meekness. And when once these hindrances are removed, these evil diseases of the soul, which were continually raising false cravings therein, and filling it with sickly appetites, the native appetite of a heaven-born spirit returns; it hungers and thirsts after righteousness: And "blessed are they which do hunger and thirst after righteousness; for they shall be filled."

2. Righteousness, as was observed before, is the image of God, the mind which was in Christ Jesus. It is every holy and heavenly temper in one; springing from, as well as terminating in, the love of God, as our Father and Redeemer, and the love of all men for his sake.

3. "Blessed are they which do hunger and thirst after" this: In order fully to understand which expression, we should observe, First, that hunger and thirst are the strongest of all our bodily appetites. In like manner this hunger in the soul, this thirst after the image of God, is the strongest of all our spiritual appetites, when it is once awakened in the heart: Yea, it swallows up all the rest in that one great desire,—to be renewed after the likeness of Him that created us. We should, Secondly, observe, that from the time we begin to hunger and thirst, those appetites do not cease, but are more and more craving and importunate, till we either eat and drink, or die. And even so, from the time that we begin to hunger and thirst after the whole mind which was in Christ, these spiritual appetites do not cease, but cry after their food with more and more importunity; nor can they possibly cease, before they are satisfied, while there is any spiritual life remaining. We may, Thirdly, observe, that hunger and thirst are satisfied with nothing but meat and drink. If you would give to him that is hungry all the world beside, all the elegance of apparel, all the trappings of state, all the treasure upon earth, yea thousands of gold and silver; if you would pay him ever so much honour;—he regards it not: All these things are then of no account with him. He would still say, "These are not the things I want; give me food, or else I die." The very same is the case with every soul that truly hungers and thirsts after righteousness. He can find no comfort in anything but this: He can be satisfied with nothing else. Whatever you offer besides, it is lightly esteemed: Whether it be riches, or honour, or pleasure, he still says, "This is not the thing which I want! Give me love, or else I die!"

4. And it is as impossible to satisfy such a soul, a soul that is athirst for God, the living God, with what the world accounts religion, as with what they account happiness. The religion of the world implies three things: (1.) The doing no harm, the abstaining from outward sin; at least from such as is scandalous, as robbery, theft, common swearing, drunkenness: (2.) The doing good, the relieving the poor; the being charitable, as it is called: (3.) The using the means of grace; at least the going to church and to the Lords Supper. He in whom these three marks are found is termed by the world a religious man. But will this satisfy him who hungers after God? No: It is not food for his soul. He wants a religion of a nobler kind, a religion higher and deeper than this. He can no more feed on this poor, shallow, formal thing, than he can "fill his belly with the east wind." True, he is careful to abstain from the very appearance of evil; he is zealous of good works; he attends all the ordinances of God: But all this is not what he longs for. This is only the outside of that religion, which he insatiably hungers after. The knowledge of God in Christ Jesus; "the life which is hid with Christ in God;" the being "joined unto the Lord in one Spirit;" the having "fellowship with the Father and the Son;" the "walking in the light as God is in the light;" the being

"purified even as He is pure;"—this is the religion, the righteousness, he thirsts after: Nor can he rest, till he thus rests in God.

5. "Blessed are they who" thus "hunger and thirst after righteousness; for they shall be filled." They shall be filled with the things which they long for; even with righteousness and true holiness. God shall satisfy them with the blessings of his goodness, with the felicity of his chosen. He shall feed them with the bread of heaven, with the manna of his love. He shall give them to drink of his pleasures as out of the river, which he that drinketh of shall never thirst, only for more and more of the water of life. This thirst shall endure for ever.

> The painful thirst, the fond desire,
> Thy joyous presence shall remove;
> But my full soul shall still require
> A whole eternity of love.

6. Whosoever then thou art, to whom God hath given to "hunger and thirst after righteousness," cry unto him that thou mayest never lose that inestimable gift,—that this divine appetite may never cease. If many rebuke thee, and bid thee hold thy peace, regard them not; yea, cry so much the more, "Jesus, Master, have mercy on me!" "Let me not live, but to be holy as thou art holy!" No more "spend thy money for that which is not bread, nor thy labour for that which satisfieth not." Canst thou hope to dig happiness out of the earth,—to find it in the things of the world? o trample under foot all its pleasures, despise its honours, count its riches as dung and dross,—yea, and all the things which are beneath the sun,—"for the excellency of the knowledge of Christ Jesus," for the entire renewal of thy soul in that image of God wherein it was originally created. Beware of quenching that blessed hunger and thirst, by what the world calls religion; a religion of form, of outward show, which leaves the heart as earthly and sensual as ever. Let nothing satisfy thee but the power of godliness, but a religion that is spirit and life; thy dwelling in God and God in thee,—the being an inhabitant of eternity; the entering in by the blood of sprinkling "within the veil," and sitting "in heavenly places with Christ Jesus."

III. 1. And the more they are filled with the life of God, the more tenderly will they be concerned for those who are still without God in the world, still dead in trespasses and sins. Nor shall this concern for others lose its reward. "Blessed are the merciful; for they shall obtain mercy."

The word used by our Lord more immediately implies the compassionate, the tender-hearted; those who, far from despising, earnestly grieve for, those that do not hunger after God.

This eminent part of brotherly love is here, by a common figure, put for the whole; so that "the merciful," in the full sense of the term, are they who love their neighbours as themselves."

2. Because of the vast importance of this love,—without which, "though we spake with the tongues of men and angels, though we had the gift of prophecy, and understood all mysteries, and all knowledge; though we had all faith, so as to remove mountains; yea, though we gave all our goods to feed the poor, and our very bodies to be burned, it would profit us nothing,"—the wisdom of God has given us, by the Apostle Paul, a full and particular account of it; by considering which we shall most clearly discern who are the merciful that shall obtain mercy.

3. "Charity," or love, (as it were to be wished it had been rendered throughout, being a far plainer and less ambiguous word,) the love of our neighbour as Christ hath loved us, "suffereth long;" is patient toward all men: It suffers all the weakness, ignorance, errors, infirmities, all the frowardness and littleness of faith, of the children of God; all the malice and wickedness of the children of the world. And it suffers all this, not only for a time, for a short season, but to the end; still feeding our enemy when he hungers; if he thirst, still giving him drink; thus continually "heaping coals of fire," of melting love, "upon his head."

4. And in every step toward this desirable end, the "overcoming evil with good," "love is kind:" (*chresteuetai*, a word not easily translated:) It is *soft, mild, benign*. It stands at the utmost distance from moroseness, from all harshness or sourness of spirit; and inspires the sufferer at once with the most amiable sweetness, and the most fervent and tender affection.

5. Consequently, "love envieth not:" It is impossible it should; it is directly opposite to that baneful temper. It cannot be, that he who has this tender affection to all, who earnestly wishes all temporal and spiritual blessings, all good things in this world and the world to come, to every soul that God hath made, should be pained at his bestowing any good gift on any child of man. If he has himself received the same, he does not grieve, but rejoice, that another partakes of the common benefit. If he has not, he blesses God that his brother at least has, and is herein happier than himself. And the greater his love, the more does he rejoice in the blessings of all mankind; the farther is he removed from every kind and degree of envy toward any creature.

6. Love *ou perpereuetai*, not vaunteth not itself; which coincides with the very next words; but rather, (as the word likewise properly imports,) *is not rash* or *hasty* in judging; it will not hastily condemn any one. It does not pass a severe sentence, on a slight or sudden view of things: It first weighs all the evidence, particularly that which is brought in favour of the accused. A true lover of his neighbour is not like the generality of men, who, even in cases of the nicest nature, see a little, presume a great deal, and so jump to the conclusion. No: he proceeds with wariness and circumspection, taking heed to every step; willingly subscribing to that rule of the ancient heathen, (o where will the modern Christian appear!) I am so far from lightly believing what one man says against another, that I will not easily believe what a man says against himself. I will always allow him second thoughts, and many times counsel too.

7. It follows, love "is not puffed up:" It does not incline or suffer any man "to think more highly of himself than he ought to think;" but rather to think soberly: Yea, it humbles the soul unto the dust. It destroys all high conceits, engendering pride; and makes us rejoice to be as nothing, to be little and vile, the lowest of all, the servant of all. They who are "kindly affectioned one to another with brotherly love," cannot but "in honour prefer one another." Those

who, having the same love, are of one accord, do in lowliness of mind "each esteem other better thanthemselves."

8. "It doth not behave itself unseemly:" It is not rude, or willingly offensive to any. It "renders to all their due; fear to whom fear, honour to whom honour;" courtesy, civility, humanity to all the world; in their several degrees "honouring all men." A late writer defines good breeding, nay, the highest degree of it, politeness, "A continual desire to please, appearing in all the behaviour." But if so, there is none so well-bred as a Christian, a lover of all mankind. For he cannot but desire to "please all men for their good to edification:" And this desire cannot be hid; it will necessarily appear in all his intercourse with men. For his "love is without dissimulation:" It will appear in all his actions and conversation; yea, and will constrain him, though without guile, "to become all things to all men, if by any means he may save some."

9. And in becoming all things to all men, "love seeketh not her own." In striving to please all men, the lover of mankind has no eye at all to his own temporal advantage. he covets no mans silver, or gold, or apparel: He desires nothing but the salvation of their souls: Yea, in some sense, he may be said, *not to seek his own* spiritual, any more than temporal, advantage; for while he is on the full stretch to save their souls from death, he, as it were, forgets himself. He does not think of himself, so long as that zeal for the glory of God swallows him up. Nay, at some times he may almost seem, through an excess of love, to give up himself, both his soul and his body; while he cries out, with Moses, "o, this people have sinned a great sin; yet now, if thou wilt forgive their sin; and if not, blot me out of the book which thou hast written;" (Exod. 32:31, 32;)—or, with St. Paul, "I could wish that myself were accursed from Christ, for my brethren, my kinsmen according to the flesh!" (Rom. 9:3.)

10. No marvel that such "love is not provoked:" *ou paroxynetai.* Let it be observed, the word *easily*, strangely inserted in the translation, is not in the original: St. Pauls words are absolute. "Love is not provoked:" It is not provoked to unkindness toward any one. occasions indeed will frequently occur; outward provocations of various kinds; but love does not yield to provocation; it triumphs over all. In all trials it looketh unto Jesus, and is more than conqueror in his love.

It is not improbable that our translators inserted that word, as it were, to *excuse* the Apostle; who, as they supposed, might otherwise appear to be wanting in the very love which he so beautifully describes. They seem to have supposed this from a phrase in the Acts of the Apostles; which is likewise very inaccurately translated. When Paul and Barnabas disagreed concerning John, the translation runs thus, "And the contention was so sharp between them, that they departed asunder." (Acts 15:39.) This naturally induces the reader to suppose, that they were equally sharp therein; that St. Paul, who was undoubtedly right, with regard to the point in question, (it being quite improper to take John with them again, who had deserted them before,) was as much provoked as Barnabas, who gave such a proof of his anger, as to leave the work for which he had been set apart by the Holy Ghost.

But the original imports no such thing; nor does it affirm that St. Paul was provoked at all. It simply says, *egeneto oun paroxysmos,* And there was a sharpness, *a paroxysm* of anger; in consequence of which Barnabas left St. Paul, took John, and went his own way. Paul then chose Silas and departed, being recommended by the brethren to the grace of God; (which is not said concerning Barnabas;) and he went through Syria and Cilicia, as he had proposed, "confirming the churches." [Acts 15:39–41] But to return.

11. Love prevents a thousand provocations which would otherwise arise, because it "thinketh no evil." Indeed the merciful man cannot avoid knowing many things that are evil, he cannot but see them with his own eyes, and hear them with his own ears. For love does not put out his eyes, so that it is impossible for him not to see that such things are done; neither does it take away his understanding, any more than his senses, so that he cannot but know that they are evil. For instance: When he sees a man strike his neighbour, or hears him blaspheme God, he cannot either question the thing done, or the words spoken, or doubt of their being evil. Yet, *ou logizetai to kakon.* The word *logizetai,* thinketh, does not refer either to our seeing and hearing, or to the first and involuntary acts of our understanding; but to our *willingly thinking* what we need not; our *inferring* evil, where it does not appear; to our *reasoning* concerning things which we do not see; our *supposing* what we have neither seen nor heard. This is what true love absolutely destroys. It tears up, root and branch, all *imagining* what we have not known. It casts out all jealousies, all evil surmisings, all readiness to believe evil. It is frank, open, unsuspicious; and, as it cannot design, so neither does it fear, evil.

12. It rejoiceth not in iniquity; common as this is, even among those who bear the name of Christ, who scruple not to rejoice over their enemy, when he falleth either into affliction, or error, or sin. Indeed, how hardly can they avoid this, who are zealously attached to any party! how difficult is it for them not to be pleased with any fault which they discover in those of the opposite party, with any real or supposed blemish, either in their principles or practice! What warm defender of any cause is clear of these? Yea, who is so calm as to be altogether free? Who does not rejoice when his adversary makes a false step, which he thinks will advantage his own cause? only a man of love. he alone weeps over either the sin or folly of his enemy, takes no pleasure in hearing or in repeating it, but rather desires that it may be forgotten for ever.

13. But he rejoiceth in the truth, wheresoever it is found; in "the truth which is after godliness;" bringing forth its proper fruit, holiness of heart, and holiness of conversation. he rejoices to find that even those who oppose him, whether with regard to opinions, or some points of practice, are nevertheless lovers of God, and in other respects unreprovable. He is glad to hear good of them, and to speak all he can consistently with truth and justice. Indeed, good in general is his glory and joy, wherever diffused throughout the race of mankind. As a citizen of the world, he claims a share in the happiness of all the inhabitants of it. Because he is a man, he is not unconcerned in the welfare of any man; but

enjoys whatsoever brings glory to God, and promotes peace and good-will among men.

14. This "love covereth all things:" (So, without all doubt, *panta stegei* should be translated; for otherwise it would be the very same with *panta hypomenei*, "endureth all things:") Because the merciful man rejoiceth not in iniquity, neither does he willingly make mention of it. Whatever evil he sees, hears, or knows, he nevertheless conceals, so far as he can without making himself "partaker of other men's sins." Wheresoever or with whomsoever he is, if he sees anything which he approves not, it goes not out of his lips, unless to the person concerned, if haply he may gain his brother. So far is he from making the faults or failures of others the matter of his conversation, that of the absent he never does speak at all, unless he can speak well. A tale-bearer, a backbiter, a whisperer, an evil-speaker, is to him all one as a murderer. He would just as soon cut his neighbour's throat, as thus murder his reputation. Just as soon would he think of diverting himself by setting fire to his neighbour's house, as of thus "scattering abroad arrows, fire-brands, and death," and saying, "Am I not in sport?"

He makes one only exception. Sometimes he is convinced that it is for the glory of God, or (which comes to the same) the good of his neighbour, that an evil should not be covered. In this case, for the benefit of the innocent, he is constrained to declare the guilty. But even here, (1.) He will not speak at all, till love, superior love, constrains him. (2.) He cannot do it from a general confused view of doing good, or promoting the glory of God, but from a clear sight of some particular end, some determinate good which he pursues. (3.) Still he cannot speak, unless he be fully convinced that this very means is necessary to that end; that the end cannot be answered, at least not so effectually, by any other way. (4.) He then doeth it with the utmost sorrow and reluctance; using it as the last and worst medicine, a desperate remedy in a desperate case, a kind of poison never to be used but to expel poison. Consequently, (5.) He uses it as sparingly as possible. And this he does with fear and trembling, lest he should transgress the law of love by speaking too much, more than he would have done by not speaking at all.

15. Love "believeth all things." It is always willing to think the best; to put the most favourable construction on everything. It is ever ready to believe whatever may tend to the advantage of any one's character. It is easily convinced of (what it earnestly desires) the innocence or integrity of any man; or, at least, of the sincerity of his repentance, if he had once erred from the way. It is glad to excuse whatever is amiss; to condemn the offender as little as possible; and to make all the allowance for human weakness which can be done without betraying the truth of God.

16. And when it can no longer believe, then love "hopeth all things." Is any evil related of any man? Love hopes that the relation is not true, that the thing related was never done. Is it certain it was?—"But perhaps it was not done with such circumstances as are related; so that, allowing the fact, there is room to hope it was not so ill as it is represented." Was the action apparently undeniably evil? Love hopes the intention was not so. Is it clear, the design was evil too?—"Yet might it

not spring from the settled temper of the heart, but from a start of passion, or from some vehement temptation, which hurried the man beyond himself." And even when it cannot be doubted, but all the actions, designs, and tempers are equally evil; still love hopes that God will at last make bare his arm, and get himself the victory; and that there shall be "joy in heaven over" this "one sinner that repenteth, more than over ninety and nine just persons that need no repentance."

17. Lastly. It "endureth all things." This completes the character of him that is truly merciful. He endureth not some, not many, things only; not most, but absolutely *all things*. Whatever the injustice, the malice, the cruelty of men can inflict, he is able to suffer. He calls nothing intolerable; he never says of anything, "This is not to be borne." No; he can not only do, but suffer, all things through Christ which strengtheneth him. And all he suffers does not destroy his love, nor impair it in the least. It is proof against all. It is a flame that burns even in the midst of the great deep. "Many waters cannot quench" his "love, neither can the floods drown it." It triumphs over all. It "never faileth," either in time or in eternity.

> In obedience to what heaven decrees,
> Knowledge shall fail, and prophecy shall cease;
> But lasting charity's more ample sway,
> Nor bound by time, nor subject to decay,
> In happy triumph shall for ever live,
> And endless good diffuse, and endless praise receive.

So shall "the merciful obtain mercy;" not only by the blessing of God upon all their ways, by his now repaying the love they bear to their brethren a thousand fold into their own bosom; but likewise by "an exceeding and eternal weight of glory," in the "kingdom prepared for them from the beginning of the world."

18. For a little while you may say, "Woe is me, that I" am constrained to "dwell with Mesech, and to have my habitation among the tents of Kedar!" You may pour out your soul, and bemoan the loss of true, genuine love in the earth: Lost indeed! You may well say, (but not in the ancient sense,) "See how *these Christians* love one another!" these Christian kingdoms, that are tearing out each other's bowels, desolating one another with fire and sword! these Christian armies, that are sending each by thousands, by ten thousands, quick into hell! these Christian nations, that are all on fire with intestine broils, party against party, faction against faction! these Christian cities, where deceit and fraud, oppression and wrong, yea, robbery and murder, go not out of their streets! these Christian families, torn asunder with envy, jealousy, anger, domestic jars, without number, without end! yea, what is most dreadful, most to be lamented of all, these Christian Churches!—Churches ("tell it not in Gath,"—but, alas! how can we hide it, either from Jews, Turks, or Pagans?) that bear the name of Christ, the Prince of Peace, and wage continual war with each other! that convert sinners by burning them alive! that are "drunk with the blood of the saints!"—Does this praise belong only to "Babylon the Great, the mother of harlots and abominations of the earth?" Nay, verily; but Reformed Churches (so called)

have fairly learned to tread in her steps. Protestant Churches too know to persecute, when they have power in their hands, even unto blood. And, meanwhile, how do they also anathematize each other! devote each other to the nethermost hell! What wrath, what contention, what malice, what bitterness, is everywhere found among them, even where they agree in essentials, and only differ in opinions, or in the circumstantials of religion! Who follows after *only* the "things that make for peace, and things wherewith one may edify another?" O God! how long? Shall thy promise fail? Fear it not, ye little flock! Against hope, believe in hope! It is your Father's good pleasure yet to renew the face of the earth. Surely all these things shall come to an end, and the inhabitants of the earth shall learn righteousness. "Nation shall not lift up sword against nation, neither shall they know war any more." "The mountains of the Lord's house shall be established on the top of the mountains;" and "all the kingdoms of the earth shall become the kingdoms of our God." "They shall not" then "hurt or destroy in all his holy mountain;" but they shall call their "walls salvation, and their gates praise." They shall all be without spot or blemish, loving one another, even as Christ hath loved us.—Be thou part of the first-fruits, if the harvest is not yet. Do thou love thy neighbor as thyself. The Lord God fill thy heart with such a love to every soul, that thou mayest be ready to lay down thy life for his sake! May thy soul continually overflow with love, swallowing up every unkind and unholy temper, till he calleth thee up into the region of love, there to reign with him for ever and ever!

23.* UPON OUR LORD'S SERMON ON THE MOUNT DISCOURSE 3

"Blessed are the pure in heart: For they shall see God.
"Blessed are the peacemakers: For they shall be called the children of God. "Blessed are they which are persecuted for righteousness' sake: For theirs is the kingdom of heaven.
"Blessed are ye, when men shall revile you, and persecute you, and shall say all manner of evil against you falsely, for my sake.
"Rejoice, and be exceeding glad: For great is your reward in heaven: For so persecuted they the Prophets which were before you."

Matt. 5:8–12.

I. 1. How excellent things are spoken of the love of our neighbour! It is "the fulfilling of the law," "the end of the commandment." Without this, all we have, all we do, all we suffer, is of no value in the sight of God. But it is that love of our neighbour which springs from the love of God: Otherwise itself is nothing worth. It behoves us, therefore, to examine well upon what foundation our love of our neighbour stands; whether it is really built upon the love of God; whether we do "love him because he first loved us;" whether we are pure in heart: For this is the foundation which shall never be moved. "Blessed are the pure in heart: For they shall see God."

2. "The pure in heart" are they whose hearts God hath "purified even as he is pure;" who are purified, through faith in the blood of Jesus, from every unholy affection; who, being "cleansed from all filthiness of flesh and spirit, perfect holiness in the" loving "fear of God." They are, through the power of his grace, purified from pride, by the deepest poverty of spirit; from anger, from every unkind or turbulent passion, by meekness and gentleness; from every desire but to please and enjoy God, to know and love him more and more, by that hunger and thirst after righteousness which now engrosses their whole soul: So that now they love the Lord their God with all their heart, and with all their soul, and mind, and strength.

3. But how little has this purity of heart been regarded by the false teachers of all ages! They have taught men barely to abstain from such outward impurities as God hath forbidden by name; but they did not strike at the heart; and by not guarding against, they in effect countenanced, inward corruptions.

A remarkable instance of this, our Lord has given us in the following words: "Ye have heard, that it was said by them of old time, Thou shalt not commit adultery;" (Matt. 5:27;) and, in explaining this, those blind leaders of the blind only insist on men's abstaining from the outward act. "But I say unto you, whosoever looketh on a woman to lust after her hath committed adultery with her already in his heart;" (Matt. 5:28;) for God requireth truth in the inward parts: He searcheth the heart, and trieth the reins; and if thou incline unto iniquity with thy heart, the Lord will not hear thee.

4. And God admits no excuse for retaining anything which is an occasion of impurity. Therefore, "if thy right eye offend thee, pluck it out, and cast it from thee: For it is profitable for thee that one of thy members should perish, and not that thy whole body should be cast into hell:" (Matt. 5:29:) If persons as dear to thee as thy right eye be an occasion of thy thus offending God, a means of exciting unholy desire in thy soul, delay not, forcibly separate from them. "And if thy right hand offend thee, cut it off, and cast it from thee: For it is profitable for thee that one of thy members should perish, and not that thy whole body should be cast into hell:" (Matt. 5:30:) If any who seem as necessary to thee as thy right hand be an occasion of sin, of impure desire; even though it were never to go beyond the heart, never to break out in word or action; constrain thyself to an entire and final parting: cut them off at a stroke: Give them up to God. Any loss, whether of pleasure, or substance, or friends, is preferable to the loss of thy soul.

Two steps only it may not be improper to take before such an absolute and final separation. First, try whether the unclean spirit may not be driven out by fasting and prayer, and by carefully abstaining from every action, and word, and look, which thou hast found to be an occasion of evil. Secondly, if thou art not by this means delivered, ask counsel of him that watcheth over thy soul, or, at least, of some who

---

* [text of the 1872 edition]

have experience in the ways of God, touching the time and manner of that separation; but confer not with flesh and blood, lest thou be "given up to a strong delusion to believe a lie."

5. Nor may marriage itself, holy and honourable as it is, be used as a pretence for giving a loose to our desires. Indeed, "it hath been said, Whosoever will put away his wife, let him give her a writing of divorcement:" And then all was well; though he alleged no cause, but that he did not like her, or liked another better. "But I say unto you, that whosoever shall put away his wife, saving for the case of fornication,' (that is, adultery; the word *porneia* signifying unchastity in general, either in the married or unmarried state,) causeth her to commit adultery, if she marry again: And whosoever shall marry her that is put away committeth adultery. (Matt 5:31, 32.)

All polygamy is clearly forbidden in these words, wherein our Lord expressly declares, that for any woman who has a husband alive, to marry again is adultery. By parity of reason, it is adultery for any man to marry again, so long as he has a wife alive, yea, although they were divorced; unless that divorce had been for the cause of adultery: In that only case there is no scripture which forbids to marry again.

6. Such is the purity of heart which God requires, and works in those who believe on the Son of his love. And blessed are they who are thus "pure in heart; for they shall see God." he will "manifest himself unto them," not only "as he doth not unto the world," but as he doth not always to his own children. he will bless them with the clearest communications of his Spirit, the most intimate "fellowship with the Father and with the Son." he will cause his presence to go continually before them, and the light of his countenance to shine upon them. It is the ceaseless prayer of their heart, "I beseech thee, show me thy glory;" and they have the petition they ask of him. They now see Him by faith, (the veil of the flesh being made as it were transparent,) even in these his lowest works, in all that surrounds them, in all that God has created and made. They see Him in the height above, and in the depth beneath; they see Him filling all in all. The pure in heart see all things full of God. They see Him in the firmament of heaven; in the moon, walking in brightness; in the sun, when he rejoiceth as a giant to run his course. They see Him "making the clouds his chariots, and walking upon the wings of the wind." They see Him "preparing rain for the earth, and blessing the increase of it; giving grass for the cattle, and green herb for the use of man." They see the Creator of all, wisely governing all, and "upholding all things by the word of his power." "o Lord our Governor, how excellent is thy name in all the world!"

7. In all his providences relating to themselves, to their souls or bodies, the pure in heart do more particularly see God. They see his hand ever over them for good; giving them all things in weight and measure, numbering the hairs of their head, making a hedge round about them and all that they have, and disposing all the circumstances of their life according to the depth both of his wisdom and mercy.

8. But in a more especial manner they see God in his ordinances. Whether they appear in the great congregation,

to "pay him the honour due unto his name," "and worship him in the beauty of holiness;" or "enter into their closets," and there pour out their souls before their "Father which is in secret;" whether they search the oracles of God, or hear the ambassadors of Christ proclaiming glad tidings of salvation; or, by eating of that bread, and drinking of that cup, "show forth his death till he come" in the clouds of heaven; in all these his appointed ways, they find such a near approach as cannot be expressed. They see him, as it were, face to face, and "talk with him, as a man talking with his friend;" a fit preparation for those mansions above, wherein they shall see him as he is.

9. But how far were they from seeing God, who, having heard "that it had been said by them of old time, Thou shalt not forswear thyself, but shalt perform unto the Lord thine oaths," (Matt. 5:33,) interpreted it thus, Thou shalt not forswear thyself, when thou swearest by the Lord Jehovah. Thou "shalt perform unto the Lord" these thine oaths;" but as to other oaths, he regardeth them not.

So the Pharisees taught. They not only allowed all manner of swearing in common conversation; but accounted even forswearing a little thing, so they had not sworn by the peculiar name of God.

But our Lord here absolutely forbids all common swearing, as well as all false swearing; and shows the heinousness of both, by the same awful consideration, that every creature is Gods, and he is everywhere present, in all, and over all. "I say unto you, Swear not at all; neither by heaven, for it is Gods throne;" (Matt. 5:34;) and, therefore, this is the same as to swear by Him who sitteth upon the circle of the heavens: "Nor by the earth; for it is his footstool;" (Matt. 5:35;) and he is as intimately present in earth as heaven: "Neither by Jerusalem; for it is the city of the great King;" and God is well known in her palaces. "Neither shalt thou swear by thy head; because thou canst not make one hair white or black;" (Matt. 5:36;) because even this, it is plain, is not thine, but Gods, the sole disposer of all in heaven and earth. "But let your communication," (Matt. 5:37,) your conversation, your discourse with each other "be, Yea, yea; Nay, nay;" a bare, serious affirming or denying; "for whatsoever is more than these cometh of evil:" *ek tou ponerou estin*, is *of the evil one*; proceedeth from the devil, and is a mark of his children.

10. That our Lord does not here forbid the "swearing in judgment and truth," when we are required so to do by a Magistrate, may appear, (1.) From the occasion of this part of his discourse,—the abuse he was here reproving,—which was false swearing and common swearing; the swearing before a Magistrate being quite out of the question.—(2.) From the very words wherein he forms the general conclusion: "Let your communication," or discourse, "be, Yea, yea; Nay, nay."—(3.) From his own example; for he answered himself upon oath, when required by a Magistrate. When the High Priest said unto him, "I adjure thee by the living God, that thou tell us whether thou be the Christ, the Son of God;" Jesus immediately answered in the affirmative, "Thou hast said;" (that is, the truth;) "nevertheless," (or rather, *moreover*,) "I say unto you, Hereafter shall ye see the Son of man sitting on the right hand of power, and coming

in the clouds of heaven." (Matt. 26:63, 64.)—(4.) From the example of God, even the Father, who, "willing the more abundantly to show unto the heirs of promise the immutability of his counsel, confirmed it by an oath." (Heb. 6:17.)—(5.) From the example of St. Paul, who we think had the Spirit of God, and well understood the mind of his Master. "God is my witness," saith he, to the Romans, "that without ceasing I make mention of you always in my prayers:" (Rom. 1:9:) To the Corinthians, "I call God to record upon my soul, that to spare you I came not as yet unto Corinth:" (2 Cor. 1:23:) And to the Philippians, "God is my record, how greatly I long after you in the bowels of Jesus Christ." (Phil. 1:8.) Hence it undeniably appears that, if the Apostle knew the meaning of his Lord's words, they do not forbid swearing on weighty occasions, even to one another: How much less before a Magistrate!—And, Lastly, from that assertion of the great Apostle, concerning solemn swearing in general: (Which it is impossible he could have mentioned without any touch of blame, if his Lord had totally forbidden it:) "Men verily swear by the greater;" by one greater than themselves; "and an oath for confirmation is to them the end of all strife." (Heb. 6:16.)

11. But the great lesson which our blessed Lord inculcates here, and which he illustrates by this example, is, that God is in all things, and that we are to see the Creator in the glass of every creature; that we should use and look upon nothing as separate from God, which indeed is a kind of practical atheism; but, with a true magnificence of thought, survey heaven and earth, and all that is therein, as contained by God in the hollow of his hand, who by his intimate presence holds them all in being, who pervades and actuates the whole created frame, and is, in a true sense, the soul of universe.

II. 1. Thus far our Lord has been more directly employed in teaching the religion of the heart. He has shown what Christians are to be. He proceeds to show, what they are to do also;—how inward holiness is to exert itself in our outward conversation. "Blessed," saith he, "are the peacemakers; for they shall be called the children of God."

2. "The peace-makers:" The word in the original is *hoi eirenopoioi*. It is well known that *eirene*, in the sacred writings, implies all manner of good; every blessing that relates either to the soul or the body, to time or eternity. Accordingly, when St. Paul, in the titles of his epistles, wishes grace and peace to the Romans or the Corinthians, it is as if he had said, "As a fruit of the free, undeserved love and favour of God, may you enjoy all blessings, spiritual and temporal; all the good things which God hath prepared for them that love him."

3. Hence we may easily learn, in how wide a sense the term peace-makers is to be understood. In its literal meaning it implies those lovers of God and man who utterly detest and abhor all strife and debate, all variance and contention; and accordingly labour with all their might, either to prevent this fire of hell from being kindled, or, when it is kindled, from breaking out, or, when it is broke out, from spreading any farther. They endeavour to calm the stormy spirits of men, to quiet their turbulent passions, to soften the minds of contending parties, and, if possible, reconcile them to each other. They use all innocent arts, and employ all their strength, all the talents which God has given them, as well to preserve peace where it is, as to restore it where it is not. It is the joy of their heart to promote, to confirm, to increase, mutual good-will among men, but more especially among the children of God, however distinguished by things of smaller importance; that as they have all "one Lord, one faith," as they are all "called in one hope of their calling," so they may all "walk worthy of the vocation wherewith they are called; with all lowliness and meekness, with long-suffering, forbearing one another in love; endeavouring to keep the unity of the Spirit in the bond of peace."

4. But in the full extent of the word, a peace-maker is one that, as he hath opportunity, "doth good unto all men;" one that, being filled with the love of God and of all mankind, cannot confine the expressions of it to his own family, or friends, or acquaintance, or party, or to those of his own opinions;—no, nor those who are partakers of like precious faith; but steps over all these narrow bounds, that he may do good to every man, that he may, some way or other, manifest his love to neighbours and strangers, friends and enemies. He doth good to them all, as he hath opportunity, that is, on every possible occasion; "redeeming the time," in order thereto; "buying up every opportunity, improving every hour, losing no moment wherein he may profit another. He does good, not of one particular kind, but good in general, in every possible way; employing herein all his talents of every kind, all his powers and faculties of body and soul, all his fortune, his interest, his reputation; desiring only, that when his Lord cometh He may say, "Well done, good and faithful servant!"

5. He doth good, to the uttermost of his power, even to the bodies of all men. He rejoices to "deal his bread to the hungry," and to "cover the naked with a garment." Is any a stranger? He takes him in, and relieves him according to his necessities. Are any sick or in prison? He visits them, and administers such help as they stand most in need of. And all this he does, not as unto man; but remembering him that hath said, "Inasmuch as ye have done it unto one of the least of these my brethren, ye have done it unto me."

6. How much more does he rejoice, if he can do any good to the soul of any man! This power, indeed, belongeth unto God. It is He only that changes the heart, without which every other change is lighter than vanity. Nevertheless, it pleases Him who worketh all in all, to help man chiefly by man; to convey his own power, and blessing, and love, through one man to another. Therefore, although it be certain that "the help which is done upon earth, God doth it himself;" yet has no man need, on this account to stand idle in his vineyard. The peace-maker cannot: He is ever labouring therein, and, as an instrument in God's hand, preparing the ground for his Master's use, or sowing the seed of the kingdom, or watering what is already sown, if haply God may give the increase. According to the measure of grace which he has received, he uses all diligence, either to reprove the gross sinner, to reclaim those who run on headlong in the broad way of destruction; or "to give light to them that sit in darkness," and are ready to "perish for lack of knowledge;" or

to "support the weak, to lift up the hands that hang down, and the feeble knees;" or to bring back and heal that which was lame and turned out of the way. Nor is he less zealous to confirm those who are already striving to enter in at the strait gate; to strengthen those that stand, that they may "run with patience the race which is set before them;" to build up in their most holy faith those that know in whom they have believed; to exhort them to stir up the gift of God which is in them, that daily growing in grace, "an entrance may be ministered unto them abundantly into the everlasting kingdom of our Lord and Saviour Jesus Christ."

7. "Blessed" are they who are thus continually employed in the work of faith and the labour of love; "for they shall be called," that is, *shall be*, (a common Hebraism,) "the children "of God." God shall continue unto them the Spirit of adoption, yea, shall pour it more abundantly into their hearts. He shall bless them with all the blessings of his children. He shall acknowledge them as sons before angels and men; "and, if sons, then heirs; heirs of God, and joint heirs with Christ."

III. 1. One would imagine such a person as has been above described, so full of genuine humility, so unaffectedly serious, so mild and gentle, so free from all selfish design, so devoted to God, and such an active lover of men, should be the darling of mankind. But our Lord was better acquainted with human nature in its present state. He therefore closes the character of this man of God with showing him the treatment he is to expect in the world. "Blessed," saith he, "are they which are persecuted for righteousness' sake; for theirs is the kingdom of heaven."

2. In order to understand this throughly, let us, First, inquire, Who are they that are persecuted? And this we may easily learn from St. Paul: "As of old, he that was born after the flesh persecuted him that was born after the Spirit, even so it is now." (Gal. 4:29.) "Yea," saith the Apostle, "and all that will live godly in Christ Jesus, shall suffer persecution." (2 Tim. 3:12.) The same we are taught by St. John: "Marvel not, my brethren, if the world hate you. We know that we have passed from death unto life, because we love the brethren." (1 John 3:13–14.) As if he had said, The brethren, the Christians, cannot be loved, but by them who have passed from death unto life. And most expressly by our Lord: "If the world hate you, ye know that it hated me before it hated you. If ye were of the world, the world would love its own; but because ye are not of the world, therefore the world hateth you. Remember the word that I said unto you, The servant is not greater than his lord. If they have persecuted me, they will also persecute you." (John 15:18.)

By all these Scriptures it manifestly appears who they are that are persecuted; namely, the righteous: He "that is born of the Spirit;" "all that will live godly in Christ Jesus;" they that are "passed from death unto life;" those who are "not of the world;" all those who are meek and lowly in heart, that mourn for God, that hunger after his likeness; all that love God and their neighbour, and therefore, as they have opportunity, do good unto all men.

3. If it be, secondly, inquired, why they are persecuted, the answer is equally plain and obvious. It is "for righteousness' sake;" because they are righteous; because they are born after the Spirit; because they "will live godly in Christ Jesus;" because they "are not of the world." Whatever may be pretended, this is the real cause: Be their infirmities more or less, still, if it were not for this, they would be borne with, and the world would love its own. They are persecuted, because they are *poor in spirit*; that is, say the world, "poor-spirited, mean, dastardly souls, good for nothing, not fit to live in the world:"—because they *mourn*: "They are such dull, heavy, lumpish creatures, enough to sink anyone's spirits that sees them! They are mere death-heads; they kill innocent mirth, and spoil company wherever they come:"—Because they are *meek*: "Tame, passive fools, just fit to be trampled upon:"—Because they *hunger and thirst after righteousness*: "A parcel of hot-brained enthusiasts, gaping after they know not what, not content with rational religion, but running mad after raptures and inward feelings:"—Because they are *merciful*, lovers of all, lovers of the evil and unthankful: "Encouraging all manner of wickedness; nay, tempting people to do mischief by impunity: and men who, it is to be feared, have their own religion still to seek; very loose in their principles:"—Because they are *pure in heart*: "Uncharitable creatures, that damn all the world, but those that are of their own sort! Blasphemous wretches, that pretend to make God a liar, to live without sin!"—Above all, because they are *peace-makers*; because they take all opportunities of doing good to all men. This is the grand reason why they have been persecuted in all ages, and will be till the restitution of all things: "If they would but keep their religion to themselves, it would be tolerable: But it is this spreading their errors, this infecting so many others, which is not to be endured. They do so much mischief in the world, that they ought to be tolerated no longer. It is true, the men do some things well enough; they relieve some of the poor: But this, too, is only done to gain the more to their party; and so, in effect, to do the more mischief!" Thus the men of the world sincerely think and speak. And the more the kingdom of God prevails, the more the peace-makers are enabled to propagate lowliness, meekness, and all other divine tempers, the more mischief is done, in their account: Consequently, the more are they enraged against the authors of this, and the more vehemently will they persecute them.

4. Let us, Thirdly, inquire, Who are they that persecute them? St. Paul answers, "He that is born after the flesh:" Everyone who is not "born of the Spirit," or, at least, desirous so to be; all that do not at least labour to "live godly in Christ Jesus;" all that are not "passed from death unto life," and, consequently, cannot "love the brethren;" "the world," that is, according to our Saviour's account, they who "know not him that sent me; they who know not God, even the loving, pardoning God, by the teaching of his own Spirit.

The reason is plain: The spirit which is in the world is directly opposite to the Spirit which is of God. It must therefore needs be, that those who are of the world will be opposite to those who are of God. There is the utmost contrariety between them, in all their opinions, their desires, designs, and tempers. And hitherto the leopard and the kid cannot lie down in peace together. The proud, because he is proud, cannot but persecute the lowly; the light and airy, those that mourn: And so in every other kind; the unlikeness of disposition (were there no other) being a perpetual ground of enmity. Therefore, were it only on this account, all the servants of the devil will persecute the children of God.

5. Should it be inquired, Fourthly, how they will persecute them, it may be answered in general, Just in that manner and measure which the wise Disposer of all sees will be most for his glory,—will tend most to his children's growth in grace, and the enlargement of his own kingdom. There is no one branch of God's government of the world which is more to be admired than this. His ear is never heavy to the threatenings of the persecutor, or the cry of the persecuted. His eye is ever open, and his hand stretched out to direct every the minutest circumstance. When the storm shall begin, how high it shall rise, which way it shall point its course, when and how it shall end, are all determined by his unerring wisdom. The ungodly are only a sword of his; an instrument which he uses as it pleaseth him, and which itself, when the gracious ends of his providence are answered, is cast into the fire.

At some rare times, as when Christianity was planted first, and while it was taking root in the earth; as also when the pure doctrine of Christ began to be planted again in our nation; God permitted the storm to rise high, and his children were called to resist unto blood. There was a peculiar reason why he suffered this with regard to the Apostles, that their evidence might be the more unexceptionable. But from the annals of the church we learn another, and a far different reason, why he suffered the heavy persecutions which rose in the second and third centuries; namely, because "the mystery of iniquity" did so strongly "work;" because of the monstrous corruptions which even then reigned in the church: These God chastised, and at the same time strove to heal, by those severe but necessary visitations.

Perhaps the same observation may be made, with regard to the grand persecution in our own land. God had dealt very graciously with our nation. He had poured out various blessings upon us: He had given us peace abroad and at home; and a King, wise and good beyond his years: And, above all, he had caused the pure light of his gospel to arise and shine amongst us. But what return did he find? "He looked for righteousness; but behold a cry!"—a cry of oppression and wrong, of ambition and injustice, of malice, and fraud, and covetousness. Yea, the cry of those who even then expired in the flames entered into the ears of the Lord of Sabaoth. It was then God arose to maintain his own cause against those that held the truth in unrighteousness. Then he sold them into the hands of their persecutors, by a judgment mixed with mercy; an affliction to punish, and yet a medicine to heal, the grievous backslidings of his people.

6. But it is seldom God suffers the storm to rise so high as torture, or death, or bonds, or imprisonment. Whereas his children are frequently called to endure those lighter kinds of persecution; they frequently suffer the estrangement of kinsfolk,—the loss of the friends that were as their own soul. They find the truth of their Lord's word (concerning the *event*, though not the *design* of his coming,) "Suppose ye that I am come to give peace on earth? I tell you, Nay; but rather division." (Luke 12:51.) And hence will naturally follow loss of business or employment, and consequently of substance. But all these circumstances likewise are under the wise direction of God, who allots to everyone what is most expedient for him.

7. But the persecution which attends *all* the children of God is that our Lord describes in the following words: "Blessed are ye, when men shall revile you, and persecute you,"—shall persecute by reviling you,—"and say all manner of evil against you, falsely, for my sake." This cannot fail; it is the very badge of our discipleship; it is one of the seals of our calling; it is a sure portion entailed on all the children of God: If we have it not, we are bastards and not sons. Straight through evil report, as well as good report, lies the only way to the kingdom. The meek, serious, humble, zealous lovers of God and man are of good report among their brethren; but of evil report with the world, who count and treat them "as the filth and offscouring of all things."

8. Indeed some have supposed that before the fullness of the Gentiles shall come in the scandal of the cross will cease; that God will cause Christians to be esteemed and loved, even by those who are as yet in their sins. Yea, and sure it is, that even now he at some times suspends the contempt as well as the fierceness of men; "he makes a man's enemies to be at peace with him for a season, and gives him favour with his bitterest persecutors. But setting aside this exempt case, the scandal of the cross is not yet ceased; but a man may say still, "If I please men, I am not the servant of Christ. Let no man therefore regard that pleasing suggestion (pleasing doubtless to flesh and blood,) that bad men only *pretend* to hate and despise them that are good, but do indeed love and esteem them in their hearts." Not so: They may employ them sometimes; but it is for their own profit. They may put confidence in them; for they know their ways are not like other men's. But still they love them not; unless so far as the Spirit of God may be striving with them. Our Saviour's words are express: "If ye were of the world, the world would love its own; but because ye are not of the world, therefore the world hateth you." Yea, (setting aside what exceptions may be made by the preventing grace or the peculiar providence, of God,) it hateth them as cordially and sincerely as ever it did their Master.

9. It remains only to inquire, How are the children of God to behave with regard to persecution? And, First, they ought not knowingly or designedly to bring it upon themselves. This is contrary, both to the example and advice of our Lord and all his Apostles; who teach us not only not to seek, but to avoid it, as far as we can, without injuring our conscience; without giving up any part of that righteousness which we are to prefer before life itself. So our Lord expressly, "When they persecute you in this city, flee ye into another," which is indeed, when it can be taken, the most unexceptionable way of avoiding persecution.

10. Yet think not that you can always avoid it, either by this or any other means. If ever that idle imagination steals into your heart, put it to flight by that earnest caution, "Remember the word that I said unto you, The servant is not greater than his Lord. If they have persecuted me, they will

also persecute you." "Be ye wise as serpents, and harmless as doves." But will this screen you from persecution? Not unless you have more wisdom than your Master, or more innocence than the Lamb of God.

Neither desire to avoid it, to escape it wholly; for if you do, you are none of his. If you escape the persecution, you escape the blessing; the blessing of those who are persecuted for righteousness' sake. If you are not persecuted for righteousness' sake, you cannot enter into the kingdom of heaven. "If we suffer with him, we shall also reign with him. But if we deny him, he will also deny us."

11. Nay, rather, "rejoice and be exceeding glad," when men persecute you for his sake; when they persecute you by reviling you, and by "saying all manner of evil against you falsely;" which they will not fail to mix with every kind of persecution: They must blacken you to excuse themselves: "For so persecuted they the Prophets which were before you!"—those who were most eminently holy in heart and life; yea, and all the righteous which ever have been from the beginning of the world. Rejoice, because by his mark also ye know unto whom ye belong. And, because great is your reward in heaven,"—the reward purchased by the blood of the covenant, and freely bestowed in proportion to your sufferings, as well as to your holiness of heart and life. Be exceeding glad;" knowing that "these light afflictions, which are but for a moment, work out for you a far more exceeding and eternal weight of glory."

12. Meantime, let no persecution turn you out of the way of lowliness and meekness, of love and beneficence. "Ye have heard" indeed "that it hath been said, An eye for an eye, and a tooth for a tooth;" (Matt. 5:38;) and your miserable teachers have hence allowed you to avenge yourselves, to return evil for evil: "But I say unto you, that ye resist not evil:"—Not thus; not by returning it in kind. "But, rather than do this, "whosoever smiteth thee on thy right cheek, turn to him the other also. And if any man will sue thee at the law, and take away thy coat, let him have thy cloak also. And whosoever shall compel thee to go a mile, go with him twain."

So invincible let thy meekness be. And be thy love suitable thereto. "Give to him that asketh thee, and from him that would borrow of thee turn not thou away." Only give not away that which is another man's, that which is not thine own. Therefore, (1.) Take care to owe no man anything: For what thou owest is not thy own, but another man's. (2.) Provide for those of thine own household: This also God hath required of thee; and what is necessary to sustain them in life and godliness is also not thine own. Then, (3.) Give or lend all that remains, from day to day, or from year to year: Only, first, seeing thou canst not give or lend to all, remember the household of faith.

13. The meekness and love we are to feel, the kindness we are to show to them which persecute us for righteousness' sake, our blessed Lord describes farther in the following verses: O that they were graven upon our hearts! "Ye have heard that it hath been said, Thou shalt love thy neighbour, and hate thy enemy:" (Matt. 5:43.) God indeed had said only the former part, "Thou shalt love thy neighbour;" the children of the

devil had added the latter, "and hate thy enemy:" "But I say unto you," (1.) "Love your enemies:" See that you bear a tender good-will to those who are most bitter of spirit against you; who wish you all manner of evil. (2.) "Bless them that curse you." Are there any whose bitterness of spirit breaks forth in bitter words? who are continually cursing and reproaching you when you are present, and "saying all evil against you" when absent? So much the rather do you bless: In conversing with them use all mildness and softness of language. Reprove them, by repeating a better lesson before them; by showing them how they ought to have spoken. And, in speaking of them, say all the good you can, without violating the rules of truth and justice. (3.) "Do good to them that hate you:" Let your actions show, that you are as real in love as they in hatred. Return good for evil. "Be not overcome of evil, but overcome evil with good." (4). If you can do nothing more, at least "pray for them that despitefully use you and persecute you." You can never be disabled from doing this; nor can all their malice or violence hinder you. Pour out your souls to God, not only for those who did this once, but now repent:—This is a little thing: "If thy brother, seven times a day, turn and say unto thee, I repent;" (Luke 17:4) that is, if, after ever so many relapses, he give thee reason to believe that he is really and throughly changed; then thou shalt forgive him, so as to trust him, to put him in thy bosom, as if he had never sinned against thee at all:—But pray for, wrestle with God for, those that do not repent, that now despitefully use thee and persecute thee. Thus far forgive them, "not until seven times only, but until seventy times seven." (Matt. 18:22.) Whether they repent or no, yea, though they appear farther and farther from it, yet show them this instance of kindness: "That ye may be the children," that ye may approve yourselves the genuine children, "of your Father which is in heaven;" who shows his goodness by giving such blessings as they are capable of, even to his stubbornest enemies; "who maketh his sun to rise on the evil and on the good, and sendeth rain on the just and on the unjust." "For if ye love them which love you, what reward have ye? Do not even the Publicans the same?" (Matt. 5:46;)—who pretend to no religion; whom ye yourselves acknowledge to be without God in the world. "And if ye salute," show kindness in word or deed to "your brethren," your friends or kinsfolk, "only; what do ye more than others?"—than those who have no religion at all? "Do not even the publicans so?" (Matt. 5:47.) Nay, but follow ye a better pattern than them. In patience, in longsuffering, in mercy, in beneficence of every kind, to all, even to your bitterest persecutors; "be ye," Christians, "perfect," in kind, though not in degree, "even as your Father which is in heaven is perfect." (Matt. 5:48.)

IV. Behold Christianity in its native form, as delivered by its great Author! This is the genuine religion of Jesus Christ! Such he presents it to him whose eyes are opened. See a picture of God, so far as he is imitable by man! A picture drawn by God's own hand: "Behold, ye despisers, and wonder, and perish!" Or rather, wonder and adore! Rather cry out, "Is this the religion of Jesus of Nazareth? the religion which I persecuted! Let me no more be found even to fight against God. Lord, what wouldst thou have me to do?" What beauty appears in the whole! How just a symmetry! What exact proportion in every part! How desirable is the happiness here described! How venerable, how lovely the holiness! This is the spirit of religion; the quintessence of it. These are indeed the fundamentals of Christianity. O that we may not be hearers of it only!—"like a man beholding his own face in a glass, who goeth his way, and straightway forgetteth what manner of man he was." Nay, but let us steadily "look into this perfect law of liberty, and continue therein." Let us not rest, until every line thereof is transcribed into our own hearts. Let us watch, and pray, and believe, and love, and "strive for the mastery," till every part of it shall appear in our soul, graven there by the finger of God; till we are "holy as He which hath called us is holy, perfect as our Father which is in heaven is perfect!"

24.* Upon our Lord's Sermon on the Mount Discourse 4

"Ye are the salt of the earth. But if the salt hath lost its savour, wherewith shall it be salted? It is thenceforth good for nothing but to be cast out, and trodden under foot of men.

"Ye are the light of the world. A city that is set on an hill cannot be hid.

"Neither do men light a candle and put it under a bushel, but on a candlestick; and it giveth light to all that are in the house.

"Let your light so shine before men that they may see your good works, and glorify your Father which is in heaven."

Matt. 5:13–16

1. The beauty of holiness, of that inward man of the heart which is renewed after the image of God, cannot but strike every eye which God hath opened,—every enlightened understanding. The ornament of a meek, humble, loving spirit, will at least excite the approbation of all those who are capable in any degree, of discerning spiritual good and evil. From the hour men begin to emerge out of the darkness which covers the giddy, unthinking world, they cannot but perceive how desirable a thing it is to be thus transformed into the likeness of him that created us. This inward religion bears the shape of God so visibly impressed upon it, that a soul must be wholly immersed in flesh and blood when he can doubt of its divine original. We may say of this, in a secondary sense, even as of the Son of God himself, that it is the "brightness of his glory, the express image of his person;" *apaugasma tes doxe autou*, the beaming forth of his eternal glory; and yet so tempered and softened, that even the children of men may herein see God and live; *charakter tes hupostaseos autou*, the character, the stamp, the living impression, of his person, who is the fountain of beauty and love, the original source of all excellency and perfection.

2. If religion, therefore, were carried no farther than this, they could have no doubt concerning it; they should have no objection against pursuing it with the whole ardour of their souls. "But why," say they, "is it clogged with other things? What need of loading it with doing and *suffering?* These are what damps the vigour of the soul, and sinks it down to earth again. Is it not enough to follow after charity; to soar upon the wings of love? Will it not suffice to worship God, who is a Spirit, with the spirit of our minds, without encumbering ourselves with outward things, or even thinking of them at all? Is it not better, that the whole extent of our thought should be taken up with high and heavenly contemplation; and that instead of busying ourselves at all about externals, we should only commune with God in our hearts?"

3. Many eminent men have spoken thus; have advised us "to cease from all outward action;" wholly to withdraw from the world; to leave the body behind us; to abstract ourselves from all sensible things; to have no concern at all about outward religion, but to *work all virtues in the will*; as the far more excellent way, more perfective of the soul, as well as more acceptable to God.

4. It needed not that any should tell our Lord of this masterpiece of the wisdom from beneath, this fairest of all the devices wherewith Satan hath ever perverted the right ways of the Lord! And o! what instruments hath he found, from time to time, to employ in this his service, to wield this grand engine of hell against some of the most important truths of God!—men that would "deceive, if it were possible, the very elect," the men of faith and love; yea, that have for a season deceived and led away no inconsiderable number of them, who have fallen in all ages into the gilded snare, and hardly escaped with the skin of their teeth.

5. But has our Lord been wanting on his part? has he not sufficiently guarded us against this pleasing delusion? has he not armed us here with armour of proof against Satan "transformed into an angel of light?" Yea, verily: he here defends, in the clearest and strongest manner, the active, patient religion he had just described. What can be fuller and plainer, than the words he immediately subjoins to what he had said of doing and suffering? "Ye are the salt of the earth: But if the salt have lost his savour, wherewith shall it be salted? It is thenceforth good for nothing but to be cast out, and trodden under foot of men. Ye are the light of the world. A city that is set on an hill cannot be hid. Neither do men light a candle and put it under a bushel, but on a candlestick; and it giveth light to all that are in the house. Let your light so shine before men, that they may see your good works, and glorify your Father which is in heaven."

In order fully to explain and enforce these important words, I shall endeavour to show, First, that Christianity is essentially a social religion; and that to turn it into a solitary one is to destroy it. Secondly, that to conceal this religion is impossible, as well as utterly contrary to the design of its Author. I shall, Thirdly, answer some objections; and conclude the whole with a practical application.

I. 1. First, I shall endeavour to show, that Christianity is essentially a social religion; and that to turn it into a solitary religion, is indeed to destroy it.

---

* [text of the 1872 ed.]

By Christianity I mean that method of worshipping God which is here revealed to man by Jesus Christ. When I say, This is essentially a social religion, I mean not only that it cannot subsist so well, but that it cannot subsist at all, without society,—without living and conversing with other men. And in showing this, I shall confine myself to those considerations which will arise from the very discourse before us. But if this be shown, then doubtless, to turn this religion into a solitary one is to destroy it.

Not that we can in any wise condemn the intermixing solitude or retirement with society. This is not only allowable but expedient; nay, it is necessary, as daily experience shows, for everyone that either already is, or desires to be, a real Christian. It can hardly be, that we should spend one entire day in a continued intercourse with men, without suffering loss in our soul, and in some measure grieving the Holy Spirit of God. We have need daily to retire from the world, at least morning and evening, to converse with God, to commune more freely with our Father which is in secret. Nor indeed can a man of experience condemn even longer seasons of religious retirement, so they do not imply any neglect of the worldly employ wherein the providence of God has placed us.

2. Yet such retirement must not swallow up all our time; this would be to destroy, not advance, true religion. For, that the religion described by our Lord in the foregoing words cannot subsist without society, without our living and conversing with other men, is manifest from hence, that several of the most essential branches thereof can have no place if we have no intercourse with the world.

3. There is no disposition, for instance, which is more essential to Christianity than meekness. Now although this, as it implies resignation to God, or patience in pain and sickness, may subsist in a desert, in a hermits cell, in total solitude; yet as it implies (which it no less necessarily does) mildness, gentleness, and long-suffering, it cannot possibly have a being, it has no place under heaven, without an intercourse with other men. So that to attempt turning this into a solitary virtue is to destroy it from the face of the earth.

4. Another necessary branch of true Christianity is peacemaking, or doing of good. That this is equally essential with any of the other parts of the religion of Jesus Christ, there can be no stronger argument to evince, (and therefore it would be absurd to allege any other,) than that it is here inserted in the original plan he has laid down of the fundamentals of his religion. Therefore, to set aside this is the same daring insult on the authority of our Great Master as to set aside mercifulness, purity of heart, or any other branch of his institution. But this is apparently set aside by all who call us to the wilderness; who recommend entire solitude either to the babes, or the young men, or the fathers in Christ. For will any man affirm that a solitary Christian (so called, though it is little less than a contradiction in terms) can be a merciful man,—that is, one that takes every opportunity of doing all good to all men? What can be more plain, than that this fundamental branch of the religion of Jesus Christ cannot possibly subsist without society, without our living and conversing with other men?

5. "But is it not expedient, however," one might naturally ask, "to converse only with good men,—only with those whom we know to be meek and merciful,—holy of heart and holy of life? Is it not expedient to refrain from any conversation or intercourse with men of the opposite character,—men who do not obey, perhaps do not believe, the gospel of our Lord Jesus Christ? The advice of St. Paul to the Christians at Corinth may seem to favour this: "I wrote unto you in an epistle not to company with fornicators." (1 Cor. 5:9) And it is certainly not advisable so to company with them, or with any of the workers of iniquity, as to have any particular familiarity, or any strictness of friendship with them. To contract or continue an intimacy with any such is no way expedient for a Christian. It must necessarily expose him to abundance of dangers and snares, out of which he can have no reasonable hope of deliverance.

But the Apostle does not forbid us to have any intercourse at all, even with the men that know not God: "For then," says he, "ye must needs go out of the world;" which he could never advise them to do. But, he subjoins, "If any man that is called a brother," that professes himself a Christian, "be a fornicator, or covetous, or an idolater, or a railer, or a drunkard, or an extortioner;" (1 Cor. 5:11;) now I have written unto you not to keep company' with him; "with such an one, no not to eat." This must necessarily imply, that we break off all familiarity, all intimacy of acquaintance with him. "Yet count him not," saith the Apostle elsewhere, "as an enemy, but admonish him as a brother;" (2 Thes. 3:15;) plainly showing that even in such a case as this we are not to renounce all fellowship with him. So that here is no advice to separate wholly, even from wicked men. Yea, these very words teach us quite the contrary.

6. Much more the words of our Lord; who is so far from directing us to break off all commerce with the world, that without it, according to his account of Christianity, we cannot be Christians at all. It would be easy to show, that some intercourse even with ungodly and unholy men is absolutely needful, in order to the full exertion of every temper which he has described as the way of the kingdom; that it is indispensably necessary, in order to the complete exercise of poverty of spirit, of mourning, and of every other disposition which has a place here, in the genuine religion of Jesus Christ. Yea, it is necessary to the very being of several of them; of that meekness, for example, which, instead of demanding "an eye for an eye, or a tooth for a tooth," doth "not resist evil," but causes us rather, when smitten "on the right cheek, to turn the other also;"—of that mercifulness, whereby "we love our enemies, bless them that curse us, do good to them that hate us, and pray for them which despitefully use us and persecute us;"—and of that complication of love and all holy tempers which is exercised in suffering for righteousness' sake. Now all these, it is clear, could have no being, were we to have no commerce with any but real Christians.

7. Indeed were we wholly to separate ourselves from sinners, how could we possibly answer that character which our Lord gives us in these very words? "Ye" (Christians, ye that are lowly, serious and meek; ye that hunger after righteousness,

that love God and man, that do good to all, and therefore suffer evil; ye) "are the salt of the earth:" It is your very nature to season whatever is round about you. It is the nature of the divine savour which is in you, to spread to whatsoever you touch; to diffuse itself, on every side, to all those among whom you are. This is the great reason why the providence of God has so mingled you together with other men, that whatever grace you have received of God may through you be communicated to others; that every holy temper, and word, and work of yours, may have an influence on lo them also. By this means a check will, in some measure, be given to the corruption which is in the world; and a small part, at least, saved from the general infection, and rendered holy and pure before God.

8. That we may the more diligently labour to season all we can with every holy and heavenly temper, our Lord proceeds to show the desperate state of those who do not impart the religion they have received; which indeed they cannot possibly fail to do, so long as it remains in their own hearts. "If the salt have lost its savour, wherewith shall it be salted? It is thenceforth good for nothing but to be cast out, and trodden under foot of men:" If ye who were holy and heavenly-minded, and consequently zealous of good works, have no longer that savour in yourselves, and do therefore no longer season others; if you are grown flat, insipid, dead, both careless of your own soul and useless to the souls of other men; wherewith shall ye be salted? How shall ye be recovered? What help? What hope? Can tasteless salt be restored to its savour? No; "it is thenceforth good for nothing but to be cast out," even as the mire in the streets, "and to be trodden under foot of men," to be overwhelmed with everlasting contempt. If ye had never known the Lord, there might have been hope,—if ye had never been "found in him:" But what can you now say to that, his solemn declaration, just parallel to what he hath here spoken? "every branch in me that beareth not fruit, he, the Father, "taketh away. He that abideth in me, and I in him, bringeth forth much fruit." "If a man abide not in me," or do not bring forth fruit. "he is cast out as a branch, and withered; and men gather them," not to plant them again, but "to cast them into the fire." (John 15:2, 5, 6.)

9. Toward those who have never tasted of the good word, God is indeed pitiful and of tender mercy. But justice takes place with regard to those who have tasted that the Lord is gracious, and have afterwards turned back "from the holy commandment" then "delivered to them." "For it is impossible for those who were once enlightened;" (Heb. 6:4) in whose hearts God had once shined, to enlighten them with the knowledge of the glory of God in the face of Jesus Christ; "who have tasted of the heavenly gift" of redemption in his blood, the forgiveness of sins; "and were made partakers of the Holy Ghost," of lowliness, of meekness, and of the love of God and man shed abroad in their hearts by the Holy Ghost which was given unto them; and "have fallen away,"— *kai parapesontas*—(here is not a supposition, but a flat declaration of matter of fact) "to renew them again unto repentance; seeing they crucify to themselves the Son of God afresh, and put him to an open shame."

But that none may misunderstand these awful words, it should be carefully observed, (1.) Who they are that are here spoken of; namely they, and they only, who were once thus "enlightened;" they only, "who did taste of" that "heavenly gift, and were" thus " 'made partakers of the Holy Ghost." So that all who have not experienced these things are wholly unconcerned in this Scripture. (2.) What that falling away is which is, here spoken of: It is an absolute, total apostasy. A believer may fall, and not fall away. He may fall and rise again. And if he should fall, even into sin, yet this case, dreadful as it is, is not desperate. For "we have an Advocate with the Father, Jesus Christ the righteous; and he is the propitiation for our sins." But let him above all things beware, lest his "heart be hardened by the deceitfulness of sin;" lest he should sink lower and lower, till he wholly fall away, till he become as salt that hath lost its savour: For if we thus sin wilfully, after we have received the experimental "knowledge of the truth, there remaineth no more sacrifice for sins; but a certain, fearful looking for of fiery indignation, which shall devour the adversaries."

II. 1. "But although we may not wholly separate ourselves from mankind, although it be granted we ought to season them with the religion which God has wrought in our hearts, yet may not this be done insensibly? May we not convey this into others in a secret and almost imperceptible manner, so that scarce anyone shall be able to observe how or when it is done?—even as salt conveys its own savour into that which is seasoned thereby, without any noise, and without being liable to any outward observation. And if so, although we do not go out of the world, yet we may lie hid in it. We may thus far keep our religion to ourselves; and not offend lo those whom we cannot help."

2. Of this plausible reasoning of flesh and blood our Lord was well aware also. And he has given a full answer to it in those words which come now to be considered; in explaining which, I shall endeavour to show, as I proposed to do in the Second place, that so long as true religion abides in our hearts, it is impossible to conceal it, as well as absolutely contrary to the design of its great Author.

And, First, it is impossible for any that have it, to conceal the religion of Jesus Christ. This our Lord makes plain beyond all contradiction, by a two-fold comparison: "Ye are the light of the world: A city set upon an hill cannot be hid." Ye Christians "are the light of the world," with regard both to your tempers and actions. Your holiness makes you as conspicuous as the sun in the midst of heaven. As ye cannot go out of the world, so neither can ye stay in it without appearing to all mankind. Ye may not flee from men; and while ye are among them, it is impossible to hide your lowliness and meekness, and those other dispositions whereby ye aspire to be perfect as your Father which is in heaven is perfect. Love cannot be hid any more than light; and least of all, when it shines forth in action, when ye exercise yourselves in the labour of love, in beneficence of every kind. As well may men think to hide a city, as to hide a Christian; yea, as well may they conceal a city set upon a hill, as a holy, zealous, active lover of God and man.

3. It is true, men who love darkness rather than light, because their deeds are evil, will take all possible pains to prove, that the light which is in you is darkness. They will say evil, all manner of evil, falsely, of the good which is in you; they will lay to your charge that which is farthest from your thoughts, which is the very reverse of all you are, and all you do. And your patient continuance in well-doing, your meek suffering all things for the Lord's sake, your calm, humble joy in the midst of persecution, your unwearied labour to overcome evil with good, will make you still more visible and conspicuous than ye were before.

4. So impossible it is, to keep our religion from being seen, unless we cast it away; so vain is the thought of hiding the light, unless by putting it out! Sure it is, that a secret, unobserved religion, cannot be the religion of Jesus Christ. Whatever religion can be concealed, is not Christianity. If a Christian could be hid, he could not be compared to a city set upon an hill; to the light of the world, the sun shining from heaven, and seen by all the world below. Never, therefore, let it enter into the heart of him whom God hath renewed in the spirit of his mind, to hide that light, to keep his religion to himself; especially considering it is not only impossible to conceal true Christianity, but likewise absolutely contrary to the design of the great Author of it.

5. This plainly appears from the following words: "Neither do men light a candle, to put it under a bushel." As if he had said, As men do not light a candle, only to cover and conceal it, so neither does God enlighten any soul with his glorious knowledge and love, to have it covered or concealed, either by prudence, falsely so called, or shame, or voluntary humility; to have it hid either in a desert, or in the world; either by avoiding men, or in conversing with them. "But they put it on a candlestick, and it giveth light to all that are in the house:" In like manner, it is the design of God that every Christian should be in an open point of view; that he may give light to all around, that he may visibly express the religion of Jesus Christ.

6. Thus hath God in all ages spoken to the world, not only by precept, but by example also. He hath "not left himself without witness," in any nation where the sound of the gospel hath gone forth, without a few who testified his truth by their lives as well as their words. These have been "as lights shining in a dark place." And from time to time they have been the means of enlightening some, of preserving a remnant, a little seed which was "counted unto the Lord for a generation." They have led a few poor sheep out of the darkness of the world, and guided their feet into the way of peace.

7. One might imagine that, where both Scripture and the reason of things speak so clearly and expressly, there could not be much advanced on the other side, at least not with any appearance of truth. But they who imagine thus know little of the depths of Satan. After all that Scripture and reason have said, so exceeding plausible are the pretences for solitary religion, for a Christian's going out of the world, or at least hiding himself in it, that we need all the wisdom of God to see through the snare, and all the power of God to escape it; so many and strong are the objections which have been brought against being social, open, active Christians.

III. 1. To answer these, was the Third thing which I proposed. And, First, it has been often objected, that religion does not lie in outward things, but in the heart, the inmost soul; that it is the union of the soul with God, the life of God in the soul of man; that outside religion is nothing worth; seeing God "delighteth not in burnt-offerings," in outward services, but a pure and holy heart is "the sacrifice he will not despise."

I answer, It is most true that the root of religion lies in the heart, in the inmost soul; that this is the union of the soul with God, the life of God in the soul of man. But if this root be really in the heart, it cannot but put forth branches. And these are the several instances of outward obedience, which partake of the same nature with the root; and consequently, are not only marks or signs, but substantial parts of religion. It is also true, that bare outside religion, which has no root in the heart, is nothing worth; that God delighteth not in such outward services, no more than in Jewish burnt-offerings; and that a pure and holy heart is a sacrifice with which he is always well pleased. But he is also well pleased with all that outward service which arises from the heart; with the sacrifice of our prayers (whether public or private,) of our praises and thanksgivings; with the sacrifice of our goods, humbly devoted to him, and employed wholly to his glory; and with that of our bodies, which he peculiarly claims, which the Apostle beseeches us, "by the mercies of God, to present unto him, a living sacrifice, holy acceptable to God."

2. A Second objection, nearly related to this, is that love is all in all; that it is "the fulfilling of the law," "the end of the commandment," of every commandment of God; that all we do, and all we suffer, if we have not charity or love, profiteth us nothing; and therefore the Apostle directs us to "follow after charity," and terms this "the more excellent way."

I answer, It is granted, that the love of God and man, arising from faith unfeigned, is all in all, the fulfilling of the law, the end of every commandment of God. It is true, that without this, whatever we do, whatever we suffer, profits us nothing. But it does not follow, that love is all in such a sense as to supersede either faith or good works. It is "the fulfilling of the law," not by releasing us from, but by constraining us to obey it. It is "the end of the commandment," as every commandment leads to and centres in it. It is allowed, that whatever we do or suffer without love, profits us nothing. But withal, whatever we do or suffer in love, though it were only the suffering reproach for Christ, or the giving a cup of cold water in his name, it shall in no wise lose its reward.

3. "But does not the Apostle direct us to 'follow after charity?' And does he not term it 'a more excellent way?' "—He does direct us to "follow after charity;" but not after that alone. His words are, "follow after charity;" and desire spiritual gifts." (1 Cor. 14:1) Yea, "follow after charity;" and desire to spend and to be spent for your brethren. "Follow after charity;" and as you have opportunity do good to all men. In the same verse also wherein he terms this, the way of love, "a more excellent way," he directs the Corinthians to desire other gifts besides it; yea, to desire them earnestly. "Covet earnestly," saith he, "the best gifts; and yet I show unto you a more excellent way." (1 Cor. 12:31.) More excellent than

what? Than the gifts of healing, of speaking with tongues, and of interpreting, mentioned in the preceding verse; but not more excellent than the way of obedience. Of this the Apostle is not speaking; neither is he speaking of outward religion at all: So that this text is quite wide of the present question.

But suppose the Apostle had been speaking of outward as well as inward religion, and comparing them together; suppose, in the comparison, he had given the preference ever so much to the latter; suppose he had preferred (as he justly might) a loving heart, before all outward works whatever; yet it would not follow that we were to reject either one or the other. No; God hath joined them together from the beginning of the world; and let not man put them asunder.

4. "But 'God is a Spirit; and they that worship him, must worship him in spirit and in truth.' And is not this enough? Nay, ought we not to employ the whole strength of our mind herein? Does not attending to outward things clog the soul, that it cannot soar aloft in holy contemplation? Does it not damp the vigour of our thought? Has it not a natural tendency to encumber and distract the mind? Whereas St. Paul would have us to be 'without carefulness', and to 'wait upon the Lord without distraction.' "

I answer, "God is a Spirit; and they that worship him, must worship him in spirit and in truth." Yea, and this is enough: We ought to employ the whole strength of our mind therein. But then I would ask, What is it to worship God, a Spirit, in spirit and in truth?' Why, it is to worship him with our spirit; to worship him in that manner which none but spirits are capable of. It is to believe in him as a wise, just, holy Being, of purer eyes than to behold iniquity; and yet merciful, gracious, and long-suffering; forgiving iniquity, and transgression and sin; casting all our sins behind his back, and accepting us in the Beloved. It is, to love him, to delight in him, to desire him, with all our heart, and mind, and soul, and strength; to imitate him we love, by purifying ourselves, even as he is pure; and to obey him whom we love, and in whom we believe, both in thought, and word, and work. Consequently, one branch of the worshipping God in spirit and in truth is, the keeping his outward commandments. To glorify him, therefore with our bodies, as well as with our spirits; to go through outward work with hearts lifted up to him; to make our daily employment a sacrifice to God; to buy and sell, to eat and drink, to his glory;—this is worshipping God in spirit and in truth, as much as the praying to him in a wilderness.

5. But if so, then contemplation is only one way of worshipping God in spirit and in truth. Therefore to give ourselves up entirely to this, would be to destroy many branches of spiritual worship, all equally acceptable to God and equally profitable, not hurtful, to the soul. For it is a great mistake, to suppose that an attention to those outward things, whereto the providence of God hath called us, is any clog to a Christian, or any hindrance at all to his always seeing Him that is invisible. It does not at all damp the ardour of his thought; it does not encumber or distract his mind; it gives him no uneasy or hurtful care, who does it all as unto the Lord; who hath learned whatsoever he doth, in word or deed, to do all in the name of the Lord Jesus; having only one eye of the soul, which moves round on outward things, and one immovably fixed on God. Learn what this meaneth, ye poor recluses, that you may clearly discern your own littleness of faith: Yea, that you may no longer judge others by yourselves, go and learn what that meaneth:—

> Thou, O Lord, in tender love
> Dost all my burdens bear;
> Lift my heart to things above,
> And fix it ever there.
> Calm on tumult's wheel I sit;
> Midst busy multitudes alone;
> Sweetly waiting at thy feet
> Till all thy will be done.

6. But the grand objection is still behind. "We appeal," say they, "to experience. Our light did shine; we used outward things many years; and yet they profited nothing. We attended on all the ordinances; but we were no better for it; nor indeed anyone else; Nay, we were the worse; for we fancied ourselves Christians for so doing, when we knew not what Christianity meant."

I allow the fact: I allow that you and ten thousand more, have thus abused the ordinances of God; mistaking the means for the end; supposing that the doing these, or some other outward works either was the religion of Jesus Christ, or would be accepted in the place of it. But let the abuse be taken away, and the use remain. Now use all outward things, but use them with a constant eye to the renewal of your soul in righteousness and true holiness.

7. But this is not all: They affirm, "Experience likewise shows, that the trying to do good is but lost labour. What does it avail to feed or clothe men's bodies, if they are just dropping into everlasting fire? And what good can any man do to their souls? If these are changed, God doth it himself. Besides, all men are either good, at least desirous so to be, or obstinately evil. Now the former have no need of us; let them ask help of God, and it shall be given them: And the latter will receive no help from us. Nay, and our Lord forbids to 'cast our pearls before swine.' "

I answer, (1.) Whether they will finally be lost or saved, you are expressly commanded to feed the hungry, and clothe the naked. If you can, and do not, whatever becomes of them, you shall go away into everlasting fire. (2.) Though it is God only changes hearts, yet he generally doth it by man. It is our part to do all that in us lies, as diligently as if we could change them ourselves, and then to leave the event to him. (3.) God, in answer to their prayers, builds up his children by each other in every good gift; nourishing and strengthening the whole "body by that which every joint supplieth." So that "the eye cannot say to the hand, I have no need of thee;" no, nor even "the head to the feet, I have no need of you." Lastly, How are you assured, that the persons before you are dogs or swine? Judge them not, until you have tried. "How knowest thou, O man, but thou mayst gain thy brother,"—but thou mayst, under God, save his soul from death? When he spurns thy love, and blasphemes the good word, then it is time to give him up to God.

8. "We have tried; we have laboured to reform sinners; and what did it avail? On many we could make no impression at all. And if some were changed for a while, yet their goodness was but as the morning dew, and they were soon as bad, nay, worse than ever: So that we only hurt them, and ourselves too; for our minds were hurried and discomposed,—perhaps filled with anger instead of love: Therefore, we had better have kept our religion to ourselves."

It is very possible this fact also may be true; that you have tried to do good, and have not succeeded; yea, that those who seemed reformed, relapsed into sin, and their last state was worse than the first. And what marvel? Is the servant above his master? But how often did He strive to save sinners, and they would not hear; or when they had followed him awhile, they turned back as a dog to his vomit! But he did not therefore desist from striving to do good: No more should you, whatever your success be. It is your part to do as you are commanded: The event is in the hand of God. You are not accountable for this. Leave it to him, who orders all things well. "In the morning sow thy seed, and in the evening withhold not thy hand: for thou knowest not whether shall prosper." (Eccles. 11:6)

But the trial hurries and frets your own soul. Perhaps it did so for this very reason, because you thought you was accountable for the event, which no man is, nor indeed can be;—or perhaps, because you was off your guard; you was not watchful over your own spirit. But this is no reason for disobeying God. Try again; but try more warily than before. Do good (as you forgive) "not seven times only, but until seventy times seven." Only be wiser by experience: Attempt it every time more cautiously than before. Be more humbled before God, more deeply convinced that of yourself you can do nothing. Be more jealous over your own spirit; more gentle, and watchful unto prayer. Thus "cast your bread upon the waters, and you shall find it again after many days."

IV. 1. Notwithstanding all these plausible pretences for hiding it, "let your light so shine before men, that they may see your good works, and glorify your Father which is in heaven." This is the practical application which our Lord himself makes of the foregoing considerations.

"Let your light so shine:"—Your lowliness of heart; your gentleness, and meekness of wisdom; your serious, weighty concern for the things of eternity, and sorrow for the sins and miseries of men; your earnest desire of universal holiness, and full happiness in God; your tender good-will to all mankind, and fervent love to your supreme Benefactor. Endeavour not to conceal this light, wherewith God hath enlightened your soul; but let it shine before men, before all with whom you are, in the whole tenor of your conversation. Let it shine still more eminently in your actions, in your doing all possible good to all men; and in your suffering for righteousness' sake, while you "rejoice and are exceeding glad, knowing that great is your reward in heaven."

2. "Let your light so shine before men, that they may see your good works:"—So far let a Christian be from ever designing or desiring to conceal his religion! On the contrary, let it be your desire, not to conceal it; not to put the light under a bushel. Let it be your care to place it "on a candlestick, that it may give light to all that are in the house." Only take heed, not to seek your own praise herein, not to desire any honour to yourselves. But let it be your sole aim, that all who see your good works may "glorify your Father which is in heaven."

3. Be this your one ultimate end in all things. With this view, be plain, open, undisguised. Let your love be without dissimulation: Why should you hide fair, disinterested love? Let there be no guile found in your mouth: Let your words be the genuine picture of your heart. Let there be no darkness or reservedness in your conversation, no disguise in your behaviour. Leave this to those who have other designs in view; designs which will not bear the light. Be ye artless and simple to all mankind; that all may see the grace of God which is in you. And although some will harden their hearts, yet others will take knowledge that ye have been with Jesus, and, by returning themselves 'to the great Bishop of their souls, "glorify your Father which is in heaven."

4. With this one design, that men may glorify God in you, go on in his name, and in the power of his might. Be not ashamed even to stand alone, so it be in the ways of God. Let the light which is in your heart shine in all good works both works of piety and works of mercy. And in order to enlarge your ability of doing good, renounce all superfluities. Cut off all unnecessary expense in food, in furniture, in apparel. Be a good steward of every gift of God, even of these his lowest gifts. Cut off all unnecessary expense of time, all needless or useless employments; and "whatsoever thy hand findeth to do, do it with thy might." In a word, be thou full of faith and love; do good; suffer evil. And herein be thou "steadfast, unmovable;" yea, "always abounding in the work of the Lord; forasmuch as thou knowest that thy labour is not in vain in the Lord."

25.* Upon our Lord's Sermon on the Mount Discourse 5

"Think not that I am come to destroy the Law or the prophets: I am not come to destroy, but to fulfil. For verily I say unto you: Till heaven and earth pass, one jot or one tittle shall in no wise pass from the law, till all be fulfilled. Whosoever therefore shall break one of these least commandments, and shall teach men so, he shall be called the least in the kingdom of heaven: but whosoever shall do and teach them, the same shall be called great in the kingdom of heaven. For verily I say unto you: That except your righteousness shall exceed the righteousness of the Scribes and Pharisees, ye shall in no case enter into the kingdom of heaven."

Matt. 5:17–20

1. Among the multitude of reproaches which fell upon Him who "was despised and rejected of men," it could not fail to be one, that He was a teacher of novelties, an introducer of *a new religion*. This might be affirmed with the more colour because many of the expressions He had used were not

common among the Jews: either they did not use them at all, or not in the same sense, not in so full and strong a meaning. Add to this, that the worshipping God "in spirit and in truth" must always appear a new religion to those who have hitherto known nothing but outside worship, nothing but the "form of godliness."

2. And it is not improbable, some might hope it was so, that He was abolishing the old religion, and bringing in another,—one which, they might flatter themselves, would be an easier way to heaven. But our Lord refutes, in these words, both the vain hopes of the one, and the groundless calumnies of the other.

I shall consider them in the same order as they lie, taking each verse for a distinct head of discourse.

I. 1. And First, "Think not that I am come to destroy the Law, or the Prophets: I am not come to destroy, but to fulfil." The ritual or ceremonial law, delivered by Moses to the children of Israel, containing all the injunctions and ordinances which related to the old sacrifices and service of the temple, our Lord indeed did come to destroy, to dissolve, and utterly abolish. To this bear all the Apostles witness; not only Barnabas and Paul, who vehemently withstood those who taught that Christians ought "to keep the law of Moses;" (Acts 15:5;) not only St. Peter, who termed the insisting on this, on the observance of the ritual law, a "tempting God," and "putting a yoke upon the neck of the disciples, which neither our fathers," saith he, "nor we, were able to bear;" but all the Apostles, elders, and brethren, being assembled with one accord, (Acts 15:22,) declared, that to command them to keep this law, was to "subvert their souls;" and that "it seemed good to the Holy Ghost" and to them, to lay no such burden upon them. (Acts 15:28.) This "hand-writing of ordinances" our Lord did blot out, take away, and nail to His cross.

2. But the moral law, contained in the Ten Commandments, and enforced by the prophets, He did not take away. It was not the design of His coming to revoke any part of this. This is a law which never can be broken, which stands fast as the faithful witness in heaven. The moral stands on an entirely different foundation from the ceremonial or ritual law, which was only designed for a temporary restraint upon a disobedient and stiff-necked people; whereas this was from the beginning of the world, being "written not on tables of stone," but on the hearts of all the children of men, when they came out of the hands of the Creator. And, however the letters once wrote by the finger of God are now in a great measure defaced by sin, yet can they not wholly be blotted out, while we have any consciousness of good and evil. Every part of this law must remain in force, upon all mankind, and in all ages; as not depending either on time or place, or any other circumstances liable to change, but on the nature of God and the nature of man, and their unchangeable relation to each other.

3. "I am not come to destroy, but to fulfil." Some have conceived our Lord to mean,—I am come to fulfil this by my entire and perfect obedience to it. And it cannot be doubted but he did, in this sense, fulfil every part of it. But this does not appear to be what He intends here, being foreign to the scope of his present discourse. Without question, his meaning in this place is, (consistently with all that goes before and follows after,)—I am come to establish it in its fullness, in spite of all the glosses of men: I am come to place in a full and clear view whatsoever was dark or obscure therein: I am come to declare the true and full import of every part of it; to show the length and breadth, the entire extent of every commandment contained therein, and the height and depth, the inconceivable purity and spirituality of it in all its branches.

4. And this our Lord has abundantly performed in the preceding and subsequent parts of the discourse before us, in which He has not introduced a new religion into the world, but the same which was from the beginning:—a religion the substance of which is, without question, as old as the creation, being coeval with man, and having proceeded from God at the very time when "man became a living soul;" (the *substance*, I say; for some circumstances of it now relate to man as a fallen creature;)—a religion witnessed to both by the Law and by the Prophets, in all succeeding generations. Yet was it never so fully explained, nor so thoroughly understood till the great Author of it Himself condescended to give mankind this authentic comment on all the essential branches of it; at the same time declaring it should never be changed, but remain in force to the end of the world.

II. 1. "For verily I say unto you," (a solemn preface, which denotes both the importance and certainty of what is spoken,) "Till heaven and earth pass, one jot or one tittle shall in no wise pass from the law till all be fulfilled."

"One jot:"—It is literally, *not one iota*, not the most inconsiderable vowel: "Or one tittle," *mia keraia*, one *corner*, or *point* of a consonant. It is a proverbial expression which signifies that no one commandment contained in the moral law, nor the least part of any one, however inconsiderable it might seem, should ever be disannulled.

Shall in no wise pass from the law: *ou me parelthei apo tou nomou*. The double negative, here used, strengthens the sense, so as to admit of no contradiction: And the word *parelthei*, it may be observed, is not barely *future*, declaring what will be; but has likewise the force of an *imperative*, ordering what *shall* be. It is a word of authority, expressing the sovereign will and power of him that spake; of him whose word is the law of heaven and earth, and stands fast for ever and ever.

one jot or one tittle shall in no wise pass till heaven and earth pass; or as it is expressed immediately after, *hews an panta genetai, till all* (or rather, *all things*) *be fulfilled*, till the consummation of all things. here is therefore no room for that poor evasion (with which some have delighted themselves greatly) that no part of the law was to pass away till *all the law* was fulfilled: But it has been fulfilled by Christ, and therefore now must pass, for the gospel to be established. Not so; the word *all* does not mean all the law, but all things in the universe; as neither has the term *fulfilled* any reference to the law, but to all things in heaven and earth.

2. From all this we may learn, that there is no contrariety at all between the law and the gospel; that there is no need for the law to pass away, in order to the establishing of the gospel.

Indeed neither of them supersedes the other, but they agree perfectly well together. Yea, the very same words, considered in different respects, are parts both of the law and of the gospel. If they are considered as commandments, they are parts of the law: if as promises, of the gospel. Thus, Thou shalt love the Lord thy God with all thy heart, when considered as a commandment, is a branch of the law; when regarded as a promise, is an essential part of the gospel; the gospel being no other than the commands of the law proposed by way of promises. Accordingly poverty of spirit, purity of heart, and whatever else is enjoined in the holy law of God, are no other, when viewed in a gospel light, than so many great and precious promises.

3. There is, therefore, the closest connexion that can be conceived between the law and the gospel. on the one hand, the law continually makes way for, and points us to the gospel; on the other, the gospel continually leads us to a more exact fulfilling of the law. The law, for instance, requires us to love God, to love our neighbour, to be meek, humble, or holy. We feel that we are not sufficient for these things; yea, that "with man this is impossible:" But we see a promise of God, to give us that love, and to make us humble, meek, and holy: We lay hold of this gospel, of these glad tidings; it is done unto us according to our faith; and "the righteousness of the law is fulfilled in us," through faith which is in Christ Jesus.

We may yet farther observe, that every command in holy writ is only a covered promise. For by that solemn declaration, "This is the covenant I will make after those days, saith the Lord; I will put my laws in your minds, and write them in your hearts," God hath engaged to give whatsoever he commands. Does he command us then to "pray without ceasing?" To "rejoice evermore?" "To be holy as He is holy?" It is enough. He will work in us this very thing. It shall be unto us according to his word.

4. But if these things are so, we cannot be at a loss what to think of those who in all ages of the Church, have undertaken to change or supersede some commands of God, as they professed, by the peculiar direction of his Spirit. Christ has here given us an infallible rule, whereby to judge of all such pretensions. Christianity, as it includes the whole moral law of God, both by way of injunction and of promise, if we will hear him is designed of God to be the last of all his dispensations. There is no other to come after this. This is to endure till the consummation of all things. of consequence, all such new revelations are of Satan, and not of God; and all pretences to another more perfect dispensation fall to the ground of course. "Heaven and earth shall pass away;" but *this* word "shall not pass away."

III. 1. "Whosoever therefore shall break one of these least commandments, and shall teach men so, he shall be called the least in the kingdom of heaven; but whosoever shall do and teach them, the same shall be called great in the kingdom of heaven."

Who, what are they that make "the preaching of the law" a character of reproach? Do they not see on whom their reproach must fall,—on whose head it must light at last? Whosoever on this ground despiseth us, despiseth Him that sent us. For did ever any man preach the law like Him, even when he came not to condemn but to save the world; when he came purposely to "bring life and immortality to light through the gospel?" Can any preach the law more expressly, more rigorously, than Christ does in these words? And who is he that shall amend them? Who is he that shall instruct the Son of God how to preach? Who will teach Him a better way of delivering the message which He hath received of the Father?

2. "Whosoever shall break one of these least commandments," or one of the least of these commandments.—"These commandments," we may observe, is a term used by our Lord as equivalent with the law, or the law and the Prophets,—which is the same thing, seeing the Prophets added nothing to the law, but only declared, explained, or enforced it, as they were moved by the Holy Ghost.

"Whosoever shall break one of these least commandments," especially if it be done wilfully or presumptuously:—**one**;—for "he that keepeth the whole law, and" thus "offends in one point, is guilty of all;" the wrath of God abideth on him, as surely as if he had broken every one. So that no allowance is made for one darling lust; no reserve for one idol; no excuse for refraining from all besides, and only giving way to one bosom sin. What God demands is an entire obedience; we are to have an eye to all His commandments; otherwise we lose all the labour we take in keeping some, and our poor souls for ever and ever.

"one of these least," or one of the least of these commandments:—Here is another excuse cut off, whereby many, who cannot deceive God, miserably deceive their own souls. "This sin," saith the sinner, "is it not a little one? Will not the Lord spare me in this thing? Surely he will not be extreme to mark this, since I do not offend in the greater matters of the law." Vain hope! Speaking after the manner of men, we may term these great, and those little commandments; but in reality they are not so. If we use propriety of speech there is no such thing as a little sin; every sin being a transgression of the holy and perfect law, and an affront on the great Majesty of heaven.

3. "And shall teach men so." In some sense it may be said that whosoever openly breaks any commandment teaches others the same; for example speaks, and many times louder than precept. In this sense, it is apparent, every open drunkard is a teacher of drunkenness; every sabbath-breaker is constantly teaching his neighbour to profane the day of the Lord. But this is not all: An habitual breaker of the law is seldom content to stop here; he generally teaches other men to do so too, by word as well as example; especially when he hardens his neck, and hateth to be reproved. Such a sinner soon commences an advocate for sin; he defends what he is resolved not to forsake; he excuses the sin which he will not leave, and thus directly teaches every sin which he commits.

"He shall be called least in the kingdom of heaven;"—that is, shall have no part therein. He is a stranger to the kingdom of heaven which is on earth; he hath no portion in that inheritance; no share of that "righteousness and peace and joy in the Holy Ghost." Nor, by consequence can he have any part in the glory which shall be revealed.

4. But if those who even thus break, and teach others to break "one of the least of these commandments shall be called least in the kingdom of heaven," shall have no part in the kingdom of Christ and of God; if even these shall be cast into "outer darkness, where is wailing and gnashing of teeth," then where will they appear whom our Lord chiefly and primarily intends in these words,—they who, bearing the character of Teachers sent from God, do nevertheless themselves break his commandments; yea, and openly teach others so to do; being corrupt both in life and doctrine?

5. These are of several sorts. Of the first sort are they who live in some wilful, habitual sin. Now, if an ordinary sinner teaches by his example, how much more a sinful Minister,—even if he does not attempt to defend, excuse, or extenuate his sin! If he does, he is a murderer indeed; yea, the murderer-general of his congregation! He peoples the regions of death. He is the choicest instrument of the prince of darkness. When he goes hence, "hell from beneath is moved to meet him at his coming." Nor can he sink into the bottomless pit without dragging a multitude after him.

6. Next to these are the good-natured, good sort of men: who live an easy, harmless life, neither troubling themselves with outward sin, nor with inward holiness; men who are remarkable neither one way nor the other, neither for religion nor irreligion who are very regular both in public and private, but do not pretend to be any stricter than their neighbours. A Minister of this kind breaks not one, or a few only, of the least commandments of God; but all the great and weighty branches of his law which relate to the power of godliness, and all that require us to "pass the time of our sojourning in fear," to "work out our salvation with fear and trembling;" to have our "loins always girt and our lights burning," to "strive," or agonize, "to enter in at the strait gate." And he teaches men so, by the whole form of his life, and the general tenor of his preaching, which uniformly tends to soothe those in their pleasing dream who imagine themselves Christians and are not; to persuade all who attend upon his ministry to sleep on and take their rest. No marvel, therefore, if both he and they that follow him wake together in everlasting burnings."

7. But above all these, in the highest rank of the enemies of the gospel of Christ, are they who openly and explicitly "judge the law" itself, and "speak evil of the law;" who teach men to break (lysai, to dissolve, to loose, to untie the obligation of) not one only, whether of the least, or of the greatest, but all the commandments at a stroke; who teach, without any cover, in so many words,—What did our Lord do with the law? he abolished it. There is but one duty, which is that of believing. All commands are unfit for our times. From any demand of the law, no man is obliged now to go one step, to give away one farthing, to eat or omit one morsel. This is, indeed, carrying matters with a high hand; this is withstanding our Lord to the face, and telling him that he understood not how to deliver the message on which he was sent. o Lord, lay not this sin to their charge! Father, forgive them; for they know not what they do!

8. The most surprising of all the circumstances that attend this strong delusion, is, that they who are given up to it, really believe that they honour Christ by overthrowing his law, and that they are magnifying his office, while they are destroying his doctrine! Yea, they honour him just as Judas did, when he said, "Hail, Master!" and kissed him. And he may as justly say to every one of them, "Betrayest thou the Son of Man with a kiss?" It is no other than betraying him with a kiss, to talk of his blood, and take away his crown; to set light by any part of his law, under pretence of advancing his gospel. Nor, indeed, can anyone escape this charge, who preaches faith in any such manner as either directly or indirectly tends to set aside any branch of obedience; who preaches Christ so as to disannul, or weaken, in anywise, the least of the commandments of God.

9. It is impossible, indeed, to have too high an esteem for "the faith of Gods elect." And we must all declare, "By grace ye are saved through faith; not of works, lest any man should boast." We must cry aloud to every penitent sinner, "Believe in the Lord Jesus Christ, and thou shalt be saved." But, at the same time, we must take care to let all men know, we esteem no faith but that which worketh by love [Gal. 5:6]; and that we are not saved by faith, unless so far as we are delivered from the power as well as the guilt of sin. And when we say, "Believe, and thou shalt be saved;" we do not mean, "Believe, and thou shalt step from sin to heaven, without any holiness coming between; faith supplying the place of holiness;" but, "Believe, and thou shalt be holy; believe in the Lord Jesus, and thou shalt have peace and power together: Thou shalt have power from Him in whom thou believest, to trample sin under thy feet; power to love the Lord thy God with all thy heart, and to serve him with all thy strength: Thou shalt have power by patient continuance in well-doing, to seek for glory, and honour, and immortality; thou shalt both do and teach all the commandments of God, from the least even to the greatest: Thou shalt teach them by thy life as well as thy words, and so be called great in the kingdom of heaven."

IV. 1. Whatever other way we teach to the kingdom of heaven, to glory, honour, and immortality, be it called the way of faith, or by any other name, it is, in truth, the way to destruction. It will not bring a man peace at the last. For thus saith the Lord, "[Verily] I say unto you, That except your righteousness shall exceed the righteousness of the Scribes and Pharisees, ye shall in no case enter into the kingdom of heaven."

The Scribes, mentioned so often in the New Testament, as some of the most constant and vehement opposers of our Lord, were not secretaries, or men employed in writing only, as that term might incline us to believe. Neither were they lawyers, in our common sense of the word; although the word nomikoi is so rendered in our translation. Their employment had no affinity at all to that of a lawyer among us. They were conversant with the laws of God, and not with the laws of man. These were their study: It was their proper and peculiar business to read and expound the law and the Prophets, particularly in the synagogues. They were the ordinary, stated preachers among the Jews. So that if the sense of the original word was attended to, we might render it, the Divines. For these were the men who made divinity their profession: and they were generally (as their name literally imports) men of letters; men of the greatest account for learning that were then in the Jewish nation.

2. The Pharisees were a very ancient sect, or body of men, among the Jews; originally so called from the Hebrew word *PRS*—which signifies to *separate* or *divide*. Not that they made any formal separation from, or division in, the national church. They were only distinguished from others by greater strictness of life, by more exactness of conversation. For they were zealous of the law in the minutest points; paying tithes of mint, anise, and cummin: And hence they were had in honour of all the people, and generally esteemed the holiest of men.

Many of the Scribes were of the sect of the Pharisees. Thus St. Paul himself, who was educated for a Scribe, first at the university of Tarsus, and after that in Jerusalem, at the feet of Gamaliel, (one of the most learned Scribes or Doctors of the law that were then in the nation,) declares of himself before the Council, "I am a Pharisee, the son of a Pharisee;" (Acts 23:6;) and before King Agrippa, "After the straitest sect of our religion, I lived a Pharisee." (Acts 26:5.) And the whole body of the Scribes generally esteemed and acted in concert with the Pharisees. Hence we find our Saviour so frequently coupling them together, as coming in many respects under the same consideration. In this place they seem to be mentioned together as the most eminent professors of religion; the former of whom were accounted the wisest,—the latter, the holiest of men.

3. What "the righteousness of the Scribes and Pharisees" really was, it is not difficult to determine. Our Lord has preserved an authentic account which one of them gave of himself: And he is clear and full in describing his own righteousness; and cannot be supposed to have omitted any part of it. He went up indeed "into the temple to pray;" but was so intent upon his own virtues, that he forgot the design upon which he came. For it is remarkable, he does not properly pray at all: He only tells God how wise and good he was. "God, I thank thee that I am not as other men are, extortioners, unjust, adulterers; or even as this publican. I fast twice in the week: I give tithes of all that I possess." His righteousness therefore consisted of three parts: First, saith he, "I am not as other men are;" I am not an extortioner, not unjust, not an adulterer; not "even as this publican." Secondly, "I fast twice in the week:" And, Thirdly, "I give tithes of all that I possess."

"I am not as other men are." This is not a small point. It is not every man that can say this. It is as if he had said,—"I do not suffer myself to be carried away by that great torrent, custom. I live not by custom, but by reason; not by the examples of men, but the word of God. I am not an extortioner, not unjust, not an adulterer; however common these sins are, even among those who are called the people of God; (extortion, in particular,—a kind of legal injustice, not punishable by any human law, the making gain of another's ignorance or necessity, having filled every corner of the land;) nor even as this publican, not guilty of any open or presumptuous sin; not an outward sinner; but a fair, honest man of blameless life and conversation."

4. "I fast twice in the week." There is more implied in this, than we may at first be sensible of. All the stricter Pharisees observed the weekly fasts; namely, every Monday and Thursday. On the former day they fasted in memory of Moses receiving on that day (as their tradition taught) the two tables of stone written by the finger of God; on the latter, in memory of his casting them out of his hand, when he saw the people dancing round the golden calf. On these days, they took no sustenance at all, till three in the afternoon; the hour at which they began to offer up the evening sacrifice in the temple. Till that hour, it was their custom to remain in the temple, in some of the corners, apartments, or courts thereof; that they might be ready to assist at all the sacrifices, and to join in all the public prayers. The time between they were accustomed to employ, partly in private addresses to God, partly in searching the Scriptures, in reading the Law and the Prophets, and in meditating thereon. Thus much is implied in, "I fast twice in the week;" the second branch of the righteousness of a Pharisee.

5. "I give tithes of all that I possess." This the Pharisees did with the utmost exactness. They would not except the most inconsiderable thing; no, not mint, anise, and cummin. They would not keep back the least part of what they believed properly to belong to God; but gave a full tenth of their whole substance yearly, and of all their increase, whatsoever it was.

Yea, the stricter Pharisees (as has been often observed by those who are versed in the ancient Jewish writings,) not content with giving one tenth of their substance to God in his priests and Levites, gave another tenth to God in the poor, and that continually. They gave the same proportion of all they had in alms as they were accustomed to give in tithes. And this likewise they ajusted with the utmost exactness; that they might not keep back any part, but might fully render unto God the things which were God's, as they accounted this to be. So that, upon the whole, they gave away, from year to year an entire fifth of all that they possessed.

6. This was "the righteousness of the Scribes and Pharisees;" a righteousness which, in many respects, went far beyond the conception which many have been accustomed to entertain concerning it. But perhaps it will be said, "It was all false and feigned; for they were all a company of hypocrites." Some of them doubtless were; men who had really no religion at all, no fear of God, or desire to please him; who had no concern for the honour that cometh of God, but only for the praise of men. And these are they whom our Lord so severely condemns, so sharply reproves, on many occasions. But we must not suppose, because many Pharisees were hypocrites, therefore all were so. Nor indeed is hypocrisy by any means essential to the character of a Pharisee. This is not the distinguishing mark of their sect. It is rather this, according to our Lord's account, "They trusted in themselves that they were righteous, and despised others." This is their genuine badge. But the Pharisee of this kind cannot be a hypocrite. He must be, in the common sense, sincere; otherwise he could not "trust in himself that he is righteous." The man

who was here commending himself to God unquestionably thought himself righteous. Consequently, he was no hypocrite; he was not conscious to himself of any insincerity. He now spoke to God just what he thought, namely, that he was abundantly better than other men.

But the example of St. Paul, were there no other, is sufficient to put this out of all question. He could not only say, when he was a Christian, "Herein do I exercise myself, to have always a conscience void of offence toward God and toward men;" (Acts 24:16;) but even concerning the time when he was a Pharisee, "Men and brethren, I have lived in all good conscience before God until this day." (Acts 23:1) He was therefore sincere when he was a Pharisee, as well when he was a Christian. He was no more a hypocrite when he persecuted the Church, than when he preached the faith which once he persecuted. Let this then be added to "the righteousness of the Scribes and Pharisees,"—a sincere belief that they are righteous, and in all things "doing God service."

7. And yet, "except your righteousness," saith our Lord, "shall exceed the righteousness of the Scribes and Pharisees, ye shall in no case enter into the kingdom of heaven." A solemn and weighty declaration, and which it behoves all who are called by the name of Christ seriously and deeply to consider. But before we inquire how our righteousness may exceed theirs, let us examine whether at present we come up to it.

First, a Pharisee was "not as other men are." In externals he was singularly good. Are we so? Do we dare to be singular at all? Do we not rather swim with the stream? Do we not many times dispense with religion and reason together, because we would not *look particular?* Are we not often more afraid of being out of the fashion, than of being out of the way of salvation? Have we courage to stem the tide?—to run counter to the world?—"to obey God rather than man?" Otherwise, the Pharisee leaves us behind at the very first step. It is well if we overtake him any more.

But to come closer. Can we use his first plea with God, which is, in substance, "I do no harm: I live in no outward sin. I do nothing for which my own heart condemns me." Do you not? Are you sure of that? Do you live in no practice for which your own heart condemns you? If you are not an adulterer, if you are not unchaste, either in word or deed, are you not unjust? The grand measure of justice, as well as of mercy, is, "Do unto others as thou wouldst they should do unto thee." Do you walk by this rule? Do you never do unto any what you would not they should do unto you, Nay, are you not grossly unjust? Are you not an extortioner? Do you not make a gain of anyone's ignorance or necessity; neither in buying nor selling? Suppose you are engaged in trade: Do you demand, do you receive, no more than the real value of what you sell? Do you demand, do you receive, no more of the ignorant than of the knowing,—of a little child, than of an experienced trader? If you do, why does not your heart condemn you? You are a barefaced extortioner! Do you demand no more than the usual price of goods of any who is in pressing want,—who must have, and that without delay, the things which you only can furnish him with? If you do, this also is flat extortion. Indeed you do not come up to the righteousness of a Pharisee.

8. A Pharisee, Secondly, (to express his sense in our common way,) used all the means of grace. As he fasted often and much, twice in every week, so he attended all the sacrifices. He was constant in public and private prayer, and in reading and hearing the Scriptures. Do you go as far as this? Do you fast much and often?—twice in the week? I fear not! Once, at least, "on all Fridays in the year?" (So our Church clearly and peremptorily enjoins all her members to do; to observe all these as well as the vigils and the forty days of Lent, as days of fasting or abstinence.) Do you fast twice in the year? I am afraid some among us cannot plead even this! Do you neglect no opportunity of attending and partaking of the Christian sacrifice? How many are they who call themselves Christians, and yet are utterly regardless of it,—yet do not eat of that bread, or drink of that cup, for months, perhaps years, together? Do you, every day, either hear the Scriptures, or read them and meditate thereon? Do you join in prayer with the great congregation, daily, if you have opportunity; if not, whenever you can; particularly on that day which you "remember to keep it holy?" Do you strive to "make opportunities?" Are you glad when they say unto you, "We will go into the house of the Lord?" Are you zealous of, and diligent in, private prayer? Do you suffer no day to pass without it? Rather are not some of you so far from spending therein (with the Pharisee) several hours in one day that you think one hour full enough, if not too much? Do you spend an hour in a day, or in a week, in praying to your Father which is in secret? yea, an hour in a month? Have you spent one hour together in private prayer ever since you was born? Ah, poor Christian! Shall not the Pharisee rise up in the judgment against thee and condemn thee? His righteousness is as far above thine, as the heaven is above the earth!

9. The Pharisee, Thirdly, paid tithes and gave alms of all that he possessed. And in how ample a manner! So that he was (as we phrase it) "a man that did much good." Do we come up to him here? Which of us is so abundant as he was in good works? Which of us gives a fifth of all his substance to God? Both of the principal and of the increase? Who of us out of (suppose) an hundred pounds a year, gives twenty to God and the poor; out of fifty, ten; and so in a larger or a smaller proportion? When shall our righteousness, in using all the means of grace, in attending all the ordinances of God, in avoiding evil and doing good, equal at least the righteousness of the Scribes and Pharisees?

10. Although if it only equalled theirs, what would that profit? "For verily I say unto you, except your righteousness shall exceed the righteousness of the Scribes and Pharisees, ye shall in no case enter into the kingdom of heaven." But how can it exceed theirs? Wherein does the righteousness of a Christian exceed that of a scribe or Pharisee? Christian righteousness exceeds theirs, First, in the extent of it. Most of the Pharisees, though they were rigorously exact in many things, yet were emboldened, by the traditions of the Elders to dispense with others of equal importance. Thus they were extremely punctual in keeping the fourth commandment,—they would not even rub an ear of corn on the Sabbath-day; but not at all in keeping the third,—making little account of light, or even false, swearing. So that their righteousness was

partial; whereas the righteousness of a real Christian is universal. He does not observe one, or some parts, of the law of God, and neglect the rest; but keeps all his commandments, loves them all, values them above gold or precious stones.

11. It may be, indeed, that some of the Scribes and Pharisees endeavoured to keep all the commandments, and consequently were, as touching the righteousness of the law, that is, according to the letter of it, blameless. But still the righteousness of a Christian exceeds all this righteousness of a Scribe or Pharisee, by fulfilling the spirit as well as the letter of the law; by inward as well as outward obedience. In this, in the spirituality of it, it admits of no comparison. This is the point which our Lord has so largely proved, in the whole tenor of this discourse. Their righteousness was external only: Christian righteousness is in the inner man. The Pharisee "cleansed the outside of the cup and the platter;" the Christian is clean within. The Pharisee laboured to present God with a good life; the Christian with a holy heart. The one shook off the leaves, perhaps the fruits, of sin; the other "lays the axe to the root," as not being content with the outward form of godliness, how exact soever it be, unless the life, the Spirit, the power of God unto salvation, be felt in the inmost soul.

Thus, to do no harm, to do good, to attend the ordinances of God (the righteousness of a Pharisee,) are all external; whereas, on the contrary, poverty of spirit, mourning, meekness, hunger and thirst after righteousness, the love of our neighbour, and purity of heart, (the righteousness of a Christian,) are all internal. And even peace-making (or doing good,) and suffering for righteousness' sake, stand entitled to the blessings annexed to them, only as they imply these inward dispositions, as they spring from, exercise, and confirm them. So that whereas the righteousness of the Scribes and Pharisees was external only, it may be said in some sense that the righteousness of a Christian is internal only: All his actions and sufferings being as nothing in themselves, being estimated before God only by the tempers from which they spring.

12. Whosoever therefore thou art, who bearest the holy and venerable name of a Christian, see, First, that thy righteousness fall not short of the righteousness of the Scribes and Pharisees. Be not thou "as other men are!" Dare to stand alone, to be "against example, singularly good." If thou "follow a multitude" at all, it must be "to do evil." Let not custom or fashion be thy guide, but reason and religion. The practice of others is nothing to thee: "Every man must give an account of himself to God." Indeed, if thou canst save the soul of another, do; but at least save one,—thy own. Walk not in the path of death because it is broad, and many walk therein. Nay, by this very token thou mayst know it. Is the way wherein thou now walkest, a broad, well-frequented, fashionable way? Then it infallibly leads to destruction. O be not thou "damned for company!" Cease from evil; fly from sin as from the face of a serpent! At least, do no harm. "He that committeth sin is of the devil." Be not thou found in that number. Touching outward sins, surely the grace of God is even now sufficient for thee. "Herein," at least, "exercise

thyself to have a conscience void of offence toward God, and toward men."

Secondly. Let not thy righteousness fall short of theirs with regard to the ordinances of God. If thy labour or bodily strength will not allow of thy fasting twice in the week, however, deal faithfully with thy own soul, and fast as often as thy strength will permit. Omit no public, no private opportunity of pouring out thy soul in prayer. Neglect no occasion of eating that bread and drinking that cup which is the communion of the body and blood of Christ. Be diligent in searching the Scriptures: read as thou mayst, and meditate therein day and night. Rejoice to embrace every opportunity of hearing "the word of reconciliation" declared by the "ambassadors of Christ," the "stewards of the mysteries of God." In using all the means of grace, in a constant and careful attendance on every ordinance of God, live up to (at least till thou canst go beyond) "the righteousness of the Scribes and Pharisees."

Thirdly. Fall not short of a Pharisee in doing good. Give alms of all thou dost possess. Is any hungry? Feed him. Is he athirst? Give him drink. Naked? Cover him with a garment. If thou hast this world's goods, do not limit thy beneficence to a scanty proportion. Be merciful to the uttermost of thy power. Why not, even as this Pharisee? Now "make thyself friends," while the time is, "of the mammon of unrighteousness," that when thou failest," when this earthly tabernacle is dissolved, "they may receive thee into everlasting habitations."

13. But rest not here. Let thy "righteousness exceed the righteousness of the Scribes and Pharisees." Be not thou content to "keep the whole law, and offend in one point." Hold thou fast all His commandments, and all "false ways do thou utterly abhor." Do all the things whatsoever He hath commanded, and that with all thy might. Thou canst do all things through Christ strengthening thee; though without Him thou canst do nothing.

Above all, let thy righteousness exceed theirs in the purity and spirituality of it. What is the exactest form of religion to thee? the most perfect outside righteousness? Go thou higher and deeper than all this! Let thy religion be the religion of the heart. Be thou poor in spirit; little, and base, and mean, and vile in thy own eyes; amazed and humbled to the dust at the "love of God which is in Christ Jesus thy Lord! Be serious: Let the whole stream of thy thoughts, words, and works, be such as flows from the deepest conviction that thou standest on the edge of the great gulf, thou and all the children of men, just ready to drop in, either into everlasting glory, or everlasting burnings! Be meek: Let thy soul be filled with mildness, gentleness, patience, long-suffering toward all men; at the same time that all which is in thee is athirst for God, the living God, longing to awake up after his likeness, and to be satisfied with it. Be thou a lover of God, and of all mankind. In this spirit, do and suffer all things. Thus "exceed the righteousness of the Scribes and Pharisees," and thou shalt be "called great in the kingdom of heaven."

26.* UPON OUR LORD'S SERMON ON THE MOUNT DISCOURSE 6

"Take heed that ye do not your alms before men, to be seen of them: Otherwise ye have no reward of your Father which is in heaven. Therefore when thou doest thine alms, do not sound a trumpet before thee, as the hypocrites do in the synagogues and in the streets, that they may have glory of men. Verily I say unto you, They have their reward. But when thou doest alms, let not thy left hand know what thy right hand doeth: That thine alms may be in secret: And thy Father, which seeth in secret, himself shall reward thee openly. And when thou prayest, thou shalt not be as the hypocrites are: For they love to pray standing in the synagogues and in the corners of the streets, that they may be seen of men. Verily I say unto you, They have their reward. But thou, when thou prayest, enter into thy closet, and when thou hast shut thy door, pray to thy Father which is in secret; and thy Father which seeth in secret, he shall reward thee openly. But when ye pray, use not vain repetitions, as the Heathen do: For they think that they shall be heard for their much speaking. Be not ye therefore like unto them: For your Father knoweth what things ye have need of, before you ask him. After this manner therefore pray ye: Our Father which art in heaven, Hallowed be thy name. Thy kingdom come. Thy will be done in earth, as it is in heaven. Give us this day our daily bread. And forgive us our debts as we forgive our debtors. And lead us not into temptation, but deliver us from evil: For thine is the kingdom, and the power, and the glory, for ever. Amen. For if ye forgive men their trespasses, your heavenly Father will also forgive you: But if ye forgive not men their trespasses, neither will your Father forgive your trespasses."

Matt. 6:1–15.

1. In the preceding chapter our Lord has described inward religion in its various branches. He has laid before us those dispositions of soul which constitute real Christianity; the inward tempers contained in that "holiness, without which no man shall see the Lord;" the affections which, when flowing from their proper fountain, from a living faith in God through Christ Jesus, are intrinsically and essentially good, and acceptable to God. He proceeds to show, in this chapter, how all our actions likewise, even those that are indifferent in their own nature, may be made holy, and good and acceptable to God, by a pure and holy intention. Whatever is done without this, he largely declares, is of no value before God. Whereas whatever outward works are thus consecrated to God, they are, in his sight, of great price.

2. The necessity of this purity of intention, he shows, First, with regard to those which are usually accounted religious actions, and indeed are such when performed with a right intention. Some of these are commonly termed works of piety; the rest, works of charity or mercy. Of the latter sort, he particularly names almsgiving; of the former, prayer and fasting. But the directions given for these are equally to be applied to every work, whether of charity or mercy.

I. 1. And, First, with regard to works of mercy. "Take heed," saith he, "that ye do not your alms before men, to be seen of them: Otherwise ye have no reward of your Father which is in heaven." "That ye do not your alms:"—Although this only is named, yet is every work of charity included, every thing which we give, or speak, or do, whereby our neighbour may be profited; whereby another man may receive any advantage, either in his body or soul. The feeding the hungry, the clothing the naked, the entertaining or assisting the stranger, the visiting those that are sick or in prison, the comforting the afflicted, the instructing the ignorant, the reproving the wicked, the exhorting and encouraging the well-doer; and if there be any other work of mercy, it is equally included in this direction.

2. "Take heed that ye do not your alms before men, to be seen of them."—The thing which is here forbidden, is not barely the doing good in the sight of men; this circumstance alone, that others see what we do, makes the action neither worse nor better; but the doing it before men, "to be seen of them," with this view from this intention only. I say, from this intention only; for this may, in some cases, be a part of our intention; we may design that some of our actions should be seen, and yet they may be acceptable to God. We may intend that our light should shine before men, when our conscience bears us witness in the Holy Ghost, that our ultimate end in designing they should see our good works, is, "that they may glorify our Father which is in heaven." But take heed that ye do not the least thing with a view to your own glory: Take heed that a regard to the praise of men have no place at all in your works of mercy. If ye seek your own glory, if you have any design to gain the honour that cometh of men whatever is done with this view is nothing worth; it is not done unto the Lord; he accepteth it not; "ye have no reward" for this "of our Father which is in heaven."

3. "Therefore when thou doest thine alms, do not sound a trumpet before thee, as the hypocrites do, in the synagogues and in the streets, that they may have praise of men."—The word synagogue does not here mean a place of worship, but any place of public resort, such as the market-place, or exchange. It was a common thing among the Jews, who were men of large fortunes, particularly among the Pharisees, to cause a trumpet to be sounded before them in the most public parts of the city, when they were about to give any considerable alms. The pretended reason for this was, to call the poor together to receive it; but the real design, that they might have praise of men. But be not thou like unto them. Do not thou cause a trumpet to be sounded before thee. Use no ostentation in doing good. Aim at the honour which cometh of God only. They who seek the praise of men have their reward: They shall have no praise of God.

4. "But when thou doest alms, let not thy left hand know what thy right hand doeth."—This is a proverbial expression, the meaning of which is,—Do it in as secret a manner as is possible; as secret as is consistent with the doing it at all, (for

---

* [text of the 1872 ed.]

it must not be left undone; omit no opportunity of doing good, whether secretly or openly,) and with the doing it in the most effectual manner. For here is also an exception to be made: When you are fully persuaded in your own mind, that by your not concealing the good which is done, either you will yourself be enabled, or others excited, to do the more good, then you may not conceal it: Then let your light appear, and "shine to all that are in the house." But, unless where the glory of God and the good of mankind oblige you to the contrary, act in as private and unobserved a manner as the nature of the thing will admit;—"that thy alms may be in secret; and thy Father which seeth in secret, he shall reward thee openly;" perhaps in the present world,—many instances of this stand recorded in all ages; but infallibly in the world to come, before the general assembly of men and angels.

II. 1. From works of charity or mercy our Lord proceeds to those which are termed works of piety. "And when thou prayest," saith he, "thou shalt not be as the hypocrites are; for they love to pray standing in the synagogues, and in the corners of the streets, that they may be seen of men."— "Thou shalt not be as the hypocrites are." Hypocrisy, then, or insincerity, is the first thing we are to guard against in prayer. Beware not to speak what thou dost not mean. Prayer is the lifting up of the heart to God: All words of prayer, without this, are mere hypocrisy. Whenever therefore thou attemptest to pray, see that it be thy one design to commune with God, to lift up thy heart to him, to pour out thy soul before him; not as the hypocrites, who love, or are wont, "to pray standing in the synagogues," the exchange, or market-places, "and in the corners of the streets," wherever the most people are, "that they may be seen of men:" This was the sole design, the motive, and end, of the prayers which they there repeated. "Verily I say unto you, They have their reward."— They are to expect none from your Father which is in heaven.

2. But it is not only the having an eye to the praise of men, which cuts us off from any reward in heaven; which leaves us no room to expect the blessing of God upon our works, whether of piety or mercy. Purity of intention is equally destroyed by a view to any temporal reward whatever. If we repeat our prayers, if we attend the public worship of God, if we relieve the poor, with a view to gain or interest, it is not a whit more acceptable to God, than if it were done with a view to praise. Any temporal view, any motive whatever on this side eternity, any design but that of promoting the glory of God, and the happiness of men for God's sake, makes every action, however fair it may appear to men, an abomination unto the Lord.

3. "But when thou prayest, enter into thy closet, and when thou hast shut the door, pray to thy Father which is in secret."—There is a time when thou art openly to glorify God, to pray, and praise him, in the great congregation. But when thou desirest more largely and more particularly to make thy requests known unto God, whether it be in the evening, or in the morning or at noon-day, "enter into thy closet, and shut the door." Use all the privacy thou canst. (Only leave it not undone, whether thou hast any closet, any privacy, or no. Pray to God, if it be possible, when none seeth but He; but, if otherwise, pray to God.) Thus "pray to thy Father which is in secret;" pour out thy heart before him; "and thy Father which seeth in secret, he shall reward thee openly."

4. "But when ye pray," even in secret, "use not vain repetitions, as the Heathen do;" *me battalogesete*. Do not use abundance of words without any meaning. Say not the same thing over and over again; think not the fruit of your prayers depends on the length of them, like the heathens; for they think they shall be heard for their much speaking.

The thing here reproved is not simply the length, any more than the shortness, of our prayers; but, First, length without meaning; speaking much, and meaning little or nothing; the using (not all repetitions; for our Lord himself prayed thrice, repeating the same words; but) vain repetitions, as the heathens did, reciting the names of their gods, over and over; as they do among Christians, (vulgarly so called,) and not among the Papists only, who say over and over the same string of prayers, without ever feeling what they speak: Secondly, the thinking to be heard for our much speaking, the fancying God measures prayers by their length, and is best pleased with those which contain the most words, which sound the longest in his ears. These are such instances of superstition and folly as all who are named by the name of Christ should leave to the heathens, to them on whom the glorious light of the gospel hath never shined.

5. Be not ye therefore like unto them.—Ye who have tasted of the grace of God in Christ Jesus are throughly convinced, your Father knoweth what things ye have need of, before ye ask him. So that the end of your praying is not to inform God, as though he knew not your wants already; but rather to inform yourselves; to fix the sense of those wants more deeply in your hearts, and the sense of your continual dependence on Him who only is able to supply all your wants. It is not so much to move God, who is always more ready to give than you to ask, as to move yourselves, that you may be willing and ready to receive the good things he has prepared for you.

III. 1. After having taught the true nature and ends of prayer, our Lord subjoins an example of it; even that divine form of prayer which seems in this place to be proposed by way of pattern chiefly, as the model and standard of all our prayers: "After this manner therefore pray ye." Whereas, elsewhere he enjoins the use of these very words: "He said unto them, When ye pray, say—." (Luke 11:2.)

2. We may observe, in general, concerning this divine prayer, First, that it contains all we can reasonably or innocently pray for. There is nothing which we have need to ask of God, nothing which we can ask without offending him, which is not included, either directly or indirectly, in this comprehensive form. Secondly, that it contains all we can reasonably or innocently desire; whatever is for the glory of God, whatever is needful or profitable, not only for ourselves, but for every creature in heaven and earth. And, indeed, our prayers are the proper test of our desires; nothing being fit to have a place in our desires which is not fit to have a place in our prayers: What we may not pray for, neither should we desire. Thirdly, that it contains all our duty to God and man; whatsoever things are pure and holy, whatsoever God

requires of the children of men, whatsoever is acceptable in his sight, whatsoever it is whereby we may profit our neighbour, being expressed or implied therein.

3. It consists of three parts,—the preface, the petitions, and the doxology, or conclusion. The preface, "our Father which art in heaven," lays a general foundation for prayer; comprising what we must first know of God, before we can pray in confidence of being heard. It likewise points out to us all those tempers with which we are to approach to God, which are most essentially requisite, if we desire either our prayers or our lives should find acceptance with him.

4. "our Father:"—If he is a Father, then he is good, then he is loving, to his children. And here is the first and great reason for prayer. God is willing to bless; let us ask for a blessing. "our Father;"—our Creator; the Author of our being; He who raised us from the dust of the earth; who breathed into us the breath of life, and we became living souls. But if he made us, let us ask, and he will not withhold any good thing from the work of his own hands. "our Father;"—our Preserver; who, day by day, sustains the life he has given; of whose continuing love we now and every moment receive life and breath and all things. So much the more boldly let us come to him, and we shall "obtain mercy, and grace to help in time of need." Above all, the Father of our Lord Jesus Christ, and of all that believe in him; who justifies us "freely by his grace, through the redemption that is in Jesus;" who hath "blotted out all our sins, and healed all our infirmities;" who hath received us for his own children, by adoption and grace; and, "because" we "are sons, hath sent forth the Spirit of his Son into" our "hearts, crying, Abba, Father;" who "hath begotten us again of incorruptible seed", and "created us anew in Christ Jesus." Therefore we know that he heareth us always; therefore we pray to him without ceasing. We pray, because we love; and "we love him because he first loved us."

5. "our Father:"—Not *mine* only who now cry unto him, but *ours* in the most extensive sense. The God and "Father of the spirits of all flesh;" the Father of angels and men: So the very Heathens acknowledged him to be, *Pater te theOn te*. The Father of the universe, of all the families both in heaven and earth. Therefore with him there is no respect of persons. He loveth all that he hath made. "He is loving unto every man, and his mercy is over all his works." And the Lords delight is in them that fear him, and put their trust in his mercy; in them that trust in him through the Son of his love, knowing they are "accepted in the Beloved." But "if God so loved us, we ought also to love one another;" yea, all mankind; seeing "God so loved the world, that he gave his only-begotten Son", even to die the death, that they "might not perish, but have everlasting life"

6. "Which art in heaven:"—High and lifted up; God over all, blessed for ever: Who, sitting on the circle of the heavens, beholdeth all things both in heaven and earth; whose eye pervades the whole sphere of created being; yea, and of uncreated night; unto whom "are known all his works", and all the works of every creature, not only "from the beginning of the world," (a poor, low, weak translation,) but *ap aionos*, from all *eternity*, from everlasting to everlasting; who constrains the host of heaven, as well as the children of men, to cry out with wonder and amazement, o the depth! the depth of the riches, both of the wisdom and of the knowledge of God! Which art in heaven: The Lord and Ruler of all, superintending and disposing all things; who art the King of kings, and Lord of lords, the blessed and only Potentate; who art strong and girded about with power, doing whatsoever pleaseth thee; the Almighty; for whensoever thou willest, to do is present with thee. In heaven: eminently there. heaven is thy throne, "the place where thine honour" particularly "dwelleth." But not there alone; for thou fillest heaven and earth, the whole expanse of space. "heaven and earth are full of thy glory. Glory be to thee, o Lord, most high!"

Therefore should we "serve the Lord with fear, and rejoice unto him with reverence." Therefore should we think, speak, and act, as continually under the eye, in the immediate presence, of the Lord, the King.

7. "hallowed be thy name."—This is the first of the six petitions, whereof the prayer itself is composed. The name of God is God himself; the nature of God, so far as it can be discovered to man. It means, therefore, together with his existence, all his attributes or perfections; His eternity, particularly signified by his great and incommunicable name, JeHoVAH, as the Apostle John translates it: *To A kai to o, arche kai telos, oon kai ho On kai ho en kai ho erchomenos,*—"the Alpha and Omega, the beginning and the end; He which is, and which was, and which is to come;"—His Fullness of Being, denoted by his other great name, *I AM THAT I AM!*—His omnipresence;—His omnipotence; who is indeed the only Agent in the material world; all matter being essentially dull and inactive, and moving only as it is moved by the finger of God; and he is the spring of action in every creature, visible and invisible, which could neither act nor exist, without the continual influx and agency of his almighty power;—His wisdom, clearly deduced from the things that are seen, from the goodly order of the universe;—His Trinity in Unity, and Unity in Trinity, discovered to us in the very first line of his written word; *bara elohim*—literally, *the Gods created*, a plural noun joined with a verb of the singular number; as well as in every part of his subsequent revelations, given by the mouth of all his holy Prophets and Apostles;—His essential purity and holiness;—and, above all, his love, which is the very brightness of his glory.

In praying that God, or his name, may "be hallowed" or glorified, we pray that he may be known, such as he is, by all that are capable thereof, by all intelligent beings, and with affections suitable to that knowledge; that he may be duly honoured, and feared, and loved, by all in heaven above and in the earth beneath; by all angels and men, whom for that end he has made capable of knowing and loving him to eternity.

8. "Thy kingdom come."—This has a close connexion with the preceding petition. In order that the name of God might be hallowed, we pray that his kingdom, the kingdom of Christ, may come. This kingdom then comes to a particular person, when he "repents and believes the gospel;" when he is taught of God, not only to know himself, but to know Jesus

Christ and him crucified. As "this is life eternal, to know the only true God, and Jesus Christ whom he hath sent;" so it is the kingdom of God begun below, set up in the believers heart; "the Lord God Omnipotent" then "reigneth," when he is known through Christ Jesus. He taketh unto himself his mighty power, that he may subdue all things unto himself. He goeth on in the soul conquering and to conquer, till he hath put all things under his feet, till "every thought is brought into captivity to the obedience of Christ."

When therefore God shall "give his Son the Heathen for hisinheritance, and the uttermost parts of the earth for his possession;" when "all kingdoms shall bow before him, and all nations shall do him service;" when "the mountain of the Lords house," the Church of Christ, "shall be established in the top of the mountains;" when "the fullness of the Gentiles shall come in, and all Israel shall be saved;" then shall it be seen, that "the Lord is King, and hath put on glorious apparel," appearing to every soul of man as King of kings, and Lord of lords. And it is meet for all those who love his appearing, to pray that he would hasten the time; that this his kingdom, the kingdom of grace, may come quickly, and swallow up all the kingdoms of the earth; that all mankind, receiving him for their King, truly believing in his name, may be filled with righteousness, and peace, and joy, with holiness and happiness,—till they are removed hence into his heavenly kingdom, there to reign with him for ever and ever. For this also we pray in those words, "Thy kingdom come:" We pray for the coming of his everlasting kingdom, the kingdom of glory in heaven, which is the continuation and perfection of the kingdom of grace on earth. Consequently this, as well as the preceding petition, is offered up for the whole intelligent creation, who are all interested in this grand event, the final renovation of all things, by Gods putting an end to misery and sin, to infirmity and death, taking all things into his own hands, and setting up the kingdom which endureth throughout all ages.

exactly answerable to this are those awful words in the prayer at the burial of the dead: "Beseeching thee, that it may please thee of thy gracious goodness, shortly to accomplish the number of thine elect, and to hasten thy kingdom: That we, with all those that are departed in the true faith of thy holy name, may have our perfect consummation and bliss, both in body and soul, in thy everlasting glory."

9. "Thy will be done in earth, as it is in heaven."—This is the necessary and immediate consequence wherever the kingdom of God is come; wherever God dwells in the soul by faith, and Christ reigns in the heart by love.

It is probable, many, perhaps the generality of men, at the first view of these words, are apt to imagine they are only an expression of, or petition for, resignation; for a readiness to suffer the will of God, whatsoever it be concerning us. And this is unquestionably a divine and excellent temper, a most precious gift of God. But this is not what we pray for in this petition; at least, not in the chief and primary sense of it. We pray, not so much for a passive, as for an active, conformity to the will of God, in saying, "Thy will be done in earth, as it is in heaven."

How is it done by the angels of God in heaven,—those who now circle his throne rejoicing? They do it *willingly*; they love his commandments, and gladly hearken to his words. It is their meat and drink to do his will; it is their highest glory and joy. They do it *continually*; there is no interruption in their willing service. They rest not day nor night, but employ every hour (speaking after the manner of men; otherwise our measures of duration, days, and nights, and hours, have no place in eternity) in fulfilling his commands, in executing his designs, in performing the counsel of his will. And they do it *perfectly*. No sin, no defect belongs to angelic minds. It is true, "the stars are not pure in his sight," even the morning-stars that sing together before him. "In his sight," that is, in comparison of Him, the very angels are not pure. But this does not imply, that they are not pure *in themselves*. Doubtless they are; they are without spot and blameless. They are altogether devoted to his will, and perfectly obedient in all things.

If we view this in another light, we may observe, the angels of God in heaven do *all* the will of God. And they do nothing else, nothing but what they are absolutely assured is his will. Again they do all the will of God *as* he willeth; in the manner which pleases him, and no other. Yea, and they do this, only *because* it is his will; for this end, and no other reason.

10. When therefore we pray, that the will of God may "be done in earth as it is in heaven," the meaning is, that all the inhabitants of the earth, even the whole race of mankind, may do the will of their Father which is in heaven, as *willingly* as the holy angels; that these may do it *continually*, even as they, without any interruption of their willing service; yea, and that they may do it *perfectly*,—that "the God of peace, through the blood of the everlasting covenant, may make them perfect in every good work to do his will, and work in them all "which is well-pleasing in his sight."

In other words, we pray that we and all mankind may do the whole will of God in all things; and nothing else, not the least thing but what is the holy and acceptable will of God. We pray that we may do the whole will of God as he willeth, in the manner that pleases him: And, lastly, that we may do it *because* it is his will; that this may be the sole reason and ground, the whole and only motive, of whatsoever we think, or whatsoever we speak or do.

11. "Give us this day our daily bread."—In the three former petitions we have been praying for all mankind. We come now more particularly to desire a supply for our own wants. Not that we are directed, even here, to confine our prayer altogether to ourselves; but this, and each of the following petitions, may be used for the whole Church of Christ upon earth.

By "bread" we may understand all things needful, whether for our souls or bodies; *ta pros zoen kai eusebeian, the things pertaining to life and godliness:* We understand not barely the outward bread, what our Lord terms the meat which perisheth; but much more the spiritual bread, the grace of God, the food which endureth unto everlasting life. It was the judgment of many of the ancient Fathers, that we are here to understand the sacramental bread also; daily received in the beginning by the whole Church of Christ, and highly esteemed, till the love of many waxed cold, as the grand channel whereby the grace of his Spirit was conveyed to the souls of all the children of God.

our daily bread. The word we render *daily* has been differently explained by different commentators. But the most plain and natural sense of it seems to be this, which is retained in almost all translations, as well ancient as modern;—what is sufficient for this day; and so for each day as it succeeds.

12. "Give us:"—For we claim nothing of right, but only of free mercy. We deserve not the air we breathe, the earth that bears, or the sun that shines upon, us. All our desert, we own, is hell: But God loves us freely; therefore, we ask him to give, what we can no more procure for ourselves, than we can merit it at his hands.

Not that either the goodness or the power of God is a reason for us to stand idle. It is his will that we should use all diligence in all things, that we should employ our utmost endeavours, as much as if our success were the natural effect of our own wisdom and strength: And then, as though we had done nothing, we are to depend on him, the giver of every good and perfect gift.

"This day:"—For we are to take no thought for the morrow. For this very end has our wise Creator divided life into these little portions of time, so clearly separated from each other, that we might look on every day as a fresh gift of God, another life, which we may devote to his glory; and that every evening may be as the close of life, beyond which we are to see nothing but eternity.

13. "And forgive us our trespasses, as we forgive them that trespass against us."—As nothing but sin can hinder the bounty of God from flowing forth upon every creature, so this petition naturally follows the former; that, all hinderances being removed, we may the more clearly trust in the God of love for every manner of thing which is good.

"our trespasses:"—The word properly signifies *our debts*. Thus our sins are frequently represented in Scripture; every sin laying us under a fresh debt to God, to whom we already owe, as it were, ten thousand talents. What then can we answer when he shall say, "Pay me that thou owest?" We are utterly insolvent; we have nothing to pay; we have wasted all our substance. Therefore, if he deal with us according to the rigour of his law, if he exact what he justly may, he must command us to be "bound hand and foot, and delivered over to the tormentors."

Indeed we are already bound hand and foot by the chains of our own sins. These, considered with regard to ourselves, are chains of iron and fetters of brass. They are wounds wherewith the world, the flesh, and the devil, have gashed and mangled us all over. They are diseases that drink up our blood and spirits, that I bring us down to the chambers of the grave. But considered, as they are here, with regard to God, they are debts, immense and numberless. Well, therefore, seeing we have nothing to pay, may we cry unto him that he would "frankly forgive' us all!

The word translated *forgive* implies either to forgive a debt, or to unloose a chain. And if we attain the former, the latter follows of course: if our debts are forgiven, the chains fall off

our hands. As soon as ever, through the free grace of God in Christ, we "receive forgiveness of sins," we receive likewise "a lot among those which are sanctified, by faith which is in him." Sin has lost its power; it has no dominion over those who "are under grace," that is, in favour with God. As "there is now no condemnation for them that are in Christ Jesus," so they are freed from sin as well as from guilt. "The righteousness of the law is fulfilled in" them, and they "walk not after the flesh, but after the Spirit."

14. "As we forgive them that trespass against us."—In these words our Lord clearly declares both on what condition, and in what degree or manner, we may look to be forgiven of God. All our trespasses and sins are forgiven us, *if* we forgive, and *as* we forgive, others. [First, God forgives us *if* we forgive others.] This is a point of the utmost importance. And our blessed Lord is so jealous lest at any time we should let it slip out of our thoughts, that he not only inserts it in the body of his prayer, but presently after repeats it twice over. "If," saith he, "ye forgive men their trespasses, your heavenly Father will also forgive you: But if ye forgive not men their trespasses, neither will your Father forgive your trespasses." (Matt. 6:14, 15.) Secondly, God forgives us *as* we forgive others. So that if any malice or bitterness, if any taint of unkindness or anger remains, if we do not clearly, fully, and from the heart, forgive all men their trespasses, we far cut short the forgiveness of our own: God cannot clearly and fully forgive us: he may show us some degree of mercy; but we will not suffer him to blot out all our sins, and forgive all our iniquities.

In the mean time, while we do not from our hearts forgive our neighbour his trespasses, what manner of prayer are we offering to God whenever we utter these words? We are indeed setting God at open defiance: we are daring him to do his worst. "Forgive us our trespasses, as we forgive them that trespass against us!" That is, in plain terms, "Do not thou forgive us at all; we desire no favour at thy hands. We pray that thou wilt keep our sins in remembrance, and that thy wrath may abide upon us." But can you seriously offer such a prayer to God? And hath he not yet cast you quick into hell?' o tempt him no longer! Now, even now, by his grace, forgive as you would be forgiven! Now have compassion on thy fellow-servant, as God hath had and will have pity on thee!

15. "And lead us not into temptation, but deliver us from evil."—"[And] lead us not into temptation." The word translated *temptation* means trial of any kind. And so the english word temptation was formerly taken in an indifferent sense, although now it is usually understood of solicitation to sin. St. James uses the word in both these senses; first, in its general, then in its restrained, acceptation. he takes it in the former sense when he saith, "Blessed is the man that endureth temptation; For when he is tried," or approved of God, "he shall receive the crown of life." (James 1:12, 13.) He immediately adds, taking the word in the latter sense, "Let no man say when he is tempted, I am tempted of God; for God cannot be tempted with evil, neither tempteth he any man. But every man is tempted, when he is *drawn away* of his own lust," or *desire, exelkomenos,* drawn out of God, in

whom alone he is safe,— *"and enticed;"* caught as a fish with a bait. Then it is, when he is thus drawn away and enticed, that he properly *"enters into temptation."* Then temptation covers him as a cloud; it overspreads his whole soul. Then how hardly shall he escape out of the snare! Therefore, we beseech God *"not to lead us into temptation,"* that is, (seeing God tempteth no man,) not to suffer us to be led into it. *"But deliver us from evil:"* Rather "from the evil one,"; *apo tou ponerouho. Poneros* is unquestionably *the wicked one,* emphatically so called, the prince and god of this world, who works with mighty power in the children of disobedience. But all those who are the children of God by faith are delivered out of his hands. He may fight against them; and so he will. But he cannot conquer, unless they betray their own souls. He may torment for a time, but he cannot destroy; for God is on their side, who will not fail, in the end, to "avenge his own elect, that cry unto him day and night." Lord, when we are tempted, suffer us not to enter into temptation! Do thou make a way for us to escape, that the wicked one touch us not!

16. The conclusion of this divine prayer, commonly called the Doxology, is a solemn thanksgiving, a compendious acknowledgement of the attributes and works of God. "For thine is the kingdom"—the sovereign right of all things that are or ever were created; yea, thy kingdom is an everlasting kingdom, and thy dominion endureth throughout all ages. "The power"—the executive power whereby thou governest all things in thy everlasting kingdom, whereby thou dost whatsoever pleaseth thee, in all places of thy dominion. "And the glory"—the praise due from every creature, for thy power, and the mightiness of thy kingdom, and for all thy wondrous works which thou workest from everlasting, and shalt do, world without end, "for ever and ever! Amen!" So be it!

I believe it will not be unacceptable to the serious reader, to subjoin

A PARAPHRASE ON THE LORD'S PRAYER

1 Father of all, whose powerful voice
Call'd forth this universal frame;
Whose mercies over all rejoice,
Through endless ages still the same.
Thou, by thy word, upholdest all;
Thy bounteous love to all is show'd,
Thou hear'st thy every creature's call,
And fillest every mouth with good.
2 In heaven thou reign'st, enthroned in light,
Nature's expanse beneath thee spread;
Earth, air, and sea before thy sight,
And hell's deep gloom are open laid.
Wisdom, and might, and love are thine:
Prostrate before thy face we fall,
Confess thine attributes divine,
An hail the Sovereign Lord of All.
3 Thee, sovereign Lord, let all confess
That moves in earth, or air, or sky
Revere thy power, thy goodness bless,
Tremble before thy piercing eye.
All ye who owe to Him your birth,

In praise your every hour employ:
Jehovah reigns! Be glad, O earth!
And shout, ye morning stars, for joy!
4 Son of thy Sire's eternal love,
Take to thyself thy mighty power;
Let all earth's sons thy mercy prove,
Let all thy bleeding grace adore.
The triumphs of thy love display;
In every heart reign thou alone;
Till all thy foes confess thy sway,
And glory ends what grace begun.
5 Spirit of grace, and health, and power,
Fountain of light and love below,
Abroad thine healing influence shower,
O'er all the nations let it flow.
Inflame our hearts with perfect love;
In us the work of faith fulfil;
So not heaven's hosts shall swifter move
Than we on earth to do thy will.
6 Father, 'tis thine each day to yield
Thy children's wants a fresh supply:
Thou cloth'st the lilies of the field,
And hearest the young ravens cry.
On thee we cast our care; we live
Through thee, who know'st our every need;
O feed us with thy grace, and give
Our souls this day the living bread!
7 Eternal, spotless Lamb of God,
Before the world's foundation slain,
Sprinkle us ever with thy blood;
O cleanse and keep us ever clean.
To every soul (all praise to Thee!)
Our bowels of compassion more:
And all mankind by this may see
God is in us; for God is love.
8 Giver and Lord of life, whose power
And guardian care for all are free;
To thee, in fierce temptation's hour,
From sin and Satan let us flee.
Thine, Lord, we are, and ours thou art;
In us be all thy goodness show'd;
Renew, enlarge, and fill our heart
With peace, and joy, and heaven, and God.
9 Blessing and honour, praise and love,
Co-equal, co-eternal Three,
In earth below, in heaven above,
By all thy works be paid to thee.
Thrice Holy! thine the kingdom is,
The power omnipotent is thine;
And when created nature dies,
Thy never-ceasing glories shine.

27. UPON OUR LORD'S SERMON ON THE MOUNT DISCOURSE 7

"Moreover when ye fast, be not, as the hypocrites, of a sad countenance. For they disfigure their faces, that they may appear unto men to fast. Verily I say unto you, They have their reward. But thou, when thou fastest, anoint

thine head, and wash thy face; That thou appear not unto men to fast, but unto thy Father which is in secret: And thy Father, which seeth in secret, shall reward thee openly."

Matthew 6:16–18.

1. It has been the endeavour of Satan, from the beginning of the world, to put asunder what God hath joined together; to separate inward from outward religion; to set one of these at variance with the other. And herein he has met with no small success among those who were "ignorant of his devices." Many, in all ages, having a zeal for God, but not according to knowledge, have been strictly attached to the "righteousness of the law," the performance of outward duties, but in the mean time wholly regardless of inward righteousness, "the righteousness which is of God by faith." And many have run into the opposite extreme, disregarding all outward duties, perhaps even "speaking evil of the law, and judging the law," so far as it enjoins the performance of them.

2. It is by this very device of Satan, that faith and works have been so often set at variance with each other. And many who had a real zeal for God have, for a time, fallen into the snare on either hand. Some have magnified faith to the utter exclusion of good works, not only from being the cause of our justification, (for we know that man is justified freely by the redemption which is in Jesus,) but from being the necessary fruit of it, yea, from having any place in the religion of Jesus Christ. Others, eager to avoid this dangerous mistake, have run as much too far the contrary way; and either maintained that good works were the cause, at least the previous condition, of justification,—or spoken of them as if they were all in all, the whole religion of Jesus Christ.

3. In the same manner have the end and the means of religion been set at variance with each other. Some well-meaning men have seemed to place all religion in attending the Prayers of the Church, in receiving the Lord's supper, in hearing sermons, and reading books of piety; neglecting, mean time, the end of all these, the love of God and their neighbour. And this very thing has confirmed others in the neglect, if not contempt, of the ordinances of God,—so wretchedly abused to undermine and overthrow the very end they were designed to establish.

4. But of all the means of grace there is scarce any concerning which men have run into greater extremes, than that of which our Lord speaks in the above-mentioned words, I mean religious fasting. How have some exalted this beyond all Scripture and reason;—and others utterly disregarded it; as it were revenging themselves by undervaluing as much as the former had overvalued it! Those have spoken of it, as if it were all in all; if not the end itself, yet infallibly connected with it: These, as if it were just nothing, as if it were a fruitless labour, which had no relation at all thereto. Whereas it is certain the truth lies between them both. It is not all, nor yet is it nothing. It is not the end, but it is a precious means thereto; a means which God himself has ordained, and in which therefore, when it is duly used, he will surely give us his blessing.

In order to set this in the clearest light, I shall endeavour to show, First, what is the nature of fasting, and what the several sorts and degrees thereof: Secondly, what are the reasons, grounds, and ends of it: Thirdly, how we may answer the most plausible objections against it: And Fourthly, in what manner it should be performed.

I. 1. I shall endeavour to show, First, what is the nature of fasting, and what the several sorts and degrees thereof. As to the nature of it, all the inspired writers, both in the Old Testament and the New, take the word *to fast* in one single sense, for not to eat, to abstain from food. This is so clear, that it would be labour lost to quote the words of David, Nehemiah, Isaiah, and the Prophets which followed, or of our Lord and his Apostles; all agreeing in this, that to fast, is, not to eat for a time prescribed.

2. To this, other circumstances were usually joined by them of old, which had no necessary connexion with it. Such were the neglect of their apparel; the laying aside those ornaments which they were accustomed to wear; the putting on mourning; the strewing ashes upon their head; or wearing sackcloth next their skin. But we find little mention made in the New Testament of any of these indifferent circumstances. Nor does it appear, that any stress was laid upon them by the Christians of the purer ages; however some penitents might voluntarily use them, as outward signs of inward humiliation. Much less did the Apostles, or the Christians contemporary with them, beat or tear their own flesh: Such discipline as this was not unbecoming the priests or worshippers of Baal. The gods of the Heathens were but devils; and it was doubtless acceptable to their devil-god, when his priests (1 Kings 18:28) "cried aloud, and cut themselves after their manner, till the blood gushed out upon them:" But it cannot be pleasing to Him, nor become His followers, who "came not to destroy men's lives, but to save them."

3. As to the degrees or measures of fasting, we have instances of some who have fasted several days together. So Moses, Elijah, and our blessed Lord, being endued with supernatural strength for that purpose, are recorded to have fasted, without intermission, "forty days and forty nights." But the time of fasting, more frequently mentioned in Scripture, is one day, from morning till evening. And this was the fast commonly observed among the ancient Christians. But beside these, they had also their half-fasts (Semijejunia, as Tertullian styles them) on the fourth and sixth days of the week, (Wednesday and Friday,) throughout the year; on which they took no sustenance till three in the afternoon, the time when they returned from the public service.

4. Nearly related to this, is what our Church seems peculiarly to mean by the term *abstinence*; which may be used when we cannot fast entirely, by reason of sickness or bodily weakness. This is the eating little; the abstaining in part; the taking a smaller quantity of food than usual. I do not remember any scriptural instance of this. But neither can I condemn it; for the Scripture does not. It may have its use, and receive a blessing from God.

5. The lowest kind of fasting, if it can be called by that name, is the abstaining from pleasant food. Of this, we have several instances in Scripture, besides that of Daniel and his

brethren, who from a peculiar consideration, namely, that they might "not defile themselves with the portion of the King's meat, nor with the wine which he drank," (a daily provision of which the King had appointed for them,) requested and obtained, of the prince of the eunuchs, pulse to eat and water to drink. (Daniel 1:8.) Perhaps from a mistaken imitation of this might spring the very ancient custom of abstaining from flesh and wine during such times as were set apart for fasting and abstinence;—if it did not rather arise from a supposition that these were the most pleasant food, and a belief that it was proper to use what was least pleasing at those times of solemn approach to God.

6. In the Jewish church there were some stated fasts. Such was the fast of the seventh month, appointed by God himself to be observed by all Israel under the severest penalty. "The Lord spake unto Moses, saying, On the tenth day of this seventh month, there shall be a day of atonement: And ye shall afflict your souls,—to make an atonement for you before the Lord your God. For whatsoever soul it be that shall not be afflicted in that same day, he shall be cut off from among his people." (Lev. 23:26.) In after-ages, several other stated fasts were added to these. So mention is made, by the Prophet Zechariah, of the fast not only "of the seventh, but also of the fourth, of the fifth, and of the tenth month." (Zech. 8:19)

In the ancient Christian Church, there were likewise stated fasts, and those both annual and weekly. Of the former sort was that before Easter; observed by some for eight-and-forty hours; by others, for an entire week; by many, for two weeks; taking no sustenance till the evening of each day: Of the latter, those of the fourth and sixth days of the week, observed (as Epiphanius writes, remarking it as an undeniable fact) *en holei tei oikoumenei, in the whole habitable earth*; at least in every place where any Christians made their abode. The annual fasts in our Church are, the forty days of Lent, the ember days at the four seasons, the Rogation days, and the Vigils or eves of several solemn festivals; the weekly, all Fridays in the year, except Christmas-day.

But beside those which were fixed, in every nation fearing God there have always been occasional fasts, appointed from time to time, as the particular circumstances and occasions of each required. So when the children of Moab, and the children of Ammon, came against Jehoshaphat to battle, Jehoshaphat set himself to seek the Lord, and proclaimed a fast throughout all Judah. (2 Chron. 20:1, 3) And so, in the fifth year of Jehoiakim the son of Josiah, in the ninth month, when they were afraid of the King of Babylon, the Princes of "Judah proclaimed a fast before the Lord, to all the people of Jerusalem." (Jer. 36:9)

And, in like manner, particular persons, who take heed unto their ways, and desire to walk humbly and closely with God, will find frequent occasion for private seasons of thus afflicting their souls before their Father which is in secret. And it is to this kind of fasting that the directions here given do chiefly and primarily refer.

II. 1. I proceed to show, in the Second place, what are the grounds, the reasons, and ends of fasting.

And, First, men who are under strong emotions of mind, who are affected with any vehement passion, such as sorrow or fear, are often swallowed up therein, and even forget to eat their bread. At such seasons they have little regard for food, not even what is needful to sustain nature, much less for any delicacy or variety; being taken up with quite different thoughts. Thus when Saul said, "I am sore distressed; for the Philistines make war against me, and God is departed from me;" it is recorded, "he had eaten no bread all the day, nor all the night." (1 Sam. 28:15, 20.) Thus those who were in the ship with St. Paul, "when no small tempest lay upon them, and all hope that they should be saved was taken away," "continued fasting, having taken nothing," no regular meal, for fourteen days together. (Acts 27:33.) And thus David, and all the men that were with him, when they heard that the people were fled from the battle, and that many of the people were fallen and dead, and Saul and Jonathan his son were dead also, "mourned, and wept, and fasted until even, for Saul and Jonathan, and for the house of Israel." (2 Sam. 1:12.)

Nay, many times they whose minds are deeply engaged are impatient of any interruption, and even loathe their needful food, as diverting their thoughts from what they desire should engross their whole attention: even as Saul, when, on the occasion mentioned before, he had "fallen all along upon the earth, and there was no strength in him," yet said, "I will not eat," till "his servants, together with the woman, compelled him."

2. here, then, is the natural ground of fasting. one who is under deep affliction, overwhelmed with sorrow for sin, and a strong apprehension of the wrath of God, would, without any rule, without knowing or considering whether it were a command of God or not, "forget to eat his bread," abstain not only from pleasant but even from needful food;—like St. Paul, who, after he was led into Damascus, "was three days without sight, and did neither eat nor drink." (Acts 9:9.) Yea, when the storm rose high; "when an horrible dread overwhelmed" one who had been without God in the world, his soul would "loathe all manner of meat;" it would be unpleasing and irksome to him; he would be impatient of anything that should interrupt his ceaseless cry, "Lord, save or I perish."

how strongly is this expressed by our Church in the first part of the Homily on Fasting!—"When men feel in themselves the heavy burden of sin, see damnation to be the reward of it, and behold, with the eye of their mind, the horror of hell, they tremble, they quake, and are inwardly touched with sorrowfulness of heart, and cannot but accuse themselves, and open their grief unto Almighty God, and call unto him for mercy. This being done seriously, their mind is so occupied, [taken up,] partly with sorrow and heaviness, partly with an earnest desire to be delivered from this danger of hell and damnation, that all desire of meat and drink is laid apart, and loathsomeness [or loathing] of all worldly things and pleasure cometh in place. So that nothing then liketh them more than to weep, to lament, to mourn, and both with words and behaviour of body to show themselves weary of life."

3. Another reason or ground of fasting is this: Many of those who now fear God are deeply sensible how often they have sinned against him, by the abuse of these lawful things. They know how much they have sinned by excess of food; how long they have transgressed the holy law of God, with regard to temperance, if not sobriety too; how they have indulged their sensual appetites, perhaps to the impairing even their bodily health,—certainly to the no small hurt of their soul For hereby they continually fed and increased that sprightly folly, that airiness of mind, that levity of temper, that gay inattention to things of the deepest concern, that giddiness and carelessness of spirit, which were no other than drunkenness of soul, which stupefied all their noblest faculties, no less than excess of wine or strong drink. To remove, therefore, the effect, they remove the cause. They keep at a distance from all excess. They abstain, as far as is possible, from what had well nigh plunged them in everlasting perdition. They often wholly refrain; always take care to be sparing and temperate in all things.

4. They likewise well remember how fulness of bread increased not only carelessness and levity of spirit, but also foolish and unholy desires, yea, unclean and vile affections. And this experience puts beyond all doubt. Even a genteel, regular sensuality is continually sensualizing the soul, and sinking it into a level with the beasts that perish. It cannot be expressed what an effect variety and delicacy of food have on the mind as well as the body; making it just ripe for every pleasure of sense, as soon as opportunity shall invite. Therefore, on this ground also, every wise man will refrain his soul, and keep it low; will wean it more and more from all those indulgences of the inferior appetites, which naturally tend to chain it down to earth, and to pollute as well as debase it Here is another perpetual reason for fasting; to remove the food of lust and sensuality, to withdraw the incentives of foolish and hurtful desires, of vile and vain affections.

5. Perhaps we need not altogether omit (although I know not if we should do well to lay any great stress upon it) another reason for fasting, which some good men have largely insisted on; namely, the punishing themselves for having abused the good gifts of God, by sometimes wholly refraining from them; thus exercising a kind of holy revenge upon themselves, for their past folly and ingratitude, in turning the things which should have been for their health into an occasion of falling. They suppose David to have had an eye to this, when he said, "I wept and chastened," or punished, "my soul with fasting;" and St. Paul, when he mentions "what revenge" godly sorrow occasioned in the Corinthians.

6. A Fifth and more weighty reason for fasting is, that it is an help to prayer; particularly when we set apart larger portions of time for private prayer. Then especially it is that God is often pleased to lift up the souls of his servants above all the things of earth, and sometimes to rap them up, as it were, into the third heavens. And it is chiefly, as it is an help to prayer, that it has so frequently been found a means, in the hand of God, of confirming and increasing, not one virtue, not chastity only, (as some have idly imagined, without any ground either from Scripture, reason, or experience,) but also seriousness of spirit, earnestness, sensibility and tenderness of conscience, deadness to the world, and consequently the love of God, and every holy and heavenly affection.

7. Not that there is any natural or necessary connexion between fasting, and the blessings God conveys thereby. But he will have mercy as he will have mercy; he will convey whatsoever seemeth him good by whatsoever means he is pleased to appoint. And he hath, in all ages, appointed this to be a means of averting his wrath, and obtaining whatever blessings we, from time to time, stand in need of.

How powerful a means this is to avert the wrath of God, we may learn from the remarkable instance of Ahab. "There was none like him who did sell himself"—wholly give himself up, like a slave bought with money—"to work wickedness." Yet when he "rent his clothes, and put sackcloth upon his flesh, and fasted, and went softly, the word of the Lord came to Elijah, saying, Seest thou how Ahab humbleth himself before me? Because he humbleth himself before me, I will not bring the evil in his days."

It was for this end, to avert the wrath of God, that Daniel sought God "with fasting, and sackcloth, and ashes." This appears from the whole tenor of his prayer, particularly from the solemn conclusion of it: "o Lord, according to all thy righteousness," or mercies, "let thy anger be turned away from thy holy mountain.—Hear the prayer of thy servant, and cause thy face to shine upon thy sanctuary that is desolate.—o Lord, hear; o Lord, forgive; o Lord, hearken and do, for thine own sake." (Dan. 9:3, 16.)

8. But it is not only from the people of God that we learn, when his anger is moved, to seek him by fasting and prayer; but even from the Heathens. When Jonah had declared, "Yet forty days and Nineveh shall be overthrown," the people of Nineveh proclaimed a fast, and put on sackcloth, from the greatest of them unto the least. "For the King of Nineveh arose from his throne, and laid his robe from him, and covered him with sackcloth, and sat in ashes. And he caused it to be proclaimed and published through Nineveh, Let neither man nor beast, herd nor flock, taste anything: Let them not feed, nor drink water:" (Not that the beast had sinned, or could repent; but that, by their example, man might be admonished, considering that, for his sin, the anger of God was hanging over all creatures:) "Who can tell if God will turn and repent, and turn away from his fierce anger, that we perish not?" And their labour was not in vain. The fierce anger of God was turned away from them. "God saw their works;" (the fruits of that repentance and faith which he had wrought in them by his Prophet;) "and God repented of the evil that he had said he would do unto them; and he did it not." (Jonah 3:4.)

9. And it is a means not only of turning away the wrath of God, but also of obtaining whatever blessings we stand in need of. So, when the other tribes were smitten before the Benjamites, "all the children of Israel went up unto the house of God, and wept, and fasted that day until even;" and then the Lord said, "Go up" again; "for to-morrow I will deliver them into thine hand." (Judges 20:26.) So Samuel gathered all Israel together, when they were in bondage to the Philistines, "and they fasted on that day" before the Lord: And when "the Philistines drew near to battle against Israel,

the Lord thundered" upon them "with a great thunder, and discomfited them; and they were smitten before Israel." (1 Sam. 7:6.) So Ezra: "I proclaimed a fast at the river Ahava, that we might afflict ourselves before our God, to seek of him a right way for us, and for our little ones; and he was entreated of us." (Ezra 8:21.) So Nehemiah: I fasted and prayed before the God of heaven, and said, Prosper, I pray thee, thy servant this day, and grant him mercy in the sight of this man:" And God granted him mercy in the sight of the king. (Neh. 1:4–11)

10. In like manner, the apostles always joined fasting with prayer when they desired the blessing of God on any important undertaking. Thus we read, (Acts 13.,) "There were in the church that was at Antioch certain Prophets and Teachers: As they ministered to the Lord and fasted," doubtless for direction in this very affair, "the Holy Ghost said, Separate me Barnabas and Saul, for the work whereunto I have called them. And when they had" a second time "fasted and prayed, and laid their hands on them, they sent them away." (Acts 13:13.)

Thus also Paul and Barnabas themselves, as we read in the following chapter, when they "returned again to Lystra, Iconium, and Antioch, confirming the souls of the disciples, and when they had ordained them Elders in every Church, and had prayed with fasting, commended them to the Lord." (Acts 14:23.)

Yea, that blessings are to be obtained in the use of this means, which are no otherwise attainable, our Lord expressly declares in his answer to his disciples, asking, "Why could not we cast him out? Jesus said unto them, Because of your unbelief: For verily I say unto you, If ye have faith as a grain of mustard-seed, ye shall say unto this mountain, Remove hence to yonder place; and it shall remove; and nothing shall be impossible unto you. Howbeit, this kind" of devils "goeth not out but by prayer and fasting:" (Matt. 17:19.)—These being the appointed means of attaining that faith whereby the very devils are subject unto you.

11. These were the appointed means: For it was not merely by the light of reason, or of natural conscience, as it is called, that the people of God have been, in all ages, directed to use fasting as a means to these ends; but they have been, from time to time, taught it of God himself, by clear and open revelations of his will. Such is that remarkable one by the Prophet Joel: "Therefore saith the Lord, Turn you to me with all your heart, and with fasting, and with weeping, and with mourning:—Who knoweth if he will return and repent, and leave a blessing behind him? Blow the trumpet in Zion, sanctify a fast, call a solemn assembly:—Then will the Lord be jealous over his land, and will pity his people. Yea, I will send you corn, and wine, and oil:—I will no more make you a reproach among the Heathen." (Joel 2:12.)

Nor are they only temporal blessings which God directs his people to expect in the use of these means. For, at the same time that he promised to those who should seek him with fasting, and weeping, and mourning, "I will restore you the years which locust hath eaten, the canker-worm, and the caterpillar, and the palmer-worm, my great army;" he subjoins, "So shall ye eat and be satisfied, and praise the name of the Lord your God.—Ye shall also know that I am in the midst of Israel, and that I am the Lord your God." And then immediately follows the great gospel promise: "I will pour out my Spirit upon all flesh; and your sons and your daughters shall prophesy, your old men shall dream dreams, and your young men shall see visions: And also upon the servants and upon the handmaids in those days will I pour out my Spirit." [Joel 2:28–29]

12. Now whatsoever reasons there were to quicken those of old, in the zealous and constant discharge of this duty, they are of equal force still to quicken us. But above all these, we have a peculiar reason for being "in fastings often;" namely, the command of Him by whose name we are called. He does not, indeed, in this place expressly enjoin either fasting, giving of alms, or prayer; but his directions *how* to fast, to give alms, and to pray, are of the same force with such injunctions. For the commanding us to do anything *thus*, is an unquestionable command to do that thing; seeing it is impossible to perform it *thus*, if it be not performed at all. Consequently, the saying, "Give alms, pray, fast" *in such a manner*, is a clear command to perform all those duties; as well as to perform them in that manner which shall in nowise lose its reward.

And this is a still farther motive and encouragement to the performance of this duty; even the promise which our Lord has graciously annexed to the due discharge of it: "Thy Father which seeth in secret shall reward thee openly." Such are the plain grounds, reasons, and ends of fasting; such our encouragement to persevere therein, notwithstanding abundance of objections which men, wiser than their Lord, have been continually raising against it.

III. 1. The most plausible of these I come now to consider. And, First, it has been frequently said, "Let a Christian fast from sin, and not from food: This is what God requires at his hands." So he does; but he requires the other also. Therefore this ought to be done, and that not left undone.

View your argument in its full dimensions; and you will easily judge of the strength of it:—

If a Christian ought to abstain from sin, then he ought not to abstain from food:

But a Christian ought to abstain from sin.

Therefore he ought not to abstain from food.

That a Christian ought to abstain from sin, is most true; but how does it follow from hence that he ought not to abstain from food? Yea, let him do both the one and the other. Let him, by the grace of God, always abstain from sin; and let him often abstain from food, for such reasons and ends as experience and Scripture plainly show to be answered thereby.

2. "But is it not better" (as it has, Secondly, been objected) "to abstain from pride and vanity, from foolish and hurtful desires, from peevishness, and anger, and discontent, than from food?" Without question, it is. But here again we have need to remind you of our Lords words: "These things ought ye to have done, and not to leave the other undone." And, indeed, the latter is only in order to the former; it is a means to that great end. We abstain from food with this view,—that, by the grace of God conveyed into our souls through

this outward means, in conjunction with all the other channels of his grace which he hath appointed, we may be enabled to abstain from every passion and temper which is not pleasing in his sight. We refrain from the one, that, being endued with power from on high, we may be able to refrain from the other. So that your argument proves just the contrary to what you designed. It proves that we ought to fast. For if we ought to abstain from evil tempers and desires, then we ought thus to abstain from food; since these little instances of self-denial are the ways God hath chose, wherein to bestow that great salvation.

3. "But we do not find it so in fact:" (This is a Third objection:) "We have fasted much and often; but what did it avail? We were not a whit better; we found no blessing therein. Nay, we have found it an hinderance rather than an help. Instead of preventing anger, for instance, or fretfulness, it has been a means of increasing them to such a height, that we could neither bear others nor ourselves." This may very possibly be the case. It is possible either to fast or pray in such a manner as to make you much worse than before; more unhappy, and more unholy. Yet the fault does not lie in the means itself, but in the manner of using it. Use it still, but use it in a different manner. Do what God commands as he commands it; and then, doubtless, his promise shall not fail: His blessings shall be withheld no longer; but, when thou fastest in secret, "He that seeth in secret shall reward thee openly."

4. "But is it not mere superstition," (so it has been, Fourthly, objected,) "to imagine that God regards such little things as these?" If you say it is, you condemn all the generations of Gods children. But will you say, These were all weak, superstitious men? Can you be so hardy as to affirm this, both of Moses and Joshua, of Samuel and David, of Jehosaphat, Ezra, Nehemiah, and all the prophets? yea, of a greater than all,—the Son of God himself? It is certain, both our Master, and all these his servants, did imagine that fasting is not a little thing, and that He who is higher than the highest doth regard it. Of the same judgment, it is plain, were all his Apostles, after they were "filled with the Holy Ghost, and with wisdom." When they had the "unction of the Holy One, teaching them all things," they still approved themselves the Ministers of God, "by fastings," as well as "by the armour of righteousness on the right hand and on the left." After "the bridegroom was taken from them, then did they fast in those days." Nor would they attempt anything (as we have seen above) wherein the glory of God was nearly concerned, such as the sending forth labourers into the harvest, without solemn fasting as well as prayer.

5. "But if fasting be indeed of so great importance, and attended with such a blessing, is it not best," say some, Fifthly, "to fast always? not to do it now and then, but to keep a continual fast? to use as much abstinence, at all times, as our bodily strength will bear?" Let none be discouraged from doing this. By all means use as little and plain food, exercise as much self-denial herein, at all times, as your bodily strength will bear. And this may conduce, by the blessing of God, to several of the great ends above-mentioned. It may be a considerable help, not only to chastity, but also to heavenly-mindedness; to the weaning your affections from things below, and setting them on things above. But this is not fasting, scriptural fasting; it is never termed so in all the Bible. It, in some measure, answers some of the ends thereof; but still it is another thing. Practise it by all means; but not so as thereby to set aside a command of God, and an instituted means of averting his judgments, and obtaining the blessings of his children.

6. Use continually then as much abstinence as you please; which, taken thus, is no other than Christian temperance; but this need not at all interfere with your observing solemn times of fasting and prayer. For instance: Your habitual abstinence or temperance would not prevent your fasting in secret, if you were suddenly overwhelmed with huge sorrow and remorse, and with horrible fear and dismay. Such a situation of mind would almost constrain you to fast; you would loathe your daily food; you would scarce endure even to take such supplies as were needful for the body, till God "lifted you up out of the horrible pit, and set your feet upon a rock, and ordered your goings." The same would be the case if you were in agony of desire, vehemently wrestling with God for his blessing. You would need none to instruct you not to eat bread till you had obtained the request of your lips.

7. Again, had you been at Nineveh when it was proclaimed throughout the city, "Let neither man nor beast, herd nor flock, taste anything: Let them not feed or drink water, but let them cry mightily unto God;"—would your continual fast have been any reason for not bearing part in that general humiliation? Doubtless it would not. You would have been as much concerned as any other not to taste food on that day. No more would abstinence, or the observing a continual fast, have excused any of the children of Israel from fasting on the tenth day of the seventh month, that shall not be afflicted," shall not fast, "in that day, he shall be cut off from among his people."

Lastly. Had you been with the brethren in Antioch, at the time when they fasted and prayed, before the sending forth of Barnabas and Saul, can you possibly imagine that your temperance or abstinence would have been a sufficient cause for not joining therein? Without doubt, if you had not, you would soon have been cut off from the Christian community. You would have deservedly been cast out from among them, as bringing confusion into the Church of God.

IV. 1. I am, in the Last place, to show in what manner we are to fast, that it may be an acceptable service unto the Lord. And, First, let it be done unto the Lord, with our eye singly fixed on Him. Let our intention herein be this, and this alone, to glorify our Father which is in heaven; to express our sorrow and shame for our manifold transgressions of his holy law; to wait for an increase of purifying grace, drawing our affections to things above; to add seriousness and earnestness to our prayers; to avert the wrath of God, and to obtain all the great and precious promises which he hath made to us in Jesus Christ.

Let us beware of mocking God, of turning our fast, as well as our prayers, into an abomination unto the Lord, by the mixture of any temporal view, particularly by seeking the praise of men. Against this our blessed Lord more peculiarly guards us in the words of the text. "Moreover when ye fast, be ye not as the hypocrites:"—Such were too many who were called the people of God; "of a sad countenance;" sour, affectedly sad, putting their looks into a peculiar form. "For they disfigure their faces," not only by unnatural distortions, but also by covering them with dust and ashes; "that they may appear unto men to fast;" this is their chief, if not only design. "Verily, I say unto you, They have their reward;" even the admiration and praise of men. "But thou, when thou fastest, anoint thy head, and wash thy face:" Do as thou art accustomed to do at other times; "that thou appear not unto men to fast;"—let this be no part of thy intention; if they know it without any desire of thine, it matters not, thou art neither the better nor the worse;—"but unto thy Father which is in secret: And thy Father, which seeth in secret, shall reward thee openly."

2. But, if we desire this reward, let us beware, Secondly of fancying we *merit* anything of God by our fasting. We cannot be too often warned of this; inasmuch as a desire to "establish our own righteousness," to procure salvation of debt and not of grace, is so deeply rooted in all our hearts. Fasting is only a way which God hath ordained, wherein we wait for his unmerited mercy; and wherein, without any desert of ours, he hath promised freely to give us his blessing.

3. Not that we are to imagine, the performing the bare outward act will receive any blessing from God. "Is it such a fast that I have chosen, saith the Lord; a day for a man to afflict his soul? Is it to bow down his head as a bulrush, and to spread sackcloth and ashes under him?" Are these outward acts, however strictly performed, all that is meant by a mans "afflicting his soul?"—"Wilt thou call this a fast, and an acceptable day to the Lord?" No, surely: If it be a mere external service, it is all but lost labour. Such a performance may possibly afflict the body; but as to the soul, it profiteth nothing.

4. Yea, the body may sometimes be afflicted too much, so as to be unfit for the works of our calling. This also we are diligently to guard against; for we ought to preserve our health, as a good gift of God. Therefore care is to be taken, whenever we fast, to proportion the fast to our strength. For we may not offer God murder for sacrifice, or destroy our bodies to help our souls.

But at these solemn seasons, we may, even in great weakness of body, avoid that other extreme, for which God condemns those who of old expostulated with him for not accepting their fasts. "Wherefore have we fasted, say they, and thou seest not?—Behold, in the day of your fast you find pleasure, saith the Lord." If we cannot wholly abstain from food, we may, at least, abstain from pleasant food; and then we shall not seek his face in vain.

5. But let us take care to afflict our souls as well as our bodies. Let every season, either of public or private fasting, be a season of exercising all those holy affections which are implied in a broken and contrite heart. Let it be a season of devout mourning, of godly sorrow for sin; such a sorrow as that of the Corinthians, concerning which the Apostle saith, "I rejoice, not that ye were made sorry, but that ye sorrowed to repentance. For ye were made sorry after a godly manner,

that ye might receive damage by us in nothing. For godly sorrow"—*he kata Theon lype*,—the sorrow which is according to God, which is a precious gift of his Spirit, lifting the soul to God from whom it flows—"worketh repentance to salvation, not to be repented of." Yea, and let our sorrowing after a godly sort work in us the same inward and outward *repentance*; the same entire change of heart, renewed after the image of God, in righteousness and true holiness; and the same change of life, till we are holy as He is holy, in all manner of conversation. Let it work in us the same *carefulness* to be found in him, without spot and blameless; the same *clearing of ourselves*, by our lives rather than words, by our abstaining from all appearance of evil; the same *indignation*, vehement abhorrence of every sin; the same *fear* of our own deceitful hearts; the same *desire* to be in all things conformed to the holy and acceptable will of God; the same *zeal* for whatever may be a means of his glory, and of our growth in the knowledge of our Lord Jesus Christ; and the same *revenge* against Satan and all his works, against all filthiness both of flesh and Spirit. (2 Cor. 7:9.)

6. And with fasting let us always join fervent prayer, pouring out our whole souls before God, confessing our sins with all their aggravations, humbling ourselves under his mighty hand, laying open before him all our wants, all our guiltiness and helplessness. This is a season for enlarging our prayers, both in behalf of ourselves and of our brethren. Let us now bewail the sins of our people; and cry aloud for the city of our God, that the Lord may build up Zion, and cause his face to shine on her desolations. Thus, we may observe, the men of God, in ancient times always joined prayer and fasting together; thus the Apostles, in all the instances cited above; and thus our Lord joins them in the discourse before us.

7. It remains only, in order to our observing such a fast as is acceptable to the Lord, that we add alms thereto; works of mercy, after our power, both to the bodies and souls of men: "With such sacrifices" also "God is well pleased." Thus the angel declares to Cornelius, fasting and praying in his house, "Thy prayers and thine alms are come up for a memorial before God." (Acts 10:4.) And this God himself expressly and largely declares: "Is not this the fast that I have chosen? to loose the bands of wickedness, to undo the heavy burdens, to let the oppressed go free, and that ye break every yoke? Is it not to deal thy bread to the hungry, and that thou bring the poor that are cast out to thy house? when thou seest the naked, that thou cover him; and that thou hide not thyself from thy own flesh? Then shall thy light break forth as the morning, and thine health shall spring forth speedily; and thy righteousness shall go before thee; the glory of the Lord shall be thy reward. Then shalt thou call, and the Lord shall answer: Thou shalt cry, and he shall say, Here I am.—If, "when thou fastest, "thou draw out thy soul to the hungry, and satisfy the afflicted soul; then shall thy light rise in obscurity, and thy darkness be as the noon-day. And the Lord shall guide thee continually, and satisfy thy soul in drought, and make fat thy bones: And thou shalt be like a watered garden, and like a spring of water, whose waters fail not." (Isa. 58:6.)

28.* Upon our Lord's Sermon on the Mount Discourse 8

"Lay not up for yourselves treasures upon earth, where moth and rust doth corrupt, and where thieves break through and steal: But lay up for yourselves treasures in heaven, where neither moth nor rust doth corrupt, and where thieves do not break through nor steal; For where your treasure is, there will your heart be also. The light of the body is the eye: if therefore thine eye be single, thy whole body shall be full of light. But if thine eye be evil, thy whole body shall be full of darkness. If therefore the light that is in thee be darkness, how great is that darkness!"

Matt. 6:19–23.

1. From those which are commonly termed religious actions, and which are real branches of true religion where they spring from a pure and holy intention and are performed in a manner suitable thereto,—our Lord proceeds to the actions of common life, and shows that the same purity of intention is as indispensably required in our ordinary business as in giving alms, or fasting, or prayer.

And without question the same purity of intention "which makes our alms and devotions acceptable must also make our labour or employment a proper offering to God. If a man pursues his business that he may raise himself to a state of honour and riches in the world, he is no longer serving God in his employment, and has no more title to a reward from God than he who gives alms that he may be seen, or prays that he may be heard of men. For vain and earthly designs are no more allowable in our employments than in our alms and devotions. They are not only evil when they mix with our good works," with our religious actions, "but they have the same evil nature when they enter into the common business of our employments. If it were allowable to pursue them in our worldly employments, it would be allowable to pursue them in our devotions. But as our alms and devotions are not an acceptable service but when they proceed frond a pure intention, so our common employment cannot be reckoned a service to him but when it is performed with the same piety of heart."

2. This our blessed Lord declares in the liveliest manner in those strong and comprehensive words which he explains, enforces, and enlarges upon, throughout this whole chapter. "The light of the body is the eye: If therefore thine eye be single, thy whole body shall be full of light: but if thine eye be evil, thy whole body shall be full of darkness." The eye is the intention: what the eye is to the body, the intention is to the soul. As the one guides all the motions of the body, so does the other those of the soul. This eye of the soul is then said to be single when it looks at one thing only; when we have no other design but to "know God, and Jesus Christ whom he hath sent,"—to know him with suitable affections, loving him as he hath loved us; to please God in all things; to serve God (as we love him) with all our heart and mind and soul and strength; and to enjoy God in all and above all things, in time and in eternity.

3. "If thine eye be" thus "single," thus fixed on God, "thy whole body shall be full of light." "Thy whole body:"—all that is guided by the intention, as the body is by the eye. All thou art, all thou doest thy desires, tempers, affections; thy thoughts, and words, and actions. The whole of these "shall be full of light;" full of true divine knowledge. This is the first thing we may here understand by light. "In his light thou shalt see light." "He which of old commanded light to shine out of darkness, shall shine in thy heart:" He shall enlighten the eyes of thy understanding with the knowledge of the glory of God. His Spirit shall reveal unto thee the deep things of God. The inspiration of the Holy One shall give thee understanding, and cause thee to know wisdom secretly. Yea, the anointing which thou receivest of him "shall abide in thee and teach thee of all things."

How does experience confirm this! Even after God hath opened the eyes of our understanding, if we seek or desire anything else than God, how soon is our foolish heart darkened! Then clouds again rest upon our souls. Doubts and fears again overwhelm us. We are tossed to and fro, and know not what to do, or which is the path wherein we should go. But when we desire and seek nothing but God, clouds and doubts vanish away. We who "were sometime darkness are now light in the Lord." The night now shineth as the day and we find "the path of the upright is light." God showeth us the path wherein we should go, and maketh plain the way before our face.

4. The Second thing which we may here understand by light, is holiness. While thou seekest God in all things thou shalt find him in all, the fountain of all holiness, continually filling thee with his own likeness, with justice, mercy, and truth. While thou lookest unto Jesus and Him alone thou shalt be filled with the mind that was in him. Thy soul shall be renewed day by day after the image of him that created it. If the eye of thy mind be not removed from him, if thou endurest "as seeing him that is invisible," and seeking nothing else in heaven or earth, then as thou beholdest the glory of the Lord thou shalt be transformed "into the same image, from glory to glory, by the Spirit of the Lord."

And it is also matter of daily experience that "by grace we are" thus "saved through faith." It is by faith that the eye of the mind is opened to see the light of the glorious love of God. And as long as it is steadily fixed thereon, on God in Christ, reconciling the world unto himself, we are more and more filled with the love of God and man, with meekness, gentleness, long-suffering; with all the fruits of holiness, which are, through Christ Jesus, to the glory of God the Father.

5. This light which fills him who has a single eye implies, Thirdly, happiness as well as holiness. Surely "light is sweet, and a pleasant thing it is to see the sun:" But how much more to see the Sun of Righteousness continually shining upon the soul! And if there be any consolation in Christ, if any comfort of love, if any peace that passeth all understanding, if any

---

* [text of the 1872 ed.]

rejoicing in hope of the glory of God, they all belong to him whose eye is single. Thus is his "whole body full of light." He walketh in the light as God is in the light, rejoicing evermore, praying without ceasing, and in everything giving thanks, enjoying whatever is the will of God concerning him in Christ Jesus.

6. "But if thine eye be evil, thy whole body shall be full of darkness." "If thine eye be evil:"—We see there is no medium between a single and an evil eye. If the eye be not single, then it is evil. If the intention in whatever we do be not singly to God, if we seek anything else, then our "mind and conscience are defiled."

Our eye therefore is evil if in anything we do we aim at any other end than God; if we have any view, but to know and to love God, to please and serve him in all things; if we have any other design than to enjoy God, to be happy in him both now and for ever.

7. If thine eye be not singly fixed on God, "thy whole body shall be full of darkness." The veil shall still remain on thy heart. Thy mind shall be more and more blinded by "the God of this world," "lest the light of the glorious gospel of Christ should shine upon thee." Thou wilt be full of ignorance and error touching the things of God, not being able to receive or discern them. And even when thou hast some desire to serve God, thou wilt be full of uncertainty as to the manner of serving him; finding doubts and difficulties on every side, and not seeing any way to escape.

Yea, if thine eye be not single, if thou seek any of the things of earth, thou shalt be full of ungodliness and unrighteousness, thy desires, tempers, affections, being all out of course, being all dark, and vile, and vain. And thy conversation will be evil as well as thy heart, not "seasoned with salt," or "meet to minister grace unto the hearers;" but idle, unprofitable, corrupt, grievous to the Holy Spirit of God.

8. Both destruction and unhappiness are in thy ways; "for the way of peace hast thou not known." There is no peace, no settled, solid peace, for them that know not God. There is no true nor lasting content for any who do not seek him with their whole heart. While thou aimest at any of the things that perish, "all that cometh is vanity;" yea, not only vanity, but "vexation of spirit," and that both in the pursuit and the enjoyment also. Thou walkest indeed in a vain shadow, and disquietest thyself in vain. Thou walkest in darkness that may be felt. Sleep on; but thou canst not take thy rest. The dreams of life can give pain, and that thou knowest; but ease they cannot give. There is no rest in this world or the world to come, but only in God, the centre of spirits.

"If the light which is in thee be darkness, how great is that darkness!" If the intention which ought to enlighten the whole soul, to fill it with knowledge, and love, and peace, and which in fact does so as long as it is single, as long as it aims at God alone—if this be darkness; if it aim at anything beside God, and consequently cover the soul with darkness instead of light, with ignorance and error, with sin and misery: O how great is that darkness! It is the very smoke which ascends out of the bottomless pit! It is the essential night which reigns in the lowest deep, in the land of the shadow of death!

9. Therefore, "lay not up for yourselves treasures upon earth, where moth and rust doth corrupt, and where thieves break through and steal." If you do, it is plain your eye is evil; it is not singly fixed on God.

With regard to most of the commandments of God, whether relating to the heart or life, the Heathens of Africa or America stand much on a level with those that are called Christians. The Christians observe them (a few only being excepted) very near as much as the Heathens. For instance: the generality of the natives of England, commonly called Christians, are as sober and as temperate as the generality of the heathens near the Cape of Good Hope. And so the Dutch or French Christians are as humble and as chaste as the Choctaw or Cherokee Indians. It is not easy to say, when we compare the bulk of the nations in Europe with those in America, whether the superiority lies on the one side or the other. At least the American has not much the advantage. But we cannot affirm this with regard to the command now before us. Here the heathen has far the pre-eminence. He desires and seeks nothing more than plain food to eat and plain raiment to put on. And he seeks this only from day to day. He reserves, he lays up nothing; unless it be as much corn at one season of the year as he will need before that season returns. This command, therefore, the heathens, though they know it not, do constantly and punctually observe. They "lay up for themselves no treasures upon earth;" no stores of purple or fine linen, of gold or silver, which either "moth or rust may corrupt", or "thieves break through and steal." But how do the Christians observe what they profess to receive as a command of the most high God? Not at all! not in any degree; no more than if no such command had ever been given to man. Even the good Christians, as they are accounted by others as well as themselves, pay no manner of regard thereto. It might as well be still hid in its original Greek for any notice they take of it. In what Christian city do you find one man of five hundred who makes the least scruple of laying up just as much treasure as he can?—of increasing his goods just as far as he is able? There are indeed those who would not do this unjustly; there are many who will neither rob nor steal; and some who will not defraud their neighbour; nay, who will not gain either by his ignorance or necessity. But this is quite another point. Even these do not scruple the thing, but the manner of it. They do not scruple the "laying up treasures upon earth," but the laying them up by dishonesty. They do not start at disobeying Christ, but at a breach of heathen morality. So that even these honest men do no more obey this command than a highwayman or a house-breaker. Nay, they never designed to obey it. From their youth up it never entered into their thoughts. They were bred up by their Christian parents, masters, and friends, without any instruction at all concerning it; unless it were this,—to break it as soon and as much as they could, and to continue breaking it to their lives' end.

10. There is no one instance of spiritual infatuation in the world which is more amazing than this. Most of these very men read or hear the Bible read,—many of them every Lord's day. They have read or heard these words an hundred times,

and yet never suspect that they are themselves condemned thereby, any more than by those which forbid parents to offer up their sons or daughters unto Moloch. O that God would speak to these miserable self-deceivers with his own voice, his mighty voice! That they may at last awake out of the snare of the devil, and the scales may fall from their eyes!

11. Do you ask what it is to "lay up treasures on earth?" It will be needful to examine this thoroughly. And let us, First, observe what is not forbidden in this command, that we may then clearly discern what is.

We are not forbidden in this command, First, to "provide things honest in the sight of all men," to provide wherewith we may render unto all their due,—whatsoever they can justly demand of us. So far from it that we are taught of God to "owe no man anything." We ought therefore to use all diligence in our calling, in order to owe no man anything: this being no other than a plain law of common justice which our Lord came "not to destroy but to fulfil."

Neither, Secondly, does he here forbid the providing for ourselves such things as are needful for the body; a sufficiency of plain, wholesome food to eat, and clean raiment to put on. Yea, it is our duty, so far as God puts it into our power, to provide these things also; to the end we may "eat our own bread," and be burdensome to no man.

Nor yet are we forbidden, Thirdly, to provide for our children, and for those of our own household. This also it is our duty to do, even upon principles of heathen morality. Every man ought to provide the plain necessaries of life both for his own wife and children, and to put them into a capacity of providing these for themselves when he is gone hence and is no more seen. I say, of providing *these*, the plain necessaries of life; not delicacies, not superfluities;—and that by their diligent labour; for it is no man's duty to furnish them any more than himself with the means either Of luxury or idleness. But if any man provides not thus far for his own children (as well as for the widows of his own house, of whom primarily St. Paul is speaking in those well-known words to Timothy), he hath practically "denied the faith, and is worse than an infidel," or Heathen.

Lastly. We are not forbidden, in these words, to lay up, from time to time what is needful for the carrying on our worldly business in such a measure and degree as is sufficient to answer the foregoing purposes;—in such a measure as, First, to owe no man anything; Secondly, to procure for ourselves the necessaries of life; and, Thirdly, to furnish those of our own house with them while we live, and with the means of procuring them when we are gone to God.

12. We may now clearly discern (unless we are unwilling to discern it) what that is which is forbidden here. It is the designedly procuring more of this world's goods than will answer the foregoing purposes; the labouring after a larger measure of worldly substance, a larger increase of gold and silver,—the laying up any more than these ends require,—is what is here expressly and absolutely forbidden. If the words have any meaning at all, it must be this; for they are capable of no other. Consequently, whoever he is that, owing no man anything, and having food and raiment for himself and his household, together with a sufficiency to carry on his worldly business so far as answers these reasonable purposes; whosoever, I say, being already in these circumstances, seeks a still larger portion on earth; he lives in an open habitual denial of the Lord that bought him. He hath practically denied the faith, and is worse than" an African or American "infidel."

13. Hear ye this, all ye that dwell in the world, and love the world wherein ye dwell. Ye may be "highly esteemed of men;" but ye are "an abomination in the sight of God." How long shall your souls cleave to the dust? How long will ye load yourselves with thick clay? When will ye awake and see that the open, speculative Heathens are nearer the kingdom of heaven than you? When will ye be persuaded to choose the better part; that which cannot be taken away from you? When will ye seek only to "lay up treasures in heaven," renouncing, dreading, abhorring all other? If you aim at "laying up treasures on earth," you are not barely losing your time and spending your strength for that which is not bread: for what is the fruit if you succeed?—You have murdered your own soul! You have extinguished the last spark of spiritual life therein! Now indeed, in the midst of life you are in death! You are a living man, but a dead Christian. "For where your treasure is, there will your heart be also." Your heart is sunk into the dust, your soul cleaveth to the ground. Your affections are set, not on things above, but on things of the earth; on poor husks that may poison, but cannot satisfy an everlasting spirit made for God. Your love your joy, your desire are all placed on the things which perish in the using. You have thrown away the treasure in heaven: God and Christ are lost! You have gained riches, and hell-fire!

14. O "how hardly shall they that have riches enter into the kingdom of God!" When our Lord's disciples were astonished at his speaking thus he was so far from retracting it that he repeated the same important truth in stronger terms than before. "It is easier for a camel to go through the eye of a needle, than for a rich man to enter into the kingdom of God." How hard is it for them whose very word is applauded not to be wise in their own eyes! How hard for them not to think themselves better than the poor, base, uneducated herd of men! How hard not to seek happiness in their riches, or in things dependent upon them; in gratifying the desire of the flesh, the desire of the eye, or the pride of life! O ye rich, how can ye escape the damnation of hell? Only, with all God all things are possible!

15. And even if you do not succeed, what is the fruit of your endeavouring to lay up treasures on earth? "They that will be rich" (*hoi boulomenoi ploutein*, they that *desire*, that *endeavour* after it, whether they succeed or no,) fall into a temptation and a snare, a gin, a trap of the devil; and into many foolish and hurtful lusts; *epithymias anoetous, desires* with which *reason hath nothing to do*, such as properly belong, not to rational and immortal beings, but only to the brute beasts which have no understanding;—which drown men in destruction and perdition, in present and eternal misery. Let us but open our eyes, and we may daily see the melancholy proofs of this,—men who, desiring, resolving to be rich, coveting after money, the root of all evil, have already

pierced themselves through with many sorrows, and anticipated the hell to which they are going!

The cautiousness with which the Apostle here speaks is highly observable. he does not affirm this absolutely of the rich: For a man may possibly be rich, without any fault of his, by an overruling Providence, preventing his own choice: But he affirms it of *hoi boulomenoi plourein, those who desire* or seek *to be rich*. Riches, dangerous as they are, do not always drown men in destruction and perdition; but the *desire of riches* does: those who calmly desire and deliberately seek to attain them, whether they do, in fact, gain the world or no, do infallibly lose their own souls. These are they that sell him who bought them with his blood, for a few pieces of gold or silver. These enter into a covenant with death and hell; and their covenant shall stand. For they are daily making themselves meet to partake of their inheritance with the devil and his angels!

16. o who shall warn this generation of vipers to flee from the wrath to come! Not those who lie at their gate, or cringe at their feet, desiring to be fed with the crumbs that fall from their tables. Not those who court their favour or fear their frown: none of those who mind earthly things. But if there be a Christian upon earth, if there be a man who hath overcome the world, who desires nothing but God, and fears none but him that is able to destroy both body and soul in hell; thou, o man of God, speak and spare not; lift up thy voice like a trumpet! Cry aloud, and show these honourable sinners the desperate condition wherein they stand! It may be, one in a thousand may have ears to hear, may arise and shake himself from the dust; may break loose from these chains that bind him to the earth, and at length lay up treasures in heaven.

17. And if it should be that one of these, by the mighty power of God, awoke and asked, What must I do to be saved? the answer, according to the oracles of God, is clear, full, and express. God doth not say to thee, "Sell all that thou hast." Indeed he who seeth the hearts of men saw it needful to enjoin this in one peculiar case, that of the young, rich ruler. But he never laid it down for a general rule to all rich men, in all succeeding generations. his general direction is, first, "Be not high minded." God seeth not as man seeth." he esteems thee not for thy riches, grandeur or equipage, for any qualification or accomplishment which is directly or indirectly owing to thy wealth, which can be bought or procured thereby. All these are with him as dung and dross: let them be so with thee also. Beware thou think not thyself to be one jot wiser or better for all these things. Weigh thyself in another balance: estimate thyself only by the measure of faith and love which God hath given thee. If thou hast more of the knowledge and love of God than he, thou art on this account, and no other, wiser and better, more valuable and honourable than him who is with the dogs of thy flock. But if thou hast not this treasure those art more foolish, more vile, more truly contemptible, I will not say, than the lowest servant under thy roof, but than the beggar laid at thy gate, full of sores.

18. Secondly. "Trust not in uncertain riches." Trust not in them for help: And trust not in them for happiness.

First. Trust not in them for help. Thou art miserably mistaken if thou lookest for this in gold or silver. These are no more able to set thee *above the world* than to set thee above the devil. Know that both the world, and the prince of this world, laugh at all such preparations against them. These will little avail in the day of trouble-even if they remain in the trying hour. But it is not certain that they will; for how oft do they "make themselves wings and fly away!" But if not, what support will they afford, even in the ordinary troubles of life? The desire of thy eyes, the wife of thy youth, thy son, thine only son, or the friend which was as thy own soul, is taken away at a stroke. Will thy riches re-animate the breathless clay, or call back its late inhabitant? Will they secure thee from sickness, diseases, pain? Do these visit the poor only? Nay, he that feeds thy flocks or tills thy ground has less sickness and pain than thou. He is more rarely visited by these unwelcome guests: and if they come there at all they are more easily driven away from the little cot than from the "cloud-topt palaces." And during the time that thy body is chastened with pain, or consumes away with pining sickness, how do thy treasures help thee? Let the poor Heathen answer,

> Ut lippum pictae tabulae, fomenta podagrum,
> Auriculas citharae collecta sorde dolentes.
> [Such help as pictures to sore eyes afford,
> As heapd-up tables to their gouty lord.]

19. But there is at hand a greater trouble than all these. Thou art to die! Thou art to sink into dust; to return to the ground from which thou wast taken, to mix with common clay. Thy body is to go to the earth as it was, while thy spirit returns to God that gave it. And the time draws on: the years slide away with a swift though silent pace. Perhaps your day is far spent: the noon of life is past, and the evening shadows begin to rest upon you. You feel in yourself sure approaching decay. The springs of life wear away apace. Now what help is there in your riches? Do they sweeten death? Do they endear that solemn hour? Quite the reverse. "o death, how bitter art thou to a man that liveth at rest in his possessions!" How unacceptable to him is that awful sentence, "This night shall thy soul be required of thee!" or will they prevent the unwelcome stroke, or protract the dreadful hour? Can they deliver your soul that it should not see death? Can they restore the years that are past? Can they add to your appointed time a month, a day, an hour, a moment?—or will the good things you have chosen for your portion here follow you over the great gulf? Not so. Naked came you into this world; naked must you return.

> Linquenda tellus, et domus, et placens
> Uxor; neque harum quas colis, arborum,
> Te, praeter invisam cupressos,
> Ulla brevem dominum sequetur!

[The following is Boscawens translation of these verses from Horace:

> Thy lands, thy dome, thy pleasing wife,
> These must thou quit; 'tis natures doom.
> No tree, whose culture charms thy life,
> Save the sad cypress, waits thy tomb.—edit.]

Surely, were not these truths too plain to be observed, because they are too plain to be denied, no man that is to die could possibly trust for help in uncertain riches.

20. And trust not in them for happiness: For here also they will be found "deceitful upon the weights." Indeed this every reasonable man may infer from what has been observed already. For if neither thousands of gold and silver, nor any of the advantages or pleasures purchased thereby, can prevent our being miserable, it evidently follows they cannot make us happy. What happiness can they afford to him who in the midst of all is constrained to cry out,

> To my new courts sad thought does still repair,
> And round my gilded roofs hangs hovering care?

Indeed experience is here so full, strong, and undeniable, that it makes all other arguments needless. Appeal we therefore to fact. Are the rich and great the only happy men? And is each of them more or less happy in proportion to his measure of riches? Are they happy at all? I had well nigh said, they are of all men most miserable! Rich man, for once, speak the truth from thy heart. Speak, both for thyself, and for thy brethren!

> Amidst our plenty something still,—
> To me, to thee, to him is wanting!
> That cruel something unpossessed
> Corrodes and leavens all the rest.

Yea, and so it will, till thy wearisome days of vanity are shut up in the night of death.

Surely then, to trust in riches for happiness is the greatest folly of all that are under the sun! Are you not convinced of this? Is it possible you should still expect to find happiness in money or all it can procure? What! Can silver and gold, and eating and drinking, and horses and servants, and glittering apparel, and diversions and pleasures (as they are called) make thee happy? They can as soon make thee immortal!

21. These are all dead show. Regard them not. Trust thou in the living God; so shalt thou be safe under the shadow of the Almighty; his faithfulness and truth shall be thy shield and buckler. He is a very present help in time of trouble such an help as can never fail. Then shalt thou say, if all thy other friends die, "The Lord liveth, and blessed be my strong helper!" He shall remember thee when thou liest sick upon thy bed; when vain is the help of man. When all the things of earth can give no support, he will "make all thy bed in thy sickness." He will sweeten thy pain; the consolations of God shall cause thee to clap thy hands in the flames. And even when this house of earth" is well nigh shaken down, when it is just ready to drop into the dust, he will teach thee to say, "O death, where is thy sting? O grave, where is thy victory? Thanks be unto God, who giveth" me "the victory, through" my "Lord Jesus Christ."

O trust in Him for happiness as well as for help. All the springs of happiness are in him. Trust in him "who giveth us all things richly to enjoy," *parechonti plousiOs panta eis apolausin.*—who, of his own rich and free mercy holds them out to us as in his own hand, that receiving them as his gift, and as pledges of his love, we may enjoy all that we possess. It is his love gives a relish to all we taste,—puts life and sweetness into all, while every creature leads us up to the great Creator, and all earth is a scale to heaven. he transfuses the joys that are at his own right hand into all he bestows on his thankful children; who, having fellowship with the Father and his Son Jesus Christ, enjoy him in all and above all.

22. Thirdly, seek not to increase in goods. Lay not up for thyself "treasures upon earth." This is a flat, positive command; full as clear as "Thou shalt not commit adultery." How then is it possible for a rich man to grow richer without denying the Lord that bought him? Yea, how can any man who has already the necessaries of life gain or aim at more, and be guiltless? "Lay not up," saith our Lord, "treasures upon earth." If, in spite of this, you do and will lay up money or goods, which "moth or rust may corrupt, or thieves break through and steal;" if you will add house to house, or field to field,—why do you call yourself a Christian? You do not obey Jesus Christ. You do not design it. Why do you name yourself by his name? "Why call ye me, Lord, Lord," saith he himself, "and do not the things which I say?"

23. If you ask, "But what must we do with our goods, seeing we have more than we have occasion to use, if we must not lay them up? Must we throw them away?" I answer: If you threw them into the sea, if you were to cast them into the fire and consume them, they would be better bestowed than they are now. You cannot find so mischievous a manner of throwing them away as either the laying them up for your posterity or the laying them out upon yourselves in folly and superfluity. Of all possible methods of throwing them away, these two are the very worst; the most opposite to the gospel of Christ, and the most pernicious to your own soul.

How pernicious to your own soul the latter of these is has been excellently shown by a late writer:—

"If we waste our money we are not only guilty of wasting a talent which God has given us, but we do ourselves this farther harm, we turn this useful talent into a powerful means of corrupting ourselves; because so far as it is spent wrong, so far it is spent in the support of some wrong temper, in gratifying some vain and unreasonable desires, which as Christians we are obliged to renounce.

"As wit and fine parts cannot be only trifled away, but will expose those that have them to greater follies, so money cannot be only trifled away, but if it is not used according to reason and religion, will make people live a more silly and extravagant life than they would have done without it. If therefore you don't spend your money in doing good to others, you must spend it to the hurt of yourself. You act like one that refuses the cordial to his sick friend which he cannot drink himself without inflaming his blood. For this is the case of superfluous money, if you give it to those who want it is a cordial; if you spend it upon yourself in something that you do not want it only inflames and disorders your mind.

"In using riches where they have no real use, nor we any real want, we only use them to our great hurt, in creating unreasonable desires, in nourishing ill tempers, in indulging in foolish passions, and supporting a vain turn of mind. For high eating and drinking, fine clothes and fine houses, state and equipage, gay pleasures and diversions, do all of them naturally hurt and disorder our heart. They are the food and nourishment of all the folly and weakness of our nature. They are all of them the support of something that ought not to be supported. They are contrary to that sobriety and piety of heart which relishes divine things. They are so many weights upon our mind, that makes us less able and less inclined to raise our thoughts and affections to things above.

"So that money thus spent is not merely wasted or lost, but it is spent to bad purposes and miserable effects; to the corruption and disorder of our hearts; to the making us unable to follow the sublime doctrines of the gospel. It is but like keeping money from the poor to buy poison for ourselves."

24. equally inexcusable are those who lay up what they do not need for any reasonable purposes:—

"If a man had hands and eyes and feet that he could give to those that wanted them; if he should lock them up in a chest instead of giving them to his brethren that were blind and lame, should we not justly reckon him an inhuman wretch? If he should rather choose to amuse himself with hoarding them up than entitle himself to an eternal reward by giving them to those that wanted eyes and hands, might we not justly reckon him mad?

"Now money has very much the nature of eyes and feet. If therefore we lock it up in chests, while the poor and distressed want it for their necessary uses, we are not far from the cruelty of him that chooses rather to hoard up the hands and eyes than to give them to those that want them. If we choose to lay it up rather than to entitle ourselves to an eternal reward by disposing of our money well, we are guilty of his madness that rather chooses to lock up eyes and hands than to make himself for ever blessed by giving them to those that want them."

25. May not this be another reason why rich men shall so hardly enter into the kingdom of heaven? A vast majority of them are under a curse, under the peculiar curse of God; inasmuch as in the general tenor of their lives they are not only robbing God continually, embezzling and wasting their Lord's goods, and by that very means corrupting their own souls; but also robbing the poor, the hungry, the naked, wronging the widow and the fatherless, and making themselves accountable for all the want, affliction, and distress which they may but do not remove. Yea, doth not the blood of all those who perish for want of what they either lay up or lay out needlessly, cry against them from the earth? O what account will they give to him who is ready to judge both the quick and the dead!

26. The true way of employing what you do not want yourselves you may, Fourthly, learn from those words of our Lord which are the counterpart of what went before: "Lay up for yourselves treasures in heaven; where neither moth nor rust doth corrupt, and where thieves do not break through and steal." Put out whatever thou canst spare upon better security than this world can afford. Lay up thy treasures in the bank of heaven; and God shall restore them in that day. "He that hath pity upon the poor lendeth unto the Lord, and look, what he layeth out, it shall be paid him again." "Place that," saith he, "unto my account. Howbeit, thou owest me thine own self besides!"

Give to the poor with a single eye, with an upright heart, and write, "So much given to God." For "Inasmuch as ye did it unto one of the least of these my brethren, ye have done it unto me."

This is the part of a "faithful and wise steward:" Not to sell either his houses or lands, or principal stock, be it more or less, unless some peculiar circumstance should require it; and not to desire or endeavour to increase it, any more than to squander it away in vanity; but to employ it wholly to those wise and reasonable purposes for which his Lord has lodged it in his hands. The wise steward, after having provided his own household with what is needful for life and godliness, makes himself friends with all that remains from time to time of the "mammon of unrighteousness; that when he fails they may receive him into everlasting habitations,"—that whensoever his earthly tabernacle is dissolved, they who were before carried into Abraham's bosom, after having eaten his bread, and worn the fleece of his flock., and praised God for the consolation, may welcome him into paradise, and to "the house of God, eternal in the heavens."

27. We "charge" you, therefore, "who are rich in this world," as having authority from our great Lord and Master, *agathoergein*, to be *habitually doing good*, to live in a course of good works. Be ye merciful as your Father which is in heaven is merciful; who doth good, and ceaseth not. Be ye merciful, how far? After your power, with all the ability which God giveth. Make this your only measure of doing good, not any beggarly maxims or customs of the world. We charge you to "be rich in good works;" as you have much, to give plenteously. "Freely ye have received; freely give;" so as to lay up no treasure but in heaven. Be ye "ready to distribute" to everyone according to his necessity. Disperse abroad, give to the poor: deal your bread to the hungry. Cover the naked with a garment, entertain the stranger, carry or send relief to them that are in prison. heal the sick; not by miracle, but through the blessing of God upon your seasonable support. Let the blessing of him that was ready to perish through pining want come upon thee. Defend the oppressed, plead the cause of the fatherless, and make the widows heart sing for joy.

28. We exhort you in the name of the Lord Jesus Christ to be "willing to communicate;" *koinonikous einai*. to be of the same spirit (though not in the same outward state) with those believers of ancient times, who remained steadfast *en tei koinoniai*, in that blessed and holy *fellowship*, wherein "none said that anything was his own, but they had all things common." Be a steward, a faithful and wise steward, of God and of the poor; differing from them in these two circumstances only, that your wants are first supplied out of the portion of your Lord's goods which remains in your hands, and that you have the blessedness of giving. Thus "lay up for yourselves a good foundation," not in the world which now is, but rather "for the time to come, that ye may lay hold on eternal life." The great foundation indeed of all the blessings of God, whether temporal or eternal, is the Lord Jesus Christ,—his righteousness and blood,—what he hath done, and what he hath suffered for us. And "other foundation," in this sense, "can no man lay;" no, not an Apostle, no, not an angel from heaven. But through his merits, whatever we do in his name is a foundation for a good

reward in the day when "every man shall receive his own reward, according to his own labour." Therefore "labour" thou "not for the meat that perisheth, but for that which endureth unto everlasting life." Therefore "whatsoever thy hand" now "findeth to do, do it with thy might." Therefore let

> No fair occasion pass unheeded by;
> Snatching the golden moments as they fly,
> Thou by few fleeting years ensure eternity!

"By patient continuance in well-doing, seek" thou "for glory and honour and immortality." In a constant, zealous performance of all good works, wait thou for that happy hour when the King shall say, "I was an hungered, and ye gave me meat; I was thirsty, and ye gave me drink. I was a stranger, and ye took me in, Naked, and ye clothed me. I was sick, and ye visited me; I was in prison, and ye came unto me.—Come, ye blessed of my Father, receive the kingdom prepared for you from the foundation of the world!"

29.* UPON OUR LORD'S SERMON ON THE MOUNT DISCOURSE 9

" 'No man can serve two masters; For either he will hate the one, and love the other; or else he will hold to the one and despise the other. Ye cannot serve God and mammon.

" 'Therefore I say unto you, Take no thought for your life, what ye shall eat, or what ye shall drink; nor yet for your body, what ye shall put on. Is not the life more than meat, and the body than raiment? Behold the fowls of the air: For they sow not, neither do they reap, nor gather into barns; yet your heavenly Father feedeth them. Are ye not much better than they? Which of you by taking thought can add one cubit unto his stature?

"And why take ye thought for raiment? Consider the lilies of the field, how they grow; they toil not, neither do they spin. And yet I say unto you, that even Solomon in all his glory was not arrayed like one of these. Wherefore, if God so clothe the grass of the field, which to-day is, and tomorrow is cast into the oven, shall he not much more clothe you, O ye of little faith? Therefore take no thought, saying, What shall we eat? or, What shall we drink? or, Wherewithal shall we be clothed? (For after all these things do the Gentiles seek:) For your heavenly Father knoweth that ye have need of all these things. But seek ye first the kingdom of God, and his righteousness; and all these things shall be added unto you.

" 'Take therefore no thought for the morrow: For the morrow shall take thought for the things of itself. Sufficient unto the day is the evil thereof.' "

Matt. 6:24–34.

1. It is recorded of the nations whom the King of Assyria, after he had carried Israel away into captivity, placed in the cities of Samaria, that "they feared the Lord, and served their own gods." "These nations," saith the inspired writer, "feared the Lord;" performed an outward service to him (a plain proof that they had a fear of God, though not according to knowledge;) "and served their graven images, both their children, and their children's children: As did their fathers, so do they unto this day. (2 Kings 17:33.)

How nearly does the practice of most modern Christians resemble this of the ancient Heathens! "They fear the Lord;" they also perform an outward service to him, and hereby show they have some fear of God; but they likewise "serve their own gods." There are those who "teach them" as there were who taught the Assyrians, "the manner of the God of the land;" the God whose name the country bears to this day, and who was once worshipped there with an holy worship: "Howbeit," they do not serve him alone; they do not fear him enough for this: But "every nation maketh gods of their own: Every nation in the cities wherein they dwell." "These nations fear the Lord;" they have not laid aside the outward form of worshipping him; but "they serve their graven images,' silver and gold, the work of men's hands: Money, pleasure, and praise, the gods of this world, more than divide their service with the God of Israel. This is the manner both of "their children and their children's children; as did their fathers, so do they unto this day."

2. But although, speaking in a loose way, after the common manner of men, those poor Heathens were said to "fear the Lord," yet we may observe the Holy Ghost immediately adds, speaking according to the truth and real nature of things, "They fear not the Lord, neither do after the law and the commandment, which the Lord commanded the children of Jacob; with whom the Lord made a covenant, and charged them, saying, Ye shall not fear other gods, nor serve them.—But the Lord your God ye shall fear; and he shall deliver you out of the hand of all your enemies."

The same judgment is passed by the unerring Spirit of God, and indeed by all the eyes of whose understanding he hath opened to discern the things of God, upon these poor Christians, commonly so called. If we speak according to the truth and real nature of things, "they fear not the Lord, neither do they serve him." For they do not "after the covenant the Lord hath made with them, neither after the law and commandment which he hath commanded them, saying, Thou shalt worship the Lord thy God, and him only shalt thou serve." "They serve other gods unto this day." And "no man can serve two masters."

3. How vain is it for any man to aim at this,—to attempt the serving of two masters! Is it not easy to foresee what must be the unavoidable consequence of such an attempt? "Either he will hate the one, and love the other; or else he will hold to the one, and despise the other." The two parts of this sentence, although separately proposed, are to be understood in connection with each other; for the latter part is a consequence of the former. He will naturally hold to him whom he loves. He will so cleave to him, as to perform to him a willing, faithful, and diligent service. And, in the meantime, he will so far at least despise the master he hates as to have little regard to his commands, and to obey them,

---

* [text of the 1872 edition]

if at all, in a slight and careless manner. Therefore, whatsoever the wise men of the world may suppose, "ye cannot serve God and mammon."

4. Mammon was the name of one of the heathen gods, who was supposed to preside over riches. It is here understood of riches themselves; gold and silver; or, in general, money; and, by a common figure of speech, of all that may be purchased thereby; such as ease, honor, and sensual pleasure.

But what are we here to understand by serving God, and what by serving mammon?

We cannot serve God unless we *believe* in him. This is the only true foundation of serving him. Therefore, believing in God, as "reconciling the world to himself through Christ Jesus," the believing in him, as a loving, pardoning God, is the first great branch of his service.

And thus to believe in God implies, to trust in him as our strength, without whom we can do nothing, who every moment endues us with power from on high, without which it is impossible to please him; as our help, our only help in time of trouble, who compasseth us about with songs of deliverance; as our shield, our defender, and the lifter up of our head above all our enemies that are round about us.

It implies, to trust in God as our happiness; as the centre of spirits; the only rest of our souls; the only good who is adequate to all our capacities, and sufficient to satisfy all the desires he hath given us.

It implies, (what is nearly allied to the other,) to trust in God as our end; to have an eye to him in all things; to use all things only as means of enjoying him; wheresoever we are, or whatsoever we do, to see him that is invisible, looking on us well-pleased, and to refer all things to him in Christ Jesus.

5. Thus to believe, is the First thing we are to understand by serving God. The Second is, to *love* him.

Now to love God in the manner the Scripture describes, in the manner God himself requires of us, and by requiring engages to work in us,—is to love him as the ONE GOD; that is, "with all our heart, and with all our soul, and with all our mind, and with all our strength;"—it is to desire God alone for his own sake; and nothing else, but with reference to him;—to rejoice in God;—to delight in the Lord; not only to seek, but find, happiness in him; to enjoy God as the chiefest among ten thousand; to rest in him, as our God and our all;—in a word, to have such a possession of God as makes us always happy.

6. A Third thing we are to understand by serving God is to *resemble* or *imitate* him.

So the ancient Father: *Optimus Dei cultus, imitari quem colis*: "It is the best worship or service of God, to imitate him you worship."

We here speak of imitating or resembling him in the spirit of our minds: For here the true Christian imitation of God begins. "God is a Spirit;" and they that imitate or resemble him must do it "in spirit and in truth."

Now God is love: Therefore, they who resemble him in the spirit of their minds are transformed into the same image. They are merciful even as he is merciful. Their soul is all love. They are kind, benevolent, compassionate, tender-hearted; and that not only to the good and gentle, but also to the froward. Yea, they are, like Him, loving unto every man, and their mercy extends to all his works.

7. One thing more we are to understand by serving God, andthat is, the *obeying* him; the glorifying him with our bodies, as well as with our spirits; the keeping his outward commandments; the zealously doing whatever he hath enjoined; the carefully avoiding whatever he hath forbidden; the performing all the ordinary actions of life with a single eye and a pure heart, offering them all in holy, fervent love, as sacrifices to God through Jesus Christ.

8. Let us consider now what we are to understand, on the other hand, by serving mammon. And, First, it implies the *trusting* in riches, in money, or the things purchasable thereby, as our strength,—the means whereby we shall perform whatever cause we have in hand; the trusting in them as our help,—by which we look to be comforted in or delivered out of trouble.

It implies the trusting in the world for happiness; the supposing that "a man's life," the comfort of his life, "consisteth in the abundance of the things which he possesseth;" the looking for rest in the things that are seen; for content, in outward plenty; the expecting that satisfaction in the things of the world, which can never be found out of God.

And if we do this, we cannot but make the world our end; the ultimate end, if not of all, at least of many, of our undertakings, many of our actions and designs; in which we shall aim only at an increase of wealth, at the obtaining pleasure or praise, at the gaining a larger measure of temporal things, without any reference to things eternal.

9. The serving mammon implies, Secondly, *loving* the world; desiring it for its own sake; the placing our joy in the things thereof, and setting our hearts upon them; the seeking (what indeed it is impossible we should find) our happiness therein; the resting with the whole weight of our souls, upon the staff of this broken reed, although daily experience shows it cannot support, but will only "enter into our hand and pierce it."

10. To *resemble*, to be *conformed* to the world, is a Third thing we are to understand by serving mammon; to have not only designs, but desires, tempers, affections, suitable to those of the world; to be of an earthly, sensual mind, chained down to the things of earth; to be self-willed, inordinate lovers of ourselves; to think highly of our own attainments; to desire and delight in the praise of men; to fear, shun, and abhor reproach; to be impatient of reproof, easy to be provoked, and swift to return evil for evil.

11. To serve mammon is, Lastly, to *obey* the world, by outwardly conforming to its maxims and customs; to walk as other men walk, in the common road, in the broad, smooth, beaten path; to be in the fashion; to follow a multitude; to do like the rest of our neighbours; that is, to do the will of the flesh and the mind, to gratify our appetites and inclinations; to sacrifice to ourselves; aim at our own ease and pleasure, in the general course both of our words and actions.

Now what can be more undeniably clear than that we cannot thus serve God and mammon?

12. Does not every man see, that he cannot *comfortably* serve both? That to trim between God and the world is the sure way to be disappointed in both, and to have no rest either in one or the other? How uncomfortable a condition must he be in, who, having the fear but not the love of God,—who, serving him, but not with all his heart,—has only the toils and not the joys of religion? He has religion enough to make him miserable, but not enough to make him happy: His religion will not let him enjoy the world, and the world will not let him enjoy God. So that, by halting between both, he loses both; and has no peace either in God or the world.

13. Does not every man see, that he cannot serve both *consistently* with himself? What more glaring inconsistency can be conceived, than must continually appear in his whole behavior, who is endeavoring to obey both these masters,—striving to "serve God and mammon?" He is indeed a "sinner that goeth two ways;" one step forward and another backward. He is continually building up with one hand, and pulling down with the other. He loves sin, and he hates it: He is always seeking, and yet always fleeing from, God. He would, and he would not. He is not the same man for one day; no, not for an hour together. He is a motley mixture of all sorts of contrarieties; a heap of contradictions jumbled in one. O be consistent with thyself one way or the other! Turn to the right hand or to the left. If mammon be God, serve thou him; if the Lord, then serve him. But never think of serving either at all, unless it be with thy whole heart.

14. Does not every reasonable, every thinking man see that he cannot *possibly* serve God and mammon? Because there is the most absolute contrariety, the most irreconcilable enmity between them. The contrariety between the most opposite things on earth, between fire and water, darkness and light, vanishes into nothing when compared to the contrariety between God and mammon. So that, in whatsoever respect you serve the one, you necessarily renounce the other. Do you believe in God through Christ? Do you trust in him as your strength, your help, your shield, and your exceeding great reward? as your happiness? your end in all, above all things? Then you cannot trust in riches. It is absolutely impossible you should, so long as you have this faith in God. Do you thus trust in riches? Then you have denied the faith. You do not trust in the living God. Do you love God? Do you seek and find happiness in him? Then you cannot love the world, neither the things of the world. You are crucified to the world, and the world crucified to you. Do you love the world? Are your affections set on things beneath? Do you seek happiness in earthly things? Then it is impossible you should love God. Then the love of the Father is not in you. Do you resemble God? Are you merciful, as your Father is merciful? Are you transformed, by the renewal of your mind, into the image of him that created you? Then you cannot be conformed to the present world. You have renounced all its affections and lusts. Are you conformed to the world? Does your soul still bear the image of the earthly? Then you are not renewed in the spirit of your mind. You do not bear the image of the heavenly. Do you obey God? Are you zealous to do his will on earth as the angels do in heaven? Then it is impossible you should obey mammon. Then you

set the world at open defiance. You trample its customs and maxims under foot, and will neither follow nor be led by them. Do you follow the world? Do you live like other men? Do you please men? Do you please yourself? Then you cannot be a servant of God. You are of your master and father, the devil.

15. Therefore, "thou shalt worship the Lord thy God; and him only shalt thou serve." Thou shalt lay aside all thoughts of obeying two masters, of serving God and mammon. Thou shalt propose to thyself no end, no help, no happiness, but God. Thou shalt seek nothing in earth or heaven but him: Thou shalt aim at nothing, but to know, to love, and enjoy him. And because this is all your business below, the only view you can reasonably have, the one design you are to pursue in all things,—"Therefore I say unto you," (as our Lord continues his discourse,) "Take no thought for your life, what ye shall eat, or what ye shall drink; nor yet for your body, what ye shall put on:"—A deep and weighty direction, which it imports us well to consider and thoroughly to understand.

16. Our Lord does not here require, that we should be utterly without thought, even touching the concerns of this life. A giddy, careless temper is at the farthest remove from the whole religion of Jesus Christ. Neither does he require us to be "slothful in business," to be slack and dilatory therein. This, likewise, is contrary to the whole spirit and genius of his religion. A Christian abhors sloth as much as drunkenness; and flees from idleness as he does from adultery. He well knows, that there is one kind of thought and care with which God is well pleased; which is absolutely needful for the due performance of those outward works unto which the providence of God has called him.

It is the will of God, that every man should labour to eat his own bread; yea, and that every man should provide for his own, for them of his own household. It is likewise his will, that we should "owe no man anything, but provide things honest in the sight of all men." But this cannot be done without taking some thought, without having some care upon our minds; yea, often, not without long and serious thought, not without much and earnest care. Consequently this care, to provide for ourselves and our household, this thought how to render to all their dues, our blessed Lord does not condemn. Yea, it is good and acceptable in the sight of God our Saviour.

It is good and acceptable to God, that we should so take thought concerning whatever we have in hand, as to have a clear comprehension of what we are about to do, and to plan our business before we enter upon it. And it is right that we should carefully consider, from time to time, what steps we are to take therein; as well as that we should prepare all things beforehand, for the carrying it on in the most effectual manner. This care, termed by some, "the care of the head," it was by no means our Lord's design to condemn.

17. What he here condemns is, the care of the heart; the anxious, uneasy care; the care that hath torment; all such care as does hurt, either to the soul or body. What he forbids is, that care which, sad experience shows, wastes the blood and drinks up the spirits; which anticipates all the misery it fears,

and comes to torment us before the time. He forbids only that care which poisons the blessings of to-day, by fear of what may be to-morrow; which cannot enjoy the present plenty, through apprehensions of future want. This care is not only a sore disease, a grievous sickness of soul, but also an heinous offence against God, a sin of the deepest dye. It is a high affront to the gracious Governor and wise Disposer of all things; necessarily implying, that the great Judge does not do right; that he does not order all things well. It plainly implies, that he is wanting, either in wisdom, if he does not know what things we stand in need of; or in goodness, if he does not provide those things for all who put their trust in him. Beware, therefore, that you take not thought in this sense: Be ye anxiously careful for nothing. Take no uneasy thought: This is a plain, sure rule, Uneasy care is unlawful care. With a single eye to God, do all that in you lies to provide things honest in the sight of all men. And then give up all into better hands; leave the whole event to God.

18. "Take no thought" of this kind, no uneasy thought, even "for your life, what ye shall eat, or what ye shall drink; nor yet for your body, what ye shall put on. Is not the life more than meat, and the body than raiment?" If then God gave you life, the greater gift, will he not give you food to sustain it? If he hath given you the body, how can ye doubt but he will give you raiment to cover it? More especially, if you give yourselves up to him, and serve him with your whole heart. "Behold," see before your eyes, "the fowls of the air: For they sow not, neither do they reap, nor gather into barns;" and yet they lack nothing; "yet your heavenly Father feedeth them. Are ye not much better than they?" Ye that are creatures capable of God, are ye not of more account in the eyes of God? of a higher rank in the scale of beings? "And which of you, by taking thought, can add one cubit to his stature?" What profit have you then from this anxious thought? It is every way fruitless and unavailing.

"And why take ye thought for raiment?" Have ye not a daily reproof wherever you turn your eyes? "Consider the lilies of the field, how they grow; they toil not, neither do they spin; and yet I say unto you, that even Solomon in all his glory was not arrayed like one of these. Wherefore, if God so clothe the grass of the field, which to-day is, and to-morrow is cast into the oven," (is cut down, burned up, and seen no more,) "shall he not much more clothe you, O ye of little faith?" you, whom he made to endure for ever and ever, to be pictures of his own eternity! Ye are indeed of little faith; otherwise ye could not doubt of his love and care; no, not for a moment.

19. "Therefore take no thought, saying, What shall we eat," if we lay up no treasure upon earth? "What shall we drink," if we serve God with all our strength, if our eye be singly fixed on him? "Wherewithal shall we be clothed," if we are not conformed to the world, if we disoblige those by whom we might be profited? "For after all these things do the Gentiles seek,"—the Heathens who know not God. But ye are sensible "your heavenly Father knoweth that ye have need of all these things." And he hath pointed out to you an infallible way of being constantly supplied therewith: "Seek ye first the kingdom of God, and his righteousness; and all these things shall be added unto you."

20. "Seek ye first the kingdom of God:"—Before ye give place to any other thought or care, let it be your concern that the God and Father of our Lord Jesus Christ (who "gave his only begotten Son," to the end that, believing in him, "ye might not perish, but have everlasting life") may reign in your heart, may manifest himself in your soul, and dwell and rule there; that he may "cast down every high thing which exalteth itself against the knowledge of God, and bring into captivity every thought to the obedience of Christ." Let God have the sole dominion over you: Let him reign without a rival: Let him possess all your heart, and rule alone. Let him be your one desire, your joy, your love; so that all that is within you may continually cry out, "The Lord God omnipotent reigneth."

"Seek the kingdom of God, and his righteousness." Righteousness is the fruit of God's reigning in the heart. And what is righteousness, but love?—the love of God and of all mankind, flowing from faith in Jesus Christ, and producing humbleness of mind, meekness, gentleness, longsuffering, patience, deadness to the world; and every right disposition of heart, toward God and toward man. And by these it produces all holy actions, whatsoever are lovely or of good report; whatsoever works of faith and labour of love are acceptable to God, and profitable to man.

"His righteousness:"—This is all his righteousness still: It is his own free gift to us, for the sake of Jesus Christ the righteous, through whom alone it is purchased for us. And it is his work; it is He alone that worketh it in us, by the inspiration of the Holy Spirit.

21. Perhaps the well observing this may give light to some other scriptures, which we have not always so clearly understood. St. Paul, speaking in his Epistle to the Romans concerning the unbelieving Jews, saith, "They, being ignorant of God's righteousness, and going about to establish their own righteousness, have not submitted themselves unto the righteousness of God." I believe this may be one sense of the words: They were "ignorant of God's righteousness," not only of the righteousness of Christ, imputed to every believer, whereby all his sins are blotted out, and he is reconciled to the favour of God: But (which seems here to be more immediately understood) they were ignorant of that inward righteousness, of that holiness of heart, which is with the utmost propriety termed God's righteousness; as being both his own free gift through Christ, and his own work, by his almighty Spirit. And because they were "ignorant" of this, they "went about to establish their own righteousness." They laboured to establish that outside righteousness which might very properly be termed their own. For neither was it wrought by the Spirit of God, nor was it owned or accepted of him. They might work this themselves, by their own natural strength; and when they had done, it was a stink in his nostrils. And yet, trusting in this, they would "not submit themselves unto the righteousness of God." Yea, they hardened themselves against that faith whereby alone it was possible to attain it. "For Christ is the end of the law for righteousness to everyone that believeth." Christ, when he said, "It is finished!" put an end to that law,—to the law of external rites and ceremonies, that he might bring in a better

righteousness through his blood, by that one oblation of himself once offered, even the image of God, into the inmost soul of everyone that believeth.

22. Nearly related to these are those words of the Apostle, in his Epistle to the Philippians: "I count all things but dung that I may win Christ;" an entrance into his everlasting kingdom; "and be found in him," believing in him, "not having mine own righteousness, which is of the law, but that which is through the faith of Christ, the righteousness which is of God by faith."—"Not having my own righteousness, which is of the law;" a barely external righteousness, the outside religion I formerly had, when I hoped to be accepted of God because I was, "touching the righteousness which is of the law, blameless;"—"but that which is through the faith of Christ, the righteousness which is of God by faith;" [Phil. 3:8–9] that holiness of heart, that renewal of the soul in all its desires, tempers, and affections, "which is of God," (it is the work of God, and not of man,) "by faith;" through the faith of Christ, through the revelation of Jesus Christ in us, and by faith in his blood; whereby alone we obtain the remission of our sins, and an inheritance among those that are sanctified.

23. "Seek ye first" this "kingdom of God" in your hearts; this righteousness, which is the gift and work of God, the image of God renewed in your souls; "and all these things shall be added unto you;" all things needful for the body; such a measure of all as God sees most for the advancement of his kingdom. These shall be added,—they shall be thrown in, over and above. In seeking the peace and the love of God, you shall not only find what you more immediately seek, even the kingdom that cannot be moved; but also what you seek not,—not at all for its own sake, but only in reference to the other. You shall find in your way to the kingdom, all outward things, so far as they are expedient for you. This care God hath taken upon himself: Cast you all your care upon Him. He knoweth your wants; and whatsoever is lacking he will not fail to supply.

24. "Therefore take no thought for the morrow." Not only, take ye no thought how to lay up treasures on earth, how to increase in worldly substance; take no thought how to procure more food than you can eat, or more raiment than you can put on, or more money than is required from day to day for the plain, reasonable purposes of life;—but take no uneasy thought, even concerning those things which are absolutely needful for the body. Do not trouble yourself now, with thinking what you shall do at a season which is yet afar off. Perhaps that season will never come; or it will be no concern of yours;—before then you will have passed through all the waves, and be landed in eternity. All those distant views do not belong to you, who are but a creature of a day. Nay, what have you to do with the morrow, more strictly speaking? Why should you perplex yourself without need? God provides for you to-day what is needful to sustain the life which he hath given you. It is enough: Give yourself up into his hands. If you live another day, he will provide for that also.

25. Above all, do not make the care of future things a pretence for neglecting present duty. This is the most fatal way of "taking thought for the morrow." And how common is it among men! Many, if we exhort them to keep a conscience void of offence, to abstain from what they are convinced is evil, do not scruple to reply, "How then must we live? Must we not take care of ourselves and of our families?" And this they imagine to be a sufficient reason for continuing in known, wilful sin. They say, and perhaps think, they would serve God now, were it not that they should, by and by, lose their bread. They would prepare for eternity; but they are afraid of wanting the necessaries of life. So they serve the devil for a morsel of bread; they rush into hell for fear of want; they throw away their poor souls, lest they should, some time or other, fall short of what is needful for their bodies!

It is not strange that they who thus take the matter out of God's hand should be so often disappointed of the very things they seek; that, while they throw away heaven to secure the things of earth, they lose the one but do not gain the other. The jealous God, in the wise course of his providence, frequently suffers this. So that they who will not cast their care on God, who, taking thought for temporal things, have little concern for things eternal, lose the very portion which they have chosen. There is a visible blast on all their undertakings; whatsoever they do, it doth not prosper; insomuch that, after they have forsaken God for the world, they lose what they sought, as well as what they sought not: They fall short of the kingdom of God, and his righteousness; nor yet are other things added unto them.

26. There is another way of "taking thought for the morrow," which is equally forbidden in these words. It is possible to take thought in a wrong manner, even with regard to spiritual things; to be so careful about what may be by and by, as to neglect what is now required at our hands. How insensibly do we slide into this, if we are not continually watching unto prayer! How easily are we carried away, in a kind of waking dream, projecting distant schemes, and drawing fine scenes in our own imagination! We think, what good we will do when we are in such a place, or when such a time is come! How useful we will be, how plenteous in good works, when we are easier in our circumstances! How earnestly we will serve God, when once such an hindrance is out of the way! Or perhaps you are now in heaviness of soul: God, as it were, hides his face from you. You see little of the light of his countenance: You cannot taste his redeeming love. In such a temper of mind, how natural is it to say, "O how I will praise God, when the light of his countenance shall be again lifted up upon my soul! How will I exhort others to praise him, when his love is again shed abroad in my heart! Then I will do thus and thus: I will speak for God in all places: I will not be ashamed of the gospel of Christ. Then I will redeem the time: I will use to the uttermost every talent I have received." Do not believe thyself. Thou wilt not do it then, unless thou doest it now. "He that is faithful in that which is little," of whatsoever kind it be, whether it be worldly substance, or the fear or love of God, "will be faithful in that which is much." But if thou now hidest one talent in the earth, thou wilt then hide five: That is, if ever they are given; but there is small reason to expect they ever will. Indeed "unto him that hath,"

that is, uses what he hath, "shall be given, and he shall have more abundantly. But from him that hath not," that is, uses not the grace which he hath already received, whether in a larger or smaller degree, "shall be taken away even that which he hath."

27. And take no thought for the temptations of to-morrow. This also is a dangerous snare. Think not, "When such a temptation comes, what shall I do? how shall I stand? I feel I have not power to resist. I am not able to conquer that enemy." Most true: You have not now the power which you do not now stand in need of. You are not able at this time to conquer that enemy; and at this time he does not assault you. With the grace you have now, you could not withstand the temptations which you have not. But when the temptation comes, the grace will come. In greater trials you will have greater strength. When sufferings abound, the consolations of God will, in the same proportion, abound also. So that, in every situation, the grace of God will be sufficient for you. He doth not suffer you "to be tempted" to-day "above that ye are able to bear;" and "in every temptation he will make a way to escape." "As thy days, so thy strength shall be."

28. "Let the morrow," therefore, "take thought for the things of itself;" that is, when the morrow comes, then think of it. Live thou to-day. Be it thy earnest care to improve the present hour. This is your own; and it is your all. The past is as nothing, as though it had never been. The future is nothing to you. It is not yours; perhaps it never will be. There is no depending on what is yet to come; for you "know not what a day may bring forth." Therefore, live to-day: Lose not an hour: Use this moment; for it is your portion. "Who knoweth the things which have been before him, or which shall be after him under the sun?" The generations that were from the beginning of the world, where are they now? Fled away: Forgotten. They were; they lived their day; they were shook off of the earth, as leaves off of their trees: They mouldered away into common dust! Another and another race succeeded; then they "followed the generation of their fathers, and shall never more see the light." Now is thy turn upon the earth. "Rejoice, O young man, in the days of thy youth! Enjoy the very, very now, by enjoying Him "whose years fail not." Now let thine eye be singly fixed on Him in "whom is no variableness neither shadow of turning!" Now give Him thy heart; now stay thyself on Him: Now be thou holy, as he is holy. Now lay hold on the blessed opportunity of doing his acceptable and perfect will! Now rejoice to "suffer the loss of all things," so thou mayest "win Christ!"

29. Gladly suffer to-day, for his name's sake, whatsoever he permits this day to come upon thee. But look not at the sufferings of to-morrow. "Sufficient unto the day is the evil thereof." Evil it is, speaking after the manner of men; whether it be reproach or want, pain or sickness; but in the language of God, all is blessing: It is a precious balm, prepared by the wisdom of God, and variously dispensed among his children, according to the various sicknesses of their souls. And he gives in one day, sufficient for that day; proportioned to the want and strength of the patient. If, therefore, thou snatchest to-day what belongs to the morrow; if thou addest this to what is given thee already, it will be more than thou canst bear: This is the way not to heal, but to destroy thy own soul. Take, therefore, just as much as he gives thee to-day: To-day, do and suffer his will! To-day, give up thyself, thy body, soul, and spirit to God, through Christ Jesus; desiring nothing, but that God may be glorified in all thou art, all thou doest, all thou sufferest; seeking nothing, but to know God, and his Son Jesus Christ, through the eternal Spirit; pursuing nothing, but to love him, to serve him, and to enjoy him at this hour, and to all eternity!

Now unto "God the Father, who hath made me and all the world;" unto "God the Son, who hath redeemed me and all mankind;" unto "God the Holy Ghost, who sanctifieth me and all the elect people of God;" be honour and praise, majesty, and dominion, for ever and ever! Amen.

30.* UPON OUR LORD'S SERMON ON THE MOUNT DISCOURSE 10

"Judge not, that ye be not judged. For with what judgment ye judge, ye shall be judged; and with what measure ye mete, it shall be measured to you again. And why beholdest thou the mote that is in thy brother's eye, but considerest not the beam that is in thine own eye? Or how wilt thou say to thy brother, Let me pull out the mote out of thine eye; and, behold, a beam is in thine own eye? Thou hypocrite, first cast out the beam out of thine own eye; and then thou shalt see clearly to cast out the mote out of thy brother's eye.

"Give not that which is holy unto the dogs, neither cast ye your pearls before swine; lest they trample them under their feet, and turn again and rend you.

"Ask, and it shall be given you; seek, and ye shall find; knock, and it shall be opened unto you. For everyone that asketh, receiveth; and he that seeketh, findeth; and to him that knocketh, it shall be opened. Or what man is there of you, who, if his son ask bread, will give him a stone? Or if he ask a fish, will give him a serpent? If ye, then, being evil, know how to give good gifts unto your children, how much more shall your Father which is in heaven give good gifts to them that ask him? Therefore all things whatsoever ye would that men should do to you, do ye even so to them; for this is the law and the prophets."

Matt. 7:1–12.

1. Our blessed Lord, having now finished his main design, having first delivered the sum of true religion, carefully guarded against those glosses of men whereby they would make the Word of God of none effect; and having, next, laid down rules touching that right intention which we are to preserve in all our outward actions, now proceeds to point out the main hindrances of this religion, and concludes all with a suitable application.

2. In the fifth chapter, our great Teacher has fully described inward religion in its various branches. He has there laid

---

* [text of the 1872 edition]

before us those dispositions of soul which constitute real Christianity; the tempers contained in that "holiness, without which no man shall see the Lord;" the affections which, when flowing from their proper fountain, from a living faith in God through Christ Jesus, are intrinsically and essentially good, and acceptable to God. In the sixth he hath shown how all our actions likewise, even those that are indifferent in their own nature, may be made holy, and good, and acceptable to God, by a pure and holy intention. Whatever is done without this he declares is of no value with God: Whereas, whatever outward works are thus consecrated to God are, in his sight, of great price.

3. In the former part of this chapter, he points out the most common and most fatal hindrances of this holiness: In the latter, he exhorts us by various motives, to break through all, and secure that prize of our high calling.

4. The first hindrance he cautions us against is judging. "Judge not, that ye be not judged." Judge not others, that ye be not judged of the Lord, that ye bring not vengeance on your own heads. "For with what judgment ye judge, ye shall be judged; and with what measure ye mete, it shall be measured to you again:"—A plain and equitable rule, whereby God permits you to determine for yourselves in what manner he shall deal with you in the judgment of the great day.

5. There is no station of life, nor any period of time, from the hour of our first repenting and believing the gospel till we are made perfect in love, wherein this caution is not needful for every child of God. For occasions of judging can never be wanting. And the temptations to it are innumerable; many whereof are so artfully disguised that we fall into the sin before we suspect any danger. And unspeakable are the mischiefs produced hereby,—always to him that judges another, thus wounding his own soul, and exposing himself to the righteous judgment of God;—and frequently to those who are judged, whose hands hang down, who are weakened and hindered in their course, if not wholly turned out of the way, and caused to turn back even to perdition. Yea, how often when this "root of bitterness springs up," are "many defiled thereby;" by reason whereof the way of truth itself is evil spoken of, and that worthy name blasphemed whereby we are called!

6. Yet it does not appear that our Lord designed this caution only, or chiefly, for the children of God; but rather for the children of the world, for the men who know not God. These cannot but hear of those who are not of the world; who follow after the religion above described; who endeavour to be humble, serious, gentle, merciful, and pure in heart; who earnestly desire such measures of these holy tempers as they have not yet attained, and wait for them in doing all good to all men, and patiently suffering evil. Whoever go but thus far cannot be hid, no more than "a city set upon a hill." And why do not those who 'see' their "good works glorify their Father which is in heaven?" What excuse have they for not treading in their steps?—for not imitating their example and being followers of them, as they are also of Christ? Why, in order to provide an excuse for themselves, they condemn those whom they ought to imitate. They spend their time in finding out their neighbour's faults, instead of amending their own. They are so busied about others going out of the way, that themselves never come into it at all; at least, never get forward, never go beyond a poor dead form of godliness without the power.

7. It is to these more especially that our Lord says, "Why beholdest thou the mote that is in thy brother's eye;"—the infirmities, the mistakes, the imprudence, the weakness of the children of God;—"but considerest not the beam that is in thine own eye?" Thou considerest not the damnable impenitence, the satanic pride, the accursed self-will, the idolatrous love of the world, which are in thyself, and which make thy whole life an abomination to the Lord. Above all, with what supine carelessness and indifference art thou dancing over the mouth of hell! And "how then," with what grace, with what decency or modesty, "wilt thou say to thy brother, Let me pull out the mote out of thine eye;"—the excess of zeal for God, the extreme of self-denial, the too great disengagement from worldly cares and employments, the desire to be day and night in prayer, or hearing the words of eternal life?—"And behold a beam is in thine own eye!" Not a mote, like one of these. "Thou hypocrite!" who pretendest to care for others, and hast no care for thy own soul; who makest a show of zeal for the cause of God, when in truth thou neither lovest nor fearest him! "First cast out the beam out of thine own eye:" Cast out the beam of impenitence! Know thyself! See and feel thyself a sinner! Feel that thy inward parts are very wickedness, that thou art altogether corrupt and abominable, and that the wrath of God abideth on thee! Cast out the beam of pride; abhor thyself; sink down as in dust and ashes; be more and more little, and mean, and base, and vile in thine own eyes! Cast out the beam of self-will! Learn what that meaneth, "If any man will come after me, let him renounce himself." Deny thyself, and take up thy cross daily. Let thy whole soul cry out, "I came down from heaven,"—for so thou didst, thou never-dying spirit, whether thou knowest it or no,—"not to do my own will, but the will of him that sent me." Cast out the beam of love of the world! Love not the world, neither the things of the world. Be thou crucified unto the world, and the world crucified unto thee. Only *use* the world, but *enjoy* God. Seek all thy happiness in him! Above all, cast out the grand beam, that supine carelessness and indifference! Deeply consider, that "one thing is needful;" the one thing which thou hast scarce ever thought of. Know and feel, that thou art a poor, vile, guilty worm, quivering over the great gulf! What art thou? A sinner born to die; a leaf driven before the wind; a vapour ready to vanish away, just appearing, and then scattered into air, to be no more seen! See this! "And then shalt thou see clearly to cast out the mote out of thy brother's eye." Then, if thou hast leisure from the concerns of thy own soul, thou shalt know how to correct thy brother also.

8. But what is properly the meaning of this word, "Judge not?" What is the judging which is here forbidden? It is not the same as evil-speaking, although it is frequently joined therewith. Evil-speaking is the relating anything that is evil concerning an absent person; whereas judging may indifferently refer either to the absent or the present. Neither

does it necessarily imply the speaking at all, but only the thinking evil of another. Not that all kind of thinking evil of others is that judging which our Lord condemns. If I see one commit robbery or murder, or hear him blaspheme the name of God, I cannot refrain from thinking ill of the robber or murderer. Yet this is not evil judging: There is no sin in this, nor anything contrary to tender affection.

9. The thinking of another in a manner that is contrary to love is that judging which is here condemned; and this maybe of various kinds. For, First, we may think another to blame when he is not. We may lay to his charge (at least in our own mind) the things of which he is not guilty; the words which he has never spoke, or the actions which he has never done. Or we may think his manner of acting was wrong, although in reality it was not. And even where nothing can justly be blamed, either in the thing itself or in the manner of doing it, we may suppose his intention was not good, and so condemn him on that ground, at the same time that he who searches the heart sees his simplicity and godly sincerity.

10. But we may not only fall into the sin of judging by condemning the innocent; but also, Secondly, by condemning the guilty to a higher degree than he deserves. This species of judging is likewise an offence against justice as well as mercy; and yet such an offence as nothing can secure us from but the strongest and tenderest affection. Without this we readily suppose one who is acknowledged to be in fault to be more in fault than he really is. We undervalue whatever good is found in him. Nay, we are not easily induced to believe that anything good can remain in him in whom we have found anything that is evil.

11. All this shows a manifest want of that love which *ou logizetai kakon, thinketh no evil;* which never draws an unjust or unkind conclusion from any premises whatsoever. Love will not infer from a persons falling once into an act of open sin that he is accustomed so to do, that he is habitually guilty of it: And if he was habitually guilty once, love does not conclude he is so still, much less, that if he is now guilty of this, therefore he is guilty of other sins also. These evil reasonings all pertain to that sinful judging which our Lord here guards us against; and which we are in the highest degree concerned to avoid, if we love either God or our own souls.

12. But supposing we do not condemn the innocent, neither the guilty any farther than they deserve; still we may not be altogether clear of the snare: For there is a Third sort of sinful judging, which is the condemning any person at all where there is not sufficient evidence. And be the facts we suppose ever so true; yet that does not acquit us. For they ought not to have been supposed, but proved; and till they were, we ought to have formed no judgment; I say, till they were; for neither are we excused; although the facts admit of ever so strong proof, unless that proof be produced before we pass sentence, and compared with the evidence on the other side. Nor can we be excused if ever we pass a full sentence before the accused has spoken for himself. even a Jew might teach us this, as a mere lesson of justice abstracted from mercy and brotherly love. Doth our law, says Nicodemus, judge any man before it hear him, and know what he doeth? (John 7:51.) Yea, a heathen could reply, when the chief of the Jewish nation desired to have judgment against his prisoner, It is not the manner of the Romans to judge "any man, before he that is accused have the accusers face to face, and have licence to answer for himself concerning the crime laid against him."

13. Indeed we could not easily fall into sinful judging were we only to observe that rule which another [Seneca] of those heathen Romans affirms to have been the measure of his own practice. "I am so far," says he, "from lightly believing every mans or any mans evidence against another, that I do not easily or immediately believe a man's evidence against himself. I always allow him second I thoughts, and many times counsel too." Go, thou who art called a Christian, and do likewise, lest the heathen rise and condemn thee in that day!

14. But how rarely should we condemn or judge one another, at least how soon would that evil be remedied, were we to walk by that clear and express rule which our Lord himself has taught us!—"If thy brother shall trespass against thee," or if thou hear or believe that he hath, "go and tell him of his fault, between him and thee alone." This is the first step thou art to take. "But if he will not hear, take with thee one or two more, that in the mouth of two or three witnesses every word may be established." This is the second step. "If he neglect to hear them, tell it unto the church," either to the overseers thereof, or to the whole congregation. Thou hast then done thy part. Then think of it no more, but commend the whole to God.

15. But supposing thou hast by the grace of God "cast the beam out of thine own eye," and dost now "clearly see the mote or the beam which is in thy brother's eye," yet beware thou dost not receive hurt thyself by endeavouring to help him. Still "give not that which is holy unto dogs." Do not lightly account any to be of this number; but if it evidently appear that they deserve the title, then "cast ye not your pearls before swine." Beware of that zeal which is not according to knowledge. For this is another great hindrance in their way who would be "perfect as their heavenly Father is perfect." They who desire this cannot but desire that all mankind should partake of the common blessing. And when we ourselves first partake of the heavenly gift, the divine "evidence of things not seen," we wonder that all mankind do not see the things which we see so plainly; and make no doubt at all but we shall open the eyes of all we have any intercourse with. hence we are for attacking all we meet without delay, and constraining them to see, whether they will or no. And by the ill success of this intemperate zeal, we often suffer in our own souls. To prevent this spending our strength in vain our Lord adds this needful caution (needful to all, but more especially to those who are now warm in their first love,) "Give not that which is holy unto the dogs, neither cast ye your pearls before swine; lest they trample them under foot, and turn again and rend you."

16. "Give not that which is holy unto the dogs." Beware of thinking that any deserve this appellation till there is full and incontestable proof, such as you can no longer resist. But when it is clearly and indisputably proved that they are unholy and wicked men, not only strangers to, but enemies

to God, to all righteousness and true holiness; "give not that which is holy," *to hagion,*—"the holy thing," emphatically so called, unto these. The holy, the peculiar doctrines of the gospel—such as were "hid from the ages and generations" of old, and are now made known to us only by the revelation of Jesus Christ and the inspiration of his Holy Spirit—are not to be prostituted unto these men, who know not if there be any Holy Ghost. Not indeed that the ambassadors of Christ can refrain from declaring them in the great congregation, wherein some of these may probably be; we must speak, whether men will hear or whether they will forbear; but this is not the case with private Christians. They do not bear that awful character; nor are they under any manner of obligation to force these great and glorious truths on them who contradict and blaspheme, who have a rooted enmity against them. Nay, they ought not so to do, but rather to lead them as they are able to bear. Do not begin a discourse with these upon remission of sins and the gift of the Holy Ghost; but talk with them in their own manner, and upon their own principles. With the rational, honourable, and unjust Epicure, reason of "righteousness, temperance, and judgment to come." This is the most probable way to make Felix tremble. Reserve higher subjects for men of higher attainments.

17. "Neither cast ye your pearls before swine." Be very unwilling to pass this judgment on any man. But if the fact be plain and undeniable, if it is clear beyond all dispute, if the swine do not endeavour to disguise themselves, but rather glory in their shame, making no pretence to purity either of heart or life, but working all uncleanness with greediness; then "cast" not ye your pearls before them. Talk not to them of the mysteries of the kingdom; of the things which eye hath not seen, nor ear heard; which of consequence, as they have no other inlets of knowledge, no spiritual senses, it cannot enter into their hearts to conceive. Tell not them of the "exceeding great and precious promises" which God hath given us in the Son of his love. What conception can they have of being made partakers of the divine nature, who do not even desire to escape the corruption that is in the world through lust? Just as much knowledge as swine have of pearls, and as much relish as they have for them, so much relish have they for the deep things of God, so much knowledge of the mysteries of the gospel, who are immersed in the mire of this world, in worldly pleasures, desires, and cares. O cast not those pearls before these, "lest they trample them under their feet!"—lest they utterly despise what they cannot understand, and speak evil of the things which they know not. Nay, it is probable this would not be the only inconvenience which would follow. It would not be strange if they were, according to their nature, to "turn again, and rend you;" if they were to return you evil for good, cursing for blessing, and hatred for your goodwill. Such is the enmity of the carnal mind against God and all the things of God. Such is the treatment you are to expect from these, if you offer them the unpardonable affront of endeavouring to save their souls from death, to pluck them as brands out of the burning.

18. And yet you need not utterly despair even of these, who, for the present, "turn again and rend you." For if all your arguments and persuasives fail, there is yet another remedy left; and one that is frequently found effectual when no other method avails; this is prayer. Therefore whatever you desire or want, either for others or for your own soul, "ask, and it shall be given you; seek, and ye shall find; knock, and it shall be opened unto you." The neglect of this is a Third grand hindrance of holiness. Still we "have not, because we ask not." O how meek and gentle, how lowly in heart, how full of love both to God and men, might ye have been at this day, if you had only asked;—if you had continued instant in prayer! Therefore, now, at least, "ask, and it shall be given unto you." Ask, that ye may throughly experience and perfectly practise the whole of that religion which our Lord has here so beautifully described. It shall then be given you, to be holy as he is holy, both in heart and in all manner of conversation. Seek, in the way he hath ordained, in searching the Scriptures, in hearing his word, in meditating thereon, in fasting, in partaking of the Supper of the Lord, and surely ye shall find: Ye shall find that pearl of great price, that faith which overcometh the world, that peace which the world cannot give, that love which is the earnest of your inheritance. Knock; continue in prayer, and in every other way of the Lord: Be not weary or faint in your mind. Press on to the mark: Take no denial: Let him not go until he bless you. And the door of mercy, of holiness, of heaven, shall be opened unto you.

19. It is in compassion to the hardness of our hearts, so unready to believe the goodness of God, that our Lord is pleased to enlarge upon this head, and to repeat and confirm what he hath spoken. "For everyone," saith he, "that asketh, receiveth;" so that none need come short of the blessing; "and he that seeketh," even everyone that seeketh, "findeth" the love and the image of God; "and to him that knocketh," to everyone that knocketh, the gate of righteousness shall be opened. So that here is no room for any to be discouraged, as though they might ask or seek or knock in vain. Only remember always to pray, to seek, to knock, and not to faint. And then the promise standeth sure. It is firm as the pillars of heaven;—yea, more firm; for heaven and earth shall pass away; but his word shall not pass away.

20. To cut off every pretence for unbelief, our blessed Lord, in the following verses, illustrates yet farther what he had said, by an appeal to what passes in our own breasts. "What man," saith he, "is there of you, whom if his son ask bread, will give him a stone?" Will even natural affection permit you to refuse the reasonable request of one you love? "Or if he ask a fish, will he give him a serpent?" Will he give him hurtful instead of profitable things? So that even from what you feel and do yourselves you may receive the fullest assurance, as on the one hand that no ill effect can possibly attend your asking, so, on the other, that it will be attended with that good effect, a full supply of all your wants. For "if ye, being evil, know I how to give good gifts unto your children, how much more shall your Father which is in heaven," who is pure, unmixed, essential goodness, "give good things to them that ask him!" or, (as he expresses it on another occasion,) "give the Holy Ghost to them that ask him?" In him are included all good things; all wisdom, peace, joy, love; the

whole treasures of holiness and happiness; all that God hath prepared for them that love him.

21. But that your prayer may have its full weight with God, see that ye be in charity with all men; for otherwise it is more likely to bring a curse than a blessing on your own head; nor can you expect to receive any blessing from God while you have not charity towards your neighbour. Therefore, let this hindrance be removed without delay. Confirm your love towards one another, and towards all men. And love them, not in word only, but in deed and in truth. "Therefore all things whatsoever ye would that men should do to you, do ye even so to them; for this is the law and the prophets."

22. This is that royal law, that golden rule of mercy as well as justice, which even the heathen Emperor caused to be written over the gate of his palace; a rule which many believe to be naturally engraved on the mind of everyone that comes into the world. And thus much is certain, that it commends itself, as soon as heard, to every man's conscience and understanding; insomuch that no man can knowingly offend against it without carrying his condemnation in his own breast.

23. "This is the law and the prophets." Whatsoever is written in that law which God of old revealed to mankind, and whatsoever precepts God has given by his holy Prophets which have been since the world began," they are all summed up in these few words, they are all contained in this short direction. And this, rightly understood, comprises the whole of that religion which our Lord came to establish upon earth.

24. It may be understood either in a positive or negative sense. If understood in a negative sense, the meaning is, "Whatever ye would not that men should do to you, do not ye unto them." Here is a plain rule, always ready at hand, always easy to be applied. In all cases relating to your neighbour, make his case your own. Suppose the circumstances to be changed, and yourself to be just as he is now. And then beware that you indulge no temper or thought, that no word pass out of your lips, that you take no step which you should have condemned in him, upon such a change of circumstances. If understood in a direct and positive sense, the plain meaning of it is, "Whatsoever you could reasonably desire of him, supposing yourself to be in his circumstances, that do, to the uttermost of your power, to every child of man."

25. To apply this in one or two obvious instances. It is clear to every man's own conscience, we would not that others should judge us, should causelessly or lightly think evil of us; much less would we that any should speak evil of us,—should publish our real faults or infirmities. Apply this to yourself. Do not unto another what you would not he should do unto you; and you will never more judge your neighbour, never causelessly or lightly think evil of anyone; much less will you speak evil; you will never mention even the real fault of an absent person, unless so far as you are convinced it is absolutely needful for the good of other souls.

26. Again: We would that all men should love and esteem us, and behave towards us according to justice, mercy, and truth.

And we may reasonably desire that they should do us all the good they can do without injuring themselves; yea, that in outward things (according to the known rule,) their superfluities should give way to our conveniencies, their conveniencies to our necessities, and their necessities to our extremities. Now then, let us walk by the same rule: Let us do unto all as we would they should do to us. Let us love and honour all men. Let justice, mercy, and truth govern all our minds and actions. Let our superfluities give way to our neighbour's conveniencies; (and who then will have any superfluities left?) our conveniencies to our neighbour's necessities; our necessities to his extremities.

27. This is pure and genuine morality. This do, and thou shalt live. "As many as walk by this rule, peace be to them, and mercy;" for they are "the Israel of God." But then be it observed, none can walk by this rule (nor ever did from the beginning of the world,) none can love his neighbour as himself, unless he first love God. And none can love God unless he believe in Christ; unless he have redemption through his blood, and the Spirit of God bearing witness with his spirit that he is a child of God. Faith, therefore, is still the root of all, of present as well as future salvation. Still we must say to every sinner, "Believe in the Lord Jesus Christ, and thou shalt be saved." Thou shalt be saved now, that thou mayst be saved for ever; saved on earth, that thou mayst be saved in heaven. Believe in him, and thy faith will work by love. Thou wilt love the Lord thy God because he hath loved thee: Thou wilt love thy neighbour as thyself: And then it will be thy glory and joy, to exert and increase this love; not barely by abstaining from what is contrary thereto, from every unkind thought, word, and action, but by showing all that kindness to every man which thou wouldst he should show unto thee.

31.* UPON OUR LORD'S SERMON ON THE MOUNT DISCOURSE 11

"Enter ye in at the strait gate: For wide is the gate, and broad is the way, which leadeth to destruction, and many there be which go in threat: Because strait is the gate, and narrow is the way, which leadeth unto life, and few there be that find it."

Mat. 7:13, 14.

1. Our Lord, having warned us of the dangers which easily beset us at our first entrance upon real religion, the hinderances which naturally arise from within, from the wickedness of our own hearts; now proceeds to apprize us of the hinderances from without, particularly ill example and ill advice. By one or the other of these, thousands, who once ran well, have drawn back unto perdition;—yea, many of those who were not novices in religion, who had made some progress in righteousness. His caution, therefore, against these he presses upon us with all possible earnestness, and repeats again and again, in variety of expressions, lest by any means we should let it slip. Thus, effectually to guard us against the former, "Enter ye in," saith he, "at the strait gate:

---

* [text of the 1872 edition]

For wide is the gate, and broad is the way, that leadeth to destruction, and many there be which go in thereat: Because strait is the gate, and narrow is the way, which leadeth unto life, and few there be that find it:" To secure us from the latter, "Beware," saith he, "of false prophets." We shall, at present, consider the former only.

2. "Enter ye in," saith our blessed Lord, "at the strait gate: For wide is the gate, and broad is the way, that leadeth to destruction, and many there be which go in thereat: Because strait is the gate, and narrow is the way, which leadeth unto life, and few there be that find it."

3. In these words we may observe, First, the inseparable properties of the way to hell: "Wide is the gate, broad the way, that leadeth to destruction, and many there be that go in thereat:" Secondly, the inseparable properties of the way to heaven: "Strait is that gate, and few there be that find it:" Thirdly, a serious exhortation grounded thereon, "Enter ye in at the strait gate."

I. 1. We may observe, First, the inseparable properties of the way to hell: "Wide is the gate, and broad is the way, that leadeth to destruction, and many there be that go in thereat."

2. Wide indeed is the gate, and broad the way, that leadeth to destruction! For sin is the gate of hell, and wickedness the way to destruction. And how wide a gate is that of sin! How broad is the way of wickedness! The "commandment" of God "is exceeding broad;" as extending not only to all our actions, but to every word which goeth out of our lips, yea, every thought that rises in our heart. And sin is equally broad with the commandment, seeing any breach of the commandment is sin. Yea, rather, it is a thousand times broader; since there is only one way of keeping the commandment; for we do not properly keep it, unless both the thing done, the manner of doing it, and all the other circumstances, are right: But there are a thousand ways of breaking every commandment; so that this gate is wide indeed.

3. To consider this a little more particularly: How wide do those parent-sins extend, from which all the rest derive their being;—that carnal mind which is enmity against God, pride of heart, self-will, and love of the world! Can we fix any bounds to them? Do they not diffuse themselves through all our thoughts, and mingle with all our tempers! Are they not the leaven which leavens, more or less, the whole mass of our affections? May we not, on a close and faithful examination of ourselves, perceive these roots of bitterness continually springing up, infecting all our words, and tainting all our actions? And how innumerable an offspring do they bring forth, in every age and nation! Even enough to cover the whole earth with darkness and cruel habitations.

4. O who is able to reckon up their accursed fruits; to count all the sins, whether against God or our neighbour, not which imagination might paint, but which may be matter of daily, melancholy experience? Nor need we range over all the earth to find them. Survey any one kingdom, any single country, or city, or town; and how plenteous is this harvest! And let it not be one of those which are still overspread with Mahometan or Pagan darkness; but of those which name the name of Christ, which profess to see the light of his glorious Gospel. Go no farther than the kingdom to which we belong, the city wherein we are now. We call ourselves Christians; yea, and that of the purest sort: We are Protestants; Reformed Christians! But alas! who shall carry on the reformation of our opinions into our hearts and lives? Is there not a cause? For how innumerable are our sins;—and those of the deepest dye! Do not the grossest abominations, of every kind, abound among us from day to day? Do not sins of every sort cover the land, as the waters cover the sea? Who can count them? Rather go and count the drops of rain, or the sands on the sea-shore. So "wide is the gate," so "broad is the way, that leadeth to destruction!"

5. "And many there are who go in at" that gate; many who walk in that way;—almost as many as go in at the gate of death, as sink into the chambers of the grave. For it cannot be denied, (though neither can we acknowledge it but with shame and sorrow of heart,) that even in this which is called a Christian country, the generality of every age and sex, of every profession and employment, of every rank and degree, high and low, rich and poor, are walking in the way of destruction. The far greater part of the inhabitants of this city, to this day, live in sin; in some palpable, habitual, known transgression of the law they profess to observe; yea, in some outward transgression, some gross, visible kind of ungodliness or unrighteousness; some open violation of their duty, either to God or man. These then, none can deny, are all in the way that leadeth to destruction. Add to these, those who have a name indeed that they live, but were never yet alive to God; those that outwardly appear fair to men, but are inwardly full of all uncleanness; full of pride or vanity, of anger or revenge, of ambition or covetousness; lovers of themselves, lovers of the world, lovers of pleasure more than lovers of God. These, indeed, may be highly esteemed of men; but they are an abomination to the Lord. And how greatly will these saints of the world swell the number of the children of hell! Yea, add all, whatever they be in other respects, whether they have more or less of the form of godliness, who, "being ignorant of God's righteousness, and seeking to establish their own righteousness," as the ground of their reconciliation to God and acceptance with him, of consequence have not "submitted themselves unto the righteousness which is of God" by faith. Now, all these things joined together in one, how terribly true is our Lord's assertion, "Wide is the gate, and broad is the way, that leadeth to destruction, and many there be who go in thereat!"

6. Nor does this only concern the vulgar herd,—the poor, base, stupid part of mankind. Men of eminence in the world, men who have many fields and yoke of oxen, do not desire to be excused from this. On the contrary, "many wise men after the flesh," according to the human methods of judging, "many mighty," in power, in courage, in riches, many "noble, are called;" called into the broad way, by the world, the flesh, and the devil; and they are not disobedient to that calling. Yea, the higher they are raised in fortune and power, the deeper do they sink into wickedness. The more blessings they have received from God, the more sins do they commit; using their honour or riches, their learning or wisdom, not as means of working out their salvation, but rather of excelling in vice, and so insuring their own destruction!

II. 1. And the very reason why many of these go on so securely in the broad way, is, because it is broad; not considering that this is the inseparable property of the way to destruction. "Many there be," saith our Lord, "which go in thereat:" for the very reason why they should flee from it, even "because strait is the gate, and narrow the way that leadeth unto life, and few there be that find it."

2. This is an inseparable property of the way to heaven. So narrow is the way that leadeth unto life, unto life everlasting,—so strait the gate,—that nothing unclean, nothing unholy, can enter. No sinner can pass through that gate, until he is saved from all his sins. Not only from his outward sins, from his evil "conversation received by tradition from his fathers." It will not suffice, that he hath "ceased to do evil" and "learned to do well:" He must not only be saved from all sinful actions, and from all evil and useless discourse; but inwardly changed, thoroughly renewed in the spirit of his mind: Otherwise he cannot pass through the gate of life, he cannot enter into glory.

3. For, "narrow is the way that leadeth unto life;" the way of universal holiness. Narrow indeed is the way of poverty of spirit; the way of holy mourning; the way of meekness; and that of hungering and thirsting after righteousness. Narrow is the way of mercifulness; of love unfeigned; the way of purity of heart; of doing good unto all men; and of gladly suffering evil, all manner of evil, for righteousness' sake.

4. "And few there be that find it." Alas! How few find even the way of heathen honesty! How few are there that do nothing to another which they would not another should do unto them! How few that are clear, before God, from acts either of injustice or unkindness! How few that do not "offend with their tongue;" that speak nothing unkind, nothing untrue! What a small proportion of mankind are innocent even of outward transgressions! And how much smaller a proportion have their hearts right before God,— clean and holy in his sight! Where are they, whom his all-searching eye discerns to be truly humble; to abhor themselves in dust and ashes, in the presence of God their Saviour; to be deeply and steadily serious, feeling their wants, and "passing the time of their sojourning with fear;" truly meek and gentle, never "overcome of evil, but overcoming evil with good;" thoroughly athirst for God, and continually painting after a renewal in his likeness? How thinly are they scattered over the earth, whose souls are enlarged in love to all mankind; and who love God with all their strength, who have given him their hearts, and desire nothing else in earth or heaven! How few are those lovers of God and man, that spend their whole strength in doing good unto all men; and are ready to suffer all things, yea, death itself, to save one soul from eternal death!

5. But while so few are found in the way of life, and so many in the way of destruction, there is great danger lest the torrent of example should bear us away with them. Even a single example, if it be always in our sight, is apt to make much impression upon us; especially when it has nature on its side, when it falls in with our own inclinations. How great then must be the force of so numerous examples, continually before our eyes; and all conspiring, together with our own hearts to carry us down the stream of nature! How difficult must it be to stem the tide, and to keep ourselves "unspotted in the world!"

6. What heightens the difficulty still more is, that they are not the rude and senseless part of mankind, at least not these alone, who set us the example, who throng the downward way, but the polite, the well-bred, the genteel, the wise, the men who understand the world, the men of knowledge, of deep and various learning, the rational, the eloquent! These are all, or nearly all, against us. And how shall we stand against these? Do not their tongues drop manna; and have they not learned all the arts of soft persuasion?—And of reasoning too; for these are versed in all controversies, and strife of words. It is therefore a small thing with them to prove, that the way is *right*, because it is *broad*; that he who follows a multitude cannot do evil, but only he who will not follow them; that your way must be *wrong*, because it is *narrow*, and because there are so few that find it. These will make it clear to a demonstration, that evil is good, and good is evil; that the way of holiness is the way of destruction, and the way of the world the only way to heaven.

7. O how can unlearned and ignorant men maintain their cause against such opponents! And yet these are not all with whom they must contend, however unequal to the task: For there are many mighty, and noble, and powerful men, as well as wise, in the road that leadeth to destruction; and these have a shorter way of confuting, than that of reason and argument. They usually apply, not to the understanding, but to the fears, of any that oppose them;—a method that seldom fails of success, even where argument profits nothing, as lying level to the capacities of all men; for all can fear, whether they can reason or no. And all who have not a firm trust in God, a sure reliance both on his power and love, cannot but fear to give any disgust to those who have the power of the world in their hands. What wonder, therefore, if the example of these is a law to all who know not God?

8. Many rich are likewise in the broad way. And these apply to the hopes of men, and to all their foolish desires, as strongly and effectually as the mighty and noble to their fears. So that hardly can you hold on in the way of the kingdom, unless you are dead to all below, unless you are crucified to the world, and the world crucified to you, unless you desire nothing more but God.

9. For how dark, how uncomfortable, how forbidding is the prospect on the opposite side! A strait gate! A narrow way! And few finding that gate! Few walking in the way! Besides, even those few are not wise men, not men of learning or eloquence. They are not able to reason either strongly or clearly: They cannot propose an argument to any advantage. They know not how to prove what they profess to believe; or to explain even what they say they experience. Surely such advocates as these will never recommend, but rather discredit, the cause they have espoused.

10. Add to this, that they are not noble, not honourable men: If they were, you might bear with their folly. They are men of no interest, no authority, of no account in the world. They are mean and base; low in life; and such as have no power, if they had the will, to hurt you. Therefore there is nothing at

all to be feared from them; and there is nothing at all to hope: For the greater part of them may say, "Silver and gold have I none;" at least a very moderate share. Nay, some of them have scarce food to eat, or raiment to put on. For this reason, as well as because their ways are not like those of other men, they are everywhere spoken against, are despised, have their names cast out as evil, are variously persecuted, and treated as the filth and offscouring of the world. So that both your fears, your hopes, and all your desires (except those which you have immediately from God,) yea, all your natural passions, continually incline you to return into the broad way.

III. 1. Therefore it is, that our Lord so earnestly exhorts, "Enter ye in at the strait gate." Or, (as the same exhortation is elsewhere expressed,) "Strive to enter in:" *Agonizesthe eiselthein*, strive as in an agony: For many, saith our Lord, shall seek to enter in, indolently strive, "and shall not be able."

2. It is true, he intimates what may seem another reason for this, for their not being able to enter in, in the words which immediately follow these. For after he had said, "Many, I say unto you, will seek to enter in, and shall not be able," he subjoins, "When once the master of the house is risen up, and hath shut to the door, and ye begin to stand without," *arxesthe exo estanai*, rather, *ye stand without*; for *arxesthe* seems to be only an elegant expletive,—"and to knock at the door, saying, Lord, Lord, open unto us; he shall answer and say unto you, I know you not: Depart from me, all ye workers of iniquity." (Luke 13:24.)

3. It may appear, upon a transient view of these words, that their delaying to seek at all, rather than their manner of seeking, was the reason why they were not able to enter in. But it comes, in effect, to the same thing. They were, therefore, commanded to depart, because they had been "workers of iniquity;" because they had walked in the broad road; in other words, because they had not agonized to "enter in at the strait gate." Probably they did *seek*, before the door was shut; but that did not suffice: And they did *strive*, after the door was shut; but then it was too late.

4. Therefore strive ye now, in this your day, to "enter in at the strait gate." And in order thereto, settle it in your heart, and let it be ever uppermost in your thoughts, that if you are in a broad way, you are in the way that leadeth to destruction. If many go with you, as sure as God is true, both they and you are going to hell! If you are walking as the generality of men walk, you are walking to the bottomless pit! Are many wise, many rich, many mighty, or noble travelling with you in the same way? By this token, without going any farther, you know it does not lead to life. Here is a short, a plain, an infallible rule, before you enter into particulars. In whatever profession you are engaged, you must be singular, or be damned! The way to hell has nothing singular in it; but the way to heaven is singularity all over. If you move but one step towards God, you are not as other men are. But regard not this. It is far better to stand alone, than to fall into the pit. Run, then, with patience the race which is set before thee, though thy companions therein are but few. They will not always be so. Yet a little while, and thou wilt "come to an innumerable company of angels, to the general assembly and Church of the first-born, and to the spirits of just men made perfect."

5. Now, then, "strive to enter in at the strait gate," being penetrated with the deepest sense of the inexpressible danger your soul is in, so long as you are in a broad way,—so long as you are void of poverty of spirit, and all that inward religion, which the many, the rich, the wise, account madness. "Strive to enter in;" being pierced with sorrow and shame for having so long run on with the unthinking crowd, utterly neglecting, if not despising, that "holiness without which no man can see the Lord." Strive, as in an agony of holy fear, lest "a promise being made you of entering into his rest," even that "rest which remaineth for the people of God," you should nevertheless "come short of it." Strive, in all the fervour of desire, with "groanings which cannot be uttered." Strive by prayer without ceasing; at all times, in all places, lifting up your heart to God, and giving him no rest, till you "awake up after his likeness" and are "satisfied with it."

6. To conclude. "Strive to enter in at the strait gate," not only by this agony of soul, of conviction, of sorrow, of shame, of desire, of fear, of unceasing prayer; but likewise by ordering thy conversation aright, by walking with all thy strength in all the ways of God, the way of innocence, of piety, and of mercy. Abstain from all appearance of evil: Do all possible good to all men: Deny thyself, thy own will, in all things, and take up thy cross daily. Be ready to cut off thy right hand, to pluck out thy right eye and cast it from thee; to suffer the loss of goods, friends, health, all things on earth, so thou mayst enter into the kingdom of heaven!

32.* UPON OUR LORD'S SERMON ON THE MOUNT DISCOURSE 12

"Beware of false prophets, which come to you in sheep's clothing, but inwardly are ravenous wolves. Ye shall know them by their fruits. Do men gather grapes of thorns, or figs of thistles? Even so every good tree bringeth forth good fruit, but a corrupt tree bringeth forth evil fruit. A good tree cannot bring forth evil fruit, neither can a corrupt tree bring forth good fruit. Every tree that bringeth not forth good fruit is hewn down and cast into the fire. Wherefore by their fruits ye shall know them."

Matt. 7:15–20.

1. It is scarce possible to express or conceive what multitudes of souls run on to destruction, because they would not be persuaded to walk in a *narrow* way, even though it were the way to everlasting salvation. And the same thing we may still observe daily. Such is the folly and madness of mankind, that thousands of men still rush on in the way to hell, only because it is a *broad* way. They walk in it themselves, because others do: Because so many perish, they will add to the number. Such is the amazing influence of example over the weak,

miserable children of men! It continually peoples the regions of death, and drowns numberless souls in everlasting perdition!

2. To warn mankind of this, to guard as many as possible against this spreading contagion, God has commanded his watchmen to cry aloud, and show the people the danger they are in. For this end he has sent his servants, the Prophets, in their succeeding generations, to point out the narrow path, and exhort all men not to be conformed to this world. But what, if the watchmen themselves fall into the snare against which they should warn others? What, if "the Prophets prophesy deceits?" if they "cause the people to err from the way?" What shall be done if they point out, as the way to eternal life, what is in truth the way to eternal death; and exhort others to walk, as they do themselves, in the broad, not the narrow way?

3. Is this and unheard-of, is it an uncommon thing? Nay, God knoweth it is not. The instances of it are almost innumerable. We may find them in every age and nation. But how terrible is this!—when the ambassadors of God turn agents for the devil!—when they who are commissioned to teach men the way to heaven do in fact teach them the way to hell! These are like the locusts of Egypt, "which eat up the residue that had escaped, that had remained after the hail." They devour even the residue of men that had escaped, that were not destroyed by ill example. It is not, therefore, without cause, that our wise and gracious Master so solemnly cautions us against them: "Beware," saith he, "of false prophets, which come to you in sheep's clothing, but inwardly they are ravening wolves."

4 A caution this of the utmost importance.—That it may the more effectually sink into our hearts, let us inquire, First, who these false prophets are: Secondly, what appearance they put on: And, Thirdly, how we may know what they really are, notwithstanding their fair appearance.

I. 1. We are, First, to inquire who these false prophets are. And this it is needful to do the more diligently, because these very men have so laboured to "wrest this scripture to their own," though not only their own, "destruction." In order, therefore, to cut off all dispute, I shall raise no dust, (as the manner of some is,) neither use any loose, rhetorical exclamations, to deceive the hearts of the simple; but speak rough, plain truths, such as none can deny, who has either understanding or modesty left, and such truths as have the closest connexion with the whole tenor of the preceding discourse: Whereas too many have interpreted these words without any regard to all that went before; as if they bore no manner of relation to the sermon in the close of which they stand.

2. By *prophets* here (as in many other passages of Scripture, particularly in the New Testament) are meant, not those who foretell things to come, but those who speak in the name of God; those men who profess to be sent of God, to teach others the way to heaven.

Those are *false* prophets, who teach a false way to heaven, a way which does not lead thither; or, (which comes in the end to the same point,) who do not teach the true.

3. Every broad way is infallibly a false one. Therefore this is one plain, sure rule, "They who teach men to walk in a broad way, a way that many walk in, are false prophets."

Again: The true way to heaven is a narrow way. Therefore this is another plain, sure rule, "They who do not teach men to walk in a narrow way, to be singular, are false prophets."

4. To be more particular: The only true way to heaven is that pointed out in the preceding sermon. Therefore they are false prophets who do not teach men to walk in this way.

Now the way to heaven pointed out in the preceding sermon is the way of lowliness, mourning, meekness, and holy desire, love of God and of our neighbour, doing good, and suffering evil for Christ's sake. They are, therefore, false prophets, who teach, as the way to heaven, any other way than this.

5. It matters not what they call that other way. They may call it faith; or good works; or faith and works; or repentance; or repentance, faith, and new obedience. All these are good words: But if, under these, or any other terms whatever, they teach men any way distinct from this, they are properly false prophets.

6. How much more do they fall under that condemnation, who speak evil of this good way;—but above all, they who teach the directly opposite way, the way of pride, of levity, of passion, of worldly desires, of loving pleasure more than God, of unkindness to our neighbour, of unconcern for good works, and suffering no evil, no persecution for righteousness' sake!

7. If it be asked, "Why, who ever did teach this, or who does teach it, as the way to heaven?" I answer, Ten thousand wise and honourable men; even all those, of whatever denomination, who encourage the proud, the trifler, the passionate, the lover of the world, the man of pleasure, the unjust or unkind, the easy, careless, harmless, useless creature, the man who suffers no reproach for righteousness' sake, to imagine he is in the way to heaven. These are false prophets in the highest sense of the word. These are traitors both to God and man. These are no other than the first-born of Satan; the eldest sons of Apollyon, the Destroyer. These are far above the rank of ordinary cut-throats; for they murder the souls of men. They are continually peopling the realms of night; and whenever they follow the poor souls whom they have destroyed, "hell shall be moved from beneath to meet them at their coming!"

II. 1. But do they come now in their own shape? By no means. If it were so, they could not destroy. You would take the alarm, and flee for your life. Therefore they put on a quite contrary appearance: (Which was the Second thing to be considered:) "They come to you in sheep's clothing, although inwardly they are ravening wolves."

2. "They come to you in sheep's clothing;" that is, with an appearance of harmlessness. They come in the most mild, inoffensive manner, without any mark or token of enmity. Who can imagine that these quiet creatures would do any hurt to any one? Perhaps they may not be so zealous and active in doing good as one would wish they were. However, you see no reason to suspect that they have even the desire to do any harm. But this is not all.

3. They come, Secondly, with an appearance of usefulness. Indeed to this, to do good, they are particularly called. They are set apart for this very thing. They are particularly commissioned to watch over your soul, and to train you up to eternal life. It is their whole business, to "go about doing good, and healing those that are oppressed of the devil." And you have been always accustomed to look upon them in this light, as messengers of God, sent to bring you a blessing.

4. They come, Thirdly, with an appearance of religion. All they do is for conscience' sake! They assure you, it is out of mere zeal for God, that they are making God a liar. It is out of pure concern for religion, that they would destroy it root and branch. All they speak is only from a love of truth, and a fear lest it should suffer; and, it may be, from a regard for the Church, and a desire to defend her from all her enemies.

5. Above all, they come with an appearance of love. They take all these pains, only for *your* good. They should not trouble themselves about you, but that they have a kindness for you. They will make large professions of their good-will, of their concern for the danger you are in, and of their earnest desire to preserve you from error, from being entangled in new and mischievous doctrines. They should be very sorry to see one who *means* so well, hurried into any extreme, perplexed with strange and unintelligible notions, or deluded into enthusiasm. Therefore it is that they advise you to keep still, in the plain middle way; and to beware of "being righteous overmuch," lest you should "destroy yourself."

III. 1. But how may we know what they really are, notwithstanding their fair appearance? This was the Third thing into which it was proposed to inquire. Our blessed Lord saw how needful it was for all men to know false prophets, however disguised. He saw, likewise, how unable most men were to deduce a truth through a long train of consequences. He therefore gives us a short and plain rule, easy to be understood by men of the meanest capacities, and easy to be applied upon all occasions: "Ye shall know them by their fruits."

2. Upon all occasions you may easily apply this rule. In order to know whether any who speak in the name of God are false or true prophets it is easy to observe, First, What are the fruits of their doctrine as to themselves? What effect has it had upon their lives? Are they holy and unblamable in all things? What effect has it had upon their hearts? Does it appear by the general tenor of their conversation that their tempers are holy, heavenly, divine? that the mind is in them which was in Christ Jesus? That they are meek, lowly, patient, lovers of God and man, and zealous of good works?

3. You may easily observe, Secondly, what are the fruits of their doctrine as to those that hear them;—in many, at least, though not in all; for the Apostles themselves did not convert all that heard them. Have these the mind that was in Christ? And do they walk as he also walked? And was it by hearing these men that they began so to do? Were they inwardly and outwardly wicked till they heard them? If so, it is a manifest proof that those are true Prophets, Teachers sent of God. But if it is not so, if they do not effectually teach either themselves or others to love and serve God, it is a manifest proof that they are false prophets; that God hath not sent them.

4. A hard saying this! How few can bear it! This our Lord was sensible of, and therefore condescends to prove it at large by several clear and convincing arguments. "Do men," says he, "gather grapes of thorns, or figs of thistles?" (Matt. 7:16.) Do you expect that these evil men should bring forth good fruit? As well might you expect that thorns should bring forth grapes, or that figs should grow upon thistles! "Every good tree bringeth forth good fruit; but a corrupt tree bringeth forth evil fruit." (Matt. 5:17.) Every true Prophet, every Teacher whom I have sent, bringeth forth the good fruit of holiness. But a false prophet, a teacher whom I have not sent, brings forth only sin and wickedness. "A good tree cannot bring forth evil fruit, neither can a corrupt tree bring forth good fruit." A true Prophet, a Teacher sent from God, does not bring forth good fruit sometimes only, but always; not accidentally, but by a kind of necessity. In like manner, a false prophet, one whom God hath not sent, does not bring forth evil fruit accidentally or sometimes only, but always, and of necessity. "Every tree that bringeth not forth good fruit is hewn down, and cast into the fire." (Verse 19.) Such infallibly will be the lot of those prophets who bring not forth good fruit, who do not save souls from sin, who do not bring sinners to repentance. "Wherefore," let this stand as an eternal rule, "By their fruits ye shall know them." (Matt. 7:20.) They who, in fact bring the proud, passionate, unmerciful, lovers of the world to be lowly, gentle, lovers of God and man,—they are true Prophets, they are sent from God, who therefore confirms their word. On the other hand, they whose hearers, if unrighteous before, remain unrighteous still, or, at least, void of any righteousness which "exceeds the righteousness of the Scribes and Pharisees,"—they are false prophets; they are not sent of God; therefore their word falls to the ground: And, without a miracle of grace, they and their hearers together will fall into the bottomless pit!

5. O "beware of these false prophets!" For though they "come in sheep's clothing, yet inwardly they are ravening wolves." They only destroy and devour the flock: They tear them in pieces, if there is none to help them. They will not, cannot, lead you in the way to heaven. How should they, when they know it not themselves? O beware they do not turn you out of the way, and cause you to "lose what you have wrought!"

6. But perhaps you will ask, "If there is such danger in hearing them, ought I to hear them at all?" It is a weighty question, such as deserves the deepest consideration, and ought not to be answered but upon the calmest thought, the most deliberate reflection. For many years I have been almost afraid to speak at all concerning it; being unable to determine one way or the other, or to give any judgment upon it. Many reasons there are which readily occur, and incline me to say, "Hear them not." And yet what our Lord speaks concerning the false prophets of his own times seems to imply the contrary. "Then spake Jesus unto the multitude, and to his disciples, saying, The Scribes and the Pharisees sit in Moses' seat,"—are the ordinary, stated Teachers in your Church: "All, therefore, whatsoever they bid you observe, that observe and do. But do not ye after their works; for they say and do not." Now, that these were false prophets, in the highest

sense, our Lord hath shown during the whole course of his ministry; as indeed he does in those very words, "They say and do not." Therefore, by their fruits his disciples could not but know them, seeing they were open to the view of all men. Accordingly, he warns them again and again, to beware of these false prophets. And yet he does not forbid them to hear even these: Nay, he, in effect, commands them so to do, in those words: "All therefore, whatsoever they bid you observe, that observe and do:" For unless they heard them, they could not know, much less observe, whatsoever they bade them do. Here, then, our Lord himself gives a plain direction, both to his Apostles and the whole multitude, in some circumstances, to hear even false prophets, known and acknowledged so to be.

7. But perhaps it will be said, "He only directed to hear them, when they read the Scripture to the congregation." I answer, at the same time that they thus read the Scripture, they generally expounded it too. And here is no kind of intimation that they were to hear the one, and not the other also. Nay, the very terms, "All things whatsoever they bid you observe," exclude any such limitation.

8. Again: Unto them, unto false prophets, undeniably such, is frequently committed (O grief to speak! for surely these things ought not so to be) the administration of the sacrament also. To direct men, therefore, not to hear them, would be, in effect, to cut them off from the ordinances of God. But this we dare not do, considering the validity of the ordinance doth not depend on the goodness of him that administers, but on the faithfulness of Him that ordained it; who will and doth meet us in his appointed ways. Therefore, on this account, likewise, I scruple to say, "Hear not even the false prophets." Even by these who are under a curse themselves, God can and doth give us his blessing. For the bread which they break, we have experimentally known to be "the communion of the body of Christ:" And the cup which God blessed, even by their unhallowed lips, was to us the communion of the blood of Christ.

9. All, therefore, which I can say, is this: in any particular case, wait upon God by humble and earnest prayer, and then act according to the best light you have: Act according to what you are persuaded, upon the whole, will be most for your spiritual advantage. Take great care that you do not judge rashly; that you do not lightly think any to be false prophets: And when you have full proof, see that no anger or contempt have any place in your heart. After this, in the presence and in the fear of God, determine for yourself. I can only say, If by experience you find that the hearing them hurts your soul, then hear them not; then quietly refrain, and hear those that profit you. If, on the other hand, you find it does not hurt your soul, you then may hear them still. Only "take heed how you hear:" Beware of them and of their doctrine. Hear with fear and trembling, lest you should be deceived, and given up, like them, to a strong delusion. As they continually mingle truth and lies, how easily may you take in both together! Hear with fervent and continual prayer to Him who alone teacheth man wisdom. And see that you bring whatever you hear "to the law and to the testimony." Receive nothing untried, nothing till it is weighed in the balance of the sanctuary: Believe nothing they say, unless it is clearly confirmed by passages of holy writ. Wholly reject whatsoever differs therefrom, whatever is not confirmed thereby. And, in particular, reject, with the utmost abhorrence, whatsoever is described as the way of salvation, that is either different from, or short of, the way our Lord has marked out in the foregoing discourse.

10. I cannot conclude without addressing a few plain words to those of whom we have now been speaking. O ye false prophets! O ye dry bones! hear ye, for once, the word of the Lord! How long will ye lie in the name of God, saying, "God hath spoken;" and God hath not spoken by you? How long will ye pervert the right ways of the Lord, putting darkness for light, and light for darkness? How long will ye teach the way of death, and call it the way of life? How long will ye deliver to Satan the souls whom ye profess to bring unto God?

11. "Woe unto you, ye blind leaders of the blind! for ye shut the kingdom of heaven against men. Ye neither go in yourselves, neither suffer ye them that are entering to go in." Them that would "strive to enter in at the strait gate," ye call back into the broad way. Them that have scarce gone one step in the ways of God, you devilishly caution against going too far. Them that just begin to "hunger and thirst after righteousness," you warn not to "be righteous overmuch." Thus you cause them to stumble at the very threshold; yea, to fall and rise no more. O wherefore do ye this? What profit is there in their blood, when they go down to the pit? Miserable profit to you! "They shall perish in their iniquity; but their blood will God require at your hands!"

12. Where are your eyes? Where is your understanding? Have ye deceived others, till you have deceived yourselves also? Who hath required this at your hands, to teach a way which ye never knew? Are you "given up to" so "strong a delusion," that ye not only teach but "believe a lie?" And can you possibly believe that God hath sent you? that ye are His messengers? Nay; if the Lord had sent you, the work of the Lord would prosper in your hand. As the Lord liveth, if ye were messengers of God, he would "confirm the word of his messengers." But the work of the Lord doth not prosper in your hand. You bring no sinners to repentance. The Lord doth not confirm your word; for you save no souls from death.

13. How can you possibly evade the force of our Lord's words,—so full, so strong, so express? How can ye evade knowing yourselves by your fruits,—evil fruits of evil trees? And how should it be otherwise? "Do men gather grapes of thorns, or figs of thistles?" Take this to yourselves, ye to whom it belongs! O ye barren trees, why cumber ye the ground? "Every good tree bringeth forth good fruit." See ye not, that here is no exception? Take knowledge, then, ye are not good trees; for ye do not bring forth good fruit. "But a corrupt tree bringeth forth evil fruit;" and so have ye done from the beginning. Your speaking, as from God, has only confirmed them that heard you in the tempers, if not works, of the devil. O take warning of Him in whose name ye speak, before the sentence he hath pronounced take place: "Every

tree which bringeth not forth good fruit, is hewn down and cast into the fire."

14. My dear brethren, harden not your hearts! You have too long shut your eyes against the light. Open them now before it is too late; before you are cast into outer darkness! Let not any temporal consideration weigh with you; for eternity is at stake. Ye have run before ye were sent. O go no farther! Do not persist to damn yourselves and them that hear you! You have no fruit of your labours. And why is this? Even because the Lord is not with you. But can you go this warfare at your own cost? It cannot be. Then humble yourselves before him. Cry unto him out of the dust, that he may first quicken *thy* soul; give *thee* the faith that worketh by love; that is lowly and meek, pure and merciful, zealous of good works, rejoicing in tribulation, in reproach, in distress, in persecution for righteousness' sake! So shall "the Spirit of glory and of Christ rest upon thee," and it shall appear that God hath sent thee. So shalt thou indeed "do the work of an Evangelist, and make full proof of thy ministry." So shall the word of God in thy mouth be "an hammer that breaketh the rocks in pieces!" It shall then be known by thy fruits that thou art a Prophet of the Lord, even by the children whom God hath given thee. And having "turned many to righteousness," thou shalt "shine as the stars for ever and ever!"

33.* Upon Our Lord's Sermon on the Mount Discourse 13

"Not everyone that saith unto me, Lord, Lord, shall enter into the kingdom of heaven; but he that doeth the will of my Father which is in heaven. Many will say to me in that day, Lord, Lord, have we not prophesied in thy name? and in thy name have cast out devils? and in thy name done many wonderful works? And then will I profess unto them, I never knew you: Depart from me, ye that work iniquity.

"Therefore whosoever heareth these sayings of mine, and doeth them, I will liken him unto a wise man, which built his house upon a rock: And the rain descended, and the floods came, and the winds blew, and beat upon that house; and it fell not: For it was founded upon a rock. And every one that heareth these sayings of mine, and doeth them not, shall be likened unto a foolish man, which built his house upon the sand: And the rain descended, and the floods came, and the winds blew, and beat upon that house; and it fell: And great was the fall of it."

Matt. 7:21–27

1. Our Divine Teacher, having declared the whole counsel of God with regard to the way of salvation, and observed the chief hindrances of those who desire to walk therein, now closes the whole with these weighty words; thereby, as it were, setting his seal to his prophecy, and impressing his whole authority on what he had delivered, that it might stand firm to all generations.

2. For thus saith the Lord, that none may ever conceive there is any other way than this, "Not everyone that saith unto me, Lord, Lord, shall enter into the kingdom of heaven; but he that doeth the will of my Father which is in heaven. Many will say to me in that day, Lord, Lord, have we not prophesied in thy name? and in thy name have cast out devils? and in thy name done many wonderful works? And then will I profess unto them, I never knew you: Depart from me, ye that work iniquity. Therefore, everyone that heareth these sayings of mine, and doeth them not, shall be likened unto a foolish man, which built his house upon the sand: And the rain descended, and the floods came, and the winds blew, and beat upon that house; and it fell: And great was the fall of it."

3. I design, in the following discourse, First, to consider the case of him who thus builds his house upon the sand: Secondly, to show the wisdom of him who builds upon a rock: And, Thirdly, to conclude with a practical application.

I. 1. And, First, I am to consider the case of him who builds his house upon the sand. It is concerning him our Lord saith, "Not everyone that saith unto me, Lord, Lord, shall enter into the kingdom of heaven." And this is a decree which cannot pass; which standeth fast for ever and ever. It therefore imports us, in the highest degree, throughly to understand the force of these words. Now what are we to understand by that expression, "That saith unto me, Lord, Lord?" It undoubtedly means, *that thinks of going to heaven by any other way than that which I have now described.* It therefore implies (to begin at the lowest point) all good words, all verbal religion. It includes whatever creeds we may rehearse, whatever professions of faith we make, whatever number of prayers we may repeat, whatever thanksgivings we read or say to God. We may speak good of his name, and declare his lovingkindness to the children of men. We may be talking of all his mighty acts, and telling of his salvation from day to day. By comparing spiritual things with spiritual we may show the meaning of the oracles of God. We may explain the mysteries of his kingdom, which have been hid from the beginning of the world. We may speak with the tongue of angels, rather than men, concerning the deep things of God. We may proclaim to sinners, "Behold the Lamb of God, who taketh away the sin of the world!" Yea, we may do this with such a measure of the power of God, and such demonstration of his Spirit, as to save many souls from death, and hide a multitude of sins. And yet it is very possible, all this may be no more than saying, "Lord, Lord." After I have thus successfully preached to others, still I myself may be a castaway. I may, in the hand of God, snatch many souls from hell, and yet drop into it when I have done. I may bring many others to the kingdom of heaven, and yet myself never enter there. Reader, if God hath ever blessed my word to thy soul, pray that he may be merciful to me a sinner!

2. The saying, "Lord, Lord," may, Secondly, imply the doing no harm. We may abstain from every presumptuous sin, from every kind of outward wickedness. We may refrain from all those ways of acting or speaking which are forbidden in holy writ. We may be able to say to all those among whom we live, "Which of you convinceth me of sin?" We may have a conscience void of any external offence, towards God and towards man. We may be clear of all uncleanness, ungodliness, and unrighteousness, as to the outward act; or,

(as the Apostle testifies concerning himself,) "touching the righteousness of the law," that is, outward righteousness, "blameless." But yet we are not hereby justified. Still this is no more than saying, "Lord, Lord;" and if we go no farther than this, we shall never "enter into the kingdom of heaven."

3. The saying, "Lord, Lord," may imply, Thirdly, many of what are usually styled good works. A man may attend the supper of the Lord, may hear abundance of excellent sermons, and omit no opportunity of partaking all the other ordinances of God. I may do good to my neighbour, deal my bread to the hungry, and cover the naked with a garment. I may be so zealous of good works as even to "give all my goods to feed the poor." Yea, and I may do all this with a desire to please God, and a real belief that I do please him thereby; (which is undeniably the case of those our Lord introduces, saying unto him, "Lord, Lord;") and still I may have no part in the glory which shall be revealed.

4. If any man marvels at this, let him acknowledge he is a stranger to the whole religion of Jesus Christ; and, in particular, to that perfect portraiture thereof which he has set before us in this discourse. For how far short is all this of that righteousness and true holiness which he has described therein! How widely distant from that inward kingdom of heaven which is now opened in the believing soul,—which is first sown in the heart as a grain of mustard-seed, but afterwards putteth forth great branches, on which grow all the fruits of righteousness, every good temper, and word, and work.

5. Yet as clearly as he had declared this, as frequently as he had repeated, that none who have not this kingdom of God within them shall enter into the kingdom of heaven; our Lord well knew that many would not receive this saying, and therefore confirms it yet again: "Many" (saith he: not one; not a few only: It is not a rare or an uncommon case) "shall say unto me in that day," not only, We have said many prayers; We have spoken thy praise; We have refrained from evil; We have exercised ourselves in doing good;—but, what is abundantly more than this, "We have prophesied in thy name; in thy name have we cast out devils; in thy name done many wonderful works." "We have prophesied;"—we have declared thy will to mankind; we have showed sinners the way to peace and glory. And we have done this "in thy name;" according to the truth of thy gospel; yea, and by thy authority, who didst confirm the word with the Holy Ghost sent down from heaven. For in or by thy name, by the power of thy word and of thy Spirit, "have we cast out devils;" out of the souls which they had long claimed as their own, and whereof they had full and quiet possession. "And in thy name," by thy power, not our own, "have we done many wonderful works;" insomuch that "even the dead heard the voice of the Son of God" speaking by us, and lived. "And then will I profess" even "unto them, I never knew you;" no, not then, when you were "casting out devils in my name:" Even then I did not know you as my own; for your heart was not right toward God. Ye were not yourselves meek and lowly; ye were not lovers of God, and of all mankind; ye were not renewed in the image of God; ye were not holy as I am holy. "Depart from me, ye" who, notwithstanding all this,

are "workers of iniquity;"—*anomia*,—Ye are transgressors of my law, my law of holy and perfect love.

6. It is to put this beyond all possibility of contradiction, that our Lord confirms it by that apposite comparison: "Every one," saith he, "who heareth these sayings of mine, and doeth them not, shall be likened unto a foolish man, which built his house upon the sand. And the rain descended, and the floods came, and the winds blew, and beat upon that house;"—as they will surely do, sooner or later, upon every soul of man; even the floods of outward affliction, or inward temptation; the storms of pride, anger, fear, or desire;—"and it fell: And great was the fall of it:" So that it perished for ever and ever. Such must be the portion of all who rest in anything short of that religion which is above described. And the greater will their fall be, because they "heard those sayings, and" yet "did them not."

II. 1. I am, Secondly, to show the wisdom of him that doeth them, that buildeth his house upon a rock. He indeed is wise, "who doeth the will of my Father which is in heaven." He is truly wise, whose "righteousness exceeds the righteousness of the Scribes and Pharisees." He is poor in spirit; knowing himself even as also he is known. He sees and feels all his sin, and all his guilt, till it is washed away by the atoning blood. He is conscious of his lost estate, of the wrath of God abiding on him, and of his utter inability to help himself, till he is filled with peace and joy in the Holy Ghost. He is meek and gentle, patient toward all men, never "returning evil for evil, or railing for railing, but contrariwise blessing," till he overcomes evil with good. His soul is athirst for nothing on earth, but only for God, the living God. He has bowels of love for all mankind, and is ready to lay down his life for his enemies. He loves the Lord his God with all his heart, and with all his mind, and soul, and strength. He alone shall enter into the kingdom of heaven, who, in this spirit, doeth good unto all men; and who, being for this cause despised and rejected of men, being hated, reproached, and persecuted, rejoices and is "exceeding glad," knowing in whom he hath believed, and being assured these light, momentary afflictions will "work out for him an eternal weight of glory."

2. How truly wise is this man! He knows himself;—an everlasting spirit, which came forth from God, and was sent down into an house of clay, not to do his own will, but the will of Him that sent him. He knows the world;—the place in which he is to pass a few days or years, not as an inhabitant, but as a stranger and sojourner, in his way to the everlasting habitations; and accordingly he uses the world as not abusing it, and as knowing the fashion of it passes away. He knows God;—his Father and his Friend, the parent of all good, the centre of the spirits of all flesh, the sole happiness of all intelligent beings. He sees, clearer than the light of the noon-day sun, that this is the end of man, to glorify Him who made him for himself, and to love and enjoy him for ever. And with equal clearness he sees the means to that end, to the enjoyment of God in glory; even now to know, to love, to imitate God, and to believe in Jesus Christ whom he hath sent.

3. He is a wise man, even in God's account; for "he buildeth his house upon a rock;" upon the Rock of Ages, the

everlasting Rock, the Lord Jesus Christ. Fitly is he so called; for he changeth not: He is "the same yesterday, and to-day, and for ever." To him both the man of God of old, and the Apostle citing his words, bear witness: "Thou, Lord, in the beginning hast laid the foundation of the earth; and the heavens are the works of thine hands: They shall perish; but thou remainest: And they all shall wax old as doth a garment; and as a vesture shalt thou fold them up, and they shall be changed: But thou art the same, and thy years shall not fail." (Heb. 1:10–12) Wise, therefore, is the man who buildeth on Him; who layeth Him for his only foundation; who builds only upon his blood and righteousness, upon what he hath done and suffered for us. On this corner-stone he fixes his faith, and rests the whole weight of his soul upon it. He is taught of God to say, "Lord, I have sinned; I deserve the nethermost hell; but I am justified freely by thy grace, through the redemption that is in Jesus Christ; and the life I now live, I live by faith in Him, who loved me, and gave himself for me:—The life I now live; namely, a divine, heavenly life; a life which is hid with Christ in God. I now live, even in the flesh, a life of love; of pure love both to God and man; a life of holiness and happiness; praising God, and doing all things to his glory."

4. Yet, let not such an one think that he shall not see war any more; that he is now out of the reach of temptation. It still remains for God to prove the grace he hath given: He shall be tried as gold in the fire. He shall be tempted not less than they who know not God: Perhaps abundantly more; for Satan will not fail to try to the uttermost those whom he is not able to destroy. Accordingly, "the rain" will impetuously descend; only at such times and in such a manner as seems good, not to the prince of the power of the air, but to Him "whose kingdom ruleth over all." "The floods," or torrents, will come; they will lift up their waves and rage horribly. But to them also, the Lord that sitteth above the water-floods, that remaineth a King for ever, will say, "Hitherto shall ye come, and no farther: Here shall your proud waves be stayed." "The winds will blow, and beat upon that house," as though they would tear it up from the foundation: But they cannot prevail: It falleth not; for it is founded upon a rock. He buildeth on Christ by faith and love; therefore, he shall not be cast down. He "shall not fear though the earth be moved, and though the hills be carried into the midst of the sea." "Though the waters thereof rage and swell, and the mountains shake at the tempest of the same;" still he "dwelleth under the defence of the Most High, and is safe under the shadow of the Almighty."

III. 1. How nearly then does it concern every child of man, practically to apply these things to himself! diligently to examine on what foundation he builds, whether on a rock or on the sand! How deeply are *you* concerned to inquire, "What is the foundation of *my* hope? Whereon do I build my expectation of entering into the kingdom of heaven? Is it not built on the sand? upon my *orthodoxy*, or right opinions, which, by a gross abuse of words, I have called *faith?* upon my having a set of notions, suppose more rational or scriptural than others have?" Alas! what madness is this! Surely this is building on the sand, or, rather, on the froth of the sea! Say, "I am convinced of this: Am I not again building my hope on what is equally unable to support it? Perhaps on my belonging to 'so excellent a church; reformed after the true Scripture model; blessed with the purest doctrine, the most primitive liturgy, the most apostolical form of government!" These are, doubtless, so many reasons for praising God, as they may be so many helps to holiness; but they are not holiness itself: And if they are separate from it, they will profit me nothing; nay, they will leave me the more without excuse, and exposed to the greater damnation. Therefore, if I build my hope upon this foundation, I am still building upon the sand.

2. You cannot, you dare not, rest here. Upon what next will you build your hope of salvation?—upon your innocence? upon your doing no harm? your not wronging or hurting anyone? Well; allow this plea to be true. You are just in all your dealings; you are a downright honest man; you pay every man his own; you neither cheat nor extort; you act fairly with all mankind; and you have a conscience towards God; you do not live in any known sin. Thus far is well: But still it is not the thing. You may go thus far, and yet never come to heaven. When all this harmlessness flows from a right principle, it is the *least part* of the religion of Christ. But in you it does not flow from a right principle, and therefore is no part at all of religion. So that in grounding your hope of salvation on this, you are still building upon the sand.

3. Do you go farther yet? Do you add to the doing no harm, the attending all the ordinances of God? Do you, at all opportunities, partake of the Lord's supper? use public and private prayer? fast often? hear and search the Scriptures, and meditate thereon? These things, likewise, ought you to have done, from the time you first set your face towards heaven. Yet these things also are nothing, being alone. They are nothing without "the weightier matters of the law." And those you have forgotten: At least, you experience them not:—Faith, mercy, and love of God; holiness of heart; heaven opened in the soul. Still, therefore, you build upon the sand.

4. Over and above all this, are you zealous of good works? Do you, as you have time, do good to all men? Do you feed the hungry, and clothe the naked, and visit the fatherless and widow in their affliction? Do you visit those that are sick? relieve them that are in prison? Is any a stranger, and you take him in? Friend, come up higher! Do you "prophesy" in the "name" of Christ? Do you preach the truth as it is in Jesus? And does the influence of his Spirit attend your word, and make it the power of God unto salvation? Does he enable you to bring sinners from darkness to light, from the power of Satan unto God? Then go and learn what thou hast so often taught, "By grace ye are saved through faith:" "Not by works of righteousness which we have done, but of his own mercy he saveth us." Learn to hang naked upon the cross of Christ, counting all thou hast done but dung and dross. Apply to him just in the spirit of the dying thief, of the harlot with her seven devils! else thou art still on the sand; and, after saving others, thou wilt lose thy own soul.

5. Lord, increase my faith, if I now believe! else, give me faith, though but as a grain of mustard-seed!—But "what doth it profit, if a man say he hath faith, and have not works? Can" that "faith save him?" O no! That faith which hath not works, which doth not produce both inward and outward holiness, which does not stamp the whole image of God on the heart, and purify us as he is pure; that faith which does not produce the whole of the religion described in the foregoing chapters, is not the faith of the gospel, not the Christian faith, not the faith which leads to glory. O beware of this, above all other snares of the devil,—of resting on unholy, unsaving faith! If thou layest stress on this, thou art lost for ever: Thou still buildest thy house upon the sand. When "the rain descends, and the floods come, it will surely fall, and great will be the fall of it."

6. Now, therefore, build thou upon a rock. By the grace of God, know thyself. Know and feel that thou wast shapen in wickedness, and in sin did thy mother conceive thee; and that thou thyself hast been heaping sin upon sin, ever since thou couldst discern good from evil. Own thyself guilty of eternal death; and renounce all hope of ever being able to save thyself. Be it all thy hope, to be washed in his blood, and purified by his Spirit, "who himself bore" all "thy sins in his own body upon the tree." And if thou knowest he hath taken away thy sins, so much the more abase thyself before him, in a continual sense of thy total dependence on him for every good thought, and word, and work, and of thy utter inability to all good unless he "water thee every moment."

7. Now weep for your sins, and mourn after God, till he turns your heaviness into joy. And even then weep with them that weep; and for them that weep not for themselves. Mourn for the sins and miseries of mankind; and see, but just before your eyes, the immense ocean of eternity, without a bottom or a shore, which has already swallowed up millions of millions of men, and is gaping to devour them that yet remain! See here, the house of God eternal in the heavens! there, hell and destruction without a covering!—and thence learn the importance of every moment, which just appears, and is gone for ever!

8. Now add to your seriousness, meekness of wisdom. Hold an even scale as to all your passions, but in particular, as to anger, sorrow, and fear. Calmly acquiesce in whatsoever is the will of God. Learn in every state wherein you are, therewith to be content. Be mild to the good: Be gentle toward all men; but especially toward the evil and the unthankful. Beware, not only of outward expressions of anger, such as calling thy brother, *Raca,* or *Thou fool;* but of every inward emotion contrary to love, though it go no farther than the heart. Be angry at sin, as an affront offered to the Majesty of heaven; but love the sinner still: Like our Lord, who "looked round about upon the Pharisees with anger, being grieved for the hardness of their hearts." He was grieved at the sinners, angry at sin. Thus be thou "angry, and sin not!"

9. Now do thou hunger and thirst, not for "the meat that perisheth, but for that which endureth unto everlasting life." Trample underfoot the world, and the things of the world; all these riches, honours, pleasures. What is the world to thee? Let the dead bury their dead; but follow thou after the image of God. And beware of quenching that blessed thirst, if it is already excited in thy soul, by what is vulgarly called religion; a poor, dull farce, a religion of form, of outside show, which leaves the heart still cleaving to the dust, as earthly and sensual as ever. Let nothing satisfy thee but the power of godliness, but a religion that is spirit and life; the dwelling in God and God in thee; the being an inhabitant of eternity; the entering in by the blood of sprinkling "within the veil," and "sitting in heavenly places with Christ Jesus!"

10. Now, seeing thou canst do all things through Christ strengthening thee, be merciful as thy Father in heaven is merciful! Love thy neighbour as thyself! Love friends and enemies as thy own soul! And let thy love be longsuffering and patient towards all men. Let it be kind, soft, benign; inspiring thee with the most amiable sweetness, and the most fervent and tender affection. Let it rejoice in the truth, wheresoever it is found; the truth that is after godliness. Enjoy whatsoever brings glory to God, and promotes peace and goodwill among men. In love, cover all things,—of the dead and the absent speaking nothing but good; believe all things which may any way tend to clear your neighbour's character; hope all things in his favour; and endure all things, triumphing over all opposition: For true love never faileth, in time or in eternity.

11. Now be thou pure in heart; purified through faith from every unholy affection; "cleansing thyself from all filthiness of flesh and spirit, and perfecting holiness in the fear of God." Being, through the power of his grace, purified from pride, by deep poverty of spirit; from anger, from every unkind or turbulent passion, by meekness and mercifulness; from every desire but to please and enjoy God, by hunger and thirst after righteousness; now love the Lord thy God with all thy heart, and with all thy strength!"

12. In a word: Let thy religion be the religion of the heart. Let it lie deep in thy inmost soul. Be thou little, and base, and mean, and vile (beyond what words can express) in thy own eyes; amazed and humbled to the dust by the love of God which is in Christ Jesus. Be serious. Let the whole stream of thy thoughts, words, and actions flow from the deepest conviction that thou standest on the edge of the great gulf, thou and all the children of men, just ready to drop in, either into everlasting glory or everlasting burnings! Let thy soul be filled with mildness, gentleness, patience, long-suffering towards all men;—at the same time that all which is in thee is athirst for God, the living God; longing to awake up after his likeness, and to be satisfied with it! Be thou a lover of God and of all mankind! In this spirit do and suffer all things! Thus show thy faith by thy works; thus "do the will of thy Father which is in heaven!" And, as sure as thou now walkest with God on earth, thou shalt also reign with him in glory!

34.* THE ORIGINAL, NATURE, PROPERTY, AND USE OF THE LAW

---

* [text from the 1872 edition]

"Wherefore the law is holy, and the commandment holy, and just, and good."

Rom. 7:12

1. Perhaps there are few subjects within the whole compass of religion so little understood as this. The reader of this Epistle is usually told, by the law St. Paul means the Jewish law; and so, apprehending himself to have no concern therewith, passes on without farther thought about it. Indeed some are not satisfied with this account; but observing the Epistle is directed to the Romans, thence infer that the Apostle in the beginning of this chapter alludes to the old Roman law. But as they have no more concern with this, than with the ceremonial law of Moses, so they spend not much thought on what they suppose is occasionally mentioned barely to illustrate another thing.

2. But a careful observer of the Apostle's discourse will not be content with theses light explications of it. And the more he weighs the words, the more convinced he will be, that St. Paul, by the law mentioned in this chapter, does not mean either the ancient law of Rome, or the ceremonial law of Moses. This will clearly appear to all who attentively consider the tenor of his discourse. He begins the chapter, "Know ye not, brethren (for I speak to them that know the law,)" to them who have been instructed therein from their youth, "that the law hath dominion over a man as long as he liveth?" (What! the law of Rome only, or the ceremonial law? No, surely; but the moral law.) "For," to give a plain instance, "the woman which hath an husband is bound by the" moral "law to her husband so long as he liveth; but if the husband be dead, she is loosed from the law of her husband. So then if, while her husband liveth, she be married to another man, she shall be called an adulteress: but if her husband be dead, she is free from that law: so that she is no adulteress, though she be married to another man." From this particular instance the Apostle proceeds to draw that general conclusion: "Wherefore, my brethren," by a plain parity of reason, "ye also are become dead to the law," the whole Mosaic institution, "by the body of Christ," offered for you, and bringing you under a new dispensation: "That ye should" without any blame "be married to another, even to him who is raised from the dead;" and hath thereby given proof of his authority to make the change; "that we should bring forth fruit unto God." And this we can do now, whereas before we could not: "for when we were in the flesh"—under the power of the flesh, that is, of corrupt nature, which was necessarily the case till we knew the power of Christ's resurrection, "the motions of sins, which were by the law,"—which were shown and inflamed by the Mosaic law, not conquered, "did work in our members,"—broke out various ways, "to bring forth fruit unto death." "But now we are delivered from the law;" from that whole moral, as well as ceremonial economy; "that being dead whereby we were held;"—that entire institution being now as it were dead, and having no more authority over us than the husband, when dead, hath over his wife: "That we should serve him,"—who died for us and rose again, "in newness of spirit;"—in a new spiritual dispensation; "and not in the oldness of the letter;"—with a bare outward service, according to the letter of the Mosaic institution (Rom. 7:1–6.)

3. The Apostle, having gone thus far in proving that the Christian had set aside the Jewish dispensation, and that the moral law itself, though it could never pass away, yet stood on a different foundation from what it did before,—now stops to propose and answer an objection: "What shall we say then? Is the law sin?" So some might infer from a misapprehension of those words, "the motions of sins, which were by the law." "God forbid!" saith the Apostle, that we should say so. Nay, the law is an irreconcilable enemy to sin; by the law: for I had not known lust," evil desire, to be sin, "except the law had said, Thou shalt not covet" (Rom. 7:7.) After opening this farther, in the four following verses, he subjoins this general conclusion, with regard more especially to the moral law, form which the preceding instance was taken: "Wherefore the law is holy, and the commandment holy, and just, and good."

4. In order to explain and enforce these deep words, so little regarded, because so little understood, I shall endeavour to show, First, the original of this law: Secondly, the nature thereof: Thirdly, the properties; that it is holy, and just, and good. And, Fourthly, the uses of it.

I. 1. I shall, first, endeavour to show the original of the moral law, often called "the law," by way of eminence. Now this is not, as some may have possibly imagined, of so late an institution as the time of Moses. Noah declared it to men long before that time, and Enoch before him. But we may trace its original higher still, even beyond the foundation of the world: to that period, unknown indeed to men, but doubtless enrolled in the annals of eternity, when "the morning stars" first "sang together," being newly called into existence. It pleased the great Creator to make these, his first-born sons, intelligent beings, that they might know him that created them. For this end he endued them with understanding, to discern truth from falsehood, good from evil; and, as a necessary result of this, with liberty,—a capacity of choosing the one and refusing the other. By this they were, likewise, enabled to offer him a free and willing service; a service rewardable in itself, as well as most acceptable to their gracious Master.

2. To employ all the faculties which he had given them, particularly their understanding and liberty, he gave the a law, a complete model of all truth, so far as is intelligible to a finite being; and of all good, so far as angelic minds were capable of embracing it. It was also the design of their beneficent Governor herein to make way for a continual increase of their happiness; seeing every instance of obedience to that law would both add to the perfection of their nature, and entitle them to an higher reward, which the righteous Judge would give in its season.

3. In like manner, when God, in his appointed time, had created a new order of intelligent beings, when he had raised man form the dust of the earth, breathed into him the breath of life, and caused him to become a living soul, endued with power to choose good or evil; he gave to this free, intelligent creature the same law as to his first-born children,—not wrote, indeed, upon tables of stone, or any corruptible

substance, but engraven on his heart by the finger of God; wrote in the inmost spirit both of men and of angels; to the intent it might never be far off, never hard to be understood, but always at hand, and always shining with clear light, even as the sun in the midst of heaven.

4. Such was the original of the law of God. With regard to man, it was coeval with his nature; but with regard to the elder sons of God, it shone in its full splendour "or ever the mountains were brought forth, or the earth and the round world were made." But it was not long before man rebelled against God, and, by breaking this glorious law, wellnigh effaced it out of his heart; the eyes of his understanding being darkened in the same measure as his soul was "alienated from the life of God." And yet God did not despise the work of his own hands; but, being reconciled to man through the Son of his love, he, in some measure, re-inscribed the law on the heart of his dark, sinful creature. "He" again "showed thee, O man, what is good," although not as in the beginning, "even to do justly, and to love mercy, and to walk humbly with thy God."

5. And this he showed, not only to our first parents, but likewise to all their posterity, by "that true light which enlightens every man that cometh into the world." But, notwithstanding this light, all flesh had, in process of time, "corrupted their way before him;" till he chose out of mankind a peculiar people, to whom he gave a more perfect knowledge of his law; and the heads of this, because they were slow of understanding, he wrote on two tables of stone, which he commanded the fathers to teach their children, through all succeeding generations.

6. And thus it is, that the law of God is now made known to them that know not God. They hear, with the hearing of the ear, the things that were written aforetime for our instruction. But this does not suffice: they cannot, by this means, comprehend the height, and depth, and length, and breadth thereof. God alone can reveal this by his Spirit. And so he does to all that truly believe, in consequence of that gracious promise made to all the Israel of God: "Behold, the days come, saith the Lord, that I will make a new covenant with the house of Israel. And this shall be the covenant that I will make; I will put My law in their inward parts, and write it in their hearts; and I will be their God, and they shall be My people" (Jer. 31:31 & c.)

II. 1. The nature of that law which was originally given to angels in heaven and man in paradise, and which God has so mercifully promised to write afresh in the hearts of all true believers, was the second thing I proposed to show. In order to which, I would first observe, that although the "law" and the "commandment" are sometimes differently taken (the commandment meaning but a part of the law,) yet, in the text they are used as equivalent terms, implying one and the same thing. But we cannot understand here, either by one or the other, the ceremonial law. It is not the ceremonial law, whereof the Apostle says, in the words above recited, "I had not known sin, but by the law:" this is too plain to need a proof. Neither is it the ceremonial law which saith, in the words immediately subjoined, "Thou shalt not covet."

Therefore the ceremonial law has no place in the present question.

2. Neither can we understand by the law mentioned in the text the Mosaic dispensation. It is true, the word is sometimes so understood; as when the Apostle says, speaking to the Galatians (Gal. 3:17,) "The covenant that was confirmed before;" namely, with Abraham, the father of the faithful, "the law," that is, the Mosaic dispensation, "which was four hundred and thirty years after, cannot disannul." But it cannot be so understood in the text; for the Apostle never bestows so high commendations as these upon that imperfect and shadowy dispensation. He nowhere affirms the Mosaic to be a spiritual law; or, that it is holy, and just, and good. Neither is it true, that God will write that law in the hearts of those whose iniquities he remembers no more. It remains, that "the law," eminently so termed, is no other than the moral law.

3. Now, this law is an incorruptible picture of the High and Holy One that inhabiteth eternity. It is he whom, in his essence, no man hath seen, or can see, made visible to men and angels. It is the face of God unveiled; God manifested to his creatures as they are able to bear it; manifested to give, and not to destroy, life—that they may see God and live. It is the heart of God disclosed to man. Yea, in some sense, we may apply to this law what the Apostle says of his Son: It is *apaugasma tes doxes, kai charakter tes hypostaseos autou the streaming forth or out-beaming of his glory, the express image of his person.*

4. If virtue, said the ancient heathen, could assume such a shape as that we could behold her with our eyes, what wonderful love would she excite in us! If virtue could do this! It is done already. The law of God is all virtues in one, in such a shape as to be beheld with open face by all those whose eyes God hath enlightened. What is the law but divine virtue and wisdom assuming a visible form? What is it but the original ideas of truth and good, which were lodged in the uncreated mind from eternity, now drawn forth and clothed with such a vehicle as to appear even to human understanding?

5. If we survey the law of God in another point of view, it is supreme, unchangeable reason; it is unalterable rectitude, it is the everlasting fitness of all things that are or ever were created. I am sensible, what a shortness, and even impropriety, there is, in these and all other human expressions, when we endeavour by these faint pictures to shadow out the deep things of God. Nevertheless, we have no better, indeed no other way, during this our infant state of existence. As we now know but "in part," so we are constrained to "prophesy," that is, speak of the things of God, "in part" also. "We cannot order our speech by reason of darkness," while we are in this house of clay. While I am "a child," I must "speak as a child:" but I shall soon "put away childish things:" for "when that which is perfect is come, that which is in part shall be done away."

6. But to return. The law of God (speaking after the manner of men) is a copy of the eternal mind, a transcript of the divine nature: Yea, it is the fairest offspring of the everlasting Father, the brightest efflux of his essential wisdom, the visible

beauty of the Most high. It is the delight and wonder of cherubim and seraphim, and all the company of heaven, and the glory and joy of every wise believer, every well-instructed child of God upon earth.

III. 1. Such is the nature of the ever-blessed law of God. I am, in the Third place, to show the properties of it: Not all; for that would exceed the wisdom of an angel; but those only which are mentioned in the text. These are three: it is holy, just, and good. And, First, the law is holy.

2. In this expression the Apostle does not appear to speak of its effects, but rather of its nature: As St. James, speaking of the same thing under another name, says, "The wisdom from above" (which is no other than this law, written in our heart) "is first pure" (Jas. 3:17;) *agne,—chaste, spotless*; eternally and essentially *holy*. And, consequently, when it is transcribed into the life, as well as the soul, it is (as the same Apostle terms it, Jas. 1:27) *threskeia kathara kai amiantos, pure religion and undefiled*; or, the pure, clean, unpolluted worship of God.

3. It is, indeed, in the highest degree, pure, chaste, clean, holy. otherwise it could not be the immediate offspring, and much less the express resemblance, of God, who is essential holiness. It is pure from all sin, clean and unspotted from any touch of evil. It is a chaste virgin, incapable of any defilement, of any mixture with that which is unclean or unholy. It has no fellowship with sin of any kind: For what communion hath light with darkness? As sin is, in its very nature, enmity to God, so his law is enmity to sin.

4. Therefore it is that the Apostle rejects with such abhorrence that blasphemous supposition, that the law of God is either sin itself, or the cause of sin. God forbid that we should suppose it is the cause of sin, because it is the discoverer of it; because it detects the hidden things of darkness, and drags them out into open day. It is true, by this means (as the Apostle observes, Rom. 7:13,) sin appears to be sin. All its disguises are torn away, and it appears in its native deformity. It is true likewise, that sin, by the commandment, becomes exceeding sinful: Being now committed against light and knowledge, being stripped even of the poor plea of ignorance, it loses its excuse, as well as disguise, and becomes far more odious both to God and man. Yea, and it is true, that "sin worketh death by that which is good;" which in itself is pure and holy. When it is dragged out to light, it rages the more: when it is restrained, it bursts out with greater violence. Thus the Apostle (speaking in the person of one who was convinced of sin, but not yet delivered from it,) "Sin, taking occasion by the commandment" detecting and endeavouring to restrain it, disdained the restraint, and so much the more "wrought in me all manner of concupiscence" (Rom. 7:8;) all manner of foolish and hurtful desire, which that commandment sought to restrain. Thus, "when the commandment came, sin revived" (Rom. 7:9;) it fretted and raged the more. But this is no stain on the commandment. Though it is abused, it cannot be defiled. This only proves that "the heart of man is desperately wicked." But "the law" of God "is holy" still.

5. And it is, Secondly, just. It renders to all their due. It prescribes exactly what is right, precisely what ought to be done, said, or thought, both with regard to the Author of our being, with regard to ourselves, and with regard to every creature which he has made. It is adapted, in all respects, to the nature of things, of the whole universe, and every individual. It is suited to all the circumstances of each, and to all their mutual relations, whether such as have existed from he beginning, or such as commenced in any following period. It is exactly agreeable to the fitnesses of things, whether essential or accidental. It clashes with none of these in any degree; nor is ever unconnected with them. If the word be taken in that sense, there is nothing arbitrary in the law of God. Although still the whole and every part thereof is totally dependent upon his will; so that, "Thy will be done," is the supreme, universal law both in earth and heaven.

6. "But is the will of God the cause of his law? Is his will the original of right and wrong? Is a thing *therefore* right, because God wills it? or does he will it because it is right?"

I fear this celebrated question is more curious than useful. And perhaps in the manner it is usually treated of, it does not so well consist with the regard that is due from a creature to the Creator and Governor of all things. It is hardly decent for man to call the supreme God to give an account to him. Nevertheless, with awe and reverence we may speak a little. The Lord pardon us if we speak amiss!

7. It seems, then, that the whole difficulty arises from considering Gods will as distinct from God: otherwise it vanishes away. For none can doubt but God is the cause of the law of God. But the will of God is God himself. It is God considered as willing thus or thus. Consequently, to say that the will of God, or that God himself, is the cause of the law, is one and the same thing.

8. Again: If the law, the immutable rule of right and wrong, depends upon the nature and fitnesses of things, and on their essential relations to each other (I do not say, their eternal relations; because the eternal relation of things existing in time, is little less than a contradiction;) if, I say, this depends on the nature and relations of things, then it must depend on God, or the will of God; because those thing themselves, with all their relations, are the works of his hands. By his will, "for his pleasure" alone, they all "are and were created."

9. And yet it may be granted (which is probably all that a considerate person would contend for,) that in every particular case, God wills this or this (suppose, that men should honour their parents,) because it is right, agreeable to the fitness of things, to the relation wherein they stand.

10. The law, then, is right and just concerning all things. And it is good as well as just. This we may easily infer from the fountain whence it flowed. For what was this, but the goodness of God? What but goodness alone inclined him to impart that divine copy of himself to the holy angels? To what else can we impute his bestowing upon man the same transcript of his own nature? And what but tender love constrained him afresh to manifest his will to fallen man either to Adam, or any of his seed, who like him were "come short of the glory of God?" Was it not mere love that moved him to publish his law after the understandings of men were darkened? and to send his prophets to declare that law to the blind, thoughtless children of men? Doubtless his goodness

it was which raised up enoch and Noah to be preachers of righteousness; which caused Abraham, his friend, and Isaac, and Jacob, to bear witness to his truth. It was his goodness alone, which, when "darkness had covered the earth, and thick darkness the people," gave a written law to Moses, and, through him, to the nation whom he had chosen. It was love which explained these living oracles by David and all the prophets that followed; until, when the fullness of time was come, he sent his only-begotten Son, "not to destroy the law, but to fulfil," confirm every jot and title thereof; till, having wrote it in the hearts of all his children, and put all his enemies under his feet, "he shall deliver up" his mediatorial "kingdom to the Father, that God may be all in all." [1 Cor. 15:28]

11. And this law, which the goodness of God gave at first, and has preserved through all ages, is, like the fountain from whence it springs, full of goodness and benignity; it is mild and kind; it is, as the Psalmist expresses it, "sweeter than honey and the honey-comb." It is winning and amiable. It includes "whatsoever things are lovely or of good report. If there be any virtue, if there be any praise" before God and his holy angels, they are all comprised in this; wherein are hid all the treasures of the divine wisdom, and knowledge, and love.

12. And it is good in its effects, as well as in its nature. As the tree is, so are its fruits. The fruits of the law of God written in the heart are "righteousness, and peace, and assurance for ever." or rather, the law itself is righteousness, filling the soul with a peace which passeth all understanding, and causing us to rejoice evermore, in the testimony of a good conscience toward God. It is to so properly a pledge, as "an earnest, of our inheritance," being a part of the purchased possession. It is God made manifest in our flesh, and bringing with him eternal life; assuring us by that pure and perfect love, that we are "sealed unto the day of redemption;" that he will "spare us as a man spareth his own son that serveth him," "in that day when he maketh up his jewels;" and that there remaineth for us "a crown of glory which fadeth not away."

IV. 1. It remains only to show, in the Fourth and last place, the uses of the law. And the First use of it, without question, is, to convince the world of sin. This is, indeed, the peculiar work of the holy Ghost; who can work it with out any means at all, or by whatever means it pleaseth him, however insufficient in themselves, or even improper, to produce such an effect. And, accordingly, some there are whose hearts have been broken in pieces in a moment, either in sickness or in health, without any visible cause, or any outward means whatever; and others (one in an age) have been awakened to a sense of the "wrath of God abiding on them, by hearing that "God was in Christ, reconciling the world unto himself." But it is the ordinary method of the Spirit of God to convict sinners by the law. It is this which, being set home on the conscience, generally breaketh the rocks in pieces. It is more especially this part of the word of God which is *zon kai energes,—quick and powerful*, full of life and energy, "and sharper than any two edged sword." This, in the hand of God and of those whom he hath sent, pierces through all the folds of a deceitful heart, and "divides asunder even the soul and the spirit;" yea, as it were, the very "joints and marrow." By

this is the sinner discovered to himself. All his fig-leaves are torn away, and he sees that he is "wretched, and poor, and miserable, and blind, and naked." The law flashes conviction on every side. He feels himself a mere sinner. He has nothing to pay. His "mouth is stopped," and he stands "guilty before God."

2. To slay the sinner is, then, the First use of the law; to destroy the life and strength wherein he trusts, and convince him that he is dead while he liveth; not only under the sentence of death, but actually dead unto God, void of all spiritual life, "dead in trespasses and sins." The Second use of it is, to bring him unto life, unto Christ, that he may live. It is true, in performing both these offices, it acts the part of a severe school-master. It drives us by force, rather than draws us by love. And yet love is the spring of all. It is the spirit of love which, by this painful means, tears away our confidence in the flesh, which leaves us no broken reed whereon to trust, and so constrains the sinner, stripped of all, to cry out in the bitterness of his soul, or groan in the depth of his heart,

> I give up every plea beside,—
> Lord, I am damn'd; but Thou hast died.

3. The Third use of the law is, to keep us alive. It is the grand means whereby the blessed Spirit prepares the believer for larger communications of the life of God.

I am afraid this great and important truth is little understood, not only by the world, but even by many whom God hath taken out of the world, who are real children of God by faith. Many of these lay it down as an unquestioned truth, that when we come to Christ, we have done with the law; and that, in this sense, "Christ is the end of the law to every one that believeth." "The end of the law:" so he is, "for righteousness," for justification, "to every one that believeth." Herein the law is at an end. It justifies none, but only brings them to Christ; who is also, in another respect, the end or scope of the law,—the point at which it continually aims. But when it has brought us to him it has yet a farther office, namely, to keep us with him. For it is continually exciting all believers, the more they see of its height, and depth, and length, and breadth, to exhort one another so much the more,—

> Closer and closer let us cleave
> To his beloved Embrace;
> Expect his fullness to receive,
> And grace to answer grace.

4. Allowing then, that every believer has done with the law, as it means the Jewish ceremonial law, or the entire Mosaic dispensation; (for these Christ hath taken out of the way;) yea, allowing we have done with the moral law, as a means of procuring our justification; for we are "justified freely by his grace, through the redemption that is in Jesus"; yet, in another sense, we have not done with this law: for it is still of unspeakable use, First, in convincing us of the sin that yet remains both in our hearts and lives, and thereby keeping us close to Christ, that his blood may cleanse us every moment; Secondly, in deriving strength from our Head into his living members, whereby he empowers them to do what his law commands; and, Thirdly, in confirming our hope of whatsoever it commands and we have not yet attained,—of

receiving grace upon grace, till we are in actual possession of the fulness of his promises.

5. How clearly does this agree with the experience of every true believer! While he cries out, "O what love have I unto thy law! all the day long is my study in it;" he sees daily, in that divine mirror, more and more of his own sinfulness. He sees more and more clearly, that he is still a sinner in all things,—that neither his heart nor his ways are right before God; and that every moment sends him to Christ. This shows him the meaning of what is written, "Thou shalt make a plate of pure gold, and grave upon it, Holiness to the Lord. And it shall be upon Aaron's forehead," (the type of our great High-Priest,) "that Aaron may bear the iniquity of the holy things, which the children of Israel shall hallow in all their holy gifts" (so far are our prayers or holy things from atoning for the rest of our sin!) "and it shall be always upon his forehead, that they may be accepted before the Lord" (Exod. 28:36, 38.)

6. To explain this by a single instance: The law says, "Thou shalt not kill;" and hereby, (as our Lord teaches,) forbids not only outward acts, but every unkind word or thought. Now, the more I look into this perfect law, the more I feel how far I come short of it; and the more I feel this, the more I feel my need of his blood to atone for all my sin, and of his Spirit to purify my heart, and make me "perfect and entire, lacking nothing."

7. Therefore I cannot spare the law one moment, no more than I can spare Christ; seeing I now want it as much to keep me to Christ, as I ever wanted it to bring me to him. Otherwise, this "evil heart of unbelief" would immediately "depart from the living God." Indeed each is continually sending me to the other,—the law to Christ, and Christ to the law. On the one hand, the height and depth of the law constrain me to fly to the love of God in Christ; on the other, the love of God in Christ endears the law to me "above gold or precious stones;" seeing I know every part of it is a gracious promise which my Lord will fulfil in its season.

8. Who art thou then, O man, that "judgest the law, and speakest evil of the law?"—that rankest it with sin, Satan, and death and sendest them all to hell together? The Apostle James esteemed judging or "speaking evil of the law" so enormous a piece of wickedness, that he knew not how to aggravate the guilt of judging our brethren more, than by showing it included this. "So now," says he, "thou art not a doer of the law, but a judge!" A judge of that which God hath ordained to judge thee! So thou hast set up thyself in the judgement-seat of Christ, and cast down the rule whereby he will judge the world! O take knowledge what advantage Satan hath gained over thee; and, for the time to come, never think or speak lightly of, much less dress up as a scarecrow, this blessed instrument of the grace of God. Yea, love and value it for the sake of him from whom it came, and of him to whom it leads. Let it be thy glory and joy, next to the cross of Christ. Declare its praise, and make it honourable before all men.

9. And if thou are thoroughly convinced that it is the offspring of God, that it is the copy of all his inimitable perfections, and that it is "holy, and just, and good," but especially to them that believe; then, instead of casting it away as a polluted thing, see that thou cleave to it more and more. Never let the law of mercy and truth, of love to God and man, of lowliness, meekness, and purity, forsake thee. "Bind it about thy neck; writ it on the table of thy heart." Keep close to the law, if thou wilt keep close to Christ; hold it fast; let it not go. Let this continually lead thee to the atoning blood, continually confirm thy hope, till all the "righteousness of the law is fulfilled in thee," and thou art "filled with all the fullness of God."

10. And if thy Lord hath already fulfilled his word, if he hath already "written his law in thy heart," then "stand fast in the liberty wherewith Christ hath made thee free." Thou art not only made free from Jewish ceremonies, from the guilt of sin, and the fear of hell (these are so far from being the whole, that they are the least and lowest part of Christian liberty;) but, what is infinitely more, from the power of sin, from serving the devil, from offending God. O stand fast in this liberty; in comparison of which, all the rest is not even worthy to be named! Stand fast in loving God with all thy heart, and serving him with all thy strength! This is perfect freedom; thus to keep his law, and to walk in all his commandments blameless. "Be not entangled again with the yoke of bondage." I do not mean of Jewish bondage; nor yet of bondage to the fear of hell: These, I trust, are far from thee. But beware of being entangled again with the yoke of sin, of any inward or outward transgression of the law. Abhor sin far more than death or hell; abhor sin itself, far more than the punishment of it. Beware of the bondage of pride, of desire, of anger; of every evil temper, or word, or work. "Look unto Jesus;" and in order thereto, look more and more into the perfect law, "the law of liberty;" and "continue therein;" so shalt thou daily "grow in grace, and in the knowledge of our Lord Jesus Christ."

35.* THE LAW ESTABLISHED THROUGH FAITH
DISCOURSE I

"Do we then make void the law through faith? God forbid: Yea, we establish the law."

Romans 3:31.

1. St. Paul, having the beginning of this Epistle laid down his general proposition, namely, that "the gospel of Christ is the power of God unto salvation to every one that believeth;"—the powerful means, whereby God makes every believer a partaker of present and eternal salvation;—goes on to show, that there is no other way under heaven whereby men can be saved. He speaks particularly of salvation from the guilt of sin, which he commonly terms justification. And that all men stood in need of this, that none could plead their own innocence, he proves at large by various arguments, addressed to the Jews as well as the Heathens. Hence he infers, (in the 19th verse of this chapter,) "that every mouth," whether of Jew or Heathen, must be "stopped" from excusing or justifying himself, "and all the world become guilty before

* (text from the 1872 edition)

God." "Therefore," saith he, by his own obedience, "by the words of the law, shall no flesh be justified in his sight." "But now the righteousness of God without the law,"—without our previous obedience thereto,—"is manifested;" "even the righteousness of God, which is by faith of Jesus Christ, unto all and upon all that believe:" "For there is no difference,"—as to their need of justification, or the manner wherein they attain it;—"for all have sinned, and come short of the glory of God;—"the glorious image of God wherein they were created: And all (who attain) "are justified freely by his grace, through the redemption that is in Jesus Christ, whom God hath set forth to be a propitiation through faith in his blood; that he might be just, and yet the justifier of him which believeth in Jesus;—"that without any impeachment to his justice, he might show him mercy for the sake of that propitiation. "Therefore we conclude," (which was the grand position he had undertaken to establish,) "that a man is justified by faith, without the works of the law." (Verses 20–28.)

2. It was easy to foresee an objection which might be made, and which has in fact been made in all ages; namely, that to say we are justified without the works of the law, is to abolish the law. The Apostle, without entering into a formal dispute, simply denies the charge. "Do we then," says he, "make void the law through faith? God forbid! Yea, we establish the law."

3. The strange imagination of some, that St. Paul, when he says, "A man is justified without the works of the law," means only ceremonial law, is abundantly confuted by these very words. For did St. Paul establish the ceremonial law? It is evident he did not. He did make void that law through faith, and openly avowed his doing so. It was the moral law only, of which he might truly say, We do not make void, but establish this through faith.

4. But all men are not herein of his mind. Many there are who will not agree to this. Many in all ages of the Church, even among those who bore the name of Christians, have contended, that "the faith once delivered to the saints" was designed to make void the whole law. They would no more spare the moral than the ceremonial law, but were for "hewing," as it were, "both in pieces before the Lord; "vehemently maintaining, "If you establish any law, Christ shall profit you nothing; Christ is become of no effect to you; ye are fallen from grace."

5. But is the zeal of these men according to knowledge? Have they observed the connexion between the law and faith? and that, considering the close connexion between them, to destroy one is indeed to destroy both?—that, to abolish the moral law, is, in truth, to abolish faith and the law together? as leaving no proper means, either of bringing us to faith, or of stirring up that gift of God in our soul.

6. It therefore behoves all who desire either to come to Christ, or to walk in him whom they have received, to take heed how they "make void the law through faith;" to secure us effectually against which, let us inquire, First, Which are the most usual ways of making "void the law through faith?" And, Secondly, how we may follow the Apostle, and by faith "establish the law."

I. 1. Let us, First, inquire, Which are the most usual ways of making void the law through faith? Now the way for a Preacher to make it all void at a stroke, is, not to preach it at all. This is just the same thing as to blot it out of the oracles of God. More especially, when it is done with design; when it is made a rule, not to preach the law; and the very phrase, "a Preacher of the law," is used as a term of reproach, as though it meant little less than an enemy of the gospel.

2. All this proceeds from the deepest ignorance of the nature, properties, and use of the law; and proves, that those who act thus, either know not Christ,—are utter strangers to living faith,—or, at least, that they are but babes in Christ, and, as such, "unskilled in the word of righteousness."

3. Their grand plea is this: That preaching the gospel, that is, according to their judgment, the speaking of nothing but the sufferings and merits of Christ, answers all the ends of the law. But this we utterly deny. It does not answer the very first end of the law, namely, the convincing men of sin; The awakening those who are still asleep on the brink of hell. There may have been here and there an exempt case. One in a thousand may have been awakened by the gospel: But this is no general rule: The ordinary method of God is, to convict sinners by the law, and that only. The gospel is not the means which God hath ordained, or which our Lord himself used, for this end. We have no authority in Scripture for applying it thus, nor any ground to think it will prove effectual. Nor have we any more ground to expect this, from the nature of the thing. "They that be whole," as our Lord himself observes, "need not a physician, but they that are sick." It is absurd, therefore, to offer a physician to them that are whole, or that at least imagine themselves so to be. You are first to convince them that they are sick; otherwise they will not thank you for your labour. It is equally absurd to offer Christ to them whose heart is whole, having never yet been broken. It is, in the proper sense, "casting pearls before swine." Doubtless "they will trample them under foot;" and it is no more than you have reason to expect, if they also "turn again and rend you."

4. "But although there is no command in Scripture, to offer Christ to the careless sinner, yet are there not scriptural precedents for it?" I think not: I know not any. I believe you cannot produce one, either from the four Evangelists, or the Acts of the Apostles. Neither can you prove this to have been the practice of any of the Apostles, from any passage in all their writings.

5. "Nay, does not the Apostle Paul say, in his former Epistle to the Corinthians, 'We preach Christ crucified?' (1:23,) and in his latter, 'We preach not ourselves, but Christ Jesus the Lord?' (4:5.)"

We consent to rest the cause on this issue; to tread in his steps, to follow his example. Only preach you just as Paul preached, and the dispute is at an end.

For although we are certain he preached Christ in as perfect a manner as the very chief of the Apostle, yet who preached the law more than St. Paul? Therefore he did not think the gospel answered the same end.

6. The very first sermon of St. Paul's which is recorded, concludes in these words: "By him all that believe are justified

from all things, from which ye could not be justified by the law of Moses. Beware therefore, lest that come upon you which is spoken of in the Prophets; Behold, ye despisers, and wonder, and perish: For I work a work in your days, a work which you will in no wise believe, though a man declare it unto you." (Acts 13:39, 40.) Now it is manifest, all this is preaching the law, in the sense wherein you understand the term; even although great part of, if not all, his hearers, were either Jews or religious proselytes, (verse 43.) and, therefore, probably many of them, in some degree at least, convicted of sin already. He first reminds them, that they could not be justified by the law of Moses, but only by faith in Christ; and then severely threatens them with the judgments of God, which is in the strongest sense, preaching the law.

7. In his next discourse, that to the Heathens at Lystra, (14·15ff.) we do not find so much as the name of Christ: The whole purport of it is, that they should "turn from those vain idols, unto the living God." Now confess the truth. Do not you think, if you had been there, you could have preached much better than he? I should not wonder if you thought too, that his *preaching so ill* occasioned his being *so ill treated*; and that his being *stoned* was a just judgment upon him for not *preaching Christ*!

8. To the gaoler indeed, when "he sprang in, and came trembling, and fell down before Paul and Silas, and said, Sirs, what must I do to be saved?" he immediately said, "Believe on the Lord Jesus Christ;" (Acts 16:29, 30;) and in the case of one so deeply convicted of sin, who would not have said the same? But to the men of Athens you find him speaking in a quite different manner; reproving their superstition, ignorance, and idolatry; and strongly moving them to repent, from the consideration of a future judgment, and of the resurrection from the dead. (17:24–31.) Likewise when Felix sent for Paul, on purpose that he might "hear him concerning the faith in Christ;" instead of preaching Christ in *your* sense, (which would probably have caused the Governor either to mock or to contradict and blaspheme,) "he reasoned of righteousness, temperance, and judgment to come," till Felix (hardened as he was) "trembled." (24:24, 25.) Go thou, and tread in his steps. Preach Christ to the careless sinner, by reasoning "of righteousness, temperance, and judgment to come!"

9. If you say, "But he preached Christ in a different manner in his Epistles:" I answer, (1.) He did not there preach at all; not in that sense wherein we speak: For preaching, in our present question, means speaking before a congregation. But, waving this, I answer, (2.) His Epistles are directed, not to unbelievers, such as those we are now speaking of, but "to the saints of God," in Rome, Corinth, Philippi, and other places. Now, unquestionably, he would speak more of Christ to these than to those who were without God in the world. And yet, (3.) Every one of these is full of the law, even the Epistles to the Romans and the Galatians; in both of which he does what you term "preaching the law," and that to believers, as well as unbelievers.

10. From hence it is plain, you know not what it is to preach Christ, in the sense of the Apostle. For doubtless St. Paul judged himself to be preaching Christ, both to Felix, and at Antioch, Lystra, and Athens: From whose example every thinking man must infer, that not only the declaring the love of Christ to sinners, but also the declaring that he will come from heaven in flaming fire, is, in the Apostle's sense, preaching Christ; yea, in the full scriptural meaning of the word. To preach Christ, is to preach what he hath revealed, either in the Old or New Testament; so that you are really preaching Christ, when you are saying, "The wicked shall be turned into hell, and all the people that forget God," as when you are saying, "Behold the Lamb of God, which taketh away the sin of the world!"

11. Consider this well;—that to preach Christ, is to preach all things that Christ hath spoken; all his promises; all his threatenings and commands; all that is written in his book; and then you will know how to preach Christ, without making void the law.

12. "But does not the greatest blessing attend those discourses wherein we peculiarly preach the merits and suffering of Christ?"

Probably when we preach to a congregation of mourners, or of believers, these will be attended with the greatest blessing; because such discourses are peculiarly suited to their state. At least, these will usually convey the most comfort. But this is not always the greatest blessing. I may sometimes receive a far greater by a discourse that cuts me to the heart, and humbles me to the dust. Neither should I receive that comfort, if I were to preach or to hear no discourses but on the sufferings of Christ. These, by constant repetition, would lose their force, and grow more and more flat and dead, till at length they would become a dull round of words, without any spirit, or life, or virtue. So that thus to preach Christ must, in process of time, make void the gospel as well as the law.

II. 1. A Second way of making void the law through faith is, the teaching that faith supersedes the necessity of holiness. This divides itself into a thousand smaller paths, and many there are that walk therein. Indeed there are few that wholly escape it; few who are convinced, we are saved by faith, but are sooner or later, more or less, drawn aside into this by-way.

2. All those are drawn into this by-way who, if it be not settled judgment that faith in Christ entirely sets aside the necessity of keeping his law; yet suppose either sets aside the necessity of keeping his law; yet suppose either, (1.) That holiness is less necessary now than it was before Christ came; or, (2.) That a less degree of it is necessary; or, (3.) That it is less necessary to believers than to others. Yea, and so are all those who, although their judgment be right in the general, yet think they may take more liberty in particular cases than they could have done before they believed. Indeed, the using the term *liberty*, in such a manner, for liberty from obedience or holiness, shows at once, that their judgment is perverted, and that they are guilty of what they imagined to be far from them; namely, of making void the law through faith, by supposing faith to supersede holiness.

3. The first plea of those who teach this expressly is, that we are now under the covenant of grace, not works; and therefore we are no longer under the necessity of performing the works of the law.

And who ever was under the covenant of works? None but Adam before the fall. He was fully and properly under that covenant which required perfect, universal obedience, as the one condition of acceptance; and left no place for pardon, upon the very least transgression. But no man else was ever under this, neither Jew nor Gentile; neither before Christ nor since. All his sons were and are under the covenant of grace. The manner of their acceptance is this: The free grace of God, through the merits of Christ, gives pardon to them that believe; that believe with such a faith as, working by love, produces all obedience and holiness.

4. The case is not, therefore, as you suppose, that men were *once* more obliged to obey God, or to work the works of his law, than they are *now*. This is a supposition you cannot make good. But we should have been obliged, if we had been under the covenant of works, to have done those works antecedent to our acceptance. Whereas now all good works, though as necessary as ever, are not antecedent to our acceptance, but consequent upon it. Therefore the nature of the covenant of grace gives you no ground, no encouragement at all, to set aside any insistence or degree of obedience; any part or measure of holiness.

5. "But are we not justified by faith, without the works of the law?" Undoubtedly we are; without the works either of the ceremonial or the moral law. And would to God all men were convicted of this! It would prevent innumerable evils; Antinomianism in particular: For generally speaking, they are the Pharisees who make the Antinomians. Running into an extreme so palpably contrary to Scripture, they occasion others to run into the opposite one. These, seeking to be justified by works, affright those from allowing any place for them.

6. But the truth lies between both. We are, doubtless, justified by faith. This is the corner-stone of the whole Christian building. We are justified without the works of the law, as any previous condition of justification; but they are an immediate fruit of that faith whereby we are justified. So that if good works do not follow our faith, even all inward and outward holiness, it is plain our faith is nothing worth; we are yet in our sins. Therefore, that we are justified by faith, even by our faith without works, is no ground for making void the law through faith; or for imagining that faith is a dispensation from any kind or degree of holiness.

7. "Nay, but does not St. Paul expressly say, 'Unto him that worketh not, but believeth on Him that justifieth the ungodly, his faith is counted for righteousness?' And does it not follow from hence, that faith is to a believer in the room, in the place, of righteousness? But if faith is in the room of righteousness or holiness, what need is there of this too?"

This, it must be acknowledged, comes home to the point, and is, indeed, the main pillar of Antinomianism. And yet it needs not a long or laboured answer. We allow, (1.) That God justifies the ungodly; him that, till that hour, is totally ungodly;—full of all evil, void of all good: (2.) That he justifies the ungodly that worketh not; that, till that moment, worketh no good work;—neither can he; for an evil tree cannot bring forth good fruit: (3.) That he justifies him by faith alone, without any goodness or righteousness preceding:

And, (4.) That faith is then counted to him for righteousness; namely, for preceding righteousness; that is, God, through the merits of Christ, accepts him that believes, as if he had already fulfilled all righteousness. But what is all this to your point? The Apostle does not say, either here or elsewhere, that this faith is counted to him for *subsequent righteousness*. He does teach that there is no righteousness *before* faith; but where does he teach that there is none *after* it? He does assert, holiness cannot *precede* justification; but not, that it need not *follow* it. St. Paul, therefore, gives you no colour for making void the law, by teaching that faith supersedes the necessity of holiness.

III. 1. There is yet another way of making void the law through faith, which is more common than either of the former. And that is, the doing it practically; the making it void in *fact*, though not in *principle*; the *living* as if faith was designed to excuse us from holiness.

How earnestly does the Apostle guard us against this, in those well-known words: "What then? Shall we sin, because we are not under the law, but under grace? God forbid:" (Rom. 6:15:) A caution which it is needful thoroughly to consider, because it is of the last importance.

2. The being "under the law," may here mean, (1.) The being obliged to observe the ceremonial law: (2.) The being obliged to conform to the whole Mosaic institution: (3.) The being obliged to keep the whole moral law, as the condition of our acceptance with God: And, (4.) The being under the wrath and curse of God; under sentence of eternal death; under a sense of guilt and condemnation, full of horror and slavish fear.

3. Now although a believer is "not without law to God, but under the law to Christ," yet from the moment he believes, he is not "under the law," in any of the preceding senses. On the contrary, he is "under grace," under a more benign, gracious dispensation. As he is no longer under the ceremonial law, nor under the Mosaic institution; as he is not obliged to keep even the moral law, as the condition of his acceptance; so he is delivered from the wrath and the curse of God, from all sense of guilt and condemnation, and from all that horror and fear of death and hell whereby he was all his life before subject to bondage. And he now performs (which while "under the law" he could not do) a willing and universal obedience. He obeys not from the motive of slavish fear, but on a nobler principle; namely, the grace of God ruling in his heart, and causing all his works to be wrought in love.

4. What then? Shall this evangelical principle of action be less powerful that the legal? Shall we be less obedient to God from filial love than we were from servile fear?

It is well if this is not a common case; if this practical Antinomianism, this unobserved way of making void the law through faith, has not infected thousands of believers.

Has it not infected you? Examine yourself honestly and closely. Do you not do now what you durst not have done when you was "under the law," or (as we commonly call it) under conviction? For instance: You durst not then indulge yourself in food: You took just what was needful, and that of the cheapest kind. Do you not allow yourself more latitude now? Do you not indulge yourself a *little* more than you did? O beware lest you "sin because you are not under the law, but under grace!"

5. When you was under conviction, you durst not indulge the lust of the eye in any degree. You would not do anything, great or small, merely to gratify your curiosity. You regarded only cleanliness and necessity, or at most very moderate convenience, either in furniture or apparel; superfluity and finery of whatever kind, as well as fashionable elegance, were both a terror and an abomination to you.

Are they so still? Is your conscience as tender now in these things as it was then? Do you still follow the same rule both in furniture and apparel, trampling all finer, all superfluity, every thing useless, every thing merely ornamental, however fashionable, underfoot? Rather, have you not resumed what you had once laid aside, and what you could not then use without wounding you conscience? And have you not learned to say, "O, I am not so scrupulous now?" I would to God you were! Then you would not *sin* thus, "because you are not under the law, but under grace!"

6. You was once scrupulous too of commending any to their face; and still more, of suffering any to commend you. It was a stab to your heart; you could not bear it; you sought the honour that cometh of God only. You could not endure such conversation; nor any conversation which was not good to the use of edifying. All idle talk, all trifling discourse, you abhorred; you hated as well as feared it; being deeply sensible of the value of time, of every precious, fleeting moment. In like manner, you dreaded and abhorred idle expense; valuing your money only less than your time, and trembling lest you should be found an unfaithful steward even of the mammon of unrighteousness.

Do you now look upon praise as deadly poison, which you can neither give nor receive but at the peril of your soul? Do you still dread and abhor all conversation which does not tend to the use of edifying; and labour to improve every moment, that it may not pass without leaving you better than it found you? Are not you less careful as to the expense both of money and time? Cannot you now lay out either, as you could not have done once? Alas! how has that "which should have been for your health, proved to you an occasion of falling!" How have you "sinned because you was not under the law, but under grace!"

7. God forbid you should any longer continue thus to "turn the grace of God into lasciviousness!" O remember how clear and strong a conviction you once had concerning all these things! And, at the same time, you was fully satisfied from whom that conviction came. The world told you, you was in a delusion; but you knew it was the voice of God. In these things you was not too scrupulous then; but you are not now scrupulous enough. God kept you longer in that painful school, that you might learn those great lessons the more perfectly. And have you forgot them already? O recollect them before it is too late! Have you suffered so many things in vain? I trust, it is not yet in vain. Now use the conviction without the pain! Practice the lesson without the rod! Let not the mercy of God weigh less with you now, than his fiery indignation did before. Is love a less powerful motive than fear? If not, let it be an invariable rule, "I will do nothing now I am 'under grace,' which I durst not have done when 'under the law.'"

8. I cannot conclude this head without exhorting you to examine yourself, likewise, touching sins of omission. Are you as clear of these, now you "are under grace," as you was when "under the law?" How diligent was you then in hearing the word of God! Did you neglect any opportunity? Did you not attend thereon day and night? Would a small hinderance have kept you away? a little business? a visitant? a slight indisposition? a soft bed? a dark or cold morning?—Did not you then fast often; or use abstinence to the uttermost of your power? Was not you much in prayer, (cold and heavy as you was,) while you was hanging over the mouth of hell? Did you not speak and not spare even for and unknown God? Did you not boldly plead his cause?—reprove sinners?—and avow the truth before an adulterous generation? And are you now a believer in Christ? Have you the faith that overcometh the world? What! and are less zealous for your Master now, than you was when you knew him not? less diligent in fasting, in prayer, in hearing his word, in calling sinners to God? O repent! See and feel your grievous loss! Remember from whence you are fallen! Bewail your unfaithfulness! Now be zealous and do the first works; lest, if you continue to "make void the law through faith," God cut you off, and appoint you your portion with the unbelievers!

36.* THE LAW ESTABLISHED THROUGH FAITH
DISCOURSE 2

"Do we then make void the law through faith? God forbid! Yea, we establish the law."

Rom. 3:31.

1. It has been shown in the preceding discourse, which are the most usual ways of making void the law through faith; namely, First, the not preaching it at all; which effectually makes it all void a stroke; and this under colour of preaching Christ and magnifying the gospel though it be, in truth, destroying both the one and the other: Secondly, the teaching (whether directly or directly,) that faith supersedes the necessity of holiness; that this less necessary now, or a less degree of it necessary, than before Christ came; that it is less necessary to us, because we believe, than otherwise it would have been; or, that Christian liberty is a liberty from any kind or degree of holiness: (So perverting those great truths, that we are now under the covenant of grace, and not of works; that a man is justified by faith, without the works of the law; and that "to him that worketh not, but believeth, his faith is counted for righteousness:") Or, Thirdly, the doing this practically; the making void the law in practice, though not in principle; the living or acting as if faith was designed to excuse us from holiness; the allowing ourselves in sin, "because we are not under the law, but under grace." It remains to inquire how we may follow a better pattern, how

---

* [text from the 1872 edition]

we may be able to say, with the Apostle, "Do we then make void the law through faith? God forbid: Yea, we establish the law."

2. We do not, indeed, establish the old ceremonial law; we know that is abolished for ever. Much less do we establish the whole Mosaic dispensation; this we know our Lord has nailed to his cross. Nor yet do we so establish the moral law, (which, it is to be feared too many do,) as if the fulfilling it, the keeping all the commandments, were the condition of our justification: If it were so, surely "in His sight should no man living be justified." But all this being allowed, we still, in the Apostle's sense, "establish the law," the moral law.

I. 1. We establish the law, First, by our doctrine; by endeavouring to preach it in its whole extent, to explain and enforce every part of it, in the same manner as our great Teacher did while upon earth. We establish it by following St. Peter's advice: "If any man speak, let him speak as the oracles of God;" as the holy men of old, moved by the Holy Ghost, spoke and wrote for our instruction; and as the Apostles of our blessed Lord, by the direction of the same Spirit. We establish it whenever we speak in his name, by keeping back nothing from them that hear; by declaring to them, without any limitation or reserve, the whole counsel of God. And in order the more effectually to establish it, we use herein great plainness of speech. "We are not as many that *corrupt* the word of God;"—kapEleuontes_, (as artful men their bad wines;) we do not *cauponize, mix, adulterate*, or *soften* it, to make it suit the taste of the hearers:—"But as of sincerity, but as of God, in the sight of God, speak we in Christ;" as having no other aim, than "by manifestation of the truth to commend ourselves to every man's conscience in the sight of God."

2. We then, by our doctrine, establish the law, when we thus openly declare it to all men; and that in the fullness wherein it is delivered by our blessed Lord and his Apostles; when we publish it in the height, and depth, and length, and breadth thereof. We then establish the law, when we declare every part of it, every commandment contained therein, not only in its full, literal sense, but likewise in its spiritual meaning; not only with regard to the outward actions, which it either forbids or enjoins, but also with respect to the inward principle, to the thoughts, desires, and intents of the heart.

3. And indeed this we do the more diligently, not only because it is of the deepest importance;—inasmuch as all the fruit, every word and work, must be only evil continually, if the tree be evil, if the dispositions and tempers of the heart be not right before God;—but likewise because as important as these things are, they are little considered or understood,—so little, that we may truly say of the law, too, when taken in its full spiritual meaning, it is "a mystery which was hid from ages and generations since the world began." It was utterly hid from the heathen world. They, with all their boasted wisdom, neither found out God, nor the law of God; not in the letter, much less in the spirit of it. "Their foolish hearts were" more and more "darkened;" while "professing themselves wise, they became fools." And it was almost equally hid, as to its spiritual meaning, from the bulk of the Jewish nation. Even these, who were so ready to declare concerning others, "this people that know not the law are cursed," pronounced their own sentence therein, as being under the same curse, the same dreadful ignorance. Witness our Lord's continual reproof of the wisest among them for their gross misinterpretations of it. Witness the supposition almost universally received among them, that they needed only to make clean the outside of the cup; that the paying tithe of mint, anise, and cummin,—outward exactness,—would atone for inward unholiness, for the total neglect both of justice and mercy, of faith and the love of God. Yea, so absolutely was the spiritual meaning of the law hidden from the wisest of them, that one of their most eminent Rabbis comments thus on those words of the Psalmist, "If I incline unto iniquity with my heart, the Lord will not hear me:" "That is," saith he, "if it be only in my heart, if I do not commit outward wickedness, the Lord will not regard it; he will not punish me unless I proceed to the outward act!"

4. But alas! the law of God, as to its inward, spiritual meaning, is not hid from the Jews or heathens only, but even from what is called the Christian world; at least, from a vast majority of them. The spiritual sense of the commandments of God is still a mystery to these also. Nor is this observable only in those lands which are overspread with Romish darkness and ignorance. But this is too sure, that the far greater part, even of those who are called *Reformed Christians* are utter strangers at this day to the law of Christ, in the purity and spirituality of it.

5. Hence it is that to this day, " 'the Scribes and Pharisees," the men who have the form but not the power of religion, and who are generally wise in their own eyes, and righteous in their own conceits,—"hearing these things, are offended;" are deeply offended, when we speak of the religion of the heart; and particularly when we show, that without this, were we to "give all our goods to feed the poor," it would profit us nothing. But offended they must be; for we cannot but speak the truth as it is in Jesus. It is our part, whether they will hear, or whether they will forbear, to deliver our own soul. All that is written in the book of God we are to declare, not as pleasing men, but the Lord. We are to declare, not only all the promises, but all the threatenings, too, which we find therein. At the same time that we proclaim all the blessings and privileges which God hath prepared for his children, we are likewise to "teach all the things whatsoever he hath commanded." And we know that all these have their use; either for the awakening those that sleep, the instructing the ignorant, the comforting the feeble-minded, or the building up and perfecting of the saints. We know that "all Scripture, given by inspiration of God is profitable," either "for doctrine," or "for reproof," either "for correction or for instruction in righteousness;" and "that the man of God," in the process of the work of God in his soul, has need of every part thereof, that he may at length "be perfect, throughly furnished unto all good works."

6. It is our part thus to preach Christ, by preaching all things whatsoever he hath revealed. We may indeed, without blame, yea, and with a peculiar blessing from God, declare the love of our Lord Jesus Christ; we may speak, in a more especial manner, of "the Lord our righteousness." We may expatiate

upon the grace of God in Christ, "reconciling the world unto himself;" we may, at proper opportunities, dwell upon his praise, as "bearing the iniquities of us all, as wounded for our transgressions, and bruised for our iniquities, that by his stripes we might be healed:"—But still we should not preach Christ, according to his word, if we were wholly to confine ourselves to this: We are not ourselves clear before God, unless we proclaim him in all his offices. To preach Christ, as a workman that needeth not to be ashamed, is to preach him, not only as our great High Priest, "taken from among men, and ordained for men, in things pertaining to God;" as such, "reconciling us to God by his blood," and "ever living to make intercession for us;"—but likewise as the Prophet of the Lord, "who of God is made unto us wisdom," who, by his word and his Spirit, is with us always, "guiding us into all truth;"—yea, and as remaining a King for ever; as giving laws to all whom he has bought with his blood; as restoring those to the image of God, whom he had first re-instated in his favour; as reigning in all believing hearts until he has "subdued all things to himself,"—until he hath utterly cast out all sin, and brought in everlasting righteousness.

II. 1. We establish the law, Secondly, when we so preach faith in Christ as not to supersede, but produce holiness; to produce all manner of holiness, negative and positive, of the heart and of the life.

In order to this, we continually declare, (what should be frequently and deeply considered by all "who would not make void the law through faith,") that faith itself, even Christian faith, the faith of God's elect, the faith of the operation of God, still is only the handmaid of love. As glorious and honourable as it is, it is not the end of the commandment. God hath given this honour to love alone: Love is the end of all the commandments of God. Love is the end, the sole end, of every dispensation of God, from the beginning of the world to the consummation of all things. And it will endure when heaven and earth flee away; for "love" alone "never faileth." Faith will totally fail; it will be swallowed up in sight, in the everlasting vision of God. But even then love,—

> Its nature and its office still the same,
> Lasting its lamp and unconsumed its flame,—
> In deathless triumph shall for ever live,
> And endless good diffuse, and endless praise receive.

2. Very excellent things are spoken of faith, and whosoever is a partaker thereof may well say with the Apostle, "Thanks be to God for his unspeakable gift." Yet still it loses all its excellence when brought into a comparison with love. What St. Paul observes concerning the superior glory of the gospel above that of the law may with great propriety be spoken of the superior glory of love above that of faith: "Even that which was made glorious hath no glory in this respect, by reason of the glory that excelleth. For if that which is done away is glorious, much more doth that which remaineth exceed in glory" Yea, all the glory of faith, before it is done away, arises hence, that it ministers to love: It is the great temporary means which God has ordained to promote that eternal end.

3. Let those who magnify faith beyond all proportion, so as to swallow up all things else, and who so totally misapprehend the nature of it as to imagine it stands in the place of love, consider farther, that as love will exist after faith, so it did exist long before it. The angels who, from the moment of their creation, beheld the face of their Father that is in heaven, had no occasion for faith, in its general notion, as it is the evidence of things not seen. Neither had they need of faith in its more particular acceptation, faith in the blood of Jesus: for he took not upon him the nature of angels, but only the seed of Abraham. There was therefore no place before the foundation of the world for faith either in the general or particular sense. But there was for love. Love existed from eternity, in God, the great ocean of love. Love had a place in all the children of God, from the moment of their creation. They received at once from their gracious Creator to exist, and to love.

4. Nor is it certain (as ingeniously and plausibly as many have descanted upon this) that faith, even in the general sense of the word, had any place in paradise. It is highly probable, from that short and uncircumstantial account which we have in Holy Writ, that Adam, before he rebelled against God, walked with him by sight and not by faith.

> For then his reason's eye was strong and clear,
> And (as an eagle can behold the sun)
> Might have beheld his Maker's face as near,
> As the' intellectual angels could have done.

He was then able to talk with him face to face, whose face we cannot now see and live; and consequently had no need of that faith whose office it is to supply the want of sight.

5. On the other hand, it is absolutely certain, faith, in its particular sense, had then no place. For in that sense it necessarily presupposes sin, and the wrath of God declared against the sinner; without which there is no need of an atonement for sin in order to the sinner's reconciliation with God. Consequently, as there was no need of an atonement before the fall, so there was no place for faith in that atonement; man being then pure from every stain of sin; holy as God is holy. But love even then filled his heart; it reigned in him without rival; and it was only when love was lost by sin, that faith was added, not for its own sake, nor with any design that it should exist any longer than until it had answered the end for which it was ordained,—namely, to restore man to the love from which he was fallen. At the fall, therefore, was added this evidence of things unseen, which before was utterly needless; this confidence in redeeming love, which could not possibly have any place till the promise was made, that "the Seed of the woman should bruise the serpent's head."

6. Faith, then, was originally designed of God to re-establish the law of love. Therefore, in speaking thus, we are not undervaluing it, or robbing it of its due praise; but on the contrary showing its real worth, exalting it in its just proportion, and giving it that very place which the wisdom of God assigned it from the beginning. It is the grand means of restoring that holy love wherein man was originally created. It follows, that although faith is of no value in itself, (as neither is any other means whatsoever,) yet as it leads to

that end, the establishing anew the law of love in our hearts; and as, in the present state of things, it is the only means under heaven for effecting it; it is on that account an unspeakable blessing to man, and of unspeakable value before God.

III. 1. And this naturally brings us to observe, Thirdly, the most important way of establishing the law; namely, the establishing it in our own hearts and lives. Indeed, without this, what would all the rest avail? We might establish it by our doctrine; we might preach it in its whole extent; might explain and enforce every part of it. We might open it in its most spiritual meaning, and declare the mysteries of the kingdom; we might preach Christ in all his offices, and faith in Christ as opening all the treasures of his love; and yet, all this time, if the law we preached were not established in our hearts, we should be of no more account before God than "sounding brass, or tinkling cymbals:" All our preaching would be so far from profiting ourselves, that it would only increase our damnation.

2. This is, therefore, the main point to be considered, How may we establish the law in our own hearts so that it may have its full influence on our lives? And this can only be done by faith.

Faith alone it is which effectually answers this end, as we learn from daily experience. For so long as we walk by faith, not by sight, we go swiftly on in the way of holiness. While we steadily look, not at the things which are seen, but at those which are not seen, we are more and more crucified to the world and the world crucified to us. Let but the eye of the soul be constantly fixed, not on the things which are temporal, but on those which are eternal, and our affections are more and more loosened from earth, and fixed on things above. So that faith, in general, is the most direct and effectual means of promoting all righteousness and true holiness; of establishing the holy and spiritual law in the hearts of them that believe.

3. And by faith, taken in its more particular meaning, for a confidence in a pardoning God, we establish his law in our own hearts in a still more effectual manner. For there is no motive which so powerfully inclines us to love God, as the sense of the love of God in Christ. Nothing enables us like a piercing conviction of this to give our hearts to him who was given for us. And from this principle of grateful love to God arises love to our brother also. Neither can we avoid loving our neighbour, if we truly believe the love wherewith God hath loved us. Now this love to man, grounded on faith and love to God, "worketh no ill to" our "neighbour." Consequently, it is, as the Apostle observes, "the fulfilling of the" whole negative "law." "For this, Thou shalt not commit adultery; Thou shalt not kill; Thou shalt not steal; Thou shalt not bear false witness; Thou shalt not covet; and if there be any other commandment, it is briefly comprehended in this saying, Thou shalt love thy neighbour as thyself." Neither is love content with barely working no evil to our neighbour. It continually incites us to do good, as we have time and opportunity; to do good, in every possible kind, and in every possible degree, to all men. It is therefore, the fulfilling of the positive, likewise, as well as of the negative, law of God.

4. Nor does faith fulfil either the negative or positive law, as to the external part only; but it works inwardly by love, to the purifying of the heart, the cleansing it from all vile affections. Everyone that hath this faith in himself, "purifieth himself, even as he is pure;"—purifieth himself from every earthly, sensual desire, from all vile and inordinate affections; yea, from the whole of that carnal mind which is enmity against God. At the same time, if it have its perfect work, it fills him with all goodness, righteousness, and truth. It brings all heaven into his soul; and causes him to walk in the light, even as God is in the light.

5. Let us thus endeavour to establish the law in ourselves; not sinning "because we are under grace," but rather using all the power we receive thereby, "to fulfil all righteousness." Calling to mind what light we received from God while his Spirit was convincing us of sin, let us beware we do not put out that light; what we had then attained let us hold fast. Let nothing induce us to build again what we have destroyed; to resume anything, small or great, which we then clearly saw was not for the glory of God, or the profit of our own soul; or to neglect anything, small or great, which we could not then neglect, without a check from our own conscience. To increase and perfect the light which we had before, let us now add the light of faith. Confirm we the former gift of God by a deeper sense of whatever he had then shown us, by a greater tenderness of conscience, and a more exquisite sensibility of sin. Walking now with joy, and not with fear, in a clear, steady sight of things eternal, we shall look on pleasure, wealth, praise-all the things of earth, as on bubbles upon the water; counting nothing important, nothing desirable, nothing worth a deliberate thought, but only what is "within the veil," where Jesus "sitteth at the right hand of God."

6. Can *you* say, "Thou art merciful to my unrighteousness; my sins thou rememberest no more?" Then for the time to come see that you fly from sin, as from the face of a serpent! For how exceeding sinful does it appear to you now! How heinous above all expression! On the other hand, in how amiable a light do you now see the holy and perfect will of God! Now, therefore, labour that it may be fulfilled, both in you, by you, and upon you! Now watch and pray that you may sin no more, that you may see and shun the least transgression of his law! You see the motes which you could not see before, when the sun shines into a dark place. In like manner you see the sins which you could not see before, now the Sun of Righteousness shines in your heart. Now, then, do all diligence to walk, in every respect, according to the light you have received! Now be zealous to receive more light daily, more of the knowledge and love of God, more of the Spirit of Christ, more of his life, and of the power of his resurrection! Now use all the knowledge, and love, and life, and power you have already attained: So shall you continually go on from faith to faith; so shall you daily increase in holy love, till faith is swallowed up in sight, and the law of love established to all eternity!

37.* THE NATURE OF ENTHUSIASM

"And Festus said with a loud voice, Paul, thou art beside thyself."

Acts 26:24.

1. And so say all the world, the men who know not God, of all that are of Paul's religion: of every one who is so a follower of him as he was of Christ. It is true, there is a sort of religion, nay, and it is called Christianity too, which may be practised without any such Imputation, which is generally allowed to be consistent with common sense,—that is, a religion of form, a round of outward duties, performed in a decent, regular manner. You may add orthodoxy thereto, a system of right opinions, yea, and some quantity of heathen morality; and yet not many will pronounce, that "much religion hath made you mad." But if you aim at the religion of the heart, if you talk of "righteousness, and peace, and joy in the Holy Ghost," then it will not be long before your sentence is passed, "Thou art beside thyself."

2. And it is no compliment which the men of the world pay you here. They, for once, mean what they say. They not only affirm, but cordially believe, that every man is beside himself who says, "the love of God is shed abroad in" his "heart by the Holy Ghost given unto him;" and that God has enabled him to rejoice in Christ "with joy unspeakable and full of glory." If a man is indeed alive to God, and dead to all things here below; if he continually sees Him that is invisible, and accordingly walks by faith, and not by sight; then they account it a clear case: beyond all dispute, "much religion hath made him mad."

3. It is easy to observe, that the determinate thing which the world account madness is, that utter contempt of all temporal things, and steady pursuit of things eternal; that divine conviction of things not seen; that rejoicing in the favour of God that happy, holy love of God; and that testimony of His Spirit with our spirit, that we are the children of God,—that is, in truth, the whole spirit, and life, and power of the religion of Jesus Christ.

4. They will, however, allow, in other respects, the man acts and talks like one in his senses. In other things, he is a reasonable man, it is in these instances only his head is touched. It is therefore acknowledged, that the madness under which he labours is of a particular kind; and accordingly they are accustomed to distinguish it by a particular name, "enthusiasm."

5. A term this, which is exceeding frequently used, which is scarce ever out of some men's mouths; and yet it is exceeding rarely understood, even by those who use it most. It may be, therefore, not unacceptable to serious men, to all who desire to understand what they speak or hear, if I endeavour to explain the meaning of this term—to show what enthusiasm is. It may be an encouragement to those who are unjustly charged therewith; and may possibly be of use to some who are justly charged with it; at least to others who might be so, were they not cautioned against it.

6. As to the word itself, it is generally allowed to be of Greek extraction. But whence the Greek word, *enthousiasmos*, is derived, none has yet been able to show. Some have endeavoured to derive it from *en theoi, in God*; because all enthusiasm has reference to him. But this is quite forced; there being small resemblance between the word derived, and those they strive to derive it from. others would derive it from *en thysiai,—in sacrifice*; because many of the enthusiasts of old were affected in the most violent manner during the time of sacrifice. Perhaps it is a fictitious word, invented from the noise which some of those made who were so affected.

7. It is not improbable, that one reason why this uncouth word has been retained in so many languages was, because men were not better agreed concerning the meaning than concerning the derivation of it. They therefore adopted the Greek word, because they did not understand it: they did not translate it into their own tongues, because they knew not how to translate it; it having been always a word of a loose, uncertain sense, to which no determinate meaning was affixed.

8. It is not, therefore, at all surprising, that it is so variously taken at this day; different persons understanding it in different senses, quite inconsistent with each other. Some take it in a good sense, for a divine impulse or impression, superior to all the natural faculties, and suspending, for the time, either in whole or in part, both the reason and the outward senses. In this meaning of the word, both the Prophets of old, and the Apostles, were proper enthusiasts; being, at divers times, so filled with the Spirit, and so influenced by Him who dwelt in their hearts, that the exercise of their own reason, their senses, and all their natural faculties, being suspended, they were wholly actuated by the power of God, and "spake" only "as they were moved by the Holy Ghost."

9. Others take the word in an indifferent sense, such as is neither morally good nor evil: thus they speak of the enthusiasm of the poets; of Homer and Virgil in particular. And this a late eminent writer extends so far as to assert, there is no man excellent in his profession, whatsoever it be, who has not in his temper a strong tincture of enthusiasm. By enthusiasm these appear to understand, all uncommon vigour of thought, a peculiar fervour of spirit, a vivacity and strength not to be found in common men; elevating the soul to greater and higher things than cool reason could have attained.

10. But neither of these is the sense wherein the word "enthusiasm" is most usually understood. The generality of men, if no farther agreed, at least agree thus far concerning it, that it is something evil: and this is plainly the sentiment of all those who call the religion of the heart "enthusiasm." Accordingly, I shall take it in the following pages, as an evil; a misfortune, if not a fault.

11. As to the nature of enthusiasm, it is, undoubtedly a disorder of the mind; and such a disorder as greatly hinders the exercise of reason. Nay, sometimes it wholly sets it aside: it not only dims but shuts the eyes of the understanding. It

---

* (text from the 1872 edition)

may, therefore, well be accounted a species of madness; of madness rather than of folly: seeing a fool is properly one who draws wrong conclusions from right premises; whereas a madman draws right conclusions, but from wrong premises. And so does an enthusiast suppose his premises true, and his conclusions would necessarily follow. But here lies his mistake: his premises are false. He imagines himself to be what he is not: and therefore, setting out wrong, the farther he goes, the more he wanders out of the way.

12. Every enthusiast, then, is properly a madman. Yet his is not an ordinary, but a religious, madness. By "religious," I do not mean, that it is any part of religion: quite the reverse. Religion is the spirit of a sound mind; and, consequently, stands in direct opposition to madness of every kind. But I mean, it has religion for its object; it is conversant about religion. And so the enthusiast is generally talking of religion, of God, or of the things of God, but talking in such a manner that every reasonable Christian may discern the disorder of his mind. Enthusiasm in general may then be described in some such manner as this: a religious madness arising from some falsely imagined influence or inspiration of God; at least, from imputing something to God which ought not to be imputed to Him, or expecting something from God which ought not to be expected from Him.

13. There are innumerable sorts of enthusiasm. Those which are most common, and for that reason most dangerous, I shall endeavour to reduce under a few general heads, that they may be more easily understood and avoided.

The first sort of enthusiasm which I shall mention, is that of those who imagine they have the grace which they have not. Thus some imagine, when it is not so, that they have redemption through Christ, "even the forgiveness of sins." These are usually such as "have no root in themselves;" no deep repentance, or thorough conviction. "Therefore they receive the word with joy." And "because they have no deepness of earth," no deep work in their heart, therefore the seed "immediately springs up." There is immediately a superficial change, which, together with that light joy, striking in with the pride of their unbroken heart, and with their inordinate self-love, easily persuades them they have already "tasted the good word of God, and the powers of the world to come."

14. This is properly an instance of the first sort of enthusiasm: it is a kind of madness, arising from the imagination that they have that grace which, in truth, they have not: so that they only deceive their own souls. Madness it may be justly termed: for the reasonings of these poor men are right, were their premises good; but as those are a mere creature of their own imagination, so all that is built on them falls to the ground. The foundation of all their reveries is this: they imagine themselves to have faith in Christ. If they had this, they would be "kings and priests to God;" possessed of a "kingdom which cannot be moved": but they have it not; consequently, all their following behaviour is as wide of truth and soberness as that of the ordinary madman who, fancying himself an earthly king, speaks and acts in that character.

15. There are many other enthusiasts of this sort. Such, for instance, is the fiery zealot for religion; or, more properly, for the opinions and modes of worship which he dignifies with that name. This man, also, strongly imagines himself to be a believer in Jesus; yea, that he is a champion for the faith which was once delivered to the saints. Accordingly, all his conduct is formed upon that vain imagination. And allowing his supposition to be just, he would have some tolerable plea for his behaviour; whereas now it is evidently the effect of a distempered brain, as well as of a distempered heart.

16. But the most common of all the enthusiasts of this kind are those who imagine themselves Christians, and are not. These abound, not only in all parts of our land, but in most parts of the habitable earth. That they are not Christians, is clear and undeniable, if we believe the oracles of God. For Christians are holy; these are unholy: Christians love God; these love the world: Christians are humble; these are proud: Christians are gentle; these are passionate; Christians have the mind which was in Christ; these are at the utmost distance from it. Consequently, they are no more Christians, than they are archangels. Yet they imagine themselves so to be; and they can give several reasons for it: for they have been *called* so ever since they can remember; they were *christened* many years ago; they embrace the *Christian opinions*, vulgarly termed the Christian or catholic faith; they use the *Christian* modes of worship, as their fathers did before them; they live what is called a good *Christian life*, as the rest of their neighbours do. And who shall presume to think or say that these men are not Christians?—though without one grain of true faith in Christ, or of real, inward holiness; without ever having tasted the love of God, or been "made partakers of the Holy Ghost!"

17. Ah poor self-deceivers! Christians ye are not. But you are enthusiasts in a high degree. Physicians, heal yourselves! But first know your disease: your whole life is enthusiasm; as being all suitable to the imagination, that you have received that grace of God which you have not. In consequence of this grand mistake, you blunder on, day by day, speaking and acting under a character which does in no wise belong to you. Hence arises that palpable, glaring inconsistency that runs through your whole behaviour; which is an awkward mixture of real Heathenism and imaginary Christianity. Yet still, as you have so vast a majority on your side, you will always carry it by mere dint of numbers, "that you are the only men in your senses, and all are lunatics who are not as you are." But this alters not the nature of things. In the sight of God, and His holy angels, yea, and all the children of God upon earth, you are mere madmen, mere enthusiasts all! Are you not? Are you not "walking in a vain shadow, a shadow of religion, a shadow of happiness? Are you not still "disquieting yourselves in vain" with misfortunes as imaginary as your happiness or religion? Do you not fancy yourselves great or good—very knowing and very wise? How long? Perhaps till death brings you back to your senses, to bewail your folly for ever and ever!

18. A second sort of enthusiasm is that of those who imagine they have such gifts from God as they have not. Thus some have imagined themselves to be endued with a power of working miracles, of healing the sick by a word or a touch, of restoring sight to the blind: yea, even of raising the dead—a

notorious instance of which is still fresh un our own history. Others have undertaken to prophesy, to foretell things to come, and that with the utmost certainty and exactness. But a little time usually convinces these enthusiasts. When plain facts run counter to their predictions, experience performs what reason could not, and sinks them down into their senses.

19. To the same class belong those who, in preaching or prayer, imagine themselves to be so influenced by the Spirit of God, as, in fact, they are not. I am sensible, indeed, that without Him we can do nothing, more especially in our public ministry; that all our preaching is utterly vain, unless it be attended with His power; and all our prayer, unless His Spirit therein help our infirmities. I know, if we do not both preach and pray by the Spirit, it is all but lost labour; seeing the help that is done upon earth He doeth it Himself, who worketh all in all. But this does not affect the case before us. Though there is a real influence of the Spirit of God, there is also an imaginary one: and many there are who mistake the one for the other. Many suppose themselves to be under that influence, when they are not, when it is far from them. And many others suppose they are more under that influence than they really are. Of this number, I fear, are all they who imagine that God dictates the very words they speak; and that, consequently, it is impossible they should speak anything amiss, either as to the matter or manner of it. It is well known how many enthusiasts of this sort also have appeared during the present century; some of whom speak in a far more authoritative manner than either St. Paul or any of the Apostles.

20. The same sort of enthusiasm, though in a lower degree, is frequently found in men of a private character. They may likewise imagine themselves to be influenced or directed by the Spirit when they are not. I allow, "if any man have not the Spirit of Christ, he is none of His;" and that if ever we either think, speak, or act aright, it is through the assistance of that blessed Spirit. But how many impute things to Him, or expect things from Him, without any rational or scriptural ground! Such are they who imagine, they either do or shall receive *particular directions* from God, not only in points of importance, but in things of no moment; in the most trifling circumstances of life. Whereas in these cases God has given us our own reason for a guide; though never excluding the secret assistance of His Spirit.

21. To this kind of enthusiasm they are peculiarly exposed, who expect to be directed of God, either in spiritual things or in common life, in what is justly called an *extraordinary* manner: I mean, by visions or dreams, by strong impressions or sudden impulses on the mind. I do not deny, that God has, of old times, manifested His will in this manner; or, that He can do so now: nay, I believe He does, in some very rare instances. But how frequently do men mistake herein! How are they misled by pride, and a warm imagination, to ascribe such impulses or impressions, dreams or visions, to God, as are utterly unworthy of Him! Now this is all pure enthusiasm; all as wide of religion, as it is of truth and soberness.

22. Perhaps some may ask, "Ought we not then to inquire what is the will of God in all things? And ought not His will to be the rule of our practice?" Unquestionably it ought. But how is a sober Christian to make this inquiry? to know what is the will of God? Not by waiting for supernatural dreams; not by expecting God to reveal it in visions; not by looking for any *particular impressions* or sudden impulses on his mind: no; but by consulting the oracles of God. "To the law and to the testimony!" This is the general method of knowing what is "the holy and acceptable will of God."

23. "But how shall I know what is the will of God, in such and such a particular case? The thing proposed is, in itself, of an indifferent nature, and so left undetermined in Scripture." I answer, the Scripture itself gives you a general rule. applicable to all particular cases: "The will of God is our sanctification." It is His will that we should be inwardly and outwardly holy; that we should be good, and do good, in every kind and in the highest degree whereof we are capable. Thus far we tread upon firm ground. This is as clear as the shining of the sun. In order, therefore, to know what is the will of God in a particular case, we have only to apply this general rule.

24. Suppose, for instance, it were proposed to a reasonable man to marry, or to enter into a new business: in order to know whether this is the will of God, being assured, "It is the will of God concerning me, that I should be as holy and do as much good as I can," he has only to enquire, "In which of these states can I be most holy, and do the most good?" And this is to be determined, partly by reason, and partly by experience. Experience tells him what advantages he has in his present state, either for being or doing good; and reason is to show, what he certainly or probably will have in the state proposed. By comparing these, he is to judge which of the two may most conduce to his being and doing good; and as far as he knows this, so far he is certain what is the will of God.

25. Meantime, the assistance of His Spirit is supposed, during the whole process of the inquiry. Indeed it is not easy to say, in how many ways that assistance is conveyed. He may bring many circumstances to our remembrance; may place others in a stronger and clearer light; may insensibly open our mind to receive conviction, and fix that conviction upon our heart. And to a concurrence of many circumstances of this kind, in favour of what is acceptable in His sight, He may superadd such an unutterable peace of mind, and so uncommon a measure of His love, as will leave us no possibility of doubting, that this, even this, is His will concerning us.

26. This is the plain, scriptural, rational way to know what is the will of God in a particular case. But considering how seldom this way is taken, and what a flood of enthusiasm must needs break in on those who endeavour to know the will of God by unscriptural, irrational ways; it were to be wished that the expression itself were far more sparingly used. The using it, as some do, on the most trivial occasions, is a plain breach of the third commandment. It is a gross way of taking the name of God in vain, and betrays great irreverence toward Him. Would it not be far better, then, to use other

expressions, which are not liable to such objections? For example: instead of saying, on any particular occasion, "I want to know what is the will of God;" would it not be better to say, "I want to know what will be most for my improvement; and what will make me most useful?" this way of speaking is clear and unexceptionable: it is putting the matter on a plain, scriptural issue, and that without any danger of enthusiasm.

27. A Third very common sort of enthusiasm (if it does not coincide with the former) is that of those who think to attain the end without using the means, by the immediate power of God. If, indeed, those means were providentially withheld, they would not fall under this charge. God can, and sometimes does, in cases of this nature, exert His own immediate power. But they who expect this when they have those means, and will not use them, are proper enthusiasts. Such are they who expect to understand the holy Scriptures, without reading them, and meditating thereon; yea, without using all such helps as are in their power, and may probably conduce to that end. Such are they who designedly speak in the public assembly without any premeditation. I say "designedly;" because there may be such circumstances as, at some times, make it unavoidable. But whoever despises that great means of speaking profitably is so far an enthusiast.

28. It may be expected that I should mention what some have accounted a Fourth sort of enthusiasm, namely, the imagining those things to be owing to the providence of God which are not owing thereto. But I doubt: I know not what things they are which are not owing to the providence of God; in ordering, or at least in governing, of which, this is not either directly or remotely concerned. I except nothing but sin; and even in the sins of others, I see the providence of God to me. I do not say His *general* providence; for this I take to be a sounding word. which means just nothing. And if there be a *particular* providence, it must extend to all persons and all things. So our Lord understood it, or He could never have said, "Even the hairs of your head are all numbered;" and, "Not a sparrow falleth to the ground without" the will of "your Father" which is in heaven. But if it be so, if God preside *universis tanquam singulis, et singulis tanquam universis*; "over the whole universe as over every single person, and over every single person as over the whole universe;" what is it (except only our own sins) which we are not to ascribe to the providence of God? So that I cannot apprehend there is any room here for the charge of enthusiasm.

29. If it be said, the charge lies here: "When you impute this to Providence, you imagine yourself the peculiar favourite of heaven": I answer, you have forgot some of the last words I spoke: *Praesidet universis tanquam singulis*. "His providence is over all men in the universe, as much as over any single person." Do you not see that he who, believing this, imputes anything which befalls him to Providence, does not therein make himself any more the favourite of heaven, than he supposes every man under heaven to be? Therefore you have no pretence, upon this ground, to charge him with enthusiasm.

30. Against every sort of this it behoves us to guard with the utmost diligence; considering the dreadful effects it has so often produced, and which, indeed, naturally result from it. Its immediate offspring is pride; it continually increases this source from whence it flows; and hereby it alienates us more and more from the favour and from the life of God. It dries up the very springs of faith and love, of righteousness and true holiness; seeing all these flow from grace: but "God resisteth the proud, and giveth grace" only "to the humble."

31. Together with pride there will naturally arise an unadvisable and unconvincible spirit. So that into whatever error or fault the enthusiast falls, there is small hope of his recovery. For reason will have little weight with him (as has been frequently and justly observed) who imagines he is led by a higher guide,—by the immediate wisdom of God. And as he grows in pride, so he must grow in unadvisableness and in stubbornness also. He must be less and less capable of being convinced, less susceptible of persuasion; more and more attached to his own judgement and his own will, till he is altogether fixed and immovable.

32. Being thus fortified both against the grace of God, and against all advice and help from man, he is wholly left to the guidance of his own heart, and of the king of the children of pride. No marvel, then, that he is daily more rooted and grounded in contempt of all mankind, in furious anger, in every unkind disposition, in every earthly and devilish temper. Neither can we wonder at the terrible outward effects which have flowed from such dispositions in all ages; even all manner of wickedness, all the works of darkness, committed by those who call themselves Christians, while they wrought with greediness such things as were hardly named even among the Heathens.

Such is the nature, such the dreadful effects, of that manyheaded monster, Enthusiasm! From the consideration of which we may now draw some plain inferences, with regard to our own practice.

33. And, first, if enthusiasm be a term, though so frequently used, yet so rarely understood, take you care not to talk of you know not what; not to use the word till you understand it. As in all other points, so likewise in this, learn to think before you speak. First know the meaning of this hard word; and then use it, if need require.

34. But if so few, even among men of education and learning, much more among the common sort of men, understand this dark, ambiguous word, or have any fixed notion of what it means; then, secondly, beware of judging or calling any man an enthusiast, upon common report. This is by no means a sufficient ground for giving any name of reproach to any man; least of all is it a sufficient ground for so black a term of reproach as this. The more evil it contains, the more cautious you should be how you apply it to any one; to bring so heavy an accusation, without full proof, being neither consistent with justice nor mercy.

35. But if enthusiasm be so great an evil, beware you are not entangled therewith yourself. Watch and pray, that you fall not into the temptation. It easily besets those who fear or love God. O beware you do not think of yourself more highly than you ought to think. Do not imagine you have attained

that grace of God which you have not attained. You may have much joy; you may have a measure of love; and yet not have living faith. Cry unto God, that He would not suffer you, blind as you are, to go out of the way; that you may never fancy yourself a believer in Christ, till Christ is revealed in you, and till His Spirit witnesses with your spirit that you are a child of God.

36. Beware you are not a fiery, persecuting enthusiast. Do not imagine that God has called you (just contrary to the spirit of Him you style your Master) to destroy men's lives, and not to save them. Never dream of forcing men into the ways of God. Think yourself, and let think. Use no constraint in matters of religion. Even those who are farthest out of the way never compel to come in by any other means than reason, truth, and love.

37. Beware you do not run with the common herd of enthusiasts, fancying you are a Christian when you are not. Presume not to assume that venerable name, unless you have a clear, scriptural title thereto; unless you have the mind which was in Christ, and walk as He also walked.

38. Beware you do not fall into the second sort of enthusiasm—fancying you have those gifts from God which you have not. Trust not in visions or dreams; in sudden impressions, or strong impulses of any kind. Remember, it is not by these you are to know what is the will of God on any particular occasion, but by applying the plain Scripture rule, with the help of experience and reason, and the ordinary assistance of the Spirit of God. Do not lightly take the name of God in your mouth; do not talk of the will of God on every trifling occasion: but let your words, as well as your actions, be all tempered with reverence and godly fear.

39. Beware, lastly, of imagining you shall obtain the end without using the means conducive to it. God can give the end without any means at all; but you have no reason to think He will. Therefore constantly and carefully use all those means which He has appointed to be the ordinary channels of His grace. Use every means which either reason or Scripture recommends, as conducive (through the free love of God in Christ) either to the obtaining or increasing any of the gifts of God. Thus expect a daily growth in that pure and holy religion which the world always did, and always will, call "enthusiasm;" but which, to all who are saved from real enthusiasm, from merely nominal Christianity, is "the wisdom of God, and the power of God;" the glorious image of the Most High; "righteousness and peace;" a "fountain of living water, springing up into everlasting life!"

38. A Caution against Bigotry

"And John answered him, saying, Master, we saw one casting out devils in Thy name: and he followeth not us: and we forbad him, because he followeth not us. But Jesus said, Forbid him not."

Mark 9:38, 39.

1. In the preceding verses we read, that after the Twelve had been disputing "which of them should be the greatest," Jesus took a little child, and set him in the midst of them, and taking him in his arms, said unto them, "Whosoever shall receive one of these little children in My name, receiveth me; and whosoever receiveth me, receiveth not me" only, "but him that sent me." Then "John answered," that is, said, with reference to what our Lord had spoken just before, "Master, we saw one casting out devils in Thy name, and we forbad him, because he followeth not us." As if he had said, "Ought we to have received him? In receiving him, should we have received thee? Ought we not rather to have forbidden him? Did not we do well therein?" "But Jesus said, Forbid him not."

2. The same passage is recited by St. Luke, and almost in the same words. But it may be asked, "What is this to us, seeing no man now *casts out devils?* Has not the power of doing this been withdrawn from the church, for twelve or fourteen hundred years? How then are *we* concerned in the case here proposed, or in our Lord's decision of it?"

3. Perhaps more nearly than is commonly imagined; the case proposed being no uncommon case. That we may reap our full advantage from it, I design to show, first, in what sense men may, and do, now cast out devils: secondly, what we may understand by, "He followeth not us." I shall, thirdly, explain our Lord's direction, "Forbid him not;" and conclude with an inference from the whole.

I. 1. I am, in the first place, to show, in what sense men may, and do, now cast out devils.

In order to have the clearest view of this, we should remember, that (according to the scriptural account) as God dwells and works in the children of light, so the devil dwells and works in the children of darkness. As the Holy Spirit possesses the souls of good men, so the evil spirit possesses the souls of the wicked. Hence it is that the Apostle terms him "the god of this world;" from the uncontrolled power he has over worldly men. Hence our blessed Lord styles him "the prince of this world;" so absolute is his dominion over it. And hence St. John: "We know that we are of God, and" all who are not of God, "the whole world," "*en toi poneroi* keitai,"—not *lieth in wickedness,* but *"lieth in the wicked one;"* lives and moves in him, as they who are not of the world do in God.

2. For the devil is not to be considered only as "a roaring lion going about seeking whom he may devour;" nor barely as a subtle enemy, who cometh unawares upon poor souls, and "leads them captive at his will;" but as he who dwelleth in them, and walketh in them; who ruleth the darkness or wickedness of this world (of worldly men and all their dark designs and actions), by keeping possession of their hearts, setting up his throne there, and bringing every thought into obedience to himself. Thus the "strong one armed keepeth his house;" and if this "unclean spirit" sometimes "go out of a man," yet he often returns with "seven spirits worse than himself, and they enter in and dwell there." Nor can he be idle in his dwelling. He is continually "working in" these "children of disobedience." he works in them with power, with mighty energy, transforming them into his own likeness, effacing all the remains of the image of God, and preparing them for every evil word and work.

3. It is, therefore, an unquestionable truth, that the god and prince of this world still possesses all who know not God.

Only the manner wherein he possesses them now differs from that wherein he did it of old time. *Then* he frequently tormented their bodies as well as souls, and that openly, without any disguise: *now* he torments their souls only (unless in some rare cases), and that as covertly as possible. The reason of this difference is plain: it was then his aim to drive mankind into superstition; therefore, he wrought as openly as he could. But it is his aim to drive us into infidelity; therefore, he works as privately as he can: for the more secret he is, the more he prevails.

4. Yet, if we may credit historians, there are countries, even now, where he works as openly as aforetime. "But why in savage and barbarous countries only? Why not in Italy, France, or England?" For a very plain reason: he knows his men, and he knows what he hath to do with each. To Laplanders he appears barefaced; because he is to fix them in superstition and gross idolatry. But with you he is pursuing a different point. He is to make you idolize yourselves; to make you wiser in your own eyes than God himself, than all the oracles of God. Now, in order to do this, he must not appear in his own shape: that would frustrate his design. No: He uses all his art to make you deny his being, till he has you safe in his own place.

5. He reigns, therefore, although in a different way, yet as absolute in one land as in the other. He has the gay Italian infidel in his teeth, as sure as the wild Tartar. But he is fast asleep in the mouth of the lion, who is too wise to wake him out of sleep. So he only plays with him for the present, and when he pleases, swallows him up!

The god of this world holds his English worshippers full as fast as those in Lapland. But it is not his business to affright them, lest they should fly to the God of heaven. The prince of darkness, therefore, does not appear, while he rules over these his willing subjects. The conqueror holds his captives so much the safer, because they imagine themselves at liberty. Thus "the strong one armed keepeth his house, and his goods are in peace;" neither the Deist nor nominal Christian suspects he is there: so he and they are perfectly at peace with each other.

6. All this while he works with energy in them. He blinds the eyes of their understanding, so that the light of the glorious gospel of Christ cannot shine upon them. He chains their souls down to earth and hell, with the chains of their own vile affections. He binds them down to the earth, by love of the world, love of money, of pleasure, of praise. And by pride, envy, anger, hate, revenge, he causes their souls to draw nigh unto hell; acting the more secure and uncontrolled, because they know not that he acts at all.

7. But how easily may we know the cause from its effects! These are sometimes gross and palpable. So they were in the most refined of the heathen nations. Go no farther than the admired, the virtuous Romans; and you will find these, when at the height of their learning and glory, "filled with all unrighteousness, fornication, wickedness, covetousness, maliciousness; full of envy, murder, debate, deceit, malignity; whisperers, backbiters, despiteful, proud, boasters, disobedient to parents, covenant-breakers, without natural affection, implacable, unmerciful."

8. The strongest parts of this description are confirmed by one whom some may think a more unexceptionable witness. I mean their brother heathen, Dion Cassius; who observes, that, before Caesar's return from Gaul, not only gluttony and lewdness of every kind were open and barefaced; not only falsehood, injustice, and unmercifulness abounded, in public courts, as well as private families; but the most outrageous robberies, rapine, and murders were so frequent in all parts of Rome, that few men went out of doors without making their wills, as not knowing if they should return alive!

9. As gross and palpable are the works of the devil among many (if not all) the modern heathens. The natural religion of the Creeks, Cherokees, Chickasaws, and all other Indians bordering on our southern settlements (not of a few single men, but of entire nations), is to torture all their prisoners from morning till night, till at length they roast them to death; and upon the slightest undesigned provocation, to come behind and shoot any of their own countrymen! Yea, it is a common thing among them, for the son, if he thinks his father lives too long, to knock out his brains; and for mother, if she is tired of her children, to fasten stones about their necks, and throw three or four of them into the river, one after another!

10. It were to be wished, that none but heathens had practised such gross, palpable works of the devil. But we dare not say so. Even in cruelty and bloodshed, how little have the Christians come behind them! And not the Spaniards or Portuguese alone, butchering thousands in South America: not the Dutch only in the East Indies, or the French in North America, following the Spaniards step by step: our own countrymen, too, have wantoned in blood, and exterminated whole nations; plainly proving thereby what spirit it is that dwells and works in the children of disobedience.

11. These monsters might almost make us overlook the works of the devil that are wrought in our own country. But, alas! we cannot open our eyes even here, without seeing them on every side. Is it a small proof of his power, that common swearers, drunkards, whoremongers, adulterers, thieves, robbers, sodomites, murderers, are still found in every part of our land? How triumphant does the prince of this world reign in all these children of disobedience!

12. He less openly, but no less effectually, works in dissemblers, tale-bearers, liars, slanderers; in oppressors and extortioners, in the perjured, the seller of his friend, his honour, his conscience, his country. And yet these may talk of religion or conscience still; of honour, virtue, and public spirit! But they can no more deceive Satan than they can God. He likewise knows those that are his: and a great multitude they are, out of every nation and people, of whom he has full possession at this day.

13. If you consider this, you cannot but see in what sense men may now also cast out devils: yea, and every Minister of Christ does cast them out, if his Lord's work prosper in his hand.

By the power of God attending his word, he brings these sinners to repentance; an entire inward as well as outward change, from all evil to all good. And this is, in a sound sense, to cast out devils, out of the souls wherein they had hitherto dwelt. The strong one can no longer keep his house. A stronger than he is come upon him, and hath cast him out, and taken possession for himself, and made it an habitation of God through his Spirit. Here, then, the energy of Satan ends, and the Son of God "destroys the works of the devil." The understanding of the sinner is now enlightened, and his heart sweetly drawn to God. His desires are refined, his affections purified; and, being filled with the Holy Ghost, he grows in grace till he is not only holy in heart, but in all manner of conversation.

14. All this is indeed the work of God. It is God alone who can cast out Satan. But he is generally pleased to do this by man as an instrument in his hand: who is then said to cast out devils in his name, by his power and authority. And he sends whom he will send upon this great work; but usually such as man would never have thought of: for "His ways are not as our ways, neither his thoughts as our thoughts." Accordingly, he chooses the weak to confound the mighty; the foolish to confound the wise; for this plain reason, that he may secure the glory to himself; that "no flesh may glory in his sight."

II. 1. But shall we not forbid one who thus "casteth out devils," if "he followeth not us"? This, it seems, was both the judgement and practice of the Apostle, till he referred the case to his Master. "We forbad him," saith he, "because he followeth not us!" which he supposed to be a very sufficient reason. What we may understand by this expression, "He followeth not us," is the next point to be considered.

The lowest circumstance we can understand thereby, is, he has no outward connexion with us. We do not labour in conjunction with each other. He is not our fellow-helper in the gospel. And indeed whensoever our Lord is pleased to send many labourers into his harvest, they cannot all act in subordination to, or connexion with, each other. Nay, they cannot be personal acquaintance with, nor be so much as known to, one another. Many there will necessarily be, in different parts of the harvest, so far from having any mutual intercourse, that they will be as absolute strangers to each other as if they had lived in different ages. And concerning any of these whom we know not, we may doubtless say, "He followeth not us."

2. A Second meaning of this expression may be,—he is not of our party. It has long been matter of melancholy consideration to all who pray for the peace of Jerusalem, that so many several parties are still subsisting among those who are all styled Christians. This has been particularly observable in our own countrymen, who have been continually dividing from each other, upon points of no moment, and many times such as religion had no concern in. The most trifling circumstances have given rise to different parties, which have continued for many generations; and each of these would be ready to object to one who was on the other side, "He followeth not us."

3. That expression may mean, Thirdly,—he differs from us in our religious opinions. There was a time when all Christians were of one mind, as well as of one heart, so great grace was upon them all, when they were first filled with the Holy Ghost! But how short a space did this blessing continue!

How soon was that unanimity lost! and difference of opinion sprang up again, even in the church of Christ,—and that not in nominal but in real Christians; nay, in the very chief of them, the Apostles themselves! Nor does it appear that the difference which then began was ever entirely removed. We do not find that even those pillars in the temple of God, so long as they remained upon the earth, were ever brought to think alike, to be of one mind, particularly with regard to the ceremonial law. It is therefore no way surprising, that infinite varieties of opinion should now be found in the Christian church. A very probable consequence of this is, that whenever we see any "casting out devils," he will be one that, in this sense, "followeth not us"—that is not of our opinion. It is scarce to be imagined he will be of our mind in all points, even of religion. He may very probably think in a different manner from us, even on several subjects of importance; such as the nature and use of the moral law, the eternal decrees of God, the sufficiency and efficacy of his grace, and the perseverance of his children.

4. He may differ from us, Fourthly, not only in opinion, but likewise in some point of practice. He may not approve of that manner of worshipping God which is practised in our congregation; and may judge that to be more profitable for his soul which took its rise from Calvin or Martin Luther. He may have many objections to that Liturgy which we approve of beyond all others; many doubts concerning that form of church government which we esteem both apostolical and scriptural. Perhaps he may go farther from us yet: he may, from a principle of conscience, refrain from several of those which we believe to be the ordinances of Christ. Or, if we both agree that they are ordained of God, there may still remain a difference between us, either as to the manner of administering those ordinances, or the persons to whom they should be administered. Now the unavoidable consequence of any of these differences will be, that he who thus differs from us must separate himself, with regard to those points, from our society. In this respect, therefore, "he followeth not us": he is not (as we phrase it) "of our Church."

5. But in a far stronger sense "he followeth not us," who is not only of a different Church, but of such a Church as we account to be in many respects anti-scriptural and anti-Christian,—a Church which we believe to be utterly false and erroneous in her doctrines, as well as very dangerously wrong in her practice; guilty of gross superstition as well as idolatry,—a Church that has added many articles to the faith which was once delivered to the saints; that has dropped one whole commandment of God, and made void several of the rest by her traditions; and that, pretending the highest veneration for, and strictest conformity to, the ancient Church, has nevertheless brought in numberless innovations, without any warrant either from antiquity or Scripture. Now, most certainly, "he followeth not us," who stands at so great a distance from us.

6. And yet there may be a still wider difference than this. He who differs from us in judgement or practice, may possibly stand at a greater distance from us in affection than in judgement. And this indeed is a very natural and a very common effect of the other. The differences which begin in

points of opinion seldom terminate there. They generally spread into the affections, and then separate chief friends. Nor are any animosities so deep and irreconcilable as those that spring from disagreement in religion. For this cause the bitterest enemies of a man are those of his own household. For this the father rises against his own children, and the children against the father; and perhaps persecute each other even to the death, thinking all the time they are doing God service. It is therefore nothing more than we may expect, if those who differ from us, either in religious opinions or practice, soon contract a sharpness, yea, bitterness towards us; if they are more and more prejudiced against us, till they conceive as ill an opinion of our persons as of our principles. An almost necessary consequence of this will be, they will speak in the same manner as they think of us. They will set themselves in opposition to us, and, as far as they are able, hinder our work; seeing it does not appear to them to be the work of God, but either of man or of the devil. He that thinks, speaks, and acts in such a manner as this, in the highest sense, "followeth not us."

7. I do not indeed conceive, that the person of whom the Apostle speaks in the text (although we have no particular account of him, either in the context, or in any other part of holy writ) went so far as this. We have no ground to suppose, that there was any material difference between him and the Apostles, much less that he had any prejudice either against them or their Master. It seems we may gather thus much from our Lord's own words, which immediately follow the text: "There is no man which shall do a miracle in My name, that can lightly speak evil of me." But I purposely put the case in the strongest light, adding all the circumstances which can well be conceived, that, being forewarned of the temptation in its full strength, we may in no case yield to it, and fight against God.

III. 1. Suppose, then, a man have no intercourse with us, suppose he be not of our party, suppose he separate from our Church, yea, and widely differ from us, both in judgement, practice, and affection; yet if we see even this man "casting out devils," Jesus saith, "Forbid him not." This important direction of our Lord I am, in the Third place, to explain.

2. If we see this man casting out devils: But it is well if, in such a case, we would believe even what we saw with our eyes, if we did not give the lie to our own senses. He must be little acquainted with human nature who does not immediately perceive how extremely unready we should be to believe that any man does cast out devils who "followeth not us" in all or most of the senses above recited: I had almost said, in any of them, seeing we may easily learn even from what passes in our own breasts, how unwilling men are to allow anything good in those who do not in all things agree with themselves.

3. "But what is a sufficient, reasonable proof, that a man does (in the sense above) cast out devils?" The answer is easy. Is there full proof, (1) That a person before us was a gross, open sinner? (2) That he is not so now? that he has broke off his sins, and lives a Christian life? And (3) That this change was wrought by his hearing this man preach? If these three points be plain and undeniable, then you have sufficient, reasonable proof, such as you cannot resist without wilful sin, that this man casts out devils.

4. Then "forbid him not." Beware how you attempt to hinder him, either by your authority, or arguments, or persuasions. Do not in any wise strive to prevent his using all the power which God has given him. If you have *authority* with him, do not use that authority to stop the work of God. Do not furnish him with *reasons* why he ought not any more to speak in the name of Jesus. Satan will not fail to supply him with these, if you do not second him therein. *Persuade* him not to depart from the work. If he should give place to the devil and you, many souls might perish in their iniquity, but their blood would God require at *your* hands.

5. "But what, if he be only a layman, who casts out devils! Ought I not to forbid him then?" Is the fact allowed? Is there reasonable proof that this man has or does cast out devils? If there is, forbid him not; no, not at the peril of your soul. Shall not God work by whom he will work? No man can do these works unless God is with him; unless God hath sent him for this very thing. But if God hath sent him, will you call him back? Will you forbid him to go?

6. "But I do not know that he is sent of God." "Now herein is a marvellous thing" (may any of the seals of his mission say, any whom he hath brought from Satan to God), "that ye know not whence this man is, and, behold, he hath opened mine eyes! If this man were not of God, he could do nothing." If you doubt the fact, send for the parents of the man: send for his brethren, friends, acquaintance. But if you cannot doubt this, if you must needs acknowledge "that a notable miracle hath been wrought" then with what conscience, with what face, can you charge him whom God hath sent, "not to speak any more in his name"?

7. I allow, that it is *highly expedient*, whoever preaches in his name should have an outward as well as an inward call, but that it is *absolutely necessary*, I deny. "Nay, is not the Scripture express? 'No man taketh this honour unto himself, but he that is called of God, as was Aaron' " (Heb. 5:4). Numberless times has this text been quoted on the occasion, as containing the very strength of the cause; but surely never was so unhappy a quotation. For, First, Aaron was not called to preach at all: he was called "to offer gifts and sacrifice for sin." That was his peculiar employment. Secondly, these men do not offer sacrifice at all, but only preach; which Aaron did not. Therefore it is not possible to find one text in all the Bible which is more wide of the point than this.

8. "But what was the practice of the apostolic age?" You may easily see in the Acts of the Apostles. In the eighth chapter we read, "There was a great persecution against the church which was at Jerusalem; and they were all scattered abroad throughout the regions of Judea and Samaria, except the Apostles" (verse 1). "Therefore they that were scattered abroad went everywhere preaching the word" (verse 4). Now, were all these outwardly called to preach? No man in his senses can think so. Here, then, is an undeniable proof, what was the practice of the apostolic age. Here you see not one,

but a multitude of lay preachers, men that were only sent of God.

9. Indeed, so far is the practice of the apostolic age from inclining us to think it was *unlawful* for a man to preach before he was ordained, that we have reason to think it was then accounted *necessary*. Certainly the practice and the direction of the Apostle Paul was, to *prove* a man before he was ordained at all. "Let these" (the deacons), says he, "first be proved; then let them use the office of a deacon" (1 Tim. 3:10). *Proved*, how? By setting them to construe a sentence of Greek and asking them a few commonplace questions? O amazing proof of a Minister of Christ! Nay; but by making a clear, open trial (as is still done by most of the Protestant Churches of Europe) not only whether their lives be holy and unblamable, but whether they have such gifts as are absolutely and indispensably necessary in order to edify the church of Christ.

10. But what if a man has these, and has brought sinners to repentance, and yet the Bishop will not ordain him? Then the Bishop does forbid him to cast out devils. But I dare not forbid him: I have published my reasons to all the world. Yet it is still insisted I ought to do it. You who insist upon it answer those reasons. I know not that any have done this yet, or even made an attempt of doing it. Only some have spoken of them as very weak and trifling: and this was prudent enough; for it is far easier to despise, at least seem to despise, an argument, than to answer it. Yet till this is done I must say, when I have reasonable proof that any man does cast out devils, whatever others do, I dare not forbid him, lest I be found even to fight against God.

11. And whosoever thou art that fearest God, "forbid him not, either directly or indirectly. There are many ways of doing this. You indirectly forbid him, if you either wholly deny, or despise and make little account of, the work which God has wrought by his hands. You indirectly forbid him, when you discourage him in his work, by drawing him into disputes concerning it, by raising objections against it, or frightening him with consequences which very possibly will never be. You forbid him when you show any unkindness toward him either in language or behaviour; and much more when you speak of him to others either in an unkind or a contemptuous manner; when you endeavour to represent him to any either in an odious or a despicable light. You are forbidding him all the time you are speaking evil of him, or making no account of his labours. O forbid him not in any of these ways; nor by forbidding others to hear him,—by discouraging sinners from hearing that word which is able to save their souls!

12. Yea, if you would observe our Lord's direction in its full meaning and extent, then remember his word: "He that is not for us is against us; and he that gathereth not with me scattereth": he that gathereth not men into the kingdom of God, assuredly scatters them from it. For there can be no neuter in this war. Every one is either on God's side, or on Satan's. Are you on God's side? Then you will not only not forbid any man that casts out devils, but you will labour, to the uttermost of your power, to forward him in the work. You will readily acknowledge the work of God, and confess the greatness of it. You will remove all difficulties and objections, as far as may be, out of his way. You will strengthen his hands by speaking honourably of him before all men, and avowing the things which you have seen and heard. You will encourage others to attend upon his word, to hear him whom God hath sent. And you will omit no actual proof of tender love, which God gives you an opportunity of showing him.

IV. 1. If we willingly fail in any of these points, if we either directly or indirectly forbid him, "because he followeth not us," then we are bigots. This is the inference I draw from what has been said. But the term "bigotry," I fear, as frequently as it is used, is almost as little understood as "enthusiasm." It is too strong an attachment to, or fondness for, our own party. opinion, church, and religion. Therefore he is a bigot who is so fond of any of these, so strongly attached to them, as to forbid any who casts out devils because he differs from himself in any or all these particulars.

2, Do *you* beware of this. Take care (1) That you do not convict yourself of bigotry, by your unreadiness to believe that any man does cast out devils, who differs from you. And if you are clear thus far, if you acknowledge the fact, then examine yourself, (2) Am I not convicted of bigotry in this, in forbidding him directly or indirectly? Do I not directly forbid him on this ground, because he is not of my party, because he does not fall in with my opinions, or because he does not worship God according to that scheme of religion which I have received from my fathers?

3. Examine yourself, Do I not indirectly at least forbid him, on any of these grounds? Am I not sorry that God should thus own and bless a man that holds such erroneous opinions? Do I not discourage him, because he is not of my Church, by disputing with him concerning it, by raising objections, and by perplexing his mind with distant consequences? Do I show no anger, contempt, or unkindness of any sort, either in my words or actions? Do I not mention behind his back, his (real or supposed) faults—his defects or infirmities? Do not I hinder sinners from hearing his word? If you do any of these things, you are a bigot to this day.

4. "Search me, O Lord, and prove me. Try out my reins and my heart! Look well if there be any way of" bigotry "in me, and lead me in the way everlasting." In order to examine ourselves thoroughly, let the case be proposed in the strongest manner. What, if I were to see a Papist, an Arian, a Socinian casting out devils? If I did, I could not forbid even him, without convicting myself of bigotry. Yea, if it could be supposed that I should see a Jew, a Deist, or a Turk, doing the same, were I to forbid him either directly or indirectly, I should be no better than a bigot still.

5. O stand clear of this! But be not content with not forbidding any that casts out devils. It is well to go thus far; but do not stop here. If you will avoid all bigotry, go on. In every instance of this kind, whatever the instrument be, acknowledge the finger of God. And not only acknowledge, but rejoice in his work, and praise his name with thanksgiving. Encourage whomsoever God is pleased to employ, to give himself wholly up thereto. Speak well of him wheresoever you are; defend his character and his mission.

Enlarge, as far as you can, his sphere of action; show him all kindness in word and deed; and cease not to cry to God in his behalf, that he may save both himself and them that hear him.

6. I need add but one caution: Think not the bigotry of another is any excuse for your own. It is not impossible, that one who casts out devils himself, may yet forbid you so to do. You may observe, this is the very case mentioned in the text. The Apostles forbade another to do what they did themselves. But beware of retorting. It is not your part to return evil for evil. Another's not observing the direction of our Lord, is no reason why you should neglect it. Nay, but let him have all the bigotry to himself. If he forbid *you*, do not you forbid *him*. Rather labour, and watch, and pray the more, to confirm your love toward him. If he speak all manner of evil of *you*, speak all manner of good (that is true) of *him*. Imitate herein that glorious saying of a great man (O that he had always breathed the same spirit!), "Let Luther call me a hundred devils; I will still reverence him as a messenger of God."

39. CATHOLIC SPIRIT

"And when he was departed thence, he lighted on Jehonadab the son of Rechab coming to meet him, and he saluted him, and said to him, Is thine heart right, as my heart is with thy heart? And Jehonadab answered: It is. If it be, give me thine hand."

2 Kings 10:15.

1. It is allowed even by those who do not pay this great debt, that love is due to all mankind, the royal law, "Thou shalt love thy neighbour as thyself," carrying its own evidence to all that hear it: and that, not according to the miserable construction put upon it by the zealots of old times, "Thou shalt love thy neighbour," thy relation, acquaintance, friend, "and hate thine enemy;" not so; "I say unto you," said our Lord, "Love your enemies, bless them that curse you, do good to them that hate you, and pray for them that despitefully use you, and persecute you; that ye may be the children," may appear so to all mankind, "of your Father which is in heaven; who maketh his sun to rise on the evil and on the good, and sendeth rain on the just and on the unjust.

2. But it is sure, there is a peculiar love which we owe to those that love God. So David: "All my delight is upon the saints that are in the earth, and upon such as excel in virtue." And so a greater than he: "A new commandment I give unto you, That ye love one another: as I have loved you, that ye also love one another. By this shall all men know that ye are My disciples, if ye have love one to another" (John 13:34, 35). This is that love on which the Apostle John so frequently and strongly insists: "This," saith he, "is the message that ye heard from the beginning, that we should love one another" (1 John 3:11). "Hereby perceive we the love of God, because he laid down his life for us: and we ought," if love should call us thereto, "to lay down our lives for the brethren" (verse 16). And again: "Beloved, let us love one another: for love is of God. He that loveth not, knoweth not God; for God is love" (4:7, 8). "Not that we loved God, but that he loved us, and

sent his Son to be the propitiation for our sins. Beloved, if God so loved us, we ought also to love one another (verses 10, 11).

3. All men approve of this; but do all men practise it? Daily experience shows the contrary. Where are even the Christians who "love one another as he hath given us commandment?" how many hindrances lie in the way! The two grand, general hindrances are, first, that they cannot all think alike and, in consequence of this, secondly, they cannot all walk alike; but in several smaller points their practice must differ in proportion to the difference of their sentiments.

4. But although a difference in opinions or modes of worship may prevent an entire external union, yet need it prevent our union in affection? Though we cannot think alike, may we not love alike? May we not be of one heart, though we are not of one opinion? Without all doubt, we may. Herein all the children of God may unite, notwithstanding these smaller differences. These remaining as they are, they may forward one another in love and in good works.

5. Surely in this respect the example of Jehu himself, as mixed a character as he was of, is well worthy both the attention and imitation of every serious Christian. "And when he was departed thence, he lighted on Jehonadab the son of Rechab coming to meet him; and he saluted him, and said to him, Is thine heart right, as my heart is with thy heart? And Jehonadab answered, It is. If it be, give me thine hand."

The text naturally divides itself into two parts:—First, a question proposed by Jehu to Jehonadab: "Is thine heart right, as my heart is with thy heart?" Secondly, an offer made on Jehonadab's answering, "It is:" "If it be, give me thine hand."

I. 1. And, first, let us consider the question proposed by Jehu to Jehonadab, "Is thine heart right, as my heart is with thy heart?"

The very first thing we may observe in these words, is, that here is no inquiry concerning Jehonadab's opinions. And yet it is certain, he held some which were very uncommon, indeed quite peculiar to himself; and some which had a close influence upon his practice; on which, likewise, he laid so great a stress, as to entail them upon his children's children, to their latest posterity. This is evident from the account given by Jeremiah many years after his death: "I took Jaazaniah and his brethren and all his sons, and the whole house of the Rechabites, ... and set before them pots full of wine, and cups, and said unto them, Drink ye wine. But they said, We will drink no wine: for Jonadab," or Jehonadab, "the son of Rechab, our father" (it would be less ambiguous, if the words were placed thus: "Jehonadab *our father, the son of* Rechab," out of love and reverence to whom, he probably desired his descendants might be called by his name), "commanded us, saying, ye shall drink no wine, neither ye, nor your sons for ever. Neither shall ye build house, nor sow seed; nor plant vineyard, nor have any: but all your days ye shall dwell in tents.... And we have obeyed, and done according to all that Jonadab our father commanded us" (Jer. 35:3–10).

2. And yet Jehu (although it seems to have been his manner both in things secular and religious, to *drive furiously*) does

not concern himself at all with any of these things, but lets Jehonadab abound in his own sense. And neither of them appears to have given the other the least disturbance touching the opinions which he maintained.

3. It is very possible, that many good men now also may entertain peculiar opinions; and some of them may be as singular herein as even Jehonadab was. And it is certain, so long as we know but *in part*, that all men will not see all things alike. It is an unavoidable consequence of the present weakness and shortness of human understanding, that several men will be of several minds in religion as well as in common life. So it has been from the beginning of the world, and so it will be "till the restitution of all things."

4. Nay, farther: although every man necessarily believes that every particular opinion which he holds is true (for to believe any opinion is not true, is the same thing as not to hold it); yet can no man be assured that all his own opinions, taken together, are true. Nay, every thinking man is assured they are not, seeing *humanum est errare et nescire*: "To be ignorant of many things, and to mistake in some, is the necessary condition of humanity." This, therefore, he is sensible, is his own case. He knows, in the general, that he himself is mistaken; although in what particulars he mistakes, he does not, perhaps he cannot, know.

5. I say "perhaps he cannot know;" for who can tell how far invincible ignorance may extend? or (that comes to the same thing) invincible prejudice?—which is often so fixed in tender minds, that it is afterwards impossible to tear up what has taken so deep a root. And who can say, unless he knew every circumstance attending it, how far any mistake is culpable? seeing all guilt must suppose some concurrence of the will; of which he only can judge who searcheth the heart.

6. Every wise man, therefore, will allow others the same liberty of thinking which he desires they should allow him; and will no more insist on their embracing his opinions, than he would have them to insist on his embracing theirs. He bears with those who differ from him, and only asks him with whom he desires to unite in love that single question, "Is thy heart right, as my heart is with thy heart?"

7. We may, secondly, observe, that here is no inquiry made concerning Jehonadab's mode of worship; although it is highly probable there was, in this respect also, a very wide difference between them. For we may well believe Jehonadab, as well as all his posterity, worshipped God at Jerusalem! whereas Jehu did not: he had more regard to state-policy than religion. And, therefore, although he slew the worshippers of Baal, and "destroyed Baal out of Israel," yet from the convenient sin of Jeroboam, the worship of the "golden calves," he "departed not" (2 Kings 10:29).

8. But even among men of an upright heart, men who desire to "have a conscience void of offence," it must needs be, that, as long as there are various opinions, there will be various ways of worshipping God; seeing a variety of opinion necessarily implies a variety of practice. And as, in all ages, men have differed in nothing more than in their opinions concerning the Supreme Being, so in nothing have they more differed from each other, than in the manner of worshipping him. Had this been only in the heathen world, it would not have been at all surprising: for we know, these "by" their "wisdom knew not God;" nor, therefore, could they know how to worship him. But is it not strange, that even in the Christian world, although they all agree in the general, "God is a Spirit; and they that worship him must worship him in spirit and in truth;" yet the particular modes of worshipping God are almost as various as among the heathens?

9. And how shall we choose among so much variety? No man can choose for, or prescribe to, another. But every one must follow the dictates of his own conscience, in simplicity and godly sincerity. He must be fully persuaded in his own mind and then act according to the best light he has. Nor has any creature power to constrain another to walk by his own rule. God has given no right to any of the children of men thus to lord it over the conscience of his brethren; but every man must judge for himself, as every man must give an account of himself to God.

10. Although, therefore, every follower of Christ is obliged, by the very nature of the Christian institution, to be a member of some particular congregation or other, some Church, as it is usually termed (which implies a particular manner of worshipping God; for "two cannot walk together unless they be agreed"); yet none can be obliged by any power on earth but that of his own conscience, to prefer this or that congregation to another, this or that particular manner of worship. I know it is commonly supposed, that the place of our birth fixes the Church to which we ought to belong; that one, for instance, who is born in England, ought to be a member of that which is styled the Church of England, and consequently, to worship God in the particular manner which is prescribed by that Church. I was once a zealous maintainer of this; but I find many reasons to abate of this zeal. I fear it is attended with such difficulties as no reasonable man can get over. Not the least of which is, that if this rule had took place, there could have been no Reformation from Popery; seeing it entirely destroys the right of private judgement, on which that whole Reformation stands.

11. I dare not, therefore, presume to impose my mode of worship on any other. I believe it is truly primitive and apostolical: but my belief is no rule for another. I ask not, therefore, of him with whom I would unite in love, Are you of my church, of my congregation? Do you receive the same form of church government, and allow the same church officers, with me? Do you join in the same form of prayer wherein I worship God? I inquire not, Do you receive the supper of the Lord in the same posture and manner that I do? nor whether, in the administration of baptism, you agree with me in admitting sureties for the baptized, in the manner of administering it; or the age of those to whom it should be administered. Nay, I ask not of you (as clear as I am in my own mind), whether you allow baptism and the Lord's supper at all. Let all these things stand by: we will talk of them, if need be, at a more convenient season, my only question at present is this, "Is thine heart right, as my heart is with thy heart?"

12. But what is properly implied in the question? I do not mean, What did Jehu imply therein? But, What should a

follower of Christ understand thereby, when he proposes it to any of his brethren?

The first thing implied is this: Is thy heart right with God? Dost thou believe his being and his perfections? his eternity, immensity, wisdom, power? his justice, mercy, and truth? Dost thou believe that he now "upholdeth all things by the word of his power?" and that he governs even the most minute, even the most noxious, to his own glory, and the good of them that love him? hast thou a divine evidence, a supernatural conviction, of the things of God? Dost thou "walk by faith not by sight?" looking not at temporal things, but things eternal?

13. Dost thou believe in the Lord Jesus Christ, "God over all, blessed for ever?" Is he revealed in thy soul? Dost thou know Jesus Christ and him crucified? Does he dwell in thee, and thou in him? Is he formed in thy heart by faith? having absolutely disclaimed all thy own works, thy own righteousness, hast thou "submitted thyself unto the righteousness of God, which is by faith in Christ Jesus? Art thou "found in him, not having thy own righteousness, but the righteousness which is by faith?" And art thou, through him, "fighting the good fight of faith, and laying hold of eternal life?"

14. Is thy faith *energoumene di agapes,—filled with the energy of love*? Dost thou love God (I do not say "above all things," for it is both an unscriptural and an ambiguous expression, but) "with all thy heart, and with all thy mind, and with all thy soul, and with all thy strength?" Dost thou seek all thy happiness in him alone? And dost thou find what thou seekest? Does thy soul continually "magnify the Lord, and thy spirit rejoice in God thy Saviour?" having learned "in everything to give thanks, dost thou find "it is a joyful and a pleasant thing to be thankful?" Is God the centre of thy soul, the sum of all thy desires? Art thou accordingly laying up thy treasure in heaven, and counting all things else dung and dross? hath the love of God cast the love of the world out of thy soul? Then thou art "crucified to the world;" thou art dead to all below; and thy "life is hid with Christ in God."

15. Art thou employed in doing, "not thy own will, but the will of him that sent thee"—of him that sent thee down to sojourn here awhile, to spend a few days in a strange land, till, having finished the work he hath given thee to do, thou return to thy Father's house? Is it thy meat and drink "to do the will of thy Father which is in heaven?" Is thine eye single in all things? always fixed on him? always looking unto Jesus? Dost thou point at him in whatsoever thou doest? in all thy labour, thy business, thy conversation? aiming only at the glory of God in all, "whatsoever thou doest, either in word or deed, doing it all in the name of the Lord Jesus; giving thanks unto God, even the Father, through him?"

16. Does the love of God constrain thee to serve him with fear, to "rejoice unto him with reverence?" Art thou more afraid of displeasing God, than either of death or hell? Is nothing so terrible to thee as the thought of offending the eyes of his glory? Upon this ground, dost thou "hate all evil ways," every transgression of his holy and perfect law; and herein "exercise thyself, to have a conscience void of offence toward God, and toward man?"

17. Is thy heart right toward thy neighbour? Dost thou love as thyself, all mankind, without exception? "If you love those only that love you, what thank have ye?" Do you "love your enemies?" Is your soul full of good-will, of tender affection, toward them? Do you love even the enemies of God, the unthankful and unholy? Do your bowels yearn over them? Could you "wish yourself" temporally "accursed" for their sake? And do you show this by "blessing them that curse you, and praying for those that despitefully use you, and persecute you?"

18. Do you show your love by your works? While you have time as you have opportunity, do you in fact "do good to all men," neighbours or strangers, friends or enemies, good or bad? Do you do them all the good you can; endeavouring to supply all their wants; assisting them both in body and soul, to the uttermost of your power?—If thou art thus minded, may every Christian say, yea, if thou art but sincerely desirous of it, and following on till thou attain, then "thy heart is right, as my heart is with thy heart."

II. 1. "If it be, give me thy hand." I do not mean, "Be of my opinion." You need not: I do not expect or desire it. Neither do I mean, "I will be of your opinion." I cannot, it does not depend on my choice: I can no more think, than I can see or hear, as I will. Keep you your opinion; I mine; and that as steadily as ever. You need not even endeavour to come over to me, or bring me over to you. I do not desire you to dispute those points, or to hear or speak one word concerning them. Let all opinions alone on one side and the other: only "give me thine hand."

2. I do not mean, "Embrace my modes of worship," or, "I will embrace yours." This also is a thing which does not depend either on your choice or mine. We must both act as each is fully persuaded in his own mind. Hold you fast that which you believe is most acceptable to God, and I will do the same. I believe the Episcopal form of church government to be scriptural and apostolical. If you think the Presbyterian or Independent is better, think so still, and act accordingly. I believe infants ought to be baptized; and that this may be done either by dipping or sprinkling. If you are otherwise persuaded, be so still, and follow your own persuasion. It appears to me, that forms of prayer are of excellent use, particularly in the great congregation. If you judge extemporary prayer to be of more use, act suitable to your own judgement. My sentiment is, that I ought not to forbid water, wherein persons may be baptized; and that I ought to eat bread and drink wine, as a memorial of my dying Master: however, if you are not convinced of this act according to the light you have. I have no desire to dispute with you one moment upon any of the preceding heads. Let all these smaller points stand aside. Let them never come into sight "If thine heart is as my heart," if thou lovest God and all mankind, I ask no more: "give me thine hand."

3. I mean, first, love me: and that not only as thou lovest all mankind; not only as thou lovest thine enemies, or the enemies of God, those that hate thee, that "despitefully use thee, and persecute thee;" not only as a stranger, as one of whom thou knowest neither good nor evil,—I am not satisfied with this,—no; "if thine heart be right, as mine with

thy heart," then love me with a very tender affection, as a friend that is closer than a brother; as a brother in Christ, a fellow citizen of the New Jerusalem, a fellow soldier engaged in the same warfare, under the same Captain of our salvation. Love me as a companion in the kingdom and patience of Jesus, and a joint heir of his glory.

4. Love me (but in a higher degree than thou dost the bulk of mankind) with the love that is *long-suffering and kind*; that is patient,—if I am ignorant or out of the way, bearing and not increasing my burden; and is tender, soft, and compassionate still; that *envieth not*, if at any time it please God to prosper me in his work even more than thee. Love me with the love that *is not provoked*, either at my follies or infirmities; or even at my acting (if it should sometimes so appear to thee) not according to the will of God. Love me so as to *think no evil* of me; to put away all jealousy and evil-surmising. Love me with the love that *covereth all things*; that never reveals either my faults or infirmities,—that *believeth all things*; is always willing to think the best, to put the fairest construction on all my words and actions,—that *hopeth all things*; either that the thing related was never done; or not done with such circumstances as are related; or, at least, that it was done with a good-intention, or in a sudden stress of temptation. And hope to the end, that whatever is amiss will, by the grace of God, be corrected; and whatever is wanting, supplied, through the riches of his mercy in Christ Jesus.

5 I mean, Secondly, commend me to God in all thy prayers; wrestle with him in my behalf, that he would speedily correct what he sees amiss, and supply what is wanting in me. In thy nearest access to the throne of grace, beg of him who is then very present with thee, that my heart may be more as thy heart, more right both toward God and toward man; that I may have a fuller conviction of things not seen, and a stronger view of the love of God in Christ Jesus; may more steadily walk by faith, not by sight; and more earnestly grasp eternal life. Pray that the love of God and of all mankind may be more largely poured into my heart; that I may be more fervent and active in doing the will of my Father which is in heaven, more zealous of good works, and more careful to abstain from all appearance of evil.

6. I mean, Thirdly, provoke me to love and to good works. Second thy prayer, as thou hast opportunity, by speaking to me, in love, whatsoever thou believest to be for my soul's health. Quicken me in the work which God has given me to do, and instruct me how to do it more perfectly. Yea, "smite me friendly, and reprove me," whereinsoever I appear to thee to be doing rather my own will, than the will of him that sent me. O speak and spare not, whatever thou believest may conduce, either to the amending my faults, the strengthening my weakness, the building me up in love, or the making me more fit, in any kind, for the Master's use.

7. I mean, Lastly, love me not in word only, but in deed and in truth. So far as in conscience thou canst (retaining still thy own opinions, and thy own manner of worshipping God), join with me in the work of God; and let us go on hand in hand. And thus far, it is certain, thou mayest go. Speak honourably wherever thou art, of the work of God, by whomsoever he works, and kindly of his messengers. And, if it be in thy power, not only sympathize with them when they are in any difficulty or distress, but give them a cheerful and effectual assistance, that they may glorify God on thy behalf.

8. Two things should be observed with regard to what has been spoken under this last head: the one, that whatsoever love, whatsoever offices of love, whatsoever spiritual or temporal assistance, I claim from him whose heart is right, as my heart is with his, the same I am ready, by the grace of God, according to my measure, to give him: the other, that I have not made this claim in behalf of myself only, but of all whose heart is right toward God and man, that we may all love one another as Christ hath loved us.

III. 1. One inference we may make from what has been said. We may learn from hence, what is a catholic spirit.

There is scarce any expression which has been more grossly misunderstood, and more dangerously misapplied, than this: but it will be easy for any who calmly consider the preceding observations, to correct any such misapprehensions of it, and to prevent any such misapplication.

For, from hence we may learn, first, that a catholic spirit is not *speculative* latitudinarianism. It is not an indifference to all opinions: this is the spawn of hell, not the offspring of heaven. This unsettledness of thought, this being "driven to and fro, and tossed about with every wind of doctrine," is a great curse, not a blessing, an irreconcilable enemy, not a friend, to true catholicism. A man of a truly catholic spirit has not now his religion to seek. He is fixed as the sun in his judgement concerning the main branches of Christian doctrine. It is true, he is always ready to hear and weigh whatsoever can be offered against his principles; but as this does not show any wavering in his own mind, so neither does it occasion any. He does not halt between two opinions, nor vainly endeavour to blend them into one. Observe this, you who know not what spirit ye are of: who call yourselves men of a catholic spirit, only because you are of a muddy understanding; because your mind is all in a mist; because you have no settled, consistent principles, but are for jumbling all opinions together. Be convinced, that you have quite missed your way; you know not where you are. You think you are got into the very spirit of Christ; when, in truth, you are nearer the spirit of Antichrist. Go, first, and learn the first elements of the gospel of Christ, and then shall you learn to be of a truly catholic spirit.

2. From what has been said, we may learn, secondly, that a catholic spirit is not any kind of *practical* latitudinarianism. It is not indifference as to public worship, or as to the outward manner of performing it. This, likewise, would not be a blessing but a curse. Far from being an help thereto, it would, so long as it remained, be an unspeakable hindrance to the worshipping of God in spirit and in truth. But the man of a truly catholic spirit, having weighed all things in the balance of the sanctuary, has no doubt, no scruple at all, concerning that particular mode of worship wherein he joins. He is clearly convinced, that *this* manner of worshipping God is both scriptural and rational. He knows none in the world which is more scriptural, none which is more rational. Therefore, without rambling hither and thither, he cleaves

close thereto, and praises God for the opportunity of so doing.

3. Hence we may, thirdly, learn, that a catholic spirit is not indifference to all congregations. This is another sort of latitudinarianism, no less absurd and unscriptural than the former. But it is far from a man of a truly catholic spirit. He is fixed in his congregation as well as his principles. He is united to one, not only in spirit, but by all the outward ties of Christian fellowship. There he partakes of all the ordinances of God. There he receives the supper of the Lord. There he pours out his soul in public prayer, and joins in public praise and thanksgiving. There he rejoices to hear the word of reconciliation, the gospel of the grace of God. With these his nearest, his best-beloved brethren, on solemn occasions, he seeks God by fasting. These particularly he watches over in love, as they do over his soul; admonishing, exhorting, comforting, reproving, and every way building up each other in the faith. These he regards as his own household; and therefore, according to the ability God has given him, naturally cares for them, and provides that they may have all the things that are needful for life and godliness.

4. But while he is steadily fixed in his religious principles in what he believes to be the truth as it is in Jesus; while he firmly adheres to that worship of God which he judges to be most acceptable in his sight; and while he is united by the tenderest and closest ties to one particular congregation,—his heart is enlarged toward all mankind, those he knows and those he does not; he embraces with strong and cordial affection neighbours and strangers, friends and enemies. This is catholic or universal love. And he that has this is of a catholic spirit. For love alone gives the title to this character: catholic love is a catholic spirit.

5. If, then, we take this word in the strictest sense, a man of a catholic spirit is one who, in the manner above-mentioned, gives his hand to all whose hearts are right with his heart: one who knows how to value, and praise God for, all the advantages he enjoys, with regard to the knowledge of the things of God, the true scriptural manner of worshipping him, and, above all, his union with a congregation fearing God and working righteousness: one who, retaining these blessings with the strictest care, keeping them as the apple of his eye, at the same time loves—as friends, as brethren in the Lord, as members of Christ and children of God, as joint partakers now of the present kingdom of God, and fellow heirs of his eternal kingdom—all, of whatever opinion or worship, or congregation, who believe in the Lord Jesus Christ; who love God and man; who, rejoicing to please, and fearing to offend God, are careful to abstain from evil, and zealous of good works. He is the man of a truly catholic spirit, who bears all these continually upon his heart; who having an unspeakable tenderness for their persons, and longing for their welfare, does not cease to commend them to God in prayer, as well as to plead their cause before men; who speaks comfortably to them, and labours, by all his words, to strengthen their hands in God. He assists them to the uttermost of his power in all things, spiritual and temporal. He is ready "to spend and be spent for them;" yea, to lay down his life for their sake.

6. Thou, O man of God, think on these things! If thou art already in this way, go on. If thou hast heretofore mistook the path, bless God who hath brought thee back! And now run the race which is set before thee, in the royal way of universal love. Take heed, lest thou be either wavering in thy judgement, or straitened in thy bowels: but keep an even pace, rooted in the faith once delivered to the saints, and grounded in love, in true catholic love, till thou art swallowed up in love for ever and ever!

[Charles Wesley's hymn, CATHOLIC LOVE, added in some editions:

Weary of all this wordy strife,
These notions, forms, and modes, and names,
To Thee, the way, the Truth, the Life,
Whose love my simple heart inflames,
Divinely taught, at last I fly,
With Thee and Thine to live and die.

Forth from the midst of Babel brought,
Parties and sects I cast behind;
Enlarged my heart, and free my thought,
Where'er the latent truth I find
The latent truth with joy to own,
And bow to Jesus' name alone.

Redeem'd by Thine almighty grace,
I taste my glorious liberty,
With open arms the world embrace,
But cleave to those who cleave to Thee;
But only in Thy saints delight,
Who walk with God in purest white.

One with the little flock I rest,
The members sound who hold the head.
The chosen few, with pardon blest
And by th' anointing Spirit led
Into the mind that was in Thee
Into the depths of Deity.

My brethren, friends, and kinsmen these
Who do my heavenly Father's will;
Who aim at perfect holiness,
And all Thy counsels to fulfil,
Athirst to be whate'er Thou art,
And love their God with all their heart.

For these, howe'er in flesh disjoin'd,
Where'er dispersed o'er earth abroad,
Unfeign'd, unbounded love I find
And constant as the life of God
Fountain of life, from thence it sprung,
As pure, as even, and as strong.

Join'd to the hidden church unknown
In this sure bond of perfectness
Obscurely safe, I dwell alone
And glory in th' uniting grace,
To me, to each believer given,
To all Thy saints in earth and heaven.
Charles Wesley]

40*. CHRISTIAN PERFECTION

"Not as though I had already attained, either were already perfect."

Phil. 3:12.

1. There is scarce any expression in Holy Writ which has given more offence than this. The word *perfect* is what many cannot bear. The very sound of it is an abomination to them. And whosoever *preaches perfection* (as the phrase is,) that is, asserts that it is attainable in this life, runs great hazard of being accounted by them worse than a heathen man or a publican.

2. And hence some have advised, wholly to lay aside the use of those expressions, "because they have given so great offence." But are they not found in the oracles of God? If so, by what authority can any Messenger of God lay them aside, even though all men should be offended? We have not so learned Christ; neither may we thus give place to the devil. Whatsoever God hath Spoken that will we speak, whether men will hear or whether they will forbear; knowing that then alone can any Minister of Christ be "pure from the blood of all men," when he hath "not shunned to declare unto them all the counsel of God." [Acts 20:26, 27]

3. We may not, therefore, lay these expressions aside, seeing they are the words of God, and not of man. But we may and ought to explain the meaning of them, that those who are sincere of heart may not err to the right hand or to the left, from the mark of the prize of their high calling. And this is the more needful to be done because in the verse already repeated the Apostle speaks of himself as not perfect: "Not," saith he, "as though I were already perfect." And yet immediately after, in the fifteenth verse, he speaks of himself, yea and many others, as perfect. "Let us," saith he, "as many as be perfect, be thus minded." [Phil. 3:15]

4. In order, therefore, to remove the difficulty arising from this seeming contradiction, as well as to give light to them who are pressing forward to the mark, and that those who are lame be not turned out of the way, I shall endeavor to show, First, in what sense Christians *are not*; and, Secondly, in what sense they *are, perfect.*

I. 1. In the first place I shall endeavor to show in what sense Christians are *not perfect.* And both from experience and Scripture it appears, First, that they are not perfect in knowledge: they are not *so* perfect in this life as to be free from ignorance. They know, it may be, in common with other men, many things relating to the present world; and they know, with regard to the world to come, the general truths which God hath revealed. They know, likewise, (what the natural man receiveth not, for these things are spiritually discerned,) "what manner of love" it is wherewith "the Father" hath loved them, "that they should be called the sons of God." [1 John 3:1] They know the mighty working of his Spirit in their hearts; [Eph. 3:16] and the wisdom of his providence, directing all their paths, [Prov. 3:6] and causing all things to work together for their good. [Rom. 8:28] Yea, they know in every circumstance of life what the Lord requireth of them, and how to keep a conscience void of offence both toward God and toward man. [Acts 24:16]

2. But innumerable are the things which they know not. Touching the Almighty himself, they cannot search him out to perfection. "Lo, these are but a part of his ways; but the thunder of his power who can understand?" [Job 26:14] They cannot understand, I will not say, how "there are Three that bear record in heaven, the Father, the Son, and the Holy Spirit, and these three are one;" [1 John 5:7] or how the eternal Son of God "took upon himself the form of a servant;" [Phil. 2:7]—but not any one attribute, not any one circumstance of the divine nature. [2 Pet. 1:4] Neither is it for them to know the times and seasons [Acts 1:7] when God will work his great works upon the earth; no, not even those which he hath in part revealed by his servants and Prophets since the world began. [see Amos 3:7] Much less do they know when God, having "accomplished the number of his elect, will hasten his kingdom;" when "the heavens shall pass away with a great noise, and the elements shall melt with fervent heat." [2 Pet. 3:10]

3. They know not the reasons even of many of his present dispensations with the sons of men; but are constrained to rest here,—Though "clouds and darkness are round about him, righteousness and judgment are the habitation of his seat." [Ps. 97:2] Yea, often with regard to his dealings with themselves, doth their Lord say unto them, "What I do, thou knowest not now; but thou shalt know hereafter." [John 13:7] And how little do they know of what is ever before them, of even the visible works of his hands!—How "he spreadeth the north over the empty place, and hangeth the earth upon nothing?" [Job 26:7] how he unites all the parts of this vast machine by a secret chain which cannot be broken? So great is the ignorance, so very little the knowledge, of even the best of men!

4. No one, then, is so perfect in this life, as to be free from ignorance. Nor, Secondly, from mistake; which indeed is almost an unavoidable consequence of it; seeing those who "know but in part" [1 Cor. 13:12] are ever liable to err touching the things which they know not. It is true, the children of God do not mistake as to the things essential to salvation: They do not "put darkness for light, or light for darkness;" [Isa. 5:20] neither "seek death in the error of their life." [Wisdom 1:12] For they are "taught of God," and the way which he teaches them, the way of holiness, is so plain, that "the wayfaring man, though a fool, need not err therein." [Isa. 35:8] But in things unessential to salvation they do err, and that frequently. The best and wisest of men are frequently mistaken even with regard to facts; believing those things not to have been which really were, or those to have been done which were not. Or, suppose they are not mistaken as to the fact itself, they may be with regard to its circumstances; believing them, or many of them, to have been quite different from what in truth, they were. And hence cannot but arise many farther mistakes. Hence they may believe either past or present actions which were or are evil, to be good; and such as were or are good, to be evil.

---

* [text of the 1872 edition]

Hence also they may judge not according to truth with regard to the characters of men; and that, not only by supposing good men to be better, or wicked men to be worse, than they are, but by believing them to have been or to be good men who were or are very wicked; or perhaps those to have been or to be wicked men, who were or are holy and unreprovable.

5. Nay, with regard to the Holy Scriptures themselves, as careful as they are to avoid it, the best of men are liable to mistake, and do mistake day by day; especially with respect to those parts thereof which less immediately relate to practice. Hence even the children of God are not agreed as to the interpretation of many places in holy writ: Nor is their difference of opinion any proof that they are not the children of God on either side; but it is a proof that we are no more to expect any living man to be infallible than to be omniscient.

6. If it be objected to what has been observed under this and the preceding head, that St. John, speaking to his brethren in the faith says, "Ye have an unction from the Holy One, and ye know all things:" (1 John 2:20:) The answer is plain: "Ye know all things that are needful for your souls' health." [cf. 3 John 2] That the Apostle never designed to extend this farther, that he could not speak it in an absolute sense, is clear, First from hence;—that otherwise he would describe the disciple as "above his Master;" seeing Christ himself, as man, knew not all things: "Of that hour," saith he, "knoweth no man; no, not the Son, but the Father only." [Mark 13:32] It is clear, Secondly, from the Apostle's own words that follow: "These things have I written unto you concerning them that deceive you;" [cf. 1 John 3:7] as well as from his frequently repeated caution, "Let no man deceive you;" [see Mark 13:5;Eph. 5:6;2 Thess. 2:3] which had been altogether needless, had not those very persons who had that unction from the Holy One [1 John 2:20] been liable, not to ignorance only, but to mistake also.

7. Even Christians, therefore, are not *so* perfect as to be free either from ignorance or error: We may, Thirdly, add, nor from infirmities.—Only let us take care to understand this word aright: Only let us not give that soft title to known sins, as the manner of some is. So, one man tells us, "Every man has his infirmity, and mine is drunkenness;" Another has the infirmity of uncleanness; another of taking God's holy name in vain; and yet another has the infirmity of calling his brother, "Thou fool," [Matt. 5:22] or returning "railing for railing." [1 Pet. 3:9] It is plain that all you who thus speak, if ye repent not, shall, with your infirmities, go quick into hell! But I mean hereby, not only those which are properly termed *bodily infirmities*, but all those inward or outward imperfections which are not of a moral nature. Such are the weakness or slowness of understanding, dulness or confusedness of apprehension, incoherency of thought, irregular quickness or heaviness of imagination. Such (to mention no more of this kind) is the want of a ready or of a retentive memory. Such in another kind, are those which are commonly, in some measure, consequent upon these; namely, slowness of speech, impropriety of language, ungracefulness of pronunciation; to which one might add a thousand nameless defects, either in conversation or behaviour. These are the infirmities which are found in the best of men, in a larger or smaller proportion. And from these none can hope to be perfectly freed till the spirit returns to God that gave it. [Eccles. 12:7]

8. Nor can we expect, till then, to be wholly free from temptation. Such perfection belongeth not to this life. It is true, there are those who, being given up to work all uncleanness with greediness, [Eph. 4:19] scarce perceive the temptations which they resist not, and so seem to be without temptation. There are also many whom the wise enemy of souls, seeing to be fast asleep in the dead form of godliness, will not tempt to gross sin, lest they should awake before they drop into everlasting burnings. I know there are also children of God who, being now justified freely, [Rom. 5:1] having found redemption in the blood of Christ, [Eph. 1:7] for the present feel no temptation. God hath said to their enemies, "Touch not mine anointed, and do my children no harm." [see 1 Chron. 16:22] And for this season, it may be for weeks or months, he causeth them to "ride on high places;" [Deut. 32:13] he beareth them as on eagles' wings, [Exod. 19:4] above all the fiery darts of the wicked one. [Eph. 6:16] But this state will not last always; as we may learn from that single consideration,—that the Son of God himself, in the days of his flesh, was tempted even to the end of his life. [Heb. 2:18;4:15;6:7] Therefore, so let his servant expect to be; for "it is enough that he be as his Master." [Luke 6:40]

9. Christian perfection, therefore, does not imply (as some men seem to have imagined) an exemption either from ignorance or mistake, or infirmities or temptations. Indeed, it is only another term for holiness. They are two names for the same thing. Thus every one that is perfect is holy, and every one that is holy is, in the Scripture sense, perfect. Yet we may, lastly, observe, that neither in this respect is there any absolute perfection on earth. There is no *perfection of degrees*, as it is termed; none which does not admit of a continual increase. So that how much soever any man hath attained, or in how high a degree soever he is perfect, he hath still need to "grow in grace," [2 Pet. 3:18] and daily to advance in the knowledge and love of God his Saviour. [see Phil. 1:9]

II. 1. In what sense, then, are Christians perfect? This is what I shall endeavor, in the Second place, to show. But it should be premised, that there are several stages in Christian life, as in natural; some of the children of God being but new-born babes; others having attained to more maturity. And accordingly St. John, in his first Epistle, (1 John 2:12.) applies himself severally to those he terms little children, those he styles young men, and those whom he entitles fathers. "I write unto you, little children," saith the Apostle, "because your sins are forgiven you:" Because thus far you have attained,—being "justified freely," you "have peace with God, through Jesus Christ." [Rom. 5:1] "I write unto you, young men, because ye have overcome the wicked one;" or (as he afterwards addeth,) "because ye are strong, and the word of God abideth in you." [1 John 2:13, 14] Ye have quenched the fiery darts of the wicked one, [Eph. 6:16] the doubts and fears wherewith he disturbed your first peace; and the witness of God, that your sins are forgiven, now abideth in your heart. "I write unto you, fathers, because ye have known him that is from the beginning." [1 John 2:13] Ye have known both the Father and the Son and the Spirit of Christ, in your inmost soul. Ye are "perfect men, being grown up to the measure of the stature of the fulness of Christ." [Eph. 4:13]

2. It is of these chiefly I speak in the latter part of this discourse: For these only are properly Christians. But even babes in Christ are in such a sense perfect, or born of God, (an expression taken also in divers senses,) as, First, not to commit sin. If any doubt of this privilege of the sons of God, the question is not to be decided by abstract reasonings, which may be drawn out into an endless length, and leave the point just as it was before. Neither is it to be determined by the experience of this or that particular person. Many may suppose they do not commit sin, when they do; but this proves nothing either way. To the law and to the testimony we appeal. "Let God be true, and every man a liar." [Rom. 3:4] By his Word will we abide, and that alone. Hereby we ought to be judged.

3. Now the Word of God plainly declares, that even those who are justified, who are born again in the lowest sense, "do not continue in sin;" that they cannot "live any longer therein;" (Rom. 6:1, 2;) that they are "planted together in the likeness of the death" of Christ; (Rom. 6:5;) that their "old man is crucified with him," the body of sin being destroyed, so that henceforth they do not serve sin; that being dead with Christ, they are free from sin; (Rom. 6:6, 7;) that they are "dead unto sin, and alive unto God;" (Rom. 6:11;) that "sin hath no more dominion over them," who are "not under the law, but under grace;" but that these, "being free from sin, are become the servants of righteousness." (Rom. 6:14, 18)

4. The very least which can be implied in these words, is, that the persons spoken of therein, namely, all real Christians, or believers in Christ, are made free from outward sin. And the same freedom, which St. Paul here expresses in such variety of phrases, St. Peter expresses in that one: (1 Pet. 4:1, 2:) "He that hath suffered in the flesh hath ceased from sin,—that he no longer should live to the desires of men, but to the will of God." For this *ceasing from sin*, if it be interpreted in the lowest sense, as regarding only the outward behaviour, must denote the ceasing from the outward act, from any outward transgression of the law.

5. But most express are the well-known words of St. John, in the third chapter of his First Epistle, verse 8: "He that committeth sin is of the devil; for the devil sinneth from the beginning. For this purpose the Son of God was manifested, that he might destroy the works of the devil. Whosoever is born of God doth not commit sin; for his seed remaineth in him: And he cannot sin because he is born of God." [1 John 3:8, 9] And those in the fifth: (1 John 5:18:) "We know that whosoever is born of God sinneth not; but he that is begotten of God keepeth himself, and that wicked one toucheth him not."

6. Indeed it is said this means only, He sinneth not *wilfully*; or he doth not commit sin *habitually*; or, *not as other men do*; or, *not as he did before.* But by whom is this said? By St. John? No. There is no such word in the text; nor in the whole chapter; nor in all his Epistle; nor in any part of his writings whatsoever. Why then, the best way to answer a bold assertion is simply to deny it. And if any man can prove it from the Word of God, let him bring forth his strong reasons.

7. And a sort of reason there is, which has been frequently brought to support these strange assertions, drawn from the examples recorded in the Word of God: "What!" say they, "did not Abraham himself commit sin,—prevaricating, and denying his wife? Did not Moses commit sin, when he provoked God at the waters of strife? Nay, to produce one for all, did not even David, 'the man after God's own heart,' commit sin, in the matter of Uriah the Hittite; even murder and adultery?" It is most sure he did. All this is true. But what is it you would infer from hence? It may be granted, First, that David, in the general course of his life, was one of the holiest men among the Jews; and, Secondly, that the holiest men among the Jews did sometimes commit sin. But if you would hence infer, that all Christians do and must commit sin as long as they live; this consequence we utterly deny: It will never follow from those premises.

8. Those who argue thus, seem never to have considered that declaration of our Lord: (Matt. 11:11:) "Verily I say unto you, Among them that are born of women there hath not risen a greater than John the Baptist: Notwithstanding he that is least in the kingdom of heaven is greater than he." I fear, indeed, there are some who have imagined "the kingdom of heaven," here, to mean the kingdom of glory; as if the Son of God had just discovered to us, that the least glorified saint in heaven is greater than any man upon earth! To mention this is sufficiently to refute it. There can, therefore, no doubt be made, but "the kingdom of heaven," here, (as in the following verse, where it is said to be taken by force.) [Matt. 11:12] or, "the kingdom of God," as St. Luke expresses it,—is that kingdom of God on earth whereunto all true believers in Christ, all real Christians, belong. In these words, then, our Lord declares two things: First, that before his coming in the flesh, among all the children of men there had not been one greater than John the Baptist; whence it evidently follows, that neither Abraham, David, nor any Jew was greater than John. Our Lord, Secondly, declares that he which is least in the kingdom of God (in that kingdom which he came to set up on earth, and which the violent now began to take by force) is greater than he:—Not a greater Prophet as some have interpreted the word; for this is palpably false in fact; but greater in the grace of God, and the knowledge of our Lord Jesus Christ. Therefore, we cannot measure the privileges of real Christians by those formerly given to the Jews. Their "ministration," (or dispensation,) we allow "was glorious;" but ours "exceeds in glory." [2 Cor. 3:7–9] So that whosoever would bring down the Christian dispensation to the Jewish standard, whosoever gleans up the examples of weakness, recorded in the Law and the Prophets, and thence infers that they who have "put on Christ" [Gal. 3:27] are endued with no greater strength, doth greatly err, neither "knowing the Scriptures, nor the power of God." [Matt. 22:29]

9. "But are there not assertions in Scripture which prove the same thing, if it cannot be inferred from those examples?

Does not the Scripture say expressly, "Even a just man sinneth seven times a day?" I answer, No. The Scripture says no such thing. There is no such text in all the Bible. That which seems to be intended is the sixteenth verse of the twenty-fourth chapter of the Proverbs the words of which are these: "A just man falleth seven times, and riseth up again." [Prov. 24:16] But this is quite another thing. For, First, the words "a day" are not in the text. So that if a just man falls seven times in his life, it is as much as is affirmed here. Secondly, here is no mention of *falling into sin* at all; what is here mentioned is *falling into temporal affliction.* This plainly appears from the verse before, the words of which are these: "Lay not wait, O wicked man, against the dwelling of the righteous; spoil not his resting place." [Prov. 24:15] It follows, "For a just man falleth seven times, and riseth up again; but the wicked shall fall into mischief." As if he had said, "God will deliver him out of his trouble; but when thou fallest, there shall be none to deliver thee."

10. "But, however, in other places," continue the objectors, "Solomon does assert plainly, 'There is no man that sinneth not;' (1 Kings 8:46;2 Chron. 6:36;) yea, "There is not a just man upon earth that doeth good, and sinneth not.' (Eccles. 7:20.)" I answer, Without doubt, thus it was in the days of Solomon. Yea, thus it was from Adam to Moses, from Moses to Solomon, and from Solomon to Christ. There was then no man that sinned not. Even from the day that sin entered into the world, there was not a just man upon earth that did good and sinned not, until the Son of God was manifested to take away our sins. It is unquestionably true, that "the heir, as long as he is a child, differeth nothing from a servant." [Gal. 4:1] And that even so they (all the holy men of old, who were under the Jewish dispensation) were, during that infant state of the Church, "in bondage under the elements of the world." [Gal. 4:3] "But when the fulness of the time was come, God sent forth his Son, made under the law, to redeem them that were under the law, that they might receive the adoption of sons;" [Gal. 4:4]—that they might receive that "grace which is now made manifest by the appearing of our Saviour, Jesus Christ, who hath abolished death, and brought life and immortality to light through the gospel." (2 Tim. 1:10.) Now, therefore, they "are no more servants, but sons." [see Gal. 4:7] So that, whatsoever was the case of those under the law, we may safely affirm with St. John, that, since the gospel was given, "he that is born of God sinneth not." [1 John 5:18]

11. It is of great importance to observe, and that more carefully than is commonly done, the wide difference there is between the Jewish and the Christian dispensation; and that ground of it which the same Apostle assigns in the seventh chapter of his Gospel. (John 7:38) After he had there related, those words of our blessed Lord, "He that believeth on me, as the Scripture hath said, out of his belly shall flow rivers of living water," he immediately subjoins, "This spake he of the Spirit," *ou emellon lambanein hoi pisteuontes eis auton, which they who should believe on him were afterwards to receive.* For the holy Ghost was not yet given, because that Jesus was not yet glorified. [John 7:39] Now, the Apostle cannot mean here, (as some have taught,) that the miracle-working power of the holy Ghost was not yet given. For this was given; our Lord had given it to all the Apostles, when he first sent them forth to preach the gospel. he then gave them power over unclean spirits to cast them out; power to heal the sick; yea, to raise the dead. [Mark 10:8] But the Holy Ghost was not yet given in his sanctifying graces, as he was after Jesus was glorified. It was then when he ascended up on high, and led captivity captive, that he received those gifts for men, yea, even for the rebellious, that the Lord God might dwell among them." [Ps. 68:18; cf. Eph. 4:8] And when the day of Pentecost was fully come, [Acts 2:1] then first it was, that they who "waited for the promise of the Father" [Acts 1:4] were made more than conquerors [Rom. 8:37] over sin by the Holy Ghost given unto them.

12. That this great salvation from sin was not given till Jesus was glorified, St. Peter also plainly testifies; where, speaking of his brethren in the flesh, as now "receiving the end of their faith, the salvation of their souls," he adds, (1 Peter 1:9, 10.) "of which salvation the Prophets have inquired and searched diligently, who prophesied of the grace" that is, the gracious dispensation, "that should come unto you: Searching what, or what manner of time the Spirit of Christ which was in them did signify, when it testified beforehand the sufferings of Christ. and the glory," the glorious salvation, "that should follow. Unto whom it was revealed, that not unto themselves, but unto us they did minister the things which are now reported unto you by them that have preached the gospel unto you with the Holy Ghost sent down from heaven;" [1 Pet. 1:12] viz., at the day of Pentecost, and so unto all generations, into the hearts of all true believers. on this ground, even "the grace which was brought unto them by the revelation of Jesus Christ," [1 Pet. 1:13] the Apostle might well build that strong exhortation, "Wherefore girding up the loins of your mind, as he which hath called you is holy, so be ye holy in all manner of conversation." [1 Pet. 1:13]

13. Those who have duly considered these things must allow, that the privileges of Christians are in no wise to be measured by what the old Testament records concerning those who were under the Jewish dispensation; seeing the fulness of times is now come; the Holy Ghost is now given; the great salvation of God is brought unto men, by the revelation of Jesus Christ. The kingdom of heaven is now set up on earth; concerning which the Spirit of God declared of old, (so far is David from being the pattern or standard of Christian perfection,) "He that is feeble among them at that day, shall be as David; and the house of David shall be as God, as the angel of the Lord before them." (Zech. 12:8.)

14. If, therefore, you would prove that the Apostles words, "He that is born of God sinneth not," [1 John 5:18] are not to be understood according to their plain, natural, obvious meaning, it is from the New Testament you are to bring your proofs, else you will fight as one that beateth the air. [1 Cor. 9:26] And the first of these which is usually brought is taken from the examples recorded in the New Testament. "The Apostles themselves," it is said, "committed sin; nay, the greatest of them, Peter and Paul: St. Paul, by his sharp contention with Barnabas; [Acts 15:39] and St. Peter, by his dissimulation at Antioch." [Gal. 2:11] Well: Suppose both

Peter and Paul did then commit sin; what is it you would infer from hence? That all the other Apostles committed sin sometimes? There is no shadow of proof in this. or would you thence infer, that all the other Christians of the apostolic age committed sin? Worse and worse: This is such an inference as, one would imagine, a man in his senses could never have thought of. or will you argue thus: "If two of the Apostles did once commit sin, then all other Christians, in all ages, do and will commit sin as long as they live?" Alas, my brother! a child of common understanding would be ashamed of such reasoning as this. Least of all can you with any colour of argument infer, that any man *must* commit sin at all. No: God forbid we should thus speak! No necessity of sinning was laid upon them. The grace of God was surely sufficient for them. And it is sufficient for us at this day. With the temptation which fell on them, there was a way to escape; as there is to every soul of man in every temptation. So that whosoever is tempted to any sin, need not yield; for no man is tempted above that he is able to bear. [1 Cor. 10:13]

15. "But St. Paul besought the Lord thrice, and yet he could not escape from his temptation." Let us consider his own words literally translated: "There was given to me a thorn to the flesh, an angel" (or messenger) "of Satan, to buffet me. Touching this, I besought the Lord thrice, that it" (or he) "might depart from me. And he said unto me, My grace is sufficient for thee: For my strength is made perfect in weakness. Most gladly, therefore, will I rather glory in" these "my weaknesses, that the strength of Christ may rest upon me. Therefore I take pleasure in weaknesses;—for when I am weak, then am I strong." [2 Cor. 12:7–10]

16. As this scripture is one of the strong-holds of the patrons of sin, it may be proper to weigh it thoroughly. Let it be observed then, First, it does by no means appear that this thorn, whatsoever it was, occasioned St. Paul to commit sin; much less laid him under any necessity of doing so. Therefore, from hence it can never be proved that any Christian must commit sin. Secondly, the ancient Fathers inform us, it was bodily pain: "a violent headache, saith Tertullian; (*De Pudic.*;) to which both Chrysostom and St. Jerome agree. St. Cyprian [*De Mortalitate*] expresses it, a little more generally, in those terms: "Many and grievous torments of the flesh and of the body." [*Carnis et corporis multa ac gravia tormenta.*] Thirdly, to this exactly agree the Apostles own words, "A thorn to the flesh to smite, beat, or buffet me." "My strength is made perfect in weakness:"— Which same word occurs no less than four times in these two verses only. But, Fourthly, whatsoever it was, it could not be either inward or outward sin. It could no more be inward stirrings, than outward expressions, of pride, anger, or lust. This is manifest, beyond all possible exception from the words that immediately follow: "Most gladly will I glory in" these "my weaknesses, that the strength of Christ may rest upon me." [2 Cor. 12:9] What! Did he glory in pride, in anger, in lust? Was it through these *weaknesses*, that the strength of Christ rested upon him? He goes on: "Therefore I take pleasure in weaknesses; for when I am weak, then am I strong;" [2 Cor. 12:10] that is, when I am weak *in body*, then am I strong *in spirit*. But will any man dare to say, "When I

am weak by pride or lust, then am I strong in spirit?" I call you all to record this day, who find the strength of Christ resting upon you, can you glory in anger, or pride, or lust? Can you take pleasure in these infirmities? Do these weaknesses make you strong? Would you not leap into hell, were it possible, to escape them? even by yourselves, then, judge, whether the Apostle could glory and take pleasure in them! Let it be, Lastly, observed, that this thorn was given to St. Paul above fourteen years before he wrote this epistle; [2 Cor. 12:2] which itself was wrote several years before he finished his course. [see Acts 20:24; 2 Tim. 4:7] So that he had after this, a long course to run, many battles to fight, many victories to gain, and great increase to receive in all the gifts of God, and the knowledge of Jesus Christ. Therefore from any spiritual weakness (if such it had been) which he at that time felt, we could by no means infer that he was never made strong; that Paul the aged, the father in Christ, still laboured under the same weaknesses; that he was in no higher state till the day of his death. From all which it appears that this instance of St. Paul is quite foreign to the question, and does in no wise clash with the assertion of St. John, "He that is born of God sinneth not." [1 John 5:18]

17. "But does not St. James directly contradict this? His words are, 'In many things we offend all, (Jas. 3:2:) And is not offending the same as committing sin?" In this place, I allow it is: I allow the persons here spoken of did commit sin; yea, that they all committed many sins. But who are the persons here spoken of? Why, those many masters or teachers whom God had not sent; (probably the same vain men who taught that faith without works, which is so sharply reproved in the preceding chapter;) [Jas. 2] not the Apostle himself, nor any real Christian. That in the word *we* (used by a figure of speech common in all other, as well as the inspired, writings) the Apostle could not possibly include himself or any other true believer, appears evidently, First, from the same word in the ninth verse:—"Therewith," saith he, "bless we God and therewith curse we men. Out of the same mouth proceedeth blessing and cursing." [Jas. 3:9] True; but not out of the mouth of the Apostle, nor of anyone who is in Christ a new creature. [2 Cor. 5:17] Secondly, from the verse immediately preceding the text, and manifestly connected with it: "My brethren, be not many masters," (or teachers,) "knowing that we shall receive the greater condemnation." "For in many things we offend all." [Jas. 3:1] *We!* Who? Not the Apostles, not true believers; but they who know they should *receive the greater condemnation*, because of those many offences. But this could not be spoke of the Apostle himself, or of any who trod in his steps, seeing "there is no condemnation to them who walk not after the flesh, but after the Spirit." [Rom. 8:2] Nay, Thirdly, the very verse itself proves, that "we offend all," cannot be spoken either of all men, or of all Christians: For in it there immediately follows the mention of a man who *offends not*, as the *we* first mentioned did; from whom, therefore, he is professedly contradistinguished, and pronounced a *perfect man.*

18. So clearly does St. James explain himself, and fix the meaning of his own words. Yet, lest any one should still remain in doubt, St. John, writing many years after St. James,

puts the matter entirely out of dispute, by the express declarations above recited. But here a fresh difficulty may arise: How shall we reconcile St. John with himself? In one place he declares, "Whosoever is born of God doth not commit sin;" [1 John 3:9] and again,—"We know that he which is born of God sinneth not:" [1 John 5:18] And yet in another he saith, "If we say that we have no sin, we deceive ourselves, and the truth is not in us;" [1 John 1:8] and again,—"If we say that we have not sinned, we make him a liar, and his word is not in us." [1 John 1:10]

19. As great a difficulty as this may at first appear, it vanishes away, if we observe, First, that the tenth verse fixes the sense of the eighth: "If we say we have no sin," in the former, being explained by, "If we say we have not sinned," in the latter verse. [1 John 1:10, 8] Secondly, that the point under present consideration is not whether we *have or have not sinned heretofore*; and neither of these verses asserts that we *do sin, or commit sin now*. Thirdly, that the ninth verse explains both the eighth and tenth. "If we confess our sins, he is faithful and just to forgive us our sins, and to cleanse us from all unrighteousness:" As if he had said, "I have before affirmed, The blood of Jesus Christ cleanseth us from all sin; but let no man say, I need it not; I have no sin to be cleansed from. If we say that we have no sin, that we have not sinned, we deceive ourselves, and make God a liar: But if we confess our sins, he is faithful and just,' not only 'to forgive our sins,' but also 'to cleanse us from all unrighteousness:' [1 John 1:8–10] that we may 'go and sin no more.' " [John 8:11]

20. St. John, therefore, is well consistent with himself, as well as with the other holy writers; as will yet more evidently appear if we place all his assertions touching this matter in one view: He declares, First, the blood of Jesus Christ cleanseth us from all sin. Secondly, no man can say, I have not sinned, I have no sin to be cleansed from. Thirdly, but God is ready both to forgive our past sins and to save us from them for the time to come. [1 John 1:7–10] Fourthly, "These things I write unto you," saith the Apostle, "that ye may not sin. But if any man" should "sin," or *have sinned*, (as the word might be rendered,) he need not continue in sin; seeing "we have an Advocate with the Father, Jesus Christ the righteous." [1 John 2:1–2] Thus far all is clear. But lest any doubt should remain in a point of so vast importance, the Apostle resumes this subject in the third chapter, and largely explains his own meaning. "Little children," saith he, "let no man deceive you:" (As though I had given any encouragement to those that continue in sin:) "He that doeth righteousness is righteous, even as He is righteous. He that committeth sin is of the devil; for the devil sinneth from the beginning. For this purpose the Son of God was manifested, that he might destroy the works of the devil. Whosoever is born of God doth not commit sin: For his seed remaineth in him; and he cannot sin, because he is born of God. In this the children of God are manifest, and the children of the devil." (1 John 3:7–10.) Here the point, which till then might possibly have admitted of some doubt in weak minds, is purposely settled by the last of the inspired writers, and decided in the clearest manner. In conformity, therefore, both to the doctrine of St. John, and to the whole tenor of the New Testament, we fix this conclusion—*A Christian is so far perfect, as not to commit sin.*

21. This is the glorious privilege of every Christian; yea, though he be but *a babe in Christ.* But it is only of those who *are strong* in the Lord, "and "have overcome the wicked one," or rather of those who "have known him that is from the beginning," [1 John 2:13, 14] that it can be affirmed they are in such a sense perfect, as, Secondly, to be freed from evil thoughts and evil tempers. First, from evil or sinful thoughts. But here let it be observed, that thoughts concerning evil are not always evil thoughts; that a thought concerning sin, and a sinful thought, are widely different. A man, for instance, may think of a murder which another has committed; and yet this is no evil or sinful thought. So our blessed Lord himself doubtless thought of, or understood the thing spoken by the devil, when he said, "All these things will I give thee, if thou wilt fall down and worship me." [Matt. 4:9] Yet had he no evil or sinful thought; nor indeed was capable of having any. And even hence it follows, that neither have real Christians: for "every one that is perfect is as his Master." (Luke 6:40) Therefore, if He was free from evil or sinful thoughts, so are they likewise.

22. And, indeed, whence should evil thoughts proceed, in the servant who is *as his Master?* "Out of the heart of man" (if at all) "proceed evil thoughts." (Mark 7:21) If, therefore, his heart be no longer evil, then evil thoughts can no longer proceed out of it. If the tree were corrupt, so would be the fruit: But the tree is good; The fruit, therefore is good also; (Matt. 22:33) our Lord himself bearing witness, "every good tree bringeth forth good fruit. A good tree cannot bring forth evil fruit," as "a corrupt tree cannot bring forth good fruit." (Matt 7:17, 18)

23. The same happy privilege of real Christians, St. Paul asserts from his own experience. "The weapons of our warfare," saith he, "are not carnal, but mighty through God to the pulling down of strongholds; casting down imaginations" (or *reasonings* rather, for so the word *logimous* signifies; all the reasonings of pride and unbelief against the declarations, promises, or gifts of God) "and every high thing that exalteth itself against the knowledge of God, and bringing into captivity every thought to the obedience of Christ." (2 Cor. 10:4.)

24. And as Christians indeed are freed from evil thoughts, so are they, Secondly, from evil tempers. This is evident from the above-mentioned declaration of our Lord himself: "The disciple is not above his Master; but every one that is perfect shall be as his Master." [Luke 6:40] He had been delivering, just before, some of the sublimest doctrines of Christianity, and some of the most grievous to flesh and blood. "I say unto you, love your enemies, do good to them which hate you;—and unto him that smiteth thee on the one cheek, offer also the other." [Luke 6:29] Now these he well knew the world would not receive; and, therefore, immediately adds, "Can the blind lead the blind? Will they not both fall into the ditch?" [Luke 6:39] As if he had said, "Do not confer with flesh and blood touching these things,—with men void of spiritual discernment, the eyes of whose understanding God hath not opened,—lest they and you perish together." In the

next verse he removes the two grand objections with which these wise fools meet us at every turn: "These things are too grievous to be borne," or, "They are too high to be attained," [Matt. 23:4] saying, " 'The disciple is not above his Master;' therefore, if I have suffered, be content to tread in my steps. And doubt ye not then, but I will fulfill my word: 'For every one that is perfect shall be as his Master.' " [Luke 6:40] But his Master was free from all sinful tempers. So, therefore, is his disciple, even every real Christian.

25. every one of these can say, with St. Paul, "I am crucified with Christ: Nevertheless I live; yet not I, but Christ liveth in me:" [Gal 2:20]—Words that manifestly describe a deliverance from inward as well as from outward sin. This is expressed both negatively, *I live not*, (my evil nature, the body of sin, is destroyed;) and positively, *Christ liveth in me*; and, therefore, all that is holy, and just, and good. Indeed, both these, *Christ liveth in me*, and *I live not*, are inseparably connected; for "what communion hath light with darkness, or Christ with Belial?" [2 Cor. 6:15]

26. He, therefore, who liveth in true believers, hath "purified their hearts by faith;" [Acts 15:9] insomuch that every one that hath Christ in him the hope of glory, [Col. 1:27] "purifieth himself, even as he is pure" (1 John 3:3.) He is purified from pride; for Christ was lowly of heart. [Matt. 11:29] He is pure from self-will or desire; for Christ desired only to do the will of his Father, and to finish his work. [John 4:34; 5:30] And he is pure from anger, in the common sense of the word; for Christ was meek and gentle, patient and long-suffering. I say, in the common sense of the word; for all anger is not evil. We read of our Lord himself, (Mark 3:5,) that he once "looked round with anger." But with what kind of anger? The next word shows, *syllypoumenos*, being, at the same time "grieved for the hardness of their hearts." [Mark 3:6] So then he was angry at the sin, and in the same moment grieved for the sinners; angry or displeased at the offence, but sorry for the offenders. With anger, yea, hatred, he looked upon the thing; with grief and love upon the persons. Go, thou that art perfect, and do likewise. Be thus angry, and thou sinnest not; [see Eph. 4:26] feeling a displacency at every offence against God, but only love and tender compassion to the offender.

27. Thus doth Jesus "save his people from their sins:" [Matt. 1:21] And not only from outward sins, but also from the sins of their hearts; from evil thoughts and from evil tempers.—"True," say some, "we shall thus be saved from our sins; but not till death; not in this world." But how are we to reconcile this with the express words of St. John?—"Herein is our love made perfect, that we may have boldness in the day of judgment. Because as he is, so are we in this world." The Apostle here, beyond all contradiction, speaks of himself and other living Christians, of whom (as though he had foreseen this very evasion, and set himself to overturn it from the foundation) he flatly affirms, that not only at or after death but *in this world* they are as their Master. (1 John 4:17.)

28. Exactly agreeable to this are his words in the first chapter of this Epistle, (1 John 1:5.) "God is light, and in him is no darkness at all. If we walk in the light,—we have fellowship one with another, and the blood of Jesus Christ his Son cleanseth us from all sin." And again, "If we confess our sins, he is faithful and just to forgive us our sins, and to cleanse us from all unrighteousness." [1 John 1:9] Now it is evident, the Apostle here also speaks of a deliverance wrought *in this world*. For he saith not, the blood of Christ will cleanse at the hour of death, or in the day of judgment, but, it "cleanseth," at the time present, "us," living Christians, "from all sin." And it is equally evident, that if *any sin* remain, we are not cleansed from *all* sin: If *any* unrighteousness remain in the soul, it is not cleansed from *all* unrighteousness. Neither let any sinner against his own soul say, that this relates to justification only, or the cleansing us from the guilt of sin. First, because this is confounding together what the Apostle clearly distinguishes, who mentions first, *to forgive us our sins*, and then *to cleanse us from all unrighteousness*. "Secondly, because this is asserting justification by works, in the strongest sense possible; it is making all inward as well as outward holiness necessarily previous to justification. For if the cleansing here spoken of is no other than the cleansing us from the guilt of sin, then we are not cleansed from guilt; that is, are not justified, unless on condition of "walking in the light, as he is in the light." [1 John 1:7] It remains, then, that Christians are saved in this world from all sin, from all unrighteousness; that they are now in such a sense perfect, as not to commit sin, and to be freed from evil thoughts and evil tempers."

29. Thus hath the Lord fulfilled the things he spake by his holy prophets, which have been since the world began;—by Moses in particular, saying, (Deut. 30:6.) I "will circumcise thine heart, and the heart of thy seed, to love the Lord thy God with all thy heart, and with all thy soul;" by David, crying out, "Create in me a clean heart, and renew a right spirit within me;" [Ps. 51:10]—and most remarkably by Ezekiel, in those words: "Then will I sprinkle clean water upon you, and ye shall be clean; From all your filthiness, and from all your idols, will I cleanse you. A new heart also will I give you, and a new spirit will I put within you;—and cause you to walk in my statutes, and ye shall keep my judgments, and do them.—Ye shall be my people, and I will be your God. I will also save you from all your uncleannesses.—Thus saith the Lord your God, In the day that I shall have cleansed you from all your iniquities,—the Heathen shall know that I the Lord build the ruined places;—I the Lord have spoken it, and I will do it." (Ezek. 36:25.)

30. "Having therefore these promises, dearly beloved," both in the Law and in the Prophets, and having the prophetic word confirmed unto us in the Gospel, by our blessed Lord and his Apostles; "let us cleanse ourselves from all filthiness of flesh and spirit, perfecting holiness in the fear of God." [2 Cor. 7:1] "Let us fear, lest" so many "promises being made us of entering into his rest," which he that hath entered into, has ceased from his own works, "any of us should come short of it." [Heb. 4:1] "This one thing let us do, forgetting those things which are behind, and reaching forth unto those things which are before, let us press toward the mark, for the prize of the high calling of God in Christ Jesus;" [Phil. 3:13, 14] crying unto him day and night, till we also are "delivered

from the bondage of corruption, into the glorious liberty of the sons of God!" [Rom. 8:21]

The Promise of Sanctification
(Ezekiel 36:25.)

By the Rev. Charles Wesley.

1 God of all power, and truth, and grace,
 Which shall from age to age endure;
Whose word, when heaven and earth shall pass,
 Remains, and stands for ever sure:
2 Calmly to thee my soul looks up,
 And waits thy promises to prove;
The object of my steadfast hope,
 The seal of thine eternal love.
3 That I thy mercy may proclaim,
 That all mankind thy truth may see,
Hallow thy great and glorious name,
 And perfect holiness in me.
4 Chose from the world, if now I stand
 Adorn'd in righteousness divine;
If, brought unto the promised land,
 I justly call the Saviour mine;
5 Perform the work thou hast begun,
 My inmost soul to thee convert:
Love me, for ever love thine own,
 And sprinkle with thy blood my heart.
6 Thy sanctifying Spirit pour,
 To quench my thirst, and wash me clean;
Now, Father, let the gracious shower
 Descend, and make me pure from sin.
7 Purge me from every sinful blot;
 My idols all be cast aside:
Cleanse me from every evil thought,
 From all the filth of self and pride.
8 Give me a new, a perfect heart,
 From doubt, and fear, and sorrow free;
The mind which was in Christ impart,
 And let my spirit cleave to thee.
9 O take this heart of stone away,
 (Thy rule it doth not, cannot own;)
In me no longer let it stay:
 O take away this heart of stone.
10 The hatred of my carnal mind
 Out of my flesh at once remove;
Give me a tender heart, resign'd,
 And pure, and fill'd with faith and love.
11 Within me thy good Spirit place,
 Spirit of health, and love and power;
Plant in me thy victorious grace,
 And sin shall never enter more.
12 Cause me to walk in Christ my Way,
 And I thy statutes shall fulfill;
In every point thy law obey.
 And perfectly perform thy will.
13 Hast thou not said, who canst not lie,
 That I thy law shall keep and do?
Lord, I believe, though men deny;
 They all are false, but thou art true.
14 O that I now, from sin released,

 Thy word might to the utmost prove!
Enter into the promised rest,
 The Canaan of thy perfect love!
15 There let me ever, ever dwell;
 By thou my God, and I will be
Thy servant: O set to thy seal!
 Give me eternal life in thee.
16 From all remaining filth within
 Let me in Thee salvation have:
From actual, and from inbred sin
 My ransom'd soul persist to save.
17 Wash out my old original stain:
 Tell me no more It cannot be,
Demons or men! The Lamb was slain
 His blood was all poured out for me!
18 Sprinkle it, Jesu, on my heart:
 One drop of thy all-cleansing blood
Shall make my sinfulness depart,
 And fill me with the life of God.
19 Father, supply my every need:
 Sustain the life thyself hast given;
Call for the corn, the living bread,
 The manna that comes down from heaven.
20 The gracious fruits of righteousness,
 Thy blessings' unexhausted store,
In me abundantly increase;
 Nor let me ever hunger more.
21 Let me no more in deep complaint
 "My leanness, O my leanness!" cry;
Alone consumed with pining want,
 Of all my Father's children I!
22 The painful thirst, the fond desire,
 Thy joyous presence shall remove;
While my full soul doth still require
 Thy whole eternity of love.
23 Holy, and true, and righteous Lord,
 I wait to prove thy perfect will;
Be mindful of thy gracious word,
 And stamp me with thy Spirit's seal!
24 Thy faithful mercies let me find,
 In which thou causest me to trust;
Give me the meek and lowly mind,
 And lay my spirit in the dust.
25 Show me how foul my heart hath been,
 When all renew'd by grace I am:
When thou hast emptied me of sin,
 Show me the fulness of my shame.
26 Open my faith's interior eye,
 Display thy glory from above;
And all I am shall sink and die,
 Lost in astonishment and love.
27 Confound, o'erpower me with thy grace:
 I would be by myself abhorr'd;
(All might, all majesty, all praise,
 All glory be to Christ my Lord!)
28 Now let me gain perfection's height!
 Now let me into nothing fall!
Be less than nothing in thy sight,

And feel that Christ is all in all!

41.* WANDERING THOUGHTS

"Bringing into captivity every thought to the obedience of Christ."

2 Cor. 5:5.

1. But will God so "bring every thought into captivity to the obedience of Christ," that no wandering thought will find a place in the mind, even while we remain in the body? So some have vehemently maintained; yea, have affirmed that none are perfected in love unless they are so far perfected in understanding, that all wandering thoughts are done away; unless not only every affection and temper be holy and just and good, but every individual thought which arises in the mind be wise and regular.

2. This is a question of no small importance. For how many of those who fear God, yea, and love him, perhaps with all their heart, have been greatly distressed on this account! How many, by not understanding it right, have not only been distressed, but greatly hurt in their souls;—cast into unprofitable, yea, mischievous reasonings, such as slackened their motion towards God, and weakened them in running the race set before them! Nay, many, through misapprehensions of this very thing, have cast away the precious gift of God. They have been induced, first, to doubt of, and then to deny, the work God had wrought in their souls; and hereby have grieved the Spirit of God, till he withdrew and left them in utter darkness!

3. How is it then, that amidst the abundance of books which have been lately published almost on all subjects, we should have none upon wandering thoughts? at least none that will at all satisfy a calm and serious mind? In order to do this in some degree, I purpose to inquire,

    I.   What are the several sorts of wandering thoughts?

    II.   What are the general occasions of them?

    III.   Which of them are sinful, and which not?

    IV.   Which of them we may expect and pray to be delivered from?

I. 1. I purpose to inquire, First, What are the several sorts of wandering thoughts? The particular sorts are innumerable; but, in general, they are of two sorts: Thoughts that wander from God; and thoughts that wander from the particular point we have in hand.

2. With regard to the former, all our thoughts are naturally of this kind: For they are continually wandering from God: We think nothing about him: God is not in all our thoughts: We are, one and all, as the Apostle observes, "without God in the world." We think of what we love; but we do not love God; therefore, we think not of him. Or, if we are now and then constrained to think of him for a time, yet as we have not pleasure therein, nay, rather, as these thoughts are not only insipid, but distasteful and irksome to us, we drive them out as soon as we can, and return to what we love to think of. So that the world, and the things of the world,—what we

shall eat, what we shall drink, what we shall put on,—what we shall see, what we shall hear, what we shall gain,—how we shall please our senses or our imagination,—takes up all our time, and engrosses all our thought. So long, therefore, as we love the world; that is, so long as we are in our natural state; all our thoughts, from morning to evening, and from evening to morning, are no other than wandering thoughts.

3. But many times we are not only "without God in the world," but also fighting against him; as there is in every man by nature a "carnal mind which is enmity against God:" No wonder, therefore, that men abound with unbelieving thoughts; either saying in their hearts, "There is no God," or questioning, if not denying, his power or wisdom, his mercy, or justice, or holiness. No wonder that they so often doubt of his providence, at least, of its extending to all events; or that, even though they allow it, they still entertain murmuring or repining thoughts. Nearly related to these, and frequently connected with them, are proud and vain imaginations. Again: Sometimes they are taken up with angry, malicious, or revengeful thoughts; at other times, with airy scenes of pleasure, whether of sense or imagination; whereby the earthly, sensual mind becomes more earthy and sensual still. Now by all these they make flat war with God: These are wandering thoughts of the highest kind.

4. Widely different from these are the other sort of wandering thoughts; in which the heart does not wander from God, but the understanding wanders from the particular point it had then in view. For instance: I sit down to consider those words in the verse preceding the text: "The weapons of our warfare are not carnal, but mighty through God." I think, "This ought to be the case with all that are called Christians. But how far is it otherwise! Look round into almost every part of what is termed the Christian world. What manner of weapons are these using? In what kind of warfare are they engaged;

    While men, like fiends, each other tear;
    In all the hellish rage of war?

See how *these* Christians love one another! Wherein are they preferable to Turks and Pagans? What abomination can be found among Mahometans or Heathens which is not found among Christians also?" And thus my mind runs off, before I am aware, from one circumstance to another. Now, all these are, in some sense, wandering thoughts: For although they do not wander from God, much less fight against him, yet they do wander from the particular point I had in view.

II. Such is the nature, such are the sorts (to speak rather usefully than philosophically) of wandering thoughts. But what are the general occasions of them? This we are, in the Second place, to consider.

1. And it is easy to observe, that the occasion of the former sort of thoughts, which oppose or wander from God, are, in general, sinful tempers. For instance: Why is not God in all the thoughts, in any of the thoughts of a natural man? For a plain reason: Be he rich or poor, learned or unlearned, he is an Atheist; (though not vulgarly so called;) he neither knows nor loves God. Why are his thoughts continually wandering

after the world? Because he is an idolater. He does not indeed worship an image, or bow down to the stock of a tree; yet is he sunk into equally damnable idolatry: He loves, that is worships, the world. He seeks happiness in the things that are seen, in the pleasures that perish in the using. Why is it that his thoughts are perpetually wandering from the very end of his being, the knowledge of God in Christ? Because he is an unbeliever; because he has no faith; or at least, no more than a devil. So all these wandering thoughts easily and naturally spring from that evil root of unbelief.

2. The case is the same in other instances: Pride, anger, revenge, vanity, lust, covetousness, every one of them occasions thoughts suitable to its own nature. And so does every sinful temper of which the human mind is capable. The particulars it is hardly possible, nor is it needful, to enumerate: It suffices to observe, that as many evil tempers as find a place in any soul, so many ways that soul will depart from God, by the worst kind of wandering thoughts.

3. The occasions of the latter kind of wandering thoughts are exceeding various. Multitudes of them are occasioned by the natural union between the soul and body. How immediately and how deeply is the understanding affected by a diseased body! Let but the blood move irregularly in the brain, and all regular thinking is at an end. Raging madness ensues; and then farewell to all evenness of thought. Yea, let only the spirits be hurried or agitated to a certain degree, and a temporary madness, a delirium, prevents all settled thought. And is not the same irregularity of thought, in a measure, occasioned by every nervous disorder? So does the "corruptible body press down the soul, and cause it to muse about many things."

4. But does it only cause this in the time of sickness or preternatural disorder? Nay, but more or less, at all times, even in a state of perfect health. Let a man be ever so healthy, he will be more or less delirious every four-and-twenty hours. For does he not sleep? And while he sleeps, is he not liable to dream? And who then is master of his own thoughts, or able to preserve the order and consistency of them? Who can then keep them fixed to any one point, or prevent their wandering from pole to pole?

5. But suppose we are awake, are we always so awake that we can steadily govern our thoughts? Are we not unavoidably exposed to contrary extremes, by the very nature of this machine, the body? Sometimes we are too heavy, too dull and languid, to pursue any chain of thought. Sometimes, on the other hand, we are too lively. The imagination, without leave, starts to and fro, and carries us away hither and thither, whether we will or no; and all this from the merely natural motion of the spirits, or vibration of the nerves.

6. Farther: How many wanderings of thought may arise from those various associations of our ideas which are made entirely without our knowledge, and independently on our choice? How these connexions are formed, we cannot tell; but they are formed in a thousand different manners. Nor is it in the power of the wisest or holiest of men to break those associations, or prevent what is the necessary consequences of them, and matter of daily observation. Let the fire but touch one end of the train, and it immediately runs on to the other.

7. Once more: Let us fix our attention as studiously as we are able on any subject, yet let either pleasure or pain arise, especially if it be intense, and it will demand our immediate attention, and attach our thought to itself. It will interrupt the steadiest contemplation, and divert the mind from its favourite subject.

8. These occasions of wandering thoughts lie within, are wrought into our very nature. But they will likewise naturally and necessarily arise from the various impulse of outward objects. Whatever strikes upon the organ of sense, the eye or ear, will raise a perception in the mind. And, accordingly, whatever we see or hear will break in upon our former train of thought. Every man, therefore, that does anything in our sight, or speaks anything in our hearing, occasions our mind to wander, more or less, from the point it was thinking of before.

9. And there is no question but those evil spirits who are continually seeking whom they may devour make use of all the foregoing occasions to hurry and distract our minds. Sometimes by one, sometimes by another, of these means, they will harass and perplex us, and, so far as God permits, interrupt our thoughts, particularly when they are engaged on the best subjects. Nor is this at all strange: They will understand the very springs of thought; and know on which of the bodily organs the imagination, the understanding, and every other faculty of the mind more immediately depends. And hereby they know how, by affecting those organs, to affect the operations dependent on them. Add to this, that they can inject a thousand thoughts, without any of the preceding means; it being as natural for spirit to act upon spirit, as for matter to act upon matter. These things being considered, we cannot admire that our thought so often wanders from any point which we have in view.

III. 1. What kind of wandering thoughts are sinful, and what not, is the Third thing to be inquired into. And, First, all those thoughts which wander from God, which leave him no room in our minds, are undoubtedly sinful. For all these imply practical Atheism; and by these we are without God in the world. And so much more are all those which are contrary to God, which imply opposition or enmity to him. Such are all murmuring, discontented thoughts, which say, in effect, "We will not have thee to rule over us;"—all unbelieving thoughts, whether with regard to his being, his attributes, or his providence. I mean, his particular providence over all things, as well as all persons, in the universe; that without which "not a sparrow falls to the ground," by which "the hairs of our head are all numbered;" for as to a general providence, (vulgarly so called,) contradistinguished from a particular, it is only a decent, well-sounding word, which means just nothing.

2. Again: All thoughts which spring from sinful tempers, are undoubtedly sinful. Such, for instance, are those that spring from a revengeful temper, from pride, or lust, or vanity. "An evil tree cannot bring forth good fruit:" Therefore if the tree be evil, so must the fruit be also.

3. And so must those be which either produce or feed any sinful temper; those which either give rise to pride or vanity, to anger or love of the world, or confirm and increase these

or any other unholy temper, passion, or affection. For not only whatever flows from evil is evil; but also whatever leads to it; whatever tends to alienate the soul from God, and to make or keep it earthly, sensual, and devilish.

4. Hence, even those thoughts which are occasioned by weakness or disease, by the natural mechanism of the body, or by the laws of vital union, however innocent they may be in themselves, do nevertheless become sinful, when they either produce or cherish and increase in us any sinful temper; suppose the desire of the flesh, the desire of the eye, or the pride of life. In like manner, the wandering thoughts which are occasioned by the words or actions of other men, if they cause or feed any wrong disposition, then commence sinful. And the same we may observe of those which are suggested or injected by the devil. When they minister to any earthly or devilish temper, (which they do, whenever we give place to them, and thereby make them our own,) then they are equally sinful with the tempers to which they minister.

5. But, abstracting from these cases, wandering thoughts, in the latter sense of the word, that is, thoughts wherein our understanding wanders from the point it has in view, are no more sinful than the motion of the blood in our veins, or of the spirits in our brain. If they arise from an infirm constitution, or from some accidental weakness or distemper, they are as innocent as it is to have a weak constitution or a distempered body. And surely no one doubts but a bad state of nerves, a fever of any kind, and either a transient or a lasting delirium, may consist with perfect innocence. And if they should arise in a soul which is united to a healthful body, either from the natural union between the body and soul, or from any of ten thousand changes which may occur in those organs of the body that minister to thought;—in any of these cases they are as perfectly innocent as the causes from which they spring. And so they are when they spring from the casual, involuntary associations of our ideas.

6. If our thoughts wander from the point we had in view, by means of other men variously affecting our senses, they are equally innocent still: For it is no more a sin to understand what I see and hear, and in many cases cannot help seeing, hearing, and understanding, than it is to have eyes and ears. "But if the devil injects wandering thoughts, are not those thoughts evil?" They are troublesome, and in that sense evil; but they are not sinful. I do not know that he spoke to our Lord with an audible voice; perhaps he spoke to his heart only when he said, "All these things will I give thee, if thou wilt fall down and worship me." But whether he spoke inwardly or outwardly, our Lord doubtless understood what he said. He had therefore a thought correspondent to those words. But was it a sinful thought? We know it was not. In him was no sin, either in action, or word, or thought. Nor is there any sin in a thousand thoughts of the same kind, which Satan may inject into any of our Lord's followers.

7. It follows that none of these wandering thoughts (whatever unwary persons have affirmed, thereby grieving whom the Lord had not grieved) are inconsistent with perfect love. Indeed, if they were, then not only sharp pain, but sleep itself, would be inconsistent with it:—Sharp pain; for whenever this supervenes, whatever we were before thinking of, it will interrupt our thinking, and of course draw our thoughts into another channel:—Yea, and sleep itself; as it is a state of insensibility and stupidity; and such as is generally mixed with thoughts wandering over the earth, loose, wild, and incoherent. Yet certainly these are consistent with perfect love: So then are all wandering thoughts of this kind.

IV. 1. From what has been observed, it is easy to give a clear answer to the last question,—What kind of wandering thoughts we may expect and pray to be delivered from.

From the former sort of wandering thoughts,—those wherein the heart wanders from God; from all that are contrary to his will, or that leave us without God in the world; every one that is perfected in love is unquestionably delivered. This deliverance, therefore, we may expect; this we may, we ought to pray for. Wandering thoughts of this kind imply unbelief, if not enmity against God; but both of these he will destroy, will bring utterly to an end. And indeed, from all sinful wandering thoughts we shall be absolutely delivered. All that are perfected in love are delivered from these; else they were not saved from sin. Men and devils will tempt them all manner of ways; but they cannot prevail over them.

2. With regard to the latter sort of wandering thoughts, the case is widely different. Till the cause is removed, we cannot in reason expect the effect should cease. But the causes or occasions of these will remain as long as we remain in the body. So long, therefore, we have all reason to believe the effects will remain also.

3. To be more particular: Suppose a soul, however holy, to dwell in a distempered body; suppose the brain be so thoroughly disordered, as that raging madness follows; will not all the thoughts be wild and unconnected as long as that disorder continues? Suppose a fever occasions that temporary madness which we term a delirium; can there be any just connexion of thought till that delirium is removed? Yea, suppose what is called a nervous disorder to rise to so high a degree as to occasion at least a partial madness; will there not be a thousand wandering thoughts? And must not these irregular thoughts continue as long as the disorder which occasions them?

4. Will not the case be the same with regard to those thoughts that necessarily arise from violent pain? They will more or less continue, while that pain continues, by the inviolable order of nature. This order, likewise, will obtain, where thoughts are disturbed, broken, or interrupted, by any defect of the apprehension, judgement, or imagination, flowing from the natural constitution of the body. And how many interruptions may spring from the unaccountable and involuntary association of our ideas! Now, all these are directly or indirectly caused by the corruptible body pressing down the mind. Nor, therefore, can we expect them to be removed till "this corruptible shall put on incorruption."

5. And then only, when we lie down in the dust, shall we be delivered from those wandering thoughts which are occasioned by what we see and hear, among those by whom we are now surrounded. To avoid these, we must go out of the world: For as long as we remain therein, as long as there are men and women round about us, and we have eyes to see and ears to hear, the things which we daily see and hear will

certainly affect our mind, and will more or less break in upon and interrupt our preceding thoughts.

6. And as long as evil spirits roam to and fro in a miserable, disordered world, so long they will assault (whether they can prevail or no) every inhabitant of flesh and blood. They will trouble even those whom they cannot destroy: They will attack, if they cannot conquer. And from these attacks of our restless, unwearied enemies, we must not look for an entire deliverance, till we are lodged "where the wicked cease from troubling, and where the weary are at rest."

7. To sum up the whole: To expect deliverance from those wandering thoughts which are occasioned by evil spirits is to expect that the devil should die or fall asleep, or, at least, should no more go about as a roaring lion. To expect deliverance from those which are occasioned by other men is to expect either that men should cease from the earth, or that we should be absolutely secluded from them, and have no intercourse with them; or that having eyes we should see, neither hear with our ears, but be as senseless as stocks or stones. And to pray for deliverance from those which are occasioned by the body is, in effect, to pray that we may leave the body: Otherwise it is praying for impossibilities and absurdities; praying that God would reconcile contradictions, by continuing our union with a corruptible body without the natural, necessary consequences of that union. It is as if we should pray to be angels and men, mortal and immortal, at the same time. Nay!—but when that which is immortal is come, mortality is done away.

8. Rather let us pray, both with the spirit and with the understanding, that all these things may work together for our good; that we may suffer all the infirmities of our nature, all the interruptions of men, all the assaults and suggestions of evil spirits, and in all be "more than conquerors." Let us pray, that we may be delivered from all sin; that both the root and branch may be destroyed; that we may be "cleansed from all pollution of flesh and spirit," from every evil temper, and word, and work; that we may "love the Lord our God with all our heart, with all our mind, with all our soul, and with all our strength;" that all the fruit of the Spirit may be found in us,—not only love, joy, peace, but also "long-suffering, gentleness, goodness, fidelity, meekness, temperance." Pray that all these things may flourish and abound, may increase in you more and more, till an abundant entrance be ministered unto you, into the everlasting kingdom of our Lord Jesus Christ!

42.* Satan's Devices

"We are not ignorant of his devices."

2 Cor. 2:11.

1. The devices whereby the subtle god of this world labours to destroy the children of God—or at least to torment whom he cannot destroy, to perplex and hinder them in running the race which is set before them—are numberless as the stars of heaven or the sand upon the sea-shore. But it is of one of them only that I now propose to speak, (although exerted in various ways,) whereby he endeavours to divide the gospel against itself, and by one part of it to overthrow the other.

2. The inward kingdom of heaven, which is set up in the heart of all that repent and believe the gospel, is no other than "righteousness and peace and joy in the Holy Ghost." Every babe in Christ knows we are made partakers of these, the very hour that we believe in Jesus. But these are only the first-fruits of his Spirit; the harvest is not yet. Although these blessings are inconceivably great, yet we trust to see greater than these. We trust to love the Lord our God, not only as we do now, with a weak though sincere affection, but "with all our heart, with all our mind, with all our soul, and with all our strength." We look for power to "rejoice evermore, to pray without ceasing, and in everything to give thanks;" knowing, "this is the will of God in Christ Jesus concerning us."

3. We expect to be "made perfect in love;" in that love which casts out all painful fear, and all desire but that of glorifying him we love, and of loving and serving him more and more. We look for such an increase in the experimental knowledge and love of God our Saviour as will enable us always "to walk in the light, as he is in the light." We believe the whole mind will be in us, "which was also in Christ Jesus;" that we shall love every man so as to be ready to lay down our life for his sake; so as, by this love, to be freed from anger, and pride, and from every unkind affection. We expect to be "cleansed from all our idols," "from all filthiness," whether "of flesh or spirit;" to be "saved from all our uncleannesses," inward or outward; to be "purified as He is pure."

4. We trust in his promise who cannot lie, that the time will surely come, when, in every word and work, we shall do his blessed will on earth, as it is done in heaven; when all our conversation shall be seasoned with salt, all meet to minister grace to the hearers; when, whether we eat or drink, or whatever we do, it shall be done to the glory of God; when all our words and deeds shall be "in the name of the Lord Jesus, giving thanks unto God, even the Father, through him."

5. Now this is the grand device of Satan, to destroy the first work of God in the soul, or at least to hinder its increase, by our expectation of that greater work. It is therefore my present design, First, to point out the several ways whereby he endeavours: this; And, secondly, to observe how we may retort these fiery darts of the wicked one, how we may rise the higher by what he intends for an occasion of our falling.

I. 1. I am, First, to point out the several ways whereby Satan endeavours to destroy the first work of God in the soul, or at least to hinder its increase by our expectation of that greater work. And, 1. He endeavours to damp our joy in the Lord by the consideration of our own vileness, sinfulness, unworthiness; added to this, that there must be a far greater change than is yet, or we cannot see the Lord. If we knew we must remain as we are even to the day of our death, we might possibly draw a kind of comfort, poor as it was, from that necessity. But as we know, we need not remain in this state, as we are assured there is a greater change to come, and that

---

* [text from the 1872 edition]

unless sin be all done away in this life we cannot see God in glory,—that subtle adversary often damps the joy we should otherwise feel in what we have already attained, by a perverse representation of what we have not attained, and the absolute necessity of attaining it. So that we cannot rejoice in what we have, because there is more which we have not. We cannot rightly taste the goodness of God, who hath done so great things for us, because there are so much greater things which as yet he hath not done. Likewise, the deeper conviction God works in us of our present unholiness, and the more vehement desire we feel in our heart of the entire holiness he hath promised, the more are we tempted to think lightly of the present gifts of God, and to undervalue what we have already received because of what we have not received.

2. If he can prevail thus far, if he can damp our joy, he will soon attack our peace also. He will suggest, "Are you fit to see God? He is of purer eyes than to behold iniquity. How then can you flatter yourself, so as to imagine he beholds you with approbation? God is holy: You are unholy. What communion hath light with darkness? How is it possible that you, unclean as you are, should be in a state of acceptance with God? You see indeed the mark, the prize of your high calling; but do you not see it is afar off? How can you presume then to think that all your sins are already blotted out? How can this be, until you are brought nearer to God, until you bear more resemblance to him?" Thus will he endeavour not only to shake your peace, but even to overturn the very foundation of it; to bring you back, by insensible degrees, to the point from whence you set out first, even to seek for justification by works, or by your own righteousness,—to make something in you the ground of your acceptance, or at least necessarily previous to it.

3. Or, if we hold fast, "Other foundation can no man lay than that which is laid, even Jesus Christ;" and, "I am justified freely by God's grace, through the redemption which is in Jesus;" yet he will not cease to urge, "But the tree is known by its fruits: And have you the fruits of justification? Is that mind in you which was in Christ Jesus? Are you dead unto sin, and alive unto righteousness? Are you made conformable to the death of Christ, and do you know the power of his resurrection?" And then, comparing the small fruits we feel in our souls with the fullness of the promises, we shall be ready to conclude: "Surely God hath not said that my sins are forgiven me! Surely I have not received the remission of my sins; for what lot have I among them that are sanctified?"

4. More especially in the time of sickness and pain he will press this with all his might: "Is it not the word of Him that cannot lie, 'Without holiness no man shall see the Lord?' But you are not holy. You know it well; you know holiness is the full image of God; and how far is this above, out of your sight? You cannot attain unto it. Therefore, all your labour has been in vain. All these things you have suffered in vain. You have spent your strength for nought. You are yet in your sins, and must therefore perish at the last." And thus, if your eye be not steadily fixed on Him who hath borne all your sins, he will bring you again under that "fear of death," whereby you was so long "subject unto bondage," and, by this means, impair, if not wholly destroy, your peace as, well as joy in the Lord.

5. But his master-piece of subtlety is still behind. Not content to strike at your peace and joy, he will carry his attempts farther yet: He will level his assault against your righteousness also. He will endeavour to shake, yea, if it be possible, to destroy the holiness you have already received by your very expectation of receiving more, of attaining all the image of God.

6. The manner wherein he attempts this, may partly appear from what has been already observed. For, First, by striking at our joy in the Lord, he strikes likewise at our holiness: Seeing joy in the Holy Ghost is a precious means of promoting every holy temper; a choice instrument of God whereby he carries on much of his work in a believing soul. And it is a considerable help not only to inward, but also to outward holiness. It strengthens our hands to go on in the work of faith, and in the labour of love; manfully to "fight the good fight of faith, and to lay hold on eternal life." It is peculiarly designed of God to be a balance both against inward and outward sufferings; to "lift up the hands that hang down, and confirm the feeble knees." Consequently, whatever damps our joy in the Lord proportionably obstructs our holiness. And therefore, so far as Satan shakes our joy he hinders our holiness also.

7. The same effect will ensue, if he can, by any means, either destroy or shake our peace. For the peace of God is another precious means of advancing the image of God in us. There is scarce a greater help to holiness than this, a continual tranquility of spirit, the evenness of a mind stayed upon God, a calm repose in the blood of Jesus. And without this, it is scarce possible to "grow in grace," and in the vital "knowledge of our Lord Jesus Christ." For all fear (unless the tender, filial fear) freezes and benumbs the soul. It binds up all the springs of spiritual life, and stops all motion of the heart toward God. And doubt, as it were, bemires the soul, so that it sticks fast in the deep clay. Therefore, in the same proportion as either of these prevail, our growth in holiness is hindered.

8. At the same time that our wise adversary endeavours to make our conviction of the necessity of perfect love an occasion of shaking our peace by doubts and fears, he endeavours to weaken, if not destroy, our faith. Indeed these are inseparably connected, so that they must stand or fall together. So long as faith subsists we remain in peace; our heart stands fast, while it believes in the Lord. But if we let go our faith, our filial confidence in a loving, pardoning God, our peace is at an end, the very foundation on which it stood being overthrown. And this is the only foundation of holiness, as well as of peace; consequently whatever strikes at this, strikes at the very root of all holiness: For without this faith, without an abiding sense that Christ loved me, and gave himself for me, without a continuing conviction that God for Christ's sake is merciful to me a sinner, it is impossible that I should love God: "We love him, because he first loved us;" and in proportion to the strength and clearness of our conviction that he hath loved us, and accepted us in his Son. And unless we love God, it is not

possible that we should love our neighbour as ourselves; nor, consequently, that we should have any right affections, either toward God, or toward man. It evidently follows, that whatever weakens our faith, must, in the same degree obstruct our holiness: And this is not only the most effectual, but also the most compendious, way of destroying all holiness; seeing it does not affect any one Christian temper, any single grace or fruit of the Spirit, but, so far as it succeeds, tears up the very root of the whole work of God.

9. No marvel, therefore, that the ruler of the darkness of this world should here put forth all his strength. And so we find by experience. For it is far easier to conceive, than it is to express, the unspeakable violence wherewith this temptation is frequently urged on them who hunger and thirst after righteousness. When they see, in a strong and clear light, on the one hand, the desperate wickedness of their own hearts,—on the other hand, the unspotted holiness to which they are called in Christ Jesus; on the one hand, the depth of their own corruption, of their total alienation from God,—on the other, the height of the glory of God, that image of the Holy One, wherein they are to be renewed; there is, many times, no spirit left in them; they could almost cry out, "With God this is impossible!" They are ready to give up both faith and hope; to cast away that very confidence, whereby they are to overcome all things, and do all things, through Christ strengthening them; whereby, "after' they have done the will of God," they are to "receive the promise."

10. And if they "hold fast the beginning of their confidence steadfast unto the end," they shall undoubtedly receive the promise of God, reaching through both time and eternity. But here is another snare laid for our feet: While we earnestly pant for that part of the promise which is to be accomplished here, "for the glorious liberty of the children of God," we may be led unawares from the consideration of the glory which shall hereafter be revealed. Our eye may be insensibly turned aside from that crown which the righteous Judge hath promised to give at that day "to all that love his appearing;" and we may be drawn away from the view of that incorruptible inheritance which is reserved in heaven for us. But this also would be a loss to our souls, and an obstruction to our holiness. For to walk in the continual sight of our goal, is a needful help in our running the race that is set before us. This it was, the having "respect unto the recompense of reward," which of old time, encouraged Moses, rather "to suffer affliction with the people of God, than to enjoy the pleasures of sin for a season; esteeming the reproach of Christ greater riches than the treasures of Egypt." Nay, it is expressly said of a greater than he, that "for the joy that was set before him, he endured the cross, and despised the shame," till he "sat down at the right hand of the throne of God." Whence we may easily infer, how much more needful for us is the view of that joy set before us, that we may endure whatever cross the wisdom of God lays upon us, and press on through holiness to glory.

11. But while we are reaching to this, as well as to that glorious liberty which is preparatory to it, we may be in danger of falling into another snare of the devil, whereby he labours to entangle the children of God. We may take too much thought for tomorrow, so as to neglect the improvement of to-day. We may so expect perfect love, as not to use that which is already shed abroad in our hearts. There have not been wanting instances of those who have greatly suffered hereby. They were so taken up with what they were to receive hereafter, as utterly to neglect what they had already received. In expectation of having five talents more, they buried their one talent in the earth. At least, they did not improve it as they might have done, to the glory of God and the good of their own souls.

12. Thus does the subtle adversary of God and man endeavour to make void the counsel of God, by dividing the gospel against itself, and making one part of it overthrow the other; while the first work of God in the soul is destroyed by the expectation of his perfect work. We have seen several of the ways wherein he attempts this by cutting off, as it were, the springs of holiness. But this he likewise does more directly by making that blessed hope an occasion of unholy tempers.

13. Thus, whenever our heart is eagerly athirst for all the great and precious promises; when we pant after the fullness of God, as the hart after the water-brook; when our soul breaketh out in fervent desire, "Why are his chariot-wheels so long a-coming?"—he will not neglect the opportunity of tempting us to murmur against God. He will use all his wisdom, and all his strength, if haply, in an unguarded hour, we may be influenced to repine at our Lord for thus delaying his coming. At least, he will labour to excite some degree of fretfulness or impatience; and, perhaps, of envy at those whom we believe to have already attained the prize of our high calling. He well knows, that, by giving way to any of these tempers, we are pulling down the very thing we would build up. By *thus* following after perfect holiness, we become more unholy than before. Yea, there is great danger that our last state should be worse than the first; like them of whom the Apostle speaks in those dreadful words, "It had been better they had never known the way of righteousness, than, after they had known it, to turn back from the holy commandment delivered to them."

14. And from hence he hopes to reap another advantage, even to bring up an evil report of the good way. He is sensible, how few are able to distinguish (and too many are not willing so to do) between the accidental abuse, and the natural tendency, of a doctrine. These, therefore, will he continually blend together, with regard to the doctrine of Christian perfection; in order to prejudice the minds of unwary men against the glorious promises of God. And how frequently, how generally, I had almost said how universally, has he prevailed herein! For who is there that observes any of these accidental ill effects of this doctrine, and does not immediately conclude, this is its natural tendency; and does not readily cry out, "See, these are the fruits (meaning the natural, necessary fruits) of such doctrine?" Not so: They are fruits which may accidentally spring from the abuse of a great and precious truth: But the abuse of this, or any other scriptural doctrine, does by no means destroy its use. Neither can the unfaithfulness of man perverting his right way, make the promise of God of none effect No: Let God be true, and every man a liar. The word of the Lord, it shall stand.

"Faithful is he that hath promised: He also will do it." Let not us then be "removed from the hope of the gospel." Rather let us observe, which was the second thing proposed: How we may retort these fiery darts of the wicked one: How we may rise the higher by what he intends for an occasion of our falling.

II. 1. And, First, does Satan endeavour to damp your joy in the Lord, by the consideration of your sinfulness; added to this, that without entire, universal holiness, no man can see the Lord? You may cast back this dart upon his own head, while through the grace of God, the more you feel of your own vileness, the more you rejoice in confident hope, that all this shall be done away. While you hold fast this hope, every evil temper you feel, though you hate it with a perfect hatred, may be a means, not of lessening your humble joy, but rather of increasing it. "This and this," may you say, "shall likewise perish from the presence of the Lord. Like as the wax melteth at the fire, so shall this melt away before his face." By this means, the greater that change is which remains to be wrought in your soul, the more may you triumph in the Lord, and rejoice in the God of your salvation, who hath done so great things for you already, and will do so much greater things than these.

2. Secondly: The more vehemently he assaults your peace with that suggestion, "God is holy; you are unholy; You are immensely distant from that holiness, without which you cannot see God: How then can you be in the favour of God? How can you fancy you are justified?"—take the more earnest heed to hold fast that, "Not by works of righteousness which I have done, I am found in him; I am accepted in the Beloved; not having my own righteousness, (as the cause, either in whole or in part, of our justification before God,) but that which is by faith in Christ, the righteousness which is of God by faith." O bind this about your neck: Write it upon the table of thy heart. Wear it as a bracelet upon thy arm, as frontlets between thine eyes: "I am 'justified freely by his grace, through the redemption that is in Jesus Christ." Value and esteem, more and more, that precious truth, "By grace we are saved through faith." Admire, more and more, the free grace of God, in so loving the world as to give "his only Son, that whosoever believeth on him might not perish, but have everlasting life." So shall the sense of the sinfulness you feel, on the one hand, and of the holiness you expect, on the other, both contribute to establish your peace, and to make it flow as a river. So shall that peace flow on with an even stream, in spite of all those mountains of ungodliness, which shall become a plain in the day when the Lord cometh to take full possession of your heart. Neither will sickness, or pain, or the approach of death, occasion any doubt or fear. You know a day, an hour, a moment with God, is as a thousand years. He cannot be straitened for time, wherein to work whatever remains to be done in your soul. And God's time is always the best time. Therefore be thou careful for nothing: Only make thy request known unto Him, and that, not with doubt or fear, but thanksgiving; as being previously assured, He cannot withhold from thee any manner of thing that is good.

3. Thirdly: The more you are tempted to give up your shield, to cast away your faith, your confidence in his love, so much the more take heed that you hold fast that whereunto you have attained; so much the more labour to stir up the gift of God which is in you. Never let that slip, "I have 'an Advocate with the Father, Jesus Christ the righteous;' and, 'The life I now live, I live by faith in the Son of God, who loved me and gave himself for me.' " Be this thy glory and crown of rejoicing. And see that no one take thy crown. Hold that fast: "I know that my Redeemer liveth, and shall stand at the latter day upon the earth;" and, "I now 'have redemption in his blood, even the forgiveness of sins.' " Thus, being filled with all peace and joy in believing, press on, in the peace and joy of faith to the renewal of thy whole soul in the image of him that created thee! Meanwhile, cry continually to God that thou mayest see that prize of thy high calling, not as Satan represents it, in a horrid dreadful shape, but in its genuine native beauty; not as something that must be, or thou wilt go to hell, but as what may be, to lead thee to heaven. Look upon it as the most desirable gift which is in all the stores of the rich mercies of God. Beholding it in this true point of light, thou wilt hunger after it more and more; thy whole soul will be athirst for God, and for this glorious conformity to his likeness; and having received a good hope of this, and strong consolation through grace, thou wilt no more be weary or faint in thy mind, but wilt follow on till thou attainest.

4. In the same power of faith, press on to glory. Indeed this is the same prospect still. God hath joined from the beginning pardon, holiness, heaven. And why should man put them asunder? O beware of this! Let not one link of the golden chain be broken. "God, for Christ's sake hath forgiven me. He is now renewing me in his own image. Shortly he will make me meet for himself, and take me to stand before his face. I, whom he hath justified through the blood of his Son, being thoroughly sanctified by his Spirit, shall quickly ascend to the 'New Jerusalem, the city of the living God.' Yet a little while, and I shall 'come to the general assembly and church of the first-born, and to God the Judge of all, and to Jesus the Mediator of the New Covenant.' How soon will these shadows flee away, and the day of eternity dawn upon me! How soon shall I drink of 'the river of the water of life, going out of the throne of God and of the Lamb! There all his servants shall praise him, and shall see his face, and his name shall be upon their foreheads. And no night shall be there; and they have no need of a candle or the light of the sun. For the Lord God enlighteneth them, and they shall reign for ever and ever.' "

5. And if you thus "taste of the good word, and of the powers of the world to come," you will not murmur against God, because you are not yet "meet for the inheritance of the saints in light." Instead of repining at your not being wholly delivered, you will praise God for thus far delivering you. You will magnify God for what he hath done, and take it as an earnest of what he will do. You will not fret against him, because you are not yet renewed, but bless him because you shall be; and because "now is your salvation" from all sin "nearer than when you" first "believed." Instead of uselessly

tormenting yourself because the time is not fully come, you will calmly and quietly wait for it, knowing that it "will come, and will not tarry." You may, therefore, the more cheerfully endure, as yet, the burden of sin that still remains in you, because it will not always remain. Yet a little while, and it shall be clean gone. Only "tarry thou the Lord's leisure:" Be strong, and "he shall comfort thy heart;" and put thou thy trust in the Lord!

6. And if you see any who appear (so far as man can judge, but God alone searcheth the hearts) to be already partakers of their hope, already "made perfect in love;" far from envying the grace of God in them, let it rejoice and comfort your heart. Glorify God for their sake! "If one member is honoured," shall not "all the members rejoice with it?" Instead of jealousy or evil surmising concerning them, praise God for the consolation! Rejoice in having a fresh proof of the faithfulness of God in fulfilling all his promises; and stir yourself up the more, to "apprehend that for which you also are apprehended of Christ Jesus!"

7. In order to this, redeem the time. Improve the present moment. Buy up every opportunity of growing in grace, or of doing good. Let not the thought of receiving more grace to-morrow, make you negligent of to-day. You have one talent now: If you expect five more, so much the rather improve that you have. And the more you expect to receive hereafter, the more labour for God now. Sufficient for the day is the grace thereof. God is now pouring his benefits upon you: Now approve yourself a faithful steward of the present grace of God. Whatever may be to-morrow, give all diligence to-day, to "add to your faith courage, temperance, patience, brotherly-kindness," and the fear of God, till you attain that pure and perfect love! Let these things be now "in you and abound!" Be not now slothful or unfruitful: "So shall an entrance be ministered into the everlasting kingdom of our Lord Jesus Christ!"

8. Lastly: If in time past you have abused this blessed hope of being holy as he is holy, yet do not therefore cast it away. Let the abuse cease, the use remain. Use it now to the more abundant glory of God, and profit of your own soul. In steadfast faith, in calm tranquility of spirit, in full assurance of hope, rejoicing evermore for what God hath done, press ye on unto perfection! Daily growing in the knowledge of our Lord Jesus Christ, and going on from strength to strength, in resignation, in patience, in humble thankfulness for what ye have attained, and for what ye shall, run the race set before you, "looking unto Jesus," till, through perfect love, ye enter into his glory!

43. THE SCRIPTURE WAY OF SALVATION

"Ye are saved through faith."

Ephesians 2:8.

1. Nothing can be more intricate, complex, and hard to be understood, than religion, as it has been often described. And this is not only true concerning the religion of the Heathens, even many of the wisest of them, but concerning the religion of those also who were, in some sense, Christians; yea, and men of great name in the Christian world; men who seemed

to be pillars thereof. Yet how easy to be understood, how plain and simple a thing, is the genuine religion of Jesus Christ; provided only that we take it in its native form, just as it is described in the oracles of God! It is exactly suited, by the wise Creator and Governor of the world, to the weak understanding and narrow capacity of man in his present state. How observable is this, both with regard to the end it proposes, and the means to attain that end! The end is, in one word, salvation; the means to attain it, faith.

2. It is easily discerned, that these two little words, I mean faith and salvation, include the substance of all the Bible, the marrow, as it were, of the whole Scripture. So much the more should we take all possible care to avoid all mistake concerning them, and to form a true and accurate judgement concerning both the one and the other.

3. Let us then seriously inquire,

  I. What is Salvation?

  II. What is that faith whereby we are saved? And,

  III. How are we saved by it?

1. I. And, first, let us inquire, What is salvation? The salvation which is here spoken of is not what is frequently understood by that word, the going to heaven, eternal happiness. It is not the soul's going to paradise, termed by our Lord, "Abraham's bosom." It is not a blessing which lies on the other side death; or, as we usually speak, in the other world. The very words of the text itself put this beyond all question: "Ye *are saved*." It is not something at a distance: it is a present thing; a blessing which, through the free mercy of God, ye are now in possession of. Nay, the words may be rendered, and that with equal propriety, "Ye *have been* saved": so that the salvation which is here spoken of might be extended to the entire work of God, from the first dawning of grace in the soul, till it is consummated in glory.

2. If we take this in its utmost extent, it will include all that is wrought in the soul by what is frequently termed "natural conscience," but more properly, "preventing grace";—all the drawings of the Father; the desires after God, which, if we yield to them, increase more and more;—all that light wherewith the Son of God "enlighteneth every one that cometh into the world;" showing every man "to do justly, to love mercy, and to walk humbly with his God";—all the convictions which His Spirit, from time to time, works in every child of man—although it is true, the generality of men stifle them as soon as possible, and after a while forget, or at least deny, that they ever had them at all.

3. But we are at present concerned only with that salvation which the Apostle is directly speaking of. And this consists of two general parts, justification and sanctification. Justification is another word for pardon. It is the forgiveness of all our sins; and, what is necessarily implied therein, our acceptance with God. The price whereby this hath been procured for us (commonly termed "the meritorious cause of our justification"), is the blood and righteousness of Christ; or, to express it a little more clearly, all that Christ hath done and suffered for us, till He "poured out His soul for the transgressors." The immediate effects of justification are, the peace of God, a "peace that passeth all understanding," and

a "rejoicing in hope of the glory of God" "with joy unspeakable and full of glory."

4. And at the same time that we are justified, yea, in that very moment, sanctification begins. In that instant we are born again, born from above, born of the Spirit: there is a *real* as well as a *relative* change. We are inwardly renewed by the power of God. We feel "the love of God shed abroad in our heart by the Holy Ghost which is given unto us"; producing love to all mankind, and more especially to the children of God; expelling the love of the world, the love of pleasure, of ease, of honour, of money, together with pride, anger, self-will, and every other evil temper; in a word, changing the earthly, sensual, devilish mind, into "the mind which was in Christ Jesus."

5. How naturally do those who experience such a change imagine that all sin is gone; that it is utterly rooted out of their heart, and has no more any place therein! How easily do they draw that inference, "I *feel* no sin; therefore, I *have* none: it does not *stir*, therefore it does not *exist*: it has no *motion*; therefore, it has no *being*!"

6. But it is seldom long before they are undeceived, finding sin was only suspended, not destroyed. Temptations return, and sin revives; showing it was but stunned before, not dead. They now feel two principles in themselves, plainly contrary to each other; "the flesh lusting against the Spirit"; nature opposing the grace of God. They cannot deny, that although they still feel power to believe in Christ, and to love God; and although His "Spirit" still "witnesses with their spirits, that they are children of God"; yet they feel in themselves sometimes pride or self-will, sometimes anger or unbelief. They find one or more of these frequently *stirring* in their heart, though not *conquering*; yea, perhaps, "thrusting sore at them that they may fall"; but the Lord is their help.

7. How exactly did Macarius, fourteen hundred years ago, describe the present experience of the children of God: "The unskilful," or unexperienced, "when grace operates, presently imagine they have no more sin. Whereas they that have discretion cannot deny, that even we who have the grace of God may be molested again. For we have often had instances of some among the brethren, who have experienced such grace as to affirm that they had no sin in them; and yet, after all, when they thought themselves entirely freed from it, the corruption that lurked within was stirred up anew, and they were wellnigh burned up."

8. From the time of our being born again, the gradual work of sanctification takes place. We are enabled "by the Spirit" to "mortify the deeds of the body," of our evil nature; and as we are more and more dead to sin, we are more and more alive to God. We so on from grace to grace, while we are careful to "abstain from all appearance of evil," and are "zealous of good works," as we have opportunity, doing good to all men; while we walk in all His ordinances blameless, therein worshipping Him in spirit and in truth; while we take up our cross, and deny ourselves every pleasure that does not lead us to God.

9. It is thus that we wait for entire sanctification; for a full salvation from all our sins,—from pride, self-will, anger, unbelief; or, as the Apostle expresses it, "go unto perfection."

But what is perfection? The word has various senses: here it means perfect love. It is love excluding sin; love filling the heart, taking up the whole capacity of the soul. It is love "rejoicing evermore, praying without ceasing, in everything giving thanks."

II. But what is faith through which we are saved? This is the second point to be considered.

1. Faith, in general, is defined by the Apostle, *oprgmaton elegchos ou blepomenon. An evidence*, a divine *evidence and conviction* (the word means both) *of things not seen*; not visible, not perceivable either by sight, or by any other of the external senses. It implies both a supernatural *evidence* of God, and of the things of God; a kind of spiritual *light* exhibited to the soul, and a supernatural *sight* or perception thereof. Accordingly, the Scripture speaks of Gods giving sometimes light, sometimes a power of discerning it. So St. Paul: God, who commanded light to shine out of darkness, hath shined in our hearts, to give us the light of the knowledge of the glory of God in the face of Jesus Christ. And elsewhere the same Apostle speaks of the eyes of our understanding being opened. By this two-fold operation of the holy Spirit, having the eyes of our soul both *opened* and *enlightened*, we see the things which the natural "eye hath not seen, neither the ear heard." We have a prospect of the invisible things of God; we see the *spiritual world*, which is all round about us, and yet no more discerned by our natural faculties than if it had no being. And we see the *eternal world*, piercing through the veil which hangs between time and eternity. Clouds and darkness then rest upon it no more, but we already see the glory which shall be revealed.

2. Taking the word in a more particular sense, faith is a divine *evidence* and *conviction* not only that "God was in Christ, reconciling the world unto himself," but also that Christ loved *me*, and gave himself for *me*. It is by this faith (whether we term it the *essence*, or rather a *property* thereof) that we *receive Christ*; that we receive Him in all His offices, as our Prophet, Priest, and King. It is by this that He is "made of God unto us wisdom, and righteousness, and sanctification, and redemption."

3. "But is this the *faith of assurance*, or *faith of adherence*?" The Scripture mentions no such distinction. The Apostle says, "There is one faith, and one hope of our calling"; one Christian, saving faith; "as there is one Lord," in whom we believe, and "one God and Father of us all." And it is certain, this faith necessarily implies an *assurance* (which is here only another word for *evidence*, it being hard to tell the difference between them) that Christ loved me, and gave Himself for me. For "he that believeth" with the true living faith "hath the witness in himself": "the Spirit witnesseth with his spirit that he is a child of God." "Because he is a son, God hath sent forth the Spirit of His Son into his heart, crying, Abba, Father"; giving him an assurance that he is so, and a childlike confidence in Him. But let it be observed, that, in the very nature of the thing, the assurance goes before the confidence. For a man cannot have a childlike confidence in God till he knows he is a child of God. Therefore, confidence, trust, reliance, adherence, or whatever else it be called, is not the

first, as some have supposed, but the second, branch or act of faith.

4. It is by this faith we are saved, justified, and sanctified; taking that word in its highest sense. But how are we justified and sanctified by faith? This is our third head of inquiry. And this being the main point in question, and a point of no ordinary importance, it will not be improper to five it a more distinct and particular consideration.

III. 1. And, first, how are we justified by faith? In what sense is this to be understood? I answer, Faith is the condition, and the only condition, of justification. It is the *condition*: none is justified but he that believes: without faith no man is justified. And it is the *only condition*: this alone is sufficient for justification. every one that believes is justified, whatever else he has or has not. In other words: no man is justified till he believes; every man when he believes is justified.

2. "But does not God command us to repent also? Yea, and to bring forth fruits meet for repentance'to cease, for instance, from doing evil, and learn to do well? And is not both the one and the other of the utmost necessity, insomuch that if we willingly neglect either, we cannot reasonably expect to be justified at all? But if this be so, how can it be said that faith is the only condition of justification?" God does undoubtedly command us both to repent, and to bring forth fruits meet for repentance; which if we willingly neglect, we cannot reasonably expect to be justified at all: therefore both repentance, and fruits meet for repentance, are, in some sense, necessary to justification. But they are not necessary in the *same sense* with faith, nor in the *same degree*. Not in the *same degree*; for those fruits are only necessary *conditionally*; if there be time and opportunity for them. otherwise a man may be justified without them, as was the *thief* upon the cross (if we may call him so; for a late writer has discovered that he was no thief, but a very honest and respectable person!); but he cannot be justified without faith; this is impossible. Likewise, let a man have ever so much repentance, or ever so many of the fruits meet for repentance, yet all this does not at all avail; he is not justified till he believes. But the moment he believes, with or without those fruits, yea, with more or less repentance, he is justified. Not in the *same sense*; for repentance and its fruits are only *remotely* necessary; necessary in order to faith; whereas faith is *immediately* necessary to justification. It remains, that faith is the only condition, which is *immediately* and *proximately* necessary to justification.

3. "But do you believe we are sanctified by faith? We know you believe that we are justified by faith; but do not you believe, and accordingly teach, that we are sanctified by our works?" So it has been roundly and vehemently affirmed for these five-and-twenty years: but I have constantly declared just the contrary; and that in all manner of ways. I have continually testified in private and in public, that we are sanctified as well as justified by faith. And indeed the one of those great truths does exceedingly illustrate the other. exactly as we are justified by faith, so are we sanctified by faith. Faith is the condition, and the only condition, of sanctification, exactly as it is of justification. It is the *condition*: none is sanctified but he that believes; with out faith no man is sanctified. And it is the *only condition*: this alone is sufficient for sanctification. every one that believes is sanctified, whatever else he has or has not. In other words, no man is sanctified till he believes: every man when he believes is sanctified.

4. "But is there not a repentance consequent upon, as well as a repentance previous to, justification? And is it not incumbent on all that are justified to be zealous of good works'? Yea, are not these so necessary, that if a man willingly neglect them he cannot reasonably expect that he shall ever be sanctified in the full sense; that is, perfected in love? Nay, can he grow at all in grace, in the loving knowledge of our Lord Jesus Christ? Yea, can he retain the grace which God has already given him? Can he continue in the faith which he has received, or in the favour of God. Do not you yourself allow all this, and continually assert it? But, if this be so, how can it be said that faith is the only condition of sanctification?"

5. I do allow all this, and continually maintain it as the truth of God. I allow there is a repentance consequent upon, as well as a repentance previous to, justification. It is incumbent on all that are justified to be zealous of good works. And there are so necessary, that if a man willingly neglect them, he cannot reasonably expect that he shall ever be sanctified; he cannot grow in grace, in the image of God, the mind which was in Christ Jesus; nay, he cannot retain the grace he has received; he cannot continue in faith, or in the favour of God. What is the inference we mist draw herefrom? Why, that both repentance, rightly understood, and the practice of all good works,—works of piety, as well as works of mercy (now properly so called, since they spring from faith), are, in some sense, necessary to sanctification.

6. I say, "repentance rightly understood"; for this must not be confounded with the former repentance. The repentance consequent upon justification is widely different from that which is antecedent to it. This implies no guilt, no sense of condemnation, no consciousness of the wrath of God. It does not suppose any doubt of the favour of God, or any "fear that hath torment." It is properly a conviction, wrought by the Holy Ghost, of the *sin* which still *remains* in our heart; of the *phronema sarkos, the carnal mind*, which "does still *remain*" (as our Church speaks) "even in them that are regenerate"; although it does no longer *reign*; it has not now dominion over them. It is a conviction of our proneness to evil, of an heart bent to backsliding, of the still continuing tendency of the flesh to lust against the spirit. Sometimes, unless we continually watch and pray, it lusteth to pride, sometimes to anger, sometimes to love of the world, love of ease, love of honour, or love of pleasure more than of God. It is a conviction of the tendency of our heart to self-will, to Atheism, or idolatry; and above all, to unbelief; whereby, in a thousand ways, and under a thousand pretenses, we are ever departing, more or less, from the living God.

7. With this conviction of the sin remaining in our hearts, there is joined a clear conviction of the sin remaining in our lives; still *cleaving* to all our words and actions. In the best of these we now discern a mixture of evil, either in the spirit, the matter, or the manner of them; something that could not

endure the righteous judgement of God, were He extreme to mark what is done amiss. Where we least suspected it, we find a taint of pride or self-will, of unbelief or idolatry; so that we are now more ashamed of our best duties than formerly of our worst sins: and hence we cannot but feel that these are so far from having anything meritorious in them, yea, so far from being able to stand in sight of the divine justice, that for those also we should be guilty before God, were it not for the blood of the covenant.

8. Experience shows that, together with this conviction of sin *remaining* in our hearts, and *cleaving* to all our words and actions; as well as the guilt which on account thereof we should incur, were we not continually sprinkled with the atoning blood; one thing more is implied in this repentance; namely, a conviction of our helplessness, of our utter inability to think one good thought, or to form one good desire; and much more to speak one word aright, or to perform one good action, but through His free, almighty grace, first preventing us, and then accompanying us every moment.

9. "But what good works are those, the practice of which you affirm to be necessary to sanctification?" First, all works of piety; such as public prayer, family prayer, and praying in our closet; receiving the supper of the Lord; searching the Scriptures, by hearing, reading, meditating; and using such a measure of fasting or abstinence as our bodily health allows.

10. Secondly, all works of mercy; whether they relate to the bodies or souls of men; such as feeding the hungry, clothing the naked, entertaining the stranger, visiting those that are in prison, or sick, or variously afflicted; such as the endeavouring to instruct the ignorant, to awaken the stupid sinner, to quicken the lukewarm, to confirm the wavering, to comfort the feeble-minded, to succour the tempted, or contribute in any manner to the saving of souls from death. This is the repentance, and these the "fruits meet for repentance," which are necessary to full sanctification. This is the way wherein God hath appointed His children to wait for complete salvation.

11. Hence may appear the extreme mischievousness of that seemingly innocent opinion, that there is no sin in a believer; that all sin is destroyed, root and branch, the moment a man is justified. By totally preventing that repentance, it quite blocks up the way to sanctification. There is no place for repentance in him who believes there is no sin either in his life or heart: consequently, there is no place for his being perfected in love, to which that repentance is indispensably necessary.

12. Hence it may likewise appear, that there is no possible danger in *thus* expecting full salvation. For suppose we were mistaken, suppose no such blessing ever was or can be attained, yet we lose nothing: nay, that very expectation quickens us in using all the talents which God has given us; yea, in improving them all; so that when our Lord cometh, He will receive His own with increase.

13. But to return. though it be allowed, that both this repentance and its fruits are necessary to full salvation; yet they are not necessary either in the same sense with faith, or in the same degree:—Not in the *same degree*; for these fruits are only necessary *conditionally*, if there be time and opportunity for them; otherwise a man may be sanctified without them. But he cannot be sanctified without faith. likewise, let a man have ever so much of this repentance, or ever so many good works, yet all this does not at all avail: he is not sanctified till he believes. But the moment he believes, with or without those fruits, yea, with more or less of this repentance, he is sanctified.—Not in the *same sense*; for this repentance and these fruits are only *remotely* necessary,—necessary in order to the continuance of his faith, as well as the increase of it; whereas faith is *immediately* and *directly* necessary to sanctification. It remains, that faith is the only condition which is *immediately* and *proximately* necessary to sanctification.

14. "But what is that faith whereby we are sanctified,—saved from sin, and perfected in love?" It is a divine evidence and conviction, first, that God hath promised it in the holy Scripture. Till we are thoroughly satisfied of this, there in no moving one step further. And one would imagine there needed not one word more to satisfy a reasonable man of this, than the ancient promise, "Then will I circumcise thy heart, and the heart of thy seed, to love the Lord they God with all thy heart, and with all thy soul, and with all thy mind." How clearly does this express the being perfected in love!—how strongly imply the being saved from all sin! For as long as love takes up the whole heart, what room is there for sin therein?

15. It is a divine evidence and conviction, secondly, that what God hath promised He is able to perform. Admitting, therefore, that "with men it is impossible" to "bring a clean thing out of an unclean," to purify the heart from all sin, and to till it with all holiness; yet this creates no difficulty in the case, seeing "with God all things are possible." And surely no one ever imagined it was possible to any power less than that of the Almighty! But if God speaks, it shall be done. God saith, "Let there be light; and there" is "light"!

16. It is, thirdly, a divine evidence and conviction that He is able and willing to do it now. And why not? Is not a moment to Him the same as a thousand years? He cannot want more time to accomplish whatever is His will. And He cannot want or stay for any more *worthiness* or *fitness* in the persons He is pleased to honour. We may therefore boldly say, at any point of time, "Now is the day of salvation!" "To-day, if ye will hear His voice, harden not your hearts!" "Behold, all things are now ready; come unto the marriage!"

17. To this confidence, that God is both able and willing to sanctify us now, there needs to be added one thing more,—a divine evidence and conviction that He doeth it. In that hour it is done: God says to the inmost soul, "According to thy faith be it unto thee!" Then the soul is pure from every spot of sin; it is clean "from all unrighteousness." The believer then experiences the deep meaning of those solemn words, "If we walk in the light as He is in the light, we have fellowship one with another, and the blood of Jesus Christ His Son cleanseth us from all sin."

18. "But does God work this great work in the soul gradually or instantaneously?" Perhaps it may be gradually wrought in some; I mean in this sense,—they do not advert to the particular moment wherein sin ceases to be. But it us infinitely desirable, were it the will of God, that it should be

done instantaneously; that the Lord should destroy sin "by the breath of His mouth," in a moment, in the twinkling of an eye. And so He generally does; a plain fact, of which there is evidence enough to satisfy any unprejudiced person. *Thou* therefore look for it every moment! Look for it in the way above described; in all those *good works* whereunto thou art "created anew in Christ Jesus." There in then no danger: you can be no worse, if you are no better, for that expectation. For were you to be disappointed of your hope, still you lose nothing. But you shall not be disappointed of your hope: it will come, and will not tarry. Look for it then every day, every hour, every moment! Why not this hour, this moment? Certainly you may look for it *now*, if you believe it is by faith. And by this token you may surely know whether you seek it by faith or by works. If by works, you want something to be done *first, before* you are sanctified. You think, I must first *be* or *do* thus or thus. Then you are seeking it by works unto this day. If you seek it by faith, you may expect it *as you are*, and expect it *now*. It is of importance to observe, that there is an inseparable connexion between these three points,— expect it *by faith*; expect it *as you are*; and expect it *now*! To deny one of them, is to deny them all; to allow one, is to allow them all. Do *you* believe we are sanctified by faith? Be true then to your principle; and look for this blessing just as you are, neither better nor worse; as a poor sinner that has still nothing to pay, nothing to plead, but "Christ *died*." And if you look for it as you are, then expect it *now*. Stay for nothing: why should you? Christ is ready; and He is all you want. He is waiting for you: He is at the door! Let your inmost soul cry out,

> Come in, come in, thou heavenly Guest!
> Nor hence again remove;
> But sup with me, and let the feast
> Be everlasting love.

44.* ORIGINAL SIN

"And God saw that the wickedness of man was great in the earth, and that every imagination of the thoughts of his heart was only evil continually."

Gen. 6:5.

1. How widely different is this from the fair pictures of human nature which men have drawn in allages! The writings of many of the ancients abound with gay descriptions of the dignity of man; whomsome of them paint as having all virtue and happiness in his composition, or, at least, entirely inhis power, without being beholden to any other being; yea, as self-sufficient, able to live on hisown stock, and little inferior to God himself.

2. Nor have Heathens alone, men who are guided in their researches by little more than the dimlight of reason, but many likewise of them that bear the name of Christ, and to whom are entrustedthe oracles of God, spoken as magnificently concerning the nature of man, as if it were all innocenceand perfection. Accounts of this kind have particularly abounded in the present century; and perhapsin

no part of the world more than in our own country. Here not a few persons of strong understanding, as well as extensive learning, have employed their utmost abilities to show, what they termed, "thefair side of human nature." And it must he acknowledged, that, if their accounts of him be just, manis still but "a little lower than the angels;" or, as the words may be more literally rendered, "alittle less than God."

3. Is it any wonder, that these accounts are very readily received by the generality of men? Forwho is not easily persuaded to think favourably of himself? Accordingly, writers of this kind aremost universally read, admired, applauded. And innumerable are the converts they have made, not onlyin the gay, but the learned world. So that it is now quite unfashionable to talk otherwise, to sayany thing to the disparagement of human nature; which is generally allowed, notwithstanding a fewinfirmities, to be very innocent, and wise, and virtuous!

4. But, in the mean time, what must we do with our Bibles?—for they will never agree with this. These accounts, however pleasing to flesh and blood, are utterly irreconcilable with the scriptural. The Scripture avers, that "by one man's disobedience all men were constituted sinners;" that "in Adamall died," spiritually died, lost the life and the image of God; that fallen, sinful Adam then "begata son in his own likeness;"—nor was it possible he should beget him in any other; for "who canbring a clean thing out of an unclean?"— that consequently we, as well as other men, were by nature"dead in trespasses and sins," "without hope, without God in the world," and therefore "children ofwrath;" that every man may say, "I was shapen in wickedness, and in sin did my mother conceive me;"that "there is no difference," in that "all have sinned and come short of the glory of God," of thatglorious image of God wherein man was originally created. And hence, when "the Lord looked down fromheaven upon the children of men, he saw they were all gone out of the way; they were altogetherbecome abominable, there was none righteous, no, not one," none that truly sought after God: Justagreeable this, to what is declared by the Holy Ghost in the words above recited, "God saw," when helooked down from heaven before, "that the wickedness of man was great in the earth;" so great, that"every imagination of the thoughts of his heart was only evil continually."

This is God's account of man: From which I shall take occasion, First, to show what men werebefore the flood: Secondly, to inquire, whether they are not the same now: And, Thirdly, to add someinferences.

I. 1. I am, First, by opening the words of the text, to show what men were before the flood. Andwe may fully depend on the account here given: For God saw it, and he cannot be deceived. He "sawthat the wickedness of man was great:"— Not of this or that man; not of a few men only; not barelyof the greater part, but of man in general; of men universally. The word includes the whole humanrace, every partaker of human nature. And it is not easy for us to compute their numbers, to tell howmany thousands and millions they were.

---

* [text from the 1872 edition]

The earth then retained much of its primeval beauty andoriginal fruitfulness. The face of the globe was not rent and torn as it is now; and spring andsummer went hand in hand. It is therefore probable, it afforded sustenance for far more inhabitantsthan it is now capable of sustaining; and these must be immensely multiplied, while men begat sonsand daughters for seven or eight hundred years together. Yet, among all this inconceivable number, only "Noah found favour with God." He alone (perhaps including part of his household) was anexception from the universal wickedness, which, by the just judgment of God, in a short time afterbrought on universal destruction. All the rest were partakers in the same guilt, as they were in thesame punishment.

2. "God saw all the imaginations of the thoughts of his heart;"—of his soul, his inward man, the spirit within him, the principle of all his inward and outward motions. He "saw all theimaginations:" It is not possible to find a word of a more extensive signification. It includeswhatever is formed, made, fabricated within; all that is or passes in the soul; every inclination, affection, passion, appetite; every temper, design, thought. It must of consequence include everyword and action, as naturally flowing from these fountains, and being either good or evil accordingto the fountain from which they severally flow.

3. Now God saw that all this, the whole thereof, was evil;—contrary to moral rectitude; contrary to the nature of God, which necessarily includes all good; contrary to the divine will, theeternal standard of good and evil; contrary to the pure, holy image of God, wherein man wasoriginally created, and wherein he stood when God, surveying the works of his hands, saw them all tobe very good; contrary to justice, mercy, and truth, and to the essential relations which each manbore to his Creator and his fellow-creatures.

4. But was there not good mingled with the evil? Was there not light intermixed with the darkness? No; none at all: "God saw that the whole imagination of the heart of man was only evil." It cannotindeed be denied, but many of them, perhaps all, had good motions put into their hearts; for theSpirit of God did then also "strive with man," if haply he might repent, more especially during thatgracious reprieve, the hundred and twenty years, while the ark was preparing. But still "in his fleshdwelt no good thing;" all his nature was purely evil: It was wholly consistent with itself, andunmixed with anything of an opposite nature.

5. However, it may still be matter of inquiry, "Was there no intermission of this evil? Were thereno lucid intervals, wherein something good might be found in the heart of man?" We are not here toconsider, what the grace of God might occasionally work in his soul; and, abstracted from this, wehave no reason to believe, there was any intermission of that evil. For God, who "saw the wholeimagination of the thoughts of his heart to be *only* evil," saw likewise, that it was alwaysthe same, that it "was only evil *continually;*" every year, every day, every hour, everymoment. He never deviated into good.

II. Such is the authentic account of the whole race of mankind which He who knoweth what is inman, who searcheth the heart and trieth the reins, hath left upon record for our instruction. Suchwere all men before God brought the flood upon the earth. We are, Secondly, to inquire, whether theyare the same now.

1. And this is certain, the Scripture gives us no reason to think any otherwise of them. On thecontrary, all the above cited passages of Scripture refer to those who lived after the flood. It wasabove a thousand years after, that God declared by David concerning the children of men, "They areall gone out of the way, of truth and holiness; "there is none righteous, no, not one." And to thisbear all the Prophets witness, in their several generations. So Isaiah, concerning God's peculiarpeople, (and certainly the Heathens were in no better condition,) "The whole head is sick, and thewhole heart faint. From the sole of the foot even unto the head there is no soundness; but wounds, and bruises, and putrifying sores." The same account is given by all the Apostles, yea, by the wholetenor of the oracles of God. From all these we learn, concerning man in his natural state, unassistedby the grace of God, that "every imagination of the thoughts of his heart is" still "evil, onlyevil," and that "continually."

2. And this account of the present state of man is confirmed by daily experience. It is true, thenatural man discerns it not: And this is not to be wondered at. So long as a man born blind continuesso, he is scarce sensible of his want: Much less, could we suppose a place where all were bornwithout sight, would they be sensible of the want of it. In like manner, so long as men remain intheir natural blindness of understanding, they are not sensible of their spiritual wants, and of thisin particular. But as soon as God opens the eyes of their understanding, they see the state they werein before; they are then deeply convinced, that "every man living," themselves especially, are, bynature, "altogether vanity;" that is, folly and ignorance, sin and wickedness.

3. We see, when God opens our eyes, that we were before *atheoi en toi kosmoi* without God, or, rather, *Atheists, in the world*. We had, by nature, no knowledge of God, no acquaintance withhim. It is true, as soon as we came to the use of reason, we learned the invisible things of God, even his eternal power and Godhead, from the things that are made. From the things that are seen weinferred the existence of an eternal, powerful Being, that is not seen. But still, although weacknowledged his being we had no acquaintance with him. As we know there is an emperor of China, whomyet we do not know; so we knew there was a King of all the earth, yet we knew him not. Indeed wecould not by any of our natural faculties. By none of these could we attain the knowledge of God. Wecould no more perceive him by our natural understanding, than we could see him with our eyes. For noone knoweth the Father but the Son, and he to whom the Son willeth to reveal him. And no one knoweththe Son but the Father, and he to whom the Father revealeth him.

4. We read of an ancient king, who, being desirous to know what was the *natural language* ofmen, in order to bring the matter to a certain issue, made the following experiment: he ordered twoinfants, as soon as they were born, to be conveyed to a place prepared for them, where they werebrought up without any instruction at all, and without ever hearing a

human voice. And what was theevent? Why that when they were at length brought out of their confinement, they spoke no language atall; they uttered only inarticulate sounds, like those of other animals. Were two infants in likemanner to be brought up from the womb without being instructed in any religion, there is little roomto doubt but (unless the grace of God interposed) the event would be just the same. They would haveno religion at all: Thy would have no more knowledge of God than the beasts of the field, than thewild asss colt. Such is natural religion, abstracted from traditional, and from the influences ofGods Spirit!

5. And having no knowledge, we can have no love of God: We cannot love him we know not. Most men *talk* indeed of loving God, and perhaps imagine they do; at least, few will acknowledge they donot love him: But the fact is too plain to be denied. No man loves God by nature, any more than hedoes a stone, or the earth he treads upon. What we love we delight in: But no man has naturally anydelight in God. In our natural state we cannot conceive how any one should delight in him. We take nopleasure in him at all; he is utterly tasteless to us. To love God! it is far above, out of oursight. We cannot, naturally, attain unto it.

6. We have by nature, not only no love, but no fear of God. It is allowed, indeed, that most menhave, sooner or later, a kind of senseless, irrational fear, properly called superstition; though theblundering epicureans gave it the name of religion. Yet even this is not natural, but acquired; chiefly by conversation or from example. By nature God is not in all our thoughts: We leave himto manage his own affairs, to sit quietly, as we imagine, in heaven, and leave us on earth to manageours; so that we have no more of the fear of God before our eyes, than of the love of God in ourhearts.

7. Thus are all men "Atheists in the world." But Atheism itself does not screen us from idolatry. In his natural state, every man born into the world is a rank idolater. Perhaps, indeed, we may notbe such in the vulgar sense of the word. We do no, like the idolatrous heathens, worship molten orgraven images. We do not bow down to the stock of a tree, to the work of our own hands. We do notpray to the angels or saints in heaven, any more than to the saints that are upon the earth. But whatthen? We have set up our idols in our hearts; and to these we bow down and worship them: We worshipourselves, when we pay that honour to ourselves which is due to God only. Therefore all pride isidolatry; it is ascribing to ourselves what is due to God alone. And although pride was not made forman, yet where is the man that is born without it? But hereby we rob god of his unalienable right, and idolatrously usurp his glory.

8. But pride is not the only sort of idolatry which we are all by nature guilty of. Satan hasstamped his own image on our heart in self-will also. "I will," said he, before he was cast out ofheaven, "I will sit upon the sides of the north;" I will do my own will and pleasure, independentlyon that of my Creator. the same does every man born into the world say, and that in a thousandinstances; nay, and avow it too, without ever blushing upon the account, without either fear orshame. Ask the man, "Why did you do this?" he answers, "Because I had a mind to it." What is thisbut, "Because it was my will;" that

is, in effect, because the devil and I agreed; because Satan andI govern our actions by one and the same principle. The will of God, mean time, is not in histhoughts, is not considered in the least degree; although it be the supreme rule of every intelligentcreature, whether in heaven or earth, resulting from the essential, unalterable relation which allcreature bear to their Creator.

9. So far we bear the image of the devil, and tread in his steps. But at the next step we leaveSatan behind; we run into an idolatry whereof he is not guilty: I mean love of the world; which isnow as natural to every man, as to love his own will. What is more natural to us than to seekhappiness in the creature, instead of the Creator? to seek that satisfaction in the works of hishands, which can be found in God only? What more natural than "the desire of the flesh?" that is, ofthe pleasure of sense in every kind? Men indeed talk magnificently of despising these low pleasures, particularly men of learning and education. They affect to sit loose to the gratification of theseappetites wherein they stand on a level with the beasts that perish. But it is mere affectation; forevery man is conscious to himself, that in this respect he is, by nature, a very beast. Sensualappetites, even those of the lowest kind, have, more or less, the dominion over him. They lead himcaptive; they drag him to and fro, in spite of his boasted reason. The man, with all his goodbreeding, and other accomplishments, has no pre-eminence over the goat: Nay, it is much to bedoubted, whether the beast has not the pre-eminence over him. Certainly he has, if we may hearken toone of their modern oracles, who very decently tells us,

once in a season beasts too taste of love;
only the beast of reason is its slave,
And in that folly drudges all the year.

A considerable difference indeed, it must be allowed, there is between man and man, arising (besidethat wrought by preventing grace) from difference of constitution and of education. But, notwithstanding this, who, that is not utterly ignorant of himself, can here cast the first stoneat another? Who can abide the test of our blessed Lords comment on the Seventh Commandment: "He thatlooketh on a woman to lust after her hath committed adultery with her already in his heart?" So thatone knows not which to wonder at most, the ignorance or the insolence of those men who speak withsuch disdain of them that are overcome by desires which every man has felt in his own breast; thedesire of every pleasure of sense, innocent or not, being natural to every child of man.

10. And so is "the desire of the eye;" the desire of the pleasures of the imagination. Thesearise either from great, or beautiful, or uncommon objects;—if the two former do not coincide withthe latter; for perhaps it would appear, upon a diligent inquiry, that neither grand nor beautifulobjects please any longer than they are new; that when the novelty of them is over, the greatestpart, at least, of the pleasure they give is over; and in the same proportion as they becomefamiliar, they become flat and insipid. But let us experience this ever so often, the same desirewill remain still. The inbred thirst continues fixed in the soul; nay, the more it is indulged, themore it increases, and incites us to follow

after another, and yet another object; although we leaveevery one with an abortive hope, and a deluded expectation. Yea,

> The hoary fool, who many days
>> Has struggled with continued sorrow,
> Renews his hope, and fondly lays
>> The desperate bet upon tomorrow!
> To-morrow comes! 'Tis noon! 'Tis night!
>> This day, like all the former, flies:
> Yet on he goes, to seek delight
>> To-morrow, till to-night he dies!

11. A third symptom of this fatal disease, the love of the world, which is so deeply rooted inour nature, is "the pride of life;" the desire of praise, of the honour that cometh of men. This thegreatest admirers of human nature allow to be strictly natural; as natural as the sight, or hearing, or any other of the external senses. And are they ashamed of it, even men of letters, men of refinedand improved understanding? So far from it that they glory therein! They applaud themselves fortheir love of applause! Yea, eminent Christians, so called, make no difficulty of adopting the sayingof the old, vain Heathen, _Animi dissoluti est et nequam negligere quid de se homines sentiant: "Notto regard what men think of us is the mark of a wicked and abandoned mind." So that to go calm andunmoved through honour and dishonour, through evil report and good report, is with them a sign of onethat is, indeed, not fit to live: "Away with such a flow from the earth!" But would one imagine thatthese men had ever heard of Jesus Christ or his Apostles; or that they knew who it was that said,"How can ye believe who receive honour one of another, and seek not the honour which cometh of Godonly?" But if this is really so, if it be impossible to believe, and consequently to please God, solong as we receive or seek honour one of another, and seek not the honour which cometh of God only; then in what a condition are all mankind! the Christians as well as Heathens! since they all seekhonour one of another! since it is as natural for them so to do, themselves being the judges, as itis to see the light which strikes upon their eye, or to hear the sound which enters their ear; yea, since they account it a sign of a virtuous mind, to seek the praise of men, and of a vicious one, tobe content with the honour that cometh of God only!

III. 1. I proceed to draw a few inferences from what has been said. And, First, from hence wemay learn one grand fundamental difference between Christianity, considered as a system of doctrines, and the most refined Heathenism. Many of the ancient Heathens have largely described the vices ofparticular men. They have spoken much against their covetousness, or cruelty; their luxury, orprodigality. Some have dared to say that "no man is born without vices of one kind or another." Butstill as none of them were apprized of the fall of man, so none of them knew of his total corruption. They knew not that all men were empty of all good, and filled with all manner of evil. They werewholly ignorant of the entire depravation of the whole human nature, of every man born into theworld, in every faculty of his soul, not so much by those particular vices which reign in particularpersons, as by the general flood of Atheism and idolatry, of pride, self-will, and love of theworld. This, therefore, is the first grand distinguishing point between Heathenism and Christianity. The one acknowledges that many men are infected with many vices, and even born with a proneness tothem; but supposes withal, that in some the natural good much over-balances the evil: The otherdeclares that all men are conceived in sin," and "shapen in wickedness;"—that hence there is inevery man a "carnal mind, which is enmity against God, which is not, cannot be, subject to" his"law;" and which so infects the whole soul, that "there dwelleth in" him, "in his flesh," in hisnatural state, "no good thing;" but "every imagination of the thoughts of his heart is evil," onlyevil, and that "continually."

2. Hence we may, Secondly, learn, that all who deny this, call it original sin, or by any othertitle, are put Heathens still, in the fundamental point which differences Heathenism fromChristianity. They may, indeed, allow, that men have many vices; that some are born with us; andthat, consequently, we are not born altogether so wise or so virtuous as we should be; there beingfew that will roundly affirm, "We are born with as much propensity to good as to evil, and thatevery man is, by nature, as virtuous and wise as Adam was at his creation." But here is the *shibboleth:* Is man by nature filled with all manner of evil? Is he void of all good? Is hewholly fallen? Is his soul totally corrupted? or, to come back to the text, is "every imagination ofthe thoughts of his heart only evil continually?" Allow this, and you are so far a Christian. Denyit, and you are but an Heathen still.

3. We may learn from hence, in the Third place, what is the proper nature of religion, of thereligion of Jesus Christ. It is *therapeia psyches*, God's method of *healing a soul* which isthus diseased. Hereby the great Physician of souls applies medicines to heal this sickness; torestore human nature, totally corrupted in all its faculties. God heals all our Atheism by theknowledge of Himself, and of Jesus Christ whom he hath sent; by giving us faith, a divine evidenceand conviction of God, and of the things of God,—in particular, of this important truth, "Christloved *me*"—and gave himself for *me*." By repentance and lowliness of heart, the deadlydisease of pride is healed; that of self-will by resignation, a meek and thankful submission to thewill of God; and for the love of the world in all its branches, the love of God is the sovereignremedy. Now, this is properly religion, "faith" thus "working by love;" working the genuine meekhumility, entire deadness to the world, with a loving, thankful acquiescence in, and conformity to, the whole will and word of God.

4. Indeed, if man were not thus fallen, there would be no need of all this. There would be nooccasion for this work in the heart, this renewal in the spirit of our mind. The superfluity ofgodliness would then be a more proper expression than the "superfluity of naughtiness." For anoutside religion, without any godliness at all, would suffice to all rational intents and purposes. It does, accordingly, suffice, in the judgment of those who deny this corruption of our nature. They make very little more of religion than the famous Mr. Hobbes did of reason. According to him, reasonis only "a well-ordered train of words:" According to them, religion is only a well-ordered train ofwords and

actions. And they speak consistently with themselves; for if the inside be not full ofwickedness, if this be clean already, what remains, but to "cleanse the outside of the cup?" Outwardreformation, if their supposition be just, is indeed the one thing needful.

5. But ye have not so learned the oracles of God. Ye know, that He who seeth what is in man givesa far different account both of nature and grace, of our fall and our recovery. Ye know that thegreat end of religion is, to renew our hearts in the image of God, to repair that total loss ofrighteousness and true holiness which we sustained by the sin of our first parent. Ye know that allreligion which does not answer this end, all that stops short of this, the renewal of our soul in theimage of God, after the likeness of Him that created it, is no other than a poor farce, and a meremockery of God, to the destruction of our own soul. O beware of all those teachers of lies, who wouldpalm this upon you for Christianity! Regard them not, although they should come unto you with all thedeceivableness of unrighteousness; with all smoothness of language, all decency, yea, beauty andelegance of expression, all professions of earnest good will to you, and reverence for the HolyScriptures. Keep to the plain, old faith, "once delivered to the saints," and delivered by the Spiritof God to our hearts. Know your disease! Know your cure! Ye were born in sin: Therefore, "ye must beborn again," born of God. By nature ye are wholly corrupted. By grace ye shall be wholly renewed. In Adam ye all died: In the second Adam, in Christ, ye all are made alive. "You that were dead in sinshath he quickened:" He hath already given you a principle of life, even faith in him who loved youand gave himself for you! Now, "go on from faith to faith," until your whole sickness be healed; andall that "mind be in you which was also in Christ Jesus!"

45.* The New Birth

"Ye must be born again."

John 3:7.

1. If any doctrines within the whole compass of Christianity may be properly termed fundamental, they are doubtless these two,—the doctrine of justification, and that of the new birth: The former relating to that great work which God does for us, in forgiving our sins; the latter, to the great work which God does *in us*, in renewing our fallen nature. In order of *time*, neither of these is before the other: in the moment we are justified by the grace of God, through the redemption that is in Jesus, we are also "born of the Spirit;" but in order of *thinking*, as it is termed, justification precedes the new birth. We first conceive his wrath to be turned away, and then his Spirit to work in our hearts.

2. How great importance then must it be of, to every child of man, throughly to understand these fundamental doctrines! From a full conviction of this, many excellent men have wrote very largely concerning justification, explaining every point relating thereto, and opening the Scriptures which treat upon it. Many likewise have wrote on the new birth: And

some of them largely enough; but yet not so clearly as might have been desired, nor so deeply and accurately; having either given a dark, abstruse account of it, or a slight and superficial one. Therefore a full, and at the same time a clear, account of the new birth, seems to be wanting still; such as may enable us to give a satisfactory answer to these three questions: First, Why must we be born again? What is the foundation of this doctrine of the new birth? Secondly, How must we be born again? What is the nature of the new birth? And, Thirdly, Wherefore must we be born again? To what end is it necessary? These questions, by the assistance of God, I shall briefly and plainly answer; and then subjoin a few inferences which will naturally follow.

I. 1. And, First, Why must we be born again? What is the foundation of this doctrine? The foundation of it lies near as deep as the creation of the world; in the scriptural account whereof we read, "And God," the three-one God, "said, Let us make man in our image, after our likeness. So God created man in his own image, in the image of God created he him:" (Gen. 1:26, 27:)—Not barely in his *natural image*, a picture of his own immortality; a spiritual being, endued with understanding, freedom of will, and various affections;—nor merely in his *political image*, the governor of this lower world, having "dominion over the fishes of the sea, and over all the earth;"—but chiefly in his *moral image*; which, according to the Apostle, is "righteousness and true holiness." (Eph. 4:24.) in this image of God was man made. "God is love:" Accordingly, man at his creation was full of love; which was the sole principle of all his tempers, thoughts, words, and actions. God is full of justice, mercy, and truth; so was man as he came from the hands of his Creator. God is spotless purity; and so man was in the beginning pure from every sinful blot; otherwise God could not have pronounced him, as well as all the other work of his hands, "very good" (Gen. 1:31.) This he could not have been, had he not been pure from sin, and filled with righteousness and true holiness. For there is no medium: If we suppose and intelligent creature not to love God, not to be righteous and holy, we necessarily suppose him not to be good at all; much less to be "very good."

2. But, although man was made in the image of God, yet he was not made immutable. This would have been inconsistent with the state of trial in which God was pleased to place him. He was therefore created able to stand, and yet liable to fall. And this God himself apprized him of, and gave him a solemn warning against it. Nevertheless, man did not abide in honour: He fell from his high estate. He "ate of the tree whereof the Lord had commanded him, Thou shalt not eat thereof." By this wilful act of disobedience to his Creator, this flat rebellion against his Sovereign, he openly declared that he would no longer have God to rule over him; That he would be governed by his own will, and not the will of Him that created him; and that he would not seek his happiness in God, but in the world, in the works of his hands. Now, God had told him before, "In the day that thou eatest" of that fruit, "thou shalt surely die." And the word of the Lord

* (text of the 1872 ed.)

cannot be broken. Accordingly, in that day he did die: He died to God,—the most dreadful of all deaths. He lost the life of God: He was separated from Him, in union with whom his spiritual life consisted. The body dies when it is separated from the soul; the soul, when it is separated from God. But this separation from God, Adam sustained in the day, the hour, he ate of the forbidden fruit. And of this he gave immediate proof; presently showing by his behaviour, that the love of God was extinguished in his soul, which was now "alienated from the life of God." Instead of this, he was now under the power of servile fear, so that he fled from the presence of the Lord. Yea, so little did he retain even of the knowledge of Him who filleth heaven and earth, that he endeavored to "hide himself from the Lord God among the trees of the garden:" (Gen. 3:8:) So had he lost both the knowledge and the love of God, without which the image of God could not subsist. Of this, therefore, he was deprived at the same time, and became unholy as well as unhappy. In the room of this, he had sunk into pride and self-will, the very image of the devil; and into sensual appetites and desires, the image of the beasts that perish.

3. If it be said, "Nay, but that threatening, 'In the day that thou eatest thereof, thou shalt surely die,' refers to temporal death, and that alone, to the death of the body only;" the answer is plain: To affirm this is flatly and palpably to make God a liar; to aver that the God of truth positively affirmed a thing contrary to truth. For it is evident, Adam did not *die* in this sense, "in the day that he ate thereof." He lived, in the sense opposite to this death, above nine hundred years after. So that this cannot possibly be understood of the death of the body, without impeaching the veracity of God. It must therefore be understood of spiritual death, the loss of the life and image of God.

4. And in Adam all died, all human kind, all the children of men who were then in Adam's loins. The natural consequence of this is, that every one descended from him comes into the world spiritually dead, dead to God, wholly dead in sin; entirely void of the life of God; void of the image of God, of all that righteousness and holiness wherein Adam was created. Instead of this, every man born into the world now bears the image of the devil in pride and self-will; the image of the beast, in sensual appetites and desires. This, then, is the foundation of the new birth,—the entire corruption of our nature. Hence it is, that, being born in sin, we must be "born again." Hence every one that is born of a woman must be born of the Spirit of God.

II. 1. But how must a man be born again? What is the nature of the new birth? This is the Second question. And a question it is of the highest moment that can be conceived. We ought not, therefore, in so weighty a concern, to be content with a slight inquiry; but to examine it with all possible care, and to ponder it in our hearts, till we fully understand this important point, and clearly see how we are to be born again.

2. Not that we are to expect any minute, philosophical account of the manner how this is done. Our Lord sufficiently guards us against any such expectation, by the words immediately following the text; wherein he reminds Nicodemus of as indisputable a fact as any in the whole compass of nature, which, notwithstanding, the wisest man under the sun is not able fully to explain. "The wind bloweth where it listeth,"—not by thy power or wisdom; "and thou hearest the sound thereof;"—thou art absolutely assured, beyond all doubt, that it doth blow; "but thou canst not tell whence it cometh, nor whither it goeth;"—the precise manner how it begins and ends, rises and falls, no man can tell. "So is every one that is born of the Spirit:"—Thou mayest be as absolutely assured of the fact, as of the blowing of the wind; but the precise manner how it is done, how the Holy Spirit works this in the soul, neither thou nor the wisest of the children of men is able to explain.

3. However, it suffices for every rational and Christian purpose, that, without descending into curious, critical inquiries, we can give a plain scriptural account of the nature of the new birth. This will satisfy every reasonable man, who desires only the salvation of his soul. The expression, "being born again," was not first used by our Lord in his conversation with Nicodemus: It was well known before that time, and was in common use among the Jews when our Saviour appeared among them. When an adult Heathen was convinced that the Jewish religion was of God, and desired to join therein, it was the custom to baptize him first, before he was admitted to circumcision. And when he was baptized, he was said to be born again; by which they meant, that he who was before a child of the devil was now adopted into the family of God, and accounted one of his children. This expression, therefore, which Nicodemus, being "a Teacher in Israel," ought to have understood well, our Lord uses in conversing with him; only in a stronger sense than he was accustomed to. And this might be the reason of his asking, "How can these things be?" They cannot be literally:—A man cannot "enter a second time into his mother's womb, and be born:"—But they may spiritually: A man may be born from above, born of God, born of the Spirit, in a manner which bears a very near analogy to the natural birth.

4. Before a child is born into the world he has eyes, but sees not; he has ears, but does not hear. He has a very imperfect use of any other sense. He has no knowledge of any of the things of the world, or any natural understanding. To that manner of existence which he then has, we do not even give the name of life. It is then only when a man is born, that we say he begins to live. For as soon as he is born, be begins to see the light, and the various objects with which he is encompassed. His ears are then opened, and he hears the sounds which successively strike upon them. At the same time, all the other organs of sense begin to be exercised upon their proper objects. He likewise breathes, and lives in a manner wholly different from what he did before. How exactly doth the parallel hold in all these instances! While a man is in a mere natural state, before he is born of God, he has, in a spiritual sense, eyes and sees not; a thick impenetrable veil lies upon them; he has ears, but hears not; he is utterly deaf to what he is most of all concerned to hear. His other spiritual senses are all locked up: He is in the same condition as if he had them not. Hence he has no knowledge of God; no intercourse with him; he is not at all acquainted with him. He has no true knowledge of the things of God,

either of spiritual or eternal things; therefore, though he is a living man, he is a dead Christian. But as soon as he is born of God, there is a total change in all these particulars. The "eyes of his understanding are opened;" (such is the language of the great Apostle;) and, He who of old "commanded light to shine out of darkness shining on his heart, he sees the light of the glory of God," his glorious love, "in the face of Jesus Christ." His ears being opened, he is now capable of hearing the inward voice of God, saying, "Be of good cheer; thy sins are forgiven thee;" "go and sin no more." This is the purport of what God speaks to his heart; although perhaps not in these very words. He is now ready to hear whatsoever "He that teacheth man knowledge" is pleased, from time to time, to reveal to him. He "feels in his heart," to use the language of our Church, "the mighty working of the Spirit of God;" not in a gross, carnal sense as the men of the world stupidly and wilfully misunderstand the expression; though they have been told again and again, we mean thereby neither more nor less than this: He feels, is inwardly sensible of, the graces which the Spirit of god works in his heart. He feels, he is conscious of, a "peace which passeth all understanding." He many times feels such a joy in God as is "unspeakable, and full of glory." He feels "the love of God shed abroad in his heart by the Holy Ghost which is given unto him;" and all his spiritual senses are then exercised to discern spiritual good and evil. By the use of these, he is daily increasing in the knowledge of God, of Jesus Christ whom he hath sent and to all the things pertaining to his inward kingdom. And now he may be properly said to live: God having quickened him by his Spirit, he is alive to God through Jesus Christ. He lives a life which the world knoweth not of, a "life which is hid with Christ in God." God is continually breathing, as it were, upon the soul; and his soul is breathing unto God. Grace is descending into his heart; and prayer and praise ascending to heaven: And by this intercourse between God and man, this fellowship with the Father and the Son, as by a kind of spiritual respiration, the life of God in the soul is sustained; and the child of God grows up, till he comes to the "full measure of the stature of Christ."

5. From hence it manifestly appears, what is the nature of the new birth. It is that great change which God works in the soul when he brings it into life; when he raises it from the death of sin to the life of righteousness. It is the change wrought in the whole soul by the almighty Spirit of God when it is "created anew in Christ Jesus;" when it is "renewed after the image of God, in righteousness and true holiness;" when the love of the world is changed into the love of God; pride into humility; passion into meekness; hatred, envy, malice, into a sincere, tender, disinterested love for all mankind. In a word, it is that change whereby the earthly, sensual, devilish mind is turned into the "mind which was in Christ Jesus." This is the nature of the new birth: "So is every one that is born of the Spirit."

III. 1. It is not difficult for any who has considered these things, to see the necessity of the new birth, and to answer the Third question, Wherefore, to what end, is it necessary that we should be born again? It is very easily discerned, that this is necessary, First, in order to holiness. For what is

holiness according to the oracles of God? Not a bare external religion, a round of outward duties, how many soever they be, and how exactly soever performed. No: Gospel holiness is no less than the image of God stamped upon the heart; it is no other than the whole mind which was in Christ Jesus; it consists of all heavenly affections and tempers mingled together in one. It implies such a continual, thankful love to Him who hath not withheld from us his Son, his only son, as makes it natural, and in a manner necessary to us, to love every child of man; as fills us "with bowels of mercies, kindness, gentleness, long-suffering:" It is such a love of God as teaches us to be blameless in all manner of conversation; as enables us to present our souls and bodies, all we are and all we have, all our thoughts, words, and actions, a continual sacrifice to God, acceptable through Christ Jesus. Now, this holiness can have no existence till we are renewed in the image of our mind. It cannot commence in the soul till that change be wrought; till, by the power of the Highest overshadowing us, we are "brought from darkness to light, from the power of Satan unto God;" that is, till we are born again; which, therefore, is absolutely necessary in order to holiness.

2. But "without holiness no man shall see the Lord," shall see the face of God in glory. Of consequence, the new birth is absolutely necessary in order to eternal salvation. Men may indeed flatter themselves (so desperately wicked and so deceitful is the heart of man!) that they may live in their sins till they come to the last gasp, and yet afterwards live with God; and thousands do really believe, that they have found a broad way which leadeth not to destruction. "What danger," say they, "can a woman be in that is so *harmless* and so *virtuous?* What fear is there that so *honest* a man, one of so strict *morality*, should miss of heaven; especially if, over and above all this, they constantly attend on church and sacrament?" One of these will ask with all assurance, "What! Shall not I do as well as my neighbours?" Yes as well as your unholy neighbours; as well as your neighbours that die in their sins! For you will all drop into the pit together, into the nethermost hell! You will all lie together in the lake of fire; "the lake of fire burning with brimstone." Then, at length, you will see (but God grant you may see it before!) the necessity of holiness in order to glory; and, consequently, of the new birth, since none can be holy, except he be born again.

3. For the same reason, except he be born again, none can be happy even in this world. For it is not possible, in the nature of things, that a man should be happy who is not holy. Even the poor, ungodly poet could tell us, *Nemo malus felix*: "no wicked man is happy." The reason is plain: All unholy tempers are uneasy tempers: Not only malice, hatred, envy jealousy, revenge, create a present hell in the breast; but even the softer passions, if not kept within due bounds, give a thousand times more pain than pleasure. Even "hope," when "deferred," (and how often must this be the case!) "maketh the heart sick;" and every desire which is not according to the will of God is liable to "pierce" us "through with many sorrows:" And all those general sources of sin—pride, self-will, and idolatry—are, in the same proportion as they

prevail, general sources of misery. Therefore, as long as these reign in any soul, happiness has no place there. But they must reign till the bent of our nature is changed, that is, till we are born again; consequently, the new birth is absolutely necessary in order to happiness in this world, as well as in the world to come.

IV. I proposed in the Last place to subjoin a few inferences, which naturally follow from the preceding observations.

1. And, First, it follows, that baptism is not the new birth: They are not one and the same thing. Many indeed seem to imagine that they are just the same; at least, they speak as if they thought so; but I do not know that this opinion is publicly avowed by any denomination of Christians whatever. Certainly it is not by any within these kingdoms, whether of the established Church, or dissenting from it. The judgment of the latter is clearly declared in the large Catechism:[Q. 163, 165.—Ed.]—Q. "What are the parts of a sacrament? A. The parts of a sacrament are two: The one an outward and sensible sign; the other, and inward and spiritual grace, thereby signified.—Q. What is baptism? A. Baptism is a sacrament, wherein Christ hath ordained the washing with water, to be a sign and seal of regeneration by his Spirit." Here it is manifest, baptism, the sign, is spoken of as distinct from regeneration, the thing signified.

In the Church Catechism likewise, the judgment of our Church is declared with the utmost clearness: "What meanest thou by this word, sacrament? A. I mean an outward and visible sign of an inward and spiritual grace. Q. What is the outward part or form in baptism? A. Water, wherein the person is baptized, in the name of the Father, Son, and Holy Ghost. Q. What is the inward part, or thing signified? A. A death unto sin, and a new birth unto righteousness." Nothing, therefore, is plainer than that, according to the Church of England, baptism is not the new birth.

But indeed the reason of the thing is so clear and evident, as not to need any other authority. For what can be more plain, than the one is a visible, the and invisible thing, and therefore wholly different from each other?—the one being an act of man, purifying the body; the other a change wrought by God in the soul: So that the former is just as distinguishable from the latter, as the soul from the body, or water from the Holy Ghost.

2. From the preceding reflections we may, Secondly, observe, that as the new birth is not the same thing with baptism, so it does not always accompany baptism: They do not constantly go together. A man my possibly be "born of water," and yet not be "born of the Spirit." There may sometimes be the outward sign, where there is not the inward grace. I do not now speak with regard to infants: It is certain our Church supposes that all who are baptized in their infancy are at the same time born again; and it is allowed that the whole Office for the Baptism of Infants proceeds upon this supposition. Nor is it an objection of any weight against this, that we cannot comprehend how this work can be wrought I infants. For neither can we comprehend how it is wrought in a person of riper years. But whatever be the case with infants, it is sure all of riper years who are baptized are not at the same time born again. "The tree is known by its fruits:" And hereby it appears too plain to be denied, that divers of those who were children of the devil before they were baptized continue the same after baptism: "for the works of their father they do:" They continue servants of sin, without any pretence either to inward or outward holiness.

3. A Third inference which we may draw from what has been observed, is, that the new birth is not the same with sanctification. This is indeed taken for granted by many; particularly by an eminent writer, in his late treatise on "The Nature and Grounds of Christian Regeneration." To wave several other weighty objections which might be made to that tract, this is a palpable one: It all along speaks of regeneration as a progressive work, carried on in the soul by slow degrees, from the time of our first turning to God. This is undeniably true of sanctification; but of regeneration, the new birth, it is not true. This is a part of sanctification, not the whole; it is the gate to it, the entrance into it. When we are born again, then our sanctification, our inward and outward holiness, begins; and thenceforward we are gradually to "grow up in Him who is our Head." This expression of the Apostle admirably illustrates the difference between one and the other, and farther points out the exact analogy there is between natural and spiritual things. A child is born of a woman in a moment, or at least in a very short time: Afterward he gradually and slowly grows, till he attains to the stature of a man. In like manner, a child is born of God in a short time, if not in a moment. But it is by slow degrees that he afterward grows up to the measure of the full stature of Christ. The same relation, therefore, which there is between our natural birth and our growth, there is also between our new birth and our sanctification.

4. One point more we may learn from the preceding observations. But it is a point of so great importance, as my excuse the considering it the more carefully, and prosecuting it at some length. What must one who loves the souls of men, and is grieved that any of them should perish, say to one whom he sees living in sabbath-breaking, drunkenness, or any other wilful sin? What can he say, if the foregoing observations are true, but, "You must be born again?" "No," says a zealous man, "that cannot be. How can you talk so uncharitably to the man? Has he not been baptized already? He cannot be born again now." Can he not be born again? Do you affirm this? Then he cannot be saved. Though he be as old as Nicodemus was, yet "except he be born again, he cannot see the kingdom of God." Therefore in saying, "He cannot be born again," you in effect deliver him over to damnation. And where lies the uncharitableness now?—on my side, or on yours? I say, he may be born again, and so become an heir of salvation. You say, "He cannot be born again:" And if so, he must inevitably perish! So you utterly block up his way to salvation, and send him to hell, out of mere charity!

But perhaps the sinner himself, to whom in real charity we say, "You must be born again," has been taught to say, "I defy your new doctrine; I need not be born again: I was born again when I was baptized. What! Would you have me deny my baptism?" I answer, First, There is nothing under heaven which can excuse a lie; otherwise I should say to an open sinner, If you have been baptized, do not own it. For how highly does this aggravate your guilt! How will it increase your damnation! Was you devoted to God at eight days old, and have you been all these years devoting yourself to the devil? Was you, even before you had the use of reason, consecrated to God the Father, the son, and the Holy Ghost? And have you, ever since you had the use of it, been flying in the face of God, and consecrating yourself to Satan? Does the abomination of desolation—the love of the word, pride, anger, lust, foolish desire, and a whole train of vile affections—stand where it ought not? Have you set up all the accursed things in that soul which was once a temple of the Holy Ghost; set apart for an "habitation of God, through the Spirit;" yea, solemnly given up to him? And do you glory in this, that you once belonged to God? O be ashamed! blush! hide yourself in the earth! Never boast more of what ought to fill you with confusion, to make you ashamed before God and man! I answer, Secondly, You have already denied your baptism; and that in the most effectual manner. You have denied it a thousand and a thousand times; and you do so still, day by day. For in your baptism you renounced the devil and all his works. Whenever, therefore, you give place to him again, whenever you do any of the works of the devil, then you deny your baptism. Therefore you deny it by every wilful sin; by every act of uncleanness, drunkenness, or revenge; by every obscene or profane word; by every oath that comes out of your mouth. Every time you profane the day of the Lord, you thereby deny your baptism; yea, every time you do any thing to another which you would not he should do to you. I answer, Thirdly, Be you baptized or unbaptized, "you must be born again;" otherwise it is not possible you should be inwardly holy; and without inward as well as outward holiness, you cannot be happy, even in this world, much less in the world to come. Do you say, "Nay, but I do no harm to any man; I am honest and just in all my dealings; I do not curse, or take the Lord's name in vain; I do not profane the Lord's day; I am no drunkard; I do not slander my neighbour, nor live in any wilful sin?" If this be so, it were much to be wished that all men went as far as you do. But you must go farther yet, or you cannot be saved: Still, "you must be born again." Do you add, "I do go farther yet; for I not only do no harm, but do all the good I can?" I doubt that fact; I fear you have had a thousand opportunities of doing good which you have suffered to pass by unimproved, and for which therefore you are accountable to God. But if you had improved them all, if you really had done all the good you possibly could to all men, yet this does not at all alter the case; still, "you must be born again." Without this nothing will do any good to your poor, sinful, polluted soul. "Nay, but I constantly attend all the ordinances of God: I keep to my church and sacrament." It is well you do: But all this will not keep you from hell, except you be born again. Go to church twice a day; go to the Lord's table every week; say ever so many prayers in private; hear ever so many good sermons; read ever so many good books; still, "you must be born again:" None of these things will stand in the place of the new birth; no, nor any thing under heaven. Let this therefore, if you have not already experienced this inward work of God,

be your continual prayer: "Lord, add this to all thy blessings,—let me be born again! Deny whatever thou pleasest, but deny not this; let me be 'born from above!' Take away whatsoever seemeth thee good,—reputation, fortune, friends, health,—only give me this, to be born of the Spirit, to be received among the children of God! Let me be born, 'not of corruptible seed, but incorruptible, by the word of God, which liveth and abideth for ever;' and then let be daily 'grow in grace, and in the knowledge of our Lord and Saviour Jesus Christ!' "

46.* THE WILDERNESS STATE

"Ye now have sorrow: But I will see you again, and your heart shall rejoice, and your joy no man taketh from you."

John 16:22.

1. After God had wrought a great deliverance for Israel, by bringing them out of the house of bondage, they did not immediately enter into the land which he had promised to their fathers; but "wandered out of the way in the wilderness," and were variously tempted and distressed. In like manner, after God has delivered them that fear him from the bondage of sin and Satan; after they are "justified freely by his grace, through the redemption that is in Jesus," yet not many of them immediately enter into "the rest which remaineth for the people of God." The greater part of them wander, more or less, out of the good way into which he hath brought them. They come, as it were, into a "waste and howling desert," where they are variously tempted and tormented: And this, some, in allusion to the case of the Israelites, have termed "a wilderness state."

2. Certain it is, that the condition wherein these are has a right the tenderest compassion. They labour under an evil and sore disease; though one that is not commonly understood; and for this very reason it is the more difficult for them to find a remedy. Being in darkness themselves, they cannot be supposed to understand the nature of their own disorder; and few of their brethren, nay, perhaps, of their teachers, know either what their sickness is, or how to heal it. So much the more need there is to inquire, First, What is the nature of this disease? Secondly, What is the cause? and, Thirdly, What is the cure of it?

I. 1. And, First, what is the nature of this disease, into which so many fall after they have believed? Wherein does it properly consist; and what are the genuine symptoms of it? It properly consists in the loss of that faith which God once wrought in their heart. They that are *in the wilderness*, have not now that divine "evidence," that satisfactory conviction "of things not seen," which they once enjoyed. They have not now that inward demonstration of the Spirit which before enabled each of them to say, "The life I live, I live by faith in the Son of God, who loved me, and gave himself for me." The light of heaven does not now "shine in their hearts," neither do they "see him that is invisible;" but darkness is again on the face of their souls, and blindness on the eyes of their understanding. The Spirit no longer "witnesses with their spirits, that they are the children of God;" neither does he continue as the Spirit of adoption, "crying" in their hearts, "Abba, Father." They have not now a sure trust in his love, and a liberty of approaching him with holy boldness. "Though he slay me, yet will I trust in him," is no more the language of their heart; but they are shorn of their strength, and become weak and feeble-minded, even as other men.

2. Hence, Secondly, proceeds the loss of love; which cannot but rise or fall, at the same time, and in the same proportion, with true, living faith. Accordingly, they that are deprived of their faith, are deprived of the love of God also. They cannot now say, "Lord, thou knowest all things, thou knowest that I love thee." They are not now happy in God, as everyone is that truly loves him. They do not delight in him as in time past, and "smell the odour of his ointments." Once, all their "desire was unto him, and to the remembrance of his name;" but now even their desires are cold and dead, if not utterly extinguished. And as their love of God is waxed cold, so is also their love of their neighbour. They have not now that zeal for the souls of men, that longing after their welfare, that fervent, restless, active desire of their being reconciled to God. They do not feel those "bowels of mercies" for the sheep that are lost,—that tender "compassion for the ignorant, and them that are out of the way." Once they were "gentle toward all men," meekly instructing such as opposed the truth; and, "if any was overtaken in a fault, restoring such an one in the spirit of meekness:" But, after a suspense, perhaps of many days, anger begins to regain its power; yea, peevishness and impatience thrust sore at them that they may fall; and it is well if they are not sometimes driven, even to "render evil for evil and railing for railing."

3. In consequence of the loss of faith and love, follows, Thirdly, loss of joy in the Holy Ghost. For if the loving consciousness of pardon be no more, the joy resulting therefrom cannot remain. If the Spirit does not witness with our spirit that we are the children of God, the joy that flowed from that inward witness must also be at an end. And, in like manner, they who once "rejoiced with joy unspeakable," "in hope of the glory of God," now they are deprived of that "hope full of immortality," are deprived of the joy it occasioned; as also of that which resulted from a consciousness of "the love of God," then "shed abroad in their hearts." For the cause being removed, so is the effect: The fountain being dammed up, those living waters spring no more to refresh the thirsty soul.

4. With loss of faith, and love, and joy there is also joined, Fourthly, the loss of that peace which once passed all understanding. That sweet tranquillity of mind, that composure of spirit, is gone. Painful doubt returns; doubt, whether we ever did, and perhaps whether we ever shall, believe. We begin to doubt, whether we ever did find in our hearts the real testimony of the Spirit; whether we did not rather deceive our own souls, and mistake the voice of nature for the voice of God. Nay, and perhaps, whether we shall ever hear his voice, and find favour in his sight. And these doubts are again joined with servile fear, with that fear which hath torment. We fear the wrath of God, even as before we believed: We fear, lest we should be cast out of his presence;

and thence sink again into that fear of death, from which we were before wholly delivered.

5. But even this is not all; for loss of peace is accompanied with loss of power. We know everyone who has peace with God, through Jesus Christ, has power over all sin. But whenever he loses the peace of God, he loses also the power over sin. While that peace remained, power also remained, even over the besetting sin, whether it were the sin of his nature, his constitution, of his education, or that of his profession; yea, and over those evil tempers and desires which, till then, he could not conquer Sin had then no more dominion over him; but he hath now no more dominion over sin. He may struggle, indeed, but he cannot overcome; the crown is fallen from his head. His enemies again prevail over him, and, more or less, bring him into bondage. The glory is departed from him, even the kingdom of God which was in his heart. He is dispossessed of righteousness, as well as of peace and joy in the Holy Ghost.

II. 1. Such is the nature of what many have termed, and not improperly, "The wilderness state." But the nature of it may be more fully understood by inquiring, Secondly, What are the causes of it? These indeed are various. But I dare not rank among these the bare, arbitrary, sovereign will of God. He "rejoiceth in the prosperity of his servants: He delighteth not to afflict or grieve the children of men." His invariable will is our sanctification, attended with "peace and joy in the Holy Ghost." These are his own free gifts; and we are assured "the gifts of God are," on his part, "without repentance." He never repenteth of what he hath given, or desires to withdraw them from us. Therefore he never *deserts* us, as some speak; it is we only that desert him.

(I.) 2. The most usual cause of inward darkness is *sin*, of one kind or another. This it is which generally occasions what is often a complication of sin and misery. And, First, sin of commission. This may frequently be observed to darken the soul in a moment; especially if it be a known, a wilful, or presumptuous sin. If, for instance, a person, who is now walking in the clear light of God's countenance, should be any way prevailed on to commit a single act of drunkenness, or uncleanness, it would be no wonder, if, in that very hour, he fell into utter darkness. It is true, there have been some very rare cases, wherein God has prevented this, by an extraordinary display of his pardoning mercy, almost in the very instant. But in general, such an abuse of the goodness of God, so gross an insult on his love, occasions an immediate estrangement from God, and a "darkness that may be felt."

3. But it may be hoped this case is not very frequent; that there are not many who so despise the riches of his goodness as, while they walk in his light, so grossly and presumptuously to rebel against him. That light is much more frequently lost by giving way to sins of omission. This, indeed, does not immediately quench the Spirit, but gradually and slowly. The former may be compared to pouring water upon a fire; the latter to withdrawing the fuel from it. And many times will that loving Spirit reprove our neglect, before he departs from us. Many are the inward checks, the secret notices, he gives, before his influences are

withdrawn. So that only a train of omissions, wilfully persisted in, can bring us into utter darkness.

4. Perhaps no sin of omission more frequently occasions this than the neglect of private prayer; the want whereof cannot be supplied by any other ordinance whatever. Nothing can be more plain, than that the life of God in the soul does not continue, much less increase, unless we use all opportunities of communing with God, and pouring out our hearts before him. If therefore we are negligent of this, if we suffer business, company, or any avocation whatever, to prevent these secret exercises of the soul, (or, which comes to the same thing, to make us hurry them over in a slight and careless manner,) that life will surely decay. And if we long or frequently intermit them, it will gradually die away.

5. Another sin of omission, which frequently brings the soul of a believer into darkness, is the neglect of what was so strongly enjoined, even under the Jewish dispensation: "Thou shalt, in anywise, rebuke thy neighbour, and not suffer sin upon him: Thou shalt not hate thy brother in thy heart." Now, if we do hate our brother in our heart, if we do not rebuke him when we see him in a fault, but suffer sin upon him, this will soon bring leanness to our own soul; seeing hereby we are partakers of his sin. By neglecting to reprove our neighbour, we make his sin our own: We become accountable for it to God: We saw his danger, and gave him no warning: So, "if he perish in his iniquity," God may justly require "his blood at our hands." No wonder then, if by thus grieving the Spirit, we lose the light of his countenance.

6. A Third cause of our losing this is, the giving way to some kind of inward sin. For example: We know, every one that is "proud in heart is an abomination to the Lord;" and that, although this pride of heart should not appear in the outward conversation. Now, how easily may a soul filled with peace and joy fall into this snare of the devil! How natural is it for him to imagine that he has more grace, more wisdom or strength, than he really has to "think more highly of himself than he ought to think!" How natural to glory in something he has received, as if he had not received it! But seeing God continually "resisteth the proud, and giveth grace" only "to the humble," this must certainly obscure, if not wholly destroy, the light which before shone on his heart.

7. The same effect may be produced by giving place to anger, whatever the provocation or occasion be; yea, though it were coloured over with the name of zeal for the truth, or for the glory of God. Indeed all zeal which is any other than the flame of love is "earthly, animal, devilish." It is the flame of wrath: It is flat, sinful anger, neither better nor worse. And nothing is a greater enemy to the mild, gentle love of God than this: They never did, they never can, subsist together in one breast. In the same proportion as this prevails, love and joy in the Holy Ghost decrease. This is particularly observable in the case of *offence*; I mean, anger at any of our brethren, at any of those who are united with us either by civil or religious ties. If we give way to the spirit of offence but one hour, we lose the sweet influences of the Holy Spirit; so that, instead of amending them, we destroy ourselves, and become an easy prey to any enemy that assaults us.

8. But suppose we are aware of this snare of the devil, we may be attacked from another quarter. When fierceness and anger are asleep, and love alone is waking, we may be no less endangered by desire, which equally tends to darken the soul. This is the sure effect of any foolish desire, any vain or inordinate affection. If we set our affection on things of the earth, on any person or thing under the sun; if we desire anything but God, and what tends to God; if we seek happiness in any creature; the jealous God will surely contend with us, for he can admit of no rival. And if we will not hear his warning voice, and return to him with our whole soul, we continue to grieve him with our idols, and running after other gods, we shall soon be cold, barren, and dry; and the god of this world will blind and darken our hearts.

9. But this he frequently does, even when we do not give way to any positive sin. It is enough, it gives him sufficient advantage, if we do not "stir up the gift of God which is in us;" if we do not agonize continually "to enter in at the strait gate;" if we do not earnestly "strive for the mastery," and "take the kingdom of heaven by violence." There needs no more than not to fight, and we are sure to be conquered. Let us only be careless or "faint in our mind," let us be easy and indolent, and our natural darkness will soon return, and overspread our soul. It is enough, therefore, if we give way to spiritual sloth; this will effectually darken the soul: It will as surely destroy the light of God, if not so swiftly, as murder or adultery.

10. But it is well to be observed, that the cause of our darkness (whatsoever it be, whether omission or commission, whether inward or outward sin) is not always nigh at hand. Sometimes the sin which occasioned the present distress may lie at a considerable distance. It might be committed days, or weeks, or months before. And that God now withdraws his light and peace on account of what was done so long ago is not (as one might at first imagine) an instance of his severity, but rather a proof of his longsuffering and tender mercy. He waited all this time if haply we would see, acknowledge, and correct what was amiss. And in default of this he at length shows his displeasure, if thus, at last, he may bring us to repentance.

(II). 1. Another general cause of this darkness is *ignorance*; which is likewise of various kinds. If men know not the Scriptures, if they imagine there are passages either in the Old or New Testament which assert, that all believers without exception, *must* sometimes be in darkness; this ignorance will naturally bring upon them the darkness which they expect. And how common a case has this been among us! How few are there that do not expect it! And no wonder, seeing they are taught to expect it; seeing their guides lead them into this way. Not only the mystic writers of the Romish Church, but many of the most spiritual and experimental in our own, (very few of the last century excepted,) lay it down with all assurance as a plain, unquestionable Scripture doctrine, and cite many texts to prove it.

2. Ignorance also of the work of God in the soul frequent occasions this darkness. Men imagine (because so they have been taught, particularly by writers of the Romish communion, whose plausible assertions too many Protestants have received without due examination) that they are not

always to walk in *luminous faith*; that this is only a *lower dispensation*; that as they rise higher they are to leave those *sensible comforts*, and to live by *naked faith* (*naked* indeed, if it be stripped both of love, and peace, and joy in the Holy Ghost!) that a state of light and joy is good, but a state of darkness and dryness is better; that it is by these alone we can be purified from pride, love of the world, and inordinate self-love; and that, therefore, we ought neither to expect nor desire to walk in the light always. Hence it is, (though other reasons may concur.) that the main body of pious men in the Romish Church generally walk in a dark uncomfortable way, and if ever they receive, soon lose the light of God.

(III). 1. A Third general cause of this darkness is *temptation*. When the candle of the Lord first shines on our head, temptation frequently flees away, and totally disappears. All is calm within; perhaps without too, while God makes our enemies to be at peace with us. It is then very natural to suppose that we shall not see war any more. And there are instances wherein this calm has continued, not only for weeks, but for months or years. But commonly it is otherwise: In a short time "the winds blow, the rains descend, and the floods arise" anew. They who know not either the Son or the Father, and consequently hate his children, when God slackens the bridle which is in their teeth, will show that hatred in various instances. As of old, "he that was born after the flesh persecuted him that was born after the Spirit, even so it is now;" the same cause still producing the same effect. The evil which yet remains in the heart will then also move afresh; anger, and many other roots of bitterness will endeavour to spring up. At the same time, Satan will not be wanting to cast in his fiery darts; and the soul will have to wrestle, not only with the world, not only "with flesh and blood, but with principalities and powers, with the rulers of the darkness of this world, with wicked spirits in high places." Now, when so various assaults are made at once, and perhaps with the utmost violence, it is not strange if it should occasion, not only heaviness, but even darkness in a weak believer;—more especially if he was not watching; if these assaults are made in an hour when he looked not for them; if he expected nothing less, but had fondly told himself,—the day of evil would return no more.

2. The force of those temptations which arise from within will be exceedingly heightened if we before thought too highly of ourselves, as if we had been cleansed from all sin. And how naturally do we imagine this during the warmth of our first love! How ready are we to believe that God has "fulfilled in us the" whole "work of faith with power!" that because we *feel* no sin, we *have* none in us; but the soul is all love! And well may a sharp attack from an enemy whom we supposed to be not only conquered but slain, throw us into much heaviness of soul; yea, sometimes, into utter darkness: Particularly when we *reason* with this enemy, instead of instantly calling upon God, and casting ourselves upon Him, by simple faith, who "alone knoweth how to deliver" his "out of temptation."

III. These are the usual causes of this second darkness. Inquire we, Thirdly, What is the cure of it?

1. To suppose that this is one and the same in all cases is a and fatal mistake; and yet extremely common, even among many, who pass for experienced Christians, yea, perhaps take upon them to be teachers in Israel, to be the guides of other souls. Accordingly, they know and use but one medicine, whatever be the cause of the distemper. They begin immediately to apply the promises; to *preach the gospel*, as they call it. To give comfort is the single point at which they aim; in order to which they say many soft and tender things, concerning the love of God to poor helpless sinners, and the efficacy of the blood of Christ. Now this is *quackery* indeed, and that of the worse sort, as it tends, if not to kill men's bodies, yet without the peculiar mercy of God, "to destroy both their bodies and souls in hell." It is hard to speak of these "daubers with untempered mortar," these promise-mongers, as they deserve. They well deserve the title, which has been ignorantly given to others: They are *spiritual mountebanks*. They do, in effect, make "the blood of the covenant an unholy thing." They vilely prostitute the promises of God by thus applying them to all without distinction. Whereas, indeed, the cure of spiritual, as of bodily diseases, must be as various as are the causes of them. The first thing, therefore, is to find out the cause; and this will naturally point out the cure.

2. For instance: Is it sin which occasions darkness? What sin? Is it outward sin of any kind? Does your conscience accuse you of committing any sin, whereby you grieve the Holy Spirit of God? Is it on this account that he is departed from you, and that joy and peace are departed with him? And how can you expect they should return, till you put away the accursed thing? "Let the wicked forsake his way;" "cleanse your hands, ye sinners;" "put away the evil of your doings;" so shall your "light break out of obscurity;" the Lord will return and "abundantly pardon."

3. If, upon the closest search, you can find no sin of commission which causes the cloud upon your soul, inquire next, if there be not some sin of omission which separates between God and you. Do you "not suffer sin upon your brother?" Do you reprove them that sin in your sight? Do you walk in all the ordinances of God? in public, family, private prayer? If not, if you habitually neglect any one of these known duties, how can you expect that the light of his countenance should continue to shine upon you? Make haste to "strengthen the things that remain;" then your soul shall live. "Today, if ye will hear his voice," by his grace supply what is lacking. When you hear a voice behind you saying, "This is the way, walk thou in it," harden not your heart; be no more "disobedient to the heavenly calling." Till the sin, whether of omission or commission, be removed, all comfort is false and deceitful. It is only skinning the wound over, which still festers and rankles beneath. Look for no peace within, till you are at peace with God; which cannot be without "fruits meet for repentance."

4. But perhaps you are not conscious of even any sin of omission which impairs your peace and joy in the Holy Ghost. Is there not then some inward sin, which as a root of bitterness, springs up in your heart to trouble you? Is not your dryness, and barrenness of soul, occasioned by your heart's

"departing from the living God?" Has not "the foot of pride come against" you? Have you not thought of yourself "more highly than you ought to think?" Have you not, in any respect, "sacrificed to your own net, and burned incense to your own drag?" Have you not ascribed your success in any undertaking to your own courage, or strength, or wisdom? Have you not boasted of something "you have received, as though you had not received it?" Have you not gloried in anything, "save the cross of our Lord Jesus Christ?" Have you not sought after or desired the praise of men? Have you not taken pleasure in it? If so, you see the way you are to take. If you have fallen by pride, "humble yourself under the mighty hand of God, and he will exalt you in due time." Have you not forced him to depart from you, by giving place to anger? Have you not "fretted yourself because of the ungodly" or "been envious against the evil-doers?" Have you not been offended at any of your brethren, looking at their (real or imagined) sin, so as to sin yourself against the great law of love, by estranging your heart from them? Then look unto the Lord, that you may renew your strength; that all this sharpness and coldness may be done away; that love and peace and joy may return together, and you may be invariably kind to each other, and "tender-hearted, forgiving one another, even as God for Christ's sake hath forgiven you." Have not you given way to any foolish desire? To any kind or degree of inordinate affection? How then can the love of God have place in your heart, till you put away your idols? "Be not deceived: God is not mocked:" He will not dwell in a divided heart. As long, therefore, as you cherish Delilah in your bosom he has no place there. It is vain to hope for a recovery of his light, till you pluck out the right eye, and cast it from you. O let there be no longer delay! Cry to Him, that he may enable you so to do! Bewail your own impotence and helplessness; and, the Lord being your helper, enter in at the strait gate; take the kingdom of heaven by violence! Cast out every idol from his sanctuary, and the glory of the Lord shall soon appear.

5. Perhaps it is this very thing, the want of striving, spiritual sloth, which keeps your soul in darkness. You dwell at ease in the land; there is no war in your coasts; and so you are quiet and unconcerned. You go on in the same even track of outward duties, and are content there to abide. And do you wonder, meantime, that your soul is dead? O stir yourself up before the Lord! Arise, and shake yourself from the dust; wrestle with God for the mighty blessing; pour out your soul unto God in prayer, and continue therein with all perseverance! Watch! Awake out of sleep; and keep awake! Otherwise there is nothing to be expected, but that you will be alienated more and more from the light and life of God.

6. If, upon the fullest and most impartial examination of yourself, you cannot discern that you at present give way either to spiritual sloth, or any other inward or outward sin, then call to mind the time that is past. Consider your former tempers, words, and actions. Have these been right before the Lord? "Commune with him in your chamber, and be still;" and desire of him to try the ground of your heart, and bring to your remembrance whatever has at any time offended the eyes of his glory. If the guilt of any unrepented sin remain on

our soul, it cannot be but you will remain in darkness, till, having been renewed by repentance, you are again washed by faith in the "fountain opened for sin and uncleanness."

7. Entirely different will be the manner of the cure, if the cause of the disease be not sin, but ignorance. It may be, ignorance of the meaning of Scripture; perhaps occasioned by ignorant commentators; ignorant, at least, in this respect, however knowing and learned they may be in other particulars. And, in this case that ignorance must be removed before we can remove the darkness arising from it. We must show the true meaning of those texts which have been misunderstood. My design does not permit me to consider all the passages of Scripture which have been pressed into this service. I shall just mention two or three, which are frequently brought to prove that all believers must, sooner or later, "walk in darkness."

8 One of these is Isaiah 50:10: "Who is among you that feareth the Lord, and obeyeth the voice of his servant, that walketh in darkness and hath no light? Let him trust in the name of the Lord and stay upon his God." But how does it appear, either from the text or context, that the person here spoken of ever had light? One who is convinced of sin, "feareth the Lord, and obeyeth voice of his servant." And him we should advise, though he was still dark of soul, and had never seen the light of God's countenance, yet to "trust in the name of the Lord, and stay upon his God." This text, therefore, proves nothing less than that believer in Christ "must sometimes *walk in darkness.*"

9. Another text which has been supposed to speak the same doctrine is Hosea 2:14: "I will allure her, and bring her into the wilderness, and speak comfortably unto her." Hence it has been inferred, that God will bring every believer *into the wilderness*, into a state of deadness and darkness. But it is certain the text speaks no such thing; for it does not appear that it speaks of particular believers at all: It manifestly refers to the Jewish nation; and, perhaps, to that only. But if it be applicable to particular persons, the plain meaning of it is this:—I will draw him by love; I will next convince him of sin; and then comfort him by pardoning mercy.

10. A third Scripture from whence the same inference has been drawn is that above recited, "Ye now have sorrow: But I will see you again, and your heart shall rejoice, and your joy no man taketh from you." This has been supposed to imply, that God would after a time withdraw himself from all believers; and that they could not, till after they had thus sorrowed, have the joy which no man could take from them. But the whole context shows that our Lord is here speaking personally to the Apostles, and no others; and that he is speaking concerning those particular events, his own death and resurrection. "A little while," says he, "and ye shall not see me;" viz., whilst I am in the grave: "And again, a little while, and ye shall see me;" when I am risen from the dead. Ye will weep and lament, and the world will rejoice: But your sorrow shall be turned into joy."—"Ye now have sorrow," because I am about to be taken from your head; "but I will see you again," after my resurrection, "and your heart shall rejoice; and your joy," which I will then give you, "no man taketh from you." All this we know was literally fulfilled in

the particular case of the Apostles. But no inference can be drawn from hence with regard to God's dealings with believers in general.

11. A fourth text (to mention no more) which has been frequently cited in proof of the same doctrine, is 1 Peter 4:12: "Beloved, think it not strange concerning the fiery trial which is to try you." But this is full as foreign to the point as the preceding. The text, literally rendered, runs thus: "Beloved, wonder not at the burning which is among you, which is for your trial." Now, however, this may be accommodated to inward trials, in a secondary sense; yet, primarily, it doubtless refers to martyrdom, and the sufferings connected with it. Neither, therefore, is this text anything at all to the purpose for which it is cited. And we may challenge all men to bring one text, either from the Old or New Testament, which is any more to the purpose than this.

12. "But is not darkness much more profitable for the soul than light? Is not the work of God in the heart most swiftly and effectually carried on during a state of inward suffering? Is not a believer more swiftly and thoroughly purified by sorrow, than by joy?—by anguish, and pain, and distress, and spiritual martyrdoms, than by continual peace?" So the Mystics teach; so it is written in their books; but not in the oracles of God. The Scripture nowhere says, that the absence of God best perfects his work in the heart! Rather, his presence, and a clear communion with the Father and the Son: A strong consciousness of this will do more an hour, than his absence in an age. Joy in the Holy Ghost will far more effectually purify the soul than the want of that joy; and the peace of God is the best means of refining the soul from the dross of earthly affections. Away then with the idle conceit, that the kingdom of God is divided against itself; that the peace of God, and joy in the Holy Ghost, are obstructive of righteousness; and that we are saved, not by faith, but by unbelief; not by hope, but by despair!

13. So long as men dream thus, they may well "walk in darkness:" Nor can the effect cease, till the cause is removed. But yet we must not imagine it will immediately cease, even when the cause is no more. When either ignorance or sin has caused darkness, one or the other may be removed, and yet the light which was obstructed thereby may not immediately return. As it is the free gift of God, he may restore it, sooner or later, as it pleases him. In the case of sin, we cannot reasonably expect that it should immediately return. The sin began before the punishment, which may, therefore, justly remain after the sin is at an end. And even in the natural course of things, though a wound cannot be healed while the dart is sticking in the flesh; yet neither is it healed as soon as that is drawn out, but soreness and pain may remain long after.

14. Lastly. If darkness be occasioned by manifold and heavy and unexpected temptations, the best way of removing and preventing this is, to teach believers always to expect temptation, seeing they dwell in an evil world, among wicked, subtle, malicious spirits, and have an heart capable of all evil. Convince them that the whole work of sanctification is not, as they imagined, wrought at once; that when they first believe the are but as new-born babes, who are gradually to grow up, and may expect many storms before they come to the full stature of Christ. Above all, let them be instructed, when the storm is upon them, not to reason with the devil, but to pray; to pour out their souls before God, and show him of their trouble. And these are the persons unto whom, chiefly, we are to apply the great and precious promises; not to the ignorant, till the ignorance is removed, much less to the impenitent sinner. To these we may largely and affectionately declare the loving kindness of God our Saviour, expatiate upon his tender mercies, which have been ever of old. Here we may dwell upon the faithfulness of God, whose "word is tried to the uttermost;" and upon the virtue of that blood which was shed for us, to "cleanse us from all sin:" And God will then bear witness to his word, and bring their souls out of trouble. He will say, "Arise, shine; for thy light is come, and the glory of the Lord is risen upon thee." Yea, and that light, if thou walk humbly and closely with God, will "shine more and more unto the perfect day."

47.* HEAVINESS THROUGH MANIFOLD TEMPTATIONS

"Now for a season, if need be, ye are in heaviness through manifold temptations."

1 Pet. 1:6.

1. In the preceding discourse I have particularly spoken of that darkness of mind into which those are often observed to fall who once walked in the light of God's countenance. Nearly related to this is the heaviness of soul which is still more common, even among believers. Indeed, almost all the children of God experience this, in an higher or lower degree. And so great is the resemblance between one and the other, that they are frequently confounded together; and we are apt to say, indifferently, "Such an one is in darkness," or "Such an one is in heaviness;"—as if they were equivalent terms, one of which implied no more than the other. But they are far, very far from it. Darkness is one thing; heaviness is another. There is a difference, yea, a wide an essential difference, between the former and the latter. And such a difference it is as all the children of God are deeply concerned to understand: Otherwise nothing will be more easy than for them to slide out of heaviness into darkness. In order to prevent this, I will endeavor to show,

    I.   What manner of persons those were to whom the Apostle says, "Ye are in heaviness."

    II.   What kind of heaviness they were in:

    III.   What were the causes: and,

    IV.   What were the ends of it. I shall conclude with some inferences.

I. 1. I am, in the first place, to show what manner of persons those were to whom the Apostle says, "Ye are in heaviness." And, first, it is beyond all dispute, that they were believers at the time the Apostle thus addressed them: For so he expressly says, (1 Pet. 1:5,) "Ye who are kept through the power of God

---

* [text from the 1872 edition]

by faith unto salvation." Again, (1 Pet. 1:7,) he mentions "the trial of their faith, much more precious than that of gold which perisheth." And yet again, (1 Pet. 1:9,) he speaks of their "receiving the end of their faith, the salvation of their souls." At the same time, therefore, that they were "in heaviness," they were possessed of living faith. Their heaviness did not destroy their faith: They still "endured, as seeing him that is invisible."

2. Neither did their heaviness destroy their peace; the "peace that passeth all understanding;" which is inseparable from true, living faith. This we may easily gather from the second verse, wherein the Apostle prays, not that grace and *peace* may be *given* them, but only that it may "be *multiplied* unto them;" that the blessing which they already enjoyed might be more abundantly bestowed upon them.

3. The persons to whom the Apostle here speaks were also full of a living hope. For thus he speaks, (1 Pet. 1:3,) "Blessed be the God and Father of our Lord Jesus Christ, who according to his abundant mercy hath begotten us again,"— me and you, all of us who are "sanctified by the Spirit," and enjoy the "sprinkling of the blood of Jesus Christ"—"unto a living hope, unto an inheritance,"—that is, unto a living hope of an inheritance, "incorruptible, undefiled, and that fadeth not away." So that, notwithstanding their heaviness, they still retained an hope full of immortality.

4. And they still "rejoiced in hope of the glory of God." They were filled with joy in the Holy Ghost. So, (1 Pet. 1:8), the Apostle, having just mentioned the final "revelation of Jesus Christ" (namely, when he cometh to judge the world,) immediately adds, "In whom, though now ye see him not," not with your bodily eyes, "yet believing, ye rejoice with joy unspeakable and full of glory." Their heaviness, therefore, was not only consistent with living hope, but also with joy unspeakable: At the same time they were thus heavy, they nevertheless rejoiced with joy full of glory.

5. In the midst of their heaviness they likewise still enjoyed the love of God, which had been shed abroad in their hearts;—"whom," says the Apostle, "having not seen, ye love." Though ye have not yet seen him face to face; yet, knowing him by faith, ye have obeyed his word, "My son, give me thy heart. "He is your God, and your love, the desire of your eyes, and your "exceeding great reward." Ye have sought and found happiness in Him; ye "delight in the Lord," and he hath given you your "hearts' desire."

6. Once more: Though they were heavy, yet were they holy; they retained the same power over sin. They were still "kept" from this, "by the power of God;" they were "obedient children, not fashioned according to their former desires;" but "as He that had called them is holy," so were they "holy in all manner of conversation." Knowing they were "redeemed by the precious blood of Christ, as a Lamb without spot and without blemish," they had, through the faith and hope which they had in God, "purified their souls by the Spirit." So that, upon the whole, their heaviness well consisted with faith, with hope, with love of God and man, with the peace of God, with joy in the Holy Ghost, with inward and outward holiness. It did no way impair, much less destroy, any part of the work of God in their hearts. It

did not at all interfere with that "sanctification of the Spirit" which is the root of all true obedience; neither with the happiness which must needs result from grace and peace reigning in the heart.

II. 1. Hence we may easily learn what kind of heaviness they were in;—the Second thing which I shall endeavor to show. The word in the original, is *lupethentes, made sorry, grieved*; from *lupe, grief* or *sorrow*. This is the constant, literal meaning of the word: And, this being observed, there is no ambiguity in the expression, nor any difficulty in understanding it. The persons spoken of here were *grieved*: The heaviness they were in was neither more nor less than *sorrow* or *grief*;—a passion which every child of man is well acquainted with.

2. It is probable our translators rendered it *heaviness* (though a less common word,) to denote two things: First, the degree, and next, the continuance, of it. It does indeed, seem that it is not a slight or inconsiderable degree of grief which is here spoken of; but such as makes a strong impression upon, and sinks deep into, the soul. Neither does this appear to be a transient sorrow, such as passes away in an hour; but rather, such as, having taken fast hold of the heart, is not presently shaken off, but continues for some time, as a settled temper, rather than a passion,—even in them that have living faith in Christ, and the genuine love of God in their hearts.

3. even in these, this heaviness may sometimes be so deep as to overshadow the whole soul; to give a colour, as it were, to all the affections; such as will appear in the whole behavior. It may likewise have an influence over the body; particularly in those that are either of a naturally weak constitution, or weakened by some accidental disorder, especially of the nervous kind. In many cases, we find the corruptible body presses down the soul. In this, the soul rather presses down the body, and weakens it more and more. Nay, I will not say that deep and lasting sorrow of heart may not sometimes weaken a strong constitution, and lay the foundation of such bodily disorders as are not easily removed: And yet, all this may consist with a measure of that faith which still worketh by love.

4. This may well be termed a fiery trial: And though it is not the same with that the Apostle speaks of in the fourth chapter [1 Pet. 4], yet many of the expressions there used concerning outward sufferings may be accommodated to this inward affliction. They cannot, indeed, with any propriety, be applied to them that are in darkness: These do not, cannot rejoice; neither is it true, that the Spirit of glory and of God resteth upon them. But he frequently doth on those that are in heaviness; so that, though sorrowful, yet are they always rejoicing.

III. 1. But to proceed to the Third point: What are the causes of such sorrow or heaviness in a true believer? The Apostle tells us clearly: "Ye are in heaviness," says he, "through manifold temptations," *poikilois, manifold*, not only many in number, but of many kinds. They may be varied and diversified a thousand ways, by the change or addition of numberless circumstances. And this very diversity and variety makes it more difficult to guard against them. Among these we may rank all bodily disorders; particularly acute diseases, and violent pain of every kind, whether affecting the whole body or the smallest part of it. It is true, some who have enjoyed uninterrupted health, and have felt none of these, may make light of them, and wonder that sickness, or pain of body, should bring heaviness upon the mind. And perhaps one in a thousand is of so peculiar a constitution as not to feel pain like other men. So hath it pleased God to show his almighty power by producing some of these prodigies of nature, who have seemed not to regard pain at all, though of the severest kind; if that contempt of pain was not owing partly to the force of education, partly to a preternatural cause, to the power either of good or evil spirits, who raised those men above the state of mere nature. But, abstracting from these particular cases, it is, in general, a just observation, that

> Pain is perfect misery, and extreme
> Quite overturns all patience.

And even where this is prevented by the grace of God, where men do "possess their souls in patience," it may, nevertheless, occasion much inward heaviness; the soul sympathizing with the body.

2. All diseases of long continuance, though less painful, are apt to produce the same effect. When God appoints over us consumption, or the chilling and burning ague, if it be not speedily removed it will not only "consume the eyes," but "cause sorrow of heart." This is eminently the case with regard to all those which are termed *nervous disorders*. And faith does not overturn the course of nature: Natural causes still produce natural effects. Faith no more hinders the *sinking of the spirits* (as it is called) in an hysteric illness than the rising of the pulse in a fever.

3. Again: When "calamity cometh as a whirlwind, and poverty as an armed man;" is this a little temptation? Is it strange if it occasion sorrow and heaviness? Although this also may appear but a small thing to those who stand at a distance, or who look, and "pass by on the other side;" yet it is otherwise to them who feel it. "having food and raiment," (indeed the latter word, *skepasmata*, implies *lodging* as well as *apparel*,) we may, if the love of God is in our hearts, "be therewith content." But what shall they do who have none of these? who, as it were, "embrace the rock for a shelter?" who have only the earth to lie upon, and only the sky to cover them? who have not a dry, or warm, much less a clean, abode for themselves and their little ones: no, nor clothing to keep themselves, or those they love next themselves, from pinching cold, either by day or night? I laugh at the stupid Heathen, crying out,

> Nil habet, Jelix paupertas durtus tn se,
> Quam quod ndiculos homines facit!

Has poverty nothing worse in it than this, that it *makes men liable to be laughed at?* It is a sign this idle poet talked by rote of the things which he knew not. Is not want of food something worse than this? God pronounced it as a curse upon man, that he should earn it "by the sweat of his brow." But how many are there in this Christian country, that toil, and labour, and sweat, and have it not at last, but struggle with weariness and hunger together? Is it not worse for one, after an hard day's labour, to come back to a poor, cold, dirty, uncomfortable lodging, and to find there not even the food which is needful to repair his wasted strength? You that live at ease in the earth, that want nothing but eyes to see, ears to hear, and hearts to understand how well God has dealt with you,—is it not worse to seek bread day by day, and find none? perhaps to find the comfort also of five or six children, crying for what he has not to give! Were it not that he is restrained by an unseen hand, would he not soon "curse God and die?" O want of bread! want of bread! Who can tell what this means unless he hath felt it himself? I am astonished it occasions no more than heaviness even in them that believe!

4. Perhaps, next to this, we may place the death of those who were near and dear unto us; of a tender parent, and one not much declined into the vale of years; of a beloved child, just rising into life, and clasping about our heart; of a friend that was as our own soul,—next the grace of God, the last, best gift of Heaven. And a thousand circumstances may enhance the distress. Perhaps the child, the friend, died in our embrace!—perhaps, was snatched away when we looked not for it! flourishing, cut down like a flower! In all these cases, we not only may, but ought to, be affected: It is the design of God that we should. He would not have us stocks and stones. He would have our affections regulated, not extinguished. Therefore,—"Nature unreproved may drop a tear." There may be sorrow without sin.

5. A still deeper sorrow we may feel for those who are dead while they live; on account of the unkindness, ingratitude, apostasy, of those who were united to us in the closest ties. Who can express what a lover of souls may feel for a friend, a brother, dead to God? for an husband, a wife, a parent, a child rushing into sin, as an horse into the battle; and, in spite of all arguments and persuasions, hasting to work out his own damnation? And this anguish of spirit may be heightened to an inconceivable degree, by the consideration, that he who is now posting to destruction once ran well in the way of life. Whatever he was in time past, serves now to no other purpose, than to make our reflections on what he is more piercing and afflictive.

6. In all these circumstances, we may be assured, our great adversary will not be wanting to improve his opportunity. He, who is always "walking about, seeking whom he may devour," will then, especially, use all his power, all his skill, if haply he may gain any advantage over the soul that is already cast down. He will not be sparing of his fiery darts, such as are most likely to find an entrance, and to fix most deeply in the heart, by their suitableness to the temptation that assaults it. He will labour to inject unbelieving, or blasphemous, or repining thoughts. He will suggest that God does not regard, does not govern, the earth; or, at least, that he does not govern it aright, not by the rules of justice and mercy. He will endeavor to stir up the heart against God, to renew our natural enmity against him. And if we attempt to fight him with his own weapons, if we begin to reason with him, more and more heaviness will undoubtedly ensue, if not utter darkness.

7. It has been frequently supposed, that there is another cause; if not of darkness, at least, of heaviness; namely, God's withdrawing himself from the soul, because it is his sovereign

will. Certainly he will do this, if we grieve his Holy Spirit, either by outward or inward sin; either by doing evil, or neglecting to do good; by giving way either to pride or anger, to spiritual sloth, to foolish desire, or inordinate affection. But that he ever withdraws himself *because he will*, merely because it is his good pleasure, I absolutely deny. There is no text in all the Bible which gives any colour for such a supposition. Nay, it is a supposition contrary, not only to many particular texts, but to the whole tenor of Scripture. It is repugnant to the very nature of God: It is utterly beneath his majesty and wisdom, (as an eminent writer strongly expresses it,) "to play at bo-peep with his creatures." It is inconsistent both with his justice and mercy, and with the sound experience of all his children.

8. One more cause of heaviness is mentioned by many of those who are termed Mystic authors. And the notion has crept in, I know not how, even among plain people who have no acquaintance with them. I cannot better explain this, than in the words of a late writer, who relates this as her own experience:—"I continued so happy in my Beloved, that, although I should have been forced to live a vagabond in a desert, I should have found no difficulty in it. This state had not lasted long, when, in effect, I found myself led into a desert. I found myself in a forlorn condition, altogether poor, wretched, and miserable. The proper source of this grief is, the knowledge of ourselves; by which we find that there is an extreme unlikeness between God and us. We see ourselves most opposite to him; and that our inmost soul is entirely corrupted, depraved, and full of all kind of evil and malignity, of the world and the flesh, and all sorts of abominations."— From hence it has been inferred, that the knowledge of ourselves, without which we should perish everlastingly, must, even after we have attained justifying faith, occasion the deepest heaviness.

9. But upon this I would observe, (1.) In the preceding paragraph, this writer says, "Hearing I had not a true faith in Christ, I offered myself up to God, and immediately felt his love." It may be so; and yet it does not appear that this was justification. It is more probable, it was no more than what are usually termed, the "drawings of the Father." And if so, the heaviness and darkness which followed was no other than conviction of sin; which in the nature of things, must precede that faith whereby we are justified. (2.) Suppose she was justified almost the same moment she was convinced of wanting faith, there was then no time for that gradually-increasing self-knowledge which uses to precede justification: In this case, therefore, it came after, and was probably the more severe, the less it was expected. (3.) It is allowed, there will be a far deeper, a far clearer and fuller knowledge of our inbred sin, of our total corruption by nature, after justification, than ever there was before it. But this need not occasion darkness of soul: I will not say, that it *must* bring us into heaviness. Were it so, the Apostle would not have used that expression, *if need be* for there would be an absolute, indispensable need of it, for all that would know themselves; that is, in effect, for all that would know the perfect love of God, and be thereby "made meet to be partakers of the inheritance of the saints in light." But this is by no means the case. On the contrary, God may increase the knowledge of ourselves to any degree, and increase in the same proportion, the knowledge of himself and the experience of his love. And in this case there would be no "desert, no misery, no forlorn condition;" but love, and peace, and joy, gradually springing up into everlasting life.

IV. 1. For what ends, then, (which was the Fourth thing to be considered,) does God permit heaviness to befall so many of his children? The Apostle gives us a plain and direct answer to this important question: "That the trial of their faith, which is much more precious than gold that perisheth, though it be tried by fire, may be found unto praise, and honour, and glory, at the revelation of Jesus Christ." (1 Pet. 1:7.) There may be an allusion to this, in that well-known passage of the fourth chapter; (Although it primarily relates to quite another thing, as has been already observed:) "Think it not strange concerning the fiery trial which is to try you: But rejoice that ye are partakers of the sufferings of Christ; that, when his glory shall be revealed, ye may likewise rejoice with exceeding great joy." (1 Pet. 4:12.)

2. Hence we learn, that the first and great end of God's permitting the temptations which bring heaviness on his children, Is the trial of their faith, which is tried by these, even as gold by the fire. Now we know, gold tried in the fire is purified thereby; is separated from its dross. And so is faith in the fire of temptation; the more it is tried, the more it is purified;—yea, and not only purified, but also strengthened, confirmed, increased abundantly, by so many more proofs of the wisdom and power, the love and faithfulness, of God. This, then,—to increase our faith,—is one gracious end of God's permitting those manifold temptations.

3. They serve to try, to purify, to confirm, and increase that living hope also, where unto "the God and Father of our Lord Jesus Christ hath begotten us again of his abundant mercy." Indeed our hope cannot but increase in the same proportion with our faith. On this foundation it stands: Believing in his name, living by faith in the Son of God, we hope for, we have a confident expectation of, the glory which shall be revealed; And, consequently, whatever strengthens our faith, increases our hope also. At the same time it increases our joy in the Lord, which cannot but attend an hope full of immortality. In this view the Apostle exhorts believers in the other chapter: "Rejoice that ye are partakers of the sufferings of Christ." On this very account, "happy are you; for the Spirit of glory and of God resteth upon you:" And hereby ye are enabled, even in the midst of sufferings, to "rejoice with joy unspeakable and full of glory."

4. They rejoice the more, because the trials which increase their faith and hope increase their love also; both their gratitude to God for all his mercies, and their good-will to all mankind. Accordingly, the more deeply sensible they are of the loving-kindness of God their Saviour, the more is their heart inflamed with love to him who "first loved us." The clearer and stronger evidence they have of the glory that shall be revealed, the more do they love Him who hath purchased it for them, and "given them the earnest" thereof "in their hearts." And this, the increase of their love, is another end of the temptations permitted to come upon them.

5. Yet another is, their advance in holiness: holiness of heart, and holiness of conversation; the latter naturally resulting from the former; for a good tree will bring forth good fruit. And all inward holiness is the immediate fruit of the faith that worketh by love. By this the blessed Spirit purifies the heart from pride, self-will, passion; from love of the world, from foolish and hurtful desires, from vile and vain affections. Beside that, sanctified afflictions have, through the grace of God, an immediate and direct tendency to holiness. Through the operation of his Spirit, they humble, more and more, and abase the soul before God. They calm and meeken our turbulent spirit, tame the fierceness of our nature, soften our obstinacy and self-will, crucify us to the world, and bring us to expect all our strength from, and to seek all our happiness in, God.

6. And all these terminate in that great end, that our faith, hope, love, and holiness "may be found," if it doth not yet appear, "unto praise" from God himself, "and honour" from men and angels, "and glory," assigned by the great Judge to all that have endured unto the end. And this will be assigned in that awful day to every man, "according to his works;" according to the work which God had wrought in his heart, and the outward works which he has wrought for God; and likewise according to what he had suffered; So that all these trials are unspeakable gain. So many ways do these "light afflictions, which are but for a moment, work out for us a far more exceeding and eternal weight of glory!"

7. Add to this the advantage which others may receive by seeing our behavior under affliction. We find by experience, example frequently makes a deeper impression upon us than precept. And what examples have a stronger influence, not only on those who are partakers of like precious faith, but even on them who have not known God, than that of a soul calm and serene in the midst of storms; sorrowful, yet always rejoicing; meekly accepting whatever is the will of God, however grievous it may be to nature; saying, in sickness and pain, "The cup which my Father hath given me, shall I not drink it?"—in loss or want, "The Lord gave; the Lord hath taken away; blessed be the name of the Lord!"

V. 1. I am to conclude with some inferences. And, First, how wide is the difference between darkness of soul, and heaviness; which, nevertheless, are so generally confounded with each other, even by experienced Christians! Darkness, or the wilderness-state, implies a total loss of joy in the Holy Ghost: Heaviness does not; in the midst of this we may "rejoice with joy unspeakable." They that are in darkness have lost the peace of God; They that are in heaviness have not; So far from it, that at the very time "peace," as well as "grace," may "be multiplied" unto them. In the former, the love of God is waxed cold, if it be not utterly extinguished; in the latter, it retains its full force, or, rather, increases daily. In these, faith itself, if not totally lost, is, however, grievously decayed: Their evidence and conviction of things not seen, particularly of the pardoning love of God, is not so clear or strong as in time past: and their trust in him is proportionably weakened: Those, though they see him not, yet have a clear, unshaken confidence in God, and an abiding evidence of that love whereby all their sins are blotted out. So that as long as

we can distinguish faith from unbelief, hope from despair, peace from war, the love of God from the love of the world, we may infallibly distinguish heaviness from darkness!

2. We may learn from hence, Secondly, that there may be need of heaviness, but there can be no need of darkness. There may be need of our being in "heaviness for a season," in order to the ends above recited; at least, in this sense, as it is a natural result of those "manifold temptations" which are needful to try and increase our faith, to confirm and enlarge our hope, to purify our heart from all unholy tempers, and to perfect us in love. And, by consequence, they are needful in order to brighten our crown, and add to our eternal weight of glory. But we cannot say, that darkness is needful in order to any of these ends. It is no way conducive to them: The loss of faith, hope, love, is surely neither conducive to holiness, nor to the increase of that reward in heaven which will be in proportion to our holiness on earth.

3. From the Apostle's manner of speaking we may gather, Thirdly, that even heaviness is not *always* needful. "Now, for a season, if need be;" So it is not needful for *all persons*; nor for any person at *all times*. God is able, he has both power and wisdom, to work, when he pleases, the same work of grace in any soul, by other means. And in some instances he does so; he causes those whom it pleaseth him to go on from strength to strength, even till they "perfect holiness in his fear," with scarce any heaviness at all; as having an absolute power over the heart of man, and moving all the springs of it at his pleasure. But these cases are rare: God generally sees good to try "acceptable men in the furnace of affliction." So that manifold temptations and heaviness, more or less, are usually the portion of his dearest children.

4. We ought, therefore, Lastly, to watch and pray, and use our utmost endeavours to avoid falling into darkness. But we need not be solicitous how to avoid so much as how to improve by heaviness. Our great care should be, so to behave ourselves under it, so to wait upon the Lord therein, that it may fully answer all the design of his love, in permitting it to come upon us; that it may be a means of increasing our faith, of confirming our hope, of perfecting us in all holiness. Whenever it comes, let us have an eye to these gracious ends for which it is permitted, and use all diligence that we may not make void the counsel of God against ourselves. Let us earnestly work together with him, by the grace which he is continually giving us, in "purifying ourselves from all pollution, both of flesh and spirit," and daily growing in the grace of our Lord Jesus Christ, till we are received into his everlasting kingdom!

48. SELF-DENIAL

"And he said to them all, If any man will come after me, let him deny himself, and take up his cross daily, and follow me."

Luke 9:23

1. It has been frequently imagined, that the direction here given related chiefly, if not wholly, to the Apostles; at least, to the Christians of the first ages, or those in a state of persecution. But this is a grievous mistake; For although our

blessed Lord is here directing his discourse more immediately to his Apostles, and those other disciples who attended him in the days of his flesh; yet, in them he speaks to us, and to all mankind, without any exception or limitation. The very reason of the thing puts it beyond dispute, that the duty which is here enjoined is not peculiar to them, or to the Christians of the early ages. It no more regards any particular order of men, or particular time, than any particular country. No: It is of the most universal nature, respecting all times, and all persons, yea, and all things; not meats and drinks only, and things pertaining to the senses. The meaning is, "If any man," of whatever rank, station, circumstances, in any nation, in any age of the world, "will" effectually "come after me, let him deny himself" in all things; let him "take up his cross" of whatever kind; yea, and that "daily; and follow me."

2. The *denying* ourselves and the *taking up our cross*, in the full extent of the expression, is not a thing of small concern: It is not expedient only, as are some of the circumstantials of religion; but it is absolutely, indispensably necessary, either to our becoming or continuing his disciples. It is absolutely necessary, in the very nature of the thing, to our coming after Him and following Him; insomuch that, as far as we do not practise it, we are not his disciples. If we do not continually deny ourselves, we do not learn of Him, but of other masters. If we do not take up our cross daily, we do not come after Him, but after the world, or the prince of the world, or our own fleshly mind. If we are not walking in the way of the cross, we are not following Him; we are not treading in his steps; but going back from, or at least wide of, Him.

3. It is for this reason, that so many Ministers of Christ, in almost every age and nation, particularly since the Reformation of the Church from the innovations and corruptions gradually crept into it, have wrote and spoke so largely on this important duty, both in their public discourses and private exhortations. This induced them to disperse abroad many tracts upon the subject; and some in our own nation. They knew both from the oracles of God, and from the testimony of their own experience, how impossible it was not to deny our Master, unless we will deny ourselves; and how vainly we attempt to follow Him that was crucified, unless we take up our cross daily.

4. But may not this very consideration make it reasonable to inquire, If much has been said and wrote on the subject already, what need is there to say or write any more? I answer, There are no inconsiderable numbers, even of people fearing God, who have not had the opportunity either of hearing what has been spoke, or reading what has been wrote, upon it. And, perhaps, if they had read much of what has been written, they would not have been so much profited. Many who have wrote, (some of them large volumes,) do by no means appear to have understood the subject. Either they had imperfect views of the very nature of it, (and then they could never explain it to others,) or they were unacquainted with the due extent of it; they did not see how exceeding broad this command is; or they were not sensible of the absolute, the indispensable necessity of it. Others speak of it in so dark, so perplexed, so intricate, so mystical a manner, as if they designed rather to conceal it from the vulgar, than to explain it to common readers. Others speak admirably well, with great clearness and strength, on the necessity of self-denial; but then they deal in generals only, without coming to particular instances, and so are of little use to the bulk of mankind, to men of ordinary capacity and education. And if some of them do descend to particulars, it is to those particulars only which do not affect the generality of men, since they seldom, if ever, occur in common life;—such as the enduring imprisonment, or tortures; the giving up, in a literal sense, their houses or lands, their husbands or wives, children, or life itself; to none of which we are called, nor are likely to be, unless God should permit times of public persecution to return. In the meantime, I know of no writer in the English tongue who has described the nature of self-denial in plain and intelligible terms, such as lie level with common understandings, and applied it to those little particulars which daily occur in common life. A discourse of this kind is wanted still; and it is wanted the more, because in every stage of the spiritual life, although there is a variety of particular hinderances of our attaining grace or growing therein, yet are all resolvable into these general ones,—either we do not deny ourselves, or we do not take up our cross.

In order to supply this defect in some degree, I shall endeavour to show, First, what it is for a man to deny himself, and what to take up his cross; and, Secondly, that if a man be not fully Christ's disciple, it is always owing to the want of this.

I. 1. I shall, First, endeavour to show, what it is for a man to "deny himself, and take up his cross daily." This is a point which is, of all others, most necessary to be considered and throughly understood, even on this account, that it is, of all others, most opposed by numerous and powerful enemies. All our nature must certainly rise up against this, even in its own defence; the world, consequently, the men who take nature, not grace, for their guide, abhor the very sound of it. And the great enemy of our souls, well knowing its importance, cannot but move every stone against it. But this is not all: Even those who have in some measure shaken off the yoke of the devil, who have experienced, especially of late years, a real work of grace in their hearts, yet are no friends to this grand doctrine of Christianity, though it is so peculiarly insisted on by their Master. Some of them are as deeply and totally ignorant concerning it, as if there was not one word about it in the Bible. Others are farther off still, having unawares imbibed strong prejudices against it. These they have received partly from outside Christians, men of a fair speech and behaviour, who want nothing of godliness but the power, nothing of religion but the spirit;—and partly from those who did once, if they do not now, "taste of the powers of the world to come." But are there any of these who do not both practise self-denial themselves, and recommend it to others? You are little acquainted with mankind, if you doubt of this. There are whole bodies of men who only do not declare war against it. To go no farther than London: Look upon the whole body of Predestinarians, who by the free mercy of God have lately been called out of the darkness of nature into the light of faith. Are they patterns of self-denial? How few of them even profess to practise it at all!

How few of them recommend it themselves, or are pleased with them that do! Rather, do they not continually represent it in the most odious colours, as if it were seeking "salvation by works," or seeking "to establish our own righteousness?" And how readily do Antinomians of all kinds, from the smooth Moravian, to the boisterous, foul-mouthed Ranter, join the cry, with their silly, unmeaning cant of *legality*, and *preaching the law!* Therefore you are in constant danger of being wheedled, hectored, or ridiculed out of this important gospel-doctrine, either by false teachers, or false brethren, (more or less beguiled from the simplicity of the gospel,) if you are not deeply grounded therein. Let fervent prayer, then, go before, accompany, and follow what you are now about to read, that it may be written in your heart by the finger of God, so as never to be erased.

2. But what is self-denial? Wherein are we to deny ourselves? And whence does the necessity of this arise? I answer, The will of God is the supreme, unalterable rule for every intelligent creature; equally binding every angel in heaven, and every man upon earth. Nor can it be otherwise: This is the natural, necessary result of the relation between creatures and their Creator. But if the will of God be our one rule of action in every thing, great and small, it follows, by undeniable consequence, that we are not to do our own will in anything. Here, therefore, we see at once the nature, with the ground and reason, of self-denial. We see the nature of self-denial: It is the denying or refusing to follow ours own will, from a conviction that the will of God is the only rule of action to us. And we see the reason thereof, because we are creatures; because "it is he that hath made us, and not we ourselves."

3. This reason for self-denial must hold, even with regard to the angels of God in heaven; and with regard to man, innocent and holy, as he came out of the hands of his Creator. But a farther reason for it arises from the condition wherein all men are since the Fall. We are all now "shapen in wickedness, and in sin did our mother conceive us." Our nature is altogether corrupt, in every power and faculty. And our will, depraved equally with the rest, is wholly bent to indulge our natural corruption. On the other hand, it is the will of God that we resist and counteract that corruption, not at some times, or in some things only, but at all times and in all things. Here, therefore, is a farther ground for constant and universal self-denial.

4. To illustrate this a little further: The will of God is a path leading straight to God. The will of man, which once ran parallel with it, is now another path, not only different from it, but in our present state, directly contrary to it: It leads from God. If, therefore, we walk in the one, we must necessarily quit the other. We cannot walk in both. Indeed, a man of *faint heart and feeble hands* may *go in two ways,* one after the other. But he cannot walk in two ways at the same time: He cannot, at one and the same time, follow his own will, and follow the will of God: He must choose the one or the other; denying God's will, to follow his own; or denying himself, to follow the will of God.

5. Now, it is undoubtedly pleasing, for the time, to follow our own will, by indulging, in any instance that offers, the corruption of our nature: But by following it in anything, we so far strengthen the perverseness of our will; and by indulging it, we continually increase the corruption of our nature. So, by the food which is agreeable to the palate, we often increase a bodily disease: It gratifies the taste, but it inflames the disorder. it brings pleasure, but it also brings death.

6. On the whole, then, to deny ourselves, is, to deny our own will, where it does not fall in with the will of God; and that however pleasing it may be. It is, to deny ourselves any pleasure which does not spring from, and lead to, God; that is, in effect, to refuse going out of our way, though into a pleasant, flowery path; to refuse what we know to be deadly poison, though agreeable to the taste.

7. And every one that would follow Christ, that would be his real disciple, must not only deny himself, but take up his cross also. A cross is anything contrary to our will, anything displeasing to our nature. So that taking up our cross goes a little farther than denying ourselves; it rises a little higher, and is a more difficult task to flesh and blood;—it being more easy to forego pleasure, than to endure pain.

8. Now, in running "the race which is set before us," according to the will of God, there is often a cross lying in the way; that is, something which is not only not joyous, but grievous; something which is contrary to our will, which is displeasing to our nature. What then is to be done? The choice is plain: Either we must take up our cross, or we must turn aside from the way of God, "from the holy commandment delivered to us;" if we do not stop altogether, or turn back to everlasting perdition!

9. In order to the healing of that corruption, that evil disease, which every man brings with him into the world, it is often needful to pluck out, as it were, a right eye, to cut off a right hand;—so painful is either the thing itself which must be done, or the only means of doing it; the parting, suppose, with a foolish desire, with an inordinate affection; or a separation from the object of it, without which it can never be extinguished. In the former kind, the tearing away such a desire or affection, when it is deeply rooted in the soul, is often like the piercing of a sword, yea, like "the dividing asunder of the soul and spirit, the joints and marrow." The Lord then sits upon the soul as a refiner's fire, to burn all the dross thereof. And this is a cross indeed; it is essentially painful; it must be so, in the very nature of the thing. The soul cannot be thus torn asunder, it cannot pass through the fire, without pain.

10. In the latter kind, the means to heal a sin-sick soul, to cure a foolish desire, an inordinate affection, are often painful, not in the nature of the thing, but from the nature of the disease. So when our Lord said to the rich young man, "Go, sell that thou hast, and give it to the poor," (as well knowing, this was the only means of healing his covetousness,) the very thought of it gave him so much pain, that "he went away sorrowful;" choosing rather to part with his hope of heaven, than his possessions on earth. This was a burden he could not consent to lift, a cross he would not take up. And in the one kind or the other, every follower of Christ will surely have need to "take up his cross daily."

11. The "taking up" differs a little from "bearing his cross." We are then properly said to "bear our cross," when we endure what is laid upon us without our choice, with meekness and resignation. Whereas, we do not properly "take up our cross," but when we voluntarily suffer what it is in our power to avoid; when we willingly embrace the will of God, though contrary to our own; when we choose what is painful, because it is the will of our wise and gracious Creator.

12. And thus it behoves every disciple of Christ to take up, as well as to bear, his cross. Indeed, in one sense, it is not *his* alone; it is common to him, and many others; seeing there is no temptation befals any man, *ei me anthropinos,*—"but such as is common to men;" such as is incident and adapted to their common nature and situation in the present world. But, in another sense, as it is considered with all its circumstances, it is his; peculiar to himself: It is prepared of God for him; it is given by God to him, as a token of his love. And if he receives it as such, and, after using such means to remove the pressure as Christian wisdom directs, lies as clay in the potter's hand; it is disposed and ordered by God for his good, both with regard to the quality of it, and in respect to its quantity and degree, its duration, and every other circumstance.

13. In all this, we may easily conceive our blessed Lord to act as the Physician of our souls, not merely "for his own pleasure, but for our profit, that we may be partakers of his holiness." If, in searching our wounds, he puts us to pain, it is only in order to heal them. He cuts away what is putrified or unsound, in order to preserve the sound part. And if we freely choose the loss of a limb, rather than the whole body should perish; how much more should we choose, figuratively, to cut off a right hand, rather than the whole soul should be cast into hell!

14. We see plainly then both the nature and ground of taking up our cross. It does not imply the *disciplining ourselves*, (as some speak;) the literally tearing our own flesh: the wearing hair-cloth, or iron-girdles, or anything else that would impair our bodily health; (although we know not what allowance God may make for those who act thus through involuntary ignorance;) but the embracing the will of God, though contrary to our own; the choosing wholesome, though bitter medicines; the freely accepting temporary pain, of whatever kind, and in whatever degree, when it is either essentially or accidentally necessary to eternal pleasure.

II. 1. I am, Secondly, to show, that it is always owing to the want either of self-denial, or taking up his cross, that any man does not throughly follow Him, is not fully a disciple of Christ.

It is true, this may be partly owing, in some cases, to the want of the means of grace; of hearing the true word of God spoken with power; of the sacraments, or of Christian fellowship. But where none of these is wanting, the great hindrance of our receiving or growing in the grace of God is always the want of denying ourselves, or taking up our cross.

2. A few instances will make this plain. A man hears the word which is able to save his soul: He is well pleased with what he hears, acknowledges the truth, and is a little affected by it; yet he remains "dead in trespasses and sins," senseless and unawakened. Why is this? Because he will not part with his bosom-sin, though he now knows it is an abomination to the Lord. He came to hear, full of lust and unholy desires; and he will not part with them. Therefore no deep impression is made upon him, but his foolish heart is still hardened: That is, he is still senseless and unawakened, because he will not deny himself.

3. Suppose he begins to awake out of sleep, and his eyes are a little opened, why are they so quickly closed again? Why does he again sink into the sleep of death? Because he again yields to his bosom-sin; he drinks again of the pleasing poison. Therefore it is impossible that any lasting impression should be made upon his heart: That is, he relapses into his fatal insensibility, because he will not deny himself.

4. But this is not the case with all. We have many instances of those who when once awakened sleep no more. The impressions once received do not wear away: They are not only deep, but lasting. And yet, many of these have not found what they seek: They mourn, and yet are not comforted. Now, why is this? It is because they do not "bring forth fruits meet for repentance;" because they do not, according to the grace they have received, "cease from evil, and do good." They do not cease from the easily besetting sin, the sin of their constitution, of their education, or of their profession; or they omit doing the good they may, and know they ought to do, because of some disagreeable circumstance attending it: That is, they do not attain faith, because they will not "deny themselves," or "take up their cross."

5. But this man did receive "the heavenly gift;" he did "taste of the powers of the world to come;" he saw "the light of the glory of God in the face of Jesus Christ;" the "peace which passeth all understanding" did "rule his heart and mind; and "the love of God was shed abroad" therein, "by the Holy Ghost which was given unto him;"—yet he is now weak as another man; he again relishes the things of earth, and has more taste for the things which are seen than for those which are not seen; the eye of his understanding is closed again, so that he cannot "see Him that is invisible;" his love is waxed cold, and the peace of God no longer rules in his heart. And no marvel: for he has again given place to the devil, and grieved the Holy Spirit of God. He has turned again unto folly, to some pleasing sin, if not in outward act, yet in heart. He has given place to pride, or anger, or desire, to self-will, or stubbornness. Or he did not stir up the gift of God which was in him; he gave way to spiritual sloth, and would not be at the pains of "praying always, and watching thereunto with all perseverance:" That is, he made shipwreck of the faith, for want of self-denial, and taking up his cross daily.

6. But perhaps he has not made shipwreck of the faith: He has still a measure of the Spirit of adoption, which continues to witness with his spirit that he is a child of God. However, he is not "going on to perfection;" he is not, as once, hungering and thirsting after righteousness, panting after the whole image and full enjoyment of God, as the hart after the water-brook. Rather he is weary and faint in his mind, and, as it were, hovering between life and death. And why is he thus, but because he hath forgotten the word of God,—"By works is faith made perfect?" He does not use all diligence in

working the works of God. He does not "continue instant in prayer," private as well as public; in communicating, hearing, meditation, fasting, and religious conference. If he does not wholly neglect some of these means, at least he does not use them all with his might. Or he is not zealous of works of charity, as well as works of piety. He is not merciful after his power, with the full ability which God giveth. He does not fervently serve the Lord by doing good to men, in every kind and in every degree he can, to their souls as well as their bodies. And why does he not continue in prayer? Because in time of dryness it is pain and grief unto him. He does not continue in hearing at all opportunities, because sleep is sweet; or it is cold, or dark, or rainy. But why does he not continue in works of mercy? Because he cannot feed the hungry, or clothe the naked, unless he retrench the expense of his own apparel, or use cheaper and less pleasing food. Beside which, the visiting the sick, or those that are in prison, is attended with many disagreeable circumstances. And so are most works of spiritual mercy; reproof, in particular. He *would* reprove his neighbour; but sometimes shame, sometimes fear, comes between: For he may expose himself, not only to ridicule, but to heavier inconveniences too. Upon these and the like considerations, he omits one or more, if not all, works of mercy and piety. Therefore, his faith is not made perfect, neither can he grow in grace; namely, because he will not deny himself, and take up his daily cross.

7. It manifestly follows, that it is always owing to the want either of self-denial, or taking up his cross, that a man does not throughly follow his Lord, that he is not fully a disciple of Christ. It is owing to this, that he who is dead in sin does not awake, though the trumpet be blown; that he who begins to awake out of sleep, yet has no deep or lasting conviction; that he who is deeply and lastingly convinced of sin does not attain remission of sins; that some who have received this heavenly gift retain it not, but make shipwreck of the faith; and that others, if they do not draw back to perdition, yet are weary and faint in their mind, and do not reach the mark of the prize of the high calling of God in Christ Jesus.

III. 1. How easily may we learn hence, that they know neither the Scripture nor the power of God, who directly or indirectly, in public or in private, oppose the doctrine of self-denial and the daily cross! How totally ignorant are these men of an hundred particular texts, as well as of the general tenor of the whole oracles of God! And how entirely unacquainted must they be with true, genuine, Christian experience;—of the manner wherein the Holy Spirit ever did, and does at this day, work in the souls of men! They may talk, indeed, very loudly and confidently, (a natural fruit of ignorance,) as though they were the only men who understood either the word of God, or the experience of his children. but their words are, in every sense, *vain words*; they are weighed in the balance, and found wanting.

2. We may learn from hence, Secondly, the real cause why not only many particular persons, but even bodies of men, who were once burning and shining lights, have now lost both their light and heat. If they did not hate and oppose, they at least lightly esteemed, this precious gospel doctrine. If they did not boldly say, *Abnegationem omnem proculcamus,*

internecioni damus-' "We trample all self-denial under foot, we devote it to destruction;" yet they neither valued it according to its high importance, nor took any pains in practising it. Hanc mystici docent,_ said that great, bad man: "The *mystic* writers teach self-denial."—No; the *inspired* writers! And God teaches it to every soul who is willing to hear his voice!

3. We may learn from hence, Thirdly, that it is not enough for a Minister of the gospel not to oppose the doctrine of self-denial, to say nothing concerning it. Nay, he cannot satisfy his duty by saying a little in favour of it. If he would, indeed, be pure from the blood of all men, he must speak of it frequently and largely; he must inculcate the necessity of it in the clearest and strongest manner; he must press it with his might, on all persons, at all times, and in all places; laying "line upon line, line upon line, precept upon precept, precept upon precept:" So shall he have a conscience void of offence; so shall he save his own soul and those that hear him.

4. Lastly: See that you apply this, every one of you, to your own soul. Meditate upon it when you are in secret: Ponder it in your heart! Take care not only to understand it throughly, but to remember it to your lives' end! Cry unto the Strong for strength, that you may no sooner understand, than enter upon the practice of it. Delay not the time, but practise it immediately, from this very hour! Practise it universally, on every one of the thousand occasions which will occur in all circumstances of life! Practise it daily, without intermission, from the hour you first set your hand to the plough, and enduring therein to the end, till your spirit returns to God!

49. THE CURE OF EVIL-SPEAKING

"If thy brother shall sin against thee, go and tell him his fault between thee and him alone: If he shall hear thee, thou hast gained thy brother. But if he will not hear, take with thee one or two more, that in the mouth of two or three witnesses every word may be established. And if he will not hear them, tell it to the Church. But if he does not hear the church, let him be to thee as an heathen man and a publican."

Matt. 18:15–17

1. "Speak evil of no man," says the great Apostle:—As plain a command as, "Thou shalt do no murder." But who, even among Christians, regards this command? Yea, how few are there that so much as understand it? What is evil-speaking? It is not, as some suppose, the same with lying or slandering. All a man says may be as true as the Bible; and yet the saying of it is evil-speaking. For evil-speaking is neither more nor less than speaking evil of an absent person; relating something evil, which was really done or said by one that is not present when it is related. Suppose, having seen a man drunk, or heard him curse or swear, I tell this when he is absent; it is evil-speaking. In our language this is also, by an extremely proper name, termed backbiting. Nor is there any material difference between this and what we usually style tale-bearing. If the tale be delivered in a soft and quiet manner (perhaps with expressions of good-will to the person, and of hope that things may not be quite so bad,) then we

call it whispering. But in whatever manner it be done, the thing is the same;—the same in substance, if not in circumstance. Still it is evil-speaking; still this command, "Speak evil of no man," is trampled under foot; if we relate to another the fault of a third person, when he is not present to answer for himself.

2. And how extremely common is this sin, among all orders and degrees of men! How do high and low, rich and poor, wise and foolish, learned and unlearned, run into it continually! Persons who differ from each other in all things else, nevertheless agree in this. How few are there that can testify before God, "I am clear in this matter; I have always set a watch before my mouth, and kept the door of my lips!" What conversation do you hear, of any considerable length, whereof evil-speaking is not one ingredient? and that even among persons who, in the general, have the fear of God before their eyes, and do really desire to have a conscience void of offence toward God and toward man.

3. And the very commonness of this sin makes it difficult to be avoided. As we are encompassed with it on every side, so, if we are not deeply sensible of the danger, and continually guarding against it, we are liable to be carried away by the torrent. In this instance, almost the whole of mankind is, as it were, in a conspiracy against us. And their example steals upon us, we know not how; so that we insensibly slide into the imitation of it. Besides, it is recommended from within as well as from without. There is scarce any wrong temper in the mind of man, which may not be occasionally gratified by it, and consequently incline us to it. It gratifies our pride, to relate those faults of others whereof we think ourselves not to be guilty. Anger, resentment, and all unkind tempers, are indulged by speaking against those with whom we are displeased; and, in many cases, by reciting the sins of their neighbors, men indulge their own foolish and hurtful desires.

4. Evil-speaking is the more difficult to be avoided, because it frequently attacks us in disguise. We speak thus out of a noble, generous (it is well if we do not say,) holy indignation, against these vile creatures! We commit sin from mere hatred of sin! We serve the devil out of pure zeal for God! It is merely in order to punish the wicked that we run into this wickedness. "So do the passions" (as one speaks) "all justify themselves," and palm sin upon us under the veil of holiness!

5. But is there no way to avoid the snare? Unquestionably there is. Our blessed Lord has marked out a plain way for His followers, in the words above recited. None, who warily and steadily walk in this path, will ever fall into evil-speaking. This rule is either an infallible preventive, or a certain cure of it. In the preceding verses, our Lord had said, "Woe to the world, because of offences,"—unspeakable misery will arise in the world from this baleful fountain: (*Offences* are all things whereby anyone is turned out of, or hindered in, the ways of God.): "For it must be that offenses come,"—Such is the nature of things; such the wickedness, folly, and weakness of mankind: "But woe to that man,"—miserable is that man, "by whom the offense cometh." "Wherefore if thy hand, thy foot, thine eye, cause thee to offend,"—if the most dear enjoyment, the most beloved and useful person, turn thee out of or hinder thee in the way, "pluck it out,"—cut them off,

and cast them from thee. But how can we avoid giving offense to some, and being offended at others? Especially, suppose they are quite in the wrong, and we see it with our own eyes? Our Lord here teaches us how: He lays down a sure method of avoiding offenses and evil-speaking together. "If thy brother shall sin against thee, go and tell him of his fault, between thee and him alone: If he will hear thee, thou hast gained thy brother. But if he will not hear thee, take with thee one or two more, that by the mouth of two or three witnesses every word may be established. And if he will not hear them, tell it to the church: But if he will not hear the Church, let him be to thee as an heathen man and a publican."

I. 1. First, "If thy brother shall sin against thee, go and tell him of his fault, between thee and him alone." The most literal way of following this first rule, where it is practicable, is the best: Therefore, if thou seest with thine own eyes a brother, a fellow Christian, commit undeniable sin, or hearest it with thine own ears, so that it is impossible for thee to doubt the fact, then thy part is plain: Take the very first opportunity of going to him; and, if thou canst have access, "tell him of his fault between thee and him alone." Indeed, great care is to be taken that this is done in a right spirit, and in a right manner. The success of a reproof greatly depends on the spirit wherein it is given. Be not, therefore, wanting in earnest prayer to God, that it may be given in a lowly spirit; with a deep, piercing conviction, that it is God alone who maketh thee to differ; and that if any good be done by what is now spoken, God doeth it himself. Pray that he would guard thy heart, enlighten thy mind, and direct thy tongue to such words as he may please to bless. See that thou speak in a meek as well as a lowly spirit; for the wrath of man worketh not the righteousness of God." If he be "overtaken in a fault," he can no otherwise be restored, than "in the spirit of meekness." If he opposes the truth, yet he cannot be brought to the knowledge thereof, but by gentleness. Still speak in a spirit of tender love, "which many waters cannot quench." If love is not conquered, it conquers all things. Who can tell the force of love?

> Love can bow down the stubborn neck,
> The stone to flesh convert;
> Soften, and melt, and pierce and break
> An adamantine heart.

Confirm, then, your love toward him, and you will thereby "heap coals of fire upon his head."

2. But see that the manner also wherein you speak be according to the Gospel of Christ. Avoid everything in look, gesture, word, and tone of voice, that savors of pride or self-sufficiency. Studiously avoid everything magisterial or dogmatical, everything that looks like arrogance or assuming. Beware of the most distant approach to disdain, overbearing, or contempt. With equal care avoid all appearance of anger; and though you use great plainness of speech, yet let there be no reproach, no railing accusation, no token of any warmth but that of love. Above all, let there be no shadow of hate or ill-will, no bitterness or sourness of expression; but use the air and language of sweetness, as well as gentleness, that all may appear to flow from love in the heart. And yet this sweetness

need not hinder your speaking in the most serious and solemn manner; as far as may be, in the very words of the oracles of God (for there are none like them,) and as under the eye of Him who is coming to judge the quick and dead.

3. If you have not an opportunity of speaking to him in person, or cannot have access, you may do it by a messenger; by a common friend, in whose prudence, as well as uprightness, you can thoroughly confide. Such a person, speaking in your name, and in the spirit and manner above described, may answer the same end, and, in a good degree, supply your lack of service. Only beware you do not feign the want of opportunity, in order to shun the cross; neither take it for granted that you cannot have access, without ever making the trial. Whenever you can speak in your own person, it is far better. But you should rather do it by another, than not at all: This way is better than none.

4. But what, if you can neither speak yourself, nor find such a messenger as you can confide in? If this is really the case, it then only remains to write. And there may be some circumstances which make this the most advisable way of speaking. One of these circumstances is, when the person with whom we have to do is of so warm and impetuous a temper as does not easily bear reproof, especially from an equal or inferior. But it may be so introduced and softened in writing as to make it far more tolerable. Besides, many will read the very same words, which they could not bear to hear. It does not give so violent a shock to their pride, nor so sensibly touch their honor. And suppose it makes little impression at first, they will, perhaps, give it a second reading, and, upon farther consideration, lay to heart what before they disregarded. If you add your name, this is nearly the same thing as going to him, and speaking in person. And this should always be done, unless it be rendered improper by some very particular reason.

5. It should be well observed, not only that this is a step which our Lord absolutely commands us to take, but that he commands us to take this step first, before we attempt any other. No alternative is allowed, no choice of anything else: This is the way; walk thou in it. It is true, he enjoins us, if need require, to take two other steps; but they are to be taken successively after this step, and neither of them before it: Much less are we to take any other step, either before or beside this. To do anything else, or not to do this, is, therefore, equally inexcusable.

6. Do not think to excuse yourself for taking an entirely different step, by saying, "Why, I did not speak to anyone, till I was so burdened that I could not refrain." You was burdened! It was no wonder you should, unless your conscience was seared; for you was under the guilt of sin, of disobeying a plain commandment of God! You ought immediately to have gone, and told "your brother of his fault between you and him alone." If you did not, how should you be other than burdened (unless your heart was utterly hardened,) while you was trampling the command of God under foot, and "hating your brother in your heart?" And what a way have you found to unburden yourself? God reproves you for a sin of omission, for not telling your brother of his fault; and you comfort yourself under His reproof by a sin of commission, by telling your brother's fault to another person! Ease bought by sin is a dear purchase! I trust in God, you will have no ease, but will be burdened so much the more, till you "go to your brother and tell him," and no one else.

7. I know but of one exception to this rule: There may be a peculiar case, wherein it is necessary to accuse the guilty, though absent, in order to preserve the innocent. For instance: You are acquainted with the design which a man has against the property or life of his neighbor. Now, the case may be so circumstanced, that there is no other way of hindering that design from taking effect, but the making it known, without delay, to him against whom it is laid. In this case, therefore, this rule is set aside, as is that of the Apostle, "Speak evil of no man:" and it is lawful, yea, it is our bounden duty, to speak evil of an absent person, in order to prevent his doing evil to others and himself at the same time. But remember, meanwhile that all evil-speaking is, in its own nature, deadly poison. Therefore if you are sometimes constrained to use it as a medicine, yet use it with fear and trembling; seeing it is so dangerous a medicine, that nothing but absolute necessity can excuse your using it at all. Accordingly, use it as seldom as possible; never but when there is such a necessity: And even then use as little of it as is possible; only so much as is necessary for the end proposed. At all other times, "go and tell him of his fault between thee and him alone."

II. 1. But what, "if he will not hear?" If he repay evil for good? If he be enraged rather than convinced? What, if he hear to no purpose, and go on still in the evil of his way? We must expect this will frequently be the case; the mildest and tenderest reproof will have no effect; but the blessing we wished for another will return into our own bosom. And what are we to do then? Our Lord has given us a clear and full direction. Then "take with thee one or two more:" This is the second step. Take one or two whom you know to be of a loving spirit, lovers of God and of their neighbor. See, likewise, that they be of a lowly spirit, and "clothed with humility." Let them also be such as are meek and gentle, patient and longsuffering; not apt to "return evil for evil, or railing for railing, but contrariwise blessing." Let them be men of understanding, such as are endued with wisdom from above; and men unbiased, free from partiality, free from prejudice of any kind. Care should likewise be taken, that both the persons and their characters be well known to him: And let those that are acceptable to him be chosen preferable to any others.

2. Love will dictate the manner wherein they should proceed, according to the nature of the case. Nor can any one particular manner be prescribed for all cases. But perhaps, in general, one might advise, before they enter upon the thing itself, let them mildly and affectionately declare that they have no anger or prejudice toward him, and that it is merely from a principle of goodwill that they now come, or at all concern themselves with his affairs. To make this the more apparent, they might then calmly attend to your repetition of your former conversation with him, and to what he said in his own defense, before they attempted to determine

anything. After this they would be better able to judge in what manner to proceed, "that by the mouth of two or three witnesses, every word might be established;" that whatever you have said may have its full force by the additional weight of their authority.

3. In order to this, may they not, (1.) Briefly repeat what you spoke, and what he answered? (2.) Enlarge upon, open, and confirm the reasons which you had given? (3.) Give weight to your reproof, showing how just, how kind, and how seasonable it was? And, lastly, enforce the advices and persuasions which you had annexed to it? And these may likewise hereafter, if need should require, bear witness of what was spoken.

4. With regard to this, as well as the preceding rule, we may observe that our Lord gives us no choice, leaves us no alternative, but expressly commands us to do this, and nothing else in the place of it. He likewise directs us when to do this; neither sooner nor later; namely, *after* we have taken the first, and *before* we have taken the third step. It is then only that we are authorized to relate the evil another has done, to those whom we desire to bear a part with us in this great instance of brotherly love. But let us have a care how we relate it to any other person, till both these steps have been taken. If we neglect to take these, or if we take any others, what wonder if we are burdened still? For we are sinners against God, and against our neighbor; and how fairly soever we may color it, yet, if we have any conscience, our sin will find us out, and bring a burden upon our soul.

III. 1. That we may be thoroughly instructed in this weighty affair, our Lord has given us a still farther direction: "If he will not hear them," then, and not till then, "tell it to the church." This is the third step. All the question is, how this word, "the church," is here to be understood. But the very nature of the thing will determine this beyond all reasonable doubt. You cannot tell it to the national Church, the whole body of men termed "the Church of England." Neither would it answer any Christian end if you could; this, therefore, is not the meaning of the word. Neither can you tell it to that whole body of people in England with whom you have a more immediate connection. Nor, indeed, would this answer any good end: The word, therefore, is not to be understood thus. It would not answer any valuable end to tell the faults of every particular member to the church (if you would so term it,) the congregation or society, united together in London. It remains that you tell it to the elder or elders of the church, to those who are overseers of that flock of Christ to which you both belong, who watch over yours and his soul, "as they that must give account." And this should be done, if it conveniently can, in the presence of the person concerned, and, though plainly, yet with all the tenderness and love which the nature of the thing will admit. It properly belongs to their office, to determine concerning the behavior of those under their care, and to rebuke, according to the demerit of the offense, "with all authority." When, therefore, you have done this, you have done all which the Word of God, or the law of love, requireth of you: You are not now partaker of his sin; but if he perish, his blood is on his own head.

2. Here, also, let it be observed, that this, and no other, is the third step which we are to take; and that we are to take it in its order after the other two; not before the second, much less the first, unless in some very particular circumstance. Indeed, in one case, the second step may coincide with this: They may be, in a manner, one and the same. The elder or elders of the church may be so connected with the offending brother, that they may set aside the necessity, and supply the place, of the one or two witnesses; so that it may suffice to tell it to them, after you have told it to your brother, "between you and him alone."

3. When you have done this, you have delivered your own soul. "If he will not hear the church," if he persist in his sin, "let him be to thee as an heathen man and a publican." You are under no obligation to think of him any more; only when you commend him to God in prayer. You need not speak of him any more, but leave him to his own Master. Indeed, you still owe to him, as to all other heathens, earnest, tender goodwill. You owe him courtesy, and, as occasion offers, all the offices of humanity. But have no friendship, no familiarity with him; no other intercourse than with an open Heathen.

4. But if this be the rule by which Christians walk, which is the land where Christians live? A few you may possibly find scattered up and down, who make a conscience of observing it. But how very few! How thinly scattered upon the face of the earth! And where is there any body of men that universally walk thereby? Can we find them in Europe? Or, to go no farther, in Great Britain or Ireland? I fear not: I fear we may search these kingdoms throughout, and yet search in vain. Alas for the Christian world! Alas for Protestants, for Reformed Christians! O, "who will rise up with me against the wicked?" "Who will take God's part" against the evil-speakers? Art thou the man? By the grace of God, wilt thou be one who art not carried away by the torrent? Art thou fully determined, God being thy helper, from this very hour to set a watch, a continual "watch, before thy mouth, and keep the door of thy lips?" From this hour wilt thou walk by this rule, "Speaking evil of no man?" If thou seest thy brother do evil, wilt thou "tell him of his fault between thee and him alone?" Afterwards, "take one or two witnesses," and then only "tell it to the church?" If this be the full purpose of thy heart, then learn one lesson well, "Hear evil of no man." If there were no hearers, there would be no speakers, of evil. And is not (according to the vulgar proverb) the receiver as bad as the thief? If, then, any begin to speak evil in thy hearing, check him immediately. Refuse to hear the voice of the charmer, charm he never so sweetly; let him use ever so soft a manner, so mild an accent, ever so many professions of goodwill for him whom he is stabbing in the dark, whom he smiteth under the fifth rib! Resolutely refuse to hear, though the whisperer complain of being "burdened till he speak." *Burdened!* thou fool! dost thou travail with thy cursed secret, as a woman travaileth with child? Go, then, and be delivered of thy burden in the way the Lord hath ordained! First, "go and tell thy brother of his fault between thee and him alone.:" next, "take with thee one or two" common friends, and tell him in their presence: If neither of these steps take effect,

then "tell it to the church." But, at the peril of thy soul, tell it to no one else, either before or after, unless in that one exempt case, when it is absolutely needful to preserve the innocent! Why shouldst thou burden another as well as thyself, by making him partaker of thy sin?

5. O that all you who bear the reproach of Christ, who are in derision called Methodists, would set an example to the Christian world, so called, at least in this one instance! Put ye away evil-speaking, talebearing, whispering: Let none of them proceed out of your mouth! See that you "speak evil of no man;" of the absent, nothing but good. If ye must be distinguished, whether ye will or no, let this be the distinguishing mark of a Methodist: "He censures no man behind his back: By this fruit ye may know him." What a blessed effect of this self-denial should we quickly feel in our hearts! How would our "peace flow as a river," when we thus "followed peace with all men!" How would the love of God abound in our own souls, while we thus confirmed our love to our brethren! And what an effect would it have on all that were united together in the name of the Lord Jesus! How would brotherly love continually increase, when this grand hindrance of it was removed! All the members of Christ's mystical body would then naturally care for each other. "If one member suffered, all would suffer with it; if one was honored, all would rejoice with it;" and everyone would love his brother "with a pure heart fervently." Nor is this all: But what an effect might this have, even on the wild unthinking world! How soon would they descry in us, what they could not find among all the thousands of their brethren, and cry (as Julian the Apostate to his heathen courtiers,) "See how these Christians love one another!" By this chiefly would God convince the world, and prepare them also for His kingdom; as we may easily learn from those remarkable words in our Lord's last, solemn prayer: "I pray for them who will believe in me, that they all may be one, as thou, Father, art in me, and I in thee; that the world may believe that thou hast sent me!" [John 17:21] The Lord hasten the time! The Lord enable us thus to love one another, not only "in word and in tongue, but in deed and in truth," even as Christ hath loved us.

50.* THE USE OF MONEY

"I say unto you, Make unto yourselves friends of the mammon of unrighteousness; that, when ye fail, they may receive you into the everlasting habitations."
Luke 16:9.

1. Our Lord, having finished the beautiful parable of the Prodigal Son, which he had particularly addressed to those who murmured at his receiving publicans and sinners, adds another relation of a different kind, addressed rather to the children of God. "He said unto his disciples," not so much to the scribes and Pharisees to whom he had been speaking before,—"There was a certain rich man, who had a steward, and he was accused to him of wasting his goods. And calling him, he said, Give an account of thy stewardship, for thou canst be no longer steward." (Luke 16:1, 2.) After reciting the method which the bad steward used to provide against the day of necessity, our Saviour adds, "His lord commended the unjust steward" namely, in this respect, that he used timely precaution; and subjoins this weighty reflection, "The children of this world are wiser in their generation than the children of light:" (Luke 16:8:) Those who seek no other portion than this world "are wiser" (not absolutely; for they are one and all the veriest fools, the most egregious madmen under heaven; but, "in their generation," in their own way; they are more consistent with themselves; they are truer to their acknowledged principles; they more steadily pursue their end) "than the children of light;"—than they who see "the light of the glory of God in the face of Jesus Christ." Then follow the words above recited: "And I,"—the only-begotten Son of God, the Creator, Lord, and Possessor of heaven and earth and all that is therein; the Judge of all, to whom ye are to "give an account of your stewardship," when ye "can be no longer stewards;" "I say unto you,"—learn in this respect, even of the unjust steward,—"make yourselves friends," by wise, timely precaution, "of the mammon of unrighteousness." "Mammon" means riches or money. It is termed "the mammon of unrighteousness," because of the unrighteous manner wherein it frequently procured, and wherein even that which was honestly procured is generally employed. "Make yourselves friends" of this, by doing all possible good, particularly to the children of God; "that, when ye fail,"—when ye return to dust, when ye have no more place under the sun,—those of them who are gone before "may receive you," may welcome you, into the "everlasting habitations."

2. An excellent branch of Christian wisdom is here inculcated by our Lord on all his followers, namely, the right use of money—a subject largely spoken of, after their manner, by men of the world; but not sufficiently considered by those whom God hath chosen out of the world. These, generally, do not consider, as the importance of the subject requires, the use of this excellent talent. Neither do they understand how to employ it to the greatest advantage; the introduction of which into the world is one admirable instance of the wise and gracious providence of God. It has, indeed, been the manner of poets, orators, and philosophers, in almost all ages and nations, to rail at this, as the grand corrupter of the world, the bane of virtue, the pest of human society. Hence nothing so commonly heard, as:

Nocens ferrum, ferroque nocentius aurum:
And gold, more mischievous than keenest steel.

Hence the lamentable complaint,

Effodiuntur opes, irritamenta malorum.
Wealth is dug up, incentive to all ill.

Nay, one celebrated writer gravely exhorts his countrymen, in order to banish all vice at once, to "throw all their money into the sea:"

… in mare proximum […]
Summi materiem mali!

But is not all this mere empty rant? Is there any solid reason therein? By no means. For, let the world be as corrupt as it will, is gold or silver to blame? "The love of money," we know, "is the root of all evil;" but not the thing itself. The fault does not lie in the money, but in them that use it. It may be used ill: and what may not? But it may likewise be used well: It is full as applicable to the best, as to the worst uses. It is of unspeakable service to all civilized nations, in all the common affairs of life: It is a most compendious instrument of transacting all manner of business, and (if we use it according to Christian wisdom) of doing all manner of good. It is true, were man in a state of innocence, or were all men "filled with the Holy Ghost," so that, like the infant Church at Jerusalem, "no man counted anything he had his own," but "distribution was made to everyone as he had need," the use of it would be superseded; as we cannot conceive there is anything of the kind among the inhabitants of heaven. But, in the present state of mankind, it is an excellent gift of God, answering the noblest ends. In the hands of his children, it is food for the hungry, drink for the thirsty, raiment for the naked: It gives to the traveller and the stranger where to lay his head. By it we may supply the place of an husband to the widow, and of a father to the fatherless. We maybe a defence for the oppressed, a means of health to the sick, of ease to them that are in pain; it may be as eyes to the blind, as feet to the lame; yea, a lifter up from the gates of death!

3. It is therefore of the highest concern that all who fear God know how to employ this valuable talent; that they be instructed how it may answer these glorious ends, and in the highest degree. And, perhaps, all the instructions which are necessary for this may be reduced to three plain rules, by the exact observance whereof we may approve ourselves faithful stewards of "the mammon of unrighteousness."

I. 1. The first of these is (he that heareth, let him understand!) "Gain all you can." Here we may speak like the children of the world: We meet them on their own ground. And it is our bounden duty to do this: We ought to gain all we can gain, without buying gold too dear, without paying more for it than it is worth. But this it is certain we ought not to do; we ought not to gain money at the expense of life, nor (which is in effect the same thing) at the expense of our health. Therefore, no gain whatsoever should induce us to enter into, or to continue in, any employ, which is of such a kind, or is attended with so hard or so long labour, as to impair our constitution. Neither should we begin or continue in any business which necessarily deprives us of proper seasons for food and sleep, in such a proportion as our nature requires. Indeed, there is a great difference here. Some employments are absolutely and totally unhealthy; as those which imply the dealing much with arsenic, or other equally hurtful minerals, or the breathing an air tainted with steams of melting lead, which must at length destroy the firmest constitution. Others may not be absolutely unhealthy, but only to persons of a weak constitution. Such are those which require many hours to be spent in writing; especially if a person write sitting, and lean upon his stomach, or remain long in an uneasy posture. But whatever it is which reason or experience shows to be destructive of health or strength, that we may not submit to; seeing "the life is more" valuable "than meat, and the body than raiment." And if we are already engaged in such an employ, we should exchange it as soon as possible for some which, if it lessen our gain, will, however not lessen our health.

2. We are, Secondly, to gain all we can without hurting our mind any more than our body. For neither may we hurt this. We must preserve, at all events, the spirit of an healthful mind. Therefore we may not engage or continue in any sinful trade, any that is contrary to the law of God, or of our country. Such are all that necessarily imply our robbing or defrauding the king of his lawful customs. For it is at least as sinful to defraud the king of his right, as to rob our fellow subjects. And the king has full as much right, to his customs as we have to our houses and apparel. Other businesses there are, which however innocent in themselves, cannot be followed with innocence now at least, not in England; such, for instance, as will not afford a competent maintenance without cheating or lying, or conformity to some custom which not consistent with a good conscience: These, likewise, are sacredly to be avoided, whatever gain they may be attended with provided we follow the custom of the trade; for to gain money we must not lose our souls. There are yet others which many pursue with perfect innocence, without hurting either their body or mind; And yet perhaps you cannot: Either they may entangle you in that company which would destroy your soul; and by repeated experiments it may appear that you cannot separate the one from the other; or there may be an idiosyncrasy,—a peculiarity in your constitution of soul, (as there is in the bodily constitution of many,) by reason whereof that employment is deadly to you, which another may safely follow. So I am convinced, from many experiments, I could not study, to any degree of perfection, either mathematics, arithmetic, or algebra, without being a Deist, if not an Atheist: And yet others may study them all their lives without sustaining any inconvenience. None therefore can here determine for another; but every man must judge for himself, and abstain from whatever he in particular finds to be hurtful to his soul.

3. We are. Thirdly, to gain all we can without hurting our neighbour. But this we may not, cannot do, if we love our neighbour as ourselves. We cannot, if we love everyone as ourselves, hurt anyone *in his substance*. We cannot devour the increase of his lands, and perhaps the lands and houses themselves, by gaming, by overgrown bills (whether on account of physic, or law, or anything else,) or by requiring or taking such interest as even the laws of our country forbid. Hereby all pawn-broking is excluded: Seeing, whatever good we might do thereby, all unprejudiced men see with grief to be abundantly overbalanced by the evil. And if it were otherwise, yet we are not allowed to "do evil that good may come." We cannot, consistent with brotherly love, sell our goods below the market price; we cannot study to ruin our neighbour's trade, in order to advance our own; much less can we entice away or receive any of his servants or workmen whom he has need of. None can gain by swallowing up his

neighbour's substance, without gaining the damnation of hell!

4. Neither may we gain by hurting our neighbour *in his body*. Therefore we may not sell anything which tends to impair health. Such is, eminently, all that liquid fire, commonly called drams or spirituous liquors. It is true, these may have a place in medicine; they may be of use in some bodily disorders; although there would rarely be occasion for them were it not for the unskillfulness of the practitioner. Therefore, such as prepare and sell them *only for this end* may keep their conscience clear. But who are they? Who prepare and sell them only for this end? Do you know ten such distillers in England? Then excuse these. But all who sell them in the common way, to any that will buy, are poisoners general. They murder His Majesty's subjects by wholesale, neither does their eye pity or spare. They drive them to hell like sheep. And what is their gain? Is it not the blood of these men? Who then would envy their large estates and sumptuous palaces? A curse is in the midst of them: The curse of God cleaves to the stones, the timber, the furniture of them. The curse of God is in their gardens, their walks, their groves; a fire that burns to the nethermost hell! Blood, blood is there: The foundation, the floor, the walls, the roof are stained with blood! And canst thou hope, O thou man of blood, though thou art "clothed in scarlet and fine linen, and farest sumptuously every day;" canst thou hope to deliver down thy *fields of blood* to the third generation? Not so; for there is a God in heaven: Therefore, thy name shall soon be rooted out. Like as those whom thou hast destroyed, body and soul, "thy memorial shall perish with thee!"

5. And are not they partakers of the same guilt, though in a lower degree, whether Surgeons, Apothecaries, or Physicians, who play with the lives or health of men, to enlarge their own gain? Who purposely lengthen the pain or disease which they are able to remove speedily? who protract the cure of their patient's body in order to plunder his substance? Can any man be clear before God who does not shorten every disorder "as much as he can," and remove all sickness and pain "as soon as he can?" He cannot: For nothing can be more clear than that he does not "love his neighbour as himself;" than that he does not "do unto others as he would they should do unto himself."

6. This is dear-bought gain. And so is whatever is procured by hurting our neighbour *in his soul*; by ministering, suppose, either directly or indirectly, to his unchastity, or intemperance, which certainly none can do, who has any fear of God, or any real desire of pleasing Him. It nearly concerns all those to consider this, who have anything to do with taverns, victualling-houses, opera-houses, play-houses, or any other places of public, fashionable diversion. If these profit the souls of men, you are clear; your employment is good, and your gain innocent; but if they are either sinful in themselves, or natural inlets to sin of various kinds, then, it is to be feared, you have a sad account to make. O beware, lest God say in that day, "These have perished in their iniquity, but their blood do I require at thy hands!"

7. These cautions and restrictions being observed, it is the bounden duty of all who are engaged in worldly business to observe that first and great rule of Christian wisdom with respect to money, "Gain all you can." Gain all you can by honest industry. Use all possible diligence in your calling. Lose no time. If you understand yourself and your relation to God and man, you know you have none to spare. If you understand your particular calling as you ought, you will have no time that hangs upon your hands. Every business will afford some employment sufficient for every day and every hour. That wherein you are placed, if you follow it in earnest, will leave you no leisure for silly, unprofitable diversions. You have always something better to do, something that will profit you, more or less. And "whatsoever thy hand findeth to do, do it with thy might." Do it as soon as possible: No delay! No putting off from day to day, or from hour to hour! Never leave anything till to-morrow, which you can do to-day. And do it as well as possible. Do not sleep or yawn over it: Put your whole strength to the work. Spare no pains. Let nothing be done by halves, or in a slight and careless manner. Let nothing in your business be left undone if it can be done by labour or patience.

8. Gain all you can, by common sense, by using in your business all the understanding which God has given you. It is amazing to observe, how few do this; how men run on in the same dull track with their forefathers. But whatever they do who know not God, this is no rule for you. It is a shame for a Christian not to improve upon *them*, in whatever he takes in hand. You should be continually learning, from the experience of others, or from your own experience, reading, and reflection, to do everything you have to do better to-day than you did yesterday. And see that you practise whatever you learn, that you may make the best of all that is in your hands.

II. 1. Having gained all you can, by honest wisdom and unwearied diligence, the second rule of Christian prudence is," Save all you can." Do not throw the precious talent into the sea: Leave that folly to heathen philosophers. Do not throw it away in idle expenses, which is just the same as throwing it into the sea. Expend no part of it merely to gratify the desire of the flesh, the desire of the eye, or the pride of life.

2. Do not waste any part of so precious a talent merely in gratifying the desires of the flesh; in procuring the pleasures of sense of whatever kind; particularly, in enlarging the pleasure of tasting. I do not mean, avoid gluttony and drunkenness only: An honest heathen would condemn these. But there is a regular, reputable kind of sensuality, an elegant epicurism, which does not immediately disorder the stomach, nor (sensibly, at least) impair the understanding. And yet (to mention no other effects of it now) it cannot be maintained without considerable expense. Cut off all this expense! Despise delicacy and variety, and be content with what plain nature requires.

3. Do not waste any part of so precious a talent merely in gratifying the desire of the eye by superfluous or expensive apparel, or by needless ornaments. Waste no part of it in curiously adorning your houses; in superfluous or expensive furniture; in costly pictures, painting, gilding, books; in elegant rather than useful gardens. Let your neighbours, who

know nothing better, do this: "Let the dead bury their dead." But "what is that to thee?" says our Lord: "Follow thou me." Are you willing? Then you are able so to do.

4. Lay out nothing to gratify the pride of life, to gain the admiration or praise of men. This motive of expense is frequently interwoven with one or both of the former. Men are expensive in diet, or apparel, or furniture, not barely to please their appetite, or to gratify their eye, their imagination, but their vanity too. "So long as thou dost well unto thyself, men will speak good of thee." So long as thou art "clothed in purple and fine linen, and farest sumptuously" every day," no doubt many will applaud thy elegance of taste, thy generosity and hospitality. But do not buy their applause so dear. Rather be content with the honour that cometh from God.

5. Who would expend anything in gratifying these desires if he considered that to gratify them is to increase them? Nothing can be more certain than this: Daily experience shows, the more they are indulged, they increase the more. Whenever, therefore, you expend anything to please your taste or other senses, you pay so much for sensuality. When you lay out money to please your eye, you give so much for an increase of curiosity,—for a stronger attachment to these pleasures which perish in the using. While you are purchasing anything which men use to applaud, you are purchasing more vanity. Had you not then enough of vanity, sensuality, curiosity before? Was there need of any addition? And would you pay for it, too? What manner of wisdom is this? Would not the literally throwing your money into the sea be a less mischievous folly?

6. And why should you throw away money upon your children, any more than upon yourself, in delicate food, in gay or costly apparel, in superfluities of any kind? Why should you purchase for them more pride or lust, more vanity, or foolish and hurtful desires? They do not want any more; they have enough already; nature has made ample provision for them: Why should you be at farther expense to increase their temptations and snares, and to pierce them through with more sorrows?

7. Do not leave it to them to throw away. If you have good reason to believe that they would waste what is now in your possession in gratifying and thereby increasing the desire of the flesh, the desire of the eye, or the pride of life at the peril of theirs and your own soul, do not set these traps in their way. Do not offer your sons or your daughters unto Belial, any more than unto Moloch. Have pity upon them, and remove out of their way what you may easily foresee would increase their sins, and consequently plunge them deeper into everlasting perdition! How amazing then is the infatuation of those parents who think they can never leave their children enough! What! cannot you leave them enough of arrows, firebrands, and death? Not enough of foolish and hurtful desires? Not enough of pride, lust, ambition vanity? not enough of everlasting burnings? Poor wretch! thou fearest where no fear is. Surely both thou and they, when ye are lifting up your eyes in hell, will have enough both of the "worm that never dieth," and of "the fire that never shall be quenched!"

8. "What then would you do, if you was in my case? If you had a considerable fortune to leave?" Whether I *would* do it or no, I know what I *ought* to do: This will admit of no reasonable question. If I had one child, elder or younger, who knew the value of money; one who I believed, would put it to the true use, I should think it my absolute, indispensable duty to leave that child the bulk of my fortune; and to the rest just so much as would enable them to live in the manner they had been accustomed to do. "But what, if all your children were equally ignorant of the true use of money?" I ought then (hard saying! who can hear it?) to give each what would keep him above want, and to bestow all the rest in such a manner as I judged would be most for the glory of God.

III. 1. But let not any man imagine that he has done anything, barely by going thus far, by "gaining and saving all he can," if he were to stop here. All this is nothing, if a man go not forward, if he does not point all this at a farther end. Nor, indeed, can a man properly be said to save anything, if he only lays it up. You may as well throw your money into the sea, as bury it in the earth. And you may as well bury it in the earth, as in your chest, or in the Bank of England. Not to use, is effectually to throw it away. If, therefore, you would indeed "make yourselves friends of the mammon of unrighteousness," add the Third rule to the two preceding. Having, First, gained all you can, and, Secondly saved all you can, Then "give all you can."

2. In order to see the ground and reason of this, consider, when the Possessor of heaven and earth brought you into being, and placed you in this world, he placed you here not as a proprietor, but a steward: As such he entrusted you, for a season, with goods of various kinds; but the sole property of these still rests in him, nor can be alienated from him. As you yourself are not your own, but his, such is, likewise, all that you enjoy. Such is your soul and your body, not your own, but God's. And so is your substance in particular. And he has told you, in the most clear and express terms, how you are to employ it for him, in such a manner, that it may be all an holy sacrifice, acceptable through Christ Jesus. And this light, easy service, he has promised to reward with an eternal weight of glory.

3. The directions which God has given us, touching the use of our worldly substance, may be comprised in the following particulars. If you desire to be a faithful and a wise steward, out of that portion of your Lord's goods which he has for the present lodged in your hands, but with the right of resuming whenever it pleases him, First, provide things needful for yourself; food to eat, raiment to put on, whatever nature moderately requires for preserving the body in health and strength. Secondly, provide these for your wife, your children, your servants, or any others who pertain to your household. If when this is done there be an overplus left, then "do good to them that are of the household of faith." If there be an overplus still, "as you have opportunity, do good unto all men." In so doing, you give all you can; nay, in a sound sense, all you have: For all that is laid out in this manner is really given to God. You "render unto God the things that are God's," not only by what you give to the poor, but also

by that which you expend in providing things needful for yourself and your household.

4. If, then, a doubt should at any time arise in your mind concerning what you are going to expend, either on yourself or any part of your family, you have an easy way to remove it. Calmly and seriously inquire, "(1.) In expending this, am I acting according to my character? Am I acting herein, not as a proprietor, but as a steward of my Lord's goods? (2.) Am I doing this in obedience to his Word? In what Scripture does he require me so to do? (3.) Can I offer up this action, this expense, as a sacrifice to God through Jesus Christ? (4.) Have I reason to believe that for this very work I shall have a reward at the resurrection of the just?" You will seldom need anything more to remove any doubt which arises on this head; but by this four-fold consideration you will receive clear light as to the way wherein you should go.

5. If any doubt still remain, you may farther examine yourself by prayer according to those heads of inquiry. Try whether you can say to the Searcher of hearts, your conscience not condemning you, "Lord, thou seest I am going to expend this sum on that food, apparel, furniture. And thou knowest, I act herein with a single eye as a steward of thy goods, expending this portion of them thus in pursuance of the design thou hadst in entrusting me with them. Thou knowest I do this in obedience to the Lord, as thou commandest, and because thou commandest it. Let this, I beseech thee, be an holy sacrifice, acceptable through Jesus Christ! And give me a witness in myself that for this labour of love I shall have a recompense when thou rewardest every man according to his works." Now if your conscience bear you witness in the Holy Ghost that this prayer is well-pleasing to God, then have you no reason to doubt but that expense is right and good, and such as will never make you ashamed.

6. You see then what it is to "make yourselves friends of the mammon of unrighteousness," and by what means you may procure, "that when ye fail they may receive you into the everlasting habitations." You see the nature and extent of truly Christian prudence so far as it relates to the use of that great talent, money. Gain all you can, without hurting either yourself or your neighbour, in soul or body, by applying hereto with unintermitted diligence, and with all the understanding which God has given you;—save all you can, by cutting off every expense which serves only to indulge foolish desire; to gratify either the desire of flesh, the desire of the eye, or the pride of life; waste nothing, living or dying, on sin or folly, whether for yourself or your children;—and then, give all you can, or, in other words, give all you have to God. Do not stint yourself, like a Jew rather than a Christian, to this or that proportion. "Render unto God," not a tenth, not a third, not half, but all that is God's, be it more or less; by employing all on yourself, your household, the household of faith, and all mankind, in such a manner, that you may give a good account of your stewardship when ye can be no longer stewards; in such a manner as the oracles of God direct, both by general and particular precepts; in such a manner, that whatever ye do may be "a sacrifice of a sweet-smelling savour to God," and that every act may be rewarded in that day when the Lord cometh with all his saints.

7. Brethren, can we be either wise or faithful stewards unless we thus manage our Lord's goods? We cannot, as not only the oracles of God, but our own conscience beareth witness. Then why should we delay? Why should we confer any longer with flesh and blood, or men of the world? Our kingdom, our wisdom is not of this world: Heathen custom is nothing to us. We follow no men any farther than they are followers of Christ. Hear ye him. Yea, to-day, while it is called to-day, hear and obey his voice! At this hour, and from this hour, do his will: Fulfil his word, in this and in all things! I entreat you, in the name of the Lord Jesus, act up to the dignity of your calling! No more sloth! Whatsoever your hand findeth to do, do it with your might! No more waste! Cut off every expense which fashion, caprice, or flesh and blood demand! No more covetousness! But employ whatever God has entrusted you with, in doing good, all possible good, in every possible kind and degree to the household of faith, to all men! This is no small part of "the wisdom of the just." Give all ye have, as well as all ye are, a spiritual sacrifice to Him who withheld not from you his Son, his only Son: So "laying up in store for yourselves a good foundation against the time to come, that ye may attain eternal life!"

51.* THE GOOD STEWARD

"Give an account of thy stewardship; for thou mayest be no longer steward."

Luke 16:2.

1. The relation which man bears to God, the creature to his Creator, is exhibited to us in the oracles of God under various representations. Considered as a sinner, a fallen creature, he is there represented as a debtor to his Creator. He is also frequently represented as a servant, which indeed is essential to him as a creature; insomuch that this appellation is given to the Son of God when, in His state of humiliation, he "took upon Him the form of a servant, being made in the likeness of men."

2. But no character more exactly agrees with the present state of man, than that of a steward. Our blessed Lord frequently represents him as such; and there is a peculiar propriety in the representation. It is only in one particular respect, namely, as he is a sinner, that he is styled a debtor; and when he is styled a servant, the appellation is general and indeterminate: But a steward is a servant of a particular kind; such a one as man is in all respects. This appellation is exactly expressive of his situation in the present world; specifying what kind of servant he is to God, and what kind of service his Divine Master expects from him.

It may be of use, then, to consider this point thoroughly, and to make our full improvement of it. In order to this, let us, First, inquire, in what respects we are now God's stewards. Let us, Secondly, observe, that when he requires our souls of us, we "can be no longer stewards." It will then only remain,

---

* [text of the 1872 edition]

as we may, in the third place, observe, to "give an account of our stewardship."

I. 1. And, first, we are to inquire, in what respects we are now God's stewards. We are now indebted to Him for all we have; but although a debtor is obliged to return what he has received, yet until the time of payment comes, he is at liberty to use it as *he* pleases. It is not so with a steward; he is not at liberty to use what is lodged in his hands as he pleases, but as his master pleases. He has no right to dispose of anything which is in his hands, but according to the will of his lord. For he is not the proprietor of any of these things, but barely entrusted with them by another; and entrusted on this express condition,—that he shall dispose of all as his master orders. Now, this is exactly the case of every man, with relation to God. We are not at liberty to use what he has lodged in our hands as we please, but as he pleases, who alone is the possessor of heaven and earth, and the Lord of every creature. We have no right to dispose of anything we have, but according to His will, seeing we are not proprietors of any of these things; they are all, as our Lord speaks, *allotria, belonging to another person*; nor is anything properly *our own*, in the land of our pilgrimage. We shall not receive *ta idia, our own things*, till we come to our own country. Eternal things only are our own: With all these temporal things we are barely entrusted by another, the Disposer and Lord of all. And he entrusts us with them on this express condition,—that we use them only as our Master's goods, and according to the particular directions which he has given us in his Word.

2. On this condition he hath entrusted us with our souls, our bodies, our goods, and whatever other talents we have received: But in order to impress this weighty truth on our hearts, it will be needful to come to particulars.

And, first, God has entrusted us with our soul, an immortal spirit, made in the image of God; together with all the powers and faculties thereof, understanding, imagination, memory, will, and a train of affections, either included in it or closely dependent upon it,—love and hatred, joy and sorrow, respecting present good and evil; desire and aversion, hope and fear, respecting that which is to come. All these St. Paul seems to include in two words, when he says, "The peace of God shall keep your hearts and minds." Perhaps, indeed, the latter word, *noemata*, might rather be rendered *thoughts*, provided we take that word in its most extensive sense, for every perception of the mind, whether active or passive.

3. Now, of all these, it is certain, we are only stewards. God has entrusted us with these powers and faculties, not that we may employ them according to our own will, but according to the express orders which he has given us; although it is true that, in doing his will, we most effectually secure our own happiness; seeing it is herein only that we can be happy, either in time or in eternity. Thus we are to use our understanding, our imagination, our memory, wholly to the glory of him that gave them. Thus our will is to be wholly given up to him, and all our affections to be regulated as he directs. We are to love and hate, to rejoice and grieve, to desire and shun, to hope and fear, according to the rule which he prescribes whose we are, and whom we are to serve in all

things. even our thoughts are not our own, in this sense; they are not at our own disposal; but for every deliberate motion of our mind we are accountable to our great Master.

4. God has, Secondly, entrusted us with our bodies (those exquisitely wrought machines, so fearfully and wonderfully made,) with all the powers and members thereof. He has entrusted us with the organs of sense; of sight, hearing, and the rest: But none of these are given us as our own, to be employed according to our own will. None of these are lent us in such a sense as to leave us at liberty to use them as we please for a season. No: We have received them on these very terms, that, as long as they abide with us, we should employ them all in that very manner, and no other, which he appoints.

5. It is on the same terms that he has imparted to us that most excellent talent of speech. Thou hast given me a tongue, says the ancient writer, that I may praise Thee therewith. For this purpose was it given to all the children of men, to be employed in glorifying God. Nothing, therefore, is more ungrateful or more absurd, than to think or say, "our tongues are our own." That cannot be, unless we have created ourselves, and so are independent on the Most High. Nay, but "it is he that hath made us, and not we ourselves;" the manifest consequence is, that he is still Lord over us, in this as in all other respects. It follows, that there is not a word of our tongue for which we are not accountable to Him.

6. To Him we are equally accountable for the use of our hands and feet, and all the members of our body. These are so many talents which are committed to our trust, until the time appointed by the Father. Until then, we have the use of all these; but as stewards, not as proprietors; to the end we should "render them, not as instruments of unrighteousness unto sin, but as instruments of righteousness unto God."

7. God has entrusted us, Thirdly, with a portion of worldly goods; with food to eat, raiment to put on, and a place where to lay our head; with not only the necessaries, but the conveniences, of life. Above all, he has committed to our charge that precious talent which contains all the rest,—money: Indeed it is unspeakably precious, if we are wise and faithful stewards of it; if we employ every part of it for such purposes as our blessed Lord has commanded us to do.

8. God has entrusted us, Fourthly, with several talents which do not properly come under any of these heads. Such is bodily strength; such are health, a pleasing person, an agreeable address; such are learning and knowledge, in their various degrees, with all the other advantages of education. Such is the influence which we have over others, whether by their love and esteem of us, or by power; power to do them good or hurt, to help or hinder them in the circumstances of life. Add to these, that invaluable talent of time, with which God entrusts us from moment to moment. Add, lastly, that on which all the rest depend, and without which they would all be curses, not blessings; namely, the grace of God, the power of his Holy Spirit, which alone worketh in us all that is acceptable in his sight.

II. 1. In so many respects are the children of men stewards of the Lord, the Possessor of heaven and earth: So large a portion of His goods, of various kinds, hath he committed to their charge. But it is not for ever, nor indeed for any considerable time: We have this trust reposed in us only during the short, uncertain space that we sojourn here below; only so long as we remain on earth, as this fleeting breath is in our nostrils. The hour is swiftly approaching, it is just at hand, when we "can be no longer stewards!" The moment the body "returns to the dust as it was, and the spirit to God that gave it," we bear that character no more; the time of our stewardship is at an end. Part of those goods wherewith we were before entrusted are now come to an end; at least, they are so with regard to us; nor are we longer entrusted with them: And that part which remains can no longer be employed or improved as it was before.

2. Part of what we were entrusted with before is at an end, at least with regard to us. What have we to do, after this life, with food, and raiment, and houses, and earthly possessions? The food of the dead is the dust of the earth; they are clothed only with worms and rottenness. They dwell in the house prepared for all flesh; their lands know them no more: All their worldly goods are delivered into other hands, and they have "no more portion under the sun."

3. The case is the same with regard to the body. The moment the spirit returns to God, we are no longer stewards of this machine, which is then sown in corruption and dishonour. All the parts and members of which it was composed lie mouldering in the clay. The hands have no longer power to move; the feet have forgot their office; the flesh, sinews, and bones, are all hastening to be dissolved into common dust.

4. Here end also the talents of a mixed nature; our strength, our health, our beauty, our eloquence, and address, our faculty of pleasing or persuading, or convincing others. Here end, likewise, all the honours we once enjoyed, all the power which was lodged in our hands, all the influence which we once had over others, either by the love or the esteem which they bore us. our love, our hatred, our desire, is perished: None regard how we were once affected toward them. They look upon the dead as neither able to help nor hurt them; so that "a living dog is better than a dead lion."

5. Perhaps a doubt may remain concerning some of the other talents wherewith we are now entrusted, whether they will cease to exist when the body returns to dust or only cease to be improvable. Indeed, there is no doubt but the kind of speech which we now use, by means of these bodily organs, will then be entirely at an end, when those organs are destroyed. It is certain, the tongue will no more occasion any vibrations in the air; neither will the ear convey these tremulous motions to the common sensory. even the *sonus exilis*, the low, shrill voice, which the poet supposes to belong to a separate spirit, we cannot allow to have a real being; it is a mere flight of imagination. Indeed, it cannot be questioned, but separate spirits have some way to communicate their sentiments to each other; but what inhabitant of flesh and blood can explain that way? What we term "speech," they cannot have: So that we can no longer be stewards of this talent when we are numbered with the dead.

6. It may likewise admit of a doubt, whether our senses will exist, when the organs of sense are destroyed. Is it not probable, that those of the lower kind will cease—the feeling, the smell, the taste—as they have a more immediate reference to the body, and are chiefly, if not wholly, intended for the preservation of it? But will not some kind of sight remain, although the eye be closed in death? And will there not be something in the soul equivalent to the present sense of hearing? Nay, is it not probable, that these will not only exist in the separate state, but exist in a far greater degree, in a more eminent manner, than now, when the soul, disentangled from its clay, is no longer "a dying sparkle in a cloudy place;" when it no longer "looks through the windows of the eye and ear;" but rather is all eye, all ear, all sense, in a manner we cannot yet conceive? And have we not a clear proof of the possibility of this, of seeing without the use of the eye, and hearing without the use of the ear? yea, and earnest of it continually? For does not the soul see, in the clearest manner, when the eye is of no use; namely, in dreams? Does she not then enjoy the faculty of hearing, without any help from the ear? But however this be, certain it is, that neither will our senses, any more than our speech, be entrusted to us in the manner they are now, when the body lies in the silent grave.

7. How far the knowledge or learning which we have gained by education will then remain, we cannot tell. Solomon indeed says, "There is no work, nor device, nor knowledge, nor wisdom, in the grave, whither thou goest." But it is evident, these words cannot be understood in an absolute sense. For it is so far from being true that there is no knowledge after we have quitted the body, that the doubt lies on the other side, whether there be any such thing as real knowledge till then; whether it be not a plain sober truth, not a mere poetical fiction, that

All these shadows which for things we take,
Are but the empty dreams, which in deaths sleep
we make;

only excepting those things which God Himself has been pleased to reveal to man. I will speak for one. After having sought for truth, with some diligence, for half a century, I am, at this day, hardly sure of anything but what I learn from the Bible. Nay, I positively affirm, I know nothing else so certainly, that I would dare to stake my salvation upon it.

So much, however, we may learn from Solomons words, that "there is no" such "knowledge or wisdom in the grave," as will be of any use to an unhappy spirit; "there is no device" there, whereby he can now improve those talents with which he was once entrusted. For time is no more; the time of our trial for everlasting happiness or misery is past. our day, the day of man, is over; the day of salvation is ended! Nothing now remains but the "day of the Lord," ushering in wide, unchangeable eternity!

8. But still, our souls, being incorruptible and immortal, of a nature "little lower than the angels" (even if we are to understand that phrase of our original nature, which may well admit of a doubt,) when our bodies are mouldered into earth, will remain with all their faculties. our memory, our understanding, will be so far from being destroyed, yea, or impaired, by the dissolution of the body, that, on the contrary, we have reason to believe, they will be inconceivably strengthened. Have we not the clearest reason to believe, that they will then be wholly freed from those

defects which now naturally result from the union of the soul with the corruptible body? It is highly probable, that, from the time these are disunited, our memory will let nothing slip; yea, that it will faithfully exhibit everything to our view which was ever committed to it. It is true, that the invisible world is, in Scripture, termed "the land of forgetfulness;" or, as it is still more strongly expressed in the old translation, "the land where all things are forgotten." They are forgotten; but by whom? Not by the inhabitants of that land, but by the inhabitants of the earth. It is with regard to them that the unseen world is "the land of forgetfulness." All things therein are too frequently forgotten by these; but not by disembodied spirits. From the time they have put off the earthly tabernacle, we can hardly think they forget anything.

9. In like manner, the understanding will, doubtless, be freed from the defects that are now inseparable from it. For many ages it has been an unquestioned maxim, *Humanum est errare et nescire*,—ignorance and mistake are inseparable from human nature. But the whole of this assertion is only true with regard to living men; and holds no longer than while "the corruptible body presses down the soul." Ignorance, indeed, belongs to every finite understanding (seeing there is none beside God that knoweth all things;) but not mistake: When the body is laid aside, this also is laid aside, for ever.

10. What then can we say to an ingenious man, who has lately made a discovery, that disembodied spirits have not only no senses (not even sight or hearing,) but no memory or understanding; no thought or perception; not so much as a consciousness of their own existence! that they are in a dead sleep from death to the resurrection! *Consanguineus lethi sopor* indeed! Such a sleep we may call "a near kinsman of death," if it be not the same thing. What can we say, but that ingenious men have strange dreams; and these they sometimes mistake for realities?

11. But to return. As the soul will retain its understanding and memory, notwithstanding the dissolution of the body, so undoubtedly the will, including all the affections, will remain in its full vigour. If our love or anger, our hope or desire, perish, it is only with regard to those whom we leave behind. To them it matters not, whether they were the objects of our love or hate, of our desire or aversion. But in separate spirits themselves we have no reason to believe that any of these are extinguished. It is more probable, that they work with far greater force, than while the soul was clogged with flesh and blood.

12. But although all these, although both our knowledge and senses, our memory and understanding, together with our will, our love, hate, and all our affections, remain after the body is dropped off; yet, in this respect, they are as though they were not—we are no longer stewards of them. The things continue, but our stewardship does not: We no more act in that capacity. even the grace which was formerly entrusted with us, in order to enable us to be faithful and wise stewards, is now no longer entrusted for that purpose. The days of our stewardship are ended.

III. 1. It now remains, that, being no longer stewards, we give an account of our stewardship. Some have imagined, this is to be done immediately after death, as soon as we enter into the world of spirits. Nay, the Church of Rome does absolutely assert this; yea, makes it an article of faith. And thus much we may allow, the moment a soul drops the body, and stands naked before God, it cannot but know what its portion will be to all eternity. It will have full in its view, either everlasting joy, or everlasting torment; as it is no longer possible to be deceived in the judgment which we pass upon ourselves. But the Scripture gives us no reason to believe, that God will then sit in judgment upon us. There is no passage in all the oracles of God which affirms any such thing. That which has been frequently alleged for this purpose seems rather to prove the contrary; namely (Heb. 9:27,) "It is appointed for men once to die, and after this the judgment:" For, in all reason, the word "once" is here to be applied to judgment as well as death. So that the fair inference to be drawn from this very text is, not that there are two judgments, a particular and a general; but that we are to be judged, as well as to die, once only: Not once immediately after death, and again after the general resurrection; but then only "when the Son of man shall come in His glory, and all His holy angels with Him." The imagination therefore of one judgment at death, and another at the end of the world, can have no place with those who make the written Word of God the whole and sole standard of their faith.

2. The time then when we are to give this account is, when the "great white throne comes down from heaven, and he that sitteth thereon, from whose face the heavens and the earth flee away, and there is found no place for them." It is then "the dead, small and great, will stand before God; and the books will be opened:"—The book of Scripture, to them who were entrusted therewith; the book of conscience to all mankind. The "book of remembrance," likewise (to use another scriptural expression,) which had been writing from the foundation of the world, will then be laid open to the view of all the children of men. Before all these, even the whole human race, before the devil and his angels, before an innumerable company of holy angels, and before God the Judge of all, thou wilt appear, without any shelter or covering, without any possibility of disguise, to give a particular account of the manner wherein thou hast employed all thy Lords goods!

3. The Judge of all will then inquire, "How didst thou employ thy soul? I entrusted thee with an immortal spirit, endowed with various powers and faculties, with understanding, imagination, memory, will, affections. I gave thee withal full and express directions, how all these were to be employed. Didst thou employ thy understanding, as far as it was capable, according to those directions; namely, in the knowledge of thyself and me—my nature, my attributes?—my works, whether of creation, of providence, or of grace?—in acquainting thyself with my word?—in using every means to increase thy knowledge thereof?—in meditating thereon day and night? Didst thou employ thy memory, according to my will, in treasuring up whatever knowledge thou hadst acquired, which might conduce to my glory, to thy own salvation, or the advantage of others? Didst thou store up therein, not things of no value, but whatever instruction thou

hadst learned from my word; and whatever experience thou hadst gained of my wisdom, truth, power, and mercy? Was thy imagination employed, not in painting vain images, much less such as nourished "foolish and hurtful desires;" but in representing to thee whatever would profit thy soul, and awaken thy pursuit of wisdom and holiness? Didst thou follow my directions with regard to thy will? Was it wholly given up to me? Was it swallowed up in mine, so as never to oppose, but always run parallel with it? Were thy affections placed and regulated in such a manner, as I appointed in my word? Didst thou give me thy heart? Didst thou not love the world, neither the things of the world? Was I the object of thy love? Was all thy desire unto me, and unto the remembrance of my name? Was I the joy of thy heart, the delight of thy soul, the chief among ten thousand? Didst thou sorrow for nothing, but what grieved my spirit? Didst thou fear and hate nothing but sin? Did the whole stream of thy affections flow back to the ocean from whence they came? Were thy thoughts employed according to my will—not in ranging to the ends of the earth, not on folly, or sin; but on whatsoever things were pure, whatsoever things were holy;' on whatsoever was conducive to my glory, and to peace and good-will among men?' "

4. Thy Lord will then inquire, "How didst thou employ the body wherewith I entrusted thee? I gave thee a tongue to praise me therewith: Didst thou use it to the end for which it was given? Didst thou employ it, not in evil speaking or idle speaking, not in uncharitable or unprofitable conversation; but in such as was good, as was necessary or useful either to thyself or others? such as always tended, directly or indirectly, to minister grace to the hearers?' I gave thee, together with thy other senses, those grand avenues of knowledge, sight, and hearing: were these employed to those excellent purposes for which they were bestowed upon thee? in bringing thee in more and more instruction in righteousness and true holiness? I gave thee hands and feet, and various members, wherewith to perform the works which were prepared for thee: were they employed, not in doing 'the will of the flesh,' of thy evil nature; or the will of the mind; (the things to which thy reason or fancy led thee;) but "the will of Him that sent" thee into the world, merely to work out thy own salvation? Didst thou present all thy members, not to sin, as instruments of unrighteousness, but to me alone, through the Son of my love, 'as instruments of righteousness?' "

5. The Lord of all will next inquire, "How didst thou employ the worldly goods which I lodged in thy hands? Didst thou use thy food, not so as to seek or place thy happiness therein, but so as to preserve thy body in health, in strength and vigour, a fit instrument for the soul? Didst thou use apparel, not to nourish pride or vanity, much less to tempt others to sin, but conveniently and decently to defend thyself from the injuries of the weather? Didst thou prepare and use thy house, and all other conveniences, with a single eye to my glory—in every point seeking not thy own honour, but mine; studying to please, not thyself, but me? once more: in what manner didst thou employ that comprehensive talent, money?—not in gratifying the desire of the flesh, the desire of the eye, or the pride of life; not squandering it away in vain expenses—the same as throwing it into the sea; not hoarding it up to leave behind thee—the same as burying it in the earth; but first supplying thy own reasonable wants, together with those of thy family; then restoring the remainder to me, through the poor, whom I had appointed to receive it; looking upon thyself as only one of that number of poor, whose wants were to be supplied out of that part of my substance which I had placed in thy hands for this purpose; leaving thee the right of being supplied first, and the blessedness of giving rather than receiving? Wast thou accordingly a general benefactor to mankind? feeding the hungry, clothing the naked, comforting the sick, assisting the stranger, relieving the afflicted, according to their various necessities? Wast thou eyes to the blind, and feet to the lame, a father to the fatherless, and an husband to the widow? And didst thou labour to improve all outward works of mercy, as means of saving souls from death?"

6. Thy Lord will farther inquire, "Hast thou been a wise and faithful steward with regard to the talents of a mixed nature which I lent thee? Didst thou employ thy health and strength, not in folly or sin, not in the pleasures which perished in the using, 'not in making provision for the flesh, to fulfil the desires thereof,' but in a vigorous pursuit of that better part which none could take away from thee? Didst thou employ whatever was pleasing in thy person or address, whatever advantages thou hadst by education, whatever share of learning, whatever knowledge of things or men, was committed thee, for the promoting of virtue in the world, for the enlargement of my kingdom? Didst thou employ whatever share of power thou hadst, whatever influence over others, by the love or esteem of thee which they had conceived, for the increase of their wisdom and holiness? Didst thou employ that inestimable talent of time, with wariness and circumspection, as duly weighing the value of every moment, and knowing that all were numbered in eternity? Above all, wast thou a good steward of my grace, preventing, accompanying, and following thee? Didst thou duly observe, and carefully improve, all the influences of my Spirit—every good desire, every measure of light, all His sharp or gentle reproofs? How didst thou profit by 'the Spirit of bondage and fear,' which was previous to 'the Spirit of adoption?' And when thou wast made a partaker of this Spirit, crying in thy heart, "Abba, Father," didst thou stand fast in the glorious liberty wherewith I made thee free? Didst thou from thenceforth present thy soul and body, all thy thoughts, thy words, and actions, in one flame of love, as a holy sacrifice, glorifying me with thy body and thy spirit? Then 'well done, good and faithful servant! enter thou into the joy of thy Lord!' "

And what will remain, either to the faithful or unfaithful steward? Nothing but the execution of that sentence which has been passed by the righteous Judge; fixing thee in a state which admits of no change through everlasting ages! It remains only that thou be rewarded, to all eternity, according to thy works.

IV. 1. From these plain considerations we may learn, First, How important is this short, uncertain day of life! How precious, above all utterance, above all conception, is every portion of it!

The least of these a serious care demands;
For though they're little, they are golden sands!

How deeply does it concern every child of man, to let none of these run to waste; but to improve them all to the noblest purposes, as long as the breath of God is in his nostrils!

2. We learn from hence, Secondly, that there is no employment of our time, no action or conversation, that is purely indifferent. All is good or bad, because all our time, as everything we have, is not our own. All these are, as our Lord speaks, *ta allotria—the property of another*, of God our Creator. Now, these either are or are not employed according to his will. If they are so employed, all is good; if they are not, all is evil. Again: it is His will, that we should continually grow in grace, and in the living knowledge of our Lord Jesus Christ. Consequently, every thought, word, and work, whereby this knowledge is increased, whereby we grow in grace, is good; and every one whereby this knowledge is not increased, is truly and properly evil.

3. We learn from hence, Thirdly, that there are no works of supererogation; that we can never do more than our duty; seeing all we have is not our own, but God's; all we can do is due to Him. We have not received this or that, or many things only, but everything from Him: therefore, everything is His due. He that gives us all, must needs have a right to all: so that if we pay Him anything less than all, we cannot be faithful stewards. And considering, "every man shall receive his own reward, according to his own labour," we cannot be wise stewards unless we labour to the uttermost of our power; not leaving anything undone which we possibly can do, but putting forth all our strength.

4. Brethren, "who is an understanding man and endued with knowledge among you?" Let him show the wisdom from above, by walking suitably to his character. If he so account of himself as a steward of the manifold gifts of God, let him see that all his thoughts, and words, and works, be agreeable to the post God has assigned him. It is no small thing, to lay out for God all which you have received from God. It requires all your wisdom, all your resolution, all your patience and constancy; far more than ever you had by nature, but not more than you may have by grace. For His grace is sufficient for you; and "all things," you know, "are possible to him that believeth." By faith, then, "put on the Lord Jesus Christ;" "put on the whole armour of God;" and you shall be enabled to glorify Him in all your words and works; yea, to bring every thought into captivity to the obedience of Christ!

Edinburgh, May 14, 1768

52**

"Who will rise up with me against the wicked?"

Ps. 94:16.

1. In all ages, men who neither feared God nor regarded man have combined together, and formed confederacies, to carry on the works of darkness. And herein they have shown themselves wise in their generation; for by this means they more effectually promoted the kingdom of their father the devil, than otherwise they could I have done. On the other hand, men who did fear God, and desire the happiness of their fellow-creatures, have, in every age, found it needful to join together, in order to oppose the works of darkness, to spread the knowledge of God their Saviour, and to promote his kingdom upon earth. Indeed He himself has instructed them so to do. From the time that men were upon the earth, he hath taught them to join together in his service, and has united them in one body by one Spirit. And for this very end he has joined them together, "that he might destroy the works of the devil;" first in them that are already united, and by them in all that care round about them.

2. This is the original design of the Church of Christ. It is a body of men compacted together, in order, first, to save each his own soul; then to assist each other in working out their salvation; and, afterwards, as far as in them lies, to save all men from present and future misery, to overturn the kingdom of Satan, and set up the kingdom of Christ. And this ought to be the continued care and endeavour of every member of his Church; otherwise he is not worthy to be called a member thereof, as he is not a living member of Christ.

3. Accordingly, this ought to be the constant care and endeavour of all those who are united together in these kingdoms, and are commonly called, *The Church of England*. They are united together for this very end, to oppose the devil and all his works, and to wage war against the world and the flesh, his constant and faithful allies. But do they, in fact, answer the end of their union? Are all who style themselves "members of the Church of England" heartily engaged in opposing the works of the devil, and fighting against the world and the flesh? Alas! we cannot say this. So far from it, that a great part, I fear the greater part of them, are themselves *the world*,—the people that know not God to any saving purpose; are indulging, day by day, instead of "mortifying the flesh, with its affections and desires;" and doing, themselves, those works of the devil, which they are peculiarly engaged to destroy.

4. There is, therefore, still need, even in this Christian county, (as we *courteously* style Great Britain,) yea, in this Christian church, (if we may give that title to the bulk of our nation,) of some to "rise up against the wicked," and join together "against the evil doers." Nay, there was never more need than there is at this day, for them "that fear the Lord to speak often together" on this very head, how they may "lift up a standard against the iniquity" which overflows the land. There is abundant cause for all the servants of God to join together against the works of the devil; with united hearts and counsels and endeavours to make a stand for God, an to

---

* [text from the 1872 edition]

* Preached before the Society for Reformation of Manners on Sunday, January 30, 1763 at the Chapel in West-Street, Seven-Dials

repress, as much as in them lies, these "floods of ungodliness."

5. For this end a few persons in London, towards the close of the last century, united together, and after a while, were termed, *The Society for Reformation of Manners*; and incredible good was done by them for near forty years. But then, most of the original members being gone to their reward, those who succeeded them grew faint in their mind, and departed from the work: So that a few years ago the Society ceased; nor did any of the kind remain in the kingdom.

6. It is a society of the same nature which has been lately formed. I purpose to show, First, the nature of their design, and the steps they have hitherto taken: Secondly, the excellency of it; with the various objections which have been raised against it: Thirdly, what manner of men they ought to be who engage in such a design: And, Fourthly, with what spirit, and in what manner, they should proceed in the prosecution of it. I shall conclude with an application both to them, and to all that fear God.

I. 1. I am, First, to show the nature of their design, and the steps they have hitherto taken.

It was on a Lord's Day, in August, 1757, that, in a small company who were met for prayer and religious conversation, mention was made of the gross and open profanation of that sacred day, by persons buying and selling, keeping open shop, tippling in alehouses, and standing or sitting in the streets, roads, or fields, vending their wares as on common days; especially in Moorfields, which was then full of them every Sunday, from one end to the other. It was considered, what method could be taken to redress these grievances; and it was agreed, that six of them should, in the morning, wait upon Sir John Fielding for instruction. They did so: He approved of the design, and directed them how to carry it into execution.

2. They first delivered petitions to the Right Honourable the Lord Mayor, and the Court of Aldermen; to the Justices sitting at Hick's Hall; and those in Westminster; and they received from all these honourable benches much encouragement to proceed.

3. It was next judged proper to signify their design to many persons of eminent rank, and to the body of the Clergy, as well as the Ministers of other denominations, belonging to the several churches and meetings in and about the cities of London and Westminster; and they had the satisfaction to meet with a hearty consent and universal approbation from them.

4. They then printed and dispersed, at their own expense, several thousand books of instruction to Constables and other Parish Officers, explaining and enforcing their several duties: And to prevent, as far as possible, the necessity of proceeding to an actual execution of the laws, they likewise printed and dispersed in all parts of the town dissuasives from Sabbath-breaking, extract from Acts of Parliament against it, and notices to the offenders.

5. The way being paved by these precautions, it was in the beginning of the year 1758, that, after notices delivered again and again, which were as often set at naught, actual informations were made to Magistrates against persons profaning the Lord's day. By this means they first cleared the streets and fields of those notorious offenders who, without any regard either to God or the king, were selling their wares from morning to night. They proceeded to a more difficult attempt, the preventing tippling on the Lord's day, spending the time in alehouses, which ought to be spent in the more immediate worship of God. Herein they were exposed to abundance of reproach, to insult and abuse of every kind; having not only the tipplers, and those who entertained them, the alehouse keepers, to contend with, but rich and honourable men, partly the landlords of those alehouse keepers, partly those who furnished them with drink, and, in general, all who gained by their sins. Some of these were not only men of substance, but men in authority; nay, in more instances than one, they were the very persons before whom the delinquents were brought. And the treatment they gave those who laid the informations naturally encouraged "the beasts of the people" to follow their example, and to use them as fellows not fit to live upon the earth. Hence they made no scruple, not only to treat them with the basest language, not only to throw at them mud or stones, or whatever came to hand, but many times to beat them without mercy, and to drag them over the stones, or through the kennels. And that they did not murder them was not for want of will; but the bridle was in their teeth.

6. Having, therefore, received help from God, they went on to restrain bakers likewise, from spending so great a part of the Lord's day in exercising the work of their calling. But many of these were more noble than the victuallers. They were so far from resenting this, or looking upon it as an affront, that several, who had been hurried down the stream of custom to act contrary to their own conscience, sincerely thanked them for their labour, and acknowledged it as a real kindness.

7. In clearing the streets, fields, and alehouses of Sabbath-breakers, they fell upon another sort of offenders, as mischievous to society as any; namely, gamesters of various kinds. Some of these were of the lowest and vilest class, commonly called gamblers; who make a trade of seizing on young and unexperienced men, and tricking them out of all their money; and after they have beggared them, they frequently teach them the same mystery of iniquity. Several nests of these they have rooted out, and constrained not a few of them honestly to earn their bread by the sweat of their brow and the labour of their hands.

8. Increasing in number and strength, they extended their views, and began, not only to repress profane swearing, but to remove out of our streets another public nuisance, and scandal of the Christian name, common prostitutes. Many of these were stopped in their mid career of audacious wickedness. And in order to go to the root of the disease, many of the houses that entertained them have been detected, prosecuted according to law, and totally suppressed. And some of the poor desolate women themselves, though fallen to

The lowest line of human infamy,

have acknowledged the gracious providence of God, and broke off their sins by lasting repentance. Several of these have been placed out, and several received into the Magdalene Hospital.

9. If a little digression may be allowed, who can sufficiently admire the wisdom of Divine Providence, in the disposal of the times and seasons so as to suit one occurrence to another? For instance: Just at a time when many of these poor creatures, being stopped in their course of sin, found a desire of leading a better life, as it were in answer to that sad question, "But if I quit the way I now am in, what can I do to live? For I am not mistress of any trade; and I have no friends that will receive me:"—I say, just at this time, God has prepared the Magdalen Hospital. Here those who have no trade, nor any friends to receive them, are received with all tenderness; yea, they may live, and that with comfort, being provided with all things that are needful "for life and godliness."

10. But to return. The number of persons brought to justice, from August, 1757, to August, 1762, is … 9,596
From thence to the present time:—

For unlawful gaming, and profane swearing	40
For Sabbath-breaking	400
Lewd women, and keepers of ill houses	550
For offering to sale obscene prints	2
In all	10,588

11. In the admission of members into the Society, no regard is had to any particular sect or party. Whoever is found, upon inquiry, to be a good man is readily admitted. And none who has selfish or pecuniary views, will long continue therein; not only because he can gain nothing thereby, but because he would quickly be a loser, inasmuch as he must commence subscriber as soon as he is a member. Indeed, the vulgar cry is, "These are all Whitefieldites." But it is a great mistake. About twenty of the constantly subscribing members are all that are in connection with Mr. Whitefield; about fifty are in connexion with Mr. Wesley; about twenty, who are of the Established Church, have no connexion with either; and about seventy are Dissenters; who make, in all, an hundred and sixty. There are, indeed, many more who assist in the work by occasional subscriptions.

II. 1. These are the steps which have been hitherto taken in prosecution of this design. I am, in the Second place, to show the excellent thereof, notwithstanding the objections which have been raised against it. Now this may appear from several considerations. And, First, from hence,—that the making an open stand against all the ungodliness and unrighteousness which overspread our land as a flood is one of the noblest ways of confessing Christ in the face of his enemies. It is

giving glory to God, and showing mankind that even in these dregs of time,

> There are, who faith prefer
> Though few, and piety to God.

And what more excellent than to render to God the honour due unto his name? To declare by a stronger proof than words, even by suffering, and running all hazards, "Verily there is a reward for the righteous; doubtless there is a God that judgeth the earth."

2. How excellent is the design to prevent in any degree the dishonour done to his glorious name, the contempt which is poured on his authority, and the scandal brought upon our holy religion by the gross, flagrant wickedness of those who are still called by the name of Christ! To stem in any degree the torrent of vice, to repress the floods of ungodliness, to remove in an leisure those occasions of blaspheming the worthy name hereby we are called, is one of the noblest designs it can possibly enter into the heart of man to conceive.

3. And as this design thus evidently tends to bring "glory to God in the highest," so it no less manifestly conduces to the establishing "peace upon earth." For as all sin directly tends both to destroy our peace with God by setting him at open defiance, to banish peace from our own breasts, and to set every man's sword against his neighbour; so whatever prevents or removes sin does in the same degree, promote peace,—both peace in our own soul, peace with God, and peace with one another. Such are the genuine fruits of this design, even in the present world. But why should we confine our views to the narrow bounds of time and space? Rather pass over these into eternity. And what fruit of it shall we find there? Let the Apostle speak: "Brethren, if one of you err from the truth, and one convert him" (not to this or that Opinion, but to God!) "let him know that he who converteth a sinner from the error of his way shall save a soul from death, and hide a multitude of sins." (Jam 5:19, 20.)

4. Nor is it to individuals only, whether those who betray other into sin or those that are liable to be betrayed and destroyed by them, that the benefit of this design redounds, but to the whole community whereof we are members. For is it not a sure observation, "righteousness exalteth a nation?" And is it not as sure on the other hand that "sin is a reproach to any people?" Yea, and bringeth down the curse of God upon them? So far therefore as righteousness in any branch is promoted, so far is the national interest advanced. So far as sin, especially open sin, is restrained, the curse and reproach are removed from us. Whoever therefore they are that labour herein, they are general benefactors. They are the truest friends of their king and country. And in the same proportion as their design takes place, there can be no doubt but God will give national prosperity, in accomplishment of his faithful word, "Them that honour me, I will honour."

5. But it is objected, "However excellent a design this is, it does not concern you. For are there not persons to whom there pressing these offenses and punishing the offenders properly belong? Are there not Constables, and other Parish Officers, who are bound by oath to this very thing?" There are. Constables and Churchwardens, in particular, are

engaged by solemn oaths to give due information against profaners of the Lord's day, and all other scandalous sinners. But if they leave it undone,—if, notwithstanding their oaths, they trouble not themselves about the matter, it concerns all that fear God, that love mankind, and that wish well to their king and country, to pursue this design with the very same vigour as if there were no such Officers existing; it being just the same thing, if they are of no use, as if they had no being.

6. "But this is only a pretence: Their real design is to get money by giving informations." So it has frequently and roundly been affirmed; but without the least shadow of truth. The contrary maybe proved by a thousand instances: No member of the Society takes any part of the money which is by the law allotted to the informer. They never did from the beginning; nor does any of them ever receive anything to suppress or withdraw their information. This is another mistake, if not wilful slander, for which there is not the least foundation.

7. "But the design is impracticable. Vice is risen to such an head that it is impossible to suppress it; especially by such means. For what can an handful of poor people do in opposition to all the world?" "With men this is impossible, but not with God." And they trust, not in themselves, but him. Be then the patrons of vice ever so strong, to him they are no more than grasshoppers. And all means are alike to Him: It is the same thing with God "to deliver by many or by few." The small number, therefore, of those who are on the Lord's side is nothing; neither the great number of those that are against him. Still He doth whatever pleaseth him; and "there is no counsel or strength against the Lord."

8. "But if the end you aim at be really to reform sinners, you choose the wrong means. It is the Word of God must effect this, and not human laws; and it is the work of Ministers, not of Magistrates; therefore, the applying to these can only produce an outward reformation. It makes no change in the heart."

It is true the Word of God is the chief, ordinary means, whereby he changes both the hearts and lives of sinners; and he does this chiefly by the Ministers of the gospel. But it is likewise true, that the Magistrate is "the minister of God;" and that he is designed of God "to be a terror to evil-doers," by executing human laws upon them. If this does not change the heart, yet to prevent outward sin is one valuable point gained. There is so much the less dishonour done to God, less scandal brought on our holy religion; less curse and reproach upon our nation; less temptation laid in the way of others; yea, and less wrath heaped up by the sinners themselves against the day of wrath.

9. "Nay, rather more; for it makes many of them hypocrites, pretending to be what they are not. Others, by exposing them to shame, and putting them to expense, are made impudent and desperate in wickedness; so that in reality none of them are any better, if they are not worse than they were before." This is a mistake all over. For, (1.) where are these hypocrites? We know none who have pretended to be what they were not. (2.) The exposing obstinate offenders to shame, and putting them to expense, does not make them desperate in offending, but afraid to offend. (3.) Some of them, far from

being worse, are substantially better, the whole tenor of their lives being changed. Yea, (4.) some are inwardly changed, even "from darkness to light, and from the power of Satan unto God."

10. "But many are not convinced that buying or selling on the Lord's day is a sin."

If they are not convinced, they ought to be: it is high time they should. The case is as plain as plain can be. For if an open, wilful breach both of the law of God and the law of the land is not sin, pray what is? And if such a breach both of divine and human laws is not to be punished because a man is not convinced it is a sin, there is an end of all execution of justice, and all men may live as they list.

11. "But *mild* methods ought to be tried first." They ought: And so they are. A mild admonition is given to every offender before the law is put in execution against him; nor is any man prosecuted till he has express notice that this will be the case unless he will prevent that prosecution by removing the cause of it. In every case the mildest method is used which the nature of the case will bear; nor are severer means ever applied, but when they are absolutely necessary to the end.

12. "Well, but after all this stir about reformation, what real good has been done?" Unspeakable good; and abundantly more than anyone could have expected in so short a time, considering the small number of the instruments, and the difficulties they had to encounter. Much evil has been already prevented, and much has been removed. Many sinners have been outwardly reformed some have been inwardly changed. The honour of him whose name we bear, so openly affronted, has been openly defended. And it is not easy to determine how many and how great blessing seven this little stand, made for God and his cause against his daring enemies, may already have derived upon our whole nation. On the whole, then, after all the objections that can be made, reasonable men may still conclude, a more excellent design could scarce ever enter into the heart of man.

III. 1. But what manner of men ought they to be who engage in such a design? Some may imagine, any that are willing to assist therein ought readily to be admitted; and that the greater the number of members, the greater will be their influence. But this is by no means true: Matter of fact undeniably proves the contrary. While the former Society for Reformation of Manners consisted of chosen members only, though neither many, rich, nor powerful, they broke through all opposition, and were eminently successful in every branch of their undertaking; but when a number of men less carefully chosen, were received into that Society, they grew less and less useful, till, by insensible degrees, they dwindled into nothing.

2. The number, therefore, of the members is no more to be attended to than the riches or eminence. This is a work of God. It is undertaken in the name of God, and for his sake. It follows, that men who neither love nor fear God have no part or lot in this matter. "Why takest thou my covenant in thy mouth?" may God say to any of these; "whereas thou" thyself "hatest to be reformed, and have cast my words behind thee?" Whoever, therefore, lives in any known sin is not fit to engage in reforming sinners: More especially if he

is guilty, in any instance, or in the least degree, of profaning the name of God, of buying, selling, or doing any unnecessary work on the Lord's day; or offending in any other of those instances which this Society is peculiarly designed to reform. No; let none who stands himself in need of this reformation presume to meddle with such an undertaking. First let him "pull the beam out of his own eye:" Let him be himself *unblamable* in all things.

3. Not that this will suffice: Everyone engaging herein, should be more than a harmless man. He should be a man of faith; having at least, such a degree of that "evidence of things not seen," as to "aim not at the things that are seen, which are temporal, but at those that are not seen, which are eternal;" such a faith as produces a steady fear of God, with a lasting resolution, by his grace, to abstain from all that he has forbidden, and to do all that he has commanded. He will more especially need that particular branch of faith,—confidence in God. It is this faith which "removes mountains;" which "quenches the violence of fire;" which breaks through all opposition; and enables one to stand against and "chase a thousand," knowing in whom his strength lies, and, even when he has "the sentence of death in himself, trusting in Him who raiseth the dead."

4. He that has faith and confidence in God, will, of consequence, be a man of courage. And such it is highly needful every man should be, who engages in this undertaking: For many things will occur in the prosecution thereof, which are terrible to nature; indeed, so terrible, that all who "confer with flesh and blood" will be afraid to encounter them. Here, therefore, true courage has its proper place, and is necessary in the highest degree. And this, faith only can supply. A believer can say,

> I fear no denial; no danger I fear;
> Nor start from the trial;—For Jesus is near.

5. To courage patience is nearly allied; the one regarding future, the other present, evils. And whoever joins in carrying on a design of this nature, will have great occasion for this. For, notwithstanding all his unblameableness, he will find himself just in Ishmael's situation,—"his hand against every man, and everyman's hand against him." And no wonder: If it be true, that "all who will live godly shall suffer persecution," how eminently must this be fulfilled in them who, not content to live godly themselves, compel the ungodly to do so too, or at least to refrain from notorious ungodliness! Is not this declaring war against all the world? setting all the children of the devil at defiance? And will not Satan himself, "the prince of this world, the ruler of the darkness" thereof, exert all his subtlety and all his force in support of his tottering kingdom? Who can expect the roaring lion will tamely submit to have the prey plucked out of his teeth? "Ye have," therefore, "need of patience; that, after ye have done the will of God, ye may receive the promise."

6. And ye have need of steadiness, that ye may "hold fast" this "profession of your faith without wavering." This also should be found in all that unite in this Society; which is not a task for a "double-minded man,"—for one that "is unstable in his ways." He that is as a reed shaken with the wind is not fit for this warfare; which demands a firm purpose of soul, a constant, determined resolution. One that is wanting in this may "set his hand to the plough;" but how soon will he "look back!" He may, indeed, "endure for a time; but when persecution or tribulation," public or private troubles, "arise because of the work, immediately he is offended."

7. Indeed, it is hard for any to persevere in so unpleasing a work, unless love overpowers both pain and fear. And, therefore, it is highly expedient, that all engaged therein have "the love of God shed abroad in their hearts;" that they should all be able to declare, "we love him, because he first loved us." The presence of Him whom their soul loveth will then make their labour light. They can then say, not from the wildness of an heated imagination, but with the utmost truth and soberness,—

> With thee conversing, I forget
> All time, and toil, and care:
> Labour is rest, and pain is sweet,
> While thou, my God, art here.

8. What adds a still greater sweetness, even to labour and pain, is the Christian "love of our neighbour." When they "love their neighbour," that is, every soul of man, "as themselves," as their own souls; when "the love of Christ constrains" them to love one another, "even as he loved us;" when, as he "tasted death for every man," so they are "ready to lay down their life for their brethren;" (including in that number every man, every soul for which Christ died,) what prospect of danger will then be able to fright them from their "labour of love?" What suffering will they not be ready to undergo to save one soul from everlasting burnings? What continuance of labour, disappointment, pain, will vanquish their fixed resolution? Will they not be

> 'Gainst all repulses steel'd, nor ever tired
> With toilsome day, or ill-succeeding night?

So love both "hopeth" and "endureth all things:" So "charity never faileth."

9. Love is necessary for all the members of such a Society, on another account likewise; even because it "is not puffed up:" It produces not only courage and patience, but humility. And O how needful is this for all who are so employed! What can be of more importance, than that they should be little and mean and base and vile in their own eyes? For, otherwise, should they think themselves anything, should they impute anything to themselves, should they admit anything of a Pharisaic spirit, "trusting in themselves that they were righteous, and despising others;" nothing could more directly tend to overthrow the whole design. For then they would not only have all the world, but also God himself, to contend with; seeing he "resisteth the proud, and giveth grace" only "to the humble." Deeply conscious, therefore, should every member of this society be of his own foolishness, weakness, helplessness; continually hanging, with his whole soul upon Him who alone hath wisdom and strength, with an unspeakable conviction that "the help which is done upon earth, God doth it himself;" and that it is He alone "who worketh in us, both to will and to do of his good pleasure."

10. One point more whoever engages in this design should have deeply impressed on his heart, namely, that "the wrath

of man worketh not the righteousness of God." Let him, therefore, learn of Him who was meek, as well as lowly; and let him abide in meekness, as well as humility: "With all lowliness and meekness," let him "walk worthy of the vocation wherewith he is called." Let them be "gentle toward all men," good or bad, for his own sake, for their sake, for Christ's sake. Are any "ignorant, and out of the way?" Let him have "compassion" upon them. Do they even oppose the word and the work of God; yea, set themselves in battle array against it? So much the more hath he need "in meekness to instruct those who thus oppose themselves;" if haply they may "escape out of the snare of the devil," and no more be "taken captive at his will."

IV. 1. From the qualifications of those who are proper to engage in such an undertaking as this I proceed to show, Fourthly, with what spirit and in what manner it ought to be pursued. First, with what spirit. Now this first regards the *motive*, which is to be preserved in every step that is taken; for if, at any time "the light which is in thee be darkness, how great is that darkness! But if thine eye be single, thy whole body shall be full of light." This is, therefore, continually to be remembered, and carried into every word and action. Nothing is to be spoke or done, either great or small, with a view to any temporal advantage; nothing with a view to the favour or esteem, the love or the praise, of men. But the intention, the eye of the mind, is always to be fixed on the glory of God and good of man.

2. But the spirit with which everything is to be done regards the *temper* as well as the motive. And this is no other than that which has been described above. For the same courage, patience, steadiness, which qualify a man for the work, are to be exercised therein. Above all let him "take the shield of faith:" This will quench a thousand fiery darts. Let him exert all the faith which God has given him, in every trying hour. And let all his doings be done in love: Never let this be wrested from him. Neither must many waters quench this love, nor the floods of ingratitude drown it. Let, likewise, that lowly mind be in him, which was also in Christ Jesus; yea, and let him "be clothed with humility," filling his heart, and adorning his whole behaviour. At the same time, let him "put on bowels of mercies, gentleness, longsuffering;" avoiding the least appearance of malice, bitterness, anger, or resentment; knowing it is our calling, not to be "overcome of evil, but to overcome evil with good." In order to preserve this humble, gentle love, it is needful to do all things with recollection of spirit; watching against all hurry, or dissipation of thought, as well as against pride, wrath, or surliness. But this can be no otherwise preserved than by "continuing instant in prayer," both before and after he comes into the field, and during the whole action; and by doing all in the spirit of sacrifice, offering all to God, through the Son of his love.

3. As to the outward manner of acting, a general rule is, Let it be expressive of these inward tempers. But to be more particular: (1.) Let every man beware not to "do evil that good may come." Therefore, "putting away all lying, let every man speak the truth to his neighbour." Use no fraud or guile, either in order to detect or to punish any man, but "by simplicity and godly sincerity" "commend yourself to men's consciences in the sight of God." It is probable that, by your adhering to these rules, fewer offenders will be convicted; but so much the more will the blessing of God accompany the whole undertaking.

4. But let innocence be joined with prudence, properly so called;—not that offspring of hell which the world calls prudence, which is mere craft, cunning, dissimulation; but with that "wisdom from above" which our Lord peculiarly recommends to all who would promote his kingdom upon earth. "Be ye therefore wise as serpents," while ye are "harmless as doves." This wisdom will instruct you how to suit your words and whole behaviour, to the persons with whom you have to do; to the time, place, and all other circumstances. It will teach you to cut off occasion of offense, even from those who seek occasion, and to do things of the most offensive nature in the least offensive manner that is possible.

5. Your manner of speaking, particularly to offenders, should be at all times deeply serious (lest it appear like insulting or triumphing over them,) rather inclining to sad; showing that you pity them for what they do, and sympathize with them in what they suffer. Let your air and tone of voice, as well as words, be dispassionate, calm, mild; yea, where it would not appear like dissimulation, even kind and friendly. In some cases, where it will probably be received as it is meant, you may profess the goodwill you bear them; but at the same time, (that it may not be thought to proceed from fear, or any wrong inclination,) professing your intrepidity, and inflexible resolution to oppose and punish vice to the uttermost.

V. 1. It remains only to make some application of what has been said, partly to you who are already engaged in this work, partly to all that fear God; and more especially to them that love as well as fear him.

With regard to you who are already engaged in this work, the First advice I would give you is, calmly and deeply to consider the nature of your undertaking. Know what you are about; be thoroughly acquainted with what you have in hand; consider the objections which are made to the whole of your undertaking; and before you proceed, be satisfied that those objections have no real weight: Then may every man act as he is fully persuaded in his own mind.

2. I advise you, Secondly, be not in haste to increase your number: And, in adding thereto, regard not wealth, rank, or any outward circumstance; only regard the qualifications above described. Inquire diligently, whether the person proposed be of an unblamable carriage, and whether he be a man of faith, courage, patience, steadiness; whether he be a lover of God and man. If so, he will add to your strength, as well as number: If not, you will lose by him more than you gain; for you will displease God. And be not afraid to purge out from among you any who do not answer the preceding character. By thus lessening your number, you will increase your strength: You will be "vessels meet for your Master's use."

3. I would, Thirdly, advise you narrowly to observe from what motive you at any time act or speak. Beware that your intention be not stained with any regard either to profit or

praise. Whatever you do, "do it to the Lord; as the servants of Christ. Do not aim at pleasing yourself in any point, but pleasing Him whose you are and whom you serve. Let your eye be single, from first to last; eye God alone in every word and work.

4. I advise you, in the Fourth place, see that you do everything in a right temper; with lowliness and meekness, with patience and gentleness, worthy the gospel of Christ. Take every step, trusting in God, and in the most tender, loving spirit you are able. Meantime, watch always against all hurry and dissipation of spirit; and pray always, with all earnestness and perseverance, that your faith fail not. And let nothing interrupt that spirit of sacrifice which you make of all you have and are, of all you suffer and do, that it may be an offering of a sweet-smelling savour to God, through Jesus Christ!

5. As to the manner of acting and speaking, I advise you to do it with all innocence and simplicity, prudence and seriousness. Add to these, all possible calmness and mildness; nay, all the tenderness which the case will bear. You are not to behave as butchers or hangmen; but as surgeons rather, who put the patient to no more pain than is necessary in order to the cure. For this purpose, each of you, likewise, has need of "a lady's hand with a lion's heart." So shall many, even of them you are constrained to punish, "glorify God in the day of visitation."

6. I exhort all of you who fear God, as ever you hope to find mercy at his hands, as you dread being found (though you knew it not) "even to fight against God," do not, on any account, reason, or pretence whatsoever, either directly or indirectly, oppose or hinder so merciful a design, and one so conducive to his glory. But this is not all: If you are lovers of mankind, if you long to lessen the sins and miseries of your fellow-creatures, can you satisfy yourselves, can you be clear before God, by barely not opposing it? Are not you also bound by the most sacred ties, "as you have opportunity to do good to all men?" And is not here an opportunity of doing good to many, even good of the highest kind? In the name of God, then, embrace the opportunity! Assist in doing this good, if no otherwise, yet by your earnest prayers for them who are immediately employed therein. Assist them, according to your ability, to defray the expense which necessarily attends it, and which, without the assistance of charitable persons, would be a burden they could not bear. Assist them, if you can without inconvenience, by quarterly or yearly subscriptions. At least, assist them *now*; use the present hour, doing what God puts into your heart. Let it not be said that you saw your brethren laboring for God, and would not help them with one of your fingers. In this way, however, "come to the help of the Lord, to the help of the Lord against the mighty!"

7. I have an higher demand upon you who love, as well as fear, God. He whom you fear, whom you love, has qualified you for promoting his work in a more excellent way. Because you love God, you love your brother also: You love, not only your friends, but your enemies; not only the friends, but even the enemies, of God. You have "put on, as the elect of God, lowliness, gentleness, long-suffering." You have faith in God, and in Jesus Christ whom he hath sent; faith which overcometh the world: And hereby you conquer both evil shame, and that "fear of man which bringeth a snare;" so that you can stand with boldness before them that despise you, and make no account of your labors. Qualified, then, as you are, and armed for the fight, will you be like the children of Ephraim, "who, being harnessed, and carrying bows, turned back in the day of battle?" Will *you* leave a few of your brethren to stand alone, against all the hosts of the aliens? O say not, "This is too heavy a cross; I have not strength or courage to bear it!" True; not of yourself: But you that believe "can do all things through Christ strengthening you." "If thou canst believe, all things are possible to him that believeth." No cross is too heavy for *him* to bear; knowing that they that "suffer with him, shall reign with him." Say not, "Nay, but I cannot bear to be *singular.*" Then you cannot enter into the kingdom of heaven. No one enters there but through the narrow way; and all that walk in this are singular. Say not, "But I cannot endure the reproach, the odious name of an informer." And did any man ever save his soul, that was not a by-word, and a proverb of reproach? Neither canst thou ever save thine, unless thou art willing that men should say all manner of evil of thee. Say not, "But if I am active in this work, I shall lose not only my reputation, but my friends, my customers, my business, my livelihood; so that I shall be brought to poverty." Thou shalt not; thou canst not: It is absolutely impossible, unless God himself chooseth it; for his "kingdom ruleth over all," and "the very hairs of thy head are all numbered." But if the wise, the gracious God choose it for thee, wilt thou murmur or complain? Wilt thou not rather say, "The cup which my Father hath given me, shall I not drink it? If you "suffer for Christ, happy are you; the Spirit of glory and of God" shall "rest upon you." Say not, "I would suffer all things, but my wife will not consent to it; and, certainly, a man ought to leave father and mother and all, and cleave to his wife." True; all but God; all but Christ: But he ought not to leave him for his wife! He is not to leave any duty undone, for the dearest relative. Our Lord himself hath said in this very sense, "If any man loveth father, or mother, or wife, or children, more than me, he is not worthy of me!" Say not, "Well, I would forsake all for Christ; but one duty must not hinder another; and this would frequently hinder my attending public worship." Sometimes it probably would. "Go, then, and learn what that meaneth, I will have mercy and not sacrifice." And whatever is lost by showing this mercy, God will repay seven-fold into thy bosom. Say not, "But I shall hurt my own soul. I am a young man; and by taking up loose women I should expose myself to temptation." Yes, if you did this in your own strength, or for your own pleasure. But that is not the case. You trust in God; and you aim at pleasing him only. And if he should call you even into the midst of a burning fiery furnace, "though thou walkest through the fire, thou shalt not be burned; neither shall the flames kindle upon thee." "True; if he called me into the furnace; but I do not see that I am called to this." Perhaps thou art not willing to see it. However, if thou wast not called before, I call thee now, in the name of Christ: Take up thy cross, and follow him!

Reason no more with flesh and blood, but now resolve to cast in thy lot with the most despised, the most infamous, of his followers; the filth and offscouring of the world! I call thee in particular, who didst once strengthen their hands, but since art drawn back. Take courage! Be strong! Fulfil their joy, by returning with heart and hand! Let it appear thou "departedst for a season, that they might receive thee again for ever." O be "not disobedient to the heavenly calling!" And, as for all of you who know whereunto ye are called, count ye all things loss, so ye may save one soul for which Christ died! And therein "take no thought for the morrow," but "cast all your care on Him that careth for you!" Commit your souls, bodies, substance, all to him, "as unto a merciful and faithful Creator!"

[After this Society had subsisted several years, and done unspeakable good, it was wholly destroyed by a verdict given against it in the King's Bench, with three hundred pounds damages. I doubt a severe account remains for the witnesses, the jury, and all who were concerned in that dreadful affair!]

53.* ON THE DEATH OF THE REV. MR. GEORGE WHITEFIELD

PREACHED AT THE CHAPEL IN TOTTENHAM-COURT ROAD AND AT THE TABERNACLE, NEAR MOORFIELDS, ON SUNDAY, NOVEMBER 18, 1770.

"Let me die the death of the righteous, and let my last end be like his!"

Num. 23:10.

1. "Let my last end be like his!" How many of you join in this wish? Perhaps there are few of you who do not, even in this numerous congregation! And O that this wish may rest upon your minds!—that it may not die away till your souls also are lodged "where the wicked cease from troubling, and where the weary are at rest!"

2. An elaborate exposition of the text will not be expected on this occasion. It would detain you too long from the sadly-pleasing thought of your beloved brother, friend, and pastor; yea, and father too: for how many are here whom he hath "begotten in the Lord!" Will it not, then, be more suitable to your inclinations, as well as to this solemnity, directly to speak of this man of God, whom you have so often heard speaking in this place?—the end of whose conversation ye know, "Jesus Christ, the same yesterday, and to-day, and for ever." And may we not,

    I.   Observe a few particulars of his life and death?

    II.   Take some view of his character? and,

    III.   Inquire how we may improve this awful providence, his sudden removal from us?

1. We may, in the first place, observe a few particulars of his life and death. He was born at Gloucester, in December, 1714, and put to a grammar-school there, when about twelve years old. When he was seventeen, he began to be seriously religious, and served God to the best of his knowledge. About eighteen he removed to the University, and was admitted at Pembroke College in Oxford; and about a year after he became acquainted with the Methodists (so called), whom from that time he loved as his own soul.

2. By them he was convinced that we "must be born again," or outward religion will profit us nothing. He joined with them in fasting on Wednesdays and Fridays; in visiting the sick and the prisoners; and in gathering up the very fragments of time, that no moment might be lost: and he changed the course of his studies; reading chiefly such books as entered into the heart of religion, and led directly to an experimental knowledge of Jesus Christ, and Him crucified.

3. He was soon tried as with fire. Not only his reputation was lost, and some of his dearest friends forsook him; but he was exercised with inward trials, and those of the severest kind. Many nights he lay sleepless upon his bed; many days, prostrate on the ground. But after he had groaned several months under "the spirit of bondage," God was pleased to remove the heavy load, by giving him "the Spirit of adoption;" enabling him through a living faith, to lay hold on "the Son of His Love."

4. However, it was thought needful, for the recovery of his health, which was much impaired, that he should go into the country. He accordingly went to Gloucester, where God enabled him to awaken several young persons. These soon formed themselves into a little society, and were some of the first-fruits of his labor. Shortly after, he began to read, twice or thrice a week, to some poor people in the town; and every day to read to and pray with the prisoners in the county jail.

5. Being now about twenty-one years of age, he was solicited to enter into holy orders. Of this he was greatly afraid, being deeply sensible of his own insufficiency. But the Bishop himself sending for him, and telling him, "Though I had purposed to ordain none under three-and-twenty, yet I will ordain you whenever you come"—and several other providential circumstances concurring—he submitted, and was ordained on Trinity Sunday, 1736. The next Sunday he preached to a crowded auditory, in the church wherein he was baptized. The week following he returned to Oxford, and took his Bachelor's degree: and he was now fully employed; the care of the prisoners and the poor lying chiefly on him.

6. But it was not long before he was invited to London, to serve the cure of a friend going into the country. He continued there two months, lodging in the Tower, reading prayers in the chapel twice a week, catechizing and preaching once, beside visiting the soldiers in the barracks and the infirmary. He also read prayers every evening at Wapping chapel, and preached at Ludgate prison every Tuesday. While he was here, letters came from his friends in Georgia, which made him long to go and help them: but not seeing his call clear, at the appointed time he returned to his little charge at Oxford, where several youths met daily at his room, to build up each other in their most holy faith.

---

* (text of the 1872 edition)

7. But he was quickly called from hence again, to supply the cure of Dummer, in Hampshire. Here he read prayers twice a day; early in the morning, and in the evening after the people came from work. He also daily catechized the children, and visited from house to house. He now divided the day into three parts, allotting eight hours for sleep and meals, eight for study and retirement, and eight for reading prayers, catechizing, and visiting the people. Is there a more excellent way for a servant of Christ and His Church? If not, who will "go and do likewise?"

8. Yet his mind still ran on going abroad; and being now fully convinced he was called of God thereto, he set all things in order, and, in January, 1737, went down to take leave of his friends in Gloucester. It was in this journey that God began to bless his ministry in an uncommon manner. Wherever he preached, amazing multitudes of hearers flocked together, in Gloucester, in Stonehouse, in Bath, in Bristol; so that the heat of the churches was scarce supportable: and the impressions made on the minds of many were no less extraordinary. After his return to London, while he was detained by General Oglethorpe, from week to week, and from month to month, it pleased God to bless his word still more. And he was indefatigable in his labor: generally on Sunday he preached four times, to exceeding large auditories; beside reading prayers twice or thrice, and walking to and fro often ten or twelve miles.

9. On December 28 he left London. It was on the 29th that he first preached without notes. December 30, he went on board; but it was above a month before they cleared the land. One happy effect of their very slow passage he mentions in April following: "Blessed be God, we now live very comfortably in the great cabin. We talk of little else but God and Christ; and scarce a word is heard among us when together, but what has reference to our fall in the first, and our new birth in the Second, Adam." It seems, likewise, to have been a peculiar providence, that he should spend a little time at Gibraltar; where both citizens and soldiers, high and low, young and old, acknowledged the day of their visitation.

10. From Sunday, May 7, 1738, till the latter end of August following, he "made full proof of his ministry" in Georgia, particularly at Savannah: he read prayers and expounded twice a day, and visited the sick daily. On Sunday he expounded at five in the morning; at ten read prayers and preached, and at three in the afternoon; and at seven in the evening expounded the Church Catechism. How much easier is it for our brethren in the ministry, either in England, Scotland, or Ireland, to find fault: with such a laborer in our Lord's vineyard, than to tread in his steps!

11. It was now that he observed the deplorable condition of many children here; and that God put into his heart the first thought of founding an Orphan-house, for which he determined to raise contributions in England, if God should give him a safe return thither. In December following, he did return to London; and on Sunday, January 14, 1739, he was ordained priest at Christ Church, Oxford. The next day he came to London again; and on Sunday, the 21st, preached twice. But though the churches were large, and crowded exceedingly, yet many hundreds stood in the churchyard, and hundreds more returned home. This put him upon the first thought of preaching in the open air. But when he mentioned it to some of his friends, they judged it to be mere madness: so he did not carry it into execution till after he, had left London. It was on Wednesday, February 21, that, finding all the church doors to be shut in Bristol (beside, that no church was able to contain one half of the congregation), at three in the afternoon he went to Kingswood, and preached abroad to near two thousand people. On Friday he preached there to four or five thousand; and on Sunday to, it was supposed, ten thousand! The number continually increased all the time he stayed at Bristol; and a flame of holy love was kindled, which will not easily be put out. The same was afterwards kindled in various parts of Wales, of Gloucestershire, and Worcestershire. Indeed, wherever he went, God abundantly confirmed the word of his messenger.

12. On Sunday, April 29, he preached the first time in Moorfields, and on Kennington Common; and the thousands of hearers were as quiet as they could have been in a church. Being again detained in England from month to month, he made little excursions into several counties, and received the contributions of willing multitudes for an Orphan-house in Georgia. The embargo which was now laid on the shipping gave him leisure for more journeys through various parts of England, for which many will have reason to bless God to all eternity. At length, on August 14, he embarked: but he did not land in Pennsylvania till October 30. Afterwards he went through Pennsylvania, the Jerseys, New York, Maryland, Virginia, North and South Carolina; preaching all along to immense congregations, with full as great effect as in England. On January 10, 1740, he arrived at Savannah.

13. January 29, he added three desolate orphans to near twenty which he had in his house before. The next day he laid out the ground for the house, about ten miles from Savannah. February 11, he took in four orphans more; and set out for Frederica, in order to fetch the orphans that were in the southern parts of the colony. In his return he fixed a school, both for children and grown persons, at Darien, and took four orphans thence. March 25, he laid the first stone of the Orphan-house; to which, with great propriety, he gave the name of Bethesda; a work for which the children yet unborn shall praise the Lord. He had now about forty orphans, so that there was near a hundred mouths to be fed daily. But he was "careful for nothing," casting his care on Him who feed the young ravens that call upon Him.

14. In April he made another tour through Pennsylvania, the Jerseys, and New York. Incredible multitudes flocked to hear, among whom were abundance of Negroes. In all places the greater part of the hearers were affected to an amazing degree. Many were deeply convinced of their lost state, many truly converted to God. In some places, thousands cried out aloud; many as in the agonies of death; most were drowned in tears; some turned pale as death; others were wringing their hands; others lying on the ground; others sinking into the arms of their friends; almost all lifting up their eyes, and calling for mercy.

15. He returned to Savannah, June 5. The next evening, during the public service, the whole congregation, young and old, were dissolved in tears: after service, several of the parishioners, and all his family, particularly the little children, returned home crying along the street, and some could not help praying aloud. The groans and cries of the children continued all night, and great part of the next day.

16. In August he set out again, and through various provinces came to Boston. While he was here, and in the neighboring places, he was extremely weak in body: yet the multitudes of hearers were so great, and the effects wrought on them so astonishing, as the oldest men then alive in the town had never seen before. The same power attended his preaching at New York, particularly on Sunday, November 2: almost as soon as he began, crying, weeping, and wailing were to be heard on every side. Many sunk down to the ground, cut to the heart; and many were filled with divine consolation. Toward the close of his journey he made this reflection: "It is the seventy-fifth day since I arrived at Rhode Island, exceeding weak in body; yet God has enabled me to preach an hundred and seventy-five times in public, besides exhorting frequently in private! Never did God vouchsafe me greater comforts: never did I perform my journeys with less fatigue, or see such a continuance of the divine presence in the congregations to whom I preached." In December he returned to Savannah, and in the March following arrived in England.

17. You may easily observe, that the preceding account is chiefly extracted from his own journals, which, for their artless and unaffected simplicity, may vie with any writings of the kind. And how exact a specimen is this of his labors both in Europe and America, for the honor of his beloved Master, during the thirty years that followed, as well as of the uninterrupted shower of blessings wherewith God was pleased to succeed his labors! Is it not much to be lamented, that anything should have prevented his continuing this account, till at least near the time when he was called by his Lord to enjoy the fruit of his labor? If he has left any papers of this kind, and his friends account me worthy of the honor, it would be my glory and joy to methodize, transcribe, and prepare them for the public view.

18. A particular account of the last scene of his life is thus given by a gentleman of Boston:—

"After being about a month with us in Boston and its vicinity, and preaching every day, he went to Old York; preached on Thursday, September 27, there; proceeded to Portsmouth, and preached there on Friday. On Saturday morning he set out for Boston; but before he came to Newbury, where he had engaged to preach the next morning, he was importuned to preach by the way. The house not being large enough to contain the people, he preached in an open field. But having been infirm for several weeks, this so exhausted his strength, that when he came to Newbury he could not get out of the ferry-boat without the help of two men. In the evening, however, he recovered his spirits, and appeared with his usual cheerfulness. He went to his chamber at nine, his fixed time, which no company could divert him from, and slept better than he had done for some weeks before. He rose at four in the morning, September 30, and went into his closet; and his companion observed he was unusually long in private. He left his closet, returned to his companion, threw himself on the bed, and lay about ten minutes. Then he fell upon his knees, and prayed most fervently to God that if it was consistent with His will, he might that day finish his Master's work. He then desired his man to call Mr. Parsons, the clergyman, at whose house he was; but, in a minute, before Mr. Parsons could reach him, died, without a sigh or groan. On the news of his death, six gentlemen set out for Newbury, in order to bring his remains hither: but he could not be moved; so that his precious ashes must remain at Newbury. Hundreds would have gone from this town to attend his funeral, had they not expected he would have been interred here.... May this stroke be sanctified to the Church of God in general, and to this province in particular!"

II. 1. We are, in the second place, to take some view of his character. A little sketch of this was soon after published in the Boston Gazette; an extract of which is subjoined:—["Little can be said of him but what every friend to vital Christianity who has sat under his ministry will attest."] "In his public labors he has, for many years, astonished the world with his eloquence and devotion. With what divine pathos did he persuade the impenitent sinner to embrace the practice of piety and virtue! [Filled with the spirit of grace, he] spoke from the heart, and, with a fervency of zeal perhaps unequalled since the day of the Apostles, [adorned the truths he delivered with the most graceful charms of rhetoric and oratory.] From the pulpit he was unrivalled in the command of an ever-crowded auditory. Nor was he less agreeable and instructive in his private conversation; happy in a remarkable ease of address, willing to communicate, studious to edify. May the rising generation catch a spark of that flame which shone, with such distinguished luster, in the spirit and practice of this faithful servant of the most high God!"

2. A more particular, and equally just, character of him has appeared in one of the English papers. It may not be disagreeable to you to add the substance of this likewise:—"The character of this truly pious person must be [deeply] impressed on the heart of every friend to vital religion. In spite of a tender [and delicate] constitution, he continued to the last day of his life, preaching with a frequency and fervor that seemed to exceed the natural strength of the most robust. Being called to the exercise of his function at an age when most young men are only beginning to qualify themselves for it, he had not time to make a very considerable progress in the learned languages. But this defect was amply supplied by a lively and fertile genius, by fervent zeal, and by a forcible and most persuasive delivery. And though in the pulpit he often found it needful by "the terrors of the Lord" to "persuade men," he had nothing gloomy in his nature; being singularly cheerful, as well as charitable and tender-hearted. He was as ready to relieve the bodily as the spiritual necessities of those that applied to him. It ought also to be observed, that he constantly enforced upon his audience every moral duty; particularly industry in their several callings, and obedience to their superiors. He endeavored, by

the most extraordinary efforts of preaching, in different places, and even in the open fields, to rouse the lower class of people from the last degree of inattention and ignorance to a sense of religion. For this, and his other labors, the name of GEORGE WHITEFIELD will long be remembered with esteem and veneration."

3. That both these accounts are just and impartial, will readily be allowed; that is, as far as they go. But they go little farther than the outside of his character. They show you the preacher, but not the man, the Christian, the saint of God. May I be permitted to add a little on this head, from a personal knowledge of near forty years? Indeed, I am thoroughly sensible how difficult it is to speak on so delicate a subject; what prudence is required to avoid both extremes, to say neither too little nor too much! Nay, I know it is impossible to speak at all, to say either less or more, without incurring from some the former, from others the latter censure. Some will seriously think that too little is said; and others, that it is too much. But without attending to this, I will speak just what I know, before Him to whom we are all to give an account.

4. Mention has already been made of his unparalleled zeal, his indefatigable activity, his tender-heartedness to the afflicted, and charitableness toward the poor. But should we not likewise mention his deep *gratitude* to all whom God had used as instruments of good to him?—of whom he did not cease to speak in the most respectful manner, even to his dying day. Should we not mention, that he had a heart susceptible of the most generous and the most tender *friendship*? I have frequently thought that this, of all others, was the distinguishing part of his character. How few have we known of so kind a temper, of such large and flowing affections! Was it not principally by this, that the hearts of others were so strangely drawn and knit to him? Can anything but love beget love? This shone in his very countenance, and continually breathed in all his words, whether in public or private. Was it not this, which, quick and penetrating as lightning, flew from heart to heart? which gave that life to his sermons, his conversations, his letters? Ye are witnesses!

5. But away with the vile misconstruction of men of corrupt minds, who know of no love but what is earthly and sensual! Be it remembered, at the same time, that he was endued with the most nice and unblemished *modesty*. His office called him to converse very frequently and largely with women as well as men; and those of every age and condition. But his whole behavior towards them was a practical comment on that advice of St. Paul to Timothy: "Entreat the elder women as mothers, the younger as sisters, with all purity."

6. Meantime, how suitable to the friendliness of his spirit was the *frankness* and *openness* of his conversation!—although it was as far removed from rudeness on the one hand, as from guile [and disguise] on the other. Was not this frankness at once a fruit and a proof of his *courage* and *intrepidity*? Armed with these, he feared not the faces of men, but "used great plainness of speech" to persons of every rank and condition, high and low, rich and poor; endeavoring only "by manifestation of the truth to commend himself to every man's conscience in the sight of God."

7. Neither was he afraid of labor or pain, any more than of "what man [could] do unto him;" being equally

  Patient in bearing ill and doing well.

And this appeared in the *steadiness* wherewith he pursued whatever he undertook for his Master's sake. Witness one instance for all,—the Orphan-house in Georgia; which he began and perfected, in spite of all discouragements. Indeed, in whatever concerned himself he was pliant and flexible. In this case he was "easy to be entreated;" easy to be either convinced or persuaded. But he was immovable in the things of God, or wherever his conscience was concerned. None could persuade, any more than affright, him to vary, in the least point, from that *integrity* which was inseparable from his whole character, and regulated all his words and actions. Herein he did

  Stand as an iron pillar strong,
  And steadfast as a wall of brass.

8. If it be inquired what was the foundation of this integrity, or of his sincerity, courage, patience, and every other valuable and amiable quality; it is easy to give the answer. It was not the excellence of his natural temper, not the strength of his understanding; it was not the force of education; no, nor the advice of his friends: it was no other than faith in a bleeding Lord; "faith of the operation of God." It was "a lively hope of an inheritance incorruptible, undefiled, and that fadeth not away." It was "the love of God shed abroad in his heart by the Holy Ghost which was given unto him," filling his soul with tender, disinterested love to every child of man. From this source arose that torrent of eloquence which frequently bore down all before it; from this, that astonishing force of persuasion which the most hardened sinners could not resist. This it was which often made his "head as waters, and his eyes a fountain of tears." This it was which enabled him to pour out his soul in prayer, in a manner peculiar to himself, with such fullness and ease united together, with such strength and variety both of sentiment and expression.

9. I may close this head with observing what an honor it pleased God to put upon His faithful servant, by allowing him to declare His everlasting gospel in so many various countries, to such numbers of people, and with so great an effect on so many of their precious souls! Have we read or heard of any person since the Apostles, who testified the gospel of the grace of God through so widely extended a space, through so large a part of the habitable world? Have we read or heard of any person who called so many thousands, so many myriads, of sinners to repentance? Above all, have we read or heard of any who has been a blessed instrument in His hand of bringing so many sinners from "darkness to light, and from the power of Satan unto God?" It is true, were we to talk thus to the gay world, we should be judged to speak as barbarians. But *you* understand the language of the country to which you are going, and whither our dear friend is gone a little before us.

III. But how shall we improve this awful providence? This is the third thing which we have to consider. And the answer to this important question is easy (may God write it in all our hearts!). By keeping close to the grand doctrines which he delivered; and by drinking into his spirit.

1. And, first, let us keep close to the grand scriptural doctrines which he everywhere delivered. There are many doctrines of a less essential nature, with regard to which even the sincere children of God (such is the present weakness of human understanding) are and have been divided for many ages. In these we may think and let think; we may "agree to disagree." But, meantime, let us hold fast the essentials of "the faith which was once delivered to the saints;" and which this champion of God so strongly insisted on, at all times, and in all places!

2. His fundamental point was, "Give God all the glory of whatever is good in man;" and, "In the business of salvation, set Christ as high and man as low as possible." With this point, he and his friends at Oxford, the original Methodists, so called, set out. Their grand principle was, there is *no power* (by nature) and *no merit* in man. They insisted, all power to think, speak, or act aright, is in and from the Spirit of Christ; and all merit is (not in man, how high soever in grace, but merely) in the blood of Christ. So he and they taught: there is no power in man, till it is given him from above, to do one good work, to speak one good word, or to form one good desire. For it is not enough to say, all men are *sick of sin*: no, we are all *"dead* in trespasses and sins." It follows, that all the children of men are, "by nature, children of wrath." We are all "guilty before God," liable to death temporal and eternal.

3. And we are all helpless, both with regard to the power and to the guilt of sin. "For who can bring a clean thing out of an unclean?" None less than the Almighty. Who can raise those that are *dead*, spiritually dead in sin? None but He who raised us from the dust of the earth. But on what consideration will He do this? "Not for works of righteousness that we have done." "The dead cannot praise Thee, O Lord;" nor do anything for the sake of which they should be raised to life. Whatever, therefore, God does, He does it merely for the sake of His well-beloved Son: "He was wounded for our transgressions, He was bruised for our iniquities." He Himself "bore" all "our sins in His own body upon the tree." He "was delivered for our offences, and was raised again for our justification." Here then is the sole meritorious cause of every blessing we do or can enjoy; in particular of our pardon and acceptance with God, of our full and free justification. But by what means do we become interested in what Christ has done and suffered? "Not by works, lest any man should boast;" but by faith alone. "We conclude," says the Apostle, "that a man is justified by faith, without the works of the law." And "to as many as" thus "receive Him, giveth He power to become the sons of God, even to those that believe in His name; who are born, not of the will of man, but of God."

4. And "except a man be" thus "born again, he cannot see the kingdom of God." But all who are thus "born of the Spirit" have "the kingdom of God within them." Christ sets up His kingdom in their hearts; "righteousness, peace, and joy in the Holy Ghost." That "mind is in them, which was in Christ Jesus," enabling them to "walk as Christ also walked." His indwelling Spirit makes them both holy in heart, and "holy in all manner of conversation." But still, seeing all this is a free gift, through the righteousness and blood of Christ, there is eternally the same reason to remember, "He that glorieth, let him glory in the Lord."

5. You are not ignorant that these are the fundamental doctrines which he everywhere insisted on. And may they not be summed up, as it were, in two words,—the new birth, and justification by faith? These let us insist upon with all boldness, at all times, and in all places;—in public (those of us who are called thereto), and at all opportunities in private. Keep close to these good, old, unfashionable doctrines, how many soever contradict and blaspheme. Go on, my brethren, in the "name of the Lord, and in the power of His might." With all care and diligence, "keep that safe which is committed to your trust;" knowing that "heaven and earth shall pass away, but this truth shall not pass away."

6. But will it be sufficient to keep close to his doctrines, how pure soever they are? Is there not a point of still greater importance than this, namely, to drink into his spirit?— herein to be a follower of him, even as he was of Christ? Without this, the purity of our doctrines would only increase our condemnation. This, therefore, is the principal thing— to copy after his spirit. And allowing that in some points we must be content to admire what we cannot imitate; yet in many others we may, through the same free grace, be partakers of the same blessing. Conscious then of your own wants and of His bounteous love, who "giveth liberally and upbraids not," cry to Him that works all in all for a measure of the same precious faith; of the same zeal and activity; the same tender-heartedness, charitableness, bowels of mercies. Wrestle with God for some degree of the same grateful, friendly, affectionate temper; of the same openness, simplicity, and godly sincerity; "love without dissimulation." Wrestle on, till the power from on high works in you the same steady courage and patience; and above all, because it is the crown of all, the same invariable integrity!

7. Is there any other fruit of the grace of God with which he was eminently endowed, and the want of which among the children of God he frequently and passionately lamented? There is one, that is, catholic love; that sincere and tender affection which is due to all those who, we have reason to believe, are children of God by faith; in other words, all those, in every persuasion, who "fear God and work righteousness." He longed to see all who had "tasted of the good word," of a true catholic spirit; a word little understood, and still less experienced, by many who have it frequently in their mouth. Who is he that answers this character? Who is the man of a catholic spirit? One who loves as friends, as brethren in the Lord, as joint partakers of the present kingdom of heaven, and fellow heirs of His eternal kingdom, all, of whatever opinion, mode of worship, or congregation, who believe in the Lord Jesus; who love God and man; who, rejoicing to please and fearing to offend God, are careful to abstain from evil, and zealous of good works. He is a man of a truly catholic spirit, who bears all these continually upon his heart; who, having an unspeakable tenderness for their persons, and an earnest desire of their welfare, does not cease to commend them to God in prayer, as well as to plead their cause before

men; who speaks comfortably to them, and labors, by all his words, to strengthen their hands in God. He assists them to the uttermost of his power, in all things, spiritual and temporal; he is ready to "spend and be spent" for them; yea, "to lay down his life for his brethren."

8. How amiable a character is this! How desirable to every child of God! But why is it then so rarely found? How is it that there are so few instances of it? Indeed, supposing we have tasted of the love of God, how can any of us rest till it is our own? Why, there is a delicate device, whereby Satan persuades thousands that they may stop short of it and yet be guiltless. It is well if many here present are not in this "snare of the devil, taken captive at his will." "O yes," says one, "I have all this love for those I believe to be children of God; but I will never believe he is a child of God, who belongs to that vile congregation! Can he, do you think, be a child of God, who holds such detestable opinions? or he that joins in such senseless and superstitious, if not idolatrous, worship?" So we may justify ourselves in one sin by adding a second to it! We excuse the want of love in ourselves by laying the blame on others! To color our own devilish temper, we pronounce our brethren children of the devil! O beware of this!—and if you are already taken in the snare, escape out of it as soon as possible! Go and learn that truly catholic love which "is not rash," or hasty in judging; that love which "thinks no evil;" which "believes and hopes all things;" which makes all the allowances for others that we desire others should make for us! Then we shall take knowledge of the grace of God which is in every man, whatever be his opinion or mode of worship: then will all that fear God be near and dear unto us "in the bowels of Jesus Christ."

9. Was not this the spirit of our dear friend? And why should it not be ours? O Thou God of love, how long shall Thy people be a by-word among the Heathen? How long shall they laugh us to scorn, and say, "See how *these* Christians love one another!" When wilt Thou roll away our reproach? Shall the sword devour for ever? How long will it be ere Thou bid Thy people return from "following each other?" Now, at least, "let all the people stand still, and pursue after their brethren no more!" But what ever others do, let all of us, my brethren, hear the voice of him that, being dead, yet speaks! Suppose ye hear him say, "Now, at least, be ye followers of me as I was of Christ! Let brother "no more lift up sword against brother, neither know ye war any more!" Rather put ye on, as the elect of God, bowels of mercies, humbleness of mild, brotherly kindness, gentleness, long-suffering, forbearing one another in love. Let the time past suffice for strife, envy, contention; for biting and devouring one another. Blessed be God, that ye have not long ago been consumed one of another! From henceforth hold ye the unity of the Spirit in the bond of peace."

10. O God, with Thee no word is impossible! Thou does whatsoever please Thee! O that Thou would cause the mantle of Thy prophet, whom Thou hast taken up, now to fall upon us that remain! "Where is the Lord God of Elijah?" Let his spirit rest upon these Thy servants! Show Thou art the God that answers by fire! Let the fire of Thy love fall on every heart! And because we love Thee, let us love one another with a "love stronger than death!" Take away from us "all anger, and wrath, and bitterness; all clamor and evil speaking!" Let Thy Spirit so rest upon us, that from this hour we may be "kind to each other, tender-hearted, forgiving one another, even as God, for Christ's sake hath forgiven us!"

An Hymn

1 Servant of God, well done!
Thy glorious warfare's past;
The battle's fought, the race is won,
And thou art crown'd at last;
Of all thy heart's desire
Triumphantly possess'd,
Lodged by the ministerial choir
In thy Redeemer's breast.
2 In condescending love,
Thy ceaseless prayer He heard;
And bade thee suddenly remove
To thy complete reward:
Ready to bring the peace,
Thy beauteous feet were shod,
When mercy sign'd thy soul's release,
And caught thee up to God.
3 With saints enthroned on high,
Thou dost thy Lord proclaim,
And still *To God salvation* cry,
Salvation to the Lamb!
O happy, happy soul!
In ecstasies of praise,
Long as eternal ages roll,
Thou seest thy Saviour's face!
4 Redeem'd from earth and pain,
Ah! when shall we ascend,
And all in Jesu's presence reign
With our translated friend?
Come, Lord, and quickly come!
And, when in Thee complete,
Receive Thy longing servants home,
To triumph at Thy feet!

SECOND SERIES

54.* ON ETERNITY

"From everlasting to everlasting thou art God."

Psalm 90:2

1. I would fain speak of that awful subject,—eternity. But how can we grasp it in our thought? It is so vast, that the narrow mind of man is utterly unable to comprehend it. But does it not bear some affinity to another incomprehensible thing,—immensity? May not space, though an unsubstantial thing, be compared with another unsubstantial thing,—duration? But what is immensity? It is boundless space. And what is eternity? It is boundless duration.
2. Eternity has generally been considered as divisible into two parts; which have been termed eternity *a parte ante,* and

---

* (text from the 1872 edition)

eternity *a parte post*,—that is, in plain English, that eternity which is past, and that eternity which is to come. And does there not seem to be an intimation of this distinction in the text? "Thou art God from everlasting:"—Here is an expression of that eternity which is past: "To everlasting:"—Here is an expression of that eternity which is to come. Perhaps, indeed, some may think it is not strictly proper to say, there is an eternity that is past. But the meaning is easily understood: We mean thereby duration which had no beginning; as by eternity to come, we mean that duration which will have no end.

3. It is God alone who (to use the exalted language of Scripture) "inhabiteth eternity," in both these senses. The great Creator alone (not any of his creatures) is "from everlasting to everlasting:" His duration alone, as it had no beginning, so it cannot have any end. On this consideration it is, that one speaks thus, in addressing Immanuel, God with us:—

> Hail, God the Son, with glory crown'd
> Ere time began to be;
> Throned with thy Sire through half the round
> Of wide eternity!

And again:—

> Hail, God the Son, with glory crown'd
> Ere time shall cease to be;
> Throned with the Father through the round
> Of whole eternity!

4. "Ere time began to be."—But what is time? It is not easy to say, as frequently as we have had the word in our mouth. We know not what it properly is. We cannot well tell how to define it. But is it not, in some sense, a fragment of eternity, broken off at both ends?—that portion of duration which commenced when the world began, which will continue as long as this world endures, and then expire for ever?—that portion of it, which is at present measured by the revolution of the sun and planets; lying (so to speak) between two eternities, that which is past, and that which is to come. But as soon as the heavens and the earth flee away from the face of Him that sitteth on the great white throne, time will be no more; but sink for ever into the ocean of eternity!

5. But by what means can a mortal man, the creature of a day, form any idea of eternity? What can we find within the compass of nature to illustrate it by? With what comparison shall we compare it? What is there that bears any resemblance to it? Does there not seem to be some sort of analogy between boundless duration and boundless space? The great Creator, the infinite Spirit, inhabits both the one and the other. This is one of his peculiar prerogatives: "Do not I fill heaven and earth, saith the Lord?"—yea, not only the utmost regions of creation, but all the expanse of boundless space! Meantime, how many of the children of men may say,

> Lo, on a narrow neck of land,
> 'Midst two unbounded seas I stand,
> Secure, insensible!
> A point of time, a moments' space,
> Removes me to that heavenly place,
> Or shuts me up in hell!

6. But leaving one of these unbounded seas to the Father of eternity, to whom alone duration without beginning belongs, let us turn our thoughts on duration without end. This is not an incommunicable attribute of the great Creator; but he has been graciously pleased to make innumerable multitudes of his creatures partakers of it. He has imparted this not only to angels, and archangels, and all the companies of heaven, who are not intended to die, but to glorify him, and live in his presences for ever; but also to the inhabitants of the earth, who dwell in houses of clay. Their bodies, indeed, are "crushed before the moth;" but their souls will never die, God made them, as an ancient writer speaks, to be "pictures of his own eternity." Indeed all spirits, we have reason to believe, are clothed with immortality; having no inward principle of corruption, and being liable to no external violence.

7. Perhaps we may go a step farther still: Is not matter itself, as well as spirit, in one sense eternal? Not indeed *a parte ante*, as some senseless philosophers, both ancient and modern, have dreamed. Not that anything had existed from eternity; seeing, if so, it must be God; yea, it must by the One God; for it is impossible there should be two Gods, or two Eternals. But although nothing beside the great God can have existed from everlasting,—none else can be eternal *a parte ante*, yet there is no absurdity in supposing that all creatures are eternal *a parte post*. All matter indeed is continually changing, and that into ten thousand forms; but that it is changeable, does in nowise imply that it is perishable. The substance may remain one and the same, though under innumerable different forms. It is very possible any portion of matter may be resolved into the atoms of which it was originally composed: But what reason have we to believe that one of these atoms ever was, or ever will be, annihilated? It never can, unless by the uncontrollable power of its almighty Creator. And is it probable that ever He will exert this power in unmaking any of the things that he hath made? In this also, God is not "a son of man that he should repent." Indeed, every creature under heaven does, and must, continually change its form, which we can now easily account for; as it clearly appears, from late discoveries, that ethereal fire enters into the composition of every part of the creation. Now, this is essentially *edax rerum*: It is the universal menstruum, the *discohere* of all things under the sun. By the force of this, even the strongest, the firmest bodies are dissolved. It appears from the experiment repeatedly made by the great Lord Bacon, that even diamonds, by a high degree of heat, may be turned into dust: and that, in a still higher degree, (strange as it may seem,) they will totally flame away. Yea, by this the heavens themselves will be dissolved; "the elements shall melt with fervent heat." But they will be only dissolved, not destroyed; they will belt, but they will not perish. Though they lose their present form, yet not a particle of them will ever lose its existence; but every atom of them will remain, under one form or other, to all eternity.

8. But still we should inquire, What is this eternity? How shall we pour any light upon this abstruse subject? It cannot be the object of our understanding. And with what comparison shall we compare it? How infinitely does it transcend all these! What are any temporal things, placed in

comparison with those that are eternal? What is the duration of the longlived oak, of the ancient castle, of Trajan's Pillar, of Pompey's Amphitheatre? What is the antiquity of the Tuscan Urns, though probably older than the foundation of Rome; yea, of the Pyramids of Egypt, suppose they have remained upwards of three thousand years;—when laid in the balance with eternity? It vanishes into nothing. Nay, what is the duration of "the everlasting hills," figuratively so called, which have remained ever since the general deluge, if not from the foundation of the world, in comparison of eternity? No more than an insignificant cipher. Go farther yet: Consider the duration, from the creation of the first-born sons of God, of Michael the Archangel in particular, to the hour when he shall be commissioned to sound his trumpet, and to utter his mighty voice through the vault of heaven, "Arise, ye dead, and come to judgement!" Is it not a moment, a point, a nothing, in comparison of unfathomable eternity? Add to this a thousand, a million of years, add a million of million of ages, "before the mountains were brought forth, or the earth and the round world were made:" What is all this in comparison of that eternity which is past? Is it not less, infinitely less, than a single drop of water to the whole ocean?—yea, immeasurably less than a day, an hour, a moment, to a million of ages! Go back a thousand millions still; yet you are no nearer the beginning of eternity.

9. Are we able to form a more adequate conception of eternity to come? In order to this, let us compare it with the several degrees of duration which we are acquainted with:— An ephemeron fly lives six hours; from six in the evening, to twelve. This is a short life compared with that of a man, which continues threescore or fourscore years; and this itself is short, if it be compared to the nine hundred and sixty-nine years of Methuselah. Yet what are these years, yea, all that have succeeded each other, from the time that the heavens, and the earth were erected, to the time when the heavens shall pass away, and the earth with the works of it shall be burned up, if we compare it to the length of that duration which never shall have an end?

10. In order to illustrate this, a late author has repeated that striking thought of St. Cyprian:—"Suppose there were a ball of sand as large as the globe of earth: suppose a grain of this sand were to be annihilated, reduced to nothing, in a thousand years: yet that whole space of duration, wherein this ball would be annihilating, at the rate of one grain in a thousand years, would bear infinitely less proportion to eternity, duration without end, than a single grain of sand would bear to all the mass!"

11. To infix this important point the more deeply in your mind, consider another comparison:—Suppose the ocean to be so enlarged, as to include all the space between the earth and the starry heavens. Suppose a drop of this were to be annihilated once in a thousand years; yet that whole space of duration, wherein this ocean would be annihilating, at the rate of one drop in a thousand years, would be infinitely less in proportion to eternity, than one drop of water to that whole ocean.

Look then at those immortal spirits, whether they are in this or the other world. When they shall have lived thousands of thousands of years, yea, millions of millions of ages, their duration will be but just begun: They will be only upon the threshold of eternity!

12. But besides this division of eternity into that which is past, and that which is to come, there is another division of eternity, which is of unspeakable importance: That which is to come, as it relates to immortal spirits, is either a happy or a miserable eternity.

13. See the spirits of the righteous that are already praising God in a happy eternity! We are ready to say, How short will it appear to those who drink of the rivers of pleasure at God's right hand! We are ready to cry out,

> A day without night
> They dwell in his sight,
> And eternity seems as a day!

But this is only speaking after the manner of men: For the measures of long and short are only applicable to time which admits of bound, and not to unbounded duration. This roles on (according to our low conceptions) with unutterable, inconceivable swiftness; if one would not rather say, it does not roll or move at all, but is one still immovable ocean.; For the inhabitants of heaven "rest not day and night," but continually cry, "Holy, holy, holy, is the Lord, the God, the Almighty, who saw, and who is, and who is to come!" And when millions of millions of ages are elapsed, their eternity is but just begun.

14. On the other hand, in what a condition are those immortal spirits who have made choice of a miserable eternity! I say, made choice; for it is impossible this should be the lot of any creature but by his own act and deed. The day is coming when every soul will be constrained to acknowledge, in the sight of men and angels,

> No dire decree of thine did seal
> Or fix the unalterable doom
> Consign my unborn soul to hell,
> Or damn me from my mother's womb.

In what condition will such a spirit be after the sentence is executed, "Depart, ye cursed, into everlasting fire, prepared for the devil and his angels!" Suppose him to be just now plunged into "the lake of fire burning with brimstone," where "they have no rest, day or night, but the smoke of their torment ascendeth up for ever and ever." "For ever and ever!" Why, if we were only to be chained down one day, yea, one hour, in a lake of fire, how amazing long would one day or one hour appear! I know not if it would not seem as a thousand years. But (astonishing thought!) after thousands of thousands, he has but just tasted of his bitter cup! After millions, it will be no nearer the end than it was the moment it began!

15. What then is he—how foolish, how mad, in how unutterable a degree of distraction—who, seeming to have the understanding of a man, deliberately prefers temporal things to eternal? who (allowing that absurd, impossible opposition, that wickedness is happiness,—a supposition utterly contrary to all reason, as well as to matter fact) prefers the happiness of a year, say a thousand years, to the happiness of eternity, in comparison of which, a thousand ages are infinitely less than a year, a day, a moment? especially when

we take this into the consideration, (which, indeed should never be forgotten,) that the refusing a happy eternity, implies the choosing of a miserable eternity: For there is not, cannot be, any medium between everlasting joy and everlasting pain. It is a vain thought which some have entertained, that death will put an end to neither the one nor the other; it will only alter the manner of their existence. But when the body "returns to the dust as it was, the spirit will return to God that gave it." Therefore, at the moment of death, it must be unspeakably happy, or unspeakably miserable: And that misery will *never* end.

> *Never!* Where sinks the soul at that dread sound?
> Into a gulf how dark, and how profound!

How often would he who had made the wretched choice wish for the death both of his soul and body! It is not impossible he might pray in some such manner as Dr. Young supposes:

> When I have writhed ten thousand years in fire,
> Ten thousand thousand, let me then expire!

16. Yet this unspeakable folly, this unutterable madness, of preferring present things to eternal, is the disease of every man born into the world, while in his natural state. For such is the constitution of our nature, that as the eye sees only such a portion of space at once, so the mind sees only such a portion of time at once. And as all the space that lies beyond that compass is invisible to the mind. So that we do not perceive either the space or the time which is at a distance from us. The eye sees distinctly the space that is near it, with the objects which it contains: In like manner, the mind sees distinctly those objects which are within such a distance of time. The eye does not see the beauties of China: They are at too great a distance: There is too great a space between us and them: There fore we are not affected by them. They are as nothing to us: It is just the same to us as if they had no being. For the same reason, the mind does not see either the beauties or the terrors of eternity. We are not at all affected by them, because they are so distant from us. On this account it is, that they appear to us as nothing: just as if they had no existence. Meantime, we are wholly taken up with things present, whether in time or space; and things appear less and less, as they are more and more distant from us, either in one respect or the other. And so it must be; such is the constitution of our nature; till nature is changed by almighty grace. but this is no manner of excuse for those who continue in their natural blindness to futurity; because a remedy for it is provided, which is found by all that seek it: Yea, it is freely given to all that sincerely ask it.

17. This remedy is faith. I do not mean that which is the faith of a Heathen, who believes that there is a God, and that he is a rewarder of them that diligently seek him; but that which is defined by the Apostle, "an evidence," or conviction "of things not seen," a divine evidence and conviction of the invisible and eternal world. This alone opens the eyes of the understanding, to see God and the things of God. This, as it were, takes away, or renders transparent, the impenetrable veil,

> Which hangs 'twixt mortal and immortal being.

When

> Faith lends its realizing light,

> The clouds disperse, the shadows fly;
> The invisible appears in sight,
> And God is seen by mortal eye.

Accordingly, a believer, in the scriptural sense, lives in eternity, and walks in eternity. His prospect is enlarged: His view is not any longer bounded by present things: No, nor by an earthly hemisphere; though it were, as Milton speaks, "ten-fold the length of this terrene." Faith places the unseen, the eternal world continually before his face. consequently, he looks not at "the things that are seen;"—

> Wealth, honour, pleasure, or what else
> This short-enduring world can give;

these are not his aim, the object of his pursuit, his desire or happiness;—but at "the things that are not seen;" at the favour, the image, and the glory of God; as well knowing that "the things which are seen are temporal,"—a vapour, a shadow, a dream that vanishes away; whereas "the things that are not seen are eternal;" real, solid, unchangeable.

18. What, then, can be a fitter employment for a wise man than to meditate upon these things? frequently to expand his thoughts "beyond the bounds of this diurnal sphere," and to expatiate above even the starry heavens, in the field of eternity? What a means might it be to confirm his contempt of the poor, little things of earth! When a man of huge possessions was boasting to his friend of the largeness of his estate, Socrates desired him to bring a map of the earth, and to point out Attica therein. When this was done, (although not very easily, as it was a small country,) he next desired Alcibiades to point out his own estate therein. When he could not do this, it was easy to observe how trifling the possessions were in which he so prided himself, in comparison of the whole earth. How applicable is this to the present case! Does any one value himself on his earthly possessions? Alas, what is the whole globe of earth to the infinity of space! A mere speck of creation. And what is the life of man, yea, the duration of the earth itself, but a speck of time, if it be compared to the length of eternity! Think of this: Let it sink into your thought, till you have some conception, however imperfect, of that

> Boundless, fathomless abyss,
> Without a bottom or a shore.

19. But if naked eternity, so to speak, be so vast, so astonishing an abject, as even to overwhelm your thought, how does it still enlarge the idea to behold it clothed with either happiness or misery! eternal bliss or pain! everlasting happiness, or everlasting misery! One would think it would swallow up every other thought in every reasonable creature. Allow me only this,—"Thou art on the brink of either a happy or miserable eternity; thy Creator bids thee now stretch out thy hand either to the one or the other;"—and one would imagine no rational creature could think on anything else. One would suppose that this single point would engross his whole attention. Certainly it ought so to do: Certainly, if these things are so, there can be but one thing needful. O let you and I, at least, whatever others do, choose that better part which shall never be taken away from us!

20. Before I close this subject, permit me to touch upon two remarkable passages in the Psalms, (one in the eighth, the other in the hundred and forty-forth,) which bear a near relation to it. The former is, "When I consider thy heavens, the work of thy fingers, the moon and the stars, which thou hast ordained; what is man, that thou art mindful of him? or the son of man, that thou visitest him?" Here man is considered as a cipher, a point, compared to immensity. The latter is, "Lord, what is man, that thou hast such respect unto him? Man is like a thing of nought His time passeth away like a shadow!" In the new translation the words are stronger still: "What is man, that thou takest knowledge of him!" Here the Psalmist seems to consider the life of man as a moment, a nothing, compared to eternity. Is not the purport of the former, "How can He that filleth heaven and earth take knowledge of such an atom as man? How is it that he is not utterly lost in the immensity of God's works?" Is not the purport of the latter, "How can He that inhabiteth eternity stoop to regard the creature of a day,—one whose life passeth away like a shadow?" Is not this a thought which has struck many serious minds, as well as it did David's, and created a kind of fear arise from a kind of supposition that God is such an one as ourselves? If we consider boundless space, or boundless duration, we shrink into nothing before it. But God is not a man. A day, and million of ages, are the same with him. Therefore, there is the same disproportion between Him and any finite being, as between Him and the creature of a day. Therefore, whenever that thought recurs, whenever you are tempted to fear lest you should be forgotten before the immense, the eternal God, remember that nothing is little or great, that no duration is long or short, before Him. Remember that God *ita praesidet singulis sicut universis, et universis sicut singulis.* That he "presides over every individual as over the universe; and the universe, as over each individual." So that you may boldly say,

> Father, how wide thy glories shine,
> Lord of the universe—and mine!
> Thy goodness watches o'er the whole,
> As all the world were but one soul;
> Yet counts my every sacred hair,
> As I remain'd thy single care!

55.* ON THE TRINITY

ADVERTISEMENT*

"There are three that bear record in heaven, the Father, the Word, and the Holy Ghost: And these three are one."
1 John 5:7.

1. Whatsoever the generality of people may think, it is certain that opinion is not religion: No, not right opinion; assent to one, or to ten thousand truths. There is a wide difference between them: Even right opinion is as distant from religion as the east is from the west. Persons may be quite right in their opinions, and yet have no religion at all; and, on the other hand, persons may be truly religious, who hold many wrong opinions. Can any one possibly doubt of this, while there are Romanists in the world? For who can deny, not only that many of them formerly have been truly religious, as Thomas a Kempis, Gregory Lopez, and the Marquis de Renty; but that many of them, even at this day, are real inward Christians? And yet what a heap of erroneous opinions do they hold, delivered by tradition from their fathers! Nay, who can doubt of it while there are Calvinists in the world,—assertors of absolute predestination? For who will dare to affirm that none of these are truly religious men? Not only many of them in the last century were burning and shining lights, but many of them are now real Christians, loving God and all mankind. And yet what are all the absurd opinions of all the Romanists in the world, compared to that one, that the God of love, the wise, just, merciful Father of the spirits of all flesh, has, from all eternity, fixed an absolute, unchangeable, irresistible, decree, that part of all mankind shall be saved, do what they will; and the rest damned, do what they can!

2. Hence, we cannot but infer, that there are ten thousand mistakes which may consist with real religion; with regard to which every candid, considerate man will think and let think. But there are some truths more important than others. It seems there are some which are of deep importance. I do not term them *fundamental* truths; because that is an ambiguous word: And hence there have been so many warm disputes about the number of *fundamentals.* But surely there are some which it nearly concerns us to know, as having a close connexion with vital religion. And doubtless we may rank among these that

contained in the words above cited: There are three that bear record in heaven, the Father, the Word, and the Holy Ghost: And these three are one.

3. I do not mean that it is of importance to believe this or that *explication* of these words. I know not that any well judging man would attempt to explain them at all. One of the best tracts which that great man, Dean Swift, ever wrote, was his Sermon upon the Trinity. Herein he shows, that all who endeavored to explain it at all, have utterly lost their way; have, above all other persons hurt the cause which they intended to promote; having only, as Job speaks, "darkened counsel by words without knowledge." It was in an evil hour that these explainers began their fruitless work I insist upon no explication at all; no, not even on the best I ever saw; I mean, that which is given us in the creed commonly ascribed to Athanasius. I am far from saying, he who does not assent to this shall without doubt perish everlastingly." For the sake of that and another clause, I, for some time, scrupled subscribing to that creed; till I considered (1.) That these sentences only relate to *wilful,* not involuntary, unbelievers; to those who, having all the means of knowing the truth, nevertheless obstinately reject it: (2.) that they relate only to the *substance* of the doctrine there delivered; not the philosophical *illustrations* of it.

4. I dare not insist upon any one's using the word Trinity, or Person. I use them myself without any scruple, because I know of none better: But if any man has any scruple

concerning them, who shall constrain him to use them? I cannot: Much less would I burn a man alive, and that with moist, green wood, for saying, Though I believe the Father is God, the Son is God, and the Holy Ghost is God; yet I scruple using the words *Trinity* and *Persons*, because I do not find those terms in the Bible." These are the words which merciful John Calvin cites as wrote by Servitus in a letter to himself. I would insist only on the direct words, unexplained, just as they lie in the text: "There are three that bear record in heaven, the Father, the Word, and the Holy Ghost: And these three are one."

5. "As they lie in the text:"—but here arises a question: Is that text genuine? Was it originally written by the Apostle, or inserted in later ages? Many have doubted of this; and, in particular, the great light of the Christian church, lately removed to the Church above, Bengelius,—the most pious, the most judicious, and the most laborious, of all the modern Commentators on the New Testament. For some time he stood in doubt of its authenticity, because it is wanting in many of the ancient copies. But his doubts were removed by three considerations: (1.) That though it is wanting in many copies, yet it is found in more; and those copies of the greatest authority:—(2.) That it is cited by a whole gain of ancient writers, from the time of St. John to that of Constantine. This argument is conclusive: For they could not have cited it, had it not been in the sacred canon:—(3.) That we can easily account for its being, after that time, wanting in many copies, when we remember that Constantine's successor was a zealous Arian, who used every means to promote his bad cause, to spread Arianism throughout the empire; in particular the erasing this text out of as many copies as fell into his hands. And he so far prevailed, that the age in which he lived is commonly styled, *Seculum Aranium,*—"the Arian age;" there being then only one eminent man who opposed him at the peril of his life. So that it was a proverb, *Athanasius contra mundum*: "Athanasius against the world."

6. But it is objected: "Whatever becomes of the text, we cannot believe what we cannot comprehend. When, therefore, you require us to believe mysteries, we pray you to have us excused."

Here is a two-fold mistake: (1.) We do not require you to believe any mystery in this; whereas; you suppose the contrary. But, (2.) You do already believe many things which you cannot comprehend.

7. To begin with the latter: You do already believe many things which you cannot comprehend. For you believe there is a *sun* over your head. But whether he stands still in the midst of his system, or not only revolves on his own axis, but rejoiceth as a giant to run his course; you cannot comprehend either one or the other: *How* he moves, or *how* he rests. By what power, what natural, mechanical power, is he upheld in the fluid either? You cannot deny the fact: Yet you cannot account for it, so as you satisfy any rational inquirer. You may indeed give us the hypothesis of Ptolemy, Tycho Brahe, Copernicus, and twenty more. I have read them over and over: I am sick of them; I care not three straws for them all.

> Each new solution but once more affords
> New change of terms, and scaffolding of words:

> In other garb my question I receive,
> And take my doubt the very same I gave.

Still I insist, the *fact* you believe, you cannot deny; but the *manner* you cannot comprehend.

8. You believe there is such a thing as *light*, whether flowing from the sun, or any other luminous body; but you cannot comprehend either its nature. or the manner wherein it flows. How does it move from Jupiter to the earth in eight minutes; two hundred thousand miles in a moment? How do the rays of the candle, brought into the room, instantly disperse into every corner? Again: Here are three candles, yet there is but one light. I explain this, and I will explain the Three-One God.

9. You believe there is such a thing as *air*. It both covers you as a garment, and,

> Wide interfused,
> Embraces round this florid earth.

But can you comprehend how? Can you give me a satisfactory account of its nature, or the cause of its properties? Think only of one, its elasticity: Can you account for this? It may be owing to electric fire attached to each particle of it; it may not; and neither you nor I can tell. But if we will not breathe it till we can comprehend it, our life is very near its period.

10. You believe there is such a thing as earth. Here you fix your foot upon it: You are supported by it. But do you comprehend what it is that supports the earth? "O, an elephant, says a Malabarian philosopher "and a bull supports him." But what supports the bull? The Indian and the Briton are equally at a loss for an answer. We know it is God that "spreadeth the north over the empty space, and hangeth the earth upon nothing. This is the fact. But how? Who can account for this? Perhaps angelic but not human creatures. I know what is plausibly said concerning the powers of projection and attraction. But spin as fine as we can, matter of fact sweeps away our cobweb hypothesis. Connect the force of projection and attraction how you can, they will never produce a circular motion. The moment the projected steel comes within the attraction of the magnet, it does not form a curve, but drops down.

11. You believe you have a *soul*. "Hold there," says the Doctor; I believe no such thing. "If *you* have an immaterial soul so have the brutes too." I will not quarrel with any that think they have; nay, I wish he could prove it: And surely I would rather allow *them* souls, than I would give up my own. In this I cordially concur in the sentiment of the honest Heathen. *Si erro, libenter erro; et me redargui valde recusem.* "If I err, I err willingly; and I vehemently refuse to be convinced of it." And I trust most of those who do not belie a Trinity are of the same mind. Permit me then to go on. You believe you have a soul connected with this house of clay. But can you comprehend how? What are the ties that unite the heavenly flame with the earthly clod? You understand just nothing of the matter. So it is; but how none can tell.

12. You surely believe you have a *body*, together with your soul, and that each is dependent on the other. Run only a thorn into your hand; immediately pain is felt in your soul. On the other side is shame felt in your soul? Instantly a blush

overspreads your cheek. Does the soul feel fear or violent anger? Presently the body trembles. These also are facts which you cannot deny; nor can you account for them.

13. I bring but one instance more: At the command of your soul, your hand is lifted up. But who is able to account for this? For the connexion between the act of the mind, and the outward actions? Nay, who can account for *muscular motion* at all; in any instance of it whatever? When one of the most ingenious Physicians in England had finished his lecture upon that head, he added, Now, gentlemen, I have told you all the discoveries of our enlightened age; and now, if you understand one jot of the matter, you understand more than I do." The short of the matter is this: Those who will not believe anything but what they can comprehend, must not believe that there is a sun in the firmament; that there is light shining around them; that there is air, though it encompasses them on every side; that there is any earth, though they stand upon it. They must not believe they have a soul; no, nor that they have a body.

14. But, secondly, as strange as it may seem. in requiring you to believe, "there arc three that bear record in heaven the Father, the Word, and the Holy Ghost: And these three are one;" you are not required to believe any mystery. Nay, that, great and good man, Dr. Peter Browne, sometime Bishop of Cork, has proved at large that the Bible does not require you to believe any mystery at all. Thee Bible barely requires you to believe such facts; not the manner of them. Now the mystery does not lie in the *fact*, but altogether in the manner. For instance: God said, let there be light: And there was light." I believe it: I believe the plain *fact*. There is no mystery at all in this. The mystery lies in the *manner* of it. But of this I believe nothing at all; nor does God require it of me.

Again: "The Word was made flesh." I Believe this fact also. There is no mystery in it; but as to the *manner how* he was made flesh, wherein the mystery lies, I know nothing about it; I believe nothing about it: It is no more the object of my faith, than it is of my understanding.

15. To apply this to the case before us: There are three that bear record in heaven: And these three are One. I believe this *fact* also, (if I may use the expression,) that God is Three and One. But the *manner how* I do not comprehend and I do not believe it. Now in this, in the *manner*, lies the mystery; and so it may; I have no concern with it: It is no object of my faith: I believe just so much as God has revealed, and no more. But this, the *manner*, he has not revealed; therefore, I believe nothing about it. But would it not be absurd in me to deny the fact, because I do not understand the manner? That is, to reject *what God has revealed*, because I do not comprehend *what he has not revealed*.

16. This is a point much to be observed. There are many things "which eye hath not seen, nor ear heard, neither hath it entered into the heart of man to conceive. Part of these God Hath "revealed to us by his Spirit:"— *"Revealed;"* that is, unveiled, uncovered: That part he requires us to believe. Part of them he has not revealed: That we need not, and indeed cannot, believe: It is far above, out of our sight.

Now, where is the wisdom of rejecting what is revealed, because we do not understand what is not revealed? of denying the *fact* which God has unveiled, because we cannot see the *manner*, which is veiled still?

17. Especially when we consider that what God has been pleased to reveal upon his head, is far from being a point of indifference, is a truth of the last importance. It enters into the very heart of Christianity: It lies at the heart of all vital religion.

Unless these Three are One, how can "all men honour the Son, even as they honour the Father?" "I know not what to do," says Socinus in a letter to his friend, with my untoward followers: They will not worship Jesus Christ. I tell them it is written, 'Let all the angels of God worship him.' They answer, However that be, if he is not God, we dare not worship him. For 'it is written, Thou shalt worship the lord thy God, and him only shalt thou serve.' "

But the thing, which I here particularly mean is this: The knowledge of the Three-One God is interwoven with all true Christian faith; with all vital religion.

I do not say that every real Christian can say with the Marquis de Renty, "I bear about with me continually an experimental verity, and a plenitude of the presence of the ever-blessed Trinity."I apprehend this is not the experience of babes," but, rather, "fathers in Christ."

But I know not how any one can be a Christian believer till he "hath," as St. John speaks, "the witness in himself;" till "the Spirit of God witnesses with his spirit, that he is a child of God;" that is, in effect, till God the holy Ghost witnesses that God the Father has accepted him through the merits of God the Son: And, having this witness, he honours the Son, and the blessed Spirit, "even as he honours the Father."

18. Not that every Christian believer *adverts* to this; perhaps, at first, not one in twenty: But if you ask any of them a few questions, you will easily find it is implied in what he believes. Therefore, I do not see how it is possible for any to have vital religion who denies that these Three are one. And all my hope for them is, not that they will he saved during their unbelief, (unless on the footing of honest Heathens, upon the plea of invincible ignorance,) but that God, before they go hence, "will bring them to the knowledge of the truth."

56*. God's Approbation of His Works

"And God saw every thing that he had made, and, behold, it was very good."

Gen. 1:31.

1. When God created the heavens and the earth, and all that is therein, at the conclusion of each day's work it is said, "And God saw that it was good." Whatever was created was good in its kind; suited to the end for which it was designed; adapted to promote the good of the whole and the glory of the great Creator. This sentence it pleased God to pass with regard to each particular creature. But there is a remarkable variation of the expression, with regard to all the parts of the

---

universe, taken in connection with each other, and constituting one system: "And God saw everything that he had made, and, behold, it was very good."

2. How small a part of this great work of God is man able to understand! But it is our duty to contemplate what he has wrought, and to understand as much of it as we are able. For "the merciful Lord," as the Psalmist observes, "hath so done his marvellous works" of creation, as well as of providence, "that they ought to be had in remembrance" by all that fear him; which they cannot well be, unless they are understood. Let us, then, by the assistance of that Spirit who giveth unto man understanding, endeavour to take a general survey of the works which God made in this lower world, as they were before they were disordered and depraved in consequence of the sin of man: We shall then easily see, that as every creature was *good* in its primeval state; so, when all were compacted in one general system, "behold, they were very good." I do not remember to have seen any attempt of this kind, unless in that truly excellent poem, (termed by Mr. Hutchinson, "That wicked farce!") Milton's "Paradise Lost."

I. 1. "In the beginning God created the matter of the heavens and the earth." (So the words, as a great man observes, may properly be translated.) He first created the four elements, out of which the whole universe was composed; earth, water, air, and fire, all mingled together in one common mass. The grossest parts of this, the earth and water, were utterly without form, till God infused a principle of motion, commanding the air to move "upon the face of the waters." In the next place, "the Lord God said, Let there be light: And there was light." Here were the four constituent parts of the universe; the true, original, simple elements. They were all essentially distinct from each other; and yet so intimately mixed together, in all compound bodies, that we cannot find any, be it ever so minute, which does not contain them all.

2. "And God saw that" every one of these "was good;" was perfect in its kind. The earth was good. The whole surface of it was beautiful in a high degree. To make it more agreeable,

> He clothed
> The universal face with pleasant green.

He adorned it with flowers of every hue, and with shrubs and trees of every kind. And every part was fertile as well as beautiful; it was no way deformed by rough or ragged rocks; it did not shock the view with horrid precipices, huge chasms, or dreary caverns; with deep, impassable morasses, or deserts of barren sand. But we have not any authority to say, with some learned and ingenious authors, that there were no mountains on the original earth, no unevenness on its surface. It is not easy to reconcile this hypothesis with those words of Moses: "The waters prevailed; and all the high hills that were under the whole heaven were covered. Fifteen cubits upward" above the highest "did the waters prevail; and the mountains were covered." (Gen. 7:19, 20.) We have no reason to believe that these mountains were produced by the deluge itself: Not the least intimation of this is given: Therefore, we cannot doubt but they existed before it.—Indeed, they answered many excellent purposes, besides greatly increasing the beauty of the creation, by a variety of prospects, which had been totally lost had the earth been one extended plain. Yet we need not suppose their sides were abrupt, or difficult of ascent. It is highly probable that they rose and fell by almost insensible degrees.

3. As to the internal parts of the earth, even to this day, we have scarce any knowledge of them. Many have supposed the centre of the globe to be surrounded with an abyss of fire. Many others have imagined it to be encompassed with an abyss of water; which they supposed to be termed in Scripture, "the great deep;" (Gen. 7:11;) all the fountains of which were broken up, in order to the General Deluge. But, however this was, we are sure all things were disposed therein with the most perfect order and harmony. Hence there were no agitations within the bowels of the globe, no violent convulsions, no concussions of the earth, no earthquakes; but all was unmoved as the pillars of heaven! There were then no such things as eruptions of fire; there were no volcanoes, or burning mountains. Neither Vesuvius, Etna, or Hecla, if they had any being, then poured out smoke and flame, but were covered with a verdant mantle from the top to the bottom.

4. The element of water, it is probable, was then mostly confined within the great abyss. In the new earth, (as we are informed by the Apostle, Rev. 21:1,) there will be "no more sea;" none covering as now the face of the earth, and rendering so large a part of it uninhabitable by man. Hence it is probable, there was no external sea in the paradisiacal earth; none, until the great deep burst the barriers which were originally appointed for it.—Indeed there was not then that need of the ocean for navigation which there is now: For either, as the poet supposes,

> Omnis tuli omnia tellus;

every country produced whatever was requisite either for the necessity or comfort of its inhabitants; or man, being then (as he will be again at the resurrection) equal to angels, was able to convey himself, at his pleasure, to any given distance; over and above that, those flaming messengers were always ready to minister to the heirs of salvation. But whether there was sea or not, there were rivers sufficient to water the earth, and make it very plenteous. These answered all the purposes of convenience and pleasure by

> Liquid lapse of murmuring stream;

to which were added gentle, genial showers, with salutary mists and exhalations. But there were no putrid lakes, no turbid or stagnating waters; but only such as

> Bore imprest
> Fair nature's image on their placid breast.

5. The element of air was then always serene, and always friendly to man. It contained no frightful meteor, no unwholesome vapours, no poisonous exhalations. There were no tempests, but only cool and gentle breezes,—

> genitabilis aura Favoni,—

fanning both man and beast, and wafting the fragrant odours on their silent wings.

6. The sun, the fountain of fire, of this great world both eye and soul, was situated at the most exact distance from the earth, so as to yield a sufficient quantity of heat (neither too little nor too much) to every part of it. God had not yet

> Bid his angels turn askance
> This oblique globe.

There was, therefore, then no country that groaned under

> The rage of Arctos, and eternal frost.

There was no violent winter, or sultry summer; no extreme, either of heat or cold. No soil was burned up by the solar heat; none uninhabitable through the want of it. Thus earth, water, air, and fire, all conspired together to the welfare and pleasure of man!

7. To the same purpose served the grateful vicissitude of light and darkness,—day and night. For as the human body, though not liable to death or pain, yet needed continual sustenance by food; so, although it was not liable to weariness, yet it needed continual reparation by sleep. By this the springs of the animal machine were wound up from time to time, and kept always fit for the pleasing labour for which man was designed by his Creator. Accordingly, "the evening and the morning were the first day," before sin or pain was in the world. The first natural day had one part dark for a season of repose; one part light for a season of labour. And even in paradise "Adam slept," (Gen. 2:21,) before he sinned: Sleep, therefore, belonged to innocent human nature. Yet I do not apprehend it can be inferred from hence, that there is either darkness or sleep in heaven. Surely there is no darkness in that city of God. Is it not expressly said, (Rev. 22:5,) "There shall be no night there?" Indeed they have no light from the sun; but "the Lord giveth them light." So it is all day in heaven, as it is all night in hell! On earth we have a mixture of both. Day and night succeed each other, till earth shall be turned to heaven. Neither can we at all credit the account given by the ancient poet, concerning sleep in heaven; although he allows "cloud-compelling Jove" to remain awake while the inferior gods were sleeping. It is pity, therefore, that our great poet should copy so servilely after the old Heathen, as to tell us,

> Sleep had seal'd
>
> All but the unsleeping eyes of God himself.

Not so: They are "before the throne of God serve him day and night," speaking after the manner of men, "in his temple;" (Rev. 7:15;) that is, without any interval. As wicked spirits are tormented day and night without any intermission of their misery; so holy spirits enjoy God day and night without any intermission of their happiness.

8. On the second day God encompassed the terraqueous globe with that noble appendage, the atmosphere, consisting chiefly of air; but replete with earthly particles of various kinds, and with huge volumes of water, sometimes invisible, sometimes visible, buoyed up by that ethereal fire, a particle of which cleaves to every particle of air. By this the water was divided ed into innumerable drops, which, descending, watered the earth, and made it very plenteous, without incommoding any of its inhabitants. For there were then no impetuous currents of air; no tempestuous winds; no furious hail; no torrents of rain; no rolling thunders, or forky lightnings. One perennial spring was perpetually smiling over the whole surface of the earth.

9. On the third day God commanded all kind of vegetables to spring out of the earth; and then, to add thereto innumerable herbs, intermixed with flowers of all hues. To these were added shrubs of every kind; together with tall and stately trees, whether for shade, for timber, or for fruit, in endless variety. Some of these were adapted to particular climates, or particular exposures; while vegetables of more general use (as wheat in particular) were not confined to one country, but would flourish almost in every climate. But among all these there were no weeds, no useless plants, none that encumbered the ground; much less were there any poisonous ones, tending to hurt any one creature; but every thing was salutary in its kind, suitable to the gracious design of its great Creator.

10. The Lord now created "the sun to rule the day, and the moon to govern the night." The sun was

> Of this great world both eye and soul:—

The *eye*, making all things visible; distributing light to every part of the system; and thereby rejoicing both earth and sky;—and the *soul*; the principle of all life, whether to vegetables or animals. Some of the uses of the moon we are acquainted with; her causing the ebbing and flowing of the sea; and influencing, with a greater or smaller degree, all the fluids in the terraqueous globe. And many other uses she may have, unknown to us, but known to the wise Creator. But it is certain she had no hurtful, no unwholesome influence on any living creature. "He made the stars also;" both those that move round the sun, whether of the primary or secondary order; or those that, being at a far greater distance, appear to us as fixed in the firmament of heaven. Whether Comets are to be numbered among the stars, and whether they were parts of the original creation, is, perhaps, not so easy to determine, at least with certainty; as we have nothing but probable conjecture, either concerning their nature or their use. We know not whether (as some ingenious men have imagined) they are ruined worlds,—worlds that have undergone a general conflagration; or whether (as others not improbably suppose) they are immense reservoirs of fluids, appointed to revolve at certain seasons, and to supply the still decreasing moisture of the earth. But certain we are that they did not either produce or portend any evil. They did not (as many have fancied since)

> From their horrid hair
>
> Shake pestilence and war.

11. The Lord God afterward peopled the earth with animals of every kind. He first commanded the waters to bring forth abundantly;—to bring forth creatures, which, as they inhabited a grosser element, so they were, in general, of a more stupid nature; endowed with fewer senses and less understanding than other animals. The bivalved shell-fish, in particular, seem to have no sense but that of feeling, unless perhaps a low measure of taste; so that they are but one degree above vegetables. And even the king of the waters, (a title which some give the whale, because of his enormous magnitude,) though he has sight added to taste and feeling, does not appear to have an understanding proportioned to his bulk. Rather, he is inferior therein not only to most birds and beasts, but to the generality of even reptiles and insects. However, none of these then attempted to devour, or in anyway hurt, one another. All were peaceful and quiet, as were the watery fields wherein they ranged at pleasure.

12. It seems the insect kinds were at least one degree above the inhabitants of the waters. Almost all these too devour one another, and every other creature which they can conquer. Indeed, such is the miserably disordered state of the world at present, that innumerable creatures can no otherwise preserve their own lives than by destroying others. But in the beginning it was not so. The paradisiacal earth afforded a sufficiency of food for all its inhabitants; so that none of them had any need or temptation to prey upon the other. The spider was then as harmless as the fly, and did not then lie in wait for blood. The weakest of them crept securely over the earth, or spread their gilded wings in the air, that wavered in the breeze, and glittered in the sun, without any to make them afraid. Meantime, the reptiles of every kind were equally harmless, and more intelligent than they; yea, one species of them "was more subtil," or knowing, "than any of the" brute creation "which God had made."

13. But, in general, the birds, created to fly in the open firmament of heaven, appear to have been of an order far superior to either insects or reptiles; although still considerably inferior to beasts; as we now restrain that word to quadrupeds, four-footed animals, which, two hundred years ago, included every kind of living creatures. Many species of these are not only endowed with a large measure of natural understanding, but are likewise capable of much improvement by art, such as one would not readily conceive. But, among all these, there were no birds or beasts of prey; none that destroyed or molested another; but all the creatures breathed, in their several kinds, the benevolence of their great Creator.

14. Such was the state of the creation, according to the scanty ideas which we can now form concerning it, when its great Author, surveying the whole system at one view, pronounced it "very good." It was good in the highest degree whereof it was capable, and without any mixture of evil. Every part was exactly suited to the others, and conducive to the good of the whole. There was "a golden chain" (to use the expression of Plato) "let down from the throne of God;" an exactly connected series of beings, from the highest to the lowest; from dead earth, through fossils, vegetables, animals, to man, created in the image of God, and designed to know, to love, and enjoy his Creator to all eternity.

II. 1. Here is a firm foundation laid, on which we may stand, and answer all the cavils of minute philosophers; all the objections which "vain men," who "would be wise," make to the goodness or wisdom of God in the creation. All these are grounded upon an entire mistake; namely, that the world is now in the same state it was at the beginning. And upon this supposition they plausibly build abundance of objections. But all these objections fall to the ground, when we observe, this supposition cannot be admitted. The world, at the beginning, was in a totally different state from that wherein we find it now. Object, therefore, whatever you please to the present state, either of the animate or inanimate creation, whether in general, or with regard to any particular instances; and the answer is ready:—These are not now as they were in the beginning. Had you therefore heard that vain King of Castile crying out, with exquisite self-sufficiency, "If I had made the world, I would have made it better than God Almighty has made it;" you might have replied, "No: God Almighty, whether you know it or not, did not make it as it is now. He himself made it better, unspeakably better, than it is at present. He made it without any blemish, yea, without any defect. He made no corruption, no destruction, in the inanimate creation. He made not death in the animal creation; neither its harbingers,—sin and pain. If you will not believe his own account, believe your brother Heathen: It was only

Post ignem aetherea domo
Subductum,

—that is, in plain English,—after man, in utter defiance of his Maker, had eaten of the tree of knowledge, that

—Macies, et nova febrium
Terris incubuit cohors;—

that a whole army of evils, totally new, totally unknown till then, broke in upon rebel man, and all other creatures, and overspread the face of the earth."

2. "Nay;" (says a bold man [Mr. S—— J——s.], who has since personated a Christian, and so well that many think him one;) "God is not to blame for either the natural or moral evils that are in the world; for he made it as well as he could; seeing evil must exist in the very nature of things." It must, *in the present nature* of things, supposing man to have rebelled against God: But evil did not exist at all in the original nature of things. It was no more the necessary result of matter, than it was the necessary result of spirit. All things then, without exception, were very good. And how should they be otherwise? There was no defect at all in the power of God, any more than in his goodness or wisdom. His goodness inclined him to make all things good; and this was executed by his power and wisdom. Let every sensible infidel, then, be ashamed of making such miserable *excuses* for his Creator. He needs none of us to make *apologies*, either for him or for his creation. "As for God, his way is perfect;" and such originally were all his works; and such they will be again, when "the Son of God" shall have "destroyed" all "the works of the devil."

3. Upon this ground, then, that "God made man upright," and every creature perfect in its kind, but that man "found out to himself many inventions" of happiness, independent on God; and that, by his apostasy from God, he threw not only himself, but likewise the whole creation, which was intimately connected with him, into disorder, misery, death;—upon this ground, I say, we do not find it difficult to

Justify the ways of God with men.

For although he left man in the hand of his own counsel, to choose good or evil, life or death; although he did not take away the liberty he had given him, but suffered him to choose death, in consequence of which the whole creation now groaneth together; yet, when we consider, all the evils introduced into the creation may work together for our good, yea, may "work out for us a far more exceeding and eternal weight of glory," we may well praise God for permitting these temporary evils, in order to our eternal good: Yea, we may well cry out, "O the depth both of the wisdom" and the goodness of God! "He hath done all things well." "Glory be unto God, and unto the Lamb, for ever and ever!"

57.* ON THE FALL OF MAN

"Dust thou are, and unto dust shalt thou return."

Gen. 3:19.

1. Why is there *pain* in the world; seeing God is "loving to every man, and his mercy is over all his works?" Because there is sin: Had there been no sin, there would have been no pain. But pain (supposing God to be just) is the necessary effect of sin. But why is there sill in the world? Because man was created in the image of God: Because he is not mere matter, a clod of earth, a lump of clay, without sense or understanding; but a spirit like his Creator, a being endued not only with sense and understanding, but also with a will exerting itself in various affections. To crown all the rest, he was endued with liberty; a power of directing his own affections and actions; a capacity of determining himself, or of choosing good or evil. Indeed, had not man been endued with this, all the rest would have been of no use: Had he not been a free as well as an intelligent being, his understanding would have been as incapable of holiness, or any kind of virtue, as a tree or a block of marble. And having this power, a power of choosing good or evil, he chose the latter: He chose evil. Thus "sin entered into the world," and pain of every kind, preparatory to death.

2. But this plain, simple account of the origin of evil, whether natural or moral, all the wisdom of man could not discover till it pleased God to reveal it to the world. Till then man was a mere enigma to himself; a riddle which none but God could solve. And in how full and satisfactory a manner has he solved it in this chapter! In such a manner, as does not indeed serve to gratify vain curiosity, but as is abundantly sufficient to answer a nobler end; to

Justify the ways of God with men.

To this great end I would, First, briefly consider the preceding part of this chapter; and then, Secondly, more particularly weigh the solemn words which have been already recited.

I. 1. In the First place let us briefly consider the preceding part of this chapter. "Now the serpent was more subtil," or intelligent, "than any beast of the field which the Lord God had made;" (Gen. 3:1;)—endued with more understanding than any other animal in the brute creation. Indeed, there is no improbability in the conjecture of an ingenious man, [The late Dr. Nicholas Robinson.] that the serpent was endued with reason, which is now the property of man. And this accounts for a circumstance which, on any other supposition, would be utterly unintelligible. How comes Eve not to be surprised, yea, startled and affrighted, at hearing the serpent *speak* and *reason*; unless she knew that reason, and speech in consequence of it, were the original properties of the serpent? Hence, without showing any surprise, she immediately enters into conversation with him. "And he said unto the woman, Yea, hath God said, Ye shall not eat of every tree of the garden?" See how he, who was a liar from the beginning, mixes truth and falsehood together! Perhaps on purpose, that she might be the more inclined to speak, in order to clear God of the unjust charge. Accordingly, the woman said unto the serpent, (Gen. 3:2,) "We may eat of the fruit of the trees of the garden: But of the tree in the midst of the garden, God hath said, Ye shall not eat of it, neither shall ye touch it, lest ye die." Thus far she appears to have been clear of blame. But how long did she continue so? "And the serpent said unto the woman, Ye shall not surely die: For God doth know that in the day ye eat thereof, your eyes shall be opened, and ye shall be as gods, knowing good and evil." (Gen. 3:4, 5.) Here sin began; namely, unbelief. "The woman was deceived," says the Apostle. She believed a lie: She gave more credit to the word of the devil, than to the word of God. And unbelief brought forth actual sin: "When the woman saw that the tree was good for food, and pleasant to the eyes, and to be desired to make one wise, she took of the fruit, and did eat;" and so completed her sin. But "the man," as the Apostle observes, "was not deceived." How then came he to join in the transgression? "She gave unto her husband, and he did eat." He sinned with his eyes open. He rebelled against his Creator, as is highly probable,

Not by stronger reason moved,
But fondly overcome with female charms.

And if this was the case, there is no absurdity in the assertion of a great man, "That Adam sinned in his heart before he sinned outwardly; before he ate of the forbidden fruit;" namely, by inward idolatry, by loving the creature more than the Creator.

2. Immediately pain followed sin. When he lost his innocence he lost his happiness. He painfully feared that God, in the love of whom his supreme happiness before consisted. "He said," (Gen. 3:10,) "I heard thy voice in the garden, and I was afraid." He fled from Him who was, till then, his desire and glory and joy. He "hid himself from the presence of the Lord God among the trees of the garden." Hid himself! What, from the all-seeing eye? the eye which, with one glance, pervades heaven and earth? See how his understanding likewise was impaired! What amazing folly was this! such as one would imagine very few, even of his posterity, could have fallen into. So dreadfully was his "foolish heart darkened" by sin, and guilt, and sorrow, and fear. His innocence was lost, and, at the same time, his happiness and his wisdom. Here is the clear, intelligible answer to that question, "How came evil into the world?"

3. One cannot but observe, throughout this whole narration, the inexpressible tenderness and lenity of the almighty Creator, from whom they had revolted, the Sovereign against whom they had rebelled. "And the Lord God called unto Adam, and said unto him, Where art thou?"—thus graciously calling him to return, who would otherwise have eternally fled from God. "And he said, I heard thy voice in the garden, and I was afraid, because I was naked." Still here is no acknowledgment of his fault, no humiliation for it. But with what astonishing tenderness does God lead him to make

---

* [text from the 1872 edition]

that acknowledgment! "And he said, Who told thee that thou wast naked?" How camest thou to make this discovery? "Hast thou eaten of the tree whereof I commanded thee that thou shouldest not eat?" "And the man said," still unhumbled, yea, indirectly throwing the blame upon GOd himself, "The woman whom thou gavest to be with me, she gave me of the tree, and I did eat." "And the Lord God," still in order to bring them to repentance, "said unto the woman, What is this that thou hast done?" (Gen. 3:13.) "And the woman said," nakedly declaring the thing as it was, "The serpent beguiled me, and I did eat." "And the Lord God said unto the serpent," to testify his utter abhorrence of sin, by a lasting monument of his displeasure, in punishing the creature that had been barely the instrument of it, "Thou art cursed above the cattle, and above every beast of the field.—And I will put enmity between thee and the woman, and between thy seed and her seed: It shall bruise thy head, and thou shalt bruise his heel." Thus, in the midst of judgment hath God remembered mercy, from the beginning of the world; connecting the grand promise of salvation with the very sentence of condemnation!

4. "Unto the woman he said, I will greatly multiply thy sorrow and," or in, "thy conception: In sorrow" or pain "thou shalt bring forth children;"—yea, above any other creature under heaven; which original curse we see is entailed on her latest posterity. "And thy desire shall be to thy husband, and he shall rule over thee." It seems, the latter part of this sentence is explanatory of the former. Was there, till now, any other inferiority of the woman to the man than that which we may conceive in one angel to another? "And unto Adam he said, Because thou hast hearkened unto the voice of thy wife, and hast eaten of the tree of which I commanded thee, saying, Thou shalt not eat of it; cursed is the ground for thy sake.—Thorns and thistles shall it bring forth unto thee:"—Useless, yea, and hurtful productions; whereas nothing calculated to hurt or give pain had at first any place in the creation. "And thou shalt eat the herb of the field:"—Coarse and vile, compared to the delicious fruits of paradise! "In the sweat of thy face shalt thou eat bread, till thou return unto the ground: For out of it wast thou taken: For dust thou art, and unto dust shalt thou return."

II. 1. Let us now, in the Second place, weigh these solemn words in a more particular manner. "Dust thou art:" But how fearfully and wonderfully wrought into innumerable fibres, nerves, membranes, muscles, arteries. veins, vessels of various kinds! And how amazingly is this dust connected with water, with inclosed, circulating fluids, diversified a thousand ways by a thousand tubes and strainers! Yea, and how wonderfully is air impacted into every part, solid, or fluid, of the animal machine; air not elastic, which would tear the machine in pieces, but as fixed as water under the pole! But all this would not avail, were not ethereal fire intimately mixed both with this earth, air, and water. And all these elements are mingled together in the most exact proportion; so that while the body is in health, no one of them predominates, in the least degree, over the others.

II. 2. Such was man, with regard to his corporeal part, as he came out of the hands of his Maker. But since he sinned, he is not only dust, but mortal, corruptible dust. And by sad experience we find, that this "corruptible body presses down the soul." It very frequently hinders the soul in its operations; and, at best, serves it very imperfectly. Yet the soul cannot dispense with its service, imperfect as it is: For an embodied spirit cannot form one thought but by the mediation of its bodily organs. For thinking is not, as many suppose, the act of a pure spirit; but the act of a spirit connected with a body, and playing upon a set of material keys. It cannot possibly, therefore, make any better music than the nature and state of its instruments allow it. Hence every disorder of the body, especially of the parts more immediately subservient to thinking, lay an almost insuperable bar in the way of its thinking justly. Hence the maxim received in all ages, *Humanum est errare et nescire*,—"Not ignorance alone,' (that belongs, more or less, to every creature in heaven and earth; seeing none is omniscient, none knoweth all things, save the Creator,) "but error, is entailed on every child of man." Mistake, as well as ignorance, is, in our present state, inseparable from humanity. Every child of man is in a thousand mistakes, and is liable to fresh mistakes every moment. And a mistake in judgment may occasion a mistake in practice; yea, naturally leads thereto. I mistake, and possibly cannot avoid mistaking the character of this or that man. I suppose him to be what be is not; to be better or worse than he really is. Upon this wrong supposition I behave wrong to him; that is, more or less affectionately than he deserves. And by the mistake which is occasioned by the defect of my bodily organs I am naturally led so to do. Such is the present condition of human nature; of a mind dependent on a mortal body. Such is the state entailed on all human spirits, while connected with flesh and blood!

3. "And unto dust thou shalt return." How admirably well has the wise Creator secured the execution of this sentence on all the offspring of Adam! It is true He was pleased to make one exception from this general rule, in a very early age of the world, in favour of an eminently righteous man. So we read, Gen. 5:23, 24, after Enoch had "walked with God" three hundred sixty and five years, "he was not; for God took him:' He exempted him from the sentence passed upon all flesh, and took him alive into heaven. Many ages after, he was pleased to make a second exception; ordering the Prophet Elijah to be taken up into heaven, in a chariot of fire,—very probably by a convoy of angels, assuming that appearance. And it is not unlikely that he saw good to make a third exception in the person of the beloved disciple. There is transmitted to us a particular account of the Apostle John's old age; but we have not any account of his death, and not the least intimation concerning it. Hence we may reasonably suppose that he did not die, but that, after he had finished his course, and "walked with God" for about a hundred years, the Lord took him, as he did Enoch; not in so open and conspicuous a manner as he did the Prophet Elijah.

4. But setting these two or three instances aside, who has been able, in the course of near six thousand years, to evade the execution of this sentence, passed on Adam and all his posterity? Be men ever so great masters of the art of healing, can they prevent or heal the gradual decays of nature? Can all

their boasted skill heal old age, or hinder dust from returning to dust? Nay, who among the greatest in masters of medicine has been able to add a century to his own years? yea, or to protract his own life any considerable space beyond the common period? The days of man, for above three thousand years, (from the time of Moses at least,) have been fixed, by a middling computation at threescore years and ten. How few are there that attain to fourscore years! Perhaps hardly one in five hundred. So little does the art of man avail against the appointment of God!

5. God has indeed provided for the execution of his own decree in the very principles of our nature. It is well known, the human body, when it comes into the world, consists of innumerable membranes exquisitely thin, that are filled with circulating fluid, to which the solid parts bear a very small proportion. Into the tubes composed of these membranes, nourishment must be continually infused; otherwise life cannot continue, but will come to an end almost as soon as it is begun. And suppose this nourishment to be liquid, which, as it flows through those fine canals, continually enlarges them in all their dimensions; yet it contains innumerable solid particles, which continually adhere to the inner surface of the vessels through which they flow; so that in the same proportion as any vessel is enlarged, it is stiffened also. Thus the body grows firmer as it grows larger, from infancy to manhood. In twenty, five-and-twenty, or thirty years, it attains its full measure of firmness. Every part of the body is then stiffened to its full degree; as much earth adhering to all the vessels, as gives the solidity they severally need to the nerves, arteries, veins, muscles, in order to exercise their functions in the most perfect manner. For twenty, or, it may be, thirty years following, although more and more particles of earth continually adhere to the inner surface of every vessel in the body, yet the stiffness caused thereby is hardly observable, and occasions little inconvenience. But after sixty years (more or less, according to the natural constitution, and a thousand accidental circumstances) the change is easily perceived, even at the surface of the body. Wrinkles show the proportion of the fluids to be lessened, as does also the dryness of the skin, through a diminution of the blood and juices, which before moistened and kept it smooth and soft. The extremities of the body grow cold, not only as they are remote from the centre of motion, but as the smaller vessels are filled up, and can no longer admit the circulating fluid. As age increases, fewer and fewer of the vessels are pervious, and capable of transmitting the vital stream; except the larger ones, most of which are lodged within the trunk of the body. In extreme old age, the arteries themselves, the grand instruments of circulation, by the continual apposition of earth, become hard, and, as it were, bony, till, having lost the power of contracting themselves, they can no longer propel the blood, even through the largest channels; in consequence of which, death naturally ensues. Thus are the seeds of death sown in our very nature! Thus from the very hour when we first appear on the stage of life, we are travelling toward death: We are preparing, whether we will or no, to return to the dust from whence we came!

6. Let us now take a short review of the whole, as it is delivered with inimitable simplicity; what an unprejudiced person might, even from hence, infer to be the word of God. In that period of duration which He saw to be most proper, (of which He alone could be the judge, whose eye views the whole possibility of things from everlasting to everlasting,) the Almighty, rising in the greatness of his strength, went forth to create the universe. "In the beginning he created," made out of nothing, "the matter of the heavens and the earth:" (So, Mr. Hutchinson observes, the original words properly signify:) Then "the Spirit" or breath "from the Lord," that is, the air, "moved upon the face of the waters." Here were earth, water, air; three of the elements, or component parts of the lower world. "And God said, Let there be light: And there was light." By his omnific word, light, that is, fire, the fourth element, sprang into being. Out of these, variously modified and proportioned to each other, he composed the whole. "The earth brought forth grass, and herb yielding seed, and the tree yielding fruit after his kind;" and then the various tribes of animals, to inhabit the waters, the air, and the earth. But the very Heathen could observe,

> Sanctius his animal, mentisque capacius aluae
> Deerat adhuc!

There was still wanting a creature of a higher rank, capable of wisdom and holiness. *Natus homo est.* So "God created man in his own image; in the image of God created he him!" Mark the emphatical repetition. God did not make him mere matter, a piece of senseless, unintelligent clay; but a spirit, like himself, although clothed with a material vehicle. As such he was endued with understanding; with a will including various affections; and with liberty, a power of using them in a right or wrong manner, of choosing good or evil. Otherwise neither his understanding nor his will would have been to any purpose; for he must have been as incapable of virtue or holiness as the stock of a tree. Adam, in whom all mankind were then contained, freely preferred evil to good. He chose to do his own will, rather than the will of his Creator. He "was not deceived," but knowingly and deliberately rebelled against his Father and his King. In that moment he lost the moral image of God, and, in part, the natural: He commenced unholy, foolish, and unhappy. And "in Adam all died:" He entitled all his posterity to error, guilt, sorrow, fear, pain, diseases, and death.

7. How exactly does matter of fact, do all things round us, even the face of the whole world, agree with this account! Open your eyes! Look round you! See darkness that may be felt; see ignorance and error; see vice in ten thousand forms; see consciousness of guilt, fear, sorrow, shame, remorse, covering the face of the earth! See misery, the daughter of sin. See, on every side, sickness and pain, inhabitants of every nation under heaven; driving on the poor, helpless sons of men, in every age, to the gates of death! So they have done well nigh from the beginning of the world. So they will do, till the consummation of all things.

8. But can the Creator despise the work of his own hands? Surely that is impossible! Hath he not then, seeing he alone is able, provided a remedy for all these evils? Yea, verily he bath! And a sufficient remedy; every way adequate to the

disease. He hath fulfilled his word: He bath given "the seed of the woman to bruise the serpent's head."—"God so loved the world, that he gave his only-begotten Son, that whosoever believeth in him might not perish, but have everlasting life." Here is a remedy provided for all our guilt: He "bore all our sins in his body on the tree." And "if any one have sinned, we have an Advocate with the Father, Jesus Christ the righteous." And here is a remedy for all our disease, all the corruption of our nature. For God hath also, through the intercession of his Son, given us his Holy Spirit, to renew us both "in knowledge," in his natural image;—opening the eyes of our understanding, and enlightening us with all such knowledge as is requisite to our pleasing God;—and also in his moral image, namely, "righteousness and true holiness." And supposing this is done, we know that "all things" will "work together for our good." We know by happy experience, that all natural evils change their nature and turn to good; that sorrow, sickness, pain, will all prove medicines, to heal our spiritual sickness. They will all be to our profit; will all tend to our unspeakable advantage; making us more largely "partakers of his holiness," while we remain on earth; adding so many stars to that crown which is reserved in heaven for us.

9. Behold then both the justice and mercy of God!—his *justice* in punishing sin, the sin of him in whose loins we were then all contained, on Adam and his whole posterity;—and his *mercy* in providing an universal remedy for an universal evil; in appointing the Second Adam to die for all who had died in the first; that, "as in Adam all died, so in Christ all" might "be made alive;" that, "as by one man's offence, judgment came upon all men to condemnation, so by the righteousness of one, the free gift" might "come upon all unto justification of life,"—"justification of *life*," as being connected with the new birth, the beginning of spiritual life, which leads us, through the life of holiness, to life eternal, to glory.

10. And it should be particularly observed, that "where sin abounded, grace does much more abound." For not as the condemnation, so is the free gift; but we may gain infinitely more than we have lost. We may now attain both higher degrees of holiness, and higher degrees of glory, than it would have been possible for us to attain. If Adam had not sinned, the Son of God had not died: Consequently that amazing instance of the love of God to man had never existed, which has, in all ages, excited the highest joy, and love, and gratitude from his children. We might have loved God the Creator, God the Preserver, God the Governor; but there would have been no place for love to God the Redeemer. This could have had no being. The highest glory and joy of saints on earth, and saints in heaven, Christ crucified, had been wanting. We could not then have praised him that, thinking it no robbery to be equal with God, yet emptied himself, took upon him the form of a servant, and was obedient to death, even the death of the cross! This is now the noblest theme of all the children of God on earth; yea, we need not scruple to affirm, even of angels, and archangels, and all the company of heaven.

"Hallelujah," they cry,

"To the King of the sky,
To the great everlasting I AM;
To the Lamb that was slain,
And liveth again,
Hallelujah to God and the Lamb!"

58. ON PREDESTINATION

"Whom he did foreknow, he also did predestinate to be conformed to the image of his Son:—Whom he did predestinate, them he also called. And whom he called, them he also justified: and whom he justified, them he also glorified."

Romans 8:29, 30.

Our beloved brother Paul," says St. Peter, "according to the wisdom given unto him hath written unto you; as also in all his Epistles, speaking in them of these things; in which are some things hard to be understood, which they that are unlearned and unstable wrest, as they do also the other Scriptures, unto their own destruction." (2 Peter 3:15, 16)

2. It is not improbable, that among those things spoken by St. Paul, which are hard to be understood, the Apostle Peter might place what he speaks on this subject in the eighth and ninth chapters of his epistle to the Romans. And it is certain not only the unlearned, but many of the most learned men in the world, and not the "unstable" only, but many who seemed to be well established in the truths of the gospel, have for several centuries, "wrested" these passages "to their own destruction."

3. "Hard to be understood" we may well allow them to be, when we consider how men of the strongest understanding, improved by all the advantages of education, have continually differed in judgment concerning them. And this very consideration, that there is so wide a difference upon the head between men of the greatest learning, sense, and piety, one might imagine would make all who now speak upon the subject exceedingly wary and self-diffident. But I know not how it is, that just the reverse is observed in every part of the Christian world. No writers upon earth appear more positive than those who write on this difficult subject. Nay, the same men, who, writing upon any other subject, are remarkably modest and humble, on this alone lay aside all self-distrust,

And speak *ex cathedrÿaa* infallible.

This is peculiarly observable of almost all those who assert the absolute decrees. But surely it is possible to avoid this: Whatever we propose, may be proposed with modesty, and with deference to those wise and good men who are of a contrary opinion; and the rather, because so much has been said already, on every part of the question, so many volumes have been written, that it is scarcely possible to say anything which has not been said before. All I would offer at present, not to the lovers of contention, but to men of piety and candour, are a few short hints, which perhaps may cast some light on the text above recited.

4. The more frequently and carefully I have considered it, the more I have been inclined to think that the apostle is not here (as many have supposed) describing a chain of causes and effects; (this does not seem to have entered into his heart;)

but simply showing *the method in which God works; the order* in which the several branches of salvation constantly follow each other. And this, I apprehend, will be clear to any serious and impartial inquirer, surveying the work of God either forward or backward; either from the beginning to the end, or from the end to the beginning.

5. And, First, let us look forward on the whole work of God in the salvation of man; considering it from the beginning, the first point, till it terminates in glory. The first point is, the foreknowledge of God. God *foreknew* those in every nation those who would believe, from the beginning of the world to the consummation of all things. but, in order to throw light upon this dark question, it should be well observed, that when we speak of God's foreknowledge, we do not speak according to the nature of things, but after the manner of men. For, if we speak properly, there is no such thing as either foreknowledge or afterknowledge in God. All time, or rather all eternity, (for the children of men,) being present to him at once, he does not know one thing in one point of view from everlasting to everlasting. As all time, with everything that exists therein, is present with him at once, so he sees at once, whatever was is, or will be, to the end of time. But observe: We must not think they are because he knows them. No: he knows them because they are. Just as I (if one may be allowed to compare the things of men with the deep things of God) now know the sun shines: Yet the sun does not shine because I know it, but I know it because he shines. My knowledge supposes the sun to shine; but does not in anywise cause it. In like manner, God knows that man sins; for he knows all things: Yet we do not sin because he knows it, but he knows it because we sin; and his knowledge supposes our sin, but does not in anywise cause it. In a word, God, looking on all ages, from the creation to the consummation, as a moment, and seeing at once whatever is in the hearts of all the children of men, knows every one that does or does not believe, in every age or nation. Yet what he knows, whether faith or unbelief, is in nowise caused by his knowledge. Men are as free in believing or not believing as if he did not know it at all.

6. Indeed, if man were not free, he could not be accountable either for his thoughts, word, or actions. If he were not free, he would not be capable either of reward or punishment; he would be incapable either of virtue or vice, of being either morally good or bad. If he had no more freedom than the sun, the moon, or the stars, he would be no more accountable than them. On supposition that he had no more freedom than them, the stones of the earth would be as capable of reward, and as liable to punishment, as man: One would be as accountable as the other. Yea, and it would be as absurd to ascribe either virtue or vice to him as to ascribe it to the stock of a tree.

7. But to proceed: "Whom he did foreknow, them he did predestinate to be conformed to the image of his Son." This is the Second step: (To speak after the manner of men: For in fact, there is nothing *before* or *after* in God:) In other words, God decrees, from everlasting to everlasting, that all who believe in the Son of his love, shall be conformed to his image; shall be saved from all inward and outward sin, into all inward and outward holiness. Accordingly, it is a plain undeniable fact all who truly believe in the name of the Son of God do now "receive the end of their faith, the salvation of their souls;" and this in virtue of the unchangeable, irreversible, irresistible decree of God,—"He that believeth shall be saved;" "he that believeth not, shall be damned."

8. "Whom he did predestinate, them he also called." This is the Third step: (Still remembering that we speak after the manner of men:) To express it a little more largely: According to his fixed decree, that believers shall be saved, those whom he foreknows as such, he calls both outwardly and inwardly,—*outwardly* by the word of his grace, and *inwardly* by his Spirit. This inward application of his word to the heart, seems to be what some term "effectual calling:" And it implies, the calling them children of God; the accepting them "in the Beloved;" the justifying them "freely by his grace, through the redemption that is in Jesus Christ."

9. "Whom he called, them he justified." This is the Fourth step. It is generally allowed that the word "justified" here is taken in a peculiar sense; that it means he made them just or righteous. He executed his decree, "conforming them to the image of his Son;" or, as we usually speak, sanctified them.

10. It remains, "whom he justified, them he also glorified." This is the Last step. Having made them "meet to be partakers of the inheritance of the saints in light," he gives them "the kingdom which was prepared for them before the world began." This is the order wherein, "according to the counsel of his will," the plan he has laid down from eternity, he saves those whom he foreknew; the true believers in every place and generation.

11. The same great work of salvation by faith, according to the foreknowledge and decree of God, may appear in a still clearer light, if we view it backward, from the end to the beginning. Suppose then you stood with the "great multitude which no man can number, out of every nation, and tongue, and kindred, and people," who "give praise unto Him that stretch upon the throne, and unto the Lamb for ever and ever;" you would not find one among them all that were entered into glory, who was not a witness of that great truth, "Without holiness no man shall see the Lord;" "not one of all that innumerable company who was not sanctified before he was glorified. By holiness he was prepared for glory; according to the invariable will of the Lord, that the crown, purchased by the blood of his son, should be given to none but those who are renewed by his Spirit. He is become "the author of eternal salvation" only "to them that obey him;" "that obey him inwardly and outwardly; that are holy in heart, and holy in all manner of conversation.

12. And could you take view of all those upon earth who are now sanctified, you would find no one of these had been sanctified till after he was called. He was first called, not only with an outward call, by the word and the messengers of God, but likewise with an inward call, by his Spirit applying his word, enabling him to believe in the only-begotten Son of God, and bearing testimony with his spirit that he was a child of God. And it was by this very means they were all sanctified. It was by a sense of the love of God shed abroad in his heart, that everyone of them was enabled to love God. Loving God,

he loved his neighbor as himself, and had power to walk in all his commandments blameless. This is a rule which admits of no exception. God calls a sinner his own, that is, justifies him, before he sanctifies. And by this very thing, the consciousness of his favour, he works in him that grateful, filial affection, from which spring every good temper, and word, and work.

13. And who are they that are thus called of God, but those whom he had before predestinated, or decreed, to "conform to the image of his Son?" This decree (still speaking after the manner of men) precedes every man's calling: Every believer was predestinated before he was called. For God calls none, but "according to the counsel of his will," according to this *orothesis*, or plan of acting, which he had laid down before the foundation of the world.

14. Once more: As all that are called were predestinated, so all whom God has predestinated he foreknew. He knew, he saw them as believers, and as such predestinated them to salvation, according to his eternal decree, "He that believeth shall be saved." Thus we see the whole process of the work of God, from the end to the beginning. Who are glorified? None but those who were first sanctified. Who are sanctified? None but those who were first justified. Who are justified? None but those who were first predestinated? Who are predestinated? None but those whom God foreknew as believers. Thus the purpose and word of God stand unshaken as the pillars of heaven:—"He that believeth shall be saved; he that believeth not shall be damned." And thus God is clear from the blood of all men; since whoever perishes, perishes by his own act and deed. "They will not come unto me," says the Savior of men; and "there is no salvation in any other." They "will not believe;" and there is no other way either to present or eternal salvation. Therefore, their blood is upon their own head; and God is still "justified in his saying" that he "willeth all men to be saved, and to come to the knowledge of his truth."

15. The sum of all is this: the almighty, all-wise God sees and knows, from everlasting to everlasting, all that is, that was, and that is to come, through one eternal *now*. With him nothing is either past or future, but all things equally present. He has, therefore, if we speak according to the truth of things, no foreknowledge, no afterknowledge. This would be ill consistent with the Apostle's words, "With him is no variableness or shadow of turning;" and with the account he gives of himself by the Prophet, "I the Lord change not." Yet when he speaks to us, knowing whereof we are made, knowing the scantiness of our understanding, he lets himself down to our capacity, and speaks of himself after the manner of men. Thus, in condescension to our weakness, he speaks of his own purpose, counsel, plan, foreknowledge. Not that God has any need of counsel, of purpose, or of planning his work beforehand. Far be it from us to impute these to the Most High; to measure him by ourselves! It is merely in compassion to us that he speaks thus of himself, as foreknowing the things in heaven or earth, and as predestinating or fore-ordaining them. But can we possibly imagine that these expressions are to be taken literally? To one who was so gross in his conceptions might he not say, "Thinkest thou I am such an one as thyself?" Not so: As the heavens are higher than the earth, so are my ways higher than thy ways. I know, decree, work, in such a manner as it is not possible for thee to conceive: But to give thee some faint, glimmering knowledge of my ways, I use the language of men, and suit myself to thy apprehensions in this thy infant state of existence.

16. What is it, then, that we learn from this whole account? It is this, and no more:—(1.) God knows all believers; (2) wills that they should be saved from sin; (3) to that end, justifies them, (4) sanctifies and (5) takes them to glory. O that men would praise the Lord for this his goodness; and that they would be content with this plain account of it, and not endeavour to wade into those mysteries which are too deep for angels to fathom!

59.* GOD'S LOVE TO FALLEN MAN

"Not as the offence, so also is the free gift."

Rom. 5:15.

1. How exceeding common, and how bitter, is the outcry against our first parent for the mischief which he not only brought upon himself, but entailed upon his latest posterity! It was by his wilful rebellion against God that "sin entered into the world." "By one man's disobedience," as the Apostle observes, the many, *hoi polloi*, as many as were then in the loins of their forefather, were made, or constituted, sinners: Not only deprived of the favour of God, but also of this image, of all virtue, righteousness, and true holiness; and sunk, partly into the image of the devil, in pride, malice, and all other diabolical tempers; partly into the image of the brute, being fallen under the dominion of brutal passions and grovelling appetites. hence also death entered into the world, with all his forerunners and attendants, pain, sickness, and a whole train of uneasy, as well as unholy passions and tempers.

2. For all this we may thank Adam, has echoed down from generation to generation. The self-same charge has been repeated in every age and every nation, where the oracles of God are known; in which alone this grand and important event has been discovered to the children of men. has not *your* heart, and probably *your* lips too, joined in the general charge? how few are there of those who believe the scriptural relation of the fall of man that have not entertained the same thought concerning our first parent; severely condemning him that, through wilful disobedience to the sole command of his Creator,

Brought death into the world, and all our woe!

3. Nay it were well if the charge rested here: But it is certain it does not. It cannot be denied that it frequently glances from Adam to his Creator. Have not thousands even of those that are called Christians, taken the liberty to call his mercy, if not his justice also, into question on this very account? Some, indeed, have done this a little more modestly, in an oblique and indirect manner; but others have thrown aside

---

* [text from the 1872 edition]

the mask, and asked, "Did not God foresee that Adam would abuse his liberty? And did he not know the baneful consequences which this must naturally have on all his posterity? And why, then, did he permit that disobedience? Was it not easy for the Almighty to have prevented it?"—He certainly did foresee the whole. This cannot be denied: For "known unto God are all his works from the beginning of the world;" rather, from all eternity, as the words *ap aionos* properly signify. And it was undoubtedly in his power to prevent it; for he hath all power both in heaven and earth. But it was known to him, at the same time, that it was best, upon the whole, not to prevent it. He knew that "not as the transgression, so is the free gift;" that the evil resulting from the former was not as the good resulting from the latter,— not worthy to be compared with it. He saw that to permit the fall of the first man was far best for mankind in general; that abundantly more good than evil would accrue to the posterity of Adam by his fall; that if "sin abounded" thereby over all the earth, yet grace "would much more abound;" yea, and that to every individual of the human race, unless it was his own choice.

4. It is exceeding strange that hardly anything has been written or at least published, on this subject; nay that it has been so little weighed or understood by the generality of Christians; especially considering that it is not a matter of mere curiosity, but a truth of the deepest importance; it being impossible, on any other principle,

> To assert a gracious Providence,
>
> And justify the ways of God with men;

and considering withal how plain this important truth is to all sensible and candid inquirers. May the Lover of men open the eyes of our understanding, to perceive clearly that, by the fall of Adam, mankind in general have gained a capacity, First, of being more holy and more happy on earth, and, Secondly, of being more happy in heaven, than otherwise they could have been!

1. And, First, mankind in general have gained, by the fall of Adam, a capacity of attaining more holiness and happiness on earth than it would have been possible for them to attain if Adam had not fallen. For if Adam had not fallen, Christ had not died. Nothing can be more clear than this; nothing more undeniable: The more thoroughly we consider the point the more deeply shall we be convinced of it. Unless all the partakers of human nature had received that deadly wound in Adam, it would not have been needful for the Son of God to take our nature upon him. Do you not see that this was the very ground of his coming into the world? "By one man sin entered into the world, and death by sin: And thus death passed upon all," through him in whom all men sinned. (Rom. 5:12.) Was it not to remedy this very thing that "the Word was made flesh," that "as in Adam all died, so in Christ all" might "be made alive?" Unless, then, many had been made sinners by the disobedience of one, by the obedience of one many would not have been made righteous: (Rom. 5:19:) So there would have been no room for that amazing display of the Son of God's love to mankind: There would have been no occasion for his being "obedient unto death, even the death of the cross." It could not then have

been said, to the astonishment of all the hosts of heaven "God so loved the world," yea, the ungodly world, which had no thought or desire of returning to him, "that he gave his Son" out of his bosom, his only-begotten Son, "to the end that whosoever believeth on him should not perish, but have everlasting life." Neither could we then have said,:God was in Christ reconciling the world to himself;" or, that he "made him to be sin," that is, a sin-offering, "for us, who knew no sin, that we might be made the righteousness of God through him." There would have been no such occasion for such "an Advocate with the Father," as "Jesus Christ the righteous;" neither for his appearing "at the right hand of God, to make intercession for us."

2. What is the necessary consequence of this? It is this: There could then have been no such thing as faith in God thus loving the world, giving his only Son for us men, and for our salvation. There could have been no such thing as faith in the Son of God, as "loving us and giving himself for us." There could have been no faith in the Spirit of God, as renewing the image of God in our hearts, as raising us from the death of sin unto the life of righteousness. Indeed the whole privilege of justification by faith could have had no existence; there could have been no redemption in the blood of Christ; neither could Christ have been "made of God unto us," either "wisdom, righteousness. sanctification" or "redemption."

3. And the same grand blank which was in our faith must likewise have been in our love. We might have loved the Author of our being, the Father of angels and men as our Creator and Preserver: We might have said, "O Lord our Governor, how excellent is thy name in all the earth!"—But we could not have loved him under the nearest and dearest relation,—as delivering up his Son for us all. We might have loved the Son of God, as being "the brightness of his Father's glory, the express image of his person;" (although this ground seems to belong rather to the inhabitants of heaven than earth;) but we could not have loved him as "bearing our sins in his own body on the tree," and "by that one oblation of himself once offered, making a full sacrifice, oblation, and satisfaction for the sins of the whole world." We could not have been "made conformable to his death," nor have known "the power of his resurrection." We could not have loved the Holy Ghost, as revealing to us the Father and the Son; as opening the eyes of our understanding; bringing us out of darkness into his marvellous light; renewing the image of God in our soul, and sealing us unto the day of redemption. So that, in truth, what is now "in the sight of God, even the Father," not of fallible men, "pure religion and undefiled," would then have had no being; inasmuch as it wholly depends on those grand principles—"By grace ye are saved through faith;" and, "Jesus Christ is of God made unto us wisdom, and righteousness, and sanctification and redemption."

4. We see then, what unspeakable advantage we derive from the fall of our first parent with regard to faith;—Faith both in God the Father, who spared not his own Son, his only Son, but "wounded him for our transgressions," and "bruised him for our iniquities:" and in God the Son, who poured out his soul for us transgressors, and washed us in his own blood. We

see what advantage we derive therefrom with regard to the love of God; both of God the Father and God the Son. The chief ground of this love, as long as we remain in the body, is plainly declared by the Apostle: "We love Him, because He first loved us." But the greatest instance of his love had never been given, if Adam had not fallen.

5. And as our faith both in God the Father and the Son, receives an unspeakable increase, if not its very being. from this grand event, as does also our love both of the Father and the Son; so does the love of our neighbour also, our benevolence to all mankind, which cannot but increase in the same proportion with our faith and love of God. For who does not apprehend the force of that inference drawn by the loving Apostle: "Beloved, if God so loved us, we ought also to love one another?" If God *SO* loved us,—observe, the stress of the argument lies on this very point: *SO loved us*, as to deliver up his only Son to die a cursed death for our salvation. Beloved, what manner of love is this wherewith God hath loved us; so as to give his *only Son*, in glory equal with the Father, in Majesty co-eternal? What manner of love is this wherewith the only-begotten Son of God hath loved us so as to *empty himself*, as far as possible, of his eternal Godhead; as to divest himself of that glory which he had with the Father before the world began; as to take upon him the form of a servant, being found in fashion as a man; and then, to humble himself still further, "being obedient unto death, even the death of the cross!" If God SO loved us, how ought we to love one another! But this motive to brotherly love had been totally wanting if Adam had not fallen. Consequently, we could not then have loved one another in so high a degree as we may now. Nor could there have been that height and depth in the command of our blessed Lord, "As I have loved you, So love one another."

6. Such gainers may we be by Adam's fall, with regard both to the love of God and of our neighbour. But there is another grand point, which, though little adverted to, deserves our deepest consideration. By that one act of our first parent, not only "sin entered into the world," but pain also, and was alike the justice but the unspeakable goodness of God. For how much good does he continually bring out of this evil! How much holiness and happiness out of pain!

7. How innumerable are the benefits which God conveys to the children of men through the channel of sufferings!—so that it might well be said, "What are termed afflictions in the language of men, are in the language of God styled blessings." Indeed, had there been no suffering in the world, a considerable part of religion, yea, and, in some respects, the most excellent part, could have had no place therein; since the very existence of it depends on our suffering; so that had there been no pain, it could have had no being. Upon this foundation, even our suffering, it is evident all our passive graces are built; yea, the noblest of all Christian graces,—love enduring all things. Here is the ground for resignation to God, enabling us to say from the heart in every trying hour, "It is the Lord: Let him do what seemeth him good:" "Shall we receive good at the hand of the Lord, and shall we not receive evil!" And what a glorious spectacle is this! Did it not constrain even a Heathen to cry out, *Ecce spectaculum Deo*

dignum! "See a sight worthy of God;" a good man struggling with adversity, and superior to it. Here is the ground for confidence in God, both with regard to what we feel, and with regard to what we should fear, were it not that our soul is calmly stayed on Him. What room could there be for trust in God if there was no such thing as pain or danger? Who might not say then, "The cup which my Father hath given me, shall I not drink it?" It is by sufferings that our faith is tried, and, therefore, made more acceptable to God. It is in the day of trouble that we have occasion to say, "Though he slay me, yet will I trust him." And this is well pleasing to God, that we should own him in the face of danger: in defiance of sorrow, sickness, pain, or death.

8. Again: Had there been neither natural nor moral evil in the world, what must have become of patience, meekness, gentleness, longsuffering? It is manifest they could have had no being; seeing all these have evil for their object. If, therefore, evil had never entered into the world, neither could these have had any place in it. For who could have returned good for evil, had there been no evil-doer in the universe? How had it been possible, on that supposition, to "overcome evil with good?" Will you say, "But all these graces might have been divinely infused into the hearts of men?" Undoubtedly they might: But if they had, there would have been no use or exercise for them. Whereas in the present state of things we can never long want occasion to exercise them: And the more they are exercised, the more all our graces are strengthened and increased. And in the same proportion as our resignation, our confidence in God, our patience and fortitude, our meekness, gentleness, and longsuffering, together with our faith, and love of God and man, increase, must our happiness increase, even in the present world.

9. Yet again: As God's permission of Adam's fall gave all his posterity a thousand opportunities of suffering, and thereby of exercising all those passive graces which increase both their holiness and happiness; so it gives them opportunities of doing good in numberless instances; of exercising themselves in various good works, which otherwise could have had no being. And what exertions of benevolence, of compassion, of godlike mercy, had then been totally prevented! Who could then have said to the Lover of men,—

> Thy Mind throughout my life be shown,
> 　While listening to the wretch's cry,
> The widow's or the orphan's groan,
> 　On mercy's wings I swiftly fly,
> The poor and needy to relieve;
> 　Myself, my all for them to give?

It is the just observation of a benevolent man,—

> All worldly joys are less
> Than that one joy of doing kindnesses.

Surely in "keeping this commandment," if to no other, "there is great reward." "As we have time, let us do good unto all men;" good of every kind, and in every degree. Accordingly, the more good we do, (other circumstances being equal,) the happier we shall be. The more we deal our bread to the hungry, and cover the naked with garments,—the more we relieve the stranger and visit them that are sick or in prison,— the more kind offices we do to those that groan under the various evils of human life,—the more comfort we receive even in the present world, the greater the recompence we have in our own bosom.

10. To sum up what has been said under this head: As the more holy we are upon earth the more happy we must be; (seeing there is an inseparable connexion between holiness and happiness;) as the more good we do to others, the more of present reward redounds into our own bosom; even as our sufferings for God lead us to rejoice in him "with joy unspeakable and full of glory;" therefore, the fall of Adam,— First, by giving us an opportunity of being far more holy, Secondly, by giving us the occasions of doing innumerable good works, which otherwise could not have been done, and, Thirdly, by putting it into our power to suffer for God, whereby "the Spirit of glory and of God resteth upon us,"— may be of such advantage to the children of men, even in the present life, as they will not thoroughly comprehend till they attain life everlasting.

11. It is then we shall be enabled fully to comprehend, not only the advantages which accrue at the present time to the sons of men by the fall of their first parent, but the infinitely greater advantages which they may reap from it in eternity. In order to form some conception of this, we may remember the observation of the Apostle: As "one star differeth from another star in glory, so also is the resurrection of the dead." The most glorious stars will undoubtedly be those who are the most holy, who bear most of that image of God wherein they were created; the next in glory to these will be those who have been most abundant in good works; and next to them, those that have suffered most, according to the will of God. But what advantages, in every one of these respects, will the children of God receive in heaven, by God's permitting the introduction of pain upon earth in consequence of sin! By occasion of this they attained many holy tempers, which other-wise could have had no being;—resignation to God; confidence in him, in times of trouble and danger; patience, meekness, gentleness, longsuffering, and the whole train of passive virtues: And on account of this superior holiness, they will then enjoy superior happiness. Again: Every one will then "receive his own reward, according to his own labour:" Every individual will be "rewarded according to his work." But the fall gave rise to innumerable good works, which could otherwise never have existed; such as ministering to the necessities of saints; yea, relieving the distressed in every kind: And hereby innumerable stars will be added to their eternal crown. Yet again: There will be an abundant reward in heaven for *suffering* as well as for *doing* the will of God: "These light affliction, which are but for a moment, work out for us a far more exceeding and eternal weight of glory." Therefore that event which occasioned the entrance of suffering into the world, has thereby occasioned to all the children of God an increase of glory to all eternity. For although the sufferings themselves will be at an end; although

> The pain of life shall then be o'er,
>> The anguish and distracting care;
> There sighing grief shall weep no more;
>> And sin shall never enter there;—

Yet the joys occasioned thereby shall never end, but flow at God's right hand for evermore.

12. There is one advantage more that we reap from Adam's fall, which is not unworthy our attention. Unless in Adam all had died, being in the loins of their first parent, every descendant of Adam, every child of man, must have personally answered for himself to God. It seems to be a necessary consequence of this, that if he had once fallen, once violated any command of God, there would have been no possibility of his rising again; there was no help, but he must have perished without remedy. For that covenant knew not to show mercy: The word was, "The soul that sinneth, it shall die." Now who would not rather be on the footing he is now,—under a covenant of mercy? Who would wish to hazard a whole eternity upon one stake? Is it not infinitely more desirable to be in a state wherein, though encompassed with infirmities, yet we do not run such a desperate risk, but if we fall, we may rise again?—wherein we may say,

> My trespass is grown up to heaven;
>> But far above the skies,
> In Christ abundantly forgiven,
>> I see thy mercies rise!

13. *In Christ!* Let me entreat every serious person once more to fix his attention here. All that has been said, all that can be said, on these subjects, centres in this point: The fall of Adam produced the death of Christ. Hear, O heavens, and give ear, O earth! Yea,

> Let earth and heaven agree,
>> Angels and men be join'd,
> To celebrate with me
>> The Saviour of mankind;
> To'adore the all-atoning Lamb,
> And bless the sound of Jesu's name!

If God had prevented the fall of man, "the Word" had never been "made flesh;" nor had we ever "seen his glory, the glory as of the only-begotten of the Father." Those mysteries never had been displayed "which the" very "angels desire to look into." Methinks this consideration swallows up all the rest, and should never be out of our thoughts. Unless "by one man judgment had come upon all men to condemnation," neither angels nor men could ever have known "the unsearchable riches of Christ."

14. See, then, upon the whole, how little reason we have to repine at the fall of our first parent; since herefrom we may derive such unspeakable advantages, both in time and eternity. See how small pretence there is for questioning the mercy of God in permitting that event to take place; since therein mercy, by infinite degrees, rejoices over judgment. Where then is the man that presumes to blame God for not preventing Adam's sin? Should we not rather bless him from the ground of the heart, for therein laying the grand scheme of man's redemption, and making way for that glorious manifestation of his wisdom, holiness, justice, and mercy? If, indeed, God had decreed, before the foundation of the world, that millions of men should dwell in everlasting burnings, because Adam sinned hundreds or thousands of years before they had a being. I know not who could thank him for this, unless the devil and his angels: Seeing, on this supposition,

all those millions of unhappy spirits would be plunged into hell by Adam's sin, without any possible advantage from it. But, blessed be God, this is not the case. Such a decree never existed. On the contrary, every one born of a woman may be an unspeakable gainer thereby: And none ever was or can be a loser but by his own choice.

15. We see here a full answer to that plausible account of the origin of evil, published to the world some years since, and supposed to be unanswerable: That it "necessarily resulted from the nature of matter, which God was not able to alter." It is very kind in this sweet-tongued orator to make an excuse for God! But there is really no occasion for it: God hath answered for himself. He made man in his own image; a spirit endued with understanding and liberty. Man, abusing that liberty, produced evil; brought sin and pain into the world. This God permitted, in order to a fuller manifestation of his wisdom, justice, and mercy, by bestowing on all who would receive it an infinitely greater happiness than they could possibly have attained if Adam had not fallen.

16. "O the depth of the riches both of the wisdom and knowledge of God!" Although a thousand particulars of "his judgments and of his ways are unsearchable" to us, and past our finding our; yet may we discern the general scheme running through time into eternity. "According to the counsel of his own will," the plan he had laid before the foundation of the world, he created the parent of all mankind in his own image; and he permitted all men to be made sinners, by the disobedience of that one man, that, by the obedience of one, all who receive the free gift may be infinitely holier and happier to all eternity.

60.* THE GENERAL DELIVERANCE

"The earnest expectation of the creature waiteth for the manifestation of the sons of God. For the creature was made subject to vanity, not willingly, but by reason of him that subjected it: Yet in hope that the creature itself also shall be delivered from the bondage of corruption, into the glorious liberty of the sons of God. For we know that the whole creation groaneth, and travaileth in pain together until now."

Rom. 8:19–22.

1. Nothing is more sure, than that as "the Lord is loving to every man," so "his mercy is over all his works;" all that have sense, all that are capable of pleasure or pain, of happiness or misery. In consequence of this, "He openeth his hand, and filleth all things living with plenteousness. He prepareth food for cattle," as well as "herbs for the children of men." He provideth for the fowls of the air, "feeding the young ravens when they cry unto him." "He sendeth the springs into the rivers, that run among the hills, to give drink to every beast of the field," and that even "the wild asses may quench their thirst." And, suitably to this, he directs us to be tender of even the meaner creatures; to show mercy to these also. "Thou shalt not muzzle the ox that treadeth out the corn:"—A custom which is observed in the eastern countries even to this day. And this is by no means contradicted by St. Paul's question: "Doth God take care for oxen?" Without doubt he does. We cannot deny it, without flatly contradicting his word. The plain meaning of the Apostle is, Is this all that is implied in the text? Hath it not a farther meaning? Does it not teach us, we are to feed the bodies of those whom we desire to feed our souls? Meantime it is certain, God "giveth grass for the cattle," as well as "herbs for the use of men."

2. But how are these Scriptures reconcilable to the present state of things? How are they consistent with what we daily see round about us, in every part of the creation? If the Creator and Father of every living thing is rich in mercy towards all; if he does not overlook or despise any of the works of his own hands; if he wills even the meanest of them to be happy, according to their degree; how comes it to pass, that such a complication of evils oppresses, yea, overwhelms them? How is it that misery of all kinds overspreads the face of the earth? This is a question which has puzzled the wisest philosophers in all ages: And it cannot be answered without having recourse to the oracles of God. But, taking these for our guide we may inquire,

    I.   What was the original state of the brute creation?

    II.   In what state is it at present? And,

    III.   In what state will it be at the manifestation of the children of God?

I. 1. We may inquire, in the First place, What was the original state of the brute creation? And may we not learn this, even from the place which was assigned them; namely, the garden of God? All the beasts of the field, and all the fowls of the air, were with Adam in paradise. And there is no question but their state was suited to their place: It was paradisiacal; perfectly happy. Undoubtedly it bore a near resemblance to the state of man himself. By taking, therefore, a short view of the one, we may conceive the other. Now, "man was made in the image of God." But "God is a Spirit:" So therefore was man. (Only that spirit, being designed to dwell on earth, was lodged in an earthly tabernacle.) As such, he had an innate principle of self-motion. And so, it seems, has every spirit in the universe; this being the proper distinguishing difference between spirit and matter, which is totally, essentially passive and inactive, as appears from a thousand experiments. He was, after the likeness of his Creator, endued with understanding; a capacity of apprehending whatever objects were brought before it, and of judging concerning them. He was endued with a will, exerting itself in various affections and passions: And, lastly, with liberty, or freedom of choice; without which all the rest would have been in vain, and he would have been no more capable of serving his Creator than a piece of earth or marble; he would have been as incapable of vice or virtue, as any part of the inanimate creation. In these, in the power of self-motion, understanding, will, and liberty, the natural image of God consisted.

2. How far his power of self-motion then extended, it is impossible for us to determine. It is probable, that he had a far higher degree both of swiftness and strength, than any of

---

* [text of the 1872 edition]

his posterity ever had, and much less any of the lower creatures. It is certain, he had such strength of understanding as no man ever since had. His understanding was perfect in its kind; capable of apprehending all things clearly, and judging concerning them according to truth, without any mixture of error. His will had no wrong bias of any sort; but all his passions and affections were regular, Being steadily and uniformly guided by the dictates of his unerring understanding; embracing nothing but good, and every good in proportion to its degree of intrinsic goodness. His liberty likewise was wholly guided by his understanding: He chose, or refused, according to its direction. Above all, (which was his highest excellence, far more valuable than all the rest put together,) he was a creature capable of God; capable of knowing, loving, and obeying his Creator. And, in fact, he did know God, did unfeignedly love and uniformly obey him. This was the supreme perfection of man; (as it is of all intelligent beings;) the continually seeing, and loving, and obeying the Father of the spirits of all flesh. From this right state and right use of all his faculties, his happiness naturally flowed. In this the essence of his happiness consisted; But it was increased by all the things that were round about him. He saw, with unspeakable pleasure, the order, the beauty, the harmony, of all the creatures; of all animated, all inanimate nature; the serenity of the skies; the sun walking in brightness; the sweetly variegated clothing of the earth; the trees, the fruits, the flowers,

>   And liquid lapse of murmuring streams.

Nor was this pleasure interrupted by evil of any kind. It had no alloy of sorrow or pain, whether of body or mind. For while he was innocent he was impassive; incapable of suffering. Nothing could stain his purity of joy. And, to crown all, he was immortal.

3. To this creature, endued with all these excellent faculties, thus qualified for his high charge, God said, "Have thou dominion over the fish of the sea, and over the fowl of the air, and over every living thing that moveth upon the earth." (Gen. 1:28.) And so the Psalmist: "Thou madest him to have dominion over the works of thy hands: Thou hast put all things under his feet: All sheep and oxen, yea, and the beasts of the field, the fowl of the air, and the fish of the sea, and whatsoever passeth through the paths of the seas." (Psalm 8:6.) So that man was God's vicegerent upon earth, the prince and governor of this lower world; and all the blessings of God flowed through him to the inferior creatures. Man was the channel of conveyance between his Creator and the whole brute creation.

4. But what blessings were those that were then conveyed through man to the lower creatures? What was the original state of the brute creatures, when they were first created? This deserves a more attentive consideration than has been usually given it. It is certain these, as well as man, had an innate principle of self-motion; and that, at least, in as high a degree as they enjoy it at this day. Again: They were endued with a degree of understanding; not less than that they are possessed of now. They had also a will, including various passions, which, likewise, they still enjoy: And they had liberty, a power of choice; a degree of which is still found in every

living creature. Nor can we doubt but their understanding too was, in the beginning, perfect in its kind. Their passions and affections were regular, and their choice always guided by their understanding

5. What then is the barrier between men and brutes? the line which they cannot pass? It was not reason. Set aside that ambiguous term: Exchange it for the plain word, understanding: and who can deny that brutes have this? We may as well deny that they have sight or hearing. But it is this: Man is capable of God; the inferior creatures are not. We have no ground to believe that they are, in any degree, capable of knowing, loving, or obeying God. This is the specific difference between man and brute; the great gulf which they cannot pass over. And as a loving obedience to God was the perfection of man, so a loving obedience to man was the perfection of brutes. And as long as they continued in this, they were happy after their kind; happy in the right state and the right use of their respective faculties. Yea, and so long they had some shadowy resemblance of even moral goodness. For they had gratitude to man for benefits received, and a reverence for him. They had likewise a kind of benevolence to each other, unmixed with any contrary temper. How beautiful many of them were, we may conjecture from that which still remains; and that not only in the noblest creatures, but in those of the lowest order. And they were all surrounded, not only with plenteous food, but with every thing that could give them pleasure; pleasure unmixed with pain; for pain was not yet; it had not entered into paradise. And they too were immortal: For "God made not death; neither hath he pleasure in the death of any living."

6. How true then is that word, "God saw everything that he had made: and behold it was very good!" But how far is this from being the present case! In what a condition is the whole lower world!—to say nothing of inanimate nature, wherein all the elements seem to be out of course, and by turns to fight against man. Since man rebelled against his Maker, in what a state is all animated nature! Well might the Apostle say of this: "The whole creation groaneth and travaileth together in pain until now." This directly refers to the brute creation In what state this is at present we are now to consider.

II. 1. As all the blessings of God in paradise flowed through man to the inferior creatures; as man was the great channel of communication, between the Creator and the whole brute creation; so when man made himself incapable of transmitting those blessings, that communication was necessarily cut off. The intercourse between God and the inferior creatures being stopped, those blessings could no longer flow in upon them. And then it was that "the creature," every creature, "was subjected to vanity," to sorrow, to pain of every kind, to all manner of evils: Not, indeed, "willingly," not by its own choice, not by any act or deed of its own; "but by reason of Him that subjected it," by the wise permission of God, determining to draw eternal good out of this temporary evil.

2. But in what respect was "the creature," every creature, then "made subject to vanity?" What did the meaner creatures

suffer, when man rebelled against God? It is probable they sustained much loss, even in the lower faculties; their vigour, strength, and swiftness. But undoubtedly they suffered far more in their understanding; more than we can easily conceive. Perhaps insects and worms had then as much understanding as the most intelligent brutes have now: Whereas millions of creatures have, at present, little more understanding than the earth on which they crawl, or the rock to which they adhere. They suffered still more in their will, in their passions; which were then variously distorted, and frequently set in flat opposition to the little understanding that was left them. Their liberty, likewise, was greatly impaired; yea, in many cases, totally destroyed. They are still utterly enslaved to irrational appetites, which have the full dominion over them. The very foundations of their nature are out of course; are turned upside down. As man is deprived of *his* perfection, his loving obedience to God; so brutes are deprived of *their* perfection, their loving obedience to man. The far greater part of them flee from him; studiously avoid his hated presence. The most of the rest set him at open defiance; yea, destroy him, if it be in their power. A few only, those we commonly term domestic animals, retain more or less of their original disposition, (through the mercy of God,) love him still, and pay obedience to him.

3. Setting these few aside, how little shadow of good, of gratitude, of benevolence, of any right temper, is now to be found in any part of the brute creation! On the contrary, what savage fierceness, what unrelenting cruelty; are invariably observed in thousands of creatures; yea, is inseparable from their natures! Is it only the lion, the tiger, the wolf, among the inhabitants of the forest and plains—the shark, and a few more voracious monsters, among the inhabitants of the waters,—or the eagle, among birds,—that tears the flesh, sucks the blood, and crushes the bones of their helpless fellow-creatures? Nay; the harmless fly, the laborious ant, the painted butterfly, are treated in the same merciless manner, even by the innocent songsters of the grove! The innumerable tribes of poor insects are continually devoured by them. And whereas there is but a small number, comparatively, of beasts of prey on the earth, it is quite otherwise in the liquid element. There are but few inhabitants of the waters, whether of the sea, or of the rivers, which do not devour whatsoever they can master: Yea, they exceed herein all the beasts of the forest, and all the birds of prey. For none of these have been ever observed to prey upon their own species:

> Saevis inter se convenit ursis:
>
> Even savage bears will not each other tear.

But the water-savages swallow up all, even of their own kind, that are smaller and weaker than themselves. Yea, such, at present, is the miserable constitution of the world, to such vanity is it now subjected, that an immense majority of creatures, perhaps a million to one, can no otherwise preserve their own lives, than by destroying their fellow-creatures!

4. And is not the very form, the outward appearance, of many of the creatures, as horrid as their dispositions? Where is the beauty which was stamped upon them when they came first out of the hands of their Creator? There is not the least trace of it left: So far from it, that they are shocking to behold! Nay, they are not only terrible and grisly to look upon, but deformed, and that to a high degree. Yet their features, ugly as they are at best, are frequently made more deformed than usual, when they are distorted by pain; which they cannot avoid, any more than the wretched sons of men. Pain of various kinds, weakness, sickness, diseases innumerable, come upon them; perhaps from within; perhaps from one another; perhaps from the inclemency of seasons; from fire, hail, snow, or storm; or from a thousand causes which they cannot foresee or prevent.

5. Thus, "as by one man sin entered into the world, and death by sin; even so death passed upon all men;" and not on man only, but on those creatures also that "did not sin after the similitude of Adam's transgression." And not death alone came upon them, but all of its train of preparatory evils; pain, and ten thousand sufferings. Nor these only, but likewise all those irregular passions, all those unlovely tempers, (which in men are sins, and even in the brutes are sources of misery,) "passed upon all" the inhabitants of the earth; and remain in all, except the children of God.

6. During this season of vanity, not only the feebler creatures are continually destroyed by the stronger; not only the strong are frequently destroyed by those that are of equal strength; but both the one and the other are exposed to the violence and cruelty of him that is now their common enemy,—man. And if his swiftness or strength is not equal to theirs, yet his art more than supplies that defect. By this he eludes all their force, how great soever it be; by this he defeats all their swiftness; and, notwithstanding their various shifts and contrivances, discovers all their retreats. He pursues them over the widest plains, and through the thickest forests. He overtakes them in the fields of air, he finds them out in the depths of the sea. Nor are the mild and friendly creatures who still own his sway, and are duteous to his commands, secured thereby from more than brutal violence; from outrage and abuse of various kinds. Is the generous horse, that serves his master's necessity or pleasure with unwearied diligence,—is the faithful dog, that waits the motion of his hand, or his eye, exempt from this? What returns for their long and faithful service do many of these poor creatures find? And what a dreadful difference is there, between What they suffer from their fellow-brutes, and what they suffer from the tyrant man! The lion, the tiger, or the shark, gives them pain from mere necessity, in order to prolong their own life; and puts them out of their pain at once: But the human shark, without any such necessity, torments them of his free choice; and perhaps continues their lingering pain till, after months or years, death signs their release.

III. 1. But will "the creature," will even the brute creation, always remain in this deplorable condition? God forbid that we should affirm this; yea, or even entertain such a thought! While "the whole creation groaneth together," (whether men attend or not,) their groans are not dispersed in idle air, but enter into the ears of Him that made them. While his creatures "travail together in pain," he knoweth all their pain, and is bringing them nearer and nearer to the birth, which shall be accomplished in its season. He seeth "the earnest expectation" wherewith the whole animated creation "waiteth for" that final "manifestation of the sons of God;" in which "they themselves also shall be delivered" (not by annihilation; annihilation is not deliverance) "from the" present "bondage of corruption, into" a measure of "the glorious liberty of the children of God."

2. Nothing can be more express: Away with vulgar prejudices, and let the plain word of God take place. They "shall be delivered from the bondage of corruption, into glorious liberty,"—even a measure, according as they are capable,—of "the liberty of the children of God." A general view of this is given us in the twenty-first chapter of the Revelation. When He that "sitteth on the great white throne" hath pronounced, "Behold, I make all things new;" when the word is fulfilled, "The tabernacle of God is with men, and they shall be his people, and God himself shall be with them and be their God;"—then the following blessing shall take place (not only on the children of men; there is no such restriction in the text; but) on every creature according to its capacity: "God shall wipe away all tears from their eyes. And there shall be no more death, neither sorrow, nor crying. Neither shall there be any more pain: For the former things are passed away."

3. To descend to a few particulars: The whole brute creation will then, undoubtedly, be restored, not only to the vigour, strength, and swiftness which they had at their creation, but to a far higher degree of each than they ever enjoyed. They will be restored, not only to that measure of understanding which they had in paradise, but to a degree of it as much higher than that, as the understanding of an elephant is beyond that of a worm. And whatever affections they had in the garden of God, will be restored with vast increase; being exalted and refined in a manner which we ourselves are not now able to comprehend. The liberty they then had will be completely restored, and they will be free in all their motions. They will be delivered from all irregular appetites, from all unruly passions, from every disposition that is either evil in itself, or has any tendency to evil. No rage will be found in any creature, no fierceness, no cruelty, or thirst for blood. So far from it that "the wolf shall dwell with the lamb, the leopard shall lie down with the kid; the calf and the young lion together; and a little child shall lead them. The cow and the bear shall feed together; and the lion shall eat straw like the ox. They shall not hurt nor destroy in all my holy mountain." (Isaiah 11:6.)

4. Thus, in that day, all the vanity to which they are now helplessly subject will be abolished; they will suffer no more, either from within or without; the days of their groaning are ended. At the same time, there can be no reasonable doubt, but all the horridness of their appearance, and all the deformity of their aspect, will vanish away, and be exchanged for their primeval beauty. And with their beauty their happiness will return; to which there can then be no obstruction. As there will be nothing within, so there will be nothing without, to give them any uneasiness: No heat or cold, no storm or tempest, but one perennial spring. In the new earth, as well as in the new heavens, there will be nothing to give pain, but everything that the wisdom and goodness of God can create to give happiness. As a recompence for what they once suffered, while under the "bondage of corruption," when God has "renewed the face of the earth," and their corruptible body has put on incorruption, they shall enjoy happiness suited to their state, without alloy, without interruption, and without end.

5. But though I doubt not that the Father of All has a tender regard for even his lowest creatures, and that, in consequence of this, he will make them large amends for all they suffer while under their present bondage; yet I dare not affirm that he has an *equal regard* for them and for the children of men. I do not believe that

He sees *with equal eyes*, as Lord of all,
A hero perish, or a sparrow fall.

By no means. This is exceeding pretty; but it is absolutely false. For though

Mercy, with truth and endless grace,
O'er all his works doth reign,
Yet chiefly he delights to bless
His favourite creature, man.

God regards his meanest creatures much; but he regards man much more. He does not *equally* regard a hero and a sparrow; the best of men and the lowest of brutes. "How *much more* does your heavenly Father care for you!" says He "who is in the bosom of his Father." Those who thus strain the point, are clearly confuted by his question, "Are not ye *much better* than they?" Let it suffice, that God regards everything that he hath made, in its own order, and in proportion to that measure of his own image which he has stamped upon it.

6. May I be permitted to mention here a conjecture concerning the brute creation? What, if it should then please the all-wise, the all-gracious Creator to raise them higher in the scale of beings? What, if it should please him, when he makes us "equal to angels," to make them what we are now,—creatures capable of God; capable of knowing and loving and enjoying the Author of their being? If it should be so, ought our eye to be evil because he is good? However this be, he will certainly do what will be most for his own glory.

7. If it be objected to all this, (as very probably it will,) "But of what use will those creatures be in that future state?" I answer this by another question, What use are they of now? If there be (as has commonly been supposed) eight thousand species of insects, who is able to inform us of what use seven thousand of them are? If there are four thousand species of fishes, who can tell us of what use are more than three thousand of them? If there are six hundred sorts of birds, who can tell of what use five hundred of those species are? If there be four hundred sorts of beasts, to what use do three hundred of them serve? Consider this; consider how little we know of even the present designs of God; and then you will not wonder that we know still less of what he designs to do in the new heavens and the new earth.

8. "But what end does it answer to dwell upon this subject, which we so imperfectly understand?" To consider so much as we do understand, so much as God has been pleased to reveal to us, may answer that excellent end—to illustrate that mercy of God which "is over all his works." And it may exceedingly confirm our belief that, much more, he "is loving

to every man." For how well may we urge our Lord's words, "Are not ye much better than they?" If, then, the Lord takes such care of the fowls of the air, and of the beasts of the field, shall he not much more take care of *you*, creatures of a nobler order? If "the Lord will save," as the inspired writer affirms, "both man and beast," in their several degrees, surely "the children of men may put their trust under the shadow of his wings!"

9. May it not answer another end; namely, furnish us with a full answer to a plausible objection against the justice of God, in suffering numberless creatures that never had sinned to be so severely punished? They could not sin, for they were not moral agents. Yet how severely do they suffer!—yea, many of them, beasts of burden in particular, almost the whole time of theirabode on earth; So that they can have no retribution here below. But the objection vanishes away, if we consider that something better remains after death for these poor creatures also; that these, likewise, shall one day be delivered from this bondage of corruption, and shall then receive an ample amends for all their present sufferings.

10. One more excellent end may undoubtedly be answered by the preceding considerations. They may encourage us to imitate Him whose mercy is over all his works. They may soften our hearts towards the meaner creatures, knowing that the Lord careth for them. It may enlarge our hearts towards those poor creatures, to reflect that, as vile as they appear in our eyes, not one of them is forgotten in the sight of our Father which is in heaven. Through all the vanity to which they are now subjected, let us look to what God hath prepared for them. Yea, let us habituate ourselves to look forward, beyond this present scene of bondage, to the happy time when they will be delivered therefrom into the liberty of the children of God.

11. From what has been said, I cannot but draw one inference, which no man of reason can deny. If it is this which distinguishes men from beasts,—that they are creatures capable of God, capable of knowing and loving and enjoying him; then whoever is "without God in the world," whoever does not know or love or enjoy God, and is not careful about the matter, does, in effect, disclaim the nature of man, and degrade himself into a beast. Let such vouchsafe a little attention to those remarkable words of Solomon: "I said in my heart concerning the estate of the sons of men,—They might see that they themselves are beasts." (Eccles. 3:18.) These sons of men are undoubtedly beasts; and that by their own act and deed; for they deliberately and wilfully disclaim the sole characteristic of human nature. It is true, they may have a share of reason; they have speech, and they walk erect; but they have not the mark, the only mark, which totally separates man from the brute creation. "That which befalleth beasts, the same thing befalleth them." They are equally without God in the world; "so that a man" of this kind "hath no pre-eminence above a beast."

12. So much more let all those who are of a nobler turn of mind assert the distinguishing dignity of their nature. Let all who are of a more generous spirit know and maintain their rank in the scale of beings. Rest not till you enjoy the privilege of humanity—the knowledge and love of God. Lift up your heads, ye creatures capable of God! Lift up your hearts to the Source of your being!

Know God, and teach your souls to know
The joys that from religion flow.

Give your hearts to Him who, together with ten thousand blessings, has given you his Son, his only Son! Let your continual "fellowship be with the Father, and with his Son, Jesus Christ!" Let God be in all your thoughts, and ye will be men indeed. Let him be your God and your All,—the desire of your eyes, the joy of your heart, and your portion for ever.

61.* THE MYSTERY OF INIQUITY

"The mystery of iniquity doth already work."

2 Thess. 2:7.

1. Without inquiring how far these words refer to any particular event in the Christian Church, I would at present take occasion from them to consider that important question,—In what manner the mystery of iniquity hath wrought among us till it hath well-nigh covered the whole earth.

2. It is certain that "God made man upright;" perfectly holy and perfectly happy: But by rebelling against God, he destroyed himself, lost the favour and the image of God, and entailed sin, with its attendant, pain, on himself and all his posterity. Yet his merciful Creator did not leave him in this helpless, hopeless state: He immediately appointed his Son, his well-beloved Son, "who is the brightness of his glory, the express image of his person," to be the Saviour of men; "the propitiation for the sins of the whole world;" the great Physician who, by his almighty Spirit, should heal the sickness of their souls, and restore them not only to the favour, but to "the image of God wherein they were created."

3. This great mystery of godliness began to work from the very time of the original promise. Accordingly, the Lamb being, in the purpose of God, "slain from the beginning of the world," from the same period his sanctifying Spirit began to renew the souls of men. We have an undeniable instance of this in Abel, who "obtained a testimony" from God "that he was righteous." (Heb. 11:4.) And from that very time all that were partakers of the same faith were partakers of the same salvation; were not only re-instated in the favour, but likewise restored to the image, of God.

4. But how exceeding small was the number of these even from the earliest ages! No sooner did "the sons of men multiply upon the face of the earth," than God, looking down from heaven, "saw that the wickedness of man was great in the earth;" so great that "every imagination of the thoughts of his heart was evil," only evil, and that "continually." (Gen. 6:1–5.) And so it remained, without any intermission, till God executed that terrible sentence, "I will destroy man whom I have created from the face of the earth." (Gen. 6:7.)

* [text of the 1872 edition]

5. Only "Noah found grace in the eyes of the Lord;" being "a just man, and perfect in his generations." Him, therefore, with his wife, his sons, and their wives, God preserved from the general destruction. And one might have imagined that this small remnant would likewise have been "perfect in their generations." But how far was this from being the case! Presently after this signal deliverance we find one of them, Ham, involved in sin, and under his father's curse. And how did "the mystery of iniquity" afterwards work, not only in the posterity of Ham, but in the posterity of Japheth; yea, and of Shem,—Abraham and his family only excepted!

6. Yea, how did it work even in the posterity of Abraham; in God's chosen people! Were not these also, down to Moses, to David, to Malachi, to Herod the Great, a faithless and stubborn generation, a "sinful nation, a people laden with iniquity," continually forsaking the Lord, and "provoking the Holy One of Israel?" And yet we have no reason to believe that these were worse than the nations that surrounded them, who were universally swallowed up in all manner of wickedness, as well as in damnable idolatries; not having the God of heaven "in all their thoughts," but working all uncleanness with greediness.

7. In the fulness of time, when iniquity of every kind, when ungodliness and unrighteousness, had spread over all nations, and covered the earth as a flood, it pleased God to lift up a standard against it by "bringing his first-begotten into the world." Now, then, one would expect "the mystery of godliness" would totally prevail over "the mystery of iniquity;" that the Son of God would be "a light to lighten the Gentiles," as well as "salvation to his people Israel." All Israel, one would think, yea, and all the earth, will soon be filled with the glory of the Lord. Nay: "The mystery of iniquity" prevailed still, well-nigh over the face of the earth. How exceeding small was the number of those whose souls were healed by the Son of God himself! "When Peter stood up in the midst of them, the number of names was about a hundred and twenty." (Acts 1:15.) And even these were but imperfectly healed; the chief of them being a little before so weak in faith that, though they did not, like Peter, forswear their Master, yet "they all forsook him and fled:" A plain proof that the sanctifying "Spirit was not" then "given, because Jesus was not glorified."

8. It was then, when he had "ascended up on high, and led captivity captive," that "the promise of the Father" was fulfilled, which they had heard from him. It was then he began to work like himself, showing that "all power was given to him in heaven and earth." "When the day of Pentecost was fully come, suddenly there came a sound from heaven, as of a rushing mighty wind, and there appeared tongues as of fire; and they were all filled with the Holy Ghost." (Acts 2:1.) In consequence of this, three thousand souls received medicine to heal their sickness, were restored to the favour and the image of God under one sermon of St. Peter's. (Acts 2:41.) "And the Lord added to them daily, "not *such as should be saved*; a manifest perversion of the text; but "such as were saved." The expression is peculiar; and so indeed is the position of the words, which run thus: "And the Lord added those that were saved daily to the church." First, they "were saved" from the power of sin; then they "were added" to the assembly of the faithful.

9. In order clearly to see how they were already saved, we need only observe the short account of them which is recorded in the latter part of the second and in the fourth chapter. "They continued steadfastly in the Apostles' doctrine, and in the fellowship, and in the breaking of bread, and in the prayers:" That is, they were daily taught by the Apostles, and had all things common, and received the Lord's supper, and attended all the public service. (Acts 2:42.) "And all that believed were together, and had all things common; and sold their possessions, and parted them to all men, as every man had need." (Acts 2:44, 45.) And again: "The multitude of them that believed," now greatly increased, "were of one heart and of one soul: Neither said any of them that aught of the things which he possessed was his own; but they had all things common." (Acts 4:32.) And yet again: "Great grace was upon them all. Neither was there any among them that lacked: For as many as were possessors of lands or houses sold them, and brought the prices of the things that were sold, and laid them at the Apostles' feet: And distribution was made unto every man according as he had need." (Acts 4:33–35.)

10. But here a question will naturally occur: "How came they to act thus, to have all things in common, seeing we do not read of any positive command to do this?" I answer, There needed no outward command: The command was written on their hearts. It naturally and necessarily resulted from the degree of love which they enjoyed. Observe! "They were of one heart, and of one soul:" And not so much as one (so the words run) said, (they could not, while their hearts so overflowed with love,) "that any of the things which he possessed was his own." And wheresoever the same cause shall prevail, the same effect will naturally follow.

11. Here was the dawn of the proper gospel day. Here was a proper Christian Church. It was now "the Sun of Righteousness" rose upon the earth, "with healing in his wings." He did now "save his people from their sins:" He "healed all their sickness." He not only taught that religion which is the true "healing of the soul," but effectually planted it in the earth; filling the souls of all that believed in him with *righteousness*,—gratitude to God, and good-will to man; attended with a *peace* that surpassed all understanding, and with joy unspeakable and full of glory.

12. But how soon did "the mystery of iniquity" work again, and obscure the glorious prospect! It began to work (not openly indeed, but covertly) in two of the Christians, Ananias and Sapphira. "They sold their possession," like the rest, and probably for the same motive; but afterwards, giving place to the devil, and reasoning with flesh and blood, they "kept back part of the price." See the first Christians, that "made shipwreck of faith and a good conscience;" the first that "drew back to perdition;" instead of continuing to "believe to the" final "salvation of the soul!" Mark the first plague which infected the Christian Church; namely, the love of money! And will it not be the grand plague in all generations, whenever God shall revive the same work? O ye believers in Christ, take warning! Whether you are yet but little children,

or young men that are strong in the faith, see the snare; your snare in particular,—that which you will be peculiarly exposed to after you have escaped from gross pollutions. "Love not the world, neither the things of the world! If any man love the world," whatever he was in times past, "the love of the Father is not" now "in him!"

13. However, this plague was stayed in the first Christian Church, by instantly cutting off the infected persons. By that signal judgment of God on the first offenders, "great fear came upon all;" (Acts 5:11;) so that, for the present at least, not one dared to follow their example. Meantime believers, men full of faith and love, who rejoiced to have all things in common, "were the more added to the Lord, multitudes both of men and women." (Acts 5:14.)

14. If we inquire in what manner "the mystery of iniquity," the energy of Satan, began to work again in the Christian Church, we shall find it wrought in quite a different way; putting on quite another shape: Partiality crept in among the Christian believers. Those by whom the distribution to everyone was made had respect of persons; largely supplying those of their own nation, while the other widows, who were not Hebrews, "were neglected in the daily administration." (Acts 6:1.) Distribution was not made to them according as everyone had need. Here was a manifest breach of brotherly love in the Hebrews; a sin both against justice and mercy: Seeing the Grecians, as well as the Hebrews, had "sold all they had, and laid the price at the Apostles' feet." See the second plague that broke in upon the Christian Church!—Partially; respect of persons; too much regard for those of our own side; and too little for others, though equally worthy.

15. The infection did not stop here, but one evil produced many more. From partiality in the Hebrews, "there arose in the Grecians a murmuring against" them; not only discontent and resentful thoughts, but words suitable thereto; unkind expressions, hard speeches, evil-speaking, and backbiting, naturally followed. And by the "root of bitterness" thus "springing up," undoubtedly "many were defiled." The Apostles indeed soon found out a means of removing the occasion of this murmuring; yet so much of the evil root remained, that God saw it needful to use a severer remedy. He let loose the world upon them all; if haply by their sufferings, by the spoiling of their goods, by pain, imprisonment, and death itself, he might at once punish and amend them. And persecution, God's last remedy for a backsliding people, had the happy effect for which he intended it. Both the partiality of the Hebrews ceased, and the murmuring of the Grecians: And "then had the churches rest, and were edified;" built up in the love of God and one another; "and, walking in the fear of the Lord, and in the comforts of the Holy Ghost, were multiplied." (Acts 9:31.)

16. It seems to have been some time after this, that "the mystery of iniquity" began to work in the form of zeal. Great troubles arose by means of some who zealously contended for circumcision, and the rest of the ceremonial law; till the Apostles and Elders put an end to the spreading evil, by that final determination,—"It seemed good unto the Holy Ghost, and to us, to lay on you no greater burden than these necessary things; that ye abstain from meats offered to idols,

and from blood, and from things strangled, and from fornication." (Acts 15:28, 29.) Yet was not this evil so thoroughly suppressed, but that it frequently broke out again; as we learn from various parts of St. Paul's Epistles, particularly that to the Galatians.

17. Nearly allied to this was another grievous evil, which at the same time sprang up in the Church;—want of mutual forbearance, and, of consequence, anger, strife, contention, variance. One very remarkable instance of this we find in this very chapter. When "Paul said to Barnabas, Let us visit the brethren where we have preached the word, Barnabas determined to take with him John;" because he was "his sister's son." "But Paul thought it not good to take him who had deserted them before." And he had certainly reason on his side. But Barnabas resolved to have his own way. *egeneto oun paroxysmos,—and there was a fit of anger.* It does not say, on St. Paul's side: Barnabas only had passion, to supply the want of reason. Accordingly he departed from the work, and went home; while St. Paul went forward "through Syria and Cilicia, confirming the churches." (Acts 15:41.)

18. The very first society of Christians at Rome were not altogether free from this evil leaven. There were "divisions and offences" among them also; (Rom. 16:17;) although, in general, they seem to have "walked in love." But how early did the "mystery of iniquity" work, and how powerfully, in the Church at Corinth! Not only schisms and heresies, animosities, fierce and bitter contentions were among them; but open, actual sins; yea, "such fornication as was not named among the Heathens." (1 Cor. 5:1.) Nay, there was need to remind them that "neither adulterers, nor thieves, nor drunkards" could "enter into the kingdom of heaven." (1 Cor. 6:9, 10.) And in all St. Paul's Epistles we meet with abundant proof, that tares grew up, with the wheat in all the Churches, and that "the mystery of iniquity" did every where, in a thousand forms, counterwork "the mystery of godliness."

19. When St. James wrote his Epistle, directed more immediately "to the twelve tribes scattered abroad," to the converted Jews, the tares sown among his wheat had produced a plentiful harvest. That grand pest of Christianity, a faith without works, was spread far and wide; filling the Church with a "wisdom from beneath," which was "earthly, sensual, devilish," and which gave rise, not only to rash judging and evil-speaking, but to "envy, strife, confusion, and every evil work." Indeed, whoever peruses the fourth and fifth chapters of this Epistle, with serious attention, will be inclined to believe, that even in this early period the tares had nigh choked the wheat, and that among most of those to whom St. James wrote, no more than the form of godliness, if so much, was left.

20. St. Peter wrote about the same time "to the strangers," the Christians, "scattered abroad through" all those spacious provinces of "Pontus, Galatia, Cappadocia, Asia" Minor, "and Bithynia." These, probably, were some of the most eminent Christians that were then in the world. Yet how exceeding far were even these from being "without spot and blemish!" And what grievous tares were here also growing up with the wheat! Some of them were "bringing in damnable heresies, even denying the Lord that bought them:" (2 Pet.

2:1.) And "many followed their pernicious ways;" of whom the Apostle gives that terrible character: "They walk after the flesh," in "the lust of uncleanness, like brute beasts, made to be taken and destroyed. Spots they are, and blemishes, while they feast with you;" (in the "feasts of charity," then celebrated throughout the whole Church:) "having eyes full of adultery, and that cannot cease from sin. These are wells without water, clouds that are carried with a tempest, for whom the mist of darkness is reserved for ever." And yet these very men were called Christians, and were even then in the bosom of the Church! Nor does the Apostle mention them as infesting any one particular church only; but as a general plague, which even then was dispersed far and wide among all the Christians to whom he wrote!

21. Such is the authentic account of "the mystery of iniquity" working even in the apostolic Churches!—an account given, not by the Jews or Heathens, but by the Apostles themselves. To this we may add the account which is given by the Head and Founder of the Church; Him "who holds the stars in his right hand;" who is "the faithful and true Witness." We may easily infer what was the state of the Church in general, from the state of the seven Churches in Asia. One of these indeed, the Church of Philadelphia, had "kept his word, and had not denied his name;" (Rev. 3:8;) the Church of Smyrna was likewise in a flourishing state: But all the rest were corrupted, more or less; insomuch that many of them were not a jot better than the present race of Christians; and our Lord then threatened, what he has long since performed, to "remove the candlestick" from them.

22. Such was the real state of the Christian Church, even during the first century; while not only St. John, but most of the Apostles were present with and presided over it. But what a mystery is this, that the All-wise, the All-gracious, the Almighty, should suffer it so to be, not in one only, but as far as we can learn, in every Christian society, those of Smyrna and Philadelphia excepted! And how came these to be excepted? Why were these less corrupted (to go no farther) than the other Churches of Asia? It seems, because they were less wealthy. The Christians in Philadelphia were not literally "increased in goods," like those in Ephesus or Laodicea; and if the Christians at Smyrna had acquired more wealth, it was swept away by persecution. So that these, having less of this world's goods, retained more of the simplicity and purity of the gospel.

23. But how contrary is this scriptural account of the ancient Christians to the ordinary apprehensions of men! We have been apt to imagine, that the Primitive Church was all excellence and perfection; answerable to that strong description which St. Peter cites from Moses: "Ye are a chosen generation, a royal priesthood, a holy nation, a peculiar people." And such, without all doubt, the first Christian Church, which commenced at the day of Pentecost, was. But how soon did the fine gold become dim! How soon was the wine mixed with water! How little time elapsed, before the "god of this world" so far regained his empire, that Christians in general were scarce distinguishable from Heathens, save by their opinions and modes of worship!

24. And if the state of the Church in the very first century was so bad, we cannot suppose it was any better in the second. Undoubtedly it grew worse and worse. Tertullian, one of the most eminent Christians of that age, has given us an account of it in various parts of his writings, whence we learn that real, internal religion was hardly found; nay, that not only the tempers of the Christians were exactly the same with those of their heathen neighbours, (pride, passion, love of the world reigning alike in both,) but their lives and manners also. The bearing a faithful testimony against the general corruption of Christians, seems to have raised the outcry against Montanus; and against Tertullian himself, when he was convinced that the testimony of Montanus was true. As to the heresies fathered upon Montanus, it is not easy to find what they were. I believe his grand heresy was, the maintaining that "without" inward and outward "holiness no man shall see the Lord."

25. Cyprian, Bishop of Carthage, in every respect an unexceptionable witness, who flourished about the middle of the third century, has left us abundance of letters, in which he gives a large and particular account of the state of religion in his time. In reading this, one would be apt to imagine, he was reading an account of the present century: So totally void of true religion were the generality both of the laity and clergy, so immersed in ambition, envy, covetousness, luxury, and all other vices, that the Christians of Africa were then exactly the same as the Christians of England are now.

26. It is true, that during this whole period, during the first three centuries, there were intermixed longer or shorter seasons wherein true Christianity revived. In those seasons the justice and mercy of God let loose the Heathens upon the Christians. Many of these were then called to resist unto blood. And "the blood of the martyrs was the seed of the Church." The apostolic spirit returned; and many "counted not their lives dear unto themselves, so they might finish their course with joy." Many others were reduced to happy poverty; and being stripped of what they had loved too well, they "remembered from whence they were fallen, and repented, and did their first works."

27. Persecution never did, never could, give any lasting wound to genuine Christianity. But the greatest it ever received, the grand blow which was struck at the very root of that humble, gentle, patient love, which is the fulfilling of the Christian law, the whole essence of true religion, was struck in the fourth century by Constantine the Great, when he called himself a Christian, and poured in a flood of riches, honours, and power upon the Christians; more especially upon the Clergy. Then was fulfilled in the Christian Church, what Sallust says of the people of Rome: *Sublata imperii aemula, non sensim, sed praecipiti cursu, a virtutibus descitum, ad vitia transcursum.* [Mr. Wesley doubtless quoted from memory; and this accounts for the slight mistake into which he has here fallen. the passage referred to does not occur in Sallust, but in Velleius Paterculus, and reads thus:—*Remoto Carthaginis metu, sublataque imperri aemula, non gradu, sed praecipiti cursu, a virtute descitum, ad vitia transcursum.* Lib. ii. cap. 1.—Edit.] Just so, when the fear of persecution was removed, and wealth and honour

attended the Christian profession, the Christians "did not gradually sink, but rushed headlong into all manner of vices." Then "the mystery of iniquity" was no more hid, but stalked abroad in the face of the sun. Then, not the golden but the iron age of the Church commenced: Then one might truly say,

> Protinus irrupit venae pejoris in aevum
> Omne nefas; fugere pudor, verumque fidesque,
> In quorum subiere locum fraudesque, dolique,
> Insidiaeque, et vis, et amor sceleratus habendi.
> At once, in that unhappy age, broke in
> All wickedness, and every deadly sin:
> Truth, modesty, and love fled far away,
> And force, and thirst of gold, claim'd universal sway,

28. And this is the event which most Christian expositors mention with such triumph! yea, which some of them suppose to be typified in the Revelation, by "the New Jerusalem coming down from heaven!" Rather say, it was the coming of Satan and all his legions from the bottomless pit: Seeing from that very time he hath set up his throne over the face of the whole earth, and reigned over the Christian as well as the Pagan world with hardly any control. Historians, indeed, tell us, very gravely, of nations, in every century, who were by such and such (*Saints* without doubt!) converted to Christianity: But still these converts practised all kinds of abominations, exactly as they did before; no way differing, either in their tempers or in their lives, from the nations that were still called Heathens. Such has been the deplorable state of the Christian Church, from the time of Constantine till the Reformation. A Christian nation, a Christian city, (according to the scriptural model,) was nowhere to be seen; but every city and country, a few individuals excepted, was plunged in all manner of wickedness.

29. Has the case been altered since the Reformation? Does "the mystery of iniquity" no longer work in the Church? No: The Reformation itself has not extended to above one third of the Western Church: so that two thirds of this remain as they were; so do the Eastern, Southern, and Northern Churches. They are as full of heathenish, or worse than heathenish, abominations, as ever they were before. And what is the condition of the Reformed Churches? It is certain that they were reformed in their opinions, as well as their modes of worship. But is not this all? Were either their tempers or lives reformed? Not at all. Indeed many of the Reformers themselves complained, that "the Reformation was not carried far enough." But what did they mean? Why, that they did not sufficiently reform the *rites* and *ceremonies* of the Church. Ye fools and blind! to fix your whole attention on the circumstantials of religion! Your complaint ought to have been, the essentials of religion were not carried far enough! You ought vehemently to have insisted on an entire change of men's *tempers* and *lives*; on their showing they had "the mind that was in Christ," by "walking as he also walked." Without this, how exquisitely trifling was the reformation of opinions and rites and ceremonies! Now, let any one survey the state of Christianity in the Reformed parts of Switzerland; in Germany, or France; in Sweden, Denmark, Holland; in Great Britain and Ireland. How little

are any of these Reformed Christians better than heathen nations! Have they more, (I will not say, communion with God, although there is no Christianity without it,) but have they more justice, mercy, or truth, than the inhabitants of China, or Indostan? O no! we must acknowledge with sorrow and shame, that we are far beneath them!

> That we, who by thy Name are named,
> The heathens unbaptized out-sin!

30. Is not this the *falling away* or *apostasy* from God, foretold by St. Paul in his Second Epistle to the Thessalonians? (2 Thess. 2:3.) Indeed, I would not dare to say, with George Fox, that this apostasy was universal; that there never were any real Christians in the world, from the days of the Apostles till his time. But we may boldly say, that wherever Christianity has spread, the apostasy has spread also; insomuch that, although there are now, and always have been, individuals who were real Christians; yet the whole world never did, nor can at this day, show a Christian country or city.

31. I would now refer it to every man of reflection, who believes the Scriptures to be of God, whether this general apostasy does not imply the necessity of a general reformation? Without allowing this, how can we possibly justify either the wisdom or goodness of God? According to Scripture, the Christian religion was designed for "the healing of the nations;" for the saving from sin by means of the Second Adam, all that were "constituted sinners" by the first. But it does not answer this end: It never did; unless for a short time at Jerusalem. What can we say, but that if it has not yet, it surely will answer it? The time is coming, when not only "all Israel shall be saved," but "the fullness of the Gentiles will come in." The time cometh, when "violence shall no more be heard in the earth, wasting or destruction within our borders;" but every city shall call her "walls Salvation, and her gates Praise;" when the people, saith the Lord, "shall be all righteous, they shall inherit the land for ever; the branch of my planting, the work of my hands, that I may be glorified." (Isa. 60:18, 21.)

32. From the preceding considerations we may learn the full answer to one of the grand objections of infidels against Christianity; namely, *the lives of Christians*. Of Christians, do you say? I doubt whether you ever knew a *Christian* in your life. When Tomo Chachi, the Indian Chief, keenly replied to those who spoke to him of being a Christian, "Why, *these* are Christians at Savannah! These are Christians at Frederica!"—the proper answer was, "No, they are not; they are no more Christians than you and Sinauky." "But are not those Christians in Canterbury, in London, in Westminster?" No: no more than they are angels. None are Christians, but they that have the mind which was in Christ, and walk as he walked. "Why, if these only are Christians," said an eminent wit, "I never saw a Christian yet." I believe it: You never did; and, perhaps, you never will; for you will never find them in the grand or the gay world. The few Christians that are upon the earth, are only to be found where *you* never look for them. Never therefore, urge this objection more: Never object to Christianity the lives or tempers of Heathens. Though they are called Christians, the name does

not imply the thing: They are as far from this as hell from heaven!

33. We may learn from hence, Secondly, the extent of the fall,—the astonishing spread of original corruption. What among so many thousands, so many millions, is there "none righteous, no, not one?" Not by nature. But including the grace of God, I will not say with the heathen poet,—

> Rari quippe boni: numero vix sunt totidem, quot
> Thebarum portae, vel divitis ostia Nili.

[The following is Gifford's translation of this quotation from Juvenal:—

> —The good are few! "the valued file"
> Scarce pass the gates of Thebes, the mouths of Nile.
> —Edit.]

As if he had allowed too much, in supposing there were a hundred good men in the Roman Empire, he comes to himself, and affirms there are hardly seven. Nay, surely, there were seven thousand! There were so many long ago in one small nation, where Elijah supposed there were none at all. But, allowing a few exceptions, we are authorized to say, "The whole world lieth in wickedness;" yea, "in the wicked one," as the words properly signify. "Yes, the whole heathen world." Yea, and the Christian too; (so called;) for where is the difference, save in a few externals? See with your own eyes! Look into that large country, Indostan. There are Christians and Heathens too. Which have more justice, mercy, and truth? the Christians or the Heathens? Which are most corrupt, infernal, devilish, in their tempers and practice? the English or the Indians? Which have desolated whole countries, and clogged the rivers with dead bodies?

> O sacred name of Christian! how profaned!

O earth, earth, earth! how dost thou groan under the villainies of thy *Christian* inhabitants!

34. From many of the preceding circumstances we may learn, Thirdly, what is the genuine tendency of riches: What a baleful influence they have had, in all ages, upon pure and undefiled religion. Not that money is an evil of itself: It is applicable to good as well as bad purposes. But, nevertheless, it is an undoubted truth, that "the love of money is the root of all evil;" and also, that the possession of riches naturally breeds the love of them. Accordingly, it is an old remark,

> Crescit amor nummi, quantum ipsa pecunia crescit:

"As money increases, so does the love of it;" and always will, without a miracle of grace. Although, therefore, other causes may concur; yet this has been, in all ages, the principal cause of the decay of true religion in every Christian community. As long as the Christians in any place were poor, they were devoted to God. While they had little of the world, they did not love the world; but the more they had of it, the more they loved it. This constrained the Lover of their souls, at various times, to unchain their persecutors; who, by reducing them to their former poverty, reduced them to their former purity. But still remember, riches have, in all ages, been the bane of genuine Christianity!

35. We may learn hence, Fourthly, how great watchfulness they need who desire to be real Christians; considering what a state the world is in! May not each of them well say,

> Into a world of ruffians sent,
> I walk on hostile ground:
> Wild human bears, on slaughter bent,
> And ravening wolves surround?

They are the more dangerous, because they commonly appear in sheep's clothing. Even those who do not pretend to religion, yet make fair professions of good-will, of readiness to serve us, and, perhaps, of truth and honesty. But beware of taking their word! Trust not any man, until he fears God! It is a great truth,

> He that fears no God, can love no friend:

Therefore stand upon your guard against every one that is not earnestly seeking to save his soul. We have need to keep both our heart and mouth as "with a bridle, while the ungodly are in our sight." Their conversation, their spirit, is infectious, and steals upon us unawares, we know not how. "Happy is the man that feareth always," in this sense also, lest he should partake of other men's sins. O "keep thyself pure!" "Watch and pray, that thou enter not into temptation!"

36. We may learn from hence, Lastly, what thankfulness becomes those who have escaped the corruption that is in the world; whom God hath chosen out of the world, to be holy and unblamable. "Who is it that maketh thee to differ?" "And what hast thou which thou hast not received?" Is it not "God" alone "who worketh in thee both to will and to do of his good pleasure?" "And let those give thanks whom the Lord hath redeemed and delivered from the hand of the enemy." Let us praise him, that he hath given us to see the deplorable state of all that are round about us, to see the wickedness which overflows the earth, and yet not be borne away by the torrent! We see the general, the almost universal contagion; and yet it cannot approach to hurt us! Thanks be unto Him "who hath delivered us from so great a death, and doth still deliver!" And have we not farther ground for thankfulness, yea, and strong consolation, in the blessed hope which God hath given us, that the time is at hand, when righteousness shall be as universal as unrighteousness is now? Allowing that "the whole creation now groaneth together" under the sin of man, our comfort is, it will not always groan: God will arise and maintain his own cause; and the whole creation shall then be delivered both from moral and natural corruption. Sin, and its consequence, pain, shall be no more: Holiness and happiness will cover the earth. Then shall all the ends of the world see the salvation of our God; and the whole race of mankind shall know, and love, and serve God, and reign with him for ever and ever!

62.* THE END OF CHRIST'S COMING

"For this purpose was the Son of God manifested, that he might destroy the works of the devil."

1 John 3:8.

---

* [text of the 1872 edition]

1. Many eminent writers, heathen as well as Christian, both in earlier and later ages, have employed their utmost labour and art in painting the beauty of virtue. And the same pains they have taken to describe, in the liveliest colours, the deformity of vice; both of vice in general, and of those particular vices which were most prevalent in their respective ages and countries. With equal care they have placed in a strong light the happiness that attends virtue, and the misery which usually accompanies vice, and always follows it. And it may be acknowledged, that treatises of this kind are not wholly without their use. Probably hereby some, on the one hand, have been stirred up to desire and follow after virtue; and some, on the other hand, checked in their career of vice,—perhaps reclaimed from it, at least for a season. But the change effected in men by these means is seldom either deep or universal: Much less is it durable; in a little space it vanishes away as the morning cloud. Such motives are far too feeble to overcome the numberless temptations that surround us. All that can be said of the beauty and advantage of virtue, and the deformity and ill effects of vice, cannot resist, and much less overcome and heal, one irregular appetite or passion.

> All these fences and their whole array,
> One cunning bosom-sin sweeps quite away.

2. There is, therefore, an absolute necessity, if ever we would conquer vice, or steadily persevere in the practice of virtue, to have arms of a better kind than these; otherwise, we may *see* what is right, but we cannot attain it. Many of the men of reflection among the very Heathens were deeply sensible of this. The language of their heart was that of Medea:—

> Video meliora, proboque;
> Deteriora sequor:

How exactly agreeing with the words of the Apostle: (Personating a man convinced of sin, but not yet conquering it:) "The good that I would, I do not; but the evil I would not, that I do!" The impotence of the human mind, even the Roman philosopher could discover: "There is in every man," says he, "this weakness;" (he might have said, this sore disease;) "*gloriae sitis*,—thirst for glory. Nature points out the disease; but nature shows us no remedy."

3. Nor is it strange, that though they sought for a remedy, yet they found none. For they sought it where it never was and never will be found, namely, in themselves; in reason, in philosophy: Broken reeds, bubbles, smoke! They did not seek it in God, in whom alone it is possible to find it. In God! No; they totally disclaim this; and that in the strongest terms. For although Cicero, one of their oracles, once stumbled upon that strange truth, *Nemo unquam vir magnus sine afflatu divino fuit*,—"There never was any great man who was not divinely inspired;" yet in the very same tract he contradicts himself, and totally overthrows his own assertion, by asking, *Quis pro virtute aut sapientia gratias dedit Deis unquam?*— "Who ever returned thanks to God for his virtue or wisdom?" The Roman poet is, if possible, more express still; who, after mentioning several outward blessings, honestly adds,—

> Haec satis est orare Jovem, qui donat et aufert;
> Det vitam, det opes: aequum mi animum ipse parabo.

> We ask of God, what he can give or take,—
> Life, wealth; but virtuous I myself will make.

4. The best of them either sought virtue partly from God and partly from themselves, or sought it from those gods who were indeed but devils, and so not likely to make their votaries better than themselves. So dim was the light of the wisest of men, till "life and immortality were brought to light by the gospel;" till "the Son of God was manifested to destroy the works of the devil!"

But what are "the works of the devil," here mentioned? How was "the Son of God manifested" to destroy them? And how, in what manner, and by what steps, does he actually "destroy" them? These three very important points we may consider in their order.

I. 1. And, First, what these works of the devil are, we learn from the words preceding and following the text: "We know that he was manifested to take away our sins." (1 John 3:5.) "Whosoever abideth in him, sinneth not: Whosoever sinneth, seeth him not, neither knoweth him." (1 John 3:6.) "He that committeth sin is of the devil; for the devil sinneth from the beginning. For this purpose was the Son of God manifested, that he might destroy the works of the devil." (1 John 3:8.) "Whosoever is born of God doth not commit sin." (1 John 3:9.) From the whole of this it appears, that "the works of the devil," here spoken of, are sin, and the fruits of sin.

2. But since the wisdom of God has now dissipated the clouds which so long covered the earth, and put an end to the childish conjectures of men concerning these things, it may be of use to take a more distinct view of these "works of the devil," so far as the oracles of God instruct us. It is true, the design of the Holy Spirit was to assist our faith, not gratify our curiosity; and therefore the account he has given in the first chapters of Genesis is exceeding short. Nevertheless, it is so clear that we may learn therefrom whatsoever it concerns us to know.

3. To take the matter from the beginning: "The Lord God" (literally, JEHOVAH, the GODS; that is, One and Three) "created man in his own image;"—in his own *natural* image, as to his better part; that is, a spirit, as God is a spirit; endued with understanding; which, if not the essence, seems to be the most essential property, of a spirit. And probably the human spirit, like the angelical, then discerned truth by intuition. Hence he named every creature, as soon as he saw it, according to its inmost nature. Yet his knowledge was limited, as he was a creature: Ignorance, therefore, was inseparable from him; but error was not; it does not appear that he was mistaken in any thing. But he was capable of mistaking, of being deceived, although not necessitated to it.

4. He was endued also with a will, with various affections; (which are only the will exerting itself various ways;) that he might love, desire, and delight in that which is good: Otherwise his understanding had been to no purpose. He was likewise endued with liberty; a power of choosing what was good, and refusing what was not so. Without this, both the will and the understanding would have been utterly useless. Indeed, without liberty, man had been so far from being a *free agent*, that he could have been no *agent* at all. For every

unfree being is purely passive; not active in any degree. Have you a sword in your hand? Does a man, stronger than you, seize your hand, and force you to wound a third person? In this you are no agent, any more than the sword: The hand is as passive as the steel. So in every possible case. He that is not free is not an agent, but a patient.

5. It seems, therefore, that every spirit in the universe, as such, is endued with *understanding*, and, in consequence, with a *will*, and with a measure of *liberty*; and that these three are inseparably united in every intelligent nature. And observe: *Liberty necessitated*, or over-ruled, is really no liberty at all. It is a contradiction in terms. It is the same as *unfree freedom*; that is, downright nonsense.

6. It may be farther observed, (and it is an important observation,) that where there is no liberty, there can be no moral good or evil, no virtue or vice. The fire warms us; yet it is not capable of virtue: It burns us; yet this is no vice. There is no virtue, but where an intelligent being knows, loves, and chooses what is good; nor is there any vice, but where such a being knows, loves, and chooses what is evil.

7. And God created man, not only in his natural, but likewise in his own *moral*, image. He created him not only "in knowledge," but also in righteousness and true holiness. As his understanding was without blemish, perfect in its kind; so were all his affections. They were all set right, and duly exercised on their proper objects. And as a free agent, he steadily chose whatever was good, according to the direction of his understanding. In so doing, he was unspeakably happy; dwelling in God, and God in him; having an uninterrupted fellowship with the Father and the Son, through the eternal Spirit; and the continual testimony of his conscience, that all his ways were good and acceptable to God.

8. Yet his liberty (as was observed before) necessarily included a power of choosing or refusing either good or evil. Indeed it has been doubted whether man could then choose evil, knowing it to be such. But it cannot be doubted, he might mistake evil for good. He was not infallible; therefore not impeccable. And this unravels the whole difficulty of the grand question, *Unde malum?* "How came evil into the world?" It came from "Lucifer, son of the morning." It was the work of the devil. "For the devil," saith the Apostle, "sinneth from the beginning;" that is, was the first sinner in the universe, the author of sin, the first being who, by the abuse of his liberty, introduced evil into the creation. He,

> —Of the first,
>
> If not the first archangel,

was self-tempted to think too highly of himself. He freely yielded to the temptation; and gave way, first to pride, then to self-will. He said, "I will sit upon the sides of the north: I will be like the Most High." He did not fall alone, but soon drew after him a third part of the stars of heaven; in consequence of which they lost their glory and happiness, and were driven from their former habitation.

9. "Having great wrath," and perhaps envy, at the happiness of the creatures whom God had newly created, it is not strange that he should desire and endeavour to deprive them of it. In order to this, he concealed himself in the serpent, who was the most subtle, or intelligent, of all the brute creatures; and, on that account, the least liable to raise suspicion. Indeed, some have (not improbably) supposed that the serpent was then endued with reason and speech. Had not Eve known he was so, would she have admitted any parley with him? Would she not have been frightened rather than deceived? as the Apostle observes she was. To deceive her, Satan mingled truth with falsehood:—"Hath God said, Ye may not eat of every tree of the garden?"—and soon after persuaded her to disbelieve God, to suppose his threatening should not be fulfilled. She then lay open to the whole temptation:—To "the desire of the flesh;" for the tree was "good for food:" To "the desire of the eyes;" for it was "pleasant to the eyes:" And to "the pride of life;" for it was "to be desired to make one wise," and consequently honoured. So unbelief begot pride: She thought herself wiser than God; capable of finding a better way to happiness than God had taught her. It begot self-will: She was determined to do her own will, not the will of Him that made her. It begot foolish desires; and completed all by outward sin: "She took of the fruit, and did eat."

10. She then "gave to her husband, and he did eat." And in that day, yea, that moment, he *died!* The life of God was extinguished in his soul. The glory departed from him. He lost the whole moral image of God,—righteousness and true holiness. He was unholy; he was unhappy; he was full of sin; full of guilt and tormenting fears. Being broke off from God, and looking upon him now as an angry Judge, "he was afraid." But how was his understanding darkened, to think he could "hide himself from the presence of the Lord among the trees of the garden!" Thus was his soul utterly dead to God! And in that day his body likewise began to die,—became obnoxious to weakness, sickness, pain; all preparatory to the death of the body, which naturally led to eternal death.

II. Such are "the works of the devil;" sin and its fruits; considered in their order and connexion. We are, in the Second place, to consider how the Son of God was manifested in order to destroy them.

1. He was manifested as the only-begotten Son of God, in glory equal with the Father, to the inhabitants of heaven before and at the foundation of the world. These "morning stars sang together," all these "sons of God shouted for joy," when they heard him pronounce, "Let there be light; and there was light;"—when he "spread the north over the empty space," and "stretched out the heavens as a curtain." Indeed, it was the universal belief of the ancient Church, that God the Father none hath seen, nor can see; that from all eternity He hath dwelt in light unapproachable; and it is only in and by the Son of his love that he hath, at any time, revealed himself to his creatures.

2. How the Son of God was manifested to our first parents in paradise it is not easy to determine. It is generally, and not improbably, supposed that he appeared to them in the form of a man, and conversed with them face to face. Not that I can at all believe the ingenious dream of Dr. Watts concerning "the glorious humanity of Christ," which he supposes to have existed before the world began, and to have been endued with I know not what astonishing powers. Nay,

I look upon this to be an exceeding dangerous, yea, mischievous hypothesis; as it quite excludes the force of very many scriptures which have been hitherto thought to prove the Godhead of the Son. And I am afraid it was the grand means of turning that great man aside from the faith once delivered to the saints;—that is, if he was turned aside; if that beautiful soliloquy be genuine which is printed among his Posthumous Works, wherein he so earnestly beseeches the Son of God not to be displeased because he cannot believe him to be co-equal and co-eternal with the Father.

3. May we not reasonably believe it was by similar appearances that He was manifested, in succeeding ages, to Enoch, while he "walked with God;" to Noah, before and after the deluge; to Abraham, Isaac, and Jacob, on various occasions; and, to mention no more, to Moses? This seems to be the natural meaning of the word: "My servant Moses is faithful in all my house.—With him will I speak mouth to mouth, even apparently, and not in dark speeches; and the similitude of Jehovah shall he behold;" namely, the Son of God.

4. But all these were only types of his grand manifestation. It was in the fulness of time (in just the middle age of the world, as a great man largely proves) that God "brought his first-begotten into the world, made of a woman," by the power of the Highest overshadowing her. He was afterwards manifested to the shepherds; to devout Simeon; to Anna, the Prophetess; and to "all that waited for redemption in Jerusalem."

5. When he was of due age for executing his priestly office, he was manifested to Israel; preaching the gospel of the kingdom of God in every town and in every city. And for a time he was glorified by all, who acknowledged that he "spake as never man spake;" that "he spake as one having authority," with all the wisdom of God and the power of God. He was manifested by numberless "signs, and wonders, and mighty works which he did," as well as by his whole life; being the only one born of a woman "who knew no sin," who, from his birth to his death, did "all things well;" doing continually "not his own will, but the will of Him that sent him."

6. After all, "behold the Lamb of God, taking away the sin of the world!" This was a more glorious manifestation of himself than any he had made before. How wonderfully was he manifested to angels and men, when he "was wounded for our transgressions;" when he "bore all our sins in his own body on the tree;" when, having "by that one oblation of himself once offered, made a full, perfect, and sufficient sacrifice, oblation, and satisfaction for the sins of the whole world," he cried out, "It is finished; and bowed his head, and gave up the ghost!" We need but just mention those farther manifestations,—his resurrection from the dead; his ascension into heaven, into the glory which he had before the world began; and his pouring out the Holy Ghost on the day of Pentecost; both of which are beautifully described in those well-known words of the Psalmist: "Thou art gone up on high, thou hast led captivity captive, and hast received gifts for men; yea, even for thine enemies, that the Lord God might dwell among" or in "them."

7. "That the Lord God might dwell in them:" This refers to a yet farther manifestation of the Son of God; even his inward manifestation of himself. When he spoke of this to his Apostles but a little before his death, one of them immediately asked, "Lord, how is it that thou wilt manifest thyself to us, and not unto the world?" By enabling us to believe in his name. For he is then inwardly manifested to us when we are enabled to say with confidence, "My Lord, and my God!" Then each of us can boldly say, "The life which I now live, I live by faith in the Son of God, who loved me and gave himself for me." [Gal. 2:20] And it is by thus manifesting himself in our hearts that he effectually "destroys the works of the devil."

III. 1. How he does this, in what manner, and by what steps, he does actually destroy them, we are now to consider. And, First, as Satan began his work in Eve by tainting her with unbelief, so the Son of God begins his work in man by enabling us to believe in him. He both opens and enlightens the eyes of our understanding. Out of darkness he commands light to shine, and takes away the veil which the "god of this world" had spread over our hearts. And we then see not by a chain of *reasoning*, but by a kind of *intuition*, by a direct view, that "God was in Christ, reconciling the world to himself, not imputing to them their former trespasses;" not imputing them to me. In that day "we know that we are of God," children of God by faith; "having redemption through the blood of Christ, even the forgiveness of sin." "Being justified by faith, we have peace with God, through our Lord Jesus Christ;"—that peace which enables us in every state therewith to be content; which delivers us from all perplexing doubts, from all tormenting fears; and in particular, from that "fear of death whereby we were all our life-time subject to bondage."

2. At the same time the Son of God strikes at the root of that grand work of the devil,—pride; causing the sinner to humble himself before the Lord, to abhor himself, as it were, in dust and ashes. He strikes at the root of self-will; enabling the humbled sinner to say in all things, "Not as I will, but as thou wilt." He destroys the love of the world; delivering them that believe in him from "every foolish and hurtful desire;" from the "desire of the flesh, the desire of the eyes, and the pride of life." He saves them from seeking, or expecting to find, happiness in any creature. As Satan turned the heart of man from the Creator to the creature; so the Son of God turns his heart back again from the creature to the Creator. Thus it is, by manifesting himself, he destroys the works of the devil; restoring the guilty outcast from God, to his favour, to pardon and peace; the sinner in whom dwelleth no good thing, to love and holiness; the burdened, miserable sinner, to joy unspeakable, to real, substantial happiness.

3. But it may be observed, that the Son of God does not destroy the whole work of the devil in man, as long as he remains in this life. He does not yet destroy bodily weakness, sickness, pain, and a thousand infirmities incident to flesh and blood. He does not destroy all that weakness of understanding, which is the natural consequence of the soul's dwelling in a corruptible body; so that still,

Humanum est errare et nescire:

"Both ignorance and error belong to humanity." He entrusts us with only an exceeding small share of knowledge, in our present state; lest our knowledge should interfere with our humility, and we should again affect to be as gods. It is to remove from us all temptation to pride, and all thought of independency, (which is the very thing that men in general so earnestly covet under the name of *liberty*.) that he leaves us encompassed with all these infirmities, particularly weakness of understanding; till the sentence takes place, "Dust thou art, and unto dust thou shalt return!"

4. Then error, pain, and all bodily infirmities cease: All these are destroyed by death. And death itself, "the last enemy" of man, shall be destroyed at the resurrection. The moment that we hear the voice of the archangel and the trump of God, "then shall be fulfilled the saying that is written, Death is swallowed up in victory." "This corruptible" body "shall put on incorruption; this mortal" body "shall put on immortality;" and the Son of God, manifested in the clouds of heaven, shall destroy this last work of the devil!

5. Here then we see in the clearest, strongest light, what is real religion: A restoration of man by Him that bruises the serpent's head [Gen. 3:15], to all that the old serpent deprived him of; a restoration not only to the favour but likewise to the image of God, implying not barely deliverance from sin, but the being filled with the fullness of God. It is plain, if we attend to the preceding considerations, that nothing short of this is Christian religion. Every thing else, whether negative or external, is utterly wide of the mark. But what a paradox is this! How little is it understood in the Christian world; yea, in this enlightened age, wherein it is taken for granted, the world is wiser than ever it was from the beginning! Among all our discoveries, who has discovered this? How few either among the learned or unlearned! And yet, if we believe the Bible, who can deny it? Who can doubt of it? It runs through the Bible from the beginning to the end, in one connected chain; and the agreement of every part of it, with every other, is, properly, the analogy of faith. Beware of taking any thing else, or anything less than this, for religion! Not *any thing else:* Do not imagine an outward form, a round of duties, both in public and private, is religion! Do not suppose that honesty, justice, and whatever is called *morality*, (though excellent in its place,) is religion! And least of all dream that orthodoxy, right opinion, (vulgarly called *faith*,) is religion. Of all religious dreams, this is the vainest; which takes hay and stubble for gold tried in the fire!

6. O do not take *any thing less than this* for the religion of Jesus Christ! Do not take part of it for the whole! What God hath joined together, put not asunder! Take no less for his religion, than the "faith that worketh by love;" all inward and outward holiness. Be not content with any religion which does not imply the destruction of all the works of the devil; that is, of all sin. We know, weakness of understanding, and a thousand infirmities, will remain, while this corruptible body remains; but sin need not remain: This is that work of the devil, eminently so called, which the Son of God was

manifested to destroy in this present life. He is able, he is willing, to destroy it now, in all that believe in him. Only be not straitened in your own bowels! Do not distrust his power, or his love! Put his promise to the proof! He hath spoken: And is he not ready likewise to perform? Only "come boldly to the throne of grace," trusting in his mercy; and you shall find, "He saveth to the uttermost all those that come to God through him!"

63.* THE GENERAL SPREAD OF THE GOSPEL

"The earth shall be full of the knowledge of the Lord, as the waters covers the sea."

Isa. 11:9.

1. In what a condition is the world at present! How does darkness, intellectual darkness, ignorance, with vice and misery attendant upon it, cover the face of the earth! From the accurate inquiry made with indefatigable pains by our ingenious countryman, Mr. Brerewood; (who travelled himself over a great part of the known world, in order to form the more exact judgment;) supposing the world to be divided into thirty parts, nineteen of them are professed Heathens, altogether as ignorant of Christ, as if he had never come into the world: Six of the remaining parts are professed Mahometans: So that only five in thirty are so much as nominally Christians!

2. And let it be remembered, that since this computation was made, many new nations have been discovered; numberless islands, particularly in the South Sea, large and well inhabited: But by whom? By Heathens of the basest sort; many of them inferior to the beasts of the field. Whether they eat men or no, (which indeed I cannot find any sufficient ground to believe,) they certainly kill all that fall into their hands. They are, therefore, more savage than lions; who kill no more creatures than are necessary to satisfy their present hunger. See the real dignity of human nature! Here it appears in its genuine purity, not polluted either by those "general corrupters, kings," or by the least tincture of religion! What will Abbe Raynal (that determined enemy to monarchy and revelation) say to this?

3. A little, and but a little, above the Heathens in religion, are the Mahometans. But how far and wide has this miserable delusion spread over the face of the earth! Insomuch that the Mahometans are considerably more in number (as six to five) than Christians. And by all the accounts which have any pretence to authenticity, these are also, in general, as utter strangers to all true religion as their four-footed brethren; as void of mercy as lions and tigers; as much given up to brutal lusts as bulls or goats. So that they are in truth a disgrace to human nature, and a plague to all that are under their iron yoke.

4. It is true, a celebrated writer (Lady Mary Wortley Montague) gives a very different character of them. With the finest flow of words, in the most elegant language, she labours to wash the Aethiop white. She represents them as many degrees above the Christians; as some of the most amiable

---

* [text of the 1872 edition]

people in the world; as possessed of all the social virtues; as some of the most accomplished of men. But I can in no wise receive her report: I cannot rely upon her authority. I believe those round about her had just as much religion as their admirer had when she was admitted into the interior parts of the Grand Seignior's seraglio. Notwithstanding, therefore, all that such a witness does or can say in their favour, I believe the Turks in general are little, if at all, better than the generality of the Heathens.

5. And little, if at all, better than the Turks, are the Christians in the Turkish dominions; even the best of them; those that live in the Morea, or are scattered up and down in Asia. The more numerous bodies of Georgian, Circassian, Mengrelian Christians, are a proverb of reproach to the Turks themselves; not only for their deplorable ignorance, but for their total, stupid, barbarous irreligion.

6. From the most authentic accounts we can obtain of the Southern Christians, those in Abyssinia, and of the Northern Churches, under the jurisdiction of the Patriarch of Moscow, we have reason to fear they are much in the same condition, both with regard to knowledge and religion, as those in Turkey. Or if those in Abyssinia are more civilized, and have a larger share of knowledge, yet they do not appear to have any more religion than either the Mahometans or Pagans.

7. The Western Churches seem to have the pre-eminence over all these in many respects. They have abundantly more knowledge: They have more scriptural and more rational modes of worship. Yet two thirds of them are still involved in the corruptions of the Church of Rome; and most of these are entirely unacquainted with either the theory or practice of religion. And as to those who are called Protestants, or Reformed, what acquaintance with it have they? Put Papists and Protestants, French and English together, the bulk of one and of the other nation; and what manner of Christians are they? Are they "holy as He that hath called them is holy?" Are they filled with "righteousness, and peace, and joy in the Holy Ghost?" Is there "that mind in them which was also in Christ Jesus?" And do they "walk as Christ also walked?" Nay, they are as far from it as hell is from heaven!

8. Such is the present state of mankind in all parts of the world! But how astonishing is this, if there is a God in heaven, and if his eyes are over all the earth! Can he despise the work of his own hand? Surely this is one of the greatest mysteries under heaven! How is it possible to reconcile this with either the wisdom or goodness of God? And what can give ease to a thoughtful mind under so melancholy a prospect? What but the consideration, that things will not always be so; that another scene will soon be opened? God will be jealous of his honour: He will arise and maintain his own cause. He will judge the prince of this world, and spoil him of his usurped dominion. He will give his Son "the Heathen for his inheritance, and the uttermost parts of the earth for his possession." "The earth shall be filled with the knowledge of the Lord, as the waters cover the sea." The loving knowledge of God, producing uniform, uninterrupted holiness and happiness, shall cover the earth; shall fill every soul of man.

9. "Impossible," will some men say, "yea, the greatest of all impossibilities, that we should see a Christian world; yea, a Christian nation, or city! How can these things be?" On one supposition, indeed, not only all impossibility, but all difficulty vanishes away. Only suppose the Almighty to act *irresistibly*, and the thing is done; yea, with just the same ease as when "God said, Let there be light; and there was light." But then, man would be man no longer: His inmost nature would be changed. He would no longer be a moral agent, any more than the sun or the wind; as he would no longer be endued with liberty,—a power of choosing, or self-determination: Consequently, he would no longer be capable of virtue or vice, of reward or punishment.

10. But setting aside this clumsy way of cutting the knot which we are not able to untie, how can all men be made holy and happy, while they continue men? While they still enjoy both the understanding, the affections, and the liberty which are essential to a moral agent? There seems to be a plain, simple way of removing this difficulty, without entangling ourselves in any subtile, metaphysical disquisitions. As God is One, so the work of God is uniform in all ages. May we not then conceive how he *will* work on the souls of men in times to come, by considering how he *does* work *now*, and how he *has* wrought in times past?

11. Take one instance of this, and such an instance as you cannot easily be deceived in. You know how God wrought in *your own* soul, when he first enabled you to say, "The life I now live, I live by faith in the Son of God, who loved me, and gave himself for me." He did not take away your understanding; but enlightened and strengthened it. He did not destroy any of your affections; rather they were more vigorous than before. Least of all did he take away your liberty; your power of choosing good or evil: He did not *force* you; but, being *assisted* by his grace, you, like Mary, *chose* the better part. Just so has he *assisted* five in one house to make that happy *choice*, fifty or five hundred in one city; and many thousands in a nation;—without depriving any of them of that liberty which is essential to a moral agent.

12. Not that I deny, that there are exempt cases, wherein

> The' o'erwhelming power of saving grace

does, for a time, work as irresistibly as lightning falling from heaven. But I speak of God's general manner of working, of which I have known innumerable instances; perhaps more within fifty years last past, than any one in England or in Europe. And with regard even to these exempt cases; although God does work irresistibly *for the time*, yet I do not believe there is any human soul in which God works irresistibly *at all times*. Nay, I am fully persuaded there is not. I am persuaded, there are no men living that have not many times "resisted the Holy Ghost," and made void "the counsel of God against themselves." Yea, I am persuaded every child of God has had, at some time, "life and death set before him," eternal life and eternal death; and has in himself the casting voice. So true is that well-known saying of St. Austin, (one of the noblest he ever uttered,) *Qui fecit nos sine nobis, non salvabit nos sine nobis*: "He that made us without ourselves, will not save us without ourselves." Now in the same manner as God has converted so many to himself without destroying their liberty, he *can* undoubtedly convert whole nations, or the whole world; and it is as easy to him to convert a world, as one individual soul.

13. Let us observe what God has done already. Between fifty and sixty years ago, God raised up a few young men, in the University of Oxford, to testify those grand truths, which were then little attended to:—That without holiness no man shall see the Lord;—that this holiness is the work of God, who worketh in us both to will and to do;—that he doeth it of his own good pleasure, merely for the merits of Christ;—that this holiness is the mind that was in Christ; enabling us to walk as he also walked;—that no man can be thus sanctified till he is justified;—and, that we are justified by faith alone. These great truths they declared on all occasions, in private and in public; having no design but to promote the glory of God, and no desire but to save souls from death.

14. From Oxford, where it first appeared, the little leaven spread wider and wider. More and more saw the truth as it is in Jesus, and received it in the love thereof. More and more found "redemption through the blood of Jesus, even the forgiveness of sins." They were born again of his Spirit, and filled with righteousness, and peace, and joy in the Holy Ghost. It afterwards spread to every part of the land, and a little one became a thousand. It then spread into North Britain and Ireland; and, a few years after into New-York, Pennsylvania, and many other provinces in America, even as high as Newfoundland and Nova-Scotia. So that, although at first this "grain of mustard—seed" was "the least of all the seeds;" yet, in a few years, it grew into a "large tree, and put forth great branches."

15. Generally, when these truths, justification by faith in particular, were declared in any large town, after a few days or weeks, there came suddenly on the great congregation,—not in a corner, at London, Bristol, Newcastle-upon-Tyne, in particular,—a violent and impetuous power, which,

> Like mighty wind or torrent fierce,
>
> Did then opposers all o'er-run.

And this frequently continued, with shorter or longer intervals, for several weeks or months. But it gradually subsided, and then the work of God was carried on by gentle degrees; while that Spirit, in watering the seed that had been sown, in confirming and strengthening them that had believed,

> Deign'd his influence to infuse,
>
> Secret, refreshing as the silent dews.

And this difference in his usual manner of working was observable not only in Great Britain and Ireland, but in every part of America, from South to North, wherever the word of God came with power.

16. Is it not then highly probable, that God will carry on his work in the same manner as he has begun? That he *will* carry it on, I cannot doubt; however Luther may affirm, that a revival of religion never lasts above a generation,—that is, thirty years; (whereas the present revival has already continued above fifty;) or however prophets of evil may say, "All will be at an end when the first instruments are removed." There will then, very probably, be a great shaking; but I cannot induce myself to think that God has wrought so glorious a work, to let it sink and die away in a few years. No: I trust, this is only the beginning of a far greater work; the dawn of "the latter day glory."

17. And is it not probable, I say, that he will carry it on in the same manner as he has begun? At the first breaking out of this work in this or that place, there may be a shower, a torrent of grace; and so at some other particular seasons, which "the Father has reserved in his own power:" But in general, it seems, the kingdom of God will not "come with observation;" but will silently increase, wherever it is set up, and spread from heart to heart, from house to house, from town to town, from one kingdom to another. May it not spread, first, through the remaining provinces; then, through the isles of North America; and, at the same time, from England to Holland, where there is already a blessed work in Utrecht, Haerlem, and many other cities? Probably it will spread from these to the Protestants in France, to those in Germany, and those in Switzerland; then to Sweden, Denmark, Russia, and all the other Protestant nations in Europe.

18. May we not suppose that the same leaven of pure and undefiled religion, of experimental knowledge and love of God, of inward and outward holiness, will afterwards spread to the Roman Catholics in Great Britain, Ireland, Holland; in Germany, France, Switzerland; and in all other countries where Romanists and Protestants live intermixed and familiarly converse with each other? Will it not then be easy for the wisdom of God to make a way for religion, in the life and power thereof, into those countries that are merely Popish; as Italy, Spain, Portugal? And may it not be gradually diffused from thence to all that name the name of Christ, in the various provinces of Turkey, in Abyssinia, yea, and in the remotest parts, not only of Europe, but of Asia, Africa, and America?

19. And in every nation under heaven, we may reasonably believe, God will observe the same order which he hath done from the beginning of Christianity. "They shall all know me, saith the Lord;" not from the greatest to the least (this is that wisdom of the world which is foolishness with God;) but "from the least to the greatest;" that the praise may not be of men, but of God. Before the end, even the rich shall enter into the kingdom of God. Together with them will enter in the great, the noble, the honourable; yea, the rulers, the princes, the kings of the earth. Last of all, the wise and learned, the men of genius, the philosophers, will be convinced that they are fools; will be "converted, and become as little children," and "enter into the kingdom of God."

20. Then shall be fully accomplished to the house of Israel, the spiritual Israel, of whatever people or nation, that gracious promise, "I will put my laws in their minds, and write them in their hearts: And I will be to them a God, and they shall be to me a people. And they shall not teach every man his neighbour, and every man his brother, saying, Know the Lord: For they shall all know me, from the least to the greatest. For I will be merciful to their unrighteousness, and their sins and their iniquities will I remember no more." Then shall "the times of" universal "refreshment come from the presence of the Lord." The grand "Pentecost" shall "fully

come," and "devout men in every nation under heaven," however distant in place from each other, shall "all be filled with the Holy Ghost;" and they will "continue steadfast in the Apostles' doctrine, and in the fellowship, and in the breaking of bread, and in prayers;" they will "eat their meat," and do all that they have to do, "with gladness and singleness of heart. Great grace will be upon them all;" and they will be "all of one heart and of one soul." The natural, necessary consequence of this will be the same as it was in the beginning of the Christian Church: "None of them will say, that aught of the things which he possesses is his own; but they will have all things common. Neither will there be any among them that want: For as many as are possessed of lands or houses will sell them; and distribution will be made to every man, according as he has need." All their desires, meantime, and passions, and tempers will be cast in one mould; while all are doing the will of God on earth, as it is done in heaven. All their "conversation will be seasoned with salt," and will "minister grace to the hearers;" seeing it will not be so much they that speak, "as the Spirit of their Father that speaketh in them." And there will be no "root of bitterness springing up," either to defile or trouble them: There will be no Ananias or Sapphira, to bring back the cursed love of money among them: There will be no partiality; no "widows neglected in the daily ministration:" Consequently, there will be no temptation to any murmuring thought, or unkind word, of one against another; while,

> They all are of one heart and soul,
> And only love informs the whole.

21. The grand stumbling-block being thus happily removed out of the way, namely, the lives of the Christians, the Mahometans will look upon them with other eyes, and begin to give attention to their words. And as their words will be clothed with divine energy, attended with the demonstration of the Spirit and of power, those of them that fear God will soon take knowledge of the Spirit whereby the Christians speak. They will "receive with meekness the engrafted word," and will bring forth fruit with patience. From them the leaven will soon spread to those who till then, had no fear of God before their eyes. Observing the *Christian dogs*, as they used to term them, to have changed their nature; to be sober, temperate, just, benevolent; and that, in spite of all provocations to the contrary; from admiring their lives, they will surely be led to consider and embrace their doctrine. And then the Saviour of sinners will say, "The hour is come; I will glorify my Father: I will seek and save the sheep that were wandering on the dark mountains. Now will I avenge myself of my enemy, and pluck the prey out of the lion's teeth. I will resume my own, for ages lost: I will claim the purchase of my blood." So he will go forth in the greatness of his strength, and all his enemies shall flee before him. All the prophets of lies shall vanish away, and all the nations that had followed them shall acknowledge the great Prophet of the Lord, "mighty in word and deed;" and "shall honour the Son, even as they honour the Father."

22. And then, the grand stumbling-block being removed from the heathen nations also, the same Spirit will be poured out upon them; even those that remain in the uttermost parts of the sea. The poor American savage will no more ask, "What are the Christians better than us?"—when they see their steady practice of universal temperance, and of justice, mercy, and truth. The Malabarian Heathen will have no more room to say, "Christian man take my wife: Christian man much drunk: Christian man kill man! *Devil-Christian!* me no Christian." Rather, seeing how far the Christians exceed their own countrymen in whatsoever things are lovely and of good report, they will adopt a very different language, and say, *Angel-Christian!* The holy lives of the Christians will be an argument they will not know how to resist: Seeing the Christians steadily and uniformly practise what is agreeable to the law written in their own hearts, their prejudices will quickly die away, and they will gladly receive "the truth as it is in Jesus."

23. We may reasonably believe, that the heathen nations which are mingled with the Christians, and those that, bordering upon Christian nations, have constant and familiar intercourse with them, will be some of the first who learn to worship God in spirit and in truth; those, for instance, that live on the continent of America, or in the islands that have received colonies from Europe. Such are likewise all those inhabitants of the East Indies that adjoin to any of the Christian settlements. To these may be added, numerous tribes of Tartars, the heathen parts of the Russias, and the inhabitants of Norway, Finland, and Lapland. Probably these will be followed by those more distant nations with whom the Christians trade; to whom they will impart what is of infinitely more value than earthly pearls, or gold and silver. The God of love will then prepare his messengers, and make a way into the polar regions; into the deepest recesses of America, and into the interior parts of Africa; yea, into the heart of China and Japan, with the countries adjoining to them. And "their sound" will then "go forth into all lands, and their voice to the ends of the earth!"

24. But one considerable difficulty still remains: There are very many heathen nations in the world that have no intercourse, either by trade or any other means, with Christians of any kind. Such are the inhabitants of the numerous islands in the South Sea, and probably in all large branches of the ocean. Now, what shall be done for these poor outcasts of men? "How shall they believe," saith the Apostle, "in Him of whom they have not heard? And how shall they hear without a preacher?" You may add, "And how shall they preach, unless they be sent?" Yea, but is not God able to send them? Cannot he raise them up, as it were, out of the stones? And can he ever want means of sending them? No: Were there no other means, he can "take them by his Spirit," as he did Ezekiel. (Ezek. 3:12,) or by his angel, as he did Philip, (Acts 8,) and set them down wheresoever it pleaseth him. Yea, he can find out a thousand ways to foolish man unknown. And he surely will: For heaven and earth may pass away; but his word shall not pass away: He will give his Son "the uttermost part of the earth for his possession."

25. And so all Israel too shall be saved. For "blindness has happened to Israel," as the great Apostle observes, (Rom. 11:25.) till the fullness of the "Gentiles be come in." Then "the Deliverer that cometh out of Sion shall turn away

iniquity from Jacob." "God hath now concluded them all in unbelief, that he may have mercy upon all." Yea, and he will so have mercy upon all Israel, as to give them all temporal with all spiritual blessings. For this is the promise: "For the Lord thy God will gather thee from all nations, whither the Lord thy God hath scattered thee. And the Lord thy God will bring thee into the land which thy fathers possessed, and thou shalt possess it. And the Lord thy God will circumcise thine heart, and the heart of thy seed, to love the Lord thy God with all thine heart, and with all thy soul." (Deut. 30:3.) Again: "I will gather them out of all countries, whither I have driven them: And I will bring them again to this place, and I will cause them to dwell safely: And I will give them one heart, and one way, that they may fear me for ever. I will put my fear in their hearts, that they shall not depart from me. And I will plant them in this land assuredly, with my whole heart and with my whole soul." (Jer. 32:37.) Yet again: "I will take you from among the Heathen, and gather you out of all countries, and will bring you into your own land. Then will I sprinkle clean water upon you, and ye shall be clean: From all your filthiness, and from all your idols, will I cleanse you. And ye shall dwell in the land that I gave to your fathers; and ye shall be my people, and I will be your God." (Ezek. 36:24.) 26. At that time will be accomplished all those glorious promises made to the Christian Church, which will not then be confined to this or that nation, but will include all the inhabitants of the earth. "They shall not hurt nor destroy in all my holy mountain." (Isaiah 11:9) "Violence shall no more be heard in thy land, wasting nor destruction within thy borders; but thou shalt call thy walls, Salvation, and thy gates Praise." Thou shalt be encompassed on every side with salvation, and all that go through thy gates shall praise God. "The sun shall be no more thy light by day; neither for brightness shall the moon give light unto thee: But the Lord shall be unto thee an everlasting light, and thy God thy glory." The light of the sun and moon shall be swallowed up in the light of His countenance, shining upon thee. "Thy people also shall be all righteous … the work of my hands, that I may be glorified." "As the earth bringeth forth her bud, and the garden causeth the things that are sown in it to spring forth; so the Lord God will cause righteousness and praise to spring forth before all the nations." (Isaiah 60:18; and 61:11.)

27. This I apprehend to be the answer, yea, the only full and satisfactory answer that can be given, to the objection against the wisdom and goodness of God, taken from the present state of the world. It will not always be thus: These things are only permitted for a season by the great Governor of the world, that he may draw immense, eternal good out of this temporary evil. This is the very key which the Apostle himself gives us in the words above recited: "God hath concluded them all in unbelief, that he might have mercy upon all." In view of this glorious event, how well may we cry out, "O the depth of the riches both of the wisdom and knowledge of God!" although for a season "his judgments were unsearchable, and his ways past finding out." (Rom. 11:32,

33.) It is enough, that we are assured of this one point, that all these transient evils will issue well; will have a happy conclusion; and that "mercy first and last will reign." All unprejudiced persons may see with their eyes, that He is already renewing the face of the earth: And we have strong reason to hope that the work he hath begun, he will carry on unto the day of the Lord Jesus; that he will never intermit this blessed work of his Spirit, until he has fulfilled all his promises, until he hath put a period to sin, and misery, and infirmity, and death; and re-established universal holiness and happiness, and caused all the inhabitants of the earth to sing together, "Hallelujah, the Lord God omnipotent reigneth!" "Blessing, and glory, and wisdom, and honour, and power, and might, be unto our God for ever and ever!" (Rev. 7:12.)

64.* THE NEW CREATION

Behold, I make all things new.

Rev. 21:5.

1. What a strange scene is here opened to our view! How remote from all our natural apprehensions! Not a glimpse of what is here revealed was ever seen in the heathen world. Not only the modern, barbarous, uncivilized Heathens have not the least conception of it; but it was equally unknown to the refined, polished Heathens of ancient Greece and Rome. And it is almost as little thought of or understood by the generality of Christians: I mean, not barely those that are nominally such, that have the form of godliness without the power; but even those that in a measure fear God, and study to work righteousness.

2. It must be allowed that after all the researches we can make, still our knowledge of the great truth which is delivered to us in these words is exceedingly short and imperfect. As this is a point of mere revelation, beyond the reach of all our natural faculties, we cannot penetrate far into it, nor form any adequate conception of it. But it may be an encouragement to those who have in any degree tasted of the powers of the world to come to go as far as we can go, interpreting Scripture by Scripture, according to the analogy of faith.

3. The Apostle, caught up in the visions of God, tells us in the first verse of the chapter, "I saw a new heaven and a new earth;" and adds, (Rev. 21:5,) "He that sat upon the throne said," (I believe the only words which he is said to utter throughout the whole book,) "Behold, I make all things new."

4. Very many commentators entertain a strange opinion that this relates only to the present state of things, and gravely tell us that the words are to be referred to the flourishing state of the Church, which commenced after the heathen persecutions. Nay, some of them have discovered that all which the Apostle speaks concerning the "new heaven and the new earth" was fulfilled when Constantine the Great poured in riches and honours upon the Christians. What a miserable way is this of making void the whole counsel of

---

* [text from the 1872 edition]

God, with regard to all that grand chain of events, in reference to his Church, yea, and to all mankind, from the time that John was in Patmos unto the end of the world! Nay, the line of this prophecy reaches farther still: It does not end with the present world, but shows us the things that will come to pass when this world is no more. For,

5. Thus saith the Creator and Governor of the universe: "Behold, I make all things new;"—all which are included in that expression of the Apostle, "A new heaven and a new earth." *A new heaven:* the original word in Genesis (Gen. 1) is in the plural number. And indeed this is the constant language of Scripture—not *heaven,* but *heavens.* Accordingly, the ancient Jewish writers are accustomed to reckon three heavens; in conformity to which, the Apostle Paul speaks of his being "caught up into the third heaven." It is this, the third heaven, which is usually supposed to be the more immediate residence of God; so far as any residence can be ascribed to his omnipresent Spirit, who pervades and fills the whole universe. It is here (if we speak after the manner of men) that the Lord sitteth upon his throne, surrounded by angels and archangels, and by all his flaming ministers.

6. We cannot think that this heaven will undergo any change, any more than its Great Inhabitant. Surely this palace of the Most High was the same from eternity, and will be, world without end. Only the inferior heavens are liable to change; the highest of which we usually call the starry heaven. This, St. Peter informs us, "is reserved unto fire, against the day of judgment and destruction of ungodly men." In that day, "being on fire," it shall, first, shrivel as a parchment scroll;" then it shall "be dissolved, and shall pass away with a great noise;" lastly, it shall "flee from the face of Him that sitteth on the throne, and there shall be found no place for it."

7. At the same time "the stars shall fall from heaven;" the secret chain being broken which had retained them in their several orbits from the foundation of the world. In the meanwhile the lower or sublunary heaven, with the elements (or principles that compose it,) "shall melt with fervent heat;" while "the earth with the works that are therein, shall be burned up." This is the introduction to a far nobler state of things, such as it has not yet entered into the heart of men to conceive,—the universal restoration, which is to succeed the universal destruction. For "we look," says the Apostle, "for new heavens and a new earth, wherein dwelleth righteousness." (2 Pet. 3:7.)

8. One considerable difference there will undoubtedly be in the starry heaven, when it is created anew: There will be no blazing stars, no comets there. Whether those horrid, eccentric orbs are half-formed planets, in a chaotic state (I speak on the supposition of a plurality of worlds;) or such as have undergone their general conflagration, they will certainly have no place in the new heaven, where all will be exact order and harmony. There may be many other differences between the heaven that now is and that which will be after the renovation: But they are above our apprehension: We must leave eternity to explain them.

9. We may more easily conceive the changes which will be wrought in the lower heaven, in the region of the air. It will be no more torn by hurricanes, or agitated by furious storms,

or destructive tempests. Pernicious or terrifying meteors will have no more place therein. We shall have no more occasion to say,

> There like a trumpet, loud and strong,
>   Thy thunder shakes our coast;
> While the red lightnings wave along,
>   The banners of thy host!

No: All will be then light, fair, serene; a lively picture of the eternal day.

10. All the elements (taking that word in the common sense, for the principles of which all natural beings are compounded) will be new indeed; entirely changed as to their qualities, although not as to their nature. Fire is at present the general destroyer of all things under the sun; dissolving all things that come within the sphere of its action, and reducing them to their primitive atoms. But no sooner will it have performed its last great office of destroying the heavens and the earth; (whether you mean thereby one system only, or the whole fabric of the universe; the difference between one and millions of worlds being nothing before the great Creator;) when, I say, it has done this, the destructions wrought by fire will come to a perpetual end. It will destroy no more: it will consume no more: it will forget its power to burn,—which it possesses only during the present state of things,—and be as harmless in the new heavens and earth as it is now in the bodies of men and other animals, and the substance of trees and flowers; in all which (as late experiments show) large quantities of ethereal fire are lodged; if it be not rather an essential component part of every material being under the sun. But it will probably retain its vivifying power, though divested of its power to destroy.

11. It has been already observed that the calm, placid air will be no more disturbed by storms and tempests. There will be no more meteors, with their horrid glare, affrighting the poor children of men. May we not add, (though at first it may sound like a paradox,) that there will be no more rain? It is observable that there was none in Paradise; a circumstance which Moses particularly mentions: (Gen. 2:5, 6:) "The Lord God had not caused it to rain upon the earth.—But there went up a mist from the earth," which then covered up the abyss of waters, "and watered the whole face of the ground," with moisture sufficient for all the purposes of vegetation. We have all reason to believe that the case will be the same when paradise is restored. Consequently there will be no more clouds or fogs; but one bright, refulgent day. Much less will there be any poisonous damps, or pestilential blasts. There will be no Sirocco in Italy; no parching or suffocating winds in Arabia; no keen north-east winds in our own country,

> Shattering the graceful locks of yon fair trees;

but only pleasing, healthful breezes,

> Fanning the earth with odoriferous wings.

12. But what change will the element of water undergo when all things are made new! It will be, in every part of the world, clear and limpid; pure from all unpleasing or unhealthful mixtures; rising here and there in crystal fountains, to refresh and adorn the earth "with liquid lapse of murmuring stream." For, undoubtedly, as there were in Paradise, there

will be various rivers gently gliding along, for the use and pleasure of both man and beast. But the inspired writer has expressly declared, "there will be no more sea." (Rev. 21:1.) We have every reason to believe, that at the beginning of the world, when God said, "Let the waters under the heaven be gathered together unto one place, and let the dry land appear," (Gen. 1:9,) the dry land spread over the face of the water, and covered it on every side. And so it seems to have done, till, in order to the general deluge which God had determined to bring upon the earth at once, "the windows of heaven were opened, and the fountains of the great deep broken up." But the sea will then retire within its primitive bounds, and appear on the surface of the earth no more. For either, indeed, will there be any more need of the sea. For either as the ancient Poet supposes,

Omnis feret omnia tellus,

—every part of the earth will naturally produce whatever its inhabitants want,—or all mankind will procure what the whole earth affords by a much easier and readier conveyance. For all the inhabitants of the earth, our Lord informs us, will then be *isaggeloi,—equal to angels*; on a level with them in swiftness, as well as strength; so that they can quick as thought, transport themselves, or whatever they want, from one side of the globe to the other.

13. But it seems, a greater change will be wrought in the earth, than even in the air and water. Not that I can believe that wonderful discovery of Jacob Behmen, which many so eagerly contend for; that the earth itself with all its furniture and inhabitants, will then be transparent as glass. There does not seem to be the least foundation for this, either in Scripture or reason. Surely not in Scripture: I know not one text in the Old or New Testament which affirms any such thing. Certainly it cannot be inferred from that text in the Revelation: (Rev. 4:6:), "And before the throne there was a sea of glass, like unto crystal." And yet, if I mistake not, this is the chief, if not the only Scripture which has been urged in favour of this opinion! Neither can I conceive that it has any foundation in reason. It has indeed been warmly alleged, that all things would be far more beautiful if they were quite transparent. But I cannot apprehend this: Yea, I apprehend quite the contrary. Suppose every part of a human body were made transparent as crystal, would it appear more beautiful than it does now? Nay, rather it would shock us above measure. The surface of the body, and in particular "the human face divine," is undoubtedly one of the most beautiful objects that can be found under heaven; but could you look through the rosy cheek, the smooth, fair forehead, or the rising bosom, and distinctly see all that lies within, you would turn away from it with loathing and horror!

14. Let us next take a view of those changes which we may reasonably suppose will then take place in the earth. It will no more be bound up with intense cold, nor parched up with extreme heat; but will have such a temperature as will be most conducive to its fruitfulness. If, in order to punish its inhabitants, God did of old

Bid his angels turn askance
This oblique lobe,

thereby occasioning violent cold on one part, and violent heat on the other; he will, undoubtedly, then order them to restore it to its original position: So that there will be a final end, on the one hand, of the burning heat which makes some parts of it scarce habitable; and, on the other of

The rage of Arctos and eternal frost.

15. And it will then contain no jarring or destructive principles within its own bosom. It will no more have any of those violent convulsions in its own bowels. It will no more be shaken or torn asunder by the impetuous force of earthquakes; and will, therefore need neither Vesuvius nor Etna, nor any burning mountains to prevent them. There will be no more horrid rocks or frightful precipices; no wild deserts, or barren sands; no impassable morasses, or unfruitful bogs, to swallow up the unwary traveller. There will, doubtless, be inequalities on the surface of the earth, which are not blemishes, but beauties. For though I will not affirm, that

Earth hath this variety from heaven,
Of pleasure situate in hill and dale;

yet I cannot think gently-rising hills will be any defect, but an ornament, of the new-made earth. And doubtless we shall then likewise have occasion to say,—

Lo, there his wondrous skill arrays
The fields in cheerful green!
A thousand herbs his hand displays,
A thousand flower between!

16. And what will the general produce of the earth be? Not thorns, briers, or thistles; not any useless or fetid weed; not any poisonous, hurtful, or unpleasant plant; but every one that can be conducive, in anywise, either to our use or pleasure. How far beyond all that the most lively imagination is now able to conceive! We shall no more regret the loss of the terrestrial Paradise, or sigh at that well-devised description of our great Poet:—

Then shall this mount
Of Paradise, by might of waves, be moved
Out of his place, push'd by the horned flood,
With all its verdure spoil'd and trees adrift,
Down the great river to the opening gulf,
And there take root, an island salt and bare!

For all the earth shall then be a more beautiful Paradise than Adam ever saw.

17. Such will be the state of the new earth with regard to the meaner, the inanimate, parts of it. But great as this change will be, it is little, it is nothing, in comparison of that which will then take place throughout all animated nature. In the living part of the creation were seen the most deplorable effects of Adam's apostasy. The whole animated creation, whatever has life, from leviathan to the smallest mite, was thereby made subject to such vanity, as the inanimate creatures could not be. They were subject to that fell monster, DEATH, the conqueror of all that breathe. They were made subject to its fore-runner, pain, in its ten thousand forms; although "God made not death, neither hath he pleasure in the death of any living." How many millions of creatures in the sea, in the air, and on every part of the earth, can now no otherwise preserve their own lives, than by taking away the

lives of others; by tearing in pieces and devouring their poor, innocent, unresisting fellow-creatures! Miserable lot of such innumerable multitudes, who, insignificant as they seem, are the offspring of one common Father; the creatures of the same God of love! It is probable not only two-thirds of the animal creation, but ninety-nine parts of a hundred, are under a necessity of destroying others in order to preserve their own life! But it shall not always be so. He that sitteth upon the throne will soon change the face of all things, and give a demonstrative proof to all his creatures that "his mercy is over all his works." The horrid state of things which at present obtains, will soon be at an end. On the new earth, no creature will kill, or hurt, or give pain to any other. The scorpion will have no poisonous sting; the adder, no venomous teeth. The lion will have no claws to tear the lamb; no teeth to grind his flesh and bones. Nay, no creature, no beast, bird, or fish, will have any inclination to hurt any other; for cruelty will be far away, and savageness and fierceness be forgotten. So that violence shall be heard no more, neither wasting or destruction seen on the face of the earth. "The wolf shall dwell with the lamb," (the words may be literally as well as figuratively understood,) "and the leopard shall lie down with the kid: They shall not hurt or destroy," from the rising up of the sun, to the going down of the same.

18. But the most glorious of all will be the change which then will take place on the poor, sinful, miserable children of men. These had fallen in many respects, as from a greater height, so into a lower depth, than any other part of the creation. But they shall "hear a great voice out of heaven, saying, Behold, the tabernacle of God is with men: And he will dwell with them, and they shall be his people, and God himself shall be their God." (Rev. 21:3, 4.) Hence will arise an unmixed state of holiness and happiness far superior to that which Adam enjoyed in Paradise. In how beautiful a manner is this described by the Apostle: "God shall wipe away all tears from their eyes; and there shall be no more death, neither sorrow, nor crying, neither shall there be any more pain: For the former things are done away!" As there will be no more death, and no more pain or sickness preparatory thereto; as there will be no more grieving for, or parting with, friends; so there will be no more sorrow or crying. Nay, but there will be a greater deliverance than all this; for there will be no more sin. And, to crown all, there will be a deep, an intimate, an uninterrupted union with God; a constant communion with the Father and his Son Jesus Christ, through the Spirit; a continual enjoyment of the Three-One God, and of all the creatures in him!

65.* THE DUTY OF REPROVING OUR NEIGHBOUR

"Thou shalt not hate thy brother in thy heart: thou shalt in any wise rebuke thy neighbour, and not suffer sin upon him."

Lev. 19:17.

A great part of the book of Exodus, and almost the whole of the book of Leviticus, relate to the ritual or ceremonial law of Moses; which was peculiarly given to the children of Israel, but was such "a yoke," says the apostle Peter, "as neither our fathers nor we were able to bear." We are, therefore, delivered from it: And this is one branch of "the liberty wherewith Christ hath made us free." Yet it is easy to observe, that many excellent moral precepts are interspersed among these ceremonial laws. Several of them we find in this very chapter: Such as, "Thou shalt not gather every grape of thy vineyard: Thou shalt leave them for the poor and stranger. I am the Lord your God." (Lev. 19:10.) Ye shall not steal, neither lie one to another. (Lev. 19:11.) "Thou shalt not defraud thy neighbour, neither rob him: The wages of him that is hired shall not abide with thee till the morning." (Lev. 19:13.) "Thou shalt not curse the deaf, nor put a stumbling-block before the blind; but shalt fear thy God: I am the Lord." (Lev. 19:14.) As if he had said, I am he whose eyes are over all the earth, and whose ears are open to their cry. "Ye shall do no unrighteousness in judgment: Thou shalt not respect the person of the poor," which compassionate men may be tempted to do; "nor honour the person of the mighty," to which there are a thousand temptations. (Lev. 19:15.) "Thou shalt not go up and down as a tale-bearer among thy people:" (Lev. 19:16:) Although this is a sin which human laws have never yet been able to prevent. Then follows, "Thou shalt not hate thy brother in thy heart: Thou shalt in anywise rebuke thy neighbour, and not suffer sin upon him." [Lev. 19:17]

In order to understand this important direction aright, and to apply it profitably to our own souls, let us consider,

    I.   What it is that we are to rebuke or reprove? What is the thing that is here enjoined?

    II.   Who are they whom we are commanded to reprove? And,

    III.   How are we to reprove them?

I. 1. Let us consider, First, What is the duty that is hereenjoined? What is it we are to rebuke or reprove? And what is it to reprove? What is it to reprove? To tell anyone of his faults; as clearly appears from the following words: "Thou shalt not suffer sin upon him." Sin is therefore the thing we are called to reprove, or rather him that commits sin. We are to do all that in us lies to convince him of his fault, and lead him into the right way.

2. Love indeed requires us to warn him, not only of sin, (although of this chiefly,) but likewise of any error which, if it were persisted in, would naturally lead to sin. If we do not "hate him in our heart," if we love our neighbour as ourselves, this will be our constant endeavour; to warn him of every evil way, and of every mistake which tends to evil.

3. But if we desire not to lose our labour, we should rarely reprove anyone for anything that is of a disputable nature, that will bear much to be said on both sides. A thing may possibly appear evil to me; therefore I scruple the doing of it; and if I were to do it while that scruple remains, I should be a sinner before God. But another is not to be judged by my conscience: To his own master he standeth or falleth.

* [text of the 1872 edition]

Therefore I would not reprove him, but for what is clearly and undeniably evil. Such, for instance, is profane cursing and swearing; which even those who practise it most will not often venture to defend, if one mildly expostulates with them. Such is drunkenness, which even a habitual drunkard will condemn when he is sober. And such, in the account of the generality of people, is the profaning of the Lord's day. And if any which are guilty of these sins for a while attempt to defend them, very few will persist to do it, if you look them steadily in the face, and appeal to their own conscience in the sight of God.

II. 1. Let us, in the Second place, consider, Who are those that we are called to reprove? It is the more needful to consider this, because it is affirmed by many serious persons, that there are some sinners whom the Scripture itself forbids us to reprove. This sense has been put on that solemn caution of our Lord, in his Sermon on the Mount: "Cast not your pearls before swine, lest they trample them under foot, and turn again and rend you." But the plain meaning of these words is, Do not offer the pearls, the sublime doctrines or mysteries of the Gospel, to those whom you know to be brutish men, immersed in sins, and having no fear of God before their eyes. This would expose those precious jewels to contempt, and yourselves to injurious treatment. But even those whom we know to be, in our Lord's sense, dogs and swine, if we saw them do, or heard them speak, what they themselves know to be evil, we ought in any wise to reprove them; else we "hate our brother in our heart."

2. The persons intended by "our neighbour" are, every child of man, everyone that breathes the vital air, all that have souls to be saved. And if we refrain from performing this office of love to any, because they are sinners above other men, they may persist in their iniquity, but their blood will God require at our hands.

3. How striking is Mr. Baxter's reflection on this head, in his "Saints' Everlasting Rest! "Suppose thou wert to meet one in the lower world, to whom thou hadst denied this of fice of love, when ye were both together under the sun; what answer couldst thou make to his upbraiding? 'At such a time and place, while we were under the sun, God delivered me into thy hands. I then did not know the way of salvation, but was seeking death in the error of my life; and therein thou sufferedst me to remain, without once endeavouring to awake me out of sleep! Hadst thou imparted to me thy knowledge, and warned me to flee from the wrath to come, neither I nor thou need ever have come into this place of torment.' "

4. Every one, therefore, that has a soul to be saved, is entitled to this good office from thee. Yet this does not imply, that it is to be done in the same degree to everyone. It cannot be denied, that there are some to whom it is particularly due. Such, in the first place, are our parents, if we have any that stand in need of it; unless we should place our consorts and our children on an equal footing with them. Next to these we may rank our brothers and sisters, and afterwards our relations, as they are allied to us in a nearer or more distant manner, either by blood or by marriage. Immediately after these are our servants, whether bound to us for a term of years or any shorter term. Lastly, such in their several degrees are our countrymen, our fellow-citizens, and the members of the same society, whether civil or religious: The latter have a particular claim to our service; seeing these societies are formed with that very design, to watch over each other for this very end, that we may not suffer sin upon our brother. If we neglect to reprove any of these, when a fair opportunity offers, we are undoubtedly to be ranked among those that "hate their brother in their heart." And how severe is the sentence of the Apostle against those who fall under this condemnation! "He that hateth his brother," though it does not break out into words or actions, "is a murderer:" And ye know," continues the Apostle, "that no murderer hath eternal life abiding in him." He hath not that seed planted in his soul, which groweth up unto everlasting life: In other words, he is in such a state, that if he dies therein, he cannot see life. It plainly follows, that to neglect this is no small thing, but eminently endangers our final salvation.

III. We have seen what is meant by reproving our brother, and who those are that we should reprove. But the principal thing remains to be considered. How, in what manner, are we to reprove them?

1. It must be allowed, that there is a considerable difficulty in performing this in a right manner: Although, at the same time, it is far less difficult to some than it is to others. Some there are who are particularly qualified for it, whether by nature, or practice, or grace. They are not encumbered either with evil shame, or that sore burden, the fear of man: They are both ready to undertake this labour of love, and skilful in performing it. To these, therefore, it is little or no cross; nay, they have a kind of relish for it, and a satisfaction therein, over and above that which arises from a consciousness of having done their duty. But be it a cross to us, greater or less, we know that hereunto we are called. And be the difficulty ever so great to us, we know in whom we have trusted; and that he will surely fulfil his word, "As thy day, so shall thy strength be."

2. In what manner, then, shall we reprove our brother, in order that our reproof may be most effectual? Let us first of all take care that whatever we do may be done in "the spirit of *love;*" in the spirit of tender good-will to our neighbour; as for one who is the son of our common Father, and one for whom Christ died, that he might be a partaker of salvation. Then, by the grace of God, love will beget love. The affection of the speaker will spread to the heart of the hearer; and you will find, in due time, that your labour hath not been in vain in the Lord.

3. Meantime the greatest care must be taken that you speak inthe spirit of *humility.* Beware that you do not think of yourself more highly than you ought to think. If you think too highly of yourself, you can scarce avoid despising your brother. And if you show, or even feel, the least contempt of those whom you reprove, it will blast your whole work, and occasion you to lose all you labour. In order to prevent the very appearance of pride, it will be often needful to be explicit on the head; to disclaim all preferring yourself before him; and at the very time you reprove that which is evil, to own and bless God for that which is good in him.

4. Great care must be taken, in the Third place, to speak in the spirit of *meekness*, as well as lowliness. The Apostle assures us that "the wrath of men worketh not the righteousness of God." Anger, though it be adorned with the name of zeal, begets anger; not love or holiness. We should therefore avoid, with all possible care, the very appearance of it. Let there be no trace of it, either in the eyes, the gesture, or the tone of voice; but let all of these concur in manifesting a loving, humble, and dispassionate spirit.

5. But all this time, see that you do not trust in yourself. Put no confidence in your own wisdom, or address, or abilities of any kind. For the success of all you speak or do, trust not in yourself, but in the great Author of every good and perfect gift. Therefore, while you are speaking, continually lift up your heart to him that worketh all in all. And whatsoever is spoken in the spirit of *prayer*, will not fall to the ground.

6. So much for the *spirit* wherewith you should speak when youreprove your neighbour. I now proceed to the *outward* manner. It has been frequently found that the prefacing a reproof with a frank profession of good-will has caused what was spoken to sink deep into the heart. This will generally have a far better effect, than that grand fashionable engineine,—flattery, by means of which the men of the world have often done surprising things. But the very same things, yea, far greater, have much oftener been effected by a plain and artless declaration of disinterested love. When you feel God has kindled this flame in your heart, hide it not; give it full vent! It will pierce like lightning. The stout, the hard-hearted, will melt before you, and know that God is with you of a truth.

7. Although it is certain that the main point in reproving is, to do it with a right spirit, yet it must also be allowed, there are several little circumstances with regard to the outward manner, which are by no means without their use, and therefore are not to be despised. One of these is, whenever you reprove, do it with great *seriousness*; so that as you really are in earnest, you may likewise appear so to be. A ludicrous reproof makes little impression, and is soon forgot; besides, that many times is taken ill, as if you ridiculed the person you reprove. And indeed those who are not accustomed to make jests, do not take it well to be jested upon. One means of giving a serious air to what you speak, is, as often as may be, to use the very words of Scripture. Frequently we find the word of God, even in a private conversation, has a peculiar energy; and the sinner, when he expects it least, feels it "sharper than a two-edged sword."

8. Yet there are some exceptions to this general rule of reproving seriously. There are some exempt cases, wherein, as a good judge of human nature observes,

> Ridiculum acri fortius—

a little well-placed raillery will pierce deeper than solid argument. But this has place chiefly, when we have to do with those who are strangers to religion. And when we condescend to give a ludicrous reproof to a person of this character, it seems we are authorized so to do, by that advice of Solomon, "Answer a fool according to his folly, lest he be wise in his own eyes."

9. The manner of the reproof may, in other respects too, be varied according to the occasion. Sometimes you may find it proper to use many words, to express your sense at large. At other times you may judge it more expedient to use few words, perhaps a single sentence; and at others, it may be advisable to use no words at all, but a gesture, a sigh, or a look, particularly when the person you would reprove is greatly your superior. And frequently, this silent kind of reproof will be attended by the power of God, and consequently, have a far better effect than a long and laboured discourse.

10. Once more: Remember the remark of Solomon, "A word spoken in season, how good is it!" It is true, if you are providentially called to reprove anyone whom you are not likely to see any more, you are to snatch the present opportunity, and to speak "in season" or "out of season;" but with them whom you have frequent opportunities of seeing, you may wait for a fair occasion. Here the advice of the poet has place. You may speak

> Si validus, si laetus erit, si denique poscet:

When he is in a good humour, or when he asks it you. Here you may catch the

> Mollia tempora fandi,—

time when his mind is in a soft, mild frame: And then God will both teach you how to speak, and give a blessing to what is spoken.

11. But here let me guard you against one mistake. It passes for an indisputable maxim, "Never attempt to reprove a man when he is intoxicated with drink." Reproof, it is said, is then thrown away, and can have no good effect. I dare not say so. I have seen not a few clear instances of the contrary. Take one: Many years ago, passing by a man in Moorfields, who was so drunk he could hardly stand, I put a paper into his hand. He looked at it, and said, "A Word—A Word to a Drunkard,—that is me,—Sir, Sir! I am wrong,—I know I am wrong,—pray let me talk a little with you." He held me by the hand a full half-hour: And I believe he got drunk no more.

12. I beseech you, brethren, by the mercies of God, do not despise poor drunkards! Have compassion on them! Be instant with them in season and out of season! Let not shame, or fear of men prevent your pulling these brands out of the burning: Many of them are self-condemned:

> Nor do they not discern the evil plight
> That they are in;

but they despair; they have no hope of escaping out of it; and they sink into it still deeper, because none else has any hope for them! "Sinners of every other sort," said a venerable old Clergyman, "have I frequently known converted to God. But an habitual drunkard I have never known converted." But I have known five hundred, perhaps five thousand. Ho! Art thou one who readest these words? Then hear thou the words of the Lord! I have a message from God unto thee, O sinner! Thus saith the Lord, Cast not away thy hope. I have not forgotten thee. He that tells thee there is no help is a liar from the beginning. Look up! Behold the Lamb of God, who taketh away the sin of the world! This day is salvation come to thy soul: Only see that thou despise not him that speaketh!

Just now he saith unto thee: "Son, be of good cheer! Thy sins are forgiven thee!"

13. Lastly: You that are diligent in this labour of love, see that you be not discouraged, although after you have used your best endeavours, you should see no present fruit. You have need of patience, and then, "after ye have done the will of God" herein, the harvest will come. Never be "weary of well-doing; in due time ye shall reap, if ye faint not." Copy after Abraham, who "against hope, still believed in hope." "Cast thy bread upon the waters; for thou shalt find it after many days."

14. I have now only a few words to add unto you, my brethren, who are vulgarly called "Methodists." I never heard or read of any considerable revival of religion which was not attended with a spirit of reproving. I believe it cannot be otherwise; for what is faith, unless it worketh by love? Thus it was in every part of England when the present revival of religion began about fifty years ago: All the subjects of that revival,—all the Methodists, so called, in every place, were reprovers of outward sin. And, indeed, so are all that "being justified by faith, have peace with God through Jesus Christ." Such they are at first; and if they use that precious gift, it will never be taken away. Come, brethren, in the name of God, let us begin again! Rich or poor, let us all arise as one man; and in any wise let every man "rebuke his neighbour, and not suffer sin upon him!" Then shall all Great Britain and Ireland know that we do not "go a warfare at our own cost:" Yea, "God shall bless us, and all the ends of the world shall fear him."

Manchester, July 28, 1787

66. THE SIGNS OF THE TIMES

"Ye can discern the face of the sky; but can ye not discern the signs of the times?"

Matthew 16:3.

1. The entire passage runs thus: "The Pharisees also, with the Sadducees, came, and tempting, desired him that he would show them a sign from heaven. He answered and said, When it is evening, ye say, It will be fair weather: for the sky is red. And in the morning, It will be foul weather to day: for the sky is red and lowering. O ye hypocrites, ye can discern the face of the sky; but can ye not discern the signs of the times?" [Matt. 16:1–3]

2. "The Pharisees also with the Sadducees came." In general, these were quite opposite to each other: but it is no uncommon thing for the children of the world to lay aside their opposition to each other, (at least for a season) and cordially to unite in opposing the children of God "And tempting;" that is, making a trial whether he was indeed sent of God; "desired him that he would show them a sign from heaven;" which they believed no false prophet was able to do. It is not improbable, they imagined, this would convince them, that he was really sent from God. "He answered and said unto them, When it is evening, ye say, It will be fair weather: for the sky is red. And in the morning, It will be foul weather today, for the sky is red and lowering." Probably there were more certain signs of fair and foul weather in their climate than there are in ours. "O ye hypocrites;" making profession of love, while you have enmity in your hearts; "ye can discern the face of the sky," and judge thereby what the weather will be; "but can ye not discern the signs of the times," when God brings his first begotten Son into the world?

3. Let us more particularly inquire, First, What were the times, whereof our Lord here speaks; and what were the signs, whereby those times were to be distinguished from all others? We may then inquire, Secondly, What are the times which we have reason to believe are *now* at hand; and how is it, that all who are called Christians, do not discern the signs of *these* times?

I. 1. Let us, in the First place, inquire, What times were those concerning which our Lord is here speaking? It is easy to answer; the times of the Messiah; the times ordained before the foundation of the world, wherein it pleased God to give his only begotten Son, to take our nature upon him, to be "found in fashion as a man," to live a life of sorrow and pain, and, at length, to be "obedient unto death, even the death of the cross," to the end that whosoever believeth on him should not perish, but have everlasting life." This was the important time the signs whereof the Pharisees and Sadducees could not discern. Clear as they were in themselves, yet so thick a veil was upon the heart of these men, that they did not discern the tokens of his coming, though foretold so long before.

2. But what were those signs of the coming of that Just One, which had been so long and so clearly foretold, and whereby they might easily have discerned those times, had not the veil been on their heart? They are many in number; but it may suffice to mention a few of them. One of the first is that pointed out in the solemn words, spoken by Jacob a little before his death: (Gen. 49:10:) "The sceptre shall not depart from Judah, nor a lawgiver from between his feet, until Shiloh come." All, both ancient and modern Jews, agree, that by Shiloh we are to understand the Messiah; who was therefore to come, according to the prophecy, "before the sceptre," that is, the sovereignty, "departed from Judah." But it did, without controversy, depart from Judah at this very time;—an infallible sign, that at this very time Shiloh, that is, the Messiah, came.

3. A Second eminent sign of those times, the times of the coming of the Messiah, is given us in the third chapter of the prophecy of Malachi: "Behold, I send my messenger, and he shall prepare my way before me: and the Lord, whom ye seek, shall suddenly come to his temple." (Mal. 3:1). How manifestly was this fulfilled, first, by the coming of John the Baptist; and then by our blessed Lord himself, "coming suddenly to his temple!" And what sign could be clearer to those that impartially considered the words of the prophet Isaiah (Isa. 40:3:) "The voice of him that crieth in the wilderness, Prepare ye the way of the Lord, make his paths straight!"

4. But yet clearer signs than these, (if any could be clearer,) were the mighty works that he wrought. Accordingly, he himself declares, "The works which I do, they testify of me." And to these he explicitly appeals in his answer to the question of John the Baptist; (not proposed, as some have

strangely imagined, from any doubt which he had himself; but from a desire of confirming his disciples, who might possibly waver, when their Master was taken from their head: "Art thou he that should come," the Messiah? "Or look we for another?" No bare verbal answer could have been so convincing, as what they saw with their own eyes. Jesus therefore referred them to this testimony: "He answered and said unto them, Go and show John the things which ye hear and see; the blind receive their sight, and the lame walk, the lepers are cleansed, and the deaf hear, the dead are raised up, and the poor have the gospel preached unto them." (Matt. 11:4, 5.)

5. But how then came it to pass, that those who were so sharp-sighted in other things, who could "discern the face of the sky," were not able to discern those signs which indicated the coming of the Messiah They could not discern them, not for want of evidence—this was full and clear,—but for want of integrity in themselves; because they were a "wicked and adulterous generation;" because the perverseness of their hearts spread a cloud over their understanding. Therefore, although the Sun of Righteousness shone bright, yet they were insensible of it. They were not willing to be convinced: Therefore they remained in ignorance. The light was sufficient; but they shut their eyes, that they might not see it: so that they were without excuse, till vengeance came upon them to the uttermost.

II. 1. We are in the Second place, to consider what are the times which we have reason to believe are *now* at hand? And how is it that all who are called Christians, do not discern the signs of *these* times?

The times which we have reason to believe are at hand, (if they are not already begun,) are what many pious men have termed, the time of "the latter-day glory;"—meaning the time wherein God would gloriously display his power and love, in the fulfilment of his gracious promise that "the knowledge of the Lord shall cover the earth, as the waters cover the sea."

2. "But are there in England, or in any part of the world, any *signs* of such a time approaching?" It is not many years since, that a person of considerable learning, as well as eminence in the Church, (then Bishop of London,) in his pastoral letter, made this observation: "I cannot imagine what persons mean, by talking of *a great work of God* at this time. I do not see any work of God now, more than has been at any other time." I believe: I believe that great man did not see any extraordinary work of God. Neither he, nor the generality of Christians, so called, saw any signs of the glorious day that is approaching. But how is this to be accounted for? How is it that those who can now "discern the face of the sky," who are not only great philosophers, but great divines, as eminent as ever the Sadducees, yea, or the Pharisees were, do not discern the signs of those glorious times, which, if not begun, are nigh even at the door?

3. We allow, indeed, that in every age of the Church, "the kingdom of God came not with observation," not with splendour and pomp, or with any of those outward circumstances which usually attend the kingdoms of this world. We allow this "kingdom of God is within us;" and that consequently, when it begins either in an individual or in a nation, it "is like a grain of mustard seed," which at first "is the least of all seeds," but nevertheless, gradually increases, till "it becomes a great tree." Or, to use the other comparison of our Lord, it is like "a little leaven, which a woman took and hid in three measures of meal, till the whole was leavened."

4. But may it not be asked, "Are there now any signs that the day of God's power is approaching?" I appeal to every candid, unprejudiced person, whether we may not, at this day, discern all those signs, (understanding the words in a spiritual sense,) to which our Lord referred to John's disciples? "The blind receive their sight:" Those who were blind from their birth, unable to see their own deplorable state, and much more to see God, and the remedy he has prepared for them in the Son of his love, now see themselves, yea, and "the light of the glory of God in the face of Jesus Christ. "The eyes of their understanding being now opened, they see all things clearly.—"The deaf hear:" Those that were before utterly deaf, to all the outward and inward calls of God, now hear, not only his providential calls, but also the whispers of his grace.—"The lame walk:" Those who never before arose from the earth, or moved one step toward heaven, are now walking in all the ways of God; yea, "running the race that is set before them."—"The lepers are cleansed:" The deadly leprosy of sin, which they brought with them into the world, and which no art of man could ever cure, is now clean departed from them. And surely never in any age or nation, since the apostles, have those words been so eminently fulfilled, "The poor have the gospel preached unto them," as it is at this day. At this day the gospel leaven, faith working by love,—inward and outward holiness,—or, (to use the terms of St. Paul,) "righteousness, and peace, and joy in the Holy Ghost"—hath so spread in various parts of Europe, particularly in England, Scotland, Ireland, in the islands, in the north and south, from Georgia to New-England and Newfoundland, that sinners have been truly converted to God, throughly changed both in heart and in life; not by tens, or by hundreds only, but by thousands, yea, by myriads! The fact cannot be denied: we can point out the persons, with their names and places of abode. And yet the wise men of the world, the men of eminence, the men of learning and renown, "cannot imagine what we mean by talking of any extraordinary work of God!" They cannot discern the signs of *these times!* They can see no sign at all of God's arising to maintain his own cause, and set up his kingdom over the earth!

5. But how may this be accounted for? How is it, that they cannot discern the signs of these times? We may account for their want of discernment on the same principle we accounted for that of the Pharisees and Sadducees; namely, that they likewise are, what those were, an "adulterous and sinful generation." If their eye was single, their whole body would be full of light: but suppose their eye be evil, their whole body must be full of darkness. Every evil temper darkens the soul; every evil passion clouds the understanding. How then can we expect, that those should be able to discern the signs of the times who are full of all disorderly passions,

and slaves to every evil temper? But this is really the case. They are full of pride: They think of themselves far more highly than they ought to think. They are vain: They "seek honour one of another, and not the honour that cometh of God only." They cherish hatred and malice in their hearts: they give place to anger, to envy, to revenge: They return evil for evil, and railing for railing. Instead of overcoming evil with good, they make no scruple of demanding an eye for an eye, and a tooth for a tooth. They "savour not the things that are of God, but the things that are of men." They set their affections, not on things above, but on things that are of the earth. They "love the creature more than the Creator:" They are "lovers of pleasure more than lovers of God." How then should they discern the signs of the times? The god of this world, whom they serve, has blinded their hearts, and covered their minds with a veil of thick darkness. Alas, what have these "souls of flesh and blood," (as one speaks) to do with God, or the things of God?

6. St. John assigns this very reason for the Jews not understanding the things of God; namely, that in consequence of their preceding sins, and wilful rejecting the light, God had now delivered them up to Satan, who blinded them past recovery. Over and over, when they might have seen, they would not; they shut their eyes against the light: And now they can not see, God having given them up to an undiscerning mind: Therefore they do not believe, because that Isaiah said, (that is, because of the reason given in that saying of Isaiah,) "He hath blinded their eyes, and hardened their hearts, that they should not see with their eyes, nor understand with their hearts, and be converted, and I should heal them." The plain meaning is, not that God did this by his own immediate power; it would be flat blasphemy to say, that God, in this sense, hardens any man; but his Spirit strives with them no longer, and then Satan hardens them effectually.

7. And as it was with them in ancient times, so it is with the present generation. Thousands of those who bear the name of Christ are now given up to an undiscerning mind. The god of this world hath so blinded their eyes, that the light cannot shine upon them; so that they can no more discern the signs of the times, than the Pharisees and Sadducees could of old. A wonderful instance of this spiritual blindness, this total inability to discern the signs of the times mentioned in Scripture, is given us in the very celebrated work of a late eminent writer; who supposes, the New Jerusalem came down from heaven, when Constantine the Great called himself a Christian. I say, *called himself a Christian*; for I dare not affirm that he *was one*, any more than Peter the Great. I cannot but believe, he would have come nearer the mark, if he had said, that it was the time when a huge cloud of infernal brimstone and smoke came up from the bottomless pit! For surely there never was a time wherein Satan gained so fatal an advantage over the Church of Christ, as when such a flood of riches, and honour, and power broke in upon it, particularly on the Clergy!

8. By the same rule, what signs would this writer have expected of the approaching conversion of the Heathens? He would doubtless, have expected a hero, like Charles of Sweden, or Frederick of Prussia, to carry fire, and sword, and Christianity, through whole nations at once! And it cannot be denied, that since the time of Constantine, many nations have been converted in this way. But could it be said concerning such conversions as these; "The kingdom of heaven cometh not with observation?" Surely every one must observe a warrior rushing through the land, at the head of fifty or sixty thousand men! But is this the way of spreading Christianity, which the author of it, the Prince of Peace, has chosen? Nay, it is not in this manner that a grain of mustard seed grows up into a great tree. It is not thus that a little leaven leavens the whole lump. Rather, it spreads by degrees farther and farther, till the whole is leavened. We may form a judgment of what will be hereafter, by what we have seen already. And this is the way wherein true Christian religion, the faith that worketh by love, has been spreading, particularly through Great Britain and its dependencies, for half a century.

9. In the same manner it continues to spread at the present time also, as may easily appear to all those whose eyes are not blinded. All those that experience in their own hearts the power of God unto salvation will readily perceive how the same religion which they enjoy, is still spreading from heart to heart. They take knowledge of the same grace of God, strongly and sweetly working on every side; and rejoice to find another and another sinner, first inquiring, "What must I do to be saved?"—and then testifying, "My soul doth magnify the Lord, and my spirit doth rejoice in God my Saviour." Upon a fair and candid inquiry, they find more and more, not only of those who had some form of religion, but of those who had no form at all, who were profligate, abandoned sinners, now entirely changed, truly fearing God and working righteousness. They observe more and more, even of these poor outcasts of men, who are inwardly and outwardly changed; loving God and their neighbour; living in the uniform practice of justice, mercy, and truth; as they have time, doing good to all men; easy and happy in their lives, and triumphant in their death.

10. What excuse, then, have any that believe the Scriptures to be the Word of God, for not discerning the signs of these times, as preparatory to the general call of the Heathens? What could God have done which he hath not done, to convince you that the day is coming, that the time is at hand, when he will fulfil his glorious promises; when he will arise to maintain his own cause, and to set up his kingdom over all the earth? What, indeed, unless he had *forced* you to believe? And this he could not do, without destroying the nature which he had given you: For he made you free agents; having an inward power of self-determination, which is essential to your nature. And he deals with you as free agents from first to last. As such, you may shut or open your eyes, as you please. You have sufficient light shining all around you; yet you need not see it unless you will. But be assured God is not well pleased with your shutting your eyes and then saying, "I cannot see." I counsel you to bestow an impartial examination upon the whole affair. After a candid inquiry into matter of fact, consider deeply, "What hath God wrought?" "Who hath seen such a thing? Who hath heard

such a thing?" Hath not a nation, as it were, been "born in a day?" How swift, as well as how deep, and how extensive a work has been wrought in the present age! And certainly, "not by might, neither by power, but by the Spirit of the Lord." For how utterly inadequate were the means! how insufficient were the instruments to work any such effect;—at least, those of which it has pleased God to make use of in the British dominions and in America! By how unlikely instruments has God been pleased to work from the beginning! "A few young raw heads," said the bishop of London, "what can they pretend to do?" They pretended to be *that* in the hand of God, that a pen is in the hand of a man. They pretended, (and do so at this day,) to do the work whereunto they are sent; to do just what the Lord pleases. And if it be his pleasure, to throw down the walls of Jericho, the strong-holds of Satan, not by the engines of war, but by the blasts of rams' horns, who shall say unto him, "What dost thou!"

11. Meantime, "blessed are your eyes, for they see: many prophets and righteous men have desired to see the things you see, and have not seen them, and to hear the things that you hear, and have not heard them." You see and acknowledge the day of your visitation; such a visitation as neither you nor your fathers had known. You may well say, "This is the day which the Lord hath made; we will rejoice and be glad therein." You see the dawn of that glorious day, whereof all the prophets have spoken. And how shall you most effectually improve this day of your visitation?

12. The first point is, see that you yourselves receive not the blessing of God in vain. Begin at the root, if you have not already. Now repent and believe the gospel! If you have believed, "look to yourselves, that ye lose not what you have wrought, but that ye receive a full reward!" Stir up the gift of God that is in you! Walk in the light, as he is in the light. And while you "hold fast that which you have attained, go on unto perfection." Yea, and when you are "made perfect in love," still, "forgetting the that are behind, press on to the mark, for the prize of the high calling of God in Christ Jesus."

13. It behoves you, in the next place to help your neighbours. "Let your light so shine before men, that they may see your good works, and glorify your Father which is in heaven." As you have time, do good unto all men, but especially unto them that are of the household of faith. Proclaim the glad tidings of salvation ready to be revealed, not only to those of your own household, not only to your relations, friends, and acquaintance, but to all whom God providentially delivers into your hands! "Ye," who already know in whom you have believed, "are the salt of the earth." Labour to season, with the knowledge and love of God, all that you have any intercourse with! "Ye are as a city set upon a hill;" ye cannot, ye ought not to be hid. "Ye are the light of the world: men do not light a candle, and put it under a bushel;" how much less the all wise God! No; let it shine to all that are in the house; all that are witnesses of your life and conversation. Above all, continue instant in prayer, both for yourselves, for all the Church of God, and for all the children of men, that they may remember themselves, and be turned unto our God, that they likewise may enjoy the gospel blessing on earth, and the glory of God in heaven!

67.* ON DIVINE PROVIDENCE

"Even the very hairs of your head are all numbered."

Luke 12:7.

1. The doctrine of divine providence has been received by wise men in all ages. It was believed by many of the eminent Heathens, not only philosophers, but orators and poets. Innumerable are the testimonies concerning it which are scattered up and down in their writings; agreeable to that well-knowing saying in Cicero, *Deorum moderamine cuncta geri*: "That all things, all events in this world, are under the management of God." We might bring a cloud of witnesses to confirm this, were any so hardy as to deny it.

2. The same truth is acknowledged at this day in most parts of the world; yea, even by those nations which are so barbarous as not to know the use of letters. So when Paustoobee, an Indian Chief, of the Chicasaw nation in North America, was asked, "Why do you think the Beloved Ones (so they term God) take care of *you*?" he answered, without any hesitation, "I was in the battle with the French; and the bullet went on this side; and this man died, and that man died; but I am alive still; and by this I know that the beloved Ones take care of me.

3. But although the ancient as well as modern Heathens had some conception of a divine providence, yet the conceptions which most of them entertained concerning it were dark, confused, and imperfect; Yea, the accounts which the most enlightened among them gave, were usually contradictory to each other. Add to this, that they were by no means assured of the truth of those very accounts: They hardly dared to affirm anything, but spoke with the utmost caution and diffidence; insomuch that what Cicero himself, the author of that noble declaration, ventures to affirm in cool blood, at the end of his long dispute upon the subject, amounts to no more than this lame and impotent conclusion: *Mihi verisimilior videbatur Cotta oratin*: "What Cotta said," (the person that argued in the defence of the being and providence of God,) *"seemed* to me *more probable* than what his opponent had advanced to the contrary."

4. And it is no wonder: For only God himself can give a clear, consistent, perfect account (that is, as perfect as our weak understanding can receive, in this our infant state of existence; or, at least, as is consistent with the designs of his government) of his manner of governing the world. And this he hath done in his written word: All the oracles of God, all the Scriptures, both of the Old Testament and the New, describe so many scenes of divine providence. It is the beautiful remark of a fine writer, "Those who object to the Old Testament in particular, that it is not a connected history of nations, but only a congeries of broken, unconnected events, do not observe the nature and design of these writings. They do not see, that Scripture is the history of

---

* (text from the 1872 edition)

God." Those who bear this upon their minds will easily perceive that the inspired writers never lose sight of it, but preserve one unbroken, connected chain from the beginning to the end. All over that wonderful book, as "life and immortality" (immortal life) is gradually "brought to light," so is Immanuel, God with us, and his kingdom ruling over all.

5. In the verses preceding the text, our Lord had been arming his disciples against the fear of man: "Be not afraid,"says he, (verse 4,)"of them that can kill the body, and after that have no more that they can do." He guards them against this fear, first, by reminding them of what was infinitely more terrible than anything which man could inflict: "Fear Him, who after he hath killed hath power to cast into hell." He guards them farther against it, by the consideration of an over-ruling providence: "Are not five sparrows sold for two farthings, and not one of them is forgotten before God?" Or, as the words are repeated by St. Matthew, with a very inconsiderable variation, (10:29, 30) "Not one of them shall fall on the ground without you Father. But the very hairs of your head are all numbered."

6. We must indeed observe, that this strong expression, through repeated by both the Evangelists, need not imply, (though if any one thinks it does, he may think so very innocently,) that God does literally number as the hairs that are on the heads of all his creatures: But it is a proverbial expression, implying, that nothing is so small or insignificant in the sight of men as not to be an object of the care and providence of God, before whom nothing is small that concerns the happiness of any of his creatures.

7. There is scarce any doctrine in the whole compass of revelation, which is of deeper importance than this. And, at the same time, there is scarce any that is so little regarded, and perhaps so little understood. Let us endeavor then, with the assistance of God, to examine it to the bottom; to see upon what foundation it stands, and what it properly implies.

8. The eternal, almighty, all-wise, all-gracious God is the Creator of heaven and earth. He called out of nothing, by his all-powerful word, the whole universe, all that is. "Thus the heavens an the earth were created, and all the hosts of them." And after he had set all things else in array, the plants after their kinds, fish and fowl, beasts and reptiles, after their kinds, "He created man after his own image." And the Lord saw that every distinct part of the universe was good. But when he saw everything he had made, all in connection with each other, "behold, it was very good."

9. And as this all-wise, all-gracious Being created all things, so he sustains all things. He is the Preserver as well as the Creator of everything that exists. "He up holdeth all things by the word of his power;" that is, by his powerful word. Now it must be that he knows everything he has made, and everything he preserves, from moment to moment; otherwise, he could not preserve it, he could not continue to it the going which he has given it. And it is nothing strange that He who is omnipresent, who "filleth heaven and earth," who is intimately present. If the eye of man discerns things at a small distance; the eye of an eagle, what is at a greater; the eye of an angle, what is at a thousand times greater distance; (perhaps taking in the surface of the earth at one view;) how shall no the eye of God see everything, through the whole extent of creation? Especially considering, that nothing is distant from Him in whom we all "live, and move, and have our being."

10. It is true, our narrow understandings but imperfectly comprehend this. But whether we comprehend it or no, we are certain that so it is. As certain as it is, that he created all things, and that he still sustains all that is created; so certain it is, that he is present, at all times, in all places; that he is above, beneath; that he "besets us behind and before," and, as it were, "lays his hand upon us." We allow, "such knowledge is too high" and wonderful for us; we "cannot attain unto it." The manner of his presence no man can explain, nor, probably, any angel in heaven. Perhaps what the ancient philosopher speaks of the soul, in regard to its residence in the body, that it is *tota in toto, et, tota in qualibet parte*, might, in some sense, be spoken of the omnipresent Spirit, in regard to the universe: That he is not only "All in the whole," but "All in every part." Be this as it may, it cannot be doubted but He sees every atom of his creation, and that a thousand times more clearly than we see the things that are close to us: Even of these we see only the surface, while He sees the inmost essence of every thing.

11. The omnipresent God sees and knows all the properties of the beings that he hath made. He knows all the connections, dependencies, and relations, and all the ways wherein one of them can affect another. In particular, he sees all the inanimate parts of the creation, whether in heaven above, or in the earth beneath. He knows how the stars, comets, or planets above influence the inhabitants of the earth beneath; what influence the lower heavens, with their magazines of fire, hail, snow, and vapors, winds, and storms, have on our planet; and what effects may be produced in the bowels of the earth by fire, air, or water; what exhalations may be raised therefrom, and what changes wrought thereby; what effects every numeral or vegetable may have upon the children of men: All these lie naked and open to the eye of the Creator and Preserver of the universe.

12. He knows all the animals of the lower world, whether beasts, birds, fishes, reptiles, or insects: He knows all the qualities and powers he hath given them, from the highest to the lowest: He knows every good angel and every evil angel in every part of his dominions; and looks from heaven upon the children of men over the whole face of the earth. He knows all the hearts of the sons of men, and understands all their thoughts: He sees what any angel, any devil, any man, either thinks, or speaks, or does; yea, and all they feel. He sees all their sufferings, with every circumstance of them.

13. And is the Creator and Preserver of the world unconcerned for what he sees therein? Does he look upon these things either with a malignant or heedless eye? Is he an Epicurean god? Does he sit at ease in the heaven, without regarding the poor inhabitants of earth? It cannot be. He hath made us, not we ourselves, and he cannot despise the work of his own hands. We are his children: And can a mother forget the children of her womb? Yea, she may forget; yet will not God forget us! On the contrary, he hath expressly

declared, that as his "eyes are over all the earth,"so he "is loving to every man, and his mercy is over all his works." Consequently, he is concerned every moment for what befalls every creature upon earth; and more especially for everything that befalls any of he children of men. It is hard, indeed, to comprehend this; nay, it is hard to believe it, considering the complicated wickedness, and the complicated misery, which we see on every side. But believe it we must, unless we will make God a liar; although it is sure, no man can comprehend it. It behoves us, then, to humble ourselves before God, and to acknowledge our ignorance. Indeed, how can we expect hat a man should be able to comprehend a worm? How much less can it be supposed, that a man can comprehend God! For how can finite measure infinite?

14. He is infinite in wisdom as well as in power: And all his wisdom is continually employed in managing all the affairs of his creation for the good of all his creatures. For his wisdom and goodness go hand in hand: They are inseparably united, and continually act in concert with Almighty power, for the real good of all his creatures. His power being equal to his wisdom and goodness, continually co-operates with them. And to him all things are possible: He doeth whatsoever pleaseth him, in heaven and earth, and in the sea, and all deep places: And we cannot doubt of his exerting all his power, as in sustaining, so in governing, all that he has made.

15. Only he that can do all things else cannot deny himself: He cannot counteract himself, or oppose his own work. Were it not for this, he would destroy all sin, with its attendant pain in a moment. He would abolish wickedness out of his whole creation, and suffer not trace of it remain. But in so doing he would counteract himself; he would altogether overturn his own work, and undo all that he has been doing since he created man upon the earth. For he created man in his own image: A spirit like himself; a spirit endued with understanding, with will or affections, and liberty; without which, neither his understanding nor his affections could have been of any use, neither would he have been capable either or vice or virtue. He could not be a moral agent, any more than a tree or a stone. If, therefore, God were thus to exert his power, there would certainly be no more vice; but it is equally certain, neither could there be any virtue in the world. Were human liberty taken away, men would be as incapable of virtue as stones. Therefore, (with reverence be it spoken,) the Almighty himself cannot do this thing. He cannot thus contradict himself, or undo what he has done. He cannot destroy out of the soul of man that image of himself wherein he make him: And without doing this, he cannot abolish sin and pain out of the world. But were it to be done, it would imply no wisdom at all; but barely a stroke of omnipotence. Whereas all the manifold wisdom of God (as well as all his power and goodness) is displayed in governing man as man; not as a stock or stone, but as an intelligent and free spirit, capable of choosing either good or evil. Herein appears the depth of the wisdom of God, in his adorable providence; in governing men, so as not to destroy either their understanding, will, or liberty. He commands all things, both in heaven and earth, to assist man in attaining the end of his being, in working out his won salvation, so far as it can be done without compulsion, without over-ruling his liberty. An attentive inquirer may easily discern, the whole frame of divine providence is so constituted as to afford man every possible help, in order to his doing good and eschewing evil, which can be done without turning man into a machine; without making him incapable of virtue or vice, reward or punishment.

16. Meantime, it has been remarked by a pious writer, that here is, as he expresses it, a three-fold circle of divine providence, over and above that which presides over the whole universe. We do not now speak of that over-ruling hand which governs the inanimate creation, which sustains the sun, moon, and stars in their stations, and guides their motions; we do not refer to his care of the animal creation, every part of which we know is under His government, "who giveth food unto the cattle, and feedeth the young ravens that call upon him;" but we here speak of that superintending providence which regards the children of men. each of these is easily distinguished from the other, by those who accurately observe the ways of God. The outermost circle includes the whole race of mankind, all the descendants of Adam, all the human creatures that are dispersed over the face of the earth. This comprises not only the Christian world, those that name the name of Christ, but the Mahometans also, who considerably out-number even the nominal Christians; yea, and the Heathens likewise, who very far out-number the Mahometans and Christians put together. "Is he the God of the Jews," says the Apostle, "and not of the Gentiles also?" And so we may say, Is he the God of the Christians, and not of the Mahometans and Heathens? Yea, doubtless of the Mahometans and Heathens also. His love is not confined: "The Lord is loving unto every man, and his mercy is over all his works." He careth for the very outcasts of men: It may truly be said,

Free as the air thy bounty streams
O'er all thy works: Thy mercies' beams
Diffusive as they sun's arise.

17. Yet it may be admitted, that He takes more immediate care of those that are comprised in the second, the smaller circle; which includes all that are called Christians, all that profess to believe in Christ. We may reasonably think that these, in some degree, honor him, at least more than the Heathens do: God does, likewise, in some measure, honor them, and has a nearer concern for them. By many instances it appears, that the prince of this world has not so full power over these as over the Heathens. The God whom they even profess to serve, does, in some measure, maintain his own cause; so that the spirits of darkness do not reign so uncontrolled over them as they do over the heathen world.

18. Within the third, the innermost circle, are contained only the real Christians; those that worship God, not in form only, but in spirit and in truth. Herein are comprised all that love God, or, at least, truly fear God and work righteousness; all in whom is the mind which was in Christ, and who walk as Christ also walked. The words of our Lord above recited peculiarly refer to these. It is to these in particular that he says, "Even the very hairs of your head are all numbered." He

sees their souls and their bodies; he takes particular notice of all their tempers, desires, and thoughts, all their words and actions. He marks all their sufferings, inward and outward, and the source whence they arise; so that we may well say,

> Thou know'st thy pains thy servants feel,
> Thou hear'st thy children's cry;
> And their best wishes to fulfil,
> Thy grace is ever nigh.

Nothing relative to these is too great, nothing too little, for His attention. He has his eye continually, as upon every individual person that is a member of this his family, so upon every circumstance that relates either to their souls or bodies; either to their inward or outward state; wherein either their present or eternal happiness in is any degree concerned.

19. But what say the wise men of the world to this? They answer, with all readiness, "Who doubts of this? We are not Atheists. We all acknowledge a providence: That is, a general providence; for, indeed the particular providence, of which some talk, we know not what to make of: Surely the little affairs of men are far beneath the regard of the great Creator and Governor or the universe! Accordingly,
"He sees with equal eyes, as Lord of all,
A hero perish, or a sparrow fall." Does he indeed? I cannot think it; because (whatever that fine poet did, or his patron, whom he so deeply despised, and yet grossly flattered) I believe the Bible; wherein the Creator and Governor of the world himself tells me quite the contrary. That he has a tender regard for the brute creatures, I know: He does, in a measure, "take care for oxen:" He "provideth food for the cattle,"as well as "herbs for the use of men." "The lions roaring after their prey, do seek their meat from God." "He openeth his hand, and filleth all things living with plenteousness."

> The various troops of sea and land
> In sense of common want agree;
> All wait on thy dispensing hand,
> And have their daily alms from thee.
> They gather what thy stores disperse,
> Without their trouble to provide:
> Thou ope'st thy hand; the universe,
> The craving world, is all supplied.

Our heavenly Father feedeth the fowls of the air: But mark! "Are no ye much better than they?" Shall he not then "much more feed you," who are pre-eminent by so much odds? He does not, in that sense, look upon *you* and *them* "with *equal* eyes;" set you on a level with *them*; least of all, does he set you on a level with brutes, in respect of life and death: "Right precious in the sight of the Lord is the death of his saints." Do you really think the death of a sparrow is equally precious in his sight? He tells us, indeed, that "not a sparrow falleth on the ground without our Father;" but he asks. at the same time, "Are ye not of more value than many sparrows?

20. But, in support of a general, in contradiction to a particular providence, the same elegant poet lays it down as an unquestionable maxim,

> The Universal Cause
> Acts not by partial, but by general laws:

Plainly meaning, that he never deviates from those general laws in favor of any particular person. This is a common supposition; but which is altogether inconsistent with the whole tenor of Scripture: For if God never deviates from these general laws, then there never was a miracle in the world; seeing every miracle is a deviation from the general laws of nature. Did the Almighty confine himself to these general laws, when he divided the Red Sea? when he commanded the waters to stand on a heap, and make a way for his redeemed to pass over? Did he act by general laws, when he caused the sun to stand still for the space of a whole day? No; nor in any of the miracles which are recorded either in the Old or New Testament.

21. But it is on supposition that the Governor of the world never deviates from those general laws, that Mr. Pope adds those beautiful lines in full triumph, as having now clearly gained the point:—

> Shall burning Etna, if a sage requires,
> Forget to thunder, and recall her fires?
> On air or sea new motions be imprest,
> O blameless Bethel! to relieve thy breast!
> When the loose mountain trembles from on high,
> Shall gravitation cease, if you go by?
> Or some old temple, nodding to its fall,
> For Chartres' head reserve the hanging wall?

We answer, If it please God to continue the life of any of his servants, he will suspend that or any other law of nature: The stone shall not fall; the fire shall not burn; the foods shall not flow; or, he will give his angels charge, and in their hands shall they bear him up, through and above all dangers!

22. Admitting then, that, in the common course of nature, God does act by general laws, he has never precluded himself from making exceptions to them, whensoever he pleases; either by suspending that law in favor of those that love him, or by employing his mighty angels: By either of which means he can deliver out of all danger them that trust in him.
"What! You expect miracles then?" Certainly I do, if I believe the Bible: For the Bible teaches me, that God hears and answers prayer: But every answer to prayer is, properly, a miracle. For if natural causes take their course, if things go on in their natural way, it is no answer at all. Gravitation therefore shall cease, that is, cease to operate, whenever the Author of it pleases. Cannot the men of the world understand these things? That is no wonder: It was observed long ago, "An unwise man doth no consider this, and a fool doth not understand these things? That is no wonder: It was observed long ago, "An unwise man doth not consider this, and a fool doth not understand it."

23. But I have not done with this same general providence yet. By the grace of God, I will sift it to the bottom: And I hope to show it is such stark-staring nonsense, as every man of sense ought to be utterly ashamed of.
You say, "You allow a *general* providence, but deny a *particular* one." And what is a general, of whatever kind it be, that includes no particulars? Is not every general necessarily made up of its several particulars? Can you instance in any general that is not? Tell me any genus, if you can, that contains no species? What is it that constitutes a genus, but

so many species added together? What, I pray, is a whole that contains no parts? Mere nonsense and contradiction! Every whole must, in the nature of things, be made up of its several parts; insomuch that if there be no parts, there can be no whole.

24. As this is a point of the utmost importance, we may consider it a little farther. What do you mean by a general providence, contradistinguished from a particle? Do you mean a providence which superintends only the larger parts of the universe? Suppose the sun, moon, and stars. Does it not regard the earth too? You allow it does. But does it not likewise regard the inhabitants of it? Else what doth the earth, an inanimate lump of matter, signify? Is not one spirit, one heir of immortality, of more value than all the earth? yea, though you add to it the sun, moon, and stars? nay, and the whole inanimate creation? Might we no say, "These shall perish; but" this "remaineth: These all shall wax old as doth a garment;" but this (it may be said in a lower sense, even of the creature) is "the same, and his "years shall not fail?"

25. Or do you mean, when you assert a general providence, distinct from a particle one, that God regards only some parts of the world, and does not regard others? What parts of it does he regard? Those without, or those within, the solar system? Or does he regard some parts of the earth, and not others? Which parts? Only those within the temperate zones? What parts then are under the care of his providence? Where will you lay the line? Do you exclude from it those that live in the torrid zone? or those that dwell within the arctic circles? Nay, rather say, "The Lord is loving to every man," and his care "is over all His works."

26. Do you mean (for we would fain find out your meaning, if you have any meaning at all) that the providence of God does indeed extend to all parts of the earth, with regard to great and singular events, such as the rise and fall of empires; but that the little concerns of this or that man are beneath the notice of the Almighty? Then you do not consider that *great* and *little* are merely relative terms, which have place only with respect to men. With regard to the Most High, man and all the concerns of men are nothing, less than nothing, before Him. And nothing is small in his sight that in any degree affects the welfare of any that fear God and work righteousness. What becomes, then, of your general providence, exclusive of a particle? Let it be for ever rejected by all rational men, as absurd, self-contradictory nonsense. We may then sum up the whole scriptural doctrine of providence in that fine saying of St. Austin, *Ita praesidet singulis sicut universis, et universis sicut singulis!*

> Father, how wide thy glories shine,
> Lord of the universe-and mine!
> Thy goodness watches o'er the whole,
> As all the world were but one soul;
> Yet keeps my every sacred hair,
> As I remain'd thy single care!

27. We may learn from this short view of the providence of God, First, to put our whole trust in Him who hath never failed them that seek him. Our blessed Lord himself makes the very use of the great truth now before us. "Fear not, therefore:" If you truly fear God, you need fear none beside.

He will be a strong tower to all that trust in him from the face of you enemies. What is there either in heaven or in earth that can harm you, while you are under the care of the Creator and Governor of heaven and earth! Let all earth and all hell combine against you; yea, the whole animate and inanimate creation; they cannot harm while God is on your side: His favorable kindness covers you as a shield.

28. Nearly allied to this confidence in God is the thankfulness we owe for his kind protection. Let those give thanks whom the Lord thus delivers from the hand of all their enemies. What an unspeakable blessing it is to be the peculiar care of Him that has all power in heaven and earth! How can we sufficiently praise him, while we are under his wings, and his faithfulness and truth are our shield and buckler!

29. But meantime we should take the utmost care to walk humbly and closely with our God. Walk *humbly*. For if you in anywise rob God of his honor, of you ascribe anything to yourself, the things which should have been for you wealth will prove to you an "occasion of falling." And walk *closely*. See that you have a conscience void of offence toward God and toward man. It is so long as you so this that you are the peculiar care of your Father which is in heaven. But let not the consciousness of his caring for you make you careless, indolent, or slothful: On the contrary, while you are penetrated with that deep truth, "The help that is done upon earth, He doeth it himself," be as earnest and diligent in the use of all the means as if you were your own protector.

Lastly: In what a melancholy condition are those who do not believe there is any providence; or, which comes to exactly the same point, not a particular one! Whatever station they are in, as long as they are in the world, they are exposed to numberless dangers which no human wisdom can foresee, and no human power can resist. And there is no help! If they trust in men, they find them "deceitful upon the weights." In many cases they cannot help; in others, they will not. But were they ever so willing, they will die: Therefore vain is the help of man and God is far above, out of their sight: They expect no help from Him. These modern (as well as the ancient) Epicureans have learned that the

> Universal Cause
> Acts not by partial, but by general laws.

He only takes care of the great globe itself; not of its puny inhabitants. He heeds not how those

> Vagrant emmets crawl
> At random on the air-suspended ball.

How uncomfortable is the situation of that man who has no father hope than this! But, on the other hand, how unspeakably *"happy* is the man that hath the Lord for his help, and whose hope is in the Lord his God!" who can say, "I have set the lord always before me; because he is on my right hand, I shall not be moved!" Therefore, "though I walk through the valley of the shadow of death, I will fear no evil: For thou art with me; thy rod and thy staff comfort me."

69.* THE IMPERFECTION OF HUMAN KNOWLEDGE

"We know in part."

1 Cor. 13:9.

1. The desire of knowledge is an universal principle in man, fixed in his inmost nature. It is not variable, but constant in every rational creature, unless while it is suspended by some stronger desire. And it is insatiable: "The eye is not satisfied with seeing, nor the ear with hearing;" neither the mind with any degree of knowledge which can be conveyed into it. And it is planted in every human soul for excellent purposes. It is intended to hinder our taking up our rest in anything here below; to raise our thoughts to higher and higher objects, more and more worthy our consideration, till we ascend to the Source of all knowledge and all excellence, the all-wise and all-gracious Creator.

2. But although our desire of knowledge has no bounds, yet our knowledge itself has. It is, indeed, confined within very narrow bounds; abundantly narrower than common people imagine, or men of learning are willing to acknowledge: A strong intimation, (since the Creator doeth nothing in vain,) that there will be some future state of being, wherein that now insatiable desire will be satisfied, and there will be no longer so immense a distance between the appetite and the object of it.

3. The present knowledge of man is exactly adapted to his present wants. It is sufficient to warn us of, and to preserve us from, most of the evils to which we are now exposed; and to procure us whatever is necessary for us in this our infant state of existence. We know enough of the nature and sensible qualities of the things that are round about us, so far as they are subservient to the health and strength of our bodies; we know how to procure and prepare our food; we know what raiment is fit to cover us; we know how build our houses, and to furnish them with all necessaries and conveniences; we know just as much as is conducive to our living comfortably in this world: But of innumerable things above, below, and round about us, we know little more than that they exist. And in this our deep ignorance is seen the goodness as well as the wisdom of God, in cutting short his knowledge on every side, on purpose to "hide pride from man."

4. Therefore it is, that by the very constitution of their nature, the wisest of men "know" but "in part." And how amazingly small a part do they know, either of the Creator, or of his works! This is a very needful but a very unpleasing theme; for "vain man would be wise." Let us reflect upon it for awhile. And may the God of wisdom and love open our eyes to discern our own ignorance!

I. 1. To begin with the great Creator himself. How astonishingly little do we know of God!—How small a part of his nature do we know! of his essential attributes! What conception can we form of his omnipresence? Who is able to comprehend how God is in this and every place? how he fills the immensity of space? If philosophers, by denying the existence of a vacuum, only meant that there is no place empty of God, that every point of infinite space is full of God, certainly no man could call it in question. But still, the fact being admitted what is omnipresence or ubiquity? Man is no more able to comprehend this, than to grasp the universe.

2. The omnipresence or immensity of God, Sir Isaac Newton endeavours to illustrate by a strong expression, by terming infinite space, "the Sensorium of the Deity." And the very Heathens did not scruple to say, "All things are full of God:" Just equivalent with his own declaration:—"Do not I fill heaven and earth? saith the Lord." How beautifully does the Psalmist illustrate this! "Whither shall I flee from thy presence? If I go into the heaven, thou art there: If I go down to hell, thou art there also. If I take the wings of the morning, and remain in the uttermost parts of the sea even there thy hand shall find me, and thy right hand shall hold me." But, in the mean time, what conception can we form, either of his eternity or immensity? Such knowledge is too wonderful for us: We cannot attain unto it.

3. A second essential attribute of God is eternity. He existed before all time. Perhaps we might more properly say, He *does exist* from everlasting to everlasting. But what is eternity? A celebrated author says, that the Divine eternity is *vitae interminabilis tota simul et perfecta possessio*: "The at once entire and perfect possession of never-ending life." But how much wiser are we for this definition? we know just as much of it as we did before. "The at once entire and perfect possession!" Who can conceive what this means?

4. If indeed God had stamped (as some have maintained) an idea of himself on every human soul, we must certainly have understood something of these, as well as his other attributes; for we cannot suppose he would have impressed upon us either a false or an imperfect idea of himself; but the truth is, no man ever did, or does now, find any such idea stamped upon his soul. The little which we do know of God, (expect what we receive by the inspiration of the Holy One,) we do not gather from any inward impression, but gradually acquire from without. "The invisible things of God," if they are known at all, "are known from the things that are made;" not from what God hath written in our hearts, but from what he hath written in all his works.

5. Hence then, from his works, particularly his works of creation, we are to learn the knowledge of God. But it is not easy to conceive how little we know even of these. To begin with those that are at a distance: Who knows how far the universe extends? What are the limits of it? The morning stars can tell, who sang together when the lines of it were stretched out, when God said, "This be thy circumference, O world!" But all beyond the fixed stars is utterly hid from the children of men. And what do we know of the fixed stars? Who telleth the number of them? even that small portion of them that, by their mingled light, form what we call, "the milky way?" And who knows the use of them? Are they so many suns that illuminate their respective planets? Or do they only minister to this, (as Mr. Hutchinson supposes,) and contribute, in

---

* (text from the 1872 edition)

some unknown way, to the perpetual circulation of light and spirit? Who knows what comets are? Are they planets not fully formed? or planets destroyed by a conflagration? Or are they bodies of a wholly different nature, of which we can form no idea? Who can tell what is the sun? Its use we know; but who knows of what substance it is composed? Nay, we are not yet able to determine, whether it be fluid or solid! Who knows what is the precise distance of the sun from the earth? Many astronomers are persuaded it is a hundred millions of miles; others, that it is only eighty-six millions, though generally accounted ninety. But equally great men say, it is no more than fifty; some of them, that it is but twelve: Last comes Dr. Rogers, and demonstrates that it is just two millions nine hundred thousand miles! So little do we know even of this glorious luminary, the eye and soul of the lower world! And just as much of the planets that surround him; yea, of our own planet, the moon. Some indeed have discovered

River and mountains on her spotty glode;

yea, have marked out all her seas and continents!—But after all, we know just nothing of the matter. We have nothing but mere uncertain conjecture concerning the nearest of all the heavenly bodies.

6. But let come to the things that are still nearer home, and inquire what knowledge we have of them. How much do we know of that wonderful body, light? How is it communicated to us? Does it flow in a continued stream from the sun? Or does the sun impel the particles next his orb, and so on and on, to the extremity of his system? Again: Does light gravitate or not? Does it attract or repel other bodies? Is it subject to the general laws which obtain in all other matter? Or is it a body *siu generis*, altogether different from all other matter? Is it the same with electric fluid, and others arrest its course? Why is the phial capable of being charged to such a point, and no farther? A thousand more questions might be asked on this head, which no man living can answer.

7. But surely we understand the air we breathe, and which encompasses us on every side. By that admirable property of elasticity, it is the general spring of nature. But is elasticity essential to air, and inseparable from it? Nay, it has lately proved, by numberless experiments, that air may be fixed, that is, divested of its elasticity, and generated or restored to it again. Therefore it is no otherwise elastic, than as it is connected with electric fire. And is not this electric or ethereal fire, the only true essential elastic in nature? Who knows by what power, dew, rain, and all other vapours rise and fall in the air? Can we account for the phenomenon of them upon the common principles? Or must we own, with a late ingenious author, that those principles are utterly insufficient; and that they cannot be rationally accounted for, but upon the principle of electricity?

8. Let us now descend to the earth which we tread upon, and which God has peculiarly given to the children of men. Do the children of men understand this? Suppose the terraqueous globe to be seven or eight thousand miles in diameter, how much of this do we know? Perhaps a mile or two of its surface: So far the art of man has penetrated. But who can inform us, what lies beneath the region of stones, metals, minerals, and other fossils? This is only a thin crust, which bears an exceeding small proportion to the whole. Who can acquaint us with the inner parts of the globe? Whereof do these consist? Is there a central fire, a grand reservoir, which not only supplies the burning mountains, but also ministers (though we know not how) to the ripening of gems and metals; yea, and perhaps to the production of vegetables, and the well-being of animals too? Or is the great deep still contained in the bowels of the earth? a central abyss of waters? Who hath seen? Who can tell? Who can give any solid satisfaction to a rational inquirer?

9. How much of the very surface of the globe is still utterly unknown to us! How very little do we know of the polar regions, either north or south, either in Europe or Asia! How little of these vast countries, the inland parts either of Africa or America! Much less do we know what is contained in the broad sea, the great abyss, which covers so large a part of the globe. Most of its chambers are inaccessible to man, so that we cannot tell how they are furnished. How little we know of those things on the dry land which fall directly under our notice! Consider even the most simple metals or stones: How imperfectly are we acquainted with their mature and properties! Who knows what it is that distinguishes metals from all other fossils? It is answered, "Why, they are heavier." Very true; but what is the cause of their being heavier? What is the specific difference between metals and stones? or between one metal and another? between gold and silver? between tin and lead? It is all mystery to the sons of men.

10. Proceed we to the vegetable kingdom. Who can demonstrate that the sap, in any vegetable, performs a regular circulation through its vessels, or that it does not? Who can point out the specific difference between one kind of plant and another? or the peculiar, internal conformation and disposition of their component parts? Yea, what man living thoroughly understands the nature and properties of any one planet under heaven?

11. With regard to animals: Are microscopic animals, so called, *real* animals or no? If they are, are they not essentially different from all other animals in the universe, as not requiring any food, not generating or being generated? Are they no animals at all, but merely inanimate particles of matter, in a state of fermentation? How totally ignorant are the most sagacious of men touching the whole affair of generation! even the generation of men. In the book of the Creator, indeed, were all our members written, "which day by day were fashioned, when as yet were none of them:" But what means was the first motion communicated to the *punctum saliens*? When, and how, was the immortal spirit superadded to the senseless clay? It is mystery all: And we can only say, "I am fearfully and wonderfully made."

12. With regard to insects, many are the discoveries which have been lately made. But how little is all that is discovered yet, in comparison of what is undiscovered! How many millions of them, by their extreme minuteness, totally escape all our inquiries! And, indeed, the minute parts of the largest animals elude our utmost diligence. have we a more complete knowledge of fishes that we have of insects? A great part, if not the greatest part, of the inhabitants of the waters are

totally concealed from us. It is probable, the species of sea-animals are full as numerous as the land-animals. But how few of them are known to us! And it is very little we know of those few. With birds we are a little better acquainted: And, indeed, it is but a little. For of very many we now hardly anything more than their outward shape. We now a few of the obvious properties of other, chiefly those that frequent our houses. But we have not a thorough, adequate knowledge even of them. How little do we now of beasts! We do not know whence the different tempers and qualities arise, not only in different species of them, but in individuals of the same species; yea, and frequently in those who spring from the same parents, the same both male and female animal. Are they mere machines? Then they are incapable either of pleasure or pain. Nay, they can have no senses; they neither see nor hear; they neither taste nor smell. Much less can they now, or remember, or move, any otherwise than they are impelled from without. But all this, as daily experiments show, is quite contrary to the matter of fact.

13. Well; but if we know nothing else, do not we now ourselves? our bodies and our souls? What is our soul? It is a spirit, we know. But what is a spirit? Here we are at a full stop. And where is the soul lodged? in the pineal gland, in the whole brain, in the heart, in the blood, in any single part of the body, or (if any one can understand those terms) "all in all, and all in every part?" How is the soul united to the body? a spirit or a clod? What is the secret, imperceptible chain that couples them together? Can the wisest of men give a satisfactory answer to any one of these plain questions? And as to our body itself, how little do we know! During a night's sleep, a healthy man perspires one part in four less when he sweats, than when he does not. Who can account for this? What is flesh? that of the muscles in particular? Are the fibres that compose it of a determinate size, so that they can be divided only so far? Or are they resolvable *in infintum?* How does a muscle act? by being inflated, and consequently shortened? But what is it inflated with? If whit blood, how and whence comes that blood? And whither does it go, the moment the muscle is relaxed? Are the nerves pervious or solid? How do they act? by vibration or transmission of the animal spirits? Who knows what the animal spirits are? Are they electric fire? What is sleep? Wherein does it consist? What is dreaming? How can we know dreams from waking thoughts? I doubt no man knows. O how little do we know even concerning the whole creation of God?

II. 1. But are we not better acquainted with his works of providence, than with his works of creation? It is one of the first principles of religion, that his kingdom ruleth over all: so that we may say with confidence, "O Lord our Governor, how excellent is thy name over all the earth!" It is a childish conceit, to suppose chance governs the world, or has any part in the government of it: No, not even in those things that, to the vulgar eye, appear to be perfectly casual. "The lot is cast to the lap; but the disposal thereof is from the Lord." Our blessed Master himself has put this matter beyond all possible doubt: "Not a sparrow," saith he, "falleth to the ground without the will of your Father which is in heaven: Yea," (to express the thing more strongly still,) "even the very hairs of you head are all numbered."

2. But although we are well apprized of this general truth, that all things are governed by the providence of God; (the very language of the heathen orator, *Deorum moderamine cuncta geri;*) yet how amazingly little do we know of the particulars contained under this general! How little do we understand of his providential dealing, either with regard to nations, or families, or individuals! There are heights and depths in all these which our understanding can in no wise fathom. We can comprehend but a small part of his ways now; the rest we shall know hereafter.

3. Even with regard to entire nations, how little do we comprehend of God's providential dealings with them! what innumerable nations in the eastern world once flourished, to the terror of all around them, and are now swept away from the face of the earth; and their memorial is perished with them! Nor has the case been otherwise in the west. In Europe also we read of many large and powerful kingdoms, of which the names only are left: The people are vanished away, and are as though they had never been. But why it has pleased the almighty Governor of the world to sweep them away with the besom of destruction we cannot tell; those who succeeded them being, many times, little better than themselves.

4. But it is not only with regard to ancient nations, that the providential dispensations of God are utterly imcomprehansible to us: The same difficulties occur now. We cannot account for his present dealings with the inhabitants of the earth. We know, "the Lord is loving unto every man, and his mercy is over all his works." But we know not how to reconcile this with the present dispensations of his providence. At this day, is not almost every part of the earth full of darkness and cruel habitations? In what a condition, in particular, is the large and populous empire of Indostan! How many hundred thousands of the poor, quiet people, have been destroyed, and their carcases left as the dung of the earth! in what a condition (though they have no English ruffians there) are the numberless islands in the Pacific Ocean! How little is their state above that of wolves and bears! And who careth either for their souls or their bodies? But does not the Father of men care for them? O mystery of providence!

5. And who cares for thousands, myriads, if not millions, of the wretched Africans? Are not whole droves of these poor sheep (human, if not rational beings!) continually driven to market, and sold, like cattle, into the vilest bondage, without any hope of delierance but by death? Who cares for those outcasts or men, the well-known Hottenots? It is true, a late writer has taken musch pains to represent them as a respectable people: But from what motive it is not easy to say; since he himself allows (a specimen of their elegance of manners) that the raw guts of sheep and other cattle are not only some of their choicest food, but also the ornaments of their arms and legs; and (a specimen of their religion) that the son is not counted a man, till he has beat his mother almost to death; and when his father grows old, he fastens him to a little hut, and leaves him there to starve! O Father

of mercies! are these the works of thy own hands, the purchase of thy Son's blood?

6. How little better is either the civil or religious state of the poor American Indians! that is, the miserable remains of them: For in some provinces not one of them is left to breathe. In Hispaniola, when the Christians came thither first, there were three millions of inhabitants. Scarce twelve thousand of them now survive. And in what condition are these, or the other Indians who are still scattered up and down in the cast continent of South or North America? Religion they have none; no public worship of any kind! God is not in all their thoughts. And most of them have no civil government at all; no laws; no magistrates; but every man does what is right in his own eyes. Therefore they are decreasing daily; and, very probably, in a century or two there will not be one them left.

7. However, the inhabitants of Europe are not in so deplorable a condition. They are in a state of civilization; they have useful laws, and are governed by magistrates; they have religion; they are Christians. I am afraid, whether they are called Christians or not, many of them have not much religion. What say you to thousands of Laplanders, or Finlanders, or Samoiedes, and Greenlanders? indeed, of all who live in high northern latitudes? Are they as civilized as sheep or oxen? To compare them with horses, or any of our domestic animals, would be doing them to much honour. Add to these, myriads of human savages that are freezing among the snow of Siberia, and as many, if not more, who are wandering up and down in the deserts of Tartary. Add thousands upon thousands of Poles and Muscovites; and of Christians, so called, from Turkey in Europe. And did "God so love" these, "that he gave his Son, his only begotten Son, to the end they might not perish, but have everlasting life?" Then why are they thus? O wonder above all wonders!

8. Is there not something equally mysterious in the divine lo dispensation with regard to Christianity itself? Who can explain why Christianity is not spread as far as sin? Why is not the medicine sent to every place where the disease is found? But alas! It is not: "The sound of it is" not now "gone forth into all lands." The poison is diffused over the whole globe; the antidote is not known in a sixth part of it. Nay, and how is it that the wisdom and goodness of God suffer the antidote itself to be so grievously adulterated, not only in Roman Catholic countries, but almost in every part of the Christian world? So adulterated by mixing it frequently with useless, frequently with poisonous ingredients, that it retains none, or at least a very small part of its original virtue. Yea, it is so thoroughly adulterated by many of those very persons whom he has sent to administer it that it adds tenfold malignity to the disease which it was designed to cure! In consequence of this there is little more mercy or truth to be found among Christians than among pagans. Nay, it has been affirmed and I am afraid truly, that many called Christians are far worse than the heathens that surround them: more profligate, more abandoned to all manner of wickedness, neither fearing God, nor regarding man! O who can comprehend this! Doth not he who is higher than the highest regard it?

9. Equally incomprehensible to us are many of the divine dispensations with regard to particular families. We cannot at all comprehend why he raises some to wealth, honour, and power and why in the meantime he depresses others with poverty and various afflictions. Some wonderfully prosper in all they take in hand, and the world pours in upon them; while others with all their labour and toil can scarce procure daily bread. And perhaps prosperity and applause continue with the former to their death; while the latter drink the cup of adversity to their life's end—although no reason appears to us either for the prosperity of the one or the adversity of the other.

10. As little can we account for the divine dispensations with regard to individuals. We know not why the lot of this man is cast in Europe, the lot of that man in the wilds of America; why one is born of rich or noble, the other of poor parents; why the father and mother of one are strong and healthy, those of another weak and diseased; in consequence of which he drags a miserable being all the days of his life, exposed to want, and pain, and a thousand temptations from which he finds no way to escape. How many are from their very infancy hedged in with such relations that they seem to have no chance (as some speak), no possibility of being useful to themselves or others? Why are they, antecedent to their own choice, entangled in such connections? Why are hurtful people so cast in their way that they know not how to escape them? And why are useful persons hid out of their sight, or snatched away from them at their utmost need? O God, how unsearchable are thy judgments or counsels! Too deep to be fathomed by our reason: and thy ways of executing those counsels not to be traced by our wisdom!

III. 1. Are we able to search out his works of grace any more than his works of providence? Nothing is more sure than that "without holiness no man shall see the Lord." Why is it then that so vast a majority of mankind are, so far as we can judge, cut off from all means, all possibility of holiness, even from their mother's womb? For instance: what possibility is there that a Hottentot, a New-Zealander, or an inhabitant of Nova-Zembla, if he lives and dies there, should ever know what holiness means? Or consequently ever attain it? Yea, but one may say: "He sinned before he was born, in a pre-existent state. Therefore he was placed here in so unfavourable a situation. And it is mere mercy that he should have a second trial." I answer: supposing such a pre-existent state, this which you call a second trial is really no trial at all. As soon as he is born into the world he is absolutely in the power of his savage parents and relations, who from the first dawn of reason train him up in the same ignorance, atheism, and barbarity with themselves. He has no chance, so to speak; he has no possibility of any better education. What trial has he then? From the time he comes into the world till he goes out of it again he seems to be under a dire necessity of living in all ungodliness lo and unrighteousness. But how is this? How can this be the case with so many millions of the souls that God has made? Art thou not the God "of all the ends of the earth, and of them that remain in the broad sea?"

2. I desire it may be observed that if this be improved into an objection against revelation it is an objection that lies full as

much against natural as revealed religion. If it were conclusive it would not drive us into Deism, but into flat Atheism. It would conclude not only against the Christian revelation but against the being of a God. And yet I see not how we can avoid the force of it but by resolving all into the unsearchable wisdom of God, together with a deep conviction of our ignorance and inability to fathom his counsels.

3. Even among us who are favoured far above these,—to whom are entrusted the oracles of God, whose word is a lantern to our feet, and a light in all our paths,—there are still many circumstances in his dispensations which are above our comprehension. We know not why he suffered us so long to go on in our own ways before we were convinced of sin. Or why he made use of this or the other instrument, and in this or the other manner. And a thousand circumstances attended the process of our conviction which we do not comprehend. We know not why he suffered us to stay so long before he revealed his Son in our hearts; or why this change from darkness to light was accompanied with such and such particular circumstances.

4. It is doubtless the peculiar prerogative of God to reserve the "times and seasons in his own power." And we cannot give any reason, why, of two persons equally athirst for salvation one is presently taken into the favour of God, and the other left to mourn for months or years. One, as soon as he calls upon God, is answered, and filled with peace and joy in believing; another seeks after him, and, it seems, with the same degree of sincerity and earnestness, and yet cannot find him, or any consciousness of his favour, for weeks, or months, or years. We know well this cannot possibly be owing to any absolute decree, consigning, one before he was born to everlasting glory, and the other to everlasting fire; but we do not know what is the reason for it: It is enough that God knoweth.

5. There is, likewise, great variety in the manner and time of God's bestowing his sanctifying grace, whereby he enables his children to give him their whole heart, which we can in no wise account for. We know not why he bestows this on some even before they ask for it; (some unquestionable instances of which we have seen;) on some after they have sought it but a few days; and yet permits other believers to wait for it perhaps twenty, thirty, or forty years; nay, and others, till a few hours, or even minutes, before their spirits return to him. For the various circumstances also which attend the fulfilling of that great promise, "I will circumcise thy heart, to love the Lord thy God with all thy heart and with all thy soul," God undoubtedly has reasons; but those reasons are generally hid from the children of men. Once more: some of those who are enabled to love God with all their heart and with all their soul, retain the same blessing, without any interruption, till they are carried to Abraham's bosom; others do not retain it, although they are not conscious of having grieved the Holy Spirit of God. This also we do not understand: We do not herein "know the mind of the Spirit."

IV. Several valuable lessons we may learn from a deep consciousness of this our own ignorance. First, we may learn hence a lesson of humility; not "to think of ourselves," particularly with regard to our understanding, "more highly than we ought to think;" but "to think soberly;" being thoroughly convinced that we are not sufficient of ourselves to think one good thought; that we should be liable to stumble at every step, to err every moment of our lives, were it not that we have "an anointing from the Holy One," which abideth "with us;" were it not that He who knoweth what is in man helpeth our infirmities; that "there is a spirit in man which giveth wisdom," and the inspiration of the Holy One which "giveth understanding."

From hence we may learn, Secondly, a lesson of faith, of confidence in God. A full conviction of our own ignorance may teach us a full trust in his wisdom. It may teach us (what is not always so easy as one would conceive it to be) to trust the invisible God farther than we can see him! It may assist us in learning that difficult lesson, to "cast down" our own "imaginations" (or *reasonings* rather, as the word properly signifies), to "cast down every high thing that exalteth itself against the knowledge of God, and bring into captivity every thought to the obedience of Christ." There are at present two grand obstructions to our forming a right judgment of the dealings of God with respect to men. The one is, there are innumerable *facts* relating to every man which we do not and cannot know. They are, at present, hid from us, and covered from our search by impenetrable darkness. The other is, we cannot see *the thoughts* of men, even when we know their actions. Still we know not their *intentions*; and without this we can but ill judge of their outward actions. Conscious of this, "judge nothing before the time" concerning his providential dispensations; till he shall bring to light "the hidden things of darkness," and manifest "the thoughts and intent of the heart."

From a consciousness of our ignorance we may learn, Thirdly, a lesson of resignation. We may be instructed to say at all times and in all instances, "Father, not as I will; but as thou wilt." This was the last lesson which our blessed Lord (as man) learnt while he was upon earth. He could go no higher than, "Not as I will, but as thou wilt," till he bowed his head and gave up the ghost. Let us also herein be made conformable to his death, that we may know the full "power of his resurrection!" [Preached at Bristol, March 5, 1784]

70.* THE CASE OF REASON IMPARTIALLY CONSIDERED

"Brethren, be not children in understanding: Howbeit in malice be ye children, but in understanding be men."
1 Cor. 14:20.

1. It is the true remark of an eminent man, who had made many observations on human nature, "If reason be against a man, a man will always be against reason." This has been confirmed by the experience of all ages. Very many have been the instances of it in the Christian as well as the heathen world; yea, and that in the earliest times. Even then there were not wanting well-meaning men who, not having much

---

* (text from the 1872 edition)

reason themselves, imagined that reason was of no use in religion; yea, rather, that it was a hinderance to it. And there has not been wanting a succession of men who have believed and asserted the same thing. But never was there a greater number of these in the Christian Church, at least in Britain, than at this day.

2. Among them that despise and vilify reason, you may always expect to find those enthusiasts who suppose the dreams of their own imagination to be revelations from God. We cannot expect that men of this turn will pay much regard to reason. Having an infallible guide, they are very little moved by the reasonings of fallible men. In the foremost of these we commonly find the whole herd of Antinomians; all that, however they may differ in other respects, agree in "making void the law through faith." If you oppose reason to these, when they are asserting propositions ever so full of absurdity and blasphemy, they will probably think it a sufficient answer to say, "O, this is your reason;" or "your carnal reason:" So that all arguments are lost upon them: They regard them no more than stubble or rotten wood.

3. How natural is it for those who observe this extreme, to run into the contrary! While they are strongly impressed with the absurdity of undervaluing reason, how apt are they to overvalue it! Accordingly, we are surrounded with those (we find them on every side) who lay it down as an undoubted principle, that reason is the highest gift of God. They paint it in the fairest colours; they extol it to the skies. They are fond of expatiating in its praise; they make it little less than divine. They are wont to describe it as very near, if not quite, infallible. They look upon it as the all-sufficient director of all the children of men; able, by its native light, to guide them into all truth, and lead them into all virtue.

4. They that are prejudiced against the Christian revelation, who do not receive the Scriptures as the oracles of God, almost universally run into this extreme: I have scarce known any exception: So do all, by whatever name they are called, who deny the Godhead of Christ. (Indeed some of these say they do not deny his Godhead; but only his supreme Godhead. Nay, this is the same thing; for in denying him to be the supreme God, they deny him to be any God at all: Unless they will assert that there are two Gods, a great one and a little one!) All these are vehement applauders of reason, as the great unerring guide. To these over-valuers of reason we may generally add men of eminently strong understanding; who, because they do know more than most other men, suppose they can know all things. But we may likewise add many who are in the other extreme; men of eminently weak understanding; men in whom pride (a very common case) supplies the void of sense; who do not suspect themselves to be blind, because they were always so.

5. Is there, then, no medium between these extremes,—undervaluing and overvaluing reason? Certainly there is. But who is there to point it out?—to mark down the middle way? That great master of reason, Mr. Locke, has done something of the kind, something applicable to it, in one chapter of his Essay concerning Human Understanding. But it is only remotely applicable to this: He does not come home to the point. The good and great Dr. Watts has wrote admirably well, both concerning reason and faith. But neither does anything he has written point out the medium between valuing it too little and too much.

6. I would gladly endeavor in some degree to supply this grand defect; to point out, First, to the under-valuers of it, what reason can do; and then to the over-valuers of it, what reason cannot do. But before either the one or the other can be done, it is absolutely necessary to define the term, to fix the precise meaning of the word in question. Unless this is done, men may dispute to the end of the world without coming to any good conclusion. This is one great cause of the numberless altercations which have been on the subject. Very few of the disputants thought of this; of defining the word they were disputing about. The natural consequence was, they were just as far from an agreement at the end as at the beginning.

I. 1. First, then, *reason* is sometimes taken for *argument*. So, "Give me a *reason* for your assertion." So in Isaiah: "Bring forth your strong *reasons*;" that is, your strong arguments. We use the word nearly in the same sense, when we say, "He has good *reasons* for what he does." It seems here to mean, He has sufficient *motives*, such as ought to influence a wise man. But how is the word to be understood in the celebrated question concerning the "reasons of things?" particularly when it is asked, *An rationes rerum sint aeternae?* "Whether the reasons of things are eternal?" Do not the "reasons of things" here mean the *relations* of things to each other? But what are the *eternal relations* of *temporal* things? of things which did not exist till yesterday? Could the relations of these things exist before the things themselves had any existence? Is not then, the talking of such relations a flat contradiction? Yea, as palpable a one as can be put into words.

2. In another acceptation of the word, reason is much the same with *understanding*. It means a faculty of the human soul; that faculty which exerts itself in three ways;—by simple apprehension, by judgement, and by discourse. *Simple apprehension* is barely conceiving a thing in the mind; the first and most simple act of understanding. *Judgment* is the determining that the things before conceived either agree with or differ from each other. *Discourse*, strictly speaking, is the motion or progress of the mind from one judgment to another. The faculty of the soul which includes these three operations I here mean by the term *reason*.

3. Taking the word in this sense, let us now impartially consider, First, What is it that reason can do? And who can deny that it can do much, very much, in the affairs of common life? To begin at the lowest point: It can direct servants how to perform the various works wherein they are employed; to discharge their duty, either in the meanest offices or in any of a higher nature. It can direct the husbandman at what time, and in what manner, to cultivate his ground; to plough, to sow, to reap, to bring in his corn, to breed and manage his cattle, and to act with prudence and propriety in every part of his employment. It can direct artificers how to prepare the various sorts of apparel, and a thousand necessaries and conveniences of life, not only for themselves and their households, but for their neighbours, whether nigh or afar off. It can direct those of higher abilities

to plan and execute works of a more elegant kind. It can direct the painter, the statuary, the musician, to excel in the stations wherein Providence has placed them. It can direct the mariner to steer his course over the bosom of the great deep. It enables those who study the laws of their country to defend the property or life of their fellow-subjects; and those who study the art of healing to cure most of the maladies to which we are exposed in our present state.

4. To ascend higher still: It is certain reason can assist us in going through the whole circle of arts and sciences; of grammar, rhetoric, logic, natural and moral philosophy, mathematics, algebra, metaphysics. It can teach whatever the skill or industry of man has invented for some thousand years. It is absolutely necessary for the due discharge of the most important offices; such as are those of Magistrates, whether of an inferior or superior rank; and those of subordinate or supreme Governors, whether of states, provinces, or kingdoms.

5. All this few men in their senses will deny. No thinking man can doubt but reason is of considerable service in all things relating to the present world. But suppose we speak of higher things,—the things of another world; what can reason do here? Is it a help or a hinderance of religion? It may do much in the affairs of men; but what can it do in the things of God?

6. This is a point that deserves to be deeply considered. If you ask, What can reason do in religion? I answer, It can do exceeding much, both with regard to the foundation of it, and the superstructure.

The foundation of true religion stands upon the oracles of God. It is built upon the Prophets and Apostles, Jesus Christ himself being the chief corner-stone. Now, of what excellent use is reason, if we would either understand ourselves, or explain to others, those living oracles! And how is it possible without it to understand the essential truths contained therein? a beautiful summary of which we have in that which is called the Apostles' Creed. Is it not reason (assisted by the Holy Ghost) which enables us to understand what the Holy Scriptures declare concerning the being and attributes of God?—concerning his eternity and immensity; his power, wisdom, and holiness? It is by reason that God enables us in some measure to comprehend his method of dealing with the children of men; the nature of his various dispensations, of the old and new covenant, of the law and the gospel. It is by this we understand (his Spirit opening and enlightening the eyes of our understanding) what that repentance is, not to be repented of; what is that faith whereby we are saved; what is the nature and the condition of justification; what are the immediate and what the subsequent fruits of it. By reason we learn what is that new birth, without which we cannot enter into the kingdom of heaven; and what that holiness is without which no man shall see the Lord. By the due use of reason we come to know what are the tempers implied in inward holiness; and what it is to be outwardly holy—holy in all manner of conversation: In other words, what is the mind that was in Christ; and what it is to walk as Christ walked.

7. Many particular cases will occur with respect to several of the foregoing articles, in which we shall have occasion for all our understanding, if we would keep a conscience void of offence. Many cases of conscience are not to be solved without the utmost exercise of our reason. The same is requisite in order to understand and to discharge our ordinary relative duties;—the duties of parents and children, of husbands and wives, and (to name no more) of masters and servants. In all these respects, and in all the duties of common life, God has given us our reason for a guide. And it is only by acting up to the dictates of it, by using all the understanding which God hath given us, that we can have a conscience void of offense towards God and towards man.

8. Here, then, there is a large field indeed, wherein reason may expatiate and exercise all its powers. And if reason can do all this, both in civil and religious things, what is it that it cannot do?

We have hitherto endeavoured to lay aside all prejudice, and to weigh the matter calmly and impartially. The same course let us take still: Let us now coolly consider, without prepossession on any side, what it is, according to the best light we have, that reason cannot do.

II. 1. And, First, reason cannot produce faith. Although it is always consistent with reason, yet reason cannot produce faith, in the scriptural sense of the word. Faith, according to Scripture, is "an evidence," or conviction, "of things not seen." It is a divine evidence, bringing a full conviction of an invisible eternal world. It is true, there was a kind of shadowy persuasion of this, even among the wiser Heathens; probably from tradition, or from some gleams of light reflected from the Israelites. Hence many hundred years before our Lord was born, the Greek Poet uttered that great truth,—

> Millions of spiritual creatures walk the earth
> Unseen, whether we wake, or if we sleep.

But this was little more than faint conjecture: It was far from a firm conviction; which reason, in its highest state of improvement, could never produce in any child of man.

2. Many years ago I found the truth of this by sad experience. After carefully heaping up the strongest arguments which I could find, either in ancient or modern authors, for the very being of a God, and (which is nearly connected with it) the existence of an invisible world, I have wandered up and down, musing with myself: "What, if all these things which I see around me, this earth and heaven, this universal frame, has existed from eternity? What, if that melancholy supposition of the old Poet be the real case,—

> oie per phullon genee, toiede kai andron;

What, if 'the generation of men be exactly parallel with the generation of leaves?' if the earth drops its successive inhabitants, just as the tree drops its leaves? What, if that saying of a great man be really true,—

> Post mortem nihil est; ipsaque mors nihil?
> Death is nothing, and nothing is after death?

How am I sure that this is not the case; that I have not followed cunningly devised fables?"—And I have pursued the thought, till there was no spirit in me, and I was ready to choose strangling rather than life.

3. But in a point of so unspeakable importance, do not depend upon the word of another; but retire for awhile from the busy world, and make the experiment yourself. Try whether *your* reason will give you a clear satisfactory evidence of the invisible world. After the prejudices of education are laid aside, produce your strong reasons for the existence of this. Set them all in array; silence all objections; and put all your doubts to flight. alas! you cannot, with all your understanding. You may repress them for a season. But how quickly will they rally again, and attack you with redoubled violence! And what can poor reason do for your deliverance? The more vehemently you struggle, the more deeply you are entangled in the toils; and you find no way to escape.

4. How was the case with that great admirer of reason, the author of the maxim above cited? I mean the famous Mr. Hobbes. None will deny that he had a strong understanding. But did it produce in him a full and satisfactory conviction of an invisible world? Did it open the eyes of his understanding, to see

Beyond the bounds of this diurnal sphere? O no! far from it! His dying words ought never to be forgotten. "Where are you going, Sir?" said one of his friends. He answered, "I am taking a leap in the dark!" and died. Just such an evidence of the invisible world can bare reason give to the wisest of men!

5. Secondly. Reason alone cannot produce hope in any child of man: I mean scriptural hope, whereby we "rejoice in hope of the glory of God:" That hope which St. Paul in one place terms, "tasting the powers of the world to come;" in another, the "sitting in heavenly places in Christ Jesus:" That which enables us to say, "Blessed be the God and Father of our Lord Jesus Christ, who hath begotten us again unto a lively hope;—to an inheritance incorruptible, undefiled, and that fadeth not away; which is reserved in heaven for us." This hope can only spring from Christian faith: Therefore, where there is not faith, there is not hope. Consequently, reason, being unable to produce faith, must be equally unable to produce hope. Experience confirms this likewise. How often have I laboured, and that with my might, to beget this hope in myself! But it was lost labour: I could no more acquire this hope of heaven, than I could touch heaven with my hand. And whoever of you makes the same attempt will find it attended with the same success. I do not deny, that a self-deceiving enthusiast may work in himself a kind of hope: He may work himself up into a lively imagination; into a sort of pleasing dream: He may "compass himself about, "as the Prophet speaks, "with sparks of his own kindling:" But this cannot be of long continuance; in a little while the bubble will surely break. And what will follow? "This shall ye have at my hand, saith the Lord, ye shall lie down in sorrow."

6. If reason could have produced a hope full of immortality in any child of man, it might have produced it in that great man whom Justin Martyr scruples not to call "a Christian before Christ." For who that was not favoured with the written word of God, ever excelled, yea, or equalled, Socrates? In what other Heathen can we find so strong an understanding, joined with so consummate virtue? But had he really this hope? Let him answer for himself. What is the conclusion of that noble apology which he made before his unrighteous judges? "And now, O judges! ye are going hence to live; and I am going hence to die: Which of these is best, the gods know; but, I suppose, no man does." *No man knows!* How far is this from the language of the little Benjamite: "I desire to depart, and to be with Christ; which is far better!" And how many thousands are there at this day, even in our own nation, young men and maidens, old men and children, who are able to witness the same good confession!

7. But who is able to do this, by the force of his reason, be it ever so highly improved? One of the most sensible and most amiable Heathens that have lived since our Lord died, even though he governed the greatest empire in the world, was the Emperor Adrian. It is his well-known saying, "A prince ought to resemble the sun: He ought to shine on every part of his dominion, and to diffuse his salutary rays in every place where he comes." And his life was a comment upon his word: Wherever he went, he was executing justice, and showing mercy. Was not he then, at the close of a long life, full of immortal hope? We are able to answer this from unquestionable authority,—from his own dying words. How inimitably pathetic!

ADRANI MORIENTIS AD ANIMAM SUAM.
"DYING ADRIAN TO HIS SOUL."

> Animula, vagula, blandula,
> Hospes, comesque corporis,
> Quae nunc abibis in loca,
> Pallidula, rigida, nudula,
> Nec, ut soles, dabis jocos!

Which to the English reader may see translated into our own language, with all the spirit of the original:—

> Poor, little, pretty, fluttering thing,
>> Must we no longer live together?
> And dost thou prune thy trembling wing,
>> To take they flight, thou know'st not whither?
> Thy pleasing vein, they humorous folly,
>> Lies all neglected, all forgot!
> And pensive, wavering, melancholy,
>> Thou hop'st, and fear'st, thou know'st not what.

8. Thirdly. Reason, however cultivated and improved, cannot produce the love of God; which is plain from hence: It cannot produce either faith or hope; from which alone this love can flow. It is then only, when we "behold" by faith "what manner of love the Father hath bestowed upon us," in giving his only Son, that we might not perish, but have everlasting life, that "the love of God is shed abroad in our heart by the Holy Ghost which is given unto us." It is only then, when we "rejoice in hope of the glory of God," that "we love Him because he first loved us." But what can cold reason do in this matter? It may present us with fair ideas; it can draw a fine picture of love: But this is only a painted fire. And farther than this reason cannot go. I made the trial for many years. I collected the finest hymns, prayers, and meditations which I could find in any language; and I said, sung, or read them over and over, with all possible seriousness and attention. But still I was like the bones in Ezekiel's vision: "The skin covered them above; but there was no breath in them."

9. And as reason cannot produce the love of God, so neither can it produce the love of our neighbour; a calm, generous, disinterested benevolence to every child of man. This earnest, steady good-will to our fellow-creatures never flowed from any fountain but gratitude to our Creator. And if this be (as a very ingenious man supposes) the very essence of virtue, it follows that virtue can have no being, unless it spring from the love of God. Therefore, as reason cannot produce this love, so neither can it produce virtue.

10. And as it cannot give either faith, hope, love, or virtue, so it cannot give happiness; since, separate from these, there can be no happiness for any intelligent creature. It is true, those who are void of all virtue may have pleasures, such as they are; but happiness they have not, cannot have. No:

> Their joy is all sadness; their mirth is all vain;
> Their laughter is madness; their pleasure is pain!

Pleasures? Shadows! dreams! fleeting as the wind! unsubstantial as the rainbow! as unsatisfying to the poor gasping soul,

> As the gay colours of an eastern cloud.

None of these will stand the test of reflection: If thought comes, the bubble breaks!

Suffer me now to add a few plain words, first to you who under-value reason. Never more declaim in that wild, loose, ranting manner, against this precious gift of God. Acknowledge "the candle of the Lord," which he hath fixed in our souls for excellent purposes. You see how many admirable ends it answers, were it only in the things of this life: Of what unspeakable use is even a moderate share of reason in all our worldly employments, from the lowest and meanest offices of life, through all the intermediate branches of business; till we ascend to those that are of the highest importance and the greatest difficulty! When therefore you despise or depreciate reason, you must not imagine you are doing God service: Least of all, are you promoting the cause of God when you are endeavouring to exclude reason out of religion. Unless you wilfully shut your eyes, you cannot but see of what service it is both in laying the foundation of true religion, under the guidance of the Spirit of God, and in raising the superstructure. You see it directs us in every point both of faith and practice: It guides us with regard to every branch both of inward and outward holiness. Do we not glory in this, that the whole of our religion is a "reasonable service?" yea, and that every part of it, when it is duly performed, is the highest exercise of our understanding?

Permit me to add a few words to you, likewise, who over-value reason. Why should you run from one extreme to the other? Is not the middle way best? Let reason do all that reason can: Employ it as far as it will go. But, at the same time, acknowledge it is utterly incapable of giving either faith, or hope, or love; and, consequently, of producing either real virtue, or substantial happiness. Expect these from a higher source, even from the Father of the spirits of all flesh. Seek and receive them, not as your own acquisition, but as the gifts of God. Lift up your hearts to Him who "giveth to all men liberally, and upbraideth not." He alone can give that faith, which is "the evidence" and conviction "of things not seen." He alone can "beget you unto a lively hope" of an inheritance eternal in the heavens; and He alone can "shed his love abroad in your heart by the Holy Ghost given unto you." Ask, therefore, and it shall be given you! Cry unto him, and you shall not cry in vain! How can you doubt? "If ye, being evil, know how to give good gifts unto your children, how much more shall your Father who is in heaven give the Holy Ghost unto them that ask him!" So shall you be living witnesses, that wisdom, holiness, and happiness are one; are inseparably united; and are, indeed, the beginning of that eternal life which God hath given us in his Son.

71.* OF GOOD ANGELS

"Are they not all ministering spirits, sent forth to minister for them who shall be heirs of salvation?"

Heb. 1:14.

1. Many of the ancient Heathens had (probably from tradition) some notion of good and evil angels. They had some conception of a superior order of beings, between men and God, whom the Greeks generally termed demons, *(knowing ones,)* and the Romans, genii. Some of these they supposed to be kind and benevolent, delighting in doing good; others, to be malicious and cruel, delighting in doing evil. But their conceptions both of one and the other were crude, imperfect, and confused; being only fragments of truth, partly delivered down by their forefathers, and partly borrowed from the inspired writings.

2. Of the former, the benevolent kind, seems to have been the celebrated demon of Socrates; concerning which so many and so various conjectures have been made in succeeding ages. "This gives me notice," said he, "every morning, of any evil which will befall me that day." A late writer, indeed, (I suppose one that hardly believes the existence of either angel or spirit,) has published a dissertation, wherein he labours to prove, that the demon of Socrates was only his reason. But it was not the manner of Socrates to speak in such obscure and ambiguous terms. If he had meant his reason, he would doubtless have said so. But this could not be his meaning: For it was impossible his reason should give him notice, every morning, of every evil which would befall him in that day. It does not lie within the province of reason, to give such notice of future contingencies. Neither does this odd interpretation in anywise agree with the inference which he himself draws from it. "My demon," says he, "did not give me notice this morning of any evil that was to befall me to-day. Therefore I cannot regard as any evil my being condemned to die." Undoubtedly it was some spiritual being: Probably one of these ministering spirits.

3. An ancient poet, one who lived several ages before Socrates, speaks more determinately on this subject. Hesiod does not scruple to say,

> Millions of spiritual creatures walk the earth unseen.

Hence, it is probable, arose the numerous tales about the exploits of their demi-gods: *Minorum Gentium.* Hence their

---

* [text from the 1872 edition]

satyrs, fauns, nymphs of every kind; wherewith they supposed both the sea and land to be filled. But how empty, childish, unsatisfactory, are all the accounts they give of them! as, indeed, accounts that depend upon broken, uncertain tradition can hardly fail to be.

4. Revelation only is able to supply this defect: This only gives us a clear, rational, consistent account of those whom our eyes have not seen, nor our ears heard; of both good and evil angels. It is my design to speak, at present, only of the former; of whom we have a full, though brief account in these words: "Are they not all ministering spirits, sent forth to minister unto them that shall be heirs of salvation?"

I. 1. The question is, according to the manner of the Apostle, equivalent to a strong affirmation. And hence we learn, First, that with regard to their essence, or nature, they are all spirits; not material beings; not clogged with flesh and blood like us; but having bodies, if any, not gross and earthly like ours, but of a finer substance; resembling fire or flame, more than any other of these lower elements. And is not something like this intimated in those words of the Psalmist: "Who maketh his angels spirits, and his ministers a flame of fire?" (Psalm 104:4.) As spirits, he has endued them with understanding, will, or affections, (which are indeed the same thing; as the affections are only the will exerting itself various ways,) and liberty. And are not these, understanding, will, and liberty, essential to, if not the essence of, a spirit?

2. But who of the children of men can comprehend what is the *understanding* of an angel? Who can comprehend how far their *sight* extends? Analogous to sight in men, though not the same; but thus we are constrained to speak through the poverty of human language. Probably not only over one hemisphere of the earth; yea, or,

      Ten-fold the length of this terrene;

or even of the solar system; but so far as to take in one view the whole extent of the creation! And we cannot conceive any defect in their perception; neither any error in their understanding. But in what manner do they use their understanding? We must in nowise imagine that they creep from one truth to another by that slow method which we call reasoning. Undoubtedly they see, at one glance, whatever truth is presented to their understanding; and that with all the certainty and clearness that we mortals see the most self-evident axiom. Who then can conceive the extent of their *knowledge?* not only of the nature, attributes, and works of God, whether of creation or providence; but of the circumstances, actions, words, tempers, yea, and thoughts, of men. For although "God" only "knows the hearts of all men," ("unto whom are known all his works,") together with the changes they undergo, "from the beginning of the world;" yet we cannot doubt but his angels know the hearts of those to whom they more immediately minister. Much less can we doubt of their knowing the thoughts that are in our hearts at any particular time. What should hinder their seeing them as they arise? Not the thin veil of flesh and blood. Can these intercept the view of a spirit? Nay,

      Walls within walls no more its passage bar,
      Than unopposing space of liquid air.

Far more easily, then, and far more perfectly, than we can read a man's thoughts in his face, do these sagacious beings read our thoughts just as they rise in our hearts; inasmuch as they see the kindred spirit, more clearly than we see the body. If this seem strange to any who had not adverted to it before, let him only consider: Suppose my spirit was out of the body, could not an angel see my thoughts, even without my uttering any words? (if words are used in the world of spirits.) And cannot that ministering spirit see them just as well now that I am in the body? It seems, therefore, to be an unquestionable truth, (although perhaps not commonly observed,) that angels know not only the words and actions, but also the thoughts, of those to whom they minister. And indeed without this knowledge, they would be very ill qualified to perform various parts of their ministry.

3. And what an inconceivable degree of *wisdom* must they have acquired by the use of their amazing faculties, over and above that with which they were originally endued, in the course of more than six thousand years! (That they have existed so long we are assured; for they "sang together when the foundations of the earth were laid.") How immensely must their wisdom have increased, during so long a period, not only by surveying the hearts and ways of men in their successive generations, but by observing the works of God, his works of creation, his works of providence, his works of grace; and, above all, by "continually beholding the face of their Father which is in heaven!"

4. What measures of *holiness*, as well as wisdom, have they derived from this inexhaustible ocean!

      A boundless, fathomless abyss,
      Without a bottom or a shore!

Are they not hence, by way of eminence, styled *the holy angels?* What goodness, what philanthropy, what love to man, have they drawn from those rivers that are at his right hand! Such as we cannot conceive to be exceeded by any but that of God our Saviour. And they are still drinking in more love from this "Fountain of living water."

5. Such is the knowledge and wisdom of the angels of God, as we learn from his own oracles. Such are their holiness and goodness. And how astonishing is their *strength!* Even a fallen angel is styled by an inspired writer, "the prince of the power of the air." How terrible a proof did he give of this power, in suddenly raising the whirlwind, which "smote the four corners of the house," and destroyed all the children of Job at once! (Job 1.) That this was his work, we may easily learn from the command to "save his life." But he gave a far more terrible proof of his strength, (if we suppose that "messenger of the Lord" to have been an evil angel, as is not at all improbable,) when he smote with death a hundred, four-score and five thousand Assyrians in one night; nay, possibly in one hour, if not one moment. Yet a strength abundantly greater than this must have been exerted by that angel (whether he was an angel of light or of darkness; which is not determined by the text) who smote, in one hour, "all the first-born of Egypt, both of man and beast." For, considering the extent of the land of Egypt, the immense populousness thereof, and the innumerable cattle fed in their houses, and grazing in their fruitful fields; the men and beasts

who were slain in that night must have amounted to several millions! And if this be supposed to have been an evil angel, must not a good angel be as strong, yea, stronger than him? For surely any good angel must have more power than even an *archangel ruined*. And what power must the "four angels" in the Revelation have, who were appointed to "keep the four winds of heaven!" There seems, therefore, no extravagance in supposing, that, if God were pleased to permit, any of the angels of light could heave the earth and all the planets out of their orbits; yea, that he could arm himself with all these elements, and crush the whole frame of nature. Indeed we do not know how to set any bounds to the strength of these first-born children of God.

6. And although none but their great Creator is omnipresent; although none beside him can ask, "Do not I fill heaven and earth?" yet, undoubtedly, he has given an immense sphere of action (though not unbounded) to created spirits. "The prince of the kingdom of Persia," (mentioned Dan. 10:13,) though probably an evil angel, seems to have had a sphere of action, both of knowledge and power, as extensive as that vast empire; and the same, if not greater, we may reasonably ascribe to the good angel whom he withstood for one-and-twenty days.

7. The angels of God have great power, in particular, over the human body; power either to cause or remove pain and diseases, either to kill or to heal. They perfectly well understand whereof we are made; they know all the springs of this curious machine, and can, doubtless, by God's permission, touch any of them, so as either to stop or restore its motion. Of this power, even in an evil angel, we have a clear instance in the case of Job; whom he "smote with sore boils" all over, "from the crown of the head to the sole of the foot." And in that instant, undoubtedly, he would have killed him, if God had not saved his life. And, on the other hand, of the power of angels to heal, we have a remarkable instance in the case of Daniel. There remained no "strength in me," said the prophet; "neither was there breath in me." "Then one came and touched me, and said, Peace be unto thee: Be strong, yea, be strong. And when he had spoken unto me, I was strengthened." (Dan. 10:17.) On the other hand, when they are commissioned from above, may they not put a period to human life? There is nothing improbable in what Dr. Parnell supposes the angel to say to the hermit, concerning the death of the child:—

> To all but thee, in fits he seem'd to go:
> And 'twas my ministry to deal the blow.

From this great truth, the heathen poets probably derived their imagination, that Iris used to be sent down from heaven to discharge souls out of their bodies. And perhaps the sudden death of many of the children of God may be owing to the ministry of an angel.

II. So perfectly are the angels of God qualified for their high office. It remains to inquire, how they discharge their office. How do they minister to the heirs of salvation?

1. I will not say, that they do not minister at all to those who, through their obstinate impenitence and unbelief, disinherit themselves of the kingdom. This world is a world of mercy, wherein God pours down many mercies, even on the evil and the unthankful. And many of these, it is probable, are conveyed even to them by the ministry of angels; especially, so long as they have any thought of God, or any fear of God before their eyes. But it is their favourite employ, their peculiar office, to minister to the heirs of salvation; to those who are now "saved by faith," or at least seeking God in sincerity.

2. Is it not their first care to minister to our souls? But we must not expect this will be done *with observation*; in such a manner, as that we may clearly distinguish their working from the workings of our own minds. We have no more reason to look for this, than for their appearing in a visible shape. Without this, they can, in a thousand ways, apply to our understanding. They may assist us in our search after truth, remove many doubts and difficulties, throw light on what was before dark and obscure, and confirm us in the truth that is after godliness. They may warn us of evil in disguise; and place what is good, in a clear, strong light. They may gently move our will to embrace what is good, and fly from that which is evil. They may, many times, quicken our dull affections, increase our holy hope or filial fear, and assist us more ardently to love Him who has first loved us. Yea, they may be sent of God to answer that whole prayer, put into our mouths by pious Bishop Ken:—

> O may thy angels, while I sleep,
> Around my bed their vigils keep;
> Their love angelical instil,
> Stop every avenue of ill!
> May they celestial joys rehearse,
> And thought to thought with me converse!

Although the manner of this we shall not be able to explain while we dwell in the body.

3. May they not minister also to us, with respect to our bodies, in a thousand ways which we do not now understand? They may prevent our falling into many dangers, which we are not sensible of; and may deliver us out of many others, though we know not whence our deliverance comes. How many times have we been strangely and unaccountably preserved, in sudden and dangerous falls! And it is well if we did not impute that preservation to chance, or to our own wisdom or strength. Not so: It was God gave his angels charge over us, and in their hands they bore us up. Indeed, men of the world will always impute such deliverances to accident or second causes. To these, possibly, some of them might have imputed Daniel's preservation in the lion's den. But himself ascribes it to the true cause: "My God hath sent his angel, and shut the lions' mouths." (Dan. 6:22.)

4. When a violent disease, supposed to be incurable, is totally and suddenly removed, it is by no means improbable that this is effected by the ministry of an angel. And perhaps it is owing to the same cause, that a remedy is unaccountably suggested either to the sick person, or some attending upon him, by which he is entirely cured.

5. It seems, what are usually called divine dreams may be frequently ascribed to angels. We have a remarkable instance of this kind related by one that will hardly be thought an enthusiast; for he was a Heathen, a Philosopher, and an Emperor: I mean Marcus Antoninus. "In his Meditations, he

solemnly thanks God for revealing to him, when he was at Cajeta, in a dream, what totally cured the bloody flux; which none of his physicians were able to heal." And why may we not suppose, that God gave him this notice by the ministry of an angel?

6. And how often does God deliver us from evil men by the ministry of his angels! overturning whatever their rage, or malice, or subtlety had plotted against us. These are about their bed, and about their path, and privy to all their dark designs; and many of them, undoubtedly, they brought to nought, by means that we think not of. Sometimes they blast their favourite schemes in the beginning; sometimes, when they are just ripe for execution. And this they can do by a thousand means that we are not aware of. They can check them in their mid-career, by bereaving them of courage or strength; by striking faintness through their loins, or turning their wisdom into foolishness. Sometimes they bring to light the hidden things of darkness, and show us the traps that are laid for our feet. In these and various other ways, they hew the snares of the ungodly in pieces.

7. Another grand branch of their ministry is, to counterwork evil angels; who are continually going about, not only as roaring lions, seeking whom they may devour, but, more dangerously still, as angels of light, seeking whom they may deceive. And how great is the number of these! Are they not as the stars of heaven for multitude? How great is their subtlety! matured by the experience of above six thousand years. How great is their strength! Only inferior to that of the angels of God. The strongest of the sons of men are but as grasshoppers before them. And what an advantage have they over us by that single circumstance, that they are invisible! As we have not strength to repel their force, so we have not skill to decline it. But the merciful Lord hath not given us up to the will of our enemies: "His eyes," that is, his holy angels, "run to and fro over all the earth." And if our eyes were opened, we should see, "they are more that are for us, than they that are against us." We should see,

> A convoy attends,
> A ministering host of invisible friends.

And whenever those assault us in soul or in body, these are able, willing, ready, to defend us; who are at least equally strong, equally wise, and equally vigilant. And who can hurt us while we have armies of angels, and the God of angels, on our side?

8. And we may make one general observation: Whatever assistance God gives to men by men, the same, and frequently in a higher degree, he gives to them by angels. Does he administer to us by men, light when we are in darkness; joy, when we are in heaviness; deliverance, when we are in danger; ease and health, when we are sick or in pain? It cannot be doubted but he frequently conveys the same blessings by the ministry of angels: Not so sensibly indeed, but full as effectually; though the messengers are not seen. Does he frequently deliver us, by means of men, from the violence and subtlety of our enemies? Many times he works the same deliverance by those invisible agents. These shut the mouths of the human lions, so that they have no power to hurt us. And frequently they join with our human friends, (although neither they nor we are sensible of it,) giving them wisdom, courage, or strength, which all their labour for us would be unsuccessful. Thus do they secretly minister, in numberless instances, to the heirs of salvation; while we hear only the voices of men, and see none but men round about us.

9. But does not the Scripture teach, "The help which is done upon earth, God doeth it himself?" Most certainly he does. And he is able to do it by his own immediate power. He has no need of using any instruments at all, either in heaven or earth. He wants not either angels or men, to fulfil the whole counsel of his will. But it is not his pleasure so to work. He never did; and we may reasonably suppose he never will. He has always wrought by such instruments as he pleases: But still it is God himself that doeth the work. Whatever help, therefore, we have, either by angels or men, is as much the work of God, as if he were to put forth his almighty arm, and work without any means at all. But he has used them from the beginning of the world: In all ages he has used the ministry both of men and angels. And hereby, especially, is seen "the manifold wisdom of God in the Church." Meantime the same glory redounds to him, as if he used no instruments at all.

10. The grand reason why God is pleased to assist men by men, rather than immediately by himself, is undoubtedly to endear us to each other by these mutual good offices, in order to increase our happiness both in time and eternity. And is it not for the same reason that God is pleased to give his angels charge over us? namely, that he may endear us and them to each other; that by the increase of our love and gratitude to them, we may find a proportionable increase of happiness, when we meet in our Father's kingdom. In the mean time, though we may not worship them, (worship is due only to our common Creator,) yet we may "esteem them very highly in love for their works' sake." And we may imitate them in all holiness; suiting our lives to the prayer our Lord himself has taught us; labouring to do his will on earth, as angels do it in heaven.

I cannot conclude this discourse better than in that admirable Collect of our Church:—

"O everlasting God, who hast ordained and constituted the services of angels and men in a wonderful manner; grant that as thy holy angels alway do thee service in heaven, so by thy appointment they may succour and defend us on earth, through Jesus Christ our Lord."

72.* OF EVIL ANGELS

"We wrestle not against flesh and blood, but against principalities, against powers, against the rulers of the darkness of this world, against wicked spirits in heavenly places."

Eph. 6:12.

1. It has been frequently observed that there are no gaps or chasms in the creation of God, but that all the parts of it are

---

admirably connected together, to make up one universal whole. Accordingly there is one chain of beings, from the lowest to the highest point, from an unorganized particle of earth or water to Michael the archangel. And the scale of creatures does not advance *per saltum*, by leaps, but by smooth and gentle degrees; although it is true, these are frequently imperceptible to our imperfect faculties. We cannot accurately trace many of the intermediate links of this amazing chain, which are abundantly too fine to be discerned either by our senses or understanding.

2. We can only observe, in a gross and general manner, rising one above another, first, inorganical earth, then minerals and vegetables in their several orders; afterwards insects, reptiles, fishes, beasts, men, and angels. Of angels indeed we know nothing with any certainty but by revelation. The accounts which are left by the wisest of the ancients, or given by the modern heathens, being no better than silly, self-inconsistent fables, too gross to be imposed even upon children. But by divine revelation we are informed that they were all created holy and happy; yet they did not all continue as they were created: Some kept, but some left, their first estate. The former of these are now good angels; the latter, evil angels. Of the former I have spoke in the preceding discourse: I purpose now to speak of the latter. And highly necessary it is that we should well understand what God has revealed concerning them, that they may gain no advantage over us by our ignorance; that we may know how to wrestle against them effectually. For "we wrestle not against flesh and blood, but against principalities, against powers, against the rulers of the darkness of this world, against wicked spirits in heavenly places."

3. This single passage seems to contain the whole scriptural doctrine concerning evil angels. I apprehend the plain meaning of it, literally translated, is this: "Our wrestling," the wrestling of real Christians, "is not" only, or chiefly, "against flesh and blood," weak men, or fleshly appetites and passions, "but against principalities, against powers,"—the mighty princes of all the infernal regions, with their combined forces: And great is their power, as is also the power of the legions they command,—"against the rulers of the world." (This is the literal meaning of the word.) Perhaps these principalities and powers remain chiefly in the citadel of their kingdom. But there are other evil spirits that range abroad, to whom the provinces of the world are committed, "of the darkness," chiefly the spiritual darkness, "of this age," which prevails during this present state of things,—"against wicked spirits"—eminently such; who mortally hate and continually oppose holiness, and labour to infuse unbelief, pride, evil desire, malice, anger, hatred, envy, or revenge—"in heavenly places;" which were once their abode, and which they still aspire after.

In prosecuting this important subject, I will endeavour to explain,

I. The nature and properties of evil angels; and,

II. Their employment.

I. 1. With regard to the First, we cannot doubt but all the angels of God were originally of the same nature. Unquestionably they were the highest order of created beings. They were spirits, pure ethereal creatures, simple and incorruptible; if not wholly immaterial, yet certainly not incumbered with gross, earthly flesh and blood. As spirits, they were endued with understanding, with affections, and with liberty, or a power of self-determination; so that it lay in themselves, either to continue in their allegiance to God, or to rebel against him.

2. And their original properties were, doubtless, the same with those of the holy angels. There is no absurdity in supposing Satan their chief, otherwise styled, "Lucifer, son of the morning," to have been at least one "of the first, if not the first Archangel." Like the other sons of the morning, they had a height and depth of understanding quite incomprehensible to us. In consequence of this they had such knowledge and wisdom, that the wisest of the children of men (had men then existed) would have been mere idiots in comparison of them. Their strength was equal to their knowledge; such as it cannot enter into our heart to conceive; neither can we conceive to how wide a sphere of action either their strength or their knowledge extended. Their number God alone can tell: Doubtless it was only less than infinite. And a third part of these stars of heaven the arch-rebel drew after him.

3. We do not exactly know, (because it is not revealed in the oracles of God,) either what was the occasion of their apostasy, or what effect it immediately produced upon them. Some have, not improbably, supposed, that when God published "the decree" (mentioned Ps. 2:6–7) concerning the kingdom of his only-begotten Son to be over all creatures, these first-born of creatures gave place to pride, comparing themselves to him;—possibly intimated by the very name of Satan, Lucifer, or Michael, which means, *Who is like God?* It may be, Satan, then first giving way to temptation, said in his heart, "I too will have my throne. 'I will sit upon the sides of the north! I will be like the Most High.' " But how did the mighty then fall! What an amazing loss did they sustain! If we allow of them all what our poet supposes concerning their chief in particular,—

> His form had not yet lost
> All its original brightness, nor appear'd
> Less than archangel ruin'd, and the excess
> Of glory obscured;

if we suppose their outward form was not entirely changed (though it must have been in a great degree; because the evil disposition of the mind must dim the lustre of the visage,) yet what an astonishing change was wrought within when angels became devils! when the holiest of all the creatures of God became the most unholy!

4. From the time that they shook off their allegiance to God, they shook off all goodness, and contracted all those tempers which are most hateful to him, and most opposite to his nature. And ever since they are full of pride, arrogance, haughtiness, exalting themselves above measure; and although so deeply depraved through their inmost frame, yet admiring their own perfections. They are full of envy, if not against God himself, (and even that is not impossible, seeing they formerly aspired after his throne,) yet against all their fellow-creatures; against the angels of God, who now enjoy

the heaven from which they fell; and much more against those worms of the earth who are now called to "inherit the kingdom." They are full of cruelty, of rage against all the children of men, whom they long to inspire with the same wickedness with themselves, and to involve in the same misery.

5. In the prosecution of this infernal design, they are diligent in the highest degree. To find out the most effectual means of putting it into execution, they apply to this end the whole force of their angelical understanding; and they second it with their whole strength, so far as God is pleased to permit. But it is well for mankind that God hath set them bounds which they cannot pass. He hath said to the fiercest and strongest of the apostate spirits, "Hitherto shalt thou come, and no farther." Otherwise, how easily and how quickly might one of them overturn the whole frame of nature! How soon would they involve all in one common ruin, or, at least, destroy man from the face of the earth! And they are indefatigable in their bad work: They never are faint or weary. Indeed, it seems no spirits are capable of weariness but those that inhabit flesh and blood.

6. One circumstance more we may learn from the Scripture concerning the evil angels: They do not wander at large, but are all united under one common head. It is he that is styled by our blessed Lord, "the prince of this world:" Yea, the Apostle does not scruple to call him, "the god of this world." He is frequently styled Satan, the adversary; being the great adversary both of God and man. He is termed "the devil," by way of eminence;—"Apollyon," or the destroyer;—"the old serpent," from his beguiling Eve under that form;—and, "the angel of the bottomless pit." We have reason to believe that the other evil angels are under his command; that they are ranged by him according to their several orders; that they are appointed to their several stations, and have, from time to time, their several works and offices assigned them. And, undoubtedly, they are connected (though we know not how; certainly not by love) both to him and to each other.

II. But what is the employment of evil angels? This is the Second point to be considered.

1. They are (remember, so far as God permits!) *kosmokratores,—governors of the world!* So that there may be more ground than we are apt to imagine for that strange expression of Satan, (Matt. 4:8–9,) when he showed our Lord "all the kingdoms of the world, and the glory of them," "All these things will I give thee, if thou wilt fall down and worship me." It is a little more particularly expressed in the fourth chapter of St. Luke: "The devil showed unto him all the kingdoms of the world in a moment of time." (Such an astonishing measure of power is still left in the prince of darkness!) "And the devil said, All this power will I give thee, and the glory of them: For that is delivered unto me; and to whomsoever I will, I give it." (Matt. 4:5, 6,) They are "the rulers of the darkness of this age;" (so the words are literally translated;) of the present state of things, during which "the whole world lieth in the wicked one." He is the element of the children of men; only those who fear God being excepted. He and his angels, in connexion with, and in subordination to him, dispose all the ignorance, all the error, all the folly,

and particularly all the wickedness of men, in such a manner as may most hinder the kingdom of God, and most advance the kingdom of darkness.

2. "But has every man a particular evil angel, as well as a good one attending him?" This has been an exceeding ancient opinion, both among the Christians, and the Jews before them: But it is much doubted whether it can be sufficiently proved from Scripture. Indeed it would not be improbable that there is a particular evil angel with every man, if we were assured there is a good one. But this cannot be inferred from those words of our Lord concerning little children: "In heaven their angels do continually see the face of their Father which is in heaven." This only proves that there are angels who are appointed to take care of little children: It does not prove that a particular angel is allotted to every child. Neither is it proved by the words of Rhoda, who, hearing the voice of Peter, said, "It is *his angel.*" We cannot infer any more from this, even suppose his angel means his guardian angel, than that Rhoda believed the doctrine of guardian angels, which was then common among the Jews. But still it will remain a disputable point, (seeing revelation determines nothing concerning it,) whether every man is attended either by a particular good or a particular evil angel.

3. But whether or no particular men are attended by particular evil spirits, we know that Satan and all his angels are continually warring against us, and watching over every child of man. They are ever watching to see whose outward or inward circumstances, whose prosperity or adversity, whose health or sickness, whose friends or enemies, whose youth or age, whose knowledge or ignorance, whose blindness or idleness, whose joy or sorrow, may lay them open to temptation. And they are perpetually ready to make the utmost advantage of every circumstance. These skilful wrestlers espy the smallest slip we make, and avail themselves of it immediately; as they also are "about our bed, and about our path, and spy out all our ways." Indeed each of them "walketh about as a roaring lion, seeking whom he may devour," or whom he may "beguile through his subtlety, as the serpent beguiled Eve." Yea, and in order to do this the more effectually, they transform themselves into angels of light. Thus,

> With rage that never ends,
> Their hellish arts they try;
> Legions of dire, malicious fiends,
> And spirits enthroned on high.

4. It is by these instruments chiefly that the "foolish hearts" of those that know not God "are darkened:" Yea, they frequently darken, in a measure, the hearts of them that do know God. The "god of this world" knows how to blind our hearts, to spread a cloud over our understanding, and to obscure the light of those truths which, at other times, shine as bright as the noonday sun. By this means he assaults our faith, our evidence of things unseen. He endeavours to weaken that hope full of immortality to which God had begotten us; and thereby to lessen, if he cannot destroy, our joy in God our Saviour. But, above all he strives to damp our love of God, as he knows this is the spring of all our religion,

and that, as this rises or falls, the work of God flourishes or decays in the soul.

5. Next to the love of God, there is nothing which Satan so cordially abhors as the love of our neighbour. He uses, therefore, every possible means to prevent or destroy this; to excite either private or public suspicions, animosities, resentment, quarrels; to destroy the peace of families or of nations; and to banish unity and concord from the earth. And this, indeed, is the triumph of his art; to embitter the poor, miserable children of men against each other, and at length urge them to do his own work, to plunge one another into the pit of destruction.

6. This enemy of all righteousness is equally diligent to hinder every good word and work. If he cannot prevail upon us to do evil, he will, if possible, prevent our doing good. He is peculiarly diligent to hinder the work of God from spreading in the hearts of men. What pains does he take to prevent or obstruct the general work of God! And how many are his devices to stop its progress in particular souls! To hinder their continuing or growing in grace, in the knowledge of our Lord Jesus Christ! To lessen, if not destroy, that love, joy, peace,—that long-suffering, gentleness, goodness,—that fidelity, meekness, temperance,—which our Lord works by his loving Spirit in them that believe, and wherein the very essence of religion consists.

7. To effect these ends, he is continually labouring, with all his skill and power, to infuse evil thoughts of every kind into the hearts of men. And certainly it is as easy for a spirit to speak to our heart, as for a man to speak to our ears. But sometimes it is exceeding difficult to distinguish these from our own thoughts; those which he injects so exactly resembling those which naturally arise in our own minds. Sometimes, indeed, we may distinguish one from the other by this circumstance:—The thoughts which naturally arise in our minds are generally, if not always, occasioned by, or at least connected with, some inward or outward circumstance that went before. But those that are preternaturally suggested have frequently no relation to or connexion (at least, none that we are able to discern) with anything which preceded. On the contrary, they shoot in, as it were, across, and thereby show that they are of a different growth.

8. He likewise labours to awaken evil passions or tempers in our souls. He endeavours to inspire those passions and tempers which are directly opposite to "the fruit of the Spirit." He strives to instil unbelief, atheism, ill-will, bitterness, hatred, malice, envy,—opposite to faith and love; fear, sorrow, anxiety, worldly care,—opposite to peace and joy; impatience, ill nature, anger, resentment,—opposite to long-suffering, gentleness, meekness; fraud, guile, dissimulation,—contrary to fidelity; love of the world, inordinate affection, foolish desires,—opposite to the love of God. One sort of evil desires he may probably raise or inflame by touching the springs of this animal machine. Endeavouring thus, by means of the body, to disturb or sully the soul.

9. And, in general, we may observe that as no good is done, or spoken, or thought, by any man, without the assistance of God, working together *in* and *with* those that believe in him; so there is no evil done, or spoke, or thought, without the assistance of the devil, "who worketh with energy," with strong, though secret power, "in the children of unbelief." Thus he "entered into Judas," and confirmed him in the design of betraying his Master; thus he "put it into the heart" of Ananias and Sapphira "to lie unto the Holy Ghost;" and, in like manner, he has a share in all the actions and words and designs of evil men. As the children of God "are workers together with God," in every good thought, or word, or action; so the children of the devil are workers together with him in every evil thought, or word, or work. So that as all good tempers, and remotely all good words and actions, are the fruit of the good Spirit; in like manner, all evil tempers, with all the words and works which spring from them, are the fruit of the evil spirit: Insomuch that all the "works of the flesh," of our evil nature, are likewise the "works of the devil."

10. On this account, because he is continually inciting men to evil, he is emphatically called "the tempter." Nor is it only with regard to his own children that he is thus employed: He is continually tempting the children of God also, and those that are labouring so to be.

> A constant watch he keeps;
> He eyes them night and day;
> He never slumbers, never sleeps,
> Lest he should lose his prey.

Indeed, the holiest of men, as long as they remain upon earth, are not exempt from his temptations. They cannot expect it; seeing "it is enough for the disciple to be as his Master:" And we know he was tempted to evil till he said, "Father, into thy hands I commend my spirit."

11. For such is the malice of the wicked one, that he will torment whom he cannot destroy. If he cannot entice men to sin, he will, so far as he is permitted, put them to pain. There is no doubt but he is the occasion, directly or indirectly, of many of the pains of mankind, which those who can no otherwise account for them lightly pass over as nervous. And innumerable accidents, as they are called, are undoubtedly owing to his agency; such as the unaccountable fright or falling of horses; the overturning of carriages; the breaking or dislocating of bones; the hurt done by the falling or burning of houses,—by storms of wind, snow, rain, or hail,—by lightning or earthquakes. But to all these, and a thousand more, this subtle spirit can give the appearance of accidents, for fear the sufferers, if they knew the real agent, should call for help on One that is stronger than him.

12. There is little reason to doubt but many diseases likewise, both of the acute and chronical kind, are either occasioned or increased by diabolical agency; particularly those that begin in an instant, without any discernible cause; as well as those that continue, and perhaps gradually increase, in spite of all the power of medicine. Here, indeed, "vain men" that "would be wise" again call in the nerves to their assistance. But is not this explaining *ignotum per ignotius*? "a thing unknown by what is more unknown?" For what do we know of the nerves themselves? Not even whether they are solid or hollow!

13. Many years ago I was asking an experienced physician, and one particularly eminent for curing lunacy, "Sir, have

you not seen reason to believe that some lunatics are really demoniacs?" He answered, "Sir, I have been often inclined to think that most lunatics are demoniacs. Nor is there any weight in that objection, that they are frequently cured by medicine: For so might any other disease occasioned by an evil spirit, if God did not suffer him to repeat the stroke by which that disease is occasioned."

14. This thought opens to us a wider scene. Who can tell how many of those diseases which we impute altogether to natural causes may be really preternatural? What disorder is there in the human frame which an evil angel may not inflict? Cannot he smite us, as he did Job, and that in a moment, with boils from the crown of the head to the sole of the foot? Cannot he with equal ease inflict any other, either external or internal malady? Could not he in a moment, by divine permission, cast the strongest man down to the ground, and make him "wallow, foaming," with all the symptoms either of an epilepsy or apoplexy? In like manner, it is easy for him to smite any one man, or every one in a city or nation, with a malignant fever, or with the plague itself, so that vain would be the help of man.

15. But that malice blinds the eyes of the wise, one would imagine so intelligent a being would not stoop so low, as it seems the devil sometimes does, to torment the poor children of men! For to him we may reasonably impute many little inconveniences which we suffer. "I believe" (said that excellent man, the Marquis de Renty, when the bench on which he sat snapped in sunder without any visible cause) "that Satan had a hand in it, making me to fall untowardly." I know not whether he may not have a hand in that unaccountable horror with which many have been seized in the dead of night, even to such a degree that all their bones have shook. Perhaps he has a hand also in those terrifying dreams which many have, even while they are in perfect health.

It may be observed, in all these instances, we usually say, "The devil;" as if there was one only; because these spirits, innumerable as they are, do all act in concert; and because we know not whether one or more are concerned in this or that work of darkness.

It remains only to draw a few plain inferences from the doctrine which has been delivered.

1. And, First, as a general preservative against all the rage, the power, and subtlety of your great adversary, put on the panoply, "the whole armour of God," universal holiness. See that "the mind be in you which was also in Christ Jesus," and that ye "walk as Christ also walked;" that ye have a "conscience void of offence toward God and toward men." So shall ye be "able to withstand" all the force and all the stratagems of the enemy: So shall ye be able to "withstand in the evil day," in the day of sore temptation, and "having done all to stand," to remain in the posture of victory and triumph.

2. To his "fiery darts,"—his evil suggestions of every kind, blasphemous or unclean, though numberless as the stars of heaven,—oppose "the shield of faith." A consciousness of the love of Christ Jesus will effectually quench them all.

Jesus hath died for *you!*
What can your faith withstand?
Believe, hold fast your shield! and who
Shall pluck you from his hand?

3. If he inject doubts whether you are a child of God, or fears lest you should not endure to the end; "take to you for a helmet the hope of salvation." Hold fast that glad word, "Blessed be the God and Father of our Lord Jesus Christ, who, according to his abundant mercy, hath begotten us again unto a living hope of an inheritance incorruptible, undefiled, and that fadeth not away." You will never be overthrown, you will never be staggered by your adversary, if you "hold fast the beginning of" this "confidence steadfast unto the end."

4. Whenever the "roaring lion, walking about and seeking whom he may devour," assaults you with all his malice, and rage, and strength, "resist" him, "steadfast in the faith." Then is the time, having cried to the Strong for strength, to "stir up the gift of God that is in you;" to summon all your faith, and hope, and love; to turn the attack in the name of the Lord, and in the power of his might; and "he will" soon "flee from you."

5. But "there is no temptation," says one, "greater than the being without temptation." When, therefore, this is the case, when Satan seems to be withdrawn, then beware lest he hurt you more as a crooked serpent, than he could do as a roaring lion. Then take care you are not lulled into a pleasing slumber; lest he should beguile you as he did Eve, even in innocence, and insensibly draw you from your simplicity toward Christ, from seeking all your happiness in Him.

6. Lastly. If he "transform himself into an angel of light," then are you in the greatest danger of all. Then have you need to beware, lest you also fall, where many mightier have been slain; then have you the greatest need to "watch and pray, that ye enter not into temptation." And if you continue so to do, the God whom you love and serve will deliver you. "The anointing of the Holy One shall abide with you, and teach you of all things." Your eye will pierce through snares, you shall "know what that holy and acceptable and perfect will of God is," and shall hold on your way, till you "grow up in all things into him that is our Head, even Christ Jesus."

73.* OF HELL

"Where their worm dieth not, and the fire is not quenched."

Mark 9:48.

1. Every truth which is revealed in the oracles of God is undoubtedly of great importance. Yet it may be allowed that some of those which are revealed therein are of greater importance than others, as being more immediately conducive to the grand end of all, the eternal salvation of men. And we may judge of their importance even from this circumstance,—that they are not mentioned once only in the sacred writings, but are repeated over and over. A remarkable instance of this we have with regard to the awful truth which

---

* [text of the 1872 edition]

is now before us. Our blessed Lord, who uses no superfluous words, who makes no "vain repetitions," repeats it over and over in the same chapter, and as it were, in the same breath. So, (Mark 9:43, 44,) "If thy hand offend thee,"—if a thing or person, as useful as a hand, be an occasion of sin, and there is no other way to shun that sin,—"cut it off: It is better for thee to enter into life maimed, than having two hands to go into hell, into the fire that shall never be quenched: Where their worm dieth not, and the fire is not quenched." So again, (Mark 9:45, 46,) "If thy foot offend thee, cut it off: It is better for thee to enter halt into life, than having two feet to be cast into hell, into the fire that shall never be quenched: Where their worm dieth not, and the fire is not quenched." And yet again, (Mark 9:47, 48,) "If thine eye"—a person or thing as dear as thine eye—"offend thee,"—hinder thy running the race which is set before thee,—"pluck it out: It is better for thee to enter into the kingdom of God with one eye, than having two eyes to be cast into hell-fire: Where their worm dieth not, and the fire is not quenched."

2. And let it not be thought, that the consideration of these terrible truths is proper only for enormous sinners. How is this supposition consistent with what our Lord speaks to those who were then, doubtless, the holiest men upon earth? "When innumerable multitudes were gathered together, he said to his disciples" (the Apostles) "first of all, I say unto you, my friends, Fear not them that can kill the body, and after that have no more that they can do. But I say unto you, Fear him, who after he hath killed hath power to cast into hell; yea, I say unto you, Fear him." (Luke 12:1–5.) Yea, fear him under this very notion,—of having power to cast into hell: That is, in effect, fear lest he should cast you into the place of torment. And this very fear, even in the children of God, is one excellent means of preserving them from it.

3. It behoves, therefore not only the outcasts of men, but even *you, his friends*, you that fear and love God, deeply to consider what is revealed in the oracles of God concerning the future state of punishment. How widely distant is this from the most elaborate accounts which are given by the heathen authors! Their accounts are (in many particulars at least) childish, fanciful, and self-inconsistent. So that it is no wonder they did not believe themselves, but only related the tales of the vulgar. So Virgil strongly intimates, when, after the laboured account he had given of the shades beneath, he sends him that had related it out at the ivory gate, through which (as he tells us) only *dreams* pass; thereby giving us to know that all the preceding account is no more than a dream. This he only insinuates; but his brother poet, Juvenal, speaks out flat and plain,—

> Esse aliquos manes, et subterranea regna,
>
> Nec pueri credunt, nisi qui nondum aere lavantur:

"Even our children do not believe a word of the tales concerning another world."

4. Here, on the contrary, all is worthy of God, the Creator, the Governor of mankind. All is awful and solemn; suitable to his wisdom and justice by whom "Tophet was ordained of old;" although originally prepared, not for the children of men, but "for the devil and his angels."

The punishment of those who, in spite of all the warnings of God, resolve to have their portion with the devil and his angels, will, according to the ancient and not improper division, be either *paena damni*,—"what they lose;" or *paena sensus*,—"what they feel." After considering these separately, I shall touch on a few additional circumstances, and conclude with two or three inferences.

I. 1. And, First, let us consider the *paena damni*,—"the punishment of loss." This commences in that very moment wherein the soul is separated from the body; in that instant, the soul loses all those pleasures, the enjoyment of which depends on the outward senses. The smell, the taste, the touch, delight no more: The organs that ministered to them are spoiled, and the objects that used to gratify them are removed far away. In the dreary regions of the dead all these things are forgotten; or, if remembered, are only remembered with pain; seeing they are gone for ever. All the pleasures of the imagination are at an end. There is no grandeur in the infernal regions; there is nothing beautiful in those dark abodes; no light but that of livid flames. And nothing new, but one unvaried scene of horror upon horror! There is no music but that of groans and shrieks; of weeping, wailing, and gnashing of teeth; of curses and blasphemies against God, or cutting reproaches of one another. Nor is there anything to gratify the sense of honour: No; they are the heirs of shame and everlasting contempt.

2. Thus are they totally separated from all the things they were fond of in the present world. At the same instant will commence another loss,—that of all the *persons* whom they loved. They are torn away from their nearest and dearest relations; their wives, husbands, parents, children; and (what to some will be worse than all this) the friend which was as their own soul. All the pleasure they ever enjoyed in these is lost, gone, vanished away: For there is no friendship in hell. Even the poet who affirms, (though I know not on what authority,)

> Devil with devil damn'd
>
> Firm concord holds,

does not affirm that there is any concord among the human fiends that inhabit the great abyss.

3. But they will then be sensible of a greater loss than that of all they enjoyed on earth. They have lost their place in Abraham's bosom, in the paradise of God. Hitherto, indeed, it hath not entered into their hearts to conceive what holy souls enjoy in the garden of God, in the society of angels, and of the wisest and best men that have lived from the beginning of the world; (not to mention the immense increase of knowledge which they will then undoubtedly receive;) but they will then fully understand the value of what they have vilely cast away.

4. But as happy as the souls in paradise are, they are preparing for far greater happiness. For paradise is only the porch of heaven; and it is there the spirits of just men are made perfect. It is in heaven only that there is the fulness of joy; the pleasures that are at God's right hand for evermore. The loss of this, by those unhappy spirits, will be the completion of their misery. They will then know and feel, that God alone is the centre of all created spirits; and, consequently, that a

spirit made for God can have no rest out of him. It seems that the Apostle had this in his view when he spoke of those "who shall be punished with everlasting destruction from the presence of the Lord." Banishment from the presence of the Lord is the very essence of destruction to a spirit that was made for God. And if that banishment lasts for ever, it is "everlasting destruction."

Such is the loss sustained by those miserable creatures, on whom that awful sentence will be pronounced: "Depart from me, ye cursed!" What an unspeakable curse, if there were no other! But, alas! this is far from being the whole: For, to the punishment of loss, will be added the punishment of sense. What they lose implies unspeakable misery, which yet is inferior to what they feel. This it is which our Lord expresses in those emphatical words: "Where their worm dieth not, and the fire is not quenched."

II. 1. From the time that sentence was pronounced upon man, "Dust thou art, and unto dust thou shalt return," it was the custom of all nations, so far as we can learn, to commit dust to dust: It seemed natural to restore the bodies of the dead to the general mother, earth. But in process of time another method obtained, chiefly among the rich and great, of burning the bodies of their relations, and frequently in a grand magnificent manner; for which purpose they erected huge funeral piles, with immense labour and expense. By either of these methods the body of man was soon restored to its parent dust. Either the worm or the fire soon consumed the well-wrought frame; after which the worm itself quickly died, and the fire was entirely quenched. But there is, likewise, a worm that belongs to the future state; and that is a worm that never dieth! and there is a fire hotter than that of the funeral pile; and it is a fire that will never be quenched!

2. The First thing intended by the worm that never dieth, seems to be a guilty conscience; including self-condemnation, sorrow, shame, remorse, and a sense of the wrath of God. May not we have some conception of this, by what is sometimes felt even in the present world? Is it not of this, chiefly, that Solomon speaks, when he says, "The spirit of a man may bear his infirmities;" his infirmities, or griefs, of any other kind; "but a wounded spirit who can bear?" Who can bear the anguish of an awakened conscience, penetrated with a sense of guilt, and the arrows of the Almighty sticking in the soul, and drinking up the spirit? How many of the stout-hearted have sunk under it, and chose strangling rather than life! And yet what are these wounds, what is all this anguish of a soul while in this present world, in comparison of those they must suffer when their souls are wholly awakened to feel the wrath of an offended God! Add to these all unholy passions; fear, horror, rage; evil desires; desires that can never be satisfied. Add all unholy tempers; envy, jealousy, malice, and revenge; all of which will incessantly gnaw the soul, as the vulture was supposed to do the liver of Tityus. To these if we add hatred of God, and all his creatures; all these united together may serve to give us some little, imperfect idea of the worm that never dieth.

3. We may observe a remarkable difference in the manner wherein our Lord speaks concerning the two parts of the future punishment. He says, "Where *their* worm dieth not," of the one; "where *the* fire is not quenched," of the other. This cannot be by chance. What then is the reason for this variation of the expression?

Does it not seem to be this? *The fire* will be the same, essentially the same, to all that are tormented therein; only perhaps more intense to some than others, according to their degree of guilt; but *their worm* will not, cannot be the same. It will be infinitely varied, according to the various kinds, as well as degrees, of wickedness. This variety will arise partly from the just judgment of God, "rewarding every man according to his works:" For we cannot doubt but this rule will take place no less in hell than in heaven. As in heaven "every man will receive his own reward," incommunicably his, according to his own labours,—that is, the whole tenor of his tempers, thoughts, words, and actions;—so undoubtedly, every man, in fact, will receive his own bad reward, according to his own bad labour. And this, likewise, will be incommunicably his own, even as his labour was. Variety of punishment will likewise arise from the very nature of the thing. As they that bring most holiness to heaven will find most happiness there; so, on the other hand, it is not only true, that the more wickedness a man brings to hell the more misery he will find there; but that this misery will be infinitely varied according to the various kinds of his wickedness. It was therefore proper to say, *the fire*, in general; but *their worm*, in particular.

4. But it has been questioned by some, whether there be any fire in hell; that is, any material fire. Nay, if there be any fire, it is unquestionably material. For what is immaterial fire? The same as immaterial water or earth! Both the one and the other is absolute nonsense, a contradiction in terms. Either, therefore, we must affirm it to be material, or we deny its existence. But if we granted them, there is no fire at all there, what would they gain thereby? seeing this is allowed, on all hands, that it is either fire or something worse. And consider this: Does not our Lord speak as if it were real fire? No one can deny or doubt of this. Is it possible then to suppose that the God of truth would speak in this manner if it were not so? Does he design to fright his poor creatures? What, with scarecrows? with vain shadows of things that have no being? O let not anyone think so! Impute not such folly to the Most High!

5. But others aver, "It is not possible that fire should burn always. For by the immutable law of nature, it consumes whatever is thrown into it. And by the same law, as soon as it has consumed its fuel, it is itself consumed; it goes out." It is most true, that in the present constitution of things, during the present laws of nature, the element of fire does dissolve and consume whatever is thrown into it. But here is the mistake: The present laws of nature are not immutable. When the heavens and the earth shall flee away, the present scene will be totally changed; and, with the present constitution of things, the present laws of nature will cease. After this great change, nothing will be dissolved, nothing will be consumed any more. Therefore, if it were true that fire consumes all things now, it would not follow that it would do the same after the whole frame of nature has undergone that vast, universal change.

6. I say, If it were true that "fire consumes all things now." But, indeed, it is not true. Has it not pleased God to give us already some proof of what will be hereafter? Is not the *Linum Asbestum*, the incombustible flax, known in most parts of Europe? If you take a towel or handkerchief made of this, (one of which may now be seen in the British Museum,) you may throw it into the hottest fire, and when it is taken out again, it will be observed, upon the nicest experiment, not to have lost one grain of its weight. Here, therefore, is a substance before our eyes, which, even in the present constitution of things, (as if it were an emblem of things to come,) may remain in fire without being consumed.

7. Many writers have spoken of other bodily torments, added to the being cast into the lake of fire. One of these, even pious Kempis, supposes that misers, for instance, have melted gold poured down their throats; and he supposes many other particular torments to be suited to men's particular sins. Nay, our great poet himself supposes the inhabitants of hell to undergo a variety of tortures; not to continue always in the lake of fire, but to be frequently,

> By harpy-footed furies, haled

into regions of ice; and then back again through extremes, by change more fierce: But I find no word, no tittle of this, not the least hint of it in all the Bible. And surely this is too awful a subject to admit of such play of imagination. Let us keep to the written word. It is torment enough to dwell with everlasting burnings.

8. This is strongly illustrated by a fabulous story, taken from one of the eastern writers, concerning a Turkish King, who, after he had been guilty of all manner of wickedness, once did a good thing: For seeing a poor man falling into a pit, wherein he must have inevitably perished, and kicking him from it, he saved his life. The story adds, that when, for his enormous wickedness, he was cast into hell, that foot wherewith he had saved the man's life was permitted to lie out of the flames. But allowing this to be a real case, what a poor comfort would it be! What, if both feet were permitted to lie out of the flames, yea, and both hands, how little would it avail! Nay, if all the body were taken out, and placed where no fire touched it, and only one hand or one foot kept in a burning fiery furnace; would the man, meantime, be much at ease? Nay, quite the contrary. Is it not common to say to a child, "Put your finger into that candle: Can you bear it even for one minute? How then will you bear hell-fire?" Surely it would be torment enough to have the flesh burnt off from only one finger. What then will it be, to have the whole body plunged into a lake of fire burning with brimstone!

III. It remains now only to consider two or three circumstances attending the never-dying worm and the unquenchable fire.

1. And, First, consider the company wherewith everyone is surrounded in that place of torment. It is not uncommon to hear even condemned criminals, in our public prisons, say, "O I wish I was hanged out of the way, rather than to be plagued with these wretches that are round about me!" But what are the most abandoned wretches upon earth, compared to the inhabitants of hell? None of these are, as yet, perfectly wicked, emptied of every spark of good; certainly not till this life is at an end; probably not till the day of judgment. Nor can any of these exert, without control, their whole wickedness on their fellow-creatures. Sometimes they are restrained by good men; sometimes even by bad. So even the tortures in the Romish Inquisition are restrained by those that employ them, when they suppose the sufferer cannot endure any more. They then order the executioners to forbear; because it is contrary to the rules of the house that a man should die upon the rack. And very frequently, when there is no human help, they are restrained by God, who hath set them their bounds which they cannot pass, and saith, "Hitherto shall ye come, and no farther." Yea, so mercifully hath God ordained, that the very extremity of pain causes a suspension of it. The sufferer faints away; and so, for a time at least, sinks into insensibility. But the inhabitants of hell are perfectly wicked, having no spark of goodness remaining. And they are restrained by none from exerting to the uttermost their total wickedness. Not by *men*; none will be restrained from evil by his companions in damnation: And not by *God*; for He hath forgotten them, hath delivered them over to the tormentors. And the devils need not fear, like their instruments upon earth, lest they should expire under the torture. They can die no more: They are strong to sustain whatever the united malice, skill, and strength of angels can inflict upon them. And their angelic tormentors have time sufficient to vary their torments a thousand ways. How infinitely may they vary one single torment,—horrible appearances! Whereby, there is no doubt, an evil spirit, if permitted, could terrify the stoutest man upon earth to death.

2. Consider, Secondly, that all these torments of body and soul are without intermission. They have no respite from pain; but "the smoke of their torment ascendeth up day and night." *Day and night!* that is, speaking according to the constitution of the present world; wherein God has wisely and graciously ordained that day and night should succeed each other: So that in every four and twenty hours there comes a

> Daily sabbath, made to rest
> Toiling man and weary beast.

Hence we seldom undergo much labour, or suffer much pain, before

> Tired nature's sweet restorer, balmy sleep,

steals upon us by insensible degrees, and brings an interval of ease. But although the damned have uninterrupted night, it brings no interruption of their pain. No sleep accompanies that darkness: Whatever either ancient or modern poets, either Homer or Milton, dream, there is no sleep either in hell or heaven. And be their suffering ever so extreme, be their pain ever so intense, there is no possibility of their fainting away; no, not for a moment.

Again: The inhabitants of earth are frequently diverted from attending to what is afflictive, by the cheerful light of the sun, the vicissitudes of the seasons, "the busy hum of men," and a thousand objects that roll around them with endless variety. But the inhabitants of hell have nothing to divert them from their torments, even for a moment:

> Total eclipse: No sun, no moon!

No change of seasons, or of companions. There is no business; but one uninterrupted scene of horror, to which they must be all attention. They have no interval of inattention or stupidity: They are all eye, all ear, all sense. Every instant of their duration, it may be said of their whole frame, that they are

> Tremblingly alive all o'er,
> And smart and agonize at every pore!

3. And of this duration there is no end! What a thought is this! Nothing but eternity is the term of their torment! And who can count the drops of rain, or the sands of the sea, or the days of eternity? Every suffering is softened, if there is any hope, though distant, of deliverance from it. But here, Hope never comes, that comes to all the inhabitants of the upper world! What! sufferings *never* to end!

> NEVER!—Where sinks the soul at that dread sound?
> Into a gulf how dark, and how profound!

Suppose millions of days, of years, of ages elapsed, still we are only on the threshold of eternity! Neither the pain of body nor of soul is any nearer an end, than it was millions of ages ago. When they are cast into *to pyr, to asbeston,* (How emphatical! *"The fire, the unquenchable,"*) all is concluded: "Their worm dieth not, and the fire is not quenched!" Such is the account which the Judge of all gives of the punishment which he has ordained for impenitent sinners. And what a counterbalance may the consideration of this be to the violence of any temptation! in particular, to the fear of man; the very use to which it is applied by our Lord himself: "Be not afraid of them that kill the body, and after that have no more that they can do. But fear Him, who after he hath killed hath power to cast into hell." (Luke 12:4, 5)

What a guard may these considerations be against any temptation from pleasure! Will you lose, for any of these poor, earthly pleasures, which perish in the using, (to say nothing of the present substantial pleasures of religion,) the pleasures of Paradise; such as "eye hath not seen, nor ear heard, neither hath it entered into our hearts to conceive?" yea, the pleasures of heaven, the society of angels, and of the spirits of just men made perfect; the conversing face to face with God your Father, your Saviour, your Sanctifier; and the drinking of those rivers of pleasure that are at God's right hand for evermore?

Are you tempted by pain, either of body or mind? O compare present things with future! What is the pain of body which you do or may endure, to that of lying in a lake of fire burning with brimstone? What is any pain of mind; any fear, anguish, sorrow, compared to the "worm that never dieth?" *That never dieth!* This is the sting of all! As for our pains on earth, blessed be God, they are not eternal. There are some intervals to relieve and there is some period to finish them. When we ask a friend that is sick, how he does; "I am in pain now," says he, "but I hope to be easy soon." This is a sweet mitigation of the present uneasiness. But how dreadful would his case be if he should answer, "I am all over pain, and I shall never be eased of it. I lie under exquisite torment of body,

and horror of soul; and I shall feel it *for ever!"* Such is the case of the damned sinners in hell. Suffer any pain, then, rather than come into that place of torment!

I conclude with one more reflection, taken from Dr. Watts,—"It demands our highest gratitude, that we who have long ago deserved this misery are not yet plunged into it. While there are thousands who have been adjudged to this place of punishment, before they had continued so long in sin as many of us have done, what an instance is it of divine goodness, that we are not under this fiery vengeance! Have we not seen many sinners, on our right and left, cut off in their sins? And what but the tender mercy of God hath spared us week after week, month after month, and given us space for repentance? What shall we render unto the Lord for all his patience and longsuffering even to this day? How often have we incurred the sentence of condemnation by our repeated rebellion against God! And yet we are still alive in his presence, and are hearing the words of hope and salvation. O let us look back and shudder at the thoughts of that dreadful precipice, on the edge of which we have so long wandered! Let us fly for refuge to the hope that is set before us, and give a thousand thanks to the divine mercy, that we are not plunged into this perdition!"

74.* OF THE CHURCH

"I beseech you that ye walk worthy of the vocation wherewith ye are called, with all lowliness and meekness, with long-suffering, forbearing one another in love; endeavouring to keep the unity of the Spirit in the bond of peace. There is one body, and one Spirit, even as ye are called in one hope of your calling; one Lord, one faith, one baptism, one God and Father of all, who is above all, and through all, and in you all."

Ephesians 4:1–6.

1. How much do we almost continually hear about the Church! With many it is matter of daily conversation. And yet how few understand what they talk of! how few know what the term means! A more ambiguous word than this, the Church, is scarce to be found in the English language. It is sometimes taken for a building, set apart for public worship: sometimes for a congregation, or body of people, united together in the service of God. It is only in the latter sense that it is taken in the ensuing discourse.

2. It may be taken indifferently for any number of people, how small or great soever. As, "where two or three are met together in his name," there is Christ; so, (to speak with St. Cyprian,) "where two or three believers are met together, there is a Church." Thus it is that St. Paul, writing to Philemon, mentions "the Church which is in his house;" plainly signifying, that even a Christian family may be termed a Church.

3. Several of those whom God hath *called out* of the world, (so the original word properly signifies,) uniting together in one congregation, formed a larger Church; as the Church at Jerusalem; that is, all those in Jerusalem whom God had so

---

* [text from the 1872 edition]

called. But considering how swiftly these were multiplied, after the day of Pentecost, it cannot be supposed that they could continue to assemble in one place; especially as they had not then any large place, neither would they have been permitted to build one. In consequence, they must have divided themselves, even at Jerusalem, into several distinct congregations. In like manner, when St. Paul, several years after, wrote to the Church in Rome, (directing his letter, "To all that are in Rome, called to be saints,") it cannot be supposed that they had any one building capable of containing them all; but they were divided into several congregations, assembling in several parts of the city.

4. The first time that the Apostle uses the word Church is in his preface to the former Epistle to the Corinthians: "Paul called to be an apostle of Jesus Christ, unto the Church of God which is at Corinth." The meaning of which expression is fixed by the following words: "To them that are sanctified in Christ Jesus; with all that, in every place," (not Corinth only; so it was a kind of circular letter,) "call upon the name of Jesus Christ our Lord, both theirs and ours." In the inscription of his second letter to the Corinthians, he speaks still more explicitly: "Unto the Church of God which is at Corinth, with all the saints that are in all Achaia." Here he plainly includes all the Churches, or Christian congregations, which were in the whole province.

5. He frequently uses the word in the plural number. So, Gal. 1:2, "Paul an apostle,—unto the Churches of Galatia;" that is, the Christian congregations dispersed throughout that country. In all these places, (and abundantly more might be cited,) the word Church or Churches means, not the buildings where the Christians assembled, (as it frequently does in the English tongue,) but the people that used to assemble there, one or more Christian congregations. But sometimes the word Church is taken in Scripture in a still more extensive meaning, as including all the Christian congregations that are upon the face of the earth. And in this sense we understand it in our Liturgy, when we say, "Let us pray for the whole state of Christ's Church militant here on earth." In this sense it is unquestionably taken by St. Paul, in his exhortation to the elders of Ephesus: (Acts 20:28:) "Take heed to the Church of God, which he has purchased with his own blood." The Church here, undoubtedly, means the catholic or universal Church; that is, all the Christians under heaven.

6. Who those are that are properly "the Church of God," the Apostle shows at large, and that in the clearest and most decisive manner, in the passage above cited; wherein he likewise instructs all the members of the Church, how to "walk worthy of the vocation wherewith they are called."

7. Let us consider, First, who are properly the Church of God? What is the true meaning of that term? "The Church at Ephesus," as the Apostle himself explains it, means, "the saints," the holy persons, "that are in Ephesus," and there assemble themselves together to worship God the Father, and his Son Jesus Christ; whether they did this in one or (as we may probably suppose) in several places. But it is the Church in general, the catholic or universal Church, which the Apostle here considers as one body: Comprehending not only the Christians in the house of Philemon, or any one family; not only the Christians of one congregation, of one city, of one province, or nation; but all the persons upon the face of the earth, who answer the character here given. The several particulars contained therein, we may now more distinctly consider.

8. "There is one Spirit" who animates all these, all the living members of the Church of God. Some understand hereby the Holy Spirit himself, the Fountain of all spiritual life; and it is certain, "if any man have not the Spirit of Christ, he is none of his." Others understand it of those spiritual gifts and holy dispositions which are afterwards mentioned.

9. "There is," in all those that have received this Spirit, "one hope;" a hope full of immortality. They know, to die is not to be lost: Their prospect extends beyond the grave. They can cheerfully say, "Blessed be the God and Father of our Lord Jesus Christ, who, according to his abundant mercy, hath begotten us again to a lively hope by the resurrection of Jesus Christ from the dead, to an inheritance incorruptible, and undefiled, and that fadeth not away."

10. "There is one Lord," who has now dominion over them, who has set up his kingdom in their hearts, and reigns over all those that are partakers of this hope. To obey him, to run the way of his commandments, is their glory and joy. And while they are doing this with a willing mind they, as it were, "sit in heavenly places with Christ Jesus."

11. "There is one faith;" which is the free gift of God, and is the ground of their hope. This is not barely the faith of a Heathen; Namely, a belief that "there is a God," and that he is gracious and just, and, consequently, "a rewarder of them that diligently seek him." Neither is it barely the faith of a devil; though this goes much farther than the former. For the devil believes, and cannot but believe, all that is written both in the Old and New Testament to be true. But it is the faith of St. Thomas, teaching him to say with holy boldness, "My Lord, and my God!" It is the faith which enables every true Christian believer to testify with St. Paul, "The life which I now live, I live by faith in the Son of God, who loved me, and gave himself for me."

12. "There is one baptism;" which is the outward sign our one Lord has been pleased to appoint, of all that inward and spiritual grace which he is continually bestowing upon his Church. It is likewise a precious means, whereby this faith and hope are given to those that diligently seek him. Some, indeed, have been inclined to interpret this in a figurative sense; as if it referred to that baptism of the Holy Ghost which the Apostles received at the day of Pentecost, and which, in a lower degree, is given to all believers: But it is a stated rule in interpreting Scripture, never to depart from the plain, literal sense, unless it implies an absurdity. And beside, if we thus understood it, it would be a needless repetition, as being included in, "There is one Spirit."

13. "There is one God and Father of all" that have the Spirit of adoption, which "crieth in their hearts, Abba, Father;" which "witnesseth" continually "with their spirits," that they are the children of God: "Who is above all,"—the Most High, the Creator, the Sustainer, the Governor of the whole

universe: "And through all,"—pervading all space; filling heaven and earth:

> Totam
>
> Mens agitans molem, et magno se corpore miscens:—

[The following is Wharton's translation of this quotation from Virgil:—

> "The general soul
>
> Lives in the parts, and agitates the whole."—Edit.]

"And in you all,"—in a peculiar manner living in you, that are one body, by one spirit:

> Making your souls his loved abode,
> The temples of indwelling God.

14. Here, then, is a clear unexceptionable answer to that question, "What is the Church?" The catholic or universal Church is, all the persons in the universe whom God hath so called out of the world as to entitle them to the preceding character; as to be "one body," united by "one spirit;" having "one faith, one hope, one baptism; one God and Father of all, who is above all, and through all, and in them all."

15. That part of this great body, of the universal Church, which inhabits any one kingdom or nation, we may properly term a National Church; as, the Church of France, the Church of England, the Church of Scotland. A smaller part of the universal Church are the Christians that inhabit one city or town; as the Church of Ephesus, and the rest of the seven Churches mentioned in the Revelation. Two or three Christian believers united together are a Church in the narrowest sense of the word. Such was the Church in the house of Philemon, and that in the house of Nymphas, mentioned Col. 4:15. A particular Church may, therefore, consist of any number of members, whether two or three, or two or three millions. But still, whether they be larger or smaller, the same idea is to be preserved. They are one body, and have one Spirit, one Lord, one hope, one faith, one baptism, one God and Father of all.

16. This account is exactly agreeable to the nineteenth Article of our Church, the Church of England: (Only the Article includes a little more than the Apostle has expressed:)
"OF THE CHURCH.
"The visible Church of Christ is a congregation of faithful men, in which the pure word of God is preached, and the sacraments be duly administered."
It may be observed, that at the same time our thirty-nine Articles were compiled and published, a Latin translation of them was published by the same authority. In this the words were *coetus credentium*; "a congregation of believers;" plainly showing that by *faithful men*, the compilers meant, men endued with *living faith*. This brings the Article to a still nearer agreement to the account given by the Apostle.
But it may be doubted whether the Article speaks of a particular Church, or of the Church universal. The title, "Of the Church," seems to have reference to the catholic Church; but the second clause of the Article mentions the particular Churches of Jerusalem, Antioch, Alexandria, and Rome. Perhaps it was intended to take in both; so to define the universal Church as to keep in view the several particular Churches of which it is composed.

17. These things being considered, it is easy to answer that question, "What is the Church of England?" It is that part, those members, of the Universal Church who are inhabitants of England. The Church of England is, that body of men in England, in whom "there is one Spirit, one hope, one Lord, one faith;" which have "one baptism," and "one God and Father of all." This and this alone is the Church of England, according to the doctrine of the Apostle.

18. But the definition of a Church, laid down in the Article, includes not only this, but much more, by that remarkable addition: "In which the pure word of God is preached, and the sacraments be duly administered." According to this definition, those congregations in which the pure Word of God (a strong expression) is not preached are no parts either of the Church of England, or the Church catholic; as neither are those in which the sacraments are not duly administered.

19. I will not undertake to defend the accuracy of this definition. I dare not exclude from the Church catholic all those congregations in which any unscriptural doctrines, which cannot be affirmed to be "the pure word of God," are sometimes, yea, frequently preached; neither all those congregations, in which the sacraments are not "duly administered." Certainly if these things are so, the Church of Rome is not so much as a part of the catholic Church; seeing therein neither is "the pure word of God" preached, nor the sacraments "duly administered." Whoever they are that have "one Spirit, one hope, one Lord, one faith, one God and Father of all," I can easily bear with their holding wrong opinions, yea, and superstitious modes of worship: Nor would I, on these accounts, scruple still to include them within the pale of the catholic Church; neither would I have any objection to receive them, if they desired it, as members of the Church of England.

II. 20. We proceed now to the second point. What is it to "walk worthy of the vocation wherewith we are called?"
It should always be remembered that the word *walk*, in the language of the Apostle, is of a very extensive signification. It includes all our inward and outward motions; all our thoughts, and words, and actions. It takes in, not only everything we do, but everything we either speak or think. It is, therefore, no small thing "to walk," in this sense of the word, "worthy of the vocation wherewith we are called;" to think, speak, and act, in every instance in a manner worthy of our Christian calling.

21. We are called to walk, First, "with all lowliness:" to have that mind in us which was also in Christ Jesus; not to think of ourselves more highly than we ought to think; to be little, and poor, and mean, and vile in our own eyes; to know ourselves as also we are known by Him to whom all hearts are open; to be deeply sensible of our own unworthiness, of the universal depravity of our nature, (in which dwelleth no good thing,)—prone to all evil, averse to all good; insomuch that we are not only sick, but dead in trespasses and sins, till God breathes upon the dry bones, and creates life by the fruit of his lips. And suppose this is done,—suppose he has now quickened us, infusing life into our dead souls; yet how much of the carnal mind remains! How prone is our heart still to depart from the living God! What a tendency to sin remains

in our heart, although we know our past sins are forgiven! And how much sin, in spite of all our endeavours, cleaves both to our words and actions! Who can be duly sensible how much remains in him of his natural enmity to God, or how far he is still alienated from God by the ignorance that is in him?

22. Yea, suppose God has now thoroughly cleansed our heart, and scattered the last remains of sin; yet how can we be sensible enough of our own helplessness, our utter inability to all good, unless we are every hour, yea, every moment, endued with power from on high? Who is able to think one good thought, or to form one good desire, unless by that Almighty power which worketh in us both to will and to do of his good pleasure? We have need even in this state of grace, to be thoroughly and continually penetrated with a sense of this. Otherwise we shall be in perpetual danger of robbing God of his honour, by glorying in something we have received, as though we had not received it.

23. When our inmost soul is thoroughly tinctured therewith, it remains that we "be clothed with humility." The word used by St. Peter seems to imply that we be covered with it as with a surtout; that we be all humility, both within and without; tincturing all we think, speak, and do. Let all our actions spring from this fountain; let all our words breathe this spirit; that all men may know we have been with Jesus, and have learned of him to be lowly in heart.

24. And being taught of Him who was meek as well as lowly in heart, we shall then be enabled to "walk with all meekness;" being taught of Him who teacheth as never man taught, to be meek as well as lowly in heart. This implies not only a power over anger, but over all violent and turbulent passions. It implies the having all our passions in due proportion; none of them either too strong or too weak; but all duly balanced with each other; all subordinate to reason; and reason directed by the Spirit of God. Let this equanimity govern your whole souls; that your thoughts may all flow in an even stream, and the uniform tenor of your words and actions be suitable thereto. In this "patience" you will then "possess your souls;" which are not our own while we are tossed by unruly passions. And by this all men may know that we are indeed followers of the meek and lowly Jesus.

25. Walk with all "longsuffering." This is nearly related to meekness, but implies something more. It carries on the victory already gained over all your turbulent passions; notwithstanding all the powers of darkness, all the assaults of evil men or evil spirits. It is patiently triumphant over all opposition, and unmoved though all the waves and storms thereof go over you. Though provoked ever so often, it is still the same,—quiet and unshaken; never being "overcome of evil," but overcoming evil with good.

26. The "forbearing one another in love" seems to mean, not only the not resenting anything, and the not avenging yourselves; not only the not injuring, hurting, or grieving each other, either by word or deed; but also the bearing one another's burdens; yea, and lessening them by every means in our power. It implies the sympathizing with them in their sorrows, afflictions, and infirmities; the bearing them up when, without our help, they would be liable to sink under their burdens; the endeavouring to lift their sinking heads, and to strengthen their feeble knees.

27. Lastly: the true members of the Church of Christ "endeavour," with all possible diligence, with all care and pains, with unwearied patience, (and all will be little enough,) to "keep the unity of the Spirit in the bond of peace;" to preserve inviolate the same spirit of lowliness and meekness, of longsuffering, mutual forbearance, and love; and all these cemented and knit together by that sacred tie,—the peace of God filling the heart. Thus only can we be and continue living members of that Church which is the body of Christ.

28. Does it not clearly appear from this whole account, why, in the ancient Creed, commonly called the Apostles', we term it the universal or catholic Church,—"the holy catholic Church?" How many wonderful reasons have been found out for giving it this appellation! One learned man informs us, "The Church is called holy, because Christ, the Head of it, is holy." Another eminent author affirms, "It is so called because all its ordinances are designed to promote holiness;" and yet another,—"because our Lord *intended* that all the members of the Church should be holy." Nay, the shortest and the plainest reason that can be given, and the only true one, is,—The Church is called *holy*, because it *is* holy, because every member thereof is holy, though in different degrees, as He that called them is holy. How clear is this! If the Church, as to the very essence of it, is a body of believers, no man that is not a Christian believer can be a member of it. If this whole body be animated by one spirit, and endued with one faith, and one hope of their calling; then he who has not that spirit, and faith, and hope, is no member of this body. It follows, that not only no common swearer, no Sabbath-breaker, no drunkard, no whoremonger, no thief, no liar, none that lives in any outward sin, but none that is under the power of anger or pride, no lover of the world, in a word, none that is dead to God, can be a member of his Church.

29. Can anything then be more absurd, than for men to cry out, *The Church! The Church!* and to pretend to be very zealous for it, and violent defenders of it, while they themselves have neither part nor lot therein, nor indeed know what the Church is? And yet the hand of God is in this very thing! Even in this his wonderful wisdom appears, directing their mistake to his own glory, and causing "the earth to help the woman." [Rev. 12:16] Imagining that they are members of it themselves, the men of the world frequently defend the Church: Otherwise the wolves that surround the little flock on every side would in a short time tear them in pieces. And for this very reason, it is not wise to provoke them more than is unavoidable. Even on this ground, let us, if it be possible, as much as lieth in us, "live peaceably with all men." Especially as we know not how soon God may call them too out of the kingdom of Satan into the kingdom of his dear Son.

30. In the mean time, let all those who are real members of the Church, see that they walk holy and unblamable in all things. "Ye are the light of the world!" Ye are "a city set upon a hill," and "cannot be hid." O "let your light shine before men!" Show them your faith by your works. Let them see, by

the whole tenor of your conversation, that your hope is all laid up above! Let all your words and actions evidence the spirit whereby you are animated! Above all things, let your love abound. Let it extend to every child of man: Let it overflow to every child of God. By this let all men know whose disciples ye are, because you "love one another."

75.* ON SCHISM

"That there might be no schism in the body."

1 Cor. 12:25.

1. If there be any word in the English tongue as ambiguous and indeterminate in its meaning as the word Church, it is one that is nearly allied to it,—the word Schism. it has been the subject of innumerable disputes for several hundred years; and almost innumerable books have been written concerning it in every part of the Christian world. A very large share of these have been published in our country; particularly during the last century, and the beginning of the present: And persons of the strongest understanding, and the most consummate learning, have exhausted all their strength upon the question, both in conversation and writing. This has appeared to be more necessary than ever, since the grand separation of the Reformed from the Romish Church. This is a charge which the members of that Church never fail to bring against all that separate from her; and which, consequently, has employed the thought and pens of the most able disputants on both sides. And Those of each side have generally, when they entered into the field, been secured of victory; supposing the strength of their arguments was so great, that it was impossible for reasonable men to resist them.

2. But it is observable, that exceeding little good has been done by all these controversies. Very few of the warmest and ablest disputants have been able to convince their opponents. After all that could be said, the Papists are Papists, and the Protestants are Protestants still. And the same success has attended those who have so vehemently disputed about separation from the Church of England. Those who separated from her were eagerly charged with schism; they as eagerly denied the charge; and scarce any were able to convince their opponents either on one side or the other.

3. One great reason why this controversy has been so unprofitable, why so few of either side have been convinced, is this: They seldom agreed as to the meaning of the word concerning which they disputed: and if they did not fix the meaning of this, if they did not define the term before they began disputing about it, they might continue the dispute to their lives' end, without getting one step forward; without coming a jot nearer to each other than when they first set out.

4. Yet it must be a point of considerable importance, or St. Paul would not have spoken so seriously of it. It is, therefore, highly needful that we should consider,

I. The nature, and,

II. The evil of it.

I. 1. It is the more needful to do this, because among the numberless books that have been written upon the subject, both by the Romanists and Protestants, it is difficult to find any that define it in a scriptural manner. The whole body of Roman Catholics define schism, a separation from the Church of Rome; and almost all our own writers define it, a separation from the Church of England. Thus both the one and the other set out wrong, and stumble at the very threshold. This will easily appear to any that calmly consider the several texts wherein the word "schism" occurs: from the whole tenor of which it is manifest, that it is not a separation *from* any Church, (whether general or particular, whether the Catholic, or any national Church,) but a separation *in* a Church.

2. Let us begin with the first verse, wherein St. Paul makes use of the word. It is the tenth verse of the first chapter of his First Epistle to the Corinthians. The Words are, "I beseech you, brethren, by the name of the Lord Jesus, that ye all speak the same thing, and that there be no schisms" (the original word is *schismata*) "among you." Can anything be more plain than that the schisms here spoken of, were not separations *from*, but divisions *in*, the Church of Corinth? Accordingly, it follows, "But that ye be perfectly united together, in the same mind and in the same judgment." You see here, that an union in mind and judgment was the direct opposite to the Corinthian schism. This, consequently, was not a separation from the Church or Christian society at Corinth' but a separation in the Church; a disunion in mind and judgment, (perhaps also affection,) among those who, notwithstanding this, continued outwardly united as before.

3. Of what nature this schism at Corinth was, is still more clearly determined (if anything can be more clear) by the words that immediately follow: "Now this I say,"—this is the schism of which I speak; you are divided into separate parties; some of you speaking in favor of one, some of another preacher,—"Every one of you saith," (verse 12,) "I am of Paul, and I of Apollos, and I of Cephas," or Peter. Who then does not see that the schism for which the Apostle here reproves the Corinthians is neither more nor less than the splitting into several parties, as they gave the preference to one or another preacher? And this species of schism there will be occasion to guard against in every religious community.

4. The second place where the Apostle uses this word is in the eighteenth verse of the eleventh chapter of this Epistle: "When ye come together in the Church," the Christian congregation, "I hear that there are division" (the original word here also is *schismata, schisms*) "among you." But what were these schisms? The Apostle immediately tells you: (Verse 20:) "When you come together," professing you design is "to cat of the Lord's Supper, every on of you taketh before another his own supper," as if it were a common meal. What then was the schism? It seems, in doing this, they divided into little parties, which cherished anger and resentment one against another, even at the solemn season.

5. May it not be observed, (to make a little digression here, for the sake of those who are troubled with needless scruples

---

on this head,) that the sin which the Apostle charges on the communicants at Corinth in this chapter is usually quite misunderstood? It was precisely this, and nothing else, "the taking one before another his own supper;' " and in such a shocking manner, that while "one was hungry, another was drunken." By doing this, he says, "ye eat and drink" (not *"damnation:"* a vile mistranslating of the word, but) *judgment*, temporal judgment, "to yourselves:" Which sometimes shortened their lives. "For this cause"—for sinning in this vile manner—"many are sick and weak among you." Observe here two things: First, What was the sin of the Corinthians? Mark is well, and remember it. It was *taking one before another his own supper*; so that while *one was hungry, another was drunken.* Secondly, What was the punishment? It was bodily weakness and sickness; which, without repentance, might end in death. But what is this to *you*? Your cannot commit *their* sin: Therefore, you cannot incur their punishment.

6. But to return. It deserves to be seriously remarked, that in this chapter the Apostle uses the word "heresies" as exactly equivalent with the word "schisms." "I hear," says he, (verse 18.) "that there are schisms among you, and I partly believe it:" He then adds, (verse 19,) "for there must be heresies" (another word for the same thing) "among you, that they which are approved among you may be made manifest." As if he had said, "The wisdom of God permits it so to be, for this end,—for the clear manifestation of those whose heart is right with him." This word, therefore, (*heresy*,) which has been so strangely distorted for many centuries, as if it meant erroneous opinions, opinions contrary to the faith delivered to the saints,—which has been made a pretense for destroying cities, depopulation countries, and shedding seas of innocent blood,—has not the least reference to opinions, whether right or wrong. It simply means, wherever it occurs in Scripture, divisions, or parties, in a religious community.

7. The third and the only remaining place in this Epistle, wherein the Apostle uses this word, is the twenty fifth verse of the twelfth chapter; where, speaking of the Church, he seems to mean the Church universal, the whole body of Christ,) he observes, "God hath tempered the body together, having given more abundant honour to that part which lacked, that there might be no schism in the body:" (Verse 24, 25:) He immediately fixes the meaning of his own words: "But that the members might have the same care one for another: And Whether one member suffer, all the members suffer with is or one member be honoured, all the members rejoice with it.: We may easily observe that the word Schism here, means the want of this tender care for each other. It undoubtedly means an alienation of affection in any of them toward their brethren; a division of heart, and parties springing therefrom, though they were still outwardly united together; though they still continued members of the same external society.

8. But there seems to be one considerable objection against the supposing heresy and schism to mean the same thing. It is said, St. Peter, in the second chapter of his Second Epistle, takes the word Heresies in a quite different sense. His words are, (verse 1,) "There shall be among you false teachers, who

will bring in damnable," or destructive, "heresies, denying the Lord that bought them." It does by no means appear that St. Peter here takes the word Heresies in any other sense that St. Paul does. Even in this passage it does not appear to have any reference to opinions, good or bad. Rather it means, They will "bring in" or occasion, destructive parties or sects, (so it is rendered in the common French translation,) who "deny the Lord that bought them:" Such sects now swarm throughout the Christian world.

9. I shall be thankful to any one who will point to me any other place in the inspired writings, where this word "Schism" is to be found. I remember only these three. And it is apparent to every impartial reader, that is does not, in any of these, mean a separation from any Church or body of Christians, whether with or without cause. So that the immense pains which have been taken both by Papists and Protestants, in writing whole volumes against Schism, as a separation, whether from the Church of Rome, or from the Church of England, exerting all their strength, and bringing all their learning, have been employed to mighty little purpose. They have been fighting with shadows of their own raising; violently combating a sin which had no existence but in their own imagination; which is to once forbidden, no, nor once mentioned, either in the Old or New Testament,

10. "But is there no sin resembling what so many learned and pious writers have termed Schism, and against which all the members of religious communities have need to be carefully guarded?: I do not doubt but there is; and I cannot tell, whether this too may not, in a remote sense, be called Schism: I mean, "A causeless separation from a body of living Christians.: There is no absurdity in taking the word in this sense, though it be not strictly scriptural. And it is certain all the members of Christian communities should be carefully guarded against it. For how little a thing soever it may seem, and how innocent soever it may be accounted, schism, even in this sense, is both evil in itself, and productive of evil consequences.

11. It is evil in itself. To separate ourselves from a body of living Christian, with whom we were before united, is a grievous breach of the law of love. It is the nature of love to unite us together; and the greater the love, the stricter the union. And while this continues in its strength, nothing can divide those whom love has united. It is only when our love grows could, that we can think of separating from our brethren. And this is certainly the case with any who willingly separate from their Christian brethren. The pretences for separation may be innumerable, but want of love is always the real cause; otherwise they would still hold the unity of he Spirit in the bound of peace. It is therefore contrary to all those commands of God, wherein brotherly love is enjoined: To that of St. Paul, "Let brotherly love continue:"—that of St. John, "My beloved children, love one another;"—and especially to that of our blessed Master, "This is my commandment, That ye love on another, as I have loved you" Yea, "By this," saith he, "shall all men know that ye are my disciples, if ye love one another."

12, And as such a separation is evil in itself, being a breach of brotherly love, so it brings forth evil fruit; it is naturally productive of the most mischievous consequences. It opens a door to all unkind tempers, both in ourselves and others. It leads directly to a whole train of evil surmising, to severe and uncharitable judging of each other. It gives occasion to offense, to anger and resentment, perhaps in ourselves as well as in our brethren; which, if not presently stopped, may issue in bitterness, malice, and settled hatred; creating a present hell wherever they are found, as a prelude to hell eternal.

13. But the ill consequences of even this species of schism do not terminate in the heart. Evil tempers cannot log remain within, before they are productive of outward fruit. Out of the abundance of the heart the mouth speaketh. As he whose heart is full of love openeth his mouth with wisdom, and in his lips there is the law of kindness; so he whose heart is full of prejudice, anger, suspicion, or any unkind temper, will surely open his mouth in a manner corresponding with the disposition of his mind. And hence will arise, if not lying and slandering, (which yet will hardly be avoided,) bitter words, tale-bearing, backbiting, and evil-speaking of every kind.

14. From evil words, form tale-bearing, backbiting and evil-speaking, how many evil works will naturally flow! Anger, jealousy, envy, wrong tempers of every kind, do not vent themselves merely in words, but push men continually to all kind of ungodly and unrighteous actions. A plentiful harvest of ail the woks of darkness may be expected to spring from this source; whereby, in the end, thousands of souls, and not a few of those who once walked in the light of God's countenance, may be turned from the way of peace, and finally drowned in everlasting perdition.

15. Well might our blessed Lord say, "Woe unto the world because of offenses:" Yet, "it must needs be, that offenses will come:" Yea, abundance of them will of necessity arise when a breach of this sort is made in any religious community; while they that leave it endeavour to justify themselves, by censuring those they separate from; and these on the other hand retort the charge, and strive to lay the blame on them. But how mightily does all this altercation grieve the Holy Spirit of God! How does it hinder his mild and gentle operations in the souls both of one and the other! Heresies and schisms (in the scriptural sense of those words) will, sooner or later, be the consequence; parties will be formed, on one and the other side, whereby the love of many will wax cold. The hunger and thirst after righteousness, after either the favor or the full image of God, together with the longing desires wherewith so many were filled of promoting the work of God in the souls of their brethren, will grow languid, and as offenses increase will gradually die away. And as the "fruit of the Spirit" withers away, "the works of the flesh" will again prevail, to the utter destruction, first of the power, and then of the very form, of religion. These consequences are not imaginary, are not built on mere conjectures, but on plain matter of fact. This has been the case again and again within these last thirty or forty year: These have been the fruits which we have seen, over and over, to be consequent on such a separation.

16. And what grievous stumbling-block must these things be to those who are without, to those who are strangers to religion, who have neither the form nor the power of godliness! How will they triumph over these once eminent Christians! How boldly ask, "What are they better than us?" How will they harden their hearts more and more against the truth, and bless themselves in their wickedness? from which, possibly, the example of the Christians might have reclaimed them, had they continued unblamable in their behavior. Such is the complicated mischief which persons separating from a Christian Church or society do, not only to themselves, but to that whole society, and the whole world in general.

17. But perhaps such persons will say, "We did not do this willingly; we were constrained to separate form that society, because we could not continue therein with a clear conscience; we could not continue without sin. I was not allowed to continue therein with breaking a commandment of God." If this was the case, you could not be blamed for separating from that society, Suppose, for instance, you were a member of the Church of Rome, and you could not remain therein without committing idolatry; without worshipping of idols, whether images, or saints and angels; then it would be your bounded duty to leave that community, totally to separate from it. Suppose you could not remain in the Church of England without doing something which the word of God forbids, or omitting something which the word of God positively commands; if this were the case, (but blessed be God it is not,) you ought to separate from the Church of England. I will make the case my own: I am now, and have been from my youth, a member and a Minister of the Church of England: And I have do desire no design to separate from it, till my soul separates from my body. Yet if I was not permitted to remain therein without omitting what God requires me to do, it would then become meet and right, and my bounden duty, to separate form it without delay. To be more particular: I know God has committed to me a dispensation of the gospel; yea, and my own salvation depends upon preaching it: "Woe is me if I preach not the gospel." If then I could not remain in the Church without omitting this, without desisting from preaching the gospel I should be under a necessity of separating from it, or losing my own soul. In like manner, if I could not continue united to any smaller society, Church, or body of Christians, without committing sin, without lying and hypocrisy, without preaching to others doctrines which I did not myself believe, I should be under an absolute necessity of separating from that society. And in all these cases the sin of separation, with all the evils consequent upon it, would not lie upon it, would not lie upon me, but upon those who constrained me to make that separation, by requiring of me such terms of communion as I could not in conscience comply with. But, setting aside this case, suppose the Church or society to which I am now united does not require me to do anything which the Scripture forbids, or to omit anything which the Scripture enjoins, it is then my indispensable duty to continue therein. And if I separate from it without any such necessity, I am just chargeable (whether I foresaw them or not) with all the evils consequent upon that separation.

18. I have spoke the more explicitly upon this head, because it is so little understood; because so may of those who profess

much religion, nay, and really enjoy a measure of it, have not the least conception of this matter, neither imagine such a separation to be any sin at all. They leave a Christian society with as much unconcern as they go out of one room into another. They give occasion to all this complicated mischief. and wipe their mouth, and say they have done no evil! Whereas they are justly chargeable, before God and man, both with an action that is evil in itself, and with all the evil consequences which may be expected to follow, to themselves, to their brethren, and to the world.

19. I entreat you, therefore, my brethren, all that fear God, and have a desire to please hem, all that wish to have a conscience void of offense toward God and toward man, think not so slightly of this matter, but consider it calmly. Do not rashly tear asunder the sacred ties which unite you to any Christian society. This indeed is not of so much consequence to *you* who are only a *nominal* Christian. For you are not now vitally united to any of the members of Christ. Though you are called a Christian, you are not really a member of any Christian Church. But if you are a living member, if you live the life that is hid with Christ in God, then take care how you tend the body of Christ by separating from your brethren. It is a thing evil in itself. It is a sore evil in its consequences. O have pity upon yourself! Have pity on your brethren. Have pity even upon the world of the ungodly! Do not lay more stumbling-blocks in the way of these for whom Christ died.

20. But if you are afraid, and that not without reason, of schism, improperly so called, how much more afraid will you be, if your conscience is tender, of schism in the proper scriptural sense! O beware, I will not say of *forming*, but of *countenancing* or *abetting* any *parties* in a Christian society! Never encourage, much less cause, either by word or action, any division therein. In the nature of things, "there must be heresies," divisions, "among you;" but keep thyself pure. Leave off contention before it be meddled with: Shun the very beginning of strife. Meddle not with them that are given to dispute, with them that love contention. I never knew that remark to fail: "He that loves to dispute, does not love God." Follow peace with all men, without which you cannot effectually follow holiness. Not only "seek peace," but "ensue it:" If it seem to flee from you, pursue it nevertheless. "Be not overcome of evil, but overcome evil with good."

21. Happy is he that attains the character of a peace-maker in the Church of God. Why should not you labor after this? Be not content, not to stir up strife; but do all that in you lies, to prevent or quench the very first spark of it. Indeed it is far easier to prevent the flame from breaking out, than to quench it afterwards. However, be not afraid to attempt even this: The God of peace is on your side. He will give you acceptable words, and will send them to the heart of the hearers. *Noli diffidere: Noli discedere*, says a pious man: *Fac quod in te est; et Deus aderit bonce tuce voluntuti.* "Do not distrust Him that has all power, that has the hearts of all men in his hand. do what in thee lies, and Good will be present,

and bring thy good desires to good effect." Never be weary of well-doing. In due time thou shalt reap if thou faint not.

76.* On Perfection

"Let us go on to perfection."

Heb. 6:1.

The whole sentence runs thus: "Therefore, leaving the principles of the doctrine of Christ, let us go on unto perfection: Not laying again the foundation of repentance from dead works, and of faith toward God;" which he had just before termed, "the first principles of the oracles of God," and "meat fit for babes," for such as have just tasted that the Lord is gracious.

That the doing of this is a point of the utmost importance the Apostle intimates in the next words: "This will we do, if God permit. For it is impossible for those who were once enlightened, and have tasted of the good word of God, and the powers of the world to come, and have fallen away, to renew them again unto repentance." As if he had said, If we do not "go on to perfection," we are in the utmost danger of "falling away;" And if we do fall away, it is "impossible" that is, exceeding hard, "to renew them again unto repentance."

In order to make this very important scripture as easy to be understood as possible I shall endeavour,

    I.   To show what perfection is;

    II.   To answer some objections to it; and,

    III.   To expostulate a little with the opposers of it.

I. I will endeavour to show what perfection is.

1. And First, I do not conceive the perfection here spoken of, to be the perfection of angels. As those glorious beings never "left their first estate," never declined from their original perfection, all their native faculties are unimpaired: Their understanding, in particular, is still a lamp of light, their apprehension of all things clear and distinct, and their judgment always true. Hence, though their knowledge is limited, (for they are creatures,) though they are ignorant of innumerable things, yet they are not liable to mistake: Their knowledge is perfect in its kind. And as their affections are all constantly guided by their unerring understanding, so all their actions are suitable thereto; so they do, every moment, not their own will, but the good and acceptable will of God. Therefore it is not possible for man, whose understanding is darkened, to whom mistake is as natural as ignorance; who cannot think at all, but by the mediation of organs which are weakened and depraved, like the other parts of his corruptible body; it is not possible, I say, for men always to think right, to apprehend things distinctly, and to judge truly of them. In consequence hereof, his affections, depending on his understanding, are variously disordered. And his words and actions are influenced, more or less, by the disorder both of his understanding and affections. It follows that no man, while in the body, can possibly attain to angelic perfection.

2. Neither can any man, while he is in a corruptible body, attain to Adamic perfection. Adam, before his fall, was

---

undoubtedly as pure, as free from sin, as even the holy angels. In like manner, his understanding was as clear as theirs, and his affections as regular. In virtue of this, as he always judged right, so he was able always to speak and act right. But since man rebelled against God, the case is widely different with him. He is no longer able to avoid falling into innumerable mistakes; consequently, he cannot always avoid wrong affections; neither can he always think, speak, and act right. Therefore man, in his present state, can no more attain Adamic than angelic perfection.

3. The highest perfection which man can attain, while the soul dwells in the body, does not exclude ignorance, and error, and a thousand other infirmities. Now, from wrong judgments, wrong words and actions will often necessarily flow: And, in some cases, wrong affections also may spring from the same source. I may judge wrong of you: I may think more or less highly of you than I ought to think; and this mistake in my judgment may not only occasion something wrong in my behaviour, but it may have a still deeper effect; it may occasion something wrong in my affection. From a wrong apprehension, I may love and esteem you either more or less than I ought. Nor can I be freed from a likableness to such a mistake while I remain in a corruptible body. A thousand infirmities, in consequence of this, will attend my spirit, till it returns to God who gave it. And, in numberless instances, it comes short of doing the will of God, as Adam did in paradise. Hence the best of men may say from the heart,

>   "Every moment, Lord, I need
>   The merit of thy death,

for innumerable violations of the Adamic as well as the angelic law." It is well, therefore, for us, that we are not now under these, but under the law of love. "Love is" now "the fulfilling of the law," which is given to fallen man. This is now, with respect to us, "the perfect law." But even against this, through the present weakness of our understanding, we are continually liable to transgress. Therefore every man living needs the blood of atonement, or he could not stand before God.

4. What is then the perfection of which man is capable while he dwells in a corruptible body? It is the complying with that kind command, "My son, give me thy heart." It is the "loving the Lord his God with all his heart, and with all his soul, and with all his mind." This is the sum of Christian perfection: It is all comprised in that one word, Love. The first branch of it is the love of God: And as he that loves God loves his brother also, it is inseparably connected with the second: "Thou shalt love thy neighbour as thyself:" Thou shalt love every man as thy own soul, as Christ loved us. "On these two commandments hang all the law and the prophets:" These contain the whole of Christian perfection.

5. Another view of this is given us in those words of the great Apostle: "Let this mind be in you, which was also in Christ Jesus." For although this immediately and directly refers to the humility of our Lord, yet it may be taken in a far more extensive sense, so as to include the whole disposition of his mind, all his affections, all his tempers, both toward God and man. Now it is certain that as there was no evil affection in him, so no good affection or temper was wanting. So that "whatsoever things are holy, whatsoever things are lovely," are all included in "the mind that was in Christ Jesus."

6. St. Paul, when writing to the Galatians, places perfection in yet another view. It is the one undivided *fruit of the Spirit*, which he describes thus: "The fruit of the Spirit is love, joy, peace; longsuffering, gentleness, goodness, fidelity," (so the word should be translated here,) "meekness, temperance." What a glorious constellation of graces is here! Now, suppose all these to be knit together in one, to be united together in the soul of a believer, this is Christian perfection.

7. Again: He writes to the Christians at Ephesus, of "putting on the new man, which is created after God, in righteousness and true holiness;" and to the Colossians, of "the new man, renewed after the image of him that created him;" plainly referring to the words in Genesis, (Gen. 1:27) "So God created man in his own image." Now, the moral image of God consists (as the Apostle observes) "in righteousness and true holiness." By sin this is totally destroyed. And we never can recover it, till we are "created anew in Christ Jesus." And this is perfection.

8. St. Peter expresses it in a still different manner, though to the same effect: "As he that hath called you is holy, so be ye holy in all manner of conversation." (1 Peter 1:15.) According to this Apostle, then, perfection is another name for universal holiness: Inward and outward righteousness: Holiness of life, arising from holiness of heart.

9. If any expressions can be stronger than these, they are those of St. Paul to the Thessalonians: (1 Thess. 5:23:) "The God of peace himself sanctify you wholly; and may the whole of you, the spirit, the soul, and the body," (this is the literal translation) "be preserved blameless unto the coming of our Lord Jesus Christ."

10. We cannot show this sanctification in a more excellent way, than by complying with that exhortation of the Apostle: "I beseech you, brethren, by the mercies of God, that ye present your bodies" (yourselves, your souls and bodies; a part put for the whole, by a common figure of speech) "a living sacrifice unto God;" to whom ye were consecrated many years ago in baptism. When what was then devoted is actually presented to God, then is the man of God perfect.

11. To the same effect St. Peter says, (1 Pet. 2:5,) "Ye are a holy priesthood, to offer up spiritual sacrifices, acceptable to God through Jesus Christ." But what sacrifices shall we offer now, seeing the Jewish dispensation is at an end? If you have truly presented yourselves to God, you offer up to him continually all your thoughts, and words, and actions, through the Son of his love, as a sacrifice of praise and thanksgiving.

12. Thus you experience that He whose name is called Jesus does not bear that name in vain: That he does, in fact, "save his people from their sins;" the root as well as the branches. And this salvation from sin, from all sin, is another description of perfection; though indeed it expresses only the least, the lowest branch of it, only the negative part of the great salvation.

II. I proposed, in the Second Place, to answer some objections to this scriptural account of perfection.

1. One common objection to it is, that there is no promise of it in the Word of God. If this were so, we must give it up; we should have no foundation to build upon: For the promises of God are the only sure foundation of our hope. But surely there is a very clear and full promise that we shall all love the Lord our God with all our hearts. So we read, (Deut. 30:6,) "Then will I circumcise thy heart, and the heart of thy seed, to love the Lord thy God with all thy heart and with all thy soul." Equally express is the word of our Lord, which is no less a promise, though in the form of a command: "Thou shalt love the Lord thy God with all thy heart, and with all thy soul, and with all thy mind." (Matt. 22:37.) No words can be more strong than these; no promise can be more express. In like manner, "Thou shalt love thy neighbour as thyself," is as express a promise as a command.

2. And indeed that general and unlimited promise which runsthrough the whole gospel dispensation, "I will put my laws in their minds, and write them in their hearts," turns all the commands into promises; and, consequently, that among the rest, "Let this mind be in you which was also in Christ Jesus." The command here is equivalent to a promise, and gives us full reason to expect that he will work in us what he requires of us.

3. With regard to the fruit of the Spirit, the Apostle, in affirming, "the fruit of the Spirit is love, joy, peace, longsuffering, gentleness, goodness, fidelity, meekness, temperance," does, in effect, affirm that the Holy Spirit actually works love, and these other tempers, in those that are led by him. So that here also, we have firm ground to tread upon, this scripture likewise being equivalent to a promise, and assuring us that all these shall be wrought in us, provided we are led by the Spirit.

4. And when the Apostle says to the Ephesians, (Eph. 4:21–24,) "Ye have been taught, as the truth is in Jesus,"—to "be renewed in the spirit of your mind," and "to put on the new man, which is created after God"—that is, after the image of God,—"in righteousness and true holiness," he leaves us no room to doubt, but God will thus "renew us in the spirit of our mind," and "create us anew" in the image of God, wherein we were at first created: Otherwise it could not be said, that this is "the truth as it is in Jesus."

5. The command of God, given by St. Peter, "Be ye holy, as he that hath called you is holy, in all manner of conversation," [1 Pet. 1:15] implies a promise that we shall be thus holy, if we are not wanting to ourselves. Nothing can be wanting on God's part: As he has called us to holiness, he is undoubtedly willing, as well as able, to work this holiness in us. For he cannot mock his helpless creatures, calling us to receive what he never intends to give. That he does call us thereto is undeniable; therefore he will give it, if we are not disobedient to the heavenly calling.

6. The prayer of St. Paul for the Thessalonians, that God would "sanctify" them throughout, and "that the whole of them, the spirit, the soul, and the body, might be preserved blameless," will undoubtedly be heard in behalf of all the children of God, as well as of those at Thessalonica. Hereby, therefore, all Christians are encouraged to expect the same blessing from "the God of peace;" namely, that they also shall be "sanctified throughout, in spirit, soul, and body;" and that "the whole of them shall be preserved blameless unto the coming of our Lord Jesus Christ." [1 Thess. 5:23]

7. But the great question is, whether there is any promise in Scripture, that we shall be *saved from sin*. Undoubtedly there is. Such is that promise, (Psalm 130:8,) "He shall redeem Israel from all his sins;" exactly answerable to those words of the angel, "He shall save his people from their sins." And surely "he is able to save unto the uttermost them that come unto God through him." Such is that glorious promise given through the Prophet Ezekiel: (Ezek. 36:25–27:) "Then will I sprinkle clean water upon you, and ye shall be clean: From all your filthiness, and from all your idols, will I cleanse you. A new heart also will I give you, and a new spirit will I put within you: And I will take away the stony heart out of your flesh, and I will give you a heart of flesh. And I will put my Spirit within you, and cause you to walk in my statutes, and ye shall keep my judgments, and do them." Such (to mention no more) is that pronounced by Zechariah, (Luke 1:73–75,) "The oath which he sware to our father Abraham, that he would grant unto us, being delivered out of the hand of our enemies," (and such, doubtless are all our sins,) "to serve him without fear, in holiness and righteousness before him, all the days of our life." The last part of this promise is peculiarly worthy of our observation. Lest any should say, "True, we shall be saved from our sins when we die," that clause is remarkably added, as if on purpose to obviate this pretence, *all the days of our life*. With what modesty then can anyone affirm, that none shall enjoy this liberty *till death?*

8. "But," say some, "this cannot be the meaning of the words; for the thing is impossible." It is impossible to men: but the things impossible with, men are possible with God. "Nay, but this is impossible in its own nature: For it implies a contradiction, that a man should be saved from all sin while he is in a sinful body."

There is a great deal of force in this objection. And perhaps we allow most of what you contend for. We have already allowed, that while we are in the body we cannot be wholly free from mistake. Notwithstanding all our care, we shall still be liable to judge wrong in many instances. And a mistake in judgment will very frequently occasion a mistake in practice. Nay, a wrong judgment may occasion something in the temper or passions which is not strictly right. It may occasion needless fear, or ill-grounded hope, unreasonable love, or unreasonable aversion. But all this is no way inconsistent with the perfection above described.

9. You say, "Yes, it is inconsistent with the last article: It cannot consist with salvation from sin." I answer, It will perfectly well consist with salvation from sin, according to that definition of sin, (which I apprehend to be the scriptural definition of it,) *a voluntary transgression of a known law.* "Nay, but all transgressions of the law of God, whether voluntary or involuntary, are sin: For St. John says, 'All *sin is a transgression of the law.*' " True, but he does not say, *All transgression of the law is sin.* This I deny: Let him prove it that can.

To say the truth, this a mere strife of words. You say none is saved from sin in *your* sense of the word; but I do not admit of that sense, because the word is never so taken in Scripture. And you cannot deny the possibility of being saved from sin, in *my* sense of the word. And this is the sense wherein the word sin is over and over taken in Scripture.

"But surely we cannot be saved from sin, while we dwell in a *sinful body.*" *A sinful body?* I pray observe, how deeply ambiguous, how equivocal, this expression is! But there is no authority for it in Scripture: The word *sinful body* is never found there. And as it is totally unscriptural, so it is palpably absurd. For no *body*, or matter of any kind, can be *sinful*: Spirits alone ares capable of sin. Pray in what part of the body should sin lodge? It cannot lodge in the skin, nor in the muscles, or nerves, or veins, or arteries; it cannot be in the bones, any more than in the hair or nails. Only the soul can be the seat of sin.

10. "But does not St. Paul himself say, 'They that are in the flesh cannot please God?'" I am afraid the sound of these words has deceived many unwary souls; who have been told, Those words, *they that are in the flesh*, mean the same as *they that are in the body*. No; nothing less. The *flesh*, in this text, no more means *the body* than it does *the soul*. Abel, Enoch, Abraham, yea, all that cloud of witnesses recited by St. Paul in the eleventh of the Hebrews, did actually please God while they were in the body, as he himself testifies. The expression, therefore, here means neither more nor less than they that are unbelievers, they that are in their natural state, they that are without God in the world.

11. But let us attend to the reason of the thing. Why cannot the Almighty sanctify the soul while it is in the body? Cannot he sanctify *you* while you are in this house, as well as in the open air? Can the walls of brick or stone hinder him? No more can these walls of flesh and blood hinder him a moment from sanctifying you throughout. He can just as easily save you from all sin in the body as out of the body.

"But has he promised thus to save us from sin while we are in the body?" Undoubtedly he has: For a promise is implied in every commandment of God: Consequently in that, "Thou shalt love the Lord thy God with all thy heart, and with all thy soul, and with all thy mind." For this and every other commandment is given, not to the dead, but to the living. It is expressed in the words above recited, that we should walk "in holiness before him all the days of our life." I have dwelt the longer on this, because it is the grand argument of those that oppose salvation from sin; and also, because it has not been so frequently and so fully answered: Whereas the arguments taken from Scripture have been answered a hundred times over.

12. But a still more plausible objection remains, taken from experience; which is, that there are no living witnesses of this salvation from sin. In answer to this, I allow,

(1.) That there are not many. Even in this sense, there are *not many fathers*. Such is our hardness of heart, such our slowness to believe what both the Prophets and Apostles have spoke, that there are few, exceeding few, true witnesses of the great salvation.

(2.) I allow that there are false witnesses, who either deceive their own souls, and speak of the things they know not, or "speak lies in hypocrisy." And I have frequently wondered, that we have not more of both sorts. It is nothing strange, that men of warm imaginations should deceive themselves in this matter. Many do the same with regard to justification: They imagine they are justified, and are not. But though many imagine it falsely, yet there are some that are truly justified. And thus, though many imagine they are sanctified, and are not, yet there are some that are really sanctified.

(3.) I allow that some who once enjoyed full salvation have now totally lost it. They once walked in glorious liberty, giving God their whole heart, "rejoicing evermore, praying without ceasing, and in everything giving thanks." But it is past. They now are shorn of their strength, and become like other men. Perhaps they do not give up their confidence; they still have a sense of his pardoning love. But cven this is frequently assaulted by doubts and fears, so that they hold it with a trembling hand.

13. "Nay, this," say some pious and sensible men, "is the very thing which we contend for. We grant, it may please God to make some of his children for a time unspeakably holy and happy. We will not deny, that they may enjoy all the holiness and happiness which you speak of. But it is only *for a time*: God never designed that it should continue to their lives' end. Consequently, sin is only suspended: It is not destroyed."

This you affirm. But it is a thing of so deep importance, that it cannot be allowed without clear and cogent proof. And where is the proof? We know that, in general, "the gifts and calling of God are without repentance." He does not repent of any gifts which he hath bestowed upon the children of men. And how does the contrary appear, with regard to this particular gift of God? Why should we imagine, that he will make an exception with respect to the most precious of all his gifts on this side heaven? Is he not as able to give it us always, as to give it once? as able to give it for fifty years, as for one day? And how can it be proved, that he is not willing to continue this his lovingkindness? How is this supposition, that he is not willing, consistent with the positive assertion of the Apostle? who, after exhorting the Christians at Thessalonica, and in them all Christians in all ages, "to rejoice evermore, pray without ceasing, and in everything give thanks,"—immediately adds, (as if on purpose to answer those who denied, not the *power*, but the *will* of God to work this in them,) "For this is the will of God concerning you in Christ Jesus." Nay, and it is remarkable, that, after he had delivered that glorious promise (such it properly is,) in the twenty-third verse, "The very God of peace shall sanctify you wholly: And the whole of you" (so it is in the original,) "the spirit, the soul, and the body, shall be preserved blameless unto the coming of the Lord Jesus Christ;" he adds again, "Faithful is he that hath called you, who also will do it." [1 Thess. 5:23–24] He *will* not only sanctify you wholly, but will preserve you in that state until he comes to receive you unto himself.

14. Agreeable to this is the plain matter of fact. Several persons have enjoyed this blessing, without any interruption, for many years. Several enjoy it at this day. And not a few have enjoyed it unto their death, as they have declared with

their latest breath; calmly witnessing that God had saved them from all sin till their spirit returned to God.

15. As to the whole head of objections taken from experience, I desire it may be observed farther, either the persons objected to have attained Christian perfection, or they have not. If they have not, whatever objections are brought against them strike wide of the mark. For they are not the persons we are talking of: Therefore, whatever they are or do is beside the question. But if they have attained it, if they answer the description given under the nine preceding articles, no reasonable objection can lie against them. They are superior to all censure; and "every tongue that riseth up against them will they utterly condemn."

16. "But I never saw one," continues the objector, "that answered my idea of perfection." It may be so. And it is probable (as I observed elsewhere) you never will. For your idea includes abundantly too much; even freedom from those infirmities which are not separable from a spirit that is connected with flesh and blood. But if you keep to the account that is given above, and allow for the weakness of human understanding, you may see at this day undeniable instances of genuine, scriptural perfection.

III. 1. It only remains, in the Third place, to expostulate a little with the opposers of this perfection.

Now permit me to ask, Why are you so angry with those who profess to have attained this? and so mad (I cannot give it any softer title) against Christian perfection?—against the most glorious gift which God ever gave to the children of men upon earth? View it in every one of the preceding points of light, and see what it contains that is either odious or terrible; that is calculated to excite either hatred or fear in any reasonable creature.

What rational objection can you have to the loving the Lord your God with all your heart? Why should you have any aversion to it? Why should you be afraid of it? Would it do you any hurt? Would it lessen your happiness, either in this world or the world to come? And why should you be unwilling that others should give him their whole heart? or that they should love their neighbours as themselves? Yea, "as Christ hath loved us?" Is this detestable? Is it the proper object of hatred? Or is it the most amiable thing under the sun? Is it proper to move terror? Is it not rather desirable in the highest degree?

2. Why are you so averse to having in you the whole "mind which was in Christ Jesus?"—all the affections, all the tempers and dispositions, which were in him while he dwelt among men? Why should you be afraid of this? Would it be any worse for you, were God to work in you this very hour all the mind that was in him? If not, why should you hinder others from seeking this blessing? or be displeased at those who think they have attained it? Is anything more lovely? anything more to be desired by every child of man?

3. Why are you averse to having the whole "fruit of the Spirit?—"love, joy, peace; longsuffering, meekness, gentleness, fidelity, goodness, temperance?" Why should you be afraid of having all these planted in your inmost soul? As "against these there is no law," so there cannot be any reasonable objection. Surely nothing is more desirable, than

that all these tempers should take deep root in your heart; nay, in the hearts of all that name the name of Christ; yea, of all the inhabitants of the earth.

4. What reason have you to be afraid of, or to entertain any aversion to the being "renewed in the" whole "image of him that created you?" Is not this more desirable than anything under heaven? Is it not consummately amiable? What can you wish for in comparison of this, either for your own soul, or for those for whom you entertain the strongest and tenderest affection? And when you enjoy this, what remains but to be "changed from glory to glory, by the Spirit of the Lord?"

5. Why should you be averse to universal holiness,—the same thing under another name? Why should you entertain any prejudice against this, or look upon it with apprehension? whether you understand by that term the being inwardly conformed to the whole image and will of God, or an outward behaviour in every point suitable to that conformity. Can you conceive anything more amiable than this? anything more desirable? Set prejudice aside, and surely you will desire to see it diffused over all the earth.

6. Is perfection (to vary the expression) the being "sanctified throughout in spirit, soul, and body?" What lover of God and man can be averse to this, or entertain frightful apprehension of it? Is it not, in your best moments, your desire to be all of a piece?—all consistent with yourself?—all faith, all meekness, and all love? And suppose you were once possessed of this glorious liberty, would not you wish to continue therein?—to be preserved "blameless unto the coming of our Lord Jesus Christ?"

7. For what cause should you that are children of God be averse to, or afraid of, presenting yourselves, your souls and bodies, as a living sacrifice, holy, acceptable to God?—to God your Creator, your Redeemer, your Sanctifier? Can anything be more desirable than this entire self-dedication to him? And is it not your wish that all mankind should unite in this "reasonable service?" Surely no one can be averse to this, without being and enemy to all mankind.

8. And why should you be afraid of, or averse to, what is naturally implied in this; namely, the offering up all our thoughts, and words, and actions, as a spiritual sacrifice to God, acceptable to him through the blood and intercession of his well-beloved Son. Surely you cannot deny that this is good and profitable to men, as well as pleasing to God. Should you not then devoutly pray that both you and all mankind may thus worship him in spirit and in truth?

9. Suffer me to ask one question more. Why should any man of reason and religion be either afraid of, or averse to, salvation from all sin? Is not sin the greatest evil on this side hell? And if so, does it not naturally follow that an entire deliverance from it is one of the greatest blessings on this side heaven? How earnestly then should it be prayed for by all the children of God! By sin I mean *a voluntary transgression of a known law.* Are you averse to being delivered from this? Are you afraid of such a deliverance? Do you then love sin, that you are so unwilling to part with it? Surely no. You do not love either the devil or his works. You rather wish to be totally

delivered from them, to have sin rooted out both of your life and your heart.

10. I have frequently observed, and not without surprise, that the opposers of perfection are more vehement against it when it is placed in this view, than in any other whatsoever. They will allow all you say of the love of God and man; of the mind which was in Christ; of the fruit of the spirit; of the image of God; of universal holiness; of entire self-dedication; of sanctification in spirit, soul, and body; yea, and of the offering up all our thoughts, words, and actions, as a sacrifice to God;—all this they will allow so we will allow sin, a little sin, to remain in us till death.

11. Pray compare this with that remarkable passage in John Bunyan's "Holy War." "When Immanuel," says he, "had driven Diabolus and all his forces out of the city of Mansoul, Diabolus preferred a petition to Immanuel, that he might have only a small part of the city. When this was rejected, he begged to have only a little room within the walls. But Immanuel answered, "He should have no place at all; no, not to rest the sole of his foot.

Had not the good old man forgot himself? Did not the force of truth so prevail over him here as utterly to overturn his own system?—to assert perfection in the clearest manner? For if this is not salvation from sin, I cannot tell what is.

12. "No," says a great man, "this is the error of errors: I hate it from my heart. I pursue it through all the world with fire and sword." Nay, why so vehement? Do you seriously think there is no error under heaven equal to this? Here is something which I cannot understand. Why are those that oppose salvation from sin (few excepted) so eager,—I had almost said, furious? Are you fighting *pro aris et focis?* "for God and your country?" for all you have in the world? for all that is near and dear unto you? for your liberty, your life? In God's name, why are you so fond of sin? What good has it ever done you? what good is it ever likely to do you, either in this world or in the world to come? And why are you so violent against those that hope for deliverance from it? Have patience with us, if we are in an error; yea, suffer us to enjoy our error. If we should not attain it, the very expectation of this deliverance gives us present comfort; yea, and ministers strength to resist those enemies which we expect to conquer. If you could persuade us to despair of that victory, we should give over the contest Now "we are saved by hope:" From this very hope a degree of salvation springs. Be not angry at those who are *felices errore suo,* "happy in their mistake." Else, be their opinion right or wrong, your temper is undeniably sinful. Bear then with *us*, as we do with *you*; and see whether the Lord will not deliver us! whether he is not able, yea, and willing "to save them to the uttermost that come unto God through him."[Tunbridge Wells, Dec. 6, 1784]

77.* SPIRITUAL WORSHIP

"This is the true God, and eternal life."

1 John 5:20.

1. In this Epistle St. John speaks not to any particular Church, but to all the Christians of that age; although more especially to them among whom he then resided. And in them he speaks to the whole Christian Church in all succeeding ages.

2. In this letter, or rather tract, (for he was present with those to whom it was more immediately directed, probably being not able to preach to them any longer, because of his extreme old age,) he does not treat directly of faith, which St. Paul had done; neither of inward and outward holiness, concerning which both St. Paul, St. James, and St. Peter, had spoken; but of the foundation of all,—the happy and holy communion which the faithful have with God the Father, Son, and Holy Ghost.

3. In the preface he describes the authority by which he wrote and spoke, (1 John 1:1–4,) and expressly points out the design of his present writing. To the preface exactly answers the conclusion of the Epistle, more largely explaining the same design, and recapitulating the marks of our communion with God, by, *"we know,"* thrice repeated. (1 John 5:18–20.)

4. The tract itself treats, First, severally, of communion with the Father; (1 John 1:5–10;) of communion with the Son; (1 John 2 and 3;) of communion with the Spirit. (1 John 4.)

Secondly, conjointly, of the testimony of the Father, Son, and Holy Ghost; on which faith in Christ, the being born of God, love to God and his children, the keeping his commandments, and victory over the world, are founded. (1 John 5:1–12.)

5. The recapitulation begins, (1 John 5:18,) "We know that he who is born of God," who sees and loves God, "sinneth not," so long as this loving faith abideth in him. "We know we are of God;" children of God, by the witness and the fruit of the Spirit; "and the whole world," all who have not the Spirit, "lieth in the wicked one." They are, and live, and dwell in him, as the children of God do in the Holy One. "We know that the Son of God is come, and hath given us" a spiritual "understanding, that we may know the true One," the faithful and true witness. "And we are in the true One," as branches in the vine. "This is the true God, and eternal life."

In considering these important words, we may inquire,

    I.   How is he the true God?
    II.   How is he eternal life? I shall then,
    III.   Add a few inferences.

I. 1. And, First, we may inquire, How is he the true God? He is "God over all, blessed for ever." "He was with God," with God the Father, "from the beginning," from eternity, "and was God. He and the Father are One;" and, consequently, "he thought it not robbery to be equal with God." Accordingly, the inspired writers give him all the titles of the most high God. They call him over and over, by the incommunicable name, JEHOVAH,—never given to any creature. They ascribe to him all the attributes and all the works of God. So that we need not scruple to pronounce him, "God of God, Light of Light, very God of very God: In glory equal with the Father, in majesty co-eternal."

---

* [text from the 1872 edition]

2. He is the true God, the only Cause, the sole Creator of all things. "By him," saith the Apostle Paul, "were created all things that are in heaven, and that are on earth,"—yea, earth and heaven themselves; but the inhabitants are named, because more noble than the house,—"visible and invisible." The several species of which are subjoined: "Whether they be thrones, or dominions, or principalities, or powers." So St. John: "All things were made by him, and without him was not anything made that was made." And, accordingly, St. Paul applies to him those strong words of the Psalmist: "Thou, Lord, in the beginning hast laid the foundation of the earth, and the heavens are the work of thy hands."

3. And as the true God, he is also the Supporter of all the things that he hath made. He beareth, upholdeth, sustaineth, all created things by the word of his power, by the same powerful word which brought them out of nothing. As this was absolutely necessary for the beginning of their existence, it is equally so for the continuance of it: Were his almighty influence withdrawn, they could not subsist a moment longer. Hold up a stone in the air; the moment you withdraw your hand, it naturally falls to the ground. In like manner, were he to withdraw his hand for a moment, the creation would fall into nothing.

4. As the true God, he is likewise the Preserver of all things. He not only keeps them in being, but preserves them in that degree of well-being which is suitable to their several natures. He preserves them in their several relations, connexions, and dependencies, so as to compose one system of beings, to form one entire universe, according to the counsel of his will. How strongly and beautifully is this expressed: *Ta panta en autoi synesteke*. By whom all things consist: or, more literally, By and in him are all things compacted into one system. he is not only the support, but also the cement, of the whole universe.

5. I would particularly remark, (what perhaps has not been sufficiently observed,) that he is the true Author of all the *motion* that is in the universe. To spirits, indeed, he has given a small degree of self-moving power, but not to matter. All matter, of whatever kind it be, is absolutely and totally inert. It does not, cannot, in any case, move itself; and whenever any part of it seems to move, it is in reality moved by something else. See that log, which, vulgarly speaking, *moves* on the sea! It is in reality *moved* by the water. The water is moved by the wind; that is, a current of air. And the air itself owes all its motion to the ethereal fire, a particle of which is attached to every particle of it. Deprive it of that fire, and it moves no longer; it is fixed: It is as inert as sand. Remove fluidity (owing to the ethereal fire intermixed with it) from water, and it has no more motion than the log. Impact fire into iron, by hammering it when red hot, and it has no more motion than fixed air, or frozen water. But when it is unfixed, when it is in its most active state, what gives motion to fire? The very heathen will tell you. It is,

> Totam
> Mens agitans molem, et magno se corpore miscens.
> [The general soul
> Lives in the parts, and agitates the whole. edit.]

6. To pursue this a little farther: We say, the moon moves round the earth; the earth and the other planets move round the sun; the sun moves round its own axis. But these are only vulgar expressions: For, if we speak the truth, neither the sun, moon, nor stars *move*. None of these move themselves: They are all *moved* every moment by the almighty hand that made them.

"Yes," says Sir Isaac [Newton], "the sun, moon, and all the heavenly bodies, do move, do gravitate, toward each other." *Gravitate*. What is that? "Why, they all *attract* each other, in proportion to the quantity of matter they contain." "Nonsense all over," says Mr. hutchinson; "jargon, self-contradiction! Can anything *act* where it is not? No; they are continually *impelled* toward each other." *Impelled!* by what? "By the subtle matter, the ether, or electric fire." But remember! be it ever so subtle, it is matter still: Consequently, it is as inert in itself as either sand or marble. It cannot therefore move itself; but probably it is the first material mover, the main spring whereby the Creator and Preserver of all things is pleased to move the universe.

7. The true God is also the Redeemer of all the children of men. It pleased the Father to lay upon him the iniquities of us all, that by the one oblation of himself once offered, when he tasted death for every man, he might make a full and sufficient sacrifice, oblation, and satisfaction for the sins of the whole world.

8. Again: The True God is the Governor of all things: "His kingdom ruleth over all." The government rests upon his shoulder, throughout all ages. He is the Lord and Disposer of the whole creation, and every part of it. And in how astonishing a manner does he govern the world! How far are his ways above human thought! How little do we know of his methods of government! only this we know, *Ita praesides singulis sicut universis, et universis sicut singulis!* "Thou presidest over each creature, as if it were the universe, and over the universe, as over each individual creature." Dwell a little upon this sentiment: What a glorious mystery does it contain! It is paraphrased in the words recited above:

> FATHER, how wide thy glories shine!
> Lord of the universe, and mine:
> Thy goodness watches over the whole,
> As all the world were but one soul;
> Yet keeps my every sacred hair,
> As I remaind thy single care!

9. And yet there is a difference, as was said before, in his providential government over the children of men. A pious writer observes, There is a three-fold circle of divine providence. The *outermost circle* includes all the sons of men; Heathens, Mahometans, Jews, and Christians. He causeth his sun to rise upon all. He giveth them rain and fruitful seasons. He pours ten thousand benefits upon them, and fills their hearts with food and gladness. With an *interior circle* he encompasses the whole visible Christian Church, all that name the name of Christ. He has an additional regard to these, and a nearer attention to their welfare. But the *innermost circle* of his providence encloses only the invisible Church of Christ: all real Christians, wherever dispersed in all corners of the earth; all that worship God (whatever

denomination they are of) in spirit and in truth. He keeps these as the apple of an eye: He hides them under the shadow of his wings. And it is to these in particular that our Lord says, "even the hairs of your head are all numbered."

10. Lastly, being the true God, he is the end of all things; according to that solemn declaration of the Apostle: (Rom. 11:36:) "of him, and through him, and to him, are all things: "*of him*, as the Creator,—*through him*, as the Sustainer and Preserver; and *to him*, as the ultimate end of all.

II. In all these senses Jesus Christ is the true God. But how is he eternal life?

1. The thing directly intended in this expression is not, that he *will be* eternal life: Although this is a great and important truth, and never to be forgotten. "He is the Author of eternal salvation to all them that obey him." He is the Purchaser of that "crown of life" which will be given to all that are "faithful unto death;" and he will be the soul of all their joys to all the saints in glory.

> The flame of angelical love
> > Is kindled at Jesuss face;
> And all the enjoyment above
> > Consists in the rapturous gaze!

2. The thing directly intended is not, that he is the resurrection; although this also is true, according to his own declaration, "I am the resurrection and the life:" Agreeable to which are St. Pauls words: "As in Adam all died, even so in Christ shall all be made alive." So that we may well say, "Blessed be the God and Father of our Lord Jesus Christ, who … hath begotten us again unto a lively hope by the resurrection of Christ from the dead, to an inheritance incorruptible, and undefiled, and that fadeth not away."

3. But waiving what he *will be* hereafter, we are here called to consider what he *is now*. He is now the life of everything that lives, in any kind or degree. He is the Source of the lowest species of life, that of *vegetables*, as being the Source of all the motion on which vegetation depends. He is the Fountain of the life of *animals*; the Power by which the heart beats, and the circulating juices flow. He is the Fountain of all the life which man possesses in common with other animals. And if we distinguish the *rational* from the animal life, he is the Source of this also.

4. But how infinitely short does all this fall of the life which is here directly intended, and of which the Apostle speaks so explicitly in the preceding verses! (1 John 5:11, 12:) "This is the testimony, that God hath given us eternal life; and this life is in his Son. He that hath the Son hath life,"—the eternal life here spoken of,—"and he that hath not the Son" of God "hath not" this "life." As if he had said, "This is the sum of the testimony which God hath testified of his Son, that God hath given us, not only a title to, but the real beginning of, eternal life: And this life is purchased by, and treasured up in, his Son; who has all the springs and the fullness of it in himself, to communicate to his body, the Church."

5. This eternal life then commences when it pleases the Father to reveal his Son in our hearts; when we first know Christ, being enabled "to call him Lord by the Holy Ghost;" when we can testify, our conscience bearing us witness in the Holy Ghost, "the life which I now live, I live by faith in the Son of God, who loved me, and gave himself for me." And then it is that happiness begins; happiness real, solid, substantial. Then it is that heaven is opened in the soul, that the proper, heavenly state commences, while the love of God, as loving us, is shed abroad in the heart, instantly producing love to all mankind; general, pure benevolence, together with its genuine fruits, lowliness, meekness, patience, contentedness in every state; an entire, clear, full acquiescence in the whole will of God; enabling us to "rejoice evermore, and in everything to give thanks."

6. As our knowledge and our love of him increase, by the same degrees, and in the same proportion, the kingdom of an inward heaven must necessarily increase also; while we "grow up in all things into Him who is our Head." And when we are *en autoi peplerOmenoi, complete in him*, as our translators render it; but more properly when we are *filled with him*; when "Christ in us, the hope of glory," is our God and our All; when he has taken the full possession of our heart; when he reigns therein without a rival, the Lord of every motion there; when we dwell in Christ, and Christ in us, we are one with Christ, and Christ with us; then we are completely happy; then we live "all the life that is hid with Christ in God;" then, and not till then, we properly experience what that word meaneth, "God is love; and whosoever dwelleth in love, dwelleth in God, and God in him."

III. I have now only to add a few inferences from the preceding observations.

1. And we may learn from hence, First, that as there is but one God in heaven above and in the earth beneath; so there is only one happiness for created spirits, either in heaven or earth. This one God made our heart for himself; and it cannot rest till it resteth in him. It is true, that while we are in the vigour of youth and health; while our blood dances in our veins; while the world smiles upon us, and we have all the conveniences, yea, and superfluities of life, we frequently have pleasing dreams, and enjoy a kind of happiness. But it cannot continue; it flies away like a shadow; and even while it does, it is not solid or substantial; it does not satisfy the soul. We still pant after something else, something which we have not. Give a man everything that this world can give, still, as Horace observed near two thousand years ago,—

> Curtae nescio quid semper abest rei.

Still,—

> Amidst our plenty something still,
> To me, to thee, to him is wanting!

That *something* is neither more nor less than the knowledge and love of God; without which no spirit can be happy either in heaven or earth.

2. Permit me to recite my own experience, in confirmation of this:—I distinctly remember, that, even in my childhood, even when I was at school, I have often said, "They say the life of a schoolboy is the happiest in the world; but I am sure I am not happy; for I am not content, and so cannot be happy." When I had lived a few years longer, being in the vigour of youth, a stranger to pain and sickness, and particularly to lowness of spirits; (which I do not remember to have felt one quarter of an hour since I was born;) having

plenty of all things, in the midst of sensible and amiable friends who loved me, and I loved them; and being in the way of life which, of all others, suited my inclinations; still I was not happy. I wondered why I was not, and could not imagine what the reason was. The reason certainly was, I did not know God; the Source of present as well as eternal happiness. What is a clear proof that I was not then happy is, that, upon the coolest reflection, I knew not one week which I would have thought it worth while to have lived over again; taking it with every inward and outward sensation, without any variation at all.

3. But a pious man affirms, "When I was young, I was happy; though I was utterly without God in the world." I do not believe you; Though I doubt not but you believe yourself. But you are deceived, as I have been over and over. Such is the condition of human life!

> Flowerets and myrtles fragrant seem to rise:
> All is at distance fair; but near at hand,
> The gay deceit mocks the desiring eyes
> With thorns, and desert heath, and barren sand.

Look forward on any distant prospect: How beautiful does it appear! Come up to it; and the beauty vanishes away, and it is rough and disagreeable. Just so is life. But when the scene is past, it resumes its former appearance; and we seriously believe, that we were then very happy, though, in reality, we were far otherwise. For as none is now, so none ever was, happy, without the loving knowledge of the true God.

4. We may learn hence, Secondly, that this happy knowledge of the true God is only another name for religion; I mean Christian religion; which, indeed, is the only one that deserves the name. Religion, as to the nature or essence of it, does not lie in this or that set of notions, vulgarly called *faith*; nor in a round of duties, however carefully *reformed* from error and superstition. It does not consist in any number of outward actions. No: it properly and directly consists in the knowledge and love of God, as manifested in the Son of his love, through the eternal Spirit. And this naturally leads to every heavenly temper, and to every good word and work.

5. We learn hence, Thirdly, that none but a Christian is happy; none but a real inward Christian. A glutton, a drunkard, a gamester may be *merry*; but he cannot be happy. The beau, the belle, may eat and drink, and rise up to play; but still they feel they are not happy. Men or women may adorn their own dear persons with all the colours of the rainbow. They may dance, and sing, and hurry to and fro, and flutter hither and thither. They may roll up and down in their splendid carriages, and talk insipidly to each other. They may hasten from one diversion to another: But happiness is not there. They are still "walking in a vain shadow, and disquieting themselves in vain." One of their own poets has truly pronounced, concerning the whole life of these sons of pleasure,

> 'Tis a dull farce, and empty show:
> Powder, and pocket-glass, and beau.

I cannot but observe of that fine writer, that he came near the mark, and yet fell short of it. In his "Solomon" (one of the noblest poems in the English tongue) he clearly shows where happiness *is not*; that it is not to be found in natural knowledge, in power, or in the pleasures of sense or imagination. But he does not show where it is to be found. He could not; for he did not know it himself. Yet he came near it when he said,

> Restore, Great Father, thy instructed son;
> And in my act may thy great will be done!

6. We learn hence, Fourthly, that every Christian is happy; and that he who is not happy is not a Christian. If, as was observed above, religion is happiness, everyone that has it must be happy. This appears from the very nature of the thing: For if religion and happiness are in fact the same, it is impossible that any man can possess the former, without possessing the latter also. He cannot have religion without having happiness; seeing they are utterly inseparable. And it is equally certain, on the other hand, that he who is not happy is not a Christian; Seeing if he was a real Christian, he could not but be happy. But I allow an exception here in favour of those who are under violent temptation; yea, and of those who are under deep nervous disorders, which are, indeed, a species of insanity. The clouds and darkness which then overwhelm the soul suspend its happiness; especially if Satan is permitted to second those disorders by pouring in his fiery darts. But, excepting these cases, the observation will hold, and it should be well attended to,—Whoever is not happy, yea, happy in God, is not a Christian.

7. Are not *you* a living proof of this? Do not you still wander to and fro, seeking rest, but finding none?—pursuing happiness, but never overtaking it? And who can blame you for pursuing it? It is the very end of your being. The great Creator made nothing to be miserable, but every creature to be happy in its kind. And upon a general review of the works of his hands he pronounced them all *very good*; which they would not have been, had not every intelligent creature, yea, everyone capable of pleasure and pain, been happy in answering the end of its creation. If *you* are now unhappy, it is because you are in an unnatural state: And shall you not sigh for deliverance from it? "The whole creation," being now "subject to vanity," "groaneth and travaileth in pain together." I blame you only, or pity you rather, for taking a wrong way to a right end; for seeking happiness where it never was, and never can be, found. You seek happiness in your fellow-creatures, instead of your Creator. But these can no more make you happy than they can make you immortal. If you have ears to hear, every creature cries aloud, "Happiness is not in me." All these are, in truth, "broken cisterns, that can hold no water." O turn unto your rest! Turn to Him in whom are hid all the treasures of happiness! Turn unto him "who giveth liberally unto all men;" and he will give you "to drink of the water of life freely."

8. You cannot find your long-sought happiness in all the pleasures of the world. Are they not "deceitful upon the weights?" Are they not lighter than vanity itself? How long will ye "feed upon that which is not bread?"—which may amuse, but cannot satisfy? You cannot find it in the religion of the world; either in opinions or a mere round of outward duties. Vain labour! Is not God a spirit, and therefore to be "worshipped in spirit and in truth?" In this alone can you find the happiness you seek; in the union of your spirit with

the Father of spirits; in the knowledge and love of Him who is the fountain of happiness, sufficient for all the souls he has made.

9. But where is He to be found? Shall we go up into heaven, or down into hell, to seek him? Shall we "take the wings of the morning" and search for him "in the uttermost parts of the sea?" Nay, *quod petis, hic est*! What a strange word to fall from the pen of a Heathen! "What you seek is here!" He is "about your bed." He is "about your path" He "besets you behind and before." He "lays his hand upon you." Lo! God is here! not afar off. Now believe and feel him near! May he now reveal himself in your heart! Know him, love him, And you are happy!.

10. Are you already happy in him? Then see that you "hold fast whereunto ye have attained!" "Watch and pray," that you may never be "moved from your steadfastness." "Look unto yourselves, that ye lose not what you have gained, but that ye receive a full reward." In so doing, expect a continual growth in grace, in the loving knowledge of our Lord Jesus Christ. Expect that the power of the Highest shall suddenly overshadow you, that all sin may be destroyed, and nothing may remain in your heart, but holiness unto the Lord. And this moment, and every moment, "present yourselves a living sacrifice, holy, acceptable to God," and "glorify him with your body and with your spirit which are God's!"

78.* SPIRITUAL IDOLATRY

"Little children, keep yourselves from idols."

1 John 5:21.

1. There are two words that occur several times in this Epistle,—*paidia* and *teknia*, both of which our translators render by the same expression, *little children*. But their meaning is very different. The former is very properly rendered *little children*; for it means, *babes in Christ*, those that have lately tasted of his love, and are, as yet, weak and unestablished therein. The latter might with more propriety be rendered, *beloved children*; as it does not denote any more than the affection of the speaker to those whom he had begotten in the Lord.

2. An ancient historian relates, that when the Apostle was so enfeebled by age as not to be able to preach, he was frequently brought into the congregation in his chair, and just uttered, Beloved children, love one another. he could not have given a more important advice. And equally important is this which lies before us; equally necessary for every part of the Church of Christ. Beloved children, keep yourselves from idols.

3. Indeed there is a close connexion between them: one cannot subsist without the other. As there is no firm foundation for the love of our brethren except the love of God, so there is no possibility of loving God except we keep ourselves from idols. But what are the idols of which the Apostle speaks? This is the First thing to be considered. We may then, in the Second place, inquire, how shall we keep ourselves from them?

I. 1. We are, First to consider, What are the idols of which the Apostle speaks? I do not conceive him to mean, at least not principally, the idols that were worshipped by the heathens. They to whom he was writing, whether they had been Jews or Heathens, were not in much danger from these. There is no probability that the Jews now converted had ever been guilty of worshipping them: As deeply given to this gross idolatry as the Israelites had been for many ages, they were hardly ever entangled therein after their return from the Babylonish captivity. From that period the whole body of Jews had shown a constant, deep abhorrence of it: And the Heathens, after they had once turned to the living God, had their former idols in the utmost detestation. They abhorred to touch the unclean thing; yea, they chose to lay down their lives rather than turn to the worship of those gods whom they now knew to be devils.

2. Neither can we reasonably suppose, that he speaks of those idols that are now worshipped in the Church of Rome; whether angels, or the souls of departed saints, or images of gold, silver, wood or stone. None of these idols were known in the Christian Church till some centuries after the time of the Apostles. once, indeed, St. John himself fell down to worship before the face of an angel that spake unto him; probably mistaking him, from his glorious appearance, for the Great Angel of the Covenant; but the strong reproof of the angel, which immediately followed, secured the Christians from imitating that bad example: " 'See thou do it not. As glorious as I appear, I am not thy Master. 'I am thy fellow-servant, and of thy brethren the Prophets: Worship God." (Rev. 22:9.)

3. Setting then pagan and Romish idols aside, what are those of which we are here warned by the Apostle? The preceding words show us the meaning of these. "This is the true God,"—the end of all the souls he has made, the centre of all created spirits;—"and eternal life,"—the only foundation of present as well as eternal happiness. To him, therefore, alone, our heart is due. And he cannot, he will not, quit his claim, or consent to its being given to any other. He is continually saying to every child of man, "My son, give me thy heart!" And to give our heart to any other is plain idolatry. Accordingly, whatever takes our heart from him, or shares it with him, is an idol; or, in other words, whatever we seek happiness in independent of God.

4. Take an instance that occurs almost every day: A person who has been long involved in the world, surrounded and fatigued with abundance of business, having at length acquired an easy fortune, disengages himself from all business, and retires into the country,—to be happy. Happy in what? Why, in taking his ease. For he intends now,

> Somno et inertibus horis
> Ducere solicitae jucunda oblivia vitae:
> To sleep, and pass away,
> In gentle inactivity the day!

Happy in eating and drinking whatever his heart desires: perhaps more elegant fare than that of the old Roman, who feasted his imagination before the treat was served up; who,

---

* [text from the 1872 edition]

before he left the town, consoled himself with the thought of "fat bacon and cabbage too!"

> Uncta satis pingui ponentur oluscula lardo!

Happy,—in altering, enlarging, rebuilding, or at least decorating, the old mansion-house he has purchased; and likewise in improving everything about it; the stables, out-houses, grounds. But, mean time, where does God come in? No where at all. He did not think about him. He no more thought of the King of heaven, than of the King of France. God is not in his plan. The knowledge and love of God are entirely out of the question. Therefore, this whole scheme of happiness in retirement is idolatry, from beginning to end.

5. If we descend to particulars, the first species of this idolatry is what St. John terms, *the desire of the flesh*. We are apt to take this in too narrow a meaning, as if it related to one of the senses only. Not so: this expression equally refers to all the outward senses. It means, the seeking happiness in the gratification of any or all of the external senses; although more particularly of the three lower senses,—tasting, smelling, and feeling. It means, the seeking happiness herein, if not in a gross, indelicate manner, by open intemperance, by gluttony or drunkenness, or shameless debauchery; yet, in a regular kind of epicurism; in a genteel sensuality; in such an elegant course of self-indulgence as does not disorder either the head or the stomach; as does not at all impair our health, or blemish our reputation.

6. But we must not imagine this species of idolatry is confined to the rich and great. In this also, "the toe of the peasant" (as our poet speaks) "treads upon the heel of the courtier." Thousands in low as well as in high life sacrifice to this idol; seeking their happiness (though in a more humble manner) in gratifying their outward senses. It is true, their meat, their drink, and the objects that gratify their other senses, are of a coarser kind. But still they make up all the happiness they either have or seek, and usurp the hearts which are due to God.

7. The second species of idolatry mentioned by the Apostle is, *the desire of the eye*: That is, the seeking happiness in gratifying the imagination; (chiefly by means of the eyes;) that internal sense, which is as natural to men as either sight or hearing. This is gratified by such objects as are either grand, or beautiful, or uncommon. But as to grand objects, it seems they do not please any longer than they are new. Were we to survey the Pyramids of egypt daily for a year, what pleasure would they then give? Nay, what pleasure does a far grander object than these,—

> The ocean rolling on the shelly shore,

give to one who has been long accustomed to it? Yea, what pleasure do we generally receive from the grandest object in the universe,—

> Yon ample, azure sky,
> Terribly large, and wonderfully bright,
> With stars unnumberd, and unmeasured light?

8. Beautiful objects are the next general source of the pleasures of the imagination: The works of nature in particular. So persons in all ages have been delighted

> With sylvan scenes, and hill and dale,
> And liquid lapse of murmuring streams.

others are pleased with adding art to nature; as in gardens, with their various ornaments: others with mere works of art; as buildings, and representations of nature, whether in statues or paintings. Many likewise find pleasure in beautiful apparel, or furniture of various kinds. But novelty must be added to beauty, as well as grandeur, or it soon palls upon the sense.

9. Are we to refer to the head of beauty, the pleasure which many take in a favourite animal? Suppose a sparrow, a parrot, a cat, a lap-dog? Sometimes it may be owing to this. At other times, none but the person pleased can find any beauty at all in the favourite. Nay, perchance it is, in the eyes of all other persons, superlatively ugly. In this case, the pleasure seems to arise from mere whim or caprice; that is, madness.

10. Must we not refer to the head of novelty, chiefly, the pleasure found in most diversions and amusements; which were we to repeat them daily but a few months would be utterly flat and insipid? To the same head we may refer the pleasure that is taken in collecting curiosities; whether they are natural or artificial, whether old or new. This sweetens the labour of the virtuoso, and makes all his labour light.

11. But it is not chiefly to novelty that we are to impute the pleasure we receive from music. Certainly this has an intrinsic beauty, as well as frequently an intrinsic grandeur. This is a beauty and grandeur of a peculiar kind, not easy to be expressed; nearly related to the sublime and the beautiful in poetry, which give an exquisite pleasure. And yet it may be allowed, that novelty heightens the pleasure which arises from any of these sources.

12. From the study of languages, from criticism, and from history, we receive a pleasure of a mixed nature. In all these, there is always something new; frequently something beautiful or sublime. And history not only gratifies the imagination in all these respects, but likewise pleases us by touching our passions; our love, desire, joy, pity. The last of these gives us a strong pleasure, though strangely mixed with a kind of pain. So that one need not wonder at the exclamation of a fine poet,—

> What is all mirth but turbulence unholy,
> When to the charms compared of heavenly melancholy?

13. The love of novelty is immeasurably gratified by experimental philosophy; and, indeed, by every branch of natural philosophy; which opens an immense field for still new discoveries. But is there not likewise a pleasure therein, as well as in mathematical and metaphysical studies, which does not result from the imagination, but from the exercise of the understanding? unless we will say, that the newness of the discoveries which we make by mathematical or metaphysical researches is one reason at least, if not the chief, of the pleasure we receive therefrom.

14. I dwell the longer on these things, because so very few see them in the true point of view. The generality of men, and more particularly men of sense and learning, are so far from suspecting that there is, or can be, the least harm in them, that they seriously believe it is matter of great praise to *give ourselves wholly to them*. Who of them, for instance, would not admire and commend the indefatigable industry of that

great philosopher who says, "I have been now eight-and-thirty years at my parish of Upminster; and I have made it clear, that there are no less than three-and-fifty species of butterflies therein: But if God should spare my life a few years longer, I do not doubt but I should demonstrate, there are five-and-fifty!" I allow that most of these studies have their use, and that it is possible to *use* without *abusing* them. But if we seek our happiness in any of these things, then it commences an *idol*. And the enjoyment of it, however it may be admired and applauded by the world, is condemned by God as neither better nor worse than damnable *idolatry*.

15. The third kind of love of the world, the Apostle speaks of under that uncommon expression, *he alazoneia ta biou*. This is rendered by our translators, *the pride of life*. It is usually supposed to mean, the pomp and splendour of those that are in high life. But has it not a more extensive sense? Does it not rather mean, the seeking happiness in the praise of men, which, above all things engenders pride? When this is pursued in a more pompous way by kings or illustrious men, we call it "thirst for glory;" when it is sought in a lower way by ordinary men, it is styled, "taking care of our reputation." In plain terms, it is seeking the honour that cometh of men, instead of that which cometh of God only.

16. But what creates a difficulty here is this: We are required not only to "give no offence to anyone," and to "provide things honest in the sight of all men," but to "please all men for their good to edification." But how difficult is it to do this, with a single eye to God! We ought to do all that in us lies, to prevent "the good that is in us from being evil spoken of." Yea, we ought to value a clear reputation, if it be given us, only less than a good conscience. But yet, if we seek our happiness therein, we are liable to perish in our idolatry.

17. To which of the preceding heads is the *love of money* to be referred? Perhaps sometimes to one, and sometimes to another; as it is a means of procuring gratifications, either for "the desire of the flesh," for "the desire of the eyes," or for "the pride of life." In any of these cases, money is only pursued in order to a farther end. But it is sometimes pursued for its own sake, without any farther view. One who is properly a miser loves and seeks money for its own sake. He looks no farther, but places his happiness in the acquiring or the possessing of it. And this is a species of idolatry distinct from all the preceding; and indeed, the lowest, basest idolatry of which the human soul is capable. To seek happiness either in gratifying this or any other of the desires above mentioned, is effectually to renounce the true God, and to set up an idol in his place. In a word, so many objects as there are in the world, wherein men seek happiness instead of seeking it in God, so many *idols* they set up in their hearts, so many species of *idolatry* they practise.

18. I would take notice of only one more, which, though it in some measure falls in with several of the preceding, yet, in many respects, is distinct from them all; I mean the idolizing a human creature. Undoubtedly it is the will of God that we should all love one another. It is his will that we should love our relations and our Christian brethren with a peculiar love; and those in particular, whom he has made particularly profitable to our souls. These we are commanded to "love fervently;" yet still "with a pure heart." But is not this "impossible with man?" to retain the strength and tenderness of affection, and yet, without any stain to the soul, with unspotted purity? I do not mean only unspotted by lust. I know this is possible. I know a person may have an unutterable affection for another without any desire of this kind. But is it without idolatry? Is it not loving the creature more than the Creator? Is it not putting a man or woman in the place of God? giving them your heart? Let this be carefully considered, even by those whom God has joined together; by husbands and wives, parents and children. It cannot be denied, that these ought to love one another tenderly: they are commanded so to do. But they are neither commanded nor permitted to love one another idolatrously. Yet how common is this! How frequently is a husband, a wife, a child, put in the place of God. How many that are accounted good Christians fix their affections on each other, so as to leave no place for God! They seek their happiness in the creature, not in the Creator. One may truly say to the other,

> I view thee, lord and end of my desires.

That is, "I desire nothing more but thee! Thou art the thing that I long for! All my desire is unto thee, and unto the remembrance of thy name." Now, if this is not flat idolatry, I cannot tell what is.

II. Having largely considered what those idols are of which the Apostle speaks, I will come now to inquire (which may be done more briefly) how we may keep ourselves from them.

1. In order to this, I would advise you, First, be deeply convinced that none of them bring happiness; that no thing, no person under the sun, no, nor the amassment of all together, can give any solid, satisfactory happiness to any child of man. The world itself, the giddy, thoughtless world, acknowledge this unawares, while they allow, nay, vehemently maintain, "No man upon earth is contented." The very same observation was made near two thousand years ago:—

> Nemo quam sibi sortem
> Seu ratio dederit, seu fors objecerit, illa
> Contentus vivat.
> Let fortune or let choice the station give
> To man, yet none on earth contented live.

And if no man upon earth is contented, it is certain no man is happy. For whatever station we are in, discontent is incompatible with happiness.

2. Indeed not only the giddy, but the thinking, part of the world allow that no man is contented; the melancholy proofs of which we see on every side, in high and low, rich and poor. And, generally, the more understanding they have, the more discontented they are. For,

> They know with more distinction to complain,
> And have superior sense in feeling pain.

It is true, every one has (to use the cant term of the day, and an excellent one it is) *his hobby-horse*, something that pleases the great boy for a few hours or days, and wherein he *hopes* to be happy! But though

> Hope blooms eternal in the human breast;
> Man never *is*, but always *to be*, blest.

Still he is walking in a vain shadow, which will soon vanish away! So that universal experience, both our own, and that of all our friends and acquaintance, clearly proves, that as God made our hearts for himself, so they cannot rest till they rest in him; that till we acquaint ourselves with him, we cannot be at peace. As "a scorner" of the wisdom of God "seeketh wisdom, and findeth it not;" so a scorner of happiness in God seeketh happiness, but findeth none.

3. When you are thoroughly convinced of this, I advise you, Secondly, stand and consider what you are about. Will you be a fool and a madman all your days? Is it not high time to come to your senses! At length, awake out of sleep, and shake yourself from the dust! Break loose from this miserable idolatry, and "choose the better part!" Steadily resolve to seek happiness where it may be found; where it cannot be sought in vain. Resolve to seek it in the true God, the fountain of all blessedness; and cut off all delay! Straightway put in execution what you have resolved! Seeing "all things are ready," "acquaint thyself now with him, and be at peace."

4. But do not either resolve, or attempt to execute your resolution, trusting in your own strength. If you do, you will be utterly foiled. You are not able to contend with the evil world, much less with your own evil heart; and least of all, with the powers of darkness. Cry, therefore, to the Strong for strength. Under a deep sense of your own weakness and helplessness, trust thou in the Lord Jehovah, in whom is everlasting strength. I advise you to cry to him for repentance in particular; not only for a full consciousness of your own impotence, but for a piercing sense of the exceeding guilt, baseness, and madness of the idolatry that has long swallowed you up. Cry for a thorough knowledge of yourself; of all your sinfulness and guiltiness. Pray that you may be fully discovered to yourself; that you may know yourself as also you are known. When once you are possessed of this genuine conviction, all your idols will lose their charms. And you will wonder, how you could so long lean upon those broken reeds, which had so often sunk under you.

5. What should you ask for next?

"Jesus, now I have lost my all,
Let me upon thy bosom fall!
Now let me see thee in thy vesture dipped in blood!
Now stand in all thy wounds confest,
And wrap me in thy crimson vest!

Hast thou not said, 'If thou canst believe, thou shalt see the glory of God?' Lord, *I would* believe! Help thou mine unbelief. And help me *now!* Help me now to enter into the rest that remaineth for the people of God; for those who give thee their heart, their whole heart; who receive thee as their God and their All. O thou that art fairer than the children of men, full of grace are thy lips! Speak that I may see thee! And as the shadows flee before the sun, so let all my idols vanish at thy presence!"

6. From the moment that you begin to experience this, fight the good fight of faith; take the kingdom of heaven by violence! Take it as it were by storm! Deny yourself every pleasure that you are not divinely conscious brings you nearer to God. Take up your cross daily: Regard no pain, if it lies in your way to him. If you are called thereto, scruple not to pluck out the right eye, and to cast it from you. Nothing is impossible to him that believeth: You can do all things through Christ that strengtheneth you. Do valiantly; and stand fast in the liberty wherewith Christ hath made you free. Yea, go on in his name, and in the power of his might, till you "know all that love of God that passeth knowledge:" And then you have only to wait till he shall call you into his everlasting kingdom!

79.* ON DISSIPATION

"This I speak—that ye may attend upon the Lord without distraction."

1 Cor. 7:35.

1. Almost in every part of our nation, more especially in the large and populous towns, we hear a general complaint among sensible persons, of the still increasing *dissipation*. It is observed to diffuse itself more and more, in the court, the city, and the country. From the continual mention which is made of this, and the continual declamations against it, one would naturally imagine that a word so commonly used was perfectly understood. Yet it may be doubted whether it be or no. Nay, we may very safely affirm that few of those who frequently use the term understand what it means. One reason of this is, that, although the thing has been long among us, especially since the time of King Charles the Second (one of the most dissipated mortals that ever breathed,) yet the word is not of long standing. It was hardly heard of fifty years ago; and not much before the present reign. So lately has it been imported: And yet it is so in every one's mouth, that it is already worn threadbare; being one of the cant words of the day.

2. Another reason why it is so little understood may be, that among the numberless writers that swarm about us, there is not one (at least whom I have seen) that has published so much as a sixpenny pamphlet concerning it. We have, indeed, one short Essay upon the subject: But exceeding few have seen it, as it stands in the midst of a volume of Essays, the author of which is little known in the world. And even this is so far from going to the bottom of the subject that it only slightly glances over it; and does not so much as give us one definition of dissipation (which I looked narrowly for) from the beginning to the end.

3. We are accustomed to speak of dissipation, as having respect chiefly, if not wholly, to the outward behaviour; to the manner of life. But it is within before it appears without: It is in the heart, before it is seen in the outward conversation. There must be a dissipated spirit, before there is a dissipated manner of life. But what is dissipation of spirit? This is the first and the grand inquiry.

4. God created all things for himself; more especially all intelligent spirits. (And indeed it seems that intelligence, in some kind or degree, is inseparable from spiritual beings; that intelligence is as essential to spirits as extension is to matter.)

---

* [text from the 1872 edition]

He made those more directly for himself, to know, love, and enjoy him. As the sun is the centre of the solar system, so (as far as we may compare material things with spiritual) we need not scruple to affirm that God is the centre of spirits. And as long as they are united to Him, created spirits are at rest: They are at rest so long, and no longer, as they "attend upon the Lord without distraction."

5. This expression of the Apostle (not to encumber ourselves at present with the particular occasion of his speaking it) is exceeding peculiar: *Pros to euprosedron toi Kyrioi*. The word which we render, *attend upon*, literally means sitting in a good posture for hearing. And therein St. Paul undoubtedly alluded to Mary sitting at the Masters feet. (Luke 10:39.) Meantime, Martha was *cumbered* with much serving: was *distracted, dissipated; periespato*. It is the very expression from whence St. Paul takes the word which we render, *without distraction*.

6. And even as much serving dissipated the thoughts of Martha, and distracted her from attending to her Lords words, so a thousand things which daily occur are apt to dissipate our thoughts, and distract us from attending to his voice who is continually speaking to our hearts: I mean, to all that listen to his voice. We are encompassed on all sides with persons and things that tend to draw us from our centre. Indeed, every creature, if we are not continually on our guard, will draw us from our Creator. The whole visible world, all we see, hear, or touch, all the objects either of our senses or understanding, have a tendency to dissipate our thoughts from the invisible world; and to distract our minds from attending to him who is both the Author and end of our being.

7. This is the more easily done, because we are all by nature *atheoi, Atheists*, in the world; and that in so high a degree that it requires no less than an almighty power to counteract that tendency to dissipation which is in every human spirit, and restore the capacity of attending to God, and fixing itself on him. For this cannot be done till we are new creatures; till we are created anew in Christ Jesus; till the same power which made the world make us a "clean heart, and renew a right spirit within us."

8. But who is he that is thus renewed? He that believeth in the name of the Son of God. He alone that believeth on the Lord Jesus Christ is thus "born of God." It is by this faith alone, that he is "created anew in," or through, "Christ Jesus;" that he is restored to the image of God wherein he was created, and again centred in God; or, as the Apostle expresses it, "joined to the Lord in one spirit." Yet even then the believer may find in himself the remains of that carnal mind, that natural tendency to rest in created good, to acquiesce in visible things, which, without continual care, will press down his soul, and draw him from his Creator. Herein the world, the men that know not God, will never fail to join; at some times with design, and at other times perhaps without design: For their very spirit is infectious, and insensibly changes ours into its own likeness. And we may be well assured, the prince of this world, the devil, will assist them with all his might. He will labour with all his strength, and, what is far more dangerous, with all his subtlety, if by any means he may draw us away from our simplicity towards Christ; from our simple adherence to him; from our union with him, through whom we are also united in one spirit to the Father.

9. But nothing is more certain than this,—that though he may tempt the strongest believer to give up his simplicity toward Christ, and scatter his thoughts and desires among worldly objects; yet he cannot force even the weakest: For the grace of God is still sufficient for him. The same grace which at first united him to God is able to continue that happy union, in spite of all the rage, and all the strength, and all the subtlety of the enemy. God has never left himself without witness that he has power to deliver them that trust in him, as out of every temptation that can assault them, so out of this in particular. He has still a little flock who do in fact, "attend upon him without distraction;" who, cleaving to him with full purpose, are not dissipated from him, no, not for a moment; but "rejoice evermore, pray without ceasing, and in everything give thanks."

10. But so far as any one yields to this temptation, so far he is *dissipated*. The original word properly signifies to *disperse*, or *scatter*. So the sun dissipates, that is, scatters, the clouds; the wind dissipates, or scatters, the dust; and, by an easy metaphor, our thoughts are said to be dissipated, when they are irregularly scattered up and down. In like manner, our desires are dissipated, when they are unhinged from God, their proper centre, and scattered to and fro among the poor, perishing, unsatisfying things of the world. And, indeed, it may be said of every man that is a stranger to the grace of God, that all his passions are dissipated,—

> Scatter'd o'er all the earth abroad,
> Immeasurably far from GOD.

11. Distraction, in St. Paul's sense, is nearly allied to, or rather the same with, dissipation: Consequently, to attend upon the Lord without distraction, is the same as to attend upon the Lord without dissipation. But whenever the mind is unhinged from God, it is so far dissipated or distracted. Dissipation then, in general, may be defined, "the uncentring the soul from God." And whatever uncentres the mind from God does properly dissipate us.

12. Hence we may easily learn what is the proper, direct meaning of that common expression,—*a dissipated man*. He is a man that is separated from God; that is disunited from his centre, whether this be occasioned by hurry of business, by seeking honour or preferment, or by fondness for diversions, for silly pleasures, so called, or for any trifle under the sun. The vulgar, it is true, commonly confine this character to those who are violently attached to women, gaming, drinking; to dancing, balls, races, or the poor, childish diversion of "running foxes and hares out of breath." But it equally belongs to the serious fool who forgets God by a close attention to any worldly employment, suppose it were of the most elegant or the most important kind. A man may be as much dissipated from God by the study of the mathematics or astronomy, as by fondness for cards or hounds. Whoever is habitually inattentive to the presence and will of his Creator, he is a dissipated man.

13. Hence we may likewise learn that a dissipated life is not barely that of a powdered beau, of a petit-maitre, a gamester, a woman-hunter, a playhouse-hunter, a fox-hunter, or a shatter-brain of any kind; but the life of an honourable statesman, a gentleman, or a merchant, that is "without God in the world." Agreeably to this, a *dissipated age* (such as is the present, perhaps beyond all that ever were, at least, that are recorded in history) is an age wherein God is generally forgotten. And *a dissipated nation* (such as England is at present in a superlative degree) is a nation, a vast majority of which have not God "in all their thoughts."

14. A plain consequence of these observations is, (what some may esteem a paradox,) that *dissipation*, in the full, general meaning of the word, is the very same thing with *ungodliness*. The name is new; but the thing is, undoubtedly almost as old as the creation. And this is, at present, the peculiar glory of England, wherein it is not equalled by any nation under heaven. We therefore speak an unquestionable truth when we say, there is not on the face of the earth another nation (at least, that we ever heard of) so perfectly *dissipated* and *ungodly*; not only so totally "without God in the world," but so openly setting him at defiance. There never was an age that we read of in history, since Julius Caesar, since Noah, since Adam, wherein dissipation or ungodliness did so generally prevail, both among high and low, rich and poor.

15. But still, blessed be God!—

> All are not lost: There be who faith
> Prefer, and piety to God!

There are some, I trust more than seven thousand, yea, or ten times that number, in England, who have not yet bowed either their knee or their heart to the god of this world; who, cleaving close to the God of heaven, are not borne away by the flood, by the general, the almost universal, torrent of dissipation or ungodliness. They are not of the mind of gentle Crispus,—

> Qui nunquam direxit brachia contra
> Torrentem,—

"who never attempted to swim against the stream." They dare swim against the stream. Each of them can truly say,

> Nec me, qui caetera, vincit
> Impetus, et rapido contrarius evehor orbi.

[The following is Addison's translation of this quotation from Ovid:—

> "I steer against their motions; nor am I
> Borne back by all the current of the sky."—Edit.]

If they cannot turn the tide back, they can at least bear an open testimony against it. They are therefore free from the blood of their ungodly countrymen: It must be upon their own head.

16. But by what means may we avoid the being carried away by the overflowing stream of dissipation? It is not difficult for those who believe the Scripture to give an answer to this question. Now, I really believe the Bible to be the Word of God; and on that supposition I answer, The radical cure of all dissipation is, the "faith that worketh by love." If, therefore, you would be free from this evil disease, first, "continue steadfast in the faith;" in that faith which brings

"the Spirit of adoption, crying in your heart, Abba, Father;" whereby you are enabled to testify, "The life which I now live, I live by faith in the Son of God; who loved me, and gave himself for me." By this faith you "see him that is invisible, and set the Lord always before you." Next, "building yourselves up in your most holy faith, keep yourselves in the love of God, waiting for the mercy of our Lord Jesus Christ unto everlasting life." And as long as you walk by this rule, you will be superior to all dissipation.

17. How exactly does this agree (though there is a difference in the expression) with that observation of pious Kempis! "Simplicity and purity are the two wings which lift the soul up to heaven. Simplicity is in the intention, purity in the affection." For what is this but (in the Apostle's language) simple "faith working by love?" By that simplicity you always see God, and by purity you love him. What is it, but having (as one of the ancients speaks) "the loving eye of the soul fixed upon God?" And as long as your soul is in this posture, dissipation can have no place.

18. It is with great judgment, therefore, that great and good Bishop Taylor, in his "Rules of Holy Living and Dying," (of whom Bishop Warburton, a person not very prone to commend, used to say, "I have no conception of a greater genius on earth than Dr. Jeremy Taylor,") premises to all his other rules those concerning purity of intention. And has he not the authority of our Lord himself so to do? who lays it down as an universal maxim, "If thine eye be single, thy whole body shall be full of light." Singly aim at God. In every step thou takest, eye Him alone. Pursue one thing: Happiness in knowing, in loving, in serving God. Then shall thy soul be full of light: Full of the light of the glory of God; of his glorious love, shining upon thee from the face of Jesus Christ.

19. Can anything be a greater help to universal holiness, than the continually seeing the light of his glory? It is no wonder, then, that so many wise and good men have recommended, to all who desire to be truly religious, the exercise of the presence of God. But in doing this, some of those holy men seem to have fallen into one mistake: (Particularly, an excellent writer of our own country, in his letters concerning "The Spirit of Prayer:") They put men, wholly unawakened, unconvinced of sin, upon this exercise, at their very entrance into religion; whereas this certainly should not be the first, but rather one of the last things. They should begin with repentance; the knowledge of themselves; of their sinfulness, guilt, and helplessness. They should be instructed next, to seek peace with God, through our Lord Jesus Christ. Then let them be taught to retain what they have received; to "walk in the light of his countenance;" yea, to "walk in the light, as he is in the light," without any darkness at all; till "the blood of Jesus Christ cleanseth" them "from all sin."

20. It was from a full conviction of the absolute necessity there is of a Christian's setting the Lord always before him that a set of young gentlemen in Oxford, who, many years ago, used to spend most of their evenings together, in order to assist each other in working out their salvation, placed that question first in their scheme of daily self-examination: "Have I been *simple* and *recollected* in all I said or did?" Have I been *simple?*—That is, setting the Lord always before me,

and doing everything with a single view of pleasing him?—*Recollected*?—that is, quickly gathering in my scattered thoughts; recovering my simplicity, if I had been in any wise drawn from it by men, or devils, or my own evil heart? By this means they were preserved from dissipation, and were enabled, each of them, to say, "By the grace of God, *this one thing I do*: (at least, it is my constant aim:) I see God, I love God, I serve God. I glorify him with my body and with my spirit."

21. The same thing seems to be intended by two uncommon words which are frequently found in the writings of those pious men who are usually styled Mystics. I mean, *Introversion*, and *Extroversion*. "Examine yourselves," says St. Paul to the Corinthians, and in them to the Christians of all ages; "know ye not that Christ is in you, except ye be reprobates?" that is, unbelievers, unable to bear the touchstone of God's word. Now, the attending to the voice of Christ within you is what they term *Introversion*. The turning the eye of the mind from him to outward things they call *Extroversion*. By this your thoughts wander from God, and you are properly dissipated: Whereas by introversion you may be always sensible of his loving presence; you continually hearken to whatever it pleases your Lord to say to your heart: And if you continually listen to his inward voice, you will be kept from all dissipation.

22. We may, Lastly, learn hence, what judgment to form of what is frequently urged in favour of the English nation, and of the present age; namely, that, in other respects, England stands on a level with other nations, and the present age stands upon a level with any of the preceding: Only it is allowed we are more *dissipated* than our neighbours; and this age is more dissipated than the preceding ages. Nay, if this is allowed, all is allowed. It is allowed that this nation is worse than any of the neighbouring nations; and that this age is worse, essentially worse, than any of the preceding ages. For as dissipation or ungodliness is the parent of all sin; of all unrighteousness; of unmercifulness, injustice, fraud, perfidy; of every possible evil temper, evil word, or evil action; so it, in effect, comprises them all. Whatsoever things are impure, whatsoever things are of evil report, whatsoever things are unholy; if there be any vice; all these are included in ungodliness, usually termed dissipation. Let not, therefore, any lover of virtue and truth say one word in favour of this monster: Let no lover of mankind once open his mouth to extenuate the guilt of it. Abhor it, as you would abhor the devil, whose offspring and likeness it is! Abhor it, as you would abhor the extinction of all virtue, and the universal prevalence of an earthly, sensual, devilish spirit; and flee from it as you would flee (if you saw it open before you) from the lake of fire burning with brimstone!

80.* ON FRIENDSHIP WITH THE WORLD

"Ye adulterers and adulteresses, know ye not that the friendship of this world is enmity with God? Whosoever therefore desireth to be a friend of the world is an enemy of God."

1. There is a passage in St. Paul's Epistle to the Romans, which has been often supposed to be of the same import with this: "Be not conformed to this world:" (Rom. 12:2:) But it has little or no relation to it; it speaks of quite another thing. Indeed the supposed resemblance arises merely from the use of the word *world* in both places. This naturally leads us to think that St. Paul means by *conformity to the world*, the same which St. James means by *friendship with the world*: whereas they are entirely different things, as the words are quite different in the original: for St. Paul's word is *aion* St. James's is *kosmos*. However, the words of St. Paul contain an important direction to the children of God. As if he had said, "Be not conformed to either the wisdom, or the spirit, or the fashions *of the age*, of either the unconverted Jews, or the Heathens, among whom ye live. You are called to show, by the whole tenor of your life and conversation, that you are 'renewed in the spirit of your mind', after the image of him that created you;' and that your rule is not the example or will of man, but 'the good, and acceptable, and perfect will of God.' "

2. But it is not strange, that St. James's caution against friendship with the world should be so little understood, even among Christians. For I have not been able to learn that any author, ancient or modern, has wrote upon the subject: No, not (so far as I have ever observed) for sixteen or seventeen hundred years. Even that excellent writer, Mr. Law, who has treated so well many other subjects, has not, in all his practical treatises, wrote one chapter upon it; no, nor said one word, that I remember, or given one caution, against it. I never heard one sermon preached upon it either before the University or elsewhere. I never was in any company where the conversation turned explicitly upon it even for one hour.

3. Yet are there very few subjects of so deep importance; few that so nearly concern the very essence of religion, the life of God in the soul; the continuance and increase, or the decay, yea, extinction of it. From the want of instruction in this respect the most melancholy consequences have followed. These indeed have not affected those who were still dead in trespasses and sins; but they have fallen heavy upon many of those who were truly alive to God. They have affected many of those called Methodists in particular; perhaps more than any other people. For want of understanding this advice of the Apostle, (I hope rather than from any contempt of it,) many among them are sick, spiritually sick, and many sleep, who were once thoroughly awakened. And it is well if they awake any more till their souls are required of them. It has appeared difficult to me to account for what I have frequently observed: many who were once greatly alive to God, whose conversation was in heaven, who had their affections on things above, not on things of the earth; though they walked in all the ordinances of God, though they still abounded in good works, and abstained from all known sin, yea, and from the appearance of evil; yet they gradually and insensibly decayed; (like Jonah's gourd, when the worm ate the root of it;) insomuch that they are less alive to God now, than they

---

* [text of the 1872 edition]

were ten, twenty, or thirty years ago. But it is easily accounted for, if we observe, that as they increased in goods, they increased in *friendship with the world;* Which, indeed, must always be the case, unless the mighty power of God interpose. But in the same proportion as they increased in this, the life of God in their soul decreased.

4. Is it strange that it should decrease, if those words are really found in the oracles of God: "Ye adulterers and adulteresses, know ye not that the friendship of the world is enmity with God?" What is the meaning of these words? Let us seriously consider. And may God open the eyes of our understanding; that, in spite of all the mist wherewith the wisdom of the world would cover us, we may discern what is the good and acceptable will of God!

5. Let us, First, consider, what it is which the Apostle here means by *the world.* He does not here refer to this outward frame of things, termed in Scripture, heaven and earth; but to the inhabitants of the earth, the children of men, or at least, the greater part of them. But what part? This is fully determined both by our Lord himself, and by his beloved disciple. First, by our Lord himself. His words are, "If the world hate you, ye know that it hated me before it hated you. If ye were of the world, the world would love its own: But because ye are not of the world, but I have chosen you out of the world, therefore the world hateth you. If they have persecuted me, they will also persecute you. And all these things will they do unto you, because they know not him that sent me." (John 15:18.) You see here *"the world"* is placed on one side, and *those who "are not of the world"* on the other. They whom God has "chosen out of the world," namely, by "sanctification of the Spirit, and belief of the truth," are set in direct opposition to those whom he hath not so chosen. Yet again: Those "who know not him that sent me," saith our Lord, who know not God, they are *"the world."*

6. Equally express are the words of the beloved disciple: "Marvel not, my brethren, if the world hate you: We know that we have passed from death unto life, because we love the brethren." (1 John 3:13, 14.) As if he had said, "You must not expect any should love you, but those that have 'passed from death unto life.' " It follows, those that are not passed from death unto life, that are not alive to God, are *"the world."* The same we may learn from those words in the fifth chapter, verse 19, "We know that we are of God, and the whole world lieth in the wicked one." [1 John 5:19] Here *"the world"* plainly means, those that are not of God, and who, consequently "Lie in the wicked one."

7. Those, on the contrary, *are of God,* who love God, or at least "fear him, and keep his commandments." This is the lowest character of those that "are of God;" who are not properly sons, but servants; who depart from evil, and study to do good, and walk in all his ordinances, because they have the fear of God in their heart, and a sincere desire to please him. Fix in your heart this plain meaning of the terms, *"the world;"* those who do not thus fear God. Let no man deceive you with vain words: It means neither more nor less than this.

8. But understanding the term in this sense, what kind of friendship may we have with the world? We may, we ought, to love them as ourselves; (for they also are included in the word *neighbour;*) to bear them real good-will; to desire their happiness, as sincerely as we desire the happiness of our own souls; yea, we are in a sense to honour them, (seeing we are directed by the Apostle to "honour all men,") as the creatures of God; nay, as immortal spirits, who are capable of knowing, of loving, and of enjoying him to all eternity. We are to honour them as redeemed by his blood who "tasted death for every man." We are to bear them tender compassion when we see them forsaking their own mercies, wandering from the path of life, and hastening to everlasting destruction. We are never willingly to grieve their spirits, or give them any pain; but, on the contrary, to give them all the pleasure we innocently can; seeing we are to "please all men for their good." We are never to aggravate their faults; but willingly to allow all the good that is in them.

9. We may, and ought, to speak to them on all occasions in the most kind and obliging manner we can. We ought to speak no evil of them when they are absent, unless it be absolutely necessary; unless it be the only means we know of preventing their doing hurt: Otherwise we are to speak of them with all the respect we can, without transgressing the bounds of truth. We are to behave to them, when present, with all courtesy, showing them all the regard we can without countenancing them in sin. We ought to do them all the good that is in our power, all they are willing to us receive from us; following herein the example of the universal Friend, our Father which is in heaven, who, till they will condescend to receive greater blessings, gives them such as they are willing to accept; "causing his sun to rise on the evil and the good, and sending" his "rain on the just and on the unjust."

10. "But what kind of friendship is it which we may not have with the world? May we not converse with ungodly men at all? Ought we wholly to avoid their company?" By no means. The contrary of this has been allowed already. If we were not to converse with them at all, "we must needs go out of the world." Then we could not show them those offices of kindness which have been already mentioned. We may, doubtless, converse with them, First, on business; in the various purposes of this life, according to that station therein, wherein the providence of God has placed us; Secondly, when courtesy requires it; only we must take great care not to carry it too far: Thirdly, when we have a reasonable hope of doing them good. But here too we have an especial need of caution, and of much prayer; otherwise, we may easily burn ourselves, in striving to pluck other brands out of the burning.

11. We may easily hurt our own souls, by sliding into a close attachment to any of them that know not God. This is the *friendship* which is "enmity with God:" We cannot be too jealous over ourselves, lest we fall into this deadly snare; lest we contract, or ever we are aware, a love of *complacence* or *delight* in them. Then only do we tread upon sure ground, when we can say with the Psalmist, "All my delight is in the saints that are upon earth, and in such as excel in virtue." We should have no *needless* conversations with them. It is our duty and our wisdom to be no oftener and no longer with

them than is strictly necessary. And during the whole time we have need to remember and follow the example of him that said, "I kept my mouth as it were with a bridle while the ungodly was in my sight." We should enter into no sort of connexion with them, farther than is absolutely necessary. When Jehoshaphat forgot this, and formed a connexion with Ahab, what was the consequence? He first lost his substance: "The ships" they sent out "were broken at Ezion-geber." And when he was not content with this warning, as well as that of the prophet Micaiah, but would go up with him to Ramoth-Gilead, he was on the point of losing his life.

12. Above all, we should tremble at the very thought of entering into a marriage-covenant, the closest of all others, with any person who does not love, or at least, fear God. This is the most horrid folly, the most deplorable madness, that a child of God can possibly plunge into; as it implies every sort of connexion with the ungodly which a Christian is bound in conscience to avoid. No wonder, then, it is so flatly forbidden of God; that the prohibition is so absolute and peremptory: "Be not unequally yoked with an unbeliever." Nothing can be more express. Especially, if we understand by the word *unbeliever*, one that is so far from being a believer in the gospel sense,—from being able to say, "The life which I now live, I live by faith in the Son of God, who loved me, and gave himself for me"—that he has not even the faith of a servant: He does not "fear God and work righteousness."

13. But for what reasons is the friendship of the world so absolutely prohibited? Why are we so strictly required to abstain from it? For two general reasons: First, because it is a sin in itself: Secondly, because it is attended with most dreadful consequences. First, it is a sin in itself; and indeed, a sin of no common dye. According to the oracles of God, friendship with the world is no less than spiritual adultery. All who are guilty of it are addressed by the Holy Ghost in those terms: "Ye adulterers and adulteresses." It is plainly violating of our marriage contract with God, by loving the creature more than the Creator; in flat contradiction to that kind command, "My son, give me thine heart."

14. It is a sin of the most heinous nature, as not only implying ignorance of God, and forgetfulness of him, or inattention to him, but positive "enmity against God." It is openly, palpably such. "Know ye not," says the Apostle, can ye possibly be ignorant of this, so plain, so undeniable a truth, "that the friendship of the world is enmity against God?" Nay, and how terrible is the inference which he draws from hence! "Therefore, whosoever will be a friend of the world,"—(the words, properly rendered, are, *Whosoever desireth to be a friend of the world*,) of men who know not God, whether he attain it or not,—is, *ipso facto*, constituted an enemy of God. This very *desire*, whether successful or not, gives him a right to that appellation.

15. And as it is a sin, a very heinous sin, in itself, so it is attended with the most dreadful consequences. It frequently entangles men again in the commission of those sins from which "they were clean escaped." It generally makes them "partakers of other men's sins," even those which they do not commit themselves. It gradually abates their abhorrence and dread of sin in general, and thereby prepares them for falling an easy prey to any strong temptation. It lays them open to all those sins of omission whereof their worldly acquaintance are guilty. It insensibly lessens their exactness in private prayer, in family duty, in fasting, in attending public service, and partaking of the Lord's Supper. The indifference of those that are near them, with respect to all these, will gradually influence them: Even if they say not one word (which is hardly to be supposed) to recommend their own practice, yet their example speaks, and is many times of more force than any other language. By this example, they are unavoidably betrayed, and almost continually, into unprofitable, yea, and uncharitable, conversation; till they no longer "set a watch before their mouth, and keep the door of their lips;" till they can join in backbiting, tale-bearing, and evil-speaking without any check of conscience; having so frequently grieved the Holy Spirit of God, that he no longer reproves them for it: Insomuch that their discourse is not now, as formerly, "seasoned with salt, and meet to minister grace to the hearers."

16. But these are not all the deadly consequences that result from familiar intercourse with unholy men. It not only hinders them from ordering their conversation aright, but directly tends to corrupt the heart. It tends to create or increase in us all that pride and self-sufficiency, all that fretfulness to resent, yea, every irregular passion and wrong disposition, which are indulged by their companions. It gently leads them into habitual self-indulgence, and unwillingness to deny themselves; into unreadiness to bear or take up any cross; into a softness and delicacy; into evil shame, and the fear of man, that brings numberless snares. It draws them back into the love of the world; into foolish and hurtful desires; into the desire of the flesh, the desire of the eyes, and the pride of life, till they are swallowed up in them. So that, in the end, the last state of these men is far worse than the first.

17. If the children of God will connect themselves with the men of the world, though the latter should not endeavour to make them like themselves, (which is a supposition by no means to be made,) yea, though they should neither design nor desire it; yet they will actually do it, whether they design it, and whether they endeavour it, or no. I know not how to account for it, but it is a real fact, that their very spirit is infectious. While you are near them, you are apt to catch their spirit, whether they will or no. Many physicians have observed, that not only the plague, and putrid or malignant fevers, but almost every disease men are liable to, are more or less infectious. And undoubtedly so are all spiritual diseases, only with great variety. The infection is not so swiftly communicated by some as it is by others. In either case, the person already diseased does not desire or design to infect another. The man who has the plague does not desire or intend to communicate his distemper to you. But you are not therefore safe: So keep at a distance, or you will surely be infected. Does not experience show that the case is the same with the diseases of the mind? Suppose the proud, the vain, the passionate, the wanton, do not desire or design to infect *you* with their own distempers; yet it is best to keep at a distance from them. You are not safe if you come too near

them. You will perceive (it is well if it be not too late) that their very breath is infectious. It has been lately discovered that there is an atmosphere surrounding every human body, which naturally affects everyone that comes within the limits of it. Is there not something analogous to this, with regard to a human spirit? If you continue long within their atmosphere, so to speak, you can hardly escape the being infected. The contagion spreads from soul to soul, as well as from body to body, even though the persons diseased do not intend or desire it. But can this reasonably be supposed? Is it not a notorious truth, that men of the world (exceeding few excepted) eagerly desire to make their companions like themselves? yea and use every means, with their utmost skill and industry, to accomplish their desire. Therefore, fly for your life! Do not play with the fire, but escape before the flames kindle upon you.

18. But how many are the pleas for friendship with the world! And how strong are the temptations to it! Such of these as are the most dangerous, and, at the same time, most common, we will consider.

To begin with one that is the most dangerous of all others, and, at the same time, by no means uncommon. "I grant," says one, "the person I am about to marry is not a religious person. She does not make any pretensions to it. She has little thought about it. But she is a beautiful creature. She is extremely agreeable, and, I think, will make me a lovely companion."

This is a snare indeed! Perhaps one of the greatest that human nature is liable to. This is such a temptation as no power of man is able to overcome. Nothing less than the mighty power of God can make a way for you to escape from it. And this can work a complete deliverance: His grace is sufficient for you. But not unless you are a worker together with him: Not unless you deny yourself, and take up your cross. And what you do, you must do at once! Nothing can be done by degrees. Whatever you do in this important case must be done at one stroke. If it is to be done at all, you must at once cut off the right hand, and cast it from you! Here is no time for conferring with flesh and blood! At once, conquer or perish!

19. Let us turn the tables. Suppose a woman that loves God is addressed by an agreeable man; genteel, lively, entertaining; suitable to her in all other respects, though not religious: What should she do in such a case? What she *should* do, if she believes the Bible, is sufficiently clear. But what *can* she do? Is not this

> A test for human frailty too severe?

Who is able to stand in such a trial? Who can resist such a temptation? None but one that holds fast the shield of faith, and earnestly cries to the Strong for strength. None but one that gives herself to watching and prayer, and continues therein with all perseverance. If she does this, she will be a happy witness, in the midst of an unbelieving world, that as "all things are possible with God," so all "things are possible to her that believeth."

20. But either a man or woman may ask, "What, if the person who seeks my acquaintance be a person of a strong natural understanding, cultivated by various learning? May not I gain much useful knowledge by a familiar intercourse with him? May I not learn many things from him, and much improve my own understanding?" Undoubtedly you may improve your own understanding, and you may gain much knowledge. But still, if he has not at least the fear of God, your loss will be far greater than your gain. For you can hardly avoid decreasing in holiness as much as you increase in knowledge. And if you lose one degree of inward or outward holiness, all the knowledge you gain will be no equivalent.

21. "But his fine and strong understanding, improved by education, is not his chief recommendation. He has more valuable qualifications than these: He is remarkably good humoured: He is of a compassionate, humane spirit; and has much generosity in his temper." On these very accounts, if he does not fear God, he is infinitely more dangerous. If you converse intimately with a person of this character, you will surely drink into his spirit. It is hardly possible for you to avoid stopping just where he stops. I have found nothing so difficult in all my life as to converse with men of this kind (*good sort of men*, as they are commonly called) without being hurt by them. O beware of them! Converse with them just as much as business requires, and no more: Otherwise (though you do not feel any present harm, yet,) by slow and imperceptible degrees, they will attach you again to earthly things, and damp the life of God in your soul.

22. It may be, the persons who are desirous of your acquaintance, though they are not experienced in religion, yet understand it well, so that you frequently reap advantage from their conversation. If this be really the case, (as I have known a few instances of the kind,) it seems you may converse with them; only very sparingly and very cautiously; Otherwise you will lose more of your spiritual life than all the knowledge you gain is worth.

23. "But the persons in question are useful to me, in carrying on my temporal business. Nay, on many occasions, they are necessary to me; so that I could not well carry it on without them." Instances of this kind frequently occur. And this is doubtless a sufficient reason for having some intercourse, perhaps frequently, with men that do not fear God. But even this is by no means a reason for your contracting an intimate acquaintance with them. And you here need to take the utmost care, "lest even by that converse with them which is necessary, while your fortune in the world increases, the grace of God should decrease in your soul."

24. There may be one more plausible reason given for some intimacy with an unholy man. You may say, "I have been helpful to him. I have assisted him when he was in trouble. And he remembers it with gratitude. He esteems and loves *me*, though he does not love God. Ought I not then to love *him*? Ought I not to return love for love? Do not even Heathens and publicans so?" I answer, You should certainly return love for love; but it does not follow that you should have any intimacy with him. That would be at the peril of your soul. Let your love give itself vent in constant and fervent prayer Wrestle with God for him. But let not your love for him carry you so far as to weaken, if not destroy, your own soul.

25. "But must I not be intimate with my relations; and that whether they fear God or not? Has not his providence recommended these to me?" Undoubtedly it has: But there are relations nearer or more distant. The nearest relations are husbands and wives. As these have taken each other for better for worse, they must make the best of each other; seeing, as God has joined the together, none can put them asunder; unless in case of adultery, or when the life of one or the other is in imminent danger. Parents are almost as nearly connected with their children. You cannot part with them while they are young; it being your duty to "train them up," with all care, "in the way wherein they should go." How frequently you should converse with them when they are grown up is to be determined by Christian prudence. This also will determine how long it is expedient for children, if it be at their own choice, to remain with their parents. In general, if they do not fear God, you should leave them as soon as is convenient. But wherever you are, take care (if it be in your power) that they do not want the necessaries or conveniences of life. As for all other relations, even brothers or sisters, if they are of the world you are under no obligation, to be intimate with them: You may be civil and friendly at a distance.

26. But allowing that "the friendship of the world is enmity against God," and consequently, that it is the most excellent way, indeed the only way to heaven, to avoid all intimacy with worldly men; yet who has resolution to walk therein? who even of those that love or fear God? for these only are concerned in the present question. A few I have known who, even in this respect, were lights in a benighted land; who did not and would not either contract or continue any acquaintance with persons of the most refined and improved understanding, and the most engaging tempers, merely because they were of the world, because they were not alive to God: Yea, though they were capable of improving them in knowledge, or of assisting them in business: Nay, though they admired and esteemed them for that very religion which they did not themselves experience: A case one would hardly think possible. but of which there are many instances at this day. Familiar intercourse even with these they steadily and resolutely refrain from, for conscience sake.

27. Go thou and do likewise, whosoever thou art that art a child of God by faith! Whatever it cost, flee spiritual adultery. Have no friendship with the world. However tempted thereto by profit or pleasure, contract no intimacy with worldly-minded men. And if thou hast contracted any such already, break it off without delay. Yea, if thy ungodly friend be dear to thee as a right eye, or useful as a right hand, yet confer not with flesh and blood, but pluck out the right eye, cut off the right hand, and cast them from thee! It is not an indifferent thing. Thy life is at stake; eternal life or eternal death. And is it not better to go into life having one eye or one hand, than having both to be cast into hell-fire? When thou knewest no better, the times of ignorance God winked at. But now thine eyes are opened, now the light is come, walk in the light! Touch not pitch, lest thou be defiled. At all events, "keep thyself pure!"

28. But whatever others do, whether they will hear, or whether they will forbear, hear this, all ye that are called Methodists! However importuned or tempted thereto, have no friendship with the world. Look round, and see the melancholy effects it has produced among your brethren! How many of the mighty are fallen! How many have fallen by this very thing! They would take no warning: They *would* converse, and that intimately, with earthly-minded men, till they "measured back their steps to earth again!" O "come out from among them!" from all unholy men, however harmless they may appear; "and be ye separate:" At least so far as to have no intimacy with them. As your "fellowship is with the Father, and with his Son Jesus Christ;" so let it be with those, and those only, who at least seek the Lord Jesus Christ in sincerity. So "shall ye be," in a peculiar sense, "my sons and my daughters, saith the Lord Almighty."

81. IN WHAT SENSE WE ARE TO LEAVE THE WORLD

"Come out from among them, and be ye separate, saith the Lord, and touch not the unclean thing; and I will receive you, And I will be to you a Father, and ye shall be my sons and daughters, saith the Lord Almighty."
2 Cor. 6:17, 18.

1. How exceeding few in the religious world have duly considered these solemn words! We have read them over and over, but never laid them to heart, or observed that they contain as plain and express a command as any in the whole Bible. And it is to be feared, there are still fewer that understand the genuine meaning of this direction. Numberless persons in England have interpreted it as a command to come out of the Established Church. And in the same sense it has been understood by thousands in the neighboring kingdoms. Abundance of sermons have been preached, and of books wrote, upon this supposition. And indeed many pious men have grounded their separation from the Church chiefly on this text. "God himself," say they, "commands us, 'Come out from among them, and be ye separate.' And it is only upon this condition that he will *receive* us, and we "shall be the sons and daughters of the Lord Almighty."

2. But this interpretation is totally foreign to the design of the Apostle, who is not here speaking of this or that church, but on quite another subject. Neither did the Apostle himself or any of his brethren draw any such inference from the words. Had they done so it would have been a flat contradiction both to the example and precept of their Master. For although the Jewish church was then full as *unclean*, as unholy, both inwardly and outwardly, as any Christian Church now upon earth, yet our Lord constantly attended the service of it. And he directed his followers in this, as in every other respect, to tread in his steps. This is clearly implied in that remarkable passage: "The scribes and Pharisees sit in Moses' seat: All therefore whatsoever they bid you observe, that observe and do; but do not ye after their works: For they say and do not." (Matt. 23:2, 3.) Even though they *themselves say and do not*, though their lives

contradict their doctrines, though they were ungodly men, yet our Lord here not only permits but requires his disciples to hear them. For he requires them to "observe and do what they say." But this could not be if they did not hear them. Accordingly the apostles, as long as they were at Jerusalem, constantly attended the public service. Therefore it is certain these words have no reference to a separation from the Established Church.

3. Neither have they any reference to the direction given by the Apostle in his first Epistle to the Corinthians. The whole passage runs thus: "I wrote unto you in an epistle, not to company with fornicators: Yet not altogether with the fornicators of this world or with the covetous, or extortioners, or with idolaters; for then must ye needs go out of the world. But now I have written unto you, not to keep company, if any man that is called a brother be a fornicator, or covetous, or an idolater, or a railer, or a drunkard, or an extortioner; with such an one, no not to eat." (1 Cor. 5:9–11.) This wholly relates to them that are members of the same Christian community. The Apostle tells them expressly, he does not give this direction, not to company with such and such persons, with regard to the Heathens, or to men in general; and adds this plain reason, "For then must ye needs go out of the world;" you could transact no business in it. "But if any man that is called a brother,"—that is connected with you in the same religious society,—"be a fornicator, or covetous, or an idolater, or a railer, or a drunkard, or an extortioner; with such an one, no not to eat." How important a caution is this! But how little is it observed, even by those that are, in other respects, conscientious Christians! Indeed some parts of it are not easy to be observed, for a plain reason,—they are not easy to be understood. I mean, it is not easy to be understood to whom the characters belong. It is very difficult, for instance, to know, unless in some glaring cases, to whom the character of an *extortioner* or of a *covetous* man belongs. We can hardly know one or the other, without seeming at least to be "busy bodies in other men's matters." And yet the prohibition is as strong concerning converse with these, as with fornicators or adulterers. We can only act in the simplicity of our hearts, without setting up for infallible judges, (still willing to be better informed,) according to the best light we have.

4. But although this direction relates only to our Christian brethren (such, at least, by outward profession;) that in the text is of a far wider extent: it unquestionably relates to all mankind. It clearly requires us to keep at a distance, as far as is practicable, from all ungodly men. Indeed it seems the word which we render *unclean thing, tou akathartou,* might rather be rendered *unclean person;* probably alluding to the ceremonial law which forbade *touching* one that was legally unclean. But even here, were we to understand the expression literally, were we to take the words in the strictest sense, the same absurdity would follow; we must needs, as the Apostle speaks, "go out of the world:" We should not be able to abide in those callings which the providence of God has assigned us. Were we not to converse at all with men of those characters, it would be impossible to transact our temporal business. So that every conscientious Christian would have nothing to do, but to flee into the desert. It would not suffice to turn recluses, to shut ourselves up in monasteries or nunneries; for even then we must have some intercourse with ungodly men, in order to procure the necessaries of life.

5. The words therefore, must necessarily be understood with considerable restriction. They do not prohibit our conversing with any man, good or bad, in the way of worldly business. A thousand occasions will occur, whereon we must converse with them in order to transact those affairs which cannot be done without them. And some of these may require us to have frequent intercourse with drunkards, or fornicators: Yea, sometimes it may be requisite for us to spend a considerable time in their company: Otherwise we should not be able to fulfil the duties of our several callings. Such conversation therefore with men, holy or unholy, is no way contrary to the Apostle's advice.

6. What is it then which the Apostle forbids? First, the conversing with ungodly men when there is no necessity, no providential call, no business, that requires it: Secondly, the conversing with them more frequently than business necessarily requires: Thirdly, the spending more time in their company than is necessary to finish our business: Above all, Fourthly, the choosing ungodly persons, however ingenious or agreeable, to be our ordinary companions, or to be our familiar friends. If any instance of this kind will admit of less excuse than others, it is that which the Apostle expressly forbids elsewhere; the being "unequally yoked with an unbeliever" in marriage; with any person that has not the love of God in their heart, or at least the fear of God before their eyes. I do not know anything that can justify this; neither the sense, wit, or beauty of the person, nor temporal advantage, nor fear of want; no, nor even the command of a parent. For if any parent command what is contrary to the Word of God, the child ought to obey God rather than man.

7. The ground of this prohibition is laid down at large in the preceding verses: "What fellowship hath righteousness with unrighteousness? What communion hath light with darkness? And what concord hath Christ with Belial? Or what part hath he that believeth with an unbeliever?" (Taking that word in the extensive sense, for him that hath neither the love nor fear of God.) "Ye are the temple of the living God: As God hath said, I will dwell in them, and walk in them: And I will be their God, and they shall be my people." It follows, "Wherefore, come out from among them;" the unrighteous, the children of darkness, the sons of Belial, the unbelievers; "and be ye separate, and touch not the unclean thing," or person, "and I will receive you."

8. Here is the sum of this prohibition to have any more intercourse with unholy men than is absolutely necessary. There can be no profitable *fellowship* between the righteous and the unrighteous; as there can be *no communion* between light and darkness,—whether you understand this of natural or of spiritual darkness. As Christ can have *no concord* with *Belial;* so a believer in him can have no concord with an unbeliever. It is absurd to imagine that any true union or concord should be between two persons, while one of them remains in darkness, and the other walks in the light. They are subjects, not only of two separate, but of two opposite

kingdoms. They act upon quite different principles; they aim at quite different ends. It will necessarily follow, that frequently, if not always, they will walk in different paths. How can they walk together, till they are agreed?—until they both serve either Christ or Belial?

9. And what are the consequences of our not obeying this direction? Of our not coming out from among unholy men? Of not being separate from them, but contracting or continuing a familiar intercourse with them? It is probable it will not immediately have any apparent, visible ill consequences. It is hardly to be expected, that it will immediately lead us into any outward sin. Perhaps it may not presently occasion our neglect of any outward duty. It will first sap the foundations of our religion: It will, by little and little damp our zeal for God; it will gently cool that fervency of spirit which attended our first love. If they do not openly oppose anything we say or do, yet their very spirit will, by insensible degrees, affect our spirit, and transfuse into it the same lukewarmness and indifference toward God and the things of God. It will weaken all the springs of our soul, destroy the vigour of our spirit, and cause us more and more to slacken our pace in running the race that is set before us.

10. By the same degrees all needless intercourse with unholy men will weaken our divine evidence and conviction of things unseen: It will dim the eyes of the soul whereby we see Him that is invisible, and weaken our confidence in him. It will gradually abate our "taste of the powers of the world to come;" and deaden that hope which before made us "sit in heavenly places with Christ Jesus." It will imperceptibly cool that flame of love which before enabled us to say, "Whom have I in heaven but thee? And there is none upon earth that I desire beside thee!" Thus it strikes at the root of all vital religion; of our fellowship with the Father and with the Son.

11. By the same degrees, and in the same secret and unobserved manner, it will prepare us to "measure back our steps to earth again". It will lead us softly, to relapse into the love of the world from which we were clean escaped; to fall gently into *the desire of the flesh*; the seeking happiness in the pleasures of sense;—*the desire of the eye*; the seeking happiness in the pleasure of imagination;—*and the pride of life*; the seeking it in pomp, in riches, or in the praise of man. And all this may be done by the assistance of the spirit who "beguiled Eve through his subtlety," before we are sensible of his attack, or are conscious of any loss.

12. And it is not only the love of the world in all its branches which necessarily steals upon us, while we converse with men of a worldly spirit farther than duty requires, but every other evil passion and temper of which the human soul is capable; in particular pride, vanity, censoriousness, evil surmising, proneness to revenge: While, on the other hand levity, gaiety, and dissipation steal upon us and increase continually. We know how all these abound in the men that know not God. And it cannot be but they will insinuate themselves into all who frequently and freely converse with them: They insinuate most deeply into those who are not apprehensive of any danger; and most of all, if they have any particular affection, if they have more love than duty requires, for those who do not love God, with whom they familiarly converse.

13. Hitherto I have supposed that the persons with whom you converse are such as we use to call *good sort of people*; such as are styled, in the cant term of the day, men of *worthy* characters;—one of the silly, insignificant words, that ever came into fashion. I have supposed them to be free from cursing, swearing, profaneness; from Sabbath-breaking and drunkenness; from lewdness, either in word or action; from dishonesty, lying, and slandering: In a word, to be entirely clear from open vice of every kind. Otherwise, whoever has even the fear of God must in any wise keep at a distance from them. But I am afraid I have made a supposition which hardly can be admitted. I am afraid, some of the persons with whom you converse more than business necessarily requires, do not deserve even the character of *good sort of men*,—are not *worthy* of anything but shame and contempt. Do not some of them live in open sin?—in cursing and swearing, drunkenness, or uncleanness? You cannot long be ignorant of this; for they take little pains to hide it. Now, is it not certain, all vice is of an infectious nature? for who can touch pitch and not be defiled? From these, therefore, you ought undoubtedly to flee as from the face of a serpent. Otherwise how soon may "evil communications corrupt good manners!"

14. I have supposed, likewise, that those unholy persons with whom you frequently converse have no desire to communicate their own spirit to *you*, or to induce *you* to follow their example. But this also is a supposition which can hardly be admitted. In many cases their interest may be advanced by your being a partaker of their sins. But supposing interest to be out of the question, does not every man naturally desire, and more or less endeavour, to bring over his acquaintance to his own opinion or party? So that, as all good men desire and endeavour to make others good, like themselves, in like manner all bad men desire and endeavour to make their companions as bad as themselves.

15. But if they do not, if we allow this almost impossible supposition, that they do not desire or use any endeavours to bring you over to their own temper and practice, still it is dangerous to converse with them. I speak not only of openly vicious men, but of all that do not love God, or at least fear him, and sincerely "seek the kingdom of God and his righteousness." Admit, such companions do not endeavour to make you like themselves; does this prove you are in no danger from them? See that poor wretch that is ill of the plague! He does not desire, he does not use the least endeavour, to communicate his distemper to you. Yet have a care! Touch him not! Nay, go not near him, or you know not how soon you may be in just the same condition. To draw the parallel: Though we should suppose the man of the world does not desire, design, or endeavour to communicate his distemper to you, yet touch him not! Come not too near him; for it is not only his reasonings or persuasions that may infect your soul, but his very breath is infectious; particularly to those who are apprehensive of no danger.

16. If conversing freely with worldly-minded men has no other ill effect upon you, it will surely, by imperceptible degrees, make you less heavenly-minded. It will give a bias to your mind which will continually draw your soul to earth. It

will incline you, without your being conscious of it, instead of being wholly transformed in the renewing of your mind, to be again conformed to this world in its spirit, in its maxims, and in its vain conversation. You will fall again into that levity and dissipation of spirit from which you had before clean escaped; into that superfluity of apparel, and into that foolish, frothy, unprofitable conversation, which was an abomination to you when your soul was alive to God. And you will daily decline from that simplicity both of speech and behaviour whereby you once adorned the doctrine of God our Saviour.

17. And if you go thus far in conformity to the world, it is hardly to be expected you will stop here. You will go farther in a short time: Having once lost your footing and begun to slide down, it is a thousand to one, you will not stop till you come to the bottom of the hill; till you fall yourself into some of those outward sins which your companions commit before your eyes or in your hearing. Hereby the dread and horror which struck you at first will gradually abate, till at length you are prevailed upon to follow their example. But suppose they do not lead you into outward sin, if they infect your spirit with pride, anger, or love of the world, it is enough: It is sufficient, without deep repentance, to drown your soul in everlasting perdition; seeing, (abstracted from all outward sin,) "to be carnally-minded is death."

18. But as dangerous as it is to converse familiarly with men that know not God, it is more dangerous still for men to converse with women of that character; as they are generally more insinuating than men, and have far greater power of persuasion; particularly if they are agreeable in their persons, or pleasing in their conversation. You must be more than man, if you can converse with such and not suffer any loss. If you do not feel any foolish or unholy desire; (and who can promise that you shall not?) yet it is scarce possible that you should not feel more or less of an improper softness, which will make you less willing and less able to persist in that habit of denying yourself, and taking up your cross daily, which constitute the character of a good soldier of Jesus Christ. And we know that not only fornicators and adulterers, but even "the soft and effeminate," the delicate followers of a self-denying Master, "shall have no part in the kingdom of Christ and of God."

19. Such are the consequences which must surely, though perhaps slowly, follow the mixing of the children of God with the men of the world. And by this means, more than by any other, yea, than by all others put together, are the people called Methodists likely to lose their strength, and become like other men. It is indeed with a good design, and from a real desire of promoting the glory of God, that many of them admit of familiar conversation with men that know not God. You have a hope of awakening them out of sleep, and persuading them to seek the things that make for their peace. But if, after a competent time of trial, you can make no impression upon them, it will be your wisdom to give them up to God; otherwise you are more likely to receive hurt from them, than to do them any good. For if you do not raise their hearts up to heaven, they will draw yours down to earth.

Therefore, retreat in time, "and come out from among them, and be ye separate."

20. But how may this be done? What is the most easy and effectual method of separating ourselves from unholy men? Perhaps a few advices will make this plain to those that desire to know and do the will of God.

First: Invite no unholy person to your house, unless on some very particular occasion. You may say, "But civility requires this, and sure, religion is no enemy to civility. Nay, the Apostle himself directs us to *be courteous*, as well as to be *pitiful*." I answer, You may be civil, sufficiently civil, and yet keep them at a proper distance. You may be courteous in a thousand instances, and yet stand aloof from them. And it was never the design of the Apostle to recommend any such courtesy as must necessarily prove a snare to the soul.

21. Secondly: On no account accept any invitation from an unholy person. Never be prevailed upon to pay a visit, unless you wish it to be repaid. It may be, a person desirous of your acquaintance will repeat the visit twice or thrice. But if you steadily refrain from returning it, the visitant will soon be tired. It is not improbable, he will be disobliged; and perhaps he will show marks of resentment. Lay your account with this, that when anything of the kind occurs you may neither be surprised nor discouraged. It is better to please God and displease man, than to please man and displease God.

22. Thirdly: it is probable, you were acquainted with men of the world before you yourself knew God. What is best to be done with regard to these? How may you most easily drop their acquaintance? First, allow a sufficient time to try whether you cannot by argument and persuasion, applied at the soft times of address, induce them to choose the better part. Spare no pains! Exert all your faith and love, and wrestle with God in their behalf. If, after all, you cannot perceive that any impression is made upon them, it is your duty gently to withdraw from them, that you be not entangled with them. This may be done in a short time, easily and quietly, by not returning their visits. But you must expect they will upbraid you with haughtiness and unkindness, if not to your face, yet behind your back. And this you can suffer for a good conscience. It is, properly, the reproach of Christ.

23. When it pleased God to give *me* a settled resolution to be, not a *nominal*, but a *real* Christian, (being then about twenty-two years of age,) my acquaintance were as ignorant of God as myself. But there was this difference: I knew my own ignorance; they did not know theirs. I faintly endeavoured to help them; but in vain. Meantime I found, by sad experience, that even their *harmless* conversation, so called, damped all my good resolutions. But how to get rid of them was the question, which I resolved in my mind again and again. I saw no possible way, unless it should please God to remove me to another College. He did so, in a manner utterly contrary to all human probability. I was elected Fellow of a College where I knew not one person. I foresaw, abundance of people would come to see me, either out of friendship, civility, or curiosity; and that I should have offers of acquaintance new and old: But I had now fixed my plan. Entering now, as it were, into a new world, I resolved to have no acquaintance by chance, but by choice; and to choose such

only as I had reason to believe would help me on in my way to heaven. In consequence of this, I narrowly observed the temper and behaviour of all that visited me. I saw no reason to think that the greater part of these truly loved or feared God. Such acquaintance, therefore, I did not choose: I could not expect they would do me any good. Therefore, when any of these came to see me, I behaved as courteously as I could. But to the question, "When will you come to see me?" I returned no answer. When they had come a few times, and found I still declined returning the visit, I saw them no more. And I bless God, this has been my invariable rule for about threescore years. I knew many reflections would follow: But that did not move me; as I knew full well, it was my calling to go "through evil report and good report".

24. I earnestly advise all of you who resolve to be, not *almost*, *but altogether Christians*, to adopt the same plan, however contrary it may be to flesh and blood. Narrowly observe, which of those that fall in your way are like-minded with yourself: Who among them have you reason to believe fears God and works righteousness. Set them down as worthy of your acquaintance: Gladly and freely converse with them at all opportunities. As to all who do not answer that character, gently and quietly let them drop. However good-natured and sensible they may be, they will do you no real service. Nay, if they did not lead you into outward sin, yet they would be a continual clog to your soul, and would hinder your running with vigour and cheerfulness the race that is set before you. And if any of your friends that did once run well "turn back from the holy commandment once delivered to them", first use every method that prudence can suggest, to bring them again into the good way. But if you cannot prevail, let them go, only still commending them unto God in prayer. Drop all familiar intercourse with them, and save your own soul.

25. I advise you, Fourthly, walk circumspectly with regard to your relations. With your parents, whether religious or not, you must certainly converse, if they desire it; and with your brothers and sisters; more especially, if they want your service. I do not know that you are under any such obligation with respect to your more distant relations. Courtesy, indeed, and natural affection, may require that you should visit them sometimes. But if they neither know nor seek God, it should certainly be as seldom as possible. And when you are with them, you should not stay a day longer than decency requires. Again: Whichsoever of them you are with at any time, remember that solemn caution of the Apostle, "Let no corrupt communication" (conversation) "come out of your mouth; but that which is good to the use of edifying, that it may minister grace to the hearers." You have no authority to vary from this rule; otherwise, you "grieve the Holy Spirit of God." And if you keep closely to it, those who have no religion will soon dispense with your company.

26. Thus it is that those who fear or love God should "come out from among" all that do not fear him. Thus in a plain scriptural sense, you should "be separate" from them; from all unnecessary intercourse with them. Yea, "touch not," saith the Lord, "the unclean thing" or person, any farther than necessity requires; "and I will receive you" into the family and household of God. "And I will be unto you a Father;" will embrace you with paternal affection; "and ye shall be unto me sons and daughters, saith the Lord Almighty." The promise is express to all that renounce the company of ungodly men; provided their spirit and conversation are, in other respects, also suitable to their duty. God does here absolutely engage to give them all the blessings he has prepared for his beloved children, both in time and eternity. Let all those, therefore, who have any regard for the favour and the blessing of God, First, beware how they contract any acquaintance, or form any connexion, with ungodly men; any farther than necessary business, or some other providential call, requires: And, Secondly, with all possible speed, all that the nature of the thing will admit, break off all such acquaintance already contracted, and all such connexions already formed. Let no pleasure resulting from such acquaintance, no gain found or expected from such connexions, be of any consideration, when laid in the balance against a clear, positive command of God. In such a case, "pluck out the right eye,"—tear away the most pleasing acquaintance,—"and cast it from thee:" Give up all thought, all design of seeking it again. "Cut off the right hand,"—absolutely renounce the most profitable connexion,—"and cast it from thee." "It is better for thee to enter into life with one eye," or one hand, "than having two, to be cast into hell-fire."

82.* ON TEMPTATION

"There hath no temptation taken you but such as is common to man: And God is faithful, who will not suffer you to be tempted above that ye are able; but will with the temptation also make a way to escape, that ye may be able to bear it."

1 Cor. 10:13.

1. In the foregoing part of the chapter, the Apostle has been reciting, on the one hand, the unparalleled mercies of God to the Israelites; and, on the other, the unparalleled ingratitude of that disobedient and gainsaying people. [1 Cor. 10:1–10] And all these things, as the Apostle observes, "were written for our ensample;" [1 Cor. 10:11] that we might take warning from them, so as to avoid their grievous sins, and escape their terrible punishment. He then adds that solemn and important caution, "Let him that thinketh he standeth, take heed lest he fall." [1 Cor. 10:12]

2. But if we observe these words attentively, will there not appear a considerable difficulty in them? "Let him that thinketh he standeth take heed lest he fall." If a man only *thinks he stands*, he is in no danger of falling. It is not possible that any one should fall, if he only *thinks he stands*. The same difficulty occurs, according to our translation, in those well-known words of our Lord, (the importance of which we may easily learn from their being repeated in the Gospel no less than eight times,) "To him that hath shall be given; but from that hath not, shall be taken away even what

he seemeth to have." "That which he *seemeth to have!*" Nay, if he only *seems to have it*, it is impossible it should taken away. None can take away from another what he only *seems to have*. What a man only seems to have, he cannot possibly lose. This difficulty may, at first, appear impossible to be surmounted. It is really so: It cannot be surmounted, if the common translation be allowed. But if we observe the proper meaning of the original word, the difficulty vanishes away. It may be allowed that the word *dokei* does (sometimes at least, in some authors) mean no more than *to seem*. But I much doubt whether it ever bears that meaning in any part of the inspired writings. By a careful consideration of every text in the New Testament wherein this word occurs, I am fully convinced, that it nowhere lessens, but every where strengthens, the sense of the word to which it is annexed. Accordingly *ho dokei echein*, does not mean, *what he seems to have*, but, on the contrary, *what he assuredly hath*. And so *ho dokon estanai*, not *he that seemeth to stand*, or he that *thinketh he standeth*, but *he that assuredly standeth*; he who standeth so fast, that he does not appear to be in any danger of falling; he that saith, like David, I shall never be moved: Thou, Lord, hast made my hill so strong. [Ps. 30:6, 7] Yet at that very time, thus saith the Lord, Be not high-minded, but fear. else shalt thou be cut off: [Rom. 11:20, 21] else shalt thou also be moved from thy steadfastness. The strength which thou assuredly hast, shall be taken away. As firmly as thou didst really stand, thou wilt fall into sin, if not into hell.

3. But lest any should be discouraged by the consideration of those who once ran well, and were afterwards overcome by temptation; lest the fearful of heart should be utterly cast down, supposing it impossible for them to stand; the Apostle subjoins to that serious exhortation, these comfortable words: There hath no temptation taken you but such as is common to man: But God is faithful, who will not suffer you to be tempted above that ye are able; but will the temptation also make a way to escape, that ye may be able to bear it. [1 Cor. 10:13]

I. 1. Let us begin with the observation which ushers in this comfortable promise: "There hath no temptation taken you but such as is common to man." our translators seem to have been sensible that this expression, *common to man*, does by means reach the force of the original word. hence they substitute another in the margin, *moderate*. But this seems to be less significant than the other, and farther from the meaning of it. Indeed it is not easy to find any word in the english tongue, which answers the word *anthropinos*. I believe the sense of it can only be expressed by some such circumlocution as this: "Such as is suited to the nature and circumstances of man; such as every man may reasonably expect, if he considers the nature of his body and his soul, and his situation in the present world." If we duly consider these, we shall not be surprised at any temptation that hath befallen us; seeing it is no other than such a creature, in such a situation, has all reason to expect.

2. Consider, First, the nature of that body with which your soul is connected. how many are the evils which it is every day, every hour, liable to! Weakness, sickness and disorders of a thousand kinds are its natural attendants. Consider the inconceivably minute fibres, threads, abundantly finer than hair, (called from thence capillary vessels,) whereof every part of it is composed; consider the innumerable multitude of equally fine pipes and strainers, all filled with circulating juice! And will not the breach of a few of these fibres, or the obstruction of a few of these tubes, particularly in the brain, or heart, or lungs, destroy our ease, health, strength, if not life itself? Now, if we observe that all pain implies temptation, how numberless must the temptations be which will beset every man, more or less, sooner or later, while he dwells in this corruptible body!

3. Consider, Secondly, the present state of the soul, as long as it inhabits the house of clay. I do not mean in its unregenerate state; while it lies in darkness and the shadow of death; under the dominion of the prince of darkness, without hope and without God in the world: No; look upon men who are raised above that deplorable state. See those who have tasted that the Lord is gracious. Yet still how weak is their understanding! how limited its extent! How confused, how inaccurate, are our apprehensions of even the things that are round about us. How liable are the wisest of men to mistake! to inform false judgments; to take falsehood for truth, and truth for falsehood; evil for good, and good for evil! What starts, what wanderings of imagination, are we continually subject to! And how many are the temptations which we have to expect even from these innocent infirmities!

4. Consider, Thirdly, what is the present situation of even those that fear God. They dwell in the ruins of a disordered world, among men that know not God, that care not for him, and whose heart is fully set in them to do evil. How many are forced to cry out, "Woe is me, that I am constrained to dwell with Mesech; to have my habitations among the tents of Kedar!" among the enemies of God and man. How immensely out-numbered are those that would do well, by them that neither fear God nor regard man! And how striking is Cowleys observation: "If a man that was armed cap-a-pie was closed in by a thousand naked Indians, their number would have them such advantage over him that it would be scarce possible for him to escape. What hope then would there be for a naked, unarmed man to escape, who was surrounded by a thousand armed men?" Now, this is the case of every good man. He is not armed either with force or fraud, and is turned out, naked as he is, among thousands that are armed with the whole armour of Satan, and provided with all the weapons which the prince of this world can supply out of the armory of hell. If then he is not destroyed, yet how must a good man be tempted in the midst of this evil world!

5. But is it only from wicked men that temptations arise to them that fear God? It is very natural to imagine this; and almost every one thinks so. Hence how many of us have said in our hearts, "o if my lot were but cast among good men, among those that loved or even feared God, I should be free from all these temptations!" Perhaps you would: Probably you would not find the same sort of temptations which you have now to encounter. But you would surely meet with temptations of some other kind, which you would find equally hard to bear. For even good men, in general, though

sin has not dominion over the, yet are not freed from the remains of it. They have still the remains of an evil heart, ever prone to "depart from the living God." They have the seeds of pride, of anger, of foolish desire; indeed, of every unholy temper. And any of these, if they do not continually watch and pray, may, and naturally will, spring up, and trouble, not themselves only, but all that are round about them. We must not therefore depend upon finding no temptation from those that fear, yea, in a measure love, God. Much less must we be surprised, if some of those who once loved God in sincerity, should lay greater temptations in our way than many of those that never knew him.

6. "But can we expect to find any temptation from those that are *perfected in love?*" This is an important question, and deserves a particular consideration. I answer, First, You may find every kind of temptation from those who *suppose* they are perfected when indeed they are not: And so you may, Secondly, from those who once really were so, but are now moved from their steadfastness. And if you are not aware of this, if you think they are still what they were once, the temptation will be harder to bear. Nay, Thirdly, even those who "stand fast in liberty wherewith Christ has made them free," [Gal. 5:1] who are now really perfect in love, may still be an occasion of temptation to *you*; for they are still encompassed with infirmities. They may be dull of apprehension; they may have natural heedlessness, or a treacherous memory; they may have too lively an imagination: And any of these may cause little improprieties, either in speech or behaviour, which, though not sinful in themselves, may try all the grace you have: especially if you impute to perverseness of will (as it is very natural to do) what is really owing to defect of memory, or weakness of understanding; if these appear to you to be voluntary mistakes, which are really involuntary. So proper was the answer which a saint of God (now in Abrahams bosom) gave me some years ago, when I said, "Jenny, surely now your mistress and you can neither of you of you be a trial to the other, as God has saved you both from sin!" "o, Sir," said she, "if we are saved from sin, we still have infirmities enough to try all the grace that God has given us!"

7. But besides evil men, do not evil spirits also continually surround us on every side? Do not Satan and his angels continually go about seeking whom they may devour? Who is out of reach of their malice and subtlety? Not the wisest or the best of the children of men. "The servant is not above his Master." If then they tempted him, will not they tempt us also? Yea, it may be, should God see good to permit, more or less, to the end of our lives. "No temptation," therefore, "hath taken us," which we had not reason to expect, either from our body or soul; either from evil spirits or evil men; yea, or even from good men, till our spirits return to God that gave them.

II. 1. Meantime, what a comfort it is to know, with the utmost certainty, that "God is faithful, who will not suffer us to be tempted above what we are able." He knoweth what our ability is, and cannot be mistaken. "He knoweth" precisely "whereof we are made: He remembereth that we are but dust." [Ps. 103:14] And we will suffer no temptation to

befal us but such as is proportioned to our strength. Not only his justice requires this, which could not punish us for not resisting any temptation if it were so disproportioned to our strength that it was impossible for us to resist it; not only his mercy,—that tender mercy which is over us, as well as over all his works,—but, above all, his faithfulness: Seeing all his words are faithful and true: and the whole tenor of his promises altogether agrees with that declaration, "As thy days, so thy strength shall be." [Deut. 33:25]

2. In that execrable slaughter-house, the Romish Inquisition, (most unfortunately called, The House of Mercy!) it is the custom of those holy butchers, while they are tearing a mans sinews upon the rack, to have the physician of the house standing by. His business is, from time to time, to observe the eyes, the pulse, and other circumstances of the sufferer, and to give notice when the torture has continued so long as it can without putting an end to his life; that it may be preserved long enough for him to undergo the residue of their tortures. But notwithstanding all the physician's care, he is sometimes mistaken; and death puts a period to the sufferings of the patient before his tormentors are aware. We may observe something like this in our own case. In whatever sufferings or temptations we are, our great Physician never departs from us. He is about our bed, and about our path. He observes every symptom of our distress, that it may not rise above our strength. And he cannot be mistaken concerning us. He sees exactly how much we can endure with our present degree of strength. And if this is not sufficient, he can increase it to whatever degree it pleases him. Nothing, therefore, is more certain, than that, in consequence of his wisdom, as well as his justice, mercy, and faithfulness, he never will, he never can, suffer us to be tempted above that we are able: Above the strength which he either hath given already, or will give as soon as we need it.

III. 1. "He will with the temptation also" (this is the Third point we are to consider) "make a way to escape, that we may be able to bear it."

The word *ekbasin*, which we render *a way of to escape*, is extremely significant. The meaning of it is nearly expressed by the English word *out-let*; but more exact by the old word *out-gate*, still frequently used by the Scottish writers. It literally means *a way out*. And this God will either find our make; which He that hath all wisdom, as well as all power in heaven and earth, can never be at a loss how to do.

2. Either he *makes a way to escape* out of the temptation, by removing the occasion of it, or *in the temptation*; that is, the occasion remaining as it was, it is a temptation no longer. First, He makes a way to escape out of the temptation, by removing the occasion of it. The histories of mankind, of the Church in particular, afford us numberless instances of this. And many have occurred in our own memory, and within the little circle of our acquaintance. One of many I think it worth while to relate, as a memorable instance of the faithfulness of God, in making a way to escape out of temptation:—Elizabeth Chadsey, then living in London, (whose daughter is living at this day, and is no dishonour to her parent,) was advised to administer to her husband, who was supposed to leave much substance behind him. But when

a full inquiry into his circumstances was made, it appeared that this supposition was utterly destitute of foundation; and that he not only left nothing at all behind him, but also was very considerably in debt. It was not long after his burial, that a person came to her house, and said, "Mrs. Chadsey, you are much indebted to your landlord, and he has sent me to demand the rent that is due to him." She answered, "Sir, I have not so much money in the world: Indeed I have none at all!" "But," said he, "have you nothing that will fetch money?" She replied, "Sir, you see all that I have. I have nothing in the house by these six little children." "Then," said he, "I must execute my writ, and carry you to Newgate. But it is a hard case. I will leave you here till to-morrow, and will go and try if I cannot persuade your landlord to give you time." He returned the next morning, and said, "I have done all I can, I have used all the arguments I could think of, but your landlord is not to be moved. He vows, if I do not carry you to prison without delay, I shall go thither myself." She answered, "You have done *your* part. The will of the Lord be done!" He said, "I will venture to make one trial more, and will come again in the morning." He came in the morning, and said, "Mrs. Chadsey, God has undertaken your cause. None can give you any trouble now; for your landlord died last night. But he has left no will; and no one knows who is heir to the estate."

3. Thus God is able to deliver out of temptations, by removing the occasion of them. But are there not temptations, the occasions of which cannot be taken away? Is it not a striking instance of this kind, which we have in a late publication? "I was walking," says the writer of the letter, "over Dover cliffs, in a calm, pleasant evening with a person whom I tenderly loved, and to whom I was to be married in a few days. While we were engaged in earnest conversation, her foot slipped, she fell down, and I saw her dashed to pieces of the beach. I lifted up my hands, and cried out. 'This evil admits of no remedy. I must now go mourning all my days! My wound is incurable. It is impossible I should ever find such another woman! One so every way fitted for me.' I added in an agony, 'This is such an affliction as even God himself cannot redress!' And just as I uttered the words, I awoke: For it was a dream!" Just so can God remove any possible temptation; making it like a dream when one waketh!

4. Thus is God able to deliver out of temptation, by taking away the very ground of it. And he is equally able to deliver in the temptation; which, perhaps, is the greatest deliverance of all. I mean, suffering the occasion to remain as it was, he will take away the bitterness of it; so that it shall not be a temptation at all, but only an occasion of thanksgiving. How many proofs of this have the children of God, even in their daily experience! How frequently are they encompassed with trouble, or visited with pain or sickness! And when they cry unto the Lord, at some times he takes away the cup from them: He removes the trouble, or sickness, or pain; and it is as though it never had been: At other times he does not make any outward change; outward trouble, or pain, or sickness continues; but the consolations of the Holy One so increase, as to over-balance them all; and they can boldly declare,

> Labour is rest, and pain is sweet,
> When thou, my God, art near.

5. An eminent instance of this kind of deliverance is that which occurs in the Life of that excellent man, the Marquis de Renty. When he was in a violent fit of the rheumatism, a friend asked him, "Sir, are you in much pain?" He answered, "My pains are extreme: But through the mercy of God, I give myself up, not to them, but to him." It was in the same spirit that my own father answered, though exhausted with a severe illness, (an ulcer in the bowels, which had given him little rest day or night, for upwards of seven months.) when I asked, "Sir, are you in pain now?" He answered, with a strong and loud voice, "God does indeed chasten me with pain; yea, all my bones with strong pain. But I thank him for all; I bless him for all; I love him for all."

6. We may observe one more instance of a somewhat similar kind, in the Life of the Marquis de Renty. When his wife, whom he very tenderly loved, was exceeding ill, and supposed to be near death, a friend took the liberty to inquire how he felt himself on the occasion. He replied, "I cannot but say, that this trial affects me in the most tender part. I am exquisitely sensible of my loss. I feel more than it is possible to express. And yet I am so satisfied, that the will of God is done, and not the will of a vile sinner, that, were it not for fear of giving offence to others, I could dance and sing!" Thus the merciful, the just, the faithful God, will, in one way or other, "in every temptation make a way to escape, that we may be able to bear it."

7. This whole passage is fruitful of instruction. Some of the lessons which we may learn from it are,

First, "Let him that most assuredly standeth, take heed lest he fall" into *murmuring*; lest he say in his hear, "Surely no one's case is like mine; no one was ever tried like *me*." Yea, ten thousand. "There was no temptation taken you," but such as is "common to man;" such as you might reasonably expect, if you considered *what you are*, a sinner born to die; a sinful inhabitant of a mortal body, liable to numberless inward and outward sufferings;—and *where you are*, in a shattered, disordered world. surrounded by evil men, and evil spirits. Consider this, and you will not repine at the common lot, the general condition of humanity.

8. Secondly. "Let him that standeth, take heed lest he fall;" lest he *tempt* God, by thinking or saying, "This is insupportable; this is too hard; I can never get through it; my burden is heavier that I can bear." Not so; unless something is too hard for God. He will not suffer you to be "tempted above that ye are able." He proportions the burden to your strength. If you want more strength, "ask, and it shall be given you."

9. Thirdly. "Let him that standeth, take heed lest he fall;" lest he tempt God by *unbelief*, by distrusting his faithfulness. Hath he said, "in every temptation he will make a way to escape?" And shall he not do it? Yea, verily;

> And far above thy thought
> His counsel shall appear,
> When fully he the work hath wrought
> That caused they needless fear.

10. Let us then receive every trial with calm resignation, and with humble confidence that He who hath all power, all wisdom, all mercy, and all faithfulness, will first support us in every temptation, and then deliver us out of all: So that in the end all things shall work together for good, and we shall happily experience, that all these things were for our profit, that we "might be partakers of his holiness."

83.* On Patience

"Let patience have its perfect work, that ye may be perfect and entire, wanting nothing."

James 1:4.

1. "My brethren," says the Apostle in the preceding verse, "count it all joy when ye fall into divers temptations." At first view, this may appear a strange direction; seeing most temptations are, "for the present, not joyous, but grievous." Nevertheless ye know by your own experience, that "the trial of your faith worketh patience:" And if "patience have its perfect work, ye shall be perfect and entire, wanting nothing."

2. It is not to any particular person, or Church, that the Apostle gives this instruction; but to all who are partakers of like precious faith, and are seeking after that common salvation. For as long as any of us are upon earth, we are in the region of temptation. He who came into the world to save his people from their sins, did not come to save them from temptation. He himself "knew no sin;" yet while he was in this vale of tears, "he suffered being tempted;" and herein also "left us an example, that we should tread in his steps." We are liable to a thousand temptations, from the corruptible body variously affecting the soul. The soul itself, encompassed as it is with infirmities, exposes us to ten thousand more. And how many are the temptations which we meet with even from the good men (such, at least, they are in part, in their general character) with whom we are called to converse from day to day! Yet what are these to the temptations we may expect to meet with from an evil world? seeing we all, in effect, "dwell with Mesech, and have our habitation in the tents of Kedar." Add to this, that the most dangerous of our enemies are not those that assault us openly. No:

> Angels our march oppose,
> Who still in strength excel:
> Our secret, sworn, eternal foes,
> Countless, invisible!

For is not our "adversary the devil, as a roaring lion," with all his infernal legions, still going "about seeking whom he may devour?" This is the case with all the children of men; yea, and with all the children of God, as long as they sojourn in this strange land. Therefore, if we do not wilfully and carelessly rush into them, yet we shall surely "fall into divers temptations;" temptations innumerable as the stars of heaven; and those varied and complicated a thousand ways. But, instead of counting this a loss, as unbelievers would do, "count it all joy; knowing that the trial of your faith," even

when it is "tried as by fire," "worketh patience." But "let patience have its perfect work, and ye shall be perfect and entire, wanting nothing."

3. But what is *Patience?* We do not now speak of a heathen virtue; neither of a natural indolence; but of a gracious temper, wrought in the heart of a believer, by the power of the Holy Ghost. It is a disposition to suffer whatever pleases God, in the manner and for the time that pleases him. We thereby hold the middle way, neither *holigorountes, despising* our sufferings, *making little* of them, passing over them lightly, as if they were owing to chance, or second causes; nor, on the other hand, *ekloumenoi, affected too much, unnerved, dissolved, sinking under them.* We may observe, the proper object of patience is suffering, either in body or mind. Patience does not imply the not *feeling* this: It is not apathy or insensibility. It is at the utmost distance from stoical stupidity; yea, at an equal distance from fretfulness or dejection. The patient believer is preserved from falling into either of these extremes, by considering, Who is the Author of all his suffering? even God his Father; What is the *motive* of his *giving us* to suffer? Not so properly his justice as his love;—and, What is the *end* of it? our profit, that we may be partakers of his holiness.

4. Very nearly related to patience is *meekness,* if it be not rather a species of it. For may it not be defined, patience of injuries; particularly affronts, reproach, or unjust censure? This teaches not to return evil for evil, or railing for railing; but contrariwise blessing. our blessed Lord himself seems to place a peculiar value upon this temper. This he peculiarly calls us to learn of him, if we would find rest for our souls.

5. But what may we understand by the *work of patience?* Let patience have its perfect work. It seems to mean, let it have its full fruit or effect. And what is the fruit which the Spirit of God is accustomed to produce hereby, in the heart of a believer? one immediate fruit of patience is peace: A sweet tranquillity of mind; a serenity of spirit, which can never be found, unless where patience reigns. And this peace often rises into joy. even in the midst of various temptations, those that are enabled in patience to possess their souls, can witness, not only quietness of spirit, but triumph and exultation. This both

> Lays the rough paths of peevish nature even,
> And opens in each breast a little heaven.

6. how lively is the account which the Apostle Peter gives not only of the peace and joy, but of the hope and love, which God works in those patient sufferers "who are kept by the power of God through faith unto salvation!" Indeed he appears herein to have an eye to this very passage of St. James: "Though ye are grieved for a season, with manifold temptations," (the very word *poikilois peirasmois,*) "that the trial of your faith" (the same expression which was used by St. James) "may be found to praise, and honour, and glory, at the revelation of Jesus Christ; whom, having not seen, ye love; in whom, though now ye see him not, yet believing, ye rejoice with joy unspeakable and full of glory." See here the

---

* [text of the 1872 edition]

peace, the joy, and the love, which, through the mighty power of God, are the fruit or "work of patience!"

7. And as peace, hope, joy, and love are the fruits of patience, both springing from, and confirmed by it, so is also rational, genuine *courage*, which indeed cannot subsist without patience. The brutal courage, or rather fierceness, of a lion may probably spring from impatience; but true fortitude, the courage of a man, springs from just the contrary temper. Christian *zeal* is likewise confirmed and increased by patience, and so is *activity* in every good work; the same Spirit inciting us to be

> Patient in bearing ill, and doing well;

making us equally willing to do and suffer the whole will of God.

8. But what is the *perfect work* of patience? Is it anything less than the "perfect love of God," constraining us to love every soul of man, "even as Christ loved us?" Is it not the whole of religion, the whole "mind which was also in Christ Jesus?" Is it not "the renewal of our soul in the image of God, after the likeness of him that created us?" And is not the fruit of this, the constant resignation of ourselves, body and spirit, to God; entirely giving up all we are, all we have, and all we love, as a holy sacrifice, acceptable unto God through the Son of his love? It seems this is "the perfect work of patience," consequent upon the trial of our faith.

9. But how does this work differ from that gracious work which is wrought in every believer, when he first finds redemption in the blood of Jesus, even the remission of his sins? Many persons that are not only upright of heart, but that fear, nay, and love God, have not spoken warily upon this head, not according to the oracles of God. They have spoken of the work of sanctification, taking the word in its full sense, as if it were quite of another kind, as if it differed entirely from that which is wrought in justification. But this is a great and dangerous mistake, and has a natural tendency to make us undervalue that glorious work of God which was wrought in us when we were justified: Whereas in that moment when we are justified freely by his grace, when we are accepted through the Beloved, we are born again, born from above, born of the Spirit. And there is as great a change wrought in our souls when we are born of the Spirit, as was wrought in our bodies when we are born of a woman. There is, in that hour, a general change from inward sinfulness, to inward holiness. The love of the creature is changed to the love of the Creator; the love of the world into the love of God. earthly desires, the desire of the flesh, the desire of the eyes, and the pride of life, are, in that instant, changed, by the mighty power of God, into heavenly desires. The whirlwind of our will is stopped in its mid career, and sinks down into the will of God. Pride and haughtiness subside into lowliness of heart; as do anger, with all turbulent and unruly passions, into calmness, meekness, and gentleness. In a word, the earthly, sensual, devilish mind, gives place to "the mind that was in Christ Jesus."

10. "Well, but what more than this can be implied in entire sanctification?" It does not imply any new *kind* of holiness: Let no man imagine this. From the moment we are justified, till we give up our spirits to God, love is the fulfilling of the law; of the whole evangelical law, which took place of the Adamic law, when the first promise of "the seed of the woman" was made. Love is the sum of Christian sanctification; it is the one *kind* of holiness, which is found, only in various *degrees*, in the believers who are distinguished by St. John into "little children, young men, and fathers." The difference between one and the other properly lies in the degree of love. And herein there is as great a difference in the spiritual, as in the natural sense, between fathers, young men, and babes.

every one that is born of God, though he be as yet only a "babe in Christ," has the love of God in his heart; the love of his neighbour; together with lowliness, meekness, and resignation. But all of these are then in a low degree, in proportion to the degree of his faith. The faith of a babe in Christ is weak, generally mingled with doubts or fears; with doubts, whether he has not deceived himself; or fear, that he shall not endure to the end. And if, in order to prevent those perplexing doubts, or to remove those tormenting fears, he catches hold of the opinion that a true believer cannot make shipwreck of the faith, experience will sooner or later show that it is merely the staff of a broken reed, which will be so far from sustaining him, that it will only enter into his hand and pierce it. But to return: In the same proportion as he grows in faith, he grows in holiness; he increases in love, lowliness, meekness, in every part of the image of God; till it pleases God, after he is thoroughly convinced of inbred sin, of the total corruption of his nature, to take it all away; to purify his heart and cleanse him from all unrighteousness; to fulfil that promise which he make first to his ancient people, and in them to the Israel of God in all ages: "I will circumcise thy heart, and the heart of thy seed, to love the Lord thy God with all thy heart, and with all thy soul."

It is not easy to conceive what a difference there is, between that which he experiences now, and that which he experienced before. Till this universal change was wrought in his soul, all his holiness was *mixed.* he was humble, but not entirely; his humility was mixed with pride: he was meek; but his meekness was frequently interrupted by anger, or some uneasy and turbulent passion. His love of God was frequently damped, by the love of some creature; the love of his neighbour, by evil surmising, or some thought, if not temper, contrary to love. His will was not wholly melted down into the will of God: But although in general he could say, "I come 'not to do my own will, but the will of him that sent me;" yet now and then nature rebelled, and he could not clearly say, "Lord, not as I will, but as thou wilt." His whole soul is now consistent with itself; there is no jarring string. All his passions flow in a continual stream, with an even tenor to God. To him that is entered into this rest, you may truly say,

> Calm thou ever art within,
> All unruffled, all serene!

There is no mixture of any contrary affections: All is peace and harmony after. Being filled with love, there is no more interruption of it, than of the beating of his heart; and continual love bringing continual joy in the Lord, he rejoices evermore. He converses continually with the God whom he loves, unto whom in everything he gives thanks. And as he now loves God with all his heart, and with all his soul, and with all his mind, and with all his strenght; so Jesus now reigns alone in his heart, the Lord of every motion there.

11. But it may be inquired, In what manner does God work this entire, this universal change in the soul of a believer? this strange work, which so many will not believe, though we declare it unto them? Does he work it gradually, by slow degrees; or instantaneously, in a moment? How many are the disputes upon this head, even among the children of God! And so there will be, after all that ever was, or ever can be said upon it. For many will still say, with the famous Jew, *Non persuadebis, etiamsi persuaseris*. That is, "Thou shalt not persuade me, though thou dost persuade me." And they will be the more resolute herein, because the Scriptures are silent upon the subject; because the point is not determined, at least not in express terms, in any part of the oracles of God. every man therefore may abound in his own sense, provided he will allow the same liberty to his neighbour; provided he will not be angry at those who differ from his opinion, nor entertain hard thoughts concerning them. Permit me likewise to add one thing more: Be the change instantaneous or gradual, see that you never rest till it is wrought in your own soul, if you desire to dwell with God in glory.

12. This premised, in order to throw what light I can upon this interesting question, I will simply relate what I have seen myself in the course of many years. Four or five and forty years ago, when I had no distinct views of what the Apostle meant by exhorting us to "leave the principles of the doctrine of Christ, and go on to perfection," two or three persons in London, whom I knew to be truly sincere, desired to give me an account of their experience. It appeared exceeding strange, being different from any that I had heard before; but exactly similar to the preceding account of entire sanctification. The next year, two or three more persons at Bristol, and two or three in Kingswood, coming to me severally, gave me exactly the same account of their experience. A few years after, I desired all those in London who made the same profession, to come to me all together at the Foundery, that I might be thoroughly satisfied. I desired that man of God, Thomas Walsh, to give us the meeting there. When we met, first one of us, and the the the other, asked them the most searching questions we could devise. They answered every one without hesitation, and with the utmost simplicity, so that we were fully persuaded, they did not deceive themselves. In the years 1759, 1760, 1761, and 1762, their numbers multiplied exceedingly, not only in London and Bristol, but in various parts of Ireland as well as england. Not trusting to the testimony of others, I carefully examined most of these myself; and in London alone I found six hundred and fifty-two members of our society who were exceedingly clear in their experience, and of whose testimony I could see no reason to doubt. I believe no year has passed since that time wherein God has not wrought the same work in many others; but sometimes in one part of England or Ireland, sometimes in another;—as "the wind bloweth where it listeth;"—and every one of these (after the most careful inquiry, I have not found one exception either in Great Britain or Ireland) has declared that his deliverance from sin was *instantaneous*; that the change was wrought in a moment. Had half of these, or one third, or one in twenty, declared it was *gradually* wrought in *them*, I should have believed this, with regard to *them*, and thought that *some* were gradually sanctified and some instantaneously. But as I have not found, in so long a space of time, a single person speaking thus; as all who believe they are sanctified, declare with one voice, that the change was wrought in a moment, I cannot but believe that sanctification is commonly, if not always, an *instantaneous* work.

13. But however that question be decided, whether sanctification, in the full sense of the word, be wrought instantaneously or gradually, how my we attain to it? "What shall *we* do," said the Jews to our Lord, "that we may work the works of God?" His answer will suit those that ask, What shall we do, that this work of God may be wrought in us? "This is the work of God, that ye believe on him whom he hath sent." on this one work all the others depend. Believe on the Lord Jesus Christ, and all has wisdom, and power, and faithfulness are engaged on thy side. In this, as in all other instances, "by grace we are saved through faith." Sanctification too is "not of works, lest any man should boast." "It is the gift of God," and is to be received by plain, simple faith. Suppose you are now labouring to "abstain from all appearance of evil," "zealous of good works," and walking diligently and carefully in all the ordinances of God; there is then only one point remaining: The voice of God to your soul is, "Believe, and be saved." [See the Sermon on "The Scripture Way of Salvation." (editors note)] First, believe that God has *promised* to save you from all sin, and to fill you with all holiness. Secondly, believe that he is *able* thus "to save to the uttermost all that come unto God through him." Thirdly, believe that he is *willing*, as well as able, to save *you* to the uttermost; to purify you from all sin, and fill up all your heart with love. Believe, Fourthly, that he is not only able, but willing to do it *now*. Not when you come to die; not at any distant time; not to-morrow, but *to-day*. He will then enable you to believe, *it is done*, according to his word: And then "patience shall have its perfect work; that ye may be perfect and entire, wanting nothing."

14. Ye shall then be perfect. The Apostle seems to mean by this expression, *teleioi*, ye shall be wholly delivered from every evil work; from every evil word; from every sinful thought; yea, from every evil desire, passion, temper; from all inbred corruption, from all remains of the carnal mind, from the body of sin; and ye shall be renewed in the spirit of your mind, in every right temper, after the image of him that created you, in righteousness and true holiness. Ye shall be *entire, holokleroi*, (The same word which the Apostle uses to the Christians in Thessalonica: [1 Thess. 5:23]) This seems to refer, not so much to the kind as to the degree of holiness; as if he had said, "Ye shall enjoy as high a degree of holiness as is consistent with your present state of pilgrimage;"—and ye shall *want nothing*; the Lord being your Shepherd, your Father, your Redeemer, your Sanctifier, your God, and your all, will feed you with the bread of heaven, and give you meat enough. He will lead you forth beside the waters of comfort, and keep you every moment: So that loving him with all your

heart, (which is the sum of all perfection,) you will "rejoice evermore, pray without ceasing, and in everything give thanks," till "an abundant entrance is ministered unto you into his everlasting kingdom!

84.* THE IMPORTANT QUESTION

"What is a man profited, if he shall gain the whole world, and lose his own soul?"

Matthew 16:26

1. There is a celebrated remark to this effect, (I think in the works of Mr. Pascal,) that if a man of low estate would speak of high things, as of what relates to kings or kingdoms, it is not easy for him to find suitable expressions, as he is so little acquainted with things of this nature; but if one of royal parentage speaks of royal things, of what concerns his own or his father's kingdom, his language will be free and easy, as these things are familiar to his thoughts. In like manner, if a mere inhabitant of this lower world speaks concerning the great things of the kingdom of God, hardly is he able to find expressions suitable to the greatness of the subject. But when the Son of God speaks of the highest things, which concern his heavenly kingdom, all his language is easy and unlaboured, his words natural and unaffected; inasmuch as, known unto him are all these things from all eternity.

2. How strongly is this remark exemplified in the passage now before us! The Son of God, the great King of heaven and earth, here uses the plainest and easiest words: But how high and deep are the things which he expresses therein! None of the children of men can fully conceive them, till, emerging out of the darkness of the present world, he commences an inhabitant of eternity.

3. But we may conceive a little of these deep things, if we consider, First, what is implied in that expression, "A man's *gaining* the whole world:" Secondly, what is implied in *losing* his own soul: We shall then, Thirdly, see, in the strongest light, what he is *profited*, who gains the whole world, and loses his own soul.

I. 1. We are, First, to consider, what is implied in a man's *gaining* the whole world. Perhaps, at the first hearing, this may seem to some equivalent with conquering the whole world. But it has no relation thereto at all: And indeed that expression involves a plain absurdity. For it is impossible any that is born of a woman should ever conquer the whole world; were it only because the short life of man could not suffice for so wild an undertaking. Accordingly no man ever did conquer the half, no, nor the tenthpart of the world. But whatever others might do, there was no danger that any of our Lord's hearers should have any thought of this. Among all the sins of the Jewish nation the desire of universal empire was not found. Even in their most flourishing times, they never sought to extend their conquests beyond the river Euphrates. And in our Lord's time, all their ambition was at an end: "The sceptre was departed from Judah;" and Judea was governed by a Roman Procurator, as a branch of the Roman Empire.

2. Leaving this, we may find a far more easy and natural sense of the expression. To gain the whole world, may properly enough imply, to gain all the pleasures which the world can give. The man we speak of may, therefore, be supposed to have gained all that will gratify his senses. In particular, all that can increase his pleasure of tasting; all the elegancies of meat and drink: Likewise, whatever can gratify his smell, or touch; all that he can enjoy in common with his fellow-brutes. He may have all the plenty and all the variety of these objects which the world can afford.

3. We may farther suppose him to have gained all that gratifies "the desire of the eyes;" whatever (by means of the eye chiefly) conveys any pleasure to the imagination. The pleasures of imagination arise from three sources: Grandeur, beauty, and novelty. Accordingly, we find by experience, our own imagination is gratified by surveying either grand, or beautiful, or uncommon objects. Let him be encompassed then with the most grand, the most beautiful, and the newest things that can anywhere be found. For all this is manifestly implied in a man's gaining the whole world.

4. But there is also another thing implied herein, which men of the most elevated spirits have preferred before all the pleasures of sense and of imagination put together; that is, honour, glory, renown:

Virum volitare per ora.

[The following is Dryden's translation of this quotation from Virgil, and of the words connected with it:—

"New ways I must attempt, my grovelling name
To raise aloft, and wing my flight to fame."—
EDIT.]

It seems, that hardly any principle in the human mind is of greater force than this. It triumphs over the strongest propensities of nature, over all our appetites and affections. If Brutus sheds the blood of his own children; if we see another Brutus, in spite of every possible obligation, in defiance of all justice and gratitude,

Cringing while he stabs his friend;

if a far greater man than either of these, Paschal Paoli, gave up ease, pleasure, everything, for a life of constant toil, pain, and alarms; what principle could support them? They might talk of *amor patriae*, the love of their country; but this would never have carried them through, had there not been also the

Laudum immensa cupido;

"the immense thirst of *praise.* "Now, the man we speak of has gained abundance of this: He is praised, if not admired, by all that are round about him. Nay, his name is gone forth into distant lands, as it were, to the ends of the earth.

5. Add to this, that he has gained abundance of wealth; that there is no end of his treasures; that he has laid up silver as the dust, and gold as the sand of the sea. Now, when a man has obtained all these pleasures, all that will gratify either the senses or the imagination; when he has gained an honourable name, and also laid up much treasure for many years; then he may be said, in an easy, natural sense of the word, to have "gained the whole world."

* [text of the 1872 ed.]

II. 1. The next point we have to consider is what is implied in a man's *losing* his own soul. But here we draw a deeper scene, and have need of a more steady attention. For it is easy to sum up all that is implied in a man's *"gaining* the whole world." but it is not easy to understand all that is implied in his "losing his own soul." Indeed none can fully conceive this, until he has passed through time into eternity.

2. The first thing which it undeniably implies is, the losing all the present pleasures of religion; all those which it affords to truly religious men, even in the present life. "If there be any consolation Christ; if any comfort of love,"—in the love of God, and of all mankind; if any "joy in the Holy Ghost;" if there be a peace of God,—a peace that passeth all understanding; if there be any rejoicing in the testimony of a good conscience toward God; it is manifest, all this is totally lost by the man that loses his own soul.

3. But the present life will soon be at an end: We know it passes away like a shadow. The hour is at hand, when the spirit will be summoned to return to God that gave it. In that awful moment,

> Leaving the old, both worlds at once they view,
> Who stand upon the threshold of the new.

And whether he looks backward or forward, how pleasing is the prospect to him that saves his soul! If he looks back, he has "the calm remembrance of the life well spent." If he looks forward, there is an inheritance incorruptible, undefiled, and that fadeth not away; and he sees the convoy of angels ready to carry him into Abraham's bosom. But how is it in that solemn hour, with the man that loses his soul? Does he look back? What comfort is there in this? He sees nothing but scenes of horror, matter of shame, remorse, and self-condemnation; a foretaste of "the worm that never dieth." If he looks forward, what does he see? No joy, no peace! No gleam of hope from any point of heaven! Some years since, one who turned back as a dog to his vomit was struck in his mid-career of sin. A friend visiting him, prayed, "Lord, have mercy upon those who are just stepping out of the body, and know not which shall meet them at their entrance into the other world, an angel or a fiend!" The sick man shrieked out with a piercing cry, "A fiend! a fiend!" and died. Just such an end, unless he die like an ox, may any man expect who loses his own soul.

4. But in what situation is the spirit of a good man, at his entrance into eternity? See,

> The convoy attends,
> The ministering host of invisible friends.

They receive the new-born spirit, and conduct him safe into Abraham's bosom, into the delights of Paradise; the garden of God, where the light of his countenance perpetually shines. It is but one of a thousand commendations of this antechamber of heaven that "there the wicked cease from troubling, there the weary are at rest." For there they have numberless sources of happiness which they could not have upon earth. There they meet with "the glorious dead of ancient days." They converse with Adam, first of men; with Noah, first of the new world; with Abraham, the friend of God; with Moses and the Prophets; with the Apostles of the Lamb; with the saints of all ages; and, above all, they are with Christ.

5. How different, alas! is the case with him who loses his own soul! The moment he steps into eternity, he meets with the devil and his angels. Sad convoy into the world of spirits! Sad earnest of what is to come! And either he is bound with chains of darkness, and reserved unto the judgment of the great day; or, at best, he wanders up and down, seeking rest, but finding none. Perhaps he may seek it (like the unclean spirit cast out of the man) in dry, dreary, desolate places; perhaps

> Where nature all in ruins lies,
> And owns her sovereign, death!

And little comfort can he find here, seeing everything contributes to increase, not remove, the fearful expectation of fiery indignation, which will devour the ungodly.

6. For even this is to him but the beginning of sorrows. Yet a little while, and he will see "the great white throne coming down from heaven, and him that sitteth thereon, from whose face the heavens and the earth flee away, and there is found no place for them." And "the dead, small and great, stand before God, and are judged, every one according to his works." "Then shall the King say to them on his right hand," (God grant he may say so to YOU!) "Come, ye blessed of my Father, inherit the kingdom prepared for you from the foundation of the world." And the angels shall tune their harps and sing, "Lift up your heads, O ye gates, and be ye lift up, ye everlasting doors, that the heirs of glory may come in." And then shall they 'shine as the brightness of the firmament, and as the stars forever and ever."

7. How different will be the lot of him that loses his own soul! No joyful sentence will be pronounced on him, but one that will pierce him through with unutterable horror: (God forbid that ever it should be pronounced on any of you that are here before God!) "Depart, ye cursed, into everlasting fire, prepared for the devil and his angels!" And who can doubt, but those infernal spirits will immediately execute the sentence; will instantly drag those forsaken of God into their own place of torment! Into those

> Regions of sorrow, doleful shades, where peace
> And rest can never dwell! Hope never comes,
> That comes to all,—

all the children of men who are on this side eternity. But not to them: The gulf is now fixed, over which they cannot pass. From the moment wherein they are once plunged into the lake of fire, burning with brimstone, their torments are not only without intermission, but likewise without end. For "they have no rest, day or night; but the smoke of their torment ascendeth up forever and ever!"

III. Upon ever so cursory a view of these things, would not anyone be astonished, that a man, that a creature endued with reason, should voluntarily choose, I say *choose;* for God forces no man into inevitable damnation; he never yet

> Consign'd one unborn soul to hell,
> Or damn'd him from his mother's womb,—

should choose thus to lose his own soul, though it were to gain the whole world! For what shall a man be profited thereby upon the whole of the account?

But a little to abate our astonishment at this, let us observe the suppositions which a man generally makes before he can reconcile himself to this fatal choice.

1. He supposes, First, that "a life of religion is a life of misery." *That religion is misery!* How is it possible that anyone should entertain so strange a thought? Do any of *you* imagine this? If you do, the reason is plain; you know not what religion is. "No! but I do, as well as you."—What is it then? "Why, the doing no harm." Not so; many birds and beasts do no harm, yet they are not capable of religion. "Then it is going to church and sacrament." Indeed it is not. This may be an excellent help to religion; and everyone who desires to save his soul should attend them at all opportunities; yet it is possible you may attend them all your days, and still have no religion at all. Religion is an higher and deeper thing than any outward ordinance whatever.

2. What is religion then? It is easy to answer, if we consult the oracles of God. According to these it lies in one single point; it is neither more nor less than love; it is love which "is the fulfilling of the law, the end of the commandment." Religion is the love of God and our neighbour; that is, every man under heaven. This love ruling the whole life, animating all our tempers and passions, directing all our thoughts, words, and actions, is "pure religion and undefiled."

3. Now, will anyone be so hardy as to say, that love is misery? Is it misery to love God? to give Him my heart who alone is worthy of it? Nay, it is the truest happiness; indeed, the only true happiness which is to be found under the sun. So does all experience prove the justness of that reflection which was made long ago, "Thou hast made us for thyself; and our heart cannot rest, until it resteth in thee." Or does anyone imagine, the love of our neighbour is misery; even the loving every man as our own soul? So far from it that, next to the love of God, this affords the greatest happiness of which we are capable. Therefore,

> Let not the Stoic boast his mind unmoved,
> The brute-philosopher, who never has proved
> The joy of loving, or of being loved.

4. So much every reasonable man must allow. But he may object: "There is more than this implied in religion. It implies not only the love of God and man; (against which I have no objection;) but also a great deal of doing and suffering. And how can this be consistent with happiness?"

There is certainly some truth in this objection. Religion does imply both doing and suffering. Let us then calmly consider, whether this impairs or heightens our happiness.

Religion implies, First, the doing many things. For the love of God will naturally lead us, at all opportunities, to converse with Him we love; to speak to him in public or private prayer; and to hear the words of his mouth, which "are dearer to us than thousands of gold and silver." It will incline us to lose no opportunity of receiving

> The dear memorials of our dying Lord;

to continue instant in thanksgiving; at morning, evening, and noon-day to praise him. But suppose we do all this, will it lessen our happiness? Just the reverse. It is plain, all these fruits of love are means of increasing the love from which they spring; and of consequence they increase our happiness in the same proportion. Who then would not join in that wish?

> Rising to sing my Saviour's praise,
> Thee may I publish all day long,
> And let thy precious word of grace
> Flow from my heart, and fill my tongue;
> Fill all my life with purest love,
> And join me to thy church above!

5. It must also be allowed, that as the love of God naturally leads to works of piety, so the love of our neighbour naturally leads all that feel it to works of mercy. It inclines us to feed the hungry; to clothe the naked; to visit them that are sick or in prison; to be as eyes to the blind, and feet to the lame; an husband to the widow, a father to the fatherless. But can you suppose, that the doing this will prevent or lessen your happiness? yea, though you did so much, as to be like a guardian angel to all that are round about you? On the contrary, it is an infallible truth, that

> All worldly joys are less
> Than that one joy of doing kindnesses.

A man of pleasure was asked some years ago, "Captain, what was the greatest pleasure you ever had?" After a little pause, he replied, "When we were upon our march in Ireland, in a very hot day, I called at a cabin on the road, and desired a little water. The woman brought me a cup of milk. I gave her a piece of silver; and the joy that poor creature expressed gave me the greatest pleasure I ever had in my life." Now, if the doing good gave so much pleasure to one who acted merely from natural generosity, how much more must it give to one who does it on a nobler principle,—the joint love of God and his neighbour! It remains, that the doing all which religion requires will not lessen, but immensely increase, our happiness.

6. "Perhaps this also may be allowed. But religion implies, according to the Christian account, not only doing, but *suffering*. And how can suffering be consistent with happiness?" Perfectly well. Many centuries ago, it was remarked by St. Chrysostom, "The Christian has his sorrows as well as his joys: But his sorrow is sweeter than joy." He may accidentally suffer loss, poverty, pain: But in all these things he is more than conqueror. He can testify,

> Labour is rest, and pain is sweet,
> While thou, my God, art here.

He can say, "The Lord gave; the Lord taketh away: Blessed be the name of the Lord!" He must suffer, more or less, reproach: For "the servant is not above his Master:" But so much the more does "the Spirit of glory and of God rest upon him." Yea, love itself will, on several occasions, be the source of suffering: The love of God will frequently produce

> The pleasing smart,
> The meltings of a broken heart.

And the love of our neighbour will give rise to sympathizing sorrow: It will lead us to visit the fatherless and widow in their affliction; to be tenderly concerned for the distressed, and to "mix our pitying tear with those that weep." But may we not well say, These are "tears that delight, and sighs that waft to heaven?" So far then are all these sufferings from either preventing or lessening our happiness, that they greatly contribute thereto, and, indeed, constitute no inconsiderable part of it. So that, upon the whole, there cannot be a more false supposition, than that a life of religion is a life of misery; seeing true religion, whether considered in its nature or its fruits, is true and solid happiness.

7. The man who chooses to gain the world by the loss of his soul, supposes, Secondly, that "a life of wickedness is a life of happiness!" *That wickedness is happiness!* Even an old heathen poet could have taught him better. Even Juvenal discovered, *Nemo malus felix*: "no wicked man is happy." And how expressly does God himself declare, "There is no peace to the wicked!" No peace of mind: And without this, there can be no happiness.

But not to avail ourselves of authority, let us weigh the thing in the balance of reason. I ask, What can make a wicked man happy? You answer, "He has gained the whole world." We allow it; and what does this imply? He has gained all that gratifies the senses: In particular, all that can please the taste; all the delicacies of meat and drink. True; but can eating and drinking make a man happy? They never did yet: And certain it is, they never will. This is too coarse food for an immortal spirit. But suppose it did give him a poor kind of happiness, during those moments wherein he was swallowing; what will he do with the residue of his time? Will it not hang heavy upon his hands? Will he not groan under many a tedious hour, and think swift-winged time flies too slow? If he is not fully employed, will he not frequently complain of lowness of spirits? an unmeaning expression; which the miserable physician usually no more understands than his miserable patient. We know there are such things as *nervous disorders*. But we know likewise, that what is commonly called nervous lowness is a secret reproof from God; a kind of consciousness that we are not in our place; that we are not as God would have us to be: We are unhinged from our proper centre.

8. To remove, or at least soothe, this strange uneasiness, let him add the pleasures of imagination. Let him bedaub himself with silver and gold, and adorn himself with all the colours of the rainbow. Let him build splendid palaces, and furnish them in the most elegant as well as costly manner. Let him lay out walks and gardens, beautified with all that nature and art can afford. And how long will these give him pleasure? Only as long as they are new. As soon as ever the novelty is gone, the pleasure is gone also. After he has surveyed them a few months, or years, they give him no more satisfaction. The man who is saving his soul, has the advantage of him in this very respect. For he can say,

> In the pleasures the rich man's possessions display,
> Unenvied I challenge my part;
> While every fair object my eye can survey
> Contributes to gladden my heart.

9. "However, he has yet another resource: *Applause, glory.* And will not this make him happy?" It will not: For he cannot be applauded by all men: No man ever was. Some will praise; perhaps many; but not all. It is certain some will blame: And he that is fond of applause, will feel more pain from the censure of one, than pleasure from the praise of many. So that whoever seeks happiness in applause will infallibly be disappointed, and will find, upon the whole of the account, abundantly more pain than pleasure.

10. But to bring the matter to a short issue. Let us take an instance of one who had gained more of this world than probably any man now alive, unless he be a sovereign prince. But did all he had gained make him happy? Answer for thyself! Then said Haman, Yet "all this profiteth me nothing, while I see Mordecai sitting in the gate." Poor Human! One unholy temper, whether pride, envy, jealousy, or revenge, gave him more pain, more vexation of spirit, than all the world could give pleasure. And so it must be in the nature of things; for all unholy tempers are unhappy tempers. Ambition, covetousness, vanity, inordinate affection, malice, revengefulness, carry their own punishment with them, and avenge themselves on the soul wherein they dwell. Indeed what are these, more especially when they are combined with an awakened conscience, but the dogs of hell, already gnawing the soul, forbidding happiness to approach? Did not even the Heathens see this? What else means their fable of Tityus, chained to a rock, with a vulture continually tearing up his breast, and feeding upon his liver? *Quid rides?* "Why do you smile?" says the poet:

> Mutato nomine, de te
> Fabula narratur.

"It is another name; but thou art the man!" Lust, foolish desire, envy, malice, or anger, is now tearing thy breast: Love of money, or of praise, hatred or revenge, is now feeding on thy poor spirit. Such happiness is in vice! So vain is the supposition that a life of wickedness is a life of happiness!

11. But he makes a Third supposition,—That he shall certainly live forty, or fifty, or threescore years. Do *you* depend upon this? On living threescore years? Who told you that you should? It is no other than the enemy of God and man: It is the murderer of souls. Believe him not; he was a liar from the beginning; from the beginning of his rebellion against God. He is eminently a liar in this: For he would not give you life, if he could. Would God permit, he would make sure work, and just now hurry you to his own place. And he cannot give you life, if he would: The breath of man is not in his hands. He is not the disposer of life and death: That power belongs to the Most High. It is possible indeed, God may, on some occasions, permit him to inflict death. I do not know but it was an evil angel who smote an hundred fourscore and five thousand Assyrians in one night: And the fine lines of our poet are as applicable to an evil as to a good spirit:—

> So when an angel, by divine command,
> Hurls death and terror over a guilty land;
> He, pleased the Almighty's order to perform,
> Rides in the whirlwind, and directs the storm.

But though Satan may sometimes inflict death, I know not that he could ever give life. It was one of his most faithful servants that shrieked out some years ago, "A week's life! A week's life! Thirty thousand pounds for a week's life!" But he could not purchase a day's life. That night God required his soul of him! And how soon may he require it of you? Are you sure of living threescore years? Are you sure of living one year, one month, one week, one day? O make haste to live! Surely the man that may die tonight should live today.

12. So absurd are all the suppositions made by him who gains the world and loses his soul. But let us for a moment imagine, that wickedness is happiness; and that he shall certainly live threescore years; and still I would ask, What is he profited, if he gain the whole world for threescore years, and then lose his soul eternally?

Can such a choice be made by any that considers what eternity is? Philip Melanchthon, the most learned of all the German Reformers, gives the following relation: (I pass no judgment upon it, but set it down nearly in his own words:) "When I was at Wirtemberg, as I was walking out one summer evening with several of my fellow-students, we heard an uncommon singing, and following the sound, saw a bird of an uncommon figure. One stepping up asked, "In the name of the Father, Son, and Holy Ghost, what art thou?" It answered, "I am a damned spirit;" and, in vanishing away, pronounced these words: "O Eternity, Eternity! who can tell the length of Eternity?" And how soon will this be the language of him who sold his soul for threescore years' pleasure! How soon would he cry out, "O Eternity, Eternity! who can tell the length of Eternity?"

13. In how striking a manner is this illustrated by one of the ancient Fathers! "Supposing there were a ball of sand as big as the whole earth. Suppose a grain of this to be annihilated in a thousand years: Which would be more eligible,—to be happy while this ball was wasting away at the rate of one grain in a thousand years, and miserable ever after?—or to be miserable, while it was wasting away at that proportion, and happy ever after?" A wise man, it is certain, could not pause one moment upon the choice; seeing all the time wherein this ball would be wasting away, bears infinitely less proportion to eternity, than a drop of water to the whole ocean, or a grain of sand to the whole mass. Allowing then that a life of religion were a life of misery; that a life of wickedness were a life of happiness; and, that a man were assured of enjoying that happiness for the term of threescore years; yet what would he be profited if he were then to be miserable to all eternity?

14. But it has been proved, that the case is quite otherwise, that religion is happiness, that wickedness is misery; and that no man is assured of living threescore days: And if so, is there any fool, any madman under heaven, who can be compared to him that casts away his own soul, though it were to gain the whole world? For what is the real state of the case? What is the choice which God proposes to his creatures? It is not, "Will you be happy threescore years, and then miserable forever, or, will you be miserable threescore years, and then happy forever?" It is not, "Will you have first a temporary heaven, and then hell eternal; or, will you have first a temporary hell, and then heaven eternal?" But it is simply this: "Will you be miserable threescore years, and miserable ever after; or, will you be happy threescore years, and happy ever after? Will you have a foretaste of heaven now, and then heaven forever; or will you have a foretaste of hell now and then hell forever? Will you have two hells, or two heavens?"

15. One would think, there needed no great sagacity to answer this question. And this is the very question which I now propose to you in the name of God. Will you be happy here and hereafter; in the world that now is, and in that which is to come? Or will you be miserable here and hereafter, in time and in eternity? What is your choice? Let there be no delay: Now take one or the other! I take heaven and earth to record this day, that I set before you life and death, blessing and cursing. O choose life! The life of peace and love now; the life of glory forever! By the grace of God, now choose that better part, which shall never be taken from you! And having once fixed your choice, never draw back; adhere to it at all events. Go on in the name of the Lord, whom ye have chosen, and in the power of his might! In spite of all opposition, from nature, from the world, from all the powers of darkness, still fight the good fight of faith, and lay hold on eternal life! And then there is laid up for you a crown, which the Lord, the righteous Judge, will give you at that day!

85.* ON WORKING OUT OUR OWN SALVATION

"Work out your own salvation with fear and trembling; For it is God that worketh in you both to will and to do of his good pleasure."

Phil. 2:12–13.

1. Some great truths, as the being and attributes of God, and the difference between moral good and evil, were known, in some measure, to the heathen world. The traces of them are to be found in all nations; So that, in some sense, it may be said to every child of man, "He hath showed thee, O man, what is good; even to do justly, to love mercy, and to walk humbly with thy God." With this truth he has, in some measure, "enlightened every one that cometh into the world." And hereby they that "have not the law," that have no written law, "are a law unto themselves." They show "the work of the law,"—the substance of it, though not the letter,—"written in their hearts," by the same hand which wrote the commandments on the tables of stone; "Their conscience also bearing them witness," whether they act suitably thereto or not.

2. But there are two grand heads of doctrine, which contain many truths of the most important nature, of which the most enlightened Heathens in the ancient world were totally ignorant; as are also the most intelligent Heathens that are now on the face of the earth; I mean those which relate to the eternal Son of God, and the Spirit of God: To the Son, giving himself to be "a propitiation for the sins of the world;" and to the Spirit of God, renewing men in that image of God wherein they were created. For after all the pains which ingenious and learned men have taken (that great man, the Chevalier Ramsay, in particular) to find some resemblance of these truths in the immense rubbish of heathen authors, the resemblance is so exceeding faint, as not to be discerned but by a very lively imagination. Beside that, even this resemblance, faint as it was, is only to be found in the discourses of a very few; and those were the most improved

---

* [text from the 1872 edition]

and deeply-thinking men, in their several generations; while the innumerable multitudes that surrounded them were little better for the knowledge of the philosophers, but remained as totally ignorant even of these capital truths as were the beasts that perish.

3. Certain it is, that these truths were never known to the vulgar, the bulk of mankind, to the generality of men in any nation, till they were brought to light by the gospel. Notwithstanding a spark of knowledge glimmering here and there, the whole earth was covered with darkness, till the Sun of Righteousness arose and scattered the shades of night. Since this day-spring from on high has appeared, a great light hath shined unto those who, till then, sat in darkness and in the shadow of death. And thousands of them in every age have known, "that God so loved the world, as to give his only Son, to the end that whosoever believeth on him should not perish, but have everlasting life." And being entrusted with the oracles of God, they have known that God hath also given us his Holy Spirit, who "worketh in us both to will and to do of his good pleasure."

4. How remarkable are those words of the Apostle, which precede these! "Let this mind be in you, which was also in Christ Jesus: Who, being in the form of God,"—the incommunicable nature of God from eternity—"counted it no act of robbery,"—(that is the precise meaning of the word,) no invasion of any other's prerogative, but his own unquestionable right,—"to be equal with God." The word implies both the *fullness* and the supreme *height* of the Godhead; to which are opposed the two words, he *emptied* and he *humbled himself.* He "emptied himself" of that divine fullness, veiled his fullness from the eyes of men and angels; "taking," and by that very act emptying himself, "the form of a servant; being made in the likeness of man," a real man, like other men. "And being found in fashion as a man,"—a common man, without any peculiar beauty or excellency,— "he humbled himself" to a still greater degree, "becoming obedient" to God, though equal with him, "even unto death; yea, the death of the cross:" The greatest instance both of humiliation and obedience. [Phil. 2:5–11]

Having proposed the example of Christ, the Apostle exhorts them to secure the salvation which Christ hath purchased for them: "Wherefore, work out your own salvation with fear and trembling; For it is God that worketh in you both to will and to do of his good pleasure."

In these comprehensive words we may observe,

I. That grand truth, which ought never to be out of our of remembrance, "It is God that worketh in us, both to will and to do of his own good pleasure."

II. The improvement we ought to make of it: "Work out your own salvation with fear and trembling."

III. The connexion between them: "It is God that worketh in you;" therefore "work out your own salvation."

I. 1. First. We are to observe that great and important truth which ought never to be out of our remembrance: "It is God that worketh in us both to will and to do of his good pleasure." The meaning of these words may be made more plain by a small transposition of them: "It is God that of his

good pleasure worketh in you both to will and to do." This position of the words, connecting the phrase, *of his good pleasure*, with the word *worketh*, removes all imagination of merit from man, and gives God the whole glory of his own work. Otherwise, we might have had some room for boasting, as if it were our own desert, some goodness in us, or some good thing done by us, which first moved God to work. But this expression cuts off all such vain conceits, and clearly shows his motive to work lay wholly in himself-in his, own mere grace, in his unmerited mercy.

2. It is by this alone he is impelled to work in man both to will and to do. The expression is capable of two interpretations; both of which are unquestionably true. First, *to will*, may include the whole of inward, *to do*, the whole of outward, religion. And if it be thus understood, it implies, that it is God that worketh both inward and outward holiness. Secondly, *to will*, may imply every good desire; *to do*, whatever results therefrom. And then the sentence means, God breathes into us every good desire, and brings every good desire to good effect.

3. The original words, *to thelein* and *to energein*, seem to favor the latter construction: *to thelein*, which we render *to will*, plainly including every good desire, whether relating to our tempers, words, or actions; to inward or outward holiness. And *to energein*, which we render *to do*, manifestly implies all that power from on high, all that energy which works in us every right disposition, and then furnishes us for every good word and work.

4. Nothing can so directly tend to hide pride from man as a deep, lasting conviction of this. For if we are thoroughly sensible that we have nothing which we have not received, how can we glory as if we had not received it? If we know and feel that the very first motion of good is from above, as well as the power which conducts it to the end; if it is God that not only infuses every good desire, but that accompanies and follows it, else it vanishes away; then it evidently follows, that he who glorieth must glory in the Lord.

II. 1. Proceed we now to the Second point: If God worketh in you, then work out your own salvation. The original word rendered, *work out*, implies the doing a thing thoroughly. *Your own*; for you yourselves must do this, or it will be left undone forever. Your *own salvation:* Salvation begins with what is usually termed (and very properly) *preventing grace*; including the first wish to please God, the first dawn of light concerning his will, and the first slight transient conviction of having sinned against him. All these imply some tendency toward life; some degree of salvation; the beginning of a deliverance from a blind, unfeeling heart, quite insensible of God and the things of God. Salvation is carried on by *convincing grace*, usually in Scripture termed *repentance*; which brings a larger measure of self-knowledge, and a farther deliverance from the heart of stone. Afterwards we experience the proper Christian salvation; whereby, through grace, we "are saved by faith;" consisting of those two grand branches, justification and sanctification. By justification we are saved from the guilt of sin, and restored to the favour of God; by sanctification we are saved from the power and root of sin, and restored to the image of God. All experience, as well as

Scripture, shows this salvation to be both instantaneous and gradual. It begins the moment we are justified, in the holy, humble, gentle, patient love of God and man. It gradually increases from that moment, as "a grain of mustard-seed, which, at first, is the least of all seeds," but afterwards puts forth large branches, and becomes a great tree; till, in another instant, the heart is cleansed, from all sin, and filled with pure love to God and man. But even that love increases more and more, till we "grow up in all things into him that is our head;" till we attain "the measure of the stature of the fullness of Christ."

2. But how are we to *work out* this salvation? The Apostle answers, "With fear and trembling." There is another passage of St. Paul wherein the same expression occurs, which may give light to this: "Servants, obey your masters according to the flesh," according to the present state of things, although sensible that in a little time the servant will be free from his master, "with fear and trembling." This is a proverbial expression, which cannot be understood literally. For what master could bear, much less require, his servant to stand trembling and quaking before him? And the following words utterly exclude this meaning: "In singleness of heart;" with a single eye to the will and providence of God; "not with eye-service, as men-pleasers; but as servants of Christ, doing the will of God from the heart;" doing whatever they do as the will of God, and, therefore, with their might. (eph. 6:5.) It is easy to see that these strong expressions of the Apostle clearly imply two things: First, that everything be done with the utmost earnestness of spirit, and with all care and caution: (Perhaps more directly referring to the former word, *meta phobou, with fear.*) Secondly, that it be done with the utmost diligence, speed, punctuality, and exactness; not improbably referring to the latter word, *meta tromou, with trembling.*

3. How easily may we transfer this to the business of life, the working out our own salvation! With the same temper, and in the same manner, that Christian servants serve their masters that are upon earth, let other Christians labour to serve their Master that is in heaven: that is, First, with the utmost earnestness of spirit, with all possible care and caution; and, secondly, with the utmost diligence, speed, punctuality, and exactness.

4. But what are the steps which the Scripture directs us to take, in the working out of our own salvation? The Prophet Isaiah gives us a general answer, touching the first steps which we are to take: "Cease to do evil; learn to do well." If ever you desire that God should work in you that faith whereof cometh both present and eternal salvation, by the grace already given, fly from all sin as from the face of a serpent; carefully avoid every evil word and work; yea, abstain from all appearance of evil. And "learn to do well:" Be zealous of good works, of works of piety, as well as works of mercy; family prayer, and crying to God in secret. Fast in secret, and "your Father which seeth in secret, he will reward you openly." "Search the Scriptures:" Hear them in public, read them in private, and meditate therein. At every opportunity, be a partaker of the Lord's Supper. "Do this in remembrance of him: and he will meet you at his own table. Let your conversation be with the children of God; and see that it "be in grace, seasoned with salt." As ye have time, do good unto all men; to their souls and to their bodies. And herein "be ye steadfast, unmovable, always abounding in the work of the Lord." It then only remains that ye deny yourselves and take up your cross daily. Deny yourselves every pleasure which does not prepare you for taking pleasure in God, and willingly embrace every means of drawing near to God, though it be a cross, though it be grievous to flesh and blood. Thus when you have redemption in the blood of Christ, you will "go on to perfection;" till "walking in the light as he is in the light," you are enabled to testify, that "he is faithful and just," not only to "forgive" your "sins," but to "cleanse" you from all unrighteousness." [1 John 1:9]

III. 1. "But," say some, "what connexion is there between the former and the latter clause of this sentence? Is there not rather a flat opposition between the one and the other? If it is God that worketh in us both to will and to do, what need is there of our working? Does not his working thus supersede the necessity of our working at all? Nay, does it not render our working impracticable, as well as unnecessary? For if we allow that God does all, what is there left for us to do?"

2. Such is the reasoning of flesh and blood. And, at first hearing, it is exceeding plausible. But it is not solid; as will evidently appear, if we consider the matter more deeply. We shall then see there is no opposition between these, "God works; therefore, do we work;" but, on the contrary, the closest connexion; and that in two respects. For, First, God works; therefore you *can* work. Secondly, God works, therefore you *must* work.

3. First. God worketh in you; therefore you *can* work: Otherwise it would be impossible. If he did not work it would be impossible for you to work out your own salvation. "With man this is impossible," saith our Lord, "for a rich man to enter into the kingdom of heaven." Yea, it is impossible for any man, for any that is born of a woman, unless God work in him. Seeing all men are by nature not only sick, but "dead in trespasses and sins," it is not possible for them to do anything well till God raises them from the dead. It was impossible for Lazarus to come forth, till the Lord had given him life. And it is equally impossible for us to *come* out of our sins, yea, or to make the least motion toward it, till He who hath all power in heaven and earth calls our dead souls into life.

4. Yet this is no excuse for those who continue in sin, and lay the blame upon their Maker, by saying, "It is God only that must quicken us; for we cannot quicken our own souls." For allowing that all the souls of men are dead in sin by *nature*, this excuses none, seeing there is no man that is in a state of mere nature; there is no man, unless he has quenched the Spirit, that is wholly void of the grace of God. No man living is entirely destitute of what is vulgarly called *natural conscience*. But this is not natural: It is more properly termed *preventing grace*. Every man has a greater or less measure of this, which waiteth not for the call of man. Every one has, sooner or later, good desires; although the generality of men stifle them before they can strike deep root, or produce any considerable fruit. Everyone has some measure of that light, some faint glimmering ray, which, sooner or later, more or

less, enlightens every man that cometh into the world. And every one, unless he be one of the small number whose conscience is seared as with a hot iron, feels more or less uneasy when he acts contrary to the light of his own conscience. So that no man sins because he has not grace, but because he does not use the grace which he hath.

5. Therefore inasmuch as God works in you, you are now able to work out your own salvation. Since he worketh in you of his own good pleasure, without any merit of yours, both to will and to do, it is possible for you to fulfil all righteousness. It is possible for you to "love God, because he hath first loved us;" and to "walk in love," after the pattern of our great Master. We know, indeed, that word of his to be absolutely true: "Without me ye can do nothing." But on the other hand, we know, every believer can say "I can do all things through Christ that strengtheneth me."

6. Meantime let us remember that God has joined these together in the experience of every believer; and therefore we must take care, not to imagine they are ever to be put asunder. We must beware of that mock humility which teacheth us to say, in excuse for our wilful disobedience, "O, I can do nothing!" and stops there, without once naming the grace of God. Pray, think twice. Consider what you say. I hope you wrong yourself; for if it be really true that you can do nothing, then you have no faith. And if you have not faith, you are in a wretched condition: You are not in a state of salvation. Surely it is not so. You can do something, through Christ strengthening you. Stir up the spark of grace which is now in you, and he will give you more grace.

7. Secondly, God worketh in you; therefore you *must* work: You must be "workers together with him," (they are the very words of the Apostle,) otherwise he will cease working. The general rule on which his gracious dispensations invariably proceed is this: "Unto him that hath shall be given; but from him that hath not,"—that does not improve the grace already given,—"shall be taken away what he assuredly hath." (So the words ought to be rendered.) Even St. Augustine, who is generally supposed to favour the contrary doctrine, makes that just remark, *Qui fecit nos sine nobis, non salvabit nos sine nobis*: "He that made us without ourselves, will not save us without ourselves." He will not save us unless we "save ourselves from this untoward generation;" unless we ourselves "fight the good fight of faith, and lay hold on eternal life; "unless we "agonize to enter in at the strait gate," "deny ourselves, and take up our cross daily," and labour by every possible means to "make our own calling and election sure."

8. "Labour" then, brethren, "not for the meat that perisheth, but for that which endureth to everlasting life." Say with our blessed Lord, though in a somewhat different sense, "My Father worketh hitherto, and I work." In consideration that he still worketh in you, be never "weary of well-doing." Go on, in virtue of the grace of God, preventing, accompanying, and following you, in "the work of faith, in the patience of hope, and in the labour of love." "Be ye steadfast and immovable, always abounding in the work of the Lord." And

"the God of peace, who brought again from the dead the great Shepherd of the sheep," (Jesus,) "make you perfect in every good work to do his will, working in you what is well-pleasing in his sight, through Jesus Christ; to whom be glory for ever and ever!"

86.* A CALL TO BACKSLIDERS

"Will the Lord absent himself for ever? And will he be no more entreated? Is his mercy clean gone for ever? And is his promise come utterly to an end for evermore?"

Ps. 77:7, 8.

1. Presumption is one grand snare of the devil, in which many of the children of men are taken. They so presume upon the mercy of God as utterly to forget his justice. Although he has expressly declared, "Without holiness no man shall see the Lord," yet they flatter themselves, that in the end God will be better than his word. They imagine they may live and die in their sins, and nevertheless "escape the damnation of hell."

2. But although there are many that are destroyed by presumption, there are still more that perish by despair. I mean, by want of hope; by thinking it impossible that they should escape destruction. Having many times fought against their spiritual enemies, and always been overcome, they lay down their arms; they no more contend, as they have no hope of victory. Knowing, by melancholy experience that they have no power of themselves to help themselves, and having no expectation that God will help them, they lie down under their burden. They no longer strive; for they suppose it is impossible they should attain.

3. In this case, as in a thousand others, "the heart knoweth its own bitterness, but a stranger intermeddleth not with his grief." It is not easy for those to know it who never felt it: For "who knoweth the things of a man, but the spirit of a man that is in him?" Who knoweth, unless by his own experience, what this sort of *wounded spirit* means? Of consequence, there are few that know how to sympathize with them that are under this sore temptation. There are few that have duly considered the case; few that are not deceived by appearances. They see men go on in a course of sin, and take it for granted, it is out of mere presumption: Whereas, in reality, it is from the quite contrary principle;—it is out of mere despair. Either they have no hope at all,—and while that is the case, they do not strive at all,—or they have some intervals of hope, and while that lasts, "strive for the mastery." But that hope soon fails: They then cease to strive, and "are taken captive of Satan at his will."

4. This is frequently the case with those that began to run well, but soon tired in the heavenly road; with those in particular who once "saw the glory of God in the face of Jesus Christ," but afterwards grieved his Holy Spirit, and made shipwreck of the faith. Indeed, many of these rush into sin, as a horse into the battle. They sin with so high an hand, as utterly to quench the Holy Spirit of God; so that he gives them up to their own heart's lusts, and lets them follow their

---

* [text from the 1872 edition]

own imaginations. And those who are thus given up may be quite stupid, without either fear, or sorrow, or care; utterly easy and unconcerned about God, or heaven, or hell; to which the god of this world contributes not a little, by blinding and hardening their hearts. But still even these would not be so careless, were it not for despair. The great reason why they have no sorrow or care is, because they have no hope. They verily believe they have so provoked God, that "he will be no more entreated."

5. And yet we need not utterly give up even these. We have known some even of the careless ones whom God has visited again, and restored to their first love. But we may have much more hope for those backsliders who are not careless, who are still uneasy;—those who fain would escape out of the snare of the devil, but think it is impossible. They are fully convinced they cannot save themselves, and believe God *will* not save them. They believe he has irrevocably "shut up his lovingkindness in displeasure." They fortify themselves in believing this, by abundance of reasons; and unless those reasons are clearly removed, they cannot hope for any deliverance.

It is in order to relieve these hopeless, helpless souls, that I propose, with God's assistance,

I. To inquire what the chief of those reasons are, some or other of which induce so many backsliders to cast away hope; to suppose that God hath forgotten to be gracious. And,

II. To give a clear and full answer to each of those reasons.

I. I am, First, to inquire, what the chief of those reasons are, which induce so many backsliders to think that God hath forgotten to be gracious. I do not say *all* the reasons; for innumerable are those which either their own evil hearts, or that old serpent, will suggest; but the chief of them;—those that are most plausible, and therefore most common.

1. The first argument which induces many backsliders to believe that "the Lord will be no more entreated," is drawn from the very reason of the thing: "If," say they, "a man rebel against an earthly prince, many times he dies for the first offence; he pays his life for the first transgression. Yet, possibly, if the crime be extenuated by some favourable circumstance, or if strong intercession be made for him, his life may be given him. But if, after a full and free pardon he were guilty of rebelling a second time, who would dare to intercede for him? He must expect no farther mercy. Now, if one rebelling against an earthly king, after he has been freely pardoned once, cannot with any colour of reason hope to be forgiven a second time; what must be the case of him that, after having been freely pardoned for rebelling against the great King of heaven and earth, rebels against him again? What can be expected, but that 'vengeance will come upon him to the uttermost' "

2. (1.) This argument, drawn from reason, they enforce by several passages of Scripture. One of the strongest of these is that which occurs in the First Epistle of St. John: (1 John 5:16.) "If any man see his brother sin a sin which is not unto death, he shall ask, and God shall give him life for them that sin not unto death. There is a sin unto death. I do not say that he shall pray for it."

Hence they argue, "Certainly, *I do not say that he shall pray for it*, is equivalent with, *I say he shall not pray for it*. So the Apostle supposes him that has committed this sin, to be in a desperate state indeed! So desperate, that we may not even pray for his forgiveness; we may not ask life for him And what may we more reasonably suppose to be a sin unto death, than a wilful rebellion after a full and free pardon?

(2). "Consider, Secondly," say they, "those terrible passages in the Epistle to the Hebrews; one of which occurs in the sixth chapter, the other in the tenth. To begin with the latter "If we sin wilfully, after we have received the knowledge of the truth, there remaineth no other sacrifice for sins; but a certain fearful looking for of judgment and fiery indignation, which shall devour the adversaries. He that despised Moses' law died without mercy: Of how much sorer punishment, suppose ye, shall he be thought worthy, who hath trodden under foot the Son of God, counted the blood of the covenant wherewith he was sanctified an unholy thing, and done despite to the Spirit of grace? For we know him that hath said, Vengeance is mine; I will recompense, saith the Lord. It is a fearful thing to fall into the hands of the living God!' (Heb. 10:26–31.) Now, is it not here expressly declared by the Holy Ghost, that our case is desperate? Is it not declared, that 'if, after we have received the knowledge of the truth,' after we have experimentally known it, 'we sin wilfully,'—which we have undoubtedly done, and that over and over,—'there remaineth no other sacrifice for sin; but a certain looking for of judgment and fiery indignation, which shall devour the adversaries?'

(3.) "And is not that passage in the sixth chapter exactly parallel with this? 'It is impossible for those that were once enlightened, and have tasted of the heavenly gift, and were made partakers of the Holy Ghost,—if they fall away,' (literally, *and have fallen away*,) 'to renew them again unto repentance: Seeing they crucify to themselves the Son of God afresh, and put him to an open shame.' (Heb. 6:4–6.)

(4.) "It is true, some are of opinion, that those words, *it is impossible*, are not to be taken literally as denoting absolute impossibility; but only a very great difficulty. But it does not appear that we have any sufficient reason to depart from the literal meaning; as it neither implies any absurdity, nor contradicts any other Scriptures. Does not this then," say they, "cut off all hope; seeing we have undoubtedly, 'tasted of the heavenly gift, and been made partakers of the Holy Ghost?' How is it possible to 'renew us again to repentance;' to an entire change both of heart and life? Seeing we have crucified to ourselves 'the Son of God afresh, and put him to an open shame.'

(5.) "A yet more dreadful passage, if possible, than this, is that in the twelfth chapter of St. Matthew: 'All manner of sin and blasphemy shall be forgiven unto men: But the blasphemy against the Holy Ghost shall not be forgiven unto men: And whosoever speaketh a word against the Son of man, it shall be forgiven him. But whosoever speaketh against the Holy Ghost, it shall not be forgiven him, neither in this world, nor in the world to come.' (Matt. 12:31, 32.) Exactly parallel to these are those words of our Lord, which are recited by St. Mark: 'Verily I say unto you, All sins shall be forgiven unto the sons of men, and blasphemies wherewith soever they blaspheme: But he that shall blaspheme against the Holy Ghost shall never be forgiven, but is in danger of eternal damnation.' (Mark 3:28, 29.)

(6.) It has been the judgment of some, that all these passages point at one and the same sin; that not only the words of our Lord, but those of St. John, concerning the 'sin unto death,' and those of St. Paul concerning 'crucifying to themselves the Son of God afresh, treading underfoot the Son of God, and doing despite to the Spirit of grace, 'all refer to the blasphemy against the Holy Ghost; the only sin that shall never be forgiven. Whether they do or no, it must be allowed that this blasphemy is absolutely unpardonable; and that, consequently, for those who have been guilty of this, God 'will be no more entreated.'

3. To confirm those arguments, drawn from reason and Scripture, they appeal to matter of fact. They ask, "Is it not a fact, that those who fall away from justifying grace, who make 'shipwreck of the faith,' that faith whereof cometh present salvation, perish without mercy? How much less can any of those escape, who fall away from sanctifying grace! who make shipwreck of that faith whereby they are cleansed from all pollution of flesh and spirit! Has there ever been an instance of one or the other of these being renewed again to repentance? If there be any instances of that, one would be inclined to believe that thought of our poet not to be extravagant:—

> "E'en Judas struggles his despair to quell,
> Hope almost blossoms in the shades of hell."

II. These are the principal arguments drawn from reason, from Scripture, and from fact, whereby backsliders are wont to justify themselves in casting away hope; in supposing that God hath utterly "shut up his lovingkindness in displeasure." I have proposed them in their full strength, that we may form the better judgment concerning them, and try whether each of them may not receive a clear, full, satisfactory answer.

1. I begin with that argument which is taken from the nature of the thing: "If a man rebel against an earthly prince, he may possibly be forgiven the first time. But if, after a full and free pardon, he should rebel again, there is no hope of obtaining a second pardon: He must expect to die without mercy. Now, if he that rebels again against an earthly king, can look for no second pardon, how can he look for mercy who rebels a second time against the great King of heaven and earth?"

2. I answer: This argument, drawn from the analogy between earthly and heavenly things, is plausible, but it is not solid; and that for this plain reason: Analogy has no place here: There can be no analogy or proportion between the mercy of any of the children of men, and that of the most high God. "Unto whom will ye liken me, saith the Lord?" Unto whom either in heaven or earth? Who, "what is he among the gods, that shall be compared unto the Lord?" "I have said, Ye are gods," saith the Psalmist, speaking to supreme magistrates. Such is your dignity and power compared to that of common men. But what are they to the God of heaven? As a bubble upon the wave. What is their power in comparison of his power? What is their mercy compared to his mercy? Hence that comfortable word, "I am God, and not man, therefore the house of Israel is not consumed." Because he is God, and not man, "therefore his compassions fail not." None then can infer, that because an earthly king will not pardon one that rebels against him a second time, therefore the King of heaven will not. Yea, he will; not until seven times only, or until seventy times seven. Nay, were your rebellions multiplied as the stars of heaven; were they more in number than the hairs of your head; yet "return unto the Lord, and he will have mercy upon you; and to our God, and he will abundantly pardon."

3. "But does not St. John cut us off from this hope, by what he says of the 'sin unto death?' Is not, 'I do not say that he shall pray for it,' equivalent with, 'I say he shall not pray for it?' And does not this imply, that God has determined not to hear that prayer? that he will not give life to such a sinner, no, not through the prayer of a righteous man?"

4. I answer: "I do not say that he shall pray for it," certainly means, he shall not pray for it. And it doubtless implies that God will not give life unto them that have sinned this sin; that their sentence is passed, and God has determined it shall not be revoked. It cannot be altered even by that "effectual fervent prayer" which, in other cases, "availeth much."

5. But I ask, First, What is the sin unto death? And, Secondly, What is the death which is annexed to it?

(1) And, First, what is the sin unto death? It is now many years since, being among a people the most experienced in the things of God of any I had ever seen, I asked some of them, What do you understand by the "sin unto death," mentioned in the First Epistle of St. John? They answered, "If anyone is sick among us, he sends for the elders of the Church; and they pray over him, and the prayer of faith saves the sick, and the Lord raises him up. And if he hath committed sins, which God was punishing by that sickness, they are forgiven him. But sometimes none of us can pray that God would raise him up. And we are constrained to tell him, We are afraid that you have sinned a sin unto death;' a sin that God has determined to punish with death; we cannot pray for your recovery. And we have never yet known an instance of such a person recovering."

(2.) I see no absurdity at all in this interpretation of the word. It seems to be one meaning (at least) of the expression, "a sin unto death;" a sin which God has determined to punish by the death of the sinner. If, therefore, you have sinned a sin of this kind, and your sin has overtaken you; if God is chastising you by some severe disease, it will not avail to pray for your life; you are irrevocably sentenced to die. But observe! This has no reference to eternal death. It does by no means imply that you are condemned to die the second death. No; it rather implies the contrary: The body is destroyed, that the soul may escape destruction. I have myself, during the course of many years, seen numerous instances of this. I have known many sinners (chiefly notorious backsliders from high degrees of holiness, and such as had given great occasion to the enemies of religion to blaspheme) whom God has cut short in the midst of their journey; yea, before they had lived out half their days: These, I apprehend, had sinned "a sin unto death;" in consequence of which they were cut off, sometimes more swiftly, sometimes more slowly, by an unexpected stroke. But in most of these cases it has been observed that "mercy rejoiced over judgment." And the persons themselves were fully convinced of the goodness as well as justice of God. They acknowledged that he destroyed the body in order to save the soul. Before they went hence, he healed their backsliding. So they died that they might live for ever.

(3.) A very remarkable instance of this occurred many years ago. young collier [coal miner] in Kingswood, near Bristol, was an eminent sinner, and afterwards an eminent saint. But, by little and little, he renewed his acquaintance with his old companions, who by degrees wrought upon him, till he dropped all his religion, and was two-fold more a child of hell than before. One day he was working in the pit with a serious young man, who suddenly stopped and cried out, "O Tommy, what a man was you once! How did your words and example provoke many to love and to good works! And what are you now? What would become of you, if you were to die as you are?" "Nay, God forbid," said Thomas, "for then I should fall into hell headlong! O let us cry to God!" They did so for a considerable time, first the one, and then the other. They called upon God with strong cries and tears, wrestling with him in mighty prayer. After some time, Thomas broke out, "Now I know God hath healed my backsliding. I know again, that my Redeemer liveth, and that he hath washed me from my sins with his own blood. I am willing to go to him." Instantly part of the pit calved in, and crushed him to death in a moment. Whoever thou art that hast sinned "a sin unto death," lay this to heart! It may be, God will require thy soul of thee in an hour when thou lookest not for it! But if he doth, there is mercy in the midst of judgment: Thou shalt not die eternally.

6. "But what say you to that other scripture, namely, the tenth of the Hebrews? Does that leave any hope to notorious backsliders, that they shall not die eternally; that they can ever recover the favour of God, or escape the damnation of hell? "If we sin wilfully after we have received the knowledge of the truth, there remaineth no other sacrifice for sins; but a certain fearful looking for of judgment and fiery indignation, which shall devour the adversaries. He that despised Moses' law died without mercy. Of how much sorer punishment, suppose ye, shall he be thought worthy, who hath trodden under foot the Son of God, and counted the blood of the covenant, wherewith he was sanctified, an unholy thing, and done despite unto the Spirit of grace?"

7. "And is not the same thing, namely, the desperate, irrecoverable state of wilful backsliders, fully confirmed by that parallel passage in the sixth chapter? "It is impossible for those who were once enlightened, and partakers of the Holy Ghost,—and have fallen away,"—so it is in the original,— "to renew them again unto repentance; seeing they crucify to themselves the Son of God afresh, and put him to an open shame.' "

8. These passages do seem to me parallel to each other, and deserve our deepest consideration. And in order to understand them it will be necessary to know, (1.) Who are the persons here spoken of; and (2.) What is the sin they had committed, which made their case nearly, if not quite, desperate.

(1.) As to the First, it will be clear to all who impartially consider and compare both these passages, that the persons spoken of herein are those, and those only, that have been justified; that the eyes of their understanding were opened and "enlightened," to see the light of the glory of God in the face of Jesus Christ. These only "have tasted of the heavenly gift," remission of sins, eminently so called. These "were made partakers of the Holy Ghost," both of the witness and the fruit of the Spirit. This character cannot, with any propriety, be applied to any but those that have been justified.

And they had been sanctified too; at least, in the first degree, as far as all are who receive remission of sins. So the second passage expressly, "Who hath counted the blood of the covenant, wherewith he was sanctifed, an unholy thing."

Hence it follows, that this Scripture concerns those alone who have been justified, and at least in part, sanctified. Therefore all of you, who never were thus "enlightened" with the light of the glory of God; all who never did "taste of the heavenly gift," who never received remission of sins; all who never "were made partakers of the Holy Ghost," of the witness and fruit of the Spirit;—in a word, all you who never were sanctified by the blood of the everlasting covenant, you are not concerned here. Whatever other passages of Scripture may condemn you, it is certain, you are not condemned either by the sixth or the tenth of the Hebrews. For both those passages speak wholly and solely of apostates from the faith which you never had. Therefore, it was not possible that you should lose it, for you could not lose what you had not. Therefore whatever judgments are denounced in these scriptures, they are not denounced against *you*. You are not the persons here described, against whom only they are denounced.

(2.) Inquire we next, What was the sin which the persons here described were guilty of? In order to understand this, we should remember, that whenever the Jews prevailed on a Christian to apostatize, they required him to declare, in express terms, and that in the public assembly, that Jesus of Nazareth was a deceiver of the people; and that he had suffered no more punishment than his crimes justly deserved. This is the sin which St. Paul, in the first passage, terms emphatically "falling away;" "crucifying the Son of God afresh, and putting him to an open shame." This is that which he terms in the second, "counting the blood of the covenant an unholy thing, treading under foot the Son of God, and doing despite to the Spirit of grace." Now, which of you has thus fallen away? Which of you has thus "crucified the Son of God afresh?" Not one: Nor has one of you thus "put him to an open shame." If you had thus formally renounced that "only sacrifice for sin," there had no other sacrifice remained; so that you must have perished without mercy. But this is not your case. Not one of you has thus renounced that sacrifice, by which the Son of God made a full and perfect satisfaction for the sins of the whole world. Bad as you are, you shudder at the thought: there fore that sacrifice still remains for you. Come then, cast away your needless fears! "Come boldly to the throne of grace." The way is still open. You shall again "obtain mercy, and find grace to help in time of need."

9. "But do not the well-known words of our Lord himself cut us off from all hope of mercy? Does he not say, 'All manner of sin and blasphemy shall be forgiven unto men: But the blasphemy against the Holy Ghost shall not be forgiven unto men. And whosoever speaketh a word against the Son of man, it shall be forgiven him: But whosoever speaketh a word against the Holy Ghost, it shall never be forgiven him; neither in this world, nor in the world to come?' Therefore, it is plain, if we have been guilty of this sin, there is no room for mercy. And is not the same thing repeated by St. Mark, almost in the same words? 'Verily I say unto you,' (a solemn preface! always denoting the great importance of that which follows,) 'All sins shall be forgiven unto the sons of men, and blasphemies wherewith soever they shall blaspheme: But he that shall blaspheme against the Holy Ghost hath never forgiveness, but is under the sentence of eternal damnation.' "

(1.) How immense is the number in every nation throughout the Christian world of those who have been more or less distressed on account of this Scripture! What multitudes in this kingdom have been perplexed above measure upon this very account! Nay, there are few that are truly convinced of sin, and seriously endeavour to save their souls, who have not felt some uneasiness for fear they had committed, or should commit, this unpardonable sin. What has frequently increased their uneasiness was, that they could hardly find any to comfort them. For their acquaintances, even the most religious of them, understood no more of the matter than themselves; and they could not find any writer who had published anything satisfactory upon the subject. Indeed, in the "Seven Sermons" of Mr. Russell, which are common among us, there is one expressly written upon it; but it will give little satisfaction to a troubled spirit. He talks *about it, and about it*, but makes nothing out: He takes much pains, but misses the mark at last.

(2.) But was there ever in the world a more deplorable proof of the littleness of human understanding, even in those that have honest hearts, and are desirous of knowing the truth! How is it possible that any one who reads his Bible, can one hour remain in doubt concerning it, when our Lord himself, in the very passage cited above, has so clearly told us what that blasphemy is? "He that blasphemeth against the Holy Ghost hath never forgiveness: Because they said, He hath an unclean spirit." (Mark 3:29–30.) This then, and this alone, (if we allow our Lord to understand his own meaning,) is the blasphemy against the Holy Ghost: *The saying, He had an unclean spirit*; the affirming that Christ wrought his miracles by the power of an evil spirit; or, more particularly, that "he cast out devils by Beelzebub, the prince of the devils." Now, have *you* been guilty of this? have *you* affirmed, that he cast out devils by the prince of devils? No more than you have cut your neighbour's throat, and set his house on fire. How marvellously then have you been afraid, where no fear is! Dismiss that vain terror; let your fear be more rational for the time to come. Be afraid of giving way to pride; be afraid of yielding to anger; be afraid of loving the world or the things of the world; be afraid of foolish and hurtful desires; but never more be afraid of committing the blasphemy against the Holy Ghost! You are in no more danger of doing this, than of pulling the sun out of the firmament.

10. Ye have then no reason from Scripture for imagining that "the Lord hath forgotten to be gracious." The arguments drawn from thence, you see, are of no weight, are utterly inconclusive. Is there any more weight in that which has been drawn from experience or matter of fact?

(1.) This is a point which may exactly be determined, and that with the utmost certainty. If it be asked, "Do any real apostates find mercy from God? Do any that have 'made shipwreck of faith and a good conscience,' recover what they have lost? Do you know, have you seen, any instance of persons who found redemption in the blood of Jesus, and afterwards fell away, and yet were restored,—'renewed again to repentance?' " Yea, verily; and not one, or an hundred only, but, I am persuaded, several thousands. In every place where the arm of the Lord has been revealed, and many sinners converted to God, there are several found who "turn back from the holy commandment delivered to them." For a great part of these "it had been better never to have known the way of righteousness." It only increases their damnation, seeing they die in their sins. But others there are who "look unto him they have pierced, and mourn," refusing to be comforted. And, sooner or later, he surely lifts up the light of his countenance upon them; he strengthens the hands that hang down, and confirms the feeble knees; he teaches them again to say, "My soul doth magnify the Lord, and my spirit rejoiceth in God my Saviour." Innumerable are the instances of this kind, of those who had fallen, but now stand upright. Indeed, it is so far from being an uncommon thing for a believer to fall and be restored, that it is rather uncommon to find any believers who are not conscious of having been backsliders from God, in a higher or lower degree, and perhaps more than once, before they were established in faith.

(2.) "But have any that had fallen from sanctifying grace been restored to the blessing they had lost?" This also is a point of experience; and we have had the opportunity of repeating our observations, during a considerable course of years, and from the one end of the kingdom to the other.

(3.) And, First, we have known a large number of persons, of every age and sex, from early childhood to extreme old age, who have given all the proofs which the nature of the thing admits, that they were "sanctified throughout;" "cleansed from all pollution of the flesh and spirit;" that they "loved the Lord their God with all their heart, and mind, and soul, and strength;" that they continually "presented" their souls and bodies "a living sacrifice, holy, acceptable to God;" in consequence of which, they "rejoiced evermore, prayed without ceasing, and in every thing gave thanks." And this, and no other, is what we believe to be true, scriptural sanctification.

(4.) Secondly. It is a common thing for those who are thus sanctified, to believe they cannot fall; to suppose themselves "pillars in the temple of God, that shall go out no more." Nevertheless, we have seen some of the strongest of them, after a time, moved from their steadfastness. Sometimes suddenly, but oftener by slow degrees, they have yielded to temptation; and pride, or anger, or foolish desires have again sprung up in their hearts. Nay, sometimes they have utterly lost the life of God, and sin hath regained dominion over them.

(5.) Yet, Thirdly, several of these, after being thoroughly sensible of their fall, and deeply ashamed before God, have been again filled with his love, and not only perfected therein, but stablished, strengthened, and settled. They have received the blessing they had before with abundant increase. Nay, it is remarkable, that many who had fallen either from justifying or from sanctifying grace, and so deeply fallen that they could hardly be ranked among the servants of God, have been restored, (but seldom till they had been shaken, as it were, over the mouth of hell,) and that very frequently in an instant, to all that they had lost. They have, at once, recovered both a consciousness of his favour, and the experience of the pure love of God. In one moment they received anew both remission of sins, and a lot among them that were sanctified.

(6.) But let not any man infer from this longsuffering of God, that he hath given any one a license to sin. Neither let any dare to continue in sin, because of these extraordinary instanced of divine mercy. This is the most desperate, the most irrational presumption, and leads to utter, irrecoverable destruction. In all my experience, I have not known one who fortified himself in sin by a presumption that God would save him at the last, that was not miserably disappointed, and suffered to die in his sins. To turn the grace of God into an encouragement to sin is the sure way to the nethermost hell!

(7.) It is not for these desperate children of perdition that the preceding considerations are designed; but for those who feel "the remembrance of their sins is grievous unto them, the burden of them intolerable." We set before these an open door of hope: Let them go in and give thanks unto the Lord; let them know that "the Lord is gracious and merciful, longsuffering, and of great goodness." "Look how high the heavens are from the earth! so far will he set their sins from them." "He will not always be chiding; neither keepeth he his anger for ever." Only settle it in your heart, *I will give all for all*, and the offering shall be accepted. Give him all your heart! Let all that is within you continually cry out, "Thou art my God, and I will thank thee; thou art my God, and I will praise thee." "This God is my God for ever and ever! He shall be my guide even unto death."

87.* The Danger of Riches

"They that will be rich fall into temptation and a snare, and into many foolish and hurtful desires, which drown men in destruction and perdition."

1 Tim. 6:9.

1. How innumerable are the ill consequences which have followed from men's not knowing, or not considering, this great truth! And how few are there even in the Christian world, that either know or duly consider it! Yea, how small is the number of those, even among real Christians, who understand and lay it to heart! Most of these too pass it very lightly over, scarce remembering there is such a text in the Bible. And many put such a construction upon it, as makes it of no manner of effect. "They that will be rich," say they, "that is, will be rich at all events, who Will be rich right or wrong; that are resolved to carry their point, to compass this end, whatever means they use to attain it; they 'fall into temptation,'" and into all the evils enumerated by the Apostle." But truly if this were all the meaning of the text, it might as well have been out of the Bible.

2. This is so far from being the whole meaning of the text, that it is no part of its meaning. The Apostle does not here speak of gaining riches unjustly, but of quite another thing: His words are to be taken in their plain obvious sense, without any restriction or qualification whatsoever. St. Paul does not say, "They that will be rich *by evil means*, by theft, robbery, oppression, or extortion; they that will be rich by fraud or dishonest art; but simply, "they that will be rich:" These, allowing, supposing the means they use to be ever so innocent, "fall into temptation and a snare, and into many foolish and hurtful desires, which drown men in destruction and perdition."

3. But who believes that? Who receives it as the truth of God? Who is deeply convinced of it? Who preaches this? Great is the company of preachers at this day, regular and irregular; but who of them all openly and explicitly, preaches this strange doctrine? It is the keen observation of a great man, "The pulpit is a fearful preacher's strong-hold." But who even in his strong-hold, has the courage to declare so unfashionable a truth? I do not remember that in threescore years I have heard one sermon preached upon this subject. And what author, within the same term, has declared it from the press? at least, in the English tongue? I do not know one. I have neither seen nor heard of any such author. I have seen two or three who just touch upon it; but none that treats of it professedly. I have myself frequently touched upon it in preaching, and twice in what I have published to the world: Once in explaining our Lord's Sermon on the Mount, and once in the discourse on the "Mammon of unrighteousness;" but I have never yet either published or preached any sermon expressly upon the subject. It is high time I should;—that I should at length speak as strongly and explicitly as I can, in order to leave a full and clear testimony behind me, whenever it pleases God to call me hence.

4. O that God would give me to speak right and forcible words; and you to receive them in honest and humble hearts! Let it not be said, "They sit before thee as my people, and they hear thy words; but they will not do them. Thou art unto them as one that hath a pleasant voice, and can play well on an instrument; for they hear thy words, but they do them not!" O that ye may "not be forgetful hearers, but doers of the word," that ye may be "blessed in your deed!" In this hope I shall endeavour,

I. To explain the Apostle's words. And,

---

* [text from the 1872 edition]

II. To apply them.

But O! "who is sufficient for these things?" Who is able to stem the general torrent? to combat all the prejudices, not only of the vulgar, but of the learned and the religious world? Yet nothing is too hard for God! Still his grace is sufficient for us. In his name, then, and by his strength I will endeavour.

I. To explain the words of the Apostle.

1. And, First, let us consider, what it is to be rich. What does the Apostle mean by this expression?

The preceding verse fixes the meaning of that: "Having food and raiment," (literally *coverings*; for the word includes lodging as well as clothes) "let us be therewith content." "But they that will be rich;" that is, who will have more than these; more than food and coverings. It plainly follows, whatever is more than these is, in the sense of the Apostle, *riches*; whatever is above the plain necessaries, or at most conveniences, of life. Whoever has sufficient food to eat, and raiment to put on, with a place where to lay his head, and something over, is *rich*.

2. Let us consider, Secondly, What is implied in that expression, "They that will be rich?" And does not this imply, First, they that desire to be rich, to have more than *food* and *coverings*; they that seriously and deliberately desire more than food to eat, and raiment to put on, and a place where to lay their head, more than the plain necessaries and conveniences of life? All, at least, who allow themselves in this desire, who see no harm in it, desire to be rich.

3. And so do, Secondly, all those that calmly, deliberately, and of set purpose *endeavour* after more than food and coverings; that aim at and endeavour after, not only so much worldly substance as will procure them the necessaries and conveniences of life, but more than this, whether to lay it up, or lay it out in superfluities. All these undeniably prove their "desire to be rich" by their endeavours after it.

4. Must we not, Thirdly, rank among those that desire to be rich, all that, in fact "lay up treasures on earth?" a thing as expressly and clearly forbidden by our Lord as either adultery or murder. It is allowed, (1.) That we are to provide necessaries and conveniences for those of our own household: (2.) That men in business are to lay up as much as is necessary for the carrying on of that business: (3.) That we are to leave our children what will supply them with necessaries and conveniences after we have left the world: and (4.) That we are to provide things honest in the sight of all men, so as to "owe no man anything." But to lay up any more, when this is done, is what our Lord has flatly forbidden. When it is calmly and deliberately done, it is a clear proof of our desiring to be rich. And thus to lay up money is no more consistent with good conscience, than to throw it into the sea.

5. We must rank among them, Fourthly, all who *possess* more of this world's goods than they use according to the will of the Donor: I should rather say, of the Proprietor; for He only *lends* them to us as Stewards; reserving the *property* of them to himself. And, indeed, he cannot possibly do otherwise, seeing they are the work of his hands; he is, and must be, the possessor of heaven and earth. This is his unalienable right; a right he cannot divest himself of. And

together with that portion of his goods which he hath lodged in our hands he has delivered to us a writing, specifying the purposes for which he has intrusted us with them. If therefore we keep more of them in our hands than is necessary for the preceding purposes, we certainly fall under the charge of "desiring to be rich." Over and above, we are guilty of burying our Lord's talent in the earth, and on that account are liable to be pronounced wicked, because unprofitable, servants.

6. Under this imputation of "desiring to be rich," fall, Fifthly, all "lovers of money." The word properly means, those that *delight in money*; those that take pleasure in it; those that seek their happiness therein; that brood over their gold and silver, bills or bonds. Such was the man described by the fine Roman painter, who broke out into that natural soliloquy:—

> … Populus me sibilat, at mihi plaudo
> Ipse domi simul ac nummos contemplor in arca.

[The following is Francis's translation of these lines from Horace:

> "Let them his on,
> While, in my own opinion fully blest,
> I count my money, and enjoy my chest."—Edit.]

If there are any vices which are not natural to man, I should imagine this is one; as money of itself does not seem to gratify any natural desire or appetite of the human mind; and as, during an observation of sixty years, I do not remember one instance of a man given up to the love of money, till he had neglected to employ this precious talent according to the will of his Master. After this, sin was punished by sin; and this evil spirit was permitted to enter into him.

7. But beside this gross sort of covetousness, the love of money, there is a more refined species of covetousness, mentioned by the great Apostle, *pleonexia*, which literally means *a desire of having more*; more than we have already. And those also come under the denomination of they that will be rich. It is true that this desire, under proper restrictions, is innocent; nay, commendable. But when it exceeds the bounds, (and how difficult is it not to exceed them!) then it comes under the present censure.

8. But who is able to receive these hard sayings? Who can believe that they are the great truths of God? Not many wise not many noble, not many famed for learning; none, indeed, who are not taught of God. And who are they whom God teaches? Let our Lord answer: If any man be willing to do his will, he shall know of the doctrine whether it be of God. Those who are otherwise minded will be so far from receiving it, that they will not be able to understand it. Two as sensible men as most in england sat down together, some time since, to read over and consider that plain discourse on, Lay not up for yourselves treasures upon earth. After much deep consideration, one of them broke out, "Positively, I cannot understand it. Pray, do *you* understand it, Mr. L.?" Mr. L. honestly replied, "Indeed, not I. I cannot conceive what Mr. W. means. I can make nothing at all of it." So utterly blind is our natural understanding touching the truth of God!

9. having explained the former part of the text, "They that will be rich," and pointed out in the clearest manner I could, the persons spoken of; I will now endeavour, God being my

helper, to explain what is spoken of them: "They fall into temptation and a snare, and into many foolish and hurtful desires, which drown men in destruction and perdition."

"They fall into temptation." This seems to mean much more than simply, "they are tempted." They *enter into the temptation*: They fall plump down into it. The waves of it compass them about, and cover them all over. of those who thus enter into temptation, very few escape out of it. And the few that do are sorely scorched by it, though not utterly consumed. If they escape at all, it is with the skin of their teeth, and with deep wounds that are not easily healed.

10. They fall, Secondly, "into a snare," the snare of the devil, which he hath purposely set in their way. I believe the Greek word properly means a gin, a steel trap, which shows no appearance of danger. But as soon as any creature touches the spring it suddenly closes; and either crushes its bones in pieces, or consigns it to inevitable ruin.

11. They fall, Thirdly, "into many foolish and hurtful desires;" *anoetous, silly, senseless, fantastic*; as contrary to reason, to sound understanding, as they are to religion; *hurtful*, both to body and soul, tending to weaken, yea, destroy every gracious and heavenly temper: Destructive of that faith which is of the operation of God; of that hope which is full of immortality; of love to God and to our neighbour, and of every good word and work.

12. But what desires are these? This is a most important question, and deserves the deepest consideration.

In general they may all be summed up in one, the desiring happiness out of God. This includes, directly, or remotely, every foolish and hurtful desire. St. Paul expresses it by "loving the creature more than the Creator;" and by being "lovers of pleasure more than lovers of God." In particular they are (to use the exact and beautiful enumeration of St. John,) "the desire of the flesh, the desire of the eyes, and the pride of life;" all of which the desire of riches naturally tends both to beget and to increase.

13. "The desire of the flesh" is generally understood in far too narrow a meaning. It does not, as is commonly supposed, refer to one of the senses only, but takes in all the pleasures of sense, the gratification of any of the outward senses. It has reference to the *taste* in particular. How many thousands do we find at this day, in whom the ruling principle is, the desire to enlarge the pleasure of tasting! Perhaps they do not gratify this desire in a gross manner, so as to incur the imputation of intemperance; much less so as to violate health or impair their understanding by gluttony or drunkenness. But they live in a genteel, regular sensuality; in an elegant epicurism, which does not hurt the body, but only destroys the soul, keeping it at a distance from all true religion.

14. experience shows that the imagination is gratified chiefly by means of the eye: Therefore, "the desire of the eyes," in its natural sense, is the desiring and seeking happiness in gratifying the imagination. Now, the imagination is gratified either by grandeur, by beauty, or by novelty: Chiefly by the last; for neither grand nor beautiful objects please any longer than they are new.

15. Seeking happiness in *learning*, of whatever kind, falls under "the desire of the eyes;" whether it be in history, languages, poetry, or any branch of natural or experimental philosophy: Yea, we must include the several kinds of learning, such as Geometry, Algebra, and Metaphysics. For if our supreme delight be in any of these, we are herein gratifying "the desire of the eyes."

16. "The pride of life" (whatever else that very uncommon expression *he alazoneia tou biou*, may mean) seems to imply chiefly, the *desire of honour*, of the esteem, admiration, and applause of men; as nothing more directly tends both to beget and cherish pride than the honour that cometh of men. And as riches attract much admiration, and occasion much applause, they proportionally minister food for pride, and so may also be referred to this head.

17. *Desire of ease* is another of these foolish and hurtful desires; desire of avoiding every cross, every degree of trouble, danger, difficulty; a desire of slumbering out life, and going to heaven (as the vulgar say) upon a feather-bed. Everyone may observe how riches first beget, and then confirm and increase, this desire, making men more and more soft and delicate; more unwilling, and indeed more unable, to "take up their cross daily;" to "endure hardship as good soldiers of Jesus Christ," and to "take the kingdom of heaven by violence."

18. Riches, either desired or possessed, naturally lead to some or other of these foolish and hurtful desires; and by affording the means of gratifying them all, naturally tend to increase them. And there is a near connexion between unholy desires, and every other unholy passion and temper. We easily pass from these to pride, anger, bitterness, envy, malice, revengefulness; to an head-strong, unadvisable, unreprovable spirit: Indeed to every temper that is earthly, sensual, or devilish. All these the desire or possession of riches naturally tends to create, strengthen, and increase.

19. And by so doing, in the same proportion as they prevail, they "pierce men through with many sorrows;" sorrows from remorse, from a guilty conscience; sorrows flowing from all the evil tempers which they inspire or increase; sorrows inseparable from those desires themselves, as every unholy desire is an uneasy desire; and sorrows from the contrariety of those desires to each other, whence it is impossible to gratify them all. And, in the end, "they drown" the body in pain, disease, "destruction," and the soul in everlasting "perdition."

II. 1. I am, in the Second place, to apply what has been said. And this is the principal point. For what avails the clearest knowledge, even of the most excellent things, even of the things of God, if it go no farther than speculation, if it be not reduced to practice? He that hath ears to hear, let him hear! And what he hears, let him instantly put in practice. O that God would give me the thing which I long for! that, before I go hence and am no more seen, I may see a people wholly devoted to God, crucified to the world, and the world crucified to them; a people truly given up to God, in body, soul, and substance! How cheerfully should I then say, "Now lettest thou thy servant depart in peace!"

2. I ask, then, in the name of God, Who of you "desire to be rich?" Which of *you* (ask your own hearts in the sight of God) seriously and deliberately desire (and perhaps applaud

yourselves for so doing, as no small instance of your *prudence*) to have more than food to eat, and raiment to put on, and a house to cover you? Who of you desires to have more than the plain necessaries and conveniences of life? Stop! Consider! What are you doing? Evil is before you! Will you rush upon the point of a sword? By the grace of God, turn and live!

3. By the same authority I ask, Who of you are *endeavouring* to be rich? to procure for yourselves more than the plain necessaries and conveniences of life? Lay, each of you, your hand to your heart, and seriously inquire, "Am I of that number? Am I labouring, not only for what I want, but for more than I want?" May the Spirit of God say to everyone whom it concerns, "Thou art the man!"

4. I ask, "Thirdly, Who of you are in fact "laying up for yourselves treasures upon earth?" increasing in goods? adding, as fast as you can, house to house, and field to field! As long as *thou* thus "dost well unto thyself, men will speak good of thee." They will call thee a wise, a prudent man! a man that *minds the main chance*. Such is, and always has been, the wisdom of the world. But God saith unto thee, " 'Thou fool!' art thou not 'treasuring up to thyself wrath against the day of wrath, and revelation of the righteous judgment of God?' "

5. Perhaps you will ask, "But do not you yourself advise, to gain all we can, and to save all we can? And is it possible to do this without both *desiring* and *endeavouring to be rich*? nay, suppose our endeavours are successful, without actually laying up treasures upon earth?" I answer, It is possible. You may gain all you can without hurting either your soul or body; you may save all you can, by carefully avoiding every needless expense; and yet never lay up treasures on earth, nor either desire or endeavour so to do.

6. Permit me to speak as freely of myself as I would of another man I *gain all I can* (namely, by writing) without hurting either my soul or body. I *save all I can*, not willingly wasting anything, not a sheet of paper, not a cup of water. I do not lay out anything, not a shilling, unless as a sacrifice to God. Yet by *giving all I can*, I am effectually secured from "laying up treasures upon earth." Yea, and I am secured from either desiring or endeavouring, it as long as I give all I can. And that I do this, I call all that know me, both friends and foes, to testify.

7. But some may say, "Whether you endeavour it or no, you are undeniably *rich*. You have more than the necessaries of life." I have. But the Apostle does not fix the charge, barely on *possessing* any quantity of goods, but on possessing more than we employ according to the will of the Donor.

Two-and-forty years ago, having a desire to furnish poor people with cheaper, shorter, and plainer books than any I had seen, I wrote many small tracts, generally a penny a-piece; and afterwards several larger. Some of these had such a sale as I never thought of; and, by this means, I unawares became rich. But I never desired or endeavoured after it. And now that it is come upon me unawares, I lay up no treasures upon earth: I lay up nothing at all. My desire and endeavour, in this respect is to "wind my bottom round the year." I cannot help leaving my books behind me whenever God calls me hence; but, in every other respect, my own hands will be my executors.

8. Herein, my brethren, let you that are rich, be even as I am. Do you that possess more than food and raiment ask: "What shall we do? Shall we throw into the sea what God hath given us?" God forbid that you should! It is an excellent talent: It may be employed much to the glory of God. Your way lies plain before your face; if you have courage, walk in it. Having *gained*, in a right sense, *all you can*, and *saved all you can*; in spite of nature, and custom, and worldly prudence, *give all you can*. I do not say, "Be a good Jew, giving a tenth of all you possess." I do not say, "Be a good Pharisee, giving a fifth of all your substance." I dare not advise you to give half of what you have; no, nor three quarters; but all! Lift up your hearts, and you will see clearly, in what sense this is to be done. If you desire to be a "faithful and a wise steward," out of that portion of your Lord's goods which he has for the present lodged in your hands, but with the right of resumption whenever it pleaseth him, (1.) Provide things needful for yourself; food to eat, raiment to put on; whatever nature moderately requires, for preserving you both in health and strength; (2.) Provide these for your wife, your children, your servants, or any others who pertain to your household. If, when this is done, there be an overplus left, then do good to "them that are of the household of faith." If there be an overplus still, "as you have opportunity, do good unto all men." In so doing, you *give all you can*; nay, in a sound sense, all you have. For all that is laid out in this manner, is really given to God. You render unto God the things that are God's, not only by what you give to the poor, but also by that which you expend in providing things needful for yourself and your household.

9. O ye Methodists, hear the word of the Lord! I have a message from God to all men; but to *you* above all. For above forty years I have been a servant to you and to your fathers. And I have not been as a reed shaken with the wind: I have not varied in my testimony. I have testified to you the very same thing from the first day even until now. But "who hath believed our report?" I fear, not many rich: I fear there is need to apply to some of *you* those terrible words of the Apostle: "Go to now, ye rich men! weep and howl for the miseries which shall come upon you. Your gold and silver is cankered, and the rust of them shall witness against you and shall eat your flesh, as it were fire." Certainly it will, unless ye both save all you can and give all you can. But who of you hath considered this since you first heard the will of the Lord concerning it? Who is now determined to consider and practise it? By the grace of God begin today!

10. O ye lovers of money, hear the word of the Lord! Suppose ye that money, though multiplied as the sand of the sea, can give happiness? Then you are "given up to a strong delusion, to believe a lie;"—a palpable lie, confuted daily by a thousand experiments. Open your eyes! Look all around you! Are the richest men the happiest? Have those the largest share of content who have the largest possessions? Is not the very reverse true? Is it not a common observation, that the richest of men are, in general, the most discontented, the most miserable? Had not the far greater part of them more content

when they had less money? Look into your breasts. If you are increased in goods, are you proportionably increased in happiness? You have more substance; but have you more content? You know that in seeking happiness from riches, you are only striving to drink out of empty cups. And let them be painted and gilded ever so finely, they are empty still.

11. O ye that *desire* or *endeavour to be rich*, hear ye the word of the Lord! Why should ye be stricken any more? Will not even experience teach you wisdom? Will ye leap into a pit with your eyes open? Why should you any more "fall into temptation"? It cannot be but temptation, will beset you, as long as you are in the body. But though it should beset you on every side, why will you *enter into* it? There is no necessity for this: it is your own voluntary act and deed. Why should you any more plunge yourselves *into a snare*, into the trap Satan has laid for you, that is ready to break your bones in pieces? to crush your soul to death? After fair warning, why should you sink any more into "foolish and hurtful desires?" desires as inconsistent with reason as they are with religion itself; desires that have done you more hurt already than all the treasures upon earth can countervail.

12. Have they not hurt you already, have they not wounded you in the tenderest part, by slackening, if not utterly destroying, your "hunger and thirst after righteousness?" Have you now the same longing that you had once, for the whole image of God? Have you the same vehement desire as you formerly had, of "going on unto perfection?" Have they not hurt you by weakening your *faith*? Have you now faith's "abiding impression, realizing things to come?" Do you endure, in all temptations, from pleasure or pain, "seeing Him that is invisible?" Have you every day, and every hour, an uninterrupted sense of his presence? Have they not hurt you with regard to your *hope*? Have you now a hope full of immortality? Are you still big with earnest expectation of all the great and precious promises? Do you now "taste the powers of the world to come?" Do you "sit in heavenly places with Christ Jesus?"

13. Have they not so hurt you, as to stab your religion to the heart? Have they not cooled (if not quenched) your *love to God*? This is easily determined. Have you the same delight in God which you once had? Can you now say,

> I nothing want beneath, above;
> Happy, happy in thy love!

I fear not. And if your love of God is in any wise decayed, so is also your love of your neighbour. You are then hurt in the very life and spirit of your religion! If you lose love, you lose all.

14. Are not you hurt with regard to your *humility*? If you are increased in goods, it cannot well be otherwise. Many will think you a better, because you are a richer, man; And how can you help thinking so yourself? especially considering the commendations which some will give you in simplicity, and many with a design to serve themselves of you.
If you are hurt in your humility it will appear by this token: You are not so easy to be teachable as you were, not so advisable; you are not so easy to be convinced, not so easy to be persuaded; you have a much better opinion of your own judgment and are more attached to your own will. Formerly one might guide you with a thread; now one cannot turn you with a cart-rope. You were glad to be admonished or reproved; but that time is past. And you now account a man your enemy because he tells you the truth. O let each of you calmly consider this, and see if it be not your own picture!

15. Are you not equally hurt with regard to your *meekness*? You had once learned an excellent lesson of him that was meek as well as lowly in heart. When you were reviled, you reviled not again. You did not return railing for railing, but contrariwise, blessing. Your love was *not provoked*, but enabled you on all occasions to overcome evil with good. Is this your case now? I am afraid not. I fear you cannot "bear all things." Alas, it may rather be said, you can bear nothing; no injury, nor even affront! How quickly are you ruffled! How readily does that occur, "What! to use *me* so! What insolence is this! How did he dare to do it! I am not now what I was once. Let him know, I am now able to defend myself." You mean, to revenge yourself. And it is much if you are not willing, as well as able; if you do not take your fellow servant by the throat.

16. And are you not hurt in your *patience* too? Does your love now "endure all things?" Do you still "in patience possess your soul," as when you first believed? O what a change is here! You have again learnt to be frequently out of humour. You are often fretful; you feel, nay, and give way to peevishness. You find abundance of things go so cross that you cannot tell how to bear them.
Many years ago I was sitting with a gentleman in London, who feared God greatly, and generally gave away, year by year, nine tenths of his yearly income. A servant came in and threw some coals on the fire. A puff of smoke came out. The baronet threw himself back in his chair and cried out, "O Mr. Wesley, these are the crosses I meet with daily!" Would he not have been less impatient, if he had had fifty, instead of five thousand, pounds a year?

17. But to return. Are not you who have been successful in your endeavours to increase in substance, insensibly sunk into softness of mind, if not of body too? You no longer rejoice to "endure hardship, as good soldiers of Jesus Christ." You no longer "rush into the kingdom of heaven, and take it as by storm." You do not cheerfully and gladly "deny yourselves, and take up your cross daily." You cannot deny yourself the poor pleasure of a little sleep, or of a soft bed, in order to hear the word that is able to save your souls! Indeed, you "cannot go out so early in the morning: besides it is dark, nay, cold, perhaps rainy too. Cold, darkness, rain, all these together,—I can never think of it." You did not say so when you were a poor man. You then regarded none of these things. It is the change of circumstances which has occasioned this melancholy change in your body and mind; You are but the shadow of what you were! What have riches done for you?

"But it cannot be expected I should do as I have done. For I am now grown old." Am not I grown old as well as you? Am not I in my seventy-eighth year? Yet by the grace of God, I do not slack my pace yet. Neither would *you*, if you were a poor man still.

18. You are so deeply hurt that you have well nigh lost your zeal for works of mercy, as well as of piety. You once pushed on through cold or rain, or whatever cross lay in your way, to see the poor, the sick, the distressed. You went about doing good, and found out those who were not able to find you. You cheerfully crept down into their cellars, and climbed up into their garrets,

> To supply all their wants,
> And spend and be spent in assisting his saints.

You found out every scene of human misery, and assisted according to your power:

> Each form of woe your generous pity moved;
> Your Saviour's face you saw, and, seeing, loved.

Do you now tread in the same steps? What hinders? Do you fear spoiling your silken coat? Or is there another lion in the way? Are you afraid of catching vermin? And are you not afraid lest the roaring lion should catch you? Are you not afraid of Him that hath said, "Inasmuch as ye have not done it unto the least of these, ye have not done it unto me?" What will follow? "Depart, ye cursed, into everlasting fire prepared for the devil and his angels!"

19. In time past how mindful were you of that word: "Thou shalt not hate thy brother in thy heart: Thou shalt in any wise reprove thy brother, and not suffer sin upon him!" You *did* reprove directly or indirectly, all those that sinned in your sight. And happy consequences quickly followed. How good was a word spoken in season! It was often as an arrow from the hand of a giant. Many a heart was pierced. Many of the stout-hearted, who scorned to hear a sermon,

> Fell down before his cross subdued,
> And felt his arrows dipped in blood.

But which of you now has that compassion for the ignorant, and for them that are out of the way? They may wander on for *you*, and plunge into the lake of fire, without let or hindrance. Gold hath steeled your hearts. You have something else to do.

> Unhelp'd, unpitied let the wretches fall.

20. Thus have I given you, O ye gainers, lovers, possessors of riches, one more (it may be the last) warning. O that it may not be in vain! May God write it upon all your hearts! Though "it is easier for a camel to go through the eye of a needle, than for a rich man to enter into the kingdom of heaven," yet the things impossible with men are possible with God." Lord, speak! and even the rich men that hear these words shall enter thy kingdom, shall "take the kingdom of heaven by violence," shall "sell all for the pearl of great price:" shall be "crucified to the world, and count all things dung, that they may win Christ!"

88.* ON DRESS

"Whose adorning let it not be that outward adorning of—wearing of gold, or of putting on of apparel; "But let it be the hidden man of the heart, in that which is not corruptible, even the ornament of a meek and quiet spirit, which is in the sight of God of great price."

1 Pet. 3:3, 4.

1. St. Paul exhorts all those who desire to "be transformed by the renewal of their minds," and to "prove what is that good and acceptable and perfect will of God," not to be "conformed to this world." [Rom. 12:2] Indeed this exhortation relates more directly to the *wisdom* of the world, which is totally opposite to his "good and acceptable and perfect will." But it likewise has a reference even to the *manners* and *customs* of the world, which naturally flow from its wisdom and spirit, and are exactly suitable thereto. And it was not beneath the wisdom of God to give us punctual directions in this respect also.

2. Some of these, particularly that in the text, descend even to the apparel of Christians. And both this text, and the parallel one of St. Paul, are as express as possible. St. Paul's words are, (1 Tim. 2:9, 10,) "I will that women adorn themselves in modest apparel; not—with gold, or pearls, or costly array; but (which becometh women professing godliness) with good works."

3. "But is it not strange," say some, "that the all-wise Spirit of God should condescend to take notice of such trifles as these? to take notice of such insignificant trifles, things of so little moment, or rather of none at all? For what does it signify, provided we take care of the soul, what the body is covered with, whether with silk or sackcloth? What harm can there be in the wearing of gold, or silver, or precious stones, or any other of those beautiful things with which God has so amply provided us? May we not apply to this what St. Paul has observed on another occasion, that 'every creature of God is good, and nothing to be rejected?' "

4. It is certain, that many who sincerely fear God have cordially embraced this opinion. And their practice is suitable thereto: They make no scruple of conformity to the world, by putting on, as often occasion offers, either gold, or pearls, or costly apparel. And indeed they are not well pleased with those that think it their duty to reject them; the using of which they apprehend to be one branch of Christian liberty. Yea, some have gone considerably farther; even so far as to make it a point to bring those who had refrained from them for some time to make use of them again, assuring them that it was mere superstition to think there was any harm in them. Nay, farther still: A very respectable person has said, in express terms, "I do not desire that any who *dress plain* should be in our society." It is, therefore, certainly worth our while to consider this matter thoroughly; seriously to inquire whether there is any harm in the putting on of gold, or jewels, or costly apparel.

5. But, before we enter on the subject, let it be observed, that slovenliness is no part of religion; that neither this, nor any text of Scripture, condemns neatness of apparel. Certainly this is a duty, not a sin. "Cleanliness is, indeed, next to godliness." Agreeably to this, good Mr. Herbert advises every one that fears God:—

> Let thy mind's sweetness have its operation
> Upon thy person, clothes, and habitation.

And surely every one should attend to this, if he would not have the good that is in him evil spoken of.

---

* [text from the 1872 edition]

6. Another mistake, with regard to apparel, has been common in the religious world. It has been supposed by some, that there ought to be no difference at all in the apparel of Christians. But neither these texts, nor any other in the book of God, teach any such thing, or direct that the dress of the master or the mistress should be nothing different from that of their servants. There may, undoubtedly, be a moderate difference of apparel between persons of different stations. And where the eye is single, this will easily be adjusted by the rules of Christian prudence.

7. Yea, it may be doubted, whether any part of Scripture forbids (at least I know not any) those in any nation that are invested with supreme authority, to be arrayed in gold and costly apparel; or to adorn their immediate attendants, or magistrates, or officers, with the same. It is not improbable, that our blessed Lord intended to give countenance to this custom when he said, without the least mark of censure or disapprobation, "Behold, those that wear gorgeous," splendid, "apparel are in kings' courts." (Luke 7:25.)

8. What is then the meaning of these scriptures? What is it which they forbid? They manifestly forbid ordinary Christians, those in the lower or middle ranks of life, to be adorned with gold, or pearls, or costly apparel. But why? What harm is there therein? This deserves our serious consideration. But it is highly expedient, or rather absolutely necessary, for all who would consider it to any purpose, as far as is possible to divest themselves of all prejudice, and to stand open to conviction: Is it not necessary, likewise, in the highest degree, that they should earnestly beseech the Father of Lights, that, "by his holy inspiration, they may think the things that are right, and, by his merciful guidance, perform the same?" Then they will not say, no, not in their hearts, (as I fear too many have done.) what the famous Jew said to the Christian, "Thou shalt not persuade me, though thou hast persuaded me."

9. The question is, What harm does it do, to adorn ourselves with gold, or pearls, or costly array, suppose you can afford it; that is, suppose it does not hurt or impoverish your family? The first harm it does, is, it engenders pride, and, where it is already, increases it. Whoever narrowly observes what passes in his own heart will easily discern this. Nothing is more natural than to think ourselves better because we are dressed in better clothes; and it is scarce possible for a man to wear costly apparel, without, in some measure, valuing himself upon it. One of the old Heathens was so well apprized of this, that, when he had a spite to a poor man, and had a mind to turn his head, he made him a present of a suit of fine clothes.

> Eutrapelus, cuicunque nocere voiebat,
>
> Vestimenta dabat pretiosa.

[The following is Boscawen's translation of this quotation from Horace:—

> Eutrapelus, whome'er he chose
>
> To ruin, deck'd in costly clothes."—EDIT.]

He could not then but imagine himself to be as much better as he was finer than his neighbour. And how many thousands, not only lords cond gentlemen, in England, but honest tradesmen, argue the same way! inferring the superior value of their persons from the value of their clothes!

10. "But may not one man be as proud, though clad in sackcloth, as another is, though clad in cloth of gold?" As this argument meets us at every turn, and is supposed to be unanswerable, it will be worth while to answer it once for all, and to show the utter emptiness of it. "May not, then, one clad in sackcloth," you ask, "be as proud as he that is clad in cloth of gold?" I answer, Certainly he may: I suppose no one doubts of it. And what inference can you draw from this? Take a parallel case. One man that drinks a cup of wholesome wine, may be as sick as another that drinks poison: But does this prove that the poison has no more tendency to hurt a man than the wine? Or does it excuse any man for taking what has a natural tendency to make him sick? Now, to apply: Experience shows that fine clothes have a natural tendency to make a man sick of pride; plain clothes have not. Although it is true, you may be sick of pride in these also, yet they have no natural tendency either to cause or increase this sickness. Therefore, all that desire to be clothed with humility, abstain from that poison.

11. Secondly. The wearing gay or costly apparel naturally tends to breed and to increase vanity. By vanity I here mean, the love and desire of being admired and praised. Every one of you that is fond of dress has a witness of this in your own bosom. Whether you will confess it before man or no, you are convinced of this before God. You know in your hearts, it is with a view to be admired that you thus adorn yourselves; and that you would not be at the pains were none to see you but God and his holy angels. Now, the more you indulge this foolish desire, the more it grows upon you. You have vanity enough by nature; but by thus indulging it, you increase it a hundred-fold. O stop! Aim at pleasing God alone, and all these ornaments will drop off.

12. Thirdly. The wearing of gay and costly apparel naturally tends to beget anger, and every turbulent and uneasy passion. And it is on this very account that the Apostle places this "outward adorning" in direct opposition to the "ornament of a meek and quiet spirit." How remarkably does he add, "which is in the sight of God of great price!"

> Than gold or pearls more precious far,
>
> And brighter than the morning star.

None can easily conceive, unless himself were to make the sad experiment, the contrariety there is between the "outward adorning," and this inward "quietness of spirit." You never can thoroughly enjoy this, while you are fond of the other. It is only while you sit loose to that "outward adorning," that you can in "patience possess your soul." Then only when you have cast off your fondness for dress, will the peace of God reign in your hearts.

13. Fourthly. Gay and costly apparel directly tends to create and inflame lust. I was in doubt whether to name this brutal appetite; or, in order to spare delicate ears, to express it by some gentle circumlocution. (Like the Dean, who, some years ago, told his audience at Whitehall, "If you do not repent, you will go to a place which I have too much manners to name before this good company.") But I think it best to speak out; since the more the word shocks your ears, the more it may arm your heart. The fact is plain and undeniable; it has this effect both on the wearer and the beholder. To the

former, our elegant poet, Cowley, addresses those fine lines:—

> The' adorning thee with so much art
>> Is but a barbarous skill;
> 'Tis like the poisoning of a dart,
>> Too apt before to kill.

That is, (to express the matter in plain terms, without any colouring,) "You poison the beholder with far more of this base appetite than otherwise he would feel." Did you not *know* this would be the natural consequence of your elegant adorning? To push the question home, Did you not *desire*, did you not *design* it should? And yet, all the time, how did you

> Set to public view
> A specious face of innocence and virtue!

Meanwhile you do not yourself escape the snare which you spread for others. The dart recoils, and you are infected with the same poison with which you infected them. You kindle a flame which, at the same time, consumes both yourself and your admirers. And it is well, if it does not plunge both you and them into the flames of hell!

14. Fifthly. The wearing costly array is directly opposite to the being adorned with good works. Nothing can be more evident than this; for the more you lay out on your own apparel, the less you have left to clothe the naked, to feed the hungry, to lodge the strangers, to relieve those that are sick and in prison, and to lessen the numberless afflictions to which we are exposed in this vale of tears. And here is no room for the evasion used before: "I may be as *humble* in cloth of gold, as in sackcloth." If you could be as humble when you choose costly as when you choose plain apparel, (which I flatly deny,) yet you could not be as beneficent,—as plenteous in good works. Every shilling which you save from your own apparel, you may expend in clothing the naked, and relieving the various necessities of the poor, whom ye "have always with you." Therefore, every shilling which you needlessly spend on your apparel is, in effect, stolen from God and the poor! And how many precious opportunities of doing good have you defrauded yourself of! How often have you disabled yourself from doing good by purchasing what you did not want! For what end did you buy these ornaments? To please God? No; but to please your own fancy, or to gain the admiration and applause of those that were no wiser than yourself. How much good might you have done with that money! and what an irreparable loss have you sustained by not doing it, if it be true that the day is at hand when "every man shall receive his own reward, according to his own labour!"

15. I pray consider this well. Perhaps you have not seen it in this light before. When you are laying out that money in costly apparel which you could have otherwise spared for the poor, you thereby deprive them of what God, the proprietor of all, had lodged in your hands for their use. If so, what you put upon yourself, you are, in effect, tearing from the back of the naked; as the costly and delicate food which you eat, you are snatching from the mouth of the hungry. For mercy, for pity, for Christ's sake, for the honour of his gospel, stay your hand! Do not throw this money away! Do not lay out on nothing, yea, worse than nothing, what may clothe your poor, naked, shivering fellow-creature!

16. Many years ago, when I was at Oxford, in a cold winter's day, a young maid (one of those we kept at school) called upon me. I said, "You seem half-starved. Have you nothing to cover you but that thin linen gown?" She said, "Sir, this is all I have!" I put my hand in my pocket; but found I had scarce any money left, having just paid away what I had. It immediately struck me, "Will thy Master say, 'Well done, good and faithful steward?' Thou hast adorned thy walls with the money which might have screened this poor creature from the cold! O justice! O mercy! Are not these pictures the blood of this poor maid?" See thy expensive apparel in the same light; thy gown, hat, head-dress! Everything about thee which cost more than Christian duty required thee to lay out is the blood of the poor! O be wise for the time to come! Be more merciful! more faithful to God and man! more abundantly *adorned* (like men and women professing godliness) *with good works!*

17. It is true, great allowance is to be made for those who have never been warned of these things, and perhaps do not know that there is a word in the Bible which forbids costly apparel. But what is *that to you?* You have been warned over and over, yea, in the plainest manner possible. And what have you profited thereby? Do not you still dress like other people of the same fortune? Is not your dress as gay, as expensive as theirs who never had any such warning? as expensive as it would have been, if you had never heard a word said about it? O how will you answer this, when you and I stand together at the judgment-seat of Christ? Nay, have not many of you grown finer as fast as you have grown richer? As you increased in substance, have you not increased in dress? Witness the profusion of ribands, gauze, or linen about your heads! What have you profited then by bearing the reproach of Christ? by being called Methodists? Are you not as fashionably dressed as others of your rank that are no Methodists? Do you ask, "But may we not as well buy fashionable things as unfashionable?" I answer, Not if they give you a bold, immodest look, as those huge hats, bonnets, head-dresses do. And not if they cost more. "But I can *afford* it." O lay aside for ever that idle, nonsensical word! No Christian can *afford* to waste any part of the substance which God has entrusted him with. How long are you to stay here? May not you to-morrow, perhaps to-night, be summoned to arise and go hence, in order to give an account of this and all your talents to the Judge of quick and dead?

18. How then can it be, that, after so many warnings, you persist in the same folly? Is it not hence? There are still among you, some that neither profit themselves by all they hear, nor are willing that others should: And these, if any of you are almost persuaded to dress as Christians, reason, and rally, and laugh you out of it. O ye pretty triflers, I entreat you not to do the devil's work any longer! Whatever ye do yourselves, do not harden the hearts of others. And you that are of a better mind, avoid these tempters with all possible care; and if you come where any of them are, either beg them to be silent on the head, or quit the room.

19. Sixthly. The putting on of costly apparel is directly opposite to what the Apostle terms, "the hidden man of the heart;" that is, to the whole "image of God" wherein we were created, and which is stamped anew upon the heart of every Christian believer;—opposite to "the mind which was in Christ Jesus," and the whole nature of inward holiness. All the time you are studying this outward adorning, the whole inward work of the Spirit stands still; or, rather, goes back, though by very gentle and almost imperceptible degrees. Instead of growing more heavenly-minded, you are more and more earthly-minded. If you once had fellowship with the Father and the Son, it now gradually declines; and you insensibly sink deeper and deeper into the spirit of the world,—into foolish and hurtful desires, and grovelling appetites. All these evils, and a thousand more, spring from that one root—indulging yourself in costly apparel.

20. Why then does not everyone that either loves or fears God, flee from it, as from the face of a serpent? Why are *you* still so conformable to the irrational, sinful customs of a frantic world? Why do you still despise the express commandment of God uttered in the plainest terms? You see the light: Why do not you follow the light of your own mind? Your conscience tells you the truth: Why do you not obey the dictates of your own conscience?

21. You answer, "Why, universal custom is against me; and I know not how to stem the mighty torrent." Not only the profane, but the religious world, run violently the other way. Look into, I do not say, the theatres, but the churches, nay, and the meetings of every denomination; (except a few old-fashioned Quakers, or the people called Moravians;) look into the congregations, in London or elsewhere, of those that are styled Gospel Ministers; look into Northampton-Chapel; yea, into the Tabernacle, or the chapel in Tottenham-Court Road; nay, look into the chapel in West-Street, or that in the City-Road; look at the very people that sit under the pulpit, or by the side of it; and are not *those that can afford it*, (I can hardly refrain from doing them the honour of naming their names,) as fashionably adorned, as those of the same rank in other places?

22. This is a melancholy truth. I am ashamed of it: But I know not how to help it. I call heaven and earth to witness this day, that it is not my fault! The trumpet has not "given an uncertain sound," for near fifty years last past. O God! thou knowest I have borne a clear and faithful testimony. In print, in preaching, in meeting the society, I have not shunned to declare the whole counsel of God. I am therefore clear of the blood of those that will not hear. It lies upon their own head.

23. I warn you once more, in the name, and in the presence of God, that the number of those that rebel against God is no excuse for their rebellion. He hath expressly told us, "Thou shalt not follow the multitude to do evil." It was said of a great, good man, he

> Fear'd not, had Heaven decreed it, to have stood
> Adverse against a world, and singly good.

Who of you desire to share in that glorious character? to stand adverse against a world? If millions condemn you, it will be enough that you are acquitted by God and your own conscience.

24. "Nay, I think," say some, "I could bear the contempt or reproach of all the world beside. I regard none but my own relations, those especially that are of my own household. My father, my mother, my brothers and sisters, (and perhaps one that is nearer than them all,) are teasing me continually." This is a trial indeed; such as very few can judge of, but those that bear it. "I have not strength to bear it." No, not of your own: Certainly you have not. But there is strength laid up for you on "One that is mighty!" His grace is sufficient for you; and he now sees your case, and is just ready to give it you. Meantime, remember his awful declaration, touching them that regard man more than God: "He that loveth father or mother, brother or sister, husband or wife, more than me, is not worthy of me."

25. But are there not some among you that did once renounce this conformity to the world, and dress, in every point, neat and plain, suitable to your profession? Why then did you not persevere therein? Why did you turn back from the good way? Did you contract an acquaintance, perhaps a friendship, with some that were still fond of dress? It is no wonder then that you was, sooner or later, moved to "measure back your steps to earth again." No less was to be expected, than that one sin would lead you on to another. It was one sin to contract a friendship with any that knew not God: For "know ye not that friendship with the world is enmity with God?" And this led you back into another, into that conformity to the world from which ye had clean escaped. But what are you to do now? Why, if you are wise, escape for your life: No delay: Look not behind you! Without loss of time, renounce the cause and the effect together! Now, to-day, before the heart is hardened by the deceitfulness of sin, cut off, at one stroke, that sinful friendship with the ungodly, and that sinful conformity to the world! Determine this day! Do not delay till to-morrow, lest you delay for ever. For God's sake, for your own soul's sake, fix your resolution now!

26. I conjure you all who have any regard for *me*, show me before I go hence, that I have not laboured, even in this respect, in vain, for near half a century. Let me see, before I die, a Methodist congregation, full as plain dressed as a Quaker congregation. Only be more consistent with yourselves. Let your dress be *cheap* as well as plain; otherwise you do but trifle with God, and me, and your own souls. I pray, let there be no costly silks among you, how grave soever they may be. Let there be no Quaker-linen,—proverbially so called, for their exquisite fineness; no Brussels lace, no elephantine hats or bonnets,—those scandals of female modesty. Be all of a piece, dressed from head to foot as persons *professing godliness*; professing to do every thing, small and great, with the single view of pleasing God.

27. Let not any of you who are rich in this world endeavour to excuse yourselves from this by talking nonsense. It is stark, staring nonsense to say, "Oh, I can *afford* this or that." If you have regard to common sense, let that silly word never come out of your mouth. No man living can *afford* to waste any part of what God has committed to his trust. None can *afford*

to throw any part of that food and raiment into the sea, which was lodged with him on purpose to feed the hungry, and clothe the naked. And it is far worse than simple waste, to spend any part of it in gay or costly apparel. For this is no less than to turn wholesome food into deadly poison. It is giving so much money to poison both yourself and others, as far as your example spreads, with pride, vanity, anger, lust, love of the world, and a thousand "foolish and hurtful desires," which tend to "pierce them through with many sorrows." And is there no harm in all this? O God, arise and maintain thy own cause! Let not men or devils any longer put out our eyes, and lead us blindfold into the pit of destruction!

28. I beseech you, every man that is here present before God, every woman, young or old, married or single, yea, every child that knows good from evil, take this to yourself. Each of you, for one, take the Apostle's advice; at least, hinder not others from taking it. I beseech you, O ye parents, do not hinder your children from following their own convictions, even though you might think they would *look prettier* if they were adorned with such gewgaws as other children wear! I beseech you, O ye husbands, do not hinder your wives! You, O ye wives, do not hinder your husbands, either by word or deed, from acting just as they are persuaded in their own minds! Above all, I conjure you, ye half-Methodists, you that trim between us and the world, you that frequently, perhaps constantly, hear our preaching, but are in no farther connexion with us; yea, and all you that were once in full connexion with us, but are not so now; whatever ye do yourselves, do not say one word to hinder others from receiving and practising the advice which has been now given! Yet a little while, and we shall not need these poor coverings; for this corruptible body shall put on incorruption. Yet a few days hence, and this mortal body shall put on immortality. In the mean time, let this be our only care, "to put off the old man,"—our old nature,—"which is corrupt,"—which is altogether evil,—and to "put on the new man, which after God is created in righteousness and true holiness." In particular, "put on, as the elect of God, bowels of mercies, kindness, gentleness, longsuffering." Yea, to sum up all in one word, "put on Christ;" that "when he shall appear, ye may appear with him in glory."

89.* THE MORE EXCELLENT WAY

"Covet earnestly the best gifts; And yet I show to you a more excellent way."

1 Cor. 12:31.

1. In the preceding verses, St. Paul has been speaking of the extraordinary gifts of the Holy Ghost; such as healing the sick, prophesying (in the proper sense of the word; that is, foretelling things to come), speaking with strange tongues, such as the speaker had never learned, and the miraculous interpretation of tongues. And these gifts the Apostle allows to be desirable; yea, he exhorts the Corinthians, at least the teachers among them (to whom chiefly, if not solely, they were wont to be given in the first ages of the Church,) to covet them *earnestly*, that thereby they might be qualified to be more useful either to Christians or heathens. "And yet," says he, "I show unto you a more excellent way;" far more desirable than all these put together, inasmuch as it will infallibly lead you to happiness both in this world and in the world to come; whereas you might have all those gifts, yea, in the highest degree, and yet be miserable both in time and eternity.

2. It does not appear that these extraordinary gifts of the Holy Ghost were common in the church for more than two or three centuries We seldom hear of them after that fatal period when the Emperor Constantine called himself a Christian, and from a vain imagination of promoting the Christian cause thereby heaped riches, and power, and honour, upon the Christians in general; but in particular upon the Christian clergy. From this time they almost totally ceased; very few instances of the kind were found. The cause of this was not (as has been vulgarly supposed,) "because there was no more occasion for them," because all the world was become Christian. This is a miserable mistake; not a twentieth part of it was then nominally Christian. The real cause was, "the love of many," almost of all Christians, so called, was "waxed cold." The Christians had no more of the Spirit of Christ than the other Heathens. The Son of Man, when he came to examine his Church, could hardly "find faith upon earth." This was the real cause why the extraordinary gifts of the Holy Ghost were no longer to be found in the Christian Church—because the Christians were turned Heathens again, and had only a dead form left.

3. However, I would not at present speak of these, of the extraordinary gifts of the Holy Ghost, but of the ordinary; and these likewise we may "covet earnestly," in order to be more useful in our generation. With this view we may covet "the gift of *convincing speech,*" in order to "sound the unbelieving heart;" and the gift of *persuasion*, to move the affections, as well as enlighten the understanding. We may covet *knowledge*, both of the word and of the works of God, whether of providence or grace. We may desire a measure of that *faith* which, on particular occasions, wherein the glory of God or the happiness of men is nearly concerned, goes far beyond the power of natural causes. We may desire an easy elocution, a pleasing address, with resignation to the will of our Lord; yea, whatever would enable us, as we have opportunity, to be useful wherever we are. These gifts we may innocently desire: but there is "a more excellent way."

4. The way of love,—of loving all men for God's sake, of humble gentle, patient love,—is that which the Apostle so admirably describes in the ensuing chapter. And without this, he assures us, all eloquence, all knowledge, all faith, all works, and all sufferings, are of no more value in the sight of God than sounding brass or a rumbling cymbal, and are not of the least avail toward our eternal salvation. Without this, all we know, all we believe, all we do, all we suffer, will profit us nothing in the great day of accounts.

5. But at present I would take a different view of the text, and point out "a more excellent way" in another sense. It is the

---

* (text from 1872 edition)

observation of an ancient writer, that there have been from the beginning two orders of Christians. The one lived an innocent life, conforming in all things, not sinful, to the customs and fashions of the world; doing many good works, abstaining from gross evils, and attending the ordinances of God. They endeavoured, in general, to have a conscience void of offence in their outward behaviour, but did not aim at any particular strictness, being in most things like their neighbours. The other sort of Christians not only abstained from all appearance of evil, were zealous of good works in every kind, and attended all the ordinances of God, but likewise used all diligence to attain the whole mind that was in Christ, and laboured to walk, in every point, as their beloved Master. In order to this they walked in a constant course of universal self-denial, trampling on every pleasure which they were not divinely conscious prepared them for taking pleasure in God. They took up their cross daily. They strove, they agonized without intermission, to enter in at the strait gate. This one thing they did, they spared no pains to arrive at the summit of Christian holiness; "leaving the first principles of the doctrine of Christ, to go on to perfection;" to "know all that love of God which passeth knowledge, and to be filled with all the fulness of God."

6. From long experience and observation I am inclined to think, that whoever finds redemption in the blood of Jesus, whoever is justified, has then the choice of walking in the higher or the lower path. I believe the Holy Spirit at that time sets before him "the more excellent way," and incites him to walk therein, to choose the narrowest path in the narrow way, to aspire after the heights and depths of holiness,—after the entire image of God. But if he does not accept this offer, he insensibly declines into the lower order of Christians. He still goes on in what may be called a good way, serving God in his degree, and finds mercy in the close of life, through the blood of the covenant.

7. I would be far from quenching the smoking flax,—from discouraging those that serve God in a low degree. But I could not wish them to stop here: I would encourage them to come up higher, without thundering hell and damnation in their ears, without condemning the way wherein they were, telling them it is the way that leads to destruction, I will endeavour to point out to them what is in every respect "a more excellent way."

8. Let it be well remembered, I do not affirm that all who do not walk in this way are in the high road to hell. But this much I must affirm, they will not have so high a place in heaven as they would have had if they had chosen the better part. And will this be a small loss,—the having so many fewer stars in your crown of glory? Will it be a little thing to have a lower place than you might have had in the kingdom of your Father? Certainly there will be no sorrow in heaven; there all tears will be wiped from our eyes; but if it were possible grief could enter there, we should grieve at that irreparable loss. Irreparable then, but not now. Now, by the grace of God, we may choose the "more excellent way." Let us now compare this, in a few particulars, with the way wherein most Christians walk.

I. To begin at the beginning of the day. It is the manner of the generality of Christians, if they are not obliged to work for their living, to rise, particularly in winter, at eight or nine in the morning after having lain in bed eight or nine, if not more hours. I do not say now (as I should have been very apt to do fifty years ago,) that all who indulge themselves in this manner are in the way to hell. But neither can I say they are in the way to heaven, denying themselves, and taking up their cross daily. Sure I am, there is "a more excellent way" to promote health both of body and mind. From an observation of more than sixty years, I have learned, that men in health require, at an average, from six to seven hours' sleep, and healthy women a little more, from seven to eight, in four-and-twenty hours. I know this quantity of sleep to be most advantageous to the body as well as the soul. It is preferable to any medicine which I have known, both for preventing and removing nervous disorders. It is, therefore, undoubtedly the most excellent way, in defiance of fashion and custom, to take just so much sleep as experience proves our nature to require; seeing this is indisputably most conducive both to bodily and spiritual health. And why should not you walk in this way? Because it is difficult? Nay, with men it is impossible. But all things are possible with God; and by his grace all things will be possible to *you*. Only continue instant in prayer, and you will find this not only possible, but easy: Yea, and it will be far easier to rise early constantly, than to do it sometimes. But then you must begin at the right end; if you rise early, you must sleep early. Impose it upon yourself, unless when something extraordinary occurs, to go to bed at a fixed hour. Then the difficulty of it will soon be over; but the advantage of it will remain for ever.

II. The generality of Christians, as soon as they rise, are accustomed to use some kind of *prayer*; and probably to use the same form still which they learned when they were eight or ten years old. Now I do not condemn those who proceed thus (though many do,) as mocking God; though they have used the same form, without any variation, for twenty or thirty years together. But surely there is "a more excellent way" of ordering our private devotions. What if you were to follow the advice given by that great and good man, Mr. Law, on this subject? Consider both your outward and inward state, and vary your prayers accordingly. For instance: Suppose your outward state is prosperous; suppose you are in a state of health, ease, and plenty, having your lot cast among kind relations, good neighbours, and agreeable friends, that love you and you them; then your outward state manifestly calls for praise and thanksgiving to God. On the other hand, if you are in a state of adversity; if God has laid trouble upon your loins; if you are in poverty, in want, in outward distress; if you are in any imminent danger; if you are in pain and sickness; then you are clearly called to pour out your soul before God in such prayer as is suited to your circumstances. In like manner you may suit your devotions to your inward state, the present state of your mind. Is your soul in heaviness, either from a sense of sin, or through manifold temptations? Then let your prayer consist of such confessions, petitions, and supplications, as are agreeable to your distressed situation of mind. On the contrary, is your soul in peace? Are you rejoicing in God? Are his consolations not small with you? Then say, with the Psalmist: "Thou art my God, and I will love thee: Thou art my God, and I will praise thee." You may, likewise, when you have time, add to your other devotions a little reading and meditation, and perhaps a psalm of praise,—the natural effusion of a thankful heart. You must certainly see that this is "a more excellent way" than the poor dry form which you used before.

III. 1. The generality of Christians, after using some prayer, usually apply themselves to the *business* of their calling. Every man that has any pretence to be a Christian will not fail to do this; seeing it is impossible that an idle man can be a good man,—sloth being inconsistent with religion. But with what view? For what end do you undertake and follow your worldly business? "To provide things necessary for myself and my family." It is a good answer as far as it goes; but it does not go far enough. For a Turk or a Heathen goes so far,—does his work for the very same ends. But a Christian may go abundantly farther: His end in all his labour is, to please God; to do, not his own will, but the will of him that sent him into the world,—for this very purpose, to do the will of God on earth as angels do in heaven. He works for eternity. He "labours not for the meat that perisheth," (this is the smallest part of his motive,) "but for that which endureth to everlasting life." And is not this "a more excellent way?"

2. Again: In what *manner* do you transact your worldly business? I trust, with diligence, whatever your hand findeth to do, doing it with all our might; in justice, rendering to all their due, in every circumstance of life; yea, and in mercy, doing unto every man what you would he should do unto you. This is well: But a Christian is called to go still farther,—to add piety to justice; to intermix prayer, especially the prayer of the heart, with all the labour of his hands. Without this all his diligence and justice only show him to be an honest Heathen; and many there are who profess the Christian religion, that go no farther than honest Heathenism.

3. Yet again: in what *spirit* do you go through your business? In the spirit of the world, or the Spirit of Christ? I am afraid thousands of those who are called good Christians do not understand the question. If you act in the Spirit of Christ you carry the end you at first proposed through all your work from first to last. You do everything in the spirit of sacrifice, giving up your will to the will of God; and continually aiming, not at ease, pleasure, or riches; not at anything "this short enduring world can give;" but merely at the glory of God. Now can anyone deny that this is the most excellent way of pursuing worldly business?

IV. 1. But these tenements of clay which we bear about us require constant reparation, or they will sink into the earth from which they were taken, even sooner than nature requires. Daily food is necessary to prevent this, to repair the constant decays of nature. It was common in the heathen world when they were about to use this, to take meat or even drink, *libare pateram Jovi,* "to pour out a little to the honour of their god;" although the gods of the Heathens were but devils, as the Apostle justly observes. "It seems," says a late writer, "there was once some such custom as this in our own country. For we still frequently see a gentleman before he sits down to dinner in his own house, holding his hat before his face, and perhaps seeming to say something; though he generally does it in such a manner that no one can tell what he says." Now what if instead of this, every head of a family, before he sat down to eat and drink, either morning, noon, or night, (for the reason of the thing is the same at every hour of the day,) was seriously to ask a blessing from God on what he was about to take? yea, and afterward, seriously to return thanks to the Giver of all his blessings? Would not this be "a more excellent way" than to use that dull farce which is worse than nothing; being, in reality, no other than mockery both of God and man?

2. As to the *quantity* of their food, good sort of men do not usually eat to excess. At least not so far as to make themselves sick with meat, or to intoxicate themselves with drink. And as to the manner of taking it, it is usually innocent, mixed with a little mirth, which is said to help digestion. So far, so good. And provided they take only that measure of plain, cheap, wholesome food, which most promotes health both of body and mind, there will be no cause of blame. Neither can I require you to take that advice of Mr. Herbert, though he was a good man:—

> Take thy meat; think it dust; then eat a bit
> And say with all, Earth to earth I commit.

This is too melancholy: it does not suit with that cheerfulness which is highly proper at a Christian meal. Permit me to illustrate this subject with a little story. The King of France one day, pursuing the chase, outrode all his company, who after seeking him some time found him sitting in a cottage eating bread and cheese. Seeing them, he cried out: "Where have I lived all my time? I never before tasted so good food in my life!" "Sire," said one of them, "you never had so good sauce before; for you were never hungry." Now it is true, hunger is a good sauce; but there is one that is better still; that is, thankfulness. Sure that is the most agreeable food which is seasoned with this. And why should not yours at every meal? You need not then cast your eye on death, but receive every morsel as a pledge of life eternal. The Author of your being gives you in this food, not only a reprieve from death, but an earnest that in a little time "death shall be swallowed up in victory."

3. The time of taking our food is usually a time of *conversation* also, as it is natural to refresh our minds while we refresh our bodies. Let us consider a little in what manner the generality of Christians usually converse together. What are the ordinary subjects of their conversation? If it is harmless (as one would hope it is), if there be nothing in it profane, nothing immodest, nothing untrue, or unkind; if there be no talebearing, backbiting, or evil-speaking, they have reason to praise God for his restraining grace. But there is more than this implied in "ordering our conversation aright." In order to this it is needful, First, that "your communication," that is, discourse or conversation, "be good;" that it be materially good, on good subjects; not fluttering about anything that occurs; for what have you to do with courts and kings? It is not your business to

Fight over the wars, reform the state; unless when some remarkable event calls for the acknowledgment of the justice or mercy of God. We *must* indeed sometimes talk of worldly things; otherwise we may as well go out of the world. But it should only be so far as is needful: Then we should return to a better subject. Secondly, let your conversation be "to the use of edifying;" calculated to edify either the speaker or the hearers, or both; to build them up, as each has particular need, either in faith, or love, or holiness. Thirdly, see that it not only gives entertainment, but, in one kind or other, "ministers grace to the hearers." Now, is not this "a more excellent way" of conversing than the harmless way above-mentioned?

V. 1. We have seen what is the "more excellent way" of ordering our conversation, as well as our business. But we cannot be always intent upon business: Both our bodies and minds require some relaxation. We need intervals of diversion from business. It will be necessary to be very explicit upon this head, as it is a point which has been much misunderstood.

2. Diversions are of various kinds. Some are almost peculiar to men, as the sports of the field-hunting, shooting, fishing, wherein not many women (I should say, ladies) are concerned. Others are indifferently used by persons of both sexes; some of which are of a more public nature, as races, masquerades, plays, assemblies, balls. Others are chiefly used in private houses, as cards, dancing, and music; to which we may add the reading of plays, novels, romances, newspapers, and fashionable poetry.

3. Some diversions indeed which were formerly in great request, are now fallen into disrepute. The nobility and gentry (in England at least) seem totally to disregard the once fashionable diversion of hawking; and the vulgar themselves are no longer diverted by men hacking and hewing each other in pieces at broad-sword. The noble game of quarter-staff, likewise, is now exercised by very few. Yea, cudgelling has lost its honour, even in Wales itself. Bear-baiting also is now very seldom seen, and bull-baiting not very often. And it seems cock-fighting would totally cease in England, were it not for two or three right honourable patrons.

4. It is not needful to say anything more of these foul *remains of Gothic barbarity*, than that they are a reproach, not only to all religion, but even to human nature. One would not pass so severe censure on the sports of the field. Let those who have nothing better to do, still run foxes and hares out of breath. Neither need much be said about horse-races, till some man of sense will undertake to defend them. It seems a great deal more may be said in defence of seeing a serious tragedy. I could not do it with a clear conscience; at least not in an English theatre, the sink of all profaneness and debauchery; but possibly others can. I cannot say quite so much for balls or assemblies, which are more reputable than masquerades, but must be allowed by all impartial persons to have exactly the same tendency. So undoubtedly have all public dancings. And the same tendency they must have, unless the same caution obtained among modern Christians which was observed among the ancient Heathens. With them men and women never danced together, but always in separate rooms. This was always observed in ancient Greece, and for several ages at Rome, where a woman dancing in company with men would have at once been set down for a prostitute. Of playing at cards I say the same as of seeing plays. I could not do it with a clear conscience. But I am not obliged to pass sentences on those that are otherwise minded. I leave them to their own Master: to him let them stand or fall.

5. But supposing these, as well as the reading of plays, novels, newspapers, and the like, to be quite innocent diversions; yet are there not more excellent ways of diverting themselves for those that love or fear God? Would men of fortune divert themselves in the open air? They may do it by cultivating and improving their lands, by planting their grounds, by laying out, carrying on, and perfecting their gardens and orchards. At other times they may visit and converse with the most serious and sensible of their neighbours; or they may visit the sick, the poor, the widows, and fatherless in their affliction. Do they desire to divert themselves in the house? They may read useful history, pious and elegant poetry, or several branches of natural philosophy. If you have time, you may divert yourself by music, and perhaps by philosophical experiments. But above all, when you have once learned the use of prayer, you will find that as

> That which yields or fills
> All space, the ambient air, wide interfused
> Embraces round this florid earth;

so will this, till through every space of life it be interfused with all your employments, and wherever you are, whatever you do, embrace you on every side. Then you will be able to say boldly:—

> With me no melancholy void,
> No moment lingers unemploy'd,
> Or unimproved below:
> My weariness of life is gone,
> Who live to serve my God alone,
> And only Jesus know.

VI. One point only remains to be considered; that is, the use of money. What is the way wherein the generality of Christians employ this? And is there not "a more excellent way?"

1. The generality of Christians usually set apart something yearly—perhaps a tenth or even one-eighth part of their income, whether it arise from yearly revenue, or from trade,—for charitable uses. Few I have known who said like Zaccheus, "Lord, the half of my goods I give to the poor." O that it would please God to multiply these friends of mankind, these general benefactors! But,

2. Besides those who have a stated rule, there are thousands who give large sums to the poor; especially when any striking instance of distress is represented to them in lively colours.

3. I praise God for all of you who act in this manner. May you never be weary of well-doing! May God restore what you give sevenfold into your own bosom! But yet I show unto you a more excellent way.

4. You may consider yourself as one in whose hands the Proprietor of heaven and earth and all things therein has lodged a part of his goods, to be disposed of according to his

direction. And his direction is, that you should look upon yourself as one of a certain number of indigent persons who are to be provided for out of that portion of His goods wherewith you are entrusted. You have two advantages over the rest: The one, that "it is more blessed to give than to receive;" the other, that you are to serve yourself first, and others afterwards. This is the light wherein you are to see yourself and them. But to be more particular: First, if you have no family, after you have provided for yourself, give away all that remains; so that

> Each Christmas your accounts may clear,
> And wind your bottom round the year.

This was the practice of all the young men at Oxford who were called Methodists. For example: One of them had thirty pounds a year. He lived on twenty-eight and gave away forty shillings. The next year receiving sixty pounds, he still lived on twenty-eight, and gave away two-and-thirty. The third year he received ninety pounds, and gave away sixty-two. The fourth year he received a hundred and twenty pounds. Still he lived as before on twenty-eight; and gave to the poor ninety-two. Was not this a more excellent way? Secondly, if you have a family, seriously consider before God, how much each member of it wants, in order to have what is needful for life and godliness. And in general, do not allow them less, nor much more, than you allow yourself. Thirdly, this being done, fix your purpose, to "gain no more." I charge you in the name of God, do not increase your substance! As it comes daily or yearly, so let it go: Otherwise you "lay up treasures upon earth." And this our Lord as flatly forbids as murder and adultery. By doing it, therefore, you would "treasure up to yourselves wrath against the day of wrath and revelation of the righteous judgement of God."

5. But suppose it were not forbidden, how can you on principles of reason spend your money in a way which God may *possibly forgive*, instead of spending it in a manner which he will *certainly reward?* You will have no reward in heaven for what you *lay up*; you will, for what you *lay out*. Every pound you put into the earthly bank is sunk: it brings no interest above. But every pound you give to the poor is put into the bank of heaven. And it will bring glorious interest; yea, and such as will be accumulating to all eternity.

6. Who then is a wise man, and endued with knowledge among you? Let him resolve this day, this hour, this moment, the Lord assisting him, to choose in all the preceding particulars the "more excellent way:" And let him steadily keep it, both with regard to sleep, prayer, work, food, conversation, and diversions; and particularly with regard to the employment of that important talent, money. Let *your* heart answer to the call of God, "From this moment, God being my helper, I will lay up no more treasure upon earth: This one thing I will do, I will lay up treasure in heaven; I will render unto God the things that are God's: I will give him all my goods, and all my heart."

90.* AN ISRAELITE INDEED

"Behold an Israelite indeed, in whom is no guile."

John 1:47.

1. Some years ago a very ingenious man, Professor Hutcheson of Glasgow, published two treatises, The Original of our Ideas of Beauty and Virtue. In the latter of these he maintains that the very essence of virtue is, the love of our fellow-creatures. He endeavours to prove, that virtue and benevolence are one and the same thing; that every temper is only so far virtuous, as it partakes of the nature of benevolence; and that all our words and actions are then only virtuous, when they spring from the same principle. "But does he not suppose gratitude, or the love of God to be the foundation of this benevolence?" By no means: Such a supposition as this never entered into his mind. Nay, he supposes just the contrary: He does not make the least scruple to aver, that if any temper or action be produced by any regard to God, or any view to a reward from him, it is not virtuous at all; and that if an action spring partly from benevolence and partly from a view to God, the more there is in it of a view to God, the less there is of virtue.

2. I cannot see this beautiful essay of Mr. Hutcheson's in any other light than as a decent, and therefore more dangerous, attack upon the whole of the Christian Revelation: Seeing this asserts the love of God to be the true foundation, both of the love of neighbour, and all other virtues; and, accordingly, places this as "the first and great commandment," on which all the rest depend, "Thou shalt love the Lord thy God will all thy heart, and with all thy mind, and with all thy soul, and with all thy strength." So that, according to the Bible, benevolence, or the love of our neighbour, is only the *second* commandment. And suppose the Scripture be of God, it is so far from being true, that benevolence alone is both the foundation and the essence of all virtue, that benevolence itself is no virtue at all, unless it spring from the love of God

3. Yet it cannot be denied, that this writer himself has a marginal note in favour of Christianity. "Who would not wish," says he, "that the Christian Revelation could be proved to be of God? Seeing it is, unquestionably, the most benevolent institution that ever appeared in the world!" But is not this, if it be considered thoroughly, another blow at the very root of that Revelation? Is it more or less than to say: "I wish it could; but in truth it cannot be proved."

4. Another ingenious writer advances an hypothesis totally different from this. Mr. Wollaston, in the book which he entitles, "The Religion of Nature Delineated," endeavours to prove, that truth is the essence of virtue, or conformableness to truth. But it seems, Mr. Wollaston goes farther from the Bible than Mr. Hutcheson himself. For Mr. Hutcheson's scheme sets aside only one of the two great commandments, namely, "Thou shalt love the Lord thy God;" whereas Mr. Wollaston sets aside both: For his hypothesis does not place the essence of virtue in either the love of God or of our neighbour.

5. However, both of these authors agree, though in different ways, to put asunder what God has joined. But St. Paul unites them together in teaching us to "speak the truth in

---

* [text from the 1872 edition]

love." And undoubtedly, both truth and love were united in him to whom He who knows the hearts of all men gives this amiable character, "Behold an Israelite indeed, in whom is no guile!"

6. But who is it, concerning whom our blessed Lord gives this glorious testimony? Who is this Nathanael, of whom so remarkable an account is given in the latter part of the chapter before us? [John 1] Is it not strange that he is not mentioned again in any part of the New Testament? He is not mentioned again under this name; but probably he had another, whereby he was more commonly called. It was generally believed by the ancients, that he is the same person who is elsewhere termed Bartholomew; one of our Lord's Apostles, and one that, in the enumeration of them, both by St. Matthew and St. Mark, is placed immediately after St. Philip, who first brought him to his Master. It is very probable, that his proper name was Nathanael,—a name common among the Jews; and that his other name, Bartholomew, meaning only the son of Ptolemy, was derived from his father, a custom which was then exceeding common among the Jews, as well as the Heathens.

7. By what little is said of him in the context he appears to have been a man of an excellent spirit; not hasty of belief, and yet open to conviction, and willing to receive the truth, from whencesoever it came. So we read, (John 1:45,) "Philip findeth Nathanael," (probably by what we term accident,) "and saith unto him, "We have found him, of whom Moses in the Law, and the Prophets, did write, Jesus of Nazareth." "Nathanael saith unto him, Can any good thing come out of Nazareth?" Has Moses spoke, or did the Prophets write, of any prophet to come from thence? "Philip saith unto him, Come and see;" and thou wilt soon be able to judge for thyself. Nathanael took his advice, without staying to confer with flesh and blood. "Jesus saw Nathanael coming, and saith, Behold an Israelite indeed, in whom is no guile!" "Nathanael saith," doubtless with surprise enough, "Whence knowest thou me?" Jesus saith, Before Philip called thee, when thou wast under the fig-tree, I saw thee." "Nathanael answered and said unto him,"—so soon was all prejudice gone!—"Rabbi, thou art the Son of God; thou art the King of Israel."

But what is implied in our Lord's character of him? "In whom is no guile." It may include all that is contained in that advice,—

> Still let thy heart be true to God,
> Thy words to it, thy actions to them both.

I. 1. We may, First, observe what is implied in having our hearts true to God. Does this imply any less than is included in that gracious command, "My son, give me thy heart?" Then only is our heart *true to God*, when we give it to him. We give him our heart, in the lowest degree, when we seek our happiness in him; when we do not seek it in gratifying "the desire of the flesh,"—in any of the pleasures of sense; nor in gratifying "the desire of the eye,"—in any of the pleasures of the imagination, arising from grand, or new, or beautiful objects, whether of nature or art; neither in "the pride of life,"—in "the honour that cometh of men," in being beloved, esteemed, and applauded by them; no, nor yet in what some term, with equal impudence and ignorance, *the main chance*, the "laying up treasures on earth." When we seek happiness in none of these, but in God alone, then we, in some sense give him our heart.

2. But in a more proper sense, we give God our heart, when we not only seek but find happiness in him. This happiness undoubtedly begins, when we begin to know him by the teaching of his own Spirit; when it pleases the Father to reveal his Son in our hearts, so that we can humbly say, "My Lord and my God;" and when the Son is pleased to reveal his Father in us, by "the Spirit of adoption, crying in our hearts, Abba Father," and "bearing his "testimony to our spirits, that we are the children of God." Then it is that "the love of God also is shed abroad in our hearts." And according to the degree of our love, is the degree of our happiness.

3. But it has been questioned, whether it is the design of God, that the happiness which is at first enjoyed by all that know and love him, should continue any longer than, as it were, the day of their espousals. In very many, we must allow, it does not; but in a few months, perhaps weeks, or even days, the joy and peace either vanishes at once, or gradually decays. Now, if God is willing that their happiness should continue, how is this to be accounted for?

4. I believe, very easily: St. Jude's exhortation, "Keep yourselves in the love of God," certainly implies that something is to be done on our part in order to its continuance. And is not this agreeable to that general declaration of our Lord, concerning this and every gift of God? "Unto him that hath shall be given, and he shall have more abundance: But from him that hath not," that is, uses it not, improves it not, "shall be taken away even that which he hath." (Luke 8:18.)

5. Indeed, part of this verse is translated in our version, "That which he seemeth to have." But it is difficult to make sense of this. For if he only *seemeth* to have this, or any other gift of God, he really hath it not. And if so, it cannot be taken away: For no man can lose what he never had. It is plain, therefore, *ho dokei echein*, ought to be rendered, *what he assuredly hath*. And it may be observed, that the word *dokeo* in various places of the New Testament does not lessen, but strengthens the sense of the word joined with it. Accordingly, whoever improves the grace he has already received, whoever increases in the love of God, will surely retain it. God will continue, yea, will give it more abundantly; Whereas, whoever does not improve this talent, cannot possibly retain it. Notwithstanding all he can do, it will infallibly be taken away from him.

II. 1. Meantime, as the heart of him that is "an Israelite indeed" is true to God, so his words are suitable thereto: And as there is no guile lodged in his heart, so there is none found in his lips. The first thing implied herein, is *veracity*,—the speaking the truth from his heart,—the putting away all wilful lying, in every kind and degree. A lie, according to a well-known definition of it, is, _falsum testimonium, cum intentione fallendi: "A falsehood, known to be such by the speaker, and uttered with an intention to deceive." But even the speaking a falsehood is not a lie, if it be not spoken with an intent to deceive.

2. Most casuists, particularly those of the Church of Rome, distinguish lies into three sorts: The First sort is malicious lies; the Second, harmless lies; the Third, officious lies: Concerning which they pass a very different judgment. I know not any that are so hardy as even to excuse, much less defend, *malicious* lies; that is, such as are told with a design to hurt any one: These are condemned by all parties. Men are more divided in their judgment with regard to *harmless* lies, such as are supposed to do neither good nor harm. The generality of men, even in the Christian world, utter them without any scruple, and openly maintain, that, if they do no harm to anyone else, they do none to the speaker. Whether they do or no, they have certainly no place in the mouth of him that is "an Israelite indeed." He cannot tell lies in jest, am more than in earnest. Nothing but truth is heard from his mouth. He remembers the express command of God to the Ephesian Christians: "Putting away lying, speak every man truth to his neighbour." (Eph. 4:25.)

3. Concerning *officious* lies, those that are spoken with a design to do good, there have been numerous controversies in the Christian Church. Abundance of writers, and those men of renown, for piety as well as learning, have published whole volumes upon the subject, and, in despite of all opposers, not only maintained them to be innocent, but commended them as meritorious. But what saith the Scripture? One passage is so express that there does not need any other. It occurs in the third chapter of the Epistle to the Romans, where the very words of the Apostle are: (Rom. 3:7, 8,) "If the truth of God hath more abounded through my lie unto his glory, why am I yet judged as a sinner?" (Will not that lie be excused from blame, for the good effect of it?) "And not rather, as we are slanderously reported, and as some affirm that we say, Let us do evil, that good may come? Whose damnation is just." Here the Apostle plainly declares, (1.) That the good effect of a lie is no excuse for it. (2.) That it is a mere slander upon Christians to say, "They teach men to do evil that good may come." (3.) That if any, in fact, do this; either teach men to do evil that good may come, or do so themselves; their damnation is just. This is peculiarly applicable to those who tell lies in order to do good thereby. It follows, that officious lies, as well as all others, are an abomination to the God of truth. Therefore, there is no absurdity, however strange it may sound, in that saying of the ancient Father, "I would not tell a wilful lie, to save the souls of the whole world."

4. The second thing which is implied in the character of "an Israelite indeed," is, *sincerity.* As veracity is opposite to lying, so sincerity is to cunning. But it is not opposite to wisdom, or discretion, which are well consistent with it. "But what is the difference between wisdom and cunning? Are they not almost, if not quite, the same thing?" By no means. The difference between them is exceeding great. Wisdom is the faculty of discerning the best ends, and the fittest means of attaining them. The end of every rational creature is God: the enjoying him in time and in eternity. The best, indeed the only, means of attaining this end, is "the faith that worketh by love." True *prudence*, in the general sense of the word, is the same thing with wisdom. *Discretion* is but another name

for prudence,—if it be not rather a part of it, as it sometimes is referred to our outward behaviour,—and means, the ordering our words and actions right. On the contrary, cunning (so it is usually termed amongst common men, but policy among the great) is, in plain terms, neither better nor worse than the art of deceiving. If therefore, it be any wisdom at all, it is "the wisdom from beneath;" springing from the bottomless pit, and leading down to the place from whence it came.

5. The two great means which cunning uses in order to deceive, are, *simulation* and *dissimulation.* Simulation is the seeming to be what we are not; dissimulation, the seeming not to be what we are; according to the old verse, *Quod non est simulo: Dissimuloque quod est.* Both the one and the other we commonly term, the "hanging out of false colours." Innumerable are the shapes that simulation puts on in order to deceive. And almost as many are used by dissimulation for the same purpose. But the man of sincerity shuns them both, and always appears exactly what he is.

6. "But suppose we are engaged with artful men, may we not use silence or reserve, especially if they ask insidious questions, without falling under the imputation of cunning?" Undoubtedly we may: Nay, we ought on many occasions either wholly to keep silence, or to speak with more or less reserve, as circumstances may require. To say nothing at all, is, in many cases, consistent with the highest sincerity. And so it is, to speak with reserve, to say only a part, perhaps a small part, of what we know. But were we to pretend it to be the whole, this would be contrary to sincerity.

7. A more difficult question than this is, "May we not speak the truth in order to deceive? like him of old, who broke out into that exclamation applauding his own ingenuity, *Hoc ego mihi puto palmarium, ut vera dicendo eos ambos fallam.* 'This I take to be my master-piece, to deceive them both by speaking the truth!" I answer, A Heathen might pique himself upon this; but a Christian could not. For although this is not contrary to veracity, yet it certainly is to sincerity. It is therefore the most excellent way, if we judge it proper to speak at all, to put away both simulation and dissimulation, and to speak the naked truth from our heart.

8. Perhaps this is properly termed, *simplicity.* It goes a little farther than sincerity itself. It implies not only, First, the speaking no known falsehood; and, Secondly, the not designedly deceiving any one; but, Thirdly, the speaking plainly and artlessly to everyone when we speak at all; the speaking as little children, in a childlike, though not a childish, manner. Does not this utterly exclude the using any *compliments?* A vile word, the very sound of which I abhor; quite agreeing with our poet:—

> It never was a good day
> Since lowly fawning was call'd compliment.

I advise men of sincerity and simplicity never to take that silly word in their mouth; but labour to keep at the utmost distance both from the name and the thing.

9. Not long before that remarkable time,

> When Statesmen sent a Prelate 'cross the seas,
> By long-famed Act of pains and penalties,

several Bishops attacked Bishop Atterbury at once, then Bishop of Rochester, and asked, "My Lord, why will you not suffer your servants to deny you, when you do not care to see company? It is not a lie for them to say your lordship is not at home; for it deceives no one: Every one knows it means only, your lordship is busy." He replied, "My Lords, if it is (which I doubt) consistent with sincerity, yet I am sure it is not consistent with that simplicity which becomes a Christian Bishop."

10. But to return. The sincerity and simplicity of him in whom is no guile have likewise an influence on his whole behaviour: They give a colour to his whole outward conversation; which, though it be far remote from everything of clownishness and ill-breeding, of roughness and surliness, yet is plain and artless, and free from all disguise, being the very picture of his heart. The truth and love which continually reign there, produce an open front, and a serene countenance; such as leave no pretence to say, with that arrogant King of Castile, "When God made man, he left one capital defect: He ought to have set a window in his breast;"—for he opens a window in his own breast, by the whole tenor of his words and actions.

11. This then is real, genuine, solid virtue. Not truth alone, nor conformity to truth. This is a property of real virtue, not the essence of it. Not love alone; though this comes nearer the mark: For *love*, in one sense, "is the fulfilling of the law." No: Truth and love united together, are the essence of virtue or holiness. God indispensably requires "truth in the inward parts," influencing all our words and actions. Yet truth itself, separate from love, is nothing in his sight. But let the humble, gentle, patient love of all mankind, be fixed on its right foundation, namely, the love of God springing from faith, from a full conviction that God hath given his only Son to die for *my* sins; and then the whole will resolve into that grand conclusion, worthy of all men to be received: "Neither circumcision availeth any thing, nor uncircumcision, but faith that worketh by love."

91.* ON CHARITY

"Though I speak with the tongues of men and of angels, and have not charity, I am become as sounding brass, or a tinkling cymbal. And though I have the gift of prophecy, and understand all mysteries, and all knowledge; and though I have all faith, so as to remove mountains, and have not charity, I am nothing. And though I bestow all my goods to feed the poor, and give my body to be burned, and have not charity, it profiteth me nothing."

1 Cor. 13:1–3.

We know, "All Scripture is given by inspiration of God," and is therefore true and right concerning all things. But we know, likewise, that there are some Scriptures which more immediately commend themselves to every man's conscience. In this rank we may place the passage before us; there are scarce any that object to it. On the contrary, the generality of men very readily appeal to it. Nothing is more common than to find even those who deny the authority of the Holy Scriptures, yet affirming, "This is my religion; that which is described in the thirteenth chapter of the Corinthians." Nay, even a Jew, Dr. Nunes, a Spanish physician, then settled at Savannah, in Georgia, used to say with great earnestness, "That Paul of Tarsus was one of the finest writers I have ever read. I wish the thirteenth chapter of his first letter to the Corinthians were wrote in letters of gold. And I wish every Jew were to carry it with him wherever he went." He judged, (and herein he certainly judged right,) that this single chapter contained the whole of true religion. It contains "whatsoever things are just, whatsoever things are pure, whatsoever things are lovely: If there be any virtue, if there be any praise," it is all contained in this.

In order to see this in the clearest light, we may consider,

      I.   What the charity here spoken of is:

      II.   What those things are which are usually put in the place of it. We may then,

      III.   Observe, that neither any of them, nor all of them put together, can supply the want of it.

I. 1. We are, First, to consider what this charity is. What is the nature and what are the properties of it? St. Paul's word is *agape*, exactly answering to the plain english word *love*. And accordingly it is so rendered in all the old translations of the Bible. So it stood in William Tyndals Bible, which, I suppose, was the first english translation of the whole Bible. So it was also in the Bible published by the authority of King henry VIII. So it was likewise, in all the editions of the Bible that were successively published in england during the reign of King edward VI., Queen elizabeth, and King James I. Nay, so it is found in the Bibles of King Charles Firsts reign; I believe, to the period of it. The first Bibles I have seen wherein the word was changed, were those printed by Roger Daniel and John Field, printers to the Parliament, in the year 1649. hence it seems probable that the alteration was made during the sitting of the Long Parliament; probably it was then the Latin word *charity* was put in the place of the English word *love*. It was in an unhappy hour this alteration was made; the ill effects of it remain to this day; and these may be observed, not only among the poor and illiterate; not only thousands of common men and women no more understand the word charity than they do the original Greek; but the same miserable mistake has diffused itself among men of education and learning. Thousands of these are misled thereby, and imagine that the charity treated of in this chapter refers chiefly, if not wholly, to outward actions, and to mean little more than almsgiving! I have heard many sermons preached upon this chapter, particularly before the University of oxford. And I never heard more than one, wherein the meaning of it was not totally misrepresented. But had the old and proper word *love* been retained, there would have been no room for misrepresentation.

2. But what kind of love is that whereof the Apostle is speaking throughout the chapter? Many persons of eminent

---

* [text from the 1872 edition]

learning and piety apprehend that it is the love of God. But from reading the whole chapter numberless times, and considering it in every light, I am thoroughly persuaded that what St. Paul is here directly speaking of is the love of our neighbour. I believe whoever carefully weighs the whole tenor of his discourse will be fully convinced of this. But it must be allowed to be such a love of our neighbour, as can only spring from the love of God. And whence does this love of God flow? only from that faith which is of the operation of God; which whoever has, has a direct evidence that, God was in Christ, reconciling the world unto himself. When this is particularly applied to his heart, so that he can say with humble boldness, The life which I now live, I live by the faith in the Son of God, who loved me, and gave himself for me; then, and not till then, the love of God is shed abroad in his heart. And this love sweetly constrains him to love every child of man with the love which is here spoken of; not with a love of esteem or of complacence; for this can have no place with regard to those who are (if not his personal enemies, yet) enemies to God and their own souls; but with a love of benevolence,—of tender good-will to all the souls that God has made.

3. But it may be asked, "If there be no true love of our neighbour, but that which springs from the love of God; and if the love of God flows from no other fountain than faith in the Son of God; does it not follow, that the whole heathen world is excluded from all possibility of salvation? Seeing they are cut off from faith; for faith cometh by hearing; and how shall they hear without a preacher?" I answer, St. Pauls words, spoken on another occasion, are applicable to this: "What the law speaketh, it speaketh to them that are under the law." Accordingly, that sentence, "he that believeth not shall be damned," is spoken of them to whom the Gospel is preached. others it does not concern; and we are not required to determine any thing touching their final state. How it will please God, the Judge of all, to deal with *them*, we may leave to God himself. But this we know, that he is not the God of the Christians only, but the God of the Heathens also; that he is "rich in mercy to all that call upon him," according to the light they have; and that "in every nation, he that feareth God and worketh righteousness is accepted of him."

4. But to return. This is the nature of that love whereof the Apostle is here speaking. But what are the properties of it,— the fruits which are inseparable from it? The Apostle reckons up many of them; but the principal of them are these.

First. "Love is not puffed up." As is the measure of love, so is the measure of humility. Nothing humbles the soul so deeply as love: It casts out all "high conceits, engendering pride;" all arrogance and overweaning; makes us little, and poor, and base, and vile in our own eyes. It abases us both before God and man; makes us willing to be the least of all, and the servants of all, and teaches us to say, "A mote in the sun-beam is little, but I am infinitely less in the presence of God."

5. Secondly, "Love is not provoked." our present English translation renders it, "is not easily provoked." But how did the word *easily* come in? There is not a tittle of it in the text: The words of the Apostle are simply these, *ou paraxynetai*. Is it not probable, it was inserted by the translators with a

design to excuse St. Paul, for fear his practice should appear to contradict his doctrine? For we read, (Acts 15:36, *et seq.*,) "And some days after, Paul said unto Barnabas, Let us go again and visit our brethren in every city where we have preached the word of the Lord, and see how they do. And Barnabas determined to take with them John, whose surname was Mark. But Paul thought not good to take with them who departed from the work. And the contention was so sharp between them that they departed asunder one from the other: And so Barnabas took Mark, and sailed unto Cyprus; and Paul chose Silas, and departed; being recommended by the brethren unto the grace of God. And he went through Syria and Cilicia, confirming the churches."

6. Would not any one think, on reading these words, that they were both equally sharp? That Paul was just as hot as Barnabas, and as much wanting in love as he? But the text says no such thing; as will be plain, if we consider first the occasion. When St. Paul proposed, that they should "again visit the brethren in every city where they had preached the word," so far they were agreed. "And Barnabas determined to take with them John," because he was his sister's son, without receiving or asking St. Paul's advice. "But Paul thought not good to take him with them who had departed from them from Pamphylia,"—whether through sloth or cowardice,— "went not with them to the work." And undoubtedly he thought right; he had reason on his side. The following words are, *egento oun paroxysmos*, literally, "and there was a fit of anger." It does not say, in St. Paul: Probably it was in Barnabas alone; who thus supplied the want of reason with passion; "so that they parted asunder." And Barnabas, resolved to have his own way, did as his nephew had done before, "departed from the work,"—"took Mark with him, and sailed to Cyprus." But Paul went on his work, "being recommended by the brethren to the grace of God;" which Barnabas seems not to have stayed for. "And he went through Syria and Cilicia, confirming the Churches." From the whole account, it does not appear that St. Paul was in any fault; that he either felt any temper, or spoke any word, contrary to the law of love. Therefore, not being in any fault, he does not need any excuse.

7. Certainly he who is full of love is "gentle towards all men." He "in meekness instructs those that oppose themselves;" that oppose what he loves most, even the truth of God, or that holiness without which no man shall see the Lord: Not knowing but "God, peradventure, may bring them to the knowledge of the truth." However provoked, he does "not return evil for evil, or railing for railing." Yea, he "blesses those that curse him, and does good to them that despitefully use him and persecute him." He "is not overcome of evil, but" always "overcomes evil with good.

8. Thirdly. "Love is longsuffering." It endures not a few affronts, reproaches, injuries; but *all things*, which God is pleased to permit either men or devils to inflict. It arms the soul with inviolable patience; not harsh stoical patience, but yielding as the air, which, making no resistance to the stroke, receives no harm thereby. The lover of mankind remembers Him who suffered for us, "leaving us an example that we might tread in his steps." Accordingly, "if his enemy hunger,

he feeds him; if he thirst, he gives him drink:" And by so doing, he "heaps coals of fire," of melting love, upon his head. "And many waters cannot quench this love; neither can the floods" of ingratitude "drown it."

II. 1. We are, Secondly, to inquire, what those things are, which, it is commonly supposed, will supply the place of love. And the first of these is eloquence; a faculty of talking well, particularly on religious subjects. Men are generally inclined to think well of one that talks well. If he speaks properly and fluently of God, and the things of God, who can doubt of his being in God's favour? And it is very natural for him to think well of himself; to have as favourable an opinion of himself as others have.

2. But men of reflection are not satisfied with this: They are not content with a flood of words; they prefer thinking before talking, and judge, one that knows much is far preferable to one that talks much. And it is certain, knowledge is an excellent gift of God; particularly knowledge of the Holy Scriptures, in which are contained all the depths of divine knowledge and wisdom. Hence it is generally thought that a man of much knowledge, knowledge of Scripture in particular, must not only be in the favour of God, but likewise enjoy a high degree of it.

3. But men of deeper reflection are apt to say, "I lay no stress upon any other knowledge, but the knowledge of God by faith. Faith is the only knowledge, which, in the sight of God, is of great price. 'We are saved by faith;' by faith alone: This is the one thing needful. He that believeth, and he alone, shall be saved everlastingly." There is much truth in this: It is unquestionably true, that "we are saved by faith:" Consequently, that "he that believeth shall be saved, and he that believeth not shall be damned."

4. But some men will say, with the Apostle James, "Show me thy faith without thy works;" (if thou canst, but indeed it is impossible;) "and I will show thee my faith by my works." And many are induced to think that good works, works of piety and mercy, are of far more consequence than faith itself, and will supply the want of every other qualification for heaven. Indeed this seems to be the general sentiment, not only of the members of the Church of Rome, but of Protestants also; not of the giddy and thoughtless, but the serious members of our own Church.

5. And this cannot be denied, our Lord himself hath said, "Ye shall know them by their fruits:" By their works ye know them that believe, and them that believe not. But yet it may be doubted, whether there is not a surer proof of the sincerity of our faith than even our works, that is, our willingly suffering for righteousness' sake: Especially if, after suffering reproach, and pain, and loss of friends and substance, a man gives up life itself; yea, by a shameful and painful death, by giving his body to be burned, rather than he would give up faith and a good conscience by neglecting his known duty.

6. It is proper to observe here, First, what a beautiful gradation there is, each step rising above the other, in the enumeration of those several things which some or other of those that are called Christians, and are usually accounted so, really believe will supply the absence of love. St. Paul begins at the lowest point, *talking well*, and advances step by step;

every one rising higher than the preceding, till he comes to the highest of all. A step above eloquence is knowledge: Faith is a step above this. Good works are a step above that faith; and even above this, is suffering for righteousness' sake. Nothing is higher than this, but Christian love; the love of our neighbour, flowing from the love of God.

7. It may be proper to observe, Secondly, that whatever passes for religion in any part of the Christian world, (whether it be a part of religion, or no part at all, but either folly, superstition, or wickedness,) may with very little difficulty be reduced to one or other of these heads. Every thing which is supposed to be religion, either by Protestants or Romanists, and is not, is contained under one or another of these five particulars. Make trial as often as you please, with anything that is called religion, but improperly so called, and you will find the rule to hold without any exception.

III. 1. I am now, in the Third place, to demonstrate, to all who have ears to hear, who do not harden themselves against conviction, that neither any one of these five qualifications, nor all of them together, will avail anything before God, without the love above described.

In order to do this in the clearest manner, we may consider them one by one. And, First, "though I speak with the tongues of men and of angels;"—with an eloquence such as never was found in men, concerning the nature, attributes, and works of God, whether of creation or providence; though I were not herein a whit behind the chief of the apostles; preaching like St. Peter, and praying like St. John;—yet unless humble, gentle, patient love, be the ruling temper of my soul, I am no better, in the judgment of God, "than sounding brass, or a rumbling cymbal." The highest eloquence, therefore, either in private conversation, or in public ministrations,—the brightest talents either for preaching or prayer,—if they were not joined with humble, meek, and patient resignation, might sink me the deeper into hell, but will not bring me one step nearer heaven.

2. A plain instance may illustrate this. I knew a young man between fifty and sixty years ago, who, during the course of several years, never endeavoured to convince any one of a religious truth, but he *was* convinced; and he never endeavoured to persuade any one to engage in a religious practice, but he was persuaded: What then? All that power of convincing speech, all that force of persuasion, if it was not joined with meekness and lowliness, with resignation and patient love, would no more qualify him for the fruition of God, than a clear voice, or a fine complexion. Nay, it would rather procure him a hotter place in everlasting burnings!

3. Secondly. "Though I have the gift of prophecy,"—of foretelling those future events which no creature can foresee; and "though I understand all" the "mysteries" of nature, of providence, and the word of God; and "have all knowledge" of things, divine or human, that any mortal ever attained to; though I can explain the most mysterious passages of Daniel, of Ezekiel, and the Revelation;—yet if I have not humility, gentleness, and resignation, "I am nothing" in the sight of God.

A little before the conclusion of the late war in Flanders, one who came from thence gave us a very strange relation. I knew not what judgment to form of this, but waited till John Haime should come over, of whose veracity I could no more doubt than of his understanding. The account he gave was this: "Jonathan Pyrah was a member of our Society in Flanders. I knew him some years, and knew him to be a man of unblamable character. One day he was summoned to appear before the Board of General Officers. One of them said, 'What is this which we hear of you? We hear you are turned prophet, and that you foretel the downfal of the bloody house of Bourbon, and the haughty house of Austria. We should be glad if you were a real prophet, and if your prophecies came true. But what sign do you give, to convince us you are so, and that your predictions will come to pass?' He readily answered, 'Gentlemen, I give you a sign: To-morrow, at twelve o'clock, you shall have such a storm of thunder and lightning as you never had before since you came into Flanders. I give you a second sign: As little as any of you expect any such thing, as little appearance of it as there is now, you shall have a general engagement with the French within three days. I give you a third sign: I shall be ordered to advance in the first line. If I am a false prophet, I shall be shot dead at the first discharge; but if I am a true prophet, I shall only receive a musket-ball in the calf of my left leg.' At twelve the next day there was such thunder and lightning as they never had before in Flanders. On the third day, contrary to all expectation, was the general battle of Fontenoy. He was ordered to advance in the first line; and, at the very first discharge, he did receive a musket-ball in the calf of his left leg."

4. And yet all this profited him nothing, either for temporal or eternal happiness. When the war was over, he returned to England; but the story was got before him: In consequence of which he was sent for by the Countess of St—s, and several other persons of quality, who were desirous to receive so surprising an account from his own mouth. He could not bear so much honour. It quite turned his brain. In a little time he ran stark mad. And so he continues to this day, living still, as I apprehend, on Wibsey Moorside, within a few miles of Leeds. [At the time of writing this sermon. He is since dead.]

5. And what would it profit a man to "have all knowledge," even that which is infinitely preferable to all other,—the knowledge of the Holy Scripture? I knew a young man about twenty years ago, who was so thoroughly acquainted with the Bible, that if he was questioned concerning any Hebrew word in the Old, or any Greek word in the New Testament, he would tell, after a little pause, not only how often the one or the other occurred in the Bible, but also what it meant in every place. His name was Thomas Walsh. [His Journal, written by himself, is extant.] Such a master of Biblic knowledge I never saw before, and never expect to see again. Yet if, with all his knowledge, he had been void of love; if he had been proud, passionate, or impatient; he and all his knowledge would have perished together, as sure as ever he was born.

6. "And though I have all faith, so that I could remove mountains."—The faith which is able to do this cannot be the fruit of vain imagination, a mere madman's dream, a system of opinions; but must be a real work of God: Otherwise it could not have such an effect. Yet if this faith does not work by love, if it does not produce universal holiness, if it does not bring forth lowliness, meekness, and resignation, it will profit me nothing. This is as certain a truth as any that is delivered in the whole oracles of God. All faith that is, that ever was, or ever can be, separate from tender benevolence to every child of man, friend or foe, Christian, Jew, Heretic, or Pagan,—separate from gentleness to all men; separate from resignation in all events, and contentedness in all conditions,—is not the faith of a Christian, and will stand us in no stead before the face of God.

7. Hear ye this, all you that are called Methodists! You, of all men living, are most concerned herein. You constantly speak of salvation by faith: And you are in the right for so doing. You maintain, (one and all,) that a man is justified by faith, without the works of the law. And you cannot do otherwise, without giving up the Bible, and betraying your own souls. You insist upon it, that we are saved by faith: And, undoubtedly, so we are. But consider, meantime, that let us have ever so much faith, and be our faith ever so strong, it will never save us from hell, unless it now save us from all unholy tempers, from pride, passion, impatience; from all arrogance of spirit, all haughtiness and overbearing; from wrath, anger, bitterness; from discontent, murmuring, fretfulness, peevishness. We are of all men most inexcusable, if, having been so frequently guarded against that strong delusion, we still, while we indulge any of these tempers, bless ourselves, and dream we are in the way to heaven!

8. Fourthly. "Although I give all my goods to the poor;"—though I divide all my real and all my personal estate into small portions, (so the original word properly signifies,) and diligently bestow it on those who, I have reason to believe, are the most proper objects;—yet if I am proud, passionate, or discontented; if I give way to any of these tempers; whatever good I may do to others, I do none to my own soul. O how pitiable a case is this! Who would not grieve that these beneficent men should lose all their labour! It is true, many of them have a reward in this world, if not before, yet after their death. They have costly and pompous funerals. They have marble monuments of the most exquisite workmanship. They have epitaphs wrote in the most elegant strain, which extol their virtues to the skies. Perhaps they have yearly orations spoken over them, to transmit their memory to all generations. So have many founders of religious houses, of colleges, alms-houses, and most charitable institutions. And it is an allowed rule, that none can exceed in the praise of the founder of his house, college, or hospital. But still what a poor reward is this! Will it add to their comfort or to their misery, suppose (which must be the case if they did not die in faith) that they are in the hands of the devil and his angels? What insults, what cutting reproaches, would these occasion, from their infernal companions! O that they were wise! that all those who are zealous of good works would put them in their proper place; would not imagine they can supply the want of holy tempers, but take care that they may spring from them!

9. How exceeding strange must this sound in the ears of most of those who are, by the courtesy of England, called Christians! But stranger still is that assertion of the Apostle, which comes in the last place: "Although I give my body to be burned, and have not love, it profiteth me nothing." Although rather than deny the faith, rather than commit a known sin, or omit a known duty, I voluntarily submit to a cruel death; "deliver up my body to be burned;" yet if I am under the power of pride, or anger, or fretfulness,—"it profiteth me nothing."

10. Perhaps this may be illustrated by an example. We have a remarkable account in the tracts of Dr. Geddes—a Civilian, who was Envoy from Queen Anne to the Court of Portugal, in the latter end of her reign. He was present at one of those _Autos de Fes, "Acts of Faith," wherein the Roman Inquisitors burned heretics alive. One of the persons who was then brought out for execution, having been confined in the dungeons of the Inquisition, had not seen the sun for many years. It proved a bright sunshiny day. Looking up, he cried out in surprise, "O how can anyone who sees that glorious luminary, worship any but the God that made it!" A friar standing by, ordered them to run an iron gag through his lips, that he might speak no more. Now, what did that poor man feel within when this order was executed? If he said in his heart, though he could not utter it with his lips, "Father, forgive them, for they know not what they do," undoubtedly the angels of God were ready to carry his soul into Abraham's bosom. But if, instead of this, he cherished the resentment in his heart which he could not express with his tongue, although his body was consumed by the flames, I will not say his soul went to paradise.

11. The sum of all that has been observed is this: Whatever I speak, whatever I know, whatever I believe, whatever I do, whatever I suffer; if I have not the faith that worketh by love, that produces love to God and all mankind, I am not in the narrow way which leadeth to life, but in the broad road that leadeth to destruction. In other words: Whatever eloquence I have; whatever natural or supernatural knowledge; whatever faith I have received from God; whatever works I do, whether of piety or mercy; whatever sufferings I undergo for conscience' sake, even though I resist unto blood: All these things put together, however applauded of men, will avail nothing before God, unless I am meek and lowly in heart, and can say in all things, "Not as I will, but as thou wilt!"

12. We conclude from the whole, (and it can never be too much inculcated, because all the world votes on the other side,) that true religion, in the very essence of it, is nothing short of holy tempers. Consequently all other religion, whatever name it bears, whether Pagan, Mahometan, Jewish, or Christian; and whether Popish or Protestant, Lutheran or Reformed; without these, is lighter than vanity itself.

13. Let every man, therefore, that has a soul to be saved see that he secure this one point. With all his eloquence, his knowledge, his faith, works, and sufferings, let him hold fast this "one thing needful." He that through the power of faith endureth to the end in humble, gentle, patient love; he, and he alone, shall, through the merits of Christ, "inherit the kingdom prepared from the foundation of the world."

92.* ON ZEAL

"It is good to be always zealously affected in a good thing."

Gal. 4:18.

1. There are few subjects in the whole compass of religion, that are of greater importance than this. For without zeal it is impossible, either to make any considerable progress in religion ourselves, or to do any considerable service to our neighbour, whether in temporal or spiritual things. And yet nothing has done more disservice to religion, or more mischief to mankind, than a sort of zeal which has for several ages prevailed, both in Pagan, Mahometan, and Christian nations. Insomuch that it may truly be said, pride, covetousness, ambition, revenge, have in all parts of the world slain their thousands; but zeal its ten thousands. Terrible instances of this have occurred in ancient times, in the most civilized heathen nations. To this chiefly were owing the inhuman persecutions of the primitive Christians; and, in later ages, the no less inhuman persecutions of the Protestants by the Church of Rome. It was zeal that kindled fires in our nation during the reign of bloody Queen Mary. It was zeal that soon after made so many provinces of France a field of blood. It was zeal that murdered so many thousand unresisting Protestants, in the never-to-be-forgotten massacre of Paris. It was zeal that occasioned the still more horrid massacre in Ireland—the like whereof, both with regard to the number of the murdered, and the shocking circumstances wherewith many of those murders were perpetrated, I verily believe never occurred before since the world began. As to the other parts of Europe, an eminent German writer has taken immense pains to search both the records in various places and the most authentic histories, in order to gain some competent knowledge of the blood which has been shed since the Reformation, and computes that, partly by private persecution, partly by religious wars, in the course of forty years, reckoning from the year 1520, above forty millions of persons have been destroyed!

2. But is it not possible to distinguish right zeal from wrong? Undoubtedly it is possible. But it is difficult; such is the deceitfulness of the human heart; so skilfully do the passions justify themselves. And there are exceeding few treatises on the subject; at least, in the English language. To this day I have seen or heard of only one sermon; and that was wrote above a hundred years ago, by Dr. Sprat, then Bishop of Rochester; so that it is now exceeding scarce.

3. I would gladly cast in my mite, by God's assistance toward the clearing up this important question, in order to enable well-meaning men, who are desirous of pleasing God, to distinguish true Christian zeal from its various counterfeits. And this is more necessary at this time than it has been for many years. Sixty years ago there seemed to be scarce any such thing as religious zeal left in the nation. People in

_____

* (text from the 1872 edition)

general were wonderfully cool and undisturbed about *that trifle, religion*. But since then, it is easy to observe, there has been a very considerable alteration. Many thousands, almost in every part of the nation, have felt a real desire to save their souls. And I am persuaded there is at this day more religious zeal in England, than there has been for a century past.

4. But has this zeal been of the right or the wrong kind? Probably both the one and the other. Let us see if we cannot separate these, that we may avoid the latter, and cleave to the former. In order to this. I would first inquire,

    I.   What is the nature of true Christian zeal?
    II.   What are the properties of it? And,
    III.   Draw some practical inferences.

I. And, First, What is the nature of zeal in general, and of true Christian zeal in particular?

1. The original word, in its primary signification, means *heat;* such as the heat of boiling water. When it is figuratively applied to the mind, it means any warm emotion or affection. Sometimes it is taken for envy. So we render it, Acts 5:17, where we read, "The High Priest, and all that were with him, were filled with envy,"—eplEsthEsan zElou_, although it might as well be rendered, *were filled with zeal*. Sometimes, it is taken for anger and indignation; sometimes, for vehement desire. And when any of our passions are strongly moved on a religious account, whether for any thing good, or against any thing which we conceive to be evil, this we term *religious zeal*.

2. But it is not all that is called religious zeal which is worthy of that name. It is not properly religious or Christian zeal, if it be not joined with charity. A fine writer (Bishop Sprat) carries the matter farther still. "It has been affirmed," says that great man, "no zeal is right, which is not charitable, but is mostly so. Charity, or love, is not only one ingredient, but the chief ingredient in its composition." May we not go further still? May we not say, that true zeal is not mostly charitable, but wholly so? that is, if we take charity, in St. Paul's sense, for love; the love of God and our neighbour. For it is a certain truth, (although little understood in the world,) that Christian zeal is all love. It is nothing else. The love of God and man fills up its whole nature.

3. Yet it is not every degree of that love to which this appellation is given. There may be some love, a small degree of it, where there is no zeal. But it is, properly, love in a higher degree. It is *fervent love*. True Christian zeal is no other than the flame of love. This is the nature, the inmost essence, of it.

II. 1. From hence it follows, that the properties of love are the properties of zeal also. Now, one of the chief properties of love is humility: "Love is not puffed up." Accordingly, this is a property of true zeal: humility is inseparable from it. As is the degree of zeal, such is the degree of humility: they must rise and fall together. The same love which fills a man with zeal for God, makes him little, and poor, and vile in his own eyes.

2. Another of the properties of love is meekness: consequently, it is one of the properties of zeal. It teaches us to be meek, as well as lowly; to be equally superior to anger or pride. Like as the wax melteth at the fire, so before this sacred flame all turbulent passions melt away, and leave the soul unruffled and serene.

3. Yet another property of love, and consequently of zeal, is unwearied patience: for "love endureth all things." It arms the soul with entire resignation to all the disposals of divine Providence, and teaches us to say, in every occurrence, "It is the Lord; let him do what seemeth him good." It enables us, in whatever state, therewith to be content; to repine at nothing, to murmur at nothing, "but in every thing to give thanks."

4. There is a Fourth property of Christian zeal, which deserves to be more particularly considered. This we learn from the very words of the Apostle, "It is good to be jealously affected always" (not to have transient touches of veal, but a steady, rooted disposition) "in a good thing: "in that which is good: for the proper object of zeal is, good in general; that is, everything that is good, really such, in the sight of God.

5. But what is good in the sight of God? What is that religion, wherewith God is always well pleased? How do the parts of this rise one above another? and what is the comparative value of them?

This is a point exceeding little considered, and therefore little understood. Positive divinity, many have some knowledge of. But few know anything of comparative divinity. I never saw but one tract upon this head; a sketch of which it may be of use to subjoin.

In a Christian believer *love* sits upon the throne which is erected in the inmost soul; namely, love of God and man, which fills the whole heart, and reigns without a rival. In a circle near the throne are all holy tempers;—longsuffering, gentleness, meekness, fidelity, temperance; and if any other were comprised in "the mind which was in Christ Jesus." In an exterior circle are all the *works of mercy*, whether to the souls or bodies of men. By these we exercise all holy tempers—by these we continually improve them, so that all these are real means of grace, although this is not commonly adverted to. Next to these are those that are usually termed works of piety—reading and hearing the word, public, family, private prayer, receiving the Lord's supper, fasting or abstinence. Lastly, that his followers may the more effectually provoke one another to love, holy tempers, and good works, our blessed Lord has united them together in one body, the church, dispersed all over the earth—a little emblem of which, of the church universal, we have in every particular Christian congregation.

6. This is that religion which our Lord has established upon earth, ever since the descent of the Holy Ghost on the day of Pentecost. This is the entire, connected system of Christianity: and thus the several parts of it rise one above another, from that lowest point, the assembling ourselves together, to the highest,—love enthroned in the heart. And hence it is easy to learn the comparative value of every branch of religion. Hence also we learn a Fifth property of true zeal. That as it is always exercised *en kaloi, in that which is good*, so it is always *proportioned* to that good, to the degree of goodness that is in its object.

7. For example. Every Christian ought, undoubtedly, to be zealous for the church, bearing a strong affection to it, and

earnestly desiring its prosperity and increase. He ought to be thus zealous, as for the church universal, praying for it continually, so especially for that particular church or Christian society whereof he himself is a member. For this he ought to wrestle with God in prayer; meantime using every means in his power to enlarge its borders, and to strengthen his brethren, that they may adorn the doctrine of God our Saviour.

8. But he should be more zealous for the ordinances of Christ than for the church itself; for prayer in public and private; for the Lord's supper, for reading, hearing, and meditating on his word; and for the much-neglected duty of fasting. These he should earnestly recommend; first, by his example; and then by advice, by argument, persuasion, and exhortation, as often as occasion offers.

9. Thus should he show his zeal for works of piety; but much more for works of mercy; seeing "God will have mercy and not sacrifice," that is, rather than sacrifice. Whenever, therefore, one interferes with the other, works of mercy are to be preferred. Even reading, hearing, prayer are to be omitted, or to be postponed, "at charity's almighty call;" when we are called to relieve the distress of our neighbour, whether in body or soul.

10. But as zealous as we are for all good works, we should still be more zealous for holy tempers; for planting and promoting, both in our own souls, and in all we have any intercourse with, lowliness of mind, meekness. gentleness, longsuffering, contentedness, resignation unto the will of God, deadness to the world and the things of the world, as the only means of being truly alive to God. For these proofs and fruits of living faith we cannot be too zealous. We should "talk of them as we sit in our house," and "when we walk by the way," and "when we lie down," and "when we rise up." We should make them continual matter of prayer; as being far more excellent than any outward works whatever: seeing those will fail when the body drops off; but these will accompany us into eternity.

11. But our choicest zeal should be reserved for love itself,— the end of the commandment, the fulfilling of the law. The church, the ordinances, outward works of every kind, yea, all other holy tempers, are inferior to this, and rise in value only as they approach nearer and nearer to it. Here then is the great object of Christian zeal. Let every true believer in Christ apply, with all fervency of spirit, to the God and Father of our Lord Jesus Christ, that his heart may be more and more enlarged in love to God and to all mankind. This one thing let him do: let him "press on to this prize of our high calling of God in Christ Jesus."

III. It remains only to draw some practical inferences from the preceding observations.

1. And, First, if zeal, true Christian zeal, be nothing but the flame of love, then *hatred*, in every kind and degree, then every sort of *bitterness* toward them that oppose us, is so far from deserving the name of zeal, that it is directly opposite to it. If zeal be only fervent love, then it stands at the utmost distance from *prejudice*, jealousy, evil surmising; seeing "love thinketh no evil." Then *bigotry* of every sort, and, above all, the spirit of *persecution*, are totally inconsistent with it. Let

not, therefore, any of these unholy tempers screen themselves under that sacred name. As all these are the works of the devil, let them appear in their own shape, and no longer under that specious disguise deceive the unwary children of God.

2. Secondly. If lowliness be a property of zeal, then pride is inconsistent with it. It is true, some degree of pride may remain after the love of God is shed abroad in the heart; as this is one of the last evils that is rooted out, when God creates all things new; but it cannot reign, nor retain any considerable power, where fervent love is found. Yea, were we to give way to it but a little, it would damp that holy fervour, and, if we did not immediately fly back to Christ. would utterly quench the Spirit.

3. Thirdly. If meekness be an inseparable property of zeal, what shall we say of those who call their auger by that name? Why, that they mistake the truth totally; that they, in the fullest sense, put darkness for light, and light for darkness. We cannot be too watchful against this delusion, because it spreads over the whole Christian world. Almost in all places, zeal and anger pass for equivalent terms; and exceeding few persons are convinced, that there is any difference between them. How commonly do we hear it said, "See how zealous the man is!" Nay, he cannot be zealous; that is impossible, for he is in a passion; and passion is as inconsistent with zeal, as light with darkness, or heaven with hell!

It were well that this point were thoroughly understood. Let us consider it a little farther. We frequently observe one that bears the character of a religious man vehemently angry at his neighbour. Perhaps he calls his brother *Raca*, or *Thou fool*. He brings a railing accusation against him. You mildly admonish him of his warmth. He answers, "It is my zeal!' No: it is your sin, and, unless you repent of it, will sink you lower than the grave. There is much such zeal as this in the bottomless pit. Thence all zeal of this kind comes; and thither it will go, and you with it, unless you are saved from it before you go hence!

4. Fourthly. If patience, contentedness, and resignation are the properties of zeal, then murmuring, fretfulness, discontent, impatience are wholly inconsistent with it. And yet how ignorant are mankind of this! How often do we see men fretting at the ungodly, or telling you they are *out of patience* with such or such things, and terming all this their zeal! O spare no pains to undeceive them! If it be possible, show them what zeal is; and convince them that all murmuring, or fretting at sin, is a species of sin, and has no resemblance of, or connexion with, the true zeal of the Gospel.

5. Fifthly. If the object of zeal be that which is good, then fervour for any *evil thing* is not Christian zeal. I instance in *idolatry*, worshipping of angels, saints, images, the cross. Although, therefore, a man were so earnestly attached to any kind of idolatrous worship, that he would even "give his body to be burned," rather than refrain from it, call this bigotry or superstition, if you please, but call it not zeal; that is quite another thing.

From the same premises it follows, that fervour for *indifferent things* is not Christian zeal. But how exceedingly common is this mistake too! Indeed one would think that men of understanding could not be capable of such weakness. But, alas! the history of all ages proves the contrary. Who were men of stronger understandings than Bishop Ridley and Bishop Hooper? And how warmly did these, and other great men of that age, dispute about the *sacerdotal vestments*! How eager was the contention for almost a hundred years, for and against wearing a *surplice*! O shame to man! I would as soon have disputed about a straw or a barley-corn. And this, indeed, shall be called zeal! And why was it not rather called wisdom or holiness?

6. It follows also, from the same premises, that fervour for *opinions* is not Christian zeal. But how few are sensible of this! And how innumerable are the mischiefs which even this species of false zeal has occasioned in the Christian world! How many thousand lives have been cast away by those who were zealous for the Romish opinions! How many of the excellent ones of the earth have been cut off by zealots, for the senseless opinion of transubstantiation! But does not every unprejudiced person see, that this zeal is "earthly, sensual, devilish;" and that it stands at the utmost contrariety to that zeal which is here recommended by the Apostle? What an excess of charity is it then which our great poet expresses, in his "Poem on the Last Day," where he talks of meeting in heaven—
Those who by mutual wounds expired,
By *zeal* for their distinct persuasions fired! Zeal indeed! What manner of zeal was this, which led them to cut one another's throats? Those who were *fired* with this spirit, and died therein, will undoubtedly have their portion, not in heaven, (only love is there,) but in the "fire that never shall be quenched."

7. Lastly. If true zeal be always proportioned to the degree of goodness which is in its object, then should it rise higher and higher according to the scale mentioned above; according to the comparative value of the several parts of religion. For instance, all that truly fear God should be zealous for the *Church*; both for the catholic or universal church, and for that part of it whereof they are members. This is not the appointment of men, but of God. He saw it was "not good for men to be alone," even in this sense. but that the whole body of his children should be "knit together, and strengthened, by that which every joint supplieth." At the same time they should be more zealous for the *ordinances* of God; for public and private prayer, for hearing and reading the word of God, and for fasting and the Lord's supper. But they should be more zealous for *works of mercy*, than even for works of piety. Yet ought they to be more zealous still for all *holy tempers*, lowliness, meekness, resignation: but most zealous of all, for that which is the sum and the perfection of religion, the *love* of God and man.

8. It remains only to make a close and honest application of these things to our own souls. We all know the general truth, that "it is good to be always zealously affected in a good thing." Let us now, every one of us, apply it to his own soul in particular.

9. Those, indeed, who are still dead in trespasses and sins have neither part nor lot in this matter; nor those that live in any open sin, such as drunkenness, Sabbath-breaking, or profane swearing. These have nothing to do with zeal; they have no business at all even to take the word in their mouth. It is utter folly and impertinence for any to talk of zeal for God, while he is doing the works of the devil. But if you have renounced the devil and all his works, and have settled it in your heart, I will "worship the Lord my God, and him only will I serve," then beware of being neither cold nor hot; then be zealous for God. You may begin at the lowest step. Be zealous for *the Church*, more especially for that particular branch thereof wherein your lot is cast. Study the welfare of this, and carefully observe all the rules of it, for conscience' sake. But, in the mean time, take heed that you do not neglect any of the *ordinances* of God; for the sake of which, in a great measure, the church itself was constituted: so that it would be highly absurd to talk of zeal for the church, if you were not more zealous for them. But are you more zealous for *works of mercy*, than even for works of piety? Do *you* follow the example of your Lord, and prefer mercy even before sacrifice? Do you use all diligence in feeding the hungry, clothing the naked, visiting them that are sick and in prison? And, above all, do you use every means in your power to save souls from death? If, as you have time, "you do good unto all men," though "especially to them that are of the household of faith," your zeal for the church is pleasing to God: but if not, if you are not "careful to maintain good works," what have you to do with the church? If you have not "compassion on your fellow-servants," neither will your Lord have pity on *you*. "Bring no more vain oblations." All your service is "an abomination to the Lord."

10. Are you better instructed than to put asunder what God has joined? than to separate works of piety from works of mercy? Are you uniformly zealous of both? So far you walk acceptably to God; that is, if you continually bear in mind, that God "searcheth the heart and reins;" that "he is a Spirit, and they that worship him must worship him in spirit and in truth;" that, consequently, no outward works are acceptable to him, unless they spring from *holy tempers*, without which no man can have a place in the kingdom of Christ and God.

11. But of all holy tempers, and above all others, see that you be most zealous for *love*. Count all things loss in comparison of this,—the love of God and all mankind. It is most sure, that if you give all your goods to feed the poor, yea, and your body to be burned, and have not humble, gentle, patient love, it profiteth you nothing. O let this be deep engraved upon your heart: "All is nothing without love!"

12. Take then the whole of religion together, just as God has revealed it in his word; and be uniformly zealous for every part of it, according to its degree of excellence. Grounding all your zeal on the one foundation, "Jesus Christ and him crucified;" holding fast this one principle, "The life I now live, I live by faith in the Son of God, who loved ME, and gave himself for ME;" proportion your zeal to the value of its object. Be calmly zealous, therefore, first, for the *Church*; "the whole state of Christ's Church militant here on earth:" and in particular for that branch thereof with which you are more immediately connected. Be more zealous for all those *ordinances* which our blessed Lord hath appointed, to continue therein to the end of the world. Be more zealous for

those *works of mercy*, those "sacrifices wherewith God is well pleased," those marks whereby the Shepherd of Israel will know his sheep at the last day. Be more zealous still for *holy tempers*, for long-suffering, gentleness, meekness, lowliness, and resignation; but be most zealous of all for *love*, the queen of all graces, the highest perfection in earth or heaven, the very image of the invisible God, as in men below, so in angels above. For "God is love; and he that dwelleth in love, dwelleth in God, and God in him."

93.* ON REDEEMING THE TIME

"Redeeming the time."

Eph. 5:16.

1. "See that ye walk circumspectly," says the Apostle in the preceding verse, "not as fools, but as wise men, redeeming the time;" saving all the time you can for the best purposes; buying up every fleeting moment out of the hands of sin and Satan, out of the hands of sloth, ease, pleasure, worldly business; the more diligently, because the present "are evil days," days of the grossest ignorance, immorality, and profaneness.

2. This seems to be the general meaning of the words. But I purpose, at present, to consider only one particular way of redeeming the time," namely, from sleep.

3. This appears to have been exceeding little considered, even by pious men. Many that have been eminently conscientious in other respects, have not been so in this. They seemed to think it an indifferent thing, whether they slept more or less; and never saw it in the true point of view, as an important branch of Christian temperance.

That we may have a more just conception hereof, I will endeavour to show,

    I.   What it is to "redeem the time" from sleep.

    II.   The evil of not redeeming it. And

    III.   The most effectual manner of doing it.

I. 1. And, First, What is it to "redeem the time" from sleep? It is, in general, to take that measure of sleep every night which nature requires, and no more; that measure which is the most conducive to the health and vigour both of the body and mind.

2. But it is objected, "One measure will not suit all men;—some require considerably more than others. Neither will the same measure suffice even the same persons at one time as at another. When a person is sick, or, if not actually so, yet weakened by preceding sickness, he certainly wants more of this natural restorative, than he did when in perfect health. And so he will when his strength and spirits are exhausted by hard or long-continued labour."

3. All this is unquestionably true, and confirmed by a thousand experiments. Whoever, therefore, they are that have attempted to fix one measure of sleep for all persons did not understand the nature of the human body, so widely different in different persons; as neither did they who imagined that the same measure would suit even the same person at all times. One would wonder, therefore, that so great a man as Bishop Taylor should have formed this strange imagination; much more, that the measure which he has assigned for the general standard should be only three hours in four-and-twenty. That good and sensible man, Mr. Baxter, was not much nearer the truth; who supposes four hours in four and twenty will suffice for any man. I knew an extremely sensible man, who was absolutely persuaded that no one living needed to sleep above five hours in twenty-four. But when he made the experiment himself, he quickly relinquished the opinion. And I am fully convinced, by an observation continued for more than fifty years, that whatever may be done by extraordinary persons, or in some extraordinary cases (wherein persons have subsisted with very little sleep for some weeks, or even months,) a human body can scarce continue in health and vigour, without at least, six hours' sleep in four-and-twenty. Sure I am, I never met with such an instance: I never found either man or woman that retained vigorous health for one year, with a less quantity of sleep than this.

4. And I have long observed, that women, in general, want a little more sleep than men; perhaps, because they are, in common of a weaker, as well as a moister, habit of body. If, therefore, one might venture to name one standard, (though liable to many exceptions and occasional alterations,) I am inclined to think this would come near to the mark: Healthy men, in general, need a little above six hours' sleep, healthy women, a little above seven, in four-and-twenty. I myself want six hours and a half, and I cannot well subsist with less.

5. If anyone desires to know exactly what quantity of sleep his own constitution requires, he may very easily make the experiment which I made about sixty years ago: I then waked every night about twelve or one, and lay awake for some time. I readily concluded that this arose from my lying longer in bed than nature required. To be satisfied, I procured an alarum, which waked me the next morning at seven; (near an hour earlier than I rose the day before,) yet I lay awake again at night. The second morning I rose at six; but, notwithstanding this, I lay awake the second night. The third morning I rose at five; but, nevertheless, I lay awake the third night. The fourth morning I rose at four; (as, by the grace of God, I have done ever since;) and I lay awake no more. And I do not now lie awake (taking the year round) a quarter of an hour together in a month. By the same experiment, rising earlier and earlier every morning, may anyone find how much sleep he really wants.

II. 1. "But why should anyone be at so much pains? What need is there of being so scrupulous? Why should we make ourselves so particular? What harm is there in doing as our neighbours do?—suppose in lying from ten till six or seven in summer, and till eight or nine in winter?"

2. If you would consider this question fairly, you will need a good deal of candour and impartiality; as what I am about to say will probably be quite new; different from anything you ever heard in your life; different from the judgment, at least from the example, of your parents and your nearest relations; nay, and perhaps of the most religious persons you ever were

---

* [text from the 1872 edition]

acquainted with. Lift up, therefore, your heart to the Spirit of truth, and beg of him to shine upon it, that without respecting any man's person, you may see and follow the truth as it in Jesus.

3. Do you really desire to know what harm there is in not redeeming all the time you can from sleep? suppose in spending therein an hour a day more than nature requires? Why, First, *it hurts your substance*; it is throwing away six hours a week which might turn to some temporal account. If you can do any work, you might earn something in that time, were it ever so small. And you have no need to throw even this away. If you do not want it yourself, give it to them that do; you know some of them that are not far off. If you are of no trade, still you may so employ the time that it will bring money, or money's worth, to yourself, or others.

4. The not redeeming all the time you can from sleep, the spending more time therein than your constitution necessarily requires, in the Second place, *hurts your health*. Nothing can be more certain than this, though it is not commonly observed, because the evil steals on you by slow and insensible degrees. In this gradual and almost imperceptible manner it lays the foundation of many diseases. It is the chief real (though unsuspected) cause of all nervous diseases in particular. Many inquiries have been made, why nervous disorders are so much more common among us than among our ancestors. Other causes may frequently concur; but the chief is, we lie longer in bed. Instead of rising at four, most of us who are not obliged to work for our bread lie till seven, eight, or nine. We need inquire no farther. This sufficiently accounts for the large increase of these painful disorders.

5. It may be observed, that most of these arise, not barely from sleeping too long, but even from what we imagine to be quite harmless, the lying too long in bed. By *soaking* (as it is emphatically called) so long between warm sheets, the flesh is, as it were, parboiled, and becomes soft and flabby." The nerves, in the mean time, are quite unstrung, and all the train of melancholy symptoms—faintness, tremors, lowness of spirits, (so called,) come on, till life itself is a burden.

6. One common effect of either sleeping too long, or lying too long in bed, is *weakness of sight*, particularly that weakness which is of the nervous kind. When I was young, my sight was remarkably weak. Why is it stronger now than it was forty years ago? I impute this principally to the blessing of God, who fits us for whatever he calls us to. But undoubtedly the outward means which he has been pleased to bless was the rising early in the morning.

7. A still greater objection to the not rising early, the not redeeming all the time we can from sleep, is, *it hurts the soul*, as well as the body; it is a sin against God. And this indeed it must necessarily be, on both the preceding accounts. For we cannot waste, or (which comes to the same thing) not improve, any part of our worldly substance, neither can we impair our own health, without sinning against Him.

8. But this fashionable intemperance does also hurt the soul in a more direct manner. It sows the seeds of foolish and hurtful desires; it dangerously inflames our natural appetites; which a person stretching and yawning in bed is just prepared to gratify. It breeds and continually increases sloth, so often objected to the English nation. It opens the way, and prepares the soul, for every other kind of intemperance. It breeds an universal softness and faintness of spirit, making us afraid of every little inconvenience, unwilling to deny ourselves any pleasure, or to take up or bear any cross. And how then shall we be able (without which we must drop into hell) to "take the kingdom of heaven by violence?" It totally unfits us for "enduring hardship as good soldiers of Jesus Christ;" and, consequently, for "fighting the good fight of faith, and laying hold on eternal life."

9. In how beautiful a manner does that great man, Mr. [William] Law treat this important subject! [Viz., Redeeming time from Sleep] Part of his words I cannot but here subjoin, for the use of every sensible reader.

"I take it for granted that every Christian who is in health is up early in the morning. For it is much more reasonable to suppose a person is up early because he is a Christian, than because he is a labourer, or a tradesman, or a servant.

"We conceive an abhorrence of a man that is in bed when he should be at his labour. We cannot think good of him, who is such a slave to drowsiness as to neglect his business for it.

"Let this, therefore, teach us to conceive how odious we must appear to God, if we are in bed, shut up in sleep, when we should be praising God; and are such slaves to drowsiness as to neglect our devotions for it.

"Sleep is such a dull, stupid state of existence, that, even among mere animals, we despise them most which are most drowsy. He, therefore, that chooses to enlarge the slothful indolence of sleep, rather than be early at his devotions, chooses the dullest refreshment of the body, before the noblest enjoyments of the soul. He chooses that state which is a reproach to mere animals, before that exercise which is the glory of angels.

10. "Besides, he that cannot deny himself this drowsy indulgence, is no more prepared for prayer when he is up, than he is prepared for fasting or any other act of self-denial. He may indeed more easily read over a form of prayer, than he can perform these duties; but he is no more disposed for the spirit of prayer, than he is disposed for fasting. For sleep thus indulged gives a softness to all our tempers, and makes us unable to relish any thing but what suits an idle state of mind, as sleep does. So that a person who is a slave to this idleness is in the same temper when he is up. Every thing that is idle or sensual pleases him. And every thing that requires trouble or self-denial, is hateful to him, for the same reason that he hates to rise.

11. "It is not possible for an epicure to be truly devout. He must renounce his sensuality, before he can relish the happiness of devotion. Now, he that turns sleep into an idle indulgence, does as much to corrupt his soul, to make it a slave to bodily appetites, as an epicure does. It does not disorder his life, as notorious acts of intemperance do; but, like any more moderate course of indulgence, it silently, and by smaller degrees, wears away the spirit of religion, and sinks the soul into dullness and sensuality.

"Self-denial of all kinds is the very life and soul of piety; but he that has not so much of it as to be able to be early at his prayers cannot think that he has taken up his cross, and is following Christ.

"What conquest has he got over himself? What right hand has he cut off? What trials is he prepared for? What sacrifice is he ready to offer to God, who cannot be so cruel to himself as to rise to prayer at such a time as the drudging part of the world are content to rise to their labour?

12. "Some people will not scruple to tell you, that they indulge themselves in sleep because they have nothing to do; and that if they had any business to rise to they would not lose so much of their time in sleep. But they must be told that they mistake the matter; that they have a great deal of business to do; they have a hardened heart to change; they have the whole spirit of religion to get. For surely he that thinks he has nothing to do, because nothing but his prayers want him, may justly be said to have the whole spirit of religion to seek.

"You must not therefore consider how small a fault it is to rise late; but how great a misery it is to want the spirit of religion, and to live in such softness and idleness as make you incapable of the fundamental duties of Christianity.

"If I was to desire you not to study the gratification of your palate, I would not insist upon the sin of wasting your money, though it is a great one; but I would desire you to renounce such a way of life, because it supports you in such a state of sensuality as renders you incapable of relishing the most essential doctrines of religion.

"For the same reason, I do not insist much upon the sin of wasting your time in sleep, though it be a great one; but I desire you to renounce this indulgence, because it gives a softness and idleness to your soul, and is so contrary to that lively, zealous, watchful, self-denying spirit, which was not only the spirit of Christ and his Apostles, and the spirit of all the saints and martyrs that have ever been among men, but must be the spirit of all those who would not sink in the common corruption of the world.

13. "Here, therefore, we must fix our charge against this practice. We must blame it, not as having this or that particular evil, but as a general habit that extends itself through our whole spirit, and supports a state of mind that is wholly wrong.

"It is contrary to piety; not as accidental slips or mistakes in life are contrary to it; but in such a manner as an ill state of body is contrary to health.

"On the other hand, if you was to rise early every morning, as an instance of self-denial, as a method of renouncing indulgence, as a means of redeeming your time and fitting your spirit for prayer, you would soon find the advantage. This method, though it seems but a small circumstance, might be a means of great piety. It would constantly keep it in your mind, that softness and idleness the bane of religion. It would teach you to exercise power over yourself, and to renounce other pleasures and tempers that war against the soul. And what is so planted and watered, will certainly have an increase from God."

III. 1. It now only remains to inquire, in the Third place, how we may redeem the time, how we may proceed in this important affair. In what manner shall we most effectually practise this important branch of temperance?

I advise all of you who are thoroughly convinced of the unspeakable importance of it, suffer not that conviction to die away, but instantly begin to act suitably to it. Only do not depend on your own strength; if you do, you will be utterly baffled. Be deeply sensible that as you are not able to do anything good of yourselves, so here, in particular, all your strength, all your resolution, will avail nothing. Whoever trusts in himself will be confounded. I never found an exception. I never knew one who trusted in his own strength that could keep this resolution for a twelve-month.

2. I advise you, Secondly, cry to the Strong for strength. Call upon Him that hath all power in heaven and earth, and believe that he will answer the prayer that goeth not out of feigned lips. As you cannot have too little confidence in yourself, so you cannot have too much in him. Then set out in faith; and surely his strength shall be made perfect in your weakness.

3. I advise you, Thirdly, add to your faith, prudence: Use the most rational means to attain your purpose. Particularly begin at the right end, otherwise you will lose your labour. If you desire to rise early, sleep early; secure this point at all events. In spite of the most dear and agreeable companions, in spite of their most earnest solicitations, in spite of entreaties, railleries, or reproaches, rigorously keep your hour. Rise up precisely at your time, and retire without ceremony. Keep your hour, notwithstanding the most pressing business: Lay all things by till the morning. Be it ever so great a cross, ever so great self-denial, keep your hour, or all is over.

4. I advise you, Fourthly, be steady. Keep your hour of rising without intermission. Do not rise two mornings, and lie in bed the third; but what you do once, do always. "But my head aches." Do not regard that. It will soon be over. "But I am uncommonly drowsy; my eyes are quite heavy." Then you must not parley; otherwise it is a lost case; but start up at once. And if your drowsiness does not go off, lie down for awhile an hour or two after. But let nothing make a breach upon this rule, rise and dress yourself at your hour.

5. Perhaps you will say, "The advice is good; but it comes too late! I have made a breach already. I did rise constantly and for a season, nothing hindered me. But I gave way by little and little, and I have now left it off for a considerable time." Then, in the name of God, begin again! Begin to-morrow; or rather to-night, by going to bed early, in spite of either company or business. Begin with more self-diffidence than before, but with more confidence in God. Only follow these few rules, and, my soul for yours, God will give you the victory. In a little time the difficulty will be over; but the benefit will last for ever.

6. If you say, "But I cannot do now as I did then; for I am not what I was: I have many disorders, my spirits are low, my hands shake; I am all relaxed,"—I answer: All these are nervous symptoms; and they all partly arise from your taking too much sleep: Nor is it probable they will ever be removed, unless you remove the cause. Therefore, on this very account, (not only to punish yourself for your folly and unfaithfulness,

but,) in order to recover your health and strength, resume your early rising. You have no other possible means of recovering, in any tolerable degree, your health both of body and mind. Do not murder yourself outright. Do not run on in the path that leads to the gates of death! As I said before, so I say again, In the name of God, this very day, set out anew. True, it will be more difficult than it was at the beginning. But bear the difficulty which you have brought upon yourself, and it will not last long. The Sun of Righteousness will soon arise again, and will heal both your soul and your body.

7. But do not imagine that this single point, rising early, will suffice to make you a Christian. No: Although that single point, the not rising, may keep you a Heathen, void of the whole Christian spirit; although this alone (especially if you had once conquered it) will keep you cold, formal, heartless, dead, and make it impossible for you to get one step forward in vital holiness, yet this alone will go but a little way to make you a real Christian. It is but one step out of many; but it is one. And having taken this, go forward. Go on to universal self-denial, to temperance in all things, to a firm resolution of taking up daily every cross whereto you are called. Go on, in a full pursuit of all the mind that was in Christ, of inward and then outward holiness; so shall you be not almost but altogether, a Christian; so shall you finish your course with joy: You shall awake up after his likeness, and be satisfied. [Jan. 20, 1782]

94.* ON FAMILY RELIGION

"As for me and my house, we will serve the Lord."
Josh. 24:15.

1. In the foregoing verses we read that Joshua, now grown old, "gathered the tribes of Israel to Shechem, and called for the elders of Israel, for their heads, for their judges and officers; and they presented themselves before the Lord." (Josh. 15:1.) And Joshua rehearsed to them the great things which God had done for their fathers; (Josh. 15:2–13;) concluding with that strong exhortation: "Now therefore fear the Lord, and serve him in sincerity and truth; and put away the gods which your fathers served on the other side the flood, (Jordan,) and in Egypt." (Josh. 15:14.) Can anything be more astonishing than this? that even in Egypt, yea, and in the wilderness, where they were daily fed, and both day and night guided by miracle, the Israelites, in general, should worship idols, in flat defiance of the Lord their God! He proceeds: "If it seemeth evil to you to serve the Lord, choose ye this day whom ye will serve; whether the gods your fathers served on the other side of the flood, or the gods of the Amorites in whose land ye dwell: But as for me and my house, we will serve the Lord."

2. A resolution this worthy of a hoary-headed saint, who had had large experience, from his youth up, of the goodness of the Master to whom he had devoted himself, and the advantages of his service. How much is it to be wished that all who have tasted that the Lord is gracious, all whom he has brought out of the land of Egypt, out of the bondage of sin,—those especially who are united together in Christian fellowship,—would adopt this wise resolution! Then would the work of the Lord prosper in our land; then would his word run and be glorified. Then would multitudes of sinners in every place stretch out their hands unto God, until "the glory of the Lord covered the land, as the waters cover the sea."

3. On the contrary, what will the consequence be, if they do not adopt this resolution?—if family religion be neglected?—if care be not taken of the rising generation? Will not the present revival of religion in a short time die away? Will it not be as the historian speaks of the Roman state in its infancy,—*res unius aetatis?*—"an event that has its beginning and end within the space of one generation?" Will it not be a confirmation of that melancholy remark of Luther's, that "a revival of religion never lasts longer than one generation?" By a generation, (as he explains himself,) he means thirty years. But, blessed be God, this remark does not hold with regard to the present instance; seeing this revival, from its rise in the year 1729, has already lasted above fifty years.

4. Have we not already seen some of the unhappy consequences of good men's not adopting this resolution? Is there not a generation arisen, even within this period, yea, and from pious parents, that know not the Lord? that have neither his love in their hearts, nor his fear before their eyes? How many of them already "despise their fathers, and mock at the counsel of their mothers!" How many are utter strangers to real religion, to the life and power of it! And not a few have shaken off all religion, and abandoned themselves to all manner of wickedness! Now, although this may sometimes be the case, even of children educated in a pious manner, yet this case is very rare: I have met with some, but not many, instances of it. The wickedness of the children is generally owing to the fault or neglect of their parents. For it is a general, though not universal rule, though is admits of some exceptions, "Train up a child in the way he should go, and when he is old he will not depart from it."

5. But what is the purport of this resolution, "I and my house will serve the Lord?" In order to understand and practice this, let us, First, inquire, what it is to "serve the Lord." Secondly, Who are included in that expression, "my house." And, Thirdly, What can we do, that we and our house my serve the Lord.

I. 1. We may inquire, First, what it is to "serve the Lord," not as a Jew, but as a Christian; not only with an outward service, (though some of the Jews undoubtedly went farther than this,) but with inward, with the service of the heart, "worshipping him in spirit in truth." The First thing implied in this service is faith; believing in the name of the Son of God. We cannot perform an acceptable service to God, till we believe on Jesus Christ whom he hath sent. Here the spiritual worship of God begins. As soon as any on had the witness in himself; as soon as he can say, "The life that I now live, I live by faith in the Son of God, who loved me, and gave himself for me;" he is able truly to "serve the Lord."

* [text from the 1872 edition]

2. As soon as he believes, he loves God, which is another thing implied in "serving the Lord." "We love him because he first loved us;" of which faith is the evidence. The love of a pardoning God is "shed abroad in our hearts, by the Holy Ghost which is given unto us." Indeed this love may admit of a thousand degrees: But still every one, as long as he believes, may truly declare before God, "Lord, thou knowest that I love thee." Thou knowest that 'my desire is unto thee, and unto the remembrance of thy name.'"

3. And if any man truly love God, he cannot but love his brother also. Gratitude to our Creator will surely produce benevolence to our fellow-creatures. If we love Him, we cannot but love one another, as Christ loved us. We feel our souls enlarged in love toward every child of man. And toward all the children of God we put on "bowels of kindness, gentleness, longsuffering, forgiving one another," if we have a complaint against any, "even as God, for Christ's sake, hath forgiven us."

4. One thing more is implied in "serving the Lord," namely, the obeying him; the steadily walking in all his ways, the doing his will from the heart. Like those, "his servants" above, "who do his pleasure, who keep his commandments, carefully avoid whatever he has forbidden, and zealously do whatever he has enjoined; studying always to have conscience void of offense toward God and toward man.

II. "I and my house will serve the Lord," will every real Christian say. But who are included in that expression, "my house?" This is the next point to be considered.

1. The person in your house that claims your first and nearest attention, is, undoubtedly, your wife; seeing you are to love her, even as Christ hath loved the Church, when he laid down his life for it, that he might "purify it unto himself, not having spot, or wrinkle, or any such thing." The same end is every husband to pursue, in all his intercourse with his wife; to use every possible means that she may be freed from every spot, and may walk unblamable in love.

2. Next to your wife are your children; immortal spirits whom God hath, for a time, entrusted to your care, that you may train them up in all holiness, and fit them for the enjoyment of God in eternity. This is a glorious and important trust; seeing on soul is of more value than all the world beside. Every child, therefore, you are to watch over with the utmost care, that, when you are called to give an account of each to the Father of Spirits, you may give your accounts with joy and not with grief.

3. Your servants, of whatever kind, you are to look upon as a kind of secondary children: These, likewise, God has committed to your charge, as one that must give account. For every one under your roof that has a soul to be saved is under every one under your roof that has a soul to be saved is under your care; not only indented servants, who are legally engaged to remain with you for a term of years; not only hired servants, whether they voluntarily contract for a longer of shorter time; but also those who serve you by the week of day: For these too are, in a measure, delivered into you hands. And it is not the will of *your* Master who is in heaven, that any of these should go out of your hands before they have received from you something more valuable than gold or silver. Yea, and you are in a degree accountable even for "the stranger that is within your gates." As you are particularly required to see that he does "no manner of work" on the Lord's day, while he is within your gates; so, by parity of reason, you are required to do all that is in your power to prevent his sinning against God in any other instance.

III. Let us inquire, in the Third place, What can we do that all these may "serve the Lord?"

1. May we not endeavour, First, to *restrain* them from all outward sin; from profane swearing; from taking the name of God in vain; from doing any needless work, or taking any pastime, on the Lord's day? This labour of love you owe even to your visitants; much more to your wife, children, and servants. The former, over whom you have the least influence, you may restrain by argument or mild persuasion. If you find that, after repeated trials, they will not yield either to one or the other, it is your bounden duty to set ceremony aside, and to dismiss them from your house. Servants also, whether by the day, or for a longer space, if you cannot reclaim, either by reasoning added to your example, or by gentle or severe reproofs, though frequently repeated, you must, in anywise, dismiss from your family, though it should be ever so inconvenient.

2. But you cannot dismiss you wife, unless for the cause of fornication, that is adultery. What can then be done, if she is habituated to any other open sin? I cannot find in the Bible that a husband has authority to strike his wife on any account, even suppose she struck him first, unless his life were in imminent danger. I never have known one instance yet of a wife that was mended thereby. I have heard, indeed, of some such instances; but as I did not see them, I do not believe them. It seems to me, all that can be done in this case is to be done partly by example, partly by argument of persuasion, each applied in such a manner as is dictated by Christian prudence. If evil can ever be overcome, it must be overcome by good. It cannot by overcome by evil: We cannot beat the devil with his own weapons. Therefore, if this evil cannot be overcome by good, we are called to suffer it. We are then called to say, "This is the cross which God hath chosen for me. He surely permits it for wise ends; 'let him do what seemeth him good.' Whenever he sees it to be best, he will remove this cup from me." Meanwhile continue in earnest prayer, knowing that with God no word is impossible; and that he will either in due time take the temptation away, or make it a blessing to your soul.

3. Your children, while they are young, you may restrain from evil, not only by advice, persuasion, and reproof, but also by *correction*; only remembering, that this means is to be used last,—not till all other have been tried, and found to be ineffectual. And even then you should take the utmost care to avoid the very appearance of passion. Whatever is done should be done with mildness; nay, indeed, with kindness too. Otherwise your own spirit will suffer loss, and the child will reap little advantage.

4. But some will tell you, "All this is lost labour: A child need not be corrected at all. Instruction, persuasion, and advice, will be sufficient for any child without correction; especially if gentle reproof be added, as occasion may require." I answer,

There may be particular instances, wherein this method may be successful. But you must not, in anywise, lay this down as an universal rule; unless you suppose yourself wiser than Solomon, or, to speak more properly wiser than God. For it is God himself, who best knoweth his own creatures, that has told us expressly, "He that spareth the rod, hateth his son: But he that loveth him chasteneth him betimes." (Prov. 13:24.) And upon this is grounded that plain commandment, directed to all that fear God, "Chasten thy son while there is hope, and let not thy soul spare for his crying." (Prov. 19:18.)

5. May we not endeavour, Secondly, to *instruct* them? to take care that every person who is under our roof have all such knowledge as is necessary to salvation? to see that our wife, servants, and children be taught all those things which belong to their eternal peace? In order to this you should provide that no only your wife, but your servants also, may enjoy all the public means of instruction. On the Lord's day in particular, you should so forecast what is necessary to be done at home, that they may have an opportunity of attending all the ordinances of God. Yea, and you should take care that they have some time every day for reading, meditation, and prayer; and you should inquire whether they do actually employ that time in the exercises for which it is allowed. Neither should any day pass without family prayer, seriously and solemnly performed.

6. You should particularly endeavour to instruct your children, early, plainly, frequently, and patiently. Instruct them *early*, from the first hour that you perceive reason begins to dawn. Truth may then begin to shine upon the mind far earlier than we are apt to suppose. And whoever watches the first openings of the understanding, may, by little and little, supply fit matter for it to work upon, and may turn the eye of the son, toward good things, as well as toward bad or trifling ones. Whenever a child begins to speak, you may be assured reason begins to work. I know no cause why a parent should not just then begin to speak of the best things, the things of God. And from that time no opportunity should be lost, of instilling all truths as they are capable of receiving.

7. But the speaking to them early will not avail, unless you likewise speak to the *plainly*. Use such words as little children may understand, just such as they use themselves. Carefully observe the few ideas which they have already, and endeavour to graft what you say upon them. To take a little example: Bid the child look up; and ask. "What do you see there?" "The sun." "See, how bright it is! Feel how warm it shines upon you hand! Look, how it makes the grass green! But God, though you cannot see him, is above the sky, and is a deal brighter than the sun! It is he, it is God that makes the grass and the flowers grow; that makes the trees green, and the fruit to come upon them! Think what he can do! He can do whatever he pleases. He can strike me or you dead in a moment! But he loves you; he loves to do you good. He loves to make you happy. Should not you then love *him*? And he will teach you how to love him."

8. While you are speaking in this, or some such manner, you should be continually lifting up your heart to God, beseeching him to open the eyes of their understanding, and to pour his light upon them. He, and he alone, can make them to differ herein from the beasts that perish. He alone can apply your words to their hearts; without which all your labour will be in vain. But whenever the Holy Ghost teaches, there is no delay in learning.

9. But if you would see the fruit of your labour, you must teach them not only early and plainly, but *frequently* too. It would be of little or no service to so it only once or twice a week. How often do you feed their bodies? Not less than three times a day. And is the soul of less value than the body? Will you not then feed this as often? If you find this a tiresome task, there is certainly something wrong in your own mind. You do not love them enough; or you do not love Him who is your Father and their Father. Humble yourself before him! Beg that he would give you more love; and love will make the labour light.

10. But it will not avail to teach them both early, plainly, and frequently, unless you *persevere* therein. Never leave off, never intermit your labour of love, till you see the fruit of it. But in order to this, you will find the absolute need of being endued with power from on high; without which, I am persuaded, none ever had, or will have, patience sufficient for the work. Otherwise, the inconceivable dullness of some children, and the giddiness or perverseness of others, would induce them to give up the irksome task, and let them follow their own imagination.

11. And suppose, after you have done this, after you have taught you children from their early infancy, in the plainest manner you could, omitting no opportunity, and persevering therein, you did not presently see any fruit of your labour, you must not conclude that there will be none. Possibly the "bread" which you have "cast upon the waters" may be "found after many days." The seed which has long remained in the ground may, at length, spring up into a plentiful harvest. Especially if you do not restrain prayer before God, if you continue instant herein with all supplication. Meantime, whatever the effect of this be upon others, your reward is with the Most High.

12. Many parents, on the other hand, presently see the fruit of the seed they have sown, and have the comfort of observing that their children grow in grace in the same proportion as they grow in years. Yet they have not done all. They have still upon their hands another task, sometimes of no small difficulty. Their children are now old enough to go to school. But to what school is it advisable to send them?

13. Let it be remembered, that I do not speak to the wild, giddy, thoughtless world, but to those that fear God. I ask, then, for what end do you send you children to school? "Why, that they may be fit to live in the world." In which world do you mean,—this or the next? Perhaps you thought of this world only; and had forgot that there is a world to come; yea, and one that will last for ever! Pray take this into your account, and send them to such masters as will keep it always before their eyes. Otherwise, to send them to school (permit me to speak plainly) is little better than sending them to the devil. At all events, then, send your boys, if you have any concern for their souls, not to any of the large public

schools, (for they are nurseries of all manner of wickedness,) but private school, kept by some pious man, who endeavours to instruct a small number of children in religion and learning together.

14. "But what shall I so with my girls?" By no means send them to a large boarding-school. In these seminaries too the children teach one another pride, vanity, affectation, intrigue, artifice, and, in short, everything which a Christian woman ought not to learn. Suppose a girl were well inclined, yet what would she do in a crowd of children, not one of whom has any thought of saving her soul in such company? especially as their whole conversation points another way, and turns upon things which one would wish she would never think of. I never yet knew a pious, sensible woman that had been bred at a large boarding-school, who did not aver, one might as well send a young maid to be bred in Drury-Lane.

15. "But where, then, shall I send my girls?" If you cannot breed them up yourself, (as my mother did, who bred up seven daughters to years of maturity,) send them to some mistress that truly fears God; one whose life is a pattern to her scholars, and who has only so many that she can watch over each as one that must give account to God. Forty years ago I did not know such a mistress in England; but you may now find several; you may find such a mistress, and such a school, at Highgate, at Deptford, near Bristol, in Chester, or near Leeds.

16. We may suppose your sons have now been long enough at school, and you are thinking of some business for them. Before you determine anything on this head, see that your eye be single. Is it so? Is it you view to please God herein? It is well if you take him into your account! But surely, if you live or fear God yourself, this will be your first consideration,—"In what business will your son be most likely to love and serve God? In what employment will he have the greatest advantage for laying up treasure in heaven?" I have been shocked above measure in observing how little this is attended to, even by pious parents! Even these consider only how he may get most money; not how he may get most holiness! Even these, upon this glorious motive, send him to a heathen master, and into family where there is not the very form, much less the power of religion! Upon this motive they fix him in a business which will necessarily expose him to such temptations as will leave him not a probability, if a possibility, of serving God. O savage parents! unnatural, diabolical cruelty.—if you believe there is another world. "But what shall I do?" Set God before your eyes, and do all things with a view to please him. Then you will find a master, of whatever profession, that loves, or at least fears, God; and you will find a family wherein is the form of religion, if not the power also. Your son may nevertheless serve the devil if he will; but it is probable he will not. And do not regard, if he get less money, provided he get more holiness. It is enough, though he have less of earthly goods, if he secure the possession of heaven.

17. There is one circumstance more wherein you will have great need of the wisdom from above. Your son or you daughter is now of age to marry, and desires your advice relative to it. Now you know what the world calls a *good match*,—one whereby much money is gained. Undoubtedly it is so, if it be true that money always brings happiness: But I doubt it is not true; money seldom brings happiness, either in this world or the world to come. Then let no man deceive you with vain words; riches and happiness seldom dwell together. Therefore, if you are wise, you will not seek riches for your children by their marriage. See that your eye be single in this also: Aim simply at the glory of God, and the real happiness of your children, both in time and eternity. It is a melancholy thing to see how Christian parents rejoice in selling their son or their daughter to a wealthy Heathen! And do you seriously call this *a good match?* Thou fool, by parity of reason, thou mayest call hell *a good lodging*, and the devil *a good master*. O learn a better lesson from a better Master! "Seek ye first the kingdom of God and his righteousness," both for thyself and thy children; "and all other things shall be added unto you."

18. It is undoubtedly true, that if you are steadily determined to walk in this path; to endeavour by every possible means, that you and your house may thus serve the Lord; that every member of you family may worship him, not only in form, but in spirit and in truth; you will have need to use all the grace, all the courage, all the wisdom which God has given you; for you will find such hinderances in the way, as only the mighty power of God can enable you to break through. You will have all the *saints of the world* to grapple with, who will think you carry things too far. You will have all the powers of darkness against you, employing both force and fraud; and, above all, the deceitfulness of your own heart; which, if you will hearken to it, will supply you with many reasons why you should be a *little more* conformable to the world. But as you have begun, go on in the name of the Lord, and in the power of his might! Set the smiling and the frowning world, with the prince thereof, at defiance. Follow reason and the oracles of God; not the fashions and customs of men. "Keep thyself pure." Whatever others do, let you and your house "adorn the doctrine of God our Saviour." Let you, your yoke-fellow, your children, and your servants, be all on the Lord's side; sweetly drawing together in one yoke, walking in all his commandments and ordinances, till every one of you "shall receive his own reward, according to his own labour!"

95.* ON THE EDUCATION OF CHILDREN

"Train up a child in the way wherein he should go: And when he is old, he will not depart from it."

Prov. 22:6.

1. We must not imagine that these words are to be understood in an absolute sense, as if no child that had been trained up in the way wherein he should go had ever departed form it. Matter of fact will by not means agree with this: So

---

far form it, that it has been a common observation, "Some of the best parents have the worst children." It is true, this might sometimes be the case, because good men have not always a good understanding; and, without this, it is hardly to be expected that they will know how to train up their children. Besides, those who are in other respects good men have often too much easiness of temper; so that they go no farther in restraining their children form evil, than an old Eli did, when he said gently, "Nay, my sons, the report I hear of you is not good." This, then, is no contradiction to the assertion; for their children are not "trained up in the way wherein they should go." But it must be acknowledged, some have been trained therein with all possible care and diligence; and yet before they were old, yea, in the strength of their years, they did utterly depart form it.

2. The words, then, must be understood with some limitation, and then they contain an unquestionable truth. It is a general, though not an universal, promise; and many have found the happy accomplishment of it. As this is the most probable method for making their children pious which any parents can take, so it generally, although not always, meets with the desired success. The God of their fathers is with their children; he blesses their endeavours; and they have the satisfaction of leaving their religion, as well as their worldly substance, to those that descend from them.

3. But what is "the way wherein a child should go?" and how shall we "train him up" therein? The ground of this is admirably well laid by Mr. Law, in his "Serious Call to a Devout Life." Part of his words are,—

"Had we continued perfect as God created the first man, perhaps the perfection of our nature had been a sufficient self-instructer for every one. But as sickness and diseases have created the necessity of medicines and physicians, so the disorders of our rational nature have introduced the necessity of education and tutors.

"And as the only end of a physician is, to restore nature to its own state, so the only end of education is, to restore our rational nature to its proper state. Education, therefore, is to be considered as reason borrowed as second-hand, which is, as far as it can, to supply the loss of original perfection. And as physic may justly be called the art of restoring health, so education should be considered in no other light, than as the art of recovering to man his rational perfection.

"This was the end pursued by the youths that attended upon Pythagoras, Socrates, and Plato. their every-day lessons and instructions were so many lectures upon the nature of man, his true end, and the right use of his faculties; upon the immortality of the soul, its relation to God; the agreeableness of virtue to the divine nature; upon the necessity of temperance, justice, mercy, and truth; and the folly of indulging our passions.

"Now, as Christianity has, as it were, new created the moral and religious world, and set everything that is reasonable, wise, holy, and desirable in its true point of light; so one would expect the education of children should be as much mended by Christianity, as the doctrines of religion are.

"As it has introduced a new state of things, and so fully informed us of the nature of man, and the end of his creation; as it has fixed all our goods and evils, taught us the means of purifying our souls, of pleasing God, and being happy eternally; one might naturally suppose that every Christian country abounded with schools, not only for teaching a few questions and answers of a catechism, but for the forming, training, and practicing children in such a course of life as the sublimest doctrines of Christianity require.

"And education under Pythagoras or Socrates had no other end, but to teach children to think and act as Pythagoras and Socrates did.

"And is it not reasonable to suppose that a Christian education should have no other end but to teach them how to think, and judge, and act according to the strictest rules of Christianity?

"At least one would suppose, that in all Christian schools, the teaching them to begin their lives in the spirit of Christianity,—in such abstinence, humility, sobriety, and devotion as Christianity requires,—should not only be more, but a hundred time more, regarded that nay or all things else.

"For those that educate us should imitate our guardian angels; suggest nothing to our minds but what is wise and holy; help us to discover every false judgement of our minds, and to subdue every wrong passion in our hearts.

"And it is as reasonable to expect and require all this benefit from a Christian education, as to require that physic should strengthen all that is right in our nature, and remove all our diseases."

4. Let it be carefully remembered all this time, that God, not man, is the physician of souls; that it is He, and none else, who giveth medicine to heal our natural sickness; that all "the help which is done upon earth, he doeth it himself;" that none of all the children of men is able to "bring a clean thing our of an unclean;" and, in a word, that "it is God who worketh in us, both to will and to do of his good pleasure." But is generally his pleasure to work by his creatures; to help man by man. He honours men to be, in a sense, "workers together with him." By this means the reward is ours, while the glory redounds to him.

5. This being premised, in order to see distinctly what is that way wherein we should train up a child, let us consider, What are the diseases of his nature? What those spiritual diseases which every one that is born of a woman brings with him into the world?

Is not the first of the *Atheism?* After all that has been so plausibly written concerning "the innate idea of God;" after all that have been said of its being common to all men, in all ages and nations; it does not appear, that man has naturally any more idea of God that any of the beasts of the field; he has no knowledge of God at all; no fear of God at all; neither is God in all his thoughts. Whatever change may afterwards be wrought, (whether by the grace of God or by his own reflection, or by education.) he is, by nature, a mere Atheist.

6. Indeed it may be said that every man is by nature, as it were, his own god. He worships himself. He is, in his own conception, absolute Lord of himself. Dryden's hero speaks only according to nature, when he says, "Myself am king of *me.*" He seeks himself in all things. He pleases himself. And why not? Who is Lord over him? *His own will* is his only law;

he does this or that because it is his good pleasure. In the same spirit as the "son of the morning" said of old time, "I will sit upon the sides of the North," he says, "*I will* do thus or thus." And do we not find sensible men on every side who are of the self-same spirit? Who if asked, "Why did you do this?" will readily answer, "Because I had a mind to it."

7. Another evil disease which every human soul brings into the world with him, is *pride*; a continual proneness to think of himself more highly than he ought to think. Every man can discern more or less of this disease in everyone—but himself. And, indeed, if he could discern it in himself, it would subsist no longer; for he would then, in consequence, think of himself just as he ought to think.

8. The next disease natural to every human soul, born with every man, is *love of the world*. Every man is, by nature, a lover of the creature, instead of the Creator; a "lover of pleasure," in every kind, "more than a lover of God." He is a slave to foolish and hurtful desires, in one kind or another; either to the "desire of the flesh, the desire of the eyes or the pride of life." "The desire of the flesh" is a propensity to seek happiness in what gratifies one or more of the outward senses. "The desire of the eyes" is a propensity to seek happiness in what gratifies internal sense, the imagination, either by things grand, or new, or beautiful. "The pride of life" seems to mean a propensity to seek happiness in what gratifies the sense of honour. To this head is usually referred "the love of money;" one of the basest passions that can have place in the human heart. But it may be doubted whether this be not an acquired rather than a natural, distemper.

9. Whether this be a natural disease or not, it is certain *anger* is. The ancient philosopher defines it, "a sense of injury received, with a desire of revenge." Now, was there ever anyone born of a woman who did not labour under this? Indeed, like other diseases of the mind, it is far more violent in some than in others. But it is *furor brevis*, as the poet speaks; it is a real, though short, madness wherever it is.

10. A *deviation from truth* is equally natural to all the children of men. One said in his haste, "All men are liars;" but we may say, upon cool reflection, All natural men will, upon a close temptation, vary from, or disguise, the truth. If they do not offend against veracity, if they do not say what is false, yet they frequently offend against *simplicity*. They use art; they hang out false colours; they practise either simulation, or dissimulation. So that you cannot say truly of any person living, till grace has altered nature, "Behold an Israelite indeed, in whom is no guile!"

11. Everyone is likewise prone, by nature, to speak or act *contrary to justice*. This is another of the diseases which we bring with us into the world. All human creatures are naturally partial to themselves, and, when opportunity, offers have more regard to their own interest or pleasure than strict justice allows. Neither is any man, by nature, *merciful* as our heavenly Father is merciful; but all, more or less, transgress that glorious rule of mercy as well as justice, "Whatsoever ye would that men should do unto you, the same do unto them."

12. Now, if these are the general diseases of human nature, is it not the grand end of education to cure them? And is it not the part of all those to whom God has entrusted the education of children, to take all possible care, first, not to increase, not to feed, any of these diseases; (as the generality of parents constantly do;) and next, to use every possible means of healing them?

13. To come to particulars. What can parents do, and mothers more especially, to whose care our children are necessarily committed in their tender years, with regard to the *Atheism* that is natural to all the children of men? How is this fed by the generality of parents, even those that love, or at least fear, God; while, in spending hours, perhaps days, with their children, they hardly name the name of God! Meantime, they talk of a thousand other things in the world that is round about them. Will not then the things of the present world, which surround these children on every side, naturally take up their thoughts, and set God at a greater distance from them (if that be possible) than he was before? Do not parents feed the atheism of their children farther, by ascribing the works of creation to *nature?* Does not the common way of talking about nature leave God quite out of the question? Do they not feed this disease, whenever they talk in the hearing of their children, of anything *happening* so or so? Of things coming by *chance?* Of good or ill *fortune?* As also when they ascribe this or that event to the wisdom or power of men; or, indeed, to any other second causes, as if these governed the world? Yea, do they not feed it unawares, while they are talking of their own wisdom, or goodness, or power to do this or that, without expressly mentioning, that all these are the gift of God? All this tends to confirm the Atheism of their children, and to keep God out of their thoughts.

14. But we are by no means clear of their blood, if we only go thus far, if we barely do not feed their disease. What can be done to cure it? From the first dawn of reason continually inculcate, God is in this and every place. God made you, and me, and the earth, and the sun, and the moon, and everything. And everything is his; heaven, and earth, and all that is therein. God orders all things: he makes the sun shine, and the wind blow, and the trees bear fruit. Nothing comes by chance; that is a silly word; there is no such thing as chance. As God made the world, so he governs the world, and everything that is in it. Not so much as a sparrow falls to the ground without the will of God. And as he governs all things, so he governs all men, good and bad, little and great. He is gives them all the power and wisdom they have. And he over-rules all. He gives us all the goodness we have; every good thought, and word, and work, are from him. Without him we can neither think anything right, or do anything right. Thus it is, we are to inculcate upon them, that God is all in all.

15. Thus may we counteract, and, by the grace of God assisting us, gradually cure, the natural Atheism of our children. But what can we do to cure their *self-will?* It is equally rooted in their nature, and is, indeed, the original idolatry, which is not confined to one age or country, but is common to all the nations under heaven. And how few parents are to be found even among Christians, even among them that truly fear God, who are not guilty in this matter!

Who do not continually feed and increase this grievous distemper in their children! To let them have their own will, does this most effectually. To let them take their own way, is the sure method of increasing their self-will sevenfold. But who has the resolution to do otherwise? One parent in a hundred! Who can be so singular, so cruel, as not, more or less, to *humour* her child? "And why should you not? What harm can there be in this, which everybody does?" The harm is, that it strengthens their will more and more, till it will neither bow to God nor man. To humour children is, as far as in us lies, to make their disease incurable. A wise parent, on the other hand, should begin to break their will the first moment it appears. In the whole art of Christian education there is nothing more important than this. The will of the parent is to a little child in the place of the will of God. Therefore studiously teach them to submit to this while they are children, that they may be ready to submit to his will when they are men. But in order to carry this point, you will need incredible firmness and resolution; for after you have once begun, you must never more give way. You must hold on still in an even course; you must never intermit your attention for one hour; otherwise you lose your labour.

16. If you are not willing to lose all the labour you have been at, to break the will of your child, to bring his will into subjection to yours, that it may be afterward subject to the will of God, there is one advice which, though little known, should be particularly attended to. It may seem a small circumstance; but it is of more consequence than one can easily imagine. It is this: Never, on any account, give a child anything that it cries for. For it is a true observation, (and you may make the experiment as often as you please,) if you give a child what he cries for you pay him for crying; and then he will certainly cry again. "But if I do not give it to him when he cries, he will scream all day long." If he does it is your own fault; for it is in your power effectually to prevent it: For no mother need suffer a child to cry aloud after it is a year old. "Why, it is impossible to hinder it." So many suppose, but it is an entire mistake. I am a witness of the direct contrary; and so are many others. My own mother had ten children, each of whom had spirit enough; yet not one of them was ever heard to cry aloud after it was a year old. A gentlewoman of Sheffield (several of whose children I suppose are alive still) assured me she had the same success with regard to her eight children. When some were objecting to the possibility of this, Mr. Parson Greenwood (well-known in the north of England) replied, "This cannot be impossible: I have had the proof of it in my own family. Nay, of more than this. I had six children by my former wife; and she suffered none of them to cry aloud after they were ten months old. And yet none of their spirits were so broken, as to unfit them for any of the offices of life." This, therefore, may be done by any woman of sense, who may thereby save herself abundance of trouble, and prevent that disagreeable noise, the squalling of young children, from being heard under her roof. But I allow, none but a woman of sense will be able to effect this; yea, and a woman of such patience and resolution as only the grace of God can give. However, this is doubtless the more excellent way: and she that is able to receive it, let her receive it!

17. It is hard to say whether self-will or *pride* be the more fatal distemper. It was chiefly pride that threw down so many of the stars of heaven, and turned angels into devils. But what can parents do in order to check this until it can be radically cured?

First. Beware of adding fuel to the flame, of feeding the disease which you should cure. Almost all parents are guilty of doing this by praising their children to their face. If you are sensible of the folly and cruelty of this, see that you sacredly abstain from it. And, in spite of either fear or complaisance, go one step farther. Not only do not encourage, but do not suffer, others to do what you dare not do yourself. How few parents are sufficiently aware of this,—or, at least, sufficiently resolute to practise it,—to check everyone at the first word, that would praise them before their face! Even those who would not on any account, *sit attentive to their own applause*, nevertheless, do not scruple to sit attentive to the applause of their children; yea, and that to their face! O consider! Is not this the spreading a net for their feet? Is it not a grievous incentive to pride, even if they are praised for what is truly praise-worthy? Is it not doubly hurtful, if they are praised for things not truly praise-worthy;—things of an indifferent nature, as sense, good-breeding, beauty, elegance of apparel? This is liable not only to hurt their heart, but their understanding also. It has a manifest and direct tendency to infuse pride and folly together; to pervert both their taste and judgment; teaching them to value what is dung and dross in the sight of God.

18. If, on the contrary, you desire without loss of time to strike at the root of their pride, teach your children as soon as possibly you can that they are fallen spirits; that they are fallen short of that glorious image of God wherein they were at first created; that they are not now, as they were once, incorruptible pictures of the God of glory; bearing the express likeness of the wise, the good, the holy Father of spirits; but more ignorant, more foolish, and more wicked, than they can possibly conceive. Show them that in pride, passion, and revenge, they are now like the devil. And that in foolish desires and grovelling appetites they are like the beasts of the field. Watch over them diligently in this respect, that whenever occasion offers you may "pride in its earliest motions find," and check the very first appearance of it.

If you ask, "But how shall I encourage them when they do well, if I am never to commend them?" I answer, I did not affirm this. I did not say, "You are never to commend them." I know many writers assert this, and writers of eminent piety. They say, to commend man is to rob God, and therefore condemn it altogether. But what say the scriptures? I read there that our Lord himself frequently commended his own disciples; and the great Apostle scruples not to commend the Corinthians, Philippians, and divers others to whom he writes. We may not therefore condemn this altogether. But I say, use it exceeding sparingly. And when you use it let it be with the utmost caution, directing them at the same moment to look upon all they have as the free gift of God, and with the deepest self-abasement to say, "Not unto us! Not unto us! But unto thy name give the praise!"

19. Next to self-will and pride, the most fatal disease with which we are born, is "love of the world." But how studiously do the generality of parents cherish this in its several branches! They cherish "the desire of the flesh," that is, the tendency to seek happiness in pleasing the outward senses, by studying to enlarge the pleasure of tasting in their children to the uttermost; not only giving them before they are weaned other things beside milk, the natural food of children; but giving them, both before and after, any sort of meat or drink that they will take. Yea, they entice them, long before nature requires it, to take wine or strong drink; and provide them with comfits, gingerbread, raisins, and whatever fruit they have a mind to. They feed in them "the desire of the eyes," the propensity to seek happiness in pleasing the imagination, by giving them pretty playthings, glittering toys, shining buckles or buttons, fine clothes, red shoes, laced hats, needless ornaments, as ribbons, necklaces, ruffles; yea, and by proposing any of these as rewards for doing their duty, which is stamping a great value upon them. With equal care and attention they cherish in them the Third branch of the love of the world, "the pride of life;" the propensity to seek their happiness in "the honour that cometh of men." Nor is the love of money forgotten; many an exhortation do they hear on *securing the main chance*; many a lecture, exactly agreeing with that of the old Heathen, _____ "Get money, honestly if you can; but if not, get money." And they are carefully taught to look on riches and honour as the reward of all their labours.

20. In direct opposition to all this, a wise and truly kind parent will take the utmost care, not to cherish in her children the desire of the flesh; their natural propensity to seek happiness in gratifying the outward senses. With this view she will suffer them to taste no food but milk, till they are weaned; which a thousand experiments show is most safely and easily done at the end of the seventh month. And then accustom them to the most simple food, chiefly of vegetables. She may inure them to taste only one kind of food, beside bread, at dinner, and constantly to breakfast and sup on milk, either cold or heated, but not boiled. She may use them to sit by her at meals; and ask for nothing, but take what is given them. She need never, till they are at least nine or ten years old, let them know the taste of tea; or use any other drink at meals but water or small beer. And they will never desire to taste either meat or drink between meals, if not accustomed thereto. If fruit, comfits, or anything of the kind be given them, let them not touch it but at meals. And never propose any of these as a reward; but teach them to look higher than this.

But herein a difficulty will arise; which it will need much resolution to conquer. Your servants, who will not understand your plan, will be continually giving little things to your children, and thereby undoing all your work. This you must prevent, if possible, by warning them when they first come into your house, and repeating the warning from time to time. If they *will* do it notwithstanding, you must turn them away. Better lose a good servant than spoil a good child.

Possibly you may have another difficulty to encounter, and one of a still more trying nature. Your mother or your husband's mother, may live with you; and you will do well to show her all possible respect. But let her on no account have the least share in the management of your children. She would undo all that you had done; she would give them their own will in all things. She would humour them to the destruction of their souls, if not of their bodies too. In fourscore years I have not met with one woman that knew how to manage grandchildren. My own mother, who governed her children so well, could never govern one grandchild. In every other point obey your mother. Give up your will to hers. But with regard to the management of your children, steadily keep the reins in your own hands.

21. A wise and kind parent will be equally cautious of feeding "the desire of the eyes" in her children. She will give them no pretty playthings, no glittering toys, shining buckles or buttons, fine or gay clothes; no needless ornaments of any kind; nothing that can attract the eye. Nor will she suffer any other person to give them what she will not give them herself. Anything of the kind that is offered may be either civilly refused, or received and laid by. If they are displeased at this, you cannot help it. Complaisance, yea, and temporal interest, must needs be set aside when the eternal interest of your children is at stake.

Your pains will be well requited, if you can inspire them early with a contempt of all finery; and, on the other hand, with a love and esteem for neat plainness of dress: Teaching them to associate the ideas of plainness and modesty; and those of a fine and a loose woman. Likewise, instil into them, as early as possible, a fear and contempt of pomp and grandeur; an abhorrence and dread of the lo love of money; and a deep conviction; that riches cannot give happiness. Wean them therefore from all these false ends; habituate them to make God their end in all things; and inure them, in all they do, to aim at knowing, loving, and serving God.

22. Again: The generality of parents feed *anger* in their children; yea, the worst part of it; that is, revenge. The silly mother says, "What hurt my child? Give me a blow for it." What horrid work is this! Will not the old murderer teach them this lesson fast enough? Let the Christian parent spare no pains to teach them just the contrary. Remind them of the words of our blessed Lord: "It was said of old, An eye for an eye, and a tooth for a tooth. But I say unto you, That ye resist not evil;" not by returning evil for evil. Rather than this, "if a man take away thy cloak, let him take thy coat also." Remind him of the words of the great Apostle: "Dearly beloved, avenge not yourselves. For it is written, Vengeance is mine: I will repay, saith the Lord."

23. The generality of parents feed and increase the natural *falsehood* of their children. How often may we hear that senseless word, "No, it was not *you*; it was not my child that did it; say, it was the cat." What amazing folly is this! Do you feel no remorse, while you are putting a lie in the mouth of your child, before it can speak plain? And do not you think, it will make good proficiency when it comes to years of

discretion? Others teach them both dissimulation and lying, by their unreasonable severity; and yet others, by admiring and applauding their ingenious lies and cunning tricks. Let the wise parent, on the contrary, teach them to "put away all lying," and both in little things and great, in jest or earnest, speak the very truth from their heart. Teach them that the author of all falsehood is the devil, who "is a liar and the father of it." Teach them to abhor and despise, not only all lying, but all equivocating, all cunning and dissimulation. Use every means to give them a love of truth,—of veracity, sincerity, and simplicity, and of openness both of spirit and behaviour.

24. Most parents increase the natural tendency to *injustice* in their children, by conniving at their wronging each other; if not laughing at, or even applauding, their witty contrivances to cheat one another. Beware of everything of this kind; and from their very infancy sow the seeds of justice in their hearts, and train them up in the exactest practice of it. If possible, teach them the love of justice, and that in the least things as well as the greatest. Impress upon their mind the old proverb: "He that will steal a penny will steal a pound." Habituate them to render unto all their due, even to the uttermost farthing.

25. Many parents connive likewise at the *ill-nature* of their children, and thereby strengthen it. But truly affectionate parents will not indulge them in any kind or degree of *unmercifulness.* They will not suffer them to vex their brothers or sisters, either by word or deed. They will not allow them to hurt, or give pain to, anything that has life. They will not permit them to rob birds' nests; much less to kill anything without necessity,—not even snakes, which are as innocent as worms, or toads, which, notwithstanding their ugliness, and the ill name they lie under, have been proved over and over to be as harmless as flies. Let them extend in its measure the rule of doing as they would be done by, to every animal whatsoever. Ye that are truly kind parents, in the morning, in the evening, and all the day beside, press upon all your children, "to walk in love, as Christ also loved us, and gave himself for us;" to mind that one point, "God is love; and he that dwelleth in love, dwelleth in God, and God in him."

96.* ON OBEDIENCE TO PARENTS

"Children, obey your parents in all things."
Col. 3:20

1. It has been a subject of controversy for many years, whether there are any innate principles in the mind of man. But it is allowed on all hands, if there be any practical principles naturally Unplanted in the soul, that "we ought to honour our parents," will claim this character almost before any other. It is enumerated among those universal principles by the most ancient authors and is undoubtedly found even among savages in the most barbarous nations. We may trace it through all the extent of Europe and Asia, through the wilds of Africa, and the forests of America. And it is not less,

but more observable in the most civilized nations. So it was first in the eastern parts of the world, which were for so many ages the seat of empire, of learning and politeness, as well as of religion. So it was afterwards in all the Grecian states, and throughout the whole Roman Empire. In this respect, it is plain, they that "have not the" written "law, are a law unto themselves," showing "the work," the substance, "of the law" to be "written in their hearts."

2. And wherever God has revealed his will to man, this law has been a part of that revelation. It has been herein opened afresh, considerably enlarged, and enforced in the strongest manner. In the Jewish revelation, the notorious breakers thereof were punishable with death. And this was one of the laws which our blessed Lord did not come to destroy, but to fulfil. Accordingly he severely reproved the Scribes and Pharisees for making it void through their traditions; clearly showing that the obligation thereof extended to all ages. It is the substance of this which St. Paul delivers to the Ephesians: (Eph. 6:1:) "Children, obey your parents in the Lord;" and again in those words to the Colossians, "Children, obey your parents in all things." [Col. 3:20]

3. It is observable, that the Apostle enforces this duty by a threefold encouragement: First. To the Ephesians he adds, "For this is right:" It is an instance of justice as well as mercy. It is no more than their due: it is what we owe to them for the very being which we have received from them. Secondly. "This is acceptable to the Lord;" it is peculiarly pleasing to the great Father of men and angels that we should pay honour and obedience to the fathers of our flesh. Thirdly. It is "the first commandment with promise;" the first to the performance whereof a peculiar promise is annexed: "that it may be well with thee, and that thy days may be long in the land which the Lord thy God giveth thee." This promise has been generally understood to include health and temporal blessings, as well as long life. And we have seen innumerable proofs, that it belongs to the Christian as well as the Jewish dispensation: Many remarkable instances of its accomplishment occur even at this day.

But what is the meaning of these words, "Children, obey your parents in all things?" I will endeavour, by the assistance of God, First, to explain, and, Then to apply them.

I. 1. First. I will endeavour to explain these words; and the rather, because so few people seem to understand them. Look round into the world, not the heathen but the Christian world, nay, the Reformed part of it; look among those that have the Scriptures in their own tongue; and who is there that appears even to have heard of this? Here and there a child obeys the parent out of fear, or perhaps out of natural affection. But how many children can you find that obey their fathers and mothers out of a sense of duty to God? And how many parents can you find that duly inculcate this duty upon their children? I doubt, a vast majority both of parents and children are totally ignorant of the whole affair. For the sake of these I will make it as plain as I can: But still I am thoroughly sensible, those that are not willing to be convinced will no more understand what I say than if I was talking Greek or Hebrew.

2. You will easily observe, that by *parents* the Apostle means both fathers and mothers, as he refers us to the Fifth Commandment, which names both the one and the other. And, however human laws may vary herein, the law of God makes no difference; but lays us under the same obligation of obeying both the one and the other.

3. But before we consider how we are to obey our parents, it may be inquired, how long we are to obey them. Are children to obey only till they run alone, till they go to school, till they can read and write, or till they are as tall as their parents, or, attain to years of discretion? Nay, if they obey only [because they cannot help it, only] because they fear to be beaten, or because otherwise they cannot procure food and raiment, what avails such obedience? Those only who obey their parents when they can live without them, and when they neither hope nor fear anything from them, shall have praise from God.

4. "But is a man that is at age, or a woman that is married, under any farther obligation to obey their parents?" With regard to marriage, although it is true that a man is to leave father and mother, and cleave unto his wife; and, by parity of reason, she is to leave father and mother, and cleave unto her husband; (in consequence of which there may be some particular cases wherein conjugal duty must take [the] place" of filial;) yet I cannot learn, either from Scripture or reason, that marriage either cancels or lessens the general obligation of filial duty. Much less does it appear that it is either cancelled or lessened by our having lived one-and-twenty years. I never understood it so in my own case. When I had lived upwards of thirty years, I looked upon myself to stand just in the same relation to my father as I did when I was ten years old. And when I was between forty and fifty, I judged myself full as much obliged to obey my mother in everything lawful, as I did when I was in my leading-strings [or hanging-sleeve coat].

5. But what is implied in, "Children, obey your parents in all things?" Certainly the First point of obedience is to do nothing which your father or mother forbids, whether it be great or small. Nothing is more plain than that the prohibition of a parent binds every conscientious child; that is, except the thing prohibited is clearly enjoined of God. Nor indeed is this all; the matter may be carried a little farther still: A tender parent may totally disapprove what he does not care flatly to forbid. What is the duty of a child in this case? How far is that disapprobation to be regarded? Whether it be equivalent to a prohibition or not, a person who would have a conscience void of offence should undoubtedly keep on the safe side, and avoid what may perhaps be evil. It is surely the more excellent way, to do nothing which you know your parents disapprove. To act otherwise seems to imply a degree of disobedience, which one of a tender conscience would wish to avoid.

6. The Second thing implied in this direction is, Do every thing which your father or mother bids, be it great or small, provided it be not contrary to any command of God. Herein God has given a power to parents, which even sovereign princes have not. The King of England, for instance, is a sovereign prince; yet he has not power to bid me do the least thing, unless the law of the land requires me so to do; for he has no power but to execute the law. The will of the king is no law to the subject. But the will of the parent is a law to the child, who is bound in conscience to submit thereto unless it be contrary to the law of God.

7. It is with admirable wisdom that the Father of spirits has given this direction, that as the strength of the parents supplies the want of strength, and the understanding of the parents the want of understanding, in their children, till they have strength and understanding of their own; so the will of the parents may [should] guide that of their children till they have wisdom and experience to guide themselves. This, therefore, is the very first thing which children have to learn,—that they are to obey their parents, to submit to their will, in all things. And this they may be inured to, long before they understand the reason of it; and, indeed, long before they are capable of understanding any of the principles of religion. Accordingly, St. Paul directs all parents to bring up their children "in the discipline and doctrine of the Lord." For their will may be broken by proper discipline, even in their early infancy; whereas it must be a considerable time after, before they are capable of instruction. This, therefore, is the first point of all: Bow down their wills from the very first dawn of reason; and, by habituating them to submit to your will, prepare them for submitting to the will of their Father which is in heaven.

8. But how few children do we find, even of six or eight years old, that understand anything of this! Indeed, how should they understand it, seeing they have none to teach them? Are not their parents, father as well as mother, full as ignorant of the matter as themselves? Whom do you find, even among religious people, that have the least conception of it? Have not you seen the proof of it with your own eyes? Have not you been present when a father or mother has said, "My child, do so or so?" The child, without any ceremony, answered peremptorily, "I won't." And the parent quietly passes it by, without any further notice. And does he or she not see, that, by this cruel indulgence, they are training up their child, by flat rebellion against their parents, to rebellion against God? Consequently they are training him up for the everlasting fire prepared for the devil and his angels! Did they duly consider this they would neither eat, nor drink, nor sleep, till they had taught him a better lesson, and made him thoroughly afraid of ever giving that diabolical answer again.

9. Let me reason this case a little farther with you parents that fear God. If you do fear God, how dare you suffer a child above a year old to say, "I will do" what you forbid, or, "I won't do" what you bid, and to go unpunished? Why do not you stop him at once, that he may never dare to say so again? Have you no bowels, no compassion for your child? No regard for his salvation or destruction? Would you suffer him to curse or swear in your presence, and take no notice of it? Why, disobedience is as certain a way to damnation as cursing and swearing. Stop him, stop him at first, in the name of God. Do not "spare the rod, and spoil the child." If you have not the heart of a tiger, do not give up your child to his

own will, that is, to the devil. Though it be pain to yourself, yet pluck your offspring out of the lion's teeth. Make them submit, that they may not perish. Break their will, that you may save their soul.

10. I cannot tell how to enforce this point sufficiently. To fix it upon your minds more strongly, permit me to add part of a letter on the subject, printed some years ago:—

"In order to form the minds of children, the first thing to be done is to conquer their will. To inform their understanding is a work of time, and must proceed by slow degrees; but the subjecting the will is a thing which must be done at once; and the sooner the better. For by our neglecting timely correction they contract a stubbornness which is hardly ever to be conquered, and never without using that severity which would be as painful to us as to the children. Therefore, I call those cruel parents who pass for kind and indulgent; who permit their children to contract habits which they know must be afterwards broken.

"I insist upon conquering the wills of children betimes; because this is the only foundation for a religious education. When this is thoroughly done, then a child is capable of being governed by the reason of its parent, till its own understanding comes to maturity.

"I cannot yet dismiss this subject. As self-will is the root of all sin and misery, so whatever cherishes this in children, ensures their after-wretchedness and irreligion; and whatever checks and mortifies it, promotes their future happiness and piety. This is still more evident if we consider that religion is nothing else but the doing the will of God, and not our own; and that self-will being the grand impediment to our temporal and eternal happiness, no indulgence of it can be trivial; no denial of it unprofitable. Heaven or hell depends on this alone. So that the parent who studies to subdue it in his children, works together with God in the saving of a soul. The parent who indulges it does the devil's work, makes religion impracticable, salvation unattainable; and does all that in him lies to damn his child, soul and body, for ever!

"This, therefore, I cannot but earnestly repeat,—break their wills betimes; begin this great work before they can run alone, before they can speak plain, or perhaps speak at all. Whatever pains it cost, conquer their stubbornness: break the will, if you would not damn the child. I conjure you not to neglect, not to delay this! Therefore, (1.) Let a child, from a year old, be taught to fear the rod and to cry softly. In order to this, (2.) Let him have nothing he cries for; absolutely nothing, great or small; else you undo your own work. (3.) At all events, from that age, make him do as he is bid, if you whip him ten times running to effect it. Let none persuade you it is cruelty to do this; it is cruelty not to do it. Break his will now, and his soul will live, and he will probably bless you to all eternity.

11. On the contrary, how dreadful are the consequences of that accursed kindness which gives children their own wills, and does not bow down their necks from their infancy! It is chiefly owing to this, that so many religious parents bring up children that have no religion at all; children that, when they are grown up, have no regard for them, perhaps set them at nought, and are ready to pick out their eyes! Why is this, but because their wills were not broken at first?—because they were not inured from their early infancy to obey their parents in all things, and to submit to their wills as to the will of God?—because they were not taught from the very first dawn of reason, that the will of their parents was, to them, the will of God; that to resist it was rebellion against God, and an inlet to all ungodliness?

II. 1. This may suffice for the explication of the text: I proceed to the application of it. And permit me, First, to apply to you that are parents, and, as such concerned to teach your children. Do you know these things yourselves? Are *you* thoroughly convinced of these important truths? Have you laid them to heart? and have you put them in practice, with regard to your own children? Have you inured them to discipline, before they were capable of instruction? Have you broken their wills from their earliest infancy; and do you still continue so to do, in opposition both to nature and custom? Did you explain to them, as soon as their understanding began to open, the reasons of your proceeding thus? Did you point out to them the will of God as the sole law of every intelligent creature; and show them it is the will of God that they should obey you in all things? Do you inculcate this over and over again till they perfectly comprehend it? O never be weary of this labour of love! and your labour will not always be in vain.

2. At least, do not teach them to disobey, by rewarding them for disobedience. Remember! you do this every time you give them anything because they cry for it. And herein they are apt scholars: If you reward them for crying, they will certainly cry again. So that there is no end, unless you make it a sacred rule, to give them nothing which they cry for. And the shortest way to do this is, never suffer them to cry aloud. Train them up to obedience in this one instance, and you will easily bring them to obey in others. Why should you not begin to-day? Surely you see what is the most excellent way; best for your child, and best for your own soul. Why then do you disobey? Because you are a coward; because you want resolution. And doubtless it requires [no small resolution to begin and persist herein. It certainly requires] no small patience, more than nature ever gave. But the grace of God is sufficient for you; you can do all things through Christ that strengtheneth you. This grace is sufficient to give you diligence, as well as resolution; otherwise laziness will be as great a hindrance as cowardice. For without much pains you cannot conquer: Nothing can be done with a slack hand; labour on; never tire, lay line upon line, till patience has its perfect work.

3. But there is another hindrance that is full as hard to be conquered as either laziness or cowardice. It is called fondness, and is usually mistaken for love: But, O, how widely different from it! It is real hate; and hate of the most mischievous kind, tending to destroy both body and soul in hell! O give not way to it any longer, no, not for a moment. Fight against it with your might! for the love of God; for the love of your children; for the love of your own soul!

4. I have one word more to say to parents; to mothers in particular. If, in spite of all the Apostle can say, you encourage your children by your example to "adorn"

themselves "with gold, or pearls, or costly apparel," you and they must drop into the pit together. But if they do it, though you set them a better example, still it is yours, as well as their fault; for if you did not put any ornament on your little child that you would not wear yourself, (which would be utter distraction, and far more inexcusable than putting it on your own arms or head), yet you did not inure them to obey you from their infancy, and teach them the duty of it, from at least two years old. Otherwise, they would not have dared to do anything, great or small, contrary to your will. Whenever, therefore, I see the fine-dressed daughter of a plain-dressed mother, I see at once the mother is defective either in knowledge or religion. Either she is ignorant of her own or her child's duty, or she has not practised what she knows.

5. I cannot dismiss this subject yet. I am pained continually at seeing religious parents suffer their children to run into the same folly of dress, as if they had no religion at all. In God's name, why do you suffer them to vary a hair's breadth from *your* example? "Why, they will do it?" They will! Whose fault is that? Why did not you break their will from their infancy? At least do it now; better late than never. It should have been done before they were two years old: It may be done at eight or ten, though with far more difficulty. However, do it now; and accept that difficulty as the just reward for your past neglect. Now, at least carry your point, whatever it costs. Be not mealy-mouthed; say not, like foolish Eli, "Nay, my children, it is no good report which I hear of you," instead of restraining them with a strong hand; but speak (though as calmly as possible, yet) firmly and peremptorily, "I will have it so;" and do as you say. Instil diligently into them the love of plain dress, and hatred of finery. Show them the reason of your own plainness of dress, and show it is equally reasonable for them. Bid defiance to indolence, to cowardice, to foolish fondness, and at all events carry your point; if you love their souls, make and keep them just as plain as yourselves. And I charge you, grandmothers before God, do not hinder your daughters herein. Do not dare to give the child anything which the mother denies. Never take the part of the children against their parent; never blame her before them. If you do not strengthen her authority, as you ought to do, at least do not weaken it; but if you have either sense or piety left, help her on in the work of real kindness

6. Permit me now to apply myself to you, children; particularly you that are the children of religious parents. Indeed if you have no fear of God before your eyes, "I have no concern with you at present; but if you have, if you really fear God, and have a desire to please him, you desire to understand all his commandments, the fifth in particular. Did you ever understand it yet? Do you now understand what is your duty to your father and mother? Do you know, at least do you consider, that by the divine appointment *their* will is law to *you?* Have you ever considered the extent of that obedience to your parents which God requires? "Children, obey your parents in all things." No exception, but of things unlawful. Have you practised your duty in this extent? Did you ever so much as intend it?

7. Deal faithfully with your own souls. Is your conscience now clear in this matter? Do you do nothing which you know to be contrary to the will either of your father or mother? Do you never do anything (though ever so much inclined to it) which he or she forbids? Do you abstain from everything which they dislike, as far as you can in conscience? On the other hand, are you careful to do whatever a parent bids? Do you study and contrive how to please them, to make their lives as easy and pleasant as you can? Whoever you are that add this to your general care to please God in all things, blessed art thou of the Lord! "Thy days shall be long in the land which the Lord thy God giveth thee."

8. But as for you who are little concerned about this matter, who do not make it a point of conscience to obey your parents in all things, but sometimes obey them, as it happens, and sometimes not; who frequently do what they forbid or disapprove, and neglect what they bid you do; suppose you awake out of sleep, that you begin to feel yourself a sinner, and begin to cry to God for mercy, is it any wonder that you find no answer, while you are under the guilt of unrepented sin? How can you expect mercy from God till you obey your parents? But suppose you have, by an uncommon miracle of mercy, tasted of the pardoning love of God, can it be expected, although you hunger and thirst after righteousness, after the perfect love of God, that you should ever attain it, ever be satisfied therewith, while you live in outward sin, in the wilful transgression of a known law of God, in disobedience to your parents? Is it not rather a wonder, that he has not withdrawn his Holy Spirit from you? that he still continues to strive with you, though you continually grieve his Spirit? O grieve him no more! By the grace of God, obey them in all things from this moment! As soon as you come home, as soon as you set foot within the door, begin an entirely new course! Look upon your father and mother with new eyes; see them as representing your Father which is in heaven: Endeavour, study, rejoice to please, to help, to obey them in all things: Behave not barely as their child, but as their servant for Christ's sake. O how will you then love one another! In a manner unknown before. God will bless you to them, and them to you: All around will feel that God is with you of a truth. Many shall see it and praise God; and the fruit of it will remain when both you and they are lodged in Abraham's bosom.

97.* ON OBEDIENCE TO PASTORS

"Obey them that have the rule over you, and submit yourselves: For they watch over your souls, as they that shall give account, that they may do this with joy, and not with grief: For that is unprofitable for you."

Heb. 13:17.

1. Exceeding few, not only among nominal Christians, but among truly religious men, have any clear conception of that important doctrine which is here delivered by the Apostle. Very many scarce think of it, and hardly know that there is any such direction in the Bible. And the greater part of those

---

* [text of the 1872 edition]

who know it is there, and imagine they follow it, do not understand it, but lean too much either to the right hand or to the left, to one extreme or the other. It is well known to what an extravagant height the Romanists in general carry this direction. Many of them believe an implicit faith is due to the doctrines delivered by those that rule over them, and that implicit obedience ought to be paid to whatever commands they give: And not much less has been insisted on by several eminent men of the Church of England: Although it is true that the generality of Protestants are apt to run to the other extreme, allowing their Pastors no authority at all, but making them both the creatures and the servants of their congregations. And very many there are of our own Church who agree with them herein; supposing the Pastors to be altogether dependent upon the people, who in their judgment have a right to direct as well as to choose their Ministers.

2. But is it not possible to find a medium between these two extremes? Is there any necessity for us to run either into one or into the other? If we set human laws out of the question, and simply attend to the oracles of God, we may certainly discover a middle path in this important matter In order thereto, let us carefully examine the words of the Apostle above recited. Let us consider,

  I. Who are the persons mentioned in the text, they "that rule over" us?

  II. Who are they whom the Apostle, directs to "obey and submit themselves" to them?

  III. What is the meaning of this direction? In what sense are they to "obey and submit" themselves? I shall then endeavour to make a suitable application of the whole.

I. 1. Consider we, first, who are the persons mentioned in the text, "they that have the rule over you?"—I do not conceive that the words of the Apostle are properly translated; because this translation makes the sentence little better the an tautology. If they "rule over you," you are certainly ruled by them; so that according to this translation you are only enjoined to do what you do already-to obey those whom you do obey. But there is another meaning of the Greek word which seems abundantly more proper: It means to *guide*, as well as to rule. And thus, it seems, it should be taken here. The direction then, when applied to our spiritual guides, is plain and pertinent.

2. This interpretation seems to be confirmed by the seventh verse, which fixes the meaning of this. "Remember them which have the rule over you, who have spoken unto you the word of God." The Apostle here shows, by the latter clause of the sentence, whom he meant in the former, Those that "were over them," were the same persons "who spoke unto them the word of God;" that is, they were their pastors, those who guided and fed this part of the flock of Christ.

3. But by whom are these guides to be appointed? And what are they Supposed to do in order to be entitled to the obedience which is here prescribed?

Volumes upon volumes have been wrote on that knotty question, *By whom are guides of souls to be appointed?* I do not intend here to enter at all into the dispute concerning church government; neither to debate whether it be advantageous or prejudicial to the interest of true religion that the church and the state should be blended together, as they have been ever since the time of Constantine, in every part of the Roman Empire where Christianity has been received. Waiving all these points (which may find employment enough for men that abound in leisure,) by "them that guide you" I mean them that do it, if not by your choice, at least by your consent; them that you willingly accept of to be your guides in the way to heaven.

4. But what are they supposed to do in order to entitle them to the obedience here prescribed?

They are supposed to go before the flock (as is the manner of the eastern shepherds to this day,) and to guide them in all the ways of truth and holiness; they are to "nourish them with the words of eternal life;" to feed them with "the pure milk of the word:" Applying it continually "for doctrine," teaching them all the essential doctrines contained therein; "for reproof," warning them if they turn aside from the way, to the right hand or to the left;—"for correction;" showing them how to amend what is amiss, and guiding them back into the way of peace;—and "for instruction in righteousness;" training them up in inward and outward holiness, "until they come to a perfect man, to the measure of the stature of the fullness of Christ."

5. They are supposed to "watch over your souls, as those that shall give account." "As those that shall give account!" How unspeakably solemn and awful are those words! May God write them upon the heart of every guide of souls! "They watch," waking while others sleep, over the flock of Christ; over the souls that he has bought with a price, that he has purchased with his own blood. They have them in their hearts both by day and by night; regarding neither sleep nor food in comparison of them. Even while they sleep their heart is waking, full of concern for their beloved children. "They watch" with deep earnestness, with uninterrupted seriousness, with unwearied care, patience, and diligence, as they that are about to give an account of every particular soul to him that standeth at the door,—to the Judge of quick and dead.

II. 1. We, Secondly, to consider who those are whom the Apostle directs to obey them that have the rule over them. And in order to determine this with certainty and clearness, we shall not appeal to human institutions, but simply (as in answering the preceding question) appeal to that decision of it which we find in the oracles of God. Indeed we have hardly occasion to go one step farther than the text itself. Only it may be proper, first, to remove out of the way some popular opinions which have been almost everywhere taken for granted, but can in no wise be proved.

2. It is usually supposed, First, that the Apostle is here directing parishioners to obey and submit themselves to the Minister of their parish. But can anyone bring the least shadow of proof for this from the Holy Scripture? Where is it written that we are bound to obey any Minister because we live in what is called his parish? "Yes," you say, "we are bound to obey every ordinance of man for the Lord's sake." True, in all things indifferent; but this is not so; it is exceeding far

from it. It is far from being a thing indifferent to me who is the guide of my soul. I dare not receive one as my guide to heaven that is himself on the high road to hell. I dare not take a wolf for my shepherd, that has not so much as sheep's clothing; that is a common swearer, an open drunkard, a notorious sabbath-breaker. And such (the more is the shame, and the more the pity!) are many parochial Ministers at this day.

3. "But are you not properly members of that congregation to which your parents belong?" I do not apprehend that I am; I know no Scripture that obliges me to this. I owe all deference to the commands of my parents, and willingly obey them in all things lawful But it is not lawful to call them Rabbi; that is, to believe or obey them implicitly. Everyone must give an account of himself to God. Therefore every man must judge for himself; especially in a point of so deep importance as this is,—the choice of a guide for his soul.

4. But we may bring this matter to a short issue by recurring to the very words of the text. They that have voluntarily connected themselves with such a pastor as answers the description given therein; such as do in fact, "watch over their souls, as they that shall give account;" such as do "nourish them up with the words of eternal life;" such as feed them as with the "pure milk of the word," and constantly apply it to them "for doctrine, for reproof, for correction, and for instruction in righteousness;"—all who have found and chosen guides of this character, of this spirit and behaviour, are undoubtedly required by the Apostle to "obey and submit themselves" to them.

III. 1. But what is the meaning of this direction? This remains to be considered. In what sense, and how far, does the Apostle direct them to "obey and submit" to their spiritual guides? If we attend to the proper sense of the two words here used by the Apostle, we may observe that the former of them *peithesthe*, (from *peitho to persuade*) refers to the understanding, the latter, *hypeikete* to the will, and outward behaviour. To begin with the former. What influence ought our spiritual guides to have over our understanding! We dare no more call our spiritual fathers Rabbi, than the fathers of our flesh. We dare no more yield implicit faith to the former than to the latter. In this sense one is our Master, (or rather Teacher,) who is in heaven. But whatever submission, of even our understanding, is short of this, we may, nay, we ought to yield to them.

2. To explain this a little farther. St. James uses a word which is nearly allied to the former of these: "The wisdom which is from above is, *eupeithes, easy to be convinced*, or to be persuaded." Now, if we ought to have and to show this wisdom toward all men, we ought to have it in a more eminent degree, and to show it upon every occasion, toward those that "watch over our souls." With regard to these, above all other men, we should be "easy to be entreated;" easily convinced of any truth, and easily persuaded to anything that is not sinful.

3. A word of nearly the same import with this is frequently used by St. Paul; namely, *epieikes.* In our translation it is more than once rendered *gentle.* But perhaps it might be more properly rendered (if the word may be allowed) *yielding;* ready to *yield,* to give up our own will, in everything that is not a point of duty. This amiable temper every real Christian enjoys, and shows in his intercourse with all men. But he shows it in a peculiar manner toward those that watch over his soul. He is not only willing to receive any instruction from them, to be convinced of anything which he did not know before; lying open to their advice, and being glad to receive admonition, or reproof; but is ready to give up his own will, whenever he can do it with a clear conscience. Whatever they desire him to do, he does; if it be not forbidden in the Word of God. Whatever they desire him to refrain from, he does so; if it be not enjoined in the Word of God. This is implied in those words of the Apostle: "Submit yourselves to them;" yield to them; give up your own will. This is meet, and right, and your bounden duty, if they do indeed watch over your souls as they that shall give account. If you do thus "obey and submit yourselves" to them, they will give an account of you "with joy, not with groaning," as they must otherwise do; for although they should be clear of your blood, yet "that would be unprofitable to you;" yea, a prelude to eternal damnation.

4. How acceptable to God was an instance of obedience somewhat similar to this! You have a large and particular account of it in the thirty-fifth chapter of Jeremiah. "The word of the Lord came to Jeremiah, saying, Go unto the house of the Rechabites, and give them wine to drink. Then I took the whole house of the Rechabites;" all the heads of their families; "and set before them pots full of wine, and said unto them, Drink ye wine. But they said, We will drink no wine: for Jonadab," a great man in the reign of Jehu, "the son of Rechab," from whom we are named, being the father of our family, "commanded us, Ye shall drink no wine, neither ye nor your sons for ever. And we have obeyed the voice of Jonadab our father, in all that he charged us." We do not know any particular reason why Jonadab gave this charge to his posterity. But as it was not sinful they gave this strong instance of gratitude to their great benefactor. And how pleasing this was to the Father of their spirits we learn from the words that follow: "And Jeremiah said unto the Rechabites, Because ye have obeyed the voice of Jonadab your father, therefore thus saith the Lord of hosts, Jonadab shall not want a man to stand before my face forever." [Jer. 35]

5. Now it is certain Christians owe full as much gratitude and obedience to those that watch over their souls as ever the house of the Rechabites owed to Jonadab the son of Rechab. And we cannot doubt but he is as well pleased with our obedience to these as ever he was with their obedience to Jonadab. If he was so well pleased with the gratitude and obedience of this people to their temporal benefactor, have we not all reason to believe he is full as well pleased with the gratitude and obedience of Christians to those who derive far greater blessings to them than ever Jonadab conveyed to his posterity?

6. It may be of use yet again to consider, In what instances is it the duty of Christians to obey and submit themselves to those that watch over their souls? Now the things which they enjoin must be either enjoined of God, or forbidden by him,

or indifferent. In things forbidden of God we dare not obey them; for we are to obey God rather than man. In things enjoined of God we do not properly obey *them*, but our common Father. Therefore, if we are to obey them at all, it must be in things indifferent. The sum is, it is the duty of every private Christian to obey his spiritual Pastor, by either doing or leaving undone anything of an indifferent nature; anything that is in no way determined in the word of God.

7. But how little is this understood in the Protestant world! at least in England and Ireland! Who is there, even among those that are supposed to be good Christians, who dreams there is such a duty as this? And yet there is not a more express command either in the Old or New Testament. No words can be more clear and plain; no command more direct and positive. Therefore, certainly none who receive the Scripture as the word of God, can live in the habitual breach of this and plead innocence. Such an instance of willful, or at least careless disobedience, must grieve the Holy Spirit of God. It cannot but hinder the grace of God from having its full effect upon the heart. It is not improbable that this very disobedience may be one cause of the deadness of many souls; one reason of their not receiving those blessings which they seek with some degree of sincerity.

8. It remains only to make a short application of what has now been delivered.

You that read this, do you apply it to yourself? Do you examine yourself thereby? Do not *you* stop your own growth in grace, if not by willful disobedience to this command; yet by a careless inattention to it, by not considering it, as the importance of it deserves? If so, you defraud yourself of many blessings which you might enjoy. Or, are you of a better mind; of a more excellent spirit? Is it your fixed resolution and your constant endeavour "to obey them that have the rule over you in the Lord;" to submit yourself as cheerfully to your spiritual as to your natural parents? Do you ask, "Wherein should I submit to them?" The answer has been given already: Not in things enjoined of God; not in things forbidden by him; but in things indifferent: In all that are not determined, one way or the other, by the oracles of God. It is true, this cannot be done, in some instances without a considerable degree of self-denial, when they advise you to refrain from something that is agreeable to flesh and blood. And it cannot be obeyed in other instances without taking up your cross; without suffering some pain or inconvenience that is not agreeable to flesh and blood. For that solemn declaration of our Lord has place here, as well as on a thousand other occasions: "Except a man deny himself, and take up his cross daily, he cannot be my disciple." But this will not affright you, if you resolve to be not only almost, but altogether, a Christian; if you determine to fight the good fight of faith, and lay hold on eternal life.

9. I would now apply myself in a more particular manner to *you* who desire *me* to watch over your souls. Do *you* make it a point of conscience to obey me, for my Master's sake? to submit yourselves to *me* in things indifferent; things not determined in the Word of God; in all things that are not enjoined, nor yet forbidden, in Scripture? Are you "easy to be entreated," as by men in general, so by me in particular?—

easy to be convinced of any truth, however contrary to your former prejudices?—and easy to be persuaded to do or forbear any indifferent thing at *my* desire? You cannot but see that all this is clearly contained in the very words of the text. And you cannot but acknowledge that it is highly reasonable for you so to do, if I do employ all my time, all my substance, all my strength both of body and soul, not in seeking my own honour, or pleasure; but in promoting your present and eternal salvation; if I do indeed "watch over your souls as one that must give account."

10. Do you then take my advice (I ask in the presence of God and all the world) with regard to *dress?* I published that advice above thirty years ago; I have repeated it a thousand times since. I have advised you not to be conformable to the world herein, to lay aside all needless ornaments, to avoid all needless expense, to be patterns of plainness to all that are round about you. Have you taken this advice? Have you all, men and women, young and old, rich and poor, laid aside all those needless ornaments which I particularly objected to? Are you all exemplarily plain in your apparel; as plain as Quakers (so called,) or Moravians? If not, if you are still dressed like the generality of people of your own rank and fortune, you declare hereby to all the world that you will not obey them that are over you in the Lord. You declare, in open defiance of God and man, that you will not *submit yourselves* to them. Many of you carry your sins on your forehead, openly and in the face of the sun. You harden your hearts against instruction and against conviction. You harden one another; especially those of you that were once convinced, and have now stifled your convictions. You encourage one another to stop your ears against the truth, and shut your eyes against the light, lest haply you should see that you are fighting against God and against your own souls. If I were now called to give an account of you, it would be "with groans, and not with joy." And sure that would be "unprofitable for you:" The loss would fall upon your own head.

11. I speak all this on supposition, (though that is a supposition not to be made,) that the Bible was silent on this head; that the Scriptures said nothing concerning *dress*, and left it to everyone's own discretion. But if all other texts were silent, this is enough: "Submit yourselves to them that are over you in the Lord." I bind this upon your consciences, in the sight of God. Were it only in obedience to this direction, you cannot be clear before God unless you throw aside all needless ornaments, in utter defiance of that tyrant of fools, *fashion*; unless you seek only to be adorned with good works, as men and women professing godliness.

12. Perhaps you will say, "This is only a little thing: it is a mere trifle." I answer, If it be, you are the more inexcusable before God and man. What! will you disobey a plain commandment of God for *a mere trifle?* God forbid! Is it a trifle to sin against God,—to set his authority at nought? Is this a little thing? Nay, remember, there can be no little sin, till we can find a little God! Meantime be assured of one thing: The more conscientiously you obey your spiritual guides, the more powerfully will God apply the word which they speak in his name to your heart! The more plentifully

will he water what is spoken with the dew of his blessing; and the more proofs will you have, it is not only they that speak, but the Spirit of your Father who speaketh in them.

98.* ON VISITING THE SICK

"I was sick, and ye visited me."

Matt. 25:36.

1. It is generally supposed, that the means of grace and the ordinances of God are equivalent terms. We commonly mean by that expression, those that are usually termed, works of piety; viz., hearing and reading the Scripture, receiving the Lord's Supper, public and private prayer, and fasting. And it is certain these are the ordinary channels which convey the grace of God to the souls of men. But are they the only means of grace? Are there no other means than these, whereby God is pleased, frequently, yea, ordinarily, to convey his grace to them that either love or fear him? Surely there are works of mercy, as well as works of piety, which are real means of grace. They are more especially such to those that perform them with a single eye. And those that neglect them, do not receive the grace which otherwise they might. Yea, and they lose, by a continued neglect, the grace which they had received. Is it not hence that many who were once strong in faith are now weak and feeble-minded? And yet they are not sensible whence that weakness comes, as they neglect none of the ordinances of God. But they might see whence it comes, were they seriously to consider St. Paul's account of all true believers: "We are his workmanship, created anew in Christ Jesus unto good works, which God hath before prepared, that we might walk therein." (Eph. 2:10.)

2. The walking herein is essentially necessary, as to the continuance of that faith whereby we are already saved grace, so to the attainment of everlasting salvation. Of this cannot doubt, if we seriously consider that these are the very words of the great Judge himself: "Come, ye blessed children of my Father, inherit the kingdom prepared for you from the foundation of the world. For I was hungry, and ye gave me meat: Thirsty, and ye gave me drink: I was a stranger, and ye took me in: Naked, and ye clothed me: I was sick, and ye visited me: I was in prison, and ye came unto me." (Matt. 25:34.) "Verily, I say unto you, Inasmuch as ye have done it to the least of these my brethren, ye have done it unto me." If this does not convince you that the continuance in works of mercy is necessary to salvation, consider what the Judge of all says to those on the left hand: "Depart, ye cursed, into everlasting fire, prepared for the devil and his angels: For I was hungry, and ye gave me no meat: Thirsty, and ye gave me no drink: I was a stranger, and ye took me not in: Naked, and ye clothed me not: Sick and in prison, and ye visited me not. Inasmuch as ye have not done it unto one of the least of these neither have ye done it unto me." You see, were it for this alone, they must "depart" from God "into everlasting punishment."

3. Is it not strange, that this important truth should be so little understood, or, at least, should so little influence the practice of them that fear God? Suppose this representation be true, suppose the Judge of all the earth speaks right, those, and those only, that feed the hungry, give drink to the thirsty, clothe the naked, relieve the stranger, visit those that are in prison, according to their power and opportunity, shall "inherit the everlasting kingdom." And those that do not shall "depart into everlasting fire, prepared for the devil and his angels'.

4. I purpose, at present, to confine my discourse to one article of these,—visiting the sick: A plain duty, which all that are in health may practise in a higher or lower degree; and which, nevertheless, is almost universally neglected, even by those that profess to love God. And touching this I would inquire,

    I.   What is implied in visiting the sick?

    II.   How is it to be performed?—And,

    III.   By whom?

I. First, I would inquire, What is the nature of this duty? What is implied in "visiting the sick?"

1. By the sick, I do not mean only those that keep their bed, or that are sick in the strictest sense. Rather I would include all such as are in a state of affliction, whether of mind or body; and that whether they are good or bad, whether they fear God or not.

2. "But is there need of visiting them in person? May we not relieve them at a distance? Does it not answer the same purpose if we send them help as if we carry it ourselves?" Many are so circumstanced that they cannot attend the sick in person; and where this is the real case it is undoubtedly sufficient for them to send help, being the only expedient they can use. But this is not properly visiting the sick; it is another thing. The word which we render *visit*, in its literal acceptation, means to *look upon*. And this, you well know, cannot be done unless you are present with them. To send them assistance is, therefore, entirely a different thing from visiting them. The former, then, ought to be done, but the latter not left undone.

"But I send a physician to those that are sick; and he can do them more good than I can." He can, in one respect; he can do them more good with regard to their bodily health. But he cannot do them more good with regard to their souls, which are of infinitely greater importance. And if he could, this would not excuse *you*: His going would not fulfil *your* duty. Neither would it do the same good to *you*, unless you saw them with your own eyes. If you do not, you lose a means of grace; you lose an excellent means of increasing your thankfulness to God, who saves you from this pain and sickness, and continues your health and strength; as well as of increasing your sympathy with the afflicted, your benevolence, and all social affections.

3. One great reason why the rich, in general, have so little sympathy for the poor, is, because they so seldom visit them. Hence it is, that, according to the common observation, one part of the world does not know what the other suffers. Many of them do not know, because they do not care to know: they keep out of the way of knowing it; and then plead their voluntary ignorances an excuse for their hardness of heart.

---

* [text of the 1872 ed.]

"Indeed, Sir," said person of large substance, "I am a very compassionate man. But, to tell you the truth, I do not know anybody in the world that is in want." How did this come to pass? Why, he took good care to keep out of their way; and if he fell upon any of them unawares "he passed over on the other side."

4. How contrary to this is both the spirit and behaviour of even people of the highest rank in a neighbouring nation! In Paris, ladies of the first quality, yea, Princesses of the blood, of the Royal Family, constantly visit the sick, particularly the patients in the Grand Hospital. And they not only take care to relieve their wants, (if they need anything more than is provided for them,) but attend on their sick beds, dress their sores, and perform the meanest offices for them. Here is a pattern for the English, poor or rich, mean or honourable! For many years we have abundantly copied after the follies of the French; let us for once copy after their wisdom and virtue, worthy the imitation of the whole Christian world. Let not the gentlewomen, or even the countesses in England, be ashamed to imitate those Princesses of the blood! Here is a fashion that does honour to human nature. It began in France; but God forbid it should end there!"

5. And if your delicacy will not permit you to imitate those truly honourable ladies, by abasing yourselves in the manner which they do, by performing the lowest offices for the sick, you may, however, without humbling yourselves so far, supply them with whatever they want. And you may administer help of a more excellent kind, by supplying their spiritual wants; instructing them (if they need such instruction) in the first principles of religion; endeavouring to show them the dangerous state they are in, under the wrath and curse of God, through sin; and pointing them to the "Lamb of God, who taketh away the sins of the world." Beside this general instruction, you might have abundant opportunities of comforting those that are in pain of body, distress of mind; you might find opportunities of strengthening the feeble-minded, quickening those that are faint and weary; and of building up those that have believed, and encouraging them to "go on to perfection." But these things you must do in your own person; you see they cannot be done by proxy. Or suppose you could give the same relief to the sick by another, you could not reap the same advantage to yourself; you could not gain that increase in lowliness, in patience, in tenderness of spirit, in sympathy with the afflicted, which you might have gained, if you had assisted them in person. Neither would you receive the same recompense in the resurrection of the just, when "every man shall receive his own reward, according to his own labour."

II. 1. I proceed to inquire, in the Second place, How are we to visit them? In what manner may this labour of love be most effectually performed? How may we do this most to the glory of God, and the benefit of our neighbour? But before ever you enter upon the work, you should be deeply convinced that you are by means sufficient for it; you have neither sufficient grace, nor sufficient understanding, to perform it in the most excellent manner. And this will convince you of the necessity of applying to the Strong for strength; and of flying to the Father of Lights, the Giver of every good gift, for wisdom; ever remembering, "there is a Spirit in man that giveth wisdom; and the inspiration of the Holy One that giveth understanding." Whenever, therefore, you are about to enter upon the work, seek his help by earnest prayer. Cry to him for the whole spirit of humility, lest if pride steal into your heart, if you ascribe anything to yourself, while you strive to save others you destroy your own soul. Before and through the work, from the beginning to the end, let your heart wait upon him for a continual supply of meekness and gentleness, of patience and longsuffering, that you may never be angry or discouraged at whatever treatment, rough or smooth, kind or unkind, you may meet with. Be not moved with the deep ignorance of some, the dullness, the amazing stupidity of others; marvel not at their peevishness or stubbornness, at their non-improvement after all the pains that you have taken; yea, at some of them turning back to perdition, and being worse than they were before. Still your record is with the Lord, and your reward with the Most High.

2. As to the particular method of treating the sick, you need not tie yourself down to any, but may continually vary your manner of proceeding as various circumstances may require. But it may not be amiss, usually, to begin with inquiring into their outward condition. You may ask whether they have the necessaries of life; whether they have sufficient food and raiment; if the weather be cold, whether they have fuel; whether they have needful attendance; whether they have proper advice, with regard to their bodily disorder; especially if it be of a dangerous kind. In several of these respects you may be able to give them some assistance yourself; and you may move those that are more able than you, to supply your lack of service. You might properly say in your own case, "To beg I am ashamed;" but never be ashamed to beg for the poor; yea, in this case, be an importunate beggar; do not easily take a denial. Use all the address, all the understanding, all the influence you have; at the same time trusting in Him that has the hearts of all men in his hands.

3. You will then easily discern, whether there is any good office which you can do for them with your own hands. Indeed, most of the things which are needful to be done, those about them can do better than you. But in some you may have more skill, or more experience, than them; and if you have, let not delicacy or honour stand in your way. Remember his word, "Inasmuch as ye have done it unto the least of these, ye have done it unto me;" and think nothing too mean to do for Him. Rejoice to be abased for his sake!

4. These little labours of love will pave your way to things greater importance. Having shown that you have a regard for their bodies, you may proceed to inquire concerning their souls. And here you have a large field before you; you have scope for exercising all the talents which God has given you. May you not begin with asking, "Have you ever considered, that God governs the world;—that his providence is over all, and over *you* in particular?—Does any thing then befall you without his knowledge,—or without his designing it for your good? He knows all you suffer; he knows all your pains; he sees all your wants. He sees not only your affliction in general, but every particular circumstance of it. Is he not looking

down from heaven, and disposing all these things for your profit? You may then inquire, whether he is acquainted with the general principles of religion. And afterwards, lovingly and gently examine, whether his life has been agreeable thereto: whether he has been an outward, barefaced sinner, or has had a form of religion. See next, whether he knows anything of the power; of worshipping God "in spirit and in truth." If he does not, endeavour to explain to him, "without holiness no man shall see the Lord;" and "except a man be born again, he cannot see the kingdom of God." When he begins to understand the nature of holiness, and the necessity of the new birth, then you may press upon him "repentance toward God, and faith in our Lord Jesus Christ."

5. When you find any of them begin to fear God, it will proper to give them, one after another, some plain tracts, as the "Instructions for Christians," "Awake, thou that sleepest," and the "Nature and Design of Christianity." At the next visit you may inquire, what they have read—what they remember,—and what they understand. And then will be the time to enforce what they understand, and, if possible, impress it on their hearts. Be sure to conclude every meeting with prayer. If you cannot yet pray without a form, you may use some of those composed by Mr. Spinckes, or any other pious writer. But the sooner you breakthrough this backwardness the better. Ask of God, and he will open your mouth.

6. Together with the more important lessons, which you endeavour to teach all the poor whom you visit, it would be a deed of charity to teach them two things more, which they are generally little acquainted with,—industry and cleanliness. It was said by a pious man, "Cleanliness is next to godliness." Indeed the want of it is a scandal to all religion; causing the way of truth to be evil spoken of. And without industry, we are neither fit for this world, nor for the world to come. With regard to both, "whatsoever thy hand findeth to do, do it with thy might."

III. 1. The Third point to be considered is, By whom is this duty to be performed? The answer is ready: By all that desire to "inherit the kingdom" of their Father, which was "prepared forth from the foundation of the world." For thus saith the Lord, "Come, ye blessed;—inherit the kingdom;—For I was sick, and ye visited me." And to those on the left hand, "Depart, ye cursed;—for I was sick, and ye visited me not." Does not this plainly imply, that as all who do this are "blessed", and shall "inherit the kingdom;" so all who do it not are "cursed," and shall "depart into everlasting fire?"

2. All, therefore, who desire to escape everlasting fire, and to inherit the everlasting kingdom, are equally concerned, according to their power, to practise this important duty. It is equally incumbent on young and old, rich and poor, men and women, according to their ability. None are so young, if they desire to save their own souls, as to be excused from assisting their neighbours. None are so poor, (unless they want the necessaries of life,) but they are called to do something, more or less, at whatever time they can spare, for the relief and comfort of their afflicted fellow-sufferers.

3. But those "who are rich in this world," who have more than the conveniences of life, are peculiarly called of God to this blessed work, and pointed out to it by his gracious Providence. As you are not under a necessity of working for your bread, you have your time at your own disposal! You may, therefore, allot some part of it every day for this labour of love. If it be practicable, it is far best to have a fixed hour; (for *any time*, we say, *is no time*;) and not to employ that time in any other business, without urgent necessity. You have likewise a peculiar advantage over many, by your station in life. Being superior in rank to them, you have the more influence on that very account. Your inferiors, of course, look up to you with a kind of reverence. And the condescension which you show in visiting them, gives them a prejudice in your favour, which inclines them to hear you with attention, and willingly receive what you say. Improve this prejudice to the uttermost for the benefit of their souls, as well as their bodies. While you are as eyes to the blind, and feet to the lame, a husband to the widow, and a father to the fatherless, see that you still keep a higher end in view, even the saving of souls from death, and that you labour to make all you say and do subservient to that great end.

4. "But have the poor themselves any part or lot in this matter? Are they any way concerned in visiting the sick? What can they give to others, who have hardly the conveniences, or perhaps necessaries, of life for themselves?" If they have not, yet they need not be wholly excluded from the blessing which attends the practice of this duty. Even those may remember that excellent rule, "Let our conveniences give way to our neighbour's necessities; and our necessities give way to our neighbour's extremities." And few are so poor, as not to be able sometimes to give "two mites;" but if they are not, if they have no money to give, may they not give what is of more value? Yea, of more value than thousands of gold and silver. If you speak "in the name of Jesus Christ of Nazareth," may not the words you speak be health to the soul, and marrow to the bones? Can you give them nothing? Nay, in administering to them the grace of God, you give them more than all this world is worth. Go on, go on, thou poor disciple of a poor Master! Do as he did in the days of his flesh! Whenever thou hast an opportunity, go about doing good, and healing all that are oppressed of the devil; encouraging them shake off his chains, and fly immediately to Him

> Who sets the prisoners free, and breaks
> The iron bondage from their necks.

Above all, give them your prayers. Pray with them; pray for them; and who knows but you may save their souls alive?

5. You that are *old*, whose feet are ready to stumble upon the dark mountains, may not you do a little more good before you go hence and are no more seen? O remember,

> 'Tis time to live, if you grow old
> Of little life the best to make,
> And manage wisely the last stake!

As you have lived many years, it may be hoped you have attained such knowledge as may be of use to others. You have certainly more knowledge of men, which is commonly learned by dear-bought experience. With what strength you have left, employ the few moments you have to spare, in ministering to those who are weaker than yourselves. Your grey hairs will not fail to give you authority, and add weight to what you speak. You may frequently urge, to increase their attention,

> Believe me, youth; for I am read in cares,
> And groan beneath the weight of more than threescore years.

You have frequently been a sufferer yourself; perhaps you are so still. So much the more give them all the assistance you can, both with regard to their souls and bodies, before they and you go to the place whence you will not return.

6. On the other hand, you that are *young* have several advantages that are almost peculiar to yourselves. You have generally a flow of spirits, and a liveliness of temper, which, by the grace of God, make you willing to undertake, and capable of performing, many good works, at which others would be discouraged. And you have your health and strength of body, whereby you are eminently qualified to assist the sick and those that have no strength. You are able to take up and carry the crosses, which may be expected to lie in the way. Employ then your whole vigour of body and mind in ministering to your afflicted brethren. And bless God that you have them to employ in so honourable a service; like those heavenly "servants of his that do his pleasure," by continually ministering to the heirs of salvation.

7. "But may not *women*, as well as men, bear a part in this honourable service?" Undoubtedly they may; nay, they ought; it is meet, right, and their bounden duty. Herein there is no difference; "there is neither male nor female in Christ Jesus."Indeed it has long passed for a maxim with many, that "women are only to be seen, not heard." And accordingly many of them are brought up in such a manner as if they were only designed for agreeable playthings! But is this doing honour to the sex? or is it a real kindness to them? No; it is the deepest unkindness; it is horrid cruelty; it is mere Turkish barbarity. And I know not how any woman of sense and spirit can submit to it. Let all you that have it in your power assert the right which the God of nature has given you. Yield not to that vile bondage any longer. You, as well as men, are rational creatures. You, like them, were made in the image of God; you are equally candidates for immortality; you too are called of God, as you have time, to "do good unto all men." Be "not disobedient to the heavenly calling." Whenever you have opportunity, do all the good you can, particularly to your poor, sick neighbour. And every one of *you* likewise "shall receive *your* own reward, according to *your* own labour."

8. It is well known, that, in the primitive Church, there were women particularly appointed for this work. Indeed there was one or more such in every Christian congregation under heaven. They were then termed Deaconesses, that is, servants; servants of the Church, and of its great Master. Such was Phebe, (mentioned by St. Paul, Rom. 16:1,) "a Deaconess of the Church of Cenchrea." It is true, most of these were women in years, and well experienced in the work of God. But were the young wholly excluded from that service? No: Neither need they be, provided they know in whom they have believed; and show that they are holy of heart, by being holy in all manner of conversation. Such a Deaconess, if she answered her picture, was Mr. Law's Miranda. Would anyone object to her visiting and relieving the sick and poor, because she was a woman; nay, and a young one too? Do any of you that are young desire to tread in her steps? Have you a pleasing form, an agreeable address? So much the better, if you are wholly devoted to God. He will use these, if your eye be single, to make your words strike the deeper. And while you minister to others, how many blessings may redound into your own bosom! Hereby your natural levity may be destroyed; your fondness for trifles cured; your wrong tempers corrected; your evil habits weakened, until they are rooted out; and you will be prepared to adorn the doctrine of God our Saviour in every future scene of life. Only be very wary, if you visit or converse with those of the other sex, lest your affections be entangled, on one side or the other, and so you find a curse instead of a blessing.

9. Seeing then this is a duty to which we are called, rich and poor, young and old, male and female, (and it would be well parents would train up their children herein, as well as in saying their prayers and going to church,) let the time past suffice that almost all of us have neglected it, as by general consent. O what need has every one of us to say, "Lord, forgive me my sins of omission!" Well, in the name of God, let us now from this day set about it with general consent. And I pray, let it never go out of your mind that this is a duty which you cannot perform by proxy; unless in one only case,—unless you are disabled by your own pain or weakness. In that only case, it suffices to send the relief which you would otherwise give. Begin, my dear brethren, begin now; else the impression which you now feel will wear off; and, possibly, it may never return! What then will be the consequence? Instead of hearing that word, "Come, ye blessed!—For I was sick, and ye visited me;" you must hear that awful sentence, "Depart, ye cursed!—For I was sick, and ye visited me not!"

99.* THE REWARD OF THE RIGHTEOUS

PREACHED BEFORE THE HUMANE SOCIETY

"Come, ye blessed of my Father, inherit the kingdom prepared for you from the foundation of the world."

Matt. 25:34.

1. Reason alone will convince every fair inquirer, that God "is a rewarder of them that diligently seek him." This alone teaches him to say, "Doubtless there is a reward for the righteous;" "there is a God that judgeth the earth." But how little information do we receive from unassisted reason touching the particulars contained in this general truth! As eye hath not seen, or ear heard, so neither could it naturally enter into our hearts to conceive the circumstances of that awful day wherein God will judge the world. No information of this kind could be given but from the great Judge himself.

---

* [text of the 1872 ed.]

And what an amazing instance of condescension it is, that the Creator, the Governor, the Lord, the Judge of all, should deign to give us so clear and particular an account of that solemn transaction! If the learned Heathen acknowledged the sublimity of that account which Moses gives of the creation, what would he have said, if he had heard this account of the Son of Man coming in his glory? Here, indeed, is no laboured pomp of words, no ornaments of language. This would not have suited either the Speaker or the occasion. But what inexpressible dignity of thought! See him "coming in the clouds of heaven; and all the angels with him!" See him "sitting on the throne of his glory, and all the nations gathered before him!" And shall he separate them, placing the good on his right hand, and the wicked on his left? "Then shall the King say:"—With what admirable propriety is the expression varied! "The Son of Man" comes down to judge the children of men. "The King" distributes rewards and punishments to his obedient or rebellious subjects:—"Then shall the King say to them on his right hand, Come, ye blessed of my Father, inherit the kingdom prepared for you from the foundation of the world."

2. "Prepared for you from the foundation of the world:"— But does this agree with the common supposition that God created man merely to supply the vacant thrones of the rebel angels? Does it not rather seem to imply, that he would have created man, though the angels had never fallen? inasmuch as he then prepared the kingdom for his human children, when he laid the foundation of the earth.

3. "Inherit the kingdom;"—as being "heirs of God, and joint heirs" with his beloved Son. It is your right; seeing I have purchased eternal redemption for all them that obey me: And ye did obey me in the days of your flesh. Ye "believed in the Father, and also in me." Ye loved the Lord your God; and that love constrained you to love all mankind. Ye continued in the faith that wrought by love. Ye showed your faith by your works. "For I was hungry, and ye gave me meat: I was thirsty, and ye gave me drink: I was a stranger, and ye took me in: Naked, and ye clothed me: I was sick, and in prison, and ye came unto me."

4. But in what sense are we to understand the words that follow? "Lord, when saw we thee hungry, and gave thee meat or thirsty, and gave thee drink?" They cannot be literally understood; they cannot answer in these very words; because it is not possible they should be ignorant that God had really wrought by them. Is it not then manifest, that these words are to be taken in a figurative sense? And can they imply any more, than that all which they have done will appear as nothing to them; will, as it were, vanish away, in view of what God their Saviour had done and suffered for them?

5. But "the King shall answer and say unto them, Verily I say unto you, Inasmuch as ye have done it to one of the least of these my brethren, ye did it unto me." What a declaration this! worthy to be had in everlasting remembrance. May the finger of the living God write it upon all our hearts! I would take occasion from hence, First, to make a few reflections on good works in general: Secondly, to consider in particular that institution for the promotion of which we are now

assembled: And, in the Third place, to make a short application.

I. 1. And, First, I would make a few reflections upon good works in general.

I am not insensible, that many, even serious people, are jealous of all that is spoken upon this subject: Nay, and whenever the necessity of good works is strongly insisted on take for granted that he who speaks in this manner is but one remove from Popery. But should we, for fear of this or of any other reproach, refrain from speaking "the truth as it is in Jesus?" Should we, on any consideration, "shun to declare the whole counsel of God?" Nay, if a false prophet could utter that solemn word, how much more may the Ministers of Christ, "We cannot go beyond the word of the Lord, to speak either more or less!"

2. Is it not to be lamented, that any who fear God should desire us to do otherwise? and that, by speaking otherwise themselves, they should occasion the way of truth to be evil spoken of? I mean, in particular, the way of salvation by faith; which, on this very account, is despised, nay, had in abomination, by many sensible men. It is now above forty years since this grand scriptural doctrine, "By grace ye are saved through faith," began to be openly declared by a few Clergymen of the Church of England. And not long after, some who heard, but did not understand, attempted to preach the same doctrine, but miserably mangled it; wresting the Scripture, and "making void the law through faith."

3. Some of these, in order to exalt the value of faith, have utterly deprecated good works. They speak of them as not only not necessary to salvation, but as greatly obstructive to it. They represent them as abundantly more dangerous than evil ones, to those who are seeking to save their souls. One cries aloud, "More people go to hell by praying, than by thieving." Another screams out, "Away with your works! Have done with your works, or you cannot come to Christ!" And this unscriptural, irrational, heathenish declamation is called, *preaching the gospel!*

4. But "shall not the Judge of all the earth" speak, as well as "do right?" Will not he "be justified in his saying, and clear when he is judged?" Assuredly he will. And upon his authority we must continue to declare, that whenever you do good to any for his sake; when you feed the hungry, give drink to the thirsty; when you assist the stranger, or clothe the naked; when you visit them that are sick or in prison; these are not *splendid sins*, as one marvellously calls them, but "sacrifices wherewith God is well pleased."

5. Not that our Lord intended we should confine our beneficence to the bodies of men. He undoubtedly designed that we should be equally abundant in works of spiritual mercy. He died "to purify unto himself a peculiar people, zealous of" *all* "good works;" zealous, above all, to "save souls from death," and thereby "hide a multitude of sins." And this is unquestionably included in St. Paul's exhortation: "As we have time, let us do good unto all men;" good in every possible kind, as well as in every possible degree. But why does not our blessed Lord mention works of spiritual mercy? He could not do it with any propriety. It was not for him to say, "I was in error, and ye convinced me; I was in sin, and

you brought me back to God." And it needed not; for in mentioning *some* he included *all* works of mercy.

6. But may I not add one thing more? (only he that heareth, let him understand:) Good works are so far from being hindrances of our salvation; they are so far from being insignificant, from being of no account in Christianity; that, supposing them to spring from a right principle, they are the perfection of religion. They are the highest part of that spiritual building whereof Jesus Christ is the foundation. To those who attentively consider the thirteenth chapter of the First Epistle to the Corinthians, it will be undeniably plain that what St. Paul there describes as the highest of all Christian graces, is properly and directly the love of our neighbour [1 Cor. 13]. And to him who attentively considers the whole tenor both of the Old and New Testament, it will be equally plain, that works springing from this love are the highest part of the religion therein revealed. Of these our Lord himself says, "Hereby is my Father glorified, that ye bring forth much fruit." Much *fruit!* Does not the very expression imply the excellency of what is so termed? Is not the tree itself for the sake of the fruit? By bearing fruit, and by this alone, it attains the highest perfection it is capable of, and answers the end for which it was planted. Who, what is he then, that is called a Christian, and can speak lightly of good works?

II. 1. From these general reflections, I proceed to consider that institution in particular, for the promotion of which we are now assembled. And in doing this, I shall, First, observe the rise of this institution; Secondly, the success; and, Thirdly, the excellency of it: After which you will give me leave to make a short application.

(I.) On the First head, the rise of this institution, I may be very brief, as a great part of you know it already.

1. One would wonder (as an ingenious writer observes) that such an institution as this, of so deep importance to mankind, should appear so late in the world. Have we anything wrote upon the subject, earlier than the tract published at Rome in the year 1637? And did not the proposal then sleep for many years? Were there any more than one or two attempts, and those not effectually pursued, till the year 1700? By what steps it has been since revived and carried into execution, we are now to inquire.

2. I cannot give you a clearer view of this, than by presenting you with a short extract from the Introduction to the "Plan and Reports of the Society," published two years ago:—

"Many and indubitable are the instances of the possibility of restoring to life persons apparently struck with sudden death, whether by an apoplexy, convulsive fits, noxious vapours, strangling, or drowning. Cases of this nature have occurred in every country. But they were considered, and *neglected,* as extraordinary phenomena from which no salutary consequence could be drawn.

3. "At length, a few benevolent gentlemen in Holland conjectured, that some at least might have been saved, had proper means been used in time; and formed themselves into a Society, in order to make a trial. Their attempts succeeded far beyond their expectations. Many were restored who must otherwise have perished. And they were, at length, enabled to extend their plan over the Seven Provinces.

"Their success instigated other countries to follow their example. In the year 1768, the Magistrates of Health at Milan and Venice issued orders for the treatment of drowned persons. The city of Hamburgh appointed a similar ordinance to be read in all the churches. In the year 1769, the Empress of Germany published an edict, extending its directions and encouragements to every case that afforded a possibility of relief. In the year 1771, the Magistrates of Paris founded an institution in favour of the drowned.

4. "In the year 1773, Dr. Cogan translated the 'Memoirs of the Society at Amsterdam,' in order to inform our countrymen of the practicability of recovering persons apparently drowned; And Mr. Hawes uniting with him, these gentlemen proposed a plan for a similar institution in these kingdoms. They were soon enabled to form a Society for this excellent purpose. The plan is this:—

"I. The Society will publish, in the most extensive manner possible, the proper methods of treating persons in such circumstances.

"II. They will distribute a premium of two guineas among the first persons who attempt to recover anyone taken out of the water as dead. And this reward will be given, even if the attempt is unsuccessful, provided it has been pursued two hours, according to the method laid down by the Society.

"III. They will distribute a premium of four guineas, where the person is restored to life.

"IV. They will give one guinea to any that admits the body into his house without delay, and furnishes the necessary accommodations.

"V. A number of medical gentlemen, living near the places where these disasters commonly happen, will give their assistance gratis."

(II.) Such was the rise of this admirable institution. With what success it has been attended, is the point which I purpose, in the next place, very briefly to consider.

And it must be allowed to be not only far greater than those who despised it had imagined, but greater than the most sanguine expectations of the gentlemen who were immediately engaged in it.

In the short space, from its first establishment in May, 1774, to the end of December, eight persons, seemingly dead, were restored to life.

In the year 1775, forty-seven were restored to life: Thirty-two of them, by the direct encouragement and assistance of the gentlemen of this Society; and the rest, by medical gentlemen and others, in consequence of their method of treatment being generally known.

In the year 1776, forty-one persons were restored to life by the assistance of this Society. And eleven cases of those who had been restored elsewhere were communicated to them.

So the number of lives preserved and restored, in two years and a half, since their first institution, amounts to one hundred and seven! Add to these those that have been since restored; and out of two hundred and eighty-four persons, who were dead, to all appearance, no less than an hundred and fifty-seven have been restored to life. Such is the *success* which has attended them in so short a time! Such a blessing has the gracious providence of God given to this infant undertaking!

(III). 1. It remains only to show the excellency of it. And this may appear from one single consideration: This institution unites together in one all the various acts of mercy. The several works of charity mentioned above are all contained in this. It comprises all corporeal (if I may so speak) and all spiritual benefits; all the instances of kindness which can be shown either to the bodies or souls of men. To show this beyond all contradiction, there needs no studied eloquence, no rhetorical colouring, but simply and nakedly to relate the thing as it is.

2. The thing attempted, and not only attempted, but actually performed, (so has the goodness of God prospered the labours of these lovers of mankind!) is no less, in a qualified sense, than restoring life to the dead. Is it any wonder, then, that the generality of men should at first ridicule such an undertaking? that they should imagine the persons who aimed at any such thing must be utterly out of their senses? Indeed, one of old said, "Why should it be thought a thing incredible with you, that God should raise the dead?" Cannot He, who bestowed life at first, just as well bestow it again? But it may well be thought a thing incredible, that *man* should raise the dead; for no human power can create life. And what human power can restore it? Accordingly, when our Lord (whom the Jews at that time supposed to be a mere man) came to the house of Jairus, in order to raise his daughter from the dead, upon the first intimation of his design, "they laughed him to scorn." "The maid," said he, "is not dead, but sleepeth." "This is rather to be called sleep than death; seeing her life is not at an end; but I will quickly awaken her out of this sleep."

3. However, it is certain, she was really dead, and so beyond all power but that of the Almighty. But see what power God has now given to man! To his name be all the praise! See with what wisdom he has endued these sons of mercy! teaching them to stop the parting soul, to arrest the spirit just quitting the breathless clay, and taking wing for eternity! Who hath seen such a thing? Who hath heard such things? Who hath read them in the annals of antiquity? Sons of men, "can these dry bones live?" Can this motionless heart beat again? Can this clotted blood flow any more? Can these dry, stiff vessels open to give it passage? Can this cold flesh resume its native warmth, or those eyes again see the sun? Surely these are such things (might one not almost say, such miracles?) as neither we, of the present generation, nor our fathers had known!

4. Consider, I entreat you, how many miracles of mercy (so to speak) are contained in one! That poor man, who was lately numbered with the dead, by the care and pains of these messengers of God, again breathes the vital air, opens his eyes, and stands up upon his feet. He is restored to his rejoicing family, to his wife, to his (late) helpless children, that he may again, by his honest labour, provide them with all the necessaries of life. See now what ye have done, ye ministers of mercy! Behold the fruit of your labour of love! Ye have been an husband to the widow, a father to the fatherless. And hereby ye have given meat to the hungry, drink to the thirsty, clothes to the naked: For hungry, thirsty, and naked these little ones must have been, had not you restored him that prevents it. You have more than relieved, you have prevented, that sickness which might naturally have arisen from their want of sufficient food to eat, or raiment to put on. You have hindered those orphans from wandering up and down, not having a place where to lay their head. Nay, and very possibly you have prevented some of them from being lodged in a dreary, comfortless prison.

5. So great, so comprehensive is the mercy which you have shown to the bodies of your fellow-creatures! But why should their souls be left out of the account? How great are the benefits you have conferred on these also! The husband has now again an opportunity of assisting his wife in things of the greatest moment. He may now again strengthen her hands in God, and help her to run with patience the race that is set before her. He may again join with her in instructing their children, and training them up in the way wherein they should go; who may live to be a comfort to their aged parents, and useful members of the community.

6. Nay, it may be, you have snatched the poor man himself, not only from the jaws of death, but from sinking lower than the waters, from the jaws of everlasting destruction. It cannot be doubted, but some of those whose lives you have restored, although they had been before without God in the world, will remember themselves, and not only with their lips, but in their lives, show forth his praise. It is highly probable, some of these (as *one* out of *ten lepers*) "will return and give thanks to God," real, lasting thanks, by devoting themselves to his honourable service.

7. It is remarkable, that several of those whom you have brought back from the margin of the grave, were intoxicated at the very time when they dropped into the water. And at that very instant (which is frequently the case) they totally lost their senses. Here therefore was no place for, no possibility of, repentance. They had not time, they had not sense, so much as to cry out, "Lord, have mercy!" So they were sinking through the mighty waters into the pit of destruction! And these instruments of divine mercy plucked them at once out of the water, and out of the fire; by the same act, delivered them from temporal and from eternal death!

8. Nay, one poor sinner (let it never be forgotten!) was just coming down from the ship, when (overtaken by the justice and mercy of God) her foot slipped, and she fell into the river. Instantly her senses were lost, so that she could not call upon God. Yet he had not forgotten her. He sent those who delivered her from death; at least from the death of the body. And who knows but she may lay it to heart, and turn from the error of her ways? Who knows, but she may be saved from the second death, and, with her deliverers, "inherit the kingdom?"

9. One point more deserves to be particularly remarked. Many of those who have been restored to life (no less than eleven out of the fourteen that were saved in a few months) were in the number of those that are a reproach to our nation,—wilful self murderers. As many of the desperate men who attempt this horrid crime are men who have had a liberal education, it is pity but they would consider those fine words,

not of a poor narrow-souled Christian, but of a generous Heathen, nay, a Roman! Let them calmly consider that beautiful passage:—

> Proxima deinde tenent maesti loca, qui sibi letum
> Insontes peperere manu, lucemque perosi
> Projecere animas. Quam vellent aethere in alto
> Nunc et pauperiem, et duros perferre labores!
> Fata obstant, tristique palus inamabilis unda
> Alligat, et novies Styx interfusa coercet.
> [Then crowds succeed, who, prodigal of breath,
> Themselves anticipate the doom of death;
> Though free from guild, they cast their lives away,
> And sad and sullen hate the golden day.
> O with what joy the wretches now would bear
> Pain, toil, and woe, to breathe the vital air!
> In vain! By fate for ever are they bound
> With dire Avernus, and the lake profound;
> And Styx, with nine wide channels, roars around!
> Mr. Pitt's Virgil.]

Fata obstant! But in favour of many, we see God has overruled fate. They are brought back over the unnavigable river. They do behold the upper skies. They see the light of the sun. O let them see the light of Thy countenance! And let them so live their few remaining days on earth, that they may live with Thee for ever!

III. 1. Permit me now to make a short application. But to whom should I direct this? Are there any here who are unhappily prejudiced against that Revelation which breathes nothing but benevolence; which contains the richest display of God's love to man, that ever was made from the foundation of the world? Yet even to *you* I would address a few words; for, if you are not Christians, you are men. You too are susceptible of kind impressions: You have the feelings of humanity. Has not your heart too glowed at that noble sentiment; worthy the heart and the lips of the highest Christian,—

> Homo sum: Humani nihil a me alienum puto!
> [This quotation from Terence is thus translated by Colman:—
> "I am a man; and all calamities
> That touch humanity come home to me."—Edit.]

Have not you also sympathized with the afflicted? How many times have you been pained at human misery? When you have beheld a scene of deep distress, has not your soul melted within you?

> And now and then a sigh you stole,
> And tears began to flow.

But is it easy for anyone to conceive a scene of deeper distress than this? Suppose you are standing by, just when the messenger comes in, and the message is delivered, "I am sorry to tell you, but you must know it; your husband is no more! He was making haste out of the vessel, and his foot slipped. It is true, after a time, his body was found; but there it lies, without any signs of life." In what a condition are now both the mother and the children! Perhaps, for a while, stupid, overwhelmed, silent; staring at each other; then bursting out into loud and bitter lamentation! Now is the time to help them, by assisting those who make it their business so to do. Now let nothing hinder you from improving the glorious opportunity! Restore the husband to his disconsolate wife, the father to his weeping children! It is true, you cannot do this in person; you cannot be upon the spot. But you may do it in an effectual manner by assisting those that are. You may now, by your generous contribution, *send* them the help which you cannot personally give. O shut not up your bowels of compassion towards them! Now open your hearts and your hands! If you have much, give plenteously; if not, give a little, with a willing mind.

2. To you who believe the Christian Revelation, I may speak in a still stronger manner. You believe, your blessed Master "left you an example, that you might tread in his steps." Now, you know his whole life was one labour of love. You know "how he went about doing good," and that without intermission; declaring to all, "My Father worketh hitherto, and I work." Is not that, then, the language of your heart?—

> Thy mind throughout my life be shown,
> While list'ning to the wretches' cry,
> The widows' and the orphans' groan,
> On mercy's wings I swiftly fly,
> The poor and helpless to relieve,
> My life, my all, for them to give.

Occasions of doing this can never be wanting; for "the poor ye have always with you." But what a peculiar opportunity does the solemnity of this day furnish you with, of "treading in his steps," after a manner which you did not before conceive? Did he say to the poor afflicted parent, (doubtless to the surprise of many,) "Weep not?" And did he surprise them still more, when he stopped her flowing tears by restoring life to her dead son, and "delivering him to his mother?" Did he (notwithstanding all that "laughed him to scorn") restore to life the daughter of Jairus? How many things of a nearly resembling sort, "if human we may liken to divine," have been done, and continue to be done daily, by these lovers of mankind! Let every one then be ambitious of having a share in this glorious work! Let every one (in a stronger sense than Mr. Herbert meant)

> Join hands with God, to make a poor man live!

By your generous assistance, be ye partakers of their work, and partakers of their joy.

3. To you I need add but one word more. Remember (what was spoken at first) the solemn declaration of Him whose ye are, and whom ye serve, coming in the clouds of heaven! While you are promoting this comprehensive charity, which contains feeding the hungry, clothing the naked, lodging the stranger; indeed all good works in one; let those animating words be written on your hearts, and sounding in your ears: "Inasmuch as ye have done it unto one of the least of these, ye have done it unto ME."

100.* ON PLEASING ALL MEN

"Let every man please his neighbour for his good to edification."

Rom. 15:2.

1. Undoubtedly the duty here prescribed is incumbent on all mankind; at least on every one of those to whom are entrusted the oracles of God. For it is here enjoined to everyone without exception that names the name of Christ. And the person whom everyone is commanded to please, is *his neighbour*, that is, every child of man. Only we are to remember here what the same Apostle speaks upon a similar occasion. "If it be possible, as much as lieth in you, live peaceably with all men." In like manner we are to please all men, if it be possible, as much as lieth in us. But strictly speaking it is not possible; it is what no man ever did, nor ever will perform. But suppose we use our utmost diligence, be the event as it may, we fulfill our duty.

2. We may farther observe in how admirable a manner the Apostle limits this direction; otherwise, were it pursued without any limitation, it might produce the most mischievous consequences. We are directed to please them *for their good*; not barely for the sake of pleasing them, or pleasing ourselves; much less of pleasing them to their hurt; which is so frequently done, indeed continually done, by those who do not love their neighbour as themselves. Nor is it only their temporal good, which we are to aim at in pleasing our neighbour; but what is of infinitely greater consequence, we are to do it *for their edification*; in such a manner as may conduce to their spiritual and eternal good. We are so to please them, that the pleasure may not perish in the using, but may redound to their lasting advantage; may make them wiser and better, holier and happier, both in time and in eternity.

3. Many are the treatises and discourses which have been published on this important subject. But all of them that I have either seen or heard were miserably defective. Hardly one of them proposed the right end: One and all had some lower design in pleasing men than to save their souls,—to build them up in love and holiness. Of consequence, they were not likely to propose the right means for the attainment of that end. One celebrated tract of this kind, entitled "The Courtier," was published in Spain about two hundred years ago, and translated into various languages. But it has nothing to do with edification, and is therefore quite wide of the mark. Another treatise, entitled "The Refined [Complete] Courtier," was published in our own country, in the reign of King Charles the Second, and, as it seems, by a retainer to his court. In this there are several very sensible advices concerning our outward behaviour; and many little improprieties in word or action are observed, whereby men displease others without intending it; but this author, likewise, has no view at all to the spiritual or eternal good of his neighbour. Seventy or eighty years ago, another book was printed in London, entitled "The Art of Pleasing." But as it was wrote in a languid manner and contained only common, trite observations, it was not likely to be of use to men of understanding, and still less to men of piety.

4. But it may be asked, Has not the subject been since treated of by a writer of a very different character? Is it not exhausted by one who was himself a consummate master of the art of pleasing? And who writing to one he tenderly loved, to a favourite son, gives him all the advice which his great understanding, improved by various learning, and the experience of many years, and much converse with all sorts of men, could suggest? I mean, the late Lord Chesterfield; the general darling of all the Irish, as well as the English nation.

5. The means of pleasing which this wise and indulgent parent continually and earnestly recommends to his darling child, and on which he doubtless formed both his tempers and outward conduct,

> Till death untimely stopped his tuneful tongue,—

were, First, *making love*, in the grossest sense, to all the married women whom he conveniently could. (Single women he advises him to refrain from, for fear of disagreeable consequences). Secondly. Constant and careful *dissimulation*; always wearing a mask; trusting no man upon earth, so as to let him know his real thoughts, but perpetually seeming to mean what he did not mean, and seeming to be what he was not. Thirdly. Well-devised *lying* to all sorts of people; speaking what was farthest from his heart; and in particular, *flattering* men, women, and children, as the infallible way of pleasing them.

It needs no great art to show, that this is not the way to please our neighbour *for his good*, or *to edification*. I shall endeavour to show, that there is a better way of doing it; and indeed a way diametrically opposite to this. It consists,

I. In removing hindrances out of the way; and
II. In using the means that directly tend to this end.

I. 1. I advise all that desire to "please their neighbour for his good to edification," First, to remove all hindrances out of the way; or, in other words, to avoid everything which tends to displease wise and good men, men of sound understanding and real piety. Now "cruelty, malice, envy, hatred, and revenge" are displeasing to all good men, to all who are endued with sound understanding and genuine piety. There is likewise another temper related to these, only in a lower kind, and which is usually found in common life, wherewith men in general are not pleased. We commonly call it *ill-nature*. With all possible care avoid all these; nay, and whatever bears any resemblance to them,—as sourness, sternness, sullenness, on the one hand; peevishness and fretfulness, on the other,—if ever you hope to "please your neighbour for his good to edification."

2. Next to cruelty, malice, and similar tempers, with the words and actions that naturally spring therefrom, nothing is more disgusting, not only to persons of sense and religion, but even to the generality of men, than pride, haughtiness of spirit, and its genuine fruit, an *assuming, arrogant, overbearing* behaviour. Even uncommon learning, joined with shining talents, will not make amends for this; but a man of eminent endowments, if he be eminently haughty, will be despised by many, and disliked by all. Of this the famous Master of Trinity College in Cambridge, was a remarkable instance. How few persons of his time had a stronger understanding, or deeper learning, than Dr. Bentley! And yet how few were less beloved! unless one who was little, if at all, inferior to him in sense or learning, and equally distant from humility,—the author of "The Divine Legation of Moses." Whoever, therefore, desires to please his

neighbour for his good, must take care of splitting upon this rock. Otherwise the same pride which impels him to seek the esteem of his neighbour, will infallibly hinder his attaining it. 3. Almost as disgustful to the generality of men as haughtiness itself, is a passionate temper and behaviour. Men of a tender disposition are afraid even to converse with persons of this spirit. And others are not fond of their acquaintance; as frequently (perhaps when they expected nothing less) meeting with shocks, which if they bear for the present, yet they do not willingly put themselves in the way of meeting with again. Hence passionate men have seldom many friends; at least, not for any length of time. Crowds, indeed, may attend them for a season, especially when it may promote their interest. But they are usually disgusted one after another, and fall off like leaves in autumn. If therefore you desire lastingly to please your neighbour for his good, by all possible means avoid violent passion.

4. Yea, and if you desire to please, even on this account, take that advice of the Apostle, "Put away all lying." It is the remark of an ingenious author, that, of all vices, *lying* never yet found an apologist, any that would openly plead in its favour, whatever his private sentiments might be. But it should be remembered, Mr. Addison went to a better world before Lord Chesterfield's Letters were published. Perhaps his apology for it was the best that ever was or can be made for so bad a cause. But, after all, the labour he has bestowed thereon, it has only "semblance of worth, not substance." It has no solidity in it; it is nothing better than a shining phantom. And as lying can never be commendable or innocent, so neither can it be pleasing; at least when it is stripped of its disguise, and appears in its own shape. Consequently, it ought to be carefully avoided by all those who wish to please their neighbour for his good to edification.

5. "But is not flattery," a man may say, "one species of lying? And has not this been allowed in all ages to be the sure means of pleasing? Has not that observation been confirmed by numerous experiments,—

> Obsequium amicos, veritas odium parat?
>
> Flattery creates friends, plain-dealing enemies?

Has not a late witty [prominent] writer, in his 'Sentimental Journal,' related some striking instances of this?" I answer, It is true: Flattery is pleasing for a while. and not only to weak minds, as the desire of praise, whether deserved or undeserved, is planted in every child of man. But it is pleasing only for a while. As soon as the mask drops off, as soon as it appears that the speaker meant nothing by his soft words, we are pleased no longer. Every man's own experience teaches him this. And we all know, that if a man continues to flatter, after his insincerity is discovered, it is disgustful, not agreeable. Therefore, even this fashionable species of lying is to be avoided, by all that are desirous of pleasing their neighbour to his lasting advantage.

6. Nay, whoever desires to do this must remember, that not only lying, in every species of it, but even dissimulation, (which is not the same with flattery, though nearly related to it,) is displeasing to men of understanding, though they have not religion. Terence represents even an old heathen, when it was imputed to him, as answering with indignation, *Simulare non est meum*: "Dissimulation is no part of my character." Guile, subtlety, cunning, the whole art of deceiving, by whatever terms it is expressed, is not accounted an accomplishment by wise men, but is, indeed, an abomination to them. And even those who practise it most, who are the greatest artificers of fraud, are not pleased with it in other men, neither are fond of conversing with those that practise it on themselves. Yea, the greatest deceivers are greatly displeased at those that play their own arts back upon them. II. Now, if cruelty, malice, envy, hatred, revenge, ill-nature; if pride and haughtiness; if irrational anger; if lying and dissimulation, together with guile, subtlety, and cunning, are all and every one displeasing to all men, especially to wise and good men, we may easily gather from hence what is the sure way to please them for their good to edification. Only we are to remember that there are those in every time and place whom we must not expect to please. We must not therefore be surprised when we meet with men who are not to be pleased any way. It is now, as it was of old when our Lord himself complained: "Whereunto shall I liken the men of this generation? They are like unto children sitting in the market-place, and saying to each other, We have piped unto you, but ye have not danced: We have mourned unto you, but ye have not wept." But leaving these forward ones to themselves, we may reasonably hope to please others by a careful and steady observation of the few directions following.

1. First. Let *love* not visit you as a transient guest, but be the constant ruling temper of your soul. See that your heart be filled at all times and on all occasions with real, undissembled benevolence; not to those only that love *you*, but to every soul of man. Let it pant in your heart; let it sparkle in your eyes, let it shine on all your actions. Whenever you open your lips, let it be with love; and let there be in your tongue the law of kindness. Your word will then distil as the rain, and as the dew upon the tender herb. Be not straitened or limited in your affection, but let it embrace every child of man. Everyone that is born of a woman has a claim to your good-will. You owe this, not to some, but to all. And let all men know that you desire both their temporal and eternal happiness, as sincerely as you do your own.

2. Secondly. If you would please your neighbour for his good, study to be *lowly* in heart. Be little and vile in your own eyes, in honour preferring others before yourself. Be deeply sensible of your own weaknesses, follies, and imperfections; as well as of the sin remaining in your heart, and cleaving to all your words and actions. And let this spirit appear in all you speak or do: "Be clothed with humility." Reject with horror that favourite maxim of the old heathen, sprung from the bottomless pit, *Tanti eris aliis, quanti tibi fueris*: "The more you value yourself, the more others will value you." Not so. On the contrary, both God and man "resist the proud:" And, as "God giveth grace to the humble," so humility, not pride, recommends us to the esteem and favour of men, especially those that fear God.

3. If you desire to please your neighbour for his good to edification you should, Thirdly, labour and pray that you may be *meek* as well as lowly in heart. Labour to be of a calm,

dispassionate temper; gentle towards all men; and let the gentleness of your disposition appear in the whole tenor of your conversation. Let all your words and all your actions be regulated thereby. Remember, likewise that advice of St. Peter: As an addition to your gentleness, be merciful; "be courteous;" be pitiful; be tenderly compassionate to all that are in distress; to all that are under any affliction of mind, body, or estate. Let

> The various scenes of human woe
> Excite your softest sympathy!

Weep with them that weep. If you can do no more, at least mix your tears with theirs; and give them healing words, such as may calm their minds, and mitigate their sorrows. But if you can, if you are able to give them actual assistance, let it not be wanting. Be as eyes to the blind, as feet to the lame, a husband to the widow and a father to the fatherless. This will greatly tend to conciliate the affection, and to give a profitable pleasure not only to those who are immediate objects of your compassion, but to others likewise that "see your good works, and glorify your Father which is in heaven."

4. And while you are pitiful to the afflicted, see that you are *courteous* toward all men. It matters not in this respect whether they are high or low, rich or poor, superior or inferior to you. No, nor even whether good or bad, whether they fear God or not. Indeed, the *mode* of showing your courtesy may vary, as Christian prudence will direct; but the thing itself is due to all; the lowest and worst have a claim to our courtesy. [But what is courtesy?] It may either be inward or outward; either a temper or a mode of behaviour. Such a mode of behaviour as naturally springs from courtesy of heart. Is this the same with good breeding, or politeness? (which seems to be only a high degree of good-breeding:) Nay, good breeding is chiefly the fruit of education; but education cannot give courtesy of heart. Mr. Addison's well-known definition of politeness seems rather to be a definition of this: "A constant desire of pleasing all men, appearing through the whole conversation." Now, this may subsist, even in a high degree, where there has been no advantage of education. I have seen as real courtesy in an Irish cabin, as could be found in St. James's or the Louvre.

5. Shall we endeavour to go a little deeper, to search into the foundation of this matter? What is the source of that desire to please which we term courtesy? Let us look attentively into our heart, and we shall soon find the answer. The same Apostle that teaches us to *be courteous*, teaches us to *honour all men*; and his Master teaches me to love all men. Join these together, and what will be the effect? A poor wretch cries to me for an alms: I look and see him covered with dirt and rags. But through these I see one that has an immortal spirit, made to know and love and dwell with God to eternity. I honour him for his Creator's sake. Lo, I see through all these rags that he is purpled over with the blood of Christ. I love him for the sake of his Redeemer. The courtesy, therefore, which I feel and show toward him is a mixture of the honour and love which I bear to the offspring of God; the purchase of his Son's blood, and the candidate for immortality This courtesy let us feel and show toward all men; and we shall please all men to their edification.

6. Once more. Take all proper opportunities of *declaring* to others the *affection* which you really feel for them. This may be done with such an air, and in such a manner, as is not liable to the imputation of flattery: And experience shows, that honest men are pleased by this, full as much as knaves are by flattery. Those who are persuaded that your expressions of good-will toward them are the language of your heart will be as well satisfied with them, as with the highest encomiums which you could pass upon them. You may judge them by yourselves, by what you feel in your own breast. You like to be honoured; but had you not rather be beloved?

7. Permit me to add one advice more. If you would please all men for their good, at all events speak to all men the very truth from your heart. When you speak, open the window of your breast: let the words be the very picture of your heart. In all company, and on all occasions, be a man of veracity. Nay, be not content with bare veracity; but "in simplicity and godly sincerity have all your conversation in the world," as "an Israelite indeed, in whom is no guile."

8. To sum up all in one word-if you would please men, please God! Let truth and love possess your whole soul. Let them be the springs of all your affections, passions, tempers; the rule of all your thoughts. Let them inspire all your discourse; continually seasoned with that salt, and meet to "minister grace to the hearers." Let all your actions be wrought in love. Never "let mercy or truth forsake thee: Bind them about thy neck." Let them be open and conspicuous to all; and "write them on the table of thy heart." "So shalt thou find favour and good understanding in the sight of God and man."

101.* THE DUTY OF CONSTANT COMMUNION* J.W.

"Do this in remembrance of me."

Luke 22:19.

It is no wonder that men who have no fear of God should never think of doing this. But it is strange that it should be neglected by any that do fear God, and desire to save their souls; And yet nothing is more common. One reason why many neglect it is, they are so much afraid of "eating and drinking unworthily," that they never think how much greater the danger is when they do not eat or drink it at all. That I may do what I can to bring these well-meaning men to a more just way of thinking, I shall,

I. show that it is the duty of every Christian to receive the Lord's Supper as often as he can; and,

II. Answer some objections.

I. I am to show that it is the duty of every Christian to receive the Lord's Supper as often as he can.

1. The First reason why it is the duty of every Christian so to do is, because it is a plain command of Christ. That this is his command, appears from the words of the text, "Do this

---

* [text of the 1872 ed.]

in remembrance of me:" By which, as the Apostles were obliged to bless, break, and give the bread to all that joined with them in holy things; so were all Christians obliged to receive those sign of Christ's body and blood. Here, therefore, the bread and wine are commanded to be received, in remembrance of his death, to the end of the world. Observe, too, that this command was given by our Lord when he was just laying down his life for our sakes. They are, therefore, as it were, his dying words to all his followers.

2. A Second reason why every Christian should do this as often as he can, is, because the benefits of doing it are so great to all that do it in obedience to him; viz., the forgiveness of our past sins and the present strengthening and refreshing of our souls. In this world we are never free from temptations. Whatever way of life we are in, whatever our condition be, whether we are sick or well, in trouble or at ease, the enemies of our souls are watching to lead us into sin. And too often they prevail over us. Now, when we are convinced of having sinned against God, what surer way have we of procuring pardon from him, than the "showing forth the Lord's death;" and beseeching him, for the sake of his Son's sufferings, to blot out all our sins?

3. The grace of God given herein confirms to us the pardon of our sins, by enabling us to leave them. As our bodies are strengthened by bread and wine, so are our souls by these tokens of the body and blood of Christ. This is the food of our souls: This gives strength to perform our duty, and leads us on to perfection. If, therefore, we have any regard for the plain command of Christ, if we desire the pardon of our sins, if we wish for strength to believe, to love and obey God, then we should neglect no opportunity of receiving the Lord's Supper; then we must never turn our backs on the feast which our Lord has prepared for us. We must neglect no occasion which the good providence of God affords us for this purpose. This is the true rule: So often are we to receive as God gives us opportunity. Whoever, therefore, does not receive, but goes from the holy table, when all things are prepared, either does not understand his duty, or does not care for the dying command of his Saviour, the forgiveness of his sins, the strengthening of his soul, and the refreshing it with the hope of glory.

4. Let every one, therefore, who has either any desire to please God, or any love of his own soul, obey God, and consult the good of his own soul, by communicating every time he can; like the first Christians, with whom the Christian sacrifice was a constant part of the Lord's day service. And for several centuries they received it almost every day: Four times a week always, and every saint's day beside. Accordingly, those that joined in the prayers of the faithful never failed to partake of the blessed sacrament. What opinion they had of any who turned his back upon it, we may learn from that ancient canon: "If any believer join in the prayers of the faithful, and go away without receiving the Lord's Supper, let him be excommunicated, as bringing confusion into the church of God."

5. In order to understand the nature of the Lord's Supper, it would be useful carefully to read over those passages in the Gospel, and in the first Epistle to the Corinthians [1 Cor. 11], which speak of the institution of it. Hence we learn that the design of this sacrament is, the continual remembrance of the death of Christ, by eating bread and drinking wine, which are the outward signs of the inward grace, the body and blood of Christ.

6. It is highly expedient for those who purpose to receive this, whenever their time will permit, to prepare themselves for this solemn ordinance by self-examination and prayer. But this is not absolutely necessary. And when we have not time for it, we should see that we have the habitual preparation which is absolutely necessary, and can never be dispensed with on any account or any occasion whatever. This is, First, a full *purpose* of heart to keep all the commandments of God; and, Secondly, a sincere *desire* to receive all his promises.

II. I am, in the Second place, to answer the common objections against constantly receiving the Lord's Supper.

1. I say *constantly* receiving; for as to the phrase of *frequent* communion, it is absurd to the last degree. If it means anything less than constant, it means more than can be proved to be the duty of any man. For if we are not obliged to communicate constantly, by what argument can it be proved that we are obliged to communicate frequently? yea, more than once a year, or once in seven years, or once before we die? Every argument brought for this, either proves that we ought to do it constantly, or proves nothing at all. Therefore, that indeterminate, unmeaning way of speaking ought to be laid aside by all men of understanding.

2. In order to prove that it is our duty to communicate constantly, we may observe that the holy communion is to be considered either, (1.), as a command of God, or, (2.) As a mercy to man.

First. As a command of God. God our Mediator and Governor, from whom we have received our life and all things, on whose will it depends whether we shall be perfectly happy or perfectly miserable from this moment to eternity, declares to us that all who obey his commands shall be eternally happy; all who not, shall be eternally miserable. Now, one of these commands is, "Do this in remembrance of me." I ask then, Why do you not do this, when you can do it if you will? When you have an opportunity before you, why do not you obey the command of God?

3. Perhaps you will say, "God does not command me to do this *as often as I can.*" That is, the words "as often as you can," are not added in this particular place. What then? Are we not to obey every command of God as often as we can? Are not all the promises of God made to those, and those only, who "give all diligence;" that is, to those who do all they can to obey his commandments? Our power is the one rule of our duty. Whatever we can do, that we ought. With respect either to this or any other command, he that, when he may obey it if he will, does not, will have no place in the kingdom of heaven.

4. And this great truth, that we are obliged to keep every command as far as we can, is clearly proved from the absurdity of the contrary opinion; for were we to allow that we are not obliged to obey every commandment of God as often as we can, we have no argument left to prove that any man is bound to obey any command at any time. For

instance: Should I ask a man why he does not obey one of the plainest commands of God, why, for instance, he does not help his parents, he might answer, "I will not do it now, but I will at another time." When that time comes, put him in mind of God's command again; and he will say, "I will obey it some time or other." Nor is it possible ever to prove that he ought to do it now, unless by proving that he ought to do it as often as he can; and therefore he ought to do it now, because he can if he will.

5. Consider the Lord's Supper, Secondly, as a mercy from God to man. As God, whose mercy is over all his works, and particularly over the children of men, knew there was but one way for man to be happy like himself; namely, by being like him in holiness; as he knew we could do nothing toward this of ourselves, he has given us certain means of obtaining his help. One of these is the Lord's Supper, which, of his infinite mercy, he hath given for this very end; that through this means we may be assisted to attain those blessings which he hath prepared for us; that we may obtain holiness on earth, and everlasting glory in heaven.

I ask, then, Why do you not accept of his mercy as often as ever you can? God now offers you his blessing;—why do you refuse it? You have now an opportunity of receiving his mercy;—why do you not receive it? You are weak:—why do not you seize every opportunity of increasing your strength? In a word: Considering this as a command of God, he that does not communicate as often as he can has no piety; considering it as a mercy, he that does not communicate as often as he can has no wisdom.

6. These two considerations will yield a full answer to all the common objections which have been made against constant communion; indeed to all that ever were or can be made. In truth, nothing can be objected against it, but upon supposition that, [at] this particular time, either the communion would be no mercy, or I am not commanded to receive it. Nay, should we grant it would be no mercy, that is not enough; for still the other reason would hold: Whether it does you any good or none, you are to obey the command of God.

7. However, let us see the particular excuses which men commonly make for not obeying it. The most common is, "I am unworthy; and 'he that eateth and drinketh unworthily, eateth and drinketh damnation to himself.' Therefore I dare not communicate, lest I should eat and drink my own damnation."

The case is this: God offers you one of the greatest mercies on this side heaven, and commands you to accept it. Why do not you accept this mercy, in obedience to his command? You say, "I am unworthy to receive it." And what then? You are unworthy to receive any mercy from God. But is that a reason for refusing all mercy? God offers you a pardon for all your sins. You are unworthy of it, it is sure, and he knows it; but since he is pleased to offer it nevertheless, will not you accept of it? He offers to deliver your soul from death: You are unworthy to live; but will you therefore refuse life? He offers to endue your soul with new strength; because you are unworthy of it, will you deny to take it? What can God

himself do for us farther, if we refuse his mercy because we are unworthy of it?

8. But suppose this were no mercy to us; (to suppose which is indeed giving God the lie; saying, that is not good for man which he purposely ordered for his good;) still I ask, Why do not you obey God's command? He says, "Do this." Why do you not? You answer, "I am unworthy to do it." What! Unworthy to obey God? Unworthy to do what God bids you do? Unworthy to obey God's command? What do you mean by this? that those who are unworthy to obey God ought not to obey him? Who told you so? If he were even "an angel from heaven, let him be accursed." If you think God himself has told you so by St. Paul, let us hear his words. They are these: "He that eateth and drinketh unworthily, eateth and drinketh damnation to himself."

Why, this is quite another thing. Here is not a word said of being unworthy to eat and drink. Indeed he does speak of eating and drinking unworthily; but that is quite a different thing; so he has told us himself. In this very chapter we are told that by eating and drinking unworthily is meant, taking the holy sacrament in such a rude and disorderly way, that one was "hungry and another drunken." But what is that to *you?* Is there any danger of *your* doing so,—of your eating and drinking *thus unworthily?* However unworthy you are to communicate, there is no fear of your communicating thus. Therefore, whatever the punishment is, of doing it thus unworthily, it does not concern *you.* You have no more reason from this text to disobey God, than if there was no such text in the Bible. If you speak of "eating and drinking unworthily" in the sense St. Paul uses the words, you may as well say, "I dare not communicate, *for fear the church should fall,"* as "for fear I should *eat and drink unworthily.*"

9. If then you fear bringing *damnation* on yourself by this, you fear where no fear is. Fear it not for eating and drinking unworthily; for that, in St. Paul's sense, ye cannot do. But I will tell you for what you shall fear damnation;—for not eating and drinking at all; for not obeying your Maker and Redeemer; for disobeying his plain command; for thus setting at nought both his mercy and authority. Fear ye this; for hear what his Apostle saith: "Whosoever shall keep the whole law, and yet offend in one point, is guilty of all." (James 2:10.)

10. We see then how weak the objection is, "I dare not receive [The Lord's Supper], because I am unworthy." Nor is it any stronger, though the reason why you think yourself unworthy is, that you have lately fallen into sin. It is true, our Church forbids those "who have done any grievous crime" to receive without repentance. But all that follows from this is, that we should repent before we come; not that we should neglect to come at all.

To say, therefore, that "a man may turn his back upon the altar because he has lately fallen into sin, that he may impose this penance upon himself," is talking without any warrant from Scripture. For where does the Bible teach to atone for breaking one commandment of God by breaking another? What advice is this,—"Commit a new act of disobedience, and God will more easily forgive the past!"

11. Others there are who, to excuse their disobedience plead that they are unworthy in another sense, that they "cannot live up to it; they cannot pretend to lead so holy a life as constantly communicating would oblige them to do." Put this into plain words. I ask, Why do not you accept the mercy which God commands you to accept? You answer, "Because I cannot live up to the profession I must make when I receive it." Then it is plain you ought never to receive it at all. For it is no more lawful to promise once what you know you cannot perform, than to promise it a thousand times. You know too, that it is one and the same promise, whether you make it every year or every day. You promise to do just as much, whether you promise ever so often or ever so seldom.

If, therefore, you cannot live up to the profession they make who communicate once a week, neither can you come up to the profession you make who communicate once a year. But cannot you, indeed? Then it had been good for you that you had never been born. For all that you profess at the Lord's table, you must both profess and keep, or you cannot be saved. For you profess nothing there but this,—that you will diligently keep his commandments. And cannot you keep up to this profession? Then you cannot enter into life.

12. Think then what you say, before you say you cannot live up to what is required of constant communicants. This is no more than is required of any communicants; yea, of everyone that has a soul to be saved. So that to say, you cannot live up to this, is neither better nor worse than renouncing Christianity. It is, in effect, renouncing your baptism, wherein you solemnly promised to keep all his commandments. You now fly from that profession. You wilfully break one of his commandments, and, to excuse yourself, say, you cannot keep his commandments: Then you cannot expect to receive the promises, which are made only to those that keep them.

13. What has been said on this pretence against constant communion, is applicable to those who say the same thing in other words: "We dare not do it, because it requires so perfect an obedience afterwards as we cannot promise to perform." Nay, it requires neither more nor less perfect obedience than you promised in your baptism. You then undertook to keep the commandments of God by his help; and you promise no more when you communicate.

14. A Second objection which is often made against constant communion, is, the having so much business as will not allow time for such a preparation as is necessary thereto. I answer: All the preparation that is absolutely necessary is contained in those words: "Repent you truly of your sins past; have faith in Christ our Saviour;" (and observe, that word is not here taken in its highest sense;) "amend your lives, and be in charity with all men; so shall ye be meet partakers of these holy mysteries." All who are thus prepared may draw near without fear, and receive the sacrament to their comfort. Now, what business can hinder you from being thus prepared?—from repenting of your past sins, from believing that Christ died to save sinners, from amending your lives, and being in charity with all men? No business can hinder you from this, unless it be such as hinders you from being in a state of salvation. If you resolve and design to follow Christ, you are fit to approach the Lord's table. If you do not design this, you are only fit for the table and company of devils.

15. No business, therefore, can hinder any man from having that preparation which alone is necessary, unless it be such as unprepares him for heaven, as puts him out of a state of salvation. Indeed every prudent man will, when he has time, examine himself before he receives the Lord's Supper. whether he repents him truly of his former sins; whether he believes the promises of God; whether he fully designs to walk in His ways, and be in charity with all men. In this, and in private prayer, he will doubtless spend all the time he conveniently can. But what is this to you who have not time? What excuse is this for not obeying God? He commands you to come, and prepare yourself by prayer, if you have time; if you have not, however, come. Make not reverence to God's command a pretence for breaking it. Do not rebel against him for fear of offending him. Whatever you do or leave undone besides, be sure to do what God bids you do. Examining yourself, and using private prayer, especially before the Lord's Supper, is good; But behold! "to obey is better than" self-examination; "and to hearken," than the prayer of an angel.

16. A Third objection against constant communion is, that it abates our reverence for the sacrament. Suppose it did? What then? Will you thence conclude that you are not to receive it constantly? This does not follow. God commands you, "Do this." You may do it now, but will not, and, to excuse yourself say, "If I do it so often, it will abate the reverence with which I do it now." Suppose it did; has God ever told you, that when the obeying his command abates your reverence to it, then you may disobey it? If he has, you are guiltless; if not, what you say is just nothing to the purpose. The law is clear. Either show that the lawgiver makes this exception, or you are guilty before him.

17. Reverence for the sacrament may be of two sorts: Either such as is owing purely to the newness of the thing, such as men naturally have for anything they are not used to; or such as is owing to our faith, or to the love or fear of God. Now, the former of these is not properly a religious reverence, but purely natural. And this sort of reverence for the Lord's Supper, the constantly receiving of it must lessen. But it will not lessen the true religious reverence, but rather confirm and increase it.

18. A Fourth objection is, "I have communicated constantly so long, but I have not found the benefit I expected." This has been the case with many well-meaning persons, and therefore deserves to be particularly considered. And consider this: First, whatever God commands us to do, we are to do because he commands, whether we feel any benefit thereby or no. Now, God commands, "Do this in remembrance of me." This, therefore, we are to do because he commands, whether we find present benefit thereby or not. But undoubtedly we shall find benefit sooner or later, though perhaps insensibly. We shall be insensibly strengthened, made more fit for the service of God, and more constant in it. At least, we are kept from falling back, and preserved from many sins and temptations: And surely this should be enough to make us receive this food as often as we can; though we do

not presently feel the happy effects of It, as some have done, and we ourselves may when God sees best.

19. But suppose a man has often been at the sacrament, and yet received no benefit. Was it not his own fault? Either he was not rightly prepared, willing to obey all the commands and to receive all the promises of God, or he did not receive it aright, trusting in God. Only see that you are duly prepared for it, and the oftener you come to the Lord's table, the greater benefit you will find there.

20. A Fifth objection which some have made against constant communion is, that "the Church enjoins it only three times a year." The words of the Church are, "Note, that every parishioner shall communicate at the least three times in the year." To this I answer, First, What, if the Church had not enjoined it at all, Is it not enough that God enjoins it? We obey the Church only for God's sake. And shall we not obey God himself? If, then, you receive three times a year because the Church commands it, receive every time you can because God commands it. Else your doing the one will be so far from excusing you for not doing the other, that your own practice will prove your folly and sin, and leave you without excuse. But, Secondly, we cannot conclude from these words, that the Church excuses him who receives only thrice a year. The plain sense of them is, that he who does not receive thrice at least, shall be cast out of the Church: But they by no means excuse him who communicates no oftener. This never was the judgment of our Church: On the contrary, she takes all possible care that the sacrament be duly administered, wherever the Common Prayer is read, every Sunday and holiday in the year.

The Church gives a particular direction with regard to those that are in Holy Orders: "In all cathedral and collegiate Churches and Colleges, where there are many Priests and Deacons, they shall all receive the communion with the Priest, every Sunday at the least."

21. It has been shown, First, that if we consider the Lord's Supper as a command of Christ, no man can have any pretence to Christian piety, who does not receive it (not once a month, but) as often as he can. Secondly, that if we consider the institution of it, as a mercy to ourselves, no man who does not receive it as often as he can has any pretence to Christian prudence. Thirdly, that none of the objections usually made, can be any excuse for that man who does not, at every opportunity obey this command and accept this mercy.

22. It has been particularly shown, First, that unworthiness is no excuse; because though in one sense we are all unworthy, yet none of us need be afraid of being unworthy in St. Paul's sense, of "eating and drinking unworthily." Secondly, that the not having time enough for preparation can be no excuse; since the only preparation which is absolutely necessary, is that which no business can hinder, nor indeed anything on earth, unless so far as it hinders our being in a state of salvation. Thirdly, that its abating our reverence is no excuse; since he who gave the command, "Do this," nowhere adds, "unless it abates your reverence." Fourthly, that our not profiting by it is no excuse; since it is our own fault, in neglecting that necessary preparation which is in our own power. Lastly, that the judgment of our own Church is quite in favour of constant communion. If those who have hitherto neglected it on any of these pretences, will lay these things to heart, they will, by the grace of God, come to a better mind, and never forsake their own mercies.

102.* OF FORMER TIMES

"Say not thou, What is the cause that the former days were better than these? for thou dost not inquire wisely concerning this."

Eccles. 7:10.

1. It is not easy to discern any connexion between this text and the context; between these words and either those that go before or those that follow after. It seems to be a detached, independent sentence, like very many in the Proverbs of Solomon: And, like them, it contains a weighty truth, which deserves a serious consideration. Is not the purport of the question this? It is not wise to inquire into the cause of a supposition, unless the supposition itself be not only true, but clearly proved so to be. Therefore, it is not wise to inquire into the cause of this supposition, that "the former days were better than these," because, common as it is, it was never yet proved, nor indeed ever can be.

2. Perhaps there are few suppositions which have passed more currently in the world than this,—that the former days were better than these; and that in several respects. It is generally supposed, that we now live in the dregs of time, when the world is, as it were, grown old; and, consequently, that everything therein is in a declining state. It is supposed, in particular, that men were, some ages ago, of a far taller stature than now; that they likewise had far greater abilities, and enjoyed a deeper and stronger understanding; in consequence of which their writings of every kind are far preferable to those of later times. Above all, it is supposed that the former generations of men excelled the present in virtue; that mankind in every age, and in every nation, have degenerated more and more; so that, at length, they have fallen from the golden into the iron age, and now justice is fled from the earth.

3. Before we consider the truth of these suppositions, let us inquire into the rise of them. And as to the general supposition, that the world was once in a far more excellent state than it is, may we not easily believe that this arose (as did all the fabulous accounts of the golden age) from some confused traditions concerning our first parents and their paradisiacal state? To this refer man of the fragments of ancient writings which men of learning have gleaned up. Therefore, we may allow that there is some truth in the supposition; seeing it is certain, the days which dam and Eve spent in Paradise were far better than any which have been spent by their descendants, or ever will be till Christ returns to reign upon earth.

4. But whence could that supposition arise, that men were formerly of a larger stature than they are now? This has been

---

* [text from the 1872 Edition]

a generally prevailing opinion, almost in all nations and in all ages. Hence near two thousand years ago, the well-known line of Virgil,—

Qualia nunc hominum producit corpora tellus.

[Thus translated by Pitt:—

"Scarce twelve strong men the ponderous mass could raise,
Such as disgrace these dark degenerate days."—Edit.]

Hence, near a thousand years before him, Homer tells us of one of his heroes throwing a stone which hardly ten men could lift,—*hoioi nyn brotoi*,—such as men are now. We allow, indeed, there have been giants in all ages, in various parts of the world. Whether the antediluians mentioned in Genesis were such or no, (which many have questioned,) we cannot doubt but Og the King of Bashan was such, as well as Goliath of Gath. Such also were many of the children (or descendants) of Anak. But it does not appear that in any age or nation men in general were larger than they are now. We are very sure they were not for many centuries past, by the tombs and coffins that have been discovered, which are exactly of the same size with those that are now in use. And in the catacombs at Rome, the niches for the dead bodies which were hewn in the rock sixteen hundred years ago are none of them six feet in length, and some a little under. Above all, the Pyramids of Egypt (that of King Cheops in particular) have, beyond all reasonable doubt, remained at least three thousand years. Yet none of the mummies (embalmed bodies) brought therefrom are above five feet ten inches long.

5. But how then came this supposition to prevail so long and so generally in the world? I know not but it may be accounted for from hence: Great and little are relative terms; and all men judge of greatness and littleness by comparing things with themselves. Therefore it is not strange, if we think men are larger now than they were when we were children. I remember a remarkable instance of this in my own case: After having left it seven years, I had a great desire to see the school where I was brought up. When I was there, I wondered that the boys were so much smaller than they used to be when I was at school. "Many of my school-fellows, ten years ago, were taller by the head than me; and few of them that are at school now reach up to my shoulders." Very true: But what was the reason of this? Indeed a very plain one: It was not because they were smaller, but because I was bigger than I was ten years before. I verily believe this is the cause, why men in general suppose the human race to decrease in stature. They remember the time when most of those round about them were both taller and bigger than themselves. Yea, and all men have done the same in their successive generations. Is it any wonder then that all should have run into the same mistake, when it has been transmitted unawares from father to son, and probably will be to the end of time.

6. But there is likewise a general supposition that the understanding of man and all his mental abilities were of a larger size in the ancient days than they are now; and that the ancient inhabitants of the earth had far greater talents than the present. Men of eminent learning have been of this mind,

and have contended for it with the utmost vehemence. It is granted that many of the ancient writers, both philosophers, poets, and historians will not easily be excelled, if equalled, by those of later ages. We may instance in Homer and Virgil, as poets; Thucydides and Livy, as historians. But this, mean time, is to be remarked concerning most of these writers; that each of them spent his whole life in composing and polishing one book. What wonder then if they were exquisitely finished, when so much labour was bestowed upon them! I doubt whether any man in Europe, or in the world, has taken so much pains in finishing any treatise: Otherwise it might possibly have equalled, if not excelled, any that went before.

7. But that the generality of men were not one jot wiser in ancient times than they are at the present time we may easily gather from the most authentic records. One of the most ancient nations concerning whom we have any certain account is the Egyptian. And what conception can we have of their understanding and learning when we reflect upon the objects of their worship? These were not only the vilest of animals, as dogs and cats, but the leeks and onions that grew in their own gardens. Indeed, I knew a great man (whose manner was to treat with the foulest abuse all that dared to differ from him: I do not mean Dr. Johnson—he was a mere courtier compared to Mr. Hutchinson) who scurrilously abused all those who are so void of common sense as to believe any such thing concerning them. He peremptorily affirms, (but without condescending to give us any proof,) that the ancient inhabitants of Egypt had a deep hidden meaning in all this. Let him believe it who can. I cannot believe it on any man bare assertion. I believe they had no deeper meaning in worshipping cats than our schoolboys have in baiting them. And I apprehend, the common Egyptians were just as wise three thousand years ago as the common ploughmen in England and Wales are at this day. I suppose their natural understanding like their stature, was on a level with ours, and their learning, their acquired knowledge, many degrees inferior to that of persons of the same rank either in France, Holland, or Germany.

8. However, did not the people of former times greatly excel us in virtue? This is the point of greatest importance;—the rest are but trifles in comparison of it. Now, is it not universally allowed, that every age grows worse and worse? Was it not observed by the old heathen poet, almost two thousand years ago,—

Aetas parentum pejor avis tulit
Nos nequiores, mox daturos
Progeniem vitiosiorem?

That is, in plain prose, "The age of our parents was more vicious—than that of our grandfathers; our age is more vicious than that of our fathers; we are worse than our fathers were, and our children will be worse than us."

9. It is certain, this has been the common cry from generation to generation. And if it is not true, whence should it arise? How can we account for it? Perhaps another remark of the same poet may help us to an answer. May it not be extracted from the general character which he gives of old men?

Difficilis, querulus, laudator temporis acti
Se puero, censor, castigatorque minorum.

[The following is Boscawen's translation of this quotation from Horace:—

> "Fastidious, peevish, prone to praise
> What pass'd when in their youthful days,
> And with severe censorious tongue
> Correct the follies of the young."—Edit.]

Is it not the common practice of old men to praise the past and condemn the present time? And this may probably operate much farther than one would at first imagine. When those that have more experience than us, and therefore we are apt to think more wisdom, are almost continually harping upon this, the degeneracy of the world; those who are accustomed from their infancy to hear how much better the world was formerly than it is now, (and so it really seemed to them when they were young, and just come into the world, and when the cheerfulness of youth gave a pleasing air to all that was round about them,) the idea of the world's being worse and worse would naturally grow up with them. And so it will be, till we, in our turn, grow peevish, fretful, discontented, and full of melancholy complaints, "How wicked the world is grown!' How much better it was when we were young, in the golden days that we can remember!"

10. But let us endeavour, without prejudice or prepossession, to take a view of the whole affair. And, upon cool and impartial consideration, it will appear that the former days were not better than these; yea, on the contrary, that these are, in many respects, beyond comparison better than them. It will clearly appear, that as the stature of men was nearly the same from the beginning of the world, so the understanding of men, in similar circumstances, has been much the same, from the time of God's bringing a flood upon the earth unto the present hour. We have no reason to believe that the uncivilized nations of Africa, America, or the South-Sea Islands, had ever a better understanding, or were in a less barbarous state than they are now. Neither, on the other hand, have we any sufficient proof that the natural understandings of men in the most civilized countries,—Babylon, Persia, Greece, or Italy,—were stronger or more improved, than those of the Germans, French, or English, now alive. Nay, have we not reason to believe, that, by means of better instruments, we have attained that knowledge of nature which few, if any, of the ancients ever attained? So that, in this respect, the advantage (and not a little one is clearly on our side: And we ought to acknowledge, with deep thankfulness to the Giver of every good gift, that the former days were not to be compared to these wherein we live.

11. But the principal inquiry still remains: Were not "the former days better than these," with regard to virtue? or, to speak more properly, religion? This deserves a full consideration.

By religion I mean the love of God and man filling the heart and governing the life. The sure effect of this is, the uniform practice of justice, mercy, and truth. This is the very essence of it; the height and depth of religion, detached from this or that opinion, and from all particular modes of worship. And I would calmly inquire, "Which of the former times were better than these, with regard to this? to the religion experienced and practised by Archbishop Fenelon, in France; Bishop Ken, in England; and Bishop Bedell, in Ireland?'

12. We need not extend our inquiry beyond the period when life and immortality were brought to light by the gospel. And it is allowed, that the days immediately succeeding the pouring out of the Holy Ghost on the day of Pentecost were better even in this respect, even with regard to religion, than any which have succeeded them.

But setting aside this short age of golden days, I must repeat the question, Which of the former days were better than the present, in every known part of the habitable world?

13. Was the former part of this century better, either in these islands or any part of the continent? I know no reason at all to affirm this. I believe every part of Europe was full as void of religion in the reign of Queen Anne as it is at this day. It is true, luxury increases to a high degree in every part of Europe: And so does the scandal of England, profaneness, in every part of the kingdom. But it is also true, that the most infernal of all vices, cruelty, does as swiftly decrease. And such instances of it as, in times past, continually occurred, are now very seldom heard of. Even in war, that savage barbarity which was everywhere practised has been discontinued for many years.

14. Was the last century more religious than this? In the former part of it there was much of the form of religion; and some undoubtedly experienced the power thereof. But how soon did the fine gold become dim! How soon was it so mingled with worldly design, and with a total contempt both of truth, justice, and mercy, as brought that scandal upon all religion which is hardly removed to this day. Was there more true religion in the preceding century, the age of the Reformation? There was doubtless in many countries a considerable reformation of religious opinions; yea, and modes of worship, which were much changed for the better, both in Germany and several other places. But it is well known that Luther himself complained with his dying breath, "The people that are called by my name (though I wish they were only called by the name of Christ) are reformed as to their opinions and modes of worship; but their tempers and lives are the same they were before." Even then both justice and mercy were so shamelessly trodden under foot that an eminent writer computes the number of those that were slaughtered, during those religious contests, to have been no less than forty millions, within the compass of forty years!

15. We may step back above a thousand years from this, without finding any better time. No historian gives us the least intimation of any such, till we come to the age of Constantine the Great. Of this period several writers have given us most magnificent accounts. Yea, one eminent author, no less a man than Dr. Newton, the late Bishop of Bristol, has been at no small pains to show, that the conversion of Constantine to Christianity, and the emoluments which he bestowed upon the Church with an unsparing hand, were the event which is signified in the Revelation by "the new Jerusalem coming down from heaven!"

16. But I cannot, in anywise subscribe to the Bishop's opinion in this matter. So far from it, that I have been long convinced, from the whole tenor of ancient history, that this very event, Constantine's calling himself a Christian, and pouring in that flood of wealth and honour [power] on the Christian Church, the Clergy in particular, was productive of more evil to the Church than all the ten persecutions put together. From the time that power, riches, and honour of all kinds were heaped upon the Christians, vice of all kinds came in like a flood, both on the Clergy and laity. From the time that the Church and State, the kingdoms of Christ and of the world, were so strangely and unnaturally blended together, Christianity and Heathenism were so thoroughly incorporated with each other, that they will hardly ever be divided till Christ comes to reign upon earth. So that, instead of fancying that the glory of the new Jerusalem covered the earth at that period, we have terrible proof that it was then, and has ever since been, covered with the smoke of the bottomless pit.

17. "However, were not the days antecedent to this,—those of the third century,—better beyond all comparison than any that followed them?" This has been almost universally believed. Few doubt but in the age before Constantine the Christian church was in its glory, worshipping God in the beauty of holiness. But was it so indeed? What says St. Cyprian, who lived in the midst of that century; a witness above all exception, and one that sealed the truth with his blood? What account does he give of what he saw with his own eyes, and heard with his own ears? Such a one as would almost make one imagine he was painting to the life, not the ancient church of Carthage, but the modern Church of Rome. According to his account, such abominations even then prevailed over all orders of men, that it was not strange God poured out his fury upon them in blood, by the grievous persecutions which followed.

18. Yea, and before this, even in the first century, even in the apostolic age, what account does St. John give of several of the churches which he himself had planted in Asia? How little were those congregations better than many in Europe at this day? Nay, forty or fifty years before that, within thirty years of the descent of the Holy Ghost, were there not such abominations in the church of Corinth as were "not even named among the Heathens?" So early did "the mystery of iniquity" begin to work in the Christian church! So little reason have we to appeal to "the former days," as though they were "better than these!"

19. To affirm this, therefore, as commonly as it is done, is not only contrary to truth, but is an instance of black ingratitude to God, and a grievous affront to his blessed Spirit. For whoever makes a fair and candid inquiry, will easily perceive that true religion has in no wise decreased, but greatly increased, in the present century. To instance in one capital branch of religion, the love of our neighbour. Is not persecution well nigh vanished from the face of the earth? In what age did Christians of various denominations show such forbearance toward each other? When before was such lenity shown by governors toward their respective subjects? not only in Great Britain and Ireland, but in France and Germany; yea, every part of Europe? Nothing like this has been seen since the time of Constantine; no, not since the time of the Apostles.

20. If it be said, "Why, this is the fruit of the general infidelity, the Deism which has overspread all Europe," I answer, Whatever be the cause, we have reason greatly to rejoice in the effect: And if the all-wise God has brought so great and universal a good out of this dreadful evil, so much the more should we magnify his astonishing power, wisdom, and goodness herein. Indeed, so far as we can judge, this was the most direct way whereby *nominal* Christians could be prepared, first, for tolerating, and afterwards, for receiving, *real* Christianity. While the governors were themselves unacquainted with it, nothing but this could induce them to suffer it. O the depth both of the wisdom and knowledge of God; causing a total disregard for all religion, to pave the way for the revival of the only religion which was worthy of God! I am not assured whether this be the case or no in France and Germany; but it is so beyond all contradiction in North-America: The total indifference of the government there, whether there be any religion or none, leaves room for the propagation of true, scriptural religion, without the least let or hindrance.

21. But above all this, while luxury and profaneness have been increasing on the one hand, on the other benevolence and compassion toward all the forms of human woe have increased in a manner not known before, from the earliest ages of the world. In proof of this we see more hospitals, infirmaries, and other places of public charity have been erected, at least in and near London, within this century, than in five hundred years before. And suppose this has been owing in part to vanity, desire of praise; yet have we cause to bless God, that so much good has sprung even from this imperfect motive.

22. I cannot forbear mentioning one instance more of the goodness of God to us in the present age. He has lifted up his standard in our islands, both against luxury, profaneness, and vice of every kind. He caused, near fifty years ago, as it were, a grain of mustard-seed to be sown near London; and it has now grown and put forth great branches, reaching from sea to sea. Two or three poor people met together, in order to help each other to be real Christians. They increased to hundreds, to thousands, to myriads, still pursuing their one point, real religion; the love of God and man ruling all their tempers, and words, and actions. Now I will be bold to say, such an event as this, considered in all its circumstances, has not been seen upon earth before, since the time that St. John went to Abraham's bosom.

23. Shall we now say, "The former days were better than these?" God forbid we should be so unwise and so unthankful! Nay, rather let us praise him all the day long; for he hath dealt bountifully with us. No "former time," since the Apostles left the earth, has been better than the present. None has been comparable to it in several respects. We are not born out of due time, but in the day of his power,—a day of glorious salvation, wherein he is hastening to renew the whole race of mankind in righteousness and true holiness. How bright hath the Sun of Righteousness already shone on

various parts of the earth! And how many gracious showers has he already poured down upon his inheritance! How many precious souls has he already gathered into his garner, as ripe shocks of corn! May we be always ready to follow them; crying in our hearts, "Come, Lord Jesus! Come quickly!" [June 27, 1787]

103. WHAT IS MAN?

"When I consider thy heaven, the work of thy fingers, the moon and stars, which thou hast ordained; what is man?"

Psalm 8:3, 4.

How often has it been observed, that the Book of Psalms is a rich treasury of devotion, which the wisdom of God has provided to supply the wants of his children in all generations! In all ages the Psalms have been of singular use to those that loved or feared God; not only to the pious Israelites, but to the children of God in all nations. And this book has been of sovereign use to the Church of God, not only while it was in its state of infancy, (so beautifully described by St. Paul in the former part to the fourth chapter to the Galatians,) but also since, in the fullness of time, "life and immortality were brought to the light by the gospel." The Christians in every age and nation have availed themselves of this divine treasure, which has richly supplied the wants, not only of the "babes in Christ," of those who were just setting out in the ways of God, but of those also who had made good progress therein; yea, of such as were swiftly advancing toward "the measure of the stature of the fullness of Christ."

The subject of this psalm is beautifully proposed in the beginning of it: "O Lord our Governor, how excellent is thy name in all the earth; who hast set thy glory above the heavens!" It celebrates the glorious wisdom and love of God, as the Creator and Governor of all things. It is not an improbable conjecture, that David wrote this psalm in a bright star-light night, while he observed the moon also "walking in her brightness;" that while he surveyed

> This fair half-round, the ample azure sky,
> Terribly large, and beautifully bright,
> With stars unnumber'd, and unmeasured light,—

he broke out, from the fullness of his heart, into the natural exultation, "When I consider thy heavens, the work of thy fingers, the moon and the stars, which thou hast ordained; what is man?" How is it possible that the Creator of these, the innumerable armies of heaven and earth, should have any regard to this speck of creation, whose time "passeth away like a shadow?"

> Thy frame but dust, thy stature but a span,
> A moment thy duration, foolish man!

"What is man?" I would consider this, First, with regard to his magnitude; and, Secondly, with regard to his duration.

I. 1. Consider we, First, What is man, with regard to his magnitude? And, in this respect, what is any one individual, compared to all the inhabitants of Great Britain? He shrinks into nothing in the comparison. How inconceivably little is one compared to eight or ten millions of people! Is he not

Lost like a drop in the unbounded main?

2. But what are all the inhabitants of Great Britain, compared to all the inhabitants of the earth? These have frequently been supposed to amount to about four hundred millions. But will this computation be allowed to be just, by those who maintain China alone to contain fifty-eight millions? If it be true, that this one empire contains little less than sixty millions, we may easily suppose that the inhabitants of the whole terraqueous globe amount to four thousand millions of inhabitants, rather than four hundred. And what is any single individual, in comparison of this number?

3. But what is the magnitude of the earth itself, compared to that of the solar system? Including, beside that vast body, the sun, so immensely larger that the earth, the whole train of primary and secondary planets; several of which (I mean, of the secondary planets, suppose that satellites or moons of Jupiter and Saturn) are abundantly larger than the whole earth?

4. And yet, what is the whole quantity of matter contained in the sun, and all those primary and secondary planets, with all the spaces comprised in the solar system, in comparison of that which is pervaded by those amazing bodies, the comets? Who but the Creator himself can "tell the number of these, and call them all by their names?" Yet what is even the orbit of a comet, and the space contained therein, to the space which is occupied by the fixed stars; which are at so immense a distance from the earth, that they appear, when they are viewed through the largest telescope, just as they do to the naked eye?

5. Whether the bounds of the creation do or do not extend beyond the region of the fixed stars, who can tell? Only the morning-stars, who sang together when the foundations thereof were laid. But it is finite, that the bounds of it are fixed, we have no reason to doubt. We cannot doubt, but when the Son of God had finished all the work which he created and made, he said,

> These be thy bounds,
> This be thy just circumference, O world!

But what is man to this?

6. We may take one step, and only one step, farther still: What is the space of the whole creation, what is all finite space that is, or can be conceived, in comparison of infinite? What is it but a point, a cipher, compared to that which is filled by him that is All in all? Think of this, and then ask, "What is man?"

7. What is man, that the great God who filleth heaven and earth, "the high and lofty One that inhabiteth eternity," should stoop so inconceivably low as to "be mindful of him?" Would not reason suggest to us, that so diminutive a creature would be overlooked by him in immensity of his works? Especially when we consider,

II. Secondly, What is man, with regard to his duration?

1. The days of man, since the last reduction of human life, which seems to have taken place in the time of Moses, (and not improbably was revealed to the man of God at the time that he made this declaration,) "are threescore years and ten." This is the general standard which God hath now appointed. "And if men be so strong," perhaps one in a hundred, "that

they come to fourscore years, yet then is their strength but labour and sorrow: So soon passeth it away, and we are gone!"

2. Now, what a poor pittance of duration is this, compared to the life of Methuselah! "And Methuselah lived nine hundred and sixty and nine years." But what are these nine hundred and sixty and nine years to the duration of an angel, which began "or ever the mountains were brought forth," or the foundations of the earth were laid? And what is the duration which has passed since the creation of angels, that which passed before they were created, to unbeginning eternity?—to that half of eternity (if one may so speak) which had then elapsed? And what are threescore years and ten to this?

3. Indeed, what proportion can there possibly be between any finite and infinite duration? What proportion is there between a thousand or ten thousand years, or ten thousand time ten thousand ages, and eternity? I know not that the inexpressible disproportion between any conceivable part of time and eternity can be illustrated in a more striking manner than it is in the well-known passage of St. Cyprian: "Suppose there was a ball of sand as large as the globe of earth, and suppose one grain of this were to be annihilated in a thousand years; yet that whole space of time wherein this ball would be annihilating, at the rate of one grain in a thousand years, would bear less, yea, unspeakably, infinitely less, proportion to eternity, than a single grain of sand would bear to that whole mass." What, then, are the seventy years of human life, in comparison of eternity? In what terms can the proportion between these be expressed? It is nothing, yea, infinitely less than nothing!

4. If, then, we add to the littleness of man the inexpressible shortness of his duration, it is any wonder that a man of reflection should sometimes feel a kind of fear, lest the great, eternal, infinite Governor of the universe should disregard so diminutive a creature as man?—a creature so every way inconsiderable, when compared either with immensity or eternity? Did not both these reflections glance through, if not dwell upon, the mind of the royal Psalmist? Thus, in contemplation of the former, he breaks out into the strong words of the text: "When I consider the heavens, the work of thy fingers, the moon and the stars which thou has ordained, What is man, that thou shouldest be mindful; or the son of man, that thou shouldest regard him?" He is, indeed, (to use St. Augustine's words,) *aliqua portio creaturæ tuæ*, "some portion of thy creation;" but *quantula portio*, "how amazingly small a portion!" How utterly beneath thy notice! It seems to be in contemplation of the latter, that he cries out in the hundred and forty-fourth Psalm, "Lord, what is man, that thou hast such respect unto him; or the son of man, that though shouldest so regard him?" "Man is like a thing of naught." Why? "His time passeth away like a shadow." In this, although in a very few places,) the new translation of the Psalms—that bound up in our Bibles—is perhaps more proper than the old,—that which we have in the Common Prayer Book. It runs thus: "Lord, what is man, that thou takest knowledge of him; or the son of man, that thou makest account of him?" According to the former translation, David seems to be amazed that the eternal God, considering the littleness of man, should have so much respect unto him, and should so much regard him: But in the latter, he seems to wonder, seeing the life of man "passeth away like a shadow," that God should take any knowledge of him at all, or make any account of him.

5. And it is natural for us to make the same reflection, and to entertain the same fear. But how may we prevent this uneasy reflection, and effectually cure this fear? First. By considering what David does not appear to have taken at all into his account; namely, that the body is not the man; that man is not only a house of clay, but an immortal spirit; a spirit made in the image of God; an incorruptible picture of the God of glory; a spirit that is of infinitely more value than the whole earth; of more value than the sun, moon, and stars, put together; yea, than the whole material creation. Consider that the spirit of man is not only of a higher order, of a more excellent nature, than any part of the visible world, but also more durable; not liable either to dissolution or decay. We know all the things "which are seen are temporal;"—of a changing, transient nature;—but "the things which are not seen" (such as is the soul of man in particular) "are eternal." "They shall perish," but the soul remaineth. "They all shall wax old as a garment;" but when heaven and earth shall pass away, the soul shall not pass away.

6. Consider, Secondly, that declaration which the Father of spirits hath made to us by the Prophet Hosea: "I am God, and not man: Therefore my compassions fail not." As if he had said, "If I were only a man, or an angel, or any finite being, my knowledge might admit of bounds, and my mercy might be limited. But 'my thoughts are not as your thoughts,' and my mercy is not as your mercy. 'As the heavens are higher than earth, so are my thoughts higher than your thoughts;' and 'my mercy,' my compassion, my ways of showing it, 'higher than your ways.' "

7. That no shadow of fear might remain, no possibility of doubting; to show what manner of regard the great eternal God bears to little, short-lived man, but especially to his immortal part; God gave his Son, "his only Son, to the end that whosoever believeth in him should not perish, but have everlasting life." See how God loved the world! The Son of God, that was "God of God, Light of Light, very God of very God," in glory equal with the Father, in majesty co-eternal, "emptied himself, took upon him the form of a servant; and, being found in fashion as a man, was obedient unto death, even the death of the cross." And all this he suffered not for himself, but "for us men and for our salvation." "He bore" all "our sins in his own body upon the tree," that "by his stripes we" might be "healed." After this demonstration of his love, is it possible to doubt any longer of God's tender regard for man; even though he was "dead in trespasses and sins?" Even when he saw us in our sins and in our blood, he said unto us. "Live!" Let us then fear no more! Let us doubt no more! "He that spared not his own Son, but delivered him up for us all, shall he not with freely give us all things?"

8. "Nay," says the philosopher, "if God so loved the world, did he not love a thousand other worlds, as well as he did this? It is now allowed that there are thousands, if not millions, of worlds, besides this in which we live. And can

any reasonable man believe that the Creator of all these, many of which are probably as large, yea, far larger than ours, would show such astonishingly greater regard to one than to all the rest?" I answer, Suppose there were millions of worlds, yet God may see, in the abyss of his infinite wisdom, reasons that do not appear to us, why he saw good to show this mercy to ours, in preference to thousands or millions of other worlds.

9. I speak this even upon the common supposition of the plurality of worlds,—a very favourite notion with all those who deny the Christian Revelation; and for this reason, because it affords them a foundation for so plausible an objection to it. But the more I consider that supposition, the more I doubt of it: Insomuch that, if it were allowed by all the philosophers in Europe, still I could not allow it without stronger proof than any I have met with yet.

10. "Nay, but is not the argument of the grey Huygens sufficient to put it beyond all doubt?—'When we view,' says that able astronomer, 'the moon through a good telescope, we clearly discover rivers and mountains on her spotted globe. Now, where rivers are, there are doubtless plants and vegetables of various kinds: And where vegetables are, there are undoubtedly animals; yea, rational ones, as on earth. It follows, then, that the moon has its inhabitants, we may easily suppose, so are all the secondary planets; and, in particular, all the satellites or moons of Jupiter and Saturn. And if the secondary planets are inhabited, why not the primary? Why should we doubt it of Jupiter and Saturn themselves, as well as Mars, Venus, and Mercury?' "

11. But do not you know, that Mr. Huygens himself, before he died, doubted of this whole hypotheses? For upon further observation he found reason to believe that the moon has no atmosphere. He observed, that in a total eclipse of the sun, on the removal of the shade from any part of the earth, the sun immediately shines bright upon it; whereas if the moon had atmosphere, would appear dim and dusky. Thus, after an eclipse of the moon, first a dusky light appears on that part of it from which the shadow of the earth removes, while that light passes that the moon has no atmosphere. Consequently, it has no clouds, no rain, no springs, no rivers; and therefore no plants or animals. But there is no proof or probability that the moon is inhabited; neither have we any proof that the other planets are. Consequently, the foundation being removed, the whole fabric falls to the ground.

12. But, you will say, "Suppose this argument fails, we may infer the same conclusion, the plurality of worlds, from the unbounded wisdom, and power, and goodness of the Creator. It was full as easy to him to create thousands or millions of worlds as one. Can any one then believe that he would exert all his power and wisdom in creating a single world? What proportion is there between this speck of creation, and the Great God that filleth the heaven and earth, while

"We know, the power of his almighty hand
Could form another world from every sand?"

13. To this boasted proof, this *argumentum palmarium* of the learned infidels, I answer, Do you expect to find any proportion between finite and infinite? Suppose God had created a thousand more worlds than there are grains of sand in the universe; what proportion would all these together bear to the infinite Creator? Still, in comparison of Him, they would be, not a thousand times, but infinitely, less than a mite compared to the universe. Have done, then, with this childish prattle about the proportion of creatures to their Creator; and leave it to the all-wise God to create what and when he pleases. For who, besides himself, "hath known the mind of the Lord? or who hath been his counselor?"

14. Suffice it then for us to know this plain and comfortable truth,—that the almighty Creator hath shown that regard to this poor little creature of a day, which he hath not shown even to the inhabitants of heaven "who kept not their first estate." He hath given us his Son, his only Son, both to live and to die for us! O let us live unto him, that we may die unto him, and live with him ever!

104.* ON ATTENDING THE CHURCH SERVICE

"The sin of the young men was very great."

1 Sam. 2:17.

1. The corruption, not only of the heathen world, but likewise of them that were called Christians, has been matter of sorrow and lamentation to pious men, almost from the time of the apostles. And hence, as early as the second century, within a hundred years of St. John's removal from the earth, men who were afraid of being partakers of other men's sins, thought it their duty to separate from them. Hence, in every age many have retired from the world, lest they should be stained with the pollutions of it. In the third century many carried this so far as to run into deserts and turn hermits. But in the following age this took another turn. Instead of turning hermits, they turned monks. Religious houses now began to be built in every Christian country; and religious communities were established, both of men and women, who were entirely secluded from the rest of mankind; having no intercourse with their nearest relations, nor with any but such as were confined, generally for life, within the same walls.

2. This spirit of literally renouncing the world, by retiring into religious houses, did not so generally prevail after the Reformation. Nay, in Protestant countries, houses of this kind were totally suppressed. But still too many serious persons (chiefly incited thereto by those that are commonly called "mystic writers") were eager to seclude themselves from the world, and run into solitude; supposing this to be the best, if not the only way, of escaping the pollution that is in the world.

3. One thing which powerfully inclined them to separate from the several churches, or religious societies, to which they had belonged, even from their infancy, was the belief that no good was to be expected from the ministration of unholy men. "What!" said they, "Can we think that a holy God will

---

* [text from the 1872 edition]

bless the ministry of wicked men? Can we imagine that they who are themselves strangers to the grace of God will manifest that grace to others? Is it to be supposed that God ever did, or ever will, work by the children of the devil? And if this cannot be supposed, ought we not to 'come out from among them and be separate?' " [2 Cor. 6:14]

4. For more than twenty years this never entered into the thought of those that were called Methodists. But as more and more who had been brought up Dissenters joined with them, the brought in more and more prejudice against the Church. In process of time, various circumstances concurred to increase and confirm it. Many had forgotten that we were all at our first setting out determined members of the Established Church. Yea, it as one of our original rules, that every member of our Society should attend the church and sacrament, unless he had been bred among Christians of any other denomination.

5. In order, therefore, to prevent others from being puzzled and perplexed, as so many have been already, it is necessary, in the highest degree, to consider this matter thoroughly; calmly to inquire, whether God ever did bless the ministry of ungodly men, and whether he does so at this hour. Here is a plain matter of fact: If God never did bless it, we ought to separate from the Church; at least where we have reason to believe that the minister is an unholy man: If he ever did bless it, and does so still, then we ought to continue therein.

6. Nineteen years ago, we considered this question in our public Conference at Leeds,—Whether the Methodists ought to separate from the Church; and after a long and candid inquiry, it was determined, *nemine contradicente*, that it was not expedient for them to separate. The reasons were set down at large, and they stand equally good at this day.

7. In order to put this matter beyond all possible dispute, I have chosen to speak from these words, which give a fair occasion of observing what the dealings of God in his Church have been, even from so early a period: For it is generally allowed that Eli lived at least a thousand years before our Lord came into the world. In the verses preceding the text we read, (1 Sam. 2:12.) "Now the sons of Eli were sons of Belial; they knew not the Lord." They were wicked to an uncommon degree. Their profane violence, with respect to the sacrifices, is related with all its shocking circumstances in the following verses. But (what was a greater abomination still) "they lay with the women that assembled at the door of the tabernacle of the congregation." (1 Sam. 2:22.) On both these accounts, "the sin of the young men was very great; and men abhorred the offering of the Lord."

8. May I be permitted to make a little digression, in order to correct a mistranslation in the twenty-fifth verse? In our translation it runs thus: "They hearkened not unto the voice of their father, because the Lord would slay them." Ought it not rather to be rendered, "Therefore the Lord was about to slay them?" [1 Sam. 2:25] As if he had said, "The Lord would not suffer their horrid and stubborn wickedness to escape unpunished; but because of that wickedness, he slew them both in one day, by the hand of the Philistines." They did not sin (as might be imagined from the common translation)

because God had determined to slay them; but God therefore determined to slay them, because they had thus sinned.

9. But to return: Their sin was the more inexcusable because they could not be ignorant of that dreadful consequence thereof, that, by reason of their enormous wickedness, "men abhorred the offering of the Lord." Many of the people were so deeply offended, that if they did not wholly refrain from the public worship, yet they attended it with pain; abhorring the Priests while they honoured the sacrifice.

10. And have we any proof that the Priests who succeeded them were more holy than them, than Hophni and Phinehas; not only till God permitted ten of the tribes to be separated from their brethren, and from the worship he had appointed; but even till Judah, as well as Israel, for the wickedness of the priests, as well as the people, were carried into captivity?

11. What manner of men they were about the time of the Babylonish captivity, we learn from various passages in the prophecy of Jeremiah: From which it manifestly appears, that people and priests wallowed in all manner of vices. And how little they were amended, after they were brought back into their own land, we may gather from those terrible words in the prophecy of Malachi: "And now, O ye priests, this commandment is for you. If ye will not hear, and if ye will not lay it to heart, to give glory unto my Name, saith the Lord of Hosts, I will send even a curse upon you, and I will curse your blessings: Yea, I have cursed them already, because ye would not lay it to heart. Behold, I will curse your seed, and I will spread dung upon your faces, even the dung of your solemn feasts; and one shall take you away with it." (Mal. 2:1–3.)

12. Such were the priests of God in their several generations, till he brought the great High Priest into the world! And what manner of men were they during the time that he ministered upon earth? A large and particular account of their character we have in the twenty-third chapter of St. Matthew; [Matt. 23] and a worse character it would be difficult to find in all the oracles of God. But may it not be said, "Our Lord does not there direct his discourse to the priests, but to the Scribes and Pharisees?" He does; but this is the same thing. For the scribes were what we now term Divines,—the public teachers of the people. And many, if not most, of the Priests, especially all the strictest sort of them, were Pharisees; so that in giving the character of the Scribes and Pharisees he gives that of the Priests also.

13. Soon after the pouring out of the Holy Ghost on the day of Pentecost, in the infancy of the Christian Church, there was indeed a glorious change. "Great grace was then upon them all," Ministers as well as people. "The multitude of them that believed were of one heart and of one soul." But how short a time did this continue! How soon did the fine gold become dim! Long before even the apostolic age expired, St. Paul himself had ground to complain, that some of his fellow-labourers had forsaken him, having "loved the present world." And not long after, St. John reproved divers of the angels, that is, the ministers, of the churches in Asia, because, even in that early period, their "works were not found perfect before God."

14. Thus did "the mystery of iniquity" begin to "work," in the Ministers as well as the people, even before the end of the apostolic age. But how much more powerfully did it work, as soon as those master-builders, the Apostles, were taken out of the way! Both Ministers and people were then farther and farther removed from the hope of the gospel. Insomuch that when St. Cyprian, about an hundred and fifty years after the death of St. John, describes the spirit and behaviour both of the laity and clergy that were round about him, one would be ready to suppose he was giving us a description of the present clergy and laity of Europe. But the corruption which had been creeping in drop by drop, during the second and third century, in the beginning of the fourth, when Constantine called himself a Christian, poured in upon the church with a full tide. And whoever reads the history of the church, from the time of Constantine to the Reformation, will easily observe that all the abominations of the heathen world, and, in following ages, of the Mahometans, overflowed every part of it. And in every nation and city the Clergy were not a whit more innocent than the laity.

15. "But was there not a very considerable change in the body of the Clergy, as well as the laity, at the time of the glorious Reformation from Popery?" Undoubtedly there was; and they were not only reformed from very many erroneous opinions, and from numberless superstitious and idolatrous modes of worship, till then prevailing over the Western Church, but they were also exceedingly reformed with respect to their lives and tempers. More of the ancient, scriptural Christianity was to be found, almost in every part of Europe. Yet notwithstanding this, all the works of the devil, all ungodliness and unrighteousness, sin of every kind, continued to prevail, both over Clergy and laity, in all parts of Christendom. Even those Clergymen who most warmly contended about the externals of religion were very little concerned for the life and power of it; for piety, justice, mercy, and truth.

16. However, it must be allowed, that ever since the Reformation, and particularly in the present century, the behaviour of the Clergy in general is greatly altered for the better. And should it be granted, that, in many parts of the Romish Church, they are nearly the same as they were before, it must be granted likewise, that most of the Protestant Clergy are far different from what they were. They have not only more learning of the most valuable kind, but abundantly much more religion: Insomuch that the English and Irish Clergy are generally allowed to be not inferior to any in Europe, for piety, as well as for knowledge.

17. And all this being allowed, what lack they yet? Can anything be laid to their charge? I wish calmly and candidly to consider this point, in the fear and in the presence of God. I am far from desiring to aggravate the defects of my brethren, or to paint them in the strongest colours. Far be it from me to treat others as I have been treated myself; to return evil for evil, or railing for railing. But, to speak the naked truth, (not with anger or contempt, as too many have done,) I acknowledge that many, if not most, of those that were appointed to minister in holy things, with whom it has been my lot to converse in almost every part of England or Ireland, for forty of fifty years last past, have not been eminent either for knowledge or piety. It has been loudly affirmed, that most of those persons now in connexion with *me*, who believe it their duty to call sinners to repentance, having been taken immediately from low trades,—tailors, shoemakers, and the like,—are a set of poor, stupid, illiterate men, that scarce know their right hand from their left: Yet I cannot but say, that I would sooner cut off my right hand, than suffer one of them to speak a word in any of our chapels, if I had not reasonable proof that he had more knowledge in the Holy Scriptures, more knowledge of himself, more knowledge of God and of the things of God, than nine in ten of the Clergymen I have conversed with, either at the Universities or elsewhere.

18. In the meantime, I gladly allow that this charge does not concern the whole body of the Clergy. Undoubtedly there are many Clergymen in these kingdoms, that are not only free from outward sin, but men of eminent learning; and, what is infinitely more, deeply acquainted with God. But still I am constrained to confess, that the far greater part of those Ministers I have conversed with for above half a century, have not been holy men, not devoted to God, not deeply acquainted either with God or themselves. It could not be said that they set their "affections on things above, not on things of the earth;" or that their desire, and the business of their lives, was, to save their own souls and those that heard them.

19. I have taken this unpleasing view of a melancholy scene,—of the character of those who have been appointed of God to be shepherds of souls for so many ages,—in order to determine this question: "Ought the children of God to refrain from his ordinances because they that administer them are unholy men?" a question with which many serious persons have been exceedingly perplexed. "Ought we not," say they, "to refrain from the ministrations of ungodly men? For is it possible that we should receive any good from the hands of those that know not God? Can we suppose, that the grace of God was ever conveyed to men by the servants of the devil?"

What saith the Scripture? Let us keep close to this, and we shall not be misled. We have seen there what manner of men most of these have been who have ministered in holy things for many ages. Two or three thousand years ago, we read, "The sons of Eli were sons of Belial; they knew not the Lord." But was this a sufficient reason for the Israelites to refrain from their administrations? It is true they "abhorred the offerings of the Lord" on their account; and yet they constantly attended them. And do you suppose that Samuel, holy as he was, ever advised them to do otherwise? Were not the priests, and public teachers, equally strangers to God, from this time to that of the Babylonish captivity? Undoubtedly they were. But did Isaiah, or any of the Prophets, exhort them, for that cause, to forsake the ordinances of God? Were they not equally ungodly from the time of the Babylonish captivity, to the coming of Christ? How clearly does this appear, were there no other proof, from the Prophecies of Jeremiah and Malachi! Yet did either

Malachi, or Jeremiah, or any other of the Prophets, exhort the people to separate themselves from these ungodly men?

20. But, to bring the matter nearer to ourselves: Never were any Priests, or public teachers, more corrupt, more totally estranged from God, than those in the days of our blessed Lord. Were they not mere whited walls? Were not those that were the best of them painted sepulchres; full of pride, lust, envy, covetousness, of all ungodliness and unrighteousness? Is not this the account which our Lord himself, who knew what was in man, gives of them? But did he therefore refrain from that public service which was performed by these very men, or did he direct his Apostles so to do? Nay, just the contrary: In consequence of which, as he constantly attended them himself, so likewise did his disciples.

21. There is another circumstance in our Lord's conduct, which is worthy of our peculiar consideration. He calls to him the twelve, and sends them forth, two by two, to preach the gospel. (Mark 6:7.) And as they did not go the warfare at their own cost, the very "devils were subject unto them." Now, one of these was Judas Iscariot. And did our Lord know that "he had a devil?" St. John expressly tells us he did. Yet he was coupled with another of the Apostles, and joined with them all in the same communion: Neither have we any reason to doubt but God blessed the labour of all his twelve ambassadors. But why did our Lord send him among them? Undoubtedly for our instruction: For a standing, unanswerable proof, that he "sendeth by whom he will send;" that he can and doth send salvation to men even by those who will not accept of it themselves.

22. Our Lord gives us farther instruction upon this head: In Matthew 23:1–3, we have those very remarkable words, "Then Jesus spoke to the multitude, and to his disciples, saying, The scribes and Pharisees sit in Moses' chair: All things, therefore, whatsoever they bid you observe, observe and do; but do not according to their works: For they say, and do not." [Matt. 23:1–3] Of these very men, he gives the blackest character in the following verses. Yet is he so far from forbidding either the multitude, or his own disciples, to attend their ministrations, that he expressly commands them so to do, even in those words, "All things whatsoever they bid you observe, observe and do." These words imply a command to hear them: For how could they "observe and do what they bid them, if they did not hear it? I pray consider this, ye that say of the successors of these ungodly men, "They say, and do not; therefore, we ought not to hear them." You see, your Master draws no such inference; nay, the direct contrary. O be not wiser than your Master! Follow his advice and do not reason against it!

23. But how shall we reconcile this with the direction given by St. Paul to the Corinthians? "If any that is called a brother be a fornicator, or covetous, or an idolater, or a railer, with such an one, no not to eat." (1 Cor. 5:11.) How is it reconcilable with that direction in his Second Epistle, (2 Cor. 6:17,) "Come out from the midst of them, and be ye separate, saith the Lord, and touch not the unclean thing?" I answer, The former passage has no relation at all to the present question. It does not concern Ministers, good or bad. The plain meaning of it is, Have no intimacy with any that is called a Christian, and lives in any open sin;—a weighty exhortation, which should be much attended to by all the children of God. As little does the other passage refer to Ministers or teachers of any kind. In this the Apostle is exhorting the children of God to break off all intercourse with the children of the devil. The words literally are, "Go out from the midst of them, and be ye separate, and touch not the unclean thing;" intimating that they could not continue united with them, without being more or less partakers of their sins. We may therefore boldly affirm, that neither St. Paul, nor any other of the inspired writers, ever advised holy men to separate from the Church wherein they were, because the Ministers were unholy.

24. Nevertheless, it is true, that many pious Christians, as was observed before, did separate themselves from the Church, some even in the second, and many more in the third, century. Some of these retired into the desert, and lived altogether alone; others built themselves houses, afterwards termed convents, and only secluded themselves from the rest of the world. But what was the fruit of this separation? The same that might easily be foreseen. It increased and confirmed, in an astonishing degree, the total corruption of the Church. The salt which was thus heaped up in a corner had effectually lost its savour. The light which was put under a bushel no longer shone before men. In consequence of this, ungodliness and unrighteousness reigned without control. The world, being given up into the hands of the devil, wrought all his works with greediness; and gross darkness, joined with all manner of wickedness, covered the whole earth.

25. "But if all this wickedness was not a sufficient reason for separating from a corrupt church, why did Calvin and Luther, with their followers, separate from the Church of Rome?" I answer, They did not properly separate from it; but were violently thrust out of it. They were not suffered to continue therein, upon any other terms than subscribing to all the errors of that Church, and joining in all their superstition and idolatry. Therefore this separation lay at *their* door. With us it was not a matter of choice, but of necessity: And if such necessity was now laid upon us, we ought to separate from any Church under heaven.

26. There were not the same reasons why various bodies of men should afterwards separate from the Church of England. No sinful terms of communion were imposed upon them; neither are at this day. Most of them separated, either because of some opinions, or some modes of worship, which they did not approve of. Few of them assigned the unholiness either of the Clergy or laity as the cause of their separation. And if any did so, it did not appear that they themselves were a jot better than those they separated from.

27. But the grand reason which many give for separating from the Church, namely, that the Ministers are unholy men, is founded on this assertion: That the ministration of evil men can do no good; that we may call the sacraments means of grace; but men who do not receive the grace of God themselves cannot convey that grace to others. So that we can never expect to receive the blessing of God through the servants of the devil.

This argument is extremely plausible, and is indeed the strongest that can be urged. Yet before you allow it to be conclusive, you should consider a few things.

28. Consider, First, Did the Jewish sacraments convey no saving grace to the hearers, because they were administered by unholy men? If so, none of the Israelites were saved from the time of Eli to the coming of Christ. For their Priests were not a whit better than ours, if they were not much worse. But who will dare to affirm this? which is no less, in effect, than to affirm, that all the children of Israel went to hell for eleven or twelve hundred years together!

29. Did the ordinances, administered in the time of our blessed Lord, convey no grace to those that attended them? Surely then the Holy Ghost would not have commended Zacharias and Elizabeth for walking in these ordinances! If the ministrations of wicked men did no good, would our Lord have commanded his followers (so far from forbidding them) to attend those of the Scribes and Pharisees? Observe, again, the remarkable words: (Matt. 23:1.) "Then spake Jesus to the multitude, and to his disciples, saying, The scribes and Pharisees sit in Moses' seat,"—are your appointed teachers; "all, therefore, whatsoever they bid you observe, that observe and do." Now, what were these Scribes and Pharisees? Were they not the vilest of men? Yet these very men he commands them to hear. This command is plainly implied in those words, "Whatsoever they command you to observe, that observe and do." For unless they heard what they said, they could not do it.

30. Consider, a little farther, the dreadful consequences of affirming that wicked Ministers do no good; that the ordinances administered by them do not convey saving grace to those that attend them. If it be so, then well nigh all the Christians from the time of the Apostles to that of the Reformation are perished! For what manner of men were well nigh all the Clergy during all those centuries? Consult the history of the church in every age, and you will find more and more proofs of their corruption. It is true, they have not been so openly abandoned since; but ever since that happy period there has been a considerable change for the better in the Clergy as well as the laity. But still there is reason to fear that even those who now minister in holy things, who are outwardly devoted to God for that purpose, (yea, and in Protestant as well as Romish countries,) are nevertheless far more devoted to the world, to riches, honour, or pleasure, (a few comparatively excepted,) than they are to God: So that in truth they are as far from Christian holiness as earth is from heaven. If then no grace is conveyed by the ministry of wicked men, in what a case is the Christian world! How hath God forgotten to be gracious! How hath he forsaken his own inheritance! O think not so! Rather say with our own Church, (though in direct opposition to the Church of Rome, which maintains, "If the Priest does not minister with a *pure intention,*" which no wicked man can do, "then the sacrament is no sacrament at all,") the unworthiness of the Minister doth not hinder the efficacy of God's ordinance. The reason is plain, because the efficacy is derived, not from him that administers, but from Him that ordains it. He does not, will not suffer his grace to be intercepted, though the messenger will not receive it himself.

31. Another consequence would follow from the supposition that no grace is conveyed by wicked Ministers; namely, that a conscientious person cannot be a member of any national Church in the world. For wherever he is, it is great odds, whether a holy Minister he stationed there; and if there be not, it is mere lost labour to worship in that congregation. But, blessed be God, this is not the case; we know by our own happy experience, and by the experience of thousands, that the word of the Lord is not bound, though uttered by an unholy minister; and the sacraments are not dry breasts, whether he that administers be holy or unholy.

32. Consider one more consequence of this supposition, should it ever be generally received. Were all men to separate from those Churches where the Minister was an unholy man, (as they ought to do, if the grace of God never did nor could attend his ministry,) what confusion, what tumults, what commotions would this occasion throughout Christendom! What evil-surmisings, heart-burnings, jealousies, envyings, must everywhere arise! What censuring, tale-bearing, strife, contention! Neither would it stop here; but from evil words the contending parties would soon proceed to evil deeds; and rivers of blood would soon be shed, to the utter scandal of Mahometans and Heathens.

33. Let us not then trouble and embroil ourselves and our neighbours with unprofitable disputations, but all agree to spread, to the uttermost of our power, the quiet and peaceable gospel of Christ. Let us make the best of whatever ministry the Providence of God has assigned us. Near fifty years ago, a great and good man, Dr. Potter, then Archbishop of Canterbury, gave me an advice for which I have ever since had occasion to bless God: "If you desire to be extensively useful, do not spend your time and strength in contending for or against such things as are of a disputable nature; but in testifying against open notorious vice, and in promoting real, essential holiness." Let us keep to this: Leaving a thousand disputable points to those that have no better business than to toss the ball of controversy to and fro, let us keep close to our point. Let us bear a faithful testimony, in our several stations, against all ungodliness and unrighteousness, and with all our might recommend that inward and outward holiness "without which no man shall see the Lord!"

105.* "ON CONSCIENCE"

"For our rejoicing is this, the testimony of our conscience."

2 Cor. 1:12.

1. How few words are there in the world more common than this, Conscience! It is in almost every one's mouth. And one would thence be apt to conclude, that no word can be found which is more generally understood. But it may be doubted whether this is the case or no; although numberless treatises have been written upon it. For it is certain, a great part of

---

those writers have rather puzzled the cause than cleared it; that they have usually "darkened counsel by uttering words without knowledge."

2. The best treatise on the subject which I remember to have seen is translated from the French of Mons. Placette, which describes in a clear and rational manner the nature and offices of conscience. But though it was published near a hundred years ago, it is in very few hands; and indeed a great part of those that have read it complain of the length of it. An octavo volume of several hundred pages, upon so plain a subject, was likely to prove a trial of patience to most persons of understanding. It seems, therefore, there is still wanting a discourse upon the subject, short, as well as clear. This, by the assistance of God, I will endeavor to supply, by showing, First, the nature of conscience; and, Then, the several sorts of it; after which, I shall conclude with a few important directions.

I. 1. And, First, I am to show the nature of conscience. This a very pious man in the last century (in his sermon on Universal Conscientiousness) describes in the following manner:—"This word, which literally signifies, *knowing with another*, excellently sets forth the scriptural motion of it. So Job: (16:19:) 'My witness is in heaven.' And so the Apostle: (Rom. 9:1:) 'I say the truth; my conscience also bearing me witness in the Holy Ghost.' In both place it is as if he had said, 'God witnesseth with my conscience. Conscience is placed in the middle, under God, and above man. It is a kind of silent reasoning of the mind, whereby those things which are judged to be right are approved of with pleasure; but those which are judged evil are disapproved of with uneasiness.' " This is a tribunal in the breast of men, to accuse sinners, and excuse them that do well.

2. To view it in a somewhat different light: Conscience, as well as the Latin word from which it is taken, and the Greek word, *syneideseos*, necessarily imply, *the knowledge of two or more things together.* Suppose the knowledge of our words and actions, and at the same time of their goodness or badness; if it be not rather the faculty whereby we know at once our actions and the quality of them.

3. Conscience, then, is that faculty whereby we are at once conscience of our own thoughts, words, and actions; and of their merit or demerit, of their being good or bad; and, consequently, deserving either praise or censure. And some pleasure generally attends the former sentence; some uneasiness the latter: But this varies exceedingly, according to education and a thousand other circumstances.

4. Can it be denied that something of this is found in every man born into the world? And does it not appear as soon as the understanding opens, as soon as reason begins to dawn? Does not every one then begin to know that there is a difference between good and evil; how imperfect soever the various circumstances of this sense of good and evil my be? Does not every man, for instance, know, unless blinded by the prejudices of education, (like the inhabitants of the Cape of Good Hope,) that it is good to honour his parents? Do not all men, however uneducated or barbarous, allow, it is right to do to others as we would have them do to us? And are not all who know this condemned in their own mind when they do anything contrary thereto? as, on the other hand, when they act suitable thereto, they have the approbation of their own conscience?

5. This faculty seems to be what is usually meant by those who speak of natural conscience; an expression frequently found is some of our best authors, but yet not strictly just. For though in one sense it may be termed natural, because it is found in all men; yet, properly speaking, it is not natural, but a supernatural gift of God, above all his natural endowments No; it is not nature, but the Son of God, that is "the true light, which enlighteneth every man that cometh into the world." So that we may say to every human creature, "He," not nature, "hath showed thee, O man, what is good." And it is his Spirit who giveth thee an inward check, who causeth thee to feel uneasy, when thou walkest in any instance contrary to the light which he hath given thee.

6. It may give a peculiar force to that beautiful passage to consider by whom and on what occasion the words were uttered. The persons speaking are Balak the King of Moab; and Balaam, then under divine impressions (it seems, then "not far from the kingdom of God, "although he afterwards so foully revolted): Probably Balak too, at that time, experienced something of the same influence. This occasioned his consulting with, or asking counsel of, Balaam,—his proposing the question to which Balaam gives so full an answer: (Micah 6:5ff.:) "O my people," saith the Prophet in the name of God, "remember what Balak the King of Moab consulted," (it seems, in the fullness of his heart,) "and what Balaam the son of Beor answered him. Wherewith," saith he, "shall I come before the Lord, and Bow myself before the high God? Shall I come before him with calves of a year old? Will the Lord by pleased with thousands of rams, or with ten thousand rivers of oil? Shall I give my first-born for my transgression? the fruit of my body for the sin of my soul?" (This the kings of Moab had actually done, on occasions of deep distress; a remarkable account of which is recorded in the third chapter of the Second Book of Kings.) To this Balaam makes that noble reply, (being, doubtless, then taught of God,) "He hath showed thee, O man, what is good; and what doth the Lord require of thee, but to do justly, to love mercy, and to walk humbly with thy God?"

7. To take a more distinct view of conscience, it appears to have a threefold office: First. It is a witness,—testifying what we have done, in though, or word, or action. Secondly. It is a judge,—passing sentence on what we have done, that it is good or evil. And, Thirdly, it, in some sort, executes the sentence, by occasioning a degree of complacency in him that does well, and a degree of uneasiness in him that does evil.

8. Professor Hutcheson, late of Glasgow, places conscience in a different light. In his Essay on the Passions," he observes, that we have several *senses*, or natural avenues of pleasure and pain, besides the five external senses. One of these he terms *the public sense*; whereby we are naturally pained at the misery of a fellow-creature, and pleased at his deliverance from it. And every man, says he, has a *moral sense*, whereby he approves of benevolence and disapproves of cruelty. Yea,

he is uneasy when he himself has done a cruel action, and pleased when he has done a generous one.

9. All this is, in some sense, undoubtedly true. But it is not true, that either the *public* or the *moral sense* (both of which are included in the term conscience) is now natural to man. Whatever may have been the case at first, while man was in a state of innocence, both the one and the other is now a branch of that supernatural gift of God which we usually style, preventing grace. But the Professor does not at all agree with this. He sets God wholly out of the question. God has nothing to do with his scheme of virtue, from the beginning to the end. So that, to say the truth, his scheme of virtue is Atheism all over. This is refinement indeed! Many have excluded God out of the World: He excludes him even out of religion!

10. But do we not mistake him? Do we take his meaning right? That it may be plain enough, that no man may mistake him, he proposes this question: "What, if a man in doing a virtuous, that is, a generous action, in helping a fellow-creature, has an eye to God, either as commanding, of as promising to reward it? Then," says he, "so far as he has an eye to God, the virtue of the action is lost. Whatever actions spring from an eye to the recompense of reward have no virtue, no moral goodness, in them." Alas! was this man called a Christian? How unjustly was he slandered with that assertion! Even Dr. Taylor, though he does not allow Christ to be God, yet does not scruple to term him, "A person of consummate *virtue*." But the Professor cannot allow him any virtue at all!

11. But to return. What is conscience, in the Christian sense? It is that faculty of the soul which, by the assistance of the grace of God, sees at one and the same time, (1.) Our own tempers and lives,—the real nature and quality of or thoughts, words, and actions; (2.) The rule whereby we are to be directed; and, (3.) The agreement or disagreement therewith. To express this a little more largely: Conscience implies, First, the faculty a man has of knowing himself; of discerning, both in general and in particular, his own tempers, thoughts, words, and actions. But this it is not possible for him to do, without the assistance of the Spirit of God. Otherwise, self-love, and, indeed, every other irregular passion, would disguise and wholly conceal him from himself. It implies, Secondly, a knowledge of the rule whereby he is to be directed in every particular; which is no other than the written word of God. Conscience implies, Thirdly, a knowledge that all his thoughts, and words, and actions are conformable to that rule. In all the offices of conscience, the "unction of the Holy One" is indispensably needful. Without this, neither could we clearly discern our lives or tempers; nor could we judge of the rule whereby we are to walk, or of our conformity of disconformity to it.

12. This is properly the account of a good conscience; which may be in other terms expressed thus: A divine consciousness of walking in all things according to the written word of God. It seems, indeed, that there can be no conscience which has not a regard to God. If you say, "Yes, there certainly may be a consciousness of having done right or wrong, without any reference to him;" I answer, This I cannot grant: I doubt whether the very words, right and wrong, according to the Christian system, do not imply, in the very idea of them, agreement and disagreement to the will and word of God. If so, there is no such thing as conscience in a Christian, if we leave God out of the question.

13. In order to the very existence of a good conscience, as well as to the continuance of it, the continued influence of the Spirit of God is absolutely needful. Accordingly, the Apostle John declares to the believers of all ages, "Ye have an unction from the Holy One, and ye know all things:" All things that are needful to your having a "conscience void of offence toward God and toward man." So he adds, "Ye have no need that any one should teach you," otherwise "than as that anointing teacheth you." That anointing clearly teacheth us those three things,—First, the true meaning of God's word; Secondly, our actions, to remembrance; and, Thirdly, the agreement of all with the commandments of God.

14. Proceed we now to consider, in the Second place, the several sorts of conscience. A good conscience has been spoken of already. This ST. Paul expresses various ways. In one place he simply terms it, a "good conscience toward God;" in another, "a conscience void of offence toward God and toward man." But he speaks still more largely in the text: "Our rejoicing is this, the testimony of our conscience, that in simplicity," with a single eye, "and godly sincerity, we have had our conversation in the world." Meantime he observes, that this was done, "not by fleshly wisdom,"—commonly called prudence,—(this never did, nor ever can produce such an effect,) "but by the grace of God;" which alone is sufficient to work this in any child of man.

15. Nearly allied to this (if it be not the same placed in another view, or a particular branch of it) is a tender conscience. One of a tender conscience is exact in observing any deviation from the word of God, whether in though, or word, or work; and immediately feels remorse and self-condemnation for it. And the constant cry of his soul is,

> O that my tender soul may fly
>   The first abhorr'd approach of ill,
> Quick as the apple of an eye
>   The slightest touch of sin to feel!

16. But sometimes this excellent quality, tenderness of conscience, is carried to an extreme. We find some who fear where no fear is; who are continually condemning themselves without cause; imagining some things to be sinful, which the Scripture nowhere condemns; and supposing other things to be their duty, which the Scripture nowhere enjoins. This is properly termed a scrupulous conscience, and is a sore evil. It is highly expedient to yield to it as little as possible; rather it is a matter of earnest prayer, that you may be delivered from this sore evil, and may recover a sound mind; to which nothing would contribute more, than the converse of a pious and judicious friend.

17. But the extreme which is opposite to this is far more dangerous. A hardened conscience is a thousand times more dangerous than a scrupulous one: That can violate a plain command of God, without any self-condemnation; either doing what he has expressly forbidden, or neglecting what he has expressly commanded; and yet without any remorse; yea,

perhaps glorying in this very hardness of heart! Many instances of this deplorable stupidity we meet with at this day; and even among people that suppose themselves to have no small share of religion. A person is doing something which the Scripture clearly forbids. You ask, "How do you dare to do this?" and are answered with perfect unconcern, "O, my heart does not condemn me." I reply, "So much the worse. I would to God it did! You would then be in a safer state than you are now. It is a dreadful thing to be condemned by the word of God, and yet not to be condemned by your own heart!" If we can break the least of the known commands of God, without any self-condemnation, it is plain that the god of this world hath hardened our hearts. If we do not soon recover from this, we shall be "past feeling," and our consciences (as St. Paul speaks) will be "seared as with a hot iron."

18. I have now only to add a few important directions. The first great point is this: Suppose we have a tender conscience, how shall we preserve it? I believe there is only one possible way of doing this, which is, to obey it. Every act of disobedience tends to blind and deaden it; to put out its eyes, that it may not see the good and the acceptable will of God; and to deaden the heart, that it may not feel self-condemnation when we act in opposition to it. And, in the contrary, every act of obedience gives to the conscience a sharper and stronger sight, and a quicker feeling of whatever offends the glorious majesty of God. Therefore, if you desire to have your conscience always quick to discern, and faithful to accuse or excuse you, if you would preserve it always sensible and tender, be sure to obey it at all events; continually listen to its admonitions, and steadily follow them. Whatever it directs you to do, according to the word of God, do; however grievous to flesh and blood. Whatever it forbids, if the prohibition be grounded on the word of God, see you do it not; however pleasing it may be to flesh and blood. The one or the other may frequently be the case. What God forbids may be pleasing to our evil nature: There you are called to deny yourself, or you deny your Master. What he enjoins may be painful to nature: There take up your cross. So true is our Lord's word: "Except a man deny himself, and take up his cross daily, he cannot be my disciple."

19. I cannot conclude this discourse better, than with an extract from Dr. Annesley's sermon on "Universal Conscientiousness." [Dr. Annesley (my mother's father) was Rector of the parish of Cripplegate.]

"Be persuaded to practise the following directions, and your conscience will continue right:—

1. "Take heed of every sin; count no sin small; and obey every command with your might. Watch against the first risings of sin, and beware of the borders of sin. Shun the very appearance of evil. Venture not upon temptation or occasions of sin.

2. "Consider yourself as living under God's eye: Live as in the sensible presence of the jealous God. Remember, all things are naked and open before him! You cannot deceive him; for he is infinite wisdom: You cannot fly from him; for he is every where: You cannot bribe him; for he is righteousness itself! Speak as knowing God hears you: Walk as knowing God besets you on every side. The Lord is with you while you are with him; that is, you shall enjoy his favourable presence while you live in his awful presence.

3. "Be serious and frequent in the examination of your heart and life. There are some duties like those parts of the body, the want of which may be supplied by other parts; but the want of these nothing can supply. Every evening review you carriage through the day; what you have done or thought that was unbecoming you character; whether you heart has been instant upon religion, and indifferent to the world. Have a special care of two portion of time; namely, morning and evening; the morning to forethink what you have to do, and the evening to examine whether you have done what you ought.

4. "Let every action have reference to your whole life, and not to a part only. Let all your subordinate ends be suitable to the great end of your living. 'Exercise yourself unto godliness.' Be as diligent in religion, as thou wouldest have thy children that go to school be in learning. Let they whole life be a preparation for heaven, like the preparation of wrestlers for the combat.

5. "Do not venture on sin because Christ hath purchased a pardon; that is a most horrible abuse of Christ. For this very reason there was no sacrifice under the law for any wilful sin; lest people should think they know the price of sins, as those do who deal in Popish indulgences.

6. "Be nothing in your own eyes: For what is it, alas! that we have to be proud of? Our very conception was sinful, our birth painful, our life toilsome, our death we know not what! But all this is nothing to the state of our soul. If we know this, what excuse have we for pride?

7. "Consult duty, not events. We have nothing to do but to mind our duty. All speculations that tend not to holiness are among your superfluities; but forebodings of what may befall you in doing your duty may be reckoned among your sins; and to venture upon sin to avoid danger is to sink the ship for fear of pirates. O how quiet, as well as holy, would our lives be, had we learned that single lesson,—to be careful for nothing, but to do our duty, and leave all consequences to God! What madness for silly dust to prescribe to infinite wisdom! to let go our work, and meddle with God's! He hath managed the concerns of the world, and of every individual person in it, without giving cause of complaint to any, for above these five thousand years. And does he now need your counsel? Nay, it is your business to mind your own duty.

8. "What advice you would give another, take yourself: The worst of men are apt enough to lay burdens on others, which if they would take on themselves they would be rare Christians.

9. "Do nothing on which you cannot pray for a blessing. Every action of a Christian that is good, is sanctified by the word and prayer. It becomes not a Christian to do anything so trivial, that he cannot pray over it. And if he would but bestow a serious ejaculation on every occurrent action, such a prayer would cut off all things sinful, and encourage all things lawful.

10. "Think, and speak, and do what you are persuaded Christ himself would do in your case, were he on earth. It becomes a Christian, rather to be an example to all, who was, and is, and ever will be, our absolute pattern. O Christians, how did Christ pray, and redeem time for prayer! How did Christ preach, out of whose mouth proceeded no other but gracious words? What time did Christ spend in impertinent discourse? How did Christ go up and down, doing good to men, and what was pleasing to God? Beloved, I commend to you these four memorials: (1.) Mind duty: (2.) What is the duty of another in your case, is your own: (3.) Do not meddle with anything, if you cannot say, The blessing of the Lord be upon it: (4.) Above all, sooner forget your Christian name, than forget to eye Christ! Whatever treatment you meet with from the world, remember him and follow his steps, 'who did no sin, neither was guile found in his mouth: Who when he was reviled, reviled not again; but committed himself to him that judgeth righteously.' "

106.* ON FAITH

"Without faith it is impossible to please him."

Heb. 11:6.

1. But what is Faith? It is a divine "evidence and conviction of things not seen;" of things which are not seen now, whether they are visible or invisible in their own nature. Particularly, it is a divine evidence and conviction of God, and of the things of God. This is the most comprehensive definition of faith that ever was or can be given; as including every species of faith, from the lowest to the highest. And yet I do not remember any eminent writer that has given a full and clear account of the several sorts of it, among all the verbose and tedious treatises which have been published upon the subject.

2. Something indeed of a similar kind has been written by that great and good man, Mr. Fletcher, in his "Treatise on the various Dispensations of the Grace of God." Herein he observes, that there are four dispensations that are distinguished from each other by the degree of light which God vouchsafes to them that are under each. A small degree of light is given to those that are under the heathen dispensation. These generally believed, "that there was a God, and that he was a rewarder of them that diligently seek him." But a far more considerable degree of light was vouchsafed to the Jewish nation; inasmuch as to them "were entrusted" the grand means of light, "the oracles of God." Hence many of these had clear and exalted views of the nature and attributes of God; of their duty to God and man; yea, and of the great promise made to our first parents, and transmitted by them to their posterity, that "the Seed of the woman should bruise the serpent's head."

3. But above both the heathen and Jewish dispensation was that of John the Baptist. To him a still clearer light was given; and he himself "a burning and shining light." To him it was given to "behold the Lamb of God, that taketh away the sin of tile world." Accordingly our Lord himself affirms, that "of

all which had been born of women," there had not till that time arisen "a greater than John the Baptist." But nevertheless he informs us, "He that is least in the kingdom of God," the Christian dispensation, "is greater than he." By one that is under the Christian dispensation, Mr. Fletcher means one that has received the Spirit of adoption; that has the Spirit of God witnessing "with his spirit, that he is a child of God."

In order to explain this still farther, I will endeavour, by the help of God,

First, To point out the several sorts of faith: And, Secondly, to draw some practical inferences.

I. In the First place, I will endeavour to point out the several sorts of faith. It would be easy, either to reduce these to a smaller number, or to divide them into a greater. But it does not appear that this would answer any valuable purpose.

1. The lowest sort of faith if it be any faith at all, is that of a Materialist,—a man who, like the late Lord Kames, believes there is nothing but matter in the universe. I say, if it be any faith at all: for, properly speaking, it is not. It is not "an evidence or conviction of God," for they do not believe there is any; neither is it "a conviction of things not seen," for they deny the existence of such. Or if, for decency's sake, they allow there is a God, yet they suppose even him to be material. For one of their maxims is, *Jupiter est quodcunque vides.* "Whatever you see, is God." *Whatever you see!* A visible, tangible god! Excellent divinity! Exquisite nonsense!

2. The Second sort of faith, if you allow a Materialist to have any, is the faith of a Deist. I mean, one who believes there is a God, distinct from matter; but does not believe the Bible. Of these we may observe two sorts. One sort are mere beasts in human shape, wholly under the power of the basest passions, and having "a downright appetite to mix with mud." Other Deists are, in most respects, rational creatures, though unhappily prejudiced against Christianity: Most of these believe the being and attributes of God; they believe that God made and governs the world; and that the soul does not die with the body, but will remain for ever in a state of happiness or misery.

3. The next sort of faith is the faith of Heathens, with which I join that of Mahometans. I cannot but prefer this before the faith of the Deists; because, though it embraces nearly the same objects, yet they are rather to be pitied than blamed for the narrowness of their faith. And their not believing the whole truth, is not owing to want of sincerity, but merely to want of light. When one asked Chicali, an old Indian Chief, "Why do not you red men know as much as us white men?" he readily answered, "Because you have the great Word, and we have not."

4. It cannot be doubted, but this plea will avail for millions of modern Heathens. Inasmuch as to them little is given, of them little will be required. As to the ancient Heathens, millions of them, likewise were savages. No more therefore will be expected of them, than the living up to the light they had. But many of them, especially in the civilized nations, we have great reason to hope, although they lived among

Heathens, yet were quite of another spirit; being taught of God, by His inward voice, all the essentials of true religion. Yea, and so was that Mahometan, and Arabian, who, a century or two ago, wrote the Life of Hai Ebn Yokdan. The story seems to be feigned; but it contains all the principles of pure religion and undefiled.

5. But, in general, we may surely place the faith of a Jew above that of a Heathen or Mahometan. By Jewish faith, I mean, the faith of those who lived between the giving of the law and the coming of Christ. These, that is, those that were serious and sincere among them, believed all that is written in the Old Testament. In particular, they believed that, in the fulness of time, the Messiah would appear, "to finish the transgression, to make an end of sin, and bring in everlasting righteousness."

6. It is not so easy to pass any judgment concerning the faith of our modern Jews. It is plain, "the veil is still upon their hearts" when Moses and the Prophets are read. The god of this world still hardens their hearts, and still blinds their eyes, "lest at any time the light of the glorious gospel" should break in upon them. So that we may say of this people, as the Holy Ghost said to their forefathers, "The heart of this people is waxed gross, and their ears are dull of hearing, and their eyes they have closed; lest they should see with their eyes, and hear with their ears, and understand with their hearts, and should be converted, and I should heal them." (Acts 28:27.) Yet it is not our part to pass sentence upon them, but to leave them to their own Master.

7. I need not dwell upon the faith of John the Baptist, any more than the dispensation which he was under; because these, as Mr. Fletcher well describes them, were peculiar to himself. Setting him aside, the faith of the Roman Catholics, in general, seems to be above that of the ancient Jews. If most of these are volunteers in faith, believing more than God has revealed, it cannot be denied that they believe all which God has revealed, as necessary to salvation. In this we rejoice on their behalf: We are glad that none of those new Articles, which they added, at the Council of Trent, "to the faith once delivered to the saints, does so materially contradict any of the ancient Articles, as to render them of no effect.

8. The faith of the Protestants, in general, embraces only those truths as necessary to salvation, which are clearly revealed in the oracles of God. Whatever is plainly declared in the Old and New Testament is the object of their faith. They believe neither more nor less than what is manifestly contained in, and provable by, the Holy Scriptures. The word of God is "a lantern to their feet, and a light in all their paths." They dare not, on any pretence, go from it, to the right hand or to the left. The written word is the whole and sole rule of their faith, as well as practice. They believe whatsoever God has declared, and profess to do whatsoever he hath commanded. This is the proper faith of Protestants: By this they will abide, and no other.

9. Hitherto faith has been considered chiefly as an evidence and conviction of such or such truths. And this is the sense wherein it is taken at this day in every part of the Christian world. But, in the mean time, let it be carefully observed, (for eternity depends upon it,) that neither the faith of a Roman Catholic, nor that of a Protestant, if it contains no more than this, no more than the embracing such and such truths, will avail any more before God, than the faith of a Mahometan or a Heathen; yea, of a Deist or Materialist. For can this "faith save him?" Can it save any man either from sin or from hell? No more than it could cave Judas Iscariot: No more than it could save the devil and his angels; all of whom are convinced that every title of Holy Scripture is true.

10. But what is the faith which is properly saving; which brings eternal salvation to all those that keep it to the end? It is such a divine conviction of God, and the things of God, as, even in its infant state, enables every one that possesses it to "fear God and work righteousness." And whosoever, in every nation, believes thus far, the Apostle declares, is "accepted of him." He actually is, at that very moment, in a state of acceptance. But he is at present only a *servant* of God, not properly a *son*. Meantime, let it be well observed, that "the wrath of God" no longer "abideth on him.'

11. Indeed, nearly fifty years ago, when the Preachers, commonly called Methodists, began to preach that grand scriptural doctrine, salvation by faith, they were not sufficiently apprized of the difference between a servant and a child of God. They did not clearly understand, that even one "who feareth God, and worketh righteousness, is accepted of him." In consequence of this, they were apt to make sad the hearts of those whom God had not made sad. For they frequently asked those who feared God, "Do you know that your sins are forgiven?" And upon their answering, "No," immediately replied, "Then you are a child of time devil." No; this does not follow. It might have been said, (and it is all that can be said with propriety,) "Hitherto you are only a *servant*, you are not a *child* of God. You have already great reason to praise God that he has called you to his honourable service. Fear not. Continue crying unto him, 'and you shall see greater things than these.' "

12. And, indeed, unless the servants of God halt by the way, they will receive the adoption of sons. They will receive the *faith* of the children of God, by his *revealing* his only begotten Son in their hearts. Thus, the faith of a child is, properly and directly, a divine conviction, whereby every child of God is enabled to testify, "The life that I now live, I live by faith the Son of God, who loved me, and gave himself for me." And whosoever hath this, the Spirit of God witnesseth with his spirit, that he is a child of God. So the Apostle writes to the Galatians: "Ye are the sons of God by faith. And because ye are sons, God hath sent forth the Spirit of his Son into your hearts, crying, Abba, Father;" that is, giving you a childlike confidence in him, together with a kind affection toward him. This then it is, that (if St. Paul was taught of God, and wrote as he was moved by the Holy Ghost) properly constitutes the difference between a servant of God, and a child of God. "He that believeth," as a child of God, "hath the witness in himself." This the servant hath not. Yet let no man discourage him; rather, lovingly exhort him to expect it every moment.

13. It is easy to observe, that all the sort of faith which we can conceive are reducible to one or other of the preceding. But let us covet the best gifts, and follow the most excellent way.

There is no reason why you should be satisfied with the faith of a Materialist, a Heathen, or a Deist; nor, indeed, with that of a servant. I do not know that God requires it at your hands. Indeed, if you have received this, you ought not to cast it away; you ought not in anywise to undervalue it but to be truly thankful for it. Yet, in the mean time, beware how you rest here: Press on till you receive the Spirit of adoption: Rest not, till that Spirit clearly witnesses with your spirit, that you are a child of God.

II. I proceed, in the Second place, to draw a few inferences from the preceding observations.

1. And I would, First, infer, in how dreadful a state, if there be a God, is a Materialist one who denies not only the "Lord that bought him," but also the Lord that made him. "Without faith it is impossible to please God." But it is impossible *he* should have any faith at all;—any conviction of any invisible world; for he believes there is no such thing;—any conviction the being of a God; for a material God is no God at all. For you cannot possibly suppose the sun or skies to be God, any more than you can suppose a God of wood or stone. And, farther, whosoever believes all things to be mere matter must, of course, believe that all things are governed by dire necessity—necessity that is as inexorable as the winds; as ruthless as the rocks as merciless as the waves that dash upon them, or the poor shipwrecked mariners! Who then shall help thee, thou poor desolate wretch, when thou art most in need of help? Winds, and seas, and rocks, and storms! Such are the best helpers which the Materialists can hope for!

2. Almost equally desolate is the case of the poor Deist, how learned, yea, how moral, soever he be. For you, likewise, though you may not advert it, are really "without God in the world." See your religion, the "Religion of nature, delineated" by ingenious Mr. Wollaston; whom I remember to have seen when I was at school, attending the public service at the Charter-house chapel. Does he found his religion upon God? Nothing less. He founds it upon truth, abstract truth. But does he not by that expression mean God? No; he sets him out of the question, and builds a beautiful castle in the air, without being beholden either to Him or his word. See your smooth-tongued orator of Glasgow, one of the most pleasing writers of the age! Has he any more to do with God, on his system, than Mr. Wollaston.? Does he deduce his "Idea of Virtue' from him, as the Father of Lights, the Source of all good? Just the contrary. He not only plans his whole theory without taking the least notice of God, but toward the close of it proposes that question, "Does the having an eye to God in an action enhance the virtue of it?' He answers, "No; it is so far from this, that if in doing a virtuous, that is, a benevolent, action, a man mingles a desire to please God, the more there is of this desire, the less virtue there is in that action?" Never before did I meet with either Jew, Turk, or Heathen who so flatly renounced God as this Christian Professor!

3. But with Heathens, Mahometans, and Jews we have at present nothing to do; only we may wish that their lives did not shame many of us that are called Christians. We have not much more to do with the members of the Church of Rome.

But we cannot doubt, that many of them, like the excellent Archbishop of Cambray, still retain (notwithstanding many mistakes) that faith that worketh by love. And how many of the Protestants enjoy this, whether members of the Church of England, or of other congregations? We have reason to believe a considerable number, both of one and the other, (and, blessed be God, an increasing number,) in every part of the land.

4. One more, I exhort you that fear God and work righteousness, you that are *servants* of God, First, flee from all sin, as from the face of a serpent; being

> Quick as the apple of an eye,
> The slightest touch of sin to feel;

and to work righteousness, to the utmost of the power you now have to abound in works both of piety and mercy: And, Secondly, continually to cry to God, that he would reveal his Son in your hearts, to the intent you may be no more *servants* but *sons*; having his love shed abroad in your hearts, and walking in "the glorious liberty of the, children of God."

5. I exhort you, Lastly, who already feel the Spirit of God witnessing with your spirit that you are the children of God, follow the advice of the Apostle: Walk in all the good works whereunto ye are created in Christ Jesus. And then, "leaving the principles of the doctrine of Christ, and not laying again the foundation of repentance from dead works, and of faith toward God," go on to perfection. Yea, and when ye have attained a measure of perfect love, when God has circumcised your hearts, and enabled you to love him with all your heart and with all your soul, think not of resting there. That is impossible. You cannot stand still; you must either rise or fall; rise higher or fail lower. Therefore the voice of God to the children of Israel, to the children of God, is, "Go forward!" "Forgetting the things that are behind, and reaching forward unto those that are before, press on to the mark, for the prize of your high calling of God in Christ Jesus!"

107. ON GOD'S VINEYARD

"What could have been done more to my vineyard, that I have not done in it? wherefore, when I looked that it should bring forth grapes, brought it forth wild grapes?"
Isa. 5:4.

The vineyard of the Lord, taking the word in its widest sense, may include the whole world. All the inhabitants of the earth may, in some sense, be called "the vineyard of the Lord;" "who hath made all nations of men, to dwell on all the face of the earth; that they might seek the Lord, if haply they may feel after him, and find him." But, in a narrower sense, the vineyard of the Lord may mean the Christian world; that is, all that name the name of Christ, and profess to obey his word. In a still narrower sense, it may be understood of what is termed the Reformed part of the Christian Church. In the narrowest of all, one may, by that phrase, "the vineyard of the Lord," mean, the body of people commonly called Methodists. In this sense I understand it now, meaning thereby that society only which began at Oxford in the year 1729, and remain united at this day. Understanding the word in this sense, I repeat the question which God proposes to the Prophet: "What could have been done more to my vineyard, that I have not done in it? wherefore, when I looked that it should bring forth grapes, brought it forth wild grapes?"

What could God have done more in this his vineyard, (suppose he had designed it should put forth great branches and spread over the earth,) which he hath not done in it,

I.   With regard to doctrine?
II.   With regard to spiritual helps?
III.   With regard to discipline? And,
IV.   With regard to outward protection?

These things being considered, I would then briefly inquire, "Wherefore, when he looked it should bring forth grapes, brought it forth wild grapes?"

I. 1. First. What could have been done in this his vineyard, which God hath not done in it? What could have been done more, with regard to doctrine? From the very beginning, from the time that four young men united together, each of them was *homo unius libri*,—"a man of one book." God taught them all, to make his "word a lantern unto their feet, and a light in all their paths." They had one, and only one, rule of judgment, with regard to all their tempers, words, and actions; namely, the oracles of God. They were one and all determined to be Bible-Christians. They were continually reproached for this very thing; some terming them, in derision, Bible-bigots; others, Bible-moths; feeding, they said, upon the Bible, as moths do upon cloth. And indeed, unto this day, it is their constant endeavour to think and speak as the oracles of God.

2. It is true, a learned man, Dr. Trapp, soon after their setting out, gave a very different account of them. "When I saw," said the Doctor, "these two books, 'The Treatise on Christian Perfection,' and 'The Serious Call to a Holy Life,' I thought, These books will certainly do mischief. And so it proved; for presently after up sprung the Methodists. So he (Mr. Law) was their parent." Although this was not entirely true, yet there was some truth in it. All the Methodists carefully read these books, and were greatly profited thereby. Yet they did by no means spring from them, but from the Holy Scriptures; being "born again," as St. Peter speaks, "by the word of God, which liveth and abideth for ever."

3. Another learned man, the late Bishop Warburton, roundly affirms, that "they were the offspring of Mr. Law and Count Zinzendorf together." But this was a greater mistake still. For they had met together several years before they had the least acquaintance with Count Zinzendorf, or even knew there was such a person in the world. And when they did know him, although they esteemed him very highly in love, yet they did not dare to follow him one step farther than they were warranted by the Scripture.

4. The book which, next to the Holy Scripture, was of the greatest use to them, in settling their judgment as to the grand point of justification by faith, was the book of Homilies. They were never clearly convinced that we are justified by faith alone, till they carefully consulted these, and compared them with the sacred writings, particularly St. Paul's Epistle to the Romans. And no Minister of the Church can, with any decency, oppose these; seeing at his ordination he subscribed to them, in subscribing the thirty-sixth Article of the Church.

5. It has been frequently observed, that very few were clear in their judgment both with regard to justification and sanctification. Many who have spoken and written admirably well concerning justification, had no clear conception, nay, were totally ignorant, of the doctrine of sanctification. Who has wrote more ably than Martin Luther on justification by faith alone? And who was more ignorant of the doctrine of sanctification, or more confused in his conceptions of it? In order to be thoroughly convinced of this, of his total ignorance with regard to sanctification, there needs no more than to read over, without prejudice, his celebrated comment on the Epistle to the Galatians. On the other hand, how many writers of the Romish Church (as Francis Sales and Juan de Castaniza, in particular) have wrote strongly and scripturally on sanctification, who, nevertheless, were entirely unacquainted with the nature of justification! insomuch that the whole body of their Divines at the Council of Trent, in their *Catechismus ad Parochos*, (Catechism which every parish Priest is to teach his people,) totally confound sanctification and justification together. But it has pleased God to give the Methodists a full and clear knowledge of each, and the wide difference between them.

6. They know, indeed, that at the same time a man is justified, sanctification properly begins. For when he is justified, he is "born again," "born from above," "born of the Spirit;" which, although it is not (as some suppose) the whole process of sanctification, is doubtless the gate of it. Of this, likewise, God has given them a full view. They know, the new birth implies as great a change in the soul, in him that is "born of the Spirit," as was wrought in his body when he was born of a woman: Not an outward change only, as from drunkenness to sobriety, from robbery or theft to honesty; (this is the poor, dry, miserable conceit of those that know nothing of real religion;) but an inward change from all unholy, to all holy tempers,—from pride to humility, from passionateness to meekness, from peevishness and discontent to patience and resignation; in a word, from an earthly, sensual, devilish mind, to the mind that was in Christ Jesus.

7. It is true, a late very eminent author, in his strange "Treatise on Regeneration," proceeds entirely on the supposition, that it is the whole gradual progress of sanctification. No; it is only the threshold of sanctification, the first entrance upon it. And as, in the natural birth, a man is born at once, and then grows larger and stronger by degrees; so in the spiritual birth, a man is born at once, and then gradually increases in spiritual stature and strength. The new birth, therefore, is the first point of sanctification, which may increase more and more unto the perfect day.

8. It is, then, a great blessing given to this people, that as they do not think or speak of justification so as to supersede sanctification, so neither do they think or speak of sanctification so as to supersede justification. They take care to keep each in its own place, laying equal stress on one and the other. They know God has joined these together, and it is not for man to put them asunder: Therefore they maintain, with equal zeal and diligence, the doctrine of free, full,

present justification, on the one hand, and of entire sanctification both of heart and life, on the other; being as tenacious of inward holiness as any Mystic, and of outward, as any Pharisee.

9. Who then is a Christian, according to the light which God hath vouchsafed to this people? He that, being "justified by faith, hath peace with God through our Lord Jesus Christ;" and, at the same time, is "born again," "born from above," "born of the Spirit;" inwardly changed from the image of the devil, to that "image of God wherein he was created:" He that finds the love of God shed abroad in his heart by the Holy Ghost which is given unto him; and whom this love sweetly constrains to love his neighbor, every man, as himself: He that has learned of his Lord to be meek and lowly in heart, and in every state to be content: He in whom is that whole mind, all those tempers, which were also in Christ Jesus: He that abstains from all appearance of evil in his actions, and that offends not with his tongue: He that walks in all the commandments of God, and in all his ordinances, blameless: He that, in all his intercourse with men, does to others as he would they should do to him; and in his whole life and conversation, whether he eats or drinks, or whatsoever he doeth, doeth all to the glory of God.

Now, what could God have done more for this his vineyard, which he hath not done in it, with regard to doctrine? We are to inquire,

II. Secondly, What could have been done which he hath not done in it, with regard to spiritual helps?

1. Let us consider this matter from the very beginning. Two young Clergymen, not very remarkable any way, of middle age, having a tolerable measure of health, though rather weak than strong, began, about fifty years ago, to call sinners to repentance. This they did, for a time, in many of the churches in and about London. But two difficulties arose: First. The churches were so crowded, that many of the parishioners could not get in. Secondly. They preached new doctrines,— that we are saved by faith, and that "without holiness no man could see the Lord." For one or other of these reasons, they were not long suffered to preach in the churches. They then preached in Moorfields, Kennington-Common, and in many other public places. The fruit of their preaching quickly appeared. Many sinners were changed both in heart and life. But it seemed this could not continue long; for every one clearly saw, these Preachers would quickly wear themselves out; and no Clergyman dared to assist them. But soon one and another, though not ordained, offered to assist them. God gave a signal blessing to their word. Many sinners were thoroughly convinced of sin, and many truly converted to God. Their assistants increased, both in number, and in the success of their labours. Some of them were learned: some unlearned. Most of them were young; a few middle-aged: Some of them were weak; some, on the contrary, of remarkably strong understanding. But it pleased God to own them all; so that more and more brands were plucked out of the burning.

2. It may be observed, that these Clergymen, all this time, had no plan at all. They only went hither and thither, wherever they had a prospect of saving souls from death. But

when more and more asked, "What must I do to be saved?" they were desired to meet all together. Twelve came the first Thursday night; forty the next; soon after, a hundred. And they continued to increase, till, three or four and twenty years ago, the London Society amounted to about 2,800.

3. "But how should this multitude of people be kept together? And how should it be known whether they walked worthy of their profession?" They were providentially led, when they were thinking on another thing, namely, paying the public debt, to divide all the people into little companies, or classes, according to their places of abode, and appoint one person in each class to see all the rest weekly. By this means it was quickly discovered if any of them lived in any known sin. If they did, they were first admonished; and, when judged incorrigible, excluded from the society.

4. This division of the people, and exclusion of those that walked disorderly, without any respect of persons, were helps which few other communities had. To these, as the societies increased, was soon added another. The stewards of the societies in each district were desired to meet the Preachers once a quarter, in some central place, to give an account of the spiritual and temporal state of their several societies. The use of these quarterly meetings was soon found to be exceeding great; in consideration of which, they were gradually spread to all the societies in the kingdom.

5. In order to increase the union between the Preachers, as well as that of the people, they were desired to meet all together in London; and, some time after, a select number of them. Afterwards, for more convenience, they met at London, Bristol, and Leeds, alternately. They spent a few days together in this general Conference, in considering what might most conduce to the general good. The result was immediately signified to all their brethren. And they soon found, that what St. Paul observes of the whole Church, may be, in a measure, applied to every part of it: "The whole body being fitly framed together and compacted by that which every joint supplieth, maketh increase of the body to the edifying of itself in love." (Eph. 4:6.)

6. That this may be the more effectually done, they have another excellent help, in the constant change of Preachers; it being their rule, that no Preacher shall remain in the same circuit more than two years together, and few of them more than one year. Some, indeed, have imagined that this was a hindrance to the work of God: But long experience, in every part of the kingdom, proves the contrary. This has always shown that the people profit less by any one person than by a variety of Preachers; while they

Used the gifts on each bestow'd,
Temper'd by the art of God.

7. Together with these helps, which are peculiar to their own society, they have all those which are enjoyed in common by the other members of the Church of England. Indeed, they have been long pressed to separate from it; to which they have had temptations of every kind. But they cannot, they dare not, they will not, separate from it, while they can remain therein with a clear conscience. It is true, if any sinful terms of communion were imposed upon them, then they would

be constrained to separate; but as this is not the case at present, we rejoice to continue therein.

8. What then could God have done more for this his vineyard, which he hath not done in it, with regard to spiritual helps? He has hardly dealt so with any other people in the Christian world. If it be said, "He could have made them a separate people, like the Moravian Brethren;" I answer, This would have been a direct contradiction to his whole design in raising them up; namely, to spread scriptural religion throughout the land, among people of every denomination, leaving every one to hold his own opinions, and to follow his own mode of worship. This could only be done effectually, by leaving these things as they were, and endeavouring to leaven the whole nation with that "faith that worketh by love."

III. 1. Such are the spiritual helps which God has bestowed on this his vineyard with no sparing hand. Discipline might be inserted among these; but we may as well speak of it under a separate head. It is certain that, in this respect, the Methodists are a highly favoured people. Nothing can be more simple, nothing more rational, than the Methodist discipline: It is entirely founded on common sense, particularly applying the general rules of Scripture. Any person determined to save his soul may be united (this is the only condition required) with them. But this desire must be evidenced by three marks: Avoiding all known sin; doing good after his power; and, attending all the ordinances of God. He is then placed in such a class as is convenient for him, where he spends about an hour in a week. And, the next quarter, if nothing is objected to him, he is admitted into the society: And therein he may continue as long as he continues to meet his brethren, and walks according to his profession.

2. Their public service is at five in the morning, and six or seven in the evening, that their temporal business may not be hindered. Only on Sunday it begins between nine and ten, and concludes with the Lord's Supper. On Sunday evening the society meets; but care is taken to dismiss them early, that all the heads of families may have time to instruct their several households. Once a quarter, the principal Preacher in every circuit examines every member of the societies therein. By this means, if the behaviour of anyone is blameable, which is frequently to be expected in so numerous a body of people, it is easily discovered, and either the offence or the offender removed in time.

3. Whenever it is needful to exclude any disorderly member out of the society, it is done in the most quiet and inoffensive manner; only by not renewing his ticket at the quarterly visitation. But in some cases, where the offence is great, and there is danger of public scandal, it is judged necessary to declare, when all the members are present, "A. B. is no longer a member of our society." Now, what can be more rational or more scriptural than this simple discipline; attended, from the beginning to the end, with no trouble, expense, or delay?

IV. 1. But was it possible, that all these things should be done without a flood of opposition? The prince of this world was not dead, nor asleep: and would he not fight, that his kingdom might not be delivered up? If the word of the Apostle be found true, in all ages and nations, "All they that will live godly in Christ Jesus shall suffer persecution;" if this be true, with regard to every individual Christian, how much more with regard to bodies of men visibly united together with the avowed design to overthrow his kingdom! And what could withstand the persecution he would not fail to stir up against a poor, defenceless, despised people, without any visible help, without money, without power, without friends?

2. In truth, the god of this world was not asleep. Neither was he idle. He *did* fight, and that with all his power, that his kingdom might not be delivered up. He "brought forth all his hosts to war." First. He stirred up the beasts of the people. They roared like lions; they encompassed the little and defenceless on every side. And the storm rose higher and higher, till deliverance came in a way that none expected. God stirred up the heart of our late gracious Sovereign to give such orders to his Magistrates as, being put in execution, effectually quelled the madness of the people. It was about the same time that a great man applied personally to His Majesty, begging that he would please to "take a course to stop these run-about Preachers." His Majesty, looking sternly upon him, answered without ceremony, like a King, "I tell you, while I sit on the throne, no man shall be persecuted for conscience' sake."

3. But in defiance of this, several who bore His Majesty's commission have persecuted them from time to time; and that under colour of law; availing themselves of what is called the Conventicle Act: One in particular, in Kent, who, some years since, took upon him to fine one of the Preachers and several of his hearers. But they thought it their duty to appeal to His Majesty's Court of King's Bench. The cause was given for the plaintiffs; who have ever since been permitted to worship God according to their own conscience.

4. I believe this is a thing wholly without precedent. I find no other instance of it, in any age of the Church, from the day of Pentecost to this day. Every opinion, right and wrong, has been tolerated, almost in every age and nation. Every mode of worship has been tolerated, however superstitious or absurd. But I do not know that true, vital, scriptural religion was ever tolerated before. For this the people called Methodists have abundant reason to praise God. In their favour he hath wrought a new thing in the earth: He hath stilled the enemy and the avenger. This then they must ascribe unto Him, the Author of their outward as well as inward peace.

V. 1. What indeed could God have done more for this his vineyard, which he hath not done in it? This having been largely showed, we may now proceed to that strong and tender expostulation: "After all that I had done, might I not have looked for the most excellent grapes? Wherefore, then, brought it forth wild grapes? Might I not have expected a general increase of faith and love, of righteousness and true holiness; yea, and of the fruit of the Spirit,—love, joy, peace, long-suffering, meekness, gentleness, fidelity, goodness, temperance?" Was it not reasonable to expect that these fruits would have overspread his whole Church? Truly, when I saw what God had done among his people between forty and fifty years ago; when I saw them warm in their first love, magnifying the Lord, and rejoicing in God their Saviour; I could expect nothing less than that all these would have lived like angels here below; that they would have walked as continually seeing Him that is invisible; having constant communion with the Father and the Son, living in eternity, and walking in eternity. I looked to see "a chosen generation, a royal priesthood, a holy nation, a peculiar people," in the whole tenor of their conversation; "showing forth His praise, who had called them into his marvellous light."

2. But, instead of this, it brought forth wild grapes,—fruit of a quite contrary nature. It brought forth error in ten thousand shapes, turning many of the simple out of the way. It brought forth enthusiasm, imaginary inspiration, ascribing to the all-wise God all the wild, absurd, self-inconsistent dreams of a heated imagination. It brought forth pride, robbing the Giver of every good gift of the honour due to his name. It brought forth prejudice, evil surmising, censoriousness, judging, and condemning one another;—all totally subversive of that brotherly love which is the very badge of the Christian profession; without which whosoever liveth is counted dead before God. It brought forth anger, hatred, malice, revenge, and every evil word and work;—all direful fruits, not of the Holy Spirit, but of the bottomless pit!

3. It brought forth likewise in many, particularly those that are increased in goods, that grand poison of souls, the love of the world; and that in all its branches: "The desire of the flesh;" that is, the seeking happiness in the pleasures of sense;—"the desire of the eyes;" that is, seeking happiness in dress, or any of the pleasures of imagination;—and "the pride of life;" that is, seeking happiness in the praise of men; or in that which ministers to all these, laying up treasures on earth. It brought forth self-indulgence of every kind, delicacy, effeminacy, softness; but not softness of the right kind, that melts at human woe. It brought such base, grovelling affections, such deep earthly-mindedness, as that of the poor Heathens, which occasioned the lamentation of their own Poet over them,—*O curvae in terras animae et coelestium inanes!*—"O souls bowed down to earth, and void of God!"

4. O ye that have riches in possession, once more hear the word of the Lord! Ye that are rich in this world, that have food to eat, and raiment to put on, and something over, are you clear of the curse of loving the world? Are you sensible of your danger? Do you feel, "How hardly will they that have riches enter into the kingdom of heaven?" Do you continue unburned in the midst of the fire? Are you untouched with the love of the world? Are you clear from the desire of the flesh, the desire of the eyes, and the pride of life? Do you "put a knife to your throat," when you sit down to meat, lest your table should be a snare to you? Is not your belly your god? Is not eating and drinking, or any other pleasure of sense, the greatest pleasure you enjoy? Do not you seek happiness in dress, furniture, pictures, gardens, or anything else that pleases the eye? Do not you grow soft and delicate; unable to bear cold, heat, the wind or the rain, as you did when you were poor? Are you not increasing in goods, laying up treasures on earth; instead of restoring to God in the poor,

not so much, or so much, but all that you can spare? Surely, "it is easier for a camel to go through the eye of a needle, than for a rich man to enter into the kingdom of heaven!"

5. But why will ye still bring forth wild grapes? What excuse can ye make? Hath God been wanting on *his* part? Have you not been warned over and over? Have ye not been fed with "the sincere milk of the word?" Hath not the whole word of God been delivered to you, and without any mixture of error? Were not the fundamental doctrines both of free, full, present justification delivered to you, as well as sanctification, both gradual and instantaneous? Was not every branch both of inward and outward holiness clearly opened, and earnestly applied; and that by Preachers of every kind, young and old, learned and unlearned? But it is well if some of you did not despise the helps which God had prepared for you. Perhaps you would hear none but Clergymen; or, at least, none but men of learning. Will you not then give God leave to choose his own messengers? to send by whom he will send? It is well if this bad wisdom was not one cause of your bringing forth wild grapes!

6. Was not another cause of it your despising that excellent help, union with a Christian society? Have you not read, "How can one be warm alone?" and, "Woe be unto him that is alone when he falleth?" But you have companions enough. Perhaps more than enough; more than are helpful to your soul. But have you enough that are athirst for God, and that labour to make you so? Have you companions enough that watch over your soul, as they that must give account; and that freely and faithfully warn you, if you take any false step, or are in danger of doing so? I fear you have few of these companions, or else you would bring forth better fruit!

7. If you are a member of the society, do you make a full use of your privilege? Do you never fail to meet your class; and that not as matter of form, but expecting that when you are met together in his name, your Lord will be in the midst of you? Are you truly thankful for the amazing liberty of conscience which is vouchsafed to you and your brethren; such as never was enjoyed before by persons in your circumstances? And are you thankful to the Giver of every good gift for the general spread of true religion? Surely, you can never praise God enough for all these blessings, so plentifully showered down upon you, till you praise him with angels and archangels, and all the company of heaven!

108.* ON RICHES

"It is easier for a camel to go through the eye of a needle, than for a rich man to enter into the kingdom of God."
Matthew 19:24.

1. In the preceding verses we have an account of a young man who came running to our Lord, and kneeling down, not in hypocrisy, but in deep earnestness of soul, and said unto him, "Good Master, what good thing shall I do, that I may have eternal life?" "All the commandments," saith he, "I have kept from my youth: What lack I yet?" Probably he had kept them in the literal sense; yet he still loved the world. And He who

---

* (text from the 1872 edition)

knew what was in man knew that, in this particular case, (for this is by no means a general rule,) he could not be healed of that desperate disease, but by a desperate remedy. Therefore he answered, "Go and sell all that thou hast, and give it to the poor; and come and follow me. But when he heard this, he went away sorrowful, for he had great possessions. So all the fair blossoms withered away! For he would not lay up treasure in heaven at so high a price! Jesus, observing this, "looked round about, and said unto his disciples," (Mark 10:23.) "How hardly shall they that have riches enter into the kingdom of God! It is easier for a camel to go through the eye of a needle, than for a rich man to enter into the kingdom of God! And they were astonished out of measure, and said among themselves, Who then can be saved?"—if it be so difficult for rich men to be saved, who have so many and so great advantages, who are frees from the cares of this world, and a thousand difficulties to which the poor are continually exposed?

2. It has indeed been supposed, he partly retracts what he had said concerning the difficulty of rich men's being saved, by what is added in the tenth chapter of St. Mark. For after he had said, (verse 23,) "How hardly shall they that have riches enter into the kingdom of God!" when "the disciples were astonished at his words, Jesus answered again," and said unto them, "How hard is it for them that trust in riches to enter into the kingdom of God!" (Verse 24.) But observe, (1.) Our Lord did not mean hereby to retract what he had said before. So far from it, that he immediately confirms it by that awful declaration, "It is easier for a camel to go through the eye of a needle, than for a rich man to enter into the kingdom of God." Observe, (2.) Both one of these sentences and the other assert the very same thing. For it is easier for a camel to go through the eye of a needle, than for those that have riches not to *trust* in them.

3. Perceiving their astonishment at this hard saying, "Jesus, looking upon them," (undoubtedly with an air of inexpressible tenderness, to prevent their thinking the case of the rich desperate,) "saith, With men it is impossible, but not with God: For with God all things are possible."

4. I apprehend, by a rich man here is meant, not only a man that has immense treasures, one that has heaped up gold as dust, and silver as the sand of the sea; but anyone that possesses more than the necessaries and conveniences of life. One that has food and raiment sufficient for himself and his family, and something over, is rich. By the kingdom of God, or of heaven, (exactly equivalent terms,) I believe is meant, not the kingdom of glory, (although that will, without question, follow,) but the kingdom of heaven, that is, true religion, upon earth. The meaning then of our Lord's assertion is this,—that it is absolutely impossible, unless by that power to which all things are possible, that a rich man should be a Christian; to have the mind that was in Christ, and to walk as Christ walked: Such are the hinderances to holiness, as well as the temptations to sin, which surround him on every side.

I. First. Such are the hinderances to holiness which surround him on every side. To enumerate all these would require a large volume: I would only touch upon a few of them.

1. The root of all religion is faith, without which it is impossible to please God. Now, whether you take this in its general acceptation, for an "evidence of things not seen," of the invisible and the eternal world, of God and the things of God, how natural a tendency have riches to darken this evidence, to prevent your attention to God and the things of God, and to things invisible and eternal! And if you take it in another sense, for a confidence; what a tendency have riches to destroy this; to make you trust, either for happiness or defence, in them, not "in the living God!" Or if you take faith, in the proper Christian sense, as a divine confidence in a pardoning God; what a deadly, what an almost insuperable, hinderance to this faith are riches! What! Can a wealthy, and consequently an honourable, man come to God as having nothing to pay? Can he lay all his greatness by, and come as a sinner, a mere sinner, the vilest of sinners; as on a level with those that feed the dogs of his flock; with that "beggar who lies at his gate full of sores?" Impossible; unless by the same power that made the heavens and the earth. Yet without doing this, he cannot, in any sense, "enter into the kingdom of God."

2. What a hinderance are riches to the very first fruit of faith,—namely, the love of God! "If any man love the world," says the Apostle, "the love of the Father is not in him." But how is it possible for a man not to love the world who is surrounded with all its allurements? How can it be that he should then hear the still small voice which says, "My son, give me thy heart?" What power, less than almighty, can send the rich man an answer to that prayer,—

> Keep me dead to all below,
> Only Christ resolved to know;
> Firm, and disengaged, and free,
> Seeking all my bliss in Thee!

3. Riches are equally a hinderance to the loving our neighbour as ourselves; that is, to the loving all mankind as Christ loved us. A rich man may indeed love them that are of his own party, or his own opinion. He may love them that love him: "Do not even Heathens," baptized or unbaptized, "the same?" But he cannot have pure, disinterested good-will to every child of man. This can only spring from the love of God, which his great possessions expelled from his soul.

4. From the love of God, and from no other fountain, true humility likewise flows. Therefore, so far as they hinder the love of God, riches must hinder humility likewise. They hinder this also in the rich, by cutting them off from that freedom of conversation whereby they might be made sensible of their defects, and come to a true knowledge of themselves. But how seldom do they meet with a faithful friend; with one that can and will deal plainly with them! And without this we are likely to grow grey in our faults; yea, to die "with all our imperfections on our head."

5. Neither can meekness subsist without humility; for "of pride" naturally "cometh contention." Our Lord accordingly directs us to learn of Him at the same time "to be meek and lowly in heart" Riches therefore are as great a hinderance to meekness as they are to humility. In preventing lowliness of mind, they of consequence prevent meekness; which increases in the same proportion as we sink in our own

esteem; and, on the contrary, necessarily decreases as we think more highly of ourselves.

6. There is another Christian temper which is nearly allied to meekness and humility; but it has hardly a name. St. Paul terms it *epieikeia*. Perhaps, till we find a better name, we may call it *yieldingness*; a readiness to submit to others, to give up our own will. This seems to be the quality which St. James ascribes to "the wisdom from above," when he styles it, which we render, *easy to be entreated; easy to be convinced* of what is true; *easy to be persuaded*. But how rarely is this amiable temper to be found in a wealthy man! I do not know that I have found such a prodigy ten times in above threescore and ten years!

7. And how uncommon a thing is it to find patience in those that have large possessions! unless when there is a counterbalance of long and severe affliction, with which God is frequently pleased to visit those he loves, as an antidote to their riches. This is not uncommon: He often sends pain, and sickness, and great crosses, to them that have great possessions. By these means, "patience has its perfect work," till they are "perfect and entire, lacking nothing,"

II. Such are some of the hinderances to holiness which surround the rich on every side. We may now observe, on the other side, what a temptation riches are to all unholy tempers.

1. And, First, how great is the temptation to Atheism which naturally flows from riches; even to an entire forgetfulness of God, as if there was no such Being in the universe. This is at present usually termed dissipation,—a pretty name, affixed by the great vulgar to an utter disregard for God, and indeed for the whole invisible world. And how is the rich man surrounded with all manner of temptations to continual dissipation! Yes, how is the art of dissipation studied among the rich and great! As Prior keenly says,—

> Cards are dealt, and dice are brought,
> Happy effects of human wit,
> That Alma may herself forget.

Say rather, that mortals may their God forget; that they may keep Him utterly out of their thoughts, who, though he sitteth on the circle of the heavens, yet is "about their bed, and about their path, and spieth out all their ways." Call this wit, if you please; but is it wisdom? O no! It is far, very far from it. Thou fool! Dost thou imagine, because thou dost not see God, that God doth not see thee? Laugh on; play on; sing on; dance on: But "for all these things God will bring thee to judgment!"

2. From Atheism there is an easy transition to idolatry; from the worship of no God to the worship of false gods: And, in fact, he that does not love God (which is his proper, and his only proper worship) will surely love some of the works of his hands; will love the creature, if not the Creator. But to how many species of idolatry is every rich man exposed! What continual and almost insuperable temptations is he under to "love the world!" and that in all its branches,—"the desire of the flesh, the desire of the eyes, and the pride of life." What innumerable temptations will he find to gratify the "desire of the flesh!" Understand this right. It does not refer to one only, but all the outward senses. It is equal idolatry to seek our happiness in gratifying any or all of these. But there is the greatest danger lest men should seek it in gratifying their taste; in a moderate sensuality; in a regular kind of Epicurism; not in gluttony or drunkenness: Far be that from them! They do not disorder the body; they only keep the soul dead,—dead to God and all true religion.

3. The rich are equally surrounded with temptations from the "desire of the eyes;" that is, the seeking happiness in gratifying the imagination, the pleasures of which the eyes chiefly minister. The objects that give pleasure to the imagination are grand, or beautiful, or new. Indeed, all rich men have not a taste for grand objects; but they have for new and beautiful things, especially for new; the desire of novelty being as natural to men as the desire of meat and drink. Now, how numerous are the temptations to this kind of idolatry, which naturally springs from riches! How strongly and continually are they solicited to seek happiness (if not in grand, yet) in beautiful houses, in elegant furniture, in curious pictures, in delightful gardens! perhaps in that trifle of all trifles,—rich or gay apparel! Yea, in every new thing, little or great, which fashion, the mistress of fools, recommends. How are rich men, of a more elevated turn of mind, tempted to seek happiness, as their various tastes lead, in poetry, history, music, philosophy, or curious arts and sciences! Now, although it is certain all these have their use, and therefore may be innocently pursued, yet the seeking happiness in any of them, instead of God, is manifest idolatry; and therefore, were it only on this account, that riches furnish him with the means of indulging all these desires, it might well be asked, "Is not the life of a rich man, above all others, a temptation upon earth?"

4. What temptation, likewise, must every rich man have to seek happiness in "the pride of life!" I do not conceive the Apostle to mean thereby pomp, or state, or equipage; so much as "the honour that cometh of men," whether it be deserved or not. A rich man is sure to meet with this: It is a snare he cannot escape. The whole city of London uses the words rich and good as equivalent terms. "Yes," say they, "he is a good man; he is worth a hundred thousand pounds." And indeed everywhere, "if thou doest well unto thyself," if thou increasest in goods, "men will speak well of thee." All the world is agreed,

> A thousand pound supplies
> The want of twenty thousand qualities.

And who can bear general applause without being puffed up,—without being insensibly induced to think of himself "more highly than he ought to think?"

5. How is it possible that a rich man should escape pride, were it only on this account,—that his situation necessarily occasions praise to flow in upon him from every quarter? For praise is generally poison to the soul; and the more pleasing, the more fatal; particularly when it is undeserved. So that well might our Poet say,—

> Parent of evil, bane of honest deeds,
> Pernicious flattery! thy destructive seeds,
> In an ill hour, and by a fatal hand,
> Sadly diffused o'er virtue's gleby land,
> With rising pride amid the corn appear,
> And check the hope and promise of the year!

And not only praise, whether deserved or undeserved, but every thing about him tends to inspire and increase pride. His noble house, his elegant furniture, his well-chosen pictures, his fine horses, his equipage, his very dress, yea, even "the embroidery plastered on his tail,"—all these will be matter of commendation to some or other of his guests, and so have an almost irresistible tendency to make him think himself a better man than those who have not these advantages.

6. How naturally, likewise, do riches feed and increase the self-will which is born in every child of man! as not only his domestic servants and immediate dependants are governed implicitly by his will, finding their account therein; but also most of his neighbours and acquaintance study to oblige him in all things: So his will being continually indulged, will of course be continually strengthened; till at length he will be ill able to submit to the will either of God or men.

7. Such a tendency have riches to beget and nourish every temper that is contrary to the love of God. And they have equal tendency to feed every passion and temper that is contrary to the love of our neighbour: Contempt, for instance, particularly of inferiors, than which nothing is more contrary to love:—Resentment of any real or supposed offence; perhaps even revenge, although God claims this as his own peculiar prerogative:—At least anger; for it immediately rises in the mind of a rich man, "What! to use *me* thus! Nay, but he shall soon know better: I am now able to do myself justice!"

8. Nearly related to anger, if not rather a species of it, are fretfulness and peevishness. But are the rich more assaulted by these than the poor? All experience shows that they are. One remarkable instance I was a witness of many years ago:—A gentleman of large fortune, while we were seriously conversing, ordered a servant to throw some coals on the fire: A puff of smoke came out: He threw himself back in his chair, and cried out, "O Mr. Wesley, these are the crosses which I meet with every day!" I could not help asking, "Pray, Sir John, are these the heaviest crosses you meet with?" Surely these crosses would not have fretted him so much, if he had had fifty, instead of five thousand, pounds a year!

9. But it would not be strange, if rich men were in general void of all good dispositions, and an easy prey to all evil ones; since so few of them pay any regard to that solemn declaration of our Lord, without observing which we cannot be his disciples: "And he said unto them all,"—the whole multitude, not unto his Apostles only,—"If any man will come after me,"—will be a real Christian,—"let him deny himself, and take up his cross daily, and follow me." (Luke 9:23.) O how hard a saying is this to those that are "at ease in the midst of their possessions!" Yet the Scripture cannot be broken. Therefore, unless a man do "deny himself" every pleasure which does not prepare him for taking pleasure in God, "and take up his cross daily,"—obey every command of God, however grievous to flesh and blood,—he cannot be a disciple of Christ; he cannot "enter into the kingdom of God."

10. Touching this important point, of denying ourselves, and taking up our cross daily, let us appeal to matter of fact; let us appeal to every man's conscience in the sight of God. How many rich men are there among the Methodists (observe, there was not one, when they were first joined together) who actually do "deny themselves and take up their cross daily?" who resolutely abstain from every pleasure, either of sense or imagination, unless they know by experience that it prepares them for taking pleasure in God? Who declines no cross, no labour or pain, which lies in the way of his duty? Who of you that are now rich, deny yourselves just as you did when you were poor? Who as willingly endure labour or pain now, as you did when you were not worth five pounds? Come to particulars. Do you fast now as often as you did then? Do you rise as early in the morning? Do you endure cold or heat, wind or rain, as cheerfully as ever? See one reason among many, why so few increase in goods, without decreasing in grace! Because they no longer deny themselves and take up their daily cross. They no longer, alas! endure hardship, as good soldiers of Jesus Christ!

11. "Go to now, ye rich men! Weep and howl for the miseries that are coming upon you;" that must come upon you in a few days, unless prevented by a deep and entire change! "The canker of your gold and silver" will be "a testimony against you," and will "eat your flesh as fire!" O how pitiable is your condition! And who is able to help you? You need more plain dealing than any men in the world, and you meet with less. For how few dare speak as plain to *you*, as they would do to one of your servants! No man living, that either hopes to gain anything by your favour, or fears to lose anything by your displeasure. O that God would give me acceptable words, and cause them to sink deep into your hearts! Many of you have known me long, well nigh from your infancy: You have frequently helped me, when I stood in need. May I not say, you loved me? But now the time of our parting is at hand: My feet are just stumbling upon the dark mountains. I would leave one word with you before I go hence; and you may remember it when I am no more seen.

12. O let your heart be whole with God! Seek your happiness in him and him alone. Beware that you cleave not to the dust! "This earth is not your place." See that you use this world as not abusing it; *use* the world, and *enjoy* God. Sit as loose to all things here below, as if you were a poor beggar. Be a good steward of the manifold gifts of God; that when you are called to give an account of your stewardship, he may say, "Well done, good and faithful servant, enter thou into the joy of thy Lord!"

THIRD SERIES

109.* WHAT IS MAN?

"What is man?"

Psa. 8:4.

1. Nay, what am I? With God's assistance, I would consider myself. Here is a curious machine, "fearfully and wonderfully made." It is a little portion of *earth*, the particles of which

---

* [text from the 1872 edition]

cohering, I know not how, lengthen into innumerable fibres, a thousand times finer than hairs. These, crossing each other in all directions, are strangely wrought into membranes; and these membranes are as strangely wrought into arteries, veins, nerves, and glands; all of which contain various fluids, constantly circulating through the whole machine.

2. In order to the continuance of this circulation, a considerable quantity of air is necessary. And this is continually taken into the habit, by an engine fitted for that very purpose. But as a particle of ethereal *fire* is connected with every particle of air, (and a particle of water too,) so both air, water, and fire are received into the lungs together; where the fire is separated from the air and water, both of which are continually thrown out; while the fire, extracted from them, is received into, and mingled with, the blood. Thus the human body is composed of all the four elements, duly proportioned and mixed together; the last of which constitutes the vital flame, whence flows the animal heat.

3. Let me consider this yet a little farther. Is not the primary use of the lungs to administer fire to the body, which is continually extracted from the air by that curious fire-pump? By inspiration it takes in the air, water, and fire together. In its numerous cells, (commonly called air-vessels,) it detaches the fire from the air and water. This then mixes with the blood; as every air-vessel has a blood-vessel connected with it: And as soon as the fire is extracted from it, the air and water air thrown out by expiration.

4. Without this spring of life, this vital fire, there could be no circulation of the blood; consequently, no motion of any of the fluids, of the nervous fluid in particular (if it be not rather, as is highly probable, this very fire we are speaking of). Therefore there could not be any sensation, nor any muscular motion. I say, there could be no circulation; for the cause usually assigned for this, namely, the force of the heart, is altogether inadequate to the supposed effect. No one supposes the force of the heart, in a strong man, to be more than equal to the weight of three thousand pounds. Whereas it would require a force equal to the weight of a hundred thousand pounds, to propel the blood from the heart through all the arteries. This can only be effected by the ethereal fire contained in the blood itself, assisted by the elastic force of the arteries through which it circulates.

5. But beside this strange compound of the four elements,—earth, water, air, and fire,—I find something in me of a quite different nature, nothing akin to any of these. I find something in me that *thinks*; which neither earth, water, air, fire, nor any mixture of them, can possibly do: Something which sees, and hears, and smells, and tastes, and feels; all which are so many modes of thinking. It goes farther: Having perceived objects by any of these senses, it forms inward ideas of them. It *judges* concerning them; it sees whether they agree or disagree with each other. It *reasons* concerning them: that is, infers one proposition from another. It reflects upon its own operations; it is endued with) imagination and memory; and any of its operations, judgment in particular, may he subdivided into many others.

6. But by what means shall I learn in what part of my body this thinking principle is lodged? Some eminent men have affirmed, that it is "all in all, and all in every part." But I learn nothing from this: They seem to be words that have no determinate meaning. Let us then appeal, in the best manner we can, to our own experience. From this I learn, that this thinking principle is not lodged in my hands, or feet, or legs, or arms. It is not lodged in the trunk of my body. Any one may be assured of this by a little reflection. I cannot conceive that it is situated in my bones, or in any part of my flesh. So far as I can judge, it seems to be situated in some part of my head; but whether in the pineal gland, or in any part of the brain, I am not able to determine.

7. But farther: This inward principle, wherever it is lodged, is capable, not only of thinking, but likewise of love, hatred, joy, sorrow, desire, fear, hope …, and a whole train of other inward emotions, which are commonly called passions or affections They are styled, by a general appellation, the will; and are mixed and diversified a thousand ways. And they seem to be the only spring of action in that inward principle I call the soul.

8. But what is my soul? It is an important question, and not easy to be resolved.

> Hear'st thou submissive, but a lowly birth,
> Some separate particles of finer earth?
> A plain effect which nature must beget,
> As motion dictates, and as atoms meet?

I cannot in anywise believe this. My reason recoils at it. I cannot reconcile myself to the thought, that the soul is either earth, water, or fire; or a composition of all of them put together; were it only for this plain reason:—All these, whether separate or compounded in any possible way, are purely *passive* still. None of them has the least power of self-motion; none of them can move itself. "But," says one, "does not that ship move?" Yes; but not of itself; it is moved by the water on which it swims. "But then the water moves." True; but the water is moved by the wind, the current of air. "But the air moves." It is moved by the ethereal fire, which is attached to every particle of it; and this fire itself is moved by the almighty Spirit, the source of all the motion in the universe. But my soul has front Him an inward principle of motion, whereby it governs at pleasure every part of the body.

9. It governs every motion of the body; only with this exception., which is a marvellous instance of the wise and gracious providence of the great Creator: There are some motions of the body, which are absolutely needful for the continuance of life; such as the dilation and contraction of the lungs, the systole and diastole of the heart, the pulsation of the arteries, and the circulation of the blood. These are not governed by me at pleasure: They do not wait the direction of my will. And it is well they do not. It is highly proper, that all the vital motions should be involuntary; going on, whether we advert to them or not. Were it otherwise, grievous inconveniences might follow. A man might put an end to his own life whenever hoe pleased, by suspending the motion of his heart, or of his lungs; or he might lose his life by mere inattention,—by not remembering, not adverting to, the circulation of his blood. But these vital motions being excepted, I direct the motion of my whole body. By a single act of my will, I put my head, eyes, hands, or any part of my

body into motion: Although I no more comprehend how I do this, than I can comprehend how the "THREE that bear record in heaven are ONE."

10. But what am *I?* Unquestionably I am something distinct from my body. It seems evident that my body is not necessarily included therein. For when my body dies, I shall not die: I shall exist as really as I did before. And I cannot but believe, this self-moving, thinking principle, with all its passions and affections, will continue to exist, although the body be mouldered into dust. Indeed at present this body is so intimately connected with the soul. that I seem to consist of both. In my present state of existence, I undoubtedly consist both of soul and body: And so I shall again, after the resurrection, to all eternity.

11. I am conscious to myself of one more property, commonly called liberty. This is very frequently confounded with the will; but is of a very different nature. Neither is it a property of the will, but a distinct property of the soul; capable of being exerted with regard to all the faculties of the soul, as well as all the motions of the body. It is a power of self-determination; which, although it does not extend to all our thoughts and imaginations, yet extends to our words and actions in general, and not with many exceptions. I am full as certain of this, that I am free, with respect to these, to speak or not to speak, to act or not to act, to do this or the contrary, as I am of my own existence. I have not only what is termed, a "liberty of contradiction,"—power to do or not to do; but what is termed, a "liberty of contrariety,"—a power to act one way, or the contrary. To deny this would be to deny the constant experience of all human kind. Every one feels that he has an inherent power to move this or that part of his body, to move it or not, and to move this way or the contrary, just as lie pleases. I can, as I choose, (and so can every one that is born of a woman,) open or shut my eyes; speak, or be silent; rise or sit down; stretch out my hand, or draw it in; and use any of my limbs according to my pleasure, as well as my whole body. And although I have not an absolute power over my own mind, because of the corruption of my own nature; yet, through the grace of God assisting me, I have a power to choose and do good, as well as evil. I am free to choose whom I will serve; and if I choose the better part, to continue therein even unto death.

12. But tell me, frighted nature, what is death?

> Blood only stopp'd, and interrupted breath?
> The utmost limit of a narrow span?
> And even of motion, which with life began?

Death is properly the separation of the soul from the body. Of this we are certain. but we are not certain (at least in many cases) of the time when this separation is made. Is it when respiration ceases? according to the well-known maxim, *Nullus spiritus, nulla vita.* "Where there is no breath, there is no life." Nay, we cannot absolutely affirm this: For many instances have been known, of those whose breath was totally lost, and yet their lives have been recovered. Is it when the heart no longer beats, or when the circulation of the blood ceases? Not so. For the heart may beat anew; and the circulation of the blood, after it is quite interrupted, may begin again. Is the soul separated from the body, when the whole body is stiff and cold as a piece of ice? But there have been several instances lately, of persons who were thus cold and stiff, and had no symptoms of life remaining, who, nevertheless, upon proper application, recovered both life and health. Therefore we can say no more, than that death is the separation of the soul and body; but in many cases God only can tell the moment of that separation.

13. But what we are much concerned to know, and deeply to consider, is, the end of life. For what end is life bestowed upon the children of me? Why were we sent into the world? For one sole end, and for no other, to prepare for eternity. For this alone we live. For this, and no other purpose, is our life either given or continued. It pleased the all-wise God, at the season which he saw best, to arise in the greatness of his strength, and create the heavens and the earth, and all things that are therein. having prepared all things for him, He "created man in his own image, after his own likeness." And what was the end of his creation? It was one, and no other,—that he might know, and love, and enjoy, and serve his great Creator to all eternity.

14. But "man, being in honour, continued not," but became lower than even the beasts that perish. He wilfully and openly rebelled against God, and cast off his allegiance to the Majesty of heaven. Hereby he instantly lost both the favour of God, and the image of God wherein lie was created. As he was then incapable of obtaining happiness by the old, God established a new covenant with man; the terms of which were no longer, "Do this and live," but, "Believe, and thou shalt be saved.' But still the end of man is one and the same; only it stands on another foundation. For the plain tenor of it is, "Believe in the Lord Jesus Christ, whom God hath given to be the propitiation for thy sins, and thou shalt be saved;" first, from the guilt of sin, having redemption through his blood; then from the power, which shall have no more dominion over thee; and then from the root of it, into the whole image of God. And being restored both to the favour and image of God, thou shalt know, love, and serve him to all eternity. So that still the end of his life, the life of every man born into the world is to know, love, and serve his great Creator.

15. And let it be observed, as thus is the end, so it is the whole and sole end, for which every man upon the face of the earth, for which every one of *you*, were brought into the world, and endued with a living soul. Remember! You were born for nothing else. You live for nothing else. Your life is continued to you upon earth, for no other purpose than this, that you may know, love, and serve God on earth, and enjoy him to all eternity. Consider! You were not created to please your senses, to gratify your imagination, to gain money, or the praise of men; to seek happiness in any created good, in anything under the sun. All this is "walking in a vain shadow;" it is leading a restless, miserable life, in order to a miserable eternity. On the contrary, you were created for this, and for no other purpose, by seeking and finding happiness in God on earth, to secure the glory of God in heaven. Therefore, let your heart continually say, "This one thing I do,"—having one thing in view, remembering why I was born, and why I am continued in life,—"I press on to the

mark." I aim at the one end of my being, God; even at "God in Christ reconciling the world to himself." He shall be my God for ever and ever, and my guide even unto death! Bradford, May 2, 1788.

110.* ON THE DISCOVERIES OF FAITH

"Now faith is the evidence of things not seen."

Heb. 11:1.

1. For many ages it has been allowed by sensible men, *Nihil est in intellectu quod non fuit prius in sensu.* That is, "There is nothing in the understanding which was not first perceived by some of the senses." All the knowledge which we naturally have is originally derived from our senses. And therefore those who want any sense cannot have the least knowledge or idea of the objects of that sense; as they that never had sight have not the least knowledge or conception of light or colours. Some indeed have of late years endeavoured to prove that we have innate ideas, not derived from any of the senses, but coeval with the understanding. But this point has been now thoroughly discussed by men of the most eminent sense and learning. And it is agreed by all impartial persons that, although some things are so plain and obvious that we can very hardly avoid knowing them as soon as we come to the use of our understanding, yet the knowledge even of these is not innate, but derived from some of our senses.

2. But there is a great difference between our senses, considered as the avenues of our knowledge. Some of them have a very narrow sphere of action, some a more extensive one. By *feeling* we discern only those objects that touch some part of our body; and consequently this sense extends only to a small number of objects. Our senses of *taste* and *smell* (which some count species of *feeling*) extend to fewer still. But on the other hand our nobler sense of *hearing* has an exceeding wide sphere of action; especially in the case of loud sounds, as thunder, the roaring of the sea, or the discharge of cannon; the last of which sounds has been frequently heard at the distance of near an hundred miles. Yet the space to which the *hearing* itself extends is small, compared to that through which the *sight* extends. The *sight* takes in at one view, not only the most unbounded prospects on earth, but also the moon, and the other planets, the sun, yea, the fixed stars; though at such an immeasurable distance, that they appear no larger through our finest telescopes than they do to the naked eye.

3. But still none of our senses, no, not the sight itself, can reach beyond the bounds of this visible world. They supply us with such knowledge of the material world as answers all the purposes of life. But as this was the design for which they were given, beyond this they cannot go. They furnish us with no information at all concerning the invisible world.

4. But the wise and gracious Governor of the worlds, both visible and invisible, has prepared a remedy for this defect. He hath appointed *faith* to supply the defect of sense; to take us up where sense sets us down, and help us over the great gulf. Its office begins where that of sense ends. Sense is an evidence of things that are seen; of the visible, the material world, and the several parts of it. Faith, on the other hand, is the "evidence of things not seen;" of the invisible world; of all those invisible things which are revealed in the oracles of God. But indeed they reveal nothing, they are a mere dead letter, if they are "not mixed with faith in those that hear them."

5. In particular, faith is an evidence to me of the existence of that unseen thing, my own soul. Without this I should be in utter uncertainty concerning it. I should be constrained to ask that melancholy question,

> Hear'st thou submissive; but a lowly birth,
> Some separate particles of finer earth?

But by faith I know it is an immortal spirit, made in the image of God; in his natural and his moral image; "an incorruptible picture of the God of glory." By the same evidence I know that I am now fallen short of the glorious image of God; yea, that I, as well as all mankind, am "dead in trespasses and sins:" So utterly dead, that "in me dwelleth no good thing;" that I am inclined to all evil, and totally unable to quicken my own soul.

6. By faith I know that, besides the souls of men there are other orders of spirits; yea, I believe that

> Millions of creatures walk the earth,
> Unseen, whether we wake, or if we sleep.

These I term angels, and I believe part of them are holy and happy, and the other part wicked and miserable. I believe the former of these, the good angels, are continually sent of God "to minister to the heirs of salvation;" who will be "equal to angels" by and by, although they are now a little inferior to them. I believe the latter, the evil angels, called in Scripture, devils, united under one head, (termed in Scripture, Satan; emphatically, the enemy, the adversary both of God and man,) either range the upper regions; whence they are called "princes of the power of the air;" or like him, walk about the earth as "roaring lions, seeking whom they may devour."

7. But I know by faith that, above all these, is the Lord Jehovah, he that is, that was, and that is to come; that is God from everlasting, and world without end; He that filleth heaven and earth; He that is infinite in power, in wisdom, in justice, in mercy, and holiness; He that created all things, visible and invisible, by the breath of his mouth, and still "upholds" them all, preserves them in being, "by the word of his power;" and that governs all things that are in heaven above, in earth beneath, and under the earth. By faith I know "there are three that bear record in heaven, the Father, the Word, and the Holy Spirit," and that "these Three are One;" that the Word, God the Son, "was made flesh," lived, and died for our salvation, rose again, ascended into heaven, and now sitteth at the right hand of the Father. By faith I know that the Holy Spirit is the giver of all spiritual life; of righteousness, peace, and joy in the Holy Ghost; of holiness and happiness, by the restoration of that image of God wherein we are created. Of all these things, faith is the evidence, the sole evidence, to the children of men.

---

* [text from the 1872 edition]

8. And as the information which we receive from our senses does not extend to the invisible world, so neither does it extend to (what is nearly related thereto) the eternal world. In spite of all the instruction which either the sight or any of the senses can afford,

> The vast, th' unbounded prospect lies before us;
> But clouds, alas! and darkness rest upon it.

Sense does not let in one ray of light, to discover "the secrets of the illimitable deep." This, the eternal world, commences at death, the death of every individual person. The moment the breath of man goeth forth he is an inhabitant of eternity. Just then time vanishes away, "like as a dream when one awaketh." And here again faith supplies the place of sense, and gives us a view of things to come: At once it draws aside the veil which hangs between mortal and immortal being. Faith discovers to us the souls of the righteous, immediately received by the holy angels, and carried by those ministering spirits into Abraham's bosom; into the delights of paradise, the garden of God, where the light of his countenance perpetually shines; where he converses, not only with his former relations, friends, and fellow-soldiers, but with the saints of all nations and all ages, with the glorious dead of ancient days, with the noble army of martyrs, the Apostles, the Prophets, the Patriarchs, Abraham, Isaac, and Jacob: Yea, above all this, he shall be with Christ, in a manner that could not be while he remained in the body.

9. It discovers, likewise, the souls of unholy men; seized the lo moment they depart from the quivering lips, by those ministers of vengeance, the evil angels, and dragged away to their own place. It is true, this is not the nethermost hell: they are not to be tormented there "before the time;" before the end of the world, when everyone will receive his just recompense of reward. Till then they will probably be employed by their bad master in advancing his infernal kingdom, and in doing all the mischief that lies in their power to the poor, feeble children of men. But still, wherever they seek rest, they will find none. They carry with them their own hell, in the worm that never dieth; in a consciousness of guilt, and of the wrath of God, which continually drinks up their spirits; in diabolical, infernal tempers, which are essential misery; and in what they cannot shake off, no, not for an hour, any more than they can shake off their own being,—that "fearful looking for of fiery indignation, which will devour God's adversaries."

10. Moreover, faith opens another scene in the eternal world; namely, the coming of our Lord in the clouds of heaven to "judge both the quick and the dead." It enables us to see the "great white throne coming down from heaven, and Him that sitteth thereon, from whose face the heavens and the earth flee away, and there is found no place for them." We see "the dead, small and great, stand before God." We see "the books opened, and the dead judged, according to the things that are written in the books." We see the earth and the sea giving up their dead, and hell (that is, the invisible world) "giving up the dead that were therein, and everyone judged according to his works.

11. By faith we are also shown the immediate consequences of the general judgment. We see the execution of that happy sentence pronounced upon those on the right hand, "Come, ye blessed of my Father, inherit the kingdom prepared for you from the foundation of the world!" After which the holy angels tune their harps, and sing, "Lift up your heads, O ye gates, and be ye lifted up, ye everlasting doors, that the heirs of glory may come in!" And then shall they drink of the rivers of pleasure that are at God's right hand for evermore. We see, likewise, the execution of that dreadful sentence, pronounced upon those on the left hand, "Depart, ye cursed, into everlasting fire, prepared for the devil and his angels." And then shall the ministers of divine vengeance plunge them into "the lake of fire burning with brimstone; where they have no rest day or night, but the smoke of their torment ascendeth up for ever and ever."

12. But beside the invisible and the eternal world, which are not seen, which are discoverable only by faith, there is a whole system of things which are not seen, which cannot be discerned by any of our outward senses. I mean, the spiritual world, understanding thereby the kingdom of God in the soul of man. "Eye hath not seen, nor ear heard this; neither can it enter into the heart of man to conceive the things of" this interior kingdom, unless God revealed them by his Spirit. The Holy Spirit prepares us for his inward kingdom, by removing the veil from our heart, and enabling us to know ourselves as we are known of him; by "convincing us of sin," of our evil nature, our evil tempers, and our evil words and actions; all of which cannot but partake of the corruption of the heart from which they spring. He then convinces us of the desert of our sins; so that our mouth is stopped, and we are constrained to plead guilty before God. At the same time, we "receive the spirit of bondage unto fear;" fear of the wrath God, fear of the punishment which we have deserved; and, above all, fear of death, lest it should consign us over to eternal death. Souls that are thus convinced feel they are so fast in prison that they cannot get forth. They feel themselves at once altogether sinful, altogether guilty, and altogether helpless. But all this conviction implies a species of faith, being "an evidence of things not seen;" nor indeed possible to be seen or known, till God reveals them unto us.

13. But still let it be carefully observed, (for it is a point of no small importance,) that this faith is only the faith of a servant, and not the faith of a son. Because this is a point which many do not clearly understand, I will endeavour to make it a little plainer. The faith of a servant implies a divine evidence of the invisible and the eternal world; yea, and an evidence of the spiritual world, so far as it can exist without living experience. Whoever has attained this, the faith of a servant, "feareth God and escheweth evil;" or, as it is expressed by St. Peter, "feareth God and worketh righteousness." In consequence of which he is in a degree, as the Apostle observes, "accepted with Him." Elsewhere he is described in those words: "He that feareth God, and keepeth his commandments." Even one who has gone thus far in religion, who obeys God out of fear, is not in any wise to be despised; seeing "the fear of the Lord is the beginning of wisdom." Nevertheless he should be exhorted not to stop there; not to rest till he attains the

adoption of sons; till he obeys out of love, which is the privilege of all the children of God.

14. Exhort him to press on, by all possible means, till he passes "from faith to faith;" from the faith of a *servant* to the faith of a *son*; from the spirit of bondage unto fear, to the spirit of childlike love: He will then have "Christ revealed in his heart," enabling him to testify, "The life that I now live in the flesh I live by faith in the Son of God, who loved *me*, and gave himself for *me*,"—the proper voice of a child of God. He will then be "born of God," inwardly changed by the mighty power of God, from "an earthly, sensual, devilish" mind, to "the mind which was in Christ Jesus." He will experience what St. Paul means by those remarkable words to the Galatians, "Ye are the sons of God by faith; and because ye are sons, God hath sent forth the Spirit of his Son into your hearts, crying, Abba, Father." "He that believeth," as a son, (as St. John observes) "hath the witness in himself." "The Spirit itself witnesses with his spirit that he is a child of God." "The love of God is shed abroad in his heart by the Holy Ghost which is given unto him."

15. But many doubts and fears may still remain, even in a child of God, while he is weak in faith; while he is in the number of those whom St. Paul terms "babes in Christ." But when his faith is strengthened, when he receives faith's abiding impression, realizing things to come; when he has received the abiding witness of the Spirit, doubts and fears vanish away. He then enjoys the plerophory, or "full assurance, of faith;" excluding all doubt, and all "fear that hath torment." To those whom he styles *young* men, St. John says, "I have written unto you, young men, because ye are strong, and the word of God abideth in you, and ye have overcome the wicked one." These, the Apostle observes in the other verse, had "the word of God abiding in them." It may not improbably mean "the pardoning word," the word which spake all their sins forgiven. In consequence of which, they have the consciousness of the divine favour, without any intermission.

16. To these more especially we may apply the exhortation of the Apostle Paul: "Leaving the first principles of the doctrine of Christ," namely, repentance and faith, "let us go on unto perfection." But in what sense are we to "leave those principles? Not absolutely; for we are to retain both one and the other, the knowledge of ourselves and the knowledge of God, unto our lives' end: But only comparatively; not fixing, as we did at first, our whole attention upon them; thinking and talking perpetually of nothing else, but either repentance or faith. But what is the "perfection" here spoken of? It is not only a deliverance from doubts and fears, but from sin; from all inward as well as outward sin; from evil desires and evil tempers, as well as from evil words and works. Yea, and it is not only a negative blessing, a deliverance from all evil dispositions implied in that expression, "I will circumcise thy heart;" but a positive one likewise; even the planting all good dispositions in their place; clearly implied in that other expression, "To love the Lord your God with all your heart, and with all your soul."

17. These are they to whom the Apostle John gives the venerable title of *Fathers*, who "have known him that is from the beginning;" the eternal Three-One God. One of these expresses himself thus: "I bear about with me an experimental verity and a plenitude of the presence of the ever-blessed Trinity." And those who are fathers in Christ, generally, though I believe not always, enjoy the plerophory, or "full assurance of hope;" having no more doubt of reigning with him in glory than if they already saw him coming in the clouds of heaven. But this does not prevent their continually increasing in the knowledge and love of God. While they "rejoice evermore, pray without ceasing, and in everything give thanks," they pray in particular, that they may never cease to watch, to deny themselves, to take up their cross daily, to fight the good fight of faith; and against the world, the devil, and their own manifold infirmities; till they are able to "comprehend, with all saints, what is the length, and breadth, and height, and depth, and to know that love of Christ which passeth knowledge;" yea, to "be filled with all the fullness of God." Yarm, June 11, 1788.

111.* ON THE OMNIPRESENCE OF GOD

"Do not I fill heaven and earth? saith the Lord."

Jer. 23:24.

1. How strongly and beautifully do these words express the omnipresence of God! And can there be in the whole compass of nature a more sublime subject? Can there be any more worthy the consideration of every rational creature? Is there any more necessary to be considered, and to be understood, so far as our poor faculties will admit? How many excellent purposes may it answer! What deep instruction may it convey to all the children of men! And more directly to the children of God.

2. How is it then that so little has been wrote on so sublime and useful a subject? It is true that some of our most eminent writers have occasionally touched upon it, and have several strong and beautiful reflections which were naturally suggested by it. But which of them has published a regular treatise, or so much as a sermon, upon the head? Perhaps many were conscious of their inability to do justice to so vast a subject. It is possible, there may some such lie hid in the voluminous writings of the last century. But if they are hid even in their own country, if they are already buried in oblivion, it is the same, for any use they are of, as if they had never been wrote.

3. What seems to be wanting still, for general use, is a plain discourse on the omnipresence or ubiquity of God. First, in some manner explaining and proving that glorious truth, "God is in this, and every place;" and Then, applying it to the consciences of all thinking men, in a few practical inferences.

I. 1. Accordingly, I will endeavour, by the assistance of his Spirit, first a little to explain the omnipresence of God; to show how we are to understand this glorious truth, "God is in this, and every place. The Psalmist, you may remember,

* [text from the 1872 edition]

speaks strongly and beautifully upon it in the hundred and thirty-ninth Psalm; observing in the most exact order, First, "God is in this place;" and Then, "God is in every place." He observes, First, "Thou art about my bed, and about my path, and spiest out all my ways." (Ps. 139:3.) "Thou hast fashioned me behind and before, and laid thine hand upon me." (Ps. 139:5) Although the *manner* thereof he could not explain; *how* it was he could not tell. "Such knowledge," says he, "is too wonderful for me: I cannot attain unto it." (Ps. 139:6) He next observes, in the most lively and affecting manner, that God is in every place. "Whither shall I go then from thy Spirit, or whither shall I go from thy presence? If I climb up into heaven, thou art there; if I go down to hell, thou art there also.' (Ps. 139:7, 8.) If I could ascend, speaking after the manner of men, to the highest part of the universe, or could I descend to the lowest point, thou art alike present both in one and the other. "If I should take the wings of the morning, and remain in the uttermost parts of the sea; even there thy hand would lead me,"—thy power and thy presence would be before me,—"and thy right hand would hold me,' seeing thou art equally in the length and breadth, and in the height and depth of the universe. Indeed thy presence and knowledge not only reach the utmost bounds of creation; but

> Thine omnipresent sight,
> Even to the pathless realms extends
> Of uncreated night.

In a word, there is no point of space, whether within or without the bounds of creation, where God is not.

2. Indeed, this subject is far too vast to be comprehended by the narrow limits of human understanding. We can only say, The great God, the eternal, the almighty Spirit, is as unbounded in his presence as in his duration and power. In condescension, indeed, to our weak understanding, he is said to dwell in heaven: but, strictly speaking, the heaven of heavens cannot contain him; but he is in every part of his dominion. The universal God dwelleth in universal space; so that we may say,

> Hail, Father! whose creating call
> Unnumber'd worlds attend!
> Jehovah, comprehending all,
> Whom none can comprehend!

3. If we may dare attempt the illustrating this a little farther, what is the space occupied by a grain of sand, compared to that space which is occupied by the starry heavens? It is as a cipher; it is nothing; it vanishes away in the comparison. What is it, then, to the whole expanse of space, to which the whole creation is infinitely less than a grain of sand? And yet this space, to which the whole creation bears no proportion at all, is infinitely less in comparison of the great God than a grain of sand, yea, a millionth part of it, bears to that whole space.

II. 1. This seems to be the plain meaning of those solemn words which God speaks of himself: "Do not I fill heaven and earth?" And these sufficiently prove his omnipresence; which may be farther proved from this consideration: God acts everywhere, and, therefore, is everywhere; for it is an utter impossibility that any being, created or uncreated, should work where it is not. God acts in heaven, in earth, and under the earth, throughout the whole compass of his creation; by sustaining all things, without which everything would in an instant sink into its primitive nothing; by governing all, every moment superintending everything that he has made; strongly and sweetly influencing all, and yet without destroying the liberty of his rational creatures. The very Heathens acknowledged that the great God governs the large and conspicuous parts of the universe; that he regulates the motions of the heavenly bodies, of the sun, moon, and stars; that he is

> Totam
> Mens agitans molem, et magno se corpore miscens:
> The all-informing soul,
> That fills, pervades and actuates the whole.

But they had no conception of his having a regard to the least things as well as the greatest; of his presiding over all that he has made, and governing atoms as well as worlds. This we could not have known unless it had pleased God to reveal it unto us himself. Had he not himself told us so, we should not have dared to think that "not a sparrow falleth to the ground, without the will of our Father which is in heaven;" and much less affirm, that "even the very hairs of our head are all numbered!"

2. This comfortable truth, that "God filleth heaven and earth," we learn also from the Psalm above recited: "If I climb up into heaven, thou art there; if I go down to hell, thou art there also. If I take the wings of the morning, and remain in the uttermost parts of the sea; even there thy hand shall lead me." The plain meaning is, If I remove to any distance whatever, thou art there; thou still besettest me, and layest thine hand upon me. Let me flee to any conceivable or inconceivable distance; above, beneath, or on any side;, it makes no difference; thou art still equally there: In thee I still "live, and move, and have my being."

3. And where no creature is, still God is there. The presence or absence of any or all creatures makes no difference with regard to him. He is equally in all, or without all. Many have been the disputes among philosophers whether there be any such thing as empty space in the universe; and it is now generally supposed that all space is full. Perhaps it cannot be proved that all space is filled with matter. But the Heathen himself will bear us witness, *Jovis omnia plena:* "All things are full of God." Yea, and space exists beyond the bounds of creation (for creation must have bounds, seeing nothing is boundless, nothing can be, but the great Creator), even that space cannot exclude Him who fills the heaven and the earth.

4. Just equivalent to this is the expression of the Apostle: (Eph. 1:23, not, as some have strangely supposed, concerning the Church, but concerning the Head of it:) "The fullness of him that filleth all in all;" *ta panta en pasin*, literally translated, +all things in all things;"—the strongest expression of universality which can possibly be conceived. It necessarily includes the last and the greatest of all things that exist. So that if any expression could be stronger, it would be stronger than even that—the "filling heaven and earth."

5. Indeed this very expression, "Do not I fill heaven and earth?" (the question being equal to the strongest affirmation), implies the clearest assertion of God's being

present everywhere and filling all space; for it is well known, the Hebrew phrase "heaven and earth," includes the whole universe; the whole extent of space, created or uncreated, and all that is therein.

6. Nay, and we cannot believe the omnipotence of God, unless we believe his omnipresence; for, seeing, as was observed before, nothing can act where it is not,—if there were any space where God was not present, he would not be able to do anything there. Therefore, to deny the omnipresence of God implies, likewise, the denial of his omnipotence. To set bounds to the one is undoubtedly to set bounds to the other also.

7. Indeed, wherever we suppose him not to be, there we suppose all his attributes to be in vain. He cannot exercise there either his justice or mercy, either his power or wisdom. In extra-mundane space, (so to speak,) where we suppose God not to be present, we must, of course, suppose him to have no duration; but as it is supposed to be beyond the bounds of the creation, so it is beyond the bounds of the Creator's power. Such is the blasphemous absurdity which is implied in this supposition.

8. But to all that is or can be said of the omnipresence of God, the world has one grand objection: They cannot see him. And this is really at the root of all their other objections. This our blessed Lord observed long ago: "Whom the world cannot receive, because they see him not." But is it not easy to reply, "Can you see the wind?" You cannot. But do you therefore deny its existence, or its presence? You say, "No; for I can perceive it by my other senses." But by which of your senses do you perceive your soul? Surely you do not deny either the existence or the presence of this! And yet it is not the object of your sight, or of any of your other senses. Suffice it then to consider that God is a Spirit, as is our soul also. Consequently, "him no man hath seen, or can see," with eyes of flesh and blood.

III. 1. But allowing that God is here, as in every place, that he is "about our bed, and about our path;" that he "besets us behind and before, and lays his hand upon us;" what inference should we draw from hence? What use should we make of this awful consideration? Is it not meet and right to humble ourselves before the eyes of his Majesty? Should we not labour continually to acknowledge his presence, "with reverence and godly fear?" not indeed with the fear of devils, that believe and tremble, but with fear of angels, with something similar to that which is felt by the inhabitants of heaven, when

> Dark with excessive bright his skirts appear,
> Yet dazzles heaven, that brightest seraphim
> Approach not, but with both wings veil their eyes.

2. Secondly. If you believe that God is about your bed, and about your path, and spieth out all your ways, then take care not to do the least thing, not to speak the least word, not to indulge the least thought, which you have reason to think would offend him. Suppose that a messenger of God, an angel, be now standing at your right hand, and fixing his eyes upon you, would you not take care to abstain from every word or action that you knew would offend him? Yea, suppose one of your mortal fellow-servants, suppose only a

holy man stood by you, would not you be extremely cautious how you conducted yourself, both in word and action? How much more cautious ought you to be when you know that not a holy man, not an angel of God, but God himself, the Holy One "that inhabiteth eternity," is inspecting your heart, your tongue, your hand, every moment; and that he himself will surely bring you into judgment for all you think, and speak, and act under the sun!

3. In particular: If there is not a word in your tongue, not a syllable you speak, but he "knoweth it altogether;" how exact should you be in "setting a watch before your mouth, and in keeping the door of your lips!" How wary does it behove you to be in all your conversation; being forewarned by your Judge, that "by your words you shall be justified, or by your words you shall be condemned!" How cautious, lest "any corrupt communication," any uncharitable, yea, or unprofitable discourse, should "proceed out of your mouth;" instead of "that which is good to the use of edifying, and meet to minister grace to the hearers!"

4. Yea, if God sees our hearts as well as our hands, and in all places; if he understandeth our thoughts long before they are clothed with words, how earnestly should we urge that petition, "Search me, O Lord, and prove me; try out my reins and my heart; look well if there be any way of wickedness in me, and lead me in the way everlasting!" Yea, how needful is it to work together with him, in "keeping our hearts with all diligence," till he hath "cast down imaginations," evil reasonings, "and everything that exalteth itself against the knowledge of God, and brought into captivity every thought to the obedience of Christ!"

5. On the other hand, if you are already listed under the great Captain of your salvation, seeing you are continually under the eye of your Captain, how zealous and active should you be to "fight the good fight of faith, and lay hold on eternal life;" "to endure hardship, as good soldiers of Jesus Christ;" to use all diligence, to "war a good warfare," and to do whatever is acceptable in his sight! How studious should you be to approve all your ways to his all-seeing eyes; that he may say to your hearts, what he will proclaim aloud in the great assembly of men and angels, "Well done, good and faithful servants!"

6. In order to attain these glorious ends, spare no pains to preserve always a deep, a continual, a lively, and a joyful sense of his gracious presence. Never forget his comprehensive word to the great father of the faithful: "I am the Almighty" (rather, the All-sufficient) "God; walk before me, and be thou perfect!" Cheerfully expect that He, before whom you stand, will ever guide you with his eye, will support you by his guardian hand, will keep you from all evil, and "when you have suffered a while, [he] will make you perfect, will stablish, strengthen, and settle you;" and then "preserve you unblameable, unto the coming of our Lord Jesus Christ!" Portsmouth, August 12, 1788

112.* THE RICH MAN AND LAZARUS

"If they hear not Moses and the Prophets, neither will they be persuaded, though one rose from the dead."

Luke 16:31.

1. How strange a paradox is this! How contrary to the common apprehension of men! Who is so confirmed in unbelief as not to think, "If one came to me from the dead, I should be effectually persuaded to repent?" But this passage affords us a more strange saying: (Luke 16:13:) "Ye cannot serve God and mammon." "No! Why not? Why cannot we serve both?" will a true servant of mammon say. Accordingly, the Pharisees, who supposed they served God, and did cordially serve mammon, *derided him: exemykterizon.* A word expressive of the deepest contempt. But he said, (Luke 16:15,) "Ye are they who justify yourselves before men; but God knoweth your hearts: And that which is highly esteemed among men, is (very commonly) an abomination before God:" A terrible proof of which our Lord subjoins in the remaining part of the chapter.

2. But is the subsequent account merely a parable, or a real history? It has been believed by many, and roundly asserted, to be a mere parable, because of one or two circumstances therein, which are not easy to be accounted for. In particular, it is hard to conceive, how a person in hell could hold conversation with one in paradise. But, admitting we cannot account for this, will it overbalance an express assertion of our Lord: "There was," says our Lord, "a certain rich man."—Was there not? Did such a man never exist? "And there was a certain beggar named Lazarus."—Was there, or was there not? Is it not bold enough, positively to deny what our blessed Lord positively affirms? Therefore, we cannot reasonably doubt, but the whole narration, with all its circumstances, is exactly true. And Theophylact (one of the ancient commentators on the Scriptures) observes upon the text, that, "according to the tradition of the Jews, Lazarus lived at Jerusalem."

I purpose, with God's assistance, First, to explain this history; Secondly, to apply it; and, Thirdly, to prove the truth of that weighty sentence with which it is concluded, namely, "If they hear not Moses and the Prophets, neither will they be persuaded, though one rose from the dead."

I. 1. And, First, I will endeavour, with God's assistance, to explain this history. "There was a certain rich man;" and, doubtless, on that very account, highly esteemed among men,—"who was clothed in purple and fine linen;" and, consequently, esteemed the more highly, both as appearing suitably to his fortune, and as an encourager of trade;—"and fared sumptuously every day." Here was another reason for his being highly esteemed,—his hospitality and generosity,—both by those who frequently sat at his table, and the tradesmen that furnished it.

2. "And there was a certain beggar;" one in the lowest line of human infamy; "named Lazarus," according to the Greek termination; in Hebrew, Eleazer. From his name we may gather, that he was of no mean family, although this branch of it was, at present, so reduced. It is probable he was well known in the city; and it was no scandal to him to be named.—"Who was laid at his gate;" although no pleasing spectacle; so that one might wonder he was suffered to lie there;—"full of sores;" of running ulcers;—"and desiring to be fed with the crumbs which fell from the rich man's table." So the complicated affliction of poverty, pain, and want of bread, lay upon him at once! But it does not appear that any creature took the least notice of the despicable wretch! Only "the dogs came and licked his sores:" All the comfort which this world afforded him!

3. But see the change! "The beggar died:" Here ended poverty and pain:—"And was carried by angels;" nobler servants than any that attended the rich man;—"into Abraham's bosom:"—So the Jews commonly termed what our blessed Lord styles paradise; the place "where the wicked cease from troubling, and where the weary are at rest;" the receptacle of holy souls, from death to the resurrection. It is, indeed, very generally supposed, that the souls of good men, as soon as they are discharged from the body, go directly to heaven; but this opinion has not the least foundation in the oracles of God: On the contrary, our Lord says to Mary, after the resurrection, "Touch me not; for I am not yet ascended to my Father" in heaven. But he had been in paradise, according to his promise to the penitent thief: "This day shalt thou be with me in paradise." Hence, it is plain, that paradise is not heaven. It is indeed (if we may be allowed the expression) the antechamber of heaven, where the souls of the righteous remain till, after the general judgment, they are received into glory.

4. But see the scene change again! "The rich man also died."—What! must rich men also die? Must they fall "like one of the people?" Is there no help? A rich man in London, some years ago, when the physician told him he must die, gnashed his teeth, and clenched his fist, and cried out vehemently, "God, God, I won't die!" But he died with the very words in his mouth.—"And was buried;" doubtless, with pomp enough, suitably to his quality; although we do not find that there was then, in all the world, that exquisite instance of human folly, that senseless, cruel mockery of a poor putrifying carcass, what we term *lying in state!*

5. And in hell he lifted up his eyes."—O, what a change! How is the mighty fallen! But the word which is here rendered hell does not always mean the place of the damned. It is, literally, *the invisible world;* and is of very wide extent, including the receptacle of separate spirits, whether good or bad. But here it evidently means, that region of hades where the souls of wicked men reside, as appears from the following words, "Being in torment;"—"in order," say some, "to atone for the sins committed while in the body, as well as to purify the soul from all its inherent sin." Just so, the eminent heathen poet, near two thousand years ago:—

Necesse est
Multa diu concreta modis inolescere miris,
Ergo exercentur poenis—
—Aliae panduntur inanes

Suspensae ad ventos: Aliis sub gurgite vasto
Infectum eluitur scelus, aut exuritur igni.

[This quotation from Virgil (Aeneid vi.737–742) is thus translated by Pitt:

"Ev'n when those bodies are to death resign'd,
Some old inherent spots are left behind;
A sullying tincture of corporeal stains
Deep in the substance of the soul remains.
Thus are her splendours dimm'd, and crusted o'er
With those dark vices that she knew before.
For this the souls a various penance pay,
To purge the taint of former crimes away.
Some in the *sweeping breezes* are refined,
And hung on high to *whiten in the wind:*
Some cleanse their stains beneath the gushing streams,
And some rise glorious from the *searching flames.*"—Edit.]

See the near resemblance between the ancient and the modern purgatory! Only in the ancient, the heathen purgatory, both fire, water, and air, were employed in expiating sin, and purifying the soul; whereas in the mystic purgatory, fire alone is supposed sufficient both to purge and expiate. Vain hope! No suffering, but that of Christ, has any power to expiate sin; and no fire, but that of love, can purify the soul, either in time or in eternity.

6. "He seeth Abraham afar off."—Far, indeed! as far as from hell to paradise! Perhaps, "ten-fold the length of this terrene." But how could this be? I cannot tell: But it is by no means incredible. For who knows "how far an angel kens," or a spirit divested of flesh and blood?—"And Lazarus in his bosom." It is well known that, in the ancient feasts among the Jews, as well as the Romans, the guests did not sit down at the table, as it is now the custom to do; but lay on couches, each having a pillow at his left side, on which he supported his elbow; and he that sat next him, on the right side, was said to lie in his bosom. It was in this sense that the Apostle John lay in his Master's bosom. Accordingly, the expression of Lazarus lying in Abraham's bosom implies that he was in the highest place of honour and happiness.

7. "And he cried, and said, Father Abraham, have mercy on me."—Thou fool! what can Abraham do? What can any creature, yea, all the creation do, to break the bars of the bottomless pit? Whoever would escape from the place of torment, let him cry to God, the Father of mercy! Nay, but the time is past! Justice now takes place, and rejoices over mercy!—"And send Lazarus, that he may dip the tip of his finger in water, and cool my tongue; for I am tormented in this flame!" How exceeding modest a request is this! He does not say, "That he may take me out of this flame." He does not ask, "That he may bring me a cup of water, or as much as he might hold in the palm of his hand;" but barely, "That he may dip" were it but "the tip of his finger in water, and cool my tongue." No! It cannot be! No mercy can enter within the shades of hell!

8. "But Abraham said, Son, remember that thou in thy lifetime receivedst thy good things, and likewise Lazarus evil things; but now he is comforted, and thou art tormented."

Perhaps these words may supply us with an answer to an important question: How came this rich man to be in hell? It does not appear that he was a wicked man, in the common sense of the word; that he was a drunkard, a common swearer, a Sabbath-breaker, or that he lived in any known sin. It is probable he was a Pharisee; and as such was, in all the outward parts of religion, blameless. How then did he come into "the place of torment?" If there was no other reason to be assigned, there is a sufficient one implied in those words, ("he that hath ears to hear, let him hear!") "Thou in thy lifetime receivedst thy good things,"—the things which thou hadst chosen for thy happiness. Thou hadst set thy affection on things beneath: And thou hadst thy reward: Thou didst receive the portion which thou hadst chosen, and canst have no portion above. "And likewise Lazarus evil things." Not *his* evil things; for he did not choose them. But they were chosen for him by the wise providence of God: And "now he is comforted, while thou art tormented."

9. "But beside all this, there is a great gulf fixed:"—A great chasm, a vast vacuity Can any tell us what this is? What is the nature, what are the bounds, of it? Nay, none of the children of men; none but an inhabitant of the invisible world.—"So that they who would pass from hence to you cannot; neither can they pass to us, that would come from thence." Undoubtedly a disembodied spirit could pass through any space whatever. But the will of God, determining that none should go across that gulf, is a bound which no creature can pass.

10. Then he said, "I pray thee therefore, father, that thou wouldst send him to my father's house; for I have five brethren; that he may testify unto them, lest they also come into this place of torment." (Luke 16:27, 28.) Two entirely different motives have been assigned for this extraordinary request. Some ascribe it wholly to self-love, to a fear of the bitter reproaches which, he might easily suppose, his brethren would pour upon him, if, in consequence of his example, and perhaps advice, they came to the same place of torment. Others have imputed it to a nobler motive. They suppose, as the misery of the wicked will not be complete till the day of judgment, so neither will their wickedness. Consequently, they believe that, till that time, they may retain some sparks of natural affection; and they, not improbably, imagine that this may have occasioned his desire to prevent their sharing his own torment.

11. "Abraham saith unto him, They have Moses and the Prophets: let them hear them." (Luke 16:29.) "And he said, Nay, father Abraham; but if one went to them from the dead, they will repent." Who would not be of the same opinion? Might not any one reasonably suppose that a message solemnly delivered by one that came from the dead must have an irresistible force? Who would not think, "I myself could not possibly withstand such a preacher of repentance?"

II. This I conceive to be the meaning of the words. I will now endeavour, with the help of God, to apply them. And I beseech you, brethren. while I am doing this, "to suffer the word of exhortation." The more closely these things are applied to your souls, the more ye may profit thereby.

1. "There was a certain rich man:"—And it is no more sinful to be rich than to be poor. But it is dangerous beyond expression. Therefore, I remind all of you that are of this number, that have the conveniences of life, and something over that ye walk upon slippery ground. Ye continually tread on snares and deaths. Ye are every moment on the verge of hell! "It is easier for a camel to go through the eye of a needle, than for you to enter in the kingdom of heaven."—"Who was clothed in purple and fine linen." And some may have a plea for this. Our Lord mentions them that "dwell in kings' houses," as wearing gorgeous, that is, splendid, apparel, and does not blame them for it. But certainly this is no plea for any that do not dwell in kings' houses. Let all of them, therefore, beware how they follow his example who is "lifting up his eyes in hell!" Let us follow the advice of the Apostle, being "adorned with good works, and with the ornament of a meek and quiet spirit."

2. "He fared sumptuously every day."—Reconcile this with religion who can. I know how plausibly the prophets of smooth things can talk in favour of hospitality; of making our friends welcome: of keeping a handsome table, to do honour to religion; of promoting trade, and the like. But God is not mocked: He will not be put off with such pretences as these. Whoever thou art that sharest in the sin of this rich man, were it no other than "faring sumptuously every day," thou shalt as surely be a sharer in his punishment, except thou repent, as if thou wert already crying for a drop of water to cool thy tongue!

3. "And there was a certain beggar named Lazarus, who was laid at his gate, full of sores, and desiring to be fed with the crumbs which fell from the rich man's table." (Luke 16:20, 21.) But it seems both the rich man and his guests were too religious to relieve *common beggars!*—a sin of which pious Mr. H. so earnestly warns his readers; and an admonition of the same kind I have read on the gate of the good city of Winchester! I wish the gentlemen who placed it there had seen a little circumstance which occurred some years since. At Epworth, in Lincolnshire, the town where I was born, a beggar came to a house in the market-place, and begged a morsel of bread, saying she was very hungry. The master bid her *be gone, for a lazy jade.* She called at a second, and begged a little small beer, saying she was very thirsty. She had much the same answer. At a third door she begged a little water; saying she was very faint. But this man also was too conscientious to encourage common beggars. The boys, seeing a ragged creature turned from door to door, began to pelt her with snow-balls. She looked up, lay down, and died! Would you wish to be the man who refused that poor wretch a morsel of bread, or a cup of water?—"Moreover the dogs came and licked his sores:" Being more compassionate than their master.—"And it came to pass, that the beggar died, and was carried of angels into Abraham's bosom." Hear this, all ye that are poor in this world. Ye that, many times, have not food to eat, or raiment to put on; ye that have not a place where to lay your head, unless it be a cold garret, or a foul and damp cellar! Ye are now reduced to "solicit the cold hand of charity." Yet lift up your load; it shall not always be thus. I love you, I pity you, I admire you, when "in patience ye possess your souls." Yet I cannot help you. But there is One that can,—the Father of the fatherless, and the Husband of the widow. "The poor crieth unto the Lord; and he heareth him, and delivereth him out of all his troubles." Yet a little while, if ye truly turn to him, his angels shall carry you into Abraham's bosom. There ye shall "hunger no more, and thirst no more;" ye shall feel no more sorrow or pain; but "the Lamb shall wipe away all tears from your eyes, and lead you forth beside fountains of living waters."

4. But see, the scene is changed! "The rich man also died." What? In spite of his riches? Probably sooner than he desired. For how just is that word, "O death, how bitter art thou to a man that is at rest in the midst of his possessions!" However, if that would be a comfort, "he was buried." But how little did it signify, whether he was laid under a lofty monument, or among

Graves with bending osier bound,
That nameless heave the crumbled ground!

And what followed? "In hell he lifted his eyes." This, it is certain, ye need not do. God does not require it of you: "He willeth not that any should perish." Ye cannot, unless by your own wilful choice,—intruding into those regions of woe, which God did not prepare for *you*, but for "the devil and his angels."

5. See the scene change again! "He seeth Abraham afar off, and Lazarus in his bosom." And he knew him; although, perhaps, he had only cast a glance at him while he "lay at his gates." Is any of you in doubt whether we shall know one another in the other world? Here your doubts may receive a full solution. If a soul in hell knew Lazarus in paradise, as far off as he was, certainly those that are together in paradise will perfectly know each other.

6. "And he cried, and said, Father Abraham, have mercy upon me!"—I do not remember, in all the Bible, any prayer made to a saint, but this. And if we observe who made it,—a man in hell,—and with what success, we shall hardly wish to follow the precedent. O let us cry for mercy to God, not to man! And it is our wisdom to cry now, while we are in the land of mercy; otherwise it will be too late!—"I am tormented in this flame!" Tormented, observe, not purified. Vain hope, that fire can purify a spirit! As well might you expect water to cleanse the soul, as fire. God forbid that you or I should make the trial!

7. And "Abraham said, Son, remember:"—Mark, how Abraham accosts a damned spirit: And shall we behave with less tenderness to any of the children of God, "because they are not of our opinion?"—"Thou in thy lifetime receivedst thy good things." O, beware it be not your case! Are not the things of the world "thy good things?"—the chief objects of thy desire and pursuit? Are they not thy chief joy? If so, thou art in a very dangerous state; in the very condition which Dives was in upon earth! Do not then dream that all is well, because thou art "highly esteemed among men;" because thou doest no harm, or doest much good, or attendest all the ordinances of God. What is all this, if thy soul cleaves to the dust; if thy heart is in the world; if thou lovest the creature more than the Creator?

8. How striking are the next words! "Beside all this, between us and you there is a great gulf fixed; so that they who would pass from us to you cannot; neither can they pass to us, that would come from thence." This was the text which occasioned the epitaph on a right honourable infidel and gamester:—

> Here lies a dicer; long in doubt
> If death could kill the soul, or not:
> Here ends his doubtfulness; at last
> Convinced;—but, ah! the die is cast!

But, blessed be God, *your* die is not cast yet. You are not passed the great gulf, but have it still in your power to choose whether you will be attended by angels or fiends when your soul quits its earthly mansion. Now stretch out your hand to eternal life or eternal death! And God says, "Be it unto thee even as thou wilt!"

9. Being repulsed in this, he makes another request: "I pray thee, send him to my father's house; for I have five brethren; that he may testify to them." It is not impossible that other unhappy spirits may wish well to the relations they have left behind them. But this is the accepted time for them, as well as for us. Let us then address them ourselves; and let us beg our living friends to give us all the help they can, without waiting for assistance from the inhabitants of another world. Let us earnestly exhort them to use the helps they have; to "hear Moses and the Prophets." We are indeed apt to think, like that unhappy spirit, "If one went to them from the dead, they will repent." "But Abraham said, If they hear not Moses and the Prophets, neither will they be persuaded though one rose from the dead."

III. 1. I am, in the Third place, to prove the truth of this weighty sentence; which I will do, First, briefly, and then more at large.

And, First, to express the matter briefly: It is certain that no human spirit, while it is in the body, can *persuade* another *to repent*; can work in him an entire change, both of heart and life; a change from universal wickedness, to universal holiness. And suppose that spirit discharged from the body, it is no more able to do this than it was before: No power less than that which created it at first can create any soul anew. No angel, much less any human spirit, whether in the body or out of the body, can bring one soul "from darkness to light, and from the power of Satan unto God." It might very possibly fright him to death, or to the belief of any speculative truth; but it could not frighten him into spiritual life. God alone can raise those that are "dead in trespasses and sins."

2. In order to prove more at large, that if men "hear not Moses and the Prophets, neither will they be" effectually "persuaded" to repent, "though one rose from the dead," I will propose a case of this kind, with all the advantages that can be conceived. Suppose, then, one that does not "hear Moses and the Prophets," that does not believe the Scripture to be of God, to be fast asleep in his bed, and suddenly to awake while the clock was just striking one. He is surprised to observe the chamber as light as if it were noon-day. He looks up, and sees one whom he perfectly knew standing at his bed-side. Though a little surprised at first, he quickly recollects himself, and has the courage to ask, "Are not you

my friend, who died at such a time?" He answers, "I am. I am come from God, with a message to *you*. You have often wished you could see one risen from the dead; and said, then you *would* repent. You have your wish; and I am ordered to inform you, you are seeking death in the error of your life. If you die in the state you are in now, you will die eternally. I warn you, in His name, that the Scriptures are the real word of God; that from the moment you die, you will be remarkably happy, or unspeakably miserable; that you cannot be happy hereafter, unless you are holy here; which cannot be, unless you are born again. Receive this call from God! Eternity is at hand. Repent, and believe the gospel!" Having spoken these words, he vanishes away; and the room is dark as it was before.

3. One may easily believe, it would be impossible for him not to be convinced for the present. He would sleep no more that night; and would, as soon as possible, tell his family what he had seen and heard. Not content with this, he would be impatient to tell it to his former companions. And, probably, observing the earnestness with which he spoke, they would not then contradict him. They would say to each other, "Give him time to cool; then he will be a reasonable man again."

4. Now, it is constantly found, that impressions made on the memory gradually decay; that they grow weaker and weaker in process of time, and the traces of them fainter and fainter. So it must be in this case; which his companions observing, would not fail to seize the opportunity. They would speak to this effect: "It was a strange account you gave us some time since; the more so, because we know *you* to be a sensible man, and not inclined to enthusiasm. But, perhaps, you have not fully considered, how difficult it is, in some cases, to distinguish our dreams from our waking thoughts. Has anyone yet been able to find out an infallible criterion between them? Is it not then possible, that you may have been asleep when this lively impression was made on your mind?" When he had been brought to think, *possibly* it might be a dream; they would soon persuade him, *probably* it was so; and not long after, to believe, it *certainly* was a dream. So little would it avail, that one came from the dead!

5. It could not be expected to be otherwise. For what was the effect which was wrought upon him? (1.) He was exceedingly frightened: (2.) This fright made way for a deeper conviction of the truth then declared: But (3.) his heart was not changed. None but the Almighty could effect this. Therefore (4.) the bias of his soul was still set the wrong way; he still loved the world, and, consequently, wished that the Scripture was not true. How easily then, as the fright wore off, would he again believe what he wished! The conclusion then is plain and undeniable. If men "hear not Moses and the Prophets, neither will they be persuaded" to repent and believe the gospel, "though one rose from the dead."

6. We may add one consideration more, which brings the matter to a full issue. Before, or about the same time, that Lazarus was carried into Abraham's bosom, another Lazarus, the brother of Martha and Mary, was actually raised from the dead. But were even those who believed the fact persuaded to repent? So far from it, that "they took counsel to kill Lazarus," as well as his Master! Away then with the fond

imagination, that those who "hear not Moses and the Prophets, would be persuaded, though on from the dead!"

7. From the whole we may draw this general conclusion. That standing revelation is the best means of rational conviction; far preferable to any of those extraordinary means which some imagine would be more effectual. It is therefore our wisdom to avail ourselves of this; to make full use of it; so that it may be a lantern to our feet, and a light in all our paths. Let us take care that our whole heart and life be conformable thereto; that it be the constant rule of all our tempers, all our words, and all our actions. So shall we preserve in all things the testimony of a good conscience toward God; and when our course is finished, we too shall be "carried by angels into Abraham's bosom." *Birmingham, March 25, 1788.*

113.* THE DIFFERENCE BETWEEN WALKING BY SIGHT, AND WALKING BY FAITH

"We walk by faith, not by sight."

2 Cor. 5:7.

1. How short is this description of real Christians! And yet how exceeding full! It comprehends, it sums up, the whole experience of those that are truly such, from the time they are born of God till they remove into Abraham's bosom. For, who are the *we* that are here spoken of? All that are true Christian believers. I say *Christian,* not *Jewish, believers.* All that are not only *servants,* but *children,* of God. All that have "the Spirit of adoption, crying in their hearts, Abba, Father." All that have "the Spirit of God witnessing with their spirits, that they are the sons of God."

2. All these, and these alone, can say, "We walk by faith, and not by sight." But before we can possibly "walk by faith," we must *live* by faith, and not by sight. And to all real Christians our Lord saith, "Because I live, ye live also:" Ye live a life which the world, whether learned or unlearned, "know not of." "You that," like the world, "were dead in trespasses and sins, hath he quickened," and made alive; given you new senses,—spiritual senses,—"senses exercised to discern spiritual good and evil."

3. In order thoroughly to understand this important truth, it may be proper to consider the whole matter. All the children of men that are not born of God "walk by sight," having no higher principle. By *sight,* that is, by *sense,* a part being put for the whole; the sight for all the senses; the rather, because it is more noble and more extensive than any, or all the rest. There are but few objects which we can discern by the three inferior senses of taste, smell, and feeling; and none of these can take any cognizance of its object, unless it be brought into a direct contact with it. Hearing, it is true, has a larger sphere of action, and gives us some knowledge of things that are distant. But how small is that distance, suppose it were fifty or a hundred miles, compared to that between the earth and the sun! And what is even this in comparison of the distance of the sun and moon and the fixed stars! Yet the sight continually takes knowledge of objects even at this amazing distance.

4. By sight we take knowledge of the visible world, from the surface of the earth to the region of the fixed stars. But what is the world visible to us, but "a speck of creation," compared to the whole universe? to the invisible world?—that part of the creation which we cannot see at all, by reason of its distance; in the place of which, through the imperfection of our senses, we are presented with an universal blank. 5. But beside these innumerable objects which we cannot see by reason of their distance, have we not sufficient ground to believe that there are innumerable others of too delicate a nature to be discerned by any of our senses? Do not all men of unprejudiced reason allow the same thing, (the small number of Materialists, or Atheists, I cannot term *men of reason,*) that there is an invisible world, naturally such, as well as a visible one? But which of our senses is fine enough to take the least knowledge of this? We can no more perceive any part of this by our sight, than by our feeling. Should we allow, with the ancient poet that,

Millions of spiritual creatures walk the earth

Unseen, both when we wake, and when we sleep;

should we allow, that the great Spirit, the Father of all, filleth both heaven and earth; yet is the finest of our senses utterly incapable of perceiving either Him or them.

6. All our external senses are evidently adapted to this external, visible world. They are designed to serve us only while we sojourn here,—while we dwell in these houses of clay. They have nothing to do with the invisible world; they are not adapted to it. And they can take no more cognizance of the eternal, than of the invisible world; although we are as fully assured of the existence of this, as of anything in the present world. We cannot think death puts a period to our being. The body indeed returns to dust; but the soul, being of a nobler nature, is not affected thereby. There is, therefore, an eternal world, of what kind soever it be. But how shall we attain the knowledge of this? What will teach us to draw aside the veil "that hangs 'twixt mortal and immortal being?" We all know, "the vast, the unbounded prospect lies before us;" but we are not constrained to add, "Yet clouds, alas! and darkness rest upon it."

7. The most excellent of our senses, it is undeniably plain, can give us no assistance herein. And what can our boasted reason do? It is now universally allowed, *Nihil est in intellectu quod non fuit prius in sensu:* "Nothing is in the understanding, which was not first perceived by some of the senses." Consequently, the understanding, having here nothing to work upon, can afford us no help at all. So that, in spite of all the information we can gain, either from sense or reason, both the invisible and eternal world are unknown to all that "walk by sight."

8. But is there no help? Must they remain in total darkness concerning the invisible and the eternal world? We cannot affirm this: Even the Heathens did not all remain in total darkness concerning them. Some few rays of light have, in all ages and nations, gleamed through the shade. Some light they

---

* [text of the 1872 ed.]

derived from various fountains touching the invisible world. "The heavens declared the glory of God," though not to their outward sight: "The firmament showed," to the eyes of their understanding, the existence of their Maker. From the creation they inferred the being of a Creator, powerful and wise, just and merciful. And hence they concluded, there must be an eternal world, a future state, to commence after the present; wherein the justice of God in punishing wicked men, and his mercy in rewarding the righteous, will be openly and undeniably displayed in the sight of all intelligent creatures.

9. We may likewise reasonably suppose, that some traces of knowledge, both with regard to the invisible and the eternal world, were delivered down from Noah and his children, both to their immediate and remote descendants. And however these were obscured or disguised by the addition of numberless fables, yet something of truth was still mingled with them, and these streaks of light prevented utter darkness. Add to this, that God never, in any age or nation, "left himself" quite "without a witness" in the hearts of men; but while he "gave them rain and fruitful seasons," imparted some imperfect knowledge of the Giver. "He is the true Light that" still, in some degree, "enlighteneth every man that cometh into the world."

10. But all these lights put together availed no farther than to produce a faint twilight. It gave them, even the most enlightened of them, no *elegchos*, no *demonstration*, no *demonstrative conviction*, either of the invisible or of the eternal world. Our philosophical poet justly terms Socrates, "The wisest of all moral men;" that is, of all that were not favoured with Divine Revelation. Yet what evidence had he of another world, when he addressed those that had condemned him to death?—"And now, O ye judges, ye are going to live, and I am going to die. Which of these is best, God knows; but I suppose no man does." Alas! What a confession is this! Is this all the evidence that poor dying Socrates had either of an invisible or an eternal world? And yet even this is preferable to the light of the great and good Emperor Adrian. Remember, ye modern Heathens, and copy after his pathetic address to his parting soul. For fear I should puzzle you with Latin, I give it you in Prior's fine translation:—

> Poor, little, pretty, fluttering thing,
>   Must we no longer live together?
> And dost thou prune thy trembling wing,
>   To take the flight, thou know'st not whither?
> Thy pleasing vein, thy humorous folly,
>   Lies all neglected, all forgot!
> And pensive, wavering, melancholy,
>   Thou hop'st and fear'st, thou know'st not what.

11. "Thou know'st not what!" True, there was no knowledge of what was to be hoped or feared after death, till "the Sun of Righteousness" arose to dispel all their vain conjectures, and "brought life and immortality," that is, immortal life, "to light, through the Gospel." Then (and not till then, unless in some rare instances) God revealed, unveiled the invisible world. He then revealed himself to the children of men. "The Father revealed the Son" in their hearts; and the Son revealed the Father. He that of old time "commanded light to shine out of darkness shined in their hearts, and enlightened them with the knowledge of the glory of God, in the face of Jesus Christ."

12. It is where sense can be of no farther use, that faith comes in to our help; it is the grand *desideratum*; it does what none of the senses can; no, not with all the helps that art hath invented. All our instruments, however improved by the skill and labour of so many succeeding ages, do not enable us to make the least discovery of these unknown regions. They barely serve the occasions for which they were formed in the present visible world.

13. How different is the case, how vast the pre-eminence, of them that "walk by faith!" God, having "opened the eyes of their understanding," pours divine light into their soul; whereby they are enabled to "see Him that is invisible," to see God and the things of God. What their "eye had not seen, nor their ear heard neither had it entered into their heart to conceive," God from time to time reveals to them, by the "unction of the Holy One, which teacheth them of all things." Having "entered into the holiest by the blood of Jesus," by that "new and living way," and being joined unto "the general assembly and church of the first-born, and unto God the Judge of all, and Jesus the Mediator of the New Covenant,"—each of these can say, "I live not, but Christ liveth in me;" [Gal. 2:20] I now live that life which "is hid with Christ in God;" "and when Christ, who is *my* life, shall appear, then *I* shall likewise appear with him in glory."

14. They that *live* by faith, *walk by faith*. But what is implied in this? They regulate all their judgments concerning good and evil, not with reference to visible and temporal things, but to things invisible and eternal. They think visible things to be of small value, because they pass away like a dream; but, on the contrary, they account invisible things to be of high value, because they will never pass away. Whatever is invisible is eternal; the things that are not seen, do not perish. So the Apostle: "The things that are seen are temporal; but the things that are not seen are eternal." Therefore, they that "walk by faith" do not desire the "things which are seen;" neither are they the object of their pursuit. They "set their affections on things above, not on things on the earth." They seek only the things which are "where Jesus sitteth at the right hand of God." Because they know, "the things that are seen are temporal," passing away like a shadow, therefore they "look not at them;" they desire them not; they account them as nothing; but "they look at the things which are not seen, that are eternal," that never pass away. By these they form their judgment of all things. They judge them to be good or evil, as they promote or hinder their welfare, not in time, but in eternity. They weigh whatever occurs in this balance: "What influence has it on my eternal state?" They regulate all their tempers and passions, all their desires, joys, and fears, by this standard. They regulate all their thoughts and designs, all their words and actions, so as to prepare them for that invisible and eternal world to which they are shortly going. They do not *dwell*, but only *sojourn* here; not looking upon earth as their home, but only

> Travelling through Immanuel's ground,

To fairer worlds on high.

15. Brethren, are *you* of this number, who are now here before God? Do *you* see "Him that is invisible?" Have you faith, living faith, the faith of a child? Can you say, "The life that I now live, I live by faith in the Son of God, who loved me, and gave himself for me"? Do you "walk by faith?" Observe the question. I do not ask, whether you curse, or swear, or profane the Sabbath, or live in any outward sin. I do not ask, whether you do good, more or less; or attend all the ordinances of God. But, suppose you are blameless in all these respects, I ask, in the name of God, by what standard do you judge of the value of things? by the visible or the invisible world? Bring the matter to an issue in a single instance. Which do you judge best,—that your son should be a pious cobbler, or a profane lord? Which appears to you most eligible,—that your daughter should be a child of God, and walk on foot, or a child of the devil, and ride in a coach-and-six? When the question is concerning marrying your daughter, if you consider her body more than her soul, take knowledge of yourself: You are in the way to hell, and not to heaven; for you walk by sight, and not by faith. I do not ask, whether you live in any outward sin or neglect; but, do you *seek* in the general tenor of your life, "the things that are above," or the things that are below? Do you "set your affection on things above," or on "things of the earth?" If on the latter, you are as surely in the way of destruction, as a thief or a common drunkard. My dear friends, let every man, every woman among you, deal honestly with yourselves. Ask your own heart, "What am I seeking day by day? What am I desiring? What am I pursuing? earth or heaven? the things that are seen, or the things that are not seen?" What is your object, God or the world? As the Lord liveth, if the world is your object, still all your religion is vain.

16. See then, my dear brethren, that from this time, at least, ye choose the better part. Let your judgment of all the things round about you be according to the real value of things, with a reference to the invisible and eternal world. See that ye judge everything fit to be pursued or shunned, according to the influence it will have on your eternal state. See that your affections, your desire, your joy, your hope, be set, not on transient objects, not on things that fly as a shadow, that pass away like a dream; but on those that are incapable of change, that are incorruptible and fade not away; those that remain the same, when heaven and earth "flee away, and there is no place found for them." See that in all you think, speak, or do, the eye of your soul be single, fixed on "Him that is invisible," and "the glories that shall be revealed." Then shall "your whole body be full of light:" Your whole soul shall enjoy the light of God's countenance; and you shall continually see the light of the glorious love of God "in the face of Jesus Christ."

17. See, in particular, that all your "desire be unto him, and unto the remembrance of his name." Beware of "foolish and hurtful desires;" such as arise from any visible or temporal thing. All these St. John warns us of, under that general term "love of the world." [1 John 2:15] It is not so much to men of the world, as to the children of God, he gives that important direction: "Love not the world, neither the things of the world." Give no place to "the desire of the flesh,"—the gratification of the outward senses, whether of the taste, or any other. Give no place to "the desire of the eye,"—the internal sense, or imagination,—by gratifying it, either by grand things, or beautiful, or uncommon. Give no place to "the pride of life,"—the desire of wealth, of pomp, or of the honour that cometh of men. St. John confirms this advice by a consideration parallel to that observation which St. Paul had made to the Corinthians: "For the world and the fashion of it passeth away." [1 John 2:16, 17] "The fashion of it"— all worldly objects, business, pleasures, cares, whatever now attracts our regard or attention—"passeth away,"—is in the very act of passing, and will return no more. Therefore desire none of these fleeting things, but that glory which "abideth for ever."

18. Observe well: This is religion, and this alone; this alone is true Christian religion; not this or that opinion, or system of opinions, be they ever so true, ever so scriptural. It is true, this is commonly called faith. But those who suppose it to be religion are given up to a strong delusion to believe a lie, and if they suppose it to be a sure passport to heaven are in the high road to hell. Observe well: Religion is not harmlessness; which a careful observer of mankind properly terms *hellish harmlessness*, as it sends thousands to the bottomless pit. It is not *morality*, excellent as that is, when it is built on a right foundation,—loving faith; but when otherwise, it is of no value in the sight of God. It is not *formality*,—the most exact observance of all the ordinances of God. This, too, unless it be built on the right foundation, is no more pleasing to God, than "the cutting off a dog's neck." No: Religion is no less than living in eternity, and walking in eternity; and hereby walking in the love of God and man, in lowliness, meekness, and resignation. This, and this alone, is that "life which is hid with Christ in God." He alone who experiences this "dwells in God, and God in him." This alone is setting the crown upon Christ's head, and doing his "will on earth as it is done in heaven."

19. It will easily be observed, that this is the very thing that men of the world call enthusiasm,—a word just fit for their purpose, because no man can tell either the meaning or even the derivation of it. If it has any determinate sense, it means a species of religious madness. Hence, when you speak your experience, they immediately cry out, "Much religion hath made thee mad." And all that you experience, either of the invisible or of the eternal world, they suppose to be only the waking dreams of a heated imagination. It cannot be otherwise, when men born blind take upon them to reason concerning light and colours. They will readily pronounce those to be insane who affirm the existence of those things whereof they have no conception.

20. From all that has been said, it may be seen, with the utmost clearness, what is the nature of that fashionable thing called *dissipation*. He that hath ears to hear, let him hear! It is the very quintessence of Atheism; it is artificial, added to natural, ungodliness. It is the art of forgetting God, of being altogether "without God in the world;" the art of excluding him, if not out of the world he has created, yet out of the minds of all his intelligent creatures. It is a total studied inattention to the whole invisible and eternal world; more

especially to death, the gate of eternity, and to the important consequences of death,—heaven and hell!

21. This is the real nature of *dissipation*. And is it so harmless a thing as it is usually thought? It is one of the choicest instruments of destroying immortal spirits that was ever forged in the magazines of hell. It has been the means of plunging myriads of souls, that might have enjoyed the glory of God, into the everlasting fire prepared for the devil and his angels. It blots out all religion at one stroke, and levels man with the beasts that perish. All ye that fear God, flee from dissipation! Dread and abhor the very name of it! Labour to have God in all your thoughts, to have eternity ever in your eye! "Look" continually, "not at the things that are seen, but at the things which are not seen." Let your hearts be fixed there, where "Christ sitteth at the right hand of God!" that whensoever he calleth you, "an entrance may be ministered unto you abundantly into his everlasting kingdom!"

London, December 30, 1788

114.* THE UNITY OF THE DIVINE BEING

"There is one God."

Mark 12:32.

1. And as there is one God, so there is one religion and one happiness for all men. God never intended there should be any more; and it is not possible there should. Indeed, in another sense, as the Apostle observes, "there are gods many, and lords many." All the heathen nations had their gods; and many, whole shoals of them. And generally, the more polished they were, the more gods they heaped up to themselves. But to us, to all that are favoured with the Christian Revelation, "there is but one God;" who declares himself, "Is there any God besides me? There is none; I know not any."

2. But who can search out this God to perfection? None of the creatures that he has made. Only some of his attributes he hath been pleased to reveal to us in his word. Hence we learn that God is an eternal Being. "His goings forth are from everlasting," and will continue to everlasting. As he ever was, so he ever will be; as there was no beginning of his existence, so there will be no end. This is universally allowed to be contained in his very name, Jehovah; which the Apostle John accordingly renders, "He that was, and that is, and that is to come." Perhaps it would be as proper to say, "He is from everlasting to everlasting."

3. Nearly allied to the eternity of God, is his omnipresence. As he exists through infinite duration, so he cannot but exist through infinite space; according to his own question, equivalent to the strongest assertion,—"Do not I fill heaven and earth? saith the Lord;" (heaven and earth in the Hebrew idiom, implying the whole universe;) which, therefore, according to his own declaration, is filled with his presence.

4. This one, eternal, omnipresent Being is likewise all—perfect. He has, from eternity to eternity, all the perfections and infinitely more than it ever did or ever can enter into the heart of man to conceive; yea, infinitely more than the angels in heaven can conceive; These perfections we usually term, the attributes of God.

5. And he is omnipotent, as well as omnipresent; there can be no more bounds to his power, than to his presence. He "hath a mighty arm; strong is his hand, and high is his right hand." He doeth whatsoever pleaseth him, in the heavens, the earth, the sea, and in all deep places. With men we know many things are impossible, but not with God: With him "all things are possible." Whensoever he willeth, to do is present with him.

6. The omniscience of God is a clear and necessary consequence of his omnipresence. If he is present in every part of the universe, he cannot but know whatever is, or is done there; according to the word of St. James, "Known unto God are all his works," and the works of every creature, "from the beginning" of the world; or rather, as the phrase literally implies, "from eternity." His eyes are not only "over all the earth, beholding the evil and the good;" but likewise over the whole creation, yea, and the paths of uncreated night. Is there any difference between his knowledge and his wisdom? If there be, is not his knowledge the more general term, (at least, according to our weak conceptions.) and his wisdom a particular branch of it; namely, the knowing the end of everything that exists, and the means of applying it to that end.

7. Holiness is another of the attributes of the almighty, all-wise God. He is infinitely distant from every touch of evil. He "is light; and in him is no darkness at all." He is a God of unblemished justice and truth; but above all is his mercy. This we may easily learn from that beautiful passage in the thirty—third and fourth chapters of Exodus: "And Moses said, I beseech thee, show me thy glory. And the Lord descended in the cloud, and proclaimed the name of the Lord,—The Lord, The Lord God, merciful and gracious, longsuffering, and abundant in goodness and truth, keeping mercy for thousands, and forgiving iniquity and transgression and sin."

8. This God is a Spirit; not having such a body, such parts or passions, as men have. It was the opinion both of the ancient Jews and the ancient Christians, that He alone is a pure Spirit, totally separate from all matter; whereas they supposed all other spirits, even the highest angels, even cherubim and seraphim, to dwell in material vehicles, though of an exceeding light and subtile substance. At that point of duration which the infinite wisdom of God saw to be most proper, for reasons which lie hid in the abyss of his own understanding, not to be fathomed by any finite mind, God "called into being all that is;" created the heavens and the earth, together with all that they contain. "All things were created by him, and without him was not any thing made that was made." He created man, in particular, after his own image, to be "a picture of his own eternity." When he had raised man from the dust of the earth, he breathed into him an immortal spirit. Hence he is peculiarly called, "The Father of our spirits;" yea, "The Father of the spirits of all flesh."

* (text from the 1872 edition)

9. He "made all things," as the wise man observes, "for himself;" "for his glory they were created." Not "as if he needed anything;" seeing "he giveth to all life, and breath, and all things." He made all things to be happy. He made man to be happy in Himself. He is the proper centre of spirits; for whom every created spirit was made. So true is that well-known saying of the ancient Fathers: *Fecisti nos ad te: et irrequietum est cor nostrum, donec requiescat in te*: "Thou has made us for thyself; and our heart cannot rest, till it resteth in thee."

10. This observation gives us a clear answer to that question in the Assembly's Catechism: "For what end did God create man?" The answer is, "To glorify and enjoy him for ever." This is undoubtedly true; but is it quite clear, especially to men of ordinary capacities? Do the generality of common people understand that expression, "To glorify God?" No; no more than they understand Greek. And it is altogether above the capacity of children; to whom we can scare ever speak plain enough. Now, is not this the very principle that should be inculcated upon every human creature,—"You are made to be happy in God," as soon as ever reason dawns? Should not every parent, as soon as a child begins to talk, or to run alone, say something of this kind: "See! what is that which shines so over your head? That we call the sun. See, how bright it is! Feel how it warms you! It makes the grass to spring, and everything to grow. But God made the sun. The sun could not shine, nor warm, nor do any good without him." In this plain and familiar way a wise parent might, many times in a day, say something of God; particularly insisting, "He made *you*; and he made you to be happy in him; and nothing else can make you happy." We cannot press this too soon. If you say, "Nay, but they cannot understand you when they are so young;" I answer, No; nor when they are fifty years old, unless God opens their understanding: And can he not do this at any age?

11. Indeed, this should be pressed on every human creature, young and old, the more earnestly and diligently, because so exceeding few, even of those that are called Christians, seem to know anything about it. Many indeed think of being happy with God in heaven; but the being happy in God on earth never entered into their thoughts. The less so, because from the time they come into the world, they are surrounded with idols. Such, in turns, are all "the things that are seen," (whereas God is not seen,) which all promise an happiness independent of God. Indeed, it is true that,

> Upright both in heart and will
> We by our God were made;
> But we turn'd from good to ill,
> And o'er the creatures stray'd;
> Multiplied our wandering thought,
> Which first was fix'd on God alone;
> In ten thousand objects sought
> The bliss we lost in one.

12. These idols, these rivals of God, are innumerable; but they may be nearly reduced to three parts. First. Objects of sense; such as gratify one or more of our outward senses. These excite the first kind of "love of the world," which St. John terms, "the desire of the flesh." Secondly. Objects of the imagination; things that gratify our fancy, by their grandeur, beauty, or novelty. All these make us fair promises of happiness, and thereby prevent our seeking it in God. This the Apostle terms, "the desire of the eyes;" whereby, chiefly, the imagination is gratified. They are, Thirdly, what St. John calls, "the pride of life." He seems to mean honour, wealth, and whatever directly tends to engender pride.

13. But suppose we were guarded against all these, are there not other idols which we have need to be apprehensive of; and idols, therefore, the more dangerous, because we suspect no danger from them? For is there any danger to be feared from our friends and relations; from the mutual endearments of husbands and wives, or of parents and children? Ought we not to bear a very tender affection to them? Ought we not to love them only less than God? Yea, and is there not a tender affection due to those whom God has made profitable to our souls? Are we not commanded to "esteem them very highly in love for their work's sake?" All this is unquestionably true; and this very thing makes the difficulty. Who is sufficient for this?—to go far enough herein, and no farther? to love them enough, and not too much? Can we love a wife, a child, a friend, well enough, without loving the creature more than the creator? Who is able to follow the caution which St. Paul gives to the Christians at Thessalonica? (1 Thess. 4:5.)

14. I wish that weighty passage (so strangely disguised in our translation) were duly considered: "Let every one of you know how to possess his vessel," his wife, "in sanctification and honour;" so as neither to dishonour God nor himself; nor to obstruct, but further, holiness. St. Paul goes on, *me en pathei epithymias*, which we render, Not in the lust of concupiscence, (What is this? It gives the english reader no conception at all. *pathos* means any *violent* or *impetuous affection. epithymia* is *desire*. By the two words the Apostle undoubtedly means vehement and impetuous affections,)—"as the Gentiles who know not God," and so may naturally seek happiness in a creature.

15. If, by the grace of God, we have avoided or forsaken all these idols, there is still one more dangerous than all the rest; that is, religion. It will easily be conceived, I mean false religion; that is, any religion which does not imply the giving of the heart to God. Such is, First, a religion of opinions; or what is called orthodoxy. Into this snare fall thousands of those who profess to hold "salvation by faith;" indeed, all of those who, by faith, mean only a system of Arminian or Calvinian opinions. Such is, Secondly, a religion of forms; of barely outward worship, how constantly soever performed; yea, though we attend the Church Service every day, and the Lord's Supper every Sunday. Such is, Thirdly, a religion of works; of seeking the favour of God by doing good to men. Such is, Lastly, a religion of Atheism; that is, every religion whereof God is not laid for the foundation. In a word, a religion wherein "God in Christ, reconciling the world unto himself," is not the Alpha and Omega, the beginning and the end, the first and the last point.

16. True religion is right tempers towards God and man. It is, in two words, gratitude and benevolence; gratitude to our Creator and supreme Benefactor, and benevolence to our

fellow creatures. In other words, it is the loving God with all our heart, and our neighbour as ourselves.

17. It is in consequence of our knowing God loves us, that we love him, and love our neighbour as ourselves. Gratitude towards our Creator cannot but produce benevolence to our fellow creatures. The love of Christ constrains us, not only to be harmless, to do no ill to our neighbour, but to be useful, to be "zealous of good works;" "as we have time, to do good unto all men;" and to be patterns to all of true, genuine morality; of justice, mercy, and truth. This is religion, and this is happiness; the happiness for which we were made. This begins when we begin to know God, by the teaching of his own Spirit. As soon as the Father of spirits reveals his Son in our hearts, and the Son reveals his Father, the love of God is shed abroad in our hearts; then, and not till then, we are happy. We are happy, first, in the consciousness of his favour, which indeed is better than life itself; next, in the constant communion with the Father, and with his Son Jesus Christ; then, in all the heavenly tempers which he hath wrought in us by his Spirit; again, in the testimony of his Spirit, that all our works please him; and, lastly, in the testimony of our own spirits, that "in simplicity and godly sincerity we have had our conversation in the world." Standing fast in this liberty from sin and sorrow, wherewith Christ hath made them free, real Christians "rejoice evermore, pray without ceasing, and in everything give thanks." And their happiness still increases as they "grow up into the measure of the stature of the fullness of Christ."

18. But how little is this religion experienced, or even thought of, in the Christian world! On the contrary, what reason have we to take up the lamentation of a dying saint, (Mr. Haliburton, of St. Andrew's in Scotland,) "O Sirs, I am afraid a kind of *rational* religion is more and more prevailing amongst us; a religion that has nothing of Christ belonging to it; nay, that has not only nothing of Christ, but nothing of God in it!" And indeed how generally does this prevail, not only among professed infidels, but also among those who call themselves Christians; who profess to believe the Bible to be the word of God! Thus our own countryman, Mr. Wollaston, in that elaborate work, "The Religion of Nature Delineated," presents us with a complete system of religion, without anything of God about it; without being beholden, in any degree, to either the Jewish or Christian revelation. Thus Monsieur Burlomachi, of Geneva, in his curious "Treatise on the Law of Nature," does not make any more use of the Bible than if he had never seen it. And thus the late Professor Hutcheson, of Glasgow, (a stranger writer than either of the other,) is so far from grounding virtue on either the fear or the love of God, that he quite shuts God out of the question; not scrupling to declare, in express terms, that a regard to God is *inconsistent with* virtue; insomuch that, if in doing a beneficent action you expect God to reward it, the virtue of the action is lost: It is then not a virtuous but a selfish action.

19. Perhaps, indeed, there are not many who carry the matter to so great a length. But how great is the number of those who, allowing religion to consist of two branches,—our duty to God, and our duty to our neighbour,—entirely forget the first part, and put the second part for the whole,—for the entire duty of man! Thus almost all men of letters, both in England, France, Germany, yea, and all the civilized countries of Europe, extol *humanity* to the skies, as the very essence of religion. To this the great triumvirate, Rousseau, Voltaire, and David Hume, have contributed all their labours, sparing no pains to establish a religion which should stand on its own foundation, independent on any revelation whatever; yea, not supposing even the being of a God. So leaving Him, if he has any being, to himself, they have found out both a religion and a happiness which have no relation at all to God, nor any dependence upon him.

20. It is no wonder that this religion should grow fashionable, and spread far and wide in the world. But call it *humanity, virtue, morality*, or what you please, it is neither better nor worse than Atheism. Men hereby wilfully and designedly put asunder what God has joined,—the duties of the first and the second table. It is separating the love of our neighbour from the love of God. It is a plausible way of thrusting God out of the world he has made. They can do the business without him; and so either drop him entirely, not considering him at all, or suppose that since

He gave things their beginning,

And set this whirligig a-spinning, he has not concerned himself with these trifles, but let every thing take its own course.

21. On the contrary, we have the fullest evidence that the eternal, omnipresent, almighty, all-wise Spirit, as he created all things, so he continually superintends whatever he has created. He governs all, not only to the bounds of creation, but through the utmost extent of space; and not only through the short time that is measured by the earth and sun, but from everlasting to everlasting. We know that as all nature, so all religion, and all happiness, depend on him; and we know that whoever teach to seek happiness without him are monsters, and the pests of society.

22. But after all the vain attempts of learned or unlearned men, it will be found, as there is but one God, so there is but one happiness, and one religion. And both of these centre in God. Both by Scripture and by experience we know that an unholy, and therefore an unhappy, man, seeking rest, but finding none, is sooner or later convinced that sin is the ground of his misery; and cries out of the deep to Him that is able to save, "God be merciful to me a sinner!" It is not long before he finds "redemption in the blood of Jesus, even the forgiveness of sins." Then "the Father reveals his Son" in his heart; and he "calls Jesus, Lord, by the Holy Ghost." And then the love of God is "shed abroad in his heart by the Holy Spirit which is given unto him." From this principle springs real, disinterested benevolence to all mankind; making him humble, meek, gentle to all men, easy to be entreated,—to be convinced of what is right, and persuaded to what is good; inviolably patient, with a thankful acquiescence in every step of his adorable providence. This is religion, even the whole mind which was also in Christ Jesus. And has any man the insolence or the stupidity to deny that this is happiness; yea, that it

Yields more of happiness below

Than victors in a triumph know?

23. There can be no doubt but from this love to God and man a suitable conversation will follow. His "communication," that is, discourse, will "be always in grace, seasoned with salt, and meet to minister grace to the hearers." He will always "open his mouth with wisdom, and there will be in his tongue the law of kindness." Hence his affectionate words will "distil as the dew, and as the rain upon the tender herb." And men will know, it is not he only that speaks, but the Spirit of the Father that speaketh in him. His actions will spring from the same source with his words; even from the abundance of a loving heart. And while all these aim at the glory of God, and tend to this one point, whatever he does, he may truly say,—

End of my every action thou,
In all things thee I see:
Accept my hallow'd labour now,
I do it as to thee!

24. He to whom this character belongs, and he alone, is a Christian. To him the one, eternal, omnipresent, all-perfect Spirit, is the "Alpha and Omega, the first and the last;" not his Creator only, but his Sustainer, his Preserver, his Governor; yea, his Father, his Savior, Sanctifier, and Comforter. This God is his God, and his All, in time and in eternity. It is the benevolence springing from this root which is pure and undefiled religion. But if it be built on any other foundation, as it is of no avail in the sight of God, so it brings no real, solid, permanent happiness to man, but leaves him still a poor, dry, indigent, and dissatisfied creature.

25. Let all therefore that desire to please God condescend to be taught of God, and take care to walk in that path which God himself hath appointed. Beware of taking half of this religion for the whole; but take both parts of it together. And see that you begin where God himself begins: "Thou shalt have no other gods before me." Is not this the first, our Lord himself being the Judge, as well as the great, commandment? First, therefore, see that ye love God; next, your neighbour,—every child of man. From this fountain let every temper, every affection, every passion flow. So shall that "mind be in you which was also in Christ Jesus." Let all your thoughts, words, and actions spring from this! So shall you "inherit the kingdom prepared for you from the beginning of the world." Preached at DUBLIN, April 9, 1789.

115.* THE MINISTERIAL OFFICE**

ONE BOOK; AND HE HAD REPEATEDLY INVITED ME TO SPEAK FULLY WHATEVER OBJECTION I HAD TO ANY THING WHICH HE PUBLISHED. I THOUGHT THAT SOME THINGS IN THAT DISCOURSE WERE NOT TO BE FOUND IN THE BOOK; AND I RESOLVED TO TELL HIM SO THE FIRST OPPORTUNITY. IT SOON OCCURRED. I RESPECTFULLY OBSERVED THAT I AGREED WITH HIM, THAT THE LORD HAD ALWAYS SENT BY WHOM HE WOULD SEND, INSTRUCTION, REPROOF, AND CORRECTION IN RIGHTEOUSNESS, TO MANKIND; AND THAT THERE WAS A REAL DISTINCTION BETWEEN THE PROPHETIC AND PRIESTLY OFFICE IN THE OLD TESTAMENT, AND THE PROPHETIC AND PASTORAL OFFICE IN THE NEW; (WHERE NO PRIESTHOOD IS MENTIONED BUT THAT OF OUR LORD;) BUT I COULD NOT THINK THAT WHAT HE HAD SAID CONCERNING THE EVANGELISTS AND THE PASTORS, OR BISHOPS, WAS AGREEABLE TO WHAT WE READ THERE; VIZ., THAT THE LATTER HAD A RIGHT TO ADMINISTER THE SACRAMENTS, WHICH THE FORMER DID NOT POSSESS. I OBSERVED, 'SIR, YOU KNOW THAT THE EVANGELISTS TIMOTHY AND TITUS WERE ORDERED BY THE APOSTLE TO ORDAIN BISHOPS IN EVERY PLACE; AND SURELY THEY COULD NOT IMPART TO THEM AN AUTHORITY WHICH THEY DID NOT THEMSELVES POSSESS.' HE LOOKED EARNESTLY AT ME FOR SOME TIME, BUT NOT WITH DISPLEASURE. HE MADE NO REPLY, AND SOON INTRODUCED ANOTHER SUBJECT. I SAID NO MORE. THE MAN OF ONE BOOK WOULD NOT DISPUTE AGAINST IT. I BELIEVE, HE SAW, HIS LOVE TO THE CHURCH, FROM WHICH HE NEVER DEVIATED

---

* [text of the 1872 Edition]
* [a.k.a. Prophets and Priests (Sermon 121 in the Bicentennial Edition)]

* [Respecting this Sermon the following information is given by Mr. Moore, in his "Life of Mr. Wesley," vol. ii., p. 339:—"I was with Mr. Wesley in London when he published that Sermon. He had encouraged me to be a man of

UNNECESSARILY, HAD, IN THIS INSTANCE, LED HIM A LITTLE TOO FAR."—EDIT.]

"No man taketh this honour unto himself but he that is called of God, as was Aaron."

Hebrews 5:4.

1. There are exceeding few texts of Holy Scripture which have been more frequently urged than this against laymen, that are neither Priests nor Deacons, and yet take upon them to preach. Many have asked, "How dare any 'take this honour to himself, unless he be called of God, as was Aaron?' " And a pious and sensible clergyman some years ago published a sermon on these words, wherein he endeavours to show that it is not enough to be inwardly called of God to preach, as many imagine themselves to be, unless they are outwardly called by men sent of God for that purpose, as Aaron was called of God by Moses.

2. But there is one grievous flaw in this argument, as often as it has been urged. "Called of God, as was Aaron!" But Aaron did not preach at all: He was not called to it either by God or man. Aaron was called to minister in holy things;—to offer up prayers and sacrifices; to execute the office of a Priest. But he was never called to be a Preacher.

3. In ancient times the office of a Priest and that of a Preacher were known to be entirely distinct. And so everyone will be convinced that impartially traces the matter from the beginning. From Adam to Noah it is allowed by all that the first-born in every family was of course the priest in that family, by virtue of his primogeniture. But this gave him no right to be a Preacher, or (in the scriptural language) a Prophet. This office not unfrequently belonged to the youngest branch of the family. For in this respect God always asserted his *right* to send by whom he *would* send.

4. From the time of Noah to that of Moses the same observation may be made. The eldest of the family was the Priest, but any other might be the Prophet. This, the office of Priest, we find Esau inherited by virtue of his birth-right, till he profanely sold it to Jacob for a mess of pottage. And this it was which he could never recover, "though he sought it carefully with tears."

5. Indeed in the time of Moses a very considerable change was made with regard to the priesthood. God then appointed that instead of the first-born in every house a whole tribe should be dedicated to him; and that all that afterwards ministered unto him as priests should be of that tribe. Thus Aaron was of the tribe of Levi. And so likewise was Moses. But he was not a Priest, though he was the greatest Prophet that ever lived before God brought his First-begotten into the world. Meantime, not many of the Levites were Prophets. And if any were, it was a mere accidental thing. They were not such as being of that tribe. Many, if not most of the Prophets (as we are informed by the ancient Jewish writers), were of the tribe of Simeon. And some were of the tribe of Benjamin or Judah, and probably of other tribes also.

6. But we have reason to believe there were, in every age, two sorts of Prophets. The extraordinary, such as Nathan, Isaiah, Jeremiah, and many others, on whom the Holy Ghost came in an extraordinary manner. Such was Amos in particular, who saith of himself: "I was no Prophet, neither a Prophet's son; but I was an herdman: And the Lord said unto me, Go, prophesy unto my people Israel." The ordinary were those who were educated in "the schools of the Prophets," one of which was at Ramah, over which Samuel presided. (1 Sam. 19:18.) These were trained up to instruct the people, and were the ordinary preachers in their synagogues. In the New Testament they are usually termed scribes, or *nomikoi*, "expounders of the law." But few, if any of them, were Priests. These were all along a different order.

7. Many learned men have shown at large that our Lord himself, and all his Apostles, built the Christian Church as nearly as possible on the plan of the Jewish. So, the great High-Priest of our profession sent apostles and evangelists to proclaim glad tidings to all the world; and then Pastors, Preachers, and Teachers, to build up in the faith the congregations that should be found. But I do not find that ever the office of an Evangelist was the same with that of a Pastor, frequently called a Bishop. He presided over the flock, and administered the sacraments: The former assisted him, and preached the Word, either in one or more congregations. I cannot prove from any part of the New Testament, or from any author of the three first centuries, that the office of an evangelist gave any man a right to act as a Pastor or Bishop. I believe these offices were considered as quite distinct from each other till the time of Constantine.

8. Indeed in that evil hour when Constantine the Great called himself a Christian, and poured in honour and wealth upon the Christians, the case was widely altered. It soon grew common for one man to take the whole charge of a congregation, in order to engross the whole pay. Hence the same person acted as Priest and Prophet, as Pastor and Evangelist. And this gradually spread more and more throughout the whole Christian Church. Yet even at this day, although the same person usually discharges both those offices, yet the office of an Evangelist or Teacher does not imply that of a Pastor, to whom peculiarly belongs the administration of the sacraments; neither among the Presbyterians, nor in the Church of England, nor even among the Roman Catholics. All Presbyterian Churches, it is well known, that of Scotland in particular, license men to preach before they are ordained, throughout that whole kingdom. And it is never understood that this appointment to preach gives them any right to administer the sacraments. Likewise in our own Church, persons may be authorized to preach, yea, may be Doctors of Divinity, (as was Dr. Alwood at Oxford, when I resided there,) who are not ordained at all, and consequently have no right to administer the Lord's Supper. Yea, even in the Church of Rome itself, if a lay-brother believes he is called to go a mission, as it is termed, he is sent out, though neither priest nor deacon, to execute that office, and not the other.

9. But may it not be thought that the case now before us is different from all these? Undoubtedly in many respects it is. Such a phenomenon has now appeared as has not appeared in the Christian world before, at least not for many ages. Two young men sowed the word of God, not only in the churches,

but likewise literally "by the high-way side;" and indeed in every place where they saw an open door, where sinners had ears to hear. They were members of the Church of England, and had no design of separating from it. And they advised all that were of it to continue therein, although they joined the Methodist society; for this did not imply leaving their former congregation, but only leaving their sins. The Churchmen might go to church still; the Presbyterian, Anabaptist, Quaker, might still retain their own opinions, and attend their own congregations. The having a real desire to flee from the wrath to come was the only condition required of them. Whosoever, therefore "feared God and worked righteousness" was qualified for this society.

10. Not long after, a young man, Thomas Maxfield, offered himself to serve them as a son in the gospel. And then another, Thomas Richards, and a little after a third, Thomas Westell. Let it be well observed on what terms we received these, viz., as Prophets, not as Priests. We received them wholly and solely to preach; not to administer sacraments. And those who imagine these offices to be inseparably joined are totally ignorant of the constitution of the whole Jewish as well as Christian Church. Neither the Romish, nor the English, nor the Presbyterian Churches, ever accounted them so. Otherwise we should never have accepted the service, either of Mr. Maxfield, Richards, or Westell.

11. In 1744, all the Methodist preachers had their first Conference. But none of them dreamed, that the being called to preach gave them any right to administer sacraments. And when that question was proposed, "In what light are we to consider ourselves?" it was answered, "As *extraordinary messengers*, raised up to provoke the *ordinary* ones to jealousy." In order hereto, one of our first rules was, given to each Preacher, you are to do *that part* of the work which we appoint." But *what work* was this? Did we ever appoint you to administer sacraments; to exercise the priestly office? Such a design never entered into our mind; it was the farthest from our thoughts: And if any Preacher had taken such a step, we should have looked upon it as a palpable breach of this rule, and consequently as a recantation of our connexion.

12. For, supposing (what I utterly deny) that the receiving you as a Preacher, at the same time gave an authority to administer the sacraments; yet it gave you no other authority than to do it, or anything else, *where I appoint.* But where did I appoint you to do this? Nowhere at all. Therefore, by this very rule you are excluded from doing it. And in doing it you renounce the first principle of Methodism, which was wholly and solely to preach the gospel.

13. It was several years after our society was formed, before any attempt of this kind was made. The first was, I apprehend, at Norwich. One of our Preachers there yielded to the importunity of a few of the people, and baptized their children. But as soon as it was known, he was informed it must not be, unless he designed to leave our Connexion. He promised to do it no more; and I suppose he kept his promise.

14. Now, as long as the Methodists keep to this plan, they cannot separate from the Church. And this is our peculiar glory. It is new upon the earth. Revolve all the histories of the Church, from the earliest ages, and you will find, whenever there was a great work of God in any particular city or nation, the subjects of that work soon said to their neighbours, "Stand by yourselves, for we are holier than you!" As soon as ever they separated themselves, either they retired into deserts, or they built religious houses; or at least formed parties, into which none was admitted but such as subscribed both to their judgment and practice. But with the Methodists it is quite otherwise: They are not a sect or party; they do not separate from the religious community to which they at first belonged. They are still members of the Church;—such they desire to live and to die. And I believe one reason why God is pleased to continue my life so long is, to confirm them in their present purpose, not to separate from the Church.

15. But, notwithstanding this, many warm men say, "Nay, but you *do* separate from the Church." Others are equally warm, because they say, I *do not*. I will nakedly declare the thing as it is.

I hold all the doctrines of the Church of England. I love her liturgy. I approve her plan of discipline, and only wish it could be put in execution. I do not knowingly vary from any rule of the Church, unless in those few instances, where I judge, and as far as I judge, there is an absolute necessity.

For instance: (1.) As few clergymen open their churches to me, I am under the necessity of *preaching abroad.*

(2.) As I know no forms that will suit all occasions, I am often under a necessity of *praying extempore.*

(3.) In order to build up the flock of Christ in faith and love, I am under a necessity of uniting them together, and of dividing them into little companies, that they may provoke one another to love and good works.

(4.) That my fellow-labourers and I may more effectually assist each other, to save our own souls and those that hear us, I judge it necessary to meet the Preachers, or at least the greater part of them, once a year.

(5.) In those Conferences we fix the stations of all the Preachers for the ensuing year.

But all this is not separating from the Church. So far from it that whenever I have opportunity I attend the Church service myself, and advise all our societies so to do.

16. Nevertheless as [to] the generality even of religious people, who do not understand my motives of acting, and who on the one hand hear me profess that I will not separate from the Church, and on the other that I do vary from it in these instances, they will naturally think I am inconsistent with myself. And they cannot but think so, unless they observe my two principles: The one, that I dare not separate from the Church, that I believe it would be a sin so to do; the other, that I believe it would be a sin not to vary from it in the points above mentioned. I say, put these two principles together, First, I will not separate from the Church; yet, Secondly, in cases of necessity I will vary from it (both of which I have constantly and openly avowed for upwards of fifty years,) and inconsistency vanishes away. I have been true to my profession from 1730 to this day.

17. "But is it not contrary to your profession to permit service in Dublin at Church hours? For what necessity is there for this? or what good end does it answer?" I believe it answers

several good ends, which could not so well be answered any other way. The First is, (strange as it may sound,) to *prevent a separation* from the Church. Many of our society were totally separated from the Church; they never attended it at all. But now they duly attend the Church every first Sunday in the month. "But had they not better attend it every week?" Yes; but who can persuade them to it? I cannot. I have strove to do it twenty or thirty years, but in vain. The Second is, the weaning them from attending Dissenting Meetings, which many of them attended constantly, but have now wholly left. The Third is, the constantly hearing that sound doctrine which is able to save their souls.

18. I wish all of you who are vulgarly termed Methodists would seriously consider what has been said. And particularly you whom God hath commissioned to call sinners to repentance. It does by no means follow from hence that ye are commissioned to baptize, or to administer the Lord's Supper. Ye never dreamed of this, for ten or twenty years after ye began to preach. Ye did not then, like Korah, Dathan, and Abiram, "seek the priesthood also." Ye knew, "no man taketh this honour unto himself, but he that is called of God, as was Aaron." O contain yourselves within your own bounds; be content with preaching the gospel; "do the work of Evangelists;" proclaim to all the world the lovingkindness of God our Saviour; declare to all, "The kingdom of heaven is at hand: Repent ye, and believe the gospel!" I earnestly advise you, abide in your place; keep your own station. Ye were, fifty years ago, those of you that were then Methodist Preachers, *extraordinary messengers* of God, not going in your own will, but *thrust out*, not to supersede, but to "provoke to jealousy" the ordinary messengers. In God's name, stop there! Both by your preaching and example provoke them to love and to good works. Ye are a new phenomenon in the earth,—a body of people who, being of no sect or party, are friends to all parties, and endeavour to forward all in heart religion, in the knowledge and love of God and man. Ye yourselves were at first called in the Church of England; and though ye have and will have a thousand temptations to leave it, and set up for yourselves, regard them not. Be Church-of-England men still; do not cast away the peculiar glory which God hath put upon you, and frustrate the design of Providence, the very end for which God raised you up.

19. I would add a few words to those serious people who are not connected with the Methodists; many of whom are of our own Church, the Church of England. And why should *ye* be displeased with us? We do you no harm; we do not design or desire to offend you in anything; we hold your doctrines; we observe your rules, more than do most of the people in the kingdom. Some of you are Clergymen. And why should *ye*, of all men, be displeased with us? We neither attack your character, nor your revenue; we honour you for "your work's sake!" If we see some things which we do not approve of, we do not publish them; we rather cast a mantle over them, and hide what we cannot commend. When ye treat us unkindly or unjustly, we suffer it. "Being reviled, we bless;" we do not return railing for railing. O let not *your* hand be upon us!

20. Ye that are rich in this world, count us not your enemies because we tell you the truth, and, it may be, in a fuller and stronger manner than any others will or dare do. Ye have therefore need of us, inexpressible need. Ye cannot buy such friends at any price. All your gold and silver cannot purchase such. Make use of us while ye may. If it be possible, never be without some of those who will speak the truth from their heart. Otherwise ye may grow grey in your sins; ye may say to your souls, "Peace, peace!" while there is no peace! Ye may sleep on, and dream ye are in the way to heaven, till ye awake in everlasting fire.

21. But whether ye will hear, or whether ye will forbear, we, by the grace of God, hold on our way; being ourselves still members of the Church of England, as we were from the beginning, but receiving all that love God in every Church as our brother, and sister, and mother. And in order to their union with us we require no unity in opinions, or in modes of worship, but barely that they "fear God and work righteousness," as was observed. Now this is utterly a new thing, unheard of in any other Christian community. In what Church or congregation beside, throughout the Christian world, can members be admitted upon these terms, without any other conditions? Point any such out, whoever can. I know none in Europe, Asia, Africa, or America! This is the glory of the Methodists, and of them alone! They are themselves no particular sect or party; but they receive those of all parties who "endeavour to do justly, and love mercy, and walk humbly with their God." Cork, May 4, 1789

116.* CAUSES OF THE INEFFICACY OF CHRISTIANITY

"Is there no balm in Gilead; is there no physician there? Why then is not the health of the daughter of my people recovered?"

Jer. 8:22

1. This question, as here proposed by the Prophet, relates only to a particular people,—the children of Israel. But I would here consider it in a general sense, with relation to all mankind. I would seriously inquire, Why has Christianity done so little good in the world? Is it not the balm, the outward means, which the great Physician has given to men, to restore their spiritual health? Why then is it not restored? You say, Because of the deep and universal corruption of human nature. Most true; but here is the very difficulty. Was it not intended, by our all-wise and almighty Creator, to be the remedy for that corruption? A universal remedy, for a universal evil? But it has not answered this intention it never did; it does not answer it at this day. The disease still remains in its full strength: Wickedness of every kind; vice, inward and outward, in all its forms, still overspreads the face of the earth.

2. O Lord God, "righteous art thou! Yet let us plead with thee." How is this? Hast thou forgotten the world thou hast

---

* [text from the 1872 edition]

made; which thou hast created for thy own glory? Canst thou despise the work of thy own hands, the purchase of thy Son's blood? Thou hast given medicine to heal our sickness; yet our sickness is not healed. Yet darkness covers the earth, and thick darkness the people; yea,

> Darkness such as devils feel,
> Issuing from the pit of hell.

3. What a mystery is this, that Christianity should have done so little good in the world! Can any account of this be given? Can any reasons be assigned for it? Does it not seem that one reason it has done so little good is this,—because it is so little known? Certainly it can do no good where it is not known. But it is not known at this day to the far greater part the inhabitants of the earth. In the last century, our ingenious and laborious countryman, Mr. Brerewood, travelled over great part of the known world on purpose to inquire, so far as was possible, what proportion the Christians bear to the Heathens and Mahometans. And, according to his computation, (probably the most accurate which has yet been made,) I suppose mankind to be divided into thirty parts, nineteen parts of these are still open Heathens, having no more knowledge of Christianity than the beasts that perish. And we may add to these the numerous nations which have been discovered in the present century. Add to these such as profess the Mahometan religion, and utterly scorn Christianity; and twenty-five parts out of thirty of mankind are not so much as nominally Christians. So then five parts of mankind out of six are totally ignorant of Christianity. It is, therefore, no wonder that five in six of mankind, perhaps nine in ten, have no advantage from it.

4. But why is it that so little advantage is derived from it to the Christian world? Are Christians any better than other men? Are they better than Mahometans or Heathens? To say the truth, it is well if they are not worse; worse than either Mahometans or Heathens. In many respects they are abundantly worse; but then they are not properly Christians. The generality of these, though they hear the Christian name, do not know what Christianity is. They no more understand it than they do Greek or Hebrew; therefore they can be no better for it. What do the Christians, so called, of the Eastern Church, dispersed throughout the Turkish dominions, know of genuine Christianity? those of the Morea, of Circassia, Mongrelia, Georgia? Are they not the very dregs of mankind? And have we reason to think that those of the Southern Church, those inhabiting Abyssinia, have any more conception than they, of "worshipping God in spirit and in truth?" Look we nearer home. See the Northern Churches; those that are under the Patriarch of Moscow. How exceedingly little do they know either of outward or inward Christianity! How many thousands, yea, myriads, of those poor savages know nothing of Christianity but the name! How little more do they know than the heathen Tartars on the one hand, or the heathen Chinese on the other!

5. But is not Christianity well known, at least, to all the inhabitants of the western world? a great part of which is eminently termed Christendom, or the land of Christians. Part of these are still members of the Church of Rome; part are termed Protestants. As to the former, Portuguese, Spaniards Italians, French, Germans, what do the hulk of them know of scriptural Christianity? Having had frequent opportunity of conversing with many of these, both at home and abroad, I am bold to affirm, that they are in general totally ignorant, both as to the theory and practice of Christianity; so that they are "perishing" by thousands "for lack of knowledge,"—for want of knowing the very first principles of Christianity.

6. "But surely this cannot be the case of the Protestants in France, Switzerland, Germany, and Holland; much less in Denmark and Sweden." Indeed I hope it is not altogether. I am persuaded, there are among them many knowing Christians; but I fear we must not think that one in ten, if one in fifty, is of this number; certainly not, if we may form a judgment of them by those we find in Great Britain and Ireland. Let us see how matters stand at our own door. Do the people of England, in general, (not the highest or the lowest; for these usually know nothing of the matter; but people of the middle rank,) understand Christianity? Do they conceive what it is? Can they give an intelligible account, either of the speculative or practical part of it? What know they of the very first principles of it?—of the natural and moral attributes of God; of his particular providence; of the redemption of man; of the offices of Christ; of the operations of the Holy Ghost; of justification; of the new birth; of inward and outward sanctification? speak of any of these things to the first ten persons you are in company with; and will you not find nine out of the ten ignorant of the whole affair? And are not most of the inhabitants of the Scotch Highlands full as ignorant as these; yea, and the common people in Ireland? (I mean the Protestants, of whom alone we are now speaking.) Make a fair inquiry, not only in the country cabins, but in the cities of Cork, Waterford, Limerick; yea, in Dublin itself. How few know what Christianity means! How small a number will you find that have any conception of the analogy of faith! of the connected chain of scripture truths, and their relation to each other,—namely, the natural corruption of man; justification by faith; the new birth; inward and outward holiness. It must be acknowledged by all competent judges, who converse freely with their neighbours in these kingdoms, that a vast majority of them know no more of these things than they do of Hebrew or Arabic. And what good can Christianity do to these, who are so totally ignorant of it?

7. However, in some parts, both of England and Ireland, scriptural Christianity is well known; especially in London, Bristol, Dublin, and almost all the large and populous cities and towns of both kingdoms. In these, every branch of Christianity is openly and largely declared; and thousands upon thousands continually hear and receive "the truth as it is in Jesus." Why is it then, that even in these parts Christianity has had so little effect? Why are the generality of the people, in all these places, Heathens still? no better than the Heathens of Africa or America, either in their tempers or in their lives? Now, how is this to be accounted for? I conceive, thus: It was a common saying among the Christians in the primitive Church, "The soul and the body make a man; the spirit and discipline make a Christian;" implying,

that none could be real Christians, without the help of Christian discipline. But if this be so, is it any wonder that we find so few Christians; for where is Christian discipline? In what part of England (to go no farther) is Christian discipline added to Christian doctrine? Now, whatever doctrine is preached, where there is not discipline, it cannot have its full effect upon the hearers.

8. To bring the matter closer still. Is not scriptural Christianity preached and generally known among the people commonly called Methodists? Impartial persons allow it is. And have they not Christian discipline too, in all the essential branches of it, regularly and constantly exercised? Let those who think any essential part of it is wanting, point it out, and it shall not be wanting long. Why then are not these altogether Christians, who have both Christian doctrine and Christian discipline? Why is not the spiritual health of the people called Methodists recovered? Why is not all that "mind in us which was also in Christ Jesus?" Why have we not learned of him our very first lesson, to be meek and lowly of heart? to say with him, in all circumstances of life, "Not as I will, but as thou wilt? I come not to do my own will, but the will of him that sent me." Why are not we "crucified to the world, and the world crucified to us;"—dead to the "desire of the flesh, the desire of the eye, and the pride of life?" Why do not all of us live "the life that is hid with Christ in God?" O why do not we, that have all possible helps, "walk as Christ also walked?" Hath he not left us an example that we might tread in his steps? But do we regard either his example or precept? To instance only in one point: Who regards those solemn words, "Lay not up for yourselves treasures upon earth?" Of the three rules which are laid down on this head, in the sermon on "The Mammon of Unrighteousness," you may find many that observe the First rule, namely, "Gain all you can." You may find a few that observe the Second, "Save all you can:" But how many have you found that observe the Third rule, "Give all you can?" Have you reason to believe, that five hundred of these are to be found among fifty thousand Methodists? And yet nothing can be more plain, than that all who observe the two first rules without the third, will be twofold more the children of hell than ever they were before.

9. O that God would enable me once more, before I go hence and am no more seen, to lift up my voice like a trumpet to those who *gain* and *save* all they can, but do not *give* all they can! Ye are the men, some of the chief men, who continually grieve the Holy Spirit of God, and in a great measure stop his gracious influence from descending on our assemblies. Many of your brethren, beloved of God, have not food to eat; they have not raiment to put on; they have not a place where to lay their head. And why are they thus distressed? Because *you* impiously, unjustly, and cruelly detain from them what your Master and theirs lodges in *your* hands on purpose to supply *their* wants! See that poor member of Christ, pinched with hunger, shivering with cold, half naked! Meantime you have plenty of this world's goods,—of meat, drink, and apparel. In the name of God, what are you doing? Do you neither fear God, nor regard man? Why do you not deal your bread to the hungry, and cover the naked with a garment? Have you

laid out in your own costly apparel what would have answered both these intentions? Did God command you so to do? Does he commend you for so doing. Did he entrust you with *his* (not *your*) goods for this end? And does he now say, "Servant of God, well done?" You well know he does not. This idle expense has no approbation, either from God, or your own conscience. But you say you can *afford* it! O be ashamed to take such miserable nonsense into your mouths! Never more litter such stupid cant; such palpable absurdity! Can any steward *afford* to be an arrant knave? to waste his Lord's goods? Can any servant *afford* to lay out his Master's money, any otherwise than his Master appoints him? So far from it, that whoever does this ought to be excluded from a Christian society.

10. "But is it possible to supply all the poor in our society with the necessaries of life?" It *was* possible once to do this, in a larger society than this. In the first Church at Jerusalem there was not any among them that lacked; but distribution was made to every one according as he had need." And we have full proof that it may be so still. It is so among the people called Quakers. Yea, and among the Moravians, so called. And why should it not be so with *us?* "Because they are ten times richer than we." Perhaps fifty times: And yet we are able enough, if we were equally willing, to do this.

A gentleman (a Methodist) told me some years since, "I shall leave forty thousand pounds among my children." Now, suppose he had left them but twenty thousand, and given the other twenty thousand to God and the poor, would God have said to him, "Thou fool?" And this would have set all the society far above want.

11. But I will not talk of giving to God, or leaving, half your fortune. You might think this to be too high a price for heaven. I will come to lower terms. Are there not a few among you that could give a hundred pounds, perhaps some that could give a thousand, and yet leave your children as much as would help them to work out their own salvation? With two thousand pounds, and not much less, we could supply the present wants of all our poor, and put them in a way of supplying their own wants for the time to come. Now, suppose this could be done, are we clear before God while it is not done? Is not the neglect of it one cause why so many are still sick and weak among you; and that both in soul and in body? that they still grieve the Holy Spirit, by preferring the fashions of the world to the commands of God? And I many times doubt whether we Preachers are not, in some measure, partakers of their sin. I am in doubt whether it is not a kind of partiality. I doubt whether it is not a great sin to keep them in our society. May it not hurt their souls, by encouraging them to persevere in walking contrary to the Bible? And may it not, in some measure, intercept the salutary influences of the blessed Spirit upon the whole community?

12. I am distressed. I know not what to do. I see what I might have done once. I might have said peremptorily and expressly, "Here I am: I and my Bible. I will not, I dare not, vary from this book, either in great things or small. I have no power to dispense with one jot or tittle what is contained therein. I am determined to be a Bible Christian, not almost,

but altogether. Who will meet me on this ground? Join me on this, or not at all." With regard to dress, in particular, I might have been as firm (and I now see it would have been far better) as either the people called Quakers, or the Moravian Brethren:—I might have said, "This is our manner of dress, which we know is both scriptural and rational. If you join with us, you are to dress as we do; but you need not join us, unless you please." But, alas! the time is now past; and what I can do now, I cannot tell.

13. But to return to the main question. Why has Christianity done so little good, even among us? among the Methodists,—among them that hear and receive the whole Christian doctrine, and that have Christian discipline added thereto, in the most essential parts of it? Plainly, because we have forgot, or at least not duly attended to, those solemn words of our Lord, "If any man will come after me, let him deny himself, and take up his cross daily, and follow me." It was the remark of a holy man, several years ago, "Never was there before a people in the Christian Church, who had so much of the power of God among them, with so little self-denial." Indeed the work of God does go on, and in a surprising manner, notwithstanding this capital defect; but it cannot go on in the same degree as it otherwise would; neither can the word of God have its full effect, unless the hearers of it "deny themselves, and take up their cross daily."

14. It would be easy to show, in how many respects the Methodists, in general, are deplorably wanting in the practice of Christian self-denial; from which, indeed, they have been continually frighted by the silly outcries of the Antinomians. To instance only in one: While we were at Oxford, the rule of every Methodist was, (unless in case of sickness,) to *fast* every Wednesday and Friday in the year, in imitation of the Primitive Church; for which they had the highest reverence. Now this practice of the Primitive Church is universally allowed. "Who does not know," says Epiphanius, an ancient writer, "that the fasts of the fourth and sixth days of the week" (Wednesday and Friday) "are observed by the Christians throughout the whole world." So they were by the Methodists for several years; by them all, without any exception; but afterwards, some in London carried this to excess, and fasted so as to impair their health. It was not long before others made this a pretence for not fasting at all. And I fear there are now thousand of Methodists, so called, both in England and Ireland, who, following the same bad example, have entirely left off fasting; who are so far from fasting twice in the week, (as all the stricter Pharisees did,) that they do not fast twice in the month. Yea, are there not some of you who do not fast one day from the beginning of the year to the end? But what excuse can there for this? I do not say for those that call themselves members of the Church of England; but for any who profess to believe the Scripture to be the word of God. Since, according to this, the man that never fasts is no more in the way to heaven, than the man that never prays.

15. But can any one deny that the members of the Church of Scotland fast constantly; particularly on their sacramental occasions? In some parishes they return only once a year; but in others, suppose in large cities, they occur twice, or even thrice, a year. Now, it is well known there is always a fast-day in the week preceding the administration of the Lord's Supper. But, occasionally looking into a book of accounts in one of their vestries, I observed so much set down *for the dinners* of the Ministers on the fast-day; and I am informed there is the same article in them all. And is there any doubt but the people fast just as their Ministers do? But what a farce is this! What a miserable burlesque upon a plain Christian duty! O that the General Assembly would have regard to the honour of their nation! Let them roll away from it this shameful reproach, by either enforcing the duty, or removing that article from their books. Let it never appear there any more! Let it vanish away for ever

16. But why is self-denial in general so little practised at present among the Methodists? Why is so exceedingly little of it to be found even in the oldest and largest societies? The more I observe and consider things, the more clearly it appears what is the cause of this in London, in Bristol, in Birmingham, in Manchester, in Leeds, in Dublin, in Cork. The Methodists grow more and more self-indulgent, because they *grow rich*. Although many of them are still deplorably poor; ("tell it not in Gath; publish it not in the streets of Askelon!") yet many others, in the space of twenty, thirty, or forty years, are twenty, thirty, yea, a hundred times richer than they were when they first entered the society. And it is an observation which admits of few exceptions, that nine in ten of these decreased in grace, in the same proportion as they increased in wealth. Indeed, according to the natural tendency of riches, we cannot expect it to be otherwise.

17. But how astonishing a thing is this! How can we understand it? Does it not seem (and yet this cannot be) that Christianity, true scriptural Christianity, has a tendency, in process of time, to undermine and destroy itself? For wherever true Christianity spreads, it must cause diligence and frugality, which), in the natural course of things, must beget riches! and riches naturally beget pride, love of the world, and every temper that is destructive of Christianity. Now, if there be no way to prevent this, Christianity is inconsistent with itself, and, of consequence, cannot stand, cannot continue long among any people; since, wherever it generally prevails, it saps its own foundation.

18. But is there no way to prevent this?—to continue Christianity among a people? Allowing that diligence and frugality must produce riches, is there no means to hinder riches from destroying the religion of those that possess them? I can see only one possible way; find out another who can. Do you gain all you can, and save all you can? Then you must, in the nature of things, grow rich. Then if you have any desire to escape the damnation of hell, *give* all you can; otherwise I can have no more hope of your salvation, than of that of Judas Iscariot.

19. I call God to record upon my soul, that I advise no more than I practise. I do, blessed be God, gain, and save, and give all I can. And so, I trust in God, I shall do, while the breath of God is in my nostrils. But what then? I count all things but loss for the excellency of the knowledge of Jesus my Lord! Still,

I give up every plea beside,—

Lord, I am damn'd! but thou hast died!
Dublin, July 2, 1789.

117.* ON KNOWING CHRIST SFTER THE FLESH

"Henceforth know we no man after the flesh; yea, though we did know Christ after the flesh, yet now henceforth know we him no more."

2 Cor. 5:16.

1. I have long desired to see something clearly and intelligibly wrote on these words. This is doubtless a point of no small importance: it enters deep into the nature of religion; and yet what treatise have we in the English language which is written upon it? Possibly there may be such; but none of them has come to my notice, no, not so much as a single sermon.'

2. This is here introduced by the Apostle in a very solemn manner. The words literally translated run thus: 'He died for all, that the who live', all who live upon the earth, 'might not henceforth from the moment they knew him, 'live unto themselves seek their own honour, or profit, or pleasure, "but unto him," in righteousness and true holiness. (2 Cor. 5:15) "So that we from this time," we that know him by faith, "know no one," either the rest of the Apostles, or you, or any other person, "after the flesh." This uncommon expression, on which the whole doctrine depends, seems to mean, we regard no man according to his former state,—his country, riches, power, or wisdom. We consider all men only in their spiritual state, and as they stand related to a better world. 'Yea, if we have known even Christ after the flesh, (which undoubtedly they had done, beholding and loving him as a man, with a natural affection,) yet now we know him so no more. We no more know him as a man, by his face, shape, voice, or manner of conversation. We no more think of him as a man, or love him under that character.

3. The meaning, then, of this strongly figurative expression appears to be no other than this. From the time that we are created anew in Christ Jesus we do not think, or speak, or act, with regard to our blessed Lord, as a mere man. We do not now use any expression with relation to Christ which may not be applied to him not only as he is man, but as he is "God over all, blessed for ever."

4. Perhaps in order to place this in a clearer light, and at the same time guard against dangerous errors, it may be well to instance in some of those that in the most plain and palpable manner "know Christ after the flesh." We may rank among the first of these the Socinians; those who flatly "deny the Lord that bought them;" who not only do not allow him to be the supreme God, but deny him to be any God at all. I believe the most eminent of these that has appeared in England, at least in the present century, was a man of great learning and uncommon abilities, Dr. John Taylor, for many years pastor at Norwich, afterwards President at the Academy at Warrington. Yet it cannot be denied that he treats our Lord with great civility; he gives him very good words; he terms him 'a very worthy personage;" yea, "a man of consummate virtue'

5. Next to these are the Arians. But I would not be thought to place these in the same rank with the Socinians. There is a considerable difference between them. For whereas the former deny Christ to be any God at all, the latter do not; they only deny him to be the great God. They willingly allow, nay, contend, that he is a little God. But this is attended with a peculiar inconvenience. It totally destroys the unity of the Godhead. For, if there be a great God and a little God, there must be two Gods. But waiving this and keeping to the point before us: all who speak of Christ as inferior to the Father, though it be ever so little, do undoubtedly "know him after the flesh;" not as "the brightness of the Father's glory, the express image of his person; as upholding," bearing up, "all things," both in heaven and earth, "by the word of his power,"—the same powerful word whereby of old time he called them all into being.

6. There are some of these who have been bold to claim that great and good man Dr. Watts, as one of their own opinion; and in order to prove him so they have quoted that fine soliloquy which is published in his posthumous works. Yet impartial men will not allow their claim without stronger proof than has yet appeared. But if he is clear of this charge, he is not equally clear of "knowing Christ after the flesh" in another sense. I was not aware of this, but read all his works with almost equal admiration, when a person of deep piety as well as judgment was occasionally remarking that some of the hymns printed in his *Horae Lyricae*, dedicated to Divine Love, were (as he phrased it) "too *amorous*, and fitter to be addressed by a lover to his fellow-mortal, than by a sinner to the most High God." I doubt whether there are not some other writers who, though they believe the Godhead of Christ, yet speak in the same unguarded manner.

7. Can we affirm that the hymns published by a late great man (whose memory I love and esteem) are free from this fault? Are they not full of expressions which strongly savour of "knowing Christ after the flesh?" Yea, and in a more gross manner than anything which was ever before published in the English tongue. What pity is it that those coarse expressions should appear in many truly spiritual hymns! How often, in the midst of excellent verses, are lines inserted which disgrace those that precede and follow! Why should not all the compositions in that book be not only as poetical, but likewise as rational and as scriptural, as many of them are acknowledged to be?

8. It was between fifty and sixty years ago that by the gracious providence of God my brother and I in our voyage to America became acquainted with the (so called) Moravian Brethren. We quickly took knowledge what spirit they were of, six-and-twenty of them being in the same ship with us. We not only contracted much esteem, but a strong affection for them. Every day we conversed with them, and consulted them on all occasions. I translated many of their hymns for the use of our own congregations. Indeed, as I durst not implicitly follow any men, I did not take all that lay before me, but selected those which I judged to be most scriptural, and most suitable to sound experience. Yet I am not sure that

---

* [text from the 1872 edition]

I have taken sufficient care to pare off every improper word or expression,—every one that may seem to border on a familiarity which does not so well suit the mouth of a worm of the earth when addressing himself to the God of heaven. I have indeed particularly endeavoured, in all the hymns which are addressed to our blessed Lord, to avoid every *fondling* expression, and to speak as to the most High God, to him that is "in glory equal with the Father, in majesty co-eternal."

9. Some will probably think that I have been over-scrupulous with regard to one particular word, which I never use myself either in verse or prose, in praying or preaching, though it is very frequently used by modern divines both of the Romish and Reformed Churches. It is the word *dear*. Many of these frequently say, both in preaching, in prayer, and in giving thanks, "Dear Lord," or "Dear Saviour;" and my brother used the same in many of his hymns, even as long as he lived. But may I not ask, Is not this using too much familiarity with the great Lord of heaven and earth? Is there any scripture, any passage either in the Old or New Testament, which justifies this manner of speaking? Does any of the inspired writers make use of it, even in the poetical Scriptures? Perhaps some would answer, "Yes, the Apostle Paul uses it. He says, "God's dear Son.'" I reply, First, This does not reach the case, for the word which we render *dear*, is not here addressed *to Christ* at all, but only spoken *of him*. Therefore it is no precedent of, or justification of, our addressing it to him. I reply, Secondly, it is not the same word. Translated literally the sentence runs, not his dear Son, but *the Son of his love*, or *his beloved Son*. Therefore I still doubt whether any of the inspired writers ever addresses the word either to the Father or the Son. Hence I cannot but advise all lovers of the Bible, if they use the expression at all, to use it very sparingly, seeing the Scripture affords neither command nor precedent for it. And surely, "if any man speak," either in preaching or prayer, he "should speak as the oracles of God."

10. Do we not frequently use this unscriptural expression, of our blessed Lord in private conversation also? And are we not then especially apt to speak of him as a mere man? Particularly when we are describing his sufferings, how easily do we slide into this! We do well to be cautious in this matter. Here is not room for indulging a warm imagination. I have sometimes almost scrupled singing (even in the midst of my brother's excellent hymn,) "That dear, disfigured face," or that glowing expression, "Drop thy warm blood upon my heart," lest it should seem to imply the forgetting I am speaking of "the Man that is my Fellow, saith the Lord of Hosts." Although he so "humbled himself as to take upon him the form of a servant, to be found in fashion as a man;" yea, though he was obedient unto death, even the death of the cross;" yet let it ever be remembered that he "thought it no robbery to be equal with God." And let our hearts still cry out, "Thou art exceeding glorious; thou art clothed with majesty and honour."

11. Perhaps some may be afraid lest the refraining from these warm expressions, or even gently checking them, should check the fervour of our devotion. It is very possible it may check, or even prevent, some kind of fervour which has passed for devotion. Possibly it may prevent loud shouting, horrid, unnatural screaming, repeating the same words twenty or thirty times, jumping two or three feet high, and throwing about the arms or legs, both of men and women, in a manner shocking not only to religion, but to common decency. But it never will check, much less prevent, true scriptural devotion. It will rather enliven the prayer that is properly addressed to him who, though he was very man, yet was very God; who, though he was born of a woman, to redeem man, yet was "God from everlasting and world without end."

12. And let it not be thought, that the knowing Christ after the flesh, the considering him as a mere man, and, in consequence using such language in public as well as private as is suitable to those conceptions of him, is a thing of a purely indifferent nature, or, however, of no great moment. On the contrary, the using this improper familiarity with God our Creator, our Redeemer, our Governor, is naturally productive of very evil fruits. And that not only in those that speak, but also to those that hear them. It has a direct tendency to abate that tender reverence due to the Lord their Governor. It insensibly damps

> That speechless awe which dares not move,
> And all the silent heaven of love

It is impossible we should accustom ourselves to this odious and indecent familiarity with our Maker, while we preserve in our minds a lively sense of what is painted so strongly in those solemn lines:—

> Dark with excessive bright his skirts appear,
> Yet dazzle heaven, that brightest seraphim
> Approach not, but with both wings veil their eyes.

13. Now, would not every sober Christian sincerely desire constantly to experience such a love to his Redeemer (seeing he is God as well as man) as is mixed with angelic fear? Is it not this very temper which good Dr. Watts so well expresses in those lines:

> Thy mercy never shall remove
> From men of heart sincere;
> Thou savest the souls whose humble love
> Is join'd with holy fear?

14. Not that I would recommend a cold, dead, formal prayer, out of which both love and desire, hope and fear, are excluded. Such seems to have been "the calm and undisturbed method of prayer," so strongly recommended by the late Bishop Hoadly, which occasioned for some years so violent a contest in the religious world. Is it not probable that the well-meaning bishop had met with some of the Mystics or Quietists (such as Madam Guion, or the Archbishop [Fenelon] of Cambray;) and that having no experience of these things he patched together a theory of his own as nearly resembling theirs as he could? But it is certain nothing is farther from apathy than real, scriptural devotion. It excites, exercises, and gives full scope to all our nobler passions; and excludes none but those that are wild, irrational, and beneath the dignity of man.

15. But how then can we account for this, that so many holy men, men of truly elevated affections, not excepting pious Kempis himself, have so frequently used this manner of speaking, these *fondling* kinds of expression; since we cannot

doubt but they were truly pious men? It is allowed they were; but we do not allow that their judgment was equal to their piety. And hence it was that their really good affections a little exceeded the bounds of reason, and led them into a manner of speaking, not authorized by the oracles of God. And surely these are the true standard, both of our affections and our language. But did ever any of the holy men of old speak thus, either in the Old or in the New Testament? Did Daniel, the "man greatly beloved," ever thus express himself to God? Or did "the disciple whom Jesus loved," and who doubtless loved his Master with the strongest affection, leave us an example of addressing him thus even when he was on the verge of glory? Even then his concluding words were not *fond*, but solemn, "Come, Lord Jesus!"

16. The sum of all is, we are to "honour the Son even as we honour the Father." We are to pay him the same worship as we pay to the Father. We are to love him with all our heart and soul; and to consecrate all we have and are, all we think, speak, and do, to the THREE-ONE GOD, Father, Son, and Spirit, world without end!

PLYMOUTH-DOCK, August 15, 1789.

118.* ON A SINGLE EYE

"If thine eye be single, thy whole body shall be full of light. But if thine eye be evil, thy whole body shall be full of darkness. Therefore, if the light that is in thee be darkness, how great is that darkness!"

Matt. 6:22, 23.

1. "Simplicity and purity," says a devout man, "are the two wings that lift the soul up to heaven: Simplicity, which is in the intention; and purity, which is in the affections." The former of these, that great and good man, Bishop Taylor, recommends with much earnestness, in the beginning of his excellent book, "Rules of Holy Living and Dying." He sets out with insisting upon this, as the very first point in true religion, and warns us, that, without this, all our endeavours after it will be vain and ineffectual. The same truth, that strong and elegant writer, Mr. Law, earnestly presses in his "Serious Call to a Devout Life"—a treatise which will hardly be excelled, if it be equalled, in the English tongue, either for beauty of expression, or for justness and depth of thought. And who can censure any follower of Christ, for laying ever so great stress on this point, that considers the manner wherein our Master recommends it, in the words above recited?

2. Let us attentively consider this whole passage, as it may be literally translated. "The eye is the lamp of the body:" And what the eye is to the body, the intention is to the soul. We may observe, with what exact propriety our Lord places simplicity of intention between worldly desires and worldly cares; either of which directly tend to destroy it. It follows, "If thine eye be single," singly fixed upon God, "thy whole body," that is, all thy soul, "shall be full of light,"—shall be filled with holiness and happiness. "But if thine eye be evil,"—not single, aiming at any other object, seeking anything beneath the sun,—"thy whole body shall be full of darkness. And if the light that is in thee be darkness, how great is that darkness!" how remote, not only from all real knowledge, but from all real holiness and happiness!

3. Considering these things, we may well cry out, "How great a thing it is to be a Christian; to be a real, inward, scriptural Christian, conformed in heart and life to the will of God! Who is sufficient for these things?" None, unless he be born of God. I do not wonder that one of the most sensible Deists should say, "I think the Bible is the finest book I ever read in my life; yet I have an insuperable objection to it: It is *too good*. It lays down such a plan of life, such a scheme of doctrine and practice, as is far too excellent for weak, silly men to aim at, or attempt to copy after." All this is most true, upon any other than the scriptural hypothesis. But this being allowed, all the difficulty vanishes into air. For if "all things are possible with God, then all things are possible to him that believeth."

4. But let us consider, First, the former part of our Lord's declaration,—"If thine eye be single, thy whole body shall be full of light;" Secondly, the latter part,—"If thine eye be evil, thy whole body shall be full of darkness;" and, Thirdly, the dreadful state of those whose eye is not single,—"If the light that is in thee be darkness, how great is that darkness!"

I. 1. And, First, "If thine eye be single, thy whole body shall be full of light." If thine eye be single; if God is in all thy thoughts; if thou art constantly aiming at Him that is invisible; if it be thy intention in all things, small and great, in all thy conversation, to please God, to do, not thy own will, but the will of Him that sent thee into the world; if thou canst say, not to any creature, but to Him that made thee for himself, "I view thee, Lord and end of my desires;"—then the promise will certainly take place: "Thy whole body shall be full of light;" thy whole soul shall be filled with the light of heaven,—with the glory of the Lord resting upon thee. In all thy actions and conversation, thou shalt have not only the testimony of a good conscience toward God, but likewise of his Spirit, bearing witness with thy spirit, that all thy ways are acceptable to him.

2. When thy whole soul is full of this light, thou wilt be able (according to St. Paul's direction to the Thessalonians) to "rejoice evermore, to pray without ceasing, and in everything to give thanks." [1 Thess. 5:16–18] For who can be constantly sensible of the loving presence of God without "rejoicing evermore?" Who can have the loving eye of his soul perpetually fixed upon God, but he will "pray without ceasing?" For his "heart is unto God without a voice, and his silence speaketh unto him." Who can be sensible that this loving Father is well-pleased with all he does and suffers, but he will be constrained "in everything to give thanks?" knowing that all things "work together for good."

3. Thus shall "his whole body be full of light." The light of knowledge is, doubtless, one thing here intended; arising from "the unction of the Holy One, which abideth with him, and teacheth him of all things,"—all the things which it is now necessary for him to know in order to please God.

---

* [text of the 1872 ed.]

Hereby he will have a clear knowledge of the divine will in every circumstance of life. Not without the means, but in the use of all those means which God has furnished him with. And, walking in this light, he cannot but "grow in grace, and in the knowledge of our Lord Jesus Christ." He will continually advance in all holiness, and in the whole image of God.

II. 1. Our Lord observes, Secondly, "If thine eye be evil, thy whole body shall be full of darkness." If it be evil, that is, not single, (for the eye which is not single is evil,) "thy whole body shall be full of darkness." It is certain there can be no medium between a single eye and an evil eye; for whenever we are not aiming at God, we are seeking happiness in some creature: And this, whatever that creature may be, is no less than idolatry. It is all one, whether we aim at the pleasures of sense, the pleasures of the imagination, the praise of men, or riches; all which St. John comprises under that general expression, "the love of the world." The eye is evil if we aim at any of these, or indeed at anything under the sun. So far as you aim at any of these, indeed, at anything beneath God, your whole soul, and the whole course of your life, will be full of darkness. Ignorance of yourselves, ignorance of your real interest, ignorance of your relation to God, will surround you with impenetrable clouds, with darkness that may be felt. And so long as the eye of your soul rests upon all or any of these, those will continue to surround your soul, and cover it with utter darkness.

2. With how many instances of this melancholy truth,—that those whose eye is not single are totally ignorant of the nature of true religion,—are we surrounded on every side! How many, even of good sort of people, of them whose lives are innocent, are as ignorant of themselves, of God, and of worshipping him in spirit and in truth, as either Mahometans or Heathens! And yet they are not any way defective in natural understanding: And some of them have improved their natural abilities by a liberal education, whereby they have laid in a considerable stock of deep and various learning. Yet how totally ignorant are they of God and of the things of God! How unacquainted both with the invisible and the eternal world! O why do they continue in this deplorable ignorance? It is the plain effect of this,—their eye is not single. They do not aim at God, he is not in all their thoughts. They do not desire or think of heaven; therefore, they sink deep as hell.

3. For this reason they are as far from real holiness as they are from valuable knowledge. It is because their eye is not single that, they are such strangers to vital religion. Let them be ever so accomplished in other respects; let them be ever so learned, ever so well versed in every branch of polite literature; yea, ever so courteous, so humane; yet if their eye is not singly fixed on God they can know nothing of scriptural religion. They do not even know what Christian holiness means; what is the entrance of it, *the new birth*, with all the circumstances attending it: They know no more of this, than do the beasts of the field. Do they repent and believe the Gospel? How much less are they "renewed in the spirit of their minds," in the image of him that created them? As they have not the least experience of this, so they have not the least conception of it. Were you to name such a thing, you might expect to hear, "Much religion hath made thee mad:" So destitute are they, whatever accomplishments they have beside, of the only religion which avails with God.

4. And till their eye is single they are as far remote from happiness as from holiness. They may now and then have agreeable dreams, from

> Wealth, honour, pleasure, or what else
> This short-enduring world can give:

But none of these can satisfy the appetite of an immortal soul. Nay, all of them together cannot give rest, which is the lowest ingredient of happiness, to a never-dying spirit, which God created for the enjoyment of himself. The hungry soul, like the busy bee, wanders from flower to flower; but it goes off from each, with an abortive hope, and a deluded expectation. Every creature cries, (some with a loud and others with a secret voice,) "Happiness is not in *me*." The height and the depth proclaim to an attentive ear, "The Creator hath not implanted in me a capacity of giving happiness: Therefore, with all thy skill and pains, thou canst not extract it from me." And indeed the more pains any of the children of men take to extract it from any earthly object, the greater will their chagrin be,—the more secure their disappointment.

5. "But although the vulgar herd of mankind can find no happiness; although it cannot be found in the empty pleasures of the world; may it not be found in learning, even by him that has not a single eye! Surely

> Content of spirit must from science flow;
> For 'tis a godlike attribute to know."

By no means. On the contrary, it has been the observation of all ages, that the men who possessed the greatest learning were the most dissatisfied of all men. This occasioned a person of eminent learning to declare, "A fool may find a kind of paradise upon earth," (although this is a grand mistake,) "but a wise man can find none." These are the most discontented, the most impatient, of men. Indeed, learning naturally effects this: "Knowledge," as the Apostle observes, "puffeth up.' But where pride is, happiness is not; they are utterly inconsistent with each other. So much ground there is for that melancholy reflection, wherever true religion is not,

> Avails it then, O Reason! to be wise?
> To see this mournful sight with quicker eyes?
> To know with more distinction to complain,
> And have superior sense in feeling pain?

III. 1. It remains to consider, in the Third place, our Lord's important question: "If the light that is in thee be darkness, how great is that darkness!" The plain meaning is, if that principle which ought to give light to thy whole soul, as the eye does to the body; to direct thy understanding, passions, affections, tempers,—all thy thoughts, words, and actions; if this principle itself be darkened,—be set wrong, and put darkness for light; how great must that darkness be! how terrible its effects!

2. In order to see this in a stronger point of view, let us consider it in a few particular instances. Begin with one of no small importance. Here is a father choosing an employment for his son. If his eye be not single; if he do not singly aim at

the glory of God in the salvation of his soul; if it be not his one consideration, what calling is likely to secure him the highest place in heaven; not the largest share of earthly treasure, or the highest preferment in the Church;—the light which is in him is manifestly darkness. And O how great is that darkness! The mistake which he is in, is not a little one, but inexpressibly great. What! do not you prefer his being a cobbler on earth, and a glorious saint in heaven, before his being a lord on earth, and a damned spirit in hell? If not, how great, unutterably great, is the darkness that covers your soul! What a fool, what a dolt, what a madman is he, how stupid beyond all expression, who judges a palace upon earth to be preferable to a throne in heaven! How unspeakably is his understanding darkened, who, to gain for his child the honour that cometh of men, will entail upon him everlasting shame in the company of the devil and his angels!

3. I cannot dismiss this subject yet, as it is of the utmost importance. How great is the darkness of that execrable wretch (I can give him no better title, be he rich or poor) who will sell his own child to the devil, who will barter her own eternal happiness for any quantity of gold or silver! What a monster would any man be accounted, who devoured the flesh of his own offspring! And is he not as great a monster who, by his own act and deed, gives her to be devoured by that roaring lion? as he certainly does (so far as is in his power) who marries her to an ungodly man. "But he is rich; but he has ten thousand pounds!" What, if it were a hundred thousand? The more the worse; the less probability will she have of escaping the damnation of hell. With what face wilt thou look upon her, when she tells thee in the realms below, "Thou hast plunged me into this place of torment. Hadst thou given me to a good man, however poor, I might have now been in Abraham's bosom. But, O! what have riches profited me? They have sunk both me and thee into hell!"

4. Are any of you that are called Methodists thus merciful to your children? Seeking to *marry them well* (as the *cant* phrase is;) that is, to sell them to some purchaser that has much money, but little or no religion? Is then the light that is in *you* also darkness? Are ye, too, regarding God less than mammon? Are ye also without understanding? Have ye profited no more by all ye have heard? Man, woman, think what you are about! Dare *you* also sell your child to the devil? You undoubtedly do this (as far as in you lies) when you marry a son or a daughter to a child of the devil; though it be one that wallows in gold and silver. O take warning in time! Beware of the gilded bait! Death and hell are hid beneath. Prefer grace before gold and precious stones; glory in heaven, to riches on earth! If you do not, you are worse than the very Canaanites. They only made their children pass "through the fire" to Moloch. You make yours *pass into the fire* that never shall be quenched, and to stay in it for ever! O how great is the darkness that causes you, after you have done this, to "wipe your mouth, and say you have done no evil!"

5. Let us consider another case, not far distant from this. Suppose a young man, having finished his studies at the University, is desirous to minister in holy things, and, accordingly, enters into orders. What is his intention in this? What is the end he proposes to himself? If his eye be single,

his one design is to save his own soul, and them that hear him; to bring as many sinners as he possibly can out of darkness into marvellous light. If, on the other hand, his eye be not single, if he aim at ease, honour, money, or preferment; the world may account him a wise man, but God says unto him, "Thou fool!" And while the light that is in him is thus darkness, "how great is that darkness!" What folly is comparable to his folly!—one peculiarly dedicated to the God of heaven, to "mind earthly things!" A worldly Clergyman is a fool above all fools, a madman above all madmen! Such vile, infamous wretches as these are the real "ground of the contempt of the Clergy." Indolent Clergymen, pleasure-taking Clergymen, money-loving Clergymen, praise-loving Clergymen, preferment-seeking Clergymen,—these are the wretches that cause the order in general to be contemned. These are the pests of the Christian world; the grand nuisance of mankind; a stink in the nostrils of God! Such as these were they who made St. Chrysostom to say, "Hell is paved with the souls of Christian Priests."

6. Take another case. Suppose a young woman, of an independent fortune, to be addressed at the same time by a man of wealth without religion, and a man of religion without wealth; in other words, by a rich child of the devil, and a poor child of God. What shall we say, if, other circumstances being equal, she prefer the rich man to the good man? It is plain, her eye is not single; therefore her foolish heart is darkened; and how great is that darkness which makes her judge gold and silver a greater recommendation than holiness! which makes a child of the devil, with money, appear more amiable to her than a child of God without it! What words can sufficiently express the inexcusable folly of such a choice? What a laughing-stock (unless she severely repent) will she be to all the devils in hell, when her wealthy companion has dragged her down to his own place of torment!

7. Are there any of you that are present before God who are concerned in any of these matters? Give me leave with "great plainness of speech," to apply to your consciences "in the sight of God." You, whom God hath entrusted with sons or daughters, is your eye single in choosing partners for them? What qualifications do you seek in your sons and daughters in law?—religion or riches? Which is your first consideration? Are you not of the old Heathen's mind,

Quaerenda pecunia primum,
Virtus post nummos?

Seek money first: Let virtue then be sought.

Bring the matter to a point. Which will you prefer? a rich Heathen, or a pious Christian?—a child of the devil, with an estate; or the child of God, without it?—a lord or gentleman, with the devil in his heart; (he does not hide it, his speech bewrayeth him;) or a tradesman, who, you have reason to believe, has Christ dwelling in his heart? O how great is that darkness which makes you prefer a child of the devil to a child of God! Which causes you to prefer the poor trash of worldly wealth, which flies as a shadow, to the riches of eternal glory!

8. I call upon you more especially who are called Methodists. In the sight of the great God, upwards of fifty years I have

ministered unto you, I have been your servant for Christ's sake. During this time I have given you many solemn warnings on this head. I now give you one more, perhaps the last. Dare any of you, in choosing your calling or situation, eye the things on earth, rather than the things above? In choosing a profession, or a companion for life, for your child, do you look at earth or heaven? And can you deliberately prefer, either for yourself or your offspring, a child of the devil with money, to a child of God without it? Why, the very Heathens cry out,

O cunae in terras animae, et caelestium inanes!

O souls, bow'd down to earth, strangers to heaven! Repent, repent of your vile earthly-mindedness! Renounce the title of Christians, or prefer, both in your own case and the case of your children, grace to money, and heaven to earth! For the time to come, at least, "let your eye be single," that your "whole body may be full of light!"

119.* ON WORLDLY FOLLY

"But God said unto him, Thou fool!"

Luke 12:20.

But one of these fools is commonly wiser in his own eyes "than seven men that can render a reason." If it were possible for a Christian, for one that has the mind which was in Christ, to despise any one, he would cordially despise those who suppose "they are the men, and wisdom shall die with them." You may see one of these, painted to the life, in the verses preceding the text. "The ground of a certain rich man," says our blessed Lord, "brought forth plenteously." (Luke 12:16.) "And he reasoned within himself, saying, What shall I do? for I have no room where to bestow my fruits. And he said, This will I do: I will pull down my barns, and build greater; and there will I bestow all my fruits and my goods. And I will say to my soul, Soul, thou hast much goods laid up for many years; take thy ease, eat, drink, and be merry. But God said unto him, Thou fool!" I propose, by the assistance of God,

I. To open and explain these few full words; and,
II. To apply them to your conscience.
I. 1. To open and explain them. A little before, our Lord had been giving a solemn caution to one who spoke to him about dividing his inheritance. "Beware of covetousness; for the life a man," that is, the happiness of it, "does not consist in the abundance of the things that he possesseth." To prove and illustrate this weighty truth, our Lord relates this remarkable story. It is not improbable, it was one that had lately occurred, and that was fresh in the memory of some that were present. "The ground of a certain rich man brought forth plenteously." The riches of the ancients consisted chiefly in the fruits of the earth. "And he said within himself, What shall I do?" The very language of want and distress! The voice of one that is afflicted, and groaning under his burden. What shalt thou do? Why, are not those at the door whom God hath appointed to receive what thou canst spare? What shalt thou do? Why, *disperse* abroad, and give to the poor. Feed the hungry. Clothe the naked. Be a father to the fatherless, and a husband to the widow. Freely thou hast received; freely give. O no! He is wiser than this comes to; he knows better than so.

2. "And he said, This will I do;"—without asking God's leave, or thinking about Him any more than if there were no God in heaven or on earth;—"I will pull down my barns, and build greater; and there will I bestow all my goods and all my fruits." *My* fruits! They are as much thine as the clouds that fly over thy head! As much as the winds that blow around thee; which, doubtless, thou canst hold in thy fists! "And I will say to my soul, Soul, thou hast much goods laid up for many years!" "Soul, thou hast much goods!" Are then corn, and wine, and oil, the goods of an immortal spirit? "Laid up for many years!" Who told thee so? Believe him not; he was a liar from the beginning. He could not prolong thy life, if he would. (God alone is the giver of life and death.) And he would not, if he could; but would immediately drag thee to his own sad abode. "Soul, take thy ease; eat, drink, and be merry!" How replete with folly and madness is every part of this wonderful soliloquy! "Eat and drink?" Will thy spirit then eat and drink? Yea, but not of earthly food. Thou wilt soon eat livid flame, and drink of the lake of fire burning with brimstone. But wilt thou then drink and be merry? "Nay, there will be no mirth in those horrid shades; those caverns will resound with no music, "but weeping, and wailing, and gnashing of teeth!"

3. But while he was applauding his own wisdom, "God said unto him, Thou fool! This night shall thy soul be required of thee. And then whose shall those things be which thou hast prepared?"

4. Let us consider his words a little more attentively. He said within himself, "What shall I do?" And is not the answer ready? Do good. Do all the good thou canst. Let thy plenty supply thy neighbour's wants; and thou wilt never want something to do. Canst thou find none that need the necessaries of life, that are pinched with cold or hunger; none that have not raiment to put on, or a place where to lay their head; none that are wasted with pining sickness; none that are languishing in prison? If you duly considered our Lord's words, "The poor have you always with you," you would no more ask, "What shall I do?"

5. How different was the purpose of this poor madman! "I will pull down my barns, and build greater; and there will I bestow all my goods." You may just as well bury them in the earth, or cast them into the sea. This will just as well answer the end for which God entrusted thee with them.

6. But let us examine a little farther the remaining part of his resolution. "I will say to my soul, Soul, thou hast much goods laid up for many years; take thy ease, eat, drink, and be merry." What, are these the goods of a never-dying spirit? As well may thy body feed on the fleeting breeze, as thy soul on earthly fruits. Excellent counsel then to such a spirit, to eat and drink! to a spirit made equal to angels, made an incorruptible picture of the God of glory, to feed not on

* [text from the 1872 edition]

corruptible things, but on the fruit of the tree of life, which grows in the midst of the paradise of God.

7. It is no marvel, then, that God should say unto him, "Thou fool!" For this terrible reason, were there no other: "This night shall thy soul be required of thee!"

> And art thou born to die,
> To lay this body down?
> And must thy trembling spirit fly
> Into a land unknown?
> —A land of deepest shade,
> Unpierced by human thought;
> The dreary regions of the dead,
> Where all things are forgot?

"And whose then shall all the things be which thou hast provided?"

II. 1. The Second thing which I proposed was, to apply these considerations; which, it is certain, are some of the most important that can enter into the heart of man. In one sense, indeed, they have been applied already; for what has been said has been all application. But I wish every one who reads or hears these words, directly to apply them to his own soul.

2. Does it not concern every one that hears,—"The ground of a certain rich man brought forth plentifully,"—to inquire, "Was this ever the case with *me*? Have I now, or have I ever heretofore had, more worldly goods given than I wanted? And what were my thoughts upon the occasion? Did I say in my heart, What shall I do? Was I distressed by my abundance? Did I think, 'I have much goods laid up for many years?' " Many years! Alas! What is thy life, if protracted to its utmost span? Is it not a vapour, that just appeareth, and vanisheth away? Say not, then, I will pull down my barns; but say to God, in the secret of thy heart, " 'Lord, save, or I perish!' See, my riches increase; let me not set my heart upon them! Thou seest I stand upon slippery ground; do thou undertake for me!

> Uphold me, Saviour, or I fall!
> O reach me forth thy gracious hand!
> Only for help on thee I call,
> Only by faith in thee I stand.

See, Lord, how greatly my substance increases! Nothing less than thy almighty power can prevent my setting my heart upon it, and being crushed lower than the grave!"

3. "I ask thee, O Lord, 'What shall I do?' " First of all, endeavour to be deeply sensible of thy danger; and make it matter of earnest and constant prayer, that thou mayest never lose that sense of it. Pray that thou mayest always feel thyself standing on the brink of a precipice. Meantime, let the language of thy heart be, "Having more means, I will do more good, by the grace of God, than ever I did before. All the additional goods which it hath pleased God to put into my hands, I am resolved to lay out, with all diligence, in additional works of mercy. And hereby I shall 'lay up for myself a sure foundation, that I may attain eternal life.' "

4. Thou no longer talkest of *thy* goods, or *thy* fruits, knowing they are not thine, but God's. The earth is the Lord's, and the fullness thereof: He is the Proprietor of heaven and earth. He cannot divest himself of his glory; he must be the Lord, the possessor, of all that is. Only he hath left a portion of his goods in thy hands, for such uses as he has specified. How long he will be pleased to lodge them with thee, thou dost not yet know; perhaps only till to-morrow, or to-night. Therefore talk not, think not, of many years. Knowest thou not, that thou art a creature of a day, that is crushed before the moth; that the breath which is in thy nostrils may be taken away at a moment's warning; that it may be resumed by him that gave it, at a time thou thinkest not of it? How knowest thou but, the next time thou liest down on thy bed, thou mayest hear, "This night shall thy soul be required of thee?"

5. Is not thy life as unstable as a cloud; fluctuating as a bubble on the water? It fleeth as it were a shadow, and never continueth in one stay. "Many years!" Who is sure of one day? And is it not an instance both of the wisdom and goodness of God, that he holds thy breath in his own hand, and deals it out from moment to moment; that thou mayest always remember, to "live each day as if it were the last?" And after the few days thou shalt have spent under the sun, how soon will it be said,

> A heap of dust is all remains of thee;
> 'Tis all thou art, and all the proud shall be!

6. Consider, again, the exquisite folly of that saying, "Soul, thou hast much goods." Are, then, the products of the earth food for a heaven-born spirit? Is there any composition of earth and water, yea, though air and fire be added thereto, which can feed those beings of a higher order? What similitude is there between those ethereal spirits, and these base-born clods of earth? Examine the rest of this wise soliloquy, and see how it will apply to yourself. "Soul, take thy ease!" O vain hope! Can ease to a spirit spring out of the ground? Suppose the soil were ever so improved, can it yield such a harvest? "Eat, drink, and be merry!" What! can thy soul eat and drink? Yea,

> Manna such as angels eat,
> Pure delights for spirits fit.

But these do not grow on earthly ground; they are only found in the Paradise of God.

7. But suppose the voice which commands life and death pronounce, "This night thy soul shall be required of thee; then whose are all those things thou hast provided?" Alas, they are not thine! Thou hast no longer any part or lot in any of the things that are under the sun. Thou hast then no more share in any of these things of earth, than if the earth and the works of it were burnt up. Naked thou camest out of thy mother's womb, and naked shalt thou return. Thou hast heaped up many things; but for what end? To leave them all behind thee! Poor shade! Thou art now stripped of all: Not even hope is left.

8. Observe the remark which our Lord has left upon the whole occurrence: "*So is* every one who layeth up treasure for himself, and is not rich toward God,"—such a fool, such an egregious madman, as it is beyond the power of language to express! However wise he may be in his own eyes, and perhaps in those of his neighbour, he is in reality the greatest fool under heaven, who heapeth up things from which he must soon be separated for ever: And whoever is seeking happiness in the things that perish is laying up treasure for

himself. This is absolutely inconsistent with *being* "rich" (or rather, *growing*) "toward God;" with obeying that scriptural command,—"My son, give me thy heart." He who is child of God can truly say.—

> All my riches are above;
> All my treasure is thy love:

He can testify, "All my desire is unto thee, and to the remembrance of thy name!"

9. Let every one who readeth these words, narrowly search his own heart. Where hast thou laid up thy treasure hitherto? Where art thou laying it up now? Art thou labouring to be rich toward God, or to lay up earthly goods? which takes up the greater part of thy thoughts? Thou that art careful for outward things, diligent in doing good, and exact in outward duties,—beware of covetousness; of decent, honourable love of money; and of a desire to lay up treasures on earth. Lay up treasure in heaven! A few days hence, thou wilt step into a land of darkness; where earthly fruits will be of no avail; where thou wilt not be capable of eating and drinking, or gratifying any of thy senses. What benefit wilt thou then receive from all thou hast laid up in this world? What satisfaction in all which thou hast treasured up,—all thou hast left behind thee? Left behind thee! What! couldest thou then take nothing with thee into the everlasting habitations? Nay then, lay up treasure, before thou go hence, which fadeth not away. Preached at Balham, February 19, 1790

120.* ON THE WEDDING GARMENT

"How camest thou in hither not having a wedding garment?

Matt. 22:12.

1. In the verses preceding the text we read, "After these things, Jesus spake to them again in parables, and said, A certain king made a supper for his son. And when the king came in to see the guests, he saw one who had not on a wedding garment. And he saith unto him, Friend, how camest thou in hither not having a wedding garment? And he was speechless. Then said the king to the servants, Bind him hand and foot, and cast him into outer darkness; there shall be weeping and gnashing of teeth."

2. Upon this parable one of our most celebrated expositors comments in the following manner:—"The design of this parable is to set forth that gracious supply made by God to men in and by the preaching of the gospel. To invite them to this, God sent forth his servants, the Prophets and Apostles."—And on these words,—"Why camest thou in hither not having a wedding garment?" he proceeds thus: "The punishment of whom ought not to discourage us, or make us turn our backs upon the holy ordinances." Certainly it ought not; but nothing of this kind can be inferred from this parable, which has no reference to the ordinances, any more than to baptism and marriage. And probably we should never have imagined it, but that the word *supper* occurred therein.

3. However, most of the English annotators have fallen into the same mistake with Mr. Burkitt. And so have thousands of their readers. Yet a mistake it certainly is; and such a mistake as has not any shadow of foundation in the text. It is true, indeed, that none ought to approach the Lord's table without habitual, at least, if not actual, preparation; that is, a firm purpose to keep all the commandments of God, and a sincere desire to receive all his promises. But that obligation cannot be inferred from this text, though it may from many other passages of Scripture. But there is no need of multiplying texts; one is as good as a thousand: There needs no more to induce any man of a tender conscience to communicate at all opportunities, than that single commandment of our Lord, "Do this in remembrance of me."

4. But whatever preparation is necessary in order to our being worthy partakers of the Lord's Supper, it has no relation at all to the "wedding garment" mentioned in this parable. It cannot: For that commemoration of his death was not then ordained. It relates wholly to the proceedings of our Lord, when he comes in the clouds of heaven to judge the quick and the dead; and to the qualifications which will then be necessary to their inheriting "the kingdom prepared for them from the foundation of the world."

5. Many excellent men, who are thoroughly apprized of this—who are convinced, the wedding garment here mentioned is not to be understood of any qualification for the Lord's Supper, but of the qualification for glory,—interpret it of the righteousness of Christ; "which," say they, "is the sole qualification for heaven; this being the only righteousness wherein any man can stand in the day of the Lord. For who," they ask, "will then dare to appear before the great God, save in the righteousness of his well-beloved Son? Shall we not then at least, if not before, find the need of having a better righteousness than our own? And what other can that be than the righteousness of God our Saviour?" The late pious and ingenious Mr. Hervey descants largely upon this; particularly in his elaborate "Dialogues between Theron and Aspasio."

6. Another elegant writer, now I trust with God, speaks strongly to the same effect in the preface to his comment on St. Paul's Epistle to the Romans: "We certainly," says he, "shall need a better righteousness than our own, wherein to stand at the bar of God in the day of judgment." I do not understand the expression. Is it scriptural? Do we read it in the Bible, either in the Old Testament or the New? I doubt it is an unscriptural, awkward phrase, Which has no determinate meaning. If you mean by that odd, uncouth question, 'In whose righteousness are you to stand at the last day?'—for *whose sake*, or *by whose merit*, do you expect to enter into the glory of God? I answer, without the least hesitation, For the sake of Jesus Christ the Righteous. It is through his merits alone that all believers are saved; that is, justified—saved from the guilt,—sanctified—saved from the nature, of sin; and glorified—taken into heaven.

---

* [text of the 1872 ed.]

7. It may be worth our while to spend a few more words on this important point. Is it possible to devise a more unintelligible expression than this,—"In what righteousness are we to stand before God at the last day?" Why do you not speak plainly, and say, *For whose sake* do you look to be saved?" Any plain peasant would then readily answer, "For the sake of Jesus Christ." But all those dark, ambiguous phrases tend only to puzzle the cause, and open a way for unwary hearers to slide into Antinomianism.

8. Is there any expression similar to this of the "wedding garment" to be found in Holy Scripture? In the Revelation we find mention made of "linen, white and clean, which is the righteousness of the saints." And this, too, many vehemently contend, means the righteousness of Christ. But how then are we to reconcile this with that passage in the seventh chapter, "They have washed their robes, and made them white in the blood of the Lamb?" Will they say, "The righteousness of Christ was washed and made white in the blood of Christ?" Away with such Antinomian jargon! Is not the plain meaning this:—It was from the atoning blood that the very righteousness of the saints derived its value and acceptableness with God?

9. In the nineteenth chapter of the Revelation, at the ninth verse, there is an expression which comes much nearer to this:—"The wedding supper of the Lamb." [Rev. 19] There is a near resemblance between this and the marriage supper mentioned in the parable. Yet they are not altogether the same: there is a clear difference between them. The supper mentioned in the parable belongs to the Church Militant; that mentioned in the Revelation, to the Church Triumphant: The one, to the kingdom of God on earth; the other, to the kingdom of God in heaven. Accordingly, in the former, there may be found those who have not a "wedding garment." But there will be none such to be found in the latter: No, not "in that great multitude which no man can number, out of every kindred, and tongue, and people, and nation." They will all be "kings and priests unto God, and shall reign with him for ever and ever."

10. Does not that expression, "the righteousness of the saints," point out what is the "wedding garment" in the parable? It is the "holiness without which no man shall see the Lord." The righteousness of Christ is doubtless necessary for any soul that enters into glory: But so is personal holiness too, for every child of man. But it is highly needful to be observed, that they are necessary in different respects. The former is necessary to *entitle* us to heaven; the latter to *qualify* us for it. Without the righteousness of Christ we could have no *claim* to glory; without holiness we could have no *fitness* for it. By the former we become members of Christ, children of God, and heirs of the kingdom of heaven. By the latter "we are made meet to be partakers of the inheritance of the saints in light."

11. From the very time that the Son of God delivered this weighty truth to the children of men,—that all who had not the "wedding garment" would be "cast into outward darkness, where are weeping and gnashing of teeth,"—the enemy of souls has been labouring to obscure it, that they might still seek death in the error of their life; and many ways has he tried to disguise the holiness without which we cannot be saved. How many things have been palmed, even upon the Christian world, in the place of this! Some of these are utterly contrary thereto, and subversive of it. Some were noways connected with or related to it; but useless and insignificant trifles. Others might be deemed to be some part of it, but by no means the whole. It may be of use to enumerate some of them, lest ye should be ignorant of Satan's devices.

12. Of the first sort, things prescribed as Christian holiness although flatly contrary thereto, is idolatry. How has this, in various shapes, been taught, and is to this day, as essential to holiness! How diligently is it now circulated in a great part of the Christian Church! Some of their idols are silver and gold, or wood and stone, "graven by art, and man's device;" some, men of like passions with themselves, particularly the Apostles of our Lord, and the Virgin Mary. To these they add numberless saints of their own creation, with no small company of angels.

13. Another thing as directly contrary to the whole tenor of true religion, is, what is diligently taught in many parts of the Christian Church; I mean the spirit of persecution; of persecuting their brethren even unto death; so that the earth has been often covered with blood by those who were called Christians, in order to "make their calling and election sure." It is true, many, even in the Church of Rome, who were taught this horrid doctrine, now seem to be ashamed of it. But have the heads of that community as openly and explicitly renounced that capital doctrine of devils, as they avowed it in the Council of Constance, and practised it for many ages? Till they have done this, they will be chargeable with the blood of Jerome of Prague, basely murdered, and of many thousands, both in the sight of God and man.

14. Let it not be said, "This does not concern us Protestants: We think and let think. We abhor the spirit of persecution; and maintain, as an indisputable truth, that every rational creature has a right to worship God as he is persuaded in his own mind." But are we true to our own principles? So far, that we do not use fire and faggot. We do not persecute unto blood those that do not subscribe to our opinions. Blessed be God, the laws of our country do not allow of this; but is there no such thing to be found in England as domestic persecution? The saying or doing anything unkind to another for following his own conscience is a species of persecution. Now, are we all clear of this? Is there no husband who, in this sense, persecutes his wife? Who uses her unkindly, in word or deed, for worshipping God after her own conscience? Do no parents thus persecute their children? no masters or mistresses, their servants? If they do this, and think they do God service therein, they must not cast the First stone at the Roman Catholics.

15. When things of an indifferent nature are represented as necessary to salvation, it is a folly of the same kind, though not of the same magnitude. Indeed, it is not a little sin to represent trifles as necessary to salvation; such as going of pilgrimages, or anything that is not expressly enjoined in the Holy Scripture. Among these we may undoubtedly rank orthodoxy, or right opinions. We know, indeed, that wrong

opinions in religion naturally lead to wrong tempers, or wrong practices; and that, consequently, it is our bounden duty to pray that we may have a right judgment in all things. But still a man may judge as accurately as the devil, and yet be as wicked as he.

16. Something more excusable are they who imagine holiness to consist in things that are only a part of it; (that is, when they are connected with the rest; otherwise they are no part of it at all;) suppose in doing no harm. And how exceeding common is this! How many take holiness and harmlessness to mean one and the same thing! whereas were a man as harmless as a post, he might be as far from holiness as heaven from earth. Suppose a man, therefore, to be exactly honest, to pay every one his own, to cheat no man, to wrong no man, to hurt no man, to be just in all his dealings; suppose a woman to be uniformly modest and virtuous in all her words and actions; suppose the one and the other to be steady practisers of morality, that is, of justice, mercy, and truth; yet all this, though it is good as far as it goes, is but a part of Christian holiness. Yea, suppose a person of this amiable character to do much good wherever he is; to feed the hungry, clothe the naked, relieve the stranger, the sick, the prisoner; yea, and to save many souls from death: it is possible he may still fall far short of that holiness without which he cannot see the Lord.

17. What, then, is that holiness which is the true "wedding garment," the only qualification for glory? "In Christ Jesus," (that is, according to the Christian institution, whatever be the case of the heathen world,) "neither circumcision availeth any thing, nor uncircumcision; but a new creation,—the renewal of the soul "in the image of God wherein it was created." In "Christ Jesus neither circumcision availeth anything, nor uncircumcision, but faith which worketh by love." [Gal. 5:6] It first, through the energy of God, worketh love to God and all mankind; and, by this love, every holy and heavenly temper,—in particular, lowliness, meekness, gentleness, temperance, and longsuffering. "It is neither circumcision,"—the attending on all the Christian ordinances,—"nor uncircumcision,"—the fulfilling of all heathen morality,—but "the keeping the commandments of God; particularly those,—"Thou shalt love the Lord thy God with all thy heart, and thy neighbour as thyself." In a word, holiness is the having "the mind that was in Christ," and the "walking as Christ walked."

18. Such has been my judgment for these threescore years, without any material alteration. Only, about fifty years ago I had a clearer view than before of justification by faith: and in this, from that very hour, I never varied, no, not an hair's breadth. Nevertheless, an ingenious man has publicly accused me of a thousand variations. I pray God, not to lay this to his charge! I am now on the borders of the grave; but, by the grace of God, I still witness the same confession. Indeed, some have supposed, that when I began to declare, "By grace ye are saved through faith," I retracted what I had before maintained: "Without holiness no man shall see the Lord." But it is an entire mistake: These scriptures well consist with each other; the meaning of the former being plainly this,— By faith we are saved from sin, and made holy. The imagination that faith *supersedes* holiness, is the marrow of Antinomianism.

19. The sum of all is this: The God of love is willing to save all the souls that he has made. This he has proclaimed to them in his word, together with the terms of salvation, revealed by the Son of his love, who gave his own life that they that believe in him might have everlasting life. And for these he has prepared a kingdom, from the foundation of the world. But he will not force them to accept of it; he leaves them in the hands of their own counsel; he saith, "Behold, I set before you life and death, blessing and cursing: Choose life, that ye may live." Choose holiness, by my grace; which is the way, the only way, to everlasting life. He cries aloud, "Be holy, and be happy; happy in this world, and happy in the world to come." "Holiness becometh his house for ever!" This is the wedding garment of all that are called to "the marriage of the Lamb." Clothed in this, they will not be found naked: "They have washed their robes and made them white in the blood of the Lamb." But as to all those who appear in the last day without the wedding garment, the Judge will say, "Cast them into outer darkness; there shall be weeping and gnashing of teeth." MADELEY, March 26, 1790

121. HUMAN LIFE A DREAM

"Even like as a dream when one awaketh; so shalt thou make their image to vanish out of the city."

Ps. 73:20.

1. Anyone that considers the foregoing verses will easily observe that the Psalmist is speaking directly of the wicked, that prosper in their wickedness. It is very common for these utterly to forget that they are creatures of a day; to live as if they were never to die; as if their present state was to endure for ever; or, at least as if they were indisputably sure that they "had much goods laid up for many years:" So that they might safely say, "Soul, take thine ease; eat, drink, and be merry." But how miserable a mistake is this! How often does God say to such a one, "Thou fool! this night shall thy soul be required of thee!" Well then may it be said of them, "O, how suddenly do they consume!"—perish, and come to a fearful end. Yea, "even like as a dream when one awaketh; so shalt thou make their image to vanish out of the city."

2. But I would at present carry this thought farther; I would consider it in a general sense, and show how near a resemblance there is between human life and a dream. An ancient poet carries the comparison farther still, when he styles life, "the dream of a shadow." And so does Cowley, when he cries out,

O life, thou nothing's younger brother!
So like, that we mistake the one for the' other!

But, setting these and all other flights of poetry aside, I would seriously inquire, wherein this resemblance lies; wherein the analogy between the one and the other does properly consist.

3. In order to this, I would inquire, First, What is a dream? You will say, "Who does not know this?" Might you not rather say, Who *does* know? Is there anything more mysterious in nature? Who is there that has not experienced

it, that has not dreamed a thousand times? Yet he is no more able to explain the nature of it, than he is to grasp the skies. Who can give any clear, satisfactory account of the parent of dreams, sleep? It is true, many physicians have attempted this, but they have attempted it in vain. They have talked learnedly about it, but have left the matter at last just as dark as it was before. They tell us some of its properties and effects; but none can tell what is the essence of it.

4. However, we know the origin of dreams, and that with some degree of certainty. There can be no doubt but some of them arise from the present constitution of the body; while others of them are probably occasioned by the passions of the mind. Again: We are clearly informed in Scripture, that some are caused by the operation of good angels; as others, undoubtedly, are owing to the power and malice of evil angels (if we may dare to suppose that there are any such now; or, at least, that they have anything to do in the world). From the same divine treasury of knowledge we learn that, on some extraordinary occasions, the great Father of spirits has manifested himself to human spirits, "in dreams and visions of the night." But which of all these arise from natural, which from supernatural, influence, we are many times not able to determine.

5. And how can we certainly distinguish between our dreams and our waking thoughts? What criterion is there by which we may surely know whether we are awake or asleep? It is true, as soon as we awake out of sleep, we know we have been in a dream, and are now awake. But how shall we know that a dream is such while we continue therein? What is a dream? To give a gross and superficial, not a philosophical, account of it: It is a series of persons and things presented to our mind in sleep, which have no being but in our own imagination. A dream, therefore, is a kind of digression from our real life. It seems to be a sort of echo of what was said or done a little when we were awake. Or, may we say, a dream is a fragment of life, broken off at both ends; not connected either with the part that goes before, or with that which follows after? And is there any better way of distinguishing our dreams from our waking thoughts, than by this very circumstance? It is a kind of parenthesis, inserted in life, as that is in a discourse, which goes on equally well either with it or without it. By this then we may infallibly know a dream,—by its being broken off at both ends; by its having no proper connection with the real things which either precede or follow it.

6. It is not needful to *prove* that there is a near resemblance between these transient dreams, and the dream of life. It may be of more use to *illustrate* this important truth; to place it in as striking a light as possible. Let us then seriously consider, in a few obvious particulars, the case of one that is just awaking out of life, and opening his eyes in eternity.

7. Let us then propose the case. Let us suppose we had now before us one that was just passed into the world of spirits. Might not you address such a new-born soul in some such manner as this? You have been an inhabitant of earth forty, perhaps fifty or sixty, years. But now God has altered his voice: "Awake, thou that sleepest!" You awake; you arise; you have no more to do with these poor transient shadows. Arise, and shake thyself from the dust! See, all is *real* here! all is permanent; all eternal! far more stable than the foundations of the earth; yea, than the pillars of that lower heaven. Now that your eyes are open, see how inexpressibly different are all the things that are now round about you! What a difference do you perceive in yourself! Where is your body,—your house of clay? Where are your limbs, your hands, your feet, your head? There they lie, cold, insensible!

> No anger, hereafter, or shame,
>   Shall redden the innocent clay;
> Extinct is the animal flame,
>   And passion is vanish'd away.

What a change is in the immortal spirit! You see everything around you; but how? Not with eyes of flesh and blood! You hear; but not by a stream of undulating air, striking on an extended membrane. You feel; but in how wonderful a manner! You have no nerves to convey the ethereal fire to the common sensory; rather, are you not now all eye, all ear, all feeling, all perception? How different, now you are throughly awake, are all the objects round about you! Where are the houses, and gardens, and fields, and cities, which you lately saw? Where are the rivers, and seas, and everlasting hills? Was it then only in a dream that our poet discovered,

> Earth hath this variety from heaven
>   Of pleasure situate in hill and dale?

Nay, I doubt all these vanished away like smoke, the moment you awoke out of the body.

8. How strange must not only the manner of existence appear, and the place wherein you are (if it may be called place; though who can define or describe the place of spirits?) but the inhabitants of that unknown region! whether they are of the number of those unhappy spirits that "kept not their first estate," or of those holy ones that still "minister to the heirs of salvation." How strange are the employments of those spirits with which you are now surrounded! How bitter are they to the taste of those that are still dreaming upon earth! "I have no relish," said one of these, (a much-applauded wit, who has lately left the body,) "for sitting upon a cloud all day long, and singing praise to God." We may easily believe him; and there is no danger of his being put to that trouble. Nevertheless, this is no trouble to them who cease not day and night, but continually sing, "Holy, holy, holy, Lord God of Sabaoth!"

9. Suppose this to be the case with any of you that are now present before God. It may be so to-morrow; perhaps to-night; perhaps this night your "soul may be required of you;" the dream of life may end, and *you* may wake into broad eternity! See, there lies the poor inanimate carcase, shortly to be sown in corruption and dishonour. But where is the immortal, incorruptible spirit? There it stands, naked before the eyes of God! Meantime, what is become of all the affairs which you have been eagerly engaged in under the sun? What profit have you reaped of all your labour and care? Does your money follow you? No; you have left it behind you;—the same thing to you as if it had vanished into air! Does your gay or rich apparel follow you? Your body is clothed with dust and rottenness. Your soul, indeed is clothed with immortality. But, O! what immortality? Is it an immortality of happiness and glory; or of shame and everlasting

contempt? Where is the honour, the pomp, of the rich and great; the applause that surrounded you? All gone; all are vanished away, "like as a shadow that departeth." "The play is over," said Monsieur Moultray, when he saw the ball pierce the temples of his dying master. [Charles XII, King of Sweden, at the siege of Frederickshall.] And what cared the courtier for this? No more than if it had been the conclusion of a farce or dance. But while the buffoon slept on and took his rest, it was not so with the monarch. Though he was not terrified with anything on earth, he would be at the very gates of hell. Vain valour! In the very article of death, he grasped the hilt of his sword! But where was he the next moment, when the sword dropped out of his hand, and the soul out of his body? Then ended the splendid dream of royalty,—of glory, of destroying cities, and of conquering kingdoms!

10. "How are the mighty fallen, and the weapons of war perished!" What are the weapons that are so terrible among *us*, to the inhabitants of eternity? How are the wise, the learned, the poet, the critic fallen, and their glory vanished away! How is the beauty fallen, the late idol of a gazing crowd! In how complete a sense are "the daughters of music brought low," and all the instruments thereof forgotten! Are you not now convinced, that (according to the Hebrew proverb) "a living dog is better than a dead lion?" For *the living know*, yea, *must* know, unless they obstinately refuse, "that they shall die; but the dead know not anything" that will avail for the ease of their pain, or to lessen their misery. Also "their hope and fear, and their desire," all are perished; all of them are fled; "they have not any portion in the things that are done under the sun!"

11. Where, indeed, is the *hope* of those who were lately laying deep schemes, and saying, "To-day, or to-morrow, we will go to such a city, and continue there a year, and traffic, and get gain?" How totally had they forgotten that wise admonition, "Ye know not what shall be on the morrow! For, what is your life? It is a vapour that appeareth awhile, and then vanisheth away!" Where is all your business? where your worldly cares, your troubles or engagements? All these things are fled away like smoke; and your soul is left. And how is it qualified for the enjoyment of this new world? Has it a relish for the objects and enjoyments of the invisible world? Are your affections loosened from things below, and fixed on things above,—fixed on that place where Jesus sitteth at the right hand of God? Then happy are ye; and when He whom ye love shall appear, "ye shall also appear with him in glory."

12. But how do you relish the company that surrounds you? Your old companions are gone; a great part of them probably separated from you never to return. Are your present companions angels of light?—ministering spirits, that but now whispered, "Sister spirit, come away! We are sent to conduct thee over that gulf into Abraham's bosom." And what are those? Some of the souls of the righteous, whom thou didst formerly relieve with "the mammon of unrighteousness;" and who are now commissioned by your common Lord to receive, to welcome you "into the everlasting habitations." Then the angels of darkness will quickly discern they have no part in you. So they must either hover at a distance, or flee away in despair. Are some of these happy spirits that take acquaintance with you, the same that travelled with you below, and bore a part in your temptations; that, together with you, fought the good fight of faith, and laid hold on eternal life? As you then wept together, you may rejoice together, you and your guardian angels perhaps, in order to increase your thankfulness for being "delivered from so great a death." They may give you a view of the realms below; those

> Regions of sorrow, doleful shades, where peace
> And rest can never dwell.

See, on the other hand, the mansions which were "prepared for you from the foundation of the world!" O what a difference between the dream that is past, and the real scene that is now present with thee! Look up! See!

> No need of the sun in that day,
> Which never is follow'd by night;
> Where Jesus's beauties display
> A pure and a permanent light!

Look down! What a prison is there! " 'Twixt upper, nether, and surrounding fire!" And what inhabitants! What horrid, fearful shapes, emblems of the rage against God and man, the envy, fury, despair, fixed within,—causing them to gnash their teeth at Him they so long despised! Meanwhile, does it comfort them to see, across the great gulf, the righteous in Abraham's bosom? What a place is that! What a "house of God, eternal in the heavens!" Earth is only His footstool; yea,

> The spacious firmament on high,
> And all the blue, ethereal sky.

Well then may we say to its inhabitants,

> Proclaim the glories of our Lord,
> Dispersed through all the heavenly street;
> Whose boundless treasures can afford
> So rich a pavement for his feet.

And yet how inconsiderable is the glory of that house, compared to that of its great Inhabitant! in view of whom all the first-born sons of light, angels, archangels, and all the company of heaven, full of light as they are full of love,

> Approach not, but with both wings veil their eyes.

13. How wonderful, then, now the dream of life is over, now you are quite awake, do all these scenes appear! Even such a sight as never entered, or could enter into your hearts to conceive! How are all those that "awake up after his likeness, now satisfied with it!" They have now a portion, real, solid, incorruptible, "that fadeth not away." Meantime, how exquisitely wretched are they who (to wave all other considerations) have chosen for their portion those transitory shadows which now are vanished, and have left them in an abyss of real misery, which must remain to all eternity!

14. Now, considering that every child of man who is yet upon earth must sooner or later wake out of this dream, and enter real life; how infinitely does it concern every one of us to attend to this before our great change comes! Of what importance is it to be continually sensible of the condition wherein we stand! How advisable, by every possible means, to connect the ideas of time and eternity! so to associate them together, that the thought of one may never recur to your mind, without the thought of the other! It is our highest wisdom to associate the ideas of the visible and invisible

world; to connect temporal and spiritual, mortal and immortal being. Indeed, in our common dreams we do not usually know we are asleep whilst we are in the midst of our dream. As neither do we know it while we are in the midst of the dream which we call life. But you may be conscious of it now! God grant you may, before you awake in a winding-sheet of fire!

15. What an admirable foundation for thus associating the ideas of time and eternity, of the visible and invisible world, is laid in the very nature of religion! For, what is religion,—I mean scriptural religion? for all other is the vainest of all dreams. What is the very root of this religion? It is Immanuel, God with us! God in man! Heaven connected with earth! The unspeakable union of mortal with immortal. For "truly our fellowship" (may all Christians say) "is with the Father and with his Son, Jesus Christ. God hath given unto us eternal life; and this life is in his Son." What follows? "He that hath the Son hath life: And he that hath not the Son of God hath not life."

16. But how shall we retain a constant sense of this? I have often thought, in my waking hours, "Now, when I fall asleep, and see such and such things, I will remember it was but a dream." Yet I could not, while the dream lasted; and probably none else can. But it is otherwise with the dream of life; which we do remember to be such, even while it lasts. And if we do forget it, (as we are indeed apt to do,) a friend may remind us of it. It is much to be wished that such a friend were always near; one that would frequently sound in our ear, "Awake, thou that sleepest, and arise from the dead!" Soon you will awake into real life. You will stand, a naked spirit, in the world of spirits, before the face of the great God! See that you now hold fast that "eternal life, which he hath given you in his Son!"

17. How admirably does this life of God branch out into the whole of religion,—I mean scriptural religion! As soon as God reveals his Son in the heart of a sinner, he is enabled to say, "The life that I now live, I live by faith in the Son of God, who loved me, and gave himself for me." He then "rejoices in hope of the glory of God," even with joy unspeakable. And in consequence both of this faith and hope, the love of God is shed abroad in his heart; which, filling the soul with love to all mankind, "is the fulfilling of the law."

18. And how wonderfully do both faith and hope and love connect God with man, and time with eternity! In consideration of this, we may boldly say,—

> Vanish then this world of shadows;
>   Pass the former things away!
> Lord, appear! appear to glad us,
>   With the dawn of endless day!
> O conclude this mortal story,
>   Throw this universe aside!
> Come, eternal King of glory,
>   Now descend, and take thy bride!

[August 1789]

122.* ON FAITH

---
* [text from the 1872 edition]

"Now faith is the evidence of things not seen."

Heb. 11:1.

1. Many times have I thought, many times have I spoke, many times have I wrote upon these words; and yet there appears to be a depth in them which I am in no wise able to fathom. Faith is, in one sense of the word, a divine conviction of God and of the things of God; in another, (nearly related to, yet not altogether the same,) it is a divine conviction of the invisible and eternal world. In this sense I would now consider,—

2. I am now an immortal spirit, strangely connected with a little portion of earth; but this is only for a while: In a short time I am to quit this tenement of clay, and to remove into another state,

> Which the living know not,
> And the dead cannot, or they may not tell!

What kind of existence shall I then enter upon, when my spirit has launched out of the body? How shall I feel myself,—perceive my own being? How shall I discern the things that are round about me, either material or spiritual objects? When my eyes no longer transmit the rays of light, how will the naked spirit *see*? When the organs of hearing are mouldered into dust, in what manner shall I hear? When the brain is of no farther use, what means of thinking shall I have? When my whole body is resolved into senseless earth, what means shall I have of gaining knowledge?

3. How strange, how incomprehensible, are the means whereby I shall then take knowledge even of the material world! Will things appear then as they do now,—of the same size, shape, and colour? Or will they be altered in any, or all these respects? How will the sun, moon, and stars appear? the sublunary heavens? the planetary heavens? the region of the fixed stars?—how the fields of ether, which we may conceive to be millions of miles beyond them? Of all this we know nothing yet. And, indeed, we need to know nothing.

4. What then can we know of those innumerable objects which properly belong to the invisible world; which mortal "eye hath not seen, nor ear heard, neither hath it entered into our heart to conceive?" What a scene will then be opened, when the regions of hades are displayed without a covering! Our English translators seem to have been much at a loss for a word to render this. Indeed, two hundred years ago, it was tolerably expressed by the word *hell*, which then signified much the same with the word *hades*, namely, the invisible world. Accordingly, by Christ descending into hell, they meant, his body remained in the grave, his soul remained in hades, (which is the receptacle of separate spirits,) from death to the resurrection. Here we cannot doubt but the spirits of the righteous are inexpressibly happy. They are, as St. Paul expresses it, "with the Lord," favoured with so intimate a communion with him as "is far better" than whatever the chief of the Apostles experienced while in this world. On the other hand, we learn from our Lord's own account of Dives and Lazarus, that the rich man, from the moment he left the world, entered into a state of torment. And "there is a great gulf fixed" in hades, between the place of the holy and that

of unholy spirits, which it is impossible for either the one or the other to pass over. Indeed, a gentleman of great learning, the Honourable Mr. [Alexander] Campbell, in his account of the Middle State, published not many years ago, seems to suppose that wicked souls may amend in hades, and then remove to a happier mansion. He has great hopes that "the rich man," mentioned by our Lord, in particular, might be purified by that penal fire, till, in process of time, he might be qualified for a better abode. But who can reconcile this with Abraham's assertion that none can pass over the "great gulf?"

5. I cannot therefore but think, that all those who are with the rich man in the unhappy division of hades, will remain there, howling and blaspheming, cursing God and looking upwards, till they are cast into "the everlasting fire, prepared for the devil and his angels." And, on the other hand, can we reasonably doubt but that those who are now in paradise, in Abraham's bosom,—all those holy souls who have been discharged from the body, from the beginning of the world, unto this day,—will be continually ripening for heaven; will be perpetually holier and happier, till they are received into "the kingdom prepared for them from the foundation of the world?"

6. But who can inform us in what part of the universe hades is situated,—this abode of both happy and unhappy spirits, till they are re-united to their bodies? It has not pleased God to reveal anything concerning it in the Holy Scripture; and, consequently, it is not possible for us to form any judgment, or even conjecture, about it. Neither are we informed, how either one or the other are employed, during the time of their abode there. Yet may we not probably suppose that the Governor of the world may sometimes permit wicked souls "to do his gloomy errands in the deep;" or, perhaps, in conjunction with evil angels, to inflict vengeance on wicked men? Or will many of them be shut up in the chains of darkness, unto the great judgment of the great day? In the mean time, may we not probably suppose, that the spirits of the just, though generally lodged in paradise, yet may sometimes, in conjunction with the holy angels, minister to the heirs of salvation? May they not

> Sometimes, on errands of love,
> Revisit their brethren below?

It is a pleasing thought, that some of these human spirits, attending us with, or in the room of, angels, are of the number of those that were dear to us while they were in the body. So that there is no absurdity in the question:

> Have ye your own flesh forgot,
> By a common ransom bought?
> Can death's interposing tide
> Spirits one in Christ divide?

But, be this as it may, it is certain human spirits swiftly increase in knowledge, in holiness, and in happiness; conversing with all the wise and holy souls that lived in all ages and nations from the beginning of the world; with angels and archangels, to whom the children of men are no more than infants; and above all, with the eternal Son of God, "in whom are hid all the treasures of wisdom and knowledge." And let it be especially considered, whatever they learn they will retain for ever. For they forget nothing. To forget is only incident to spirits that are clothed with flesh and blood.

7. But how will this material universe appear to a disembodied spirit? Who can tell whether any of these objects that surround us will appear the same as they do now? And if we know so little of these, what can we now know concerning objects of a quite different nature? concerning the spiritual world? It seems it will not be possible for us to discern them at all, till we are furnished with senses of a different nature, which are not yet opened in our souls. These may enable us both to penetrate the inmost substance of things, whereof we now discern only the surface; and to discern innumerable things, of the very existence whereof we have not now the least perception. What astonishing scenes will then discover themselves to our newly-opening senses! Probably fields of ether, not only ten fold, but ten thousand fold, "the length of this terrene." And with what variety of furniture, animate and inanimate! How many orders of beings, not discovered by organs of flesh and blood! perhaps thrones, dominions, princedoms, virtues, powers!—whether of those that retain their first habitations and primeval strength, or of those that, rebelling against their Creator, have been cast out of heaven! And shall we not then, as far as angel's ken, survey the bounds of creation, and see every place where the Almighty

> Stopp'd his rapid wheels, and said,—
> "This be thy just circumference, O world?"

Yea, shall we not be able to move, quick as thought, through the wide realms of uncreated night? Above all, the moment we step into eternity, shall we not feel ourselves swallowed up of Him who is in this and every place,—who filleth heaven and earth? It is only the veil of flesh and blood which now hinders us from perceiving, that the great Creator cannot but fill the whole immensity of space. He is every moment above us, beneath us, and on every side. Indeed, in this dark abode, this land of shadows, this region of sin and death, the thick cloud which is interposed between conceals him from our sight. But the veil will disappear; and he will appear in unclouded majesty, "God over all, blessed for ever!"

8. How variously are the children of men employed in this world! In treading over "the paths they trod six thousand years before!" But who knows how we shall be employed after we enter that visible world? A little of it we may conceive, and that without any doubt, provided we keep to what God himself has revealed in his word, and what he works in the hearts of his children. Let us consider, First, what may be the employment of unholy spirits from death to the resurrection. We cannot doubt but the moment they leave the body, they find themselves surrounded by spirits of their own kind, probably human as well as diabolical. What power God may permit these to exercise over them, we do not distinctly know. But it is not improbable, he may suffer Satan to employ them, as he does his own angels, in inflicting death, or evils of various kinds, on the men that know not God: For this end they may raise storms by sea or by land; they may shoot meteors through the air; they may occasion earthquakes; and, in numberless ways, afflict those whom they are not suffered to destroy. Where they are not permitted to take away life, they may inflict various diseases;

and many of these, which we judge to be natural, are undoubtedly diabolical. I believe this is frequently the case with lunatics. It is observable, that many of those mentioned in Scripture, who are called lunatics by one of the Evangelists, are termed demoniacs by another. One of the most eminent Physicians I ever knew, particularly in cases of insanity, the late Dr. [Thomas] Deacon, was clearly of opinion that this was the case with many, if not most, lunatics. And it is no valid objection to this, that these diseases are so often cured by natural means; for a wound inflicted by an evil spirit might be cured as any other, unless that spirit was permitted to repeat the blow.

9. May not some of these evil spirits be likewise employed, in conjunction with evil angels, in tempting wicked men to sin, and in procuring occasions for them? yea, and in tempting good men to sin, even after they have escaped the corruption that is in the world? Herein, doubtless, they put forth all their strength; and greatly glory if they conquer. A passage in an ancient author may greatly illustrate this: (Although I apprehend, he did not intend that we should take it literally:) "Satan summoned his powers, and examined what mischief each of them had done. One said, 'I have set a house on fire, and destroyed all its inhabitants.' Another said, 'I have raised a storm at sea, and sunk a ship; and all on board perished in the waters.' Satan answered, 'Perhaps those that were burnt or drowned were saved.' A third said, 'I have been forty years tempting a holy man to commit adultery; and I have left him asleep in his sin.' Hearing this, Satan rose to do him honour; and all hell resounded with his praise." Hear this, all ye that imagine you cannot fall from grace!

10. Ought not we then to be perpetually on our guard against those subtle enemies? Though we see them not,—

> A constant watch they keep;
> They eye us night and day;
> And never slumber, never sleep,
> Lest they should lose their prey.

Herein they join with "the rulers of the darkness," the intellectual darkness, "of this world,"—the ignorance, wickedness, and misery diffused through it,—to hinder all good, and promote all evil! To this end they are continually "working with energy in the children of disobedience." Yea, sometimes they work by them those *lying wonders* that might almost deceive even the children of God.

11. But meantime, how may we conceive the inhabitants of the other part of hades, the souls of the righteous, to be employed? It has been positively affirmed by some philosophical men, that spirits have no place. But they do not observe, that if it were so, they must be omnipresent,—an attribute which cannot be allowed to any but the Almighty Spirit. The abode of these blessed spirits the ancient Jews were used to term Paradise,—the same name which our Lord gave it, telling the penitent thief, "This day shalt thou be with me in paradise." Yet in what part of the universe this is situated who can tell, or even conjecture, since it has not pleased God to reveal anything concerning it? But we have no reason to think they are confined to this place; or, indeed, to any other. May we not rather say, that, "servants of his," as well as the holy angels, they "do his pleasure;" whether among the inhabitants of earth, or in any other part of his dominions? And as we easily believe that they are swifter than the light; even as swift as thought; they are well able to traverse the whole universe in the twinkling of an eye, either to execute the divine commands, or to contemplate the works of God. What a field is here opened before them! And how immensely may they increase in knowledge, while they survey his works of creation or providence, or his manifold wisdom in the Church! What depth of wisdom, of power, and of goodness do they discover in his methods of "bringing many sons to glory!" Especially while they converse on any of these subjects, with the illustrious dead of ancient days! with Adam, first of men; with Noah, who saw both the primeval and the ruined world; with Abraham, the friend of God; with Moses, who was favoured to speak with God, as it were, "face to face;" with Job, perfected by sufferings; with Samuel, David, Solomon, Isaiah, Daniel, and all the Prophets; with the Apostles, the noble army of Martyrs, and all the saints who have lived and died to the present day; with our elder brethren, the holy angels, cherubim, seraphim, and all the companies of heaven; above all the name of creature owns, with Jesus, the Mediator of the new covenant! Meantime, how will they advance in holiness; in the whole image of God, wherein they were created; in the love of God and man; gratitude to their Creator, and benevolence to all their fellow-creatures! Yet it does not follow, (what some earnestly maintain,) that this general benevolence will at all interfere with that peculiar affection which God himself implants for our relations, friends, and benefactors. O no! had you stood by his bed-side, when that dying saint was crying out, "I have a father and a mother gone to heaven;" (to paradise, the receptacle of happy spirits;) "I have ten brothers and sisters gone to heaven; and now I am going to them that am the eleventh! Blessed be God that I was born!" would you have replied, "What, if you are going to them? They will be no more to you than any other persons; for you will not know them." *Not know them!* Nay, does not all that is in you recoil at that thought? Indeed, sceptics may ask, "How do disembodied spirits know each other?" I answer plainly, I cannot tell: But I am certain that they do. This is as plainly proved from one passage of Scripture as it could be from a thousand. Did not Abraham and Lazarus know each other in hades, even afar off? even though they were fixed on different sides of the "great gulf?" Can we doubt, then, whether the souls that are together in paradise shall know one another? The Scripture, therefore, clearly decides this question. And so does the very reason of the thing; for we know, every holy temper which we carry with us into paradise will remain in us for ever. But such is gratitude to our benefactors. This, therefore, will remain for ever. And this implies, that the knowledge of our benefactors will remain, without which it cannot exist.

12. And how much will that add to the happiness of those spirits which are already discharged from the body, that they are permitted to minister to those whom they have left behind! An indisputable proof of this we have in the twenty-second chapter of the Revelation. When the Apostle fell down to worship the glorious spirit which he seems to have

mistaken for Christ, he told him plainly, "I am of thy fellow-servants, the Prophets;" [Rev. 22] not God, not an angel, not a human spirit. And in how many ways may they "minister to the heirs of salvation!" Sometimes by counteracting wicked spirits whom we cannot resist, because we cannot see them; sometimes by preventing our being hurt by men, or beasts, or inanimate creatures. How often may it please God to answer the prayer of good Bishop Ken!—

> O may thine angels, while I sleep,
> Around my bed their vigils keep;
> Their love angelical instil;
> Stop all the avenues [consequence] of ill!
> May they celestial joys rehearse,
> And thought to thought with me converse;
> Or, in my stead, the whole night long,
> Sing to my God a grateful song!

And may not the Father of spirits allot this office jointly to angels, and human spirits waiting to be made perfect?

13. It may indeed be objected that God has no need of any subordinate agents, of either angelical or human spirits, to guard his children in their waking or sleeping hours; seeing "He that keepeth Israel doth neither slumber nor sleep." And certainly, he is able to preserve them by his own immediate power; yea, and he is able, by his own immediate power, without any instruments at all, to supply the wants of all his creatures both in heaven and earth. But it is, and ever was, his pleasure, not to work by his own immediate power only, but chiefly by subordinate means, from the beginning of the world. And how wonderfully is his wisdom displayed in adjusting all these to each other! So that we may well cry out, "O Lord, how manifold are thy works! In wisdom hast thou made them all."

14. This we know, concerning the whole frame and arrangement of the visible world. But how exceeding little do we now know concerning the invisible! And we should have known still less of it, had it not pleased the Author of both worlds to give us more than natural light, to give us "his word to be a lantern to our feet, and a light in all our paths." And holy men of old, being assisted by his Spirit, have discovered many particulars of which otherwise we should have had no conception.

15. And without revelation, how little certainty of invisible things did the wisest of men obtain! The small glimmerings of light which they had were merely conjectural. At best they were only a faint, dim twilight, delivered from uncertain tradition; and so obscured by heathen fables, that it was but one degree better than utter darkness.

16. How uncertain the best of these conjectures was, may easily be gathered from their own accounts. The most finished of all these accounts, is that of the great Roman poet. Where observe how warily he begins, with that apologetic preface,—*Sit mihi fas audita loqui?*—"May I be allowed to tell what I have heard?" And, in the conclusion, lest anyone should imagine he believed any of these accounts, he sends the relater of them out of hades by the *ivory gate*, through which, he had just informed us, that only dreams and shadows pass,—a very plain intimation, that all which has gone before, is to be looked upon as a dream!

17. How little regard they had for all these conjectures, with regard to the invisible world, clearly appears from the words of his brother poet; who affirms, without any scruple,—

> Esse aliquos manes, et subterranea regna
> Nec pueri credunt.

"That there are ghosts, or realms below, not even a man [boy] of them now believes."

So little could even the most improved reason discover concerning the invisible and eternal world! The greater cause have we to praise the Father of Lights, who hath opened the eyes of our understanding, to discern those things which could not be seen by eyes of flesh and blood; that He who of old time shined out of darkness, hath shined in our hearts, and enlightened us with the light of the glory of God, in the face of Jesus Christ, "the author and finisher of our faith;" "by whom he made the worlds;" by whom he now sustains whatever he hath made; for,

> Till nature shall her Judge survey,
> The King Messiah reigns.

These things we have believed upon the testimony of God, the Creator of all things, visible and invisible; by this testimony we already know the things that now exist, though not yet seen, as well as those that will exist in their season, until this visible world will pass away, and the Son of Man shall come in his glory.

18. Upon the whole, what thanks ought we to render to God, who has vouchsafed this "evidence of things unseen" to the poor inhabitants of earth, who otherwise must have remained in utter darkness concerning them! How invaluable a gift is even this imperfect light, to the benighted sons of men! What a relief is it to the defects of our senses, and consequently, of our understanding; which can give us no information of anything, but what is first presented by the senses! But hereby a new set of senses (so to speak) is opened in our souls; and, by this means,

> The things unknown to feeble sense,
>   Unseen by reason's glimmering ray,
> With strong, commanding evidence,
>   Their heavenly origin display.
> Faith lends its realizing light:
>   The clouds disperse, the shadows fly;
> The' Invisible appears in sight,
>   And GOD is seen by mortal eye!

London, Jan. 17, 1791 [probably Wesley's last sermon]

123.* THE DECEITFULNESS OF THE HUMAN HEART

"The heart of man is deceitful above all things, and desperately wicked: Who can know it?"

Jer. 17:9.

1. The most eminent of the ancient Heathens have left us many testimonies of this. It was indeed their common opinion that there was a time when men in general were

---

* [text from the 1872 edition]

virtuous and happy; this they termed the "golden age." And the account of this was spread through almost all nations. But it was likewise generally believed that this happy age had expired long ago; and that men are now in the midst of the "iron age." At the commencement of this, says the poet,—

> Irrumpit venae pejoris in aeuum
> Omne nefas: fugere pudor, verumque, fidesque
> In quorum subiere locum, fraudesque, dolique
> Insidiaeque, et vis, et amor sceleratus habendi.
> Immediately broke in,
> With a full tide, all wickedness and sin:
> Shame, truth, fidelity, swift fled away;
> And cursed thirst of gold bore unresisted sway.

2. But how much more knowing than these old Pagans are the present generation of Christians! How many laboured panegyrics do we now read and hear on the Dignity of Human Nature. One eminent preacher, in one of his sermons, preached and printed a few years ago, does not scruple to affirm, First, that men in general (if not every individual) are very wise; Secondly, that men in general are very virtuous; and Thirdly, that they are very happy: And I do not know that anyone yet has been so hardy as to controvert the assertion.

3. Nearly related to them were the sentiments of an ingenious gentleman who, being asked, "My Lord, what do you think of the Bible?" answered, "I think it is the finest book I ever read in my life. Only that part of it which indicates the mediatorial scheme, I do not understand; for I do not conceive there is any need of a Mediator between God and man. If indeed," continued he, "I was a sinner, then I should need a Mediator; but I do not conceive I am. It is true, I often act wrong, for want of more understanding: And I frequently *feel* wrong tempers, particularly proneness to anger; but I cannot allow this to be a sin; for it depends on the motion of my blood and spirits, which I cannot help. Therefore it cannot be a sin; or, if it be, the blame must fall, not on *me*, but on him that made me." The very sentiments of pious Lord Kames, and modest Mr. Hume!

4. Some years ago, a charitable woman discovered that there was no sinner in the world but the devil. "For," said she, "he *forces* men to act as they do; therefore they are unaccountable: The blame lights on Satan." But these more enlightened gentlemen have discovered that "there is no sinner in the world but God! For he *forces* men to think, speak, and act as they do; therefore the blame lights on God alone. Satan, avaunt! It may be doubted whether he himself ever uttered so fond a blasphemy as this!

5. But, whatever unbaptized or baptized infidels may say concerning the innocence of mankind, He that made man, and that best knows what he has made, gives a very different account of him. He informs us that "the heart of man," of all mankind, of every man born into the world, "is desperately wicked;" and that it is "deceitful above all things:" So that we may well ask, "Who can know it?"

I. 1. To begin with this: "The heart of man is desperately wicked." In considering this, we have no need to refer to any particular sins; these are no more than the leaves, or, at most, the fruits, which spring from that evil tree;) but rather to the general root of all. See how this was first planted in heaven itself, by "Lucifer, son of the morning;"—till then undoubtedly "one of the first, if not the first archangel:" "Thou saidst, I will sit upon the side of the north." See self-will, the first-born of Satan! "I will be like the Most High." See pride, the twin sister of self-will. Here was the true origin of evil. Hence came the inexhaustible flood of evils upon the lower world. When Satan had once transfused his own self-will and pride into the parents of mankind, together with a new species of sin,—love of the world, the loving the creature above the Creator,—all manner of wickedness soon rushed in; all ungodliness and unrighteousness; shooting out into crimes of every kind; soon covering the whole face of the earth with all manner of abominations. It would be an endless task to enumerate all the enormities that broke out. Now the fountains of the great deep were broken up. The earth soon became a field of blood: Revenge, cruelty, ambition, with all sorts of injustice, every species of public and private wrongs, were diffused through every part of the earth. Injustice, in ten thousand forms, hatred, envy, malice, blood-thirstiness, with every species of falsehood, rode triumphant; till the Creator, looking down from heaven, would be no more entreated for an incorrigible race, but swept them off from the face of the earth. But how little were the following generations improved by the severe judgment! They that lived after the flood do not appear to have been a whit better than those that lived before it. In a short time, probably before Noah was removed from the earth, all unrighteousness prevailed as before.

2. But is there not a God in the world? Doubtless there is: And it is "He that hath made us, not we ourselves." He made us gratuitously, of his own mere mercy; for we could merit nothing of him before we had a being. It is of his mercy that he made us at all; that he made us sensible, rational creatures, and above all, creatures capable of God. It is this, and this alone, which puts the essential difference between men and brutes. But if he has made us, and given us all we have, if we owe all we are and have to him; then surely he has a right to all we are and have,—to all our love and obedience. This has been acknowledged by almost all who believed themselves to be his creatures, in all ages and nations. But a few years ago a learned man frankly confessed: "I could never apprehend that God's having created us, gave him any title to the government of us; or, that his having created us, laid us under any obligation to yield him our obedience." I believe that Dr. Hutcheson was the first man that ever made any doubt of this; or that ever doubted, much less denied, that a creature was obliged to obey his Creator. If Satan ever entertained this thought, (but it is not probable he ever did,) it would be no wonder he should rebel against God, and raise war in heaven. And hence would enmity against God arise in the hearts of men also; together with all the branches of ungodliness which abound therein at this day. Hence would naturally arise the neglect of every duty which we owe to him as our Creator, and all the passions and hopes which are directly opposite to every such duty.

3. From the devil the spirit of independence, self-will, and pride, productive of all ungodliness and unrighteousness,

quickly infused themselves into the hearts of our first parents in paradise. After they had eaten of the tree of knowledge, wickedness and misery of every kind rushed in with a full tide upon the earth, alienated us from God, and made way for all the rest. Atheism, (now fashionably termed dissipation,) and idolatry, love of the world, seeking happiness in this or that creature, covered the whole earth.

> Upright both in heart and will,
> We by our God were made;
> But we turn'd from good to ill,
> And o'er the creatures stray'd;
> Multiplied our wandering thought,
> Which first was fix'd on God alone;
> In ten thousand objects sought
> The bliss we lost in one.

4. It would be endless to enumerate all the species of wickedness, whether in thought, word, or action, that now overspread the earth, in every nation, and city, and family. They all centre in this,—Atheism, or idolatry; pride, either thinking of themselves more highly than they ought to think, or glorying in something which they have received, as though they had not received it; independence and self-will,—doing their own will, not the will of Him that made them. Add to this, seeking happiness out of God, in gratifying the desire of the flesh, the desire of the eye, and the pride of life. Hence it is a melancholy truth that (unless when the Spirit of God has made the difference) all mankind now, as well as four thousand years ago, "have corrupted their ways before the Lord; and every imagination of the thought of man's heart is evil, only evil, and that continually." However therefore men may differ in their outward ways, (in which, undoubtedly, there are a thousand differences,) yet in the inward root, the enmity against God, Atheism, pride, self-will, and idolatry, it is true of all, that "the heart of man," of every natural man, "is desperately wicked."

5. But if this be the case, how is it that everyone is not conscious of it? For who should "know the things of a man, like the spirit of a man that is in him?" Why is it that so few know themselves? For this plain reason: Because the heart is not only "desperately wicked," but "deceitful above all things." So deceitful, that we may well ask, "Who can know it?" Who, indeed, save God that made it? By his assistance we may, in the Second place, consider this,—the deceitfulness of man's heart.

II. 1. It is deceitful above all things;" that is, in the highest degree, above all that we can conceive. So deceitful, that the generality of men are continually deceiving both themselves and others. How strangely do they deceive themselves, not knowing either their own tempers or characters, imagining themselves to be abundantly better and wiser than they are! The ancient poet supposes there is no exception to this rule,—"that no man is willing to know his own heart." *Ut nemo in sese tentat descendere, nemo*! None but those who are taught of God!

2. And if men thus deceive themselves, is it any wonder that they deceive others also, and that we so seldom find "an Israelite indeed, in whom there is no guile?" In looking over my books, some years ago, I found the following memorandum: "I am this day thirty years old; and till this day I know not that I have met with one person of that age, except in my father's house, who did not use guile, more or less."

3. This is one of the sorts of desperate wickedness which cleaves to the nature of every man, proceeding from those fruitful roots,—self-will, pride, and independence on God. Hence springs every species of vice and wickedness; hence every sin against God, our neighbour, and ourselves. Against God,—forgetfulness and contempt of God, of his name, his day, his word, his ordinances; Atheism on the one hand, and idolatry on the other; in particular, love of the world, the desire of the flesh, the desire of the eyes, and the pride of life; the love of money, the love of power, the love of ease, the love of the "honour that cometh of men," the love of the creature more than the Creator, the being lovers of pleasure more than lovers of God:—Against our neighbour, ingratitude, revenge, hatred, envy, malice, uncharitableness.

4. Hence there is in the heart of every child of man, an inexhaustible fund of ungodliness and unrighteousness, so deeply and strongly rooted in the soul, that nothing less than almighty grace can cure it. From hence naturally arises a plentiful harvest of all evil words and works; and to complete the whole, that complex of all evils,—

> —That foul monster, War, that we meet,
> Lays deep the noblest work of the creation;
> Which wears in vain its Maker's glorious image,
> Unprivileged from thee!

In the train of this fell monster are murder, adultery, rape, violence, and cruelty of every kind. And all these abominations are not only found in Mahometan or Pagan countries, where their horrid practice may seem to be the natural result of equally horrid principles; but in those that are called Christian countries, yea, in the most knowing and civilized states and kingdoms. And let it not be said, "This is only the case in Roman Catholic countries." Nay, we that are called Reformed are not one whit behind them in all manner of wickedness. Indeed, no crime ever prevailed among the Turks or Tartars, which we here cannot parallel in every part of Christendom. Nay, no sin ever appeared in heathen or papal Rome, which is not found at this day in Germany, France, Holland, England, and every other Protestant as well as popish country. So that it might now be said, with as much truth and as few exceptions, of every court in Europe, as it was formerly in the court of Saul: "There is none righteous, no not one; they are altogether become abominable: There is none that understandeth, and seeketh after God."

5. But is there no exception as to the wickedness of man's heart? Yes, in those that are born of God. "He that is born of God keepeth himself, and that wicked one toucheth him not." God has "purified his heart by faith," so that his wickedness is departed from him. "Old things are passed away, and all things" in him "are become new." So that his heart is no longer desperately wicked, but "renewed in righteousness and true holiness." Only let it be remembered, that the heart, even of a believer, is not wholly purified when he is justified. Sin is then overcome, but it is not rooted out; it is conquered, but not destroyed. Experience shows him,

First, that the roots of sin, self-will, pride, and idolatry, remain still in his heart. But as long as he continues to watch and pray, none of them can prevail against him. Experience teaches him, Secondly, that sin (generally pride or self-will) cleaves to his best actions: So that, even with regard to these, he finds an absolute necessity for the blood of atonement.

6. But how artfully does this conceal itself, not only from others, but even from ourselves! Who can discover it in all the disguises it assumes, or trace it through all its latent mazes? And if it be so difficult to know the heart of a good man, who can know the heart of a wicked one, which is far more deceitful? No unregenerate man, however sensible, ever so experienced, ever so wise in his generation. And yet these are they who pique themselves upon "knowing the world," and imagine they see through all men. Vain men! One may boldly say they "know nothing yet as they ought to know." Even that politician in the late reign neither knew the heart of himself or of other men, whose favourite saying was: "Do not tell me of your virtue, or religion: I tell you, every man has his price." Yes, Sir R[obert]; every man like you; everyone that sells himself to the devil.

7. Did that right honourable wretch, compared to whom Sir R[obert] was a saint, know the heart of man,—he that so earnestly advised his own son, "never to speak the truth, to lie or dissemble as often as he speaks, to wear a mask continually?" that earnestly counselled him, "not to debauch *single women*," (because some inconveniences might follow,) "but always married women?" Would one imagine this grovelling animal ever had a wife or a married daughter of his own? O rare Lord C[hesterfield]! Did ever man so well deserve, though he was a Peer of the realm, to die by the side of Newgate? Or did ever book so well deserve to be burned by the common hangman, as his Letters? Did Mr. David Hume, lower, if possible, than either of the former, know the heart of man? No more than a worm or a beetle does. After "playing so idly with the darts of death," do you now find it a laughing matter? What think you now of Charon? Has he ferried you over Styx? At length he has taught you to know a little of your own heart! At length you know it is a fearful thing to fall into the hands of the living God!

8. One of the ablest champions of infidelity (perhaps the most elegant, and the most decent writer that ever produced a system of religion without being in the least obliged to the Bible for it) breaks out in the fullness of his heart: "Who would not wish that there was full proof of the Christian revelation, since it is undoubtedly the most benevolent system that ever appeared in the world!" Might he not add a reason of another kind,—Because without this man must be altogether a mystery to himself? Even with the help of Revelation, he knows exceeding little; but without it, he would know abundantly less, and nothing with any certainty. Without the light which is given us by the oracles of God, how could we reconcile his greatness with his meanness? While we acknowledged, with Sir John Davies,—

> I know my soul has power to know all things,
> Yet is she blind, and ignorant of all:
> I know I'm one of nature's little kings·
> Yet to the least and vilest things in thrall.

9. Who then knoweth the hearts of all men? Surely none but He that made them. Who knoweth his own heart? Who can tell the depth of its enmity against God? Who knoweth how deeply it is sunk into the nature of Satan?

III. 1. From the preceding considerations, may we not learn, First, "He that trusteth in his own heart is a fool?" For who that is wise would trust one whom he knows to be "desperately wicked?" especially, whom he hath known, by a thousand experiments, to be "deceitful above all things"? What can we expect, if we still trust a known liar and deceiver, but to be deceived and cheated to the end?

2. We may hence, in the Second place, infer the truth of that other reflection of Solomon: "Seest thou a man that is wise in his own eyes? there is more hope of a fool than of him." For at what a distance from wisdom must that man be who never suspected his want of it? And will not his thinking so well of himself prevent his receiving instruction from others? Will he no be apt to be displeased at admonition, and to construe reproof into reproach? Will he not therefore be less ready to receive instruction than even one that has little natural understanding? Surely no fool is so incapable of amendment as one that imagines himself to be wise. He that supposes himself not to need a physician, will hardly profit by his advice.

3. May we not learn hence, Thirdly, the wisdom of that caution, "Let him who thinketh he standeth take heed lest he fall?" Or, to render the text more properly,) "Let him that assuredly standeth take heed lest he fall." How firmly soever he may stand, he has still a deceitful heart. In how many instances has he been deceived already! And so he may again. Suppose he be not deceived now, does it follow that he never will? Does he not stand upon slippery ground? And is he not surrounded with snares? Into which he may fall and rise no more?

4. Is it not wisdom for him that is now standing, continually to cry to God, "Search me, O Lord, and prove me; try out my reins and my heart! Look well, if there be any way of wickedness in me, and lead me in the way everlasting?" Thou alone, O God, "knowest the hearts of all the children of men:" O show thou me what spirit I am of, and let me not deceive my own soul! Let me not "think of myself more highly than I ought to think." But let me always "think soberly, according as thou hast given me the measure of faith!"

Halifax, April 21, 1790

124.* THE HEAVENLY TREASURE IN EARTHEN VESSELS

"We have this treasure in earthen vessels."

2 Cor. 4:7.

1. How long was man a mere riddle to himself! For how many ages were the wisest of men utterly unable to reveal the mystery, to reconcile the strange inconsistencies, in him,—

---

* [text from the 1872 edition]

the wonderful mixture of good and evil, of greatness and littleness, of nobleness and baseness [barrenness]? The more deeply they considered these things the more they were entangled. The more pains they took, in order to clear up the subject, the more they were bewildered in vain, uncertain conjectures.

2. But what all the wisdom of man was unable to do, was in due time done by the wisdom of God. When it pleased God to give an account of the origin of things, and of man in particular, all the darkness vanished away, and the clear light shone. "God said, Let us make man in our own image." It was done. In the image of God man was made. Hence we are enabled to give a clear, satisfactory account of the greatness, the excellency, the dignity of man. But "man, being in honour" did not continue therein, but rebelled 20 against his sovereign Lord. Hereby he totally lost, not only the favour, but likewise the image of God. And "in Adam all died." For fallen "Adam begat a son in his own likeness." And hence we are taught to give a clear, intelligible account of the littleness and baseness of man. He is sunk even below the beasts that perish. Human nature now is not only sensual but devilish. There is in every man born into the world, (what is not in any part of the brute creation; no beast is fallen so low,) a "carnal mind, which is enmity," direct enmity, "against God."

3. By considering, therefore, these things in one view,—the creation and the fall of man,—all the inconsistencies of his nature are easily and fully understood. The greatness and littleness, the dignity and baseness, the happiness and misery, of his present state, are no longer a mystery, but clear consequences of his original state and his rebellion against God. This is the key that opens the whole mystery, that removes all the difficulty, by showing what God made man at first, and what man has made himself. It is true, he may regain a considerable measure of "the image of God wherein he was created:" But still, whatever we regain, we shall "have this treasure in earthen vessels."

In order to have a clear conception of this, we may inquire, First, what is "the treasure" which we now have; and, in the Second place, consider how "we have this treasure in earthen vessels."

I. 1. And, First, let us inquire, What is this treasure which Christian believers have? I say, believers; for it is of these directly that the Apostle is here speaking. Part of this they have, in common with other men, in the remains of the image of God. May we not include herein, First, an immaterial principle, a spiritual nature, endued with understanding, and affections, and a degree of liberty; of a self-moving, yea, and self-governing power? (otherwise we were mere machines, stocks, and stones)? And, Secondly, all that is vulgarly called natural conscience; implying some discernment of the difference between moral good and evil, with an approbation of one, and disapprobation of the other, by an inward monitor excusing or accusing? Certainly, whether this is natural or superadded by the grace of God, it is found, at least in some small degree, in every child of man. Something of this is found in every human heart, passing

sentence concerning good and evil, not only in all Christians, but in all Mahometans, all Pagans, yea, the vilest of savages.

2. May we not believe, that all Christians, though but nominally such, have sometimes at least, some desire to please God, as well as some light concerning what does really please him, and some convictions when the are sensible of displeasing him? Such treasure have all the children of men, more or less, even when they do not yet know God.

3. But it is not these of whom the Apostle is here speaking; neither is this the treasure which is the subject of his discourse. The persons concerning whom he is here speaking are those that are born of God; those that, "being justified by faith," have now redemption in the blood of Jesus, even the forgiveness of sins; those who enjoy that peace of God which passeth all understanding; whose soul doth magnify the Lord, and rejoice in him with joy unspeakable; and who feel the "love of God shed abroad in their hearts by the Holy Ghost, which is given unto them." This, then, is the treasure which they have received;—a faith of the operation of God; a peace which sets them above the fear of death, and enables them in everything to be content; an hope full of immortality, whereby they already "taste of the powers of the world to come;" the love of God shed abroad in their hearts with love to every child of man, and a renewal in the whole image of God, in all righteousness and true holiness. This is properly and directly the treasure concerning which the Apostle is here speaking.

II. 1. But this, invaluable as it is, "we have in earthen vessels." The word is exquisitely proper, denoting both the brittleness of the vessels, and the meanness of the matter they are made of. It directly means, what we term earthenware; china, porcelain, and the like. How weak, how easily broken in pieces! Just such is the case with a holy Christian. We have the heavenly treasure in earthly, mortal, corruptible bodies. "Dust thou art," said the righteous Judge to his rebellious creature, till then incorruptible and immortal, "and to dust thou shalt return." How finely (but with what a mixture of light and darkness) does the heathen poet touch upon this change! *Post ignem etherea domo subduxerat,*—"After man had stolen fire from heaven," (what an emblem of forbidden knowledge!) *macies et nova febrium,*—that unknown army of consumptions, fevers, sickness, pain of every kind, fixed their camp upon earth, which till then they could no more have entered than they could scale heaven; and all tended to introduce and pave the way for the last enemy, death. From the moment that awful sentence was pronounced the body received the sentence of death in itself; if not from the moment our first parents completed their rebellion by eating of the forbidden fruit. May we not probably conjecture that there was some quality naturally in this, which sowed the seeds of death in the human body, till then incorruptible and immortal? Be this as it may, it is certain that, from this time, "the corruptible body has pressed down the soul." And no marvel, seeing the soul, during its vital union with the body, cannot exert any of its operations, any otherwise than in union with the body, with its bodily organs. But all of these are more debased and depraved by the fall of man, than we can possibly conceive; and the brain, on which the soul more directly depends, not less than the rest of the body. Consequently, if these instruments, by which the soul works, are disordered, the soul itself must be hindered in its operations. Let a musician be ever so skilful, he will make but poor music if his instrument be out of tune. From a disordered brain (such as is, more or less, that of every child of man) there will necessarily arise confusedness of apprehension, showing itself in a thousand instances; false judgment, the natural result thereof, and wrong inferences; and from these, innumerable mistakes will follow, in spite of all the caution we can use. But mistakes in the judgment will frequently give occasion to mistakes in practice; they will naturally cause our speaking wrong in some instances, and acting wrong in others; nay, they may occasion not only wrong words or actions, but wrong tempers also. If I judge a man to be better than he really is; in consequence I really love him more than he deserves. If I judge another to be worse than he really is; I shall, in consequence, love him less than he deserves. Now both these are wrong tempers. Yet possibly it may not be in my power to avoid either the one or the other.

2. Such are the unavoidable consequences of "having these treasures in earthen vessels." Not only death, and its forerunners,—sickness, weakness, and pain, and a thousand infirmities,—but likewise error, in ten thousand shapes, will be always ready to attack us. Such is the present condition of humanity! Such is the state of the wisest men! Lord, "what is man, that thou art still mindful of him; or the son of man, that thou regardest him?"

3. Something of this great truth, that the "corruptible body presses down the soul,"—is strongly expressed in those celebrated lines of the ancient poet. Speaking of the souls of men he says:

> Igneus est ollis vigor, et coelestis origo
> Semnibus; quantum non noxia corpora tardant,
> Terrenique hebetant artus, moribundaque membra.
> These seeds of heavenly fire,
> With strength innate, would to their source aspire,
> But that their earthly limbs obstruct their flight,
> And check their soaring to the plains of light.

4. But suppose it pleased the all-wise Creator, for the sin of man, to suffer the souls of men in general to be weighed down in this miserable manner by their corruptible body; why does he permit the excellent treasure which he has entrusted to his own children, to be still lodged in these poor earthen vessels?" Would not this question naturally occur to any reflecting mind? Perhaps it would; and therefore the Apostle immediately furnishes us with a full answer: God has done this, that "the excellency of the power might be of God, and not of us;" that it might be undeniably plain to whom that excellent power belonged; that no flesh might glory in his sight; but that all who have received this treasure might continually cry, "Not unto us, but unto thee, O Lord, be the praise, for thy name and for thy truth's sake."

5. Undoubtedly this was the main design of God in this wonderful dispensation; to humble man, to make and keep him little and poor, and base, and vile, in his own eyes. And whatever we suffer hereby, we are well repaid, if it be a means of "hiding pride from man;" of laying us low in the dust, even then, when we are most in danger of being lifted up by the excellent gifts of God!

6. Nay, if we suffer hereby, from the mean habitation of the immortal spirit; if pain, sickness, and numberless other afflictions beside, to which we should not otherwise have been liable, assault us on every side, and at length bear us down into the dust of death; what are we losers by this? Losers! No, "In all these things we are more than conquerors, through him that loved us." Come on then, disease, weakness, pain,—afflictions, in the language of men. Shall we not be infinite gainers by them? Gainers for ever and ever! seeing "these light afflictions, which are but for a moment, work out for us a far more exceeding and eternal weight of glory!"

7. And are we not, by the consciousness of our present weakness, effectually taught wherein our strength lies? How loud does it proclaim, "Trust in the Lord Jehovah; for in him is everlasting strength!" Trust in Him who suffered a thousand times more than ever you can suffer! Hath he not all power in heaven and in earth? Then, what though

> The heavenly treasure now we have
> In a vile house of clay!
> Yet He shall to the utmost save,
> And keep it to that day.

Potto, June 17, 1790

125.* ON LIVING WITHOUT GOD

"Without God in the world."

Eph. 2:12.

1. Perhaps these words might be more properly translated, *Atheists in the world.* This seems to be a little stronger expression than "without God in the world," which sounds nearly negative, and does not necessarily imply any more than the having no fellowship or intercourse with God. On the contrary, the word Atheist is commonly understood to mean something positive,—the not only disclaiming any intercourse with him, but denying his very being.

2. The case of these unhappy men may be much illustrated by a late incident, the truth of which cannot reasonably be doubted, there having been so large a number of eye-witnesses. An ancient oak being cut down, and split through the midst, out of the very heart of the tree crept a large toad, and walked away with all the speed he could. Now how long, may we probably imagine, had this creature continued there? It is not unlikely it might have remained in its nest above a hundred years. It is not improbable it was nearly, if not altogether, coeval with the oak; having been some way or other enclosed therein at the time that it was planted. It is not therefore unreasonable to suppose that it had lived that strange kind of life at least a century. We say, *it had lived;* But what manner of life! How desirable! How enviable! As Cowley says:

---

* [text from the 1872 edition]

O life, most precious and most dear!

O life, that Epicures would long to share!

Let us spend a few thoughts upon so uncommon a case, and make some improvement of it.

3. This poor animal had organs of sense; yet it had not any sensation. It had eyes, yet no ray of light ever entered its black abode. From the very first instant of its existence there, it was shut up in impenetrable darkness. It was shut up from the sun, moon and stars, and from the beautiful face of nature; indeed, from the whole visible world, as much as if it had no being.

4. As no air could penetrate its sable recess, it consequently could have no *hearing*. Whatever organs it was provided with, they could be of no use; seeing no undulating air could find a way through the walls that surrounded it. And there is no reason to believe that it had any sense analogous to those either of *smelling* or *tasting*. In a creature which did not need any food these could have been of no possible use. Neither was there any way whereby the objects of smell or taste could make their approach to it. It must be very little, if at all, that it could be acquainted even with the general sense,—that of *feeling:* As it always continued in one unvaried posture amidst the parts that surrounded it, all of these being immovably fixed could make no new impression upon it. So that it had only one feeling from hour to hour, and from day to day, during its whole duration.

5. And as this poor animal was destitute of *sensation*, it must have equally been destitute of *reflection*. Its head (of whatever sort it was,) having no materials to work upon, no ideas of sensation of any kind, could not produce any degree of *reflection*. It scarce, therefore could have any *memory*, or any *imagination*. Nor could it have any locative *power*, while it was so closely bound in on every side. If it had in itself some springs of motion, yet it was impossible that power should be exerted, because the narrowness of its cavern could not allow of any change of place.

6. How exact a parallel may be drawn between this creature (hardly to be called an animal) and a man that is "without God in the world!" Such as are a vast majority of even those that are called Christians! I do not mean that they are Atheists, in the common sense of the word. I do not believe that these are so numerous as many have imagined. Making all the inquiry and observation I could for upwards of fifty years, I could not find twenty who seriously disbelieved the being of a God; nay, I have found only two of these (to the best of my judgment) in the British Islands: Both of these then lived in London, and had been of this persuasion many years. But several years before they were called to appear before God, both John S—— and John B—— were fully convinced that there is a God; and, what is more remarkable, they were first convinced that he is a terrible, and then that he is a merciful God. I mention these two accounts to show not only that there are real literal Atheists in the world; but also, that even then, if they will condescend to ask it, they may find "grace to help in time of need."

7. But I do not mean such as these when I speak of those who are Atheists or "without God in the world;" but of such as are only practical Atheists; as have not God in all their thoughts; such as have not acquainted themselves with him, neither have any fellowship with him; such as have no more intercourse with God, or the invisible world, than this animal had with the visible. I will endeavour to draw the parallel between these. And may God apply it to their hearts!

8. Every one of these is in exactly such a situation with regard to the invisible as the toad was in respect to the visible world. That creature had undoubtedly a sort of life, such as it was. It certainly had all the internal and external parts that are essential to animal life; and, without question, it had suitable juices, which kept up a kind of circulation. This was a life indeed! And exactly such a life is that of the Atheist, the man "without God in the world." What a thick veil is between him and the invisible world, which, with regard to him, is as though it had no being! He has not the least perception of it; not the most distant idea. He has not the least sight of God, the intellectual Sun; nor any the least attraction toward him, or desire to have any knowledge of his ways. Although His light be gone forth into all lands, and His sound unto the end of the world, yet he *heareth* no more thereof than of the fabled music of the spheres. He *tastes* nothing of the goodness of God or the powers of the world to come. He does not *feel* (as our Church speaks) the working of the Holy Spirit in his heart. In a word, he has no more intercourse with a knowledge of the spiritual world, than this poor creature had of the natural, while shut up in its dark enclosure.

9. But the moment the Spirit of the Almighty strikes the heart of him that was till then without God in the world, it breaks the hardness of his heart, and creates all things new. The Sun of Righteousness appears, and shines upon his soul, showing him the light of the glory of God in the face of Jesus Christ. He is in a new world. All things round him are become new, such as it never before entered into his heart to conceive. He sees, so far as his newly-opened eyes can bear the sight,

The opening heavens around him shine,

With beams of sacred bliss.

He sees that he has "an Advocate with the Father, Jesus Christ the righteous;" and that he has "redemption in his blood, the remission of his sins." He sees "a new way that is opened into the holiest by the blood of Jesus;" and his "light shineth more and more unto the perfect day."

10. By the same gracious stroke, he that before had ears but heard not is now made capable of *hearing*. He hears the voice that raiseth the dead,—the voice of Him that is "the resurrection and the life." He is no longer deaf to his invitations or commands, to his promises or threatenings; but gladly hears every word that proceeds out of his mouth, and governs thereby all his thoughts, words, and actions.

11. At the same time, he receives other spiritual senses, capable of discerning spiritual good and evil. He is enabled to *taste*, as well as to see, how gracious the Lord is. He enters into the holiest by the blood of Jesus, and tastes of the powers of the world to come. He finds Jesus' love far better than wine; yea, sweeter than honey or the honey-comb. He knows what that meaneth: "All thy garments smell of myrrh, aloes, and cassia." He *feels* the love of God shed abroad in his heart by the Holy Ghost which is given unto him; or, as our

Church expresses it, "feels the workings of the Spirit of God in his heart." Meantime, it may easily be observed, that the substance of all these figurative expressions is comprised in that one word *faith*, taken in its widest sense; being enjoyed, more or less, by everyone that believes in the name of the Son of God. This change, from spiritual death to spiritual life, is properly the new birth; all the particulars whereof are admirably well expressed by Dr. Watts in one verse:

> Renew my eyes, open my ears,
> And form my soul afresh;
> Give me new passions, joys and fears,
> And turn the stone to flesh!

12. But before this universal change there may be many partial changes in a natural man, which are frequently mistaken for it, whereby many say, "Peace, peace!" to their souls, when there is no peace. There may be not only a considerable change in the life, so as to refrain from open sin, yea, the easily besetting sin; but also a considerable change of tempers, conviction of sin, strong desires, and good resolutions. And here we have need to take great care, not, on the one hand, to despise the day of small things; nor, on the other, to mistake any of these partial changes for that entire, general change, the new birth; that total change from the image of the earthly Adam into the image of the heavenly, from an earthly, sensual, devilish mind, into the mind that was in Christ.

13. Settle it therefore in your hearts, that however you may be changed in many other respects, yet in Christ Jesus, that is, according to the Christian institution, nothing will avail without the whole mind that was in Christ, enabling you to walk as Christ walked. Nothing is more sure than this: "If any man be in Christ," a true believer in him, "he is a new creature: Old things," in him, "are passed away; all things are become new."

14. From hence we may clearly perceive the wide difference there is between Christianity and morality. Indeed nothing can be more sure than that true Christianity cannot exist without both the inward experience and outward practice of justice, mercy, and truth; and this alone is given in morality. But it is equally certain that all morality, all the justice, mercy, and truth which can possibly exist without Christianity, profiteth nothing at all, is of no value in the sight of God, to those that are under the Christian dispensation. Let it be observed, I purposely add, "to those that are under the Christian dispensation," because I have no authority from the Word of God "to judge those that are without." Nor do I conceive that any man living has a right to sentence all the heathen and Mahometan world to damnation. It is far better to leave them to him that made them, and who is "the Father of the spirits of all flesh;" who is the God of the Heathens as well as the Christians, and who hateth nothing that he hath made. But meantime this is nothing to those that name the name of Christ:—all those, being under the law, the Christian law, shall undoubtedly be judged thereby; and, of consequence, unless those be so changed as was the animal above mentioned, unless they have new senses, ideas, passions, tempers, they are no Christians. However just, true, or merciful they may be, they are but Atheists still!

15. Perhaps there may be some well-meaning persons who carry this farther still; who aver, that whatever change is wrought in men, whether in their hearts or lives, yet if they have not clear views of those capital doctrines, the fall of man, justification by faith, and of the atonement made by the death of Christ, and of his righteousness transferred to them, they can have no benefit from his death. I dare in no wise affirm this. Indeed I do not believe it. I believe the merciful God regards the lives and tempers of men more than their ideas. I believe he respects the goodness of the heart rather than the clearness of the head; and that if the heart of a man be filled (by the grace of God, and the power of his Spirit) with the humble, gentle, patient love of God and man, God will not cast him into everlasting fire prepared for the devil and his angels because his ideas are not clear, or because his conceptions are confused. Without holiness, I own, "no man shall see the Lord;" but I dare not add, "or clear ideas."

16. But to return to the text. Let me entreat all of you who are still "without God in the world," to consider with all your humanity, benevolence, virtue, you are still

> Inclusi tenebris, et carcere caeco:
> Inclosed in darkness and infernal shade.

My dear friends! you do not see God. You do not see the Sun of righteousness. You have no fellowship with the Father, or with his Son, Jesus Christ. You never heard the voice that raiseth the dead. Ye know not the voice of your Shepherd. Ye have not received the Holy Ghost. Ye have no spiritual senses. You have your old, natural ideas, passions, joys, and fears; you are not new creatures. O cry to God, that he may rend the veil which is still upon your hearts; and which gives you occasion to complain,—

> O dark, dark, dark, I still must say,
> Amidst the blaze of gospel-day!

O that you may this day hear his voice, who speaketh as never man spake, saying, "Arise, shine, for thy light is come, and the glory of the Lord is risen upon thee!" Is it not *his* voice that crieth aloud, "Look unto me, and be thou saved?" He saith, "Lo! I come!" Even so, Lord Jesus! Come quickly!

Rotherham, July 6, 1790

126.* ON THE DANGER OF INCREASING RICHES

"If riches increase, set not thine heart upon them."

Ps. 62:10.

1. From that express declaration of our Lord, "It is easier for a camel to go through the eye of a needle, than for a rich man to enter into the kingdom of heaven," we may easily learn, that none can *have* riches without being greatly endangered by them. But if the danger of barely having them is so great, how much greater is the danger of *increasing* them! This danger is great even to those who receive what is transmitted to them by their forefathers; but it is abundantly greater to those who acquire them by their skill and industry.

---

* [text from the 1872 edition]

Therefore, nothing can be more prudent than this caution: "If riches increase, set not thine heart upon them."

2. It is true, riches, and the increase of them, are the gift of God. Yet great care is to be taken, that what is intended for a blessing, do not turn into a curse. To prevent which, it is highly expedient to consider seriously,

I. What is meant by riches; and when they may be said to increase.

II. What is implied in setting our hearts upon them; and how we may avoid it.

I. Consider, First, what is here meant by riches. Indeed some may imagine that it is hardly possible to mistake the meaning of this common word. Yet, in truth, there are thousands in this mistake; and many of them quite innocently. A person of note, hearing a sermon preached upon this subject several years since, between surprise and indignation broke out aloud, "Why does he talk about riches here? There is no rich man at Whitehaven, but Sir James L——r." And it is true there was none but he that had forty thousand pounds a year, and some millions in ready money. But a man may be rich that has not a hundred a year, nor even one thousand pounds in cash. Whosoever has food to eat, and raiment to put on, with something over, is rich. Whoever has the necessaries and conveniences of life for himself and his family, and a little to spare for them that have not, is properly a rich man; unless he is a miser, a lover of money, one that hoards up what he can and ought to give to the poor. For it so, he is a poor man still, though he has millions in the bank; yea, he is the poorest of men; for

> The beggars but a common lot deplore;
> The rich poor man's emphatically poor.

2. But here an exception may be made. A person may have more than necessaries and conveniences for his family, and yet not be rich. For he may be in debt; and his debts may amount to more than he is worth. But if this be the case, he is not a rich man, how much money soever he has in his hands. Yea, a man of business may be afraid that this is the real condition of his affairs, whether it be or no; and then he cannot be so charitable as he would, for fear of being unjust. How many that are engaged in trade, are in this very condition! those especially that trade to a very large amount; for their affairs are frequently so entangled, that it is not possible to determine, with any exactness, how much they are worth, or, indeed, whether they are worth anything or nothing. Should we not make a fair allowance for them?

3. And beware of forming a hasty judgment concerning the fortune of others. There may be secrets in the situation of a person, which few but God are acquainted with. Some years since, I told a gentleman, "Sir, I am afraid you are covetous." He asked me, "What is the reason of your fear?" I answered, "A year ago, when I made a collection for the expense of repairing the Foundery, you subscribed five guineas. At the subscription made this year you subscribed only half a guinea." He made no reply; but after a time asked, "Pray, Sir, answer me a question: Why do you live upon potatoes?" (I did so between three and four years.) I replied, "It has much conduced to my health." He answered, "I believe it has. But did you not do it likewise to save money?" I said, "I did; for

what I save from my own meat, will feed another that else would have none." "But, Sir", said he, "if this be your motive you may save much more. I know a man that goes to the market at the beginning of every week: There he buys a pennyworth of parsnips, which he boils in a large quantity of water. The parsnips serve him for food, and the water for drink, the ensuing week So his meat and drink together cost him only a penny a week." This he constantly did, though he had then two hundred pounds a year, to pay the debts which he had contracted before he knew God! And this was he, whom I had set down for a covetous man!

4. But there are those who are conscious before God that they are rich. And, doubtless, some among *you* are of the number. You have more of the goods of this world than is needful either for yourself or your family. Let each consider for himself. Do *your* riches increase? Do not you understand that plain expression? Have you not more money, or more of money's worth, than you had ten or twenty years ago, or at this time last year? If you keep any account, you can easily know this. Indeed you ought to know; otherwise, you are not a good steward, even in this respect, of the mammon of unrighteousness. And every man, whether engaged in trade or not, ought to know whether his substance lessens or increases.

5. But many have found out a way never to be rich, though their substance increase ever so much. It is this: As fast as ever money comes in, they lay it out, either in land, or enlarging their business. By this means, each of these, keeping himself bare of money, can still say, "I am not rich;" yea, though he has ten, twenty, a hundred times more substance than he had some years ago. This may be explained by a recent case: A gentleman came to a merchant in London, a few years since, and told him, "Sir, I beg you will give me a guinea for a worthy family that is in great distress." He replied, "Really, Mr. M., I cannot well afford to give you it just now; but if you will call upon me when I am worth ten thousand pounds, upon such an occasion I will give you ten guineas." Mr. M., after some time, called upon him again, and said, "Sir, I claim your promise; now you are worth ten thousand pounds." He replied, "That is very true: But I assure you, I cannot spare one guinea so well as I could then."

6. It is possible for a man to cheat himself by this ingenious device. And he may cheat other men; for as long "as thou doest good unto thyself, men will speak well of thee." "A right *good man*," says the Londoner, "he is worth a plum" (a hundred thousand pounds). But, alas! he cannot deceive God; and he cannot deceive the devil. Ah, no! The curse of God is upon thee already, and on all that thou hast. And to-morrow, when the devil seizes thy soul, will he not say, "What do all thy riches profit thee?" Will they purchase a pillow for thy head, in the lake of fire burning with brimstone? Or will they procure thee a cup of "water to cool thy tongue," while thou art tormented in that flame?" O follow the wise direction here given! that God may not say unto thee, "Thou fool!"

7. This shift, therefore, will not avail. It will not be any protection, either against the wrath of God, or the malice and power of the devil. Thou art convicted already of "setting thy

heart" upon thy riches, if thou layest all thou hast above the conveniences of life, on adding money to money, house to house, or field to field, without giving at least a tenth of thine income (the Jewish proportion) to the poor. By whatsoever means thy riches increase, whether with or without labour; whether by trade, legacies, or any other way; unless thy charities increase in the same proportion; unless thou givest a full tenth of thy substance, of thy fixed and occasional income; thou dost undoubtedly set thy heart upon thy gold, and it will "eat thy flesh as fire!"

8. But O! who can convince a rich man that he sets his heart upon riches? For considerably above half a century I have spoken on this head, with all the plainness that was in my power. But with how little effect! I doubt whether I have, in all that time, convinced fifty misers of covetousness. When the lover of money was described ever so clearly, and painted in the strongest colours, who applied it to himself? To whom did God, and all that knew him, say, "Thou art the man!" If he speaks to any of you that are present, O do not stop your ears! Rather say, with Zaccheus, "Behold, Lord, the half of my goods I give to the poor; and if I have done any wrong to any man, I restore fourfold." He did not mean that he had done this in time past; but that he determined to do so for the time to come. I charge thee before God, thou lover of money, to "go and do likewise!"

9. I have a message from God unto thee, O rich man! whether thou wilt hear, or whether thou wilt forbear. Riches have increased with thee; at the peril of thy soul, "set not thine heart upon them!" Be thankful to Him that gave thee such a talent, so much power of doing good. Yet dare not to rejoice over them, but with fear and trembling. *Cave ne inhaereas,* says pious Kempis, *ne capiaris et pereas:* "Beware thou cleave not unto them, lest thou be entangled and perish." Do not make them thy end, thy chief delight, thy happiness, thy God! See that thou expect not happiness in money, nor anything that is purchasable thereby; in gratifying either the desire of the flesh, the desire of the eyes, or the pride of life.

10. But let us descend to particulars; and see that each of you deal faithfully with his own soul. If any of you have now twice, thrice, or four times as much substance as when you first saw my face, faithfully examine yourselves, and see if you do not set your hearts, if not directly on money or riches themselves, yet on some of the things that are purchasable thereby; which comes to the same thing. All those the Apostle John includes under that general name, *the world*; and the desire of them, or to seek happiness in them, under that form, "the love of the world." This he divides into three branches, "the desire of the flesh, the desire of the eyes, and the pride of life." Fairly examine yourselves with regard to these. And, First, as to "the desire of the flesh." I believe this means the seeking of happiness in the things that gratify the senses. To instance in one: Do not you seek your happiness in enlarging the pleasure of *tasting*. To be more particular: Do you not *eat* more plentifully, or more delicately, than you did ten or twenty years ago? Do not you use more *drink*, or drink of a more *costly* kind, than you did then? Do you sleep on as hard a bed as you did once, suppose your health will bear it? To touch on one point more: do you *fast* as often, now you are

rich, as you did when you was poor? Ought you not, in all reason, to do this rather more often than more seldom? I am afraid your own heart condemns you. You are not clear in this matter.

11. The Second branch of the love of the world, "the desire of the eyes," is of a wider extent. We may understand thereby, the seeking our happiness in gratifying the imagination, (which is chiefly done by means of the eyes,) by grand, or new, or beautiful objects;—If they may not all be reduced to one head; since neither grand nor beautiful objects are pleasing when the novelty of them is gone. But are not the veriest trifles pleasing as long as they are new? Do not some of you, on the score of novelty, seek no small part of your happiness in that trifle of trifles—dress? Do not you bestow more money, or (which is the same) more time or pains, upon it than you did once? I doubt this is not done to please God. Then it pleases the devil. If you laid aside your needless ornaments some years since,—ruffles, necklaces, spider-caps, ugly, unbecoming bonnets, costly linen, expensive laces,—have you not, in defiance of religion and reason, taken to them again?

12. Perhaps you say you can now *afford* the expense. This is the quintessence of nonsense. Who gave you this addition to your fortune; or (to speak properly) *lent* it to you? To speak more properly still, who lodged it for a time in your hands as his stewards; informing you at the same time for what purposes he entrusted you with it? And can you *afford* to waste your Lord's goods, for every part of which you are to give an account; or to expend them in any other way than that which he hath expressly appointed? Away with this vile, diabolical cant! Let it never more come out of your lips. This *affording* to rob God is the very cant of hell. Do not you know that God entrusted you with that money (all above what buys necessaries for your families) to feed the hungry, to clothe the naked, to help the stranger, the widow, the fatherless; and, indeed, as far as it will go, to relieve the wants of all mankind? How can you, how dare you, defraud your Lord, by applying it to any other purpose? When he entrusted you with a little, did he not entrust you with it that you might lay out all that little in doing good? And when he entrusted you with more, did he not entrust you with that additional money that you might do so much the more good, as you had more ability? Had you any more right to waste a pound, a shilling, or a penny, than you had before? You have, therefore, no more right to gratify the desire of the flesh, or the desire of the eyes, now than when you was a beggar. O no! do not make so poor a return to your beneficent Lord! Rather, the more he entrusts you with, be so much the more careful to employ every mite as he hath appointed.

13. Ye angels of God, ye servants of his, that continually do his pleasure! our common Lord hath entrusted you also with talents far more precious than gold and silver, that you may minister in your various offices to the heirs of salvation. Do not you employ every mite of what you have received, to the end for which it was given you? And hath he not directed us to do his will on earth, as it is done by you in heaven? Brethren, what are we doing! Let us awake! Let us arise! Let us imitate those flaming ministers! Let us employ our whole

soul, body and substance, according to the will of our Lord! Let us render unto God the things that are God's; even all we are, and all we have!

14. Most of those who when riches increase set their hearts upon them, do it indirectly in some of the preceding instances. But there are others who do this more directly; being, properly, "lovers of money;" who love it for its own sake; not only for the sake of what it procures. But this vice is very rarely found in children or young persons; but only, or chiefly, in the old,—in those that have the least need of money, and the least time to enjoy it. Might not this induce one to think, that in many cases it is a penal evil; that it is a sin-punishing evil; that when a man has, for many years, hid his precious talent in the earth, God delivers him up to Satan, to punish by the inordinate love of it? Then it is that he is more and more tormented by that *auri sacra fames*, "that execrable hunger after gold" which can never be satisfied. No: It is most true, as the very Heathen observes, *Crescit amor nummi, quantum ipsa pecunia crescit*,—"As money, so the love of money, grows; it increases in the same proportion." As in a dropsy, the more you drink, the more you thirst; till that unquenchable thirst plunge you into the fire which ever shall be quenched!

15. "But is there no way," you may ask, "either to prevent or to cure this dire disease?" There is one preventative of it, which is also a remedy for it; and I believe there is no other under heaven. It is this. After you have *gained* (with the cautions above given) *all you can*, and *saved all you can*, wanting for nothing; spend not one pound, one shilling, or one penny, to gratify either the desire of the flesh, the desire of the eyes, or the pride of life; or indeed, for any other end than to please and glorify God. Having avoided this rock on the right hand, beware of that on the left. Secondly. *Hoard nothing*. Lay up no treasure on earth, but *give all you can*; that is, all you have. I defy all the men upon earth, yea, all the angels in heaven, to find any other way of extracting the poison from riches.

16. Let me add one word more. After having served you between sixty and seventy years; with dim eyes, shaking hands, and tottering feet, I give you one more advice before I sink into the dust. Mark those words of St. Paul: "Those that desire" or endeavour "to be rich," that moment "fall into temptation." Yea, a deep gulf of temptation, out of which nothing less than almighty power can deliver them. "They fall into a snare"—the word properly means *a steel trap*, which instantly crushes the animal, taken therein, *to pieces*;—"and into divers foolish and hurtful desires, which plunge men into destruction and perdition." You, above all men, who now prosper in the world, never forget these awful words! How unspeakably slippery is your path! How dangerous every step! The Lord God enable you to see your danger, and make you deeply sensible of it! O may you "awake up after his likeness, and be satisfied with it!"

17. Permit me to come a little closer still. Perhaps I may not trouble you any more on this head. I am pained for you that are "rich in this world." Do you give all you can? You who receive five hundred pounds a year, and spend only two hundred, do you give three hundred back to God? If not, you certainly rob God of that three hundred. You that receive two hundred, and spend but one, do you give God the other hundred? If not, you rob him of just so much. "Nay, may I not do what I will with *my own*?" Here lies the ground of your mistake. It is not your *own*. It cannot be, unless you are Lord of heaven and earth. "However, I must provide for my children." Certainly. But how? By making them rich? Then you will probably make them Heathens, as some of you have done already. "What shall I do, then?" Lord, speak to their hearts! else the Preacher speaks in vain. Leave them enough to live on, not in idleness and luxury, but by honest industry. And if you have not children, upon what scriptural or rational principle can you leave a groat behind you more than will bury you? I pray consider, what are you the better for what you leave behind you? What does it signify, whether you leave behind you ten thousand pounds, or ten thousand shoes and boots? O leave nothing behind you! Send all you have before you into a better world! Lend it, lend it all unto the Lord, and it shall be paid you again! Is there any danger that *his* truth should fail? It is fixed as the pillars of heaven. Haste, haste, my brethren, haste! lest you be called away before you settled what you have on this security! When this is done, you may boldly say, "Now I have nothing to do but to die! Father, into thy hands I commend my spirit! Come, Lord Jesus! Come quickly!"

Bristol, September 21, 1790.

FOURTH SERIES

127.* THE TROUBLE AND REST OF GOOD MEN***

---

* [text from the 1872 edition]
* Preached at St. Mary's in Oxford, on Sunday, Sept. 21, 1735
* Published at the request of several of the hearers
* [This appears to have been the first Sermon that Mr. Wesley ever committed to the press. It was preached about a month before he sailed for Georgia; and published the same year by C. Rivington, in St. Paul's Church-Yard. After remaining out of print upwards of ninety years, it is here republished as an authentic, and not uninteresting, specimen of his preaching at the time when he left his native country to convert Heathens; and, as he states, learned in the ends of the earth, what he least suspected, that he had never been converted himself. The reader will observe that while the Sermon displays great seriousness and zeal, it exhibits a very inadequate view of real Christianity. The Preacher attributes the sanctification of human nature, in a great measure, to personal sufferings; assumes that the body is the seat of moral evil; and that sin exists in the best of Christians till they obtain deliverance by the hand of death. With what ability and success he afterwards opposed these unevangelical principles, and taught the doctrine of present salvation from all sin, by faith in Jesus Christ, is well known to all who are conversant with his Works, and especially with his Journal and Sermons. Viewed in connexion with his subsequent writings, this Sermon is of considerable importance, as it serves very strikingly to illustrate the change which took place in his religious sentiments previously to his entrance upon that astonishing career of ministerial labour and usefulness, by which he was so eminently

"There the wicked cease from troubling, and there the weary be at rest."

Job 3:17.

When God at first surveyed all the works he had made, "behold, they were very good." All were perfect in beauty, and man, the lord of all, was perfect in holiness. And as his holiness was, so was his happiness. Knowing no sin, he knew no pain. But when sin was conceived, it soon brought forth pain; the whole scene was changed in a moment. He now groaned under the weight of a mortal body, and, what was far worse, a corrupted soul. That "spirit" which could have borne all his other "infirmities" was itself "wounded," and sick unto death. Thus, "in the day wherein he sinned, he began to "die;" and thus "in the midst of life we are in death;" yea, "the whole creation groaneth together," "being in bondage to sin," and therefore to misery.

The whole world is, indeed, in its present state, only one great infirmary. All that are therein are sick of sin; and their one business there is to be healed. And for this very end, the great Physician of souls is continually present with them; marking all the diseases of every soul, and "giving medicines to heal its sickness." These medicines are often painful, too: Not that God willingly afflicts his creatures, but he allots them just as much pain as is necessary to their health; and for that reason—because it is so.

The pain of cure must, then, be endured by every man, as well as the pain of sickness. And herein is manifest the infinite wisdom of Him who careth for us, that the very sickness of those with whom he converses may be a great means of every man's cure. The very wickedness of others is, in a thousand ways, conducive to a good man's holiness. They trouble him, it is true; but even that trouble is "health to his soul, and marrow to his bones." He suffers many things from them; but it is to this end, that he may be "made perfect through" those "sufferings."

But as perfect holiness is not found on earth, so neither is perfect happiness. [In this life adult Christians are saved from all sin, and are made perfect in love. See Mr. Wesley's "Plain Account of Christian Perfection."—Edit.] Some remains of our disease will ever be felt, and some physic be necessary to heal it. Therefore we must be, more or less, subject to the pain of cure, as well as the pain of sickness. And, accordingly, neither do "the wicked" here "cease from troubling," nor can "the weary be at rest."

Who, then will "deliver" us "from the body of this death?" Death will deliver us. Death shall set those free in a moment, who "were all their life-time subject to bondage." Death shall destroy at once the whole body of sin, [This doctrine, that we are saved from sin by death, is nowhere taught in sacred Scripture, as Mr. Wesley afterwards perceived, and demonstrated in the treatise just mentioned, and in several of his Sermons.—Edit.] and therewith of its companion,—pain. And therefore, "there the wicked cease from troubling, and there the weary be at rest."

The Scriptures give us no account of the *place* where the souls of the just remain from death to the resurrection; but we have an account of their *state* in these words: In explaining which I shall consider,

I. How the wicked do here trouble good men; and,
II. How the weary are there at rest."
[I.] Let us consider, First, how the "wicked" here "trouble" good men. And this is a spacious field. Look round the world; take a view of all the troubles therein: How few are there whereof the wicked are not the occasion! "From whence come wars and fightings among you?" Whence all the ills that embitter society; that often turn that highest of blessings into a curse, and make it "good for man to be alone?" "Come they not hence," from self-will, pride, inordinate affection? in one word, from wickedness? And can it be otherwise, so long as it remains upon earth? As well may "the Ethiopian change his skin," as a wicked man cease to trouble both himself and his neighbour, but especially good men: Inasmuch as, while he is wicked he is continually injuring either them, or himself, or God.

First. Wicked men trouble those who serve God, by the injuries they do them. As at first, "he that was born after the flesh persecuted him that was born after the Spirit, even so it is now." And so it must be, till all things are fulfilled; "till heaven and earth pass away," "all that will live godly in Christ Jesus shall suffer persecution." For there is an irreconcilable enmity between the Spirit of Christ, and the spirit of the world. If the followers of Christ "were of the world, the world would love its own: But because they are not of the world, therefore the world hateth them." And this hatred they will not fail to show by their words: They will "say all manner of evil against them falsely;" "they will find out many inventions" whereby even "the good that is in them may be evil spoken of," and in a thousand instances lay to their charge the ill that they know not. From words in due time they proceed to deeds; treating the servants as their forefathers did their Master; wronging and despitefully using them in as many ways as fraud can invent and force accomplish.

[2.] It is true, these troubles sit heaviest upon those who are yet weak in the faith; and the more of the Spirit of Christ any man gains, the lighter do they appear to him. So that to him who is truly renewed therein, who is full of the knowledge and love of God, all the wrongs of wicked men are not only no evils, but are matter of real and solid joy. But still, though he rejoices for his own sake, he cannot but grieve for theirs. "He hath great heaviness and continual sorrow in" his "heart, for" his "brethren according to the flesh," who are thus "treasuring up to themselves wrath against the day of wrath, and revelation of the righteous judgment of God." His eyes weep for them in secret places; he is horribly afraid for them; yea, he "could even wish to be accursed" himself, so they might inherit a blessing. And thus it is, that they who can not only slight, but rejoice in the greatest injury done to *them,*

---

distinguished. As a perfect antidote to the doctrinal mistakes which it contains, the reader is referred to the admirable Sermon, entitled, "The Scripture Way of Salvation," [43] (Sermons, vol. 2, p. 43.)—Edit.]

yet are troubled at that which wicked men do to themselves and the grievous misery that attends them.

[3.] How much more are they troubled at the injuries wicked men are continually offering to God! This was the circumstance which made the contradiction of sinners so severe a trial to our Lord himself: "He that despiseth me, despiseth Him that sent me." And how are these despisers now multiplied upon earth! Who fear not the Son, neither the Father. How are we surrounded with those who blaspheme the Lord and his Anointed; either reviling the whole of his glorious gospel, or making him a liar as to some of the blessed truths which he hath graciously revealed therein! How many of those who profess to believe the whole, yet, in effect preach another gospel; so disguising the most essential doctrines thereof by their new interpretations, as to retain the words only, but nothing of "the faith once delivered to the saints!" How many who have not yet made shipwreck of the faith are strangers to the fruits of it! It hath not purified their hearts; it hath not overcome the world; they are yet "in the gall of bitterness, and in the bond of iniquity." They are still "lovers of themselves," "lovers of the world," "lovers of pleasure," and not "lovers of God." Lovers of God? No. He "is not in all their thoughts!" They delight not in Him, they do not thirst after Him; they do not rejoice in doing his will, neither make their boast of his praise! O faith, working by love, whither art thou fled? Surely the Son of man did once plant thee upon earth. Where then art thou now? Among the wealthy? No. "The deceitfulness of riches" there "chokes the word, and it becometh unfruitful." Among the poor? No. "The cares of the world" are there, so that it bringeth forth no fruit to perfection. However, there is nothing to prevent its growth among those who have neither poverty nor riches:"—Yes; "the desire of other things." And experience shows, by a thousand melancholy examples, that the allowed desire of anything, great or small, otherwise than as a means to the one thing needful, will by degrees banish the care of that out of the soul, and unfit it for every good word or work.

Such is the trouble—not to descend to particulars, which are endless—that wicked men [continually] occasion to the good. Such is the state of all good men while on earth: But it is not so with their souls in paradise. In the moment wherein they are loosed from the body they know pain no more. Though they are not yet possessed of the "fullness of joy," yet all grief is done away. For "there the wicked cease from troubling; and there the weary be at rest."

II. 1. "There the weary are at rest"—which was the Second thing to be considered,—not only from those evils which prudence might have prevented, or piety removed, even in this life; but from those which were inseparable therefrom, which were their unavoidable portion on earth. They are now at rest, whom wicked men would not suffer to rest before: For into the seat of the spirits of just men, none but the spirits of the just can enter. They are at length hid from the scourge of the tongue: Their name is not here cast out as evil. Abraham, Isaac, and Jacob, and the Prophets, do not revile, or separate them from their company. They are no longer despitefully used, and persecuted; neither do they groan under the hand of the oppressor. No injustice, no malice, no fraud is there; they are all "Israelites indeed, in whom there is no guile." There are no sinners against their own souls; therefore there is no painful pity, no fear for them. There are no blasphemers of God or of his word; no profaners of his name or of his Sabbaths; no denier of the Lord that bought him; none that trample upon the blood of his everlasting covenant: In a word, no earthly or sensual, no devilish spirit; none who do not love the Lord their God with all their heart.

2. There, therefore, "the weary are at rest" from all the troubles which the wicked occasioned; and, indeed, from all the other evils which are necessary in this world, either as the consequence of sin, or for the cure of it. They are at rest, in the First place, from bodily pain. In order to judge of the greatness of this deliverance, let but those who have not felt it take a view of one who lies on a sick or death bed. Is this he that was "made a little lower than the angels?" How is the glory departed from him! His eye is dim and heavy; his cheek pale and wan; his tongue falters; [his hand trembles;] his breast heaves and pants; his whole body is now distorted, and writhed to and fro; now moist, and cold, and motionless, like the earth to which it is going. And yet, all this which you see is but the shadow of what he feels. You see not the pain that tears his heart, that shoots through all his veins, and chases the flying soul through every part of her once-loved habitation. Could we see this, too, how earnestly should we cry out: "O sin, what hast thou done! To what hast thou brought the noblest part of the visible creation! Was it for this the good God made man?" O no! Neither will he suffer it long. Yet a little while, and all the storms of life shall be over, and thou shalt be gathered into the storehouse of the dead; and "there "the weary are at rest."

3. They "are at rest" from all these infirmities and follies which they could not escape in this life. They are no longer exposed to the delusions of sense, or the dreams of imagination. They are not hindered from seeing the noblest truths, by inadvertence; nor do they ever lose the sight they have once gained, by inattention. They are not entangled with prejudice, nor ever misled by hasty or partial views of the object: And, consequently, no error is there. O blessed place, where truth alone can enter! truth unmixed, undisguised, enlightening every man who cometh into the world! where there is no difference of opinions; but all think alike; all are of one heart, and of one mind: Where that offspring of hell, controversy, which turneth this world upside down, can never come: Where those who have been sawn asunder thereby, and often cried out in the bitterness of their soul, "Peace, peace!" shall find what they then sought in vain, even a peace which none taketh from them.

4. And yet all this, inconceivably great as it is, is the least part of their deliverance. For in the moment wherein they shake off the flesh, they are delivered, not only from the troubling of the wicked, not only from pain and sickness, from folly and infirmity; but also from all sin. A deliverance this, in sight of which all the rest vanish away. This is the triumphal song which everyone heareth when he entereth the gates of paradise:—"Thou, being dead, sinnest no more. Sin hath no more dominion over thee. For in that thou diedst, thou

diedst unto sin once; but in that thou livest, thou livest unto God." [The sentiment which is here again expressed, that it is death which destroys sin in the human heart, though couched in the language of an Apostle, is a branch of that philosophical Mysticism which Mr. Wesley entertained at this early period of his life, and which he afterwards renounced for the scriptural doctrine of salvation by faith. According to the New Testament, every believer is already delivered from the dominion of sin; and the Bible never represents the entire sanctification of our nature as effected by death. It is the work of the Holy Spirit; and is not suspended upon the dissolution of the body; but upon the exercise of a steadfast faith in the almighty Saviour.—Edit.]

5. There then "the weary be at rest." The blood of the Lamb hath healed all their sickness, hath washed them throughly from their wickedness, and cleansed them from their sin. The disease of their nature is cured; they are at length made whole; they are restored to perfect soundness. They no longer mourn the "flesh lusting against the Spirit;" the "law in their members" is now at an end, and no longer "wars against the law of their mind, and brings them into captivity to the law of sin." There is no root of bitterness left; no remains even of that sin which did "so easily beset them;" no forgetfulness of "Him in whom they live, move, and have their being;" no ingratitude to their gracious Redeemer, who poured out his soul unto the death for them; no unfaithfulness to that blessed Spirit who so long bore with their infirmities. In a word, no pride, no self-will is there; so that they who are thus "delivered from the bondage of corruption" may indeed say one to another, and that in an emphatical sense, "Beloved, now we are the children of God; and it doth not yet appear what we shall be; but we shall be like him; for we shall see him as he is."

6. Let us view a little more nearly the state of a Christian at his entrance into the other world. Suppose "the silver cord" of life just "loosed," and "the wheel broken at the cistern;" the heart can now beat no more; the blood ceases to move; the last breath flies off from the quivering lips, and the soul springs forth into eternity. What are the thoughts of such a soul, that has just subdued her last enemy, death? That sees the body of sin lying beneath her, and is new born into the world of spirits? How does she sing, " 'O death, where is thy sting? O grave, where is thy victory? Thanks be unto God,' who hath given me 'the victory, through our Lord Jesus Christ!' O happy day, wherein I shall begin to live! wherein I shall taste my native freedom! When I was 'born of a woman' I had 'but a short time to live,' and that time was 'full of misery;' that corruptible body pressed me down, and enslaved me to sin and pain. But the snare is broken, and I am delivered. Henceforth I know them no more. That head is no more an aching head: Those eyes shall no more run down with tears: That heart shall no more pant with anguish or fear; be weighed down with sorrow or care: Those limbs shall no more be racked with pain: Yea, 'sin hath no more dominion over' me. At length, I have parted from thee, O my enemy; and I shall see thy face no more! I shall never more

be unfaithful to my Lord, or offend the eyes of his glory: I am no longer that wavering, fickle, self-inconsistent creature, sinning and repenting, and sinning again. No. I shall never cease, day or night, to love and praise the Lord my God, with all my heart, and with all my strength. But what are ye? Are 'all these ministering spirits sent forth to minister to' one 'heir of salvation?' Then, dust and ashes, farewell! I hear a voice from heaven saying, 'Come away, and rest from thy labours. Thy warfare is accomplished, thy sin is pardoned; and the days of thy mourning are ended.' "

7. My brethren, these truths need little application. Believe ye that these things are so? What then hath each of you to do, but to "lay aside every weight, and run with patience the race set before him?" To "count all things" else "but dung" and dross; especially those grand idols, learning and reputation, if they are pursued in any other measure, or with any other view, than as they conduce to the knowledge and love of God? to have this "one thing" continually in thine heart, "when thou sittest in thine house, and when thou walkest by the way, and when thou liest down, and when thou risest up?"—to have thy "loins" ever "girt," and "thy light burning?"—to serve the Lord thy God with all thy might; if by any means, when He requireth thy soul of thee, perhaps in an hour when thou lookest not for Him, thou mayst enter "where the wicked cease from troubling, and where the weary are at rest."

128.* FREE GRACE*

To The Reader:

Nothing but the strongest conviction, not only that what is here advanced is "the truth as it is in Jesus," but also that I am indispensably obliged to declare this truth to all the world, could have induced me openly to oppose the sentiments of those whom I esteem for their work's sake: At whose feet may I be found in the day of the Lord Jesus!

Should any believe it his duty to reply hereto, I have only one request to make,—Let whatsoever you do, be done inherently, in love, and in the spirit of meekness. Let your very disputing show that you have "put on, as the elect of God, bowel of mercies, gentleness, longsuffering; "that even according to this time it may be said, "See how these Christians love one another!"

Whereas a pamphlet entitled, "Free Grace Indeed," has been published against this Sermon; this is to inform the publisher, that I cannot answer his tract till he appears to be more in earnest. For I dare not speak of "the deep things of God" in the spirit of a prize-fighter or a stage-player.

> "He that spared not his own Son, but delivered him up
> for us all, how
> shall he not with him also freely give us all things?"
>
> Rom. 8:32

1. How freely does God love the world! While we were yet sinners, "Christ died for the ungodly." While we were "dead in our sin," God "spared not his own Son, but delivered him up for us all." And how freely with him does he "give us all things!" Verily, FREE GRACE is all in all!

---

2. The grace or love of God, whence cometh our salvation, is FREE IN ALL, and FREE FOR ALL.

3. First. It is free in all to whom it is given. It does not depend on any power or merit in man; no, not in any degree, neither in whole, nor in part. It does not in anywise depend either on the good works or righteousness of the receiver; not on anything he has done, or anything he is. It does not depend on his endeavors. It does not depend on his good tempers, or good desires, or good purposes and intentions; for all these flow from the free grace of God; they are the streams only, not the fountain. They are the fruits of free grace, and not the root. They are not the cause, but the effects of it. Whatsoever good is in man, or is done by man, God is the author and doer of it. Thus is his grace free in all; that is, no way depending on any power or merit in man, but on God alone, who freely gave us his own Son, and "with him freely giveth us all things.

4. But it is free for ALL, as well as IN ALL. To this some have answered, "No: It is free only for those whom God hath ordained to life; and they are but a little flock. The greater part of God hath ordained to death; and it is not free for them. Them God hateth; and, therefore, before they were born, decreed they should die eternally. And this he absolutely decreed; because so was his good pleasure; because it was his sovereign will. Accordingly, they are born for this,—to be destroyed body and soul in hell. And they grow up under the irrevocable curse of God, without any possibility of redemption; for what grace God gives. he gives only for this, to increase, not prevent, their damnation."

5. This that decree of predestination. But methinks I hear one say, "This is not the predestination which I hold: I hold only the election of grace. What I believe is not more than this,—that God, before the foundation of the world, did elect a certain number of men to be justified, sanctified, and glorified. Now, all these will be saved, and none else; for the rest of mankind God leaves to themselves: So they follow the imaginations of their own hearts, which are only evil continually, and, waxing worse and worse, are at length justly punished with everlasting destruction."

6. Is this all the predestination which you hold? Consider; perhaps this is not all. Do not you believe God ordained them to this very thing" If so, you believe the whole degree; you hold predestination in the full sense which has been above described. But it may be you think you do not. Do not you then believe, God hardens the hearts of them that perish: Do not you believe, he (literally) hardened Pharaoh's heart; and that for this end he raised him up, or created him? Why, this amounts to just the same thing. If you believe Pharaoh, or any one man upon earth, was created for this end,—to be damned,—you hold all that has been said of predestination. And there is no need you should add, that God seconds his degree, which is supposed unchangeable and irresistible, by hardening the hearts of those vessels of wrath whom that decree had before fitted for destruction.

7. well, but it may be you do not believe even this; you do not hold any decree of reprobation; you do not think God decrees any man to be damned, not hardens, irresistibly fits him, for damnation; you only say, "God eternally decreed, that all being dead in sin, he would say to some of the dry bones, Live, and to others he would not; that, consequently, these should be made alive, and those abide in death,—these should glorify God by their salvation, and those by their destruction."

8. Is not this what you mean by the election of grace? If it be, I would ask one or two question: Are any who are not thus elected saved? or were any, from the foundation of the world? Is it possible any man should be saved unless he be thus elected? If you say, "No," you are but where you was; you are not got one hair's breadth farther; you still believe, that, in consequence of an unchangeable, irresistible decree of God, the greater part of mankind abide in death, without any possibility of redemption; inasmuch as none can save them but God, and he will not save them. You believe he hath absolutely decreed not to save them; and what is this but decreeing to damn them? It is, in effect, neither more not less; it comes to the same thing; for if you are dead, and altogether unable to make yourself alive, then, if God has absolutely decreed he will make only others alive, and not you, he hath absolutely decreed your everlasting death; you are absolutely consigned to damnation. So then, though you use softer words than some, you mean the self-same thing; and God's decree concerning the election of grace, according to your account of it, amounts to neither more not less than what others call God's decree of reprobation.

9. Call it therefore by whatever name you please, election, preterition, predestination, or reprobation, it comes in the end to the same thing. The sense of all is plainly this,—by virtue of an eternal, unchangeable, irresistible decree of God, on part of mankind are infallibly saved, and the rest infallibly damned; it being impossible that any of the former should be damned. or that any of the latter should be saved.

10. But if this be so, then is all preaching vain. It is needless to them that are elected; for they, whether with preaching or without, will infallibly be saved. Therefore, the end of preaching—to save should—is void with regard to them; and it is useless to them that are not elected, for they cannot possibly be saved: They, whether with preaching or without, will infallibly be damned. The end of preaching is therefore void with regard to them likewise; so that in either case our preaching is vain, as you hearing is also vain.

11. This then, is a plain proof that the doctrine of predestination is not a doctrine of God, because it makes void the ordinance of God; and God is not divided against himself. A Second is, that it directly tends to destroy that holiness which is the end of all the ordinances of God. I do not say, none who hold it are holy; (for God is of tender mercy to those who are unavoidably entangled in errors of any kind;) but that the doctrine itself,—that every man is either elected or not elected from eternity, and that the one must inevitably be saved, and the other inevitably damned,— has a manifest tendency to destroy holiness in general; for it wholly takes away those first motives to follow after it, so frequently proposed in Scripture, the hope of future reward and fear of punishment, the hope of heaven and fear of hell. That these shall go away into everlasting punishment, and those into life eternal, is not motive to him to struggle for life

who believes his lot is cast already; it is not reasonable for him so to do, if he thinks he is unalterably adjudged either to life or death. You will say, "But he knows not whether it is life or death." What then?—this helps not the matter; for if a sick man knows that he must unavoidably die, or unavoidably recover, though he knows not which, it is unreasonable for him to take any physic at all. He might justly say, (and so I have heard some speak, both in bodily sickness and in spiritual,) "If I am ordained to life, I shall live; if to death, I shall live; so I need not trouble myself about it." So directly does this doctrine tend to shut the very gate of holiness in general,—to hinder unholy men from ever approaching thereto, or striving to enter in thereat.

12. as directly does this doctrine tend to destroy several particular branches of holiness. Such are meekness and love,—love, I mean, of our enemies,—of the evil and unthankful. I say not, that none who hold it have meekness and love; (for as is the power of God, so is his mercy;) but that it naturally tends to inspire, or increase, a sharpness or eagerness of temper, which is quite contrary to the meekness of Christ; as then especially appears, when they are opposed on this head. And it as naturally inspires contempt or coldness towards those whom we suppose outcast form God. "O but," you say. "I suppose no particular man a reprobate." You mean you would not if you could help it: But you cannot help sometimes applying your general doctrine to particular persons: The enemy of souls will apply it for you. You know how often he has done so. But you rejected the thought with abhorrence. True; as soon as you could; but how did it sour and sharpen your spirit in the mean time! you well know it was not the spirit of love which you then felt towards that poor sinner, whom you supposed or suspected, whether you would or no, to have been hated of God from eternity.

13. Thirdly. This doctrine tends to destroy the comfort of religion, the happiness of Christianity. This is evident as to all those who believe themselves to be reprobated, or who only suspect or fear it. All the great and precious promises are lost to them; they afford them no ray of comfort: For they are not the elect of God; therefore they have neither lot nor portion in them. This is an effectual bar to their finding any comfort or happiness, even in that religion whose ways are designed to be "ways of pleasantness, and all her paths peace."

14. And as to you who believe yourselves the elect of God, what is your happiness? I hoe, not a notion, a speculative belief, a bare opinion of any kind; but a feeling possession of God in your heart, wrought in you by the Holy Ghost, or, the witness of God's Spirit with your spirit that you are a child of God. This, otherwise termed "the full assurance of faith,: is the true ground of a Christian's happiness. And it does indeed imply a full assurance that all your past sins are forgiven, and that you are now a child of God. But it does not necessarily imply a full assurance of our future perseverance. I do not say this is never joined to it, but that it is not necessarily implied therein; for many have the one who have not the other.

15. Now, this witness of the Spirit experience shows to be much obstructed by this doctrine; and not only in those who, Believing themselves reprobated, by this belief thrust it far

from them, but even in them that have tasted of that good gift, who yet have soon lost it again, and fallen back into doubts, and fears, and darkness,—horrible darkness, that might be felt! And I appeal to any of you who hold this doctrine, to say, between God and your own hearts, whether you have not often a return of doubts and fears concerning your election or perseverance! If you ask, "Who has not?" I answer, Very few of those that hold this doctrine; but many, very many, of those that hold it not, in all parts of the earth;—many of these have enjoyed the uninterrupted witness of his Spirit, the continual light of his countenance, from the moment wherein they first believed, for many months or years, to this day.

16. That assurance of faith which these enjoy excludes all doubt and fear, It excludes all kinds of doubt and fear concerning their future perseverance; though it is not properly, as was said before, an assurance of what is future, but only of what now is. And this needs not for its support a speculative belief, that whoever is once ordained to life must live; for it is wrought from hour to hour, by the mighty power of God, "by the Holy Ghost which is given unto them." And therefore that doctrine is not of God, because it tends to obstruct, if not destroy, this great work of the Holy Ghost, whence flows the chief comfort of religion, the happiness of Christianity.

17. Again: How uncomfortable a thought is this, that thousands and millions of men, without any preceding offense or fault of theirs, were unchangeably doomed to everlasting burnings! How peculiarly uncomfortable must it be to those who have put on Christ! to those who, being filled with bowels of mercy, tenderness, and compassion, could even "wish themselves accursed for their brethren's sake!"

18. Fourthly. This uncomfortable doctrine directly tends to destroy our zeal for good works. And this it does, First, as it naturally tends (according to what was observed before) to destroy our love to the greater part of mankind, namely, the evil and unthankful. For whatever lessens our love, must go far lessen our desire to do them good. This it does, Secondly, as it cuts off one of the strongest motives to all acts of bodily mercy, such as feeding the hungry, clothing the naked, and the like,—viz., the hope of saving their souls from death. For what avails it to relieve their temporal wants, who are just dropping into eternal fire? "Well; but run and snatch them as brands out of the fire.: Nay, this you suppose impossible. They were appointed thereunto, you say, from eternity, before they had done either good or evil. you believe it is the will of God they should die. And "who hath resisted his will?" But you say you do not know whether these are elected or not. What then? If you know they are the one or the other,—that they are either elected or not elected,—all your labour is void and vain. In either case, your advice, reproof, or exhortation is as needless and useless as our preaching. It is needless to them that are elected; for they will infallibly be saved without it. It is useless to them that are not elected; for with or without it they will infallibly be damned; therefore you cannot consistently with your principles take any pains about their salvation. Consequently, those principles directly tend to destroy you zeal for good works; for all good works;

but particularly for the greatest of all, the saving of souls from death.

19. But, Fifthly, this doctrine not only tends to destroy Christian holiness, happiness, and good works, but hath also a direct and manifest tendency to overthrow the whole Christian Revelation. The point which the wisest of the modern unbelievers most industriously labour to prove, is, that the Christian Revelation is not necessary. They well know, could they once show this, the conclusion would be too plain to be denied, "If it be not necessary, it is not true," Now, this fundamental point you give up. For supposing that eternal, unchangeable decree, one part of mankind must be saved, though the Christian Revelation were not in being, and the other part of mankind must be damned, notwithstanding that Revelation. And what would an infidel desire more? You allow him all he asks. In making the gospel thus unnecessary to all sorts of men, you give up the whole Christian cause. "O tell it not in Gath! lest the daughters of the uncircumcised rejoice; "lest the sons of unbelief triumph!

20. And as this doctrine manifestly and directly tends to overthrow the whole Christian Revelation, so it does the same thing, by plain consequence, in making that Revelation contradict itself. For it is grounded on such an interpretation of some texts (more or fewer it matters not) as flatly contradicts all the other texts, and indeed the whole scope and tenor of Scripture. For instance: The assertors of this doctrine interpret that text of Scripture, "Jacob have I loved, but Esau have I hated," as implying that God in a literal sense hated Esau, and all the reprobated, from eternity. Now, what can possibly be a more flat contradiction than this, not only to the whole scope and tenor of Scripture, but also to all those particular texts which expressly declare, "God is love?" Again: They infer from that text, "I will have mercy on whom I will have mercy," (Romans 4:15) that God is love only to some men, viz., the elect, and that he hath mercy for those only; flatly contrary to which is the whole tenor of Scripture, as is that express declaration in particular, "The Lord is loving unto every man; and his mercy is over all his works." (Psalm 145:9.) Again: They infer from that and the like texts, "It is not of him that willeth, nor of him that runneth, but of God that showeth mercy,: that he showeth mercy only to those to whom he had respect from all eternity. Nay, but who replieth against God now? You now contradict the whole oracles of God, which declare throughout, "God is no respecter of persons:' (Acts 10:34) "There is no respect of persons with him." (Rom. 2:11.) Again: from that text, "The children being not yet born, neither having done any good or evil, that the purpose of God according to election might stand, not of works, but of him that calleth; it was said unto her," unto Rebecca, "The elder shall serve the younger;"you infer, that our being predestinated, or elect, no way depends on the foreknowledge of God. Flatly contrary to this are all the scriptures; and those in particular, "Elect according to the foreknowledge of God;" (1 Peter 1:2;) "Whom he did foreknow, he also did predestinate." (Rom. 8:29.)

21. And "the same Lord over all is rich" in mercy "to all that call upon him:" (Romans 10:12:) But you say, "No; he is such only to those for whom Christ died. And those are not all, but only a few, whom God hath chosen out of the world; for he died not for all, but only for those who were 'chosen in him before the foundation of the world.' " (Eph. 1:4.) Flatly contrary to your interpretation of these scriptures, also, is the whole tenor of the New Testament; as are in particular those texts:—"Destroy not him with thy meat, for whom Christ died," (Rom. 14:15,)—a clear proof that Christ died, not only for those that are saved, but also for them that perish: He is "the Saviour of the world;" (John 4:42;) He is "the Lamb of God that taketh away the sins of the world;" (John 1:29;) "He is the propitiation, not for our sins only, but also for the sins of the whole world;" (1 John 2:2;) "He," the living God, "is the Savior of all men;" (1 Timothy 4:10;) "He gave himself a ransom for all;" (1 Tim. 2:6;) "He tasted death for every man." (Heb. 2:9.)

22. If you ask, "Why then are not all men saved?" the whole law and the testimony answer, First, Not because of any decree of God; not because it is his pleasure they should die; for, As I live, saith the Lord God," I have no pleasure in the death of him that dieth." (Ezek. 18:3, 32.) Whatever be the cause of their perishing, it cannot be his will, if the oracles of God are true; for they declare, "He is not willing that any should perish, but that all should come to repentance;" (2 Pet. 3:9;) "He willeth that all men should be saved." And they, Secondly, declare what is the cause why all men are not saved, namely, that they will not be saved: So our Lord expressly, "Ye will not come unto me that ye may have life." (John 5:40.) "The power of the Lord is present to heal" them, but they will not be healed. "They reject the counsel," the merciful counsel, "of God against themselves," as did their stiff-necked forefathers. And therefore are they without excuse; because God would save them, but they will not be saved: This is the condemnation, "How often would I have gathered you together, and ye would not!" (Matt. 23:37.)

23. Thus manifestly does this doctrine tend to overthrow the whole Christian Revelation, by making it contradict itself; by giving such an interpretation of some texts, as flatly contradicts all the other texts, and indeed the whole scope and tenor of Scripture;—an abundant proof that it is not of God. But neither is this all: For, Seventhly, it is a doctrine full of blasphemy; of such blasphemy as I should dread to mention, but that the honour of our gracious God, and the cause of his truth, will not suffer me to be silent. In the cause of God, then, and from a sincere concern for the glory of his great name, I will mention a few of the horrible blasphemies contained in this horrible doctrine. But first, I must warn every one of you that hears, as ye will answer it at the great day, not to charge me (as some have done) with blaspheming, because I mention the blasphemy of others. And the more you are grieve with them that do thus blaspheme, see that ye "confirm your love towards them: the more, and that your heart's desire, and continual prayer to God, be, "Father, forgive them; for they know not what they do!"

24. This premised, let it be observed, that this doctrine represents our blessed Lord, "Jesus Christ the righteous," "the only begotten Son of the Father, full of grace and truth," as an hypocrite, a deceiver of the people, a man void of common sincerity. For it cannot be denied, that he everywhere speaks

as if he was willing that all men should be saved. Therefore, to say he was not willing that all men should be saved, is to represent him as a mere hypocrite and dissembler. It cannot be denied that the gracious words which came out of his mouth are full of invitations to all sinners. To say, then, he did not intend to save all sinners, is to represent him as a gross deceiver of the people. You cannot deny that he says, "Come unto me, all ye that are weary and heavy laden." If, then, you say he calls those that cannot come; those whom he knows to be unable to come; those whom he can make able to come, but will not; how is it possible to describe greater insincerity? You represent him as mocking his helpless creatures, by offering what he never intends to give. You describe him as saying on thing, and meaning another; as pretending the love which his had not. Him, in "whose mouth was no guile," you make full of deceit, void of common sincerity;—then especially, when, drawing nigh the city, He wept over it, and said, "O Jerusalem, Jerusalem, thou killest the prophets, and stonest them that are sent unto thee; how often *would* I have gathered thy children together,—and *ye would not,*" *ethelesakai ouk ethelesate.* Now, if you say, *they would,* but *he would not,* you represent him (which who could hear?) as weeping crocodiles' tears; weeping over the prey which himself had doomed to destruction!

25. Such blasphemy this, as one would think might make the ears of a Christian to tingle! But there is yet more behind; for just as it honours the Son, so doth this doctrine honour the Father. It destroys all his attributes at once: It overturns both his justice, mercy, and truth; yea, it represents the most holy God as worse than the devil, as both more false, more cruel, and more unjust. More *false*; because the devil, liar as he is, hath never said, "He willeth all men to be saved:" More *unjust*, because the devil cannot, if he would, be guilty of such injustice as you ascribe to God, when you say that God condemned millions of souls to everlasting fire, prepared for the devil and his angels, for continuing in sin, which, for want of that grace *he will not* give them, they cannot avoid: And more *cruel*; because that unhappy spirit "seeketh rest and findeth none;" so that his own restless misery is a kind of temptation to him to tempt others. But God resteth in his high and holy place; so that to suppose him, of his own mere motion, of his pure will and pleasure, happy as he is, to doom his creatures, whether they will or no, to endless misery, is to impute such cruelty to him as we cannot impute even to the great enemy of God and man. It is to represent the high God (he that hath ears to hear let him hear!) as more cruel, false, and unjust than the devil!

26. This is the blasphemy clearly contained in *the horrible decree* of predestination! And here I fix my foot. On this I join issue with every assertor of it. You represent God as worse than the devil; more false, more cruel, more unjust. But you say you will prove it by scripture. Hold! What will you prove by Scripture? that God is worse than the devil? I cannot be. Whatever that Scripture proves, it never an prove this; whatever its true meaning be. This cannot be its true meaning. Do you ask, "What is its true meaning then?" If I say, "I know not," you have gained nothing; for there are many scriptures the true sense whereof neither you nor I shall know till death is swallowed up in victory. But this I know, better it were to say it had no sense, than to say it had such a sense as this. It cannot mean, whatever it mean besides, that the God of truth is a liar. Let it mean what it will it cannot mean that the Judge of all the world is unjust. No scripture can mean that God is not love, or that his mercy is not over all his works; that is, whatever it prove beside, no scripture can prove predestination.

27. This is the blasphemy for which (however I love the persons who assert it) I abhor the doctrine of predestination, a doctrine, upon the supposition of which, if one could possibly suppose it for a moment, (call it election, reprobation, or what you please, for all comes to the same thing,) one might say to our adversary, the devil, "Thou fool, why dost thou roar about any longer? Thy lying in wait for souls is as needless and useless as our preaching. Hearest thou not, that God hath taken thy work out of thy hands; and that he doeth it much more effectually? Thou, with all thy principalities and powers, canst only so assault that we may resist thee; but He can irresistibly destroy both body and soul in hell! Thou canst only entice; but his unchangeable decrees, to leave thousands of souls in death, compels them to continue in sin, till they drop into everlasting burnings. Thou temptest; He forceth us to be damned; for we cannot resist his will. Thou fool, why goest thou about any longer, seeking whom thou mayest devour? Hearest thou not that God is the devouring lion, the destroyer of souls, the murderer of men" Moloch caused only children to pass though the fire: and that fire was soon quenched; or, the corruptible body being consumed, its torment was at an end; but God, thou are told, by his eternal decree, fixed before they had done good or evil, causes, not only children of a span long, but the parents also, to pass through the fire of hell, the 'fire which never shall be quenched; and the body which is cast thereinto, being now incorruptible and immortal, will be ever consuming and never consumed, but 'the smoke of their torment,' because it is God's good pleasure, 'ascendeth up for ever and ever.' "

28. O how would the enemy of God and man rejoice to hear these things were so! How would he cry aloud and spare not! How would he lift up his voice and say, "To your tents, O Israel! Flee from the face of this God, or ye shall utterly perish! But whither will ye flee? Into heaven? He is there, Down to hell? He is there also. Ye cannot flee from an omnipresent, almighty tyrant. And whether ye flee or stay, I call heaven, his throne, and earth, his footstool, to witness against you, ye shall perish, ye shall die eternally. Sing, O hell, and rejoice, ye that are under the earth! For God, even the mighty God, hath spoken, and devoted to death thousands of souls, form the rising of the sun unto the going down thereof! Here, O death, is they sting! They shall not, cannot escape; for the mouth of the Lord hath spoken it. Here, O grave is thy victory Nations yet unborn, or ever they have done good or evil are doomed never to see the light of life, but thou shalt gnaw upon them for ever and ever! Let all those morning stars sing together, who fell with Lucifer, son of the morning! Let all the sons of hell shout for joy! For the decree is past, and who shall disannul it?"

29. Yea, the decree is past; and so it was before the foundation of the world. But what decree? Even this: "I will set before the sons of men 'life and death, blessing cursing.' And the soul that chooseth life shall live, as the soul that chooseth death shall die." This decree whereby "whom God did foreknow, he did predestinate," was indeed from everlasting; this, whereby all who suffer Christ to make them alive are "elect according to the foreknowledge of God," now standeth fast, even as the moon, and as the faithful witnesses in heaven; and when heaven and earth shall pass away, yet this shall not pass away; for it is as unchangeable and eternal as is the being of God that gave it. This decree yields the strongest encouragement to abound in all good works and in all holiness; and it is a well-spring of joy, of happiness also, to our great and endless comfort. This is worthy of God; it is every way consistent with all the perfections of his nature. It gives us the noblest view both of his justice, mercy, and truth. To this agrees the whole scope of the Christian Revelation, as well as all the parts thereof. To this Moses and all the Prophets bear witness, and our blessed Lord and all his Apostles Thus Moses, in the name of his Lord: "I call heaven and earth to record against you this day, that I have set before you life and death, blessing and cursing; therefore choose life, that thou and thy seed may live." Thus Ezekiel: choose life, that thou and thy seed may live;"Thus Ezekiel: (To cite one Prophet for all:) "The soul that sinneth, it shall die: The son shall not bear" eternally, "the iniquity of the father. The righteousness of the righteous shall be upon him, and the wickedness of the wicked shall be upon him." (18:20.) Thus our blessed Lord: "If any man thirst, let him come unto me and drink." (John 7:37.) Thus his great Apostle, St. Paul: (Acts 17:30:) "God commandeth all men everywhere to repent;—"all men everywhere;" every man in every place, without any exception either of place or person. Thus St. James: "If any of you lack wisdom, let him ask of God, who giveth to all men liberally, and upbraideth not, and it shall be given him." (James 1:5.) Thus St. Peter: (2 Pet. 3:9:) "The Lord is not willing that any should perish, but that all should come to repentance." And thus St. John: "If any man sin, we have an Advocate with the Father; and he is the propitiation for our sins; and not for ours only, but for the sins of the whole world." (1 John 2:1, 2.)

30. O hear ye this, ye that forget God! Ye cannot charge your death upon him! " 'Have I any pleasure at all that the wicked should die?' saith the Lord God." (Ezek. 18:23ff.) "Repent, and turn from all your transgressions; so iniquity shall not be your ruin. Cast away from you all your transgressions where by ye have transgressed,—for why will ye die, O house of Israel? For I have no pleasure in the death of him that dieth, saith the Lord God. Wherefore turn yourselves, and live ye." "As I live, saith the Lord God, I have no pleasure in the death of the wicked.—Turn ye, turn ye from your evil ways; for why will ye die, O house of Israel?" (Ezekiel 33:11.)

129.* THE CAUSE AND CURE OF EARTHQUAKES*

O come hither, and behold the works of the Lord; what destruction he hath brought upon the earth!

Ps. 46:8.

Of all the judgments which the righteous God inflicts on sinners here, the most dreadful and destructive is an earthquake. This he has lately brought on our part of the earth, and thereby alarmed our fears, and bid us "prepare to meet our God!" The shocks which have been felt in divers places, since that which made this city tremble, may convince us that the danger is not over, and ought to keep us still in awe; seeing "his anger is not turned away, but his hand is stretched out still." (Isa. 10:4.)

That I may fall in with the design of Providence at this awful crisis, I shall take occasion from the words of my text,

    I.   To show that earthquakes are the works of the Lord, and He only bringeth this destruction upon the earth:

    II.   Call you to behold the works of the Lord, in two or three terrible instances: And,

    III.   Give you some directions suitable to the occasion.

I. I am to show you that earthquakes are the works of the Lord, and He only bringeth this destruction upon the earth. Now, that God is himself the Author, and sin the *moral* cause, of earthquakes, (whatever the natural cause may be,) cannot be denied by any who believe the Scriptures; for these are they which testify of Him, that it is God" which removeth the mountains, and overturneth them in his anger; which shaketh the earth out of her place, and the pillars thereof tremble." (Job 9:5, 6.) "He looketh on the earth, and it trembleth he toucheth the hills, and they smoke." (Ps. 104:32.) "The hills melted like wax at the presence of the Lord, at the presence of the Lord of the whole earth." (Ps. 97:5.) "The mountains quake at him, and the hills melt. Who can stand before his indignation, and who can abide in the fierceness of his anger? His fury is poured out like fire, and the rocks are thrown down by him." (Nahum 1:5, 6.) Earthquakes are set forth by the inspired writers as God's proper judicial act, or the punishment of sin: Sin is the cause, earthquakes the effect, of his anger. So the Psalmist: "The earth trembled and quaked; the very foundations also of the hills shook, and were removed, because he was wroth" (Ps. 18:7.) So the Prophet Isaiah: "I will punish the world for their evil,—and will lay low the haughtiness of the terrible:— Therefore I will shake the heavens, and the earth shalt remove out of her place, in the wrath of the Lord of host, and in the day of his fierce anger." (Isa. 13:11, 13.) And again. "Behold, the Lord maketh the earth empty; and maketh it waste, and turneth it upside down," (in the original, *perverteth the face thereof,*) "and scattereth abroad the inhabitants thereof. For the windows from on high are open, and the foundations of the earth do shake. The earth is utterly broken down, the earth is clean dissolved, the earth is moved exceedingly. The earth shall reel to and fro like a drunkard, and shall be removed like a cottage; and the transgression thereof shall be heavy upon it; and it shall fall and not rise again." (Isa. 24:1,

* [text from the 1872 edition]

|* [First published in the year 1750.]

18–20.) "Tremble, thou earth, at the presence of the God of Jacob." (Ps. 114:7.) "thou shalt be visited of the Lord of hosts with thunder, and with earthquake, and great noise." (Isa. 29:6.)

Nothing can be more express than these scripture testimonies, which determine both the cause and author of this terrible calamity. But reason, as well as faith, doth sufficiently assure us it must be the punishment of sin, and the effect of that curse which was brought upon the earth by the original transgression. Steadfastness must be no longer looked for in the world, since innocency is banished thence: But we cannot conceive that the universe would have been disturbed by these furious accidents during the state of original righteousness. Wherefore should God's anger have armed the elements against his faithful subjects? Wherefore should he have overthrown all his works to destroy innocent men? or why overwhelmed the inhabitants of the earth with the ruins thereof, if they had not been sinful? why buried those in the bowels of the earth who were not to die? Let us then conclude, both from Scripture and reason, that earthquakes are God's *strange works* of judgment—the proper effect and punishment of sin. I proceed,

II. To set before you these works of the Lord in two or three terrible instances.

In the year 1692 there happened in Sicily one of the most dreadful earthquakes in all history. It shook the whole island and not only that, but Naples and Malta shared in the shock. It was impossible for any one to keep on their legs on the dancing earth: Nay, those who lay on the ground were tossed from side to side, as on a rolling billow. High walls leaped from their foundations several paces.

The mischief it did is amazing: Fifty-four cities and towns, besides an incredible number of villages, were almost entirely destroyed. Catania, one of the most famous, ancient, and flourishing cities in the kingdom, the residence of several monarchs, and an university, had the greatest share in the judgment. Father Anth. Serrvoita, being on his way thither, a few miles from the city observed a black cloud like night hovering over it; and there arose from the mouth of Etna great spires of flame, which spread all around. The sea, all on a sudden, began to roar, and rise in billows; the birds flew about astonished; the cattle ran crying in the fields; and there was a blow as if all the artillery in the world had been discharged at once!

His and his companions' horses stopped short, trembling; so that they were forced to alight. They were no sooner off; but they were lifted from the ground above two palms; when, casting his eyes towards Catania, he was astonished to see nothing but a thick cloud of dust in the air. This was the scene of their calamity; for of the magnificent Catania there is not the least footstep to be seen. Of eighteen thousand nine hundred and fourteen inhabitants, eighteen thousand perished therein: In the several cities and towns sixty thousand were destroyed out of two hundred and fifty-four thousand nine hundred!

In the same year, 1692, on June 7, was the earthquake in Jamaica. It threw down most of the houses, churches, sugar-works, mills, and bridges throughout the island; tore the rocks and mountains, reducing some of them to plains; destroyed whole plantations, and threw them into the sea; and, in two minutes time, shook down and destroyed nine-tenths of the town of Port Royal; the houses sunk outright thirty or forty fathom deep!

The earth, opening, swallowed up people; and they rose in other streets; some in the midst of the harbour, (being driven up again by the sea which rose in those breaches,) and so wonderfully escaped.

Of all wells, from one fathom to six or seven, the water flew out of the top with a vehement motion. While the houses on one side of the street were swallowed up, on the other they were thrown into heaps. The sand in the street rose like waves of the sea, lifting up every body that stood on it, and immediately dropping down into pits; and at the same instant, a flood of water, breaking in, rolled them over and over, while catching hold of beams and rafters to save themselves.

Ships and sloops in the harbour were overset and lost. A vessel, by the motion if the sea and sinking of the wharf, was driven over the tops of many houses, and sunk there.

The earthquake was attended with a hollow rumbling sound, like that of thunder. In less than a minute, three quarters of the houses, and the ground they stood on, with the inhabitants, were quite sunk under water, and the little part left behind was no better than a heap of rubbish!

The shock was so violent that it threw people down on their knees or their faces, as they were running about for shelter; the ground heaved and swelled like a rolling sea; and several houses, still standing were shuffled and moved some yards out of their places; a whole street is said to be twice as broad now as before.

In many places the earth would crack, and open and shut quick and fast, of which openings, two or three hundred might be seen at a time; in some whereof the people were swallowed up; others the closing earth caught by the middle, and squeezed to death; and in that manner they were left buried with only their heads above ground; some heads the dogs ate!

The Minister of the place, in his account, saith, that such was the desperate wickedness of the people, that he was afraid to continue among them; that on the day of the earthquake some sailors and others fell to breaking open and rifling warehouses, and houses deserted, while the earth trembled under them, and the houses fell upon them in the act; that he met many swearing and blaspheming; and that the common harlots, who remained still upon the place, were as drunken and impudent as ever.

While he was running towards the Fort, a wide open place, to save himself, he saw the earth open and swallow up a multitude of people; and the sea mounting in upon them over the fortifications, it likewise destroyed their large burying-place, and washed away the carcases out of their graves, dashing their tombs to pieces. The whole harbour was covered with dead bodies, floating up and down without burial!

As soon as the violent shock was over, he desired all people to join with him in prayer. Among them were several Jews, who kneeled and answered as they did, and were heard even to call upon Jesus Christ. After he had spent an hour and an half with them in prayer, and exhortations to repentance, he was desired to retire to some ship in the harbour, and, passing over the tops of some houses which lay level with) the water, got first into a canoe, and then into a long-boat, which put him on board a ship.

The larger openings swallowed up houses; and out of some would issue whole rivers of water, spouted up a great height into the air, and threatening a deluge to that part which the earthquake spared. The whole was attended with offensive smells, and the noise of falling mountains. The sky in a minutes time was turned dull and red, like a glowing oven. Scarce a planting-house or sugar-work was left standing in all Jamaica. A great part of them was swallowed up, houses, trees, people, and all at one gape; in the place of which afterwards appeared great pools of water, which, when dried up, left nothing but sand, without any mark that ever tree or plant had been thereon.

About twelve miles from the sea, the earth gaped, and spouted out, with a prodigious force, vast quantities of water into the air. But the greatest violence was among the mountains and rocks. Most of the rivers were stopped for twenty-four hours, by the falling of the mountains; till, swelling up, they made themselves new channels, tearing up trees, and all they met with, in their passage.

A great mountain split, and fell into the level ground, and covered several settlements, and destroyed the people there. Another mountain, having made several leaps or moves, overwhelmed [a] great part of a plantation lying a mile off. Another large high mountain, near a day's journey over, was quite swallowed up, and where it stood is now a great lake some leagues over.

After the great shake, those who escaped got on board ships in the harbour, where many continued above two months; the shakes all that time being so violent, and coming so thick, sometimes two or three in an hour, accompanied with frightful noises, like a ruffling wind, or a hollow rumbling thunder, with brimstone blasts, that they durst not come ashore. The consequence of the earthquake was, a general sickness from the noisome vapours, which swept away above three thousand persons.

On the 28th of October, 1746, half an hour past ten at night, Lima, the capital city of Peru, was destroyed by an earthquake, which extended an hundred leagues northward and as many more to the south, all along the sea-coast. The destruction did not so much as give time for fright; for, at one and the same instant, the noise, the shock, and the ruin were perceived. In the space of four minutes, during which the greatest force of the earthquake lasted, some found themselves buried under the ruins of the falling houses; and others crushed to death in the streets by the tumbling of the walls, which fell upon them as they ran here and there. Nevertheless, the greater part of the inhabitants (who were computed near sixty thousand) were providentially preserved, either in the hollow places which the ruins left, or on the top of the very ruins themselves, without knowing how they got up thither. For no person, at such a season, had time for deliberation; and supposing he had, there was no place of retreat: For the parts which seemed most firm sometimes proved the weakest; on the contrary the weakest, at intervals, made the greatest resistance; and the consternation was such, that no one thought himself secure, till he had made his escape out of the city.

The earth struck against the buildings with such violence, that every shock beat down the greatest part of them; and these, tearing along with them vast weights in their fall, (especially the churches and high houses,) completed the destruction of everything they encountered with, even of what the earth-quake had spared. The shocks, although instantaneous, were yet successive; and at intervals men were transported from one place to another, which was the means of safety to some, while the utter impossibility of moving preserved others.

There were seventy-four churches, besides chapels, and fourteen monasteries, with as many more hospitals and infirmaries, which were in all instant reduced to a ruinous heap, and their immense riches buried in the earth! But though scarce twenty houses were left standing, yet it does not appear that the number of the dead amounted to much more than one thousand one hundred and forty-one persons; seventy of whom were patients in an hospital, who were buried by the roof falling upon them as they lay in their beds, no person being able to give them any assistance.

Callao, a sea-port town, two leagues distant from Lima, was swallowed up by, the sea in the same earthquake. It vanished out of sight in a moment; so that not the least sight of it now appears.

Some few towers, indeed, and the strength of its walls, for a time, endured the whole force of the earthquake: But scarcely had its poor inhabitants begun to recover their first fright which the dreadful ruin had occasioned, when, suddenly, the sea began to swell, and, rising to a prodigious height, rushed furiously forward, and overflowed, with so vast a deluge of water, its ancient bounds, that, foundering most of the ships which were at anchor in the port, and lifting the rest above the height of the walls and towers, it drove them on and left them on dry ground far beyond the town. At the same time, it tore up from the foundations everything therein of houses and buildings, excepting the two gates, and here and there some small fragments of the walls themselves, which, as registers of the calamity, are still to be seen among the ruins and the waters,—a dreadful monument of what they were!

In this raging flood were drowned all the inhabitants of the place, about five thousand persons. Such as could lay hold on any pieces of timber, floated about for a considerable time; but those fragments, for want of room, were continually striking against each other, and so beat off those who had clung to them.

About two hundred, mostly fishermen and sailors, saved themselves. They declared that the waves in their retreat surrounded the whole town, without leaving any means for preservation; ad that, in the intervals, when the violence of the inundation was a little abated, they heard the most mournful cries and shrieks of those who perished. Those, likewise, who were on board the ships, which, by the elevation of the sea, were carried quite over the town, had the opportunity of escaping. Of twenty-three ships in the port at the time of the earthquake, four were stranded, and all the rest foundered. The few persons who saved themselves upon planks were several times driven about as far as the island of St. Lawrence, more than two leagues from the fort. At last some of them were cast upon the sea-shore, others upon the island, and so were preserved.

In these instances we may behold and see the works of the Lord, and how "terrible he is in his doings toward the children of me." (Ps. 66:5.) Indeed, nothing can be so affecting as this judgment of earthquakes when it comes unexpectedly as a thief in the night;—"when hell enlarges herself, and open her mouth without measure; and their glory, and their multitude, and their pomp, and he that rejoiceth, descent into it;" (Isa. 5:14;)—when there is no time to flee, or method to escape, or possibility to resist;—when no sanctuary or refuge remains; no shelter is to be found in the highest towers or lowest caverns;—when the earth opens on a sudden, and becomes the grave of whole families, streets, and cities; and effects this in less time than you are able to tell the story of it; either sending out a flood of waters to drown, or vomiting out flames of fire to consume them, or closing again upon them, that they die by suffocation or famine, if not by the ruins of their own dwelling;—when parents and children, husbands and wives, masters and servants, magistrates, Ministers, and people, without distinction, in the midst of health, and peace, and business, are buried in a common ruin, and pass all together into the eternal world: and there is only the difference of a few hours or minutes between a famous city and none at all!

Now, if war be a terrible evil, how much more an earthquake, which, in the midst of peace, brings a worse evil than the extremity of war! If a raging pestilence be dreadful, which sweeps away thousands in a day, and ten thousands in a night; if a consuming fire be an amazing judgment; how much more astonishing is this, whereby houses, and inhabitants, towns, and cities, and countries, are all destroyed at one stroke in a few minutes! Death is the only presage of such a judgment, without giving leisure to prepare for another world, or opportunity to look for any shelter in this. For a man to feel the earth, which hangeth upon nothing, (but as some vast ball in the midst of a thin yielding air,) totter under him, must fill him with secret fright and confusion. History informs us of the fearful effects of earthquakes in all ages; where you may see rocks torn in pieces; mountains not cast down only, but removed; hills raised, not out of valleys only, but out of seas; fires breaking out of waters; stones and cinders belched up; rivers changed; seas dislodged; earth opening; towns swallowed up; and many such-like hideous events!

Of all divine animadversions, there is none more horrid, more inevitable, than this. For where can we think to escape danger, if the most solid thing in all the world shakes? If that which sustains all other things threaten us with sinking under our feet, what sanctuary shall we find from an evil that encompasses us about? And whither can we withdraw, if the gulfs which open themselves shut up our passages on every side?

With what horror are men struck when they hear the earth groan; when her trembling succeeds her complaints; when houses are loosened from their foundations; when the roofs fall upon their heads, and the pavement sinks under their feet! What hope, when fear cannot he fenced by flight! In other evils there is some way to escape; but an earthquake incloses what it overthrows, and wages war with whole provinces; and sometimes leaves nothing behind it to inform posterity of its outrages. More insolent than fire, which spares rocks; more cruel than the conqueror, who leaves walls; more greedy than the sea, which vomits up shipwrecks; it swallows and devours whatsoever it overturns. The sea itself is subject to its empire, and the most dangerous storms are those occasioned by earthquakes.

I come, in the Third and last place, to give you some directions suitable to the occasion. And this is the more needful, because ye know not how soon the late earthquake, wherewith God hath visited us, may return, or whether He may not enlarge as well as repeat its commission. Once, yea, twice, hath the Lord warned us, that he is arisen to shake terribly the earth. Wherefore, 1. Fear God, even that God can in a moment cast both body and soul into hell! "Enter into the rock, and hide thee in the dust, for fear of the Lord, and for the glory of his majesty." (Isa. 1:10.) Ought we not all to cry out, "Great and marvellous are thy works, Lord God Almighty! Who shall not fear thee, O Lord, and glorify thy name? for thy judgments are made manifest!" (Rev. 15:3, 4.) God speaks to your hearts, as in subterranean thunder, "The Lord's voice crieth unto the city,—Hear the rod, and who hath appointed it." (Mic. 6:9.) He commands you to take notice of his power and justice. "Come and see!" (Rev. 6:5,) while a fresh seal is opening; yea, "come and see the works of God; his is terrible in his doings towards the children of men." (Ps. 66:5.)

When he makes the mountains tremble, and the earth shake, shall not our hearts be moved? "Fear ye not me? saith the Lord; and will ye not tremble at my presence?" (Jer. 5:22.) Will ye not fear me, who can open the windows of heaven above, or break up the fountains of the deep below, and pour forth whole floods of vengeance when I please?—who can "rain upon the wicked snares, fire and brimstone, and an horrible tempest;" (Ps. 11:6;) or kindle those streams and exhalations in the bowels and caverns of the earth, and make them force their way to the destruction of towns, cities, and countries? who can thus suddenly turn a fruitful land into a barren wilderness; an amazing spectacle of desolation and ruin?

"Shall a trumpet be blown in the city, and the people not be afraid? Shall there be evil in a city, and the Lord hath not done it." "The lion hath roared; who will not fear? With God is terrible majesty; men do therefore fear him." Some *do*; and all *ought*. O that his fear might this moment fall upon all you who hear these words; constraining every one of you to cry out, "My flesh trembleth for fear of thee; and I am afraid of thy judgments!" (Ps. 109:10.) O that all might see, now His hand is lifted up, as in act to strike; is stretched out still; and shakes his rod over a guilty land, a people fitted for destruction! For is not this the nation to be visited? And "shall not I wait for these things? saith the Lord; and shall not my soul be avenged on such a nation as this?" (Jer. 5:9.) What but national repentance can prevent national destruction?

"O consider this, ye that forget God, lest he pluck you away, and there be none to deliver you!" (Ps. 50:22.) That iniquity may not be your ruin, repent! This is the Second advice I would offer you; or, rather, the First enforced upon you farther, and explained. Fear God, and depart from evil; repent, and bring forth fruits meet for repentance; break off our sins this moment. "Wash ye, make you clean; put away the evil of your doings from before mine eyes; cease to do evil; learn to do well," saith the Lord. (Isa.:16, 17.)

"Except ye repent, ye shall all likewise perish." (Luke 13:3.)

"Therefore now, saith the Lord," who is not willing any should perish, "turn ye unto me with all your heart, and with fasting, and with weeping, and with mourning; and rend your heart, and not your garments, and turn unto the Lord your God; for he is gracious and merciful, slow to anger, and of great kindness, and repenteth him of the evil. Who knoweth if he will return and repent, and leave a blessing behind him?" (Joel 2:12–14.)

"Who knoweth?" A question which should make you tremble. God is weighing you in the balance, and, as it were, considering whether to save or to destroy! "Say unto the children of Israel, Ye are a stiff-necked people: I will come up into the midst of thee in a moment, and consume thee; therefore now put off thy ornaments from thee, that I may know what to do unto thee." (Exod. 33:5.)

God waits to see what effect his warnings will have upon you. He pauses on the point of executing judgment, and cries, "How shall I give thee up?" (Hos. 11:8) Or, "Why should ye be stricken any more?" (Isa. 1:5.) He hath no pleasure in the death of him that dieth. He would not bring to pass his strange act, unless your obstinate impenitence compel him. "Why will you die, O house of Israel?" (Ezek. 18:31.) God warns you of the approaching judgment, that ye may take warning, and escape it by timely repentance. He lifts up his hand, and shakes it over you, that ye may see it, and prevent the stroke. He tells you, "Now is the axe laid unto the root of the trees:" (Matt. 3:10:) Therefore repent; bring forth good fruit; and ye shall not be hewn down, and cast into the fire. O do not despise the riches of his mercy, but let it lead you to repentance! "Account that the longsuffering of the Lord is salvation." (2 Pet. 3:15.) Harden not your hearts, but turn to Him that smites you; or, rather, threatens to smite, that ye may turn and be spared!

How slow is the Lord to anger! how unwilling to punish! By what leisurely steps does he come to take vengeance! How many lighter afflictions before the final blow!

Should he beckon the man on the red horse to return, and say, "Sword, go through this land;" can we complain he gave us no warning? Did not the sword first bereave abroad; and did we not then see it within our borders? Yet the merciful God said, "Hitherto shalt thou come, and no further;" he stopped the invaders in the midst of our land, and turned them back again, and destroyed them.

Should he send the man on the pale horse, whose name is Death, and the pestilence destroy thousands and ten thousands of us; can we deny that first he warned us by the raging mortality among our cattle?

So, if we provoke him to lay waste our earth, and turn it upside down, and overthrow us, as he overthrew Sodom and Gomorrah; shall we not have procured this unto ourselves? Had we no reason to expect any such calamity; no previous notice; no trembling of the earth before it clave; no shock before it opened its mouth? Did he set no examples of so terrible a judgment before our eyes? Had we never heard of the destruction of Jamaica, or Catania, or that of Lima, which happened but yesterday? If we perish at last, we perish without excuse; for what could have been done more to save us?

Yes; thou hast now another call to repentance, another offer of mercy, whosoever thou art that hearest these words. In the name of the Lord Jesus, I warn thee once more, as a watchman over the house of Israel, to flee from the wrath to come! I put thee in remembrance (if thou hast so soon forgotten it) of the late awful judgment, whereby God shook thee over the mouth of hell! Thy body he probably awoke by it; but did he awake thy soul? The Lord was in the earthquake, and put a solemn question to thy conscience: "Art thou ready to die?" "Is thy peace made with God?" Was the earth just now to open its mouth, and swallow thee up, what would become of thee? Where wouldest thou be? in Abraham's bosom, or lifting up thine eyes in torment? Hadst thou perished by the late earthquake, wouldest thou not have died in thy sins, or rather gone down quick into hell? Who prevented thy damnation? it was the Son of God! O fall down, and worship him! Give Him the glory of thy deliverance; and devote the residue of thy days to his service! This is the Third advice I would give you: Repent and believe the gospel. Believe on the Lord Jesus, and ye shall yet be saved. Kiss the Son, lest he be angry, and ye perish. Repentance *alone* will profit you nothing; neither do ye repent, unless ye confess with broken hearts the most damnable of all your sins, your unbelief; your having rejected, or not accepted, Jesus Christ as your only Saviour. Neither can ye repent unless he himself gives the power; unless his Spirit convince you of sin, because ye believe not in Him.

Till ye repent of your unbelief, all your good desires and promises are vain, and will pass away as a morning cloud. The vows which ye make in a time of trouble, ye will forget and break as soon as the trouble is over and the danger past.

But shall ye escape for your wickedness, suppose the earthquake should not return? God will never want ways and means to punish impenitent sinners. He hath a thousand other judgments in reserve; and if the earth should not open its mouth, yet ye shall surely at last be swallowed up in the bottomless pit of hell!

Wouldest thou yet escape that eternal death? Then receive the sentence of death in thyself, thou miserable self-destroyed sinner! Know thy want of living, saving, divine faith! Groan under thy burden of unbelief, and refuse to be comforted till thou hear Him of his own mouth say, "Be of good cheer, thy sins be forgiven thee."

I cannot take it for granted, that all men have faith; or speak to the sinners of this land as to believers in Jesus Christ. For where are the fruits of faith? Faith worketh by love; faith overcometh the world; faith purifieth the heart; faith, in the smallest measure, removeth mountains. If thou canst believe, all things are possible to thee. If thou art justified by faith, thou hast peace with God, and rejoicest in hope of his glorious appearing.

He that believeth hath the witness in himself; hath the earnest of heaven in his heart; hath love stronger than death. Death to a believer has lost its sting; "therefore will he not fear, though the earth be removed, and though the mountains be carried into the midst of the sea." (Ps. 46:2.) For he knows in whom he has believed; and that "neither life nor death shall be able to separate him from the love of God which is in Christ Jesus his Lord."

Dost thou *so* believe? Prove thy own self by the infallible word of God. If thou hast not the fruits, effects, or inseparable properties of faith, thou hast not faith. Come, then, to the Author and Finisher of faith, confessing thy sins, and the root of all—thy unbelief, till he forgive thee thy sins, and cleanse thee from all unrighteousness. Come to the Friend of sinners, weary and heavy laden, and he will give thee pardon! Cast thy poor desperate soul on his dying love! Enter into the rock, the ark, the city of refuge! Ask, and thou shalt receive faith and forgiveness together. He waited to be gracious. He hath spared thee for this very thing; that thine eyes might see his salvation. Whatever judgments come in these latter days, yet whosoever shall call on the name of the Lord Jesus hall be delivered.

Call upon Him now, O sinner! and continue instant in prayer, till he answer thee in peace and power! Wrestle for the blessing! Thy life, thy soul, is at stake! Cry mightily unto Him,—"Jesus, thou Son of David, have mercy on me "God he merciful unto me a sinner!" Lord, help me! Help my unbelief! Save, or I perish! Sprinkle my troubled heart! Wash me throughly in the fountain of thy blood; guide me by thy Spirit; sanctify me throughout, and receive me up into glory! "Now to God the Father …

130.* NATIONAL SINS AND MISERIES*

"Lo, I have sinned, and I have done wickedly: But these sheep, what have they done?"

2 Sam. 24:17.

1. The chapter begins, "And again the anger of the Lord was kindled against Israel, and he moved David against them to say, Go, number Israel and Judah." *"Again;"*—it had been kindled against them but a few years before; in consequence of which "there had been a famine in the land three years, year after year," (2 Sam. 21:1,) till David inquired of the Lord, and was taught the way of appeasing it. We are not informed, in what particular manner Israel had now offended God; by what particular cause his anger was kindled, but barely with the effect. "He moved David against them to say, Go, number Israel and Judah." *"He,"*—not God! Beware how you impute this to the fountain of love and holiness! It was not God, but Satan, who thus moved David. So the parallel Scripture expressly declares: "And Satan stood up against Israel, and provoked David to number Israel." (1 Chron. 21:1.) Satan stood before God, to accuse David and Israel, and to beg God's permission to tempt David. Standing is properly the accuser's posture before the tribunals of men; and therefore the Scripture, which uses to speak of the things of God after the manner of men, represents Satan as appearing in this posture before the tribunal of God. "And David said to Joab, and to the rulers of the people, Go, number Israel, from Beersheba even to Dan; and bring the number of them to me, that I may know it." (2 Sam. 23:2.)

2. It does not clearly appear wherein the sin of thus numbering the people consisted. There is no express prohibition of it in any of the Scriptures which were then extant. Yet we read, "The king's word was abominable to Joab," (2 Sam. 23:6,) who was not a man of the tenderest conscience, so that he expostulated with David before he obeyed. "Joab answered, Why doth my lord require this thing?" "Why will he be a cause of trespass"—of punishment or calamity,—"to Israel?" God frequently punishes a people for the sins of their rulers, because they are generally partakers of their sins, in one kind or other. And the righteous Judge takes this occasion of punishing them for all their sins. In this, Joab was right; for after they were numbered, it is said, "And God was displeased with this thing." Yea, "David's heart smote him, and he said unto the Lord, I have sinned greatly in that I have done: and now, I beseech thee, O Lord, take away the iniquity of thy servant." (2 Sam. 24:10). Did not the sin lie in the motive on which the thing was done? Did he not do it in the pride of his heart? Probably out of a principle of vanity and ostentation; glorying not in God, but in the number of his people.

3. In the sequel we find that even Joab was for once a true prophet: David was a cause of trespass, of punishment, to Israel. His sin, added to all the sins of the people, filled up the measure of their iniquities. So "the Lord sent a pestilence upon Israel, from the morning," wherein Gad the prophet gave David his choice of war, famine, or pestilence, "unto the evening of the third day. And there died of the people from Dan unto Beersheba, seventy thousand men." (2 Sam. 24:15.) "And when David saw the angel that smote the people,"—who appeared in the form of a man with a drawn sword in his hand, to convince him the more fully, that this plague was immediately from God,—"he said, Lo, I have sinned, I have done wickedly: but these sheep, what have they done?"

4. Is there not in several respects, a remarkable resemblance between the case of Israel and our own? General wickedness then occasioned a general visitation; and does not the same

---

* [text from the 1872 edition]

* Preached at St. Matthew's, Bethnal-Green, on Sunday, November 12, 1775, for the benefit of the Widows and Orphans of the Soldiers who lately fell, near Boston, in New-England

cause now produce the same effect? We likewise have sinned, and we are punished; and perhaps these are only the beginning of sorrows. Perhaps the angel is now stretching out his hand over England to destroy it. O that the Lord would at length say to him that destroyeth, "It is enough; stay now thine hand!"

5. That vice is the parent of misery, few deny; it is confirmed by the general suffrage of all ages. But we seldom bring this home to ourselves; when we speak of sin as the cause of misery, we usually mean, the sin of other people, and suppose *we* suffer, because *they* sin. But need we go so far? Are not our own vices sufficient to account for all our sufferings? Let us fairly and impartially consider this; let us examine our own hearts and lives. We all suffer: and we have all sinned. But will it not be most profitable for us, to consider every one his own sins, as bringing sufferings both on himself and others; to say, "Lo, I have sinned, I have done wickedly; but these sheep, what have they done?"

I. 1. Let us inquire, First, what they suffer; and, afterwards, What is the cause of these sufferings? That the people suffer, none can deny;—that they are afflicted in a more than ordinary manner. Thousands and tens of thousands are at this day deeply afflicted through want of business. It is true that this want is in some measure removed in some large and opulent towns. But it is also true, that this is far, very far, from being the general case of the kingdom. Nothing is more sure than that thousands of people in the west of England, throughout Cornwall in particular, in the north, and even in the midland counties, are totally unemployed. Hence those who formerly wanted nothing, are now in want of all things. They are so far from the plenty they once enjoyed that they are in the most deplorable distress, deprived not only of the conveniences, but most of the necessaries of life. I have seen not a few of these wretched creatures, within little more than an hundred miles of London, standing in the streets with pale looks, hollow eyes, and meager limbs; or creeping up and down like walking shadows. I have known families, who a few years ago lived in an easy, genteel manner, reduced to just as much raiment as they had on, and as much food as they could gather in the field. To this one or other of them repaired once a day, to pick up the turnips which the cattle had left; which they boiled, if they could get a few sticks, or otherwise ate them raw. Such is the want of food to which many of our countrymen are at this day reduced by want of business!

2. Grievous enough is this calamity, which multitudes every day suffer. But I do not know whether many more do not labour under a still more grievous calamity. It is a great affliction to be deprived of bread; but it is a still greater to be deprived of our senses. And this is the case with thousands upon thousands of our countrymen at this day. Wide-spread poverty (though not in so high a degree) I have seen several years ago. But so widespread a lunacy I never saw, nor, I believe the oldest man alive. Thousands of plain, honest people throughout the land are driven utterly out of their senses, by means of the poison which is so diligently spread through every city and town in the kingdom. They are screaming out for liberty while they have it in their hands,

while they actually possess it; and to so great an extent, that the like is not known in any other nation under heaven; whether we mean civil liberty, a liberty of enjoying all our legal property,—or religious liberty, a liberty of worshipping God according to the dictates of our own conscience. Therefore all those who are either passionately or dolefully crying out, "Bondage! Slavery!" while there is no more danger of any such thing, than there is of the sky falling upon their head, are utterly distracted; their reason is gone; their intellects are quite confounded. Indeed, many of these have lately recovered their senses; yet are there multitudes still remaining, who are in this respect as perfectly mad as any of the inhabitants of Bedlam.

3. Let not anyone think, this is but a small calamity which has fallen upon our land. If you saw, as I have seen, in every county, city, town, men who were once of a calm, mild, friendly temper, mad with party-zeal, foaming with rage against their quiet neighbours, ready to tear out one another's throats, and to plunge their swords into each other's bowels; if you had heard men who once feared God and honoured the king, now breathing out the bitterest invectives against him, and just ripe, should any occasion offer, for treason and rebellion; you would not then judge this to be a little evil, a matter of small moment, but one of the heaviest judgments which God can permit to fall upon a guilty land.

4. Such is the condition of Englishmen at home. And is it any better abroad? I fear not. From those who are now upon the spot, I learn that in our colonies also many are causing the people to drink largely of the same deadly wine; thousands of whom are thereby inflamed more and more, till their heads are utterly turned, and they are mad to all intents and purposes. Reason is lost in rage; its small still voice is drowned by popular clamour. Wisdom is fallen in the streets. And where is the place of understanding? It is hardly to be found in these provinces. Here is *slavery*, real slavery indeed, most properly so called. For the regular, legal, constitutional form of government is no more. Here is real, not imaginary, bondage: Not the shadow of English liberty is left. Not only no *liberty of the press* is allowed,—none dare print a page, or a line, unless it be exactly conformable to the sentiments of our lords, the people,—but *no liberty of speech*. Their *tongue is* not *their own.* None must dare to utter one word, either in favour of King George, or in disfavour of the idol they have set up,—the new, illegal, unconstitutional government, utterly unknown to us and to our forefathers. Here is no *religious liberty*; no liberty of conscience for them that "honour the king," and whom, consequently, a sense of duty prompts them to defend from the vile calumnies continually vented against him. Here is no *civil liberty*; no enjoying the fruit of their labour, any further than the populace pleases. A man has no security for his trade, his house, his property, unless he will swim with the stream. Nay, he has no security for his life, if his popular neighbour has a mind to cut his throat: For there is no law; and no legal magistrate to take cognizance of offences. There is the gulf of tyranny,—of arbitrary power on one hand, and of anarchy on the other. And, as if all this were not misery enough, see likewise the fell monster, war! But who can describe the

complicated misery which is contained in this? Hark! the cannons roar! A pitchy cloud covers the face of the sky. Noise, confusion, terror, reign over all! Dying groans are on every side. The bodies of men are pierced, torn, hewed in pieces; their blood is poured on the earth like water! Their souls take their flight into the eternal world; perhaps into everlasting misery. The ministers of grace turn away from the horrid scene; the ministers of vengeance triumph. Such already has been the face of things in that once happy land where peace and plenty, even while banished from great part of Europe, smiled for near an hundred years.

5. And what is it which drags on these poor victims into the field of blood? It is a great phantom, which stalks before them, which they are taught to call, *liberty!* It is this

> Which breathes into their hearts stern love of war,
> And thirst of vengeance, and contempt of death.

Real liberty, meantime, is trampled underfoot, and is lost in anarchy and confusion.

6. But which of these warriors all the while considered the wife of his youth, that is now left a disconsolate widow,—perhaps with none that careth for her; perhaps deprived of her only comfort and support, and not having where to lay her head? Who considered his helpless children, now desolate orphans,—it may be, crying for bread, while their mother has nothing left to give them but her sorrows and her tears?

II. 1. And yet "these sheep, what have they done," although all this is come upon them? "Suppose ye that they are sinners above other men, because they suffer such things? I tell you, Nay; but except ye repent, ye shall all likewise perish." It therefore behoves us to consider our own sins;—the cause of all our sufferings. It behoves each of us to say, "Lo, I have sinned; I have done wickedly."

2. The time would fail, should I attempt to enumerate all the ways wherein we have sinned; but in general, this is certain:—

> The rich, the poor, the high, the low,
>> Have wander'd from his mild command;
> The floods of wickedness o'erflow,
>> And deluge all the guilty land:
> People and Priest lie drown'd in sin,
>> And Tophet yawns to take them in.

How innumerable are the violations of justice among us! Who does not adopt the old maxim, *Si possis, recte; si non, quocunque modo rem:* "If you can get money honestly, do; but, however, get money?" Where is mercy to be found, if it would stand in opposition to interest? How few will scruple, for a valuable consideration, to oppress the widow or fatherless? And where shall we find truth? Deceit and fraud go not out of our streets. Who is it that speaks the truth from his heart? Whose words are the picture of his thoughts? Where is he that has "put away all lying," that never speaks what he does not mean? Who is ashamed of this? Indeed it was once said, and even by a statesman, "All other vices have had their patrons; but lying is so base, so abominable a vice, that never was anyone found yet who dared openly to plead for it." Would one imagine this writer lived in a Court? yea, and that in the present century? Did not he himself, then, as well as all his brother-statesmen, plead for a trade of deliberate lying? Did he not plead for the innocence, yea, and the necessity, of employing *spies?*—the vilest race of liars under the sun? Yet who ever scrupled using them, but Lord Clarendon?

3. O truth, whither art thou fled? How few have any acquaintance with thee! Do not we continually tell lies for the nonce, without gaining thereby either profit or pleasure? Is not even our common language replete with falsehood? Above a hundred years ago the poet complained,

> It never was good day
> Since lowly fawning was called compliment.

What would he have said had he lived a century later, when that art was brought to perfection?

4. Perhaps there is one palpable evidence of this which is not usually attended to. If you blame a man in many other respects, he is not much affronted. But if you say he is a liar, he will not bear it; he takes fire at once. Why is this? Because a man can bear to be blamed when he is conscious of his own innocence. But if you say he is a liar, you touch a sore spot: he is guilty, and therefore cannot bear it.

5. Is there a character more despicable than even that of a liar? Perhaps there is; even that of an epicure. And are we not a generation of epicures? Is not our *belly* our *god?* Are not eating and drinking our chief delight, our highest happiness? Is it not the main study (I fear, the only study) of many honourable men to enlarge the pleasure of tasting? When was luxury (not in food only, but in dress, furniture, equipage) carried to such an height in Great Britain ever since it was a nation? We have lately extended the British empire almost over the globe. We have carried our laurels into Africa, into Asia, into the burning and the frozen climes of America. And what have we brought thence? All the elegance of vice which either the eastern or western world could afford.

6. Luxury is constantly the parent of sloth. Every glutton will, in due time, be a drone. The more of meat and drink he devours, the less taste will he have for labour. This degeneracy of the Britons from their temperate, active forefathers, was taken notice of in the last century. But if Mr. Herbert then said,

> O England, full of sin, but most of sloth!

what would he have said now? Observe the difference between the last and the present century, only in a single instance: In the last, the Parliament used to meet *hora quinta, ante meridiem,* "at five in the morning!" Could these Britons look out of their graves, what would they think of the present generation?

7. Permit me to touch on one article more, wherein, indeed, we excel all the nations upon earth. Not one nation under the canopy of heaven can vie with the English in profaneness. Such a total neglect, such an utter contempt of God, is nowhere else to be found. In no other streets, except in Ireland, can you hear on every side,

> The horrid oath, the direful curse,
> That latest weapon of the wretch's war,
> And blasphemy, sad comrade of despair!

8. Now let each of us lay his hand upon his heart and say, " 'Lord, is it I?' Have I added to this flood of unrighteousness and ungodliness, and thereby to the misery of my

countrymen? Am not I guilty in any of the preceding respects? And do not *they* suffer because *I* have sinned?" If we have any tenderness of heart, any bowels of mercies, any sympathy with the afflicted, let us pursue this thought till we are deeply sensible of *our* sins, as one great cause of *their* sufferings.

9. But now the plague is begun, and has already made such ravages both in England and America, what can *we* do, in order that it may be stayed? How shall we stand "between the living and the dead?" Is there any better way to turn aside the anger of God, than that prescribed by St. James: "Purge your hands, ye sinners, and purify your hearts, ye double-minded?" First. "Purge your hands." Immediately put away the evil of your doings. Instantly flee from sin, from every evil word and work, as from the face of a serpent. "Let no corrupt communication proceed out of your mouth;" no uncharitable, no unprofitable, conversation. Let no guile be found in your mouth: Speak to every man the truth from your heart. Renounce every way of acting, however gainful, which is contrary either to justice or mercy. Do to everyone as, in parallel circumstances, you would wish he should do unto you. Be sober, temperate, active; and in every word and work, labour to have a conscience void of offence toward God and toward man. Next, through the almighty grace of Him that loved you, and gave himself for you, "purify your hearts by faith." Be no longer double-minded, halting between earth and heaven, striving to serve God and mammon. Purify your hearts from pride,—humbling yourselves under the mighty hand of God; from all party-zeal, anger, resentment, bitterness, which now, especially, will easily beset you; from all prejudice, bigotry, narrowness of spirit; from impetuosity, and impatience of contradiction; from love of dispute, and from every degree of an unmerciful or implacable temper. Instead of this *earthly, devilish wisdom*, let "the wisdom from above" sink deep into your hearts; that "wisdom" which "is first pure," then "peaceable, easy to be entreated,"—convinced, persuaded, or appeased,—"full of mercy and good fruits; without partiality,"—embracing all men; "without hypocrisy," genuine and unfeigned. Now, if ever, "putting away with all malice, all clamour," (railing,) "and evil-speaking: Be ye kind one to another," to all your brethren and countrymen,—"tender-hearted" to all that are in distress; "forgiving one another, even as God for Christ's sake hath forgiven you."

10. And "now let my counsel be acceptable to" you, to every one of you present before God. "Break off thy sins by repentance, and thy iniquities by showing mercy to the poor, if it may be a lengthening of thy tranquility,"—of what degree of it still remains among us. Show mercy more especially to the poor widows, to the helpless orphans, of your countrymen who are now numbered among the dead, who fell among the slain in a distant land. Who knoweth but the Lord will yet be entreated, will calm the madness of the people, will quench the flames of contention, and breathe into all the spirit of love, unity, and concord? Then brother shall not lift up sword against brother, neither shall they know war any more. Then shall plenty and peace flourish in our land, and all the inhabitants of it be thankful for the innumerable blessings which they enjoy, and shall "fear God, and honour the king."

London, Nov. 7, 1775

131.* THE LATE WORK OF GOD IN NORTH AMERICA

"The appearance was as it were a wheel in the middle of a wheel."

Ezek. 1:16.

1. Whatever may be the primary meaning of this mysterious passage of Scripture, many serious Christians, in all ages have applied it in a secondary sense, to the manner wherein the adorable providence of God usually works in governing the world. They have judged this expression manifestly to allude to the complicated wheels of his providence, adapting one event to another, and working one thing by means of another. In the whole process of this, there is an endless variety of wheels within wheels. But they are frequently so disposed and complicated, that we cannot understand them at first sight; nay, we can seldom fully comprehend them till they are explained by the event.

2. Perhaps no age ever afforded a more striking instance of this kind than the present does, in the dispensations of divine providence with respect to our colonies in North-America. In order to see this clearly, let us endeavour, according to the measure of our weak understanding,

First, to trace each wheel apart: And,

Secondly, to consider both, as they relate to and answer each other.

I. And, First, we are to trace each wheel apart.

It is by no means my design to give a particular detail of the late transactions in America; but barely to give a simple and naked deduction of a few well-known facts.

I know this is a very delicate subject; and that it is difficult, if not impossible, to treat it in such a manner as not to offend any, particularly those who are warmly attached to either party. But I would not willingly offend; and shall therefore studiously avoid all keen and reproachful language, and use the softest terms I can, without either betraying or disguising the truth.

1. In the year 1736 it pleased God to begin a work of grace in the newly planted colony of Georgia, then the southernmost of our settlements on the continent of America. To those English who had settled there the year before, were then added a body of Moravians, so called; and a larger body who had been expelled from Germany by the Archbishop of Salzburg. These were men truly fearing God and working righteousness. At the same time there began an awakening among the English, both at Savannah and Frederica; many inquiring what they must do to be saved, and "bringing forth fruits meet for repentance."

2. In the same year there broke out a wonderful work of God in several parts of New-England. It began in Northampton, and in a little time appeared in the adjoining towns. A

---

* [text from the 1872 edition]

particular and beautiful account of this was published by Mr. Edwards, Minister of Northampton. Many sinners were deeply convinced of sin, and many truly converted to God. I suppose there had been no instance in America of so swift and deep a work of grace, for an hundred years before; nay, nor perhaps since the English settled there.

3. The following year, the work of God spread by degrees from New-England towards the south. At the same time it advanced by slow degrees, from Georgia towards the north. In a few souls it deepened likewise; and some of them witnessed a good confession, both in life and in death.

4. In the year 1738 Mr. Whitefield came over to Georgia, with a design to assist me in preaching, either to the English or the Indians. But as I was embarked for England before he arrived, he preached to the English altogether, first in Georgia, to which his chief service was due, then in South and North Carolina, and afterwards in the intermediate provinces, till he came to New-England. And all men owned that God was with him, wheresoever he went; giving a general call to high and low, rich and poor, to "repent, and believe the gospel." Many were not disobedient to the heavenly calling: They did repent and believe the gospel. And by his ministry a line of communication was formed, quite from Georgia to New-England.

5. Within a few years he made several more voyages to America, and took several more journeys through the provinces. And in every journey he found fresh reason to bless God, who still prospered the work of his hands; there being more and more, in all the provinces, who found his word to be "the power of God unto salvation."

6. But the last journey he made, he acknowledged to some of his friends, that he had much sorrow and heaviness in his heart, on account of multitudes who for a time ran well, but afterwards "drew back unto perdition." Indeed, in a few years, the far greater part of those who had once "received the word with joy," yea, had "escaped the corruption that is in the world," were "entangled again and overcome." Some were like those who received the seed on stony ground, which "in time of temptation withered away." Others were like those who "received it among thorns: "the thorns" soon "sprang up, and choked it." Insomuch that he found exceeding few who "brought forth fruit to perfection." A vast majority had entirely "turned back from the holy commandment delivered to them."

7. And what wonder! for it was a true saying, which was common in the ancient Church, "The soul and the body make a man; and the spirit and discipline make a Christian." But those who were more or less affected by Mr. Whitefield's preaching had no discipline at all. They had no shadow of discipline; nothing of the kind. They were formed into no societies: They had no Christian connection with each other, nor were ever taught to watch over each other's souls. So that if any fell into lukewarmness, or even into sin, he had none to lift him up: He might fall lower and lower, yea, into hell, if he would, for who regarded it?

8. Things were in this state when about eleven years ago I received several letters from America, giving a melancholy account of the state of religion in most of the colonies, and earnestly entreating that some of our Preachers would come over and help them. It was believed they might confirm many that were weak or wavering, and lift up many that were fallen; nay, and that they would see more fruit of their labours in America than they had done either in England or Ireland.

9. This was considered at large in our yearly Conference at Bristol, in the year 1769: And two of our Preachers willingly offered themselves; viz., Richard Boardman and Joseph Pillmoor. They were men well reported of by all, and (we believed) fully qualified for the work. Accordingly, after a few days spent in London, they cheerfully went over. They laboured first in Philadelphia and New-York; afterwards in many other places: And everywhere God was eminently with them, and gave them to see much fruit of their labour. What was wanting before was now supplied: Those who were desirous to save their souls were no longer a rope of sand, but clave to one another, and began to watch over each other in love. Societies were formed, and Christian discipline introduced in all its branches. Within a few years after, several more of the Preachers were willing to go and assist them. And God raised up many natives of the country who were glad to act in connexion with them; till there were two-and-twenty Travelling Preachers in America, who kept their circuits as regularly as those in England.

10. The work of God then not only spread wider, particularly in North Carolina, Maryland, Virginia, Pennsylvania, and the Jerseys, but sunk abundantly deeper than ever it had done before. So that at the beginning of the late troubles there were three thousand souls connected together in religious societies; and a great number of these witnessed that the Son of God hath power on earth to forgive sin.

11. But now it was that a bar appeared in the way, a grand hindrance to the progress of religion. The immense trade of America, greater in proportion than even that of the mother-country, brought in an immense flow of wealth; which was also continually increasing. Hence both merchants and tradesmen of various kinds accumulated money without end, and rose from indigence to opulent fortunes, quicker than any could do in Europe. Riches poured in upon them as a flood, and treasures were heaped up as the sand of the sea. And hence naturally arose unbounded plenty of all the necessaries, conveniences, yea, and superfluities, of life.

12. One general consequence of this was pride. The more riches they acquired, the more they were regarded by their neighbours as men of weight and importance: And they would naturally see themselves in at least as fair a light as their neighbours saw them. And, accordingly, as they rose in the world, they rose in their opinion of themselves. As it is generally allowed,

> A thousand pound supplies
> The want of twenty thousand qualities;

so, the richer they grew, the more admiration they gained, and the more applause they received. Wealth then bringing in more applause, of course brought in more pride, till they really thought themselves as much wiser, as they were wealthier, than their neighbours.

13. Another natural consequence of wealth was luxury, particularly in food. We are apt to imagine nothing can

exceed the luxurious living which now prevails in Great Britain and Ireland. But alas! what is this to that which lately prevailed in Philadelphia, and other parts of North America? A merchant or middling tradesman there kept a table equal to that of a nobleman in England; entertaining his guests with ten, twelve, yea, sometimes twenty dishes of meat at a meal! And this was so far from being blamed by any one, that it was applauded as generosity and hospitality.

14. And is not idleness naturally joined with "fullness of bread?" Doth not sloth easily spring from luxury? It did so here in an eminent degree; such sloth as is scarce named in England. Persons in the bloom of youth, and in perfect health, could hardly bear to put on their own clothes. The slave must be called to do this, and that, and everything: It is too great labour for the master or mistress. It is a wonder they would be at the pains of putting meat into their own mouths. Why did they not imitate the lordly lubbers in China, who are fed by a slave standing on each side?

15. Who can wonder, if sloth alone beget wantonness? Has it not always had this effect? Was it not said near two thousand years ago,

> Quaeritur, Aegisthus quare sit factus adulter?
>
> In promptu causa est; Desidiosus erat.

[The following is Tate's translation of this quotation from Ovid:—

> "The adulterous lust that did Aegisthus seize,
> And brought on murder, sprang from wanton ease."—Edit.]

And when sloth and luxury are joined together, will they not produce an abundant offspring? This they certainly have done in these parts. I was surprised a few years ago at a letter I received from Philadelphia, wherein were (nearly) these words: "You think the women in England (many of them, I mean) do not abound in chastity. But yet the generality of your women, if compared with ours, might almost pass for vestal virgins." Now this complication of pride, luxury, sloth, and wantonness, naturally arising from vast wealth and plenty, was the grand hindrance to the spreading of true religion through the cities of North-America.

II. Let us now see the other wheel of divine providence.

1. It may reasonably be supposed that the colonies in New-England had, from their very beginning, an hankering after independency. It could not be expected to be otherwise, considering their families, their education, their relations, and the connections they had formed before they left their native country. They were farther inclined to it by the severe and unjust treatment which many of them had met with in England. This might well create in them a fear lest they should meet with the like again, a jealousy of their governors, and a desire of shaking off that dependence, to which they were never thoroughly reconciled. The same spirit they communicated to their children, from whom it descended to the present generation. Nor could it be effaced by all the favours and benefits which they continually received from the English Government.

2. This spirit generally prevailed, especially in Boston, as early as the year 1737. In that year, my brother, being detained there some time, was greatly surprised to hear almost in every company, whether of Ministers, gentlemen, merchants, or common people, where anything of the kind was mentioned, "We must be independent! We will be independent! We will bear the English yoke no longer! We will be our own governors!" This appeared to be even then the general desire of the people; although it is not probable that there was at that time any formed design. No; they could not be so vain as to think they were able to stand alone against the power of Great Britain.

3. A gentleman who was there in the following year observed the same spirit in every corner of the town: "Why should these *English* blockheads rule over us?" was then the common language. And as one encouraged another herein, the spirit of independency rose higher and higher, till it began to spread into the other colonies bordering upon New-England. Nevertheless the fear of their troublesome neighbours, then in possession of Canada, kept them within bounds, and for a time prevented the flame from breaking out. But when the English had removed that fear from them, when Canada was ceded to the king of Great Britain, the desire then ripened into a formed design; only a convenient opportunity was wanting.

4. It was not long before that opportunity appeared. The Stamp-Act was passed, and sent over to America. The malcontents saw and pressed their advantage; they represented it as a common cause; and by proper emissaries spread their own spirit through another and another colony. By inflammatory papers of every kind, they stirred up the minds of the people. They vilified, first, the English Ministry, representing them, one and all, as the veriest wretches alive, void of all honesty, honour, and humanity. By the same methods they next inflamed the people in general against the British Parliament, representing them as the most infamous villains upon earth, as a company of base, unprincipled hirelings. But still they affected to reverence the King, and spoke very honourably of him. Not long; a few months after, they treated him in the same manner they had done his ministers and his Parliament.

5. Matters being now, it was judged, in sufficient forwardness, an association was formed between the northern and southern colonies; both took up arms, and constituted a supreme power which they termed the Congress. But still they affirmed, their whole design was to secure their liberty; and even to insinuate that they aimed at anything more, was said to be quite cruel and unjust. But in a little time they threw off the mask, and boldly asserted their own independency. Accordingly, Dr. Witherspoon, President of the College in New-Jersey, in his address to the Congress (added to a Fast-Sermon, published by him, August 3, 1776,) uses the following words:—"It appears now, in the clearest manner, that till very lately those who seemed to take the part of America, in the British Parliament, never did it on American principles. They either did not understand, or were not willing to admit, the extent of our claim. Even the great Lord Chatham's Bill for Reconciliation would not have been accepted here, and did not materially differ from what the Ministry would have consented to." Here it is avowed, that

their claim was independency; and that they would accept of nothing less.

6. By this open and avowed defection from, and defiance of, their mother-country, (whether it was defensible or not, is another question,) at least nine parts in ten of their immense trade to Europe, Asia, Africa, and other parts of America were cut off at one stroke. In lieu of this they gained at first, perhaps, an hundred thousand pounds a year by their numerous privateers. But even then, this was, upon the whole, no gain at all; for they lost as many ships as they took. Afterwards they took fewer and fewer; and in the meantime they lost four or five millions yearly, (perhaps six or seven,) which their trade brought them in. What was the necessary consequence of this? Why, that, as the fountain of their wealth was dammed up, the streams of it must run lower and lower, till they were wholly exhausted; so that at present these provinces are no richer than the poorest parts either of Scotland or Ireland.

7. Plenty declined in the same proportion as wealth, till universal scarcity took place. In a short time there was everywhere felt a deep want, not only of the superfluities, not only of the common conveniences, but even of the necessaries, of life. Wholesome food was not to be procured but at a very advanced price. Decent apparel was not to be had, not even in the large towns. Not only velvets, and silks, and fashionable ornaments, (which might well be spared,), but even linen and woollen clothes, were not to be purchased at any price whatsoever.

8. Thus have we observed each of these wheels apart;—on the one hand, trade, wealth, pride, luxury, sloth, and wantonness spreading far and wide, through the American provinces; on the other, the spirit of independency diffusing itself from north to south.

Let us now observe how each of these wheels relates to, and answers, the other; how the wise and gracious providence of God uses one to check the course of the other, and even employs (if so strong an expression may be allowed) Satan to cast out Satan. Probably, that subtle spirit hoped, by adding to all those other vices the spirit of independency, to have overturned the whole work of God, as well as the British Government, in North-America. But he that sitteth in heaven laughed him to scorn, and took the wise in his own craftiness. By means of this very spirit, there is reason to believe, God will overturn every hindrance of that work.

9. We have seen, how by the breaking out of this spirit, in open defiance of the British Government, an effectual check was given to the trade of those colonies. They themselves, by a wonderful stroke of policy, threw up the whole trade of their mother-country, and all its dependencies; made an Act, that no British ship should enter into any of their harbours; nay, they fitted out numberless privateers, which seized upon all the British ships they could find. The King's ships seized an equal number of theirs. So their foreign trade too was brought almost to nothing. Their riches died away with their trade, especially as they had no internal resources; the flower of their youth, before employed in husbandry, being now drawn off into their armies, so that the most fruitful lands were of no use, none being left to till the ground. And when

wealth fled away, (as was before observed,) so did plenty too;—abundance of all things being succeeded by scarcity of all things.

10. The wheel now began to move within the wheel. The trade and wealth of the Americans failing, the grand incentives of pride failed also; for few admire or flatter the poor. And, being deserted by most of their admirers, they did not altogether so much admire themselves; especially when they found, upon the trial, that they had grievously miscalculated their own strength; which they had made no doubt would be sufficient to carry all before it. It is true, many of them still exalted themselves; but others were truly and deeply humbled.

11. Poverty, and scarcity consequent upon it, struck still more directly at the root of their luxury. There was no place now for that immoderate superfluity either of food or apparel. They sought no more, and could seldom obtain, so much as plain food, sufficient to sustain nature. And they were content if they could procure coarse apparel, to keep them clean and warm. Thus they were reduced to the same condition their forefathers were in when the providence of God brought them into this country. They were nearly in the same outward circumstances. Happy, if they were likewise in the same spirit!

12. Poverty and want struck at the root of sloth also. It was now no time to say, "A little more sleep, a little more slumber, a little more folding of the hands to rest." If a man would not work now, it was plain he could not eat. All the pains he could take were little enough to procure the bare necessaries of life: Seeing, on the one hand, so few of them remained, their own armies having swept away all before them; and, on the other, what remained bore so high a price, that exceeding few were able to purchase them.

13. Thus, by the adorable providence of God, the main hindrances of his work are removed. And in how wonderful a manner;—such as it never could have entered into the heart of man to conceive! Those hindrances had been growing up and continually increasing for many years. What God foresaw would prove the remedy grew up with the disease; and when the disease was come to its height, then only began to operate. Immense trade, wealth, and plenty begot and nourished proportionable pride, and luxury, and sloth, and wantonness. Meantime the same trade, wealth, and plenty begot or nourished the spirit of independency. Who would have imagined that this evil disease would lay a foundation for the cure of all the rest? And yet so it was. For this spirit, now come to maturity, and disdaining all restraint, is now swiftly destroying the trade, and wealth, and plenty whereby it was nourished, and thereby makes way for the happy return of humility, temperance, industry, and chastity. Such unspeakable good does the all-wise God bring out of all this evil! So does "the fierceness of man," of the Americans, "turn to his praise," in a very different sense from what Dr. Witherspoon supposes!

14. May we not observe, how exactly in this grand scene of providence, one wheel answers to the other? The spirit of independency, which our poet so justly terms,

The glorious fault of angels and of gods,

(that is, in plain terms, of devils,) the same which so many call liberty, is over-ruled by the justice and mercy of God, first to punish those crying sins, and afterwards to heal them. He punishes them by poverty, coming as an armed man, and over-running the land; by such scarcity as has hardly been known there for an hundred years past; by want of every kind, even of necessary clothing, even of bread to eat. But with what intent does he do this? Surely that mercy may rejoice over judgment. He punishes that he may amend, that he may first make them sensible of their sins, which anyone that has eyes to see may read in their punishment; and then bring them back to the spirit of their forefathers, the spirit of humility, temperance, industry, chastity; yea, and a general willingness to hear and receive the word which is able to save their souls. "O the depth, both of the wisdom and knowledge of God! How unsearchable are his judgments, and his ways past finding out!"—unless so far as they are revealed in his word, and explained by his providence.

15. From these we learn that the spiritual blessings are what God principally intends in all these severe dispensations. He intends they should all work together for the destruction of Satan's kingdom, and the promotion of the kingdom of his dear Son; that they should all minister to the general spread of "righteousness, and peace, and joy in the Holy Ghost." But after the inhabitants of these provinces are brought again to "seek the kingdom of God, and his righteousness," there can be no doubt, but all other things, all temporal blessings, will be added unto them. He will send through all the happy land, with all the necessaries and conveniences of life, not independency, (which would be no blessing, but an heavy curse, both to them and their children,) but liberty, real, legal liberty; which is an unspeakable blessing. He will superadd to Christian liberty, liberty from sin, true civil liberty; a liberty from oppression of every kind; from illegal violence; a liberty to enjoy their lives, their persons, and their property; in a word, a liberty to be governed in all things by the laws of their country. They will again enjoy true British liberty, such as they enjoyed before these commotions: Neither less nor more than they have enjoyed from their first settlement in America. Neither less nor more than is now enjoyed by the inhabitants of their mother country. If their mother-country had ever designed to deprive them of this, she might have done it long ago; and that this was never done, is a demonstration that it was never intended. But God permitted this strange dread of imaginary evils to spread over all the people that he might have mercy upon all, that he might do good to all, by saving them from the bondage of sin, and bringing them into "the glorious liberty of the children of God!"

132.* ON LAYING THE FOUNDATION OF THE NEW CHAPEL, NEAR THE CITY-ROAD, LONDON

PREACHED ON MONDAY, APRIL 21, 1777

* [text of the 1872 ed.]

"According to this time it shall be said,—What hath God wrought!"

Num. 23:23.

1. We need not now inquire, in what sense this was applicable to the children of Israel. It may be of more use to consider in what sense the words are applicable to ourselves;—how far the people of England have reason to say, "According to this time, what hath God wrought!"

2. A great man, indeed, who I trust is now in a better world, Dr. Gibson, late Lord Bishop of London, in one of his Charges to his Clergy, flatly denies that God has wrought any "extraordinary work" in our nation;—nay, affirms, that to imagine any such thing is no better than downright enthusiasm. It is so, if his Lordship's supposition is true,—if God has not wrought any extraordinary work; but if he really has, then we may believe and assert it, without incurring any such imputation.

3. Yet a still greater man of a neighbouring nation, a burning and a shining light, equally eminent in piety and in learning, partly confirmed the Bishop's supposition; for Bengelius, being asked why he placed the grand revival of religion so late as the year 1836, replied, "I acknowledge all the prophecies would incline me to place it a century sooner; but an insurmountable difficulty lies in the way: I cannot reconcile this to matter of fact; for I do not know of any remarkable work of God which has been wrought upon earth between the years 1730 and 1740." This is really surprising. It is strange that sensible men should know so little of what is done at so small a distance. How could so great a man be ignorant of what was transacted no farther off than England?—especially considering the accounts then published in Germany, some of which were tolerably impartial; nay, considering the particular account which I had sent, as early as the year 1742, to one well known through all the empire, Pastor (afterwards Superintendent) Steinmetz.

4. But has there, indeed, been any extraordinary work of God wrought in England during this century? This is an important question: It is certainly worthy of our serious consideration; and it is capable of being answered to the full satisfaction of every fair inquirer. He may easily be informed, what work it is, and in what manner it has been wrought. It is true, I am in one respect an improper person to give this information; as it will oblige me frequently to speak of myself, which may have the appearance of ostentation: But, with regard to this, I can only cast myself upon the candour of my hearers, being persuaded they will put the most favourable construction upon what is not a matter of choice, but of necessity. For there is no other person, if I decline the task, who can supply my place,—who has a perfect knowledge of the work in question, from the beginning of it to this day. We may consider, First, the rise and progress of this work: Secondly, the nature of it.

I. 1. As to the rise of it. In the year 1725, a young student at Oxford was much affected by reading Kempis's "Christian Pattern," and Bishop Taylor's "Rules of Holy Living and

Dying." He found an earnest desire to live according to those rules, and to flee from the wrath to come. He sought for some that would be his companions in the way, but could find none; so that, for several years, he was constrained to travel alone, having no man either to guide or to help him. But in the year 1729, he found one who had the same desire. They then endeavoured to help each other; and, in the close of the year, were joined by two more. They soon agreed to spend two or three hours together every Sunday evening. Afterwards they sat two evenings together, and, in a while, six evenings, in the week; spending that time in reading the Scriptures, and provoking one another to love and to good works.

2. The regularity of their behaviour gave occasion to a young gentleman of the college to say, "I think we have got a new set of *Methodists*,"—alluding to a set of Physicians, who began to flourish at Rome about the time of Nero, and continued for several ages. The name was new and quaint; it clave to them immediately; and from that time, both those four young gentlemen, and all that had any religious connection with them, were distinguished by the name of *Methodists*.

3. In the four or five years following, another and another were added to the number, till, in the year 1735, there were fourteen of them who constantly met together. Three of these were Tutors in their several Colleges; the rest, Bachelors of Arts or Under-graduates. They were all precisely of one judgment, as well as of one soul; all tenacious of order to the last degree, and observant, for conscience' sake, of every rule of the Church, and every statute both of the University and of their respective Colleges. They were all orthodox in every point; firmly believing, not only the Three Creeds, but whatsoever they judged to be the doctrine of the Church of England, as contained in her Articles and Homilies. As to that practice of the Apostolic Church, (which continued till the time of Tertullian, at least in many Churches,) the having all things in common, they had no rule, nor any formed design concerning it; but it was so in effect. and it could not be otherwise; for none could want anything that another could spare. This was the infancy of the work. They had no conception of anything that would follow. Indeed, they took "no thought for the morrow," desiring only to live today.

4. Many imagined that little society would be dispersed, and Methodism (so called) come to an end, when, in October, 1735, my brother, Mr. Ingham, and I, were induced, by a strange chain of providences, to go over to the new colony in Georgia. Our design was to preach to the Indian nations bordering upon that province; but we were detained at Savannah and Frederica, by the importunity of the people, who, having no other Ministers, earnestly requested that we would not leave them. After a time, I desired the most serious of them to meet me once or twice a week at my house. Here were the rudiments of a Methodist society; but, notwithstanding this, both my brother and I were as vehemently attached to the Church as ever, and to every rubric of it; insomuch that I would never admit a Dissenter to the Lord's Supper, unless he would be re-baptized. Nay, when the Lutheran Minister of the Saltzburgers at Ebenezer, being at Savannah, desired to receive it, I told him, I did not dare to administer it to him, because I looked upon him as unbaptized; as I judged baptism by laymen to be invalid: And such I counted all that were not episcopally ordained.

5. Full of these sentiments, of this zeal for the Church, (from which, I bless God, he has now delivered me,) I returned to England in the beginning of February, 1738. I was now in haste to retire to Oxford, and bury myself in my beloved obscurity; but I was detained in London, week after week, by the Trustees for the Colony of Georgia. In the meantime, I was continually importuned to preach in one and another church; and that not only morning, afternoon, and night, on Sunday, but on week-days also. As I was lately come from a far country, vast multitudes flocked together; but in a short time, partly because of those unwieldy crowds, partly because of my unfashionable doctrine, I was excluded from one and another church, and, at length, shut out of all! Not daring to be silent, after a short struggle between honour and conscience, I made a virtue of necessity, and preached in the middle of Moorfields. Here were thousands upon thousands, abundantly more than any church could contain; and numbers among them, who never went to any church or place of public worship at all. More and more of them were cut to the heart, and came to me all in tears, inquiring with the utmost eagerness, what they must do to be saved. I said, "If all of you will meet on Thursday evening, I will advise you as well as I can." The first evening about twelve persons came; the next week, thirty or forty. When they were increased to about an hundred, I took down their names and places of abode, intending, as often as it was convenient, to call upon them at their own houses. Thus, without any previous plan or design, began the Methodist society in England,—a company of people associating together, to help each other to work out their own salvation.

6. The next spring we were invited to Bristol and Kingswood; where, likewise, Societies were quickly formed. The year following we went to Newcastle-upon-Tyne, and preached to all the colliers and keelmen round it. In 1744, we went through Cornwall, as far as Sennen, near the Land's End; and, in the compass of two or three years more, to almost every part of England. Some time after, we were desired to go over to Ireland; and, in process of time, to every county therein. Last of all, we were invited to Musselburgh, Glasgow, and several other parts of Scotland. But it was in Edinburgh, Glasgow, Dundee, Arbroath, and Aberdeen, that we saw the greatest fruit of our labour.

II. 1. Such was the rise, and such has been the progress, of Methodism, from the beginning to the present time. But you will naturally ask, "What is Methodism? What does this new word mean? Is it not a new religion?" This is a very common, nay, almost an universal, supposition; but nothing can be more remote from the truth. It is a mistake all over. Methodism, so called, is the old religion, the religion of the Bible, the religion of the primitive Church, the religion of the Church of England. This old religion, (as I observed in the "Earnest Appeal to Men of Reason and Religion,") is "no other than love, the love of God and of all mankind; the loving God with all our heart, and soul, and strength, as having first loved us,—as the fountain of all the good we have received, and of all we ever hope to enjoy; and the loving every soul which God hath made, every man on earth as our own soul. This love is the great medicine of life; the neverfailing remedy for all the evils of a disordered world; for all the miseries and vices of men. Wherever this is, there are virtue and happiness going hand in hand; there is humbleness of mind, gentleness, long-suffering, the whole image of God; and, at the same time, a 'peace that passeth all understanding,' with 'joy unspeakable and full of glory.' This religion of love, and joy, and peace, has its seat in the inmost soul; but is ever showing itself by its fruits, continually springing up, not only in all innocence, (for love worketh no ill to his neighbour,) but, likewise, in every kind of beneficence,—spreading virtue and happiness all around it."

2. This is the religion of the Bible, as no one can deny who reads it with any attention. It is the religion which is continually inculcated therein, which runs through both the Old and New Testament. Moses and the Prophets, our blessed Lord and his Apostles, proclaim with one voice, "Thou shalt love the Lord thy God with all thy soul, and thy neighbour as thyself." The Bible declares, "Love is the fulfilling of the Law," "the end of the commandment,"—of all the commandments which are contained in the oracles of God. The inward and outward fruits of this love are also largely described by the inspired writers; so that whoever allows the Scripture to be the Word of God, must allow this to be true religion.

3. This is the religion of the primitive Church, of the whole Church in the purest ages. It is clearly expressed, even in the small remains of Clemens Romanus, Ignatius, and Polycarp; it is seen more at large in the writings of Tertullian, Origen, Clemens Alexandrinus, and Cyprian; and, even in the fourth century, it was found in the works of Chrysostom, Basil, Ephrem Syrus, and Macarius. It would be easy to produce "a cloud of witnesses," testifying the same thing; were not this a point which no one will contest, who has the least acquaintance with Christian antiquity.

4. And this is the religion of the Church of England; as appears from all her authentic records, from the uniform tenor of her Liturgy, and from numberless passages in her Homilies. The scriptural, primitive religion of love, which is now reviving throughout the three kingdoms, is to be found in her Morning and Evening Service, and in her daily, as well as occasional, Prayers; and the whole of it is beautifully summed up in that one comprehensive petition, "Cleanse the thoughts of our hearts by the inspiration of thy Holy Spirit, that we may perfectly love thee, and worthily magnify thy holy name."

5. Permit me to give a little fuller account, both of the progress and nature of this religion, by an extract from a treatise which was published many years ago:—[Farther Appeal, Part III.]

"Just at the time when we wanted little of filling up the measure of our iniquities, two or three Clergymen of the Church of England began vehemently to call sinners to repentance. Many thousands gathered together to hear them; and, in every place where they came, many began to show such concern for religion as they never had done before. Many were in a short time deeply convinced of the number and heinousness of their sins, of their evil tempers, of their inability to help themselves, and of the insignificancy of their outside religion. And from this repentance sprung fruits meet for repentance; the whole form of their life was changed. They 'ceased to do evil, and learned to do well.' Neither was this all; but over and above this outward change they began to experience inward religion; the love of God was shed abroad in their hearts, which they enjoy to this day. They 'love Him, because he first loved us;' and this love constrains them to love all mankind, and inspires them with every holy and heavenly temper, with the mind which was in Christ. Hence it is that they are now uniform in their behaviour, unblamable in all manner of conversation; and in whatsoever state they are, they have learned therewith to be content. Thus they calmly travel on through life, never repining, or murmuring, or dissatisfied, till the hour comes that they shall drop this covering of earth, and return to the Father of spirits."

6. This revival of religion has spread to such a degree, as neither we nor our fathers had known. How *extensive* has it been! There is scarce a considerable town in the kingdom, where some have not been made witnesses of it. It has spread to every age and sex, to most orders and degrees of men; and even to abundance of those who, in time past, were accounted monsters of wickedness.

Consider the *swiftness* as well as extent of it. "In what age has such a number of sinners been recovered in so short a time from the error of their ways? When has true religion, I will not say since the Reformation, but since the time of Constantine the Great, made so large a progress in any nation, within so small a space? I believe hardly can either ancient or modern history afford a parallel instance.

7. "We may likewise observe the *depth* of the work so extensively and swiftly wrought. Multitudes have been throughly convinced of sin; and, shortly after, so filled with joy and love, that whether they were in the body, or out of the body, they could hardly tell; and, in the power of this love, they have trampled underfoot whatever the world accounts either terrible or desirable, having evidenced, in the severest trials, an invariable and tender good-will to mankind, and all the fruits of holiness. Now so deep a repentance, so strong a faith, so fervent love, and so unblemished holiness, wrought in so many persons in so short a time, the world has not seen for many ages.

8. "No less remarkable is the *purity* of the religion which has extended itself so deeply and swiftly: I speak particularly as to the doctrines held by those who are the subjects of it. Those of the Church of England, at least, must acknowledge this; for where is there a body of people, who, number for number, so closely adhere to the doctrines of the Church?

"Nor is their religion more pure from heresy than it is from *superstition*. In former times, wherever any unusual religious concern has appeared, there has sprung up with it a zeal for things that were no part of religion. But it has not been so in the present case; no stress has been laid on anything, as though it was necessary to salvation, but what is plainly contained in the word of God. And of the things contained therein, the stress laid on each has been in proportion to the nearness of its relation to what is there laid down as the sum of all,—the love of God and our neighbour. So pure, both from superstition and error, is the religion which has lately spread in this nation.

9. "It is likewise *rational*. It is as pure from enthusiasm as from superstition. It is true the contrary has been continually affirmed; but to affirm is one thing, to prove is another. Who will prove that it is enthusiasm to love God, yea, to love him with all our heart? Who is able to make good this charge against the love of all mankind? (I do but just touch on the general heads.) But if you cannot make it good, own this religion to be sober, manly, rational, divine.

10. "It is also pure from *bigotry*. Those who hold it are not bigoted to opinions. They would hold right opinions; but they are peculiarly cautious not to rest the weight of Christianity there. They have no such overgrown fondness for any opinions, as to think those alone will make them Christians; or to confine their affection, or esteem, to those that agree with them therein. Nor are they bigoted to any particular branch even of practical religion; they are not attached to one point more than another; they aim at uniform, universal obedience. They contend for nothing circumstantial, as if it were essential to religion; but for everything in its own order.

11. "They dread that *bitter zeal*, that spirit of *persecution*, which has so often accompanied the spirit of reformation. They do not approve of using any kind of violence, on any pretence, in matters of religion. They allow no method of bringing any to the knowledge of the truth, except the methods of reason and persuasion; and their practice is consistent with their profession. They do not, in fact, hinder their dependents from worshipping God, in every respect, according to their own conscience."

But if these things are so, may we not well say, "What hath God wrought!" For such a work, if we consider the *extensiveness* of it, the *swiftness* with which it has spread, the *depth* of the religion so swiftly diffused, and its *purity* from all corrupt mixtures, we must acknowledge cannot easily be paralleled, in all these concurrent circumstances, by anything that is found in the English annals, since Christianity was first planted in this island.

12. It may throw considerable light upon the nature of this work, to mention one circumstance more, attending the present revival of religion, which, I apprehend, is quite peculiar to it. I do not remember to have either seen, heard, or read of anything parallel. It cannot be denied that there have been several considerable revivals of religion in England since the Reformation. But the generality of the English nation were little profited thereby; because they that were the subjects of those revivals, Preachers as well as people, soon separated from the Established Church, and formed themselves into a distinct sect. So did the Presbyterians first; afterwards, the Independents, the Anabaptists, and the Quakers: And after this was done, they did scarce any good, except to their own little body. As they chose to separate from the Church, so the people remaining therein separated from them, and generally contracted a prejudice against them. But these were immensely the greatest number; so that, by that unhappy separation, the hope of a general, national reformation was totally cut off.

13. But it is not so in the present revival of religion. The Methodists (so termed) know their calling. They weighed the matter at first, and, upon mature deliberation, determined to continue in the Church. Since that time, they have not wanted temptations of every kind to alter their resolution. They have heard abundance said upon the subject, perhaps all that can be said: They have read the writings of the most eminent pleaders for separation, both in the last and present century: They have spent several days in a General Conference upon this very question, "Is it *expedient* (supposing, not granting, that it is *lawful*) to separate from the Established Church?" But still they could see no sufficient cause to depart from their first resolution. So that their fixed purpose is, let the Clergy or laity use them well or ill, by the grace of God, to endure all things, to hold on their even course, and to continue in the Church, maugre men or devils, unless God permits them to be thrust out.

14. Near twenty years ago, immediately after their solemn consultation on the subject, a Clergyman, who had heard the whole, said, with great earnestness, "In the name of God, let nothing move you to recede from this resolution. God is with you, of a truth; and so he will be, while you continue in the Church: But whenever the Methodists leave the Church, God will leave them." Lord, what is man! In a few months after, Mr. Ingham himself left the Church, and turned all the societies under his care into congregations of Independents. And what was the event? The same that he had foretold!—They swiftly mouldered into nothing. Some years after, a person of honour told me, "This is the peculiar glory of the Methodists: However convenient it might be, they will not, on any account or pretence whatever, form a distinct sect or party. Let no one rob you of this glorying." I trust none will, as long as I live. But the giver of this advice entirely forgot it in a very short time, and has, almost ever since, been labouring to form Independent congregations.

15. This has occasioned many to ask, "Why do you say the Methodists form no distinct party,—that they do not leave the Church? Are there not thousands of Methodists who have, in fact, left the Church; who never attend the Church Service; never receive the Lord's Supper there; nay, who speak against the Church, even with bitterness, both in public and private; yea, who appoint and frequent meetings for divine service at the same hour? How, then, can you affirm that the Methodists do not leave the Church?"

I am glad of so public an opportunity of explaining this; in order to which, it will be necessary to look back some years. The Methodists at Oxford were all one body, and, as it were, one soul; zealous for the religion of the Bible, of the primitive church, and, in consequence, of the Church of England; as they believed it to come nearer the scriptural and primitive plan than any other national Church upon earth.

When my brother and I returned from Georgia, we were in the same sentiments. And at that time we and our friends were the only persons to whom that innocent name was affixed. Thus far, therefore, all the Methodists were firm to the Church of England.

16. But a good man who met with us when we were at Oxford, while he was absent from us, conversed much with Dissenters, and contracted strong prejudices against the Church: I mean Mr. Whitefield: And not long after he totally separated from us. In some years, William Cudworth and several others separated from him, and turned Independents; as did Mr. Maxfield and a few more, after separating from us. Lastly, a school was set up near Trevecka, in Wales; and almost all who were educated there, (except those that were ordained, and some of them too,) as they disclaimed all connexion with the Methodists, so they disclaimed the Church also: Nay, they spoke of it, upon all occasions, with exquisite bitterness and contempt.

Now, let every impartial person judge whether we are accountable for any of these. None of these have any manner of connexion with the original Methodists. They are branches broken off from the tree: If they break from the Church also, we are not accountable for it.

These, therefore, cannot make our glorying void, that we do not, will not, form any separate sect, but from principle remain, what we always have been, true members of the Church of England.

17. Brethren, I presume the greater part of you also are members of the Church of England. So, at least, you are called; but you are not so indeed, unless you are witnesses of the religion above described. And are you really such? Judge not one another; but every man look into his own bosom. How stands the matter in your own breast? Examine your conscience before God. Are you an happy partaker of this scriptural, this truly primitive, religion? Are you a witness of the religion of love? Are you a lover of God and all mankind? Does your heart glow with gratitude to the Giver of every good and perfect gift, the Father of the spirit flesh, who giveth you life, and breath, and all things; who hath given you his Son, his only Son, that you "might not perish, but have everlasting life?" Is your soul warm with benevolence to all mankind? Do you long to have all men virtuous and happy? And does the constant tenor of your life and conversation bear witness of this? Do you "love, not in word" only, "but in deed and in truth?" Do you persevere in the "work of faith, and the labour of Love?" Do you "walk in love, as Christ also loved us, and gave himself for us?" Do you, as you have time, "do good unto all men;" and in as high a degree as you are able? *Whosoever* thus "doeth the will of my Father which is in heaven, the same is my brother, and sister, and mother." Whosoever thou art, whose heart is herein as my heart, give me thine hand! Come, and let us magnify the Lord together, and labour to promote his kingdom upon earth! Let us join hearts and hands in this blessed work, in striving to bring glory to God in the highest, by establishing peace and good-will among men, to the uttermost of our power! First. Let our hearts be joined herein; let us unite our wishes and prayers; let our whole soul pant

after a general revival of pure religion and undefiled, the restoration of the image of God, pure love, in every child of man! Then let us endeavour to promote, in our several stations, this scriptural, primitive religion; let us, with all diligence, diffuse the religion of love among all we have any intercourse with; let us provoke all men, not to enmity and contention, but to love and to good works; always remembering those deep words, (God engrave them on all our hearts!) "God is love; and he that dwelleth in love dwelleth in God, and God in him!"

133.* Preached on Occasion of the Death of the Rev. Mr. John Fletcher, Vicar of Madeley, Shropshire*

"Mark the perfect man, and behold the upright: For the end of that man is peace."

Ps. 37:37.

In the preceding verses, taken together with this, there is a beautiful contrast between the death of a wicked and that of a good man. "I myself," says the Psalmist, "have seen the ungodly in great power, and flourishing like a green bay tree. I went by and lo, he was gone: I sought him, but his place could nowhere be found." Dost thou desire to be found happy, both in life and in death? Then "keep innocency, and take heed unto the thing that is right; for that shall bring a man peace at the last." The words are rendered in the new translation, with far more force and elegance: "Mark the perfect man, and behold the upright: For the end of that man is peace." It is not improbable that David, while he uttered these words, had a particular instance before his eyes. Such an instance was that of the great and good man whom God has not long ago taken to himself.

In discoursing on these words I purpose, First, briefly to inquire, Who is the person that is here spoken of, "the perfect, the upright man." I will endeavour, Secondly, to explain the promise, "That shall bring a man peace at the last;" or, as it is expressed in the other version, "The end of that man is peace." I will then, with the divine assistance, show a little more at large, in how glorious a manner it was fulfilled in the end of that "perfect and upright man" who has been lately removed from us.

I. 1. I am, First, briefly to inquire who is the person that is here spoken of, "the upright and perfect man." In speaking on this head, I shall not endeavour to describe the character of an upright Jew, such as David himself was, or any of those holy men that lived under the Mosaic dispensation: It more nearly imports us to consider such an upright man as are those that live under the Christian dispensation; such as have lived and died since "life and immortality" have been "brought to light by the gospel."

2. In this sense, he is a perfect and upright man who believes in the name of the Son of God; he is one in whom it has pleased the Father to reveal the Son of his love, and who, consequently, is able to declare, "The life that I now live, I live by faith in the Son of God; who loved me, and gave

---

* [text from the 1872 edition]

himself for me." He is one that finds "the Spirit of God witnessing with his spirit, that he is a child of God," and unto whom Jesus Christ is made of God "wisdom, and righteousness, and sanctification, and redemption."

3. This faith will undoubtedly work by love. Accordingly, every Christian believer has "the love of God shed abroad in his heart, by the Holy Ghost which is given unto him." And, loving God, he loves his brother also; his good-will extends to every child of man. By this, as well as by the fruits of love,—lowliness, meekness, and resignation,—he shows that there is the same "mind in him which was in Christ Jesus."

4. As to his outward behaviour, the upright Christian believer is blameless and unreprovable. He is holy, as Christ that has called him is holy, in all manner of conversation; ever labouring to "have a conscience void of offence toward God and toward man." He not only avoids all outward sin, but "abstains from all appearance of evil." He steadily walks in all the public and private ordinances of the Lord blameless. He is zealous of good works; as he hath time, doing good, in every kind and degree, to all men. And in the whole course of his life he pursues one invariable rule,—"whether he eats or drinks, or whatever he does, to do all to the glory of God.

II. And surely "the end of this man is peace;" the meaning of which words we are now, in the Second place, to consider. I do not conceive this immediately to refer to that glorious peace which is prepared for him in the presence of God to all eternity; but rather to that which he will enjoy in the present world, before his spirit returns to God that gave it. Neither does it seem directly to refer to outward peace, or deliverance from outward trouble; although it is true, many good men, who have been long buffeted by adversity, and troubled on every side, have experienced an entire deliverance from it, and enjoyed a remarkable calm before they went hence. But this seems chiefly to refer to inward peace; even that "peace of God which passeth all understanding." Therefore it is no wonder that it cannot be fully and adequately expressed in human language. We can only say, it is an unspeakable calmness and serenity of spirit, a tranquillity in the blood of Christ, which keeps the souls of believers, in their latest hour, even as a garrison keeps a city; which keeps not only their hearts, all their passions and affections, but also their minds, all the motions of their understanding and imagination, and all the workings of their reason, in Christ Jesus. This peace they experienced in a higher or lower degree, (suppose they continued in the faith,) from the time they first found redemption in the blood of Jesus, even the forgiveness of sins. But when they have nearly finished their course, it generally flows as a river, even in such a degree as it had not before entered into their hearts to conceive. A remarkable instance of this, out of a thousand, occurred many years ago:—Enoch Williams, one of the first of our Preachers that was stationed at Cork, (who had received this peace when he was eleven years old, and never lost it for an hour,) after he had rejoiced in God with joy unspeakable during the whole course of his illness, was too much exhausted to speak many words, but just said, "Peace! peace!" and died.

III. So was the Scripture fulfilled. But it was far more gloriously fulfilled in that late eminent servant of God; as will clearly appear if we consider a few circumstances, First, of his life, and Secondly, of his triumphant death.

1. Indeed we have, as yet, but a very imperfect knowledge of his life. We know little more of his early years, than that he was from his infancy so remarkably regardless of food, that he would scarce take enough to sustain life; and that he had always much of the fear of God, and a real sense of religion. He was born September 12, in the year 1729, at Nyon, in Switzerland, of a very reputable family. He went through the usual course of academical studies in the University of Geneva. One of his uncles, who was at that time a General Officer in the Imperial service, then invited him into the same service, promising to procure him a commission. But just as he came into Germany, the war was at an end. Being so far on his way, he was then invited into Holland by another uncle, who had, a little before been desired by a correspondent in England to procure a tutor for a gentleman's sons. He asked Mr. Fletcher whether he was willing to go into England and undertake this office. He consented, and accordingly went over to England, and undertook the care of Mr. Hill's two sons, at Tern, in Shropshire; and he continued in that office till the young gentlemen went to the University.

2. When Mr. Hill went up to London, to attend the Parliament, he took his lady and Mr. Fletcher with him. While they were dining at St. Alban's, he walked out into the town, but did not return till the coach was set out for London. However, a saddle-horse being left, he came after, and overtook them on the same evening. Mrs. Hill asking him why he stayed behind, he said, "I was walking through the market-place, and I heard a poor old woman talk so sweetly of Jesus Christ, that I knew not how the time past away." "I will be hanged," said Mrs. Hill, "if our tutor does not turn Methodist by and by!" "Methodist, Madam," said he, "pray what is that?" She replied, "Why, the Methodists are a people that do nothing but pray. They are praying all day and all night." "Are they?" said he, "then, with the help of God, I will find them out, if they be above ground." He did, not long after, find them out, and had his desire, being admitted into the society. While he was in town, he met in Mr. Richard Edwards's class, and lost no opportunity of meeting. And he retained a peculiar regard for Mr. Edwards to the day of his death.

3. It was not long before he was pressed in spirit to call sinners to repentance. Seeing the world all around him lying in wickedness, he found an earnest desire

> To pluck poor brands out of the fire,
> To snatch them from the verge of hell.

And though he was yet far from being perfect in the English tongue, particularly with regard to the pronunciation of it, yet the earnestness with which he spake, seldom to be seen in England, and the unspeakably tender affection to poor, lost sinners which breathed in every word and gesture, made so deep an impression on all that heard that very few went empty away.

4. About the year 1753, (being now of a sufficient age,) he was ordained Deacon and Priest, and soon after presented to the little living of Madeley, in Shropshire. This, he had

frequently said, was the only living which he ever desired to have. He was ordained at Whitehall, and the same day, being informed that I had no one to assist me at West-street chapel, he came away as soon as ever the ordination was over, and assisted me in the administration of the Lord's Supper. And he was now doubly diligent in preaching, not only in the chapels of West-street and Spitalfields, but wherever the providence of God opened a door to proclaim the everlasting gospel. This he did frequently in French, (as well as in English,) of which all judges allowed him to be a complete master.

5. Hence he removed into the Vicarage-house at Madeley. Here he was fully employed among his parishioners, both in the town and in Madeley-Wood, a mile or two from it,—a place much resembling Kingswood, almost wholly inhabited by poor colliers [coal miners], and their numerous families. These forlorn ones (little wiser than the beasts that perish) he took great pains to reform and instruct. And they are now as judicious and as well-behaved a people as most of their station in the three kingdoms.

6. But after some time he was prevailed upon by the Countess of Huntingdon to leave his beloved retreat, and remove into Wales, in order to superintend her school at Trevecka. This he did with all his power, instructing the young men both in learning and philosophy; till he received a letter from the Countess, together with the circular letter signed by Mr. Shirley, summoning all that feared God in England to meet together at Bristol at the time of the Methodist Conference, "in order to bear testimony against the dreadful heresy contained in the Minutes of the preceding Conference." Her Ladyship declared, that all who did not absolutely renounce those eight propositions which were contained in the Minutes of that Conference must immediately leave her house. Mr. Fletcher was exceedingly surprised at this peremptory declaration. He spent the next day in fasting and prayer, and in the evening wrote to her Ladyship that he not only could not utterly renounce, but must entirely approve of, all those eight propositions; and therefore had obeyed her order, by leaving her house and returning to his own at Madeley.

7. That circular letter was the happy occasion of his writing those excellent "Checks to Antinomianism," in which one knows not which to admire most, the purity of the language, (such as a foreigner scarce ever wrote before,) the strength and clearness of the argument, or the mildness and sweetness of the spirit which breathes throughout the whole; insomuch that I nothing wonder at a clergyman that was resolved never to part with his dear decrees, who, being pressed to read them, replied, "No, I will never read Mr. Fletcher's writings; for if I did, I should be of his mind." He now likewise wrote several other valuable tracts. Meantime, he was more abundant in his ministerial labours, both in public and private; visiting his whole parish, early and late, in all weathers; regarding neither heat nor cold, rain nor snow, whether he was on horseback or on foot. But this insensibly weakened his constitution, and sapped the foundation of his health; which was still more effectually done by his intense and uninterrupted studies, at which he frequently continued with scarce any intermission, fourteen, fifteen, or sixteen hours a day. Meantime, he did not allow himself necessary food. He seldom took any regular meals, unless he had company; but twice or thrice in four and twenty hours ate some bread and cheese, or fruit; instead of which he sometimes took a draught of milk, and then wrote on again. When one reproved him for this, for not allowing himself a sufficiency of necessary food, he replied, with surprise, "Not allow myself food? Why, our food seldom costs my housekeeper and me less than two shillings a week!"

8. Being informed that his health was greatly impaired, I judged nothing was so likely to restore it as a long journey: So I proposed his taking a journey with me into Scotland, to which he willingly consented. We set out in spring, and after travelling eleven or twelve hundred miles, returned to London in autumn. I verily believe, had he travelled with me a few months longer, he would have quite recovered his health; but being stopped by his friends, he quickly relapsed, and fell into a true pulmonary consumption.

9. But this sickness was not unto death; it was only sent that the glory of the Lord might appear. During the whole course of it, he remained at Newington, and was visited by persons of all ranks; and they all marvelled at the grace of God that was in him. In all his pain, no complaint came out of his mouth; but his every breath was spent, either in praising God, or exhorting and comforting his neighbour.

10. When nothing else availed, he was advised to take a journey by sea and by land into his own country. He did this in company with Mr. Ireland, a well-tried and faithful friend, who loved him as a brother, and thought no pains ill bestowed, if he could preserve so valuable a life. He resided in his own country about a year, and was a blessing to all that were round about him. Being much recovered, he spent some months in France, and then returned in perfect health to Madeley.

11. In the year 1781, with the full approbation of all his friends, he married Miss Bosanquet; of whom, as she is still alive, I say no more at present, than that she was the only person in England whom I judged to be worthy of Mr. Fletcher. By her tender and judicious care his health was confirmed more and more; and I am firmly convinced, that had he used this health in travelling all over the kingdom, five, or six, or seven months every year, (for which never was man more eminently qualified; no, not Mr. Whitefield himself,) he would have done more good than any other man in England. I cannot doubt but this would have been the more excellent way. However, though he did not accept of this honour, he did abundance of good in that narrower sphere of action which he chose; and was a pattern well worthy the imitation of all the parochial Ministers in the kingdom.

12. His manner of life during the time that he and his wife lived together, it may be most satisfactory to give in her own words:—

"It is no little grief to me that my dearly beloved husband has left no account of himself in writing; and I am not able to give many particulars of a life the most angelical I have ever known.

"He was born at Nyon, in the Canton of Berne, in Switzerland. In his infancy he discovered a lively genius, and great tenderness of heart. One day, having offended his father, who threatened to correct him, he kept himself at a distance in the garden, till, seeing his father approach, and fearing his anger would be renewed by the sight of him he ran away; but he was presently struck with a deep remorse, thinking, 'What! Do I run away from my father? What a wicked wretch! It may be, I may live to grow up and have a son that will run away from me!" And it was some years before the impression of sorrow, then made upon him, wore off.

"When he was about seven years old, he was reproved by his nurse-maid saying, 'You are a naughty boy, and the devil takes all such.' After he was in bed, he began to reflect on her words: His heart smote him, and he said, 'I am a naughty boy; and perhaps God will let the devil fetch me away." He got up on the bed and for a considerable time wrestled with God in prayer; till he felt such a sense of the love of God as made him quite easy."

Part of the next paragraph I omit, being nearly the same with what I inserted before.

"When he entered Mr. Hill's family, he did not know Christ in his heart. One Sunday evening, as he was writing some music, the servant came in to make up the fire, and, looking at him said, 'Sir, I am very sorry to see you so employed on the Lord's day.' He immediately put away his music, and from that hour, became a strict observer of that holy day.

"Not long after, he met with a person who asked him to go with her and hear the Methodists. He readily consented. The more he heard, the more uneasy he grew; and, doubling his diligence, he hoped by *doing much* to render himself acceptable to God; till one day hearing Mr. Green, he was convinced he did not know what true faith was. This occasioned many reflections in his mind. 'Is it possible,' said he, 'that I, who have made divinity my study, and have received *the premium of piety* (so called) from the University for my writings on divine subjects,—that I should still be so ignorant as not to know what faith is?' But the more he examined, the more he was convinced: Then sin revived, and hope died away. He now sought by the most rigorous austerities, to conquer an evil nature, and bring heaven-born peace into his soul. But the more he struggled, the more he was convinced that all his fallen soul was sin; and that nothing but a revelation of the love of Jesus could make him a Christian. For this he groaned with unwearied assiduity; till one day, after much wrestling with God, lying prostrate on his face before the throne, he felt the application of the blood of Jesus. Now his bonds were broken, and his free soul began to breathe a pure air. Sin was beneath his feet, and he could triumph in the Lord, the God of his salvation.

"From this time he walked valiantly in the ways of God; and, thinking he had not leisure enough in the day, he made it a constant rule to sit up two nights in a week for reading, prayer, and meditation; in order to sink deeper" into that communion with God which was become his soul's delight. Meantime he took only vegetable food; and for above six months, lived wholly on bread, with milk-and-water.

"Not withstanding the nights he sat up, he made it a rule never to sleep as long as he could possibly keep awake. For this purpose he always took a candle and book to bed with him; but one night, being overcome of sleep before he had put out the candle, he dreamed his curtains, pillow, and cap were on fire, without doing him any harm. And so it was: In the morning part of his curtains, pillow, and cap were burnt. But not an hair of his head was singed. So did God give his angels charge over him!

"Some time after, he was favoured with a particular manifestation of the love of God; so powerful, that it appeared to him as if body and soul would be separated. Now all his desires centred in one, that of devoting himself to the service of his precious Master. This he thought he could do best by entering into Orders. God made his way plain, and he soon after settled in Madeley. He received this parish as from the immediate hand of God, and unweariedly laboured therein, and in the adjacent places, till he had spent himself in his Master's service, and was ripening fast for glory. Much opposition he met with for many years, and often his life was in danger. Sometimes he was inwardly constrained to warn obstinate sinners that if they did not repent, the hand of God would cut them off. And the event proved the truth of the prediction. But, notwithstanding all their opposition, many were the seals of his ministry.

"He had an earnest desire that the pure gospel should remain among his people after he was taken away. For this purpose he surmounted great difficulties in building the house in Madeley-Wood. He not only saved for it the last farthing he had, but when he was abroad, proposed to let the Vicarage-house; designing at his return, to live in a little cottage near it, and appropriating the rent of it for clearing that house.

"Since the time I had the honour and happiness of living with him, every day made me more sensible of the mighty work of the Spirit upon him. The fruits of this were manifest in all his life and conversation; but in nothing more than in his meekness and humility. It was a meekness which no affront could move; an humility which loved to be unknown, forgotten, and despised. [I think this was going to an extreme.] How hard is it to find an eminent person who loves an equal! But his delight was in preferring others to himself. It appeared so natural in him, that it seemed as his meat to set everyone before himself. He spake not of the fault of an absent person but when necessary; and then with the utmost caution. He made no account of his own labours; and perhaps carried to an extreme his dislike of hearing them mentioned.

"Patience is the daughter of humility. In him it discovered itself in a manner which I wish I could either describe or imitate. It produced in him a ready mind to embrace every cross with alacrity and pleasure. And for the good of his neighbour, (the poor in particular,) nothing seemed hard, nothing wearisome. When I have been grieved to call him out of his study, from his closet-work, two or three times in an hour, he would answer, "O, my dear, never think of that; it matters not what we do, so we are always ready to meet the will of God; it is only conformity to this which makes any employment excellent.""

"He had a singular love for the lambs of the flock,—the children; and applied himself with the greatest diligence to their instruction, for which he had a peculiar gift: and this populous parish found him full exercise for it. The poorest met with the same attention from him as the rich. For their sakes he almost grudged himself necessaries, and often expressed a pain in using them, while any of his parish wanted them.

"But while I mention his meekness and love, let me not forget the peculiar favour of his Master in giving him the most firm and resolute *courage*. In reproving sin and daring sinners, he was a "son of thunder;" and regarded neither fear nor favour, when he had a message from God to deliver.

"With respect to his communion with God, it is much to be lamented that we have no account of it from his own pen. But thus far I can say, it was his constant care to keep an uninterrupted sense of the divine presence. In order to this he was slow of speech, and had the exactest government of his words. To this he was so inwardly attentive, as sometimes to appear stupid to those who knew him not; though few conversed in a more lively manner when he judged it would be for the glory of God. It was his continual endeavour to draw up his own and every other spirit to an immediate intercourse with God; and all his intercourse with me was so mingled with prayer and praise, that every employment and every meal, was, as it were, perfumed therewith. He often said, 'It is a very little thing so to hang upon God by faith as to feel no departure from him. But I want to be filled with the fullness of his Spirit.' 'I feel," said he, 'sometimes such gleams of light, as it were wafts of heavenly air, as seem ready to take my soul with them to glory.' A little before his last illness, when the fever began to rage among us, he preached a sermon on the duty of visiting the sick, wherein he said: 'What do you fear? Are you afraid of catching the distemper and dying! O, fear it no more! What an honour to die in your Master's work! If permitted to me, I should account it a singular favour.' In his former illness he wrote thus: 'I calmly wait, in unshaken resignation, for the full salvation of God; ready to venture on his faithful love, and on the sure mercies of David. His time is best, and is my time. Death has lost its sting; and, I bless God, I know not what hurry of spirits is, or unbelieving fears.'

"For his last months, he scarce ever lay down or rose up without these words in his mouth:—

> I nothing have, I nothing am;
> My treasure's in the bleeding Lamb,
> Both now and evermore.

"In one of the letters which he wrote some time since to his dear people of Madeley, some of his words are, "I leave this blessed island for awhile, but I trust I shall never leave the kingdom of God,—the shadow of Christ's cross,—the clefts of the Rock, smitten and pierced for us. There I meet you in spirit; thence, I trust, I shall joyfully leap into the ocean of eternity, to go and join those ministering spirits who wait on the heirs of salvation. And if I am no more allowed to minister to you on earth, I rejoice at the thought that I shall perhaps be allowed to accompany the angels who, if you abide in the faith, will be commissioned to carry you into Abraham's bosom.'

"The thought enlivens my faith! Lord give me to walk in his steps! Then shall I see him again, and my heart shall rejoice, and we shall eternally behold the Lamb together. Faith brings near the welcome moment! And now he beckons me away, and Jesus bids me come!"

I know not that anything can or need be added to this, but Mrs. Fletcher's account of his death, which follows also in her own words:—

"For some time before his late illness he was particularly penetrated with the nearness of eternity. There was scarce an hour in which he was not calling upon us to drop every thought and every care, that we might attend to nothing but drinking deeper into God. We spent much time in wrestling with God, and were led in a peculiar manner to abandon our whole selves into the hands of God, to do or suffer whatever was pleasing to him.

On Thursday, August 4, he was employed in the work of God from three in the afternoon till nine at night. When he came home he said, 'I have taken cold.' On Friday and Saturday he was not well, but seemed uncommonly drawn out in prayer. On Saturday night his fever appeared very strong. I begged him not to go to church in the morning; but he told me, 'It was the will of the Lord;' in which case I never dared to persuade. In reading Prayers, he almost fainted away. I got through the crowd and entreated him to come out of the desk. But he let me and others know, in his sweet manner, that we were not to interrupt the order of God. I then retired to my pew, where all around me were in tears. When he was a little refreshed by the windows being opened, he went on; and then preached with a strength and recollection that surprised us all.

"After sermon he went up to the communion-table with these words, 'I am going to throw myself under the wings of the cherubim, before the mercy-seat.' The service held till near two. Sometimes he could scarce stand, and was often obliged to stop. The people were deeply affected; weeping was on every side. Gracious Lord! how was it my soul was kept so calm in the midst of the most tender feelings? Notwithstanding his extreme weakness, he gave out several verses of hymns, and lively sentences of exhortation. When service was over, we hurried him to bed, where he immediately fainted away. He afterward dropped into a sleep for some time, and, on waking, cried out, with a pleasant smile, 'Now, my dear, thou seest I am no worse for doing the Lord's work: He never fails me when I trust in him." Having got a little dinner, he dozed most of the evening, now and then waking full of the praises of God. At night his fever returned, though not violent; but his strength decreased amazingly. On Monday and Tuesday we had a little paradise together: He lay on a couch in the study, and, though often changing posture, was sweetly pleasant, and frequently slept a good while. When awake he delighted in hearing me read hymns and tracts on faith and love. His words were all animating, and his patience beyond expression. When he had any nauseous medicines to take, he seemed to enjoy the cross, according to a word he used often to repeat, that we are to seek a perfect conformity to the will of God, and leave him to give us what comfort he saw good. I asked him, whether he had any advice to leave me, if he should be taken from me: He replied, 'I have nothing particular to say: The Lord will open all before thee.' I said, 'Have you any conviction that God is about to take you?' He said, 'No; not in particular; only I always see death so inexpressibly near that we both seem to stand on the very verge of eternity.' While he slept a little I besought the Lord, if it was his good pleasure, to spare him to me a little longer; but my prayer seemed to have no wings, and I could not help mingling continually therewith, 'Lord, give me perfect resignation.' This uncertainty made me tremble, lest God was going to put into my hand the bitter cup which he lately threatened my husband. Some weeks before, I myself was ill of the fever. My husband then felt the whole parting scene, and struggled for perfect resignation. He said: 'O Polly, shall I ever see the day when thou must be carried out to bury? How will the little things which thy tender care has prepared for me in every part of the house,—how will they wound and distress me! How is it? I think I feel jealousy! I am jealous of the worms. I seem to shrink at giving my dear Polly to the worms!'

"Now all these reflections returned upon my heart with the weight of a millstone. I cried to the Lord, and those words were deeply impressed on my spirit, "Where I am, there shall my servants be, that they may behold my glory.' This promise was full of comfort to my soul. I saw that in Christ's immediate presence was our home, and that we should find our re-union in being deeply centred in him. I received it as a fresh marriage for eternity. As such I trust for ever to hold it. All that day, whenever I thought of that expression, 'to behold my glory,' it seemed to wipe away every tear, and was as the ring whereby we were joined anew.

"Awaking some time after he said: 'Polly, I have been thinking it was Israel's fault that they asked for *signs*. We will not do so; but abandoning our whole selves into the hands of God, we will lie patiently before him, assured that he will do all things well.'

" 'My dear love,' said I, 'if ever I have done or said anything to grieve thee, how will the remembrance wound my heart, shouldst thou be taken from me!'

"He entreated and charged me, with inexpressible tenderness, not to allow the thought; declaring his thankfulness for our union, in a variety of words written on my heart as with the adamantine pen of friendship, deeply dipped in blood.

"On Wednesday, after groaning all day under the weight of the power of God, he told me he had received such a manifestation of the full meaning of those words, 'God is love,' as he could never be able to tell. 'It fills me,' said he, 'every moment. O Polly, my dear Polly, God is love! Shout, shout aloud! I want a gust of praise to go to the ends of the earth! But it seems as if I could not speak much longer. Let us fix on a sign between ourselves,' (tapping me twice with his fingers;) '—now I mean, God is love; and we will draw each other into God. Observe! By this we will draw each other into God!"

"Sally coming in, he cried out: "O Sally, God is love! Shout, both of you. I want to hear you shout his praise.' All this time,

the medical friend, who diligently attended him hoped he was in no danger; as he had no bad head-ache, much sleep, without the least delirium, and an almost regular pulse. So was the disease, though commissioned to take his life, restrained by the power of God!

"On Thursday his speech began to fail. While he was able, he spoke to all that came in his way. Hearing a stranger was in the house, he ordered her to be called up, though uttering two sentences almost made him faint. To his friendly doctor he would not be silent while he had any power of speech; saying, 'O Sir, you take much thought for my body; give me leave to take thought for your soul.' When I could scarce understand anything he said, I spoke these words, 'God is love.' Instantly, as if all his powers were awakened, he broke out in a rapture, 'God is love! love! love! O for that gust of praise I want to sound!'—Here his voice again failed. He suffered many ways, but with such patience as none but those then present can conceive. If I named his sufferings, he would smile, and make the sign.

"On Friday, finding his body covered with spots, I felt a sword pierce through my soul. As I was kneeling by his side, with my hand in his, entreating the Lord to be with us in this tremendous hour, he strove to say many things, but could not; pressing my hand, and often repeating the sign. At last he breathed out, 'Head of the Church, be Head to my wife!' When, for a few moments, I was forced to leave him, Sally said to him, 'My dear master, do you know me?' He replied, 'Sally, God will put his right hand under you.' She added, 'O my dear master, should you be taken away, what a disconsolate creature will my poor dear mistress be!' He replied, 'God will be her all in all.' He had always delighted much in these words,—

> Jesu's blood, through earth and skies,
> Mercy, free, boundless mercy! cries.

Whenever I repeated them to him he would answer, "Boundless! boundless! boundless!' He now added, though with great difficulty,

> Mercy's full power I *soon* shall prove,
> Loved with an everlasting love.

"On Saturday afternoon his fever seemed quite off; and a few friends standing near the bed, he reached his hand to each, and, looking on a Minister, said, 'Are you ready to assist to-morrow?' His recollection surprised us, as the day of the week had not been named in his room. Many believed he would recover; and one said, 'Do you think the Lord will raise you up?' He strove to answer, saying, 'Raise me in the resur'— meaning in the resurrection. To another, asking the same question, he said, 'I leave it all to God.'

"In the evening the fever returned with violence, and the mucus falling on his throat almost strangled him. It was supposed the same painful emotion would grow more and more violent to the last. As I felt this exquisitely, I cried to the Lord to remove it; and, glory be to his name, he did. From that time, it returned no more. As night drew on, I perceived him dying very fast. His fingers could hardly make the sign (which he scarce ever forgot,) and his speech seemed quite gone. I said, 'My dear creature, I ask not for myself, *I know thy soul*; but for the sake of others, if Jesus is very present with thee, lift thy right hand.' He did. 'If the prospect of glory sweetly opens before thee, repeat the sign.' He immediately raised it again; and, in half a minute, a second time: He then threw it up, as if he would reach the top of the bed. After this, his dear hands moved no more; but on my saving, 'Art thou in much pain?' he answered, 'No.' From this time, he lay in a kind of sleep, though with his eyes open and fixed. For the most part he sat upright against pillows, with his head a little inclining to one side; and so remarkably composed and triumphant was his countenance, that the least trace of death was scarce discernible in it.

"Twenty-four hours he was in this situation, breathing like a person in common sleep. About thirty-five minutes past ten, on Sunday night, August 14th, his precious soul entered into the joy of his Lord, without one struggle or groan, in the fifty-sixth year of his age.

"And here I break off my mournful story: But on my bleeding heart the fair picture of his heavenly excellence will be for ever drawn. When I call to mind his ardent zeal, his laborious endeavours to seek and save the lost, his diligence in the employment of his time, his Christ-like condescension toward me, and his uninterrupted converse with heaven,—I may well be allowed to add, my loss is beyond the power of words to paint. I have gone through deep waters; but all my afflictions were nothing compared to this. Well: I want no pleasant prospect, but upwards; nor anything whereon to fix my hope, but immortality.

"On the 17th, [18th] his dear remains were deposited in Madeley churchyard, amid the tears and lamentations of thousands. The service was performed by the Rev. Mr. Hatton, Rector of Waters-Upton, whom God enabled to speak in a pathetic manner to his weeping flock. In the conclusion, at my request, he read the following paper:

"As it was the desire of my beloved husband to be buried in this plain manner, so, out of tenderness he begged that I might not be present: And in all things I would obey him.

"Permit me then, by the mouth of a friend, to bear my open testimony, to the glory of God, that I who have known him in the most perfect manner, am constrained to declare, that I never knew anyone walk so closely in the ways of God as he did. The Lord gave him a conscience tender as the apple of an eye. He literally preferred the interest of everyone to his own.

"He was rigidly just, but perfectly loose from all attachment to the world. He shared *his all* with the poor, who lay so close to his heart that at the approach of death, when he could not speak without difficulty, he cried out: 'O my poor! what will become of my poor?' He was blessed with so great a degree of humility, as is scarce to be found. I am witness, how often he has rejoiced in being treated with contempt. Indeed, it seemed the very food of his soul to be little and unknown. When he desired me to write a line to his brother, if he died; I replying, 'I will write him all the Lord's dealings with thee;' 'No, no," said he, 'write nothing about me. I only desire to be forgotten. *God is all.*'

His zeal for souls I need not tell *you*. Let the labours of twenty-five years and a martyr's death in the conclusion, imprint it on your hearts. His diligent visitation of the sick occasioned the fever which, by God's commission, tore him from you and me. And his vehement desire to take his last leave of you, with dying lips and hands, gave, it is supposed, the finishing stroke, by preparing his blood for putrefaction. Thus has he lived and died your servant; and will any of you refuse to meet him at God's right hand in that day?

"He walked with death always in sight. About two months ago he came to me and said, 'My dear love, I know not how it is, but I have a strange impression death is very near us, as if it would be some sudden stroke upon one of us. And it draws out all my soul in prayer, that we may be ready.' He then broke out: 'Lord, prepare the soul thou wilt call! And Oh, stand by the poor disconsolate one that shall be left behind!'

"A few days before his departure, he was filled with love in an uncommon manner; saying to me, 'I have had such a discovery of the depth of that word, *God is love*, I cannot tell thee half. O shout his praise!' The same he testified, as long as he had a voice, and continued to testify to the end, by a most lamb-like patience, in which he smiled over death, and set his last seal to the glorious truths he had so long preached among you.

"Three years, nine months, and two days, I have possessed my heavenly—minded husband; but now the sun of my earthly joy is set for ever, and my soul filled with an anguish which only finds its consolation in a total resignation to the will of God. When I was asking the Lord, if he pleased, to spare him to me a little longer, the following promise was impressed on my mind with great power: (In the accomplishment of which I look for our re-union:)—'Where I am, there shall my servants be, that they may behold my glory.' Lord, hasten the hour.

There is little need of adding any farther character of this man of God to the foregoing account, given by one who wrote out of the fullness of her heart. I would only observe, that for many years I despaired of finding any inhabitant of Great Britain, that could stand in any degree of comparison with Gregory Lopez or Monsieur de Renty. But let any impartial person judge, if Mr. Fletcher was at all inferior to them. Did he not experience as deep communion with God, and as high a measure of inward holiness, as was experienced either by one or the other of those burning and shining lights? And it is certain his outward holiness shone before men with full as bright a lustre as theirs. But if any should attempt to draw a parallel between them, there are two circumstances that deserve consideration. One is, we are not assured that the writers of *their* lives did not extenuate, if not suppress, what was amiss in them; and some things amiss we are assured there were, viz., many touches of superstition, and some of idolatry, in worshipping saints, the Virgin Mary in particular: But I have not suppressed or extenuated anything in Mr. Fletcher's character; for, indeed, I knew nothing that was amiss,—nothing that needed to be extenuated, much less suppressed. A second circumstance is, that the writers of *their* lives could not have so full a knowledge of them, as both Mrs. Fletcher and I had of Mr. Fletcher; being eye and ear witnesses of his whole conduct. Consequently, we know that his life was not sullied with any mixture of either idolatry or superstition. I was intimately acquainted with him for above thirty years; I conversed with him morning, noon, and night, without the least reserve, during a journey of many hundred miles. And in all that time I never heard him speak one improper word nor saw him do an improper action.—To conclude: Many exemplary men have I known, holy in heart and life, within fourscore years, but one equal to him I have not known,—one so inwardly and outwardly devoted to God. So unblamable a character in every respect I have not found either in Europe or America; and I scarce expect to find another such on this side of eternity.

But it is possible we all may be such as he was: Let us then endeavour to follow him as he followed Christ!

Norwich, October 24, 1785

FIFTH SERIES

134.* TRUE CHRISTIANITY DEFENDED*

"How is the faithful city become an harlot!"

Isa. 2:21.

1. "When I bring the sword upon a land, saith the Lord, if the watchman blow the trumpet, and warn the people; then whosoever heareth the sound of the trumpet, and taketh not warning; if the sword come and take him away, his blood shall be upon his own head. But if the watchman see the sword come, and blow not the trumpet, and the people be not warned; if the sword come, and take away any person from among them, he is taken away in his iniquity, but his blood will I require at the watchman's hand." (Ezek. 33:2–6.)

2. It cannot be doubted, but that word of the Lord is come unto every Minister of Christ also. "So thou, O son of man, I have set thee a watchman unto the house of Israel: Therefore thou shalt hear the word at my mouth, and warn them from me. When I say unto the wicked, O wicked man, thou shalt surely die: If thou dost not speak to warn the wicked from his way, that wicked man shall die in his iniquity; but his blood will I require at thine hand."

3. Nor ought any man, therefore, to be accounted our enemy because he telleth us the truth: The doing of which is indeed an instance of love to our neighbour, as well as of obedience to God. Otherwise, few would undertake so thankless a task: For the return they will find, they know already. The Scripture must be fulfilled: "Me the world hateth," saith our Lord, "because I testify of it that the deeds thereof are evil."

4. It is from a full, settled conviction, that I owe this labour of love to my brethren, and to my tender parent, [alma mater: The University of Oxford] by whom I have been nourished for now more than twenty years, and from whom, under God, I have received those advantages of which I trust I shall retain a grateful sense till my spirit returns to God who gave

it; it is, I say, from a full conviction that love and gratitude, as well as that dispensation of the gospel wherewith I am entrusted, require it of me, that even I have undertaken to speak on a needful, though unwelcome, subject. I would indeed have wished that some more acceptable person would have done this. But should all hold their peace, the very stones would cry out, "How is the faithful city become an harlot!"

5. How faithful she was once to her Lord, to whom she had been betrothed as a chaste virgin, let not only the writings of her sons, which shall be had in honour throughout all generations, but also the blood of her martyrs, speak;—a stronger testimony of her faithfulness than could be given by words, even

By all the speeches of the babbling earth.

But how is she now become an harlot! How hath she departed from her Lord! How hath she denied him, and listened to the voice of strangers! both,

I. In respect of doctrine; and,

II. Of practice.

I. In respect of doctrine.

1. It cannot be said that all our writers are setters forth of strange doctrines. There are those who expound the oracles of God by the same Spirit wherewith they were written; and who faithfully cleave to the solid foundation which our Church hath laid agreeable thereto; touching which we have His word who cannot lie, that "the gates of hell shall not prevail against it." There are those also, (blessed be the Author of every good gift!) who, as wise master-builders, build thereon, not hay or stubble, but gold and precious stones,—but that charity which never faileth.

2. We have likewise cause to give thanks to the Father of Lights, for that he hath not left himself without witness; but that there are those who now preach the gospel of peace, the truth as it is in Jesus. But how few are these in comparison of those (*hoi kapeleuontes*) who *adulterate* the word of God! how little wholesome food have we for our souls, and what abundance of poison! how few are there that, either in writing or preaching, declare the genuine gospel of Christ, in the simplicity and purity wherewith it is set forth in the venerable records of our own Church! And how are we inclosed on every side with those who, neither knowing the doctrines of our Church, nor the Scriptures, nor the power of God, have found out to themselves inventions wherewith they constantly corrupt others also!

3. I speak not now of those (prototokoi tou Satana_) *first-born of Satan*, the Deists, Arians, or Socinians. These are too infamous among us to do any great service to the cause of their master. But what shall we say of those who are accounted the pillars of our Church, and champions of our faith; who, indeed, betray that Church, and sap the very foundations of the faith we are taught thereby?

---

* [text from the 1872 edition]

* [The following Sermon was found in a mutilated manuscript among Mr. Wesley's papers. It is dated June 24, 1741. A Latin copy of the same Discourse has also been discovered. Mr. Pawson, with great care, copied the former, and I have supplied the deficiencies out of the latter. On collating both Sermons, I find several variations, and though not of any great importance, yet sufficient, in my judgment, to vindicate the propriety of translating and publishing the Latin one, not merely as a matter of curiosity, but of utility. The Sermon, no doubt, was written with the design of being preached before the University of Oxford; but whether it ever were preached there, cannot be determined. A. Clarke.]

4. But how invidious a thing it is to show this! Who is sufficient to bear the weight of prejudice which must necessarily follow the very mention of such a charge against men of so established a character? nay, and who have, indeed, in many other respects, done great service to the Church of God? Yet must every faithful Minister say, God forbid that I should accept any mans person! I dare not give any man flattering tithes, nor spare any that corrupt the Gospel. In so doing my Maker would soon take me away.

5. Let me, however, be as short as may be upon this head; and I will instance only in two or three men of renown, who have endeavoured to sap the very foundation of our Church, by attacking its fundamental, and, indeed, the fundamental doctrine of all Reformed Churches; viz., justification by faith alone.

one of these, and one of the highest station in our Church, hath written and printed, before his death, several sermons, expressly to prove, that not *faith alone*, but *good works* also, are necessary in order to justification. The unpleasing task of quoting particular passages out of them is superseded by the very title of them; which is this: The Necessity of Regeneration, (which he at large proves to imply holiness both of heart and life,) in order to Justification. [Tillotson's Sermons, Vol. 1.]

6. It may appear strange to some, that an angel of the Church of God, (as the great Shepherd terms the overseers of it,) and one so highly esteemed both in our own and many other nations, should coolly and calmly thus speak. But o, what is he in comparison of the great Bishop Bull! Who shall be able to stand, if this eminent scholar, Christian, and Prelate, in his youth wrote and published to the world, and in his riper years defended, the positions that follow?

"A man is said (*ex ergon dikaioutai*) *to be justified by works*; because good works are the condition, according to the divine appointment, established in the gospel covenant, requisite and necessary to a man's justification; that is, to his obtaining remission of sins through Christ." BULLI *Harm. Apost.*, p. 4.

A little after, being about to produce testimonies in proof of this proposition, he says, "The first class of these shall be those who speak of good works in a general sense, as the requisite and necessary condition of justification." Then follow certain texts of Scripture; after which he adds, "Who does not believe that in these scriptures there is an abundance of good works required, which if a man do not perform, he is altogether excluded from the hope of pardon, and remission of sins?"—Ibid., p. 6.

Having introduced some other things, he adds, "Besides *faith*, there is no one but may see that *repentance* is required as necessary to justification. Now, repentance is not one work alone, but is, as it were, a collection of many others: For in its compass the following works are comprehended:—(1.) Sorrow on account of sin: (2.) Humiliation under the hand of God: (3.) Hatred to sin: (4.) Confession of sin: (5.) Ardent supplication of the divine mercy: (6.) The love of God: (7.) Ceasing from sin: (8.) Firm purpose of new obedience: (9.) Restitution of ill-gotten goods: (10.) Forgiving our neighbour his transgressions against us: (11.) Works of beneficence, or alms-giving. How much these things avail to procure remission of sins from God is sufficiently evident from Dan. 4:27; where the Prophet gives this wholesome advice to Nebuchadnezzar, who was at that time cleaving to his sins: 'Redeem [The Bishop translates *PRQ*—*peruk*, with the Vulgate, *redeem*, or *buy off* but the proper and literal meaning is, *break off.* A.C.] your sins by alms-giving, and your iniquities by showing mercy to the poor.' "—Ibid., p. 10.

7. To instance in one point more: All the Liturgy of the Church is full of petitions for that holiness without which, the Scripture everywhere declares, no man shall see the Lord. And these are all summed up in those comprehensive words which we are supposed to be so frequently repeating: "Cleanse the thoughts of our hearts by the inspiration of thy Holy Spirit, that we may perfectly love thee, and worthily magnify thy holy name." It is evident that in the last clause of this petition, all outward holiness is contained: Neither can it be carried to a greater height, or expressed in stronger terms. And those words, "Cleanse the thoughts of our hearts," contain the negative branch of inward holiness; the height and depth of which is purity of heart, by the inspiration of God's Holy Spirit. The remaining words, "that we may perfectly love thee," contain the positive part of holiness; seeing this love, which is the fulfilling of the law, implies the whole mind that was in Christ.

8. But how does the general stream of writers and Preachers (let me be excused the invidious task of instancing in particular persons) agree with this doctrine? Indeed, not at all. Very few can we find who simply and earnestly enforce it. But very many who write and preach as if Christian holiness, or religion, were a purely negative thing; as if, not to curse or swear, not to lie or slander, not to be a drunkard, a thief, or a whoremonger, not to speak or do evil, was religion enough to entitle a man to heaven! How many, if they go something further than this, describe it only as an outward thing; as if it consisted chiefly, if not wholly, in doing good, (as it is called,) and using the means of grace! Or, should they go a little farther still, yet what do they add to this poor account of religion? Why, perhaps, that a man should be orthodox in his opinions, and have a zeal for the constitution in Church and state. And this is all: This is all the religion they can allow, without degenerating into enthusiasm! So true it is, that the faith of a devil, and the life of a Heathen, make up what most men call a *good Christian!*

9. But why should we seek further witnesses of this? Are there not many present here who are of the same opinion? who believe that a good moral man, and a good Christian, mean the same thing? that a man need not trouble himself any further, if he only practises as much Christianity as was written over the Heathen Emperor's gate,—"Do as thou wouldest be done unto;" especially if he be not an infidel, or a heretic, but believes all that the Bible and the Church say is true?

10. I would not be understood, as if I despised these things, as if I undervalued right opinions, true morality, or a zealous regard for the constitution we have received from our fathers. Yet what are these things, being alone? What will they profit

us in that day? What will it avail to tell the Judge of all) "Lord, I was not as other men were; not unjust, not an adulterer, not a liar, not an immoral man?" Yea, what will it avail, if we have done all good, as well as done no harm,—if we have given all our goods to feed the poor,—and have not charity? How shall we then look on those who taught us to sleep on and take our rest, though "the love of the Father was not in us?" or who, teaching us to seek salvation by works, cut us off from receiving that faith freely, whereby alone the love of God could have been shed abroad in our hearts?

To these miserable corrupters of the gospel of Christ, and the poison they have spread abroad, is chiefly owing,

II. Secondly, that general corruption in practice as well as in doctrine. There is hardly to be found (O tell it not in Gath, publish it not in the streets of Askelon!) either the form of godliness, or the power! So is "the faithful city become an harlot!"

1. With grief of heart I speak it, and not with joy, that scarcely is the form of godliness seen among us. We are all indeed called to be saints, and the very name of Christians means no less. But who has so much as the appearance? Take any one you meet; take a second, a third, a fourth, or the twentieth. Not one of them has even the appearance of a saint, any more than of an angel. Observe his look, his air, his gesture! Does it breathe nothing but God? Does it bespeak a temple of the Holy Ghost? Observe his conversation; not an hour only, but day by day. Can you gather from any outward sign, that God dwelleth in his heart? that this is an everlasting spirit, who is going to God? Would you imagine that the blood of Christ was shed for that soul, and had purchased everlasting salvation for it; and that God was now waiting till that salvation should be wrought out with fear and trembling?

2. Should it be said, "Why, what signifies the form of godliness?" we readily answer, Nothing, if it be alone. But the absence of the form signifies much. It infallibly proves the absence of the power. For though the form may be without the power, yet the power cannot be without the form. Outward religion may be where inward is not; but if there is none without, there can be none within.

3. But it may be said, "We have public prayers both morning and evening in all our Colleges." It is true; and it were to be wished that all the members thereof; more especially the elder, those of note and character, would, by constantly attending them, show how sensible they are of the invaluable privilege. But have all who attend them the form of godliness? Before those solemn addresses to God begin, does the behaviour of all who are present show that they know before whom they stand? What impression appears to be left on their minds when those holy offices are ended? And even during their continuance, can it be reasonably inferred from the tenor of their outward behaviour, that their hearts are earnestly fixed on Him who standeth in the midst of them? I much fear, were a Heathen, who understood not our tongue, to come into one of these our assemblies, he would suspect nothing less than that we were pouring out our hearts before the Majesty of heaven and earth. What then shall we say, (if indeed "God is not mocked,") but, "What a man soweth, that also shall he reap?"

4. "On Sundays, however," say some, "it cannot be denied that we have the form of godliness, having sermons preached both morning and afternoon, over and above the morning and evening Service." But do we keep the rest of the Sabbath-day holy? Is there no needless visiting upon it? no trifling, no impertinence of conversation? Do neither you yourself do any unnecessary work upon it, nor suffer others over whom you have any power, to break the laws of God and man herein? If you do, even in this you have nothing whereof to boast. But herein also you are guilty before God.

5. But if we have the form of godliness on one day in a week, is there not on other days what is quite contrary thereto? Are not the best of our conversing hours spent in foolish talking and jesting, which are not convenient? nay, perhaps, in wanton talking too; such as modest ears could not hear? Are there not many among us found to eat and drink with the drunken? And if so, what marvel is it that our profaneness should also go up into the heavens, and our oaths and curses into the ears of the Lord of Sabaoth?

6. And even as to the hours assigned for study, are they generally spent to any better purpose? Not if they are employed in reading (as is too common) plays, novels, or idle tales, which naturally tend to increase our inbred corruption, and heat the furnace of our unholy desires seven times hotter than it was before? How little preferable is the laborious idleness of those who spend day after day in gaming or diversions, vilely casting away that time the value of which they cannot know, till they are passed through it into eternity!

7. Know ye not then so much as this, you that are called moral men, that all idleness is immorality; that there is no grosser dishonesty than sloth; that every voluntary blockhead is a knave? He defrauds his benefactors, his parents, and the world; and robs both God and his own soul. Yet how many of these are among us! How many lazy drones, as if only *fruges consumere nati!* "born to eat up the produce of the soil." How many whose ignorance is not owing to incapacity, but to mere laziness! How few, (let it not seem immodest that even such a one as I should touch on that tender point,) of the vast number who have it in their power, are truly learned men Not to speak of the other eastern tongues, who is there that can be said to understand Hebrew? Might I not say, or even Greek? A little of Homer or Xenophon we may still remember; but how few can readily read or understand so much as a page of Clemens Alexandrinus, Chrysostom, or Ephrem Syrus? And as to philosophy, (not to mention mathematics, or the abstruser branches of it,) how few do we find who have laid the foundation,—who are masters even of logic; who thoroughly understand so much as the rules of syllogizing; the very doctrine of the moods and figures! O what is so scarce as learning, save religion!

8. And indeed learning will be seldom found without religion; for temporal views, as experience shows, will very rarely suffice to carry one through the labour required to be a thorough scholar. Can it then be dissembled, that there is too often a defect in those to whom the care of youth is

entrusted? Is that solemn direction sufficiently considered, (Statut. p. 7,) "Let the tutor diligently instruct those scholars committed to his care in strict morality; and especially in the first principles of religion, and in the articles of doctrine?" And do they, to whom this important charge is given, labour diligently to lay this good foundation? to fix true principles of religion in the minds of youth entrusted with them by their lectures? to recommend the practice thereof by the powerful and pleasing influence of their example? to enforce this by frequent private advice, earnestly and strongly inculcated? to observe the progress, and carefully inquire into the behaviour, of every one of them? in a word, to watch over their souls as they that must give account?

9. Suffer me, since I have begun to speak upon this head, to go a little farther. Is there sufficient care taken that they should know and keep the statutes which we are all engaged to observe? How then is it that they are so notoriously broken every day? To instance only in a few:

It is appointed, as to divine offices and preaching, "That ALL shall publicly attend:—Graduates and scholars shall attend punctually, and continue till all be finished with due reverence from the beginning to the end." (P. 181.)

It is appointed, "That scholars of every rank shall abstain from all kinds of play where money is contended for; such as cards, dice, and bowls; nor shall they be present at public games of this nature." (P. 157.)

It is appointed, "That all (the sons of noblemen excepted) shall accustom themselves to black or dark-coloured clothing; and that they shall keep at the utmost distance from pomp and extravagance." (P. 157.)

It is appointed, "That scholars of every rank shall abstain from alehouses, inns, taverns, and from every place within the city where wine, or any other kind of liquor, is ordinarily sold." (P. 164.)

10. It will be objected, perhaps, that "these are but little things." Nay, but perjury is not a little thing; nor, consequently, the wilful breach of any rule which we have solemnly sworn to observe. Surely those who speak thus have forgotten those words: "Thou shalt pledge thy faith to observe all the statutes of this University. So help thee God, and the holy Inspired Gospels of Christ!" (P. 229.)

11. But is this oath sufficiently considered by those who take it; or any of those prescribed by public authority? Is not this solemn act of religion, the calling God to record on our souls, commonly treated as a slight thing? in particular by those who swear by the living God, that "neither entreaties nor reward, neither hatred nor friendship, neither hope nor fear, induce them to give a testimony to any unworthy person?" (P. 88;) and by those who swear, "I know this person to be meet and fit in morals and knowledge for that high degree to which he is presented?" (P. 114.)

12. Yet one thing more. We have all testified before God, "that all and every the Articles of our Church, as also the Book of Common Prayer, and the ordaining of Bishops, Priests, and Deacons, are agreeable to the word of God." And, in so doing, we have likewise testified, "that both the First and the Second Book of Homilies doth contain godly and wholesome doctrine." But upon what evidence have many of us declared this? Have we not affirmed the thing we know not. If so, however true they may happen to be, we are found false witnesses before God. Have the greater part of us ever used any means to know whether these things are so or not? Have we ever, for one hour, seriously considered the Articles to which we have subscribed? If not, how shamefully do we elude the design of the very compilers, who compiled them "to remove difference of opinion, and to establish unanimity in the true religion!"

13. Have we half of us read over the Book of Common Prayer, and of ordaining Bishops, Priests, and Deacons? If not, what is it we have so solemnly confirmed? In plain terms, we cannot tell. And as to the two Books of Homilies, it is well if a tenth part of those who have subscribed to them, I will not say, had considered them before they did this, but if they have even read them over to this day! Alas, my brethren! How shall we reconcile these things even to common honesty, to plain heathen morality? So far are those who do them, nay, and perhaps defend them too, from having even the form of Christian godliness!

14. But, waving all these things, where is the power? Who are the living witnesses of this? Who among us (let God witness with our hearts) experimentally knows the force of inward holiness? Who feels in himself the workings of the Spirit of Christ, drawing up his mind to high and heavenly things? Who can witness,—"The thoughts of my heart God hath cleansed by the inspiration of his Holy Spirit?" Who knoweth that "peace of God which passeth all understanding?" Who is he that "rejoiceth with joy unspeakable and full of glory?" Whose "affections are set on things above, not on things of the earth?" Whose "life is hid with Christ in God?" Who can say, "I am crucified with Christ; yet I live; yet not I, but Christ liveth in me; and the life that I now live in the body, I live by the faith of the Son of God, who loved me, and gave himself for me?" In whose heart is the "love of God shed abroad, by the Holy Ghost which is given unto him?"

15. Is not almost the very notion of this religion lost? Is there not a gross overflowing ignorance of it? Nay, is it not utterly despised? Is it not wholly set at nought, and trodden under foot? Were any one to witness these things before God, would he not be accounted a madman, an enthusiast? Am not I unto you a barbarian who speak thus? My brethren, my heart bleeds for you. O that you would at length take knowledge, and understand that these are the words of truth and soberness! O that you knew, at least in this your day, the things that make for your peace!

16. I have been a messenger of heavy tidings this day. But the love of Christ constraineth me; and to me it was the less grievous, because for you it was safe. I desire not to accuse the children of my people. Therefore, neither do I speak thus in the ears of them that sit on the wall; but to you I endeavour to speak the truth in love, as a faithful Minister of Jesus Christ. And I can now "call you to record this day, that I am pure from the blood of all men. For I have not shunned to declare unto you all the counsel of God."

17. May the God of all grace, who is longsuffering, of tender mercy, and repenteth him of the evil, fix these things in your hearts, and water the seed he hath own with the dew of

heaven! May he correct whatsoever he seeth amiss in us! May he supply whatsoever is wanting! May he perfect that which is according to his will; and so establish, strengthen, and settle us, that this place may again be a faithful city to her Lord; yea, the praise of the whole earth!

135.* ON MOURNING FOR THE DEAD*

"Now he is dead, wherefore should I fast? Can I bring him back again? I shall go to him, but he shall not return to me."

2 Sam. 12:23.

The resolution of a wise and good man, just recovering the use of his reason and virtue, after the bitterness of soul he had tasted from the hourly expectation of the death of a beloved son, is comprised in these few but strong words. He had fasted and wept, and lay all night upon the earth, and refused not only comfort, but even needful sustenance, whilst the child was still alive, in hopes that God would be gracious, as well in that as in other instances, and reverse the just sentence he had pronounced. When it was put in execution, in the death of the child, he arose and changed his apparel, having first paid his devotions to his great Master, acknowledging, no doubt, the mildness of his severity, and owning, with gratitude and humility, the obligation laid upon him, in that he was not consumed, as well as chastened, by his heavy hand; he then came into his house, and behaved with his usual composure and cheerfulness. The reason of this strange alteration in his proceedings, as it appeared to those who were ignorant of the principles upon which he acted, he here explains, with great brevity, but in the most beautiful language, strength of thought, and energy of expression: "Now he is dead, wherefore should I fast? Can I bring him back again? I shall go to him, but he shall not return to me." "To what end," saith the resigned mourner, "should I fast, now the child is dead? Why should I add grief to grief; which, being a volunteer, increases the affliction I already sustain? Would it not be equally useless to him and me? Have my tears or complaints the power to refix his soul in her decayed and forsaken mansion? Or, indeed, would he wish to change, though the power were in his hands, the happy regions of which lie is now possessed, for this land of care, pain, and misery? O vain thought! Never can he, never will he, return to me: Be it my comfort, my constant comfort, when my sorrows bear hard upon me, that I shall shortly, very shortly, go to him! that I shall soon awake from this tedious dream of life, which will soon be at an end; and then shall I gaze upon him; then shall I behold him again, and behold him with that perfect love, that sincere and elevated affection, to which even the heart of a parent is here a stranger! when the Lord God shall wipe away all tears from my eyes; and the least part of my happiness shall be that the sorrow of absence shall flee away!"

The unprofitable and bad consequences, the sinful nature, of profuse sorrowing for the dead, are easily deduced from the former part of this reflection; in the latter, we have the strongest motives to enforce our striving against it,—a remedy exactly suited to the disease,—a consideration which, duly applied, will not fail, either to prevent this sorrow, or rescue us from this real misfortune.

Grief, in general, is the parent of so much evil, and the occasion of so little good to mankind, that it may be justly wondered how it found a place in our nature. It was, indeed, of man's own, not of God's creation; who may permit, but never was the author of, evil. The same hour gave birth to grief and sin, as the same moment will deliver us from both. For neither did exist before human nature was corrupted, nor will it continue when that is restored to its ancient perfection. Indeed, in this present state of things, that wise Being, who knows well how to extract good out of evil, has shown us one way of making this universal frailty highly conducive both to our virtue and happiness. Even grief, if it lead us to repentance, and proceed from a serious sense of our faults, is not to be repented of; since those who thus sow in tears shall reap in joy. If we confine it to this particular occasion, it does not impair, but greatly assist, our imperfect reason; pain, either of body or mind, acting quicker than reflection, and fixing more deeply in the memory any circumstance it attends.

From the very nature of grief; which is an uneasiness in the mind on the apprehension of some present evil, it appears, that its arising in us, on any other occasion than that of sin, is entirely owing to our want of judgment. Are any of those accidents, in the language of men termed misfortunes, such as reproach, poverty, loss of life, or even of friends, real evils? So far from it, that, if we dare believe our Creator, they are often positive blessings. They all work together for our good. And our Lord accordingly commands us, even when the severest loss, that of our reputation, befals us, if it is in a good cause, as it must be our own fault if it be not, to "rejoice, and be exceeding glad."

But what fully proves the utter absurdity of almost all our grief; except that for our own failings, is, that the occasion of it is always past before it begins. To recal what has already been, is utterly impossible, and beyond the reach of Omnipotence itself. Let those who are fond of misery, if any such there be, indulge their minds in this fruitless inquietude. They who desire happiness will have a care how they cherish such a passion, as is neither desirable in itself; nor serves to any good purpose, present or future.

If any species of this unprofitable passion be more particularly useless than the rest, it is that which we feel when we sorrow for the dead. We destroy the health of our body, and impair the strength of our minds, and take no price for those invaluable blessings; we give up our present, without any prospect of future, advantage; without any probability of either recalling them hither, or profiting them where they are. As it is an indifferent proof of our wisdom, it is still a worse of our affection for the dead. It is the property of envy, not of love, to repine at another's happiness; to weep, because all tears are wiped from their eyes. Shall it disturb us, who call

---

* [text from the 1872 edition]

* Preached at Epworth, January 11, 1726, at the Funeral of John Griffith: A Hopeful Young Man.

ourselves his friends, that a weary wanderer has at length come to his wished-for home? Nay, weep we rather for ourselves, who still want that happiness; even to whom that rest appeareth yet in prospect.

Gracious is our God and merciful, who, knowing what is in man, that *passion*, when it has conquered reason, always takes the appearance of it, lest we should be misled by this appearance, adds the sanction of his unerring commands to the natural dictates of our own understanding. The judgment, perhaps, might be so clouded by passion, as to think it reasonable to be profuse in our sorrow at parting from a beloved object; but Revelation tells us, that all occurrences of life must be borne with patience and moderation,—otherwise we lay a greater weight on our own souls than external accidents can do without our concurrence, with humility,—because from the offended justice of God we might well have expected he would have inflicted much worse, and with resignation,—because we know, whatsoever happens is for our good; and although it were not, we are not able to contend with, and should not therefore provoke, Him that is stronger than we.

Against this fault, which is inconsistent with those virtues, and, therefore, tacitly forbidden in the precepts that enjoin them, St. Paul warns us in express words: "I would not have you to be ignorant, brethren, concerning them which are asleep; that ye sorrow not, even as others who have no hope. For if we believe that Jesus died and rose again, even so them also who sleep in Jesus will God bring with him:— Wherefore, comfort one another with these words." (1 Thess. 4:13, 14, 18.) And these, indeed, are the only words which can give lasting comfort to a spirit whom such an occasion hath wounded. Why should I be so unreasonable, so unkind, as to desire the return of a soul now in happiness to me,—to this habitation of sin and misery; since I know that the time will come, yea, is now at hand, when, in spite of the great gulf fixed between us, I shall shake off these chains and go to him?

What he was, I am both unable to paint in suitable colours, and unwilling to attempt it. Although the chief; at least the most common, argument for those laboured encomiums on the dead, which for many years have so much prevailed among us, is, that there can be no suspicion of flattery; yet we all know, that the pulpit, on those occasions, has been so frequently prostituted to those servile ends, that it is now no longer capable of serving them. Men take it for granted, that what is there said are words of course; that the business of the speaker is to describe the beauty, not the likeness, of the picture; and, so it be only well drawn, he cares not whom it resembles: In a word, that his business is to show his own wit, not the generosity of his friend, by giving him all the virtues he can think on.

This, indeed, is an end that is visibly served in those ill-timed commendations; of what other use they are, it is hard to say. It is of no service to the dead to celebrate his actions; since he has the applause of God and his holy angels, and also that of his own conscience. And it is of very little use to the living; since he who desires a pattern may find enough proposed as such in the sacred writings. What! must one be raised from the dead to instruct him, whilst Moses, the Prophets, and the blessed Jesus are still presented to his view in those everlasting tables? Certain it is, that he who will not imitate these, would not be converted, though one literally rose from the dead.

Let it suffice to have paid my last duty to him, (whether he is now hovering over these lower regions, or retired already to the mansions of eternal glory,) by saying, in a few plain words, such as were his own, and were always agreeable to him, that he was to his parents an affectionate, dutiful son; to his acquaintance, an ingenuous, cheerful, good-natured companion; and to me, a well-tried, sincere friend.

At such a loss, if considered without the alleviating circumstances, who can blame him that drops a tear? The tender meltings of a heart dissolved with fondness, when it reflects on the several agreeable moments which have now taken their flight never to return, give an authority to some degree of sorrow. Nor will human frailty permit an ordinary acquaintance to take his last leave of them without it. Who then can conceive, much less describe, the strong emotion, the secret workings of soul which a parent feels on such an occasion? None, surely, but those who are parents themselves; unless those few who have experienced the power of friendship; than which human nature, on this side of the grave, knows no closer, no softer, no stronger tie!

At the tearing asunder of these sacred bands, well may we allow, without blame, some parting pangs; but the difficulty is, to put as speedy a period to them as reason and religion command us. What can give us sufficient ease after that rupture, which has left such an aching void in our breasts? What, indeed, but the reflection already mentioned, which can never be inculcated too often,—that we are hastening to him ourselves; that, pass but a few years, perhaps hours, which will soon be over, and not only this, but all other desires will be satisfied; when we shall exchange the gaudy shadow of pleasure we have enjoyed, for sincere, substantial, untransitory happiness?

With this consideration well imprinted in our minds, it is far better, as Solomon observes, to go to the house of mourning, than to the house of feasting The one embraces the soul, disarms our resolution, and lays us open to an attack: The other cautions us to recollect our reason, and stand upon our guard and infuses that noble steadiness, and seriousness of temper, which it is not in the power of an ordinary stroke to discompose. Such objects naturally induce us to lay it to heart, that the next summons may be our own; and that since death is the end of all men without exception, it is high time for the living to lay it to heart.

If we are, at any time, in danger of being overcome by dwelling too long on the gloomy side of this prospect, to the giving us pain, the making us unfit for the duties and offices of life, impairing our faculties of body or mind,—which proceedings, as has been already shown, are both absurd, unprofitable, and sinful; let us immediately recur to the bright side, and reflect, with gratitude as well as humility, that our time passeth away like a shadow; and that, when we awake from this momentary dream, we shall then have a clearer view of that latter day in which our Redeemer shall stand upon the earth; when this corruptible shall put on incorruption, and this mortal shall be clothed with immortality; and when we shall sing, with the united choirs of men and angels, "O death, where is thy sting? O grave, where is thy victory?"

136.* On Corrupting the Word of God*

"We are not as many, who corrupt the word of God: But as of sincerity, but as of God, in the sight of God speak we in Christ."

2 Cor. 2:17.

[1.] Many have observed, that nothing conduces more to a Preacher's success with those that hear him, than a general good opinion of his sincerity. Nothing gives him a greater force of persuasion than this; nothing creates either a greater attention in the hearers or a greater disposition to improve. When they really believe he has no end in speaking, but what he fairly carries in view, and that he is willing that they should see all the steps he takes for the attainment of that end,—it must give them a strong presumption, both that what he seeks is good, and the method in which he seeks it.

[2.] But how to possess them with this belief is the question. How shall we bring them to take notice of our sincerity, if they do not advert to it of themselves? One good way, however common, is, frankly and openly to profess it. There is something in these professions, when they come from the heart, strongly insinuating into the hearts of others. The persons of any generosity that hear them find themselves almost forced to believe them; and even those who believe them not are obliged in prudence, not to let their incredulity appear, since it is a known rule,—the honester any man is, the less apt is he to suspect another. The consequence whereof is plain: Whoever without proof, is suspicious of his neighbour's sincerity, gives a probable proof that he judges of *his* heart from the falseness of his own.

[3.] Would not any man be tempted to suspect his integrity, who, without proof, suspected the want of it in another, that had fairly and openly professed the principles on which he acted? Surely none, but who himself corrupted the word of God, or wished that it were corrupted, could lightly suspect either St. Paul of doing it, or any that after him should use his generous declaration: "We are not as many, who corrupt the word of God: But as of sincerity, but as of God, in the sight of God speak we in Christ."

[4.] Not that the Apostle, any more than his followers in preaching the gospel, desires they should wholly rely on his words; for afterwards he appeals to his actions to confirm them. And those who in this can imitate him need not entreat men to believe their sincerity. If our works bear the stamp of it, as well as our words, both together will speak so loudly and plainly, every unprejudiced person must understand that we speak in Christ, as in sincerity, and that in so doing we consider we are in the sight of that God whose commission we bear.

[5.] Those whom the Apostle accuses of the contrary practice, of corrupting the word of God, seem to have been Jews, who owning Jesus to be Christ, and his gospel to be divine, yet adulterated it, by intermingling with it the law of Moses, and their own traditions. And in doing this, their principal view was to make a gain of Christ; which, consequently, laid them under a necessity of concealing the end they proposed, as well as the means they used to obtain it. On the contrary, those who intend the good of mankind, are by no means concerned to hide their intentions. If the benefit we propose in speaking be to ourselves, it is often our interest to keep it private. If the benefit we propose be to others, it is always our interest to make it public; and it is the interest both of ourselves and others, to make public those marks of distinction whence may clearly be known who corrupt the word of God, and who preach it in sincerity.

[I. 1.] The First and great mark of one who corrupts the word of God, is, introducing into it human mixtures; either the errors [heresies] of others, or the fancies of his own brain. To do this, is to corrupt it in the highest degree; to blend with the oracles of God, impure dreams, fit only for the mouth of the devil! And yet it has been so frequently done, that scarce ever was any erroneous [heretical] opinion either invented or received, but Scripture was quoted to defend it. [2.] And when the imposture was too bare-faced, and the text cited for it appeared too plainly either to make against it, or to be nothing to the purpose, then recourse has usually been had to a Second method of corrupting it, by mixing it with false interpretations. And this is done, sometimes by repeating the words wrong; and sometimes by repeating them right, but putting a wrong sense upon them; one that is either strained and unnatural, or foreign to the writer's intention in the place from whence they are taken; perhaps contrary either to his intention in that very place, or to what he says in some other part of his writings. And this is easily effected: Any passage is easily perverted, by being recited singly, without any of the preceding or following verses. By this means it may often seem to have one sense, when it will be plain, by observing what goes before and what follows after, that it really has the direct contrary: For want of observing which, unwary souls are liable to be tossed about with every wind of doctrine, whenever they fall into the hand of those who have enough of wickedness and cunning, thus to adulterate what they preach, and to add now and then a plausible comment to make it go down the more easily.

[3.] A Third sort of those who corrupt the Word of God, though in a lower degree than either of the former, are those who do so, not by adding to it, but taking from it; who take either of the spirit or substance of it away, while they study to prophesy only smooth things, and therefore palliate and colour what they preach, to reconcile it to the taste of the hearers. And that they may do this the better, they commonly let those parts go that will admit of no colouring. They wash their hands of those stubborn texts that will not bend to their purpose, or that too plainly touch on the reigning vices of the place where they are. These they exchange for those more soft and tractable ones, that are not so apt to give offence. Not one word must be said of the tribulation and anguish

---

* [text from the 1872 edition]

denounced against sinners in general; much less of the unquenchable fire, which, if God be true, awaits several of those particular offences that have fallen within their own notice. These tender parts are not to be touched without danger by them who study to recommend themselves to men; or, if they are, it must be with the utmost caution, and a nice evasion in reserve. But they safely may thunder against those who are out of their reach, and against those sins which they suppose none that hear them are guilty of. No one takes it to heart, to hear those practices laid open which he is not concerned in himself. But when the stroke comes home, when it reaches his own case, then is he, if not convinced, displeased, or angry, and out of patience.

These are the methods of those corrupters of the word, who act in the sight of men, not of God. He trieth the hearts, and will receive no service in which the lips only are concerned. But their words have no intercourse with their thoughts. Nor is it proper for them that they should. For if their real intention once appeared, it must make itself unsuccessful. They purpose, it is true, to do good by the gospel of Christ; but it is to themselves, not to others. Whereas they that use sincerity in preaching the gospel, in the good of others seek their own. And that they are sincere, and speak as commissioned officers, in the sight of Him whose commission they bear, plainly appears from the direct contrariety between their practice, and that of the dissemblers above described.

[II. 1.] First. Consider, it is not their own word they preach, but the word of Him that sent them. They preach it genuine and unmixed. As they do not only profess, but really believe, that, "if any man add unto the word of God, He will add unto him all the plagues that are written in it," they are fearful of doing it in the least instance. You have the gospel from them, if in a less elegant manner, yet fair, and as it is; without any mixture of errors [heresy] to pollute it, or misinterpretation to perplex it; [2.] explained in the most natural, obvious manner, by what precedes and what follows the place in question; and commented on by the most sure way, the least liable to mistake or corruption, the producing of those parallel places that express the same thing the more plainly.

[3.] In the next place, they are as cautious of taking from, as of adding to, the word they preach. They dare no more, considering in whose sight they stand, say less, than [or] more, than He has assigned them. They must publish, as proper occasions offer, all that is contained in the oracles of God; whether smooth or otherwise, it matters nothing, since it is unquestionably true, and useful too: "For all Scripture is given by inspiration of God; and is profitable either for doctrine, or reproof, or correction, or instruction in righteousness,"—either to teach us what we are to believe or practise, or for conviction of error, reformation of vice. They know that there is nothing superfluous in it, relating either to faith or practice; and therefore they preach all parts of it, though those more frequently and particularly which are more particularly wanted where they are. They are so far from abstaining to speak against any vice because it is fashionable and in repute in the place Providence has allotted them; but for that very reason they are more zealous in testifying against it. They are so far from abstaining from speaking for any virtue because it is unfashionable and in disrepute where they are placed, that they therefore the more vigorously recommend it.

[4.] Lastly. They who speak in sincerity, and as in the sight of Him who deputes them, show that they do so, by the manner in which they speak. They speak with plainness and boldness, and are not concerned to palliate their doctrine, to reconcile it to the tastes of men. They endeavour to set it always in a true light, whether it be a pleasing one or not. They will not, they dare not, soften a threatening, so as to prejudice its strength, neither represent sin in such mild colours as to impair its native blackness. Not that they do not choose mildness, when it is likely to be effectual. Though they know "the terrors of the Lord," they desire rather to "persuade men." This method they use, and love to use it, with such as are capable of persuasion. With such as are not, they are obliged, if they will be faithful, to take the severer course. Let the revilers look to that; it harms not them: and if they are blamed or reviled for so doing, let the revilers look to that: Let the hearers accommodate themselves to the word; the word is not, in this sense, to be accommodated to the hearers. The Preacher of it would be no less in fault, in a slavish obsequiousness on one side, than in an unrelenting sternness on the other.

[III. 1.] If, then, we have spoken the word of God, the genuine unmixed word of God, and that only; if we have put no unnatural interpretation upon it, but [have] taken the known phrases in their common, obvious sense,—and when they were less known, explained scripture by scripture; if we have spoken the whole word, as occasion offered, though rather the parts which seemed most proper to give a check to some fashionable vice, or to encourage the practice of some unfashionable virtue; and if we have done this plainly and boldly, though with all the mildness and gentleness that the nature of the subject will bear;—then, believe ye our works, if not our words; or rather, believe them both together. Here is all a Preacher can do; all the evidence that he either can or need give of his good intentions. There is no way but this to show he speaks as of sincerity, as commissioned by the Lord, and as in his sight. If there be any who, after all this, will not believe that it is his concern, not our own, we labour for; that our first intention in speaking, is to point him the way to happiness, and to disengage him from the great road that leads to misery; we are clear of the blood of that man;—it rests on his own head. For thus saith the Lord, who hath set us as watchmen over the souls of our countrymen and brethren: "If thou warn the wicked of his way to turn from it;"—much more if we use all methods possible to convince him that the warning is of God;—"if he do not turn from his way,"—which certainly he will not, if he do not believe that we are in earnest,—"he shall die in his iniquity, but thou hast delivered thine own soul."[Section numbers (and other bracketed insertions of more significant textual variants) follow the Bicentennial Edition.]

137.* ON THE RESURRECTION OF THE DEAD**

"But some man will say, how are the dead raised up? and with what body do they come?"

1 Cor. 15:35.

The Apostle having, in the beginning of this chapter, firmly settled the truth of our Saviour's resurrection, adds, "Now if Christ be preached that he rose from the dead, how say some among you, that there is no resurrection of the dead?" It cannot now any longer seem impossible to you that God should raise the dead; since you have so plain an example of it in our Lord, who was dead and is alive; and the same power which raised Christ must also be able to quicken our mortal bodies.

"But some man will say, How are the dead raised up? And with what body do they come?" How can these things be? How is it possible that these bodies should be raised again, and joined to their several souls, which many thousands of years ago were either buried in the earth, or swallowed up in the sea, or devoured by fire?—which have mouldered into the finest dust,—that dust scattered over the face of the earth, dispersed as far as the heavens are wide;—nay, which has undergone ten thousand changes, has fattened the earth, become the food of other creatures, and these again the food of other men? How is it possible that all these little parts, which made up the body of Abraham, should be again ranged together, and, unmixed with the dust of other bodies, be all placed in the same order and posture that they were before, so as to make up the very self-same body which his soul at his death forsook? Ezekiel was indeed, in a vision, set down in a valley full of dry bones, "and he heard a noise, and behold a shaking, and the bones came together, bone to his bone; the sinews and the flesh came upon them, and the skin covered them above, and breath came into them, and they lived, and stood upon their feet." This might be in a vision. But that all this, and much more, should in time come to pass; that our bones, after they are crumbled into dust, should really become living men; that all the little parts whereof our bodies were made, should immediately, at a general summons, meet again, and every one challenge and possess its own place, till at last the whole be perfectly rebuilt; that this, I say, should be done, is so incredible a thing, that we cannot so much as have any notion of it. And we may observe, that the Gentiles were most displeased with this article of the Christian faith; it was one of the last things the Heathens believed; and it is to this day the chief objection to Christianity, "How are the dead raised up? With what body do they come?" In my discourse on these words, I shall do three things:—

I. I shall show, that the resurrection of the self-same body that died and was buried, contains nothing in it incredible or impossible.

II. I shall describe the difference which the Scripture makes between the qualities of a glorified and a mortal body.

III. I shall draw some inferences from the whole.

I. I shall show, that the resurrection of the self-same body that died, contains nothing in it incredible or impossible.

But before I do this, it may be proper to mention some of the reasons upon which this article of our faith is built.

And, 1. The plain notion of a resurrection requires, that the self-same body that died should rise again. Nothing can be said to be raised again, but that very body that died. If God give to our souls at the last day a new body, this cannot be called the resurrection of our body; because that word plainly implies the fresh production of what was before.

2. There are many places of Scripture that plainly declare it. St. Paul, in the 53d verse of this chapter, tells us that "this corruptible must put on incorruption, and this mortal must put on immortality." [1 Cor. 15:53] Now, by this mortal, and this corruptible, can only be meant, that body which we now carry about with us, and shall one day lay down in the dust.

The mention which the Scripture makes of the places where the dead shall rise, further shows, that the same body which died shall rise. Thus we read in Daniel: "Those that sleep in the dust of the earth shall awake; some to everlasting life, and some to shame and everlasting contempt." And, we may likewise observe, that the very phrase, of *sleep* and *awake*, implies, that when we rise again from the dead, our bodies will be as much the same as they are when we awake from sleep. Thus, again, our Lord affirms, (John 5:28, 29,) "The hour is coming in which all that are in the graves shall hear his voice, and shall come forth; they that have done good to the resurrection of life, and they that have done evil to the resurrection of damnation." Now, if the same body do not rise again, what need is there of opening the graves at the end of the world? The graves can give up no bodies but those which were laid in them. If we were not to rise with the very same bodies that died, then they might rest for ever. To this we need only add that of St. Paul: "The Lord shall change this vile body, that it may be fashioned like unto his glorious body. Now, this vile body can be no other than that with which we are flow clothed, which must be restored to life again.

That in all this there is nothing incredible or impossible, I shall show by proving these three things:—1. That it is possible for God to keep and preserve unmixed, from all other bodies, the particular dust into which our several bodies are dissolved, and can gather and join it again, how far soever dispersed asunder. 2. That God can form that dust so gathered together, into the same body as it was before. 3. That when he hath formed this body, he can enliven it with the same soul that before inhabited it.

1. God can distinguish and keep unmixed from all other bodies the particular dust into which our several bodies are dissolved, and can gather it together and join it again, how far soever dispersed asunder. God is infinite both in knowledge and power. He knoweth the number of the stars, and calleth them all by their names; he can tell the number of the sands on the sea-shore: And is it at all incredible, that He should distinctly know the several particles of dust into which the bodies of men are mouldered, and plainly discern to whom they belong, and the various changes they have

---

* [text from the 1872 edition]

undergone? Why should it be thought strange, that He, who at the first formed us, whose eyes saw our substance yet being imperfect, from whom we were not hid when we were made in secret, and curiously wrought in the lowest parts of the earth, should know every part of our bodies, and every particle of dust whereof we were composed? The artist knows every part of the watch which he frames; and if it should fall in pieces, and the various parts of it lie in the greatest disorder and confusion, yet he can soon gather them together, and as easily distinguish one from another, as if every one had its particular mark. He knows the use of each, and can readily give it its proper place, and put them all exactly in the same figure and order they were before. And can we think that the Almighty Builder of the world, whose workmanship we are, does not know whereof we are made, or is not acquainted with the several parts of which this earthly tabernacle is composed? All these lay in one vast heap at the creation, till he separated them one from another, and framed them into those distinct bodies whereof this beautiful world consists. And why may not the same Power collect the ruins of our corrupted bodies, and restore them to their former condition? All the parts into which men's bodies are dissolved, however they seem to us carelessly scattered over the face of the earth, are yet carefully laid up by God's wise disposal till the day of the restoration of all things. They are preserved in the waters and fires, in the birds and beasts, till the last trumpet shall summon them to their former habitation.

"But," say they, "it may sometimes happen that several men's bodies may consist of the self-same matter. For the bodies of men are often devoured by other animals, which are eaten by other men. Nay, there are nations which feed upon human flesh; consequently, they borrow a great part of their bodies from other men. And if that which was part of one man's body becomes afterwards part of another man's, how can both rise at the last day with the same bodies they had before?" To this it may easily be replied, that a very small part of what is eaten turns to nourishment, the far greater part goes away according to the order of nature. So that it is not at all impossible for God, who watches over and governs all this, so to order things, that what is part of one man's body, though eaten by another, shall never turn to his nourishment; or, if it does, that it shall wear off again, and, some time before his death, be separated from him, so that it may remain in a capacity of being restored at the last day to its former owner.

2. God can form this dust, so gathered together, into the same body it was before. And that it is possible, all must own who believe that God made Adam out of the dust of the earth. Therefore, the bodies of men being dust after death, it is no other than it was before; and the same power that at the first made it of dust, may as easily re-make it, when it is turned into dust again. Nay, it is no more wonderful than the forming a human body in the womb, which is a thing we have daily experience of; and is doubtless as strange an instance of divine power as the resurrection of it can possibly be. And were it not so common a thing, we should be as hardly brought to think it possible that such a beautiful fabric as the body of man is, with nerves and bones, flesh and veins, blood, and the several other parts whereof it consists, should be formed as we know it is; as now we are, that hereafter it should be rebuilt when it has been crumbled into dust. Had we only heard of the wonderful production of the bodies of men, we should have been as ready to ask, "How are men made, and with what bodies are they born?" as now, when we hear of the resurrection, "How are the dead raised up, and with what bodies do they come?"

3. When God hath raised this body, he can enliven it with the same soul that inhabited it before. And this we cannot pretend to say is impossible to be done; for it has been done already. Our Saviour himself was dead, rose again, and appeared alive to his disciples and others, who had lived with him many years, and were then fully convinced that he was the same person they had seen die upon the cross.

Thus have I shown that the resurrection of the same body is by no means impossible to God; that what he hath promised he is able also to perform, by that "mighty power by which he is able to subdue all things to himself." Though, therefore, we cannot exactly tell the manner how it shall be done, yet this ought not in the least to weaken our belief of this important article of our faith. It is enough, that He to whom all things are possible hath passed his word that he will raise us again. Let those who presume to mock at the glorious hope of all good men, and are constantly raising objections against it, first try their skill upon the various appearances of nature. Let them explain everything which they see happen in this world, before they talk of the difficulties of explaining the resurrection. Can they tell me how their own bodies were fashioned and curiously wrought? Can they give me a plain account, by what orderly steps this glorious stately structure, which discovers so much workmanship and rare contrivance, was at first created? How was the first drop of blood made; and how came the heart, and veins, and arteries to receive it? Of what, and by what means, were the nerves and fibres made? What fixed the little springs in their due places, and fitted them for the several uses for which they now serve? How was the brain distinguished from the other parts of the body, and filled with spirits to move and animate the whole? How came the body to be fenced with bones and sinews, to be clothed with skin and flesh, distinguished into various muscles? Let them but answer these few questions about the mechanism of our own bodies, and I will answer all the difficulties concerning the resurrection of them. But if they cannot do this without having recourse to the infinite power and wisdom of the FIRST CAUSE, let them know that the same power and wisdom can re-animate it, after it is turned into dust; and that there is no reason for our doubting concerning the thing because there are some circumstances belonging to it which we cannot perfectly comprehend or give a distinct account of.

II. I now proceed to the Second thing I proposed; which was, to describe the difference the Scripture makes between the qualities of a mortal and of a glorified body.

The change which shall be made in our bodies at the resurrection, according to the Scripture account, will consist chiefly in these four things:—1. That our bodies shall be raised immortal and incorruptible. 2. That they shall be raised in glory. 3. That they shall be raised in power. 4. That they shall be raised spiritual bodies.

1. The body that we shall have at the resurrection shall be immortal and incorruptible: "For this corruptible must put on incorruption, and this mortal must put on immortality." Now, these words, *immortal* and *incorruptible*, not only signify that we shall die no more, (for in that sense the damned are immortal and incorruptible,) but that we shall be perfectly free from all the bodily evils which sin brought into the world; that our bodies shall not be subject to sickness, or pain, or any other inconveniences we are daily exposed to. This the Scripture calls "the redemption of our bodies,"—the freeing them from all their maladies. Were we to receive them again, subject to all the frailties and miseries which we are forced to wrestle with, I much doubt whether a wise man, were he left to his choice, would willingly take his again;—whether he would not choose to let his still lie rotting in the grave, rather than to be again chained to such a cumbersome clod of earth. Such a resurrection would be, as a wise Heathen calls it, "a resurrection to another sheep." It would look more like a redemption to death again, than a resurrection to life.

The best thing we can say of this house of earth, is, that it is a ruinous building, and will not be long before it tumbles into dust; that it is not our home,—we look for another "house, eternal in the heavens;" that we shall not always be confined here, but that in a little time we shall be delivered from the bondage of corruption, from this burden of flesh, into the glorious liberty of the sons of God. What frail things these bodies of ours are! How soon are they disordered! To what a troop of diseases, pains, and other infirmities are they constantly subject! And how does the least distemper disturb our minds, and make life itself a burden! Of how many parts do our bodies consist! and if one of these be disordered, the whole man suffers. If but one of these slender threads, whereof our flesh is made up be stretched beyond its due proportion, or fretted by any sharp humour, or broken, what torment does it create! Nay, when our bodies are at the best, what pains do we take to answer their necessities, to provide for their sustenance, to preserve them in health, and to keep them tenantable, in some tolerable fitness for our souls' use! And what time we can spare from our labour is taken up in rest, and refreshing our jaded bodies, and fitting them for work again. How are we forced, even naturally, into the confines of death; even to cease to be;—at least to pass so many hours without any useful or reasonable thoughts, merely to keep them in repair! But our hope and comfort are, that we shall shortly be delivered from this burden of flesh: When "God shall wipe away all tears from our eyes, and there shall be no more death, neither sorrow, nor crying, neither shall there be any more pain; for the former things are passed away." O when shall we arrive at that happy hand where no complaints were ever heard, where we shall all enjoy uninterrupted health both of body and mind, and never more be exposed to any of those inconveniences that disturb our present pilgrimage. When we shall have once passed from death unto life, we shall be eased of all the troublesome care of our bodies, which now takes up so much of our time and thoughts. We shall be set, now undergo to support our lives. Yon robes of light, with which we shall be clothed at the resurrection of the just will not stand in need of those careful provisions which it is so troublesome to us here either to procure or to be without. But then, as our Lord tells us, those who shall be accounted worthy to obtain that world "neither marry nor are given in marriage, neither can they die any more, but they are equal to the angels." Their bodies are neither subject to disease, nor want that daily sustenance which these mortal bodies cannot be without. "Meats for the belly, and the belly for meats; but God will destroy both it and them." This is that perfect happiness which all good men shall enjoy in the other world,—a mind free from all trouble and guilt, in a body free from all pains and diseases. Thus our mortal bodies shall he raised immortal. They shall not only be always preserved from death, (for so these might be, if God pleased,) but the nature of them shall be wholly changed, so that they shall not retain the same seeds of mortality;—they cannot die any more.

2. Our bodies shall he raised in glory. "Then shall the righteous shine as the sun in the kingdom of their Father." A resemblance of this we have in the lustre of Moses's face, when he had conversed with God on the mount. His face shone so bright, that the children of Israel were afraid to come near him, till he threw a veil over it. And that extraordinary majesty of Stephen's face seemed to be an earnest of his glory. "All that sat in the council, looking steadfastly on him, saw his face as it had been the face of an angel." How then, if it shone so gloriously even on earth, will it shine in the other world, when his, and the bodies of all the saints, are made like unto Christ's glorious body! How glorious the body of Christ is, we may guess from his transfiguration. St. Peter, when he saw this, when our Lord's face shone as the sun, and his raiment became shining and white as snow, was so transported with joy and admiration, that he knew not what he said. When our Saviour discovered but a little of that glory which he now possesses, and which in due time he will impart to his followers, yet that little of it made the place seem a paradise; and the disciples thought that they could wish for nothing better than always to live in such pure light, and enjoy so beautiful a sight. "It is good for us to be here: Let us make three tabernacles;"—here let us fix our abode for ever. And if they thought it so happy only to be present with such heavenly bodies, and to behold them with their eyes, how much happier must it be to dwell in such glorious mansions, and to be themselves clothed with so much brightness!

This excellency of our heavenly bodies will probably arise, in great measure, from the happiness of our souls. The unspeakable joy that we then shall feel will break through our bodies, and shine forth in our countenances; as the joy of the soul, even in this life, has some influence upon the countenance, by rendering it more open and cheerful: So Solomon tells us, "A man's wisdom makes his face to shine." Virtue, as it refines a man's heart, so it makes his very looks more cheerful and lively.

3. Our bodies shall be raised in power. This expresses the sprightliness of our heavenly bodies, the nimbleness of their motion, by which they shall be obedient and able instruments of the soul. In this state, our bodies are no better than clogs and fetters, which confine and restrain the freedom of the soul. The corruptible body presses down the soul, and the earthly tabernacle weighs down the mind. Our dull, sluggish, inactive bodies are often unable, or backward, to obey the commands of the soul. But in the other life, "they that wait upon the Lord shall renew their strength; they shall mount up with wings as eagles; they shall run, and not be weary; they shall walk, and not faint:" Or, as another expresses it, "they shall run to and fro like sparks among the stubble." The speed of their motion shall be like that of devouring fire in stubble; and the height of it, above the towering of an eagle; for they shall meet the Lord in the air when he comes to judgment, and mount up with him into the highest heaven. This earthly body is slow and heavy in all its motions, listless and soon tired with action. But our heavenly bodies shall be as fire; as active and as nimble as our thoughts are.

4. Our bodies shall be raised spiritual bodies. Our spirits are now forced to serve our bodies, and to attend their leisure, and do greatly depend upon them for most of their actions. But our bodies shall then wholly serve our spirits, and minister to them, and depend upon them. So that, as by "a natural body" we understand one fitted for this lower, sensible world for this earthly state; so "a spiritual body" is one that is suited to a spiritual state, to an invisible world, to the life of angels. And, indeed, this is the principal difference between a mortal and a glorified body. This flesh is the most dangerous enemy we have: We therefore deny and renounce it in our baptism. It constantly tempts us to evil. Every sense is a snare to us. All its lusts and appetites are inordinate. It is ungovernable, and often rebels against reason. The law in our members wars against the law of our mind. When the spirit is willing, the flesh is weak; so that the best of men are forced to keep it under, and use it hardly, lest it should betray them into folly and misery. And how does it hinder us in all our devotions! How soon does it jade our minds when employed on holy things! How easily, by its enchanting pleasures, does it divert them from those noble exercises! But when we have obtained the resurrection unto life, our bodies will be spiritualized, purified, and refined from their earthly grossness; then they will be fit instruments for the soul in all its divine and heavenly employment; we shall not be weary of singing praises to God through infinite ages.

Thus, after what little we have been able to conceive of it, it sufficiently appears, that a glorified body is infinitely more excellent and desirable than this vile body. The only thing that remains is,

III. To draw some inferences from the whole. And, First, from what has been said, we may learn the best way of preparing ourselves to live in those heavenly bodies; which is, by cleansing ourselves more and more from all earthly affections, and weaning ourselves from this body, and all the pleasures that are peculiar to it. We should begin in this life to loosen the knot between our souls and this mortal flesh; to refine our affections, and raise them from things below to things above; to take 'off our thoughts, and disengage them from present and sensible things, and accustom ourselves to think of, and converse with, things future and invisible; that so our souls, when they leave this earthly body, may be prepared for a spiritual one, as having beforehand tasted spiritual delights, and being in some degree acquainted with the things which we then shall meet with. A soul wholly taken up with this earthly body is not fit for the glorious mansions above. A sensual mind is so wedded to bodily pleasures, that it cannot enjoy itself without them; and it is not able to relish any other, though infinitely to be preferred before them. Nay, such as follow the inclinations of their fleshly appetites, are so far unfit for heavenly joys, that they would, esteem it the greatest unhappiness to he clothed with a spiritual body. It would be like clothing a beggar in the robes of a king. Such glorious bodies would be uneasy to them, they would not know what to do in them, they would be glad to retire and put on their rags again. But when we are washed from the guilt of our sins, and cleansed from all filthiness of flesh and spirit, by faith in the Lord Jesus Christ, then we shall long to be dissolved, and to be with our exalted Saviour; we shall be always ready to take wing for the other world, where we shall at last have a body suited to our spiritual appetites.

2. From hence we may see how to account for the different degrees of glory in the heavenly world. For although all the children of God shall have glorious bodies, yet the glory of them all shall not be equal. "As one star differeth from another star in glory, so also is the resurrection of the dead." They shall all shine as stars; but those who, by a constant diligence in well-doing, have attained to a higher measure of purity than others, shall shine more bright than others. They shall appear as more glorious stars. It is certain that the most heavenly bodies will be given to the most heavenly souls; so that this is no little encouragement to us to make the greatest progress we possibly can in the knowledge and love of God, since the more we are weaned from the things of the earth now, the more glorious will our bodies be at the resurrection.

3. Let this consideration engage us patiently to bear whatever troubles we may be exercised with in the present life. The time of our eternal redemption draweth nigh. Let us hold out a little longer, and all tears hall be wiped from our eyes, and we shall never sigh nor sorrow any more. And how soon shall we forget all we endured in this earthly tabernacle, when once we are clothed with that house which is from above! We are now but on our journey towards home, and so must expect to struggle with many difficulties; but it will not he long ere we come to our journey's end, and that will make amends for all. We shall then be in a quiet and safe harbour, out of the reach of all storms and dangers. We shall then be at home in our Father's house, no longer exposed to the inconveniences which, so long as we abide abroad in these tents, we are subject to. And let us not forfeit all this happiness, for want of a little more patience. Only let us hold out to the end, and we shall receive an abundant recompence for all the trouble arid uneasiness of our passage which shall be endless rest and peace.

Let this especially, fortify us against the fear of death: It is now disarmed, and can do us no hurt. It divides us, indeed, from this body awhile; but it is only that we may receive it again more glorious. As God, therefore, said once to Jacob, "Fear not to go down into Egypt, for I will go down with thee, and will surely bring thee up again;" so may I say to all who are born of God, "Fear not to go down into the grave; lay down your heads in the dust; for God will certainly bring you up again, and that in a much more glorious manner." Only "be ye steadfast and unmovable, always abounding in the work of the Lord;" and then let death prevail over, and pull down, this house of clay; since God hath undertaken to rear it up again, infinitely more beautiful, strong, and useful.

138.* ON GRIEVING THE HOLY SPIRIT

"Grieve not the Holy Spirit of God, whereby ye are sealed unto the day of redemption."

Eph. 4:30.

There can be no point of greater importance to him who knows that it is the Holy Spirit which leads us into all truth and into all holiness, than to consider with what temper of soul we are to entertain his divine presence; so as not either to drive him from us, or to disappoint him of the gracious ends for which his abode with us is designed; which is not the amusement of our understanding, but the conversion and entire sanctification of our hearts and lives.

These words of the Apostle contain a most serious and affectionate exhortation to this purpose. "Grieve. not the Holy Spirit of God, whereby ye are sealed unto the day of redemption."

The title "holy," applied to the Spirit of God, does not only denote that he is holy in his own nature, but that he makes us so; that he is the great fountain of holiness to his church; the Spirit from whence flows all the grace and virtue, by which the stains of guilt are cleansed, and we are renewed in all holy dispositions, and again bear the image of our Creator. Great reason, therefore, there was for the Apostle to give this solemn charge concerning it, and the highest obligation lies upon us all to consider it with the deepest attention; which that we may the more effectually do, I shall inquire,

      I.   In what sense the Spirit of God is said to be grieved at the sins of men:

      II.   By what kind of sin he is more especially grieved.

      III.   I shall endeavour to show the force of the Apostle's argument against grieving the Holy Spirit,— "By whom we are sealed to the day of redemption."

I. I am, First, to inquire, in what sense the Spirit of God may be said to be grieved with the sins of men. There is not anything of what we properly call passion in God. But there is something of an infinitely higher kind: Some motions of his will, which are more strong and vigorous than can be conceived by men; and although they have not the nature of human passions, yet will answer the ends of them. By grief, therefore, we are to understand, a disposition in God's will,

flowing at once from his boundless love to the persons of men, and his infinite abhorrence of their sins. And in this restrained sense it is here applied to the Spirit of God in the words of the Apostle.

And the reasons for which it is peculiarly applied to him are, First, because he is more immediately present with us; Second, because our sins are so many contempts of this highest expression of his love, and disappoint the Holy Spirit in his last remedy; and, Third, because, by this ungrateful dealing, we provoke him to withdraw from us.

1. We are said to grieve the Holy Spirit by our sins, because of his immediate presence with us. They are more directly committed under his eye, and are, therefore, more highly offensive to him. He is pleased to look upon professing Christians as more peculiarly separated to his honour; nay, we are so closely united to him, that we are said to be "one spirit with him;" and, therefore, every sin which we now commit, besides its own proper guilt, carries in it a fresh and infinitely high provocation. "Know ye not your own selves," saith St. Paul, "that your bodies are the temples of the Holy Ghost?" And how are they so, but by his inhabitation and intimate presence with our souls? When, therefore, we set up the idols of earthly inclinations in our hearts, (which are properly his altar,) and bow down ourselves to serve those vicious passions which we ought to sacrifice to his will,—this must needs be, in the highest degree, offensive and grievous to him. "For what concord is there between" the Holy Spirit "and Belial? or what agreement hath the temple of God with idols?"

2. We grieve the Holy Spirit by our sins, because they are so many contempts of the highest expression of his love, and disappoint him in his last remedy whereby he is pleased to endeavour our recovery. And thus every sin we now commit is done in despite of all his powerful assistances, in defiance of his reproofs,—an ungrateful return for infinite lovingkindness!

As the Holy Spirit is the immediate minister of God's will upon earth, and transacts all the great affairs of the Church of Christ,—if while he pours out the riches of his grace upon us, be finds them all unsuccessful, no wonder if he appeals to all the world, in the words of the Prophet, against our ingratitude: "And now, O ye men of Judah, judge between me and my vineyard. What could have been done more to my vineyard that I have not done in it? Wherefore, when I looked that it should bring forth grapes, brought it forth wild grapes?" These, and many more such, which we meet with in the Holy Scriptures, are the highest expressions of the deepest concern; such as imply the utmost unwillingness to deal severely even with those whom yet, by all the wise methods of his grace, he could not reform. The Holy Spirit here represents himself as one who would be glad to spare sinners if he could; and therefore we may be sure it is grievous to him that by their sins they will not suffer him.

For men thus to disappoint the Holy Spirit of Love,—for that too is his peculiar title,—to make him thus wait that he may be gracious, and pay attendance on us through our

---

* (Written in the year 1733)

whole course of folly and vanity, and to stand by, and be a witness of our stubbornness, with the importunate offers of infinite kindness in his hands,—is a practice of such a nature that no gracious mind can hear the thoughts of it. It is an argument of God's unbounded mercy, that he is pleased to express, that he is only grieved at it; that his indignation does not flame out against those who are thus basely ungrateful, and consume them in a moment.

It was such ingratitude as this in the Jews, after numberless experiences of his extraordinary mercies towards them, that made infinite love, at last, turn in bitterness to reward them according to their doings; as we find the account given by the Prophets, in the most affecting and lively manner. And surely, considering the much greater obligations he hath laid on us, who enjoy the highest privileges, we may be sure that our sinful and untoward behaviour will, at last, be as great as the mercies we have abused.

There is no doubt but God observes all the sons of men, and his wrath abides on every worker of iniquity. But it is the unfaithful professor who has known his pardoning love, that grieves his Holy Spirit; which implies a peculiar baseness in our sins. A man may be provoked, indeed, by the wrongs of his enemy; but he is properly grieved by the offences of his friend. And, therefore, besides our other obligations, our very near relation to God, as being his friends and children, would, if we had a spark of gratitude in our souls, be a powerful restraint upon us, in preserving us from evil.

3. But if arguments of this kind are not strong enough to keep us from grieving our best Friend, the Holy Spirit of God, let us consider, that, by this ungrateful conduct, we shall provoke him to withdraw from us.

The truth of this, almost all who have ever tasted of the good gifts of the Holy Spirit must have experienced. It is to be hoped that we have had, some time or other, so lively a sense of his holy influence upon us, as that when we have been so unhappy as to offend him, we could easily perceive the change in our souls, in that darkness, distress, and despondency which more especially follow the commission of wilful and presumptuous sins. At those seasons, the blessed Spirit retired and concealed his presence from us, we were justly left to a sense of our own wretchedness and misery, till we humbled ourselves before the Lord, and by deep repentance and active faith obtained a return of divine mercy and peace.

And the more frequently we offend him, the more we weaken his influences in our souls. For frequent breaches will necessarily occasion estrangement between us; and it is impossible that our intercourse with him can be cordial, when it is disturbed by repeated interruptions. So a man will forgive his friend a great many imprudences, and some wilful transgresions; but to find him frequently affronting him, all his kindness will wear off by degrees; and the warmth of his affection, even towards him who had the greatest share of it, will die away; as he cannot but think that such a one does not any longer either desire or deserve to maintain a friendship with him.

II. I come now to consider by what kinds of sin the Holy Spirit is more especially grieved. These sins are, in general], such as either at first wholly disappoint his grace of its due effect upon our souls, or are afterwards directly contrary to his gracious and merciful assistances. Of the former sort, I shall only mention, at present, inconsiderateness; of the latter, sins of presumption.

The First I shall mention, as being more especially grievous to the Holy Spirit, is inconsiderateness and inadvertence to his holy motions within us. There is a particular frame and temper of soul, a sobriety of mind, without which the Spirit of God will not concur in the purifying of our hearts. It is in our power, through his preventing and assisting grace, to prepare this in ourselves; and he expects we should, this being the foundation of all his after-works. Now, this consists in preserving our minds in a cool and serious disposition, in regulating and calming our affections, and calling in and checking the inordinate pursuits of our passions after the vanities and pleasures of this world; the doing of which is of such importance, that the very reason why men profit so little under the most powerful means, is, that they do not look enough within themselves, they do not observe and watch the discords and imperfections of their own spirit nor attend with care to the directions and remedies which the Holy Spirit is always ready to suggest. Men are generally lost in the hurry of life, in the business or pleasures of it, and seem to think that their regeneration, their new nature, will spring and grow up within them, with as little care and thought of their own as their bodies were conceived and have attained their full strength and stature; whereas, there is nothing more certain than that the Holy Spirit will not purify our nature, unless we carefully attend to his motions, which are lost upon us while, in the Prophet's language, we "scatter away our time,"—while we squander away our thoughts upon unnecessary things, and leave our spiritual improvement, the one thing needful, quite unthought of and neglected.

There are many persons who, in the main of their lives, are regular in their conversation, and observe the means of improvement, and attend upon the holy sacrament with exactness; who yet, in the intervals of their duties, give too great liberty to their thoughts, affections, and discourse: They seem to adjourn the great business of salvation to the next hour of devotion. If these professors lose so much in their spiritual estate for want of adjusting and balancing their accounts, what then must we think of those who scarce ever bestow a serious thought upon their eternal welfare? Surely there is not any temper of mind less a friend to the spirit of religion, than a thoughtless and inconsiderate one, that, by a natural succession of strong and vain affections shuts out everything useful from their souls, till, at length, they are overtaken by a fatal lethargy; they lose sight of all danger, and become insensible of divine convictions; and, in consequence, quite disappoint all the blessed means of restoration. If, therefore, we measure the Holy Spirit's concern at the sins of men by the degrees of his disappointment, we may conclude, that there is no state of mind that grieves him more, unless that of actual wickedness.

Presumptuous sins are, indeed, in the highest manner offensive to the Holy Spirit of God. They are instances of open enmity against him, and have all the guilt of open rebellion. The wilful sinner is not ignorant or surprised, but knowingly fights against God's express commandment, and the lively, full, and present conviction of his own mind and conscience; so that this is the very standard of iniquity. And all other kinds of sins are more or less heinous, as they are nearer or farther off from sins of this dreadful nature; inasmuch as these imply the greatest opposition to God's will, contempt of his mercy, and defiance of his justice. This, if any thing can, doubtless, must so grieve him as to make him wholly withdraw his gracious presence.

III. I come now to show the force of the Apostle's argument against grieving the Holy Spirit,—Because we "are sealed to the day of redemption."

By "the day of redemption" may be meant, either the time of our leaving these bodies at death, or, of our taking them again at the general resurrection. Though here it probably means the latter; in which sense the Apostle uses the word in another place: "Waiting for the adoption, to wit, the redemption of our bodies." And to this day of redemption we are sealed by the Holy Spirit these three ways:—

1. By receiving his real stamp upon our souls; by being made the partakers of the divine nature.

2. By receiving him as a mark of God's property; as a sign that we belong to Christ. And,

3. As an earnest and assurance to our own spirits, that we have a title to eternal happiness.

And, First, we are sealed by the Holy Spirit of God, by our receiving his real stamp upon our souls; being made the partakers of the divine nature, and "meet for the inheritance of the saints in light." This is, indeed, the design of his dwelling in us, to heal our disordered souls, and to restore that image of his upon our nature, which is so defaced by our original and actual corruptions. And until our spirits are, in some measure, thus renewed, we can have no communion with him. For "if we say that we have fellowship with him, and walk in darkness, we lie, and do not the truth." But by the renewal of our minds in the image of Him that created us, we are still more capable of his influences; and by means of a daily intercourse with him, we are more and more transformed into his likeness, till we are satisfied with it.

This likeness to God, this conformity of our will and affections to his will, is, properly speaking, holiness; and to produce this in us, is the proper end and design of all the influences of the Holy Spirit. By means of his presence with us, we receive from him a great fulness of holy virtues; we take such features of resemblance in our spirits as correspond to his original perfections. And thus we are sealed by him, in the first sense, by way of preparation for our day of redemption.

And since we are so, and our new nature thus grows up under the same power of his hands, what do we, when we grieve him by our sins, but undo and destroy his work? We frustrate his designs by breaking down the fences which he had been trying to raise against the overflowings of corruption; so that, at last, we entirely defeat all his gracious measures for our salvation.

2. We are sealed by the Holy Spirit unto the day of redemption, as a sign of God's property in us, and as a mark that we belong to Christ. And this is, by his appointment, the condition and security of that future happiness, into which he will admit none but those who have received the Spirit of his Son into their hearts. But in whomsoever he finds this mark and character, when he shall come to judge the world, these will he take to himself, and will not suffer the destroyer to hurt them. To this very purpose the Prophet Malachi, speaking of those who feared God, says, "They shall be mine, saith the Lord, in the day when I make up my jewels;"—that is to say, when I set my seal and mark upon them;—"and I will spare them, as a man spareth his own son that serveth him."

Now, if the Holy Spirit be the sign, the seal, and the security of our salvation, then, by grieving him by our sins, we break up this seal with our own hands, we cancel our firmest security, and, as much as in us lies, reverse our own title to eternal life.

Besides this, the Holy Spirit within us is the security of our salvation; he is likewise an earnest of it, and assures our spirits that we have a title to eternal happiness. "The Spirit of God beareth witness with our spirits that we are the children of God." And in order that this inward testimony may be lively and permanent, it is absolutely necessary to attend carefully to the secret operation of the Holy Spirit within us; who, by infusing his holy consolations into our souls, by enlivening our drooping spirits, and giving us a quick relish of his promises, raises bright and joyous sensations in us, and gives a man, beforehand, a taste of the bliss to which he is going. In this sense, God is said, by the Apostle to the Corinthians, to have "sealed us, and to have given the earnest of his Spirit in our hearts;" and that earnest, not only by way of confirmation of our title to happiness, but as an actual part of that reward at present, the fulness of which we expect hereafter.

139.* ON LOVE*

"Though I bestow all my goods to feed the poor, and though I give my body to be burned, and have not love, it profiteth me nothing."

1 Cor. 13:3.

[1.] There is great reason to fear that it will hereafter be said of most of you who are here present, that this scripture, as well as all those you have heard before, profited you nothing. Some, perhaps, are not serious enough to attend to it; some who do attend, will not believe it; some who do believe it, will yet think it a hard saying, and so forget it as soon as they can; and, of those few who receive it gladly for a time, some, having no root of humility, or self-denial, when persecution ariseth because of the word, will, rather than suffer for it, fall away. Nay, even of those who attend to it, who believe, remember, yea, and receive it so deeply into their hearts, that it both takes root there, endures the heat of temptation, and begins to bring forth fruit, yet will not *all* bring forth fruit

---

* [text from the 1872 edition]

* Preached at Savannah, February 20, 1736

unto perfection. The cares or pleasures of the world, and the desire of other things, (perhaps not felt till then,) will grow up with the word, and choke it.

[2.] Nor am I that speak the word of God any more secure from these dangers than you that hear it. I, too, have to bewail "an evil heart of unbelief." And whenever God shall suffer persecution to arise, yea, were it only the slight one of reproach, I may be the first that is offended. Or, if I be enabled to sustain this, yet, should he let loose the cares of the world upon me, or should he cease to guard me against those pleasures that do not lead to him, and the desire of other things [than knowing and loving him], I should surely be overwhelmed, and, having preached to others, be myself a castaway.

[3.] Why then do I speak this word at all? Why? Because a dispensation of the gospel is committed to me: And, though what I shall do to-morrow I know not, to-day I will preach the gospel. And with regard to you, my commission runs thus: "Son of man, I do send thee to them; and thou shalt say unto them, Thus saith the Lord God;—whether they will hear, or whether they will forbear."

[4.] Thus saith the Lord God, "Whosoever thou art who wilt enter into life, keep the commandments." (In order to this, "believe in the Lord Jesus Christ, and thou shalt be saved.") "Forsake not the assembling together, as the manner of some is." In secret, likewise, "pray to thy Father who seeth in secret," and "pour out thy heart before him." Make my word "a lantern to thy feet, and a light unto thy paths." Keep it "in thy heart, and in thy mouth, when thou sittest in thy house, when thou walkest by the way, when thou liest down, and when thou risest up." "Turn unto me with fasting," as well as prayer; and, in obedience to thy dying Redeemer, by eating that bread and drinking that cup, "show ye forth the Lord's death till he comes." By the power thou shalt through these means receive from on high, do all the things which are enjoined in the Law, and avoid all those things which are forbidden therein, knowing that if ye offend in one point, ye are guilty of all." "To do good also, and to distribute, forget not;"—yea, while you have time, do all the good you can unto all men. Then "deny thyself, take up thy cross daily;" and, if called thereto, "resist unto blood." And when each of you can say, "All this have I done," then let him say to himself farther, (words at which not only such as Felix alone, but the holiest soul upon earth might tremble,) "Though I bestow all my goods to feed the poor, and though I give my body to be burned, and have not love, it profiteth me nothing."

It concerns us all, therefore, in the highest degree, to know,

    I.   The full sense of those words, "Though I bestow all my goods to feed the poor, and though I give my body to be burned;"

    II.   The true meaning of the word *love*; and,

    III.   In what sense it can be said, that without love all this profiteth us nothing.

I. As to the First: It must be observed that the word used by St. Paul properly signifies, *To divide into small pieces, and then to distribute what has been so divided*; and, consequently, it implies, not only divesting ourselves at once of all the worldly goods we enjoy, either from a fit of distaste to the world, or a sudden start of devotion, but an act of choice, and that choice coolly and steadily executed. It may imply, too, that this be done not out of vanity, but in part from a right principle; namely, from a design to perform the command of God, and a desire to obtain his kingdom. It must be farther observed, that the word *give* signifies, actually to deliver a thing according to agreement; and, accordingly, it implies, like the word preceding, not a hasty, inconsiderate action, but one performed with open eyes and a determined heart, pursuant to a resolution before taken. The full sense of the words, therefore, is this; which he that hath ears to hear, let him hear: "Though I should give all the substance of my house to feed the poor; though I should do so upon mature choice and deliberation; though I should spend my life in dealing it out to them with my own hands, yea, and that from a principle of obedience; though I should suffer, from the same view, not only reproach and shame, not only bonds and imprisonment, and all this by my own continued act and deed, not accepting deliverance, but, moreover, death itself,—yea, death inflicted in a manner the most terrible to nature; yet all this, if I have not love, (the love of God, and the love of all mankind, 'shed abroad in my heart by the Hold Ghost given unto me,') it profiteth me nothing."

II. Let us inquire what this love is,—what is the true meaning of the word? We may consider it either as to its properties or effects: And that we may be under no possibility of mistake, we will not at all regard the judgment of men, but go to our Lord himself for an account of the nature of love; and, for the effects of it, to his inspired Apostle.

The love which our Lord requires in all his followers, is the love of God and man;—of God, for his own, and of man, for God's sake. Now, what is it to love God, but to delight in him, to rejoice in his will, to desire continually to please him, to seek and find our happiness in him, and to thirst day and night for a fuller enjoyment of him?

As to the measure of this love, our Lord hath clearly told us, "Thou shalt love the Lord thy God with all thy heart." Not that we are to love or delight in none but him: For he hath commanded us, not only to love our neighbour, that is, all men, as ourselves;—to desire and pursue their happiness as sincerely and steadily as our own,—but also to love many of his creatures in the strictest sense; to delight in them, to enjoy them: Only in such a manner and measure as we know and feel, not to indispose but to prepare us for the enjoyment of Him. Thus, then, we are called to love God with all our heart.

The effects or properties of this love, the Apostle describes in the chapter before us. And all these being infallible marks whereby any man may judge of himself, whether he hath this love or hath it not, they deserve our deepest consideration. "Love suffereth long," or is longsuffering. If thou love thy neighbour for God's sake, thou wilt bear long with his infirmities: If he want wisdom, thou wilt pity and not despise him: If he be in error, thou wilt mildly endeavour to recover him, without any sharpness or reproach: If he be overtaken in a fault, thou wilt labour to restore him in the spirit of meekness: And if, haply, that cannot be done soon, thou wilt have patience with him; if God, peradventure, may bring him, at length to the knowledge and love of the truth. In all provocations, either from the weakness or malice of men, thou wilt show thyself a pattern of gentleness and meekness; and, be they ever so often repeated, wilt not be overcome of evil, but overcome evil with good. Let no man deceive you with vain words: He who is not thus long-suffering, hath not love.

Again: "Love is kind." Whosoever feels the love of God and man shed abroad in his heart, feels an ardent and uninterrupted thirst after the happiness of all his fellow-creatures. His soul melts away with the very fervent desire which he hath continually to promote it; and out of the abundance of the heart his mouth speaketh. In his tongue is the law of kindness. The same is impressed on all his actions. The flame within is continually working itself away, and spreading abroad more and more, in every instance of good-will to all with whom he hath to do. So that whether he thinks or speaks, or whatever he does, it all points to the same end,—the advancing, by every possible way, the happiness of all his fellow-creatures. Deceive not, therefore, your own souls: He who is not thus kind, hath not love.

Farther: "Love envieth not." This, indeed, is implied, when it is said, "Love is kind." For kindness and envy are inconsistent: They can no more abide together than light and darkness. If we earnestly desire *all* happiness to *all*, we cannot be grieved at the happiness of any. The fulfilling of our desire will be sweet to our soul; so far shall we be from being pained at it. If we are always doing what good we can for our neighbour, and wishing we could do more, it is impossible that we should repine at an good he receives: Indeed, it will be the very joy of our heart. However, then, we may flatter ourselves, or one another, he that envieth hath not love.

It follows, "Love vaunteth not itself;" or rather, is not rash or hasty in judging: For this is indeed the true meaning of the word. As many as love their neighbour for God's sake, will not easily receive an ill opinion of any to whom they wish all good, spiritual as well as temporal. They cannot condemn him even in their heart without evidence; nor upon slight evidence neither; nor, indeed upon any, without first, if it be possible, having him and his accuser face to face, or at the least acquainting him with the accusation, and letting him speak for himself. Every one of you feels that he cannot but act thus, with regard to one whom he tenderly loves. Why, then, he who doth not act thus hath not love.

I only mention one more of the properties of this love: "Love is not puffed up." You cannot wrong one you love: Therefore, if you love God with all your heart, you cannot so wrong him as to rob him of his glory, by taking to yourself what is due to him only. You will own that all you are, and all you have, is his; that without him you can do nothing; that he is your light and your life, your strength and your all; and that you are nothing, yea, less than nothing, before him. And if you love your neighbour as yourself, you will not be able to prefer yourself before him. Nay, you will not be able to despise any one, any more than to hate him. [Nay, you will think every man better than yourself.] As the wax melteth away before the fire, so doth pride melt away before love. All haughtiness, whether of heart, speech, or behaviour, vanishes away where love prevails. It bringeth down the high looks of him who boasted in his strength, and maketh him as a little child; diffident of himself, willing to hear, glad to learn, easily convinced, easily persuaded. And whosoever is otherwise minded, let him give up all vain hope: He is puffed up, and so hath not love.

III. It remains to inquire, in what sense it can be said that "though I bestow all my goods to feed the poor, yea, though I give my body to be burned, and have not love, it profiteth me nothing."

The chief sense of the words is, doubtless, this: That whatsoever we do, and whatsoever we suffer, if we are not renewed in the spirit of our mind, by "the love of God shed abroad in our hearts by the Holy Ghost given unto us," we cannot enter into life eternal. None can enter there, unless in virtue of covenant which God hath given unto man in the Son of his love.

But, because general truths are less apt to affect us, let consider one or two particulars, with regard to which all we can do or suffer, if we have not love, profiteth us nothing. And, First, all without this profiteth not, so as to make life happy; nor, Secondly, so as to make death comfortable.

And, First, without love nothing can so profit us as to make our lives happy. By happiness I mean, not a slight, trilling pleasure, that perhaps begins and ends in the same hour; but such a state of well-being as contents the soul, and gives it a stead, lasting satisfaction. But that nothing without love can profit us, as to our present happiness, will appear from this single consideration: You cannot want it, in any one single instance, without pain; and the more you depart from it, the pain is the greater. Are you wanting in longsuffering? Then, so far as you fall short of this, you fall short of happiness. The more the opposite tempers—anger, fretfulness, revenge—prevail, the more unhappy you are. You know it; you feel it; nor can the storm be allayed, or peace ever return to your soul, unless meekness, gentleness, patience, or, in one word, love, take possession of it. Does any man find in himself ill-will, malice, envy, or any other temper opposite to kindness? Then is misery there; and the stronger the temper, the more miserable he is. If the slothful man may be said to eat his own flesh, much more the malicious, or envious. His soul is the very type of hell;—full of torment as well as wickedness. He hath already the worm that never dieth, and he is hastening to the fire that never can be quenched. Only as yet the great gulf is not fixed between him and heaven. As yet there is a Spirit ready to help his infirmities; who is still willing, if he stretch out his hands to heaven, and bewail his ignorance and misery, to purify his heart from vile affections, and to renew it in the love of God, and so lead him by present, up to eternal, happiness.

Secondly. Without love, nothing can make death comfortable.

By comfortable I do not mean stupid, or senseless. I would not say, he died comfortably who died by an apoplexy, or by the shot of a cannon, any more than he who, having his conscience seared, died as unconcerned as the beasts that beasts that perish. Neither do I believe you would envy any one the comfort of dying raving mad. But, by a comfortable death, I mean, a calm passage out of life, full of even, rational peace and joy. And such a death, all the acting and all the suffering in the world cannot give, without love.

To make this still more evident, I cannot appeal to your own experience; but I may to what we have seen, and to the experience of others. And two I have myself seen going out of this life in what I call a comfortable manner, though not with equal comfort. One had evidently more comfort than the other, because he had more love.

I attended the first during a great part of his last trial, as well as when he yielded up his soul to God. He cried out, "God doth chasten me with strong pain; but I thank him for all; I bless him for all; I love him for all!" When asked, not long before his release, "Are the consolations of God small with you?" he replied aloud, "No, no, no!" Calling all that were near him by their names, he said, "Think of heaven, talk of heaven: All the time is lost when we are not thinking of heaven." Now, this was the voice of love; and, so far as that prevailed, all was comfort, peace, and joy. But as his love was not perfect, so neither was his comfort. He intervals of [anger or] fretfulness, and therein of misery; giving by both an incontestable proof that love can sweeten both life and death. So when that is either absent from, or obscured in, the soul, there is no peace or comfort there.

It was in this place that I saw the other good soldier of Jesus Christ grappling with his last enemy, death. And it was, indeed, a spectacle worthy to be seen, of God, and angels, and men. Some of his last breath was spent in a psalm of praise to Him who was then giving him the victory; in assurance whereof be began triumph even in the heat of the battle. When he was asked, "Hast thou the love of God in thy heart?" he lifted up his eyes and hands, and answered, "Yes, yes!" with the whole strength he had left. To one who inquired if he was afraid of the devil, whom he had just mentioned as making his last attack upon him, he replied, "No, no: My loving Saviour hath conquered every enemy: He is with me. I fear nothing." Soon after, he said, "The way to our loving Saviour is sharp, but it is short." Nor was it long before he fell into a sort of slumber, wherein his soul sweetly returned to God that gave it.

Here, we may observe, was no mixture of any passion or temper contrary to love; therefore, there was no misery; perfect love casting out whatever might have occasioned torment. And whosoever thou art who hast the like measure of love, thy last end shall be like his.[Section numbers in brackets follow the Bicentennial Edition.]

140.* ON PUBLIC DIVERSIONS

"Shall a trumpet be blown in the city, and the people not be afraid? shall there be evil in the city, and the Lord hath not done it?"

Amos 3:6.

It is well if there are not too many here who are too nearly concerned in these words of the Prophet; the plain sense of which seems to be this: Are there any men in the world so stupid and senseless, so utterly void of common reason, so careless of their own and their neighbours' safety or destruction, as when an alarm of approaching judgments is given, to show no signs of apprehension? to take no care in order to prevent them, but go on as securely as if no alarm had been given? Do not all men know that whatsoever evil befals them, it befalls them either by God's appointment; and that he designs every evil of this life to warn men to avoid still greater evils? that he suffers these lighter marks of his displeasure, to awaken mankind, so that they may shun his everlasting vengeance, and be timely advised, by feeling a part of it, so to change their ways that his whole displeasure may not arise?

I intend, speaking on this subject, to show, First, that there is no evil in any place but the hand of the Lord is in it. Secondly. That every uncommon evil is the trumpet of God blown in that place, so that the people may take warning. Thirdly. To consider whether, after God hath blown his trumpet in this place, we have been duly afraid.

I am, First, to show, in few words, that there is no evil in any place but the hand of the Lord is therein. No evil, that is, no affliction or calamity, whether of a public or of a private nature, whether it concerns only one, or a few persons, or reaches to many, or to all, of that place where it comes. Whatever circumstance occasions loss or pain to any man, or number of men, may in that respect be called an evil; and of such evils the Prophet speaks in these words.

Of such evils, we are to believe, that they never happen but by the knowledge and permission of God. And of every such evil we may say, that the Lord hath done it, either by his own immediate power, by the strength of his own right hand, or by commanding, or else suffering, it to be done by those his servants that do his pleasure. For the Lord is King, be the people never so impatient; yea, the great King of all the earth. Whatsoever, therefore, is done in all the earth, (sin only excepted,) he doeth it himself. The Lord God Omnipotent still reigneth; and all things are so subject unto him, that his will must be done, whether we agree to it or not, as in heaven, so also upon earth. Not only his blessed angels, but all things, serve him in all places of his dominion; those wicked spirits which rule the darkness of this world, and those men who are like them, he rules by constraint; the senseless and brute parts of the creation, by nature; and those men who are like God, by choice. But, however it be, with or without their own choice, they all act in obedience to his will; and particularly so, when, in judgment, he remembers mercy, and permits a smaller evil that he may prevent greater. Then, at least, we are to acknowledge the hand of God in whatsoever instruments he makes use of. It makes little difference whether he executes his purpose by the powers of heaven or hell, or by the mistakes, carelessness, or malice of men. If a destroying angel marches forth against a town or country, it is God who empowers him to destroy. If bad men distress one or more of their fellow-creatures, the ungodly are a sword of his. If fire, hail, wind, or storm be let loose upon the earth, yet they only fulfil his word. So certain it is, that there is no evil in any place which the Lord, in this sense, hath not done.

---

* [text from the 1872 edition]

I am to prove, Secondly, that every uncommon evil is the trumpet of God blown in that place where it comes, that the people may take warning.

Every private affliction is doubtless the voice of God, whereby he calls upon that person to flee to him for succour. But if any extraordinary affliction occurs, especially when many persons are concerned in it, we may not only say that in this God speaks to us, but that the God of glory thundereth. This voice of the Lord is in power! This voice of the Lord is full of majesty! This demands the deepest attention of all to whom it comes. This loudly claims the most serious consideration, not only of those to whom it is peculiarly sent, but of all those that are round about them. This, like a voice from heaven, commands that all people should be afraid, should tremble at the presence of God! that everyone should feel and show that religious fear, that sacred awe, of the majesty of God, which is both the beginning and perfection of wisdom; that fear which should make them haste to do whatsoever the Lord their God commands them, and careful not to turn aside from it to the right hand or the left.

It is needless to use many words to prove this, after what has been proved already. For if there be no evil in any place which the Lord hath not done, and if he doth not willingly send evil on any place, but only to warn them to avoid greater evils; then it is plain, that, wherever any evil is, it is the trumpet of God blown in that place, to the end that the people may be so afraid as not to continue in anything that displeaseth him. Then it is plain, that, in every such merciful evil, God speaks to this effect: "O that there were such an heart in this people, that they would fear me, and keep my commandments always; that it might be well with them, and their children after them!"

Thirdly, What signs we have manifested of this wise and grateful fear, I am now to consider more at large.

First. Let us consider how God hath blown his trumpet in this place; and, Secondly, whether we have been duly afraid. Let us consider, First, how God hath blown his trumpet among us of this place. And that it might never be forgotten, it were much to be wished, not only that parents would tell their children, to the intent that their posterity might know it, and the children that are yet unborn; but also, that it were written in our public register, for a standing memorial to all generations; that in the very week, and on the very day, when that diversion which hath had a considerable share in turning the Christian world upside down, was to have been brought in hither also, such a fire broke out, as neither we nor our fathers had seen in this place; a fire which soon spread itself not over one only, but over several dwelling-houses; which so went forth in the fury of its strength, that it soon prevailed over the weak resistance made against it, and left only so much standing of most of those buildings over which it prevailed, as might serve to quicken our remembrance of it. Let it be told, that those who came prepared for another prospect, were entertained with *that* of devouring flames! a prospect which continued during the whole time of the intended diversion, and which was but too plainly to be seen, together with the fiery pillars of smoke which increased its horror, from the very place which had been pitched upon for the scene of this diversion.

This is the bare matter of fact. And even from this, let any one, in whom is the spirit of a man, judge, whether the trumpet of God hath not sufficiently sounded among us of this place! And doth this trumpet give an uncertain sound? How would you have God speak more plainly? Do you desire that the Lord should also thunder out of heaven, and give hail-stones, and coals of fire? Nay, rather let us say, "It is enough! Speak no more, Lord; for thy servants hear! Those to whom thou hast most severely spoken are afraid, and do seek thee with their whole heart. They resolve not to prolong the time, but even *now*, by thy gracious assistance, to look well if there be any way of wickedness in them, and to turn their feet unto the way everlasting; to renounce everything that is evil in thy sight; yea, the sin that doth the most easily beset them; and to use their whole diligence for the time to come, to make their calling and election sure. Those to whom thou hast spoken by the misfortune of their neighbours are likewise afraid at thy tokens, and own that it was thy mere goodness, that they, too, and their substance, were not consumed. They likewise firmly purpose in themselves to make the true use of thy merciful warning; to labour more and more, day by day, to purge themselves from all sin, from every earthly affection, that they may be fit to stand in the presence of that God who is himself 'a consuming fire!' "

But have we indeed been thus duly afraid? This is now to be considered. And because we cannot see the hearts of others, let us form our judgment from their actions, which will be best done by a plain relation, of which everyone that hears it can easily tell whether it be true or false.

In the day following that on which the voice of God had so dreadfully commanded us to exchange our mirth for sadness, the diversion which that had broken off was as eagerly begun anew. Crowds of people flocked out of that very town where the destruction had been wrought the day before, and rushed by the place of desolation to the place of entertainment! Here you might see the ground covered with heaps of ruins, mingled with yet unquenched fire; a little way off, as thickly covered with horses and men, pressing on to see another new sight. On this side were the mourners bewailing the loss of their goods, and the necessities of their families; on the other, the feasters delighting themselves with the sport they had gained. Surely, such a mixture of mirth and sadness, of feasting and mourning, of laughing and weeping, hath not been seen from the day in which our forefathers first came up into this land, until yesterday.

Such is the fear we have shown of the wrath of God! Thus have we been afraid after he had blown his trumpet among us! These are the signs we have given of our resolution to avoid whatever is displeasing in his sight! Hereby we have proved how we design to avoid that diversion in particular, which he hath given us so terrible a reason to believe is far from being pleasing to him! Not that this is the only reason we have to believe so. Besides this last melancholy argument against it, we have so many others, as any serious Christian would find it a hard task to answer. But I have only time to mention slightly a few of the consequences that were never yet separated from it.

Before I mention these, it is not necessary for me to say whether the diversion is sinful in itself, simply considered, or not. If anyone can find a race which has none of these consequences, let him go to it in the name of God. Only, till he finds one which does not give occasion to these or the like villanies, let him who nameth the name of Christ have a care of any way encouraging them.

One thing more I would have observed, that it is so far from being uncharitable to warn well-meaning people of the tendency of these diversions, that the more clearly and strongly anyone represents it to them, the more charitable to them he is. This may be made plain by a very easy comparison. You see the wine when it sparkles in the cup, and are going to drink of it. I tell you there is poison in it! and, therefore, beg you to throw it away. You answer, "The wine is harmless in itself." I reply, Perhaps it is so; but still if it be mixed with what is not harmless, no one in his senses, if he knows it at least, unless he could separate the good from the bad, will once think of drinking it. If you add, "It is not poison to me, though it be to others;" then I say, Throw it away for thy brother's sake, lest thou embolden him to drink also. Why should thy strength occasion thy weak brother to perish, for whom Christ died? Now let anyone judge which is the uncharitable person: He who pleads against the wine or the diversion, for his brother's sake; or he who pleads against the life of his brother, for the sake of the wine or the diversions.

All the doubt there can be is: "Is there poison in this diversion which is supposed to be harmless in itself?" To clear this up, let us, First, observe the notorious lying that is always joined with it; the various kinds of over-reaching and cheating; the horrid oaths and curses that constantly accompany it, wherewith the name of our Lord God, blessed for ever, is blasphemed. When or where was this diversion ever known without these dreadful consequences? Who was ever one day present at one of these entertainments, without being himself a witness to some of these? And surely these alone, had we no other ill consequences to charge upon this diversion, are enough, till a way is found to purge it from them, to make both God and all wise men to abhor it.

But, over and above these, we charge it, Secondly, with affording the fairest means to exercise and to increase covetousness. This it done by the occasion it gives to all who please to lay wagers with one another, which commonly brings so strong a desire of possessing what is another's, as will hardly cease when that one point is decided; but will be exceedingly likely to leave such a thirst in the mind, as not all the winning in the world will satisfy. And what amends can the trifling sport of a thousand people make for one soul thus corrupted and ruined? Therefore, on this account too, till a way is known to secure all that frequent it from this danger, well may this sport itself be an abomination to Him who values one soul more than the whole world.

May we not well fear, that it is an abomination to the Lord because of a Third effect of it? because it is so apt to inflame those passions which he so earnestly commands us to quench? because many people are so heated on such occasions, as they never ought to be on any occasion? supposing it possible that a man might be angry, and not sin; yet hardly upon such occasions, or in such a degree as those who are angry upon such occasions commonly are. This consequence, too, let him separate from such a diversion, who would prevent its being displeasing to God.

Till this be done, let no one say, "What hurt is there in a horse-race?" But if any should still ask that question, we can answer yet more particularly, Are you a young person who desires to go to it? Then it is likely you go either to see or to be seen; to admire other fine sights, or to be admired yourself. The hurt of this is, it nourishes that friendship which is enmity with God. It strengthens those affections which are already too strong,—the desire of the eye, and the pride of life. All such diversions as these are the noblest instruments the devil has to fill the mind with earthly, sensual, devilish passions; to make you of a light and trifling spirit; in a word, to make you a lover of pleasure more than a lover of God. Are you, who desire to go to it, advanced in years, and, therefore, less subject to such temptations? Take heed that your hearts deceive you not. But be it as you suppose, hath it not done you hurt enough, if it has hindered any of you from partaking of the blessed sacrament? if by preventing either that serious examination or that private devotion which you wisely use before you come to it, has occasioned your neglecting to come to this holy table; and so not only disobeying a plain command of God, but likewise losing all those inestimable advantages which are there reached out to them who obey him? Are you a rich man that desire to go? Then you have probably given something towards it. That is, you have thrown away that seed which might have borne fruit to eternity! You have thrown away a part of that talent, which had you rightly improved, you might have been an everlasting gainer by it! You have utterly lost what God himself, had you lent it to him, would richly have repaid you. For you have given to those who neither need, nor perhaps thank you for it; which if you had bestowed upon your helpless brethren, your blessed Redeemer would have esteemed it as done unto himself, and would have treated you accordingly at the great day. Are you a poor man, who have gone or given anything to this diversion? Then it has done you most hurt of all. It has made you throw away, for an idle sport abroad, what your wife and family wanted at home. If so, you have denied the faith, and are far worse than an infidel. But suppose it cost you no money, was it not hurt enough if it cost you any of your time? What had you to do to run after trifling diversions, when you ought to have been employed in honest labour? Surely if the rich think, God hath given them more than they want, (though it will be well if they do not one day think otherwise,) yet *you* have no temptation to think so. Sufficient for your day is the labour thereof.

I have but a few words to add,—and those I speak not to them who are unwilling to hear, whose affections are set upon this world, and therefore their eyes are blinded by it; but I speak to them in whom is an understanding heart, and a discerning spirit;—who, if they have formerly erred, are now resolved, by the grace of God, to return no more to the error of their ways; but for the time come, not only to avoid, but also earnestly to oppose, whatsoever is contrary to the will of God. To these I say, Are ye young? So much the rather scorn all employments that are useless, but much more if they are sinful; For you are they, whose wisdom and glory it is to remember your Creator in the days of your youth. Are you elder? So much the rather bestow all the time which you can spare from the necessary business of this life, in preparing yourself and those about you for their entrance into a better life. For your day is far spent, your night is at hand. Redeem therefore the little time you have left. Are you rich? Then you have particular reason to labour that you may be rich in good works: For you are they to whom much is given, not to throw away, but to use well and wisely; and of you much shall be required. Are ye poor? Then you have particular reason to work with your hands, that you may provide for your own household. Nor when you have done this have you done all; for then you are to labour that you may give to him that needeth,—not to him that needeth diversions, but to him that needeth the necessaries of nature,—that needeth clothes to cover him, food to support his life, or a house where to lay his head.

What remains, but that we labour, one and all, young and old, rich and poor, to wipe off the past scandal from our town and people? First, by opposing to the utmost, for the time to come, by word and deed, among our friends, and all we have to do with, this unhappy diversion, which has such terribly hurtful consequences; by doing all we possibly can to hinder its coming among us any more. And, Secondly, by showing all the mercy we can to our afflicted neighbours, according as God hath prospered us; and by this timely relief of them, laying up for ourselves a good foundation against the day of necessity. Thirdly, by our constant attendance on God's public service and blessed sacrament, and our watchful, charitable, and pious life. Thus giving the noblest proof before men and angels, that although, even after we were troubled, we went wrong, yet, upon more deeply considering how God hath blown his trumpet among us, we were afraid. We then shall say with an awakened heart, Behold, the Lord our God hath showed us his glory and his greatness, and we have heard his voice out of the midst of the fire. Now, therefore, while time is, let us put away far from us every accursed thing: "For if we hear this voice of the Lord our God any more, then we shall die."

141.* On the Holy Spirit*

"Now the Lord is that Spirit."

2 Cor. 3:17.

The Apostle had been showing how the gospel ministry was superior to that of the law: The time being now come when types and shadows should be laid aside, and we should be invited to our duty by the manly and ingenuous motives of a clear and full revelation, open and free on God's part, and not at all disguised by his ambassadors. But what he chiefly insists upon is, not the *manner*, but the *subject* of their ministry: "Who hath made us able ministers," saith he, "of the New Testament: Not of the letter, but of the Spirit: For the letter killeth, but the Spirit giveth life." Here lies the great difference between the two dispensations: That the law was indeed *spiritual* in its demands, requiring a life consecrated to God in the observance of many rules; but, not conveying spiritual assistance, its effect was only to kill and mortify man, by giving him to understand, that he must needs be in a state of great depravity, since he found it so difficult to obey God; and that, as particular deaths were by that institution inflicted for particular sins, so death, in general, was but the consequence of his universal sinfulness. But the ministration of the New Testament was that of a "Spirit which giveth life;"—a Spirit, not only promised, but actually conferred; which should both enable Christians now to live unto God, and fulfil precepts even more spiritual than the former; and restore them hereafter to perfect life, after the ruins of sin and death. The incarnation, preaching, and death of Jesus Christ were designed to represent, proclaim, and purchase for us this gift of the Spirit; and therefore says the Apostle, "The Lord is that Spirit," or the Spirit.

This description of Christ was a proper inducement to Jews to believe on him; and it is still a necessary instruction to Christians, to regulate their expectations from him. But [we] think this age has made it particularly necessary to be well assured what Christ is to us: When that question is so differently resolved by the pious but weak accounts of some pretenders to *faith* on one hand, and by the clearer, but not perfectly Christian, accounts of some pretenders to *reason* on the other: While some derive from him a "righteousness of God," but in a sense somewhat improper and figurative; and others no more than a charter of pardon, and a system of morality: While some so interpret the gospel, as to place the holiness they are to be saved by in something divine, hut exterior to themselves; and others, so as to place it in things really within themselves, but not more than human. Now, the proper cure of what indistinctness there is one way, and what infidelity in the other, seems to be contained in the doctrine of my text: "The Lord is that Spirit."

In treating of which words, I will consider,

    I.   The nature of our fall in Adam; by which it will appear, that if "the Lord" were not "that Spirit," he could not be said to save or redeem us from our fallen condition.

    II.   I will consider the person of Jesus Christ; by which it will appear that "the lord is that Spirit." And,

    III.   I will inquire into the nature and operations of the Holy Spirit, as bestowed upon Christians.

I. I am to consider the nature of our fall in Adam.

Our first parents did enjoy the presence of the Holy Spirit; for they were created in the image and likeness of God, which was no other than his Spirit. By that he communicates himself to his creatures, and by that alone they can bear any likeness to him. It is, indeed, his life in them; and so properly

---

* [text from the 1872 edition]

|* Preached at St. Mary's, Oxford, on Whitsunday, 1736.

divine, that, upon this ground, angels and regenerate men are called his children.

But when man would not be guided by the Holy Spirit, it left him. When be would be wise in his own way, and in his own strength, and did not depend in simplicity upon his heavenly Father, the seed of a superior life was recalled from him. For he was no longer fit to be formed into a heavenly condition, when he had so unworthy a longing for, or rather dependence upon, an earthly fruit, which he knew God would not bless to him; no longer fit to receive supernatural succours, when he could not be content with his happy state towards God, without an over-curious examination into it.

Then he found himself forsaken of God, and left to the poverty, weakness, and misery of his own proper nature. He was now a mere animal, like unto other creatures made of flesh and blood, but only possessed of a larger understanding; by means of which he should either be led into greater absurdities than they could be guilty of, or else be made sensible of his lost happiness, and put into the right course for regaining it; that is, if he continued a careless apostate, he should love and admire the goods of this world, the adequate happiness only of animals; and, to recommend them and dissemble their defects, add all the ornament to them that his superior wit could invent. Or else (which is indeed more above brutes, but no nearer the perfection of man as a partaker of God, than the other) he should frame a new world to himself in theory; sometimes by warm imaginations, and sometimes by cool reasonings, endeavour to aggrandize his condition and defend his practice, or at least divert himself from feeling his own meanness and disorder.

If, on the other hand, he should be willing to find out the miseries of his fall, his understanding might furnish him with reasons for constant mourning, for despising and denying himself; might point out the sad effects of turning away from God and losing his Spirit, in the shame and anguish of a nature at variance with itself; thirsting after immortality, and yet subject to death; approving righteousness, and yet taking pleasure in things inconsistent with it; feeling an immense want of something to perfect and satisfy all it faculties, and yet neither able to know what that mighty thing is, otherwise than from its present defects, nor how to attain it, otherwise than by going contrary to its present inclinations.

Well might Adam now find himself *naked*; nothing less than God was departed from him. Till then he had experienced nothing but the goodness and sweetness of God; a heavenly life spread itself through his whole frame, as if he were not made of dust; his mind was filled with angelic wisdom; a direction from above took him by the hand; he walked and thought uprightly, and seemed not to be a child or novice in divine things. But now he had other things to experience; something in his soul that he did not find, nor need to fear, while he was carried on straight forward by the gentle gale of divine grace; something in his body that he could not see nor complain of; while that body was covered with glory. He feels there a self-displeasure, turbulence, and confusion; such as is common to other spirits who have lost God: He sees here causes of present shame and a future dissolution; and a strong engagement to that grovelling life which is common to animals that never enjoyed the divine nature.

The general character, therefore, of man's present state is death,—a death from God, whereby we no longer enjoy any intercourse with him, or happiness in him; we no longer shine with his glory, or act with his powers. It is true, while we have a being, *"in him* we must live, and move, and have our being;" but this we do now, not in a *filial* way, but only in a *servile* one, as all, even the meanest creatures, exist in him. It is one thing to receive from God an ability to walk and speak, eat and digest,—to be supported by his hand as a part of this earthly creation, and upon the same terms with it, for farther trial or vengeance; and another, to receive from him a life which is his own likeness,—to have within us something which is not of this creation, and which is nourished by his own immediate word and power.

Yet this is not the whole that is implied in man's sin. For he is not only inclined himself to all the sottishness of appetite, and all the pride of reason, but he is fallen under the tutorage of the *evil* one, who mightily furthers him in both. The state he was at first placed in, was a state of the most simple subjection to God, and this entitled him to drink of his Spirit; but when he, not content to be actually in Paradise, under as full a light of God's countenance as he was capable of; must know good and evil, and be satisfied upon rational grounds whether it was best for him to be as he was, or not; when, disdaining to be directed as a child, he must weigh every thing himself; and seek better evidence than the voice of his Maker and the seal of the Spirit in his heart; then he not only obeyed, but became like to, that eldest son of pride, and was unhappily entitled to frequent visits, or rather a continued influence, from him. As life was annexed to his keeping the command, and, accordingly, that Spirit, which alone could form it unto true life, dwelt in his body; so, being sentenced to death for his transgression, he was now delivered unto "him who has the power of death, that, is, the devil," whose hostile and unkindly impressions promote death and sin at once.

This being the state of man, if God should send him a Redeemer, what must that Redeemer do for him? Will it he sufficient for him to be the promulgator of a new law,—to give us a set of excellent precepts? No: If we could keep them, that alone would not make us happy. A good conscience brings a man the happiness of being consistent with himself; but not that of being raised above himself into God; which every person will find, after all, is the thing he wants. Shall he be the fountain of an *imputed* righteousness, and procure the tenderest favour to all his followers? This is also not enough. Though a man should be allowed to be righteous, and be exempt from all punishment, yet if he is as really enslaved to the corruptions of nature, as endued with these privileges of redemption, he can hardly make himself easy; and whatever favour he can receive from God, here or hereafter, without a communication of himself; it is neither the cure of a spirit fallen, nor the happiness of one reconciled. Must not then our Redeemer be (according to the character which St. John, his forerunner, gave of him) one that "baptizeth with the Holy Ghost,"—the Fountain and

Restorer of that to mankind, whereby they are restored to their first estate, and the enjoyment of God? And this is a presumptive argument that "the Lord is that Spirit."

II. But it will appear more plainly that he is so, from the Second thing proposed; which was the consideration of the person of Jesus Christ.

He was one to whom "God gave not the Spirit by measure: but in him dwelt all the fulness of the Godhead bodily; and of his fulness we have all received, and grace for grace."

Indeed, all the communications of the Godhead, which any creatures could receive, were always from him as the Word of God; but all that mankind now in an earthly state were to receive, must be from him by means of that body, at first mortal, like unto theirs, and then glorious "in the likeness of God," which he took upon him for their sake.

In the beginning, the heavenly Word,—being a Spirit that issued from the Father, and the Word of his power,—made man an image of immortality, according to the likeness of the Father; but he who had been made in the image of God, afterwards became mortal, when the more powerful Spirit was separated from him. To remedy this, the Word became Man, that man by receiving the adoption might become a son of God once more; that the light of the Father might rest upon the flesh of our Lord, and come bright from thence unto us; and so man, being encompassed with the light of the Godhead, might be carried into immortality. When he was incarnate and became man, he recapitulated in himself all generations of mankind, making himself the centre of our salvation, that what we lost in Adam, even the image and likeness of God, we might receive in Christ Jesus. By the Holy Ghost coming upon Mary, and the power of the highest overshadowing her, the incarnation or Christ was wrought, and a new birth, whereby man should be born of God, was shown; that as by our first birth we did inherit death, so by this birth we might inherit life.

This is no other than what St. Paul teaches us: "The first man, Adam, was made a living soul, but the Second Adam was made a quickening spirit." All that the first man possessed of himself, all that he has transmitted to us, is "a living soul;" a nature endued with an animal life, and receptive of a spiritual. But the Second Adam is, and was made to us, "a quickening spirit;" by a strength from him as our Creator, we were at first raised above ourselves; by a strength from him as our Redeemer, we shall again live unto God.

In him is laid up for us that supplement to our nature, which we shall find the need of sooner or later; and that it cannot be countervailed by any assistance from the creatures, or any improvement of our own faculties: For we were made to be happy only in God; and all our labours and hopes, while we do not thirst after our deified state,—to partake as truly of God as we do of flesh and blood, to be glorified in his nature, as we have been dishonoured in our own,—are the labours and hopes of those who utterly mistake themselves.

The divine wisdom knew what was our proper consolation, though we did not. What does more obviously present itself in the Saviour of the world, than an union of man with God?—an union attended with all the propriety of behaviour that *we* are called to, as candidates of the Spirit; such as walking with God in singleness of heart, perfect self-renunciation, and a life of sufferings,—an union which submitted to the necessary stages of our progress; where the divine life was hid, for the most part, in the secret of the soul till death; in the state of separation, comforted the soul, but did not raise it above the intermediate region of Paradise; at the resurrection, clothed the body with heavenly qualities, and the powers of immortality; and at last raised it to the immediate presence and right hand of the Father.

Christ is not only God above us; which may keep us in awe, but cannot save; but he is Immanuel, God with us, and in us. As he is the Son of God, God must be where he is; and as he is the Son of man, he will be with mankind; the consequence of this is, that in the future age "the tabernacle of God will be with men," and he will show them his glory; and, at present, he will *dwell* in their hearts by faith in his Son.

I hope it sufficiently appears, that "the Lord is that Spirit." Considering what we are, and what we have been, nothing less than the receiving that Spirit again would be redemption to us; and considering who that heavenly person was that was sent to be our Redeemer, we can expect nothing less from him.

III. I proceed now to the Third thing proposed, viz., to inquire into the nature and operations of the Holy Spirit, as bestowed upon Christians.

And here I shall pass by the particular extraordinary gifts vouchsafed to the first ages for the edification of the Church and only consider what the Holy Spirit is to every believer, for his personal sanctification and salvation. It is not granted to every one to raise the dead, and heal the sick. What is most necessary is, to be sure, as to ourselves, that we are "passed from death unto life;" to keep our bodies pure and undefiled, and let them reap that health which flows from a magnanimous patience, and the serene joys of devotion. The Holy Spirit has enabled men to speak with tongues, and to prophesy; but the light that most necessarily attends it is a light to discern the fallacies of flesh and blood, to reject the irreligious maxims of the world, and to practice those degrees of trust in God and love to men, whose foundation is not so much in the present appearances of things, as in some that are yet to come. The object which this light brings us most immediately to know is ourselves; and by virtue of this, one that is born of God, and has a lively hope may indeed see far into the ways of Providence, and farther yet into the holy Scriptures; for the holy Scriptures, excepting some accidental and less necessary parts, are only a history of that new man which he himself is; and Providence is only a wise disposal of events for the awakening of particular persons, and ripening the world in general for the coming of Christ's kingdom.

But I think the true notion of the Spirit is, that it is some portion of, as well as preparation for, a life in God, which we are to enjoy hereafter. The gift of the Holy Spirit looks full to the resurrection; for then is the life of God completed in us.

Then, after man has passed through all the *penalties* of sin, the drudgery and vanity of human life, the painful reflections of an awakened mind, the infirmities and dissolution of the body, and all the sufferings and mortifications a just God shall lay in his way; when, by this means, he is come to know God and himself, he may safely be entrusted with true life, with the freedom and ornaments of a child of God; for he will no more arrogate anything to himself. Then shall the Holy Spirit be fully bestowed, when the flesh shall no longer resist it, but be itself changed into an angelical condition, being clothed upon with the incorruption of the Holy Spirit; when the body which, by being born with the soul, and living through it, could only be called an animal one, shall now become spiritual, whilst by the Spirit it rises into eternity. Everything in Christianity is some kind of anticipation of something that is to be at the end of the world. If the Apostles were to preach by their Master's command, "that the kingdom of God drew nigh;" the meaning was, that from henceforth all men should fix their eyes on that happy time, foretold by the Prophets, when the Messiah should come and restore all things; that by renouncing their worldly conversation, and submitting to the gospel institution, they should fit themselves for, hasten, that blessing. "Now are we the sons of God," as St. John tells us; and yet what he imparts to us at present will hardly justify that title, without taking in that fulness of his image which shall then be displayed in us, when we shall be "the children of God, by being the children of the resurrection."

True believers, then, are entered upon a life, the *sequel* of which they know not; for it is "a life hid with Christ in God." He, the forerunner, hath attained the end of it, being gone unto the Father; but we can know no more of it than appeared in him while he was upon earth. And even that, we shall not know but by following his steps; which if we do, we shall be so strengthened and renewed day by day in the inner man, that we shall desire no comfort from the present world through a sense of "the joy set before us;" though, as to the outward man, we shall be subject to distresses and decays, and treated as the offscouring of all things.

Well may a man ask his own heart, whether it is able to admit the Spirit of God. For where that divine Guest enters, the laws of another world must be observed: The body must be given up to martyrdom, or spent in the Christian warfare, as unconcernedly as if the soul were already provided of its house from heaven; the goods of this world must be parted with as freely, as if the last fire were to seize them to-morrow; our neighbour must be loved as heartily as if he were washed from all his sins, and demonstrated to be a child of God by the resurrection from the dead. The fruits of this Spirit must not be mere moral virtues, calculated for the comfort and decency of the present life; but holy dispositions, suitable to the instincts of a superior life already begun.

Thus to press forward, whither the promise of life calls him,—to turn his back upon the world, and comfort himself in God,—every one that has faith perceives to be just and necessary, and forces himself to do it: Every one that has hope, does it gladly and eagerly, though not without difficulty; but he that has love does it with ease and singleness of heart.

The state of love, being attended with "joy unspeakable and full of glory," with rest from the passions and vanities of man, with the integrity of an unchangeable judgment, and an undivided will, is, in a great measure, its own reward; yet not so as to supersede the desire of another world. For though such a man, having a free and insatiable love of that which is good, may seldom have need formally to propose to himself the hopes of retribution, in order to overcome his unwillingness to his duty; yet surely he must long for that which is best of all; and feel a plain attraction towards that country in which he has his place and station already assigned him; and join in the earnest expectation of all creatures, which wait for the manifestation of the sons of God. For now we obtain but some part of his Spirit, to model and fit us for incorruption, that we may, by degrees, be accustomed to receive and carry God within us; and, therefore, the Apostle calls it, "the earnest of the Spirit;' that is, a part of that honour which is promised us by the Lord. If, therefore, the earnest, abiding in us, makes us spiritual even now, and that which is mortal is, as it were, swallowed up of immortality; how shall it be when, rising again, we shall see him face to face? when all our members shall break to forth into songs of triumph, and glorify Him who hath raised them from the dead, and granted them everlasting life? For if this earnest or pledge, embracing man into itself, makes him now cry, "Abba, Father;" what shall the whole grace of the Spirit do, when, being given at length to believers, it shall make us like unto God, and perfect us through the will of the Father?

And thus I have done what was at first proposed: I have considered the nature of our fall in Adam; the person of Jesus Christ; and the operations of the Holy Spirit in Christians.

The only inference I will draw from what has been said, and principally from the account of man's fall, shall be, the reasonableness of those precepts of self-denial, daily suffering, and renouncing the world, which are so peculiar to Christianity, and which are the only foundation whereon the other virtues, recommended in the New Testament, can be practised or attained, in the sense there intended.

This inference is so natural, that I could not help anticipating it in some measure all the while. One would think it should be no hard matter to persuade a creature to abhor the badges of his misery; to dislike a condition or mansion which only banishment and disgrace have assigned him; to trample on the grandeur, refuse the comforts, and suspect the wisdom of a life whose nature it is to separate him from his God.

Your Saviour bids you "hate your own life." If you ask the reason, enter into your heart, see whether it be holy, and full of God; or whether, on the other hand, many things that are contrary to him are wrought there, and it is become a plantation of the enemy. Or, if this is too nice an inquiry, look upon your body. Do you find there the brightness of an angel, all the vigour of immortality? If not, be sure your soul is in the same degree of poverty, nakedness, and absence from God. It is true, your soul may sooner he re-admitted to some rays of the light of God's countenance, than your body can; but if you would take any step at all towards it, to dislike your present self must be the first.

You want a reason why you should renounce the world. Indeed you cannot see the prince of it walking up and down, "seeking whom he may devour;" and you may be so far ignorant of his devices, as not to know that they take place, as well in the most specious measures of business and learning, as in the wildest pursuits of pleasure. But this, however, you cannot but see, that the world is not still a paradise of God, guarded and ennobled with the light of glory; it is, indeed, a place where God has determined he will not appear to you at best, but leave you in a state of hope, that you shall see his face when this world is dissolved.

However, there is a way to rescue ourselves, in great measure, from the ill consequences of our captivity; and our Saviour has taught us that way. It is by suffering. We must not only "suffer many things," as he did, and so enter into our glory; but we must also suffer many things, that we may get above our corruption at present, and enjoy the Holy Spirit.

The world has no longer any power over us, than we have a quick relish of its comforts; and suffering abates that. Suffering is, indeed, a direct confutation of the pretences which the flattering tempter gains us by: For I am in human life; and if that life contains such soft ease, ravishing pleasure, glorious eminence, as you promise, why am I thus? Is it because I have not yet purchased riches to make me easy, or the current accomplishments to make me considerable. Then I find that all the comfort you propose is by leading me off from myself; but I will rather enter deep into my own condition, bad as it is: Perhaps I shall be nearer to God, the Eternal Truth, in feeling sorrows and miseries that are personal and real, than in feeling comforts that are not so. I begin already to find that all my grievances centre in one point: There is always at the bottom one great loss or defect, which is not the want of friends or gold, of health or philosophy. And the abiding sense of this may possibly become a prayer in the ears of the Most High;—a prayer not resulting from a set of speculative notions, but from the real, undissembled state of all that is within me; nor, indeed, so explicit a prayer as to describe the thing I want, but, considering how strange a want mine is, as explicit a one as I can make. Since, then, suffering opens me a door of hope, I will not put it from me as long as I live: It helps me to a true discovery of one period of my existence, though it is a low one; and bids fairer for having some connexion with a more glorious period that may follow, than the arts of indulgence, the amusements of pride and sloth, and all the dark policy of this world, which wage war with the whole truth, that man must know and feel, before he can look towards God. It may be, while I continue on the cross, I shall, like my Saviour, put off "principalities and powers;" recover myself more and more from the subjection I am indeed in (which he only seemed to be) to those wicked rulers, and to "triumph over them in it." At least, it shall appear, in the day when God shall visit, that my heart, though grown unworthy of his residence, was too big to be comforted by any of his creatures; and was kept for him, as a place originally sacred, though for the present unclean.

But supposing that our state does require of us to "die daily,"—to sacrifice all that this present life can boast of, or is delighted with, before we give up life itself; supposing also, that in the hour we do somewhat of this kind, we receive light and strength from God, to grow superior to our infirmities, and are carried smoothly towards him in the joy of the Holy Ghost; yet how can a man have such frequent opportunities of suffering? Indeed, martyrdoms do not happen in every age, and some days of our lives may pass without reproaches from men; we may be in health, and not want food to eat and raiment to put on; (though health itself, and nutrition itself, oblige us to the pain of a constant correction of them;) yet still, the love of God and heavenly hope will not want something to oppress them in this world.

Let a man descend calmly into his heart, and see if there be no root of bitterness springing up; whether, at least, his thoughts, which are ever in motion, do not sometimes sally out into projects suggested by pride, or sink into indolent trifling, or be entangled in mean anxiety. Does not he find a motion of anger, or of gaiety, leavening him in an instant throughout; depriving him of the meekness and steady discernment he laboured after? Or, let him but conceive at any time, that unfeigned obedience, and watchful zeal, and dignity of behaviour, which, is suitable, I do not say to an angel, but to a sinner that has "a good hope through grace," and endeavour to work himself up to it; and if he find no sort of obstacle to this within him, he has indeed then no opportunity of suffering. In short, if he is such an abject sort of creature, as will, unless grace should do him a perpetual violence, relapse frequently into a course of thinking and acting entirely without God; then he can never want occasions of suffering, but will find his own nature to he the same burden to him, as that "faithless and perverse generation" was to our Saviour, of whom he said, "How long shall I be with you? How long shall I suffer you?"

I will conclude all with that excellent Collect of our Church:—"O God, who in all ages hast taught the hearts of thy faithful people, by sending to them the light of thy Holy Spirit; grant us by the same Spirit to have a right judgment in all things, and evermore to rejoice in his holy comfort, through the merits of Jesus Christ our Saviour; who liveth and reigneth with thee, in the unity of the same Spirit, one God, world without end. Amen."

ABOUT CROSSREACH PUBLICATIONS

Thank you for choosing CrossReach Publications.

Hope. Inspiration. Trust.

These three words sum up the philosophy of why CrossReach Publications exist. To create inspiration for the present thus inspiring hope for the future, through trusted authors from previous generations.

We are *non-denominational* and *non-sectarian*. We appreciate and respect what every part of the body brings to the table and believe everyone has the right to study and come to their own conclusions. We aim to help facilitate that end.

We aspire to excellence. If we have not met your standards please contact us and let us know. We want you to feel satisfied with your product. Something for everyone. We publish quality books both in presentation and content from a wide variety of authors who span various doctrinal positions and traditions, on a wide variety of Christian topics that will teach, encourage, challenge, inspire and equip.

We're a family-based home-business. A husband and wife team raising 8 kids. If you have any questions or comments about our publications email us at:

CrossReach@outlook.com

Don't forget you can follow us on Facebook and Twitter, (links are on the copyright page above) to keep up to date on our newest titles and deals.

BESTSELLING TITLES FROM CROSSREACH[1]

How to Be Filled with the Holy Spirit
A. W. Tozer

Before we deal with the question of how to be filled with the Holy Spirit, there are some matters which first have to be settled. As believers you have to get them out of the way, and right here is where the difficulty arises. I have been afraid that my listeners might have gotten the idea somewhere that I had a how-to-be-filled-with-the-Spirit-in-five-easy-lessons doctrine, which I could give you. If you can have any such vague ideas as that, I can only stand before you and say, "I am sorry"; because it isn't true; I can't give you such a course. There are some things, I say, that you have to get out of the way, settled.

God Still Speaks
A. W. Tozer

Tozer is as popular today as when he was living on the earth. He is respected right across the spectrum of Christianity, in circles that would disagree sharply with him doctrinally. Why is this? A. W. Tozer was a man who knew the voice of God. He shared this experience with every true child of God. With all those who are called by the grace of God to share in the mystical union that is possible with Him through His Son Jesus.
Tozer fought against much dryness and formality in his day. Considered a mighty man of God by most Evangelicals today, he was unconventional in his approach to spirituality and had no qualms about consulting everyone from Catholic Saints to German Protestant mystics for inspiration on how to experience God more fully.
Tozer, just like his Master, doesn't fit neatly into our theological boxes. He was a man after God's own heart and was willing to break the rules (man-made ones that is) to get there.
Here are two writings by Tozer that touch on the heart of this goal. Revelation is Not Enough and The Speaking Voice. A bonus chapter The Menace of the Religious Movie is included.
This is meat to sink your spiritual teeth into. Tozer's writings will show you the way to satisfy your spiritual hunger.

What We Are In Christ
E. W. Kenyon

I was surprised to find that the expressions "in Christ," "in whom," and "in Him" occur more than 130 times in the New Testament. This is the heart of the Revelation of Redemption given to Paul.
Here is the secret of faith—faith that conquers, faith that moves mountains. Here is the secret of the Spirit's guiding us into all reality. The heart craves intimacy with the Lord Jesus and with the Father. This craving can now be satisfied.
Ephesians 1:7: "In whom we have our redemption through his blood, the remission of our trespasses according to the riches of his grace."
It is not a beggarly Redemption, but a real liberty in Christ that we have now. It is a Redemption by the God Who could

---

[1] Buy from CrossReach Publications for quality and price. We have a full selection of titles in print and eBook. All available on the Amazon and Createspace stores. You can see our full selection just by searching for CrossReach Publications in the search bar!

say, "Let there be lights in the firmament of heaven," and cause the whole starry heavens to leap into being in a single instant. It is Omnipotence beyond human reason. This is where philosophy has never left a footprint.

Claiming Our Rights
E. W. Kenyon

There is no excuse for the spiritual weakness and poverty of the Family of God when the wealth of Grace and Love of our great Father with His power and wisdom are all at our disposal. We are not coming to the Father as a tramp coming to the door begging for food; we come as sons not only claiming our legal rights but claiming the natural rights of a child that is begotten in love. No one can hinder us or question our right of approach to our Father. Satan has Legal Rights over the sinner that God cannot dispute or challenge. He can sell them as slaves; he owns them, body, soul and spirit. But the moment we are born again... receive Eternal Life, the nature of God,—his legal dominion ends.

Christ is the Legal Head of the New Creation, or Family of God, and all the Authority that was given Him, He has given us: (Matthew 28:18), "All authority in heaven," the seat of authority, and "on earth," the place of execution of authority. He is "head over all things," the highest authority in the Universe, for the benefit of the Church which is His body.

The Two Babylons
Alexander Hislop

Fully Illustrated High Res. Images. Complete and Unabridged. Expanded Seventh Edition. This is the first and only seventh edition available in a modern digital edition. Nothing is left out! New material not found in the first six editions!!! Available in eBook and paperback edition exclusively from CrossReach Publications.

"In his work on "The Two Babylons" Dr. Hislop has proven conclusively that all the idolatrous systems of the nations had their origin in what was founded by that mighty Rebel, the beginning of whose kingdom was Babel (Gen. 10:10)."—A. W. Pink, The Antichrist (1923)

There is this great difference between the works of men and the works of God, that the same minute and searching investigation, which displays the defects and imperfections of the one, brings out also the beauties of the other. If the most finely polished needle on which the art of man has been expended be subjected to a microscope, many inequalities, much roughness and clumsiness, will be seen. But if the microscope be brought to bear on the flowers of the field, no such result appears. Instead of their beauty diminishing, new beauties and still more delicate, that have escaped the naked eye, are forthwith discovered; beauties that make us appreciate, in a way which otherwise we could have had little conception of, the full force of the Lord's saying, "Consider the lilies of the field, how they grow; they toil not, neither do they spin: and yet I say unto you, That even Solomon, in all his glory, was not arrayed like one of these." The same law appears also in comparing the Word of God and the most finished productions of men. There are spots and blemishes in the most admired productions of human genius. But the more the Scriptures are searched, the more minutely they are studied, the more their perfection appears; new beauties are brought into light every day; and the discoveries of science, the researches of the learned, and the labours of infidels, all alike conspire to illustrate the wonderful harmony of all the parts, and the Divine beauty that clothes the whole. If this be the case with Scripture in general, it is especially the case with prophetic Scripture. As every spoke in the wheel of Providence revolves, the prophetic symbols start into still more bold and beautiful relief. This is very strikingly the case with the prophetic language that forms the groundwork and corner-stone of the present work. There never has been any difficulty in the mind of any enlightened Protestant in identifying the woman "sitting on seven mountains," and having on her forehead the name written, "Mystery, Babylon the Great," with the Roman apostacy.

Elementary Geography
Charlotte Mason

This little book is confined to very simple "reading lessons upon the Form and Motions of the Earth, the Points of the Compass, the Meaning of a Map: Definitions."

It is hoped that these reading lessons may afford intelligent teaching, even in the hands of a young teacher. Children should go through the book twice, and should, after the second reading, be able to answer any of the questions from memory.

Who Moved the Stone?
Frank Morison

This study is in some ways so unusual and provocative that the writer thinks it desirable to state here very briefly how the book came to take its present form.

In one sense it could have taken no other, for it is essentially a confession, the inner story of a man who originally set out to write one kind of book and found himself compelled by the sheer force of circumstances to write another.

It is not that the facts themselves altered, for they are recorded imperishably in the monuments and in the pages of human history. But the interpretation to be put upon the facts underwent a change. Somehow the perspective shifted—not suddenly, as in a flash of insight or inspiration, but slowly, almost imperceptibly, by the very stubbornness of the facts themselves.

The book as it was originally planned was left high and dry, like those Thames barges when the great river goes out to meet the incoming sea. The writer discovered one day that not only could he no longer write the book as he had once conceived it, but that he would not if he could.

To tell the story of that change, and to give the reasons for it, is the main purpose of the following pages.

The Person and Work of the Holy Spirit
R. A. Torey

Before one can correctly understand the work of the Holy Spirit, he must first of all know the Spirit Himself. A frequent source of error and fanaticism about the work of the Holy Spirit is the attempt to study and understand His work without first of all coming to know Him as a Person.

It is of the highest importance from the standpoint of worship that we decide whether the Holy Spirit is a Divine Person, worthy to receive our adoration, our faith, our love, and our entire surrender to Himself, or whether it is simply an influence emanating from God or a power or an illumination that God imparts to us. If the Holy Spirit is a person, and a Divine Person, and we do not know Him as such, then we are robbing a Divine Being of the worship and the faith and the love and the surrender to Himself which are His due.

In His Steps
Charles M. Sheldon

The sermon story, In His Steps, or "What Would Jesus Do?" was first written in the winter of 1896, and read by the author, a chapter at a time, to his Sunday evening congregation in the Central Congregational Church, Topeka, Kansas. It was then printed as a serial in The Advance (Chicago), and its reception by the readers of that paper was such that the publishers of The Advance made arrangements for its appearance in book form. It was their desire, in which the author heartily joined, that the story might reach as many readers as possible, hence succeeding editions of paper-covered volumes at a price within the reach of nearly all readers.

The story has been warmly and thoughtfully welcomed by Endeavor societies, temperance organizations, and Y. M. C. A. 's. It is the earnest prayer of the author that the book may go its way with a great blessing to the churches for the quickening of Christian discipleship, and the hastening of the Master's kingdom on earth.

Charles M. Sheldon.
Topeka, Kansas,
November, 1897.

Christianity and Liberalism
J. Gresham Machen

The purpose of this book is not to decide the religious issue of the present day, but merely to present the issue as sharply and clearly as possible, in order that the reader may be aided in deciding it for himself. Presenting an issue sharply is indeed by no means a popular business at the present time; there are many who prefer to fight their intellectual battles in what Dr. Francis L. Patton has aptly called a "condition of low visibility." Clear-cut definition of terms in religious matters, bold facing of the logical implications of religious views, is by many persons regarded as an impious proceeding. May it not discourage contribution to mission boards? May it not hinder the progress of consolidation, and produce a poor showing in columns of Church statistics? But with such persons we cannot possibly bring ourselves to agree. Light may seem at times to be an impertinent intruder, but it is always beneficial in the end. The type of religion which rejoices in the pious sound of traditional phrases, regardless of their meanings, or shrinks from "controversial" matters, will never stand amid the shocks of life. In the sphere of religion, as in other spheres, the things about which men are agreed are apt to be the things that are least worth holding; the really important things are the things about which men will fight.

Made in the USA
Middletown, DE
29 August 2023